POLITICAL DISSENT

POLITICAL DISSENT

An International Guide to Dissident, Extra-Parliamentary,
Guerrilla and Illegal Political Movements

A KEESING'S REFERENCE PUBLICATION

Compiled and written by Henry W. Degenhardt

General editor: Alan J. Day

Gale Research Company
Detroit

POLITICAL DISSENT. AN INTERNATIONAL GUIDE TO
DISSIDENT, EXTRA-PARLIAMENTARY, GUERRILLA AND
ILLEGAL POLITICAL MOVEMENTS

Published by Longman Group Limited, Longman House,
Burnt Mill, Harlow, Essex CM20 2JE, United Kingdom

Distributed exclusively in the United States and possessions,
Canada and Mexico by Gale Research Company,
Book Tower, Detroit, Michigan 48226, USA

ISBN 0 582 90255 X (Longman)
    0 8103 2050 9 (Gale)

Library of Congress Catalog Card Number: 83-14096

First published 1983

British Library Cataloguing in Publication Data
Degenhardt, Henry W.
  1. Political ethics
  I. Title   II. Day, Alan J.
  320′.025   JA79

ISBN 0 582 90255 X

Library of Congress Cataloging in Publication Data
Degenhardt, Henry W.
  Political dissent.
  (A Keesing's reference publication)
  Bibliography: p. 529
  Includes indexes.
  1. Government, Resistance to—Societies, etc.—Handbooks, manuals, etc.
I. Day, Alan J. II. Title. III Series.
JC328.3.D43 1983   322.4′2′025   83-14096

ISBN 0-8103-2050-9
ISBN 0-582-90255-X (Longman)

Typeset by Dawson & Goodall Limited, The Mendip Press, Bath BA1 1EN
Printed and bound in Great Britain by William Clowes Limited, Beccles and London

The Keesing's Reference Publications (KRP) series has been developed as an adjunct to Keesing's Contemporary Archives (KCA), the international news reference service which over the last half-century has built up an unrivalled reputation for the accuracy and objectivity of its presentation of world events. The KRP titles draw on the editorial resources of KCA as well as on other relevant information sources.

Contents

INTRODUCTION

"Political dissent" has, in the title of this book, been used to embrace various kinds of expression of political opposition outside the legal structure of the state concerned, i.e. forces which constitute an actual or potential threat to the stability of the state. (Legal political parties have been described in *Political Parties of the World* published earlier in the Keesing's Reference Publications series.)

The most obvious dissent of this kind has been that expressed by acts of violence committed by members of political movements, such violence having become an increasingly significant feature of the international scene over the last 10 or 15 years. These acts of violence have ranged from bank robberies with the aim of raising funds for revolutionary purposes, the taking of hostages in order to extort ransom and/or political concessions, and the hijacking of aircraft for similar purposes, to open warfare, either in the countryside (where terrain may favour protracted guerrilla war) or in cities, with the object of overthrowing existing regimes in the hope of replacing them with new ones providing greater social justice. Some of these activities, however, appear to have had no clear political object other than to "destabilize" the existing regime or simply to create an atmosphere of terror, e.g. by the assassination of prominent persons and the use of explosives to destroy buildings, trains or railway stations.

Small subversive groups included in this book have often been able to create effects quite out of proportion to their numerical strength. Although active, in many cases, over a period of years, they may fail to gain mass support (as did Che Guevara's revolutionary movement among Bolivian peasants in 1967), and they may eventually be overcome by security forces and disintegrate. The most spectacular of such groups have been the (revolutionary communistic) Red Army Faction in West Germany (the Baader-Meinhof group), the United Red Army of Japan and the Red Brigades of Italy.

Notwithstanding a number of exceptions in the 1970s where the principle of saving life was placed above the interests of the state, the majority of governments have insisted on refusing any compromise with terrorist organizations and have often rejected their demands even at the risk of lives being lost. In particular, Israel has steadfastly refused to make any concessions to Palestinian demands backed by violence and has, on the contrary, made every effort to suppress such attacks or has undertaken retaliatory action. Moreover, in recent years many governments have entered into various bilateral and multilateral agreements designed to curb the activities of terrorists and to facilitate the bringing of such persons to justice (e.g. by means of extradition arrangements).

Among the movements described in the present volume, those which are historically the oldest are the anti-colonialist national liberation movements such as those of the Republic of South Africa and Namibia, the anti-Israeli movements in the Middle East (which in the absence of a recognized state of Palestine have been covered in a chapter on "Palestinian Movements") and the revolutionary movements against military dictatorships in Latin America, which are at the same time strongly hostile to the United States. A recent addition to this type of movement are the various organizations offering armed resistance to the Soviet occupation of Afghanistan.

Threats to the territorial integrity of certain countries have arisen out of the activities of separatist movements based in ethnic or religious minorities. The many minority groups displaying such tendencies include Eritreans and Somalis in Ethiopia, Kurds in Iran, Iraq and Turkey, Armenians in Turkey, Moslems in the Philippines, Basques in Spain, Corsicans in France and Albanians in Yugoslavia. Such groups may also use violence to further aims more limited than secession, e.g. internal autonomy.

On the other hand many dissenting movements or individuals have adopted non-violent policies. In East European countries, and in particular in the Soviet Union, dissent has been most strongly expressed by individuals such as Dr Andrei Sakharov, the Medvedev brothers, Alexander Solzhenitsyn and others, whose ideas are also presented in this book. In addition, attention has been given to movements such as the Czechoslovak reform programme which came to an end with the Soviet inter-vention in 1968, the "Charter 77" movement in Czechoslovakia and the unique development of an independent trade union movement (Solidarity) in Poland.

Other organizations which have been described or listed in this book include illegal Communist parties (whether of orthodox, Trotskyist, Maoist or any other persuasion), as well as governments-in-exile (most of them dating back to regimes in power before World War II) and organizations of human rights activists (especially in the Soviet Union and in some Latin American countries). Religious dissent had been covered where it appears to have come into conflict with the authority of the state, an important strand of this type of dissent being the fundamentalist movements which have come to the fore in many Islamic countries in the wake of the 1979 revolution in Iran.

Dissent movements have been listed according to countries grouped under broad geographical headings. For each country the prevailing political set-up is summarized in an introduction in which relevant internal security developments, such as attempted coups, are described. In the entries which follow, the aim has been to describe the leadership, history, objects and activities of movements and the ideas of leading individual dissenters. Revolutionary or liberation movements which have come to power (e.g. in Nicaragua or Zimbabwe) have not been dealt with in this book, and the operation of the maxim that "today's terrorists may become tomorrow's governments" is likely to mean that at least some of those which are covered will have to be excluded from a future edition.

It should be noted that a reference book of this kind will inevitably be incomplete in certain respects owing to the difficulty of compiling precise information on movements and organizations of a clandestine nature. It is also likely that between the time of going to press and the date of publication of the volume new groups will have emerged, or those covered will have undergone changes of leadership or of policy orientation. Such is the unavoidable hazard which besets any reference book of the present kind.

Users of this work should also be aware that no attempt has been made to cover the numerous "one issue" pressure groups which are such a prominent feature of the political scene, at least in the industrialized countries. Such groups, including the various "peace" and anti-nuclear-weapons movements and the "green" ecologist lobby, have become so numerous in recent years that they merit a separate volume. For present purposes they are excluded because they have not, so far, presented a challenge to the legal structure of the states in which they operate.

The information presented in this volume is based on the resources of *Keesing's Contemporary Archives* (KCA), and every effort has been made to match the standards of accuracy, detachment and impartiality characteristic of KCA. The separate indexes of organizations and of personal names will serve to enhance the usefulness of this reference work. The select bibliography may encourage the user to embark on further studies of particular subjects of his or her choice in the general area of political dissent.

Thanks are due for co-operation in the compilation of this book to Colin F. Hansen, for producing the index of names, and to Christine Stewart-Morgan, for typing many of the entries. Thanks are also due for the permissions granted by Macmillan Publishers of London and by Alfred A. Knopf Inc. of New York to reproduce an extract from the book *Ten Years after Ivan Denisovich* by Zhores Medvedev, defining Alexander Solzhenitsyn's view of literature (see page 48).

June 1983   *HWD*

Abbreviations used in this book are the following:

ch.	= chairman	pres.	= president
g.s.	= general secretary	s.g.	= secretary-general
l.	= leader	sec.	= secretary

1. EASTERN EUROPE AND THE USSR

Albania

Capital: Tirana

Pop. 2,770,000

The Socialist People's Republic of Albania is, under its Constitution adopted by the People's Assembly in December 1976, "the state of the dictatorship of the proletariat" exercised in effect by the Albanian Party of Labour, which is "the sole directing political power in state and society". The single-chamber People's Assembly of 250 members (the supreme legislative body) is elected every four years on a single list of candidates nominated by the Democratic Front mass organization controlled by the party. The Albanian regime claims to be the sole guardian of true Marxism-Leninism and is opposed to all other forms of communism, notably those of the Soviet bloc, China, Yugoslavia and the Euro-communist parties.

Since Albania has remained almost totally closed to the outside world, little reliable evidence has emerged as to the existence or otherwise of internal opposition groups. In September 1982 a top party official referred to internal opponents of the Government as being linked to "external, imperialist revisionist enemies"; but such pronouncements were thought to refer to a power struggle within the regime (arising from the death in unclear circumstances of the long-time Prime Minister, Mehmet Shehu, in December 1981) rather than to any internal anti-communist movement as such. Moreover, there appears to have been little resistance by religious believers to the complete suppression of all religion since 1967—apart from occasional reports of imprisonment, ill-treatment or execution of priests and other believers, and the survival of a number of Moslem customs (Islam having been the religion of the majority of Albania's inhabitants).

Outside Albania, however, emigré groups opposed to the Tirana regime have continued to be sporadically active, notably those associated with the aspiration to bring about a restoration of the Albanian monarchy.

External Movements

Monarchist Movement

Leadership. Mbret Shquiparvet Leka ("King Leka I of the Albanians").

Mbret Shquiparvet Leka is the son of ex-King Zog (who fled from Albania in 1939, was deposed in absentia in 1946 and died in 1961) and styles himself "King Leka I of the Albanians". In March 1977 he was reported to have told a press conference in New York that he was training guerrilla forces to harass the Albanian Government and that a number of guerrillas had already entered the country. Arms were found in his possession when he was in Thailand in April 1977 and again when he was in Madrid in January 1979, when he was quoted as having said that he was pledged "to fight hard to help my country escape from communist dictatorship". Expelled from Spain in February 1979, he lived for a period in Rhodesia (Zimbabwe)

and eventually settled in South Africa with his Australian-born wife Susan after an interim stay in Egypt.

In a statement made in Paris on Sept. 29, 1982, "King" Leka said that an attempted armed invasion of Albania a few days earlier had been carried out by a "National Liberation Army" of his supporters but added that he had personally refused to be associated with the operation because of its "suicidal" nature. According to the Albanian authorities, the abortive invasion had occurred on the night of Sept. 25-26, when "a gang of criminal Albanian emigrés" had made an armed landing on the Albanian coast (the precise location being unspecified); the group had been discovered at daybreak and within five hours had been "totally liquidated" by the Albanian Army. No details were given as to the strength of the group, but the Albanian authorities claimed (i) that the infiltrators had been equipped with automatic rifles, pistols, binoculars, a radio transmitter, disguises and quantities of foreign and local currency, and (ii) that they had been led by "the bandit Xhevdet Mustafa", who was subsequently described as a "well-known criminal" active in emigré circles (although his name was unfamiliar to Western experts).

In the absence of further clarification or confirmation, some Western observers suggested that the alleged invasion was a device used by the Albanian Government to explain the elimination of an internal opposition group. In this context they referred to persistent rumours that the death in December 1981 of Mehmet Shehu (Prime Minister since 1954) had not been a suicide as officially announced but rather the result of a violent struggle for power with Enver Hoxha, the party leader. Soon after the alleged invasion attempt the latter on Nov. 10 denounced Shehu as "one of the most dangerous traitors and enemies" of Albania, claiming that he had worked since before World War II for the US, Yugoslav and Soviet intelligence services in turn.

National Organization of the Legality Movement

Leadership. Ydriz Basha i Novosejt (pres.).

This small group of exiled opponents of the Tirana regime has made its existence known from time to time in communications to the Western press. In a letter published in the French daily *Le Monde* on April 21, 1976, its president claimed that there were four forced-labour camps and "terrible political prisons" in Albania.

Bulgaria

Capital: Sofia   Pop. 8,900,000

In the People's Republic of Bulgaria the Communist Party plays, in terms of the 1971 Constitution, the leading role in the state, holding 272 seats in the 400-member single-chamber National Assembly. Of the remaining seats in the Assembly, 100 are held by the Bulgarian Agrarian People's Union (the country's only other legal party). All candidates for elections, however, are nominated by the Fatherland Front mass organization, which is controlled by the Communist Party. The ruling party has closely followed the political line of the Communist Party of the Soviet Union.

There has been little evidence of activities by political opposition or human rights groups inside Bulgaria, whereas externally exiled opponents of the Sofia regime are grouped within a number of organizations.

Internal Opposition

ABD—Declaration 78

According to the Vienna daily *Die Presse* of April 3, 1978, an anonymous group calling itself "ABD" had distributed a manifesto on alleged violations of human rights in Bulgaria. This six-point manifesto, called "Declaration 78", was quoted as calling for the cessation of violations of human and civil rights, non-interference in people's private lives, a free press and free art, freedom of choice and of criticism, freedom of religion, the abolition of censorship, the right to emigrate and the opening of frontiers, an improvement in social security and the standard of living, and the replacement of the existing official trade unions by independent employees' organizations to defend "the genuine interests of the workers".

On May 21, 1978, it was reported that a banner reading "Down with communism" had been displayed from a building in Sofia, while leaflets of similar content were being distributed by unknown activists who escaped before police intervened.

External Movements

Social Democratic Party of Bulgaria

Leadership. Stefan Tabakov (ch.).

The Social Democratic Party of Bulgaria was founded in 1891 and became a left-wing member of the pre-1914 Second International. The breakaway of the revolutionary wing in 1919 to form the Bulgarian Communist Party left the Social Democrats in a weakened position, but they nevertheless played a prominent role in the anti-Nazi resistance during World War II, for most of which Bulgaria was allied to Germany. With the Communists, left-wing Agrarians and other groups, the party participated in the Fatherland Front which seized power in September 1944 with the backing of the Red Army. Pressure for a merger with the Communist Party then developed, but its formal accomplishment in October 1947 was preceded by the departure into exile of those surviving Social Democrats who wished to preserve the party's non-communist identity.

The exiled party currently has its headquarters in Vienna and is a consultative member of the Socialist International as well as a constituent party of the Socialist Union of Central and Eastern Europe (SUCEE). The party chairman is also vice-chairman of a Bulgarian National Committee in exile.

Bulgarian Social Democratic Union

Based in Munich, this ostensibly social democratic group was in December 1978 accused by Stefan Tabakov (chairman of the exiled Social Democratic Party) of being linked with the Bulgarian secret service. In particular, Tabakov alleged that the Union's vice-chairman had hired a Bulgarian to make an attempt on his (Tabakov's) life on the model of the murder of Georgi Markov, a Bulgarian employee of the British Broadcasting Corporation who was killed in London in September 1978.

Collective for the Support of the Bulgarian People's Struggle (Collectif de Soutien de la Lutte du Peuple Bulgare)

The aim of this organization, which is based in Paris, is to support political prisoners in Bulgaria. In an appeal of March 1979 it mentioned in particular Kristo Kolev Yordanov (68), a trade unionist said to have spent more than 30 years in Bulgarian prisons, and Dr Peter Kondorgersky (74), a heart patient.

In a dossier on Bulgaria issued in December 1976, the International Committee against Repression (Comité International contre la Répression), also based in Paris, estimated the number of persons held for political reasons in concentration camps, prisons and mental hospitals (of which two were mentioned specifically) as totalling 20,000. The Committee described conditions in the camps as "impossible", with prisoners being often beaten, under-fed and ill-treated.

Civil Rights Group

Dimiter Tshabdarov, a member of this Vienna-based group, alleged in Vienna on Feb. 23, 1977, that 28,000 people were in prison and concentration camps in Bulgaria for political reasons. At the same time the group appealed to the leaders of the French, Italian and Spanish Communist parties for support for the civil rights cause in Bulgaria.

4

Czechoslovakia

Capital: Prague   Pop. 15,400,000

The Czechoslovak Socialist Republic has since Jan. 1, 1969, been a federal socialist republic comprising the Czech Socialist Republic and the Slovak Socialist Republic, each of them with its own Government and National Council (unicameral Parliament, with 200 deputies in the Czech Council and 150 in the Slovak Council). There is a Federal Government and a bicameral Federal Assembly consisting of a directly elected House of the People and a House of Nations elected by the Czech and the Slovak National Councils. Direct elections consist of the endorsement of a list of candidates nominated by the National Front, a mass organization embracing the Communist Party and also the Czechoslovak People's Party, the Czechoslovak Socialist Party, the Slovak Freedom Party, the Slovak Reconstruction Party, trade unions and youth organizations.

Since 1948 the Czechoslovak Communist Party has been the leading political force in the country, although with varying political programmes. Early in 1968 a new Central Committee with Alexander Dubcek as First Secretary embarked on a liberalization programme (also known as the "Prague Spring" and designed to bring about "socialism with a human face"). However, in the view of the Communist Party leaders of the Soviet Union (and also those of Bulgaria, the German Democratic Republic, Hungary and Poland) this programme was liable to lead to the detachment of Czechoslovakia from the "socialist community". The subsequent intervention by forces of these five Warsaw Pact member countries in August 1968 entailed the abandonment of the liberalization programme and the progressive removal of Dubcek from all positions of power in 1969-70. Since April 1969 the party has, under the leadership of Dr Gustáv Husák, been guided by the need to maintain "friendly relations with the Soviet Union and other socialist countries", without whose aid in August 1968 (as stated by Dr Husák on May 25, 1972) "the power of the working class of the country would have been overthrown". (Details of the 1968 reform programme and its aftermath are given at the end of this country section.)

In the decade following the suppression of the Prague Spring, the activities of dissident elements within Czechoslovakia became increasingly centred on campaigns for the full observance by the Government of human and civil rights in terms of international covenants to which Czechoslovakia was a contracting party. In the late 1970s groups were formed inside the country to promote such campaigns, which also received backing from various external organizations opposed to the Communist regime in Prague.

Internal Opposition

Charter 77

Leadership. Radim Palous, Anna Marvanova and Ladislav Liss (spokesmen). The group's founding spokesmen from January 1977 were Prof. Jirí Hajek, Dr Václav Havel and Prof. Jan Patocka (who died in March 1977) joined from September 1977 by Prof. Ladislav Hejdanek and Marta Kubisova.

Subsequent spokesmen were Prof. Václav Benda, Zdena Tominova and Jirí Dienstbier (1979); Milos Rejchrt and Marie Hromadkova (1980); Václav Maly, Dr Bedrich Placak and Prof. Jaroslav Sabata (1981).

The official publication in Czechoslovakia on Oct. 13, 1976, of the UN Covenants on Civil and Political Rights and on Economic, Social and Cultural Rights (which after their ratification by Czechoslovakia in December

1975 had entered into force on March 23, 1976) gave rise to the drafting of a manifesto by a new movement calling itself "Charter 77". While the manifesto, dated Jan. 1, 1977, was not published in Czechoslovakia, copies of it were sent to the Government and to its initial 242 signatories (who increased to about 800 by mid-1977 and later to over 1,000), and it was printed in West German newspapers (in translation) on Jan. 6-7, 1977, whereupon police action was taken against a number of its signatories.

After welcoming the fact that Czechoslovakia had acceded to the covenants, the manifesto continued as follows:

"At the same time their publication urgently reminds us that in our country many fundamental civil rights—regrettably—exist only on paper. The right of free expression of opinion, as guaranteed by Article 19 of the first covenant, for instance, is quite illusory. Tens of thousands of citizens are prevented from working in their professions merely because they hold views at variance with the official ones. Moreover, they often become the targets of all kinds of discrimination and chicanery by the authorities and social organizations; being deprived of any possibility of defending themselves, they become in effect victims of apartheid. Hundreds of thousands of other citizens are deprived of 'freedom from fear' (see the preamble of the first covenant) because they are forced to live in constant danger of losing their jobs or other facilities should they express their opinion.

The Right to Education. "Contrary to Article 13 of the second covenant which guarantees the right to education for everybody, innumerable young people are refused admission to higher education merely because of their views or even the views of their parents. Countless citizens have to live in fear that, if they express themselves in accordance with their convictions, they themselves or their children may be deprived of the right to education.

"Insistence on the right 'to seek, receive and impart information and ideas of all kinds, regardless of frontiers, either orally, in writing or in print [or] in the form of art' (Paragraph 2, Article 19 of the first covenant) is persecuted not only outside the courts but also by the courts themselves, often under the pretext of criminal indictment (as evidenced, inter alia, by the trials of young musicians).

Freedom of Expression of Opinion and Freedom of Conscience. "The freedom of public expression of opinions is suppressed as a result of the central administration of all media and of the publishing and cultural institutions. Neither any political, philosophical or scientific view nor any artistic expression can be published if it deviates in the slightest degree from the narrow framework of official ideology or aesthetics; public criticism of manifestations of social crises is made impossible; it is out of the question to conduct a public defence against untrue and defamatory assertions in official propaganda organs (there is in practice no legal protection against 'attacks on honour and reputation' as explicitly guaranteed in Article 17 of the first covenant); false accusations cannot be refuted, and any attempt to obtain a remedy or rectification from the courts is futile; and in the field of intellectual or cultural work no open discussion is possible. Many who are active in academic and cultural affairs, and other citizens, are being discriminated against merely because years ago they published or openly expressed views which are condemned by the existing political power.

"Freedom of conscience, expressly guaranteed in Article 18 of the first covenant, is systematically limited by arbitrary acts of those in power—by curtailing the activities of the clergy who are constantly threatened by withdrawal or loss of the state's permission enabling them to exercise their functions; by reprisals affecting, in respect of their livelihood or otherwise, persons who express their religious convictions in word or deed; and by the suppression of religious instruction, etc.

Absolute Power of Authorities. "The limitation, and often the complete suppression, of a series of civil rights is effected by a system of de facto subordination of all institutions and organizations in the state to the political directives of the ruling party's apparatus and the decisions of despotically influential individuals. The Constitution of Czechoslovakia, other laws and legal norms regulate neither the contents, the form nor the application of such decisions; they are mainly taken behind closed doors, often merely verbally; they are unknown to citizens in general and cannot be checked by them; their authors are responsible to no one except themselves and their own hierarchy; but they exert a decisive influence on the activities of legislative and executive organs in the administration of the state, the courts, trade unions, professional and all other social organizations, other political parties, enterprises, works, institutions, authorities, schools and other establishments—their orders taking precedence even before the law.

"If, in the interpretation of their rights and duties, organizations or citizens come into conflict with the directives they cannot appeal to any impartial arbitrator because there is none. All these facts seriously limit the rights resulting from Articles 21 and 22 of the first covenant (on freedom of assembly and the prohibition of any restriction of exercising this freedom), as well as from Article 25 (equality of the right to take part in the conduct of public affairs) and from Article 26 (equality before the law). This state of affairs prevents workers and other employees from establishing trade unions and other organizations and freely to apply the right to strike (Paragraph 1, Article 8 of the second covenant) in order to protect their economic and social interests without any restriction.

"Further civil rights, including the express prohibition of 'arbitrary interference with privacy, family, home or correspondence' (Article 17 of the first covenant), are also gravely violated by the fact that the Ministry of the Interior controls the lives of citizens in various ways, e.g. by telephone tapping, observation of homes, control of mail, personal surveillance, searches of homes, and the establishment of a network of informers from among the population (often recruited by means of unlawful threats or by promises), etc. In such cases the Ministry often interferes with employers' decisions, inspires discriminatory acts by authorities and organizations, exerts influence on the organs of justice and also directs propaganda campaigns through the media. These activities are not regulated by laws, they are secret and the citizen has no defence against them.

"In cases of politically motivated prosecutions the investigative and court organs violate the rights of the defendants and their defence, as guaranteed by Article 14 of the first covenant and also by Czechoslovak laws. In our prisons persons thus convicted are treated in a manner which violates their human dignity, endangers their health and aims at breaking them morally.

"Generally violations are also carried out in respect of Paragraph 2, Article 12, of the first covenant, which guarantees a citizen's right freely to leave his country; under the pretext of 'protecting national security' (Paragraph 3) this right is tied to various unlawful conditions. There is arbitrary procedure also in the granting of entry visas to nationals of foreign states, many of whom cannot visit Czechoslovakia because, for instance, they have had professional or friendly contacts with persons discriminated against in our country.

"Many citizens draw attention—either privately, at their place of work, or in public (which in practice is possible only in foreign media)—to the systematic violation of human rights and democratic freedoms and demand remedies in concrete cases; in most instances, however, their voice finds no echo or they become targets of official investigations.

The Object of Charter 77. "The responsibility for maintaining civil rights in the country lies, of course, above all with the political power and the state—but not exclusively. Every person has his share of responsibility for the general conditions and thus for the observance of the codified covenants, which is obligatory not only for governments but also for all citizens. The feeling of such co-responsibility, the belief in the meaningfulness of civil commitments and the will to carry them out, as well as the general need to find new and more effective expression for them, has given us the idea of forming Charter 77, the establishment of which is announced today.

"Charter 77 is a free, informal and open community of persons of varying convictions, religions and professions, joined together by the will to work individually and collectively for respect for civil and human rights in our country and in the world—those rights which are granted to man by the two codified international covenants, by the Final Act of the Helsinki conference [i.e. the 1975 Conference on Security and Co-operation in Europe (CSCE)], by numerous other documents opposing war, the use of force and social and intellectual oppression, and which have been expressed succinctly in the UN Universal Declaration of Human Rights.

"Charter 77 is based on the solidarity and friendship of people who are motivated by a common concern for the fate of the ideals to which they have attached, and are still attaching, their lives and their work.

"Charter 77 is no organization, and has no statutes, no permanent organs and no organized membership. Everyone belongs to it who agrees with its idea, takes part in its work and supports it.

"Charter 77 is no base for oppositional political activity. It wishes to serve the common interest, as do many similar civic initiatives in various countries of the West and the East. It therefore does not intend to draw up its own programmes for political or social reforms or changes but wants to conduct, within its sphere of activity, a constructive dialogue with the political and state authorities, in particular by drawing attention to various concrete cases in which human and civil rights are infringed, by preparing their documentation, proposing solutions, submitting various general suggestions aimed at strengthening these rights and their guarantees, and acting as a mediator in situations of conflict which may be caused by unlawful measures.

"Charter 77 emphasizes, by its symbolic name, that it is created at the beginning of the year which has been declared the year of the rights of political prisoners, and in the course of which the Belgrade conference is to review the fulfilment of the Helsinki obligations.

"As signatories of this manifesto we entrust Prof. Jiří Hajek, Dr Václav Havel and Prof. Jan Patocka with the task of acting as spokesmen for Charter 77. These spokesmen are empowered to represent Charter 77 before state and other organizations, before the public in our country and in the world, and by their signature they guarantee the authenticity of Charter 77 documents. They will find in us, and in other citizens who will join us, collaborators who, together with them, will support the necessary actions, undertake specific tasks and share all responsibility with them.

"We believe that Charter 77 will contribute to enabling all citizens of Czechoslovakia to work and live as free human beings."

Prof. Hajek (a former Foreign Minister) said on Jan. 7, 1977, that the purpose of the manifesto was to put the international covenants on human rights into practice and claimed that the initiative was "fully within the framework of the Czechoslovak Constitution" and was not meant to be "a political action or a basis for opposition activity". Late in January 1977 it was reported that Prof. Hajek and Prof. Patocka had asked the Government in an open letter to declare whether the organs of the state were bound by the Covenant on Civil and Political Rights and, if so, why "the defenders of civil rights" were "subjected to repression and discrimination, and publicly insulted and defamed".

Dr Zdenek Mlynar (a former Communist Party secretary) declared on Jan. 17, 1977 (in an open letter addressed to leaders of Communist and Socialist parties in the West), inter alia: "I am a Communist, and I am convinced that socialism must give people more political and civil rights than capitalism. I thus share the conviction which many European Communist parties represent today, behaving accordingly. For this I am publicly branded as a traitor to socialism and an agent of imperialism." Prof. Hajek stated in a television interview broadcast in Vienna on Feb. 7 that the signatories of the manifesto, who regarded themselves as Marxists, felt that respect for the civil rights covenant would mean, on the one hand, "a deepening of the Czechoslovak socialist system towards democracy, humanism and greater efficiency" and, on the other hand, "a contribution to progress of détente in Europe".

However, the public prosecutor in Prague told Prof. Hajek on Jan. 31, 1977, that his movement contravened Article 4 of the Czechoslovak Constitution, under which the Communist Party was established as the "leading force" in society and the state. Prof. Hajek said later that he did not deny this role and that the manifesto was "a lawful expression of the right of citizens to petition the Government".

Charter 77 was strongly attacked by *Rudé Právo*, the Communist Party's organ, which inter alia stated on Feb. 5, 1977, that the signatories of the manifesto were "objectively playing a sorry role in the actions of rabid anti-communism" and that their objectives were "to disrupt the peaceful climate in the country, to divert attention from the problems of the capitalist countries beset by unemployment, inflation and an economic, social and moral bankruptcy, to inculcate in the people of the West the fear of socialism, and to obstruct international détente". Despite such attacks, Charter 77 expanded its activities and subsequently issued a number of documents describing alleged violations of human rights in Czechoslovakia.

A statement said to have been written by Prof. Patocka on March 8, 1977 (shortly before his death), contained inter alia the following passages: "The legal character of the Charter, the fact that its aim is to foster an unconditional and publicly accountable legality, the obvious refusal of the authorities to accept this principle of the equality of the citizen before the law, their refusal to conduct a dialogue about the issues involved, has given us a considerable political advantage and forced our adversary to seek new methods in his struggle against us. . . . We are convinced that there is no one in the world who does not know that the Helsinki accords *must* be accepted if we are to escape a future of major wars and minor conflicts. But it is only now that we have come to realize just how terribly long a road it is going to be, and we know it thanks to the Charter."

Shortly after a meeting on March 1, 1977, with the then Dutch Foreign Minister, Max van der Stoel, during a visit by the latter to Prague, Prof. Patocka had been interrogated by police for more than 10 hours and was thereafter taken to hospital, where he died on March 13, two days after suffering a cerebral haemorrhage. In his memory Charter 77 supporters subsequently established the "Jan Patocka Alternative University" to promote teaching and learning independent of the government-controlled system. Inspired principally by Dr Julius Tomin and Prof. Radim Palous (both philosophers), the Alternative University developed close contacts with Western academics, several of whom assisted in its seminars. However, by mid-1980 the enterprise appeared to have been effectively suppressed amid constant harassment by the authorities of its members and also of visiting academics from the West.

A number of signatories of the "Charter 77" manifesto were given prison sentences in 1979-81, while others were allowed to leave the country, many of the latter being subsequently deprived of their Czechoslovak citizenship. Such developments and other forms of harassment by the Czechoslovak authorities reduced the scope of the movement's activities, although it continued in being and celebrated its fifth anniversary in January 1982. In two appeals issued in the course of 1982 to coincide with sessions of the Madrid follow-up meeting of the CSCE, the Charter 77 spokesmen (i) urged the

Czechoslovak Government in March to adopt a document guaranteeing freedom of religion, and (ii) called in October for the release of all political prisoners in the country.

Committee for the Defence of Persons Unjustly Persecuted (VONS)

Leadership. Rudolf Battek, Dr Václav Havel, Dr Gertruda Sekaninova-Carterova.

This Committee was formed in May 1978 as an offshoot of the Charter 77 movement (see separate entry) with the specific purpose of mobilizing support for Charter signatories and others whose activities had brought them into direct conflict with the Czechoslovak authorities. VONS is affiliated to the International Federation of Human Rights.

Members of VONS were co-signatories (with Prof. Ladislav Hejdanek and Marta Kubisova, then spokesmen for Charter 77) of an open letter addressed on Nov. 6, 1978, to the heads of states who had signed the 1975 Helsinki Final Act and also to Dr Kurt Waldheim (then UN Secretary-General) stating that Charter supporters were being "subjected to the most diverse provocations, accused of acts which they have not committed, arrested . . . and detained for months contrary to legal provisions in force". The letter asserted that "an atmosphere of fear" reigned in Czechoslovakia and that "most people dare not express their true opinions", and called on the addressees to put pressure on the Prague regime to "fulfil their human rights obligations under the Helsinki agreement".

Prison sentences were subsequently imposed on VONS members for subversive activities (in some cases allegedly in collaboration with foreign agents as follows: on Dr Havel (4½ years), Petr Uhl (five years), Prof. Václav Benda, Otta Bednarova and Jiří Dienstbier (three years each), all on Oct. 23, 1979 (all sentences being confirmed on appeal on Dec. 20, 1980); on Albert Cerny (3½ years) on Nov. 28, 1979 (confirmed on appeal on March 28, 1980); on Rudolf Battek (7½ years, reduced on appeal to 5½ years, with an additional three years of official "surveillance"); and on Jan Litomisky (three years) on Oct. 26, 1981. Mrs Bednarova was released because of ill-health on Sept. 26, 1980.

Plastic People of the Universe

Leadership. Ivan Jirous.

During the early 1970s this rock music group became the focus of aspirations to an alternative life style among young people and was accordingly regarded as subversive by the authorities. Its leader, Ivan Jirous, was sent to prison on four occasions between 1973 and 1982, most recently in July 1982, when he received a 3½-year prison sentence and two years' official "surveillance" and three associates lesser terms (these sentences being upheld on appeal in September 1982). Jirous had been arrested in November 1981 and charged with participating in the editorship of the underground cultural review *Vokno* ("Window") and also with illegal possession of drugs. During the 1982 trial a Prague University professor advised the court that "the culture of 1968" was being propagated by *Vokno*, which was thus "paving the way to counter-revolution".

Revolutionary Socialist Party

Established in 1968 as the Revolutionary Youth Movement, this organization was described as "clandestine and subversive" and inspired by the writings Trotsky and by the West European "New Left" when 19 of its members were brought to trial in March 1971. The charge was that its members had written, recopied and distributed numerous tracts and manifestos described as "ultra-left propaganda" and that they had actively taken part in preparing demonstrations held in Prague on Aug. 21, 1969 (the first anniversary of the Soviet-led invasion). Of the defendants, 16 were sentenced to terms of imprisonment ranging from one to four years (the latter sentence being imposed on the chief defendant, Petr Uhl).

Socialist Movement of Czechoslovak Citizens

In a document issued in September 1973 this group expressed the view that Czechoslovakia would "by its stagnation and the paralysis of its internal development constantly poison the atmosphere in Europe..., divide the international communist movement and contribute to fragmenting the anti-imperialist forces"; that the main causes of stagnation were the exclusion of thousands of skilled specialists, the suppression of all initiative except "initiative ordered from above", investment in projects with no future and "a return to the outdated system of command management"; and that the first need was to overcome "negative and undiscriminating attitudes of the majority of our people towards the Soviet Union". The document also called upon the Soviet leaders to show that they wanted to make good the consequences of the 1968 invasion.

External Movements

Committee for the Defence of Liberties in Czechoslovakia

Leadership. Artur London.

This Paris-based organization of exiled dissidents and their supporters campaigns specifically for the release of political prisoners in Czechoslovakia and for the ending of official persecution of Charter 77 activists. In November 1982 the Committee organized a protest petition for presentation to the Czechoslovak embassy in Paris to mark the 30th anniversary of the 1952 show trial of Rudolf Slansky and 13 other former Communist Party leaders accused of being "Trotskyist-Titoist-Zionist-bourgeois-nationalist traitors and enemies of the Czechoslovak people".

Artur London (a former Deputy Foreign Minister) had been a defendant in the 1952 trial and was one of three sentenced to life imprisonment (the other 11 being sentenced to death and executed). Following Nikita Khrushchev's denunciation of Stalin at the 20th congress of the Soviet Communist Party in February 1956, London was released from prison and rehabilitated in April of that year (most of those executed in 1952 being posthumously rehabilitated in 1963).

Czechoslovak People's Party

This party has continued to exist in exile since the advent of Communist rule in Czechoslovakia and is a member of the Christian Democratic World Union.

Czechoslovak Social Democratic Party

Leadership. Vilem Bernard (ch.).

Having disputed the leadership of the workers' movement with the Communists in the inter-war period, the Czechoslovak Social Democrats participated in the Communist-dominated National Bloc of Working People formed in 1945 and thereafter came under intense pressure to accept a merger with the Soviet-backed Communists as the latter gradually established full control of the state apparatus. A campaign of violence and intimidation against Social Democrats in 1946-47 led to the formal merger of the party with the Communists on April 1, 1948, but those Social Democrats who escaped into exile have always maintained that the "unification" was carried out against the wishes of most party members. In exile the Czech Social Democratic Party has consistently stood for the re-establishment of full party pluralism in Czechoslovakia, where it claims to have retained extensive underground support. During the 1968 "Prague Spring" a proposal that a Social Democratic Party should be reconstituted was rejected by the Communist Party then led by Alexander Dubcek.

The exiled Social Democratic Party is a consultative member of the Socialist International as well as a constituent party of the Socialist Union of Central and Eastern Europe (SUCEE).

1968 Reform Programme

"Prague Spring" Action Programme

The 1968 reform programme of the "Prague Spring" was set out in a 24,000-word "action programme" published by the Czechoslovak Communist Party on April 9, 1968. The main aim, it was stated, was to "reform the whole political system so as to permit . . . the combination of a broad democracy with a scientific, highly qualified management, the strengthening of the social order, the stabilization of socialist relations, and the maintenance of social discipline". At the same time the basic structure of the political system "must provide firm guarantees against a return to the old methods of subjectivism and high-handedness from a position of power".

The Communist Party of Czechoslovakia would "use every means to develop such forms of political life as will ensure the expression of the direct will of the working class and all working people in political decision-making in our country". The National Front as a whole, and its components, "must have independent rights and their own responsibility for the management of our country and society. . . ."

In a long section on the role of the Communist Party it was stated inter alia that the party should be based on the voluntary support of the people; it did not fulfil its function by ruling over society but by "serving faithfully the free and progressive development of society". After emphasizing that the party's authority must be renewed, not by orders but by the deeds and work of its members, the programme stated: "The leading role of the party was too often understood in the past as a monopolistic concentration of power in the hands of the party organs. . . . This weakened the initiative and responsibilities of the state and of economic and social institutions, damaged the authority of the party, and made it impossible for the party to fulfil its basic tasks. The party must fight . . . for the voluntary support of a majority within the framework of the democratic rules of a socialist state. . . ."

In the constitutional sphere, assurances were given that freedom of assembly would be implemented "this year"; that censorship before publication would be eliminated; that the rehabilitation of people who had been the victims of judicial injustice in the past would be accelerated; that freedom of minority interests and opinions, as well as other freedoms, would be guaranteed more exactly; and that the "constitutional freedom of movement, in particular travel by our citizens abroad, must be guaranteed by law". In the latter connexion it was stated that Czechoslovak citizens should have "the legal right to long-term or permanent sojourn abroad'', although in the interests of the state it would be necessary by law to prevent a ''brain drain'' of certain categories of specialists. Freedom of assembly and association must also be ''legally guaranteed and applied to various religious denominations''.

Another section of the programme said that the security police would limit their activities solely to matters involving the security of the state. ''Every citizen not guilty in this respect,'' it was stated, ''must feel sure that his political convictions and opinions do not become the subject of attention by the state security. Its organs may not be used to solve questions of internal policy.''

On relations between the Czechs and the Slovaks, the programme said: ''Our Republic, as a joint state of two equal nations— Czechs and Slovaks—must ensure that the constitutional arrangement of relations between our fraternal nations and the status of all other nationalities of Czechoslovakia develops as demanded by the strengthening of the unity of the state, the development of the nations and nationalities themselves, and in keeping with the needs of socialism.'' To this end a constitutional law would be passed which would ''embody the principle of a symmetrical arrangement'' and which would, ''on the basis of full equality, solve the status of Slovak national bodies in the nearest future''. A statute would also be worked out for the other nationalities in Czechoslovakia—Hungarians, Poles, Ukrainians, and Germans—which would ''guarantee the possibilities of their national life and the development of their national individuality''.

The ''basic orientation of Czechoslovak foreign policy'', it was stated, was ''alliance and co-operation with the Soviet Union and other socialist countries . . . on the basis of mutual respect, sovereignty and equality, and international solidarity''.

After saying that Czechoslovak society had entered a new stage of development since the end of the 1950s, the document stated that the present stage of development was marked by the following characteristics:

(1) Antagonistic classes no longer existed, and the main feature of internal development was becoming ''the process of rapprochement of all social groups of our society''.

(2) Existing methods of management and the orientation of the national economy had become outdated, and urgent changes were required having intensive economic growth as their objective.

(3) It was necessary to ''prepare the country's link-up with the process of the scientific technical revolution in the world'', a task which would require ''especially intensive co-operation between workers and peasants and the intelligentsia and which will lay great demands on people's knowledge and qualifications. . . .''

(4) An ''open exchange of views and the democratization of the whole social and political system is becoming literally a condition of the dynamics of socialist society. . . .''

''2,000 Words'' Manifesto

A call for speeding up the proposed reforms was made in a document known as the ''2,000 Words'' and published on June 27, 1968, in four Czechoslovak newspapers. It was written by Ludvik Vaculik, a well-known writer, and signed by 70 persons, most of them intellectuals. It was also published in the West in translation, and the version which appeared in *The Times Literary Supplement* (of London) on July 18, 1968, contained the following passages:

''The first threat to our national life was the war. Then came other evil days, and events menacing to the nation's spiritual wellbeing and character. It was with high hopes that most of the nation welcomed the socialist programme. But its direction fell into the hands of the wrong people. It would not have mattered so much that they lacked adequate experience in affairs of state, factual knowledge, or philosophical education, if only they had had enough common prudence and decency to listen to the opinion of others and agree to being gradually replaced by more able men.

''After enjoying great popular confidence immediately after the war, the Communist Party by degrees bartered this confidence away for office, till it had all the offices and nothing else. We have to say this, and it is well known to those of us who are Communists and who are as disappointed as the rest at the way things turned out. The leaders' mistaken policies transformed a political party and an alliance based on ideas into an organization for exerting power, one which proved highly attractive to egotists itching to wield authority, to cowards with an eye to the main chance, to people with bad consciences. The influx of members such as these affected the character and behaviour of the party, whose internal arrangements made it impossible—short of scandalous incidents—for honest members to gain influence and adapt it continuously to modern conditions. Many Communists fought against this decline, but they did not manage to prevent what ensued.

''Conditions inside the Communist Party served as pattern and cause for identical conditions in the state. The party's association with the state robbed it of the asset of separation from executive power. No one criticized the activities of the state and of the economic bodies. Parliament forgot how to hold proper debates, the Government forgot how to govern properly, and managers how to manage properly. Elections lost their significance, the law carried no weight. We could not trust our representatives on any committee or, if we could, there was no point in asking them for anything because they were powerless. Worse still, we could scarcely trust one another. Personal and collective honour decayed. Honesty was a useless virtue, assessment by merit unheard of. Most people accordingly lost interest in public affairs. . . .

"We all of us bear responsibility for the present state of affairs. But those of us who are communists bear more than others, and those who acted as component parts, or as instruments, of unchecked power bear most of all. It was the power of a self-willed band of men, spreading out through the party apparatus into every district and community. It was this apparatus which decided what might and might not be done, which ran the co-operative farms for the co-operative farmers, ran the factories for the workers, and ran the National Committees for the public. No organizations, not even communist ones, were really controlled by their own members. The chief sin and deception of these rulers was to have represented their own whims as the 'will of the workers'. Were we to accept this pretence, we would have to blame the workers today for the decline of our economy, for crimes committed against the innocent, for the introduction of censorship to prevent anyone writing about these things; the workers would be to blame for misconceived investments, trading losses and the housing shortage.

"Obviously no sensible person will believe the working class responsible for such things. We all know, and every worker knows especially well, that he had virtually no say in deciding anything. Working-class functionaries were given their voting instructions by somebody else. While many workers imagined that they were the rulers, it was a specially trained stratum of party and state officials who ruled in their name. In effect it was these men who stepped into the shoes of the deposed ruling class and themselves came to constitute the new authority.

"Let us in fairness say that some of them long ago realized the bad trick history had played. We can recognize such individuals today by the way they are rectifying old wrongs, making good their blunders, handing back powers of decision to rank-and-file party members and members of the public, setting limits to the authority and size of the bureaucracy. They share our opposition to backward views among party members. But a large proportion of officials have been resistant to change and are still influential. They still wield the instruments of power, especially at district and community level,

where they can employ them in secret and without fear of prosecution.

"Since the start of this year we have been experiencing a regenerative process of democratization. It started inside the Communist Party. We have to say this, and it is well known even to those Communists amongst us who no longer had hopes of anything good emerging from that quarter. It must also be added, of course, that there was nowhere else where the process could have started. For after 20 years the Communists were alone able to conduct some sort of political existence: it was only Communist criticism which had any impact on courses of action; it was only the opposition inside the Communist Party which had the privilege of contact with antagonistic views. The effort and initiative now displayed by democratically-minded Communists, then, is only a partial repayment of the debt owed by the entire party to the non-Communists whom it had been holding down in a position of inequality. No thanks, accordingly, are due to the Communist Party, though perhaps it should be granted that the party is making an honest effort at the eleventh hour to save its own honour and the nation's.

"The regenerative process introduces nothing particularly new into our life. It revives ideas and topics, many of which are older than the errors of our socialism, while others, having arisen below the surface of visible history, should long ago have found expression but were instead repressed.

"Let us not foster the illusion that it is the power of truth which now makes such ideas victorious. Their victory has been due rather to the weakness of the old leaders, evidently debilitated in advance by 20 years of rule with no one standing in their way. All the defects hidden in the foundations and ideology of the system must clearly have reached their full maturity. So let us not overestimate the effect of the writers' and students' criticisms. The source of social changes is the economy. The true word makes its mark only when it is spoken under conditions that have been properly prepared. Properly prepared conditions —in our context, that must unfortunately include the whole impoverishment of our society and the complete collapse of the old system of government, under which a certain sort of politicians calmly and quietly compromised themselves at our expense. Truth, then, is not winning the day; truth is merely what remains when everything else has been frittered away. So there is no reason for national jubilation; simply for fresh hope. . . .

"To begin with, we shall oppose the view sometimes heard that a democratic revival can be achieved without the Communists, or even in opposition to them. This would be unjust, and foolish too. The Communists have their organizations ready built, and in these we must support the progressive wing. They have their experienced officials, and they still have in their hands, after all, the crucial levers and press-buttons. On the other hand they have come before the public with their Action Programme. This is a programme for the first evening-out of the crassest inequalities, and no one else has a programme in such specific detail. We must demand that they produce local action programmes in public in every district and community. Then the issue will suddenly revolve around very ordinary and long-awaited acts of justice. . . .

"There has been great alarm recently over the prospect of foreign forces intervening in our development. Whatever superior forces may face us, all we can do is to stick to our own positions, behave decently, and start nothing ourselves. We can show our Government that we will stand by it, with weapons if need be, if it will do what we give it a mandate to do. And we can assure our allies that we shall observe our treaties of alliance, friendship, and trade. Irritable reproaches and ill-argued suspicions on our part can only make things harder for our Government, and bring no benefit to ourselves. In any case, the only way we can achieve relations of equality is to improve our domestic situation and carry the regenerative process so far as to elect one day statesmen with enough courage, honour and political sagacity to create such relations and keep them so. But this is a problem that faces all governments of small countries everywhere.

"This spring a great opportunity came to us again, as it came after the end of the war. Again we have the chance to take into our own hands our common cause—which for working purposes we call socialism—and give it a form more appropriate to our once good reputation, and to that fairly good opinion we originally had of ourselves. The spring is over and will never return. By winter we shall know all."

Suppression of Reform Movement

The Soviet-led invasion of Czechoslovakia in August 1968 forced the abandonment of the reform programme, while the replacement of Dubcek as party leader by Dr Husak in April 1969 marked the beginning of concerted action by the authorities to remove all traces of the Prague Spring in terms both of its supporters and of the liberalization measures introduced during Dubcek's brief ascendancy.

As a protest against the Soviet intervention, Jan Palach (a 21-year-old student) burned himself to death in Prague on Jan. 17, 1969, after writing down that he had been a member of a group which demanded the immediate abolition of censorship and the prohibition of the distribution of *Zpravy* (a Soviet-sponsored propaganda publication). His death was followed by mass demonstrations and demands for the restoration of democratic liberties.

Anti-Soviet demonstrations took place in several localities in Czechoslovakia on March 28-29, 1969 (following the defeat of a Soviet ice hockey team by a Czechoslovak one), the resultant disorders being condemned by the Government and the Communist Party in a statement issued on April 2, 1969, saying that a "psychosis nourished by anti-Soviet and anti-socialist forces for political ends" had been "fanned by irresponsible articles and transmissions in the press and on radio and television"; that there had been "more or less open invectives against the Soviet Union" and against the Communist Party and its leaders through both the written and the spoken word; and that this had created "an atmosphere in contradiction with the Government's efforts to achieve a normalization of life in Czechoslovakia". Further disturbances occurred on Aug. 19-20, 1969 (the first anniversary of the 1968 Soviet-led invasion), when five persons were killed and (in Prague alone) 1,377 were arrested.

After his removal from all political posts in the period 1969-70, Dubcek repeatedly defended his own position. In a letter published in Italy on March 13, 1974, he wrote inter alia that Czechoslovakia was "ruled by a system of personal power from the top to the bottom"; that the Government had lost "what counts most in the work of a Leninist-type party—the confidence of the masses in the party"; and that he was still unable to understand how false reports about his liberalization plans could have been accepted as true in Moscow. He concluded: "We [i.e. his wife and he himself] have no rancour towards the party, its movement and its ideas. They are stronger than the obstacles along the path which will nevertheless still lead onward. We have not let ourselves be discouraged."

In a letter written to the Czechoslovak Federal Assembly on Oct. 28, 1974 (according to the Stockholm *Dagens Nyheter* of April 13, 1975), Dubcek claimed that in the party there was no democracy; that no attempt was made to gain a majority by discussion; that the courts were "totally dependent" on the Ministry of the Interior; and that it was "impossible to speak of legality when the judiciary can express no opposition". He also claimed that the "compromise policy" adopted in November 1968 might have succeeded had it not been for the "sectarian opportunism" adopted by Dr Husák (his successor as First Secretary of the party) with his "dogmatic and divisive tactics under the pretext of struggling against counter-revolution". He added that during the entire invasion period not a single counter-revolutionary had been arrested, but "hundreds of thousands of loyal Communists, many of them veterans of the wartime resistance . . . were branded as anti-Soviet and punished". He dismissed as nonsense the allegation that the "Prague Spring" was a return to capitalism. Claiming that the working class in Czechoslovakia knew that it was "being manipulated", he wrote: "It is necessary consciously to overcome this system, to thwart it through legal means and to prevent its perpetuation and existence", and he condemned the misuse of power and the violation of socialist principles as "a violation of human rights".

Dr Husák, however, called this letter "a falsification of history" in which Dubcek had slandered "the state, the party and parliamentary bodies" and had worked his way to "the position of a traitor". On Aug. 17, 1975, Dubcek was reported to have been expelled from his trade union because of his letter of October 1974.

At the first congress of the Czech Writers' Union (founded in 1971), held in Prague on May 31, 1972, the newly-elected chairman stated that writers who had been "the organizers of the revisionists' anti-socialist actions" (during 1968) could not become members of the union. Moreover, the eighth congress of the Central Council of the Czechoslovak Revolutionary Trade Union Movement, which opened in Prague on July 12, 1972, annulled all documents and resolutions of the previous congress (held in March 1969, shortly before the fall of Dubcek), including the right of workers to strike. The Council's chairman, Karel Hoffmann, denounced "right-wing deviationist opportunism" and declared that the March 1969 congress had given "anti-socialist forces" a last opportunity for "an open political manifestation".

Legislation to empower the Government to restrict more effectively the influence of Dubcek's followers and other dissenters was passed in 1973-74. In amendments to the penal code approved by the Federal Assembly on April 25, 1973, the existing maximum prison sentence of 15 years was increased to 25 years for "capital" crimes, including "anti-socialist" activities; the existing law against spreading false information abroad was expanded to cover also "untrue reports" about Czechoslovakia's international status and foreign policy; and any person found guilty of such charges would not only be imprisoned for up to three years but would also lose his property by confiscation. The amendment also introduced "protective surveillance" which could be ordered by a court and involved the control, through the security services, of the movement of persons who had served prison sentences.

Under a bill which came into force on July 1, 1974, the police were empowered to "infringe the rights and freedom of citizens if required for the protection of the social system and the socialist state, for public order or for the safety of persons or property".

The writer Václav Havel, who had supported the 1968 reforms and who later became a leading member of the Charter 77 movement (see below), wrote in an open letter handed to Western correspondents in Prague in mid-April 1975 that there was "an ever-deepening crisis in our society" based on "fear, corruption and apathy". He continued: "Our present rulers actually offer bribes to those whom they want to win over to their side. . . . The prerequisite to any advancement, or even retention of one's current position, is an assent to lie to oneself, to betray one's friends and to deceive one's employers." He held Dr Husák personally responsible for the "paralysis of our cultural activity" and "the drastic suppression of our history", as well as for "ceaselessly degrading human dignity, for the puny sake of protecting your own power".

In a 90-page dossier presented in Vienna on May 24, 1976, by Jiři Starek (a former cultural attaché at the Czechoslovak embassy in Austria) it was asserted that, since November 1970, 7,000 army officers had been expelled from the Czechoslovak Communist Party and had lost their posts; that 2,000 others dismissed had been regarded as "right-wing deviationists"; that 2,000 journalists had been "purged" and several thousand academics had been prevented from continuing their work; and that entry to the country's only theological seminary had been restricted, at first to 16 young people a year and from 1974 onwards to 26.

German Democratic Republic

Capital: East Berlin   Pop. 17,000,000

Under a Constitution adopted in 1968 the "supreme organ of state power" in the German Democratic Republic (GDR) is the unicameral Parliament (People's Chamber or *Volkskammer*) of 500 seats filled by members of the (Communist) Socialist Unity Party (SED), as well as by members of four other parties and of mass organizations. The *Volkskammer* elects a Council of State (whose Chairman is in effect the head of state) and a Council of Ministers (Cabinet). Real power, however, is held by the Politburo of the Central Committee of the SED.

There has been no organized internal opposition in recent years, but criticism of the regime has been expressed occasionally by small groups and by some dissident intellectuals. There has been freedom of worship for both the Protestant Churches (of some 8,000,000 members) and the Roman Catholic Church (with about 1,300,000). The Protestant Churches in particular have accepted the existing social and political order as "ordained by God" and have increasingly co-operated with the authorities since 1978, though not without criticizing the introduction of compulsory military education in schools as from Sept. 1, 1978.

In 48 amendments to the GDR penal code, passed by the *Volkskammer* on June 28, 1979, and in force from Aug. 1 of that year, increased prison sentences were provided for internal security offences, and new offences were introduced for the collection and communication of "treasonable" secret or non-secret information and "possessing illegal connexions" with a view to communicating critical material to the foreign press and to publishing abroad books or manuscripts not registered with the GDR authorities.

According to a statement issued by a West Berlin Working Group for Human Rights on June 15, 1981, the number of political prisoners held in the GDR was about 4,500. In November 1979 the group had stated that since 1949 there had been some 100,000 political trials in the GDR, with 167 persons being condemned to death and 590 to life imprisonment.

Dissenting Marxists

Robert Havemann

Prof. Robert Havemann of the Humboldt University of East Berlin was suspended in 1964 after he had tried to give Marxism a liberal interpretation; in December 1965 he was dismissed from the position of head of a research institution after he had called for the new foundation of the (then banned) Communist Party in West Germany and at the same time the creation of an opposition in the GDR. After he had expressed support for Wolf Biermann (a singer who had on Nov. 16, 1976, been refused permission to return to the GDR after giving a concert on West German television), Prof. Havemann was kept under house arrest from Nov. 26, 1976, until May 9, 1979.

During 1981 Prof. Havemann issued several political appeals. On June 22 he called, in an open letter to Helmut Schmidt, then West German Chancellor, for the opening of talks in disarmament with the GDR and the Soviet Union in order to demonstrate to President Reagan of the USA that the latter's European allies were not willing to put up with delays in this matter. On July 3 he was reported to have called for the abolition of the Politburo of the SED, which he called "the source of all evil" in the country.

In a letter addressed to President Brezhnev of the Soviet Union in October 1981, Prof. Havemann called for the conclusion of a peace treaty and the withdrawal of all occupation

15

troops from both parts of Germany; this, he said, would be possible if the USA were to remove its forces from West Germany. He argued that if the USSR agreed to negotiate mutual troop withdrawals and to freeze the number of medium-range missiles currently directed against Western Europe, no West German Government would further insist on stationing US nuclear weapons on its territory. The letter was signed by 27 other GDR citizens and about 150 public figures in West Germany (including four Social Democratic members of Parliament).

Rudolf Bahro

Rudolf Bahro, the author of a theoretical study of GDR communism, was charged with high treason for allowing his book to be published in West Germany and was on June 30, 1978, sentenced to eight years in prison. He was, however, released under an amnesty in October 1979, left for West Germany and was subsequently deprived of his GDR citizenship. In an interview published in *Der Spiegel* in the same month, he described himself as a Marxist and claimed that there existed in the GDR, even among high-ranking party officials, a strong tendency towards the political road which he had described in his book *Die Alternative*.

Stefan Heym

Stefan Heym, a prominent writer, was in May 1979 fined 9,000 marks and expelled from the Writers' Federation for having had a novel published in West Germany. Allowed to leave the GDR temporarily, he said in Amsterdam in November 1979: "We must strive for a form of socialism in which critical literature is tolerated. As long as writers in the GDR risk five years' imprisonment when they publish a book in the West which is considered harmful, a great silence will continue to reign in East Germany." In May 1980 he was allowed to leave for West Germany for good.

Other Opposition Activities

Uwe Reimann, of Görlitz (on the Polish border), was in December 1978 given a 33-month prison sentence for "anti-state agitation", i.e. for distributing copies of a manifesto of an alleged opposition group within the SED (which had been reprinted in *Der Spiegel* of Hamburg); he was, however, released in March 1979 and allowed to leave for West Germany. He had also been active in protesting against the introduction of military education in schools.

In March 1980 it was reported that leaflets headed "Oppositional Newspaper in the GDR" and calling for the withdrawal of Soviet occupation troops from Afghanistan and the GDR had been distributed in East Berlin.

In a pamphlet, reproduced in *Der Spiegel* on Aug. 3, 1981, and allegedly distributed in the GDR, the officials of the SED were criticized for serving as "spearhead against the democratic forces" in the Warsaw Pact countries; for suppressing "independent thought in all fields"; and for driving "thousands into prison and emigration". At the same time the anonymous authors of the pamphlet demanded the observance of fundamental human rights, including freedom of conscience, association, speech and assembly, the release of all political prisoners and a general amnesty, as well as free, secret and equal elections with free nomination of candidates.

Human rights activists given severe prison sentences have included Dr Werner Schädicke, a medical practitioner of Leipzig, who had in 1972 written letters and tracts calling for the implementation of human rights, including the right to emigrate; sentenced to six years in prison for "anti-state activities" in 1974, he was released in November 1979.

Those sentenced for activities against the state have included Rolf Mainz (to 4½ years in April 1977 and to another five years later, but released to West Germany on Dec. 22, 1978) and Herbert Balzer (to 4½ years on Dec. 3, 1977). Raimund Bäurich, described as a "non-party evangelical Christian", was in June 1980 given a five-year hard-labour sentence for alleged "anti-state agitation"; he had previously been imprisoned from 1977 until December 1979, when he had been amnestied.

Günter and Leni Prager, a married couple convicted of collecting and sending to the West information likely to tarnish the image of the GDR, were reported in November 1979 to have been sentenced to 3½ years in prison each. They had sent to West German newspapers reports of food supply difficulties in Dresden, and they had earlier made some 50 applications for permission to emigrate to West Germany.

Bernd and Gerdi Sobe, another married couple, were sentenced in Dresden on April 29, 1980, to 5½ and 4½ years in prison respectively for "treasonable communication of information" after they had referred to alleged "serious violations of human rights in the GDR" in letters addressed to the UN Secretary-General, the UN Human Rights Commission and the West German trade union federation *(Deutscher Gewerkschaftsbund)*.

On May 1, 1980, Günter Weinhold (an engineer) was arrested in Dresden after having, at a May Day parade, displayed a banner reading: "Everyone is free to leave his country; so are we." He had for three years unsuccessfully applied for permission to leave for West Germany.

Andreas Koburg was sentenced in Potsdam on Aug. 8, 1980, to four years in prison for spreading news harmful to the international reputation of the GDR by requesting the International Committee of the Red Cross to send a delegation to the GDR to examine conditions in prisons; he had himself been sentenced to 18 months in August 1978 but had been released under the 1979 amnesty and had thereafter described some of his experiences.

In August 1981 Dr Wilhelm Kock was reported to have been sentenced to four years in prison for having given financial aid to Solidarity, the independent trade union organization in Poland. A number of other persons were also prosecuted for expressing support for Solidarity.

The Rev. Klaus-Detlef Beck was on Sept. 8, 1981 given a suspended prison sentence of 18 months for "forming an association for pursuing illegal objectives" by proposing that would-be emigrants should stage a sit-in at the office of the permanent representative of West Germany in East Berlin.

Dissent within the Churches

The leaders of the Protestant Churches in the GDR were greatly disturbed by the suicide of two of their pastors in 1976 and 1978 respectively.

The Rev. Oskar Brüsewitz set himself on fire at Zeitz (south of Leipzig) on Aug. 18, 1976, and died four days later; he was said to have acted in protest against "the suppression of youth" by communism. A church spokesman declared on Aug. 22 that the impediments and restrictions imposed on young Christians and on church life had repeatedly been discussed with the state authorities and that a Government which had signed the Helsinki Final Act could expect to be asked to what extent it was ready to observe freedom of religion and of conscience.

The Rev. Rolf Guenther burnt himself to death in his church at Falkenstein (near Plauen) on Sept. 17, 1978, allegedly in apparent despair at the lack of Christian piety in his community; it was also alleged that he had wished to protest against compulsory military education in the (state-controlled) schools of the GDR.

In a petition to the Government the Roman Catholic Bishops' Conference had on June 12, 1978, objected to the measure as "education for hatred", and on Sept. 24 of that year the Protestant Churches also protested against the "idealization of military life and the minimization of the consequences of war" resulting from the introduction of such military education.

Hungary

Capital: Budapest   Pop. 10,710,000

The People's Republic of Hungary, in which de facto power is held by the Politburo of the Central Committee of the Hungarian Socialist Workers' Party, has a Presidential Council (whose Chairman is the head of state), a Council of Ministers under a Prime Minister and a 352-member National Assembly elected for a five-year term, with election candidates having to be supporters of the Patriotic People's Front, a mass organization dominated by the party. The regime set up in the wake of the repression of the 1956 rising has become one of the most liberal among the East European communist states as regards economic, social and cultural policy.

A new civil code, which came into effect on March 1, 1978, provided inter alia, in accordance with the Constitution, for the protection of human rights, which were not to be infringed by discrimination on grounds of sex, race, nationality or denomination, by violations of the freedom of conscience, by unlawful restrictions of personal liberty, or by offences against corporal integrity, health, honour or human dignity. The protection of the privacy of mail, of personal and business secrets and of the home were reaffirmed.

There is no organized opposition group in Hungary. Dissent among intellectuals has been kept within limits imposed by the authorities without extreme measures of repression.

Dissent among Intellectuals

Some of the dissenting intellectuals were members of the "Budapest School" founded by the Marxist philosopher Georgy Lukacs (who died in 1971) and adopted ideas of the West European "New Left", describing the societies of East European countries as "no longer capitalist and not socialist either but controlled by bureaucracies". In January 1973 these intellectuals were officially described as "pseudo-revolutionaries" and "petty-bourgeois romantics" who "objectively" played a "reactionary role". Some of them were subsequently allowed to leave the country. One of them, Ferenc Fehér, announced on Jan. 20, 1977, that some 28 Hungarian intellectuals had sent a letter to the Czechoslovak "Charter 77" group to express solidarity with it and to protest against government reprisals against its members.

The sentences imposed in Prague on Oct. 23, 1979, on six members of VONS (see page 9) led to a protest by 184 Hungarian intellectuals and the sending of two petitions to János Kádár, the First Secretary of the Hungarian Socialist Workers' Party (HSWP)—these documents being signed by 252 persons altogether. A small number subsequently withdrew their signatures under pressure from the authorities who threatened them with dismissal from their posts.

In May 1981 there was in clandestine circulation a dossier compiled by 77 intellectuals in memory of István Bibó (a former Peasant Party politician and historian, who had died in 1979), containing criticism of conditions in Hungary. The dossier was commented upon by two members of the Central Committee of the HSWP, who reported that its joint authors fell into four distinct groups: (i) those whose views were neither of interest nor dangerous; (ii) those who were "traitors" and denied their socialist past; (iii) those who had a scientific and moderate approach; and (iv) those who merely recorded expressions of faith in opposition to the regime. The second of these groups regarded the whole development in Hungary and other "central European" states since 1945 as illegal, as it had been imposed by the Soviets and had never been legitimized by a social contract with the people; this group also stated that in the 1956 rising the people had attempted to restore the multi-party system which had existed until 1948.

Early in September 1981 "a limited group" of the intelligentsia was accused of "ideological confusion" in *Partelet,* the monthly theoretical organ of the Central Committee of the HSWP. While this "ideological confusion", the journal declared, constituted "no political problem, for Hungary's society is mature enough to emerge victorious from this struggle", no opportunity would be given to points of view hostile to the regime.

Exiled Parties

Social Democratic Party of Hungary

Leadership. Andor Bolcsfoldi (g.s.).

Having been prominent in the pre-war opposition to the Horthy dictatorship, the Hungarian Social Democrats participated in the Communist-dominated Government formed in April 1945 after the liberation of Hungary by the Red Army. The left wing of the party merged with the Communists in June 1948, but surviving elements opposed to the merger maintained the party's existence in exile. Following the October 1956 Hungarian uprising, the exiled party's then chairman, Anna Kéthly, was invited to become a member of the coalition Government formed by Imre Nagy but was unable to reach Hungary before the suppression of the revolution by Soviet forces in early November. Thereafter the exiled party included many of the 1956 generation of Hungarian refugees.

The Hungarian Social Democratic Party is a consultative member of the Socialist International and also a constituent party of the Socialist Union of Central and Eastern Europe (SUCEE).

People's Democratic Party

In exile since the Communists came to full power in the late 1940s, this party is affiliated to the Christian Democratic World Union.

Poland

Capital: Warsaw   Pop. 35,700,000

The Polish People's Republic is, under its Constitution as amended in February 1976, "a socialist state" in which the role of "the leading political force in the building of socialism" is vested in the Polish United Workers' Party (PUWP). The PUWP dominates a National Unity Front (NUF), of which the other members are the United Peasants' Party, the Democratic Party, the "social organizations of the working people" and "the patriotic associations of all citizens" (including the Roman Catholic *Znak* and *Pax* groups). The 1976 constitutional amendments also contained the provision that the state would "strengthen friendship and co-operation with the USSR and other socialist states". While supreme power is exercised by the Politburo of the Central Committee of the PUWP, the authority of the Republic is vested in the 460-member Diet *(Sejm)* elected by universal adult suffrage for a four-year term on a single list of the NUF. The official results of elections held on March 23, 1980, showed that 98.87 per cent of the electorate had taken part in the vote and that 99.52 per cent of the valid votes had been cast for the list of the NUF.

For the first time in any country of the Soviet bloc there emerged in Poland during 1980-81 a workers' movement which succeeded in creating a strong independent trade union federation. This new "Solidarity" movement effectively replaced the existing official trade union organization controlled by the state and confronted the Government with demands of an increasingly political nature, which were eventually seen as a threat to the regime. The movement was supported by a number of smaller groups, some of which were openly anti-communist.

The free trade union movement was also supported by the Roman Catholic Church, of which the vast majority of the population are practising members and which took part in some of the negotiations between the Solidarity leaders on the one hand and representatives of the Government and the PUWP on the other. These negotiations resulted in major concessions by the authorities but by the end of 1981 an impasse was reached between the two sides and on Dec. 13, 1981, a state of martial law was declared and power was assumed by a Military Council of National Salvation led by Gen. Wojciech Jaruzelski, who had earlier become Chairman of the Council of Ministers (Prime Minister) and First Secretary of the Central Committee of the PUWP. On Oct. 8, 1982, the *Sejm* effectively dissolved the Solidarity movement by adopting legislation which created the framework for the replacement of all existing unions by new and more closely controlled bodies. Although martial law was suspended on Dec. 31, 1982, some of its remaining provisions were transferred to the penal code and shortly afterwards the first of the new officially-sanctioned trade unions came into being.

Free Trade Union Movement

Solidarity *(Solidarnosc)*

Leadership. Lech Walesa (ch.).

The Solidarity movement arose out of the formation, early in 1980, of various independent workers' committees, strike committees and finally trade unions. An important event at the beginning of these developments was the holding of a service of commemoration in the Gdansk shipyard on Dec. 18, 1979, for workers killed by troops during demonstrations and strikes in 1970 (against major price increases) in Gdansk, Gdynia and Szczecin; the service, called by students and dissident

19

groups, was attended by some 4,000 persons, although many dissidents—including members of the Social Self-Defence Committee (KOR—see separate entry)—were arrested before and during the service. Some 25 workers at the Elektromontaz plant were dismissed for taking part in the service, and the staff of this plant thereupon formed, on Jan. 25, 1980, a five-member "workers committee" including Lech Walesa (who had been one of the organizers of the 1970 demonstrations and had since lost his job) to campaign for the reinstatement of the 25 workers.

Strikes which began during July-September 1980 as wage disputes soon assumed overtly political dimensions as the strikers called for the legalization of independent trade unions, the lifting of censorship in the Polish press, the release of imprisoned dissidents, the strengthening of the position of the Roman Catholic Church and changes in government priorities in social welfare. In August the strikers began to form inter-factory strike committees to negotiate directly with the authorities on demands covering, in addition to those on pay and working conditions, the disbandment of the official trade unions, the erection of a monument to the workers killed in 1970 and publication of all the workers' demands in the mass media.

By Aug. 23, 1980, the Government began to negotiate with the inter-factory committees, and on Aug. 30 an agreement was reached in Gdansk between an inter-factory committee led by L. Walesa and a government delegation led by Mieczyslaw Jagielski (a Deputy Premier), with the committee explicitly acknowledging the undisputed "leading force" represented by the Polish United Workers' Party (PUWP), while the Government, in addition to consenting to a new wage agreement, expressed readiness to recognize legitimate new unions which could be based on the strike committees, to introduce within three months a bill moderating the censorship laws and to permit the broadcasting of Roman Catholic church services on Sundays. A similar agreement was signed in Szczecin, and by Sept. 1 both regions were largely back to normal working. However, industrial unrest continued to spread elsewhere, in particular among coal miners in Silesia, with whose inter-factory committee agreement was reached on Sept. 3.

Solidarity was formally established at a conference held on Sept. 18, 1980, in Gdansk by some 250 delegates of unofficial trade unions formed in many areas during September 1980. On Sept. 24 Solidarity applied for the registration of its statutes by the Warsaw district court, but the court objected to Solidarity's statement that the holding of a major trade union post was incompatible with political office. Describing this statement as a breach of human and political rights, the court insisted that Solidarity should incorporate in its statute a specific recognition of the PUWP as the only "leading political force"—as had earlier been agreed by the Gdansk inter-factory committee at the end of August. Solidarity responded that its acceptance of the Polish Constitution was itself a guarantee of recognition of the role of the PUWP. When the presiding judge eventually announced the recognition of Solidarity, he added a statement amending several of the union's statutes, including those relating to the right to strike, and inserted among the statutes the disputed clause of recognition of the PUWP. Solidarity accepted the registration but not the amendments and applied to the Supreme Court for their annulment.

On Oct. 27, 1980, Solidarity presented new demands to the Prime Minister (Jozef Pinkowski), with an ultimatum threatening a national strike unless negotiations were begun immediately—on the reversal of the Warsaw district court's decision, the granting of greater access of Solidarity to the media, the right to a trade union newspaper, the implementation of all agreed but outstanding wage increases and the cessation of alleged harassment by local bodies. Following a further threat of a general strike the Supreme Court pronounced in favour of Solidarity on Nov. 10; as proposed by the latter, the recognition of the PUWP was incorporated in the annexe to the statutes.

It was announced on Nov. 17, 1980, that further disputes in Gdansk had been settled at a meeting between Solidarity and Stanislaw Kania (who had succeeded Edward Gierek as First Secretary of the PUWP on Sept. 6, 1980), and on Nov. 24 it was announced that Solidarity had been allotted a weekly hour-long broadcast on Warsaw radio.

The national co-ordinating commission of Solidarity announced on Dec. 10, 1980, that it had formed a "committee for the defence of those prosecuted for their convictions" to campaign for the release of political prisoners, which it described as "vital for the restoration of an atmosphere of confidence between the authorities and society". However, during early January 1981 Solidarity failed to reach agreement with the Government over its demand for a five-day working week. On Jan. 7 Solidarity militants declared every Saturday work-free and threatened strike action if any worker were penalized for taking any Saturday off. Following further strike threats "preliminary agreement" was reached on Jan. 30 on three issues—the free Saturday, access to the media and the registration of Rural Solidarity (see separate entry).

Under the final agreement reached on Jan. 31, 1981, between the Government and Solidarity the latter accepted (i) the norm of a 40-hour week and an eight-hour working day as a target; (ii) 38 work-free Saturdays during

1981; (iii) an interim government proposal for what amounted to a 42-hour working week (for which details were worked out on Feb. 18) and (iv) the publication of a nationally-distributed weekly newspaper of Solidarity (in addition to its three existing weeklies) and time to be allowed for Solidarity programmes on radio and television. However, these new agreements did not lead to immediate industrial peace.

Following his appointment as Prime Minister, Gen. Wojciech Jaruzelski called, on Feb. 12, 1981, on Solidarity members to resist agitators proposing "false anarchistic paths contrary to socialism" and stressed the Government's determination to "bar the way" to those who were striving "to achieve counter-revolution".

In a "resolution concerning the aims and methods of the union, dated Feb. 12, 1981, Solidarity accused the Government inter alia of having held up progress on the proposed laws on the trade unions and on the revision of censorship, and of having arrested activists in alleged violation of the Gdansk agreement. The resolution, however, also condemned "local and regional strikes pursuing disparate aims without the consent of the national co-ordinating commission, often against its advice" and "sometimes provoked by advocates of confrontation among those in authority as a means of disrupting our unity", which "would mean the destruction of our movement and would herald a period of uncontrolled social conflict".

On Feb. 13, 1981, the national co-ordinating commission of Solidarity indicated its willingness to comply with a request by Gen. Jaruzelski for "three months of honest work, 90 days of calm, to put some order into the economy". An official Solidarity spokesman said on Feb. 16 that Solidarity would support the new Government as long as it was offered a genuine partnership; he also denied PUWP allegations that Solidarity was attempting to supplant the party as the country's leading political force.

During March 1981 regional Solidarity committees took action over specific issues, e.g. in Lodz over the dismissal of five Solidarity members from a hospital and in Radom (on March 11) over several matters, including the charges against Jacek Kuron (the KOR chairman) and a demand for the dismissal of officials said to have been involved in the suppression of the 1976 riots.

At a meeting of the national co-ordinating commission of Solidarity in Bydgoszcz on March 23-24, 1981, L. Walesa was strongly criticized by J. Kuron and Karol Modzelewski (press spokesman for Solidarity) for his "autocratic" handling of the negotiations with the Government over the occupation (on March 16) of the United Peasant Party's headquarters in Bydgoszcz by members of Rural Solidarity. The meeting decided (i) to declare a four-hour national strike on March 27; (ii) to seek immediate new negotiations with the Government; and (iii) to call an indefinite general strike starting on March 31 unless such negotiations proved successful. S. Kania called this decision "a call for self-annihilation" and accused Solidarity of turning a local incident into a "national catastrophe". Talks between the Government and Solidarity on March 25 ended inconclusively after the Minister of Justice had failed to present a report on the Bydgoszcz incident as demanded by Solidarity, and the four-hour warning strike was observed by some 13,000,000 workers on March 27, 1981, bringing virtually the whole country's industry and communications to a standstill.

In the Soviet Union, the German Democratic Republic, Czechoslovakia and Hungary the latest strike action was strongly condemned as serving counter-revolutionary forces, and Tass (the official Soviet news agency) stated on March 29, 1981, that there was now "an open struggle" between Solidarity and the Polish state. However, on March 30 it was announced that agreement had been reached between Solidarity and the Government on the handling of the Bydgoszcz incident. Under this agreement the Government undertook (i) to withdraw police units from Bydgoszcz, (ii) to set up a special commission to examine the farmers' case for union recognition and (iii) to pay in full all workers who had taken part in the strike of March 27, while Solidarity undertook (i) to suspend the strike alert for March 31, (ii) to halt any other occupations or activities creating tensions and (iii) to set up mechanisms for the solution of local disputes without resorting to national strike action.

L. Walesa described the March 30 agreement as "a 70 to 80 per cent success" and thanked the Pope for his assistance (by having written to Cardinal Wyszinski, the Polish Primate, on the subject and having appealed for a peaceful settlement of the dispute). Although the national co-ordinating commission of Solidarity again severely criticized L. Walesa on March 31 for not having insisted on the formal registration of Rural Solidarity. L. Walesa firmly declared on April 11 that he would not resign as chairman of Solidarity as long as the possibility of "adventurism and irresponsibility" continued in the organization. The commission had earlier (on March 31) decided by 25 votes to four with six abstentions to call off the planned general strike.

On April 14, 1981, Solidarity issued a draft policy statement in which it argued that either rationing should be introduced for most goods or the "price mechanism" should be brought into play to reduce excess spending power (but with lower-income groups receiving additional assistance), and that luxury goods should be more heavily taxed and a progressive system of income tax should be introduced. It also declared its readiness to withhold all wage claims until the end of 1981, and described its aim as the achievement of social egalitarianism and its basic task as being to defend the working people and to ensure that the state also adhered to this principle. Moreover, the statement called for the observance of civil liberties such as "the right to profess one's own views, freedom of speech and the printed word, the right to honest information and to assemblies and free associations" and for the limitation of censorship measures. It attributed Poland's crisis to bureaucracy and the lack of democratic processes under previous administrations but claimed that "the severe economic crisis, the outbreak of social protest [in 1980] and the establishment of Solidarity [had] paved the way for reform and renewal". Proposals for such reform included "more autonomy for individual concerns, which should have more freedom to determine manning levels", and "an active policy of job creation by the state", which should form a fund for the aid of the unemployed and the retraining of displaced workers. It emphasized that Solidarity was "the main guarantee of the renewal process" but at the same time "must be determined and ready to make sacrifices".

The emergence of Solidarity in Poland was strongly opposed in the Soviet Union. The journal *Literaturnaya Gazeta* declared on May 13, 1981, that Solidarity had achieved nothing positive but had links with the "totalitarian, terrorist organization KOR" (the Social Self-Defence Committee) and was "a social movement following aims which have nothing to do with trade unionism but which are by their objective content political aims". The Central Committee of the Communist Party of the Soviet Union (CPSU), on June 7, accused the PUWP leadership of failure to control the "anti-socialist forces" in Poland and of allowing the latter to take control of the party's "horizontal structures" reform movement. (This movement within the PUWP consisted of various groups such as the Movement for Horizontal Consultations created in Gdansk in November 1980 to link like-minded party organizations in a "horizontal", i.e. not vertical or hierarchical, structure.) In a statement by the CPSU Central Committee, published on June 9, 1981, and dealing with the "profound crisis" in Poland which had "spread across the country's entire political and economic life", the need was stressed "to oppose in a determined manner any attempts by the enemies of socialism to take advantage of the difficulties". However, it was conceded that the PUWP had been "falling back step by step under the pressure of internal counter-revolution supported by im-

perialist foreign centres of subversion" and that "the enemies of socialist Poland" had been "gaining control of one position after another", with counter-revolution "using Solidarity's extremist faction as a strike force" and with "a wave of anti-communism and anti-Sovietism" developing.

The Central Committee of the PUWP approved on June 11, 1981, a resolution stating that politically motivated strikes were inadmissible and that partnership with Solidarity was acceptable only as long as the relationship was "based on socialist principles". During the ninth congress of the PUWP on July 14-20, 1981, the party's then First Secretary, S. Kania, declared inter alia that the PUWP saw positive elements in Solidarity and was ready to work with it, although there was concern over that element in Solidarity which attempted to turn it into a political party, "an opposition party in respect of the socialist state"; he claimed that this destructive element was being encouraged by KOR and "other opponents of socialism".

Increases in food prices by an average 100 per cent on July 22, 1981, were followed by violent protest demonstrations and strikes which the Central Committee of the PUWP described, on Aug. 12, as "a great danger to peace". On the same day Solidarity leaders called for a two-month voluntary suspension of all strikes and demonstrations—but this call was not followed by all regional sections of the organization. The national co-ordinating commission of Solidarity also suggested that members should volunteer to work on eight (normally work-free) Saturdays to aid the failing economy. At this time there was a succession of Warsaw Pact military manoeuvres near Poland's border and in the Baltic Sea, and on Sept. 1 S. Kania and Gen. Jaruzelski (then Prime Minister) had a meeting with four Soviet generals.

Internal unrest nevertheless continued. On Aug. 17, 1981, Solidarity called a two-day occupation and strike affecting most printing presses in protest against its inability to use the state-controlled media in answering criticism by the Government and the PUWP. The action virtually stopped all distribution of newspapers, and L. Walesa had some difficulty in preventing the organization's militant branches in Lodz, Wroclaw, Cracow and Lublin from continuing the action, which was formally ended on Aug. 20. Further Solidarity demands, for such things as uncensored coverage of the forthcoming congress of the movement, were rejected by S. Kania on Aug. 26.

L. Walesa had declared at a rally in Gdansk on Aug. 14, 1981 (the first anniversary of the outbreak of the shipyard strike): "We do not want to overthrow the power of the state. Let the Government govern the country, and we will govern ourselves in the factories." In a televised statement on Sept. 1 he said, however, that the authorities were "losing social acceptance" and that the situation was forcing Solidarity "to assume responsibility for the fate of the country".

Evidence of further disagreement emerged on Sept. 2-3, 1981, when the national coordinating commission of Solidarity accused the Government of retreating from the implementation of the agreements of August 1980 on censorship and the media. The Central Committee of the PUWP, approving a draft of the self-management bill, rejected Solidarity's demands for more extensive powers regarding the appointment of managers. On Sept. 4 S. Kania affirmed that the authorities were willing to declare a state of emergency.

Solidarity held its first national congress in two stages in Gdansk on Sept. 5-10 and Sept. 20-Oct. 7, 1981 (by which time it was said to have nearly 10,000,000 members). It re-elected L. Walesa as its chairman and approved a large number of resolutions. It was, however, still in dispute with the Government on (i) self-management in commercial enterprises, including procedures for appointing and dismissing managers; (ii) censorship and Solidarity's disputed claim to free and uncensored access to the mass media; (iii) government proposals for economic reform; (iv) the reduction of the meat ration from 3.7 to 3.0 kg per month; and (v) proposed food and tobacco price rises.

At the opening of the congress the minister in charge of trade union affairs (Stanislaw Ciosek) stated that the state structures were initiating and assimilating socialist renewal and stressed the need for Solidarity to co-operate with the Government but within "the political framework for the existence of any kind of organization" based on respect for (i) the principle of social ownership of the means of production; (ii) the constitutional role of the PUWP as the leading force in Polish society; (iii) the inviolability of Poland's international alliance; and (iv) Solidarity's undertaking not to play the role of a political party.

In the national co-ordination commission's report to the congress, presented on Sept. 6, it was stated that the winning of the right to free Saturdays had been a major success but that efforts to secure fair wage settlements had only limited success; that Solidarity had so far taken no direct action on economic matters but that the proven inefficiency of the Government now necessitated a more active economic strategy for the movement; that the authorities' monopoly of broadcasting systems encroached upon the rights of society as a whole; that Solidarity was the object of virulent, hostile and often slanderous propaganda; that Solidarity's access to the mass media was one of the basic conditions for stability and social calm in Poland; and that union consultation on the creation

of self-management systems in enterprises was a political prerequisite for the achievement of Solidarity's other major aims.

On Sept. 8, 1981, the congress issued a call to the *Sejm* to hold a national referendum before creating the proposed self-management law, failing which Solidarity would conduct its own referendum and even, if necessary, ignore the law after its approval by the *Sejm*. Also on Sept. 8 the congress approved a "message to the working people of Eastern Europe" stating inter alia (according to *Trybuna Ludu,* the organ of the PUWP): "We assure you that, despite the lies disseminated in your countries, we are a genuine, 10,000,000-strong representative organ of workers, created as a result of workers' strikes. . . . We support those of you who have decided to take the difficult path of struggle for a free trade union movement. . . . We believe that soon your representatives and ours will be able to meet and exchange experiences as trade unionists."

Finally the first stage of the congress issued, on Sept. 10, a programmatic declaration which contained the following paragraphs (according to the Polish press): "Solidarity's supreme goal is the creation of dignified living conditions in a Poland which is economically and politically sovereign. It is intended to create a life free from poverty, exploitation, fear and lies in a society organized on the principles of democracy and the rule of law. Today the nation expects: first, an improvement in food supplies, through the establishment of a control over their production, distribution and pricing, in co-operation with Rural Solidarity; secondly, an economic reform, through the creation of authentic workers' self-management, the elimination of the party's right to make senior appointments, and the introduction of effective economic mechanisms; thirdly, truth, through public control of the mass media and the removal of lies from Polish schools and culture; fourthly, democracy, through the holding of free elections to the *Sejm* and people's councils [i.e. organs of local government in the provinces—voivodships—on which issue the congress passed a separate resolution on Sept. 10]; fifthly, justice, through the ensurance of the equality of all before the law, the release of those imprisoned for their beliefs and the defence of those repressed for publishing or union activities; sixthly, saving the threatened health of the nation by protecting the natural environment, increasing health spending and guaranteeing the rights of handicapped people in society; and seventhly, coal for the population and for industry, through guarantees of appropriate living and working conditions."

The congress's first stage (ending on Sept. 19, 1981) gave rise to strong criticism from sections of the PUWP, whose Warsaw branch executive stated on Sept. 11 that Solidarity was developing into a political and social movement aiming at a counter-revolutionary change of the system. Some PUWP members urged the banning of Solidarity, thus engendering a further polarization of positions. A Solidarity bulletin claimed on Sept. 15 that the deputies to the *Sejm* had been undemocratically elected (as they had been presented mainly on uncontested lists), and J. Kuron, the KOR chairman, said on Sept. 16 that until free elections could be held power should be taken over by a "committee of national salvation" composed of the PUWP, other parties, the Church and the trade unions; he added that the PUWP as a whole was "completely and utterly paralysed" and that "sooner or later a situation will be reached in which nothing can be done with this Government".

The Politburo of the PUWP stated on the same day (Sept. 16, 1981) that the party would use all means to prevent a political takeover, but on Sept. 23 Stefan Olszowski, a hard-line member of the Politburo, said that a broad-based national front could be formed, including Solidarity and church representatives as well as those of political parties. On Sept. 25 the *Sejm* unanimously approved new laws on state enterprises and on workers' self-management, laying down inter alia that factory directors could not be appointed or dismissed without approval by both the management and the workers' councils (except in certain cases of key or strategic importance). The approval of these laws by the Government was severely criticized at the second part of the Solidarity congress, but L. Walesa repudiated those Solidarity members who "would like to overthrow everything, the *Sejm* included", and added that "within five years they would have replaced the system with greater totalitarianism than the present system".

On Oct. 7, 1981, the Solidarity congress approved overwhelmingly an eight-chapter programme in which it described itself "not only as the force able to protest but also as the force which desires to build a Poland which will be just for everybody" and as "the only guarantor for society" which would, however, have to act gradually to maximize its public support. Rejecting the Government's programme for economic stabilization because it failed to mobilize several important reserves in the economy and did not enjoy public confidence, Solidarity insisted on the abolition of centralized management of the economy and on its separation from political authority. The programme advocated the creation of a "social council for national economy" to "size up the Government's economic policy, the economic situation and economic legislation". It supported the right to work and called for measures to redeploy

labour rather than resorting to dismissals. It declared that democracy should be based "on the principles of philosophical, social, political and cultural pluralism"; that there should be "genuine and freely-elected workers' and territorial self-government bodies"; and that state legislation should guarantee the maintenance of basic civil liberties and respect the equality of all before the law. Democracy, it was postulated, should arise from the rule of the majority and a respect for the beliefs of the minority, and the interests of the workers were to be achieved primarily through negotiations, and only in the second instance through strikes. To ensure the survival of Poland through the coming winter, an "anti-crisis agreement" was needed, with Solidarity seeking an "honest and loyal dialogue" with the authorities in the best interests of Poland and all its citizens.

The second stage of the congress also decided (on Sept. 28) that Solidarity should have a centralized union structure (in accordance with a proposal by L. Walesa), with a 107-member national commission comprising 69 regionally-elected members (each representing 140,000 members) and the heads of the 38 regional chapters; the national commission itself would elect a 19-member presidium headed by the overall chairman of the organization.

On Oct. 16, 1981, S. Kania accused right-wing groups within Solidarity of deliberately obstructing every step taken by the Government to alleviate the crisis and of being the chief impediment to the implementation of the agreements of August 1980; he called on Solidarity to ban all strikes and to work on all Saturdays throughout the winter. Solidarity, however, rejected the first of these demands on Oct. 20 as contrary to its rights under international law. The Solidarity presidium had on Sept. 19 called for the suspension of "all unjustified strikes and those called before all possible means of agreement had been exhausted" but added on Sept. 20 that it could not agree to any negotiations on the content of the August 1980 accords and that it would not refrain from "any statutory permitted actions aimed at giving full effect to the social contracts concluded with the Government and ratified by the *Sejm*".

Despite an appeal by Solidarity to its members on Oct. 22, 1981, to avoid any further protest actions, strikes broke out in several areas, and on Oct. 23 the national coordinating commission called for a one-hour national strike on Oct. 28 in protest against alleged harassment of Solidarity officials by the authorities; it also threatened further selective "active strikes" unless by the end of October steps had been taken to improve the meat supply situation and to set up the proposed "social council for the national economy". The one-hour strike called for

Oct. 28 was generally observed throughout the country.

During the remaining weeks of October 1981 there were a number of incidents involving clashes between police and Solidarity members. On Oct. 30 the national co-ordinating commission called on Solidarity members to end all unco-ordinated local strikes—but some of these strikes nevertheless continued for a few days longer. On Nov. 3 the national co-ordinating commission called on workers to take control of their workplaces if necessary rather than to stop all production by striking. A meeting of the national co-ordinating commission held on Nov. 4, 1981, called for (i) for formulation of draft regulations for a revision of the procedures governing elections to the *Sejm* and the people's councils; (ii) the foundation of a social council to implement them; and (iii) the implementation of true self-management in factories.

By this time the Polish economic crisis had reached unprecedented proportions. On Nov. 12 it was officially stated that during the first 10 months of 1981 labour productivity had fallen by 14 per cent, the level of industrial production by 10 per cent, that of coal production by 20 per cent, that of construction by 21 per cent and that of exports by 15 per cent, while wages had increased by 25 per cent. At the same time L. Walesa appealed to workers in Western countries to exert pressure on their respective governments for the speeding-up of emergency aid to Poland because, he said, the political and economic reforms in Poland were in danger of collapse owing to "dangerous social tensions and spontaneous outbursts of popular anger". L. Walesa did not have whole-hearted support from some sections of Solidarity, however—as evidenced when Andrzei Gwiazda and 14 other members of the Gdansk regional executive resigned on Nov. 23 in protest against what they called his "excessively moderate" attitude towards the Government.

On Nov. 28, 1981, the PUWP Central Committee approved a call made by Gen. Jaruzelski (who had succeeded S. Kania as First Secretary of the PUWP on Oct. 18) for the development of an emergency powers law which would give the Government full powers for safeguarding the population and the economy. On Nov. 30 the Council of Ministers approved a series of bills to expedite the realization of the reforms due to be implemented in January 1982, but Solidarity rejected these measures as inadequately prepared and creating a "socially dangerous situation".

A new confrontation was created by a serious incident which began on Nov. 25, 1981, when, with the support of Solidarity, some 30 trainee firemen occupied a fire officers' training academy in Warsaw, demanding the "demilitarization" of the academy; on Dec. 2, however, armed police cleared the trainees out of the building.

At a meeting of the Solidarity presidium and regional heads in Radom on Dec. 3, 1981, L. Walesa was reported to have said that "confrontation" was inevitable and that Solidarity was aware that it was dismantling the system. J. Kuron was said to have stated that "total negation of the so-called government provisional pre-reform system and the state of emergency should become the field of confrontation" and also to have called for the preparation of "action to overpower the authorities". Militant Solidarity members were said to have called for the creation of a "so-called worker militia" armed with helmets and batons, its first task being the "liberation" of the radio and the television headquarters, and for the immediate establishment of a "social council for the national economy" to act as a "provisional national government".

On Dec. 4, 1981, the Solidarity presidium issued a statement in which it laid down conditions for achieving a national accord, including (i) the cessation of anti-union repression, (ii) the passage of a law on trade unions in a version approved by Solidarity, (iii) the holding of democratic elections to local and provincial councils and (iv) the establishment of the "social council for the national economy". Following a meeting with Archbishop Glemp, L. Walesa stated at a Solidarity presidium meeting on Dec. 10 that he had written evidence of a campaign by the authorities to provoke confrontation but that Solidarity would "not retreat any more" and would respond with strike action if the *Sejm* accepted either the trade union law or the emergency powers law.

Early in December 1981 the Polish authorities claimed to have conclusive evidence that Solidarity leaders were planning a deliberate confrontation with the Government with the ultimate aim of overthrowing it. Earlier, the Army had been strengthened by the extension of national service by two months on Oct. 16, and Gen. Florian Siwicki, the Army Chief of Staff, became a candidate member of the PUWP Politburo on Oct. 28.

At a meeting of Solidarity's national co-ordinating commission in Gdansk on Dec. 11-12, 1981, it was proposed to conduct a national referendum on Jan. 15, 1982, with the particular aim of obtaining a vote of no confidence in the Government. During the following night the armed forces detained virtually the whole Solidarity leadership (including L. Walesa) and on Dec. 13 the Council of State (exercising collectively the functions of the head of state) announced the introduction of a state of martial law and the creation of a Military Council of Salvation.

This Council and the Council of Ministers subsequently issued a number of decrees which in effect (i) banned all trade union and most other organized non-governmental activities; (ii) abolished the right to strike; (iii) provided for the internment of up to 6,000 persons in specially-erected internment camps; (iv) declared a large part of the economy to be under military discipline; (v) made work compulsory for most men; (vi) set up "summary trial" courts for dealing with infringements of martial law; (vii) closed down all except the official news media and most communications links, as well as closing the national frontiers and airspace; and (viii) reformed the higher education system. Among other measures taken by the authorities was an increase by about 300 per cent in retail prices of fuel and most staple foods with effect from Feb. 1, 1982.

In announcing the imposition of martial law (a "state of war"), Gen. Jaruzelski said that "a group of people presenting a threat to the safety of the state", including Solidarity activists and also activists of illegal anti-state organizations, had been interned. Although Solidarity was not officially banned, all gatherings were prohibited, all publications were subjected to prior censorship and the right of workers to organize and carry out "strikes of any nature whatsoever and demonstrations" were suspended.

Solidarity was reported to have set up, immediately after the declaration of martial law, a provisional executive to direct operations in the absence of its interned leaders and to produce a bulletin. However, strikes by Solidarity members in Gdansk ended on Dec. 15, 1981, and a rally in Warsaw on Dec. 17 was put down by troops with water cannon, one person being killed. There were also reports of several clashes between striking workers and troops, with seven miners being shot dead by troops near Katowice on Dec. 17. On Dec. 29, however, Poland was officially reported to be free of strikes.

During the first few weeks of martial law the Roman Catholic Church continued to press for the resumption of three-party negotiations between Solidarity, the Government and the Church. Gen. Jaruzelski said on Dec. 25, 1981, that the independent trade unions would continue to play a role in Poland's affairs.

At the end of January 1982 the total of martial law detainees was officially given as 4,177, held in 24 different camps. This figure included a number of former office-bearers in the PUWP and the Government who were held for alleged abuse of power while in office. Several Solidarity activists were sentenced to terms of imprisonment for from three to nine years for organizing strikes after Dec. 13, 1981. L. Walesa, who had also been detained, was formally interned on Jan. 26,

1982; in a letter (published in *Le Monde* on Feb. 1) he claimed that there was a campaign for his "gradual elimination" from the political arena.

A "Solidarity resistance committee" describing itself as the acting leadership of the union stated early in February 1982 that the organization's members would not attempt to negotiate independently with the authorities, as trade union unity was essential at this time. Thereafter there were frequent reports of Solidarity supporters being arrested for illegal trade union activities and the only two Solidarity presidium members still at large (Zbigniew Bujak and Wladyslaw Frasyniuk) called repeatedly for continued public resistance. On April 12, 1982, an unofficial Solidarity radio transmitter began weekly broadcasts in Warsaw, demanding a resumption of dialogue between the Government, the Church and the trade unions, the restoration of Solidarity and the release of martial law detainees. A resurgence of disturbances in May 1982, particularly in Warsaw and Cracow, coincided with an appeal by underground Solidarity leaders for protest actions on May 13 to mark the fifth month of martial law.

The Polish television network announced on July 11, 1982, that "Radio Solidarity" had been dissolved after the discovery and confiscation on July 8 of a set of broadcasting equipment and the arrest of a number of people. However, "Radio Solidarity" broadcast again on July 13, when it announced a two-month break in transmissions (the station's organizer, Zbigniew Romaszewski, having gone underground). A further "Radio Solidarity" transmitter was seized on Aug. 30.

It was reported on July 13, 1982, that underground Solidarity bulletins had called for the temporary suspension of strikes and protest actions in order to facilitate the rapid resumption of dialogue with the authorities; however, the PUWP daily organ *Trybuna Ludu* replied on July 15 that there could be "no agreement with the enemies of socialism, with the anti-socialist underground, and with those who still have not set aside the strike weapons, who distribute hostile publications and who encourage young people to demonstrate".

Social tensions worsened again at the beginning of August 1982, following the failure of the authorities to respond positively to the offer of negotiations with Solidarity, and on Aug. 1 a new appeal for mass resistance was launched by Zbigniew Bujak, who delivered a tape-recorded message to some 15,000 people attending a ceremony in a Warsaw cemetery to commemorate the Polish uprising of 1944. Z. Bujak's message coincided with a new leaflet campaign by Solidarity's acting leadership for the restoration of the union's rights, the release of all remaining detainees and the ending of martial law. *Trybuna Ludu* dismissed the new appeals on Aug. 3 as "dreams", but added that such unrealistic expectations could still endanger social calm, and on Aug. 12 the ("hard-line") army newspaper *Zolnierz Wolnosci* demanded a new crackdown on the opponents of the regime.

A major rally involving some 10,000 people was held on Aug. 13, 1982, outside the PUWP headquarters in Gdansk, but was dispersed by police using tear gas and water cannon; other rallies were reported on the same day in Warsaw, Wroclaw and Cracow. Heavy contingents of police and militia then moved into Gdansk in preparation for the second anniversary (on Aug. 16) of the forming of the Gdansk inter-factory strike committee (which had led to the ultimate foundation of Solidarity), but no incidents were reported there, although a demonstration of some 2,000 people took place on the same day in Warsaw.

Leaflets distributed by Solidarity in late August 1982 called for a nationwide protest, including strikes, to mark the second anniversary of the Gdansk agreement. Although the extent to which this call was followed remained unclear because of the severance of telephone links in many parts of the country, it became clear that major protests had taken place in several cities, notably Lubin, where five people were killed in several days of clashes with government riot squads (the "Zomos").

On Oct. 8, 1982, the *Sejm* approved two laws on trade unions which effectively dissolved all existing unions and created the framework for new and more closely controlled unions to replace them. The new legislation was intended primarily to dismantle Solidarity, whose underground leadership nevertheless affirmed that the union would continue in existence and called a one-day protest strike for Nov. 10, to be followed by a general strike in early 1983. However, the Nov. 10 action attracted only limited support, and amid a general easing of social tensions L. Walesa was released from internment on Nov. 12. During his detention the Solidarity chairman had been kept completely isolated from the public in remote locations but had reportedly refused to make any accommodation with the authorities. His wife had reported in March 1982 that he had refused an offer to be allowed to emigrate permanently from Poland.

On the basis of plans outlined by Gen. Jaruzelski on Dec. 12, martial law was suspended on Dec. 31, 1982—the Government thereby relinquishing its powers inter alia to intern people without trial, to impose curfews and to ban public meetings. The Government nevertheless retained the right to reimpose martial law at any time, while certain martial law provisions were institutionalized within the penal code, notably specifications that workers or students who stirred up unrest could be dismissed and also that military courts would continue to try those accused of major economic or social crimes. At the same time, seven members of the Solidarity presidium were excluded from a general release of political detainees, as were some 1,500 others who (according to a government statement on Jan. 4, 1983) had been convicted or were awaiting trial for political crimes.

On Jan. 3, 1983, the first of the new trade unions created under the October 1982 legislation came into being, it being officially stated that 2,500 such unions had been legally registered and that a further 4,000 applications were pending. Under the new regulations each new union could represent only one workplace or factory and strikes of a "political" character were banned. The acting Solidarity leadership had consistently condemned the new union regulations and had refused to enter into any discussions with the Government during their formulation.

L. Walesa himself, having returned to his home in Gdansk, came under various forms of pressure from the authorities in late 1982 and early 1983, including official inquiries into alleged irregularities in Solidarity's finances under his chairmanship and also in his own tax returns. On Dec. 16 he was prevented from delivering a speech at a rally in Gdansk to commemorate the 1970 food price demonstrations, having intended (according to a text pre-released to Western correspondents) to assert that the spirit of Solidarity remained alive and that "given time and different methods" the movement would achieve ultimate victory.

Rural Solidarity (Independent Self-Governing Trade Union for Private Farmers)

Leadership. Jan Kulaj (ch.).

Rural Solidarity was established in December 1980 as the (uncollectivized) Polish peasants' counterpart to the independent Solidarity trade union organization of industrial workers which had emerged earlier in the year. After an application for its registration had been deferred by the Warsaw district court on Dec. 30, 1980, farmers embarked on protest action involving the occupation of local government offices and agricultural strikes in various areas and the setting-up of a national strike committee in Rzeszow (southeastern Poland) on Jan. 12, 1981. Stanislaw Kania, then First Secretary of the PUWP, had said at a meeting of the United Peasants' Party (UPP) on Jan. 11 that there was "no room in the Polish countryside for a political opposition of an anti-socialist character".

A preliminary agreement reached on Jan.

30, 1981, between the Government and the national co-ordinating commission of Solidarity covered also the registration of Rural Solidarity. The Supreme Court, on the other hand, ruled on Feb. 10, 1981, that there was no legal basis for recognizing the organization as a trade union but that it could be registered as an association. The farmers thereupon threatened to withhold their produce from the market unless 60 specific demands were met, mainly on the level of state investment in agriculture. On Feb. 19 (after the appointment of Gen. Wojciech Jaruzelski as First Secretary of the PUWP), Rural Solidarity was granted (i) the right to private ownership of land (to be formalized in new provisions to be inserted in the Constitution), (ii) equality of treatment of private and state farms and (iii) increased government investment in agriculture. The organization's basic structure and policy were established at a meeting of 490 delegates in Poznan on March 8-9, 1981.

In an incident in Bydgoszcz, where police broke up the occupation of provincial council offices on March 19-20, 1981, by protesting farmers, the latter's leader, Jan Rulewski, was seriously injured; the incident led to two-hour protest strikes by Solidarity members in Szczecin, Torun, Grudziadz and Bydgoszcz on March 20, when Lech Walesa, the Solidarity chairman, expressed his personal opposition to a general strike (for which he was severely criticized at a meeting of Solidarity's national co-ordinating committee in Bydgoszcz on March 23).

On April 17, 1981, it was announced that the Government had reached a 10-point agreement with the private farmers and had undertaken (i) to create by May 10 the legal basis for registration of Rural Solidarity, (ii) to incorporate the farmers' rights in the new trade union law and (iii) to adopt no disciplinary measures against those occupying party offices. The farmers in turn agreed to call off all protest actions. The Warsaw district court finally registered Rural Solidarity as an "Independent Self-Governing Trade Union for Private Farmers" on May 12. J. Kulaj claimed that it represented some 2,500,000 of Poland's 3,500,000 private farmers (who worked on about 70 per cent of all agricultural land and produced about 80 per cent of the country's agricultural output). The *Sejm* had on May 6 almost unanimously approved the proposed amendments to the trade union bill.

On Aug. 17, 1981, Rural Solidarity was, under an agreement with the Ministry of Agriculture, awarded a share in the rural development fund, but on Aug. 28 Rural Solidarity called on its members to withhold tax contributions in protest against the Government's alleged failure to approve the agreement and its alleged intention of re-negotiating it so as to include the official Polish Union of Agricultural Circles and Organizations (PZKiOR).

Under the martial law regime proclaimed on Dec. 13, 1981, Rural Solidarity was suspended (along with the urban free trade union movement) and its leader, J. Kulaj, interned. After the latter had undertaken to avoid resistance to the Government and to co-operate with the UPP, he was released from detention in late April 1982. Nevertheless, some 3,000 farmers participated in a rally in Warsaw on May 12, 1982, to commemorate the first anniversary of the legalization of Rural Solidarity.

Under legislation adopted by the *Sejm* on Oct. 8, 1982, creating the framework for new and more closely controlled workers' organizations, Rural Solidarity was effectively replaced by new organizations which lacked the essential character of trade unions. The Government argued that trade unions of private landowners existed in no country in the world and that landowners' associations with the character of agricultural chambers were a more normal form of organization for private farmers. Events since the registration of Rural Solidarity, it maintained, had shown that a complete reform of the system for the representation of farmers was required, since "the ambitions and the selfish interests of the leading groups became predominant, and a significant role was played by the influences, and not infrequently the pressures, exerted by external centres alien to the interests of the countryside".

The legislation specified that the names of the national, provincial and parish organizations grouped within the PZKiOR would be changed in order to incorporate the word "Farmers", thus emphasizing that the PZKiOR represented farmers (both state and private) as well as other rural groups. It was stated that the new organizations were regarded as the appropriate forum of activity for members of Rural Solidarity. As in the case of its industrial counterpart, however, the Rural Solidarity organization appeared to have continued widespread popular support notwithstanding its effective dissolution.

Other Groupings

Amnesty International, Polish Section

Leadership. Adam Wojciechowski (ch.).

The chairman of this group was on March 30, 1980, sentenced to two months' imprisonment for distributing leaflets recommending that the public should boycott the elections to the *Sejm* which were held on March 23 that year (and in which 98.87 per cent of the electorate were officially stated to have taken part).

Armed Forces of Underground Poland

This group emerged on Feb. 18, 1982, when a policeman was killed in Warsaw and nine members of the group (including a Roman Catholic priest) were arrested. Eight of those arrested were on Sept. 9, 1982, sentenced to imprisonment for terms of from two to 25 years; no details of the composition and aims of the group were disclosed.

Club for a Self-Governed Republic—Freedom, Justice, Independence

Leadership. Jacek Kuron (ch.).

The chairman of this Club had previously been chairman of the Social Self-Defence Council (KOR—see separate entry). Its foundation meeting on Nov. 22, 1981, was broken up by police who seized a document, signed by some 40 people, including Janusz Onyskiewicz (a member of the presidium of Solidarity), and stating inter alia: "The belief that the movement of social protest would lead quickly to the emergence of a democratic and independent state has shown itself to be an illusion. What has happened is that the totalitarian power, subjected to the pressures of an independent organization, has become paralysed in the sphere of government."

The authors of the document therefore considered it "essential to create ideological political formations" which were to become "the nuclei of future political parties in a democratic state". While the document did not openly attack Poland's links with the Soviet Union, it claimed that the model of Polish-Soviet relations evolved during the Stalinist era was still in practice and "deprived Poles of their civic rights", as it severely limited their right to self-determination.

The authors of the document also stated their belief that armed Soviet intervention in Poland was unlikely but that since August 1980 the Polish people had "undermined the model of relations with the Soviet Union and must develop a new relationship based on their newly-found national identity and on the principles of national sovereignty". The signatories of the document undertook to form similar clubs at their places of work or residence.

Trybuna Ludu, the organ of the PUWP, stated on Nov. 25, 1981, that the foundation of the club had been deliberately timed by those extremist Solidarity leaders who were frustrated by the moderate line taken by Lech Walesa (the Solidarity chairman) in such a way as to upset the talks between Solidarity and the Government. Detained after the imposition of martial law on Dec. 13, 1981, J. Kuron at first called for continued peaceful protest against martial law but by April 1982 he was advocating a "mass operation" to overthrow the authorities, involving a "co-ordinated attack on all centres of power and information".

Committee for the Defence of Prisoners of Conscience

A national conference of this Committee, held in Radom on Nov. 21, 1981, was attended by some 80 delegates. The conference had been declared illegal by the Ministry of Justice, which had denied that there were any political prisoners in Poland.

Confederation for an Independent Poland (KPN)

Leadership. Robert Leszek Moczulski (ch.).

This organization, which the Polish authorities regarded as an anti-Soviet movement, was to have announced on Feb. 27, 1980, that it intended to nominate candidates for the election to the *Sejm* to be held on March 23, 1980, for which all official candidates were nominated by the National Unity Front dominated by the PUWP. However, its planned meeting was banned by the authorities and two of its leaders were arrested. On Dec. 17, 1980, the KPN announced the temporary suspension of its activities in view of the country's "dangerous situation".

On March 6, 1981, four leading KPN members—R. L. Moczulski, Romuald Szeremitiewow, Tadeusz Stanski and Tadeusz Jandziszak—were formally charged with seeking the violent overthrow of Poland's constitutional system. During the trial R. L. Moczulski was reported to have told the court on July 3 that he rejected the legitimacy of the Yalta agreement (by which the Allies had laid down the post-war boundaries in Europe) and of the Polish People's Republic, and that he supported the concept of a "Greater Poland" (including eastern territories which had become part of the Soviet Union in 1945). Following the imposition of martial law on Dec. 13, 1981, the four were all convicted on Oct. 8, 1982, and sentenced to prison terms of seven years (R. L. Moczulski), five years (R. Szeremitiewow and T. Stanski) and two years' suspended (T. Jandziszak).

At the first congress of the free trade union movement Solidarity (held in September-October 1981) the KPN had advocated the extensive reprivatization of agriculture and commerce. The military newspaper *Zolnierz Wolnosci* had accused the KPN on Nov. 25, 1981, of setting up a paramilitary wing.

Confederation of Independent Trade Unions

This Confederation was reported to have been founded on Jan. 8, 1981, by 19 independent unions affiliated to neither the official trade union movement nor to Solidarity.

Movement for the Defence of Human and Civil Rights of Man

Leadership. Robert Leszek Moczulski, Andrzej Czuma (spokesmen).

Established on March 27, 1977, this Movement had among its 18 founding members Gen. (rtd.) Mieczyslav Boruta-Spiechowicz, Zbigniew Sikulski, Adam Wojciechowski (the Polish representative of Amnesty International), three members of the Workers' Defence Committee (WDC) and three Roman Catholic priests. The WDC was, however, on June 8, 1977, reported to have broken off relations with the Movement because it doubted the latter's authenticity.

The spokesmen of the Movement declared at its foundation that they would seek changes in Polish laws to bring them into line with the UN Covenants on Civil and Political Rights and on Economic, Social and Cultural Rights ratified by the Polish Government on March 3, 1977, and that they hoped to work in co-operation, and not in confrontation, with the authorities. The Movement was on March 28, 1977, condemned as "anti-Polish" by the editor-in-chief of *Trybuna Ludu,* the organ of the PUWP, who denied that Poland's existing laws were not in line with UN declarations and covenants. The political tendency of the Movement (which had a publication called *Opina*) was said to be Christian democratic; its leader was also chairman of the anti-Soviet Confederation of Independent Poland (see separate entry).

Katowice Marxist-Leninist Seminar

This group of hard-line Communists, created as the "Katowice Forum" within the ruling PUWP, issued a statement and four resolutions on May 15, 1981, condemning certain developments in the party. In its declaration the Forum stated that the "political disarmament" of the PUWP had been in progress for some years and that this was partly responsible for the party's failure to deal effectively with the disturbances of August 1980 leading to the recognition of Solidarity. The party had, the declaration said, been under "alien ideological influences" with the result that "the entire party and the individual members [had] lost the ideo-political and programmatic compass for the struggle for socialism".

In its resolutions the Forum asserted (i) that "revisionism and right-wing opportunism", "bourgeois-liberal and Trotskyist-Zionist views, nationalism, agrarianism, clericalism, anti-class solidarity and anti-Soviet views and moods cultivated by the right wing" were gaining such ground that there was a "threat of a revisionist coup d'état" with the passive consent of the PUWP leadership; (ii) that the dominance of

the right-wing views in the party had obscured the erosion and discrediting of the organs of public order by organizations such as Solidarity; (iii) that Poland was threatened by "anarchy, counter-revolution and anti-Soviet psychosis" (which it must oppose as part of its internationalist duty); and (iv) that the mass media had actively assisted in attacks on the ideological unity of the party and its statutory structure.

The resolutions of the Forum were, however, condemned by numerous party delegates and in particular by the Politburo (on June 2, 1981), which described the Forum's statement as "harmful" in the present situation.

In a statement published on July 6, 1981, the Katowice Forum called for the non-recognition of those delegates to a PUWP congress who had not been elected in accordance with party statutes, and it claimed that the party was in danger of losing its working-class base and that this fact had been ignored by the party press which was "infiltrated by extremists".

On Sept. 30, 1981, the Forum announced that it had been reconstituted as the Katowice Marxist-Leninist Seminar, whose declared aim was to lead the struggle for the consolidation of the PUWP. The press of the German Democratic Republic (GDR) published, on Nov. 6, an open letter sent by the Seminar to the Socialist Unity Party (SED) of the GDR, calling for assistance in countering the increased support for private enterprise in Poland.

Polish Home Army of Resistance

The name of this group was used by four terrorists who temporarily occupied the Polish embassy in Berne (Switzerland) on Sept. 6, 1982, threatening to blow the building up—including themselves and 13 hostages—unless the Polish authorities lifted the state of martial law in Poland. The incident was ended on Sept. 9 when Swiss anti-riot police stormed the embassy and arrested four men, the hostages being freed without injury. Solidarity spokesmen in Poland disclaimed any connexion with the group and described the incident as a possible "provocation" by the Polish authorities.

Social Self-Defence Committee (SSDC or KOR)

Leadership. Jacek Kuron (ch.).

KOR was established on Oct. 3, 1977, and replaced an earlier Workers' Defence Committee (WDC), which had been formed on Sept. 23, 1976, and had, without being officially recognized, given financial aid to the families of workers who had been dismissed or imprisoned after strikes and demonstrations against rises in food prices announced on June 24, 1976, but withdrawn on the following day. Early in 1977 the WDC began to challenge the official attitude to the question of human rights. Although Edward Gierek (then First Secretary of the PUWP) had stated that no action would be taken against the WDC, several of its members were in January 1977 fined for "illegal collection of funds".

In May 1977 WDC supporters accused the Civic Militia of having killed a student in Cracow on May 7 after he had collected signatures for a petition calling for a commission of inquiry into the prosecution of workers on charges arising out of riotous demonstrations. (Students in Cracow subsequently formed a new solidarity committee to replace the existing official student organization.) Also in May 1977 five WDC members were detained without trial for three months; after writing a letter to the prosecutor-general appealing for their release, Prof. Edward Lipinski, the doyen of Poland's economists and a WDC member, was expelled from the PUWP. The five WDC members were, however, released on July 23, 1977; the charges against one of them were withdrawn; and five workers imprisoned in connexion with riots were released.

When the majority of the WDC members decided to replace the organization by KOR, the latter's objects were listed as the collection of information regarding political, racial or religious repression as well as any violation of human or civic rights and also the provision of moral and legal aid to victims of arbitrary bureaucratic measures. The 23 founder members of KOR included Prof. Lipinski, Jerzy Andrzejewski and (Mrs) Halina Mikolajska. On Oct. 20, 1977, a new independent monthly called *Glos* ("Voice") published a "Declaration of the Democratic Movement" signed by 110 persons, including five members of KOR. Claiming that the existing decay of authority was caused by the fact that citizens were deprived of their rights and the state of its sovereignty, the declaration stated that there was "a large social base to undertake a social struggle for democracy and independence in a lasting way and on a broad scale". The declaration called for freedom of belief, speech, assembly and work, and for the application of the UN covenants on human rights, which would require basic legal changes in Poland, including the liberalization of education, trade unions and science and the creation of a consumers' movement.

Adam Michnik, a leading member of KOR, declared in October 1977 that the "Democratic Movement" was not an opposition in the traditional sense and did not want power but action in defence of civic and human rights and for the extension of democratic freedom. He also took the line that in terms of the 1975 Final Act of the Helsinki Conference on Security and Co-operation in Europe (CSCE) respect for human rights was no longer "the internal affair of each country" but was an international problem. In August 1978 KOR entered into a co-operation agreement with the Charter 77 movement in Czechoslovakia.

During the strikes for higher wages in July 1980 J. Kuron, writing in KOR's journal *Robotnik* ("The Worker"), advised strikers on how to conduct wage negotiations but warned them against carrying disputes on to the streets, as this had caused armed confrontations in 1970 and 1976. Nevertheless, workers in a number of enterprises campaigned not only for the right to elect independent delegates to the official trade unions but also for the right of their unofficial "workers' committees" to form interfactory organizations which would negotiate directly with the authorities on such issues as a complete revision of the trade union system in Poland. During August 1980 shipyard workers in Gdansk and Szczecin, after striking and occupying the shipyards, achieved considerable concessions in this respect (see separate entry for Solidarity). Negotiations between a Gdansk strike committee led by Lech Walesa and a government commission led by Mieczyslaw Jagielski (a Deputy Premier) led to the conclusion of a wage agreement and government recognition of legitimate new unions as well as other government concessions, while the strike committee explicitly acknowledged that the PUWP remained the undisputed "leading force" in the country. A similar agreement was reached in Szczecin, and after parliamentary approval of these agreements work was back to normal in both regions by Sept. 1, 1980. KOR, on the other hand, warned workers (in *Robotnik* on Oct. 19, 1980) that the actions of certain elements among them appeared likely to provoke Soviet armed intervention in Poland.

By February 1981 KOR was increasingly attacked in the press (not only in Poland but more especially in that of the Soviet Union, the German Democratic Republic and Czechoslovakia) for alleged subversive propaganda links with right-wing groups in London and elsewhere with the aim of undermining the stability of Polish society through its extremists' involvement with Solidarity, the independent trade union movement. J. Kuron and A. Michnik were strongly attacked during a debate in the PUWP Central Committee in February 1981, and on March 5 J. Kuron was arrested and formally charged with "publicly defaming the Polish nation, the Polish People's Republic, the state system and its highest organ". However, he was released after undertaking to present himself to the authorities twice a week. A. Michnik was arrested on March 12, and on June 24 *Pravda* (the organ of the Central Committee of the Communist Party of the Soviet Union) claimed to have documentary evidence that he had been in contact with Western spies working in Eastern Europe, according to two women who had in March 1979 defected from West to East Germany.

At the end of the second part of the first congress held by Solidarity, Prof. Edward Lipinski announced on Sept. 28, 1981, that KOR considered its work as completed and had therefore decided to dissolve itself, the struggle for an independent Poland having now been taken over by "the strong arm of Solidarity".

Exiled Movements

Since the establishment of Communist rule after World War II a number of Poland's former political parties have continued to exist in exile, as does a "Polish government in exile" established in London following the German conquest of Poland in 1939.

Polish Christian Labour Party

Leadership. Konrad Sieniewicz (g.s.).

This party was formed in 1937 as a merger of two formations with roots in 19th-century Polish politics (the National Workers' Party and the Christian Democratic Party). It formed part of the London-based government in exile during World War II, following which it was forced to suspend its activities in Poland in July 1946. The exiled party, now based in Rome, is affiliated to the Christian Democratic World Union.

Polish Socialist Party

Leadership. Stanislaw Wasik (ch.); Tadeusz Prokopowicz (g.s.).

This historic Polish party formed part of the London-based government in exile during World War II, after which it continued as an exiled party in rejection of the forcible merger with the Communist Party instituted in Poland in December 1948. The exiled party is a member of the Socialist International and a constituent party of the Socialist Union of Central and Eastern Europe (SUCEE).

Romania

Capital: Bucharest   Pop. 22,200,000

In the Socialist Republic of Romania the Communist Party has the leading role, as reaffirmed in the 1965 Constitution. There is a Grand National Assembly elected for a five-year term by all citizens above the age of 18 years and from one or more candidates in single-member constituencies. Authority is exercised in part through the Front of Socialist Democracy and Unity, a popular front organization, the National Council of which acts as a consultative body to the Council of Ministers (the Government). For the national minorities there are also two consultative National Councils, one Hungarian and the other German.

Ultimate power is in the hands of a 15-member Permanent Bureau of the Executive Political Committee of the Central Committee of the Romanian Communist Party. The Bureau is presided over by President Ceausescu, who is also head of state and General Secretary of the party.

Government is strongly centralized, and there is no evidence of the existence of organized groups of dissenters (except for an attempt to set up an independent trade union). Civil rights are limited and emigration is strictly controlled, with the result that there have been a number of cases of illegal emigration and of defections.

Human Rights Activists

Following the publication of the "Charter 77" manifesto in Czechoslovakia there appeared in Paris, on Feb. 9, 1977, the text of a letter signed by eight Romanian intellectuals who declared their solidarity with the manifesto and with the peoples of Eastern Europe who, they claimed, were under "foreign occupation". The signatories stated in particular: "The Romanian occupation of Romania is even more painful and more efficient than a foreign occupation. We all live under the same boot, the same violation of elementary rights, the same lies. Poverty, economic chaos, demagogy, insecurity and terror reign everywhere." This letter subsequently received support from 128 other Romanians.

The eight signatories of the letter declared, in another letter addressed to the 35 Governments which had signed the Helsinki Final Accord of 1975 and released in Belgrade on Feb. 15, 1977, that Romania's commitment to respect for human rights and freedom of movement and of information, as laid down in the Constitution and the international conventions signed by the Romanian Government, were "nothing but empty words".

President Ceausescu thereupon, in a speech on Feb. 17, 1977, attacked "traitors who denigrate their country to please their masters and to pocket large amounts of money" and claimed that there was "intensified activity by certain neo-fascist circles" abroad and that Western countries were even supporting "outcasts and traitors by granting them funds and facilities ... to agitate against the Helsinki resolutions, détente, peace and co-operation in Europe".

Among the authors of the two letters, Paul Goma (a writer) was on March 16, 1977, quoted as saying that there were in Romania four mental hospitals where opponents of the regime were detained, and this allegation was said to have been confirmed by Dr Ion Viana, a psychiatrist who had drawn attention to such "misuse of psychiatry" in October 1976.

Goma was arrested early in April, expelled from the Writers' Union on April 22, but allowed to leave the country five months later. At a press conference in Paris on Nov. 24, 1977, he made a strong attack on the Romanian regime, asserting inter alia that labour camps had been reopened; that psychiatric internment methods had been reactivated; that thousands of people had been forcibly displaced, among them 4,000 miners; that he himself had been ill-treated during his imprisonment in April-May 1977; and that Elena Ceausescu (the President's wife and a member of the Permanent Bureau of the Communist Party's Central Committee) had ordered the destruction of a church in Bucharest and the withdrawal from libraries of all books about and pictures of churches. Goma was one of three Romanian émigrés to whom parcel bombs were addressed from Madrid in February 1981.

A leading figure among those who expressed concern at the situation of ethnic minorities in Romania was Carol Kiraly, a Romanian of Hungarian extraction and a former high-ranking official of the Romanian Communist Party, who repeatedly made allegations of repression of minority groups. In an open letter sent to the party leadership in December 1977 (and published in the West in January 1978) he alleged that Hungarians in Romania (who according to official statistics numbered 1,700,000) were subject to discrimination and that this form of oppression "in violation of Romania's Constitution" included the closure of Hungarian universities and schools (such as the closure of the Hungarian section of the University of Cluj in Transylvania in 1977), the suppression of the Hungarian language and the appointment of Romanians to nearly all key positions in towns with Hungarian majorities. He stated that there was "a wide gap" between the Government's theory and its practice regarding its policies on ethnic groups and that "forced assimilation" was being applied to all minority groups in the country (principally Hungarians, Germans and Serbs).

Following talks with government ministers and officials, Kiraly was obliged to abandon his campaign and agreed, on Feb. 11, 1978, to move to the remote Transylvanian town of Caransebes, but he was reported to have refused to renounce his appeal and to declare that his letter was a fake or a fabrication of the (US) Central Intelligence Agency and Radio Free Europe. In March 1978 he was removed from his post as vice-president of the Hungarian National Council but he remained a member of the Communist Party. The Romanian Government branded him as a traitor and denied all allegations of repression of minorities. At meetings of the Hungarian and German National Councils in Bucharest on March 13-14, 1978, the presidents of these two Councils emphasized that there was "full equality of rights of all citizens in the country without distinction as to nationality".

While C. Kiraly had claimed that his letter had the support of some 16 prominent Romanians, it was reported on April 24, 1978, that three leading members of the Hungarian community had sent separate appeals to the Romanian leadership protesting against the Government's alleged discriminatory policies towards the minority groups and demanding a number of improvements. In particular Prof. Lajos Takacs (who was an alternate member of the Communist Party's Central Committee and a former chancellor of the University of Cluj, and who was re-elected vice-president of the Hungarian National Council on March 13, 1978) made 18 demands for improvements, which included (i) the allocation of increased powers to the Hungarian National Council in order to enable it to select and delegate the representatives of the group to local and central bodies, (ii) the creation in the Romanian Parliament of a permanent commission responsible for matters concerned with the minorities, and

(iii) the drawing-up of a new statute for the various nationalities in the country. He also asked for the Hungarian language to be used on a much wider scale, complaining that almost half of the Hungarian pupils in secondary and vocational schools were being educated in the Romanian language only. These demands do not appear to have elicited any public reaction by the Government.

Free Trade Union of Romanian Workers

Leadership. Ion Cana; Gheorghe Brasoveanu; Nicolae Dascalu.

Following its establishment, this union published a manifesto in which it called for the legalization of unofficial trade unions and for the implementation of the right to free association.

In April 1979 the union, in an open letter to President Ceausescu, protested against the frequent arrests of its members. These included I. Cana and G. Brasoveanu (an economist), said to be confined in psychiatric institutions in March 1979, and N. Dascalu, who succeeded them as chairman of the union and who was in June 1979 sentenced to 18 months in prison for allegedly passing state secrets to Amnesty International. In addition Fr Gheorghe Calciu-Dumitreus was imprisoned in June 1979 for alleged involvement with the union (as reported on June 13, 1980).

(The official Romanian trade unions admitted in November 1980 that they had not always adequately represented the interests of the workers. In a paper published by the central council of the unions on Nov. 16 it was stated inter alia that, although the unions enjoyed the right of co-determination in all economic affairs and organizations, this right had not always been observed, to the disadvantage of the workers.)

Exiled Party

Social Democratic Party

Leadership. Eugenie Boeuve Voinea (Paris rep.).

Originally founded in 1893, the Romanian Social Democratic Party was split when the left wing broke away in 1921 to form the Communist Party. Following the Social Democratic-Communist merger of October 1947, opposition Social Democrats were progressively outlawed, but those who escaped from the country maintained the party's existence in exile.

The Romanian Social Democratic Party is a consultative member of the Socialist International and a constituent party of the Socialist Union of Central and Eastern Europe (SUCEE).

Union of Soviet Socialist Republics (USSR)

Capital: Moscow   Pop. 265,500,000

The USSR (Soviet Union) is, under its 1977 Constitution, "a socialist state of the whole people" in which "the Communist Party of the Soviet Union (CPSU) is the leading and guiding force of Soviet society and the nucleus of its political system, of all state and public organizations". The USSR comprises 15 Union Republics, by far the largest of which is the Russian Soviet Federative Socialist Republic (RSFSR). There are also Autonomous Republics (16 within the RSFSR and four in three other Union Republics) and Autonomous Regions (five within the RSFSR and three in three other Union Republics). There are Supreme Soviets (Parliaments) for the USSR and for each of the Union Republics, the Autonomous Republics and the Autonomous Regions. There is a USSR Council of Ministers headed by a Chairman (Prime Minister) and there are Councils of Ministers in each Union Republic.

There are no officially recognized opposition organizations, but a number of groups have been established from time to time to campaign for the observance of civil rights. The principal documents cited by such groups are the 1948 Universal Declaration of Human Rights (on the adoption of which the Soviet Union had abstained from voting), the 1967 International Covenants on Economic, Social and Cultural Rights and on Civil and Political Rights (the ratification of which by the Soviet Union was announced on Sept. 26, 1973), and also the Final Act of the 1975

Helsinki Conference on Security and Co-operation in Europe (CSCE), of which the Soviet Union was a signatory.

The Soviet Union has always emphasized that the rights specified in the above-mentioned covenants could be restricted in the interests of internal security, public order, public health or morals, and the rights and freedoms of others; it has not ratified an additional protocol to the Covenant on Civil and Political Rights empowering a Human Rights Committee to consider communications from citizens of a signatory state complaining of violations of the covenant.

The task of ensuring internal security is carried out by the State Security Committee (*Komitet Gosudarstvennoye Bezhopasnosty,* KGB), the secret police first set up after the 1917 October Revolution and successively known as the Cheka, the GPU, the NKVD (Public Security Department), the MVD (a tribunal with powers to deal with political offenders, abolished in 1953) and thereafter the KGB.

The civil rights groups formed in the Soviet Union have included a Soviet section of the London-based Amnesty International; the "Helsinki Group" (to monitor fulfilment of the civil rights provisions of the CSCE Final Act); independent trade unions; organizations propagating autonomy for national minorities and the prevention of their Russification; groups campaigning for freedom of religious worship; and other groups, in particular among Jews, calling for freedom to emigrate. A number of intellectuals have proposed various forms of changes in the country's political and social system and demanded freedom of expression for writers and artists. An important role in the activities of these "dissidents" has been played by privately produced typescripts circulated as unauthorized publications known as *samizdat*.

Penalties to which dissenters are exposed range from expulsion from official bodies (such as the Writers' Union of the CPSU), dismissal from employment and restriction to a certain locality ("internal exile") to imprisonment in penal institutions, including labour camps of varying degrees of severity, and to internment in psychiatric hospitals—or a combination of these forms of punishment. A number of dissidents have been deprived of their nationality, allowed to emigrate or even expelled from the USSR.

Although the cause of dissenters in the Soviet Union has received considerable attention in the West, it has also been pointed out that it has not elicited widespread response in the USSR. In a survey on *Dissent in the USSR—Politics, Ideology and People,* published in 1975 by the Johns Hopkins University Press, Walter O'Connor came to the following conclusion: "Dissent and dissenters may be a natural product of over 50 years of Soviet history, but just as natural is their failure to strike a responsive chord among the masses. The interest in freedom and the rule of law is not broad enough, is not sufficiently a 'mass' interest, to make its accommodation critical."

Civil Rights Movements

Details are given below of groups which have been active in the Soviet Union in the field of civil and human rights. An important activity of this movement was the publication of the *Chronicle of Current Events,* which appeared regularly—at first every two months—from April 30, 1968, onwards in *samizdat*, i.e. as self-published literature issued in typescript of not more than 10 copies (which was not subject to censorship). The principal function of the *Chronicle* was to record developments in the civil rights movement and in particular trials and other official action affecting dissenters. Those found guilty of producing or distributing copies of the *Chronicle* were liable to severe penalties, and mere possession of a copy was also a punishable offence.

Action Group for the Defence of Civil Rights in the USSR

On May 20, 1969, the 15 civil rights activists who had formed this Group—who included Pyotr Yakir and Anatoly Levitin-Krasnov—as well as 39 other persons (among them Alexander Yessenin-Volpin, Zenaida Grigorenko and Vyacheslav Chornovil) signed an appeal to the United Nations Commission for Human Rights to review the question of the alleged violation of civil rights in the

Soviet Union. The appeal contained the following passage:

"We, the signers of this letter, deeply disturbed by the increasing political persecutions in the Soviet Union, and perceiving in this a return to the Stalin era when our entire country was gripped by terror, appeal to the UN Human Rights Commission to defend the human rights being trampled on in our country. We appeal to the United Nations because our protests and complaints, addressed for a number of years to the higher state and judicial instances in the Soviet Union, have received no response of any kind. The hope that our voice might be heard, that the authorities would cease the lawless acts which we have constantly pointed out—this hope has been exhausted. Therefore we appeal to the United Nations, believing that the defence of human rights is the sacred duty of this organization."

Referring to specific trials, including those of Sinyavsky, Daniel, Bukovsky, Ginsburg and others (see section on "Prominent Dissidents" below), the appeal stated that they had been held "with gross violations of procedural norms, above all of the principles of publicity and of the impartiality of the judicial inquiry". It condemned as "especially inhuman" the placing of normal persons in psychiatric hospitals because of their political convictions and stated that recent arrests suggested that "the Soviet punitive organs" had "resolved once and for all to suppress the activity of persons protesting against arbitrariness in our country".

On Oct. 1, 1969, it was stated in a letter to U Thant, then UN Secretary-General, signed by 46 persons (including A. Yessenin-Volpin, Natalya Gorbanyevskaya, Viktor Krassin, Z. Grigorenko and P. Yakir) that the Action Group's appeal to the UN Commission for Human Rights had led to further police repression of its authors. The signatories appealed to U Thant to use his personal influence "to intervene against human rights violations in our country and to take steps to present this issue before the UN Human Rights Commission for consideration".

Amnesty International, Soviet Section

The chairmanship of the Soviet Section of Amnesty International was held by Dr Valentin Turchin (a physicist) from 1974 to 1977; he was temporarily detained in February 1977 and arrived in Vienna on Oct. 14 of that year, having been granted permission to leave the USSR for Israel (although he was not a Jew). He was succeeded as chairman of the Section by Georgy Vladimov, a writer who was in 1978 denied permission to attend an Amnesty International annual congress in England.

In July 1977 Maj.-Gen. Pyotr Grigorenko, a leading human rights activist, claimed that the Soviet authorities had agreed on a plan to liquidate all human rights groups in the USSR, including the Amnesty International section. On Nov. 3, 1977, the Section appealed to the authorities to abolish the death penalty (which was still applicable to treason, murder, rape and "economic crimes").

Committee for Human Rights

This Committee was set up in November 1970 by Dr Andrei Sakharov, Dr Andrei Tverdokhlebov and Dr Valery Chalidze, with Alexander Solzhenitsyn as a corresponding member. The Committee's main object was to make representations to the authorities on alleged violations of human rights and to appeal for clemency towards persons convicted of anti-state activities. In 1971 Dr Igor Shafarevich was elected to the Committee; Alexander Galich, a writer, was associated with it as a corresponding member, and Alexander Yessenin-Volpin (a mathematician) and B. I. Zuckermann as experts. In July 1971 the Committee was affiliated to the International League for the Rights of Man based in New York, and it issued its own typewritten journal *Social Problems*.

A. Galich was expelled from the Writers' Union on Dec. 29, 1971, for allowing his works to be published abroad and encouraging Jews to emigrate to Israel. Dr Chalidze was on Nov. 16, 1972, allowed to travel to the United States to give a number of lectures but on Dec. 13 of that year he was informed that he had been deprived of his Soviet nationality.

Cultural Information Group

The formation of a group to gather and disseminate information on "violations by the authorities of international agreements on culture" was announced on May 3, 1978, by Oskar Rabin and Iosif Kiblitsky (both artists) as well as Boris Amarantov (a mime), Leonid Pinsky (a literary critic) and Yury Mikhailov (a poet).

Public Group to assist the Fulfilment of the Helsinki Accords in the Soviet Union ("Helsinki Group")

The formation of a Public Group to assist the Fulfilment of the Helsinki Accords—i.e. the Final Act of the Conference on Security and Co-operation in Europe (CSCE) signed in Helsinki on Aug. 1, 1975—was announced on May 13, 1976, by nine persons. This so-called "Helsinki Group" included as its leader Dr Yury Orlov (a physicist) and also Maj.-Gen. (rtd.) Pyotr Grigorenko, Anatoly Marchenko and Yelena Bonner Sakharova (the wife of Dr Andrei Sakharov).

In a document issued late in July 1976 the Group maintained that the USSR had no intention of fulfilling its international obligations in the humanitarian field; that there had been no improvement in the granting of permission to emigrate; and that, although concessions had been made to those dissidents who were best known in the West, repression was perhaps more rigorous than before against those who obtained no publicity. The document gave details of persons arrested for political offences since the Helsinki conference (some of them having been sent to mental hospitals). Further such details were supplied by the Group in a document issued on Oct. 30, 1976.

The Soviet interpretation of the provisions of the CSCE Final Act was given in an article published in *Pravda* on Dec. 25, 1975, and entitled "Peaceful Coexistence and Social Progress". In this article it was stated inter alia: "We reject categorically the demands for so-called liberalization of the regime [in the Soviet Union] because those who talk about human rights and so-called pluralism of a political system want to force these notions in their bourgeois interpretation upon us." The Western idea of pluralism, it was stated, did not give expression to the interests of the various social strata but served their division and the formation of political opposition, which jeopardized the revolutionary achievements of the workers and advocated "freedom of all forces, including the anti-socialist ones", and this was not acceptable to the Soviet Union. Those who propagated human rights in the USSR were said to be interested not in "the free development of the individual in all directions" but only in using human rights "for action against the socialist system".

In March 1977 the Moscow group was joined by two new members—Dr Yury Mnyukh (a physicist) and Prof. Nahum Meiman (a mathematician). The latter became acting chairman of the group (as announced on Nov. 7, 1977) after Maj.-Gen. Grigorenko, who had been chairman between February and November 1977, had left for the United States. Dr Mnyukh and his wife were, during the same year, allowed to leave the country for Israel.

During 1976-77 branches of the Helsinki Group were set up (i) in Armenia in April 1977 by Edvard Arutunian (an economist), Robert Nazarian (an engineer) and Samuel Ossian (a student); (ii) in Georgia by Dr Zviad Gamsakhurdia (a writer) and Merab Kostava (a musicologist); (iii) in Lithuania, where members included Viktoras Piatkus (a Lithuanian nationalist and Roman Catholic); and (iv) in the Ukraine by Maj.-Gen. Grigorenko, Mikola Rudenko (a writer) and Olexy Tikhy (a teacher), the leadership of this branch subsequently passing to Oles Berdnyk (a writer). However, these branches had all been suppressed by the authorities by 1981 and most of their active members sentenced to various terms of imprisonment for "anti-Soviet agitation and propaganda".

As regards the original Moscow group, by early 1982 virtually all its founding members had been either imprisoned, exiled or sent into internal exile. In view of this constant pressure, Yelena Bonner Sakharova announced on Sept. 8, 1982, that the Helsinki Group had been disbanded—a decision which was regarded as a significant victory for the Soviet authorities in their campaign against political dissent.

Working Committee to investigate the Use of Psychiatry for Political Purposes

This Committee was established as a sub-committee of the Public Group to assist the Fulfilment of the Helsinki Accords in the Soviet Union (the "Helsinki Group"). In a book entitled *Punitive Medicine* (which reached the West in 1977), a prominent member of the group, Alexander Podrabinek, listed some 200 cases of political dissidents being held in mental institutions in the Soviet Union. On Aug. 15, 1978, Podrabinek was sentenced to five years' internal exile for "spreading fabrications known to be false".

The Soviet practice of confining political dissidents to mental hospitals had become more widely known in the West from 1966 onwards. According to an issue of the *Chronicle of Current Events* which reached the West in January 1970, the first mental hospital for political prisoners was established before World War II at Kazan (about 400 miles east of Moscow), two others were set up after the war and three more such institutions were created between 1965 and 1968. At the Serbsky Institute of Forensic Psychiatry in Moscow a "special diagnosis" department was set up with the alleged purpose of providing medical justification for decisions taken by the KGB. Political "patients" in these hospitals were kept in the same cells as mentally disordered persons who had committed serious crimes (such as murder or rape) and some inmates who had feigned mental illness to escape from labour camps found the conditions in these institutions so bad that they begged to be returned to the camps.

Alexander Solzhenitsyn claimed in a French television appeal on April 11, 1975, that the number of people held in lunatic asylums in the USSR included 7,000 persons whose crime was "not to think the same thoughts as those in power" and who were being injected with substances which caused suffering and gradually destroyed their brains.

According to a statement made in London on Aug. 31, 1977, by Dr Avtandil Papiashvili, a psychiatrist from Tbilisi (Soviet Georgia) who had been granted political asylum in Austria, the Soviet practice was largely based on theories of Dr Andrei Snezhnevsky, director of the Soviet Institute of Psychiatry in

Moscow, which "with little proof" widened the boundaries of schizophrenia with the result that it could be "scientifically" diagnosed in mentally healthy people. On the other hand Prof. Edvard A. Babayan, leader of a Soviet delegation at the sixth congress of the World Psychiatric Association (held in Honolulu on Aug. 28-Sept. 3, 1977), emphasized (on Aug. 30) the "humanitarian character" of Soviet laws on psychiatry. He maintained that to exclude errors every patient was examined by at least six or seven psychiatrists before being interned in a psychiatric clinic, and denied that any healthy person had ever been placed in a mental hospital in the Soviet Union.

Psychiatrists who did not co-operate with the KGB were also liable to be tried. Thus Dr Anatoly Barabanov (one of seven psychiatrists who, according to an announcement by Amnesty International in London on March 6, 1978, had refused to collaborate in the imprisonment of dissidents in hospitals) was arrested in 1976 for his sympathetic attitude towards inmates at the Sychovka Special Psychiatric Hospital in Moscow and was later said to have been confined in a maximum-security psychiatric hospital near the Chinese border. Moreover, Dr Anatoly Koryagin was in May 1981 sentenced to seven years of imprisonment to be followed by five years of exile for "anti-Soviet agitation and propaganda" after he had communicated to the West the results of his examination of a number of "dissidents" whom he had found sane.

The work of the Working Committee finally came to an end on July 21, 1981, when its last active member, Feliks Serebrov, was sentenced to four years' hard labour to be followed by five years' internal exile for "anti-Soviet agitation and propaganda". (On Oct. 17, 1977, he had been sentenced to one year in a strict-regime labour camp for using an incomplete work pass.)

The Soviet practice had earlier been condemned by medical organizations outside the Soviet Union, in particular by the world psychiatric congress held in Honolulu in 1977. Following continued opposition to the practice by the World Psychiatric Association, the Soviet section of this organization withdrew from it in February 1983.

Prominent Dissidents

Although during the early 1960s there had been public denunciation of the "personality cult" and of repression under Stalin's regime, trials continued to be held of persons for their activities arising out of political dissent; such actions by the authorities increased during the 1970s in the context of the development of groups calling for the observance of civil and human rights in the Soviet Union.

State prosecutors frequently laid charges of infringement of Article 70 of the penal code of the Russian Soviet Federative Socialist Republic (RSFSR) which stated: "Agitation or propaganda carried on for the purpose of subverting or weakening Soviet power . . . or circulating for the same purpose slanderous fabrications which defame the Soviet state and social system, or circulating or preparing or keeping, for the same purpose, literature of such content, shall be punished by deprivation of freedom for a term of six months to seven years and by exile for a term of two to five years." Corresponding provisions are contained in the penal codes of the other constituent republics of the USSR. The "deprivation of freedom" usually consisted of detention in labour camps with regimes of varying severity, and "exile" meant restriction in internal exile at a remote locality for a period following that of imprisonment. From the mid-1970s, moreover, the Soviet authorities increasingly resorted to the policy of allowing prominent dissidents to leave the country and then depriving them of their Soviet nationality.

The cases of some of the more prominent dissidents against whom action has been taken by the Soviet authorities in recent years are described below.

Andrei Amalrik

Andrei Amalrik, an historian and dramatist, was on Nov. 12, 1970, sentenced at Sverdlovsk to three years in a strict-regime labour camp for defaming the Soviet state. He was reported to have stated, before sentence was passed, that he wished to refute the allegation that his statements were directed against his country and his people, and he attributed his trial to "the cowardice of a regime that regards as a danger the spreading of any thought or idea alien to its top bureaucrats". Amalrik had in 1965 been sentenced to 2½ years' exile for "parasitism" (i.e. being without regular employment). On July 16, 1973, he was sentenced to three years in a labour camp for "slandering the Soviet state", but this sentence was, on Nov. 13, 1973, commuted to three years' internal exile at Magadan (Siberia), where he was given employment at a scientific institute.

During 1975-76 he was on several occasions temporarily arrested for visiting Moscow without permission, but on June 23, 1976, he was granted a visa for Israel, and he reached the Netherlands (with his wife) on July 15 of that year.

Amalrik declared repeatedly that he would continue his activities in the cause of human rights. On June 29, 1976, he was quoted as saying that "the democratic movement" in the Soviet Union had changed "both the climate in our society" and the idea formed abroad of this society; that without the movement there would have been no schism among communist parties, since protest against repression had made it evident that such repression existed; and that without the movement there would probably have been no possibility of emigration from the Soviet Union.

Amalrik admitted that progress in the Soviet Union would be very much slower than he had forecast in an essay entitled "Will the Soviet Union survive until 1984?" which he had written in 1969. In this essay he had ruled out the possibility of increasing liberalization inside the Soviet Union but had suggested that the regime would collapse between 1980 and 1985 as the result of a major military defeat or the outbreak of strikes or armed clashes—although the process might be delayed if the armed forces took control. He had also forecast the attainment of independence by the non-Russian nationalities, either peacefully or by force.

In 1977 Amalrik endeavoured to induce the French and West German Governments to make representations to the Soviet Union on the human rights issue. He died in France in 1980.

Vladimir Borisov

Vladimir Borisov, a founder-member of the Committee for Human Rights in 1970 (see section on Civil Rights Movements above) had been detained at a psychiatric hospital in Leningrad in 1964-68 and again in 1969 because of activities on behalf of the civil rights movement. He was rearrested on Dec. 25, 1976, and again taken to a mental hospital in Leningrad but on Jan. 18, 1977, he was reported to have been declared sane. On March 5 of that year he was again released (having spent nine of the 13 previous years in mental hospitals); later in 1977 he refused an offer of permission to leave for Israel. He became one of the founder members of the Free Interprofessional Association of Soviet Workers (SMOT), established in October 1978 (see section on Free Trade Unions below), was again arrested in August 1979 and on June 22, 1980, was deported to Vienna.

Vladimir Bukovsky

Vladimir Bukovsky, a biologist and poet born in 1943, was committed to a mental hospital in 1962 after he had published a poem in a clandestine magazine, and again in 1965 for organizing a protest demonstration against the arrest of Sinyavsky and Daniel (see below), and in this connexion he was sentenced to three years' imprisonment on Sept. 1, 1967.

After his release he condemned, in an interview with a US journalist in 1970, the practice of detaining dissidents in mental hospitals. On March 29, 1971, he was arrested and again taken to a psychiatric hospital, but was declared sane and was tried for attempting to persuade two army officers to transmit information abroad, trying to smuggle printing equipment into the country in order to disseminate "subversive material" and circulating "slanderous" information on the Soviet social and political system. He denied these charges but was sentenced, on Jan. 5, 1972, to two years in prison and five years in a strict-regime labour camp, this sentence being upheld by the Supreme Court of the RSFSR on Feb. 22, 1972.

From his prison Bukovsky was in December 1975 reported to have sent a letter to Alexei Kosygin, then Chairman of the USSR Council of Ministers, to protest against the policy of Russification which had led to the detention of "numerous Armenians, Lithuanians, Ukrainians, Jews, Tartars and others in concentration camps and prisons".

On Dec. 18, 1976, Bukovsky was exchanged in Zurich against Luis Corvalán Lepe, the secretary-general of the Chilean Communist Party who had been held in detention in Chile since September 1973, after an agreement on such an exchange had been reached between the respective Governments.

Speaking in Zurich on Dec. 19, 1976, Bukovsky described the exchange as "an extraordinary event" because it meant that for the first time the Soviet Union had officially recognized that it held political prisoners. He also expressed the view that the Helsinki agreements (of the CSCE) had been "a Soviet manoeuvre" to achieve unilateral disarmament of the West and to prevent Western human rights campaigners from "interfering" in the internal affairs of the Soviet Union. Since the agreement, he said, the life of political prisoners in the Soviet Union had become very much more difficult, and he himself intended to devote all his energy to the cause of such prisoners in the USSR and throughout the world.

On March 1, 1977, Bukovsky was received by Vice-President Walter Mondale and President Carter in Washington, where the US President was stated to have given assurances that his commitment to the concept of human rights was permanent and to have added that he would like his public declarations to be productive and not harmful and to "convince our own nation and countries other than the Soviet Union that we wish to support the freedom of the individual and the right to free expression of opinion".

Yuli Daniel

Yuli Daniel, a translator and author who had used the pseudonym Nikolai Arzhak, was given a five-year labour camp sentence on Feb. 14, 1966, after being tried together with Andrei Sinyavsky (see below) on charges of smuggling and publishing abroad works "actively used in the ideological struggle against the Soviet Union" and also of "disseminating slanderous works".

In defence of his book *Moscow Calling,* a fantasy written in 1960-61 and describing "a day of permissible murder" proclaimed by the Soviet Government, Daniel said that its idea was that "man must remain human . . . and be true to himself and take no part in anything against which his conscience revolts" (such as the establishment of a new personality cult, which he feared to be imminent). He was expelled from the Writers' Union on Feb. 22, 1966.

Yury Galanskov

Yury Galanskov, a poet, was on Jan. 12, 1968, sentenced to 12 years' hard labour for working with and for the People's Labour Union (see section on External Organizations below), allegedly since 1962. He had been expelled from Moscow University in 1961 for contributing a poem to an underground review, and in 1966 he had edited *Phoenix 66,* a clandestine magazine in which he attacked the Soviet writer Mikhail Sholokov for defending the Sinyavsky-Daniel trial. On Nov. 2, 1972, he was reported to have died in Camp 3 of the Mordovian complex of labour camps (300 miles south-east of Moscow).

Alexander Ginsburg

Alexander Ginsburg, a writer, was on Jan. 12, 1968, sentenced to seven years' hard labour on charges of collecting information and distributing anti-Soviet literature for the People's Labour Union (see section on External Organizations below). He had been involved in the publication of clandestine journals and books, including a review called *Syntax* in 1960 and a "white book" on the trial of Sinyavsky and Daniel in 1966. Following his release on Jan. 22, 1972, after serving a two-year prison sentence on charges of fraud, he became, in 1976, the administrator of a fund set up by Alexander Solzhenitsyn to aid political prisoners and their families in the Soviet Union.

On July 13, 1978, he was sentenced at Kaluga (100 miles south of Moscow) to eight years in a special-regime labour camp for anti-Soviet activities and propaganda, involving in 1973-77 engagement in subversive activities and the receipt of money from abroad with which he was accused of having "financed hostile activities of criminal elements, including professional murderers, former members of gangs and henchmen of the German fascists"; he was also charged with having, "in order to undermine and weaken the Soviet system . . . , systematically produced and circulated documents containing slanderous inventions discrediting the Soviet state and social system". Conducting

his own defence, Ginsburg said in a final speech on July 13 that he did not consider himself guilty and did not ask for mercy. He admitted that he had prepared and distributed literature banned by the Soviet authorities but claimed for himself the right to freedom of conscience as laid down in the Universal Declaration of Human Rights.

Anatoly Kuznetsov

Anatoly Kuznetsov was a novelist whose books *Babi Yar* (published in 1966) and *The Fire* (published in 1969) were strongly criticized by the Soviet authorities. In *Babi Yar,* which dealt with the massacre of Kiev Jews by the Germans in 1941, he was said to have concentrated too much on the Jewish victims of the Nazis and to have paid too much attention to those Soviet citizens who collaborated with the Germans. In *The Fire,* it was alleged, he had depicted Soviet workers as "cynics, scoundrels, fiddlers and alcoholics".

Kuznetsov arrived in Britain on July 24, 1969, and was on July 30 granted permission to remain in Britain indefinitely. Giving reasons for leaving his country, he wrote in a statement published in *The Sunday Telegraph* on Aug. 3, 1969, that during 25 years of writing not a single one of his works (which had been sold in millions of copies) had been printed in the Soviet Union as he had written it. He stated in particular: "For political reasons the Soviet censorship and the editors shorten, distort and violate my words to the point of making them completely unrecognizable. Or they do not permit them to be published at all. . . . Artistic freedom in the Soviet Union has been reduced to the 'freedom' to praise the Soviet system and the Communist Party and to urge people to fight for communism. The theoretical basis for this is an article which Lenin wrote 60 years ago on 'The Party Organization and Party Literature', which laid down that every writer is a propagandist for the party. His job is to receive slogans and orders from the party and make propaganda out of them."

Kuznetsov went on to explain that he could no longer carry on without seeing his works in the form in which he had written them, and he dissociated himself from everything which had been published under his name in the USSR or elsewhere in translation from Soviet editions, since these publications were not really his own books. He was expelled from the Writers' Union early in August 1969.

Anatoly Marchenko

Anatoly Marchenko, a writer, was on Aug. 21, 1968, sentenced to one year's imprisonment for visiting Moscow without the necessary permission. He had earlier signed a protest against Soviet pressure exerted on Czechoslovakia, and in his book *My Testimony* he had described conditions in the Potma labour camp where he had been a prisoner in 1960-66. On July 4, 1969, he was sentenced to a further three years for "slandering the Soviet state and social system". He was released on July 28, 1971, and subsequently lived in exile at Tarusa (some 60 miles south of Moscow) where he was arrested on Feb. 26, 1975. On March 31 of that year he was sentenced to four years in strict exile for failing to comply with the conditions of his existing exile by joining his wife in Moscow, and he was subsequently transferred to Chuna (near Bratsk in Siberia). In December 1974 he had formally renounced his Soviet citizenship and applied for permission to emigrate to the United States.

Vladimir Maximov

Vladimir Maximov, born in 1932, had his first verse published in 1956, and his novel *Man Alive* was in 1965 made into a play and performed in Moscow. He became an editor of the journal *October,* in which stories, novels and plays of his were published, but in 1967 he was removed from the journal's editorial board and the journal published no further works by him. His novel *Seven Days of Creation,* purporting to give a truthful picture of Soviet working-class life, was published in West Germany in 1971. In 1973 he was expelled from the Writers' Union for allowing an "anti-Soviet" firm to publish his books, among them his novel *Quarantine.*

Together with Dr Andrei Sakharov, Dr Igor Shafarevich and the writers Alexander Galich and Vladimir Voinovich, he signed, on Jan. 6, 1974, a statement in defence of Alexander Solzhenitsyn, defending an author's right to publish what his conscience dictated as "one of the most basic in civilized society". He also signed a statement issued by Dr Sakharov on Feb. 14, 1974, demanding that Solzhenitsyn should be allowed to work freely; that *The Gulag Archipelago* should be published together with all documents giving a full picture of security police activities; and that an international tribunal should be set up to investigate the crimes committed. He was subsequently allowed to leave the country for France, and from 1974 onwards was editor of the dissident magazine *Kontinent* published in West Germany.

Roy Medvedev

Dr Roy A. Medvedev, born in 1925, was a historian and sociologist and was head of a department at the Research Institute of Vocational Education at the Academy of Pedagogical Sciences of the USSR in 1960-70, but from 1972 onwards he was a free-lance author.

Of his book *Let History Judge* (on the history and implications of Stalinism) he submitted a first version to the State Publishing House for Political Literature *(Gospolitizdat)* and to the Central Committee of the CPSU in mid-1964, by which time several books criticizing Stalin were withdrawn (while in 1965 eulogies of Stalin began to reappear in connexion with the 20th anniversary of the victory over Nazi Germany). In this book (published in Britain in March 1972) Dr Medvedev attempted to analyse the origins and consequences of Stalinism, which he regarded as a perversion of Leninism. It was based on material collected from many survivors of Stalin's purges (but not on official archives, to which he had been denied access) and gave a detailed description of the purges, with biographical data on hundreds of victims, of the functioning of the security police and of the system of concentration camps.

In another book, *Socialism and Democracy 1972* (reported to be circulating in *samizdat* in August 1972), he reviewed Soviet achievements and failures, problems of civil liberties and the conflicting neo-Stalinist and democratic currents inside the CPSU.

In reply to Dr Sakharov's statement published in France on Oct. 7, 1973 (see below), Dr Medvedev expressed his views in a statement issued on Nov. 7 and entitled "The Problems of Democratization and Détente". He maintained that democratization would have to come from Soviet society, including its present and future leaders; that the intellectuals were too weak to bring it about, and workers and peasants remained politically passive; and that those inside the party and the state apparatus who realized the need for change were mainly at the lower level and exercised little influence. He therefore felt that any move towards democracy had to result from "initiatives coming from above and supported from below" (just as the denunciation of Stalin by the 20th CPSU congress in 1956 had been the result of a complex struggle at the top).

Acknowledging that pressure from abroad could produce some effect, he stated that Soviet dissidents should look for support primarily to left-wing circles in the West because the right-wing parties were "seeking not so much to facilitate the victory of 'socialism with a human face' as to compromise both communism and socialism as a whole and thus deliver a blow first of all to the left-wing forces in their own country". In the long run, he felt, international détente would promote the broadening of democratic rights and freedoms in the USSR.

Early in March 1975 he issued, as editor-in-chief, an unauthorized journal, *20th Century,* as an ostensible renewal of *Politchesky Dnevnik* ("Political Diary"), issued in the late 1960s by "liberal socialists". The basic aim of the new journal was stated to be "a combination of socialism and democracy". The journal also published the prison camp memoirs of Dmitri P. Vitkovsky.

Dr Medvedev's views on the "intellectual opposition" in the Soviet Union were set out in an article in *The Guardian* (of London) on May 14, 1975. He distinguished three movements of this opposition: (i) that of the "liberal Marxists" advocating democratic and humanitarian socialism, (ii) that standing for the spiritual renovation of society on the basis of religion and (iii) that of the various nationalistic groups—the first of these being to him "the most important and the most promising". Although, he wrote, underground literature *(samizdat)* had "shrunk considerably" as a result of "administrative repression" it was through Western media that the views of Soviet dissidents became better known to the people in the Soviet Union. Western opinion, however, could not have a decisive importance, and substantial change could only be achieved by the country's internal forces. In the long run, agreements between Western governments and the Soviet Union might become "quite a weighty factor of change in the USSR", but "only the establishment of a wide and solid system of co-operation and of economic interdependence between East and West will increase the effectiveness of the influence of Western opinion on the political atmosphere in the USSR".

He also wrote: "Many people imagine that there is complete uniformity within the Soviet establishment both as regards the Soviet system as well as its management which is said to operate without any 'feed-back'. This view is schematic and false. . . . In one form or another . . . 'feed-back' exists. . . . On the majority of shortcomings in Soviet life, including separate outbursts of mass dissatisfaction among workers in the provinces, the Soviet leadership is much better informed than the rank and file."

Dr Medvedev distinguished three main trends in the Soviet leadership—"a group of reactionaries led by Mikhail Suslov", who wanted "a stiffening of internal policy" and opposed "any rapprochement or co-operation with their capitalist neighbours"; the more moderate politicians whose aim was "stability", led by "Brezhnev, Andropov, Grechko, Gromyko, Kosygin and Podgorny", who had been victorious over "the Suslov group and the Shelepin and Semichastny group who were the main organizers of Khrushchev's dismissal"; and the "technocrats", comparatively younger leaders who wanted "to modernize the management of the economy and science" and would like to have "closer links with the West and a more tolerant internal policy". Dr Medvedev foresaw "a possible alliance between these tech-nocrats and the main representatives of the 'moderate' group".

Of the political and religious statements made by Solzhenitsyn and also his letter to Soviet leaders published in 1974 (see below) Dr Medvedev claimed that they had caused most dissidents "undoubted disappointment". Early in June 1977 Dr Medvedev alleged that measures taken by the Soviet authorities against leading human rights activists were "not routine actions of the KGB" but had been "sanctioned at the highest party level" (i.e. by the Politburo of the CPSU) in the autumn of 1976 in order to sever the dissidents' contacts with the West.

In January 1983 it was reported that the Moscow public prosecutor had warned Dr Medvedev that, unless he discontinued his "anti-state activities", he would be arrested.

Zhores Medvedev

Dr Zhores (Jaurès) A. Medvedev (twin brother of Dr Roy Medvedev) was a biologist and worked at the National Institute for Medical Research in London from 1973 onwards. A book written by him on the history of the genetic debate concerning the theories of Trofim D. Lysenko was circulated in *samizdat* from 1962 onwards. (Lysenko had propounded the theory that hereditary changes could be induced in plants and animals by environmental influences and had wielded virtually dictatorial powers in Soviet biological and genetic studies under Stalin and partly under Khrushchev until he was dismissed in 1965.) In his book (published in English in 1969 under the title *The Rise and Fall of T.D. Lysenko*) Dr Medvedev offered a scientific criticism of the theories of Lysenko and his followers. After Khrushchev had made it clear, in July 1962, that he fully supported Lysenko's enterprises, Dr Medvedev tried to withdraw the *samizdat* copies of his book, but this proved impossible. The book was highly praised by Alexander Solzhenitsyn.

After he had had his book published in the United States and had also protested against restrictions on communications between Soviet and foreign scientists, Dr Medvedev was removed from his post as director of a biological laboratory in 1969 and was temporarily held in a psychiatric hospital at Kaluga in May-June 1970. His experiences in that hospital were described in a book entitled *A Question of Madness* (published in Britain in 1971), written in collaboration with his brother. In the book psychiatrists were said to have diagnosed him as suffering from "poor adaptation to his social environment", "paranoid delusions of reforming society" and "a split personality, expressed in the need to combine scientific work in his field with publicist activities".

In January 1973 Dr Medvedev was granted permission to carry out research in London for a year, but while in New York he was, on Aug. 7, 1973, informed that he had been deprived of his Soviet citizenship and his passport was seized. Tass, the official Soviet news agency, stated on Aug. 8 that these steps had been taken because Dr Medvedev had "fabricated, sent to the West and spread slanderous materials discrediting the Soviet state, social system and people".

Of the intellectual dissidents in the Soviet Union, Dr Medvedev said in London on Nov. 13, 1973, that a group of them, including Dr Sakharov, wanted to make the Soviet Union a kind of Western democracy and give it a mixed (capitalist and socialist) economy, but that this group had little support inside the country and had therefore started to appeal to foreign countries to set preconditions for their co-operation with the USSR as a means of inducing change (e.g. the Jackson amendment to the US trade reform legislation, which would require countries receiving preferences to give undertakings on the freedom of emigration, in particular of Jews). Dr Medvedev claimed that there was in the Soviet Union a more moderate group of dissidents, supported by most scientists, who endorsed demands for democratization as long as it did not mean a complete change in Soviet society and the demands were put forward within the existing legal system.

Valentyn Moroz

Dr Valentyn Moroz, a Ukrainian historian, was on Nov. 18, 1970, sentenced (on a charge of "anti-Soviet agitation and propaganda") to three years in a special-regime labour camp and five years' exile after he had written a *Report from the Beria Reserve* while serving a four-year sentence in a labour camp in 1966-69, and also other works in which he advocated the preservation of Ukrainian national traditions. In the aforementioned *Report* he had inter alia expressed the view that "individuality" was "one of the chief factors in the whole development of mankind"; that intellect was "an individual matter"; that the history of progress was "the history of the development of individuality"; that "the so-called masses create nothing"; and that the KGB had the task of suppressing individuality and creating uniformity ("normality") of thought. Dr Moroz was released to the West on April 27, 1979, in an exchange of five Soviet citizens against two other Soviet citizens convicted of spying in the United States.

Yury Orlov

Dr Yury Orlov, former chairman of the Helsinki Group, was on May 18, 1978, sentenced to seven years in a hard-labour camp and five years in internal exile for "anti-Soviet agitation and propaganda". Evidence produced by the prosecution included documents said to have been prepared by Dr Orlov and to have been disseminated through anti-Soviet publications and broadcast by Radio Liberty (the US station based in West Germany), the (West German) Deutsche Welle, the (official US) Voice of America, the British Broadcasting Corporation and Radio Roma; the documents were also said to have been handed to Western correspondents in Moscow and sent to foreign governments and organizations.

During the trial no witnesses for the defence were allowed to testify but Dr Orlov said in his own defence on May 15 that he accepted responsibility for the documents concerned but refused to plead guilty to anti-Soviet propaganda, as the information distributed by his group was neither false nor defamatory. He declared that his motive had been humanitarian and not political; he criticized the "ideological intolerance" prevailing in the Soviet Union and leading to "cultural stagnation"; and he added that without such tolerance there could be no peaceful coexistence or genuine détente.

The Orlov verdict was strongly condemned in Western countries, especially in the United States, France and West Germany, as a violation of the Helsinki agreements. In September 1979 Dr Orlov succeeded in smuggling out of his labour camp a 20-page report (published in the Western press) alleging that the current total of inmates of Soviet prisons and labour camps had reached 5,000,000.

Andrei Sakharov

One of the foremost civil rights activists in the Soviet Union has been Dr Andrei D. Sakharov, an eminent physicist, involved in the foundation, in November 1970, of the Committee for Human Rights and, in May 1976, of the Public Group to assist the Fulfilment of the Helsinki Accords in the Soviet Union (the Helsinki Group). He has taken a leading part in numerous campaigns for the release of political prisoners and for the rights of national and religious minorities, and has expressed his reformist democratic socialist convictions on a number of occasions.

Dr Sakharov, born in 1921, began his studies at the Lomonosov State University in Moscow in 1939 but volunteered for active service in 1940. After continuing his studies by correspondence he was called to Moscow for direct studies and subsequently worked, among others, under Prof. Peter L. Kapitsa on the secret "super complex project" as an assistant at its "ignition cycle", i.e. the first proposed Soviet atomic fission. After working as an assistant of Prof. Lev D. Landau (the 1962 Nobel Physics Prize winner) he became, in 1945, assistant at, and later director of, the Lebedev Physical Institute of the Soviet Academy of Sciences. After 1947 he became, with Dr Igor Tamm (1958 Nobel Prize winner), the "father of the Soviet atom bomb", and following the explosion of the first Soviet hydrogen bomb in 1953 he was unanimously elected a full member of the Academy of Sciences. (In Nikita Khrushchev's posthumously published memoirs it was stated that Dr Sakharov had in vain appealed for the cancellation of the explosion of the hydrogen bomb and for an end to further tests of the bomb.) In 1963 he took part in the drafting of the partial nuclear test-ban treaty signed in August of that year.

He lost his post at the State Committee for Atomic Energy (but remained a member of the Academy of Sciences) after he had expressed his "Reflections on Progress, Peaceful Coexistence and Intellectual Freedom" which were circulated in manuscript in Moscow and published in *The New York Times* on July 22, 1968. In the first part of this essay, entitled "Dangers", he questioned the "loud demands that the intelligentsia should subordinate its strivings to the will and interests of the working class" because this meant "subordination to the will of the [Communist] party or more specifically to the party's central apparatus and officials" who, he said, might "not always express the genuine interests of the working class as a whole and the genuine interests of progress, rather than their own caste interests". He called for disarmament and in particular for a moratorium on the construction of "senselessly expansive missile systems"; for a massive programme of technical and economic assistance (through a 15-year tax of 20 per cent of national income of developed nations) to avert "the growing threat of hunger in the poorer part of the world"; and for an end to police regimes, stating in particular that under Stalin "at least 10 to 15 million people perished in the torture chambers of the NKVD [secret police] and in camps for exiled kulaks and so-called semi-kulaks and their families" and in camps "without the right of correspondence". He claimed that in 1936-39 alone more than 1,200,000 party members (more than half the membership) had been arrested; that only 30,000 of them had regained freedom; and that 600,000 had been shot and the others had been tortured and had died in camps. He called for a "complete exposure" of Stalinism; strongly supported the appeal made by Alexander Solzhenitsyn for the abolition of censorship (see below); and condemned the Sinyavsky-Daniel trial (see above) and also any "backsliding into anti-semitism in our appointments policy".

In the second part of his essay, called "The Basis for Hope", Dr Sakharov maintained that the Soviet Union was "catching up with the United States only in some of the old traditional industries, which are no longer as important as they used to be for the United States (e.g. coal and steel)", but that in some of the newer fields (e.g. automation, computers, petro-chemicals and industrial research and development) the Soviet Union was "not only lagging behind but also growing more slowly, so that a complete victory of our economy in the next few decades is unlikely". He added: "The continuing economic progress being achieved under capitalism should be a fact of great theoretical significance for any non-dogmatic Marxist. It is precisely this fact that lies at the basis of peaceful coexistence, and it suggests, in principle, that if capitalism ever runs into an economic blind alley it will not necessarily have to leap into a desperate military adventure. Both capitalism and socialism are capable of long-term development, borrowing positive elements from each other and actually coming closer to each other in a number of essential elements."

In collaboration with Roy Medvedev (see above) and Dr Valentin A. Turchin (a physicist), Dr Sakharov issued, on March 19, 1970, an open letter to the Soviet leaders, maintaining that greater freedom was essential to the country's economic progress. In this letter it was stated that the Soviet Union was falling behind the West economically and technically because of "anti-democratic traditions and norms of public life which appeared during Stalin's period" and had "not been completely liquidated". The letter proposed that the leadership itself should introduce a programme of democratization—to include free access to information, broadcasts and books from the West; more contacts with people in other countries; an amnesty for political prisoners; publication of proceedings at political trials; public control of places of imprisonment; measures to make courts less susceptible to political pressure; abolition of the system of internal passports; more autonomy for economic enterprises; greater expenditure on education; introduction of a press law; greater use of electoral procedure in promoting party and government officials; expansion of the rights of the Supreme Soviet; and freedom for the nationalities deported by Stalin to return to their homelands.

On June 23, 1972, Dr Sakharov released to Western press correspondents the text of a programme of reform which he had sent to Leonid Brezhnev (then General Secretary of the Central Committee of the CPSU) on March 5, 1971, and of a recently written postscript. The programme contained the following proposals: (i) an amnesty for all persons imprisoned for political or religious reasons or for trying to leave the country; (ii) the abolition of secret trials and a review of all sentences passed "in violation of the right to know''; (iii) clarification of the regulations under which dissidents were detained in mental hospitals; (iv) a new press law based on the right to know; (v) the ending of the jamming of foreign broadcasts; (vi) free access to foreign literature; (vii) freedom of international travel and emigration; (viii) abolition of the death penalty; (ix) a committee to protect arrested persons against physical methods of pressure such as starvation and beating; (x) the abolition of single-candidate elections; (xi) popular selection of Government and party leaders; (xii) provision for the recall of officials at all levels in case of unsuitability; and (xiii) recognition of the right of any Republic to secede from the Soviet Union if it so desired.

In his postscript Dr Sakharov developed the ideas which he had put forward in his "Reflections on Progress, Peaceful Coexistence and Intellectual Freedom" in 1968. In his view it would be "possible to overcome the tragic contradictions and dangers of our epoch only through the convergence of capitalism and the socialist system". In the socialist countries, he said, "total ideological freedom" was "essential, as well as a radical reform of education and the abolition of all forms of ideological persecution", and "the system of privileges" would have to be "eliminated in all sectors". He expressed his alarm at the fact that "after a period of largely illusory liberalization" there was once again "an extension of restrictions on ideological freedom, of efforts to cut off all sources of information not controlled by the state, of persecution for political and ideological reasons, and a deliberate worsening of the problems of national minorities" and also the "crushing of religion". He claimed inter alia that the Soviet Union had the highest ratio of military expenditure with relation to national income, i.e. "more than 40 per cent".

In a letter published in the Paris L'Express on Oct. 7, 1973, Dr Sakharov declared that he fully supported all efforts, including proposed measures of arms limitations, to avert the danger of a nuclear war which, he said, was "the matter of foremost concern for all humanity". He also supported the "strengthening of economic, cultural and scientific links between East and West" but he did not share the optimism of some Western circles on the consequences of economic contacts for the democratization of Soviet society. He expressed his conviction that "real détente and real rapprochement" implied greater "mutual confidence and reciprocal understanding and a greater opening of society, public information and democratic control". He also declared that he was "in favour of a gradual improvement of the Soviet state within the framework of the existing regime", and he added that "the adoption of measures within the limits of real possibilities, such as a complete amnesty for political prisoners and freedom of emigration, would create a new atmosphere more favourable to the process of détente".

On Oct. 21, 1974, Dr Sakharov handed to Western reporters in Moscow an open letter addressed to the US Senator Henry M. Jackson, Dr Henry Kissinger (the US Secretary of State) and the US Congress, stating that any liberalization measures concerning emigration from the Soviet Union—as had been demanded by Senator Jackson in an amendment to US trade reform legislation—would not become effective until such measures were incorporated in Soviet law. He therefore suggested certain changes in the law, including the introduction of the right to readmission to the Soviet Union after emigrating; the relaxation of restrictions on temporary visits abroad; the formal abrogation of an education tax on emigrants (which had already been suspended); and the granting of a right of appeal against refusal of permission to emigrate.

Following the signature of the Final Act of the Conference on Security and Co-operation in Europe (CSCE) in Helsinki on Aug. 1, 1975, Dr Sakharov and 31 other Soviet dissidents, in a letter released in Moscow on Sept. 9, 1975, appealed to the Presidium of the USSR Supreme Soviet for a total political amnesty which should cover "all people sentenced for ideology, political views and activity, for religious convictions and for demanding the recognition of human rights", as well as those sentenced on criminal charges which in fact had arisen from their political beliefs. (An amnesty declared on May 7, 1975, had not applied to prisoners convicted of "particularly dangerous state crimes".)

On Oct. 9, 1975, the 1975 Nobel Peace Prize was awarded to Dr Sakharov for his "personal and fearless effort in the cause of peace among mankind" and for fighting "not only against the abuse of power and violations of human dignity in all its forms" but also "with equal vigour . . . for the ideal of a state founded on the principle of justice for all". The Nobel Prize citation described his aims as "demilitarization, democratization of society in all countries, and a more rapid pace of social progress", aims through which he had become "the spokesman for the conscience of mankind, which the world so sorely needs today".

In Moscow the Peace Prize award to Dr Sakharov was officially denounced in strong terms, Tass (the official news agency) calling him, on Oct. 10, "an anti-patriot and an opponent of peaceful coexistence" who had come out "against expansion of international economic ties and against relaxation of international tensions". In a statement issued on Oct. 25 a total of 72 members of the Academy of Sciences asserted that Dr Sakharov's activity had been aimed at undermining the cause of peace and peaceful relations on equal terms and at instigating distrust among nations, and they declared the award to be "unacceptable to the real peace supporters".

Dr Sakharov was not allowed to travel to Oslo to receive his prize, on the grounds that he possessed state secrets and his journey would therefore constitute a security risk. After Dr Sakharov's wife (Mrs Yelena Bonner Sakharova) had received his Nobel Prize on his behalf in Oslo, she read, on Dec. 11, 1975, a speech prepared by him in which he mentioned by name a total of 118 "prisoners of conscience" held in the Soviet Union.

In a book entitled *My Country and the World,* published outside the Soviet Union in October 1975, Dr Sakharov again called for sweeping reforms to the Soviet system. Although he emphasized that he did not want to blacken his country's image, he claimed that conditions in the USSR were far worse than those in the West with its economic recession, oil crisis and unemployment. He attributed the poor state of the Soviet economy largely to excessive military expenditure and "secret as well as overt expansion throughout the world"; to bureaucratic mismanagement; and to expenditure to safeguard a higher standard of living for the privileged élite. He claimed that the consumption of alcohol (to "drown people's sorrows") was three times as high as in Tsarist times; that low wages forced many women to do heavy work which was destroying their health; that there was not enough money to feed children adequately; and that crime was increasing steadily. The reforms for which he called included the introduction of a mixed economy and of social democracy.

On Jan. 21, 1977, Dr Sakharov appealed to President Carter of the United States to intervene in favour of political prisoners in the Soviet Union and Western Europe, of whom he named 15 specifically. In a statement of Jan. 27 the US State Department referred to Dr Sakharov as "an outspoken champion of human rights in the Soviet Union" and declared: "Any attempt by the Soviet authorities to intimidate Dr Sakharov conflicts with accepted international standards in the field of human rights." On Feb. 17, 1977, Dr Sakharov announced that he had received a reply from President Carter reaffirming the United States' "firm commitment to promote respect for human rights not only in our country but also abroad" and declaring: "We shall use our good offices to seek the release of prisoners of conscience, and we will continue our efforts to shape a world responsive to human aspirations in which nationals of differing cultures and histories can live side by side in peace and justice."

On Jan. 2, 1980, Dr Sakharov called on the United Nations and the Soviet Union to work out an arrangement for the withdrawal of the Soviet forces which had entered Afghanistan a week earlier, pointing out that there might follow "a chain reaction" with unpredictable consequences in an age of nuclear weapons. Following his signature, on Jan. 21, of a statement (published on Jan. 24) by the Helsinki Group in Moscow, protesting against the Soviet intervention in Afghanistan (for which, the statement said, the Soviet Government had no popular support at home or abroad), Dr Sakharov was arrested on Jan. 22, deprived of all state awards and official honours and removed from Moscow to internal exile in Gorky (an industrial city about 300 miles east of Moscow and permanently closed to foreigners).

On Jan. 23, 1980, *Izvestia* accused Dr Sakharov of "subversive activities" against the state and of treason, alleging that he had given foreign agents important state secrets, including defence information, and that he had allowed himself to be used by foreign mass media for undermining Soviet socialism. On Jan. 28 Mrs Bonner Sakharova presented Western journalists with a statement from Dr Sakharov, describing the *Izvestia* article as slander and adding a list of what he called current examples of Soviet aggression. In a second statement brought to Moscow on Feb. 4 he claimed to have received death threats and suggestions that he would be removed to a psychiatric institution. He had by then been banned from making telephone calls, and police interrogated all visitors to his flat, which was situated opposite the police station in Gorky. He was also prohibited from leaving the town, meeting foreigners and communicating with people abroad (including his children and grandchildren in the United States). On March 4 he was effectively excluded from the Academy of Sciences.

Dr Sakharov's removal to Gorky was followed by strong protests not only by most Western Governments and many scientific organizations, but also by the Communist parties of France, Italy, Norway and Spain. In a letter smuggled out of Gorky and published in *The New York Times* on June 8, 1980, Dr Sakharov appealed for the broadest boycott of the 1980 Olympic Games due to be held in Moscow.

Notwithstanding numerous international protests against Dr Sakharov's continued banishment, he was at the end of 1982 still confined to his enforced residence at Gorky.

Anatoly Shcharansky

Anatoly Shcharansky, a computer specialist and member of the Helsinki Group in Moscow, was sentenced in Moscow on July 14, 1978, to three years in a "close-confinement" prison and a further 10 years in a strict-regime labour camp (slightly less harsh than the "special-regime" camp punishment imposed on Alexander Ginsburg—see page 40) for (i) high treason and espionage, for which he was given a 13-year sentence, and (ii) anti-Soviet agitation and propaganda, for which the penalty was seven years—these sentences to run concurrently.

Shcharansky had been dismissed from his post after applying for permission to leave for Israel in 1973. He had been arrested on March 15, 1977, and on Oct. 28 of that year Tass had stated that he had been charged with helping a foreign state to pursue hostile activities against the Soviet Union, and had called him "a traitor of his motherland". Shcharansky, as well as Prof. Alexander Lerner and Dr Vladimir Slepak, had been denounced as "spies" working for the (US) Central Intelligence Agency (CIA) in *Izvestia* on March 4, 1977. President Carter of the United States stated on June 13 that he was completely convinced that Shcharansky had never worked for the CIA.

Shcharansky, who conducted his own defence, said in his final statement before the court on July 13, 1978, that what had been deemed to be espionage represented efforts which he had made, and which he had not concealed, to disclose information which was not of a secret nature and which was accessible to everybody. He retraced the history of Zionism and the upsurge of emigration from the USSR, calling this development an historical process in which the Jews had begun to seek their identity and to opt not for assimilation but for emigration to their newly-created fatherland, and he added that he was "happy to go to prison in the cause of human rights and Jewish liberation" and that he had refused "to co-operate with the investigation with the aim of liquidating the Jewish emigration movement".

Despite continuing protests against A. Shcharansky's detention and the conditions under which he was held in a labour camp there was, at the end of 1982, no indication that he might be released.

Andrei Sinyavsky

Andrei D. Sinyavsky, who had written books under the name of Abram Tertz, was on Feb. 14, 1966, sentenced (together with Yuli Daniel—see above) to seven years in a labour camp for smuggling and publishing abroad under pseudonyms works "actively used in the ideological struggle against the Soviet Union" and for "disseminating slanderous works". After his release in June 1971, with remission for good conduct, he arrived in Paris on Aug. 10, 1973, having been granted permission to accept a teaching post at the University of Paris.

Alexander Solzhenitsyn

Alexander I. Solzhenitsyn (born in 1918) joined the Army in 1941, was commissioned in 1942 and served in World War II as an artillery commander, being twice decorated for bravery. However, after criticizing Stalin in a private letter, he served eight years in a forced-labour camp in 1945-53, followed by exile in Siberia until 1956. He was officially rehabilitated in 1957, and he subsequently taught physics in Ryazan.

His first book, *One Day in the Life of Ivan Denisovich,* a detailed account of life in a prison camp under Stalin, was published in the progressive Moscow journal *Novy Mir* (edited by Alexander Tvardovsky) in November 1962. Among his further books, *The First Circle* (a novel) and *Cancer Ward* (based on his experiences in prison, where he was suffering from cancer, which was later cured) were published in the United States and Britain without his approval. It was later claimed by the (official) Writers' Union of the USSR that these works, "taken abroad illegally and published there, have been used by reactionary circles in the West for anti-Soviet purposes".

Solzhenitsyn had written *One Day in the Life of Ivan Denisovich* in 1956-58 but had made no effort to have it published until the 22nd Congress of the CPSU, held in October 1961, had publicly revealed Stalin's repressions. Publication of the book was approved by the Presidium of the Central Committee of the CPSU in November 1962. This decision was somewhat unexpected since the book *Not by Bread Alone* by Vladimir Dudintsev, dealing with the theme of illegal repression, had been criticized in 1957, and Boris Pasternak's *Doctor Zhivago* had been condemned as being "anti-Soviet" in 1958.

The book was read by millions of people in the Soviet Union, over 750,000 copies being printed in one edition alone in January 1963. Its publication was followed by the submission to publishers of a large number of typescripts describing life in Stalin's camps, in exile and in prisons, and many other subjects relating to the Stalinist repression. However, efforts made by Tvardovsky to have the censorship lifted failed, and Nikita Khrushchev (the First Secretary of the Central Committee of the CPSU) issued a warning that the publication of "prison camp" writing should be treated with extreme caution so as not to damage the prestige of the party. As a result of this warning the publication of many works was stopped at the editorial stage.

Early in 1965 the Central Committee of the CPSU found out that *Miniature Stories* (a series of short stories by Solzhenitsyn) had been published by *Grani,* a quarterly Russian-language journal issued by the (anti-Soviet) People's Labour Union (NTS—see section on External Organizations below) in Frankfurt (West Germany). They had been circulating from hand to hand in the Soviet Union but had not been accepted for publication by *Novy Mir*. Although Solzhenitsyn had not been aware of the appearance of these stories in *Grani*, he was liable to be charged with anti-Soviet activities for having dealings with the NTS. (Great risk was incurred by any Soviet writer who decided to bring to the notice of the public any work which had no chance of being passed by the Soviet censor and whose works appeared in the anti-Soviet émigré press or were published abroad even under copyright arrangements with reputable publishers.)

Later in 1965 *One Day in the Life of Ivan Denisovich* began to be denounced by certain CPSU leaders. N. G. Egorychev, a first secretary of the Moscow party committee, wrote in the journal *Kommunist* (No. 3, March 1965) that from the ideological and the artistic points of view the book was "unquestionably suspect". From 1966 onwards Solzhenitsyn was no longer mentioned by Soviet literary critics (except in *Novy Mir*), and by the end of that year he had been successfully prevented from giving talks about his writings. At a search at the flat of a friend of Solzhenitsyn's in Moscow, the KGB confiscated, on Sept. 11, 1965, typescript copies of *The First Circle* and also literary papers going back 15-20 years, which Solzhenitsyn had left there after collecting them from the office of *Novy Mir*, whose editor had told him that early publication of any of his works was unlikely.

In an appeal to the Fourth Soviet Writers' Congress (held in May 1967)—an appeal which was not read to the congress—Solzhenitsyn called inter alia for the abolition of censorship and defined his view of literature as follows: "Literature cannot develop in between categories of 'permitted' and 'not permitted', 'about this you may write' and 'about this you may not'. Literature that is not the breath of contemporary society, that dares not transmit the pains and fears of that society, that does not warn in time against threatening moral and social dangers—such literature does not deserve the name of literature; it is only a façade. Such literature loses the confidence of its own people, and its published works are used as wastepaper instead of being read. Our literature has lost the leading role it played at the end of the last century and the beginning of this one, and it has lost the brilliance of experimentation that distinguished it in the 1920s. To the entire world the literary life of our country now appears immeasurably more colourless, trivial and inferior than it actually is—than it would be if it were not confined and hemmed in. If the world had access to all the uninhibited fruits of our literature, if it were enriched by our own spiritual experience, the whole artistic evolution of the world would move along in a different way, acquiring a new stability and attaining even a new artistic threshold." (Quoted from Zhores Medvedev, *Ten Years after Ivan Denisovich*, Macmillan, 1972, and Alfred A. Knopf Inc.)

In his appeal Solzhenitsyn also gave details of the persecution to which he had been subjected by the KGB and alleged that more than 600 writers who were guilty of no crime had been "left to their fate in prisons and camps" by the leadership of the Writers' Union.

On Nov. 4, 1969, Solzhenitsyn was expelled from the Writers' Union on the grounds that his name and works had been used for anti-Soviet propaganda and he had not publicly condemned this propaganda. He responded by writing an open letter to the Union's secretariat, stating inter alia that it was "time to remember that first of all we belong to humanity, that man is distinguishable from animals by thought and speech, and that man should naturally be free". He continued: "Public proclamation of the facts, in an honest and complete manner—that is the prime condition for the health of any society, including our own. Whoever does not want that for his country does not want to cure it of its sickness, but only to drive it inward and produce putrefaction." The secretariat's reply was to the effect that his letter proved his stand "in positions which are alien to our people and their literature" and that nobody was going to prevent him from going "where his anti-Soviet works and letters are always received with such delight".

On Oct. 8, 1970, Solzhenitsyn was awarded the Nobel Prize for Literature for that year "for the ethical force with which he has pursued the indispensable tradition of Russian literature". In the official address given on Dec. 10, 1970, setting out the reasons for the award, it was pointed out that the vitality of his books sprang "not least from the feeling that roots his being to his country and its destiny" and that they revealed "a profound, decisive identification with the country whose life provided their subject matter and for whose life they are essential". It was also recalled that *Pravda* had welcomed the appearance of *One Day in the Life of Ivan Denisovich* by writing that at times it called to mind "Tolstoy's artistic power" and that "a writer with a rare talent" had "come into our literature", whose "remarkable story" was of "profound humanity".

Solzhenitsyn himself decided not to travel to Stockholm to receive his prize because he feared that the Soviet authorities would not allow him to return home after the ceremony. He therefore request that the prize should be handed to him at a ceremony to be held at the Swedish embassy in Moscow, but this request was not acceded to by the Swedish Government. When Solzhenitsyn had arranged that the prize should be handed to him at the flat of his (second) wife in Moscow by Dr Karl Ragnar Gierow, the secretary of the Royal Swedish Academy (which had awarded the prize), the latter was refused an entry visa by the USSR authorities.

In June 1971 Solzhenitsyn had a further book—*August 1914,* dealing with the defeat of the Russian Army at Tannenberg at the beginning of World War I and constituting the first part of a proposed trilogy on the downfall of the Tsarist regime—published in Russian in Paris, after his request for permission to publish it in the Soviet Union had been ignored. In *Literaturnaya Gazeta,* the organ of the Writers' Union, the book was on Jan. 12, 1972, described as "very helpful for anti-Soviet elements of every description", and later it was alleged in the journal that he had allowed the work to be printed abroad by an organization with former Nazi connexions.

On March 30, 1972, Solzhenitsyn explained to two US correspondents that he was exposed to constant official harassment, as everyone who visited his house was closely followed, and some of his visitors had been dismissed from their posts, his telephone was tapped, his conversation recorded and his correspondence opened, while slanderous statements were being made about his private life.

In May 1972 Solzhenitsyn circulated a Lenten Letter to the (Orthodox) Patriarch of Moscow accusing the Church leaders of conniving at the destruction of Christianity in the Soviet Union. He recalled that the Patriarch had, in his Christmas message, appealed to Russians living abroad to inculcate in their children a love of the Church but had not made a similar appeal to Christians inside the USSR. He also listed official acts of persecution of religion, including action taken in May 1966 against two priests (Nikolai Eshliman and Gleb Yakunin, who had protested against state interference in ecclesiastical affairs), who were forbidden to administer the sacraments; the imprisonment of Archbishop Yermogen of Kaluga (the only archbishop to oppose the closing of churches in his diocese in 1965); the demolition or ruination beyond repair or profanation of churches; the ban on the ringing of church bells; and the need to bring in copies of the Gospel from abroad. He concluded by asking: "Is there anything at all which the Church has defended?"

Following the publication in Paris of the first two of seven parts of Solzhenitsyn's major work *The Gulag Archipelago* on Dec. 28, 1973, the author was on Feb. 13, 1974, expelled from the USSR and deprived of his Soviet citizenship.

Gulag is the abbreviated form of the Russian name of the Main Administration of Labour Camps which was responsible for the organization of these camps (between 1934 and 1960) "geographically scattered like an archipelago". In a summary of his autobiography, included in the book, Solzhenitsyn states that it was between 1945 and 1956, when he was in prison or in labour camps, that he came to abandon his communist beliefs under the influence of his fellow prisoners who were of many shades of political and religious opinion.

In his book Solzhenitsyn distinguished three peak periods for the number of people held in camps in the Soviet Union: (i) 1929-31, during the enforced collectivization of the land and the "liquidation" of the kulaks (when he estimated that 15,000,000 peasants were arrested and deported); (ii) 1934-39, the period of the great purges beginning with the assassination of Sergei Kirov in Leningrad in 1934; and (iii) 1944-46, when entire population groups such as the Kalmucks and the Crimean Tartars were sent to Siberia. The largest number of camp inmates at any one time was, according to Solzhenitsyn, about 12,000,000, of whom not more than half were political prisoners.

A controversial passage in the book (which led to the condemnation of Solzhenitsyn as a "traitor" in the Soviet press) was that relating to the Soviet General Andrei Vlasov, who had during World War II formed an anti-Soviet force from Soviet prisoners of war held by the Germans; this force had fought against the Soviet forces but had, according to Solzhenitsyn, later changed sides and had in April 1945 expelled the Germans from Prague. Solzhenitsyn condemned the action of the Americans in forcing the Vlasov forces to surrender to the Soviet authorities, who hanged Gen. Vlasov and sent his followers to labour camps. Solzhenitsyn also maintained that since the 1917 October revolution millions of people had been executed—far more than under the Tsars.

The Gulag Archipelago was written between 1958 and 1968, but its author decided not to publish it because some 200 former prisoners mentioned in it were still alive. However, in April 1973 the KGB succeeded in tracing the woman who had typed the book and extracted from her the whereabouts of a copy, whereafter she hanged herself. Solzhenitsyn, who had already sent another copy of the book abroad, thereupon authorized its publication in the West.

On Nov. 14, 1974, it was announced by Prof. Igor Shafarevich (a mathematician and candidate member of the Soviet Academy of Sciences) that a book called *From under the Rubble,* compiled by Solzhenitsyn and himself, was about to be published in Russian in Paris with the object of showing, in essays written by Soviet dissidents on Russia's future, what possibilities existed for dissidents to work for changes while still living in the Soviet Union. In this book (published in

English in the United States and Britain in 1975) Solzhenitsyn praised Dr Sakharov's "Reflections on Progress, Peaceful Coexistence and Intellectual Freedom" (of 1968), inter alia for "shattering the Marxist myth that capitalism brings the productive forces to an impasse" or "always leads to the absolute pauperization of the working class", but criticized him for rejecting only Stalinism and not socialism itself and for underrating the role of nationalism—which according to Solzhenitsyn has "revealed inexhaustible strength and vitality" during the 20th century. Solzhenitsyn further rejected the whole tradition of the pre-revolutionary Russian intelligentsia favouring Western liberalism—i.e. political freedom—as the main objective. He stated in particular: "The Western democracies today are in a state of political crisis and spiritual confusion. Today, more than at any time in the past century, it ill becomes us to see our country's *only* way out in the Western parliamentary system." Solzhenitsyn concluded that for the people of the Soviet Union "the absolutely essential task" was "not political liberation" but "the liberation of our souls from participating in the lie forced upon us" by the existing regime, and that it was up to each individual to take this "moral step within his power"— failing which he would never be able "to justify himself to the living, or to posterity, or to his friends, or to his children".

Solzhenitsyn himself, in broadcasts made in March and April 1976, issued "a warning to the Western world" and denounced what he called "the tragic enfeeblement of Europe" vis-à-vis the Soviet Union. In a television interview broadcast by the British Broadcasting Corporation of March 1, 1976, he declared that the West was "on the verge of collapse created by its own hand"; that the Soviet Politburo would not have the power to refuse starting a new war because the existing Soviet war economy would have to be changed to a normal peace economy, which, he claimed, would require "an agonizing change"; that the West had "given up all its world positions" and had thereby strengthened "tyranny in our country"; that the speed of the West's capitulation had "so rapidly overtaken the pace of our moral regeneration" that at this moment the Soviet Union could "move only along one path—the flourishing road of totalitarianism".

Solzhenitsyn's assertions were publicly rejected not only by the Soviet authorities but also by Roy Medvedev, who (as reported on March 14, 1976) described them as "reinforcing the most reactionary quarters" in Moscow and also as "disastrous for Western society", seeing that "even total isolation of the Western countries from the Soviet Union" could "not lead to the death of the Soviet regime which Solzhenitsyn hates so much".

He added that Solzhenitsyn was "deeply mistaken" in claiming that he was speaking for the majority of the Russian people, and that he had in fact broken off all personal and business relations with his former friends and the people who once shared his ideas.

On Sept. 8, 1976, Solzhenitsyn was granted permanent residence in the United States. Earlier the policy platform of the (US) Republican Party, as approved on Aug. 18, 1976, had been expanded, at the suggestion of Ronald Reagan (who was then a rival candidate for the party's presidential nomination in 1976) by the addition of a paragraph on "morality in foreign policy" in which it was stated inter alia: "We recognize and commend the great beacon of human courage and morality, Alexander Solzhenitsyn, for his compelling message that we must face the world with no illusions about the nature of tyranny. Ours will be a foreign policy that keeps this ever in mind. . . . In pursuing détente we must not grant unilateral favours with only the hope of getting future favours in return. Agreements that are negotiated, such as the one signed in Helsinki [i.e. the Final Act of the 1975 Conference on Security and Co-operation in Europe] must not take away from those who do not have freedom the hope of one day gaining it."

Geli Snegiryov

Geli Snegiryov (a writer and film producer, expelled from the CPSU and the Writers' Union in 1974) announced in a letter to the Government, written early in July 1977 (after the trial of two Ukrainian civil rights activists) that he was renouncing his Soviet citizenship; asserting that he considered the 1977 Constitution of the USSR to be "a lie from beginning to end", and that he did not wish to remain the citizen of a state which had "destroyed the elite of my Ukrainian people, the best part of its peasantry and the intelligentisia".

In open letters published in Paris in July 1977 Snegiryov asked President Carter of the United States inter alia to tell Brezhnev: "The human rights of your citizens are not your internal affair. . . . The problem concerns the whole world . . . because, if we allow you to deceive us in matters of human rights, you will also deceive us in other matters."

On July 17, 1977, he challenged Brezhnev (in an open letter) to carry out a seven-day programme for reforming the Soviet state by (i) ordering the publication of a "true book" on the "60 years of our shame" which had brought the state to "the brink of economic and spiritual collapse", (ii) dissolving the KGB; (iii) disbanding the Army (but "keeping your rockets"); (iv) stripping Marxism of its "aura of dogma"; (v) dissolving co-operative and state farms—but "not in a hurry";

(vi) convincing the peasants that after taking over the land they would not again be deprived of it; and (vii) permitting emigration and allowing the constituent republics to leave the USSR.

Snegiryov was subsequently arrested (as announced by his wife on Sept. 25, 1977), and on April 12, 1978, *Literaturnaya Gazeta* (the official organ of the USSR Writers' Union) reprinted a letter previously published in a Ukrainian newspaper, in which Snegiryov repudiated his links with dissidents, renounced his past and stated that his "criminal activities" had done "serious harm" to his country. On April 20, however, Okhana Meshko (a member of the Helsinki Group in the Ukraine) denied that Snegiryov had written such a letter and stated that he had been force-fed during a 29-day hunger strike and had asked to be transferred from a prison isolation ward to a hospital. He died on Dec. 28, 1978, at the age of 51, in a Kiev hospital where he had been kept under guard by the KGB.

Free Trade Unions

Free Interprofessional Association of Soviet Workers (SMOT)

The creation of this Association was disclosed on Oct. 29, 1978, by eight persons who claimed that it had 100 members. However, the authorities soon took action against SMOT members, among them Lev Volokhonsky (a founder member), sentenced on June 12, 1979, to two years in a labour camp for "spreading anti-Soviet slander"; Anatoly Pozdniakov, arrested on Sept. 10, 1979, tried on Oct. 30 and transferred to a psychiatric hospital; Vladimir Borisov, arrested in August 1979, sent to a psychiatric hospital and expelled from the Soviet Union on June 22, 1980; Mark Morozov, arrested on Nov. 2, 1978, and subsequently exiled to Vorkuta (northern Urals) for five years (for spreading "anti-Soviet fabrications"), and on Jan. 13, 1981, sentenced to eight years' hard labour (for spreading "anti-Soviet propaganda"); Mikhail Sokolov, sentenced on April 1, 1980, to three years in a labour camp for "hooliganism" (after allegedly making derogatory remarks about President Brezhnev); and Vselovod Kuyakin (who had also been involved in the formation of the Free Trade Union of Soviet Workers—see separate entry), arrested on April 22, 1981, and sentenced on Dec. 27 of that year to one year in a labour camp and five years' internal exile for "anti-Soviet agitation and propaganda".

Mrs Albina Yakoreva, a SMOT organizer expelled from the Soviet Union, stated in Vienna on Aug. 8, 1982, that SMOT had increased significantly during the last year, that it had 300 active members and 1,500 sympathizers and that 21 new branches had been set up during 1982 alone.

Free Trade Union of Soviet Workers

An attempt to set up a free trade union (outside the established official trade union organization) was begun late in 1977 by a group of workers who had been dismissed after protesting unsuccessfully against alleged unsatisfactory working conditions and corruption. The protest was first made public in an open letter signed by 72 workers from 42 different cities castigating "the plundering of socialist property, bad conditions of work, low pay, high injury rates and low quality production'. In November 1977 seven of the signatories gave a press conference to Western journalists to explain their action. One of them, Vladimir Klebanov, was arrested on Dec. 19 and was subsequently sent to psychiatric hospitals. Another, Valentin T. Poplavsky, disclosed on Feb. 21, 1978, that 43 persons had on Feb. 1 drawn up a charter for a "Free Trade Union of Soviet Workers" which claimed to have 200 members and was to base itself on existing declarations and conventions on human rights.

In a letter to the Soviet authorities, dated April 13, 1978, the group applied for registration as an organization whose aim was to "contribute to the full and complete application of all laws and Soviet regulations governing labour relations, to enable workers to be protected and to assure citizens of the possibility of legal aid in the solution of labour conflicts"; it was also claimed in the letter that the setting up of such a trade union was not contrary to Soviet law.

However, on May 12, 1978, V. T. Poplavsky was sentenced to one year in a labour camp for "parasitism" (i.e. being without regular employment), and during 1979 it became clear that the attempt to set up such a trade union had failed, as official action had been taken not only against the above two, but also against three other members. After the committee on freedom of association of the International Labour Organization (ILO) had on Feb. 21, 1978, requested the USSR to supply details of the alleged arrest of the five office-bearers, the Soviet Government was on March 29 reported to have replied that the persons mentioned were not workers but "parasites" and "deviates" and that the examination of their case by the ILO was "illegal and inadmissible".

The Baltic Republics

The incorporation into the Soviet Union of the Baltic republics of Estonia, Latvia and Lithuania in 1940 has not been officially recognized by most Western nations, and the former independent Governments of these three states are still represented by legations in London. In that the three countries had formerly been part of the Tsarist empire, the Soviet Government regarded their post-World War I independence as an aberration from historical legality.

On the occasion of the 40th anniversary of the 1939 Soviet-German non-aggression pact—which led to the Soviet annexation of the three Baltic republics—45 Estonian, Latvian and Lithuanian citizens published an appeal to the United Nations, the Soviet Union and the two (East and West) German Governments to revoke that pact on the grounds that secret protocols attached to it had enabled the Soviet Union to occupy the three Baltic republics in the following year. The signatories also called for the withdrawal of "foreign" (i.e. Soviet) troops from these republics. Of the signatories, Vitalda Skuodis (a Lithuanian geologist) was on Jan. 14, 1980, reported to have been arrested, and Prof. Juri Kukk (an Estonian chemistry lecturer deprived of his post in September 1979 after applying for permission to emigrate to Sweden) was arrested on March 13, 1980; on Jan. 8, 1981, the latter was sentenced to two years in a labour camp, together with Mart Niklus, who was given 10 years in a special-regime labour camp and five years' internal exile for "defaming the Soviet system" and "anti-Soviet propaganda".

ESTONIA

On Oct. 1 and 3, 1980, some 2,000 students and school pupils demonstrated in Tallinn for "freedom for Estonia" and displayed the (banned) Estonian flag; some 150 were detained but more demonstrations took place on Oct. 5 and 10, and it was reported that more than 1,000 students had subsequently been expelled from their places of learning. In March 1981 two Estonian pupils were sent to labour camps for burning Soviet flags. After further disturbances in October 1982 several persons were sentenced to up to three years in labour camps.

LATVIA

In an open letter which reached the West in February 1972, a group of 17 veteran Latvian Communists appealed to the leaders of Western Communist parties to persuade the Soviet leaders to abandon their policy of Russification of the Baltic peoples. The signatories of the letter, who claimed to have fought against the pre-war Latvian regime and against the Germans, alleged that Leninism was "being used as a cover for Great Russian chauvinism" and that forcible Russification had become one of the principal aims of the Soviet leaders. They stated that Latvians had been deported to other parts of the USSR and Russians had been set-

tled in Latvia, with the result that the proportion of Latvians in the population was falling and the use of the Latvian language was in decline.

They also claimed that of the 1,500 employees of the Latvian Ministry of the Interior only 300 knew the Latvian language; that about two-thirds of the radio and television programmes broadcast from Riga were in Russian; that the first secretary of the Latvian party never spoke Latvian; and that many of his assistants did not speak the language. They also pointed out that all schools and cultural organizations which had existed before 1940 for Estonians, Germans, Jews, Lithuanians and Poles had been abolished.

LITHUANIA

In addition to the activities of Roman Catholics (forming the majority of the population in Lithuania) in pursuit of the right to practise their religion (see section on Religious Opposition below), nationalist or separatist feelings continued to persist in Lithuania, as was admitted in *Pravda* on Jan. 24, 1969.

Four Lithuanians were on Dec. 30, 1974, reported to have been sentenced to terms of imprisonment in labour camps for duplicating "anti-Soviet writings", namely Pyatras Plumpa (eight years), Povilas Petromis (four years), Virgilius Yangelis (two years) and Ionas Stashaitis (one year).

Balys Gayauskas, who had before 1973 served a 15-year prison sentence for nationalist activities, was sentenced in Vilnius on April 14, 1978, to 10 years in a labour camp and five years' internal exile for "anti-Soviet activities" after he had distributed monies from the Solzhenitsyn fund for the families of imprisoned dissidents.

Viktoras Piatkus, a Roman Catholic, was sentenced in Vilnius on July 13, 1978, to three years in prison and seven years in a labour camp as well as five years' internal exile for "anti-Soviet agitation and propaganda" and "organization of anti-Soviet activities", inter alia by disseminating documents of the Helsinki Group in Lithuania and inciting young people to homosexuality. He was said to have previously spent 16 years in prison and to have only recently begun to "pose as a champion of human rights".

Other Nationalities

United National Party of Armenia

An attempt to organize this party, with the object of separating the Soviet Socialist Republic of Armenia from the Soviet Union and reunifying it with former Armenian areas in Turkey and in Soviet Azerbaijan, was made by several Armenians who were tried in 1973-

74. In particular Bagrad Shakhverdian (an engineer) was in December 1973 sentenced to five years' hard labour and two years' exile, while Aratat Movmasian (a bus driver) was given a 3½-year prison sentence, for alleged nationalist activities. On Nov. 13, 1974, it was reported that 11 Armenians had, in separate trials, been sentenced to from two to seven years in prison for organizing the party, and on Nov. 22 Paruir Arakian (who had already served a four-year sentence in 1969-73 for "anti-Soviet activity) was sentenced in Yerevan to seven years in prison and three years' internal exile for helping to form the party.

Crimean Tartars

During World War II the Soviet Government forcibly deported (in May 1944) over 200,000 Tartars from the Crimea, where they had lived for centuries, to Uzbekistan and Kazakhstan, on the grounds that they had collaborated with the Germans; the Crimean Tartar Republic was abolished and all vestiges of its existence were destroyed. According to the Tartars' own estimate, 110,000 of them, or over 26 per cent, died of thirst or suffocation during the three to four months long journey to Central Asia (whereas the Soviet authorities put the death toll at "only" 22 per cent).

Following the denunciation of Stalin's mass deportations by Nikita Khrushchev in 1956, the Tartars began a campaign for their rehabilitation and their return to the Crimea. As a result two decrees of the USSR Supreme Soviet were signed on Sept. 5, 1967, by President Podgorny, stating that (i) the fact that "a certain section" of the Tartar population had collaborated with the Germans should not be used to blame the entire Tartar people, especially as a new generation had entered the work and political life of the people, and (ii) the Tartars were free to live anywhere in the Soviet Union and to return to the Crimea if they so wished.

However, of 6,000 Tartars who thereupon travelled to the Crimea only a few were allowed to settle there, with the result that the Tartars launched a new agitation. This led to clashes with police and troops near Tashkent (Uzbekistan) on April 21, 1968, and to the arrest, on May 16-18, of some 800 Tartars who had come to Moscow to ask for an official inquiry into the above clashes. Trials which followed included those of Gomer Bayev (a Tartar engineer), sentenced to two years in prison at Simferopol (Crimea) on April 29, 1969; Prof. Rollan Kadiyev (a physicist), Izzet Khairov (also a physicist), Reshat Bairamov and Ridvan Gafarov (both electrical engineers), each given four years in a labour camp in Tashkent on Aug. 5, 1969; and six others sentenced to a year in prison on the same occasion.

Ilya Gabai, a poet who was imprisoned in 1969-72 for taking part in the agitation on behalf of the Crimean Tartars, committed suicide in Moscow on Oct. 20, 1973, after being questioned in connexion with the underground *Chronicle of Current Events*.

In the following years, however, up to October 1978 some 16,600 Tartar families were allowed to return to the Crimea, but 700 others were considered to be illegally resident in the Crimea and were reported to have been arrested, with their houses being demolished. Some of the Tartars were involved in demonstrations against the eviction, and at least two committed suicide. Some 200 who tried in Moscow on March 15, 1979, to submit to the USSR Supreme Soviet a petition calling for the unhampered return of their people to the Crimea were arrested and forcibly taken back to Tashkent.

Of the activists among the Crimean Tartars, Mustafa Dzhemilev (Abduldzhemil) was sentenced in Omsk on April 15, 1976, to 2½ years in a strict-regime labour camp for "spreading anti-state propaganda", this sentence being confirmed by the Supreme Court of the RSFSR on May 25, 1976. On March 6, 1979, he was sentenced to four years' internal exile for having disregarded conditions imposed upon him after his release on Dec. 22, 1977. In February 1979 he renounced his Soviet citizenship and applied for permission to emigrate.

A cousin of his, Rechat Dzhemilev, who was a spokesman for the Crimean Tartars, was in July 1979 sentenced to three years' imprisonment for "spreading slanderous fabrications", and another Tartar, Mamedi Chobanov, was on July 12, 1979, sentenced to three years in a labour camp for "anti-Soviet propaganda".

Georgian Nationalists

Among Georgian nationalists Vladimir Zhvaniya was, on Feb. 4, 1977, reported to have been condemned to death for having planted bombs at three government buildings, according to his own testimony "in the cause of the struggle against the Russification of Georgia"; he was executed on Jan. 13, 1978.

Germans

In West Germany it was estimated in 1980 that some 100,000 persons claiming to be ethnic Germans had applied for visas to enable them to travel to the Federal Republic of Germany (whereas the Soviet authorities gave their number as only 10,000). According to a report by Dr Sakharov on Aug. 8, 1979, a group of 18 ethnic Germans had been sentenced to imprisonment in Frunze (Kirghizia), two of them to two years in a labour camp each for "hooliganism". In the early 1980s arrests were reported from time to time of ethnic Germans demonstrating against the refusal of the authorities to grant them permission to emigrate, notably two groups protesting in Red Square (Moscow) in August and November 1981 respectively.

An Association of Germans in Estonia was early in 1974 reported to have asked for official recognition. In a secret journal *Re Patria* issued by two Estonian Germans, the right to emigrate was demanded and reference was made to a demonstration said to have been held in Moscow on Feb. 11, 1974, by Soviet Germans demanding freedom to emigrate.

Ukrainian Nationalists

Activities by Ukrainian nationalists directed mainly against the Russification of the Ukraine have led to trials of such activists on various charges on a number of occasions.

In the spring of 1966 trials took place in Kiev, Lvov, Ivano-Frankoist, and Tarnopol of 30 Ukrainian intellectuals, of whom 20 were sentenced to imprisonment for up to six years. According to a report on these trials, drawn up by Vyacheslav Chornovil (a journalist and then an official of the Young Communist League) and submitted to the first secretary of the Ukrainian Communist Party, the only offence proved against them was that they had discussed ways of defending Ukrainian culture against forcible Russification and had possessed books on this question, some of them dating back to before the 1917 October Revolution.

V. Chornovil also maintained that Article 62 of the Ukrainian criminal code, under which the accused had been sentenced, completely negated the freedom guaranteed to citizens by the Constitution of the USSR, with the result that it seemed possible to classify as "slanderous fabrications" all statements which did not coincide with official directives.

V. Chornovil was consequently tried in Lvov in November 1967 for "anti-Soviet activities" and sentenced to three years in prison, which were later reduced to 18 months. In February 1973 he was, also in Lvov, sentenced to seven years in a strict-regime labour camp and five years' internal exile for "anti-Soviet agitation and propaganda" and on suspicion of involvement in the publication of *The Ukrainian Herald,* an underground journal.

Levko Lukyanenko (a lawyer) was sentenced at Gorodnya (Ukraine) on July 20, 1978, to 10 years in a special-regime labour camp and five years' internal exile for "anti-Soviet agitation". He had been arrested at Chernigov on Dec. 12, 1977, having previously been condemned to death in 1961 for treason and for trying to set up a "Marxist" group propagating self-determination for the Ukraine, this sentence having been com-

muted to 15 years in a severe-regime labour camp.

Yuri Badzyo (a Ukrainian historian) was sentenced on Dec. 25, 1979, to seven years in a labour camp and five years' internal exile for "slandering the Soviet Union"; he had written a book on Russo-Ukrainian relations, accusing the Soviet leadership of attempting to eliminate non-Russian cultures within the Soviet Union's post-war boundaries.

Religious Opposition

In a decree issued after the 1917 October Revolution and probably formulated by Lenin, it was laid down that it was illegal "to restrain or limit freedom of conscience" and that every citizen was entitled to "profess any religion or none at all". The Constitution of 1918 recognized the right of all citizens to conduct religious and anti-religious propaganda. However, in the late 1920s pressure on the Churches increased and a 1929 law restraining religious associations was sporadically enforced. During the 1941-45 war, on the other hand, Stalin made concessions to the Churches in order to gain their support.

Under the administration of Nikita Khrushchev a determined campaign was conducted against all religious groups in 1960-64. In terms of a 1961 decree the administration of places of worship was transferred from the local clergy to parish councils consisting of laymen (which might be dissolved and the churches closed if the membership fell below 20). As a result some 10,000 churches were reported to have been closed between 1961 and 1964 and the number of theological seminaries reduced from eight in 1959 to three in 1964.

Thereafter it was officially admitted that the anti-religious campaign had been counter-productive, and measures against religious minorities were less stringent than before. They included the outlawing of whole denominations; the enforced merging with other denominations; the enforced closure of legally existing places of worship; state control of all places of worship through registration regulations; the legal provision that no religious association (parish) was a person at law; arbitrary distinctions in recognizing central representative bodies; restrictions on local and national church congresses; libelling in the press without the right of reply; the suppression of old religious customs; and discrimination against believers at places of work and in housing, education and public life.

The 1929 law was amended by a decree of June 23, 1975 (published in November 1975), with the result of abolishing the state's obligation to provide alternative premises for church buildings confiscated by the state and also the concession allowing parents to give religious instruction to their children (these provisions of the 1929 law having already been disregarded in practice).

According to an official Soviet source quoted in March 1977, there were then some 1,200 groups of religious dissenters "with anti-Soviet tendencies" existing illegally and refusing to register with the authorities.

ORTHODOX CHURCH

According to a report published on Dec. 17, 1970, by the (British) Minority Rights Group (a research and information unit), the Orthodox Church in the Soviet Union had the allegiance of some 30,000,000 people. Trials of dissenting Orthodox Christians have frequently been reported, notably in connexion with the appearance of unauthorized publications, and the authorities have also taken action against members of Orthodox seminars. Against this background, organizations in defence of freedom of religion have been formed by members of the Orthodox Church on various occasions.

All-Russian Social Christian Union for the Liberation of the People

This Union, formed in 1964, was said to consist of about 60 intellectuals who sought a synthesis of Christianity, Marxism and Russian nationalism and the establishment of a socialist republic with a freely elected President and Parliament, subject to control by an assembly of representatives of the Russian Orthodox Church. A number of members of the organization, launched in Leningrad and with contacts with similar groups in the Ukraine and at Sverdlovsk, Tomsk and Irkutsk, were charged with treason and in November 1967 their leader, Prof. Igor Ogurtsov (a specialist in Tibetan studies), was sentenced to 20 years' imprisonment, two other members were given 13 years each and a fourth eight years, while at a trial of other members which ended in April 1968 prison sentences ranged from one to six years.

Christian Committee for the Defence of Believers' Rights

Founding members of this organization of adherents to the unofficial Orthodox Church included (i) Lev Regelson, who was on Sept. 24, 1980, convicted of producing and distributing, in 1974-79, material slandering the USSR and of "maintaining criminal contacts with Western journalists" and given a suspended sentence of five years after confessing his "guilt" and expressing repentance; and (ii) Viktor Kapitanchuk, who was similarly given a five-year suspended sentence on Oct. 9, 1980 (see also below).

Committee for the Defence of Believers in the Soviet Union

This Committee was established in December 1976 by three members of the Russian Orthodox Church—the Rev. Gleb Yakunin, Varsonofy Haibulin (a former priest) and Viktor Kapitanchuk—in order to "co-operate with public and state organizations" in dealing with grievances of believers in the USSR, on the basis of their belief that the freedom of religion guaranteed by the Constitution was widely disregarded. Fr Yakunin was arrested on Nov. 1, 1979, and on Aug. 28, 1980, he was sentenced in Moscow to five years in a labour camp, to be followed by five years' internal exile, for "anti-Soviet agitation". V. Kapitanchuk was arrested on March 12, 1980; he was also involved in the founding of the Christian Committee for the Defence of Believers' Rights (see separate entry) and was on Oct. 9, 1980, given a five-year suspended sentence after pleading guilty to "anti-Soviet agitation and propaganda".

ROMAN CATHOLIC CHURCH

The Roman Catholic Church was estimated, in the 1970s, to have about 3,000,000 members in the Soviet Union, most of them in Lithuania, where they constituted about 85 per cent of the population.

The trial of two Lithuanian Catholic priests—Fr Juozas Zdebskis and Fr P. Bubnis, each of whom was sentenced on Nov. 11, 1971, to one year's detention under a 1966 decree making it illegal to give formal religious instruction to minors—led to mass protests and the signing by 17,054 Lithuanian Catholics in December 1971 and January 1972 of a petition sent to Leonid Brezhnev (then General Secretary of the CPSU) and also Dr Kurt Waldheim (then UN Secretary-General) asking the Government of the USSR "to secure for us freedom of conscience which is guaranteed by the Constitution of the USSR but which up to the present does not exist in practice". In the petition it was pointed out inter alia that two bishops had been exiled for an unspecified period without trial; that Catholics were often dismissed from their employment solely because of their religion; that believers were not allowed to restore burned-out churches even at their own expense; and that private religious education was forbidden, while atheism was "compulsorily inculcated".

The funeral, on May 18, 1972, of a Catholic worker who had burned himself to death in Kaunas on May 14, was followed by demonstrations calling for "freedom for Lithuania" and leading to clashes with police and subsequent prison sentences for a number of rioters.

The Ukrainian Catholic Church was forcibly incorporated in the Orthodox Church in

1946 but continued to lead a clandestine existence. Of its leading clerics, Joseph Slipyj-Kobernickyj-Dyckowsky, Archbishop of Lvov and Metropolitan of Halyc, was deported to Siberia in 1945 but released to the Vatican in 1963. In 1963 he was recognized by the Holy See as the Major Archbishop of the Ukrainian Rite Catholic Church, and he was created a Cardinal in 1965. Before the Roman Catholic Bishops' Synod in Rome he stated in 1974 that any priest who secretly read mass in the Soviet Union was "being sentenced to three years' hard labour in Siberia". (In fact the Ukrainian Archbishop Basil Welytschovsky had been given such a sentence on March 27, 1970.)

In a letter sent to the Synod by the Association for the Patriarchal System in the Ukrainian Catholic Church and published on Oct. 21, 1974, it was alleged that the clergy and laity of this Church were exposed to "terrible persecution" by the Communist regime in the Soviet Union, and the Congregation for the Eastern Churches and the Roman Curia were accused of abandoning their "Church-in-exile" in order to improve relations with Moscow. However, on March 27, 1980, the Pope nominated Mgr Myroslav Ivan Lubachivsky as head of the Ukrainian Catholic Church in succession to Cardinal Slipyj.

As detailed below, Roman Catholics in the Soviet Union have formed a number of organizations to defend freedom of religion and of worship, although without constituting any serious political challenge to the Communist regime.

Catholic Committee for the Defence of Believers

This Committee was established in November 1978 by the Rev. Alfonsas Svareinkas and four other Lithuanian Roman Catholic priests. It decided to co-operate closely with the (Orthodox) Committee for the Defence of Believers in the Soviet Union (see separate entry). The Committee was to protest in particular against the closure of monasteries and of religious publishing and printing houses and the refusal to allow the Roman Catholic community to express itself on radio and television. Fr Svareinkas claimed that of 628 churches in Lithuania 95 per cent were without a priest; that there were only 711 priests as against 1,500 before World War II; and that the number of young people admitted to the Kaunas seminary was half that of the priests who died.

Association for the Patriarchal System in the Ukrainian Catholic Church

This Association was formed to oppose the officially recognized Roman Catholic Church in the Ukraine.

OTHER CHRISTIAN GROUPS

Council of Churches of the Evangelical Christians and Baptists (Initsiatniki)

This organization broke away from the officially tolerated All-Union Council of Evangelical Christians-Baptists (representing more than 500,000 Baptists in the Soviet Union) as it rejected the Soviet authorities' right to oversee religious affairs. It was therefore totally outlawed and its members were prosecuted for "distributing religious propaganda and perverting the minds of children". Between 1961 and 1964 over 200 dissident Baptists were sentenced to imprisonment for up to 10 years, and although most of them were released after the dismissal of N. Khrushchev in 1964 more Baptists were arrested in 1966-67. Letters sent in May and June by five wives of imprisoned Baptists to President Podgorny and U Thant (then UN Secretary-General) were accompanied by a list of 202 Baptist prisoners, of whom 169 had been sentenced in 1967.

In October 1974 it was reported that a clandestine bible printing works had been uncovered in Riga (Latvia), with 15,000 copies of the New Testament and 16 tons of paper being seized. (Some 220,000 copies of the New Testament were said to have been distributed from Riga in 1973, against only 10,000 bibles having been printed for the whole of the Soviet Union by official permission of the Soviet authorities in that year.)

Pastor Georgi P. Vins, a leading member of the outlawed Council, was on Jan. 31, 1975, sentenced to five years in prison and another five years in exile for unauthorized religious activity. As a result of negotiations between the Carter Administration in the United States and the Soviet authorities, Pastor Vins was, on April 27, 1979, exchanged in New York, together with four other imprisoned Soviet citizens, against two Soviet citizens sentenced in the United States for espionage. Pastor Vins said in the United States on April 24, 1980, that there were then 60 Baptist ministers imprisoned in the USSR, against 35 at the beginning of 1980. Further arrests of Baptists were reported later in 1980 on various charges, including alleged violation of the laws on the separation of church and state.

Committee for the Right to Free Emigration (Pentecostalists)

This Committee was established in Moscow by a group of Pentecostalists, as announced by them on June 29, 1979. It had been reported on Feb. 24, 1977, that the unofficial Pentecostalist Pastor Nikolai Goretai of a village in the north-western Caucasus had stated that applications for permission to emigrate to any country where they might be "able to practise their religion freely'' had been made to the USSR Supreme Soviet by 90 persons in his village and by 525 in other Pentecostal communities in the USSR, but that the Emigration Office had refused the applications. On March 24, 1977, he claimed that there were 484 Pentecostalists at Nakhodka (near Vladivostok) and more than 500 elsewhere who wished to emigrate.

It was later estimated that during the year 1979 some 30,000 Pentecostalists had applied for exit visas; however, the Soviet authorities announced in February 1980 that no such visas would be issued.

After attempting for 17 years to obtain permission to emigrate, seven Pentecostalists entered the US embassy in Moscow on June 27, 1978, and were allowed to remain there; despite repeated Western appeals on their behalf six of them were still living there at the end of 1982, the Soviet authorities having refused to allow them to emigrate.

On Nov. 25, 1980, Pastor Goretai was reported to have been sentenced to seven years in a labour camp and five years' internal exile for "anti-Soviet agitation and propaganda". (He had already served a five-year sentence in a labour camp and five years in internal exile imposed in 1961.)

In 1981-82 sentences were passed on a number of Pentecostalists in the Ukraine. They included five who were said to have applied for permission to emigrate and to have renounced their Soviet citizenship, and who were on Aug. 5, 1981, reported to have been convicted of anti-Soviet slander in Dnepropetrovsk, four of them being sentenced to five years in a labour camp and five years' internal exile, and the fifth to three years in prison and three years in exile. Among others Pavel Achtyorev was on Feb. 4, 1982, sentenced to seven years in a labour camp and five years in exile for printing "slanderous" publications.

Free Adventists

The spiritual leader of this group of Seventh-Day Adventists, Vladimir Shelkov (83), was on March 23, 1979, sentenced in Tashkent to five years in a strict-regime labour camp and to confiscation of his house for alleged spreading of false information designed to discredit the Soviet system (after he had previously served 23 years in prisons or banishment) and he died on Jan. 27, 1980. Four other members of the group were sentenced to from two years suspended to five years in a strict-regime labour camp. During 1981 a number of Seventh-Day Adventists were sentenced to from two to five years' detention in a labour camp, inter alia for circulating illegal leaflets, a five-year sentence being imposed on Rostislav Galetsky, a senior minister of the sect, accused of transmitting "slanderous material" to the Western press and of contravening the Soviet laws on the formation of religious sects (as reported on April 5).

Jehovah's Witnesses (Watchtower Society)

This sect, whose members are conscientious objectors to military service, is banned in the Soviet Union. From time to time (e.g. on April 18, 1975) it was reported that members had been sentenced to imprisonment for practising their religion.

JEWISH COMMUNITY

Against the Jewish religion a sustained campaign was officially pursued in the Soviet Union between 1948 and 1953, although after Stalin's death in the latter year a more liberal policy was adopted. In 1961, however, Khrushchev's Government launched an attack on Jewish culture and religious observances. According to official Soviet figures the number of synagogues fell from 450 in 1956 to 96 in 1963. Dr Nahum Goldmann, then president of the World Jewish Congress, stated on Feb. 17, 1964, that there were only one rabbinical seminary with four students in the USSR; that there were no rabbis under 70 years old; that only one (limited) edition of the Jewish prayer book had been printed in the past 40 years; and that no Hebrew bibles were available. The baking of *matzoh* (unleavened bread for Passover) was forbidden between 1961 and 1965.

In 1965, however, the authorities again adopted a more liberal attitude. The admission of 30 students to the rabbinical seminary was permitted; the printing of 10,000 copies of the Jewish prayer book was allowed; and the number of Yiddish books published was increased. The Soviet press recalled that Lenin had demanded "a tireless struggle" against anti-semitism, and a number of Soviet Jews were allowed to emigrate in 1965-66.

In an article in *Izvestia* (the daily organ of the USSR Supreme Soviet) it was stated early in January 1977 that "militant anti-communists" were "advocating the departure of Jews from our united multinational society" and "the creation of a ramified network of circles to study Hebrew in order to 'bring closer spiritually' the young people to 'God's chosen country' and its state religion [i.e. to Israel]". Zionists, the article continued, planned to establish "direct and permanent contacts between Jewish religious communities in the USSR and Zionist centres abroad" and while anti-semitism was "banned in the Soviet Union by law" Zionists would never "be allowed to propagate racialism in the Soviet Union unpunished".

Official action was accordingly taken against Zionist activities and the private tuition of Hebrew, but the number of Jews permitted to leave the country (which had risen to over 34,500 in 1973 and had been reduced thereafter to 13,222 in 1975, 14,261 in 1976 and 16,737 in 1977) was allowed to rise again (to 28,864 in 1978 and 51,320 in 1979). Thereafter it fell drastically to 21,471 in 1980 and 9,400 in 1981. Those who continued to be refused exit visas included scientists as well as human rights activists.

Among the latter, Dr Viktor Brailovsky, editor of the underground journal *Jews in the USSR,* was on June 18, 1981, sentenced to five years' internal exile for "anti-Soviet slander", after his co-editor, Igor Gubermann, had on March 20, 1980, been sentenced to five years in a strict-regime labour camp for allegedly receiving stolen icons.

Other Internal Opposition Groups

Free Republican Party

A young Ukrainian who gave his name as Vladislav Davydenko and who appeared in Britain in September 1969 after stowing away on a ship which had left Leningrad on Aug. 23, claimed to be a member of this party which, he said, had about 3,000 members, including high-ranking army officers.

Group for Establishing Trust between the USSR and the USA

The formation of this Group was announced in Moscow on June 4, 1982, by a group of 11 intellectuals, whose spokesman, Sergei Batovrin, explained that the Group sought "the participation of the Soviet and the American public, on equal terms, in the dialogue between politicians" on questions of disarmament; he also claimed that the official Soviet "Peace Committee" served only to echo the Communist Party's policy. All the 11 intellectuals involved were subsequently subjected to restrictions, S. Batovrin being arrested on Aug. 6 (for evading military service) and subsequently confined in a psychiatric hospital until Sept. 7. (It appeared that the official intention was to keep the members of the Group away from an officially-approved "Peace March 1982" mainly organized by women's disarmament movements from Scandinavian countries for the second half of July 1982.)

"New Left" Movement

A "New Left" Movement described as "anarcho-syndicalist" and calling for "socialism with a human face" emerged in Leningrad in 1976. The editors of its underground journal *Perspectives*—Arkadi Tsurkov and Alexander Skobov, both students—were temporarily arrested in 1976 and rearrested in 1979. In the latter year A. Tsurkov was, on April 13, sentenced to five years in a strict-

regime labour camp and two years' exile for "anti-Soviet propaganda", while A. Skobov was declared "not responsible" by the Serbsky Institute of Psychiatry in Moscow.

External Organizations

Action Front for the Liberation of the Baltic Countries

This group claimed responsibility for bomb attacks made in Paris on the Soviet embassy on April 5, 1977 and on the offices of two Soviet organizations seven days later.

International Committee for the Defence of Human Rights in the Soviet Union

In a report published by this Brussels-based Committee on Feb. 26, 1973, it was estimated that there were some 10,000 political prisoners (out of a total of at least 1,000,000 prisoners) held in Soviet labour camps (excluding remand or penal prisons and psychiatric prison hospitals), with many of these camps being in remote areas and political prisoners being concentrated in the most severe camps, in Mordovia and Vladimir (east of Moscow).

Organization of Ukrainian Nationalists

This right-wing Organization was held responsible for sending to the Soviet Union foreign agents (usually of Ukrainian descent) to contact Ukrainians inside the Soviet Union. In the newspaper *Pravda Ukrainy* it was alleged that three writers (one of them being Vyacheslav Chornovil—see section on Other Nationalities above) had been associated with such an agent.

Peasants' Party of Latvia

This exiled formation is affiliated to the Christian Democratic World Union.

People's Labour Union *(Narodno Trudovoi Soyuz,* NTS)

The NTS was founded as an anti-Soviet organization by Russian émigrés in Belgrade in 1930. It began to infiltrate agents into the Soviet Union in 1937. During World War II it collaborated with the Germans in occupied Soviet territory but it later aroused the suspicions of the German authorities who arrested many of its members. In the 1950s, when it was based in Frankfurt (West Germany), it resumed its infiltration of agents and propaganda into the Soviet Union. The Soviet authorities have repeatedly claimed to have seized NTS publications found in the possession of dissidents (such as Vladimir Bukovsky and Alexander Ginsburg) and also of foreign "tourists". The NTS was also said to have recruited persons of Russian extraction to visit the Soviet Union in order to obtain copies of books and other documents for publication outside the Soviet Union.

Social Democratic Party of Latvia

Leadership. Bruno Kalnins (ch.).

This party in exile is a member of the Socialist Union of Eastern Europe (SUCEE) and a consultative member of the Socialist International. Inside the Soviet Republic of Latvia, Dr Fricis Menders (84), a former leader of the party, was on Nov. 1, 1969, sentenced to five years in a labour camp for "defaming the Soviet state" after he had reportedly supplied a manuscript to a US historian who was collecting material for a study of the 1917-18 revolutionary period in Latvia. Dr Menders had been deported to Siberia by the Tsarist authorities in 1906 and had later been sentenced to 10 years in a labour camp in 1948. On June 11, 1981, Juris Burmeistar, said to be the party's underground leader, was reported to have been sentenced to 15 years in a labour camp for "treason", together with D. A. Limanis, who was given a 10-year sentence.

Social Democratic Party of Lithuania

Leadership. J. Skorubskas (ch.).

This party in exile is a member of the Socialist Union of Central and Eastern Europe (SUCEE) and a consultative member of the Socialist International.

Socialist Party of Estonia

Leadership. Johannes Mihkelson (ch.).

This party in exile is a member of the Socialist Union of Central and Eastern Europe (SUCEE) and a consultative member of the Socialist International.

Ukrainian Liberation Front

Members of this Front claimed responsibility for a bomb attack on the Luxembourg offices of Aeroflot (the Soviet national airline) on Nov. 11, 1980. (In Paris a Ukrainian group set fire to two cars belonging to the Soviet embassy on Nov. 24, 1981.)

Union of Christian Democrats of Lithuania

This exiled formation is a member of the Christian Democratic World Union.

World Congress of Free Ukrainians

Dr Valentyn Moroz (the Ukrainian nationalist who reached the United States in the exchange of April 27, 1979, against two Soviet citizens convicted of spying—see section on Prominent Dissidents above) regarded the above Congress as most representative of the 3,000,000 Ukrainians in emigration (of whom 2,000,000 were in the United States), and he called, on May 18, 1979, for observer status to be granted to the Congress by the United Nations.

Yugoslavia

Capital: Belgrade

Pop. 22,262,000

The Socialist Federal Republic of Yugoslavia, in which effective power is exercised by the League of Communists of Yugoslavia (LCY), is composed of six socialist republics (Bosnia and Herzegovina, Croatia, Macedonia, Montenegro, Serbia and Slovenia) and two autonomous provinces (Kosovo—known as Kosovo-Metohija until 1968—and Vojvodina), both being parts of Serbia. Under the 1974 Constitution there is, at federal level, a Federal Assembly elected for a four-year term and consisting of (i) a Federal Chamber composed of delegates of self-managing organizations and communities and of socio-political organizations and (ii) a Chamber of Republics and Provinces consisting of delegates of the elected Republican and Provincial Assemblies. All election candidates are subject to screening by the Socialist Alliance of the Working People of Yugoslavia, an overall political organization under the leadership of the LCY. All elections take place under the delegate system laid down in the 1974 Constitution.

The principal (illegal) political groups in opposition to the existing regime in Yugoslavia are as follows: (i) Albanian nationalists, partly supported by the Government of the Socialist People's Republic of Albania; (ii) Croatian nationalists, supported largely by Croatian émigré organizations, including remnants of the *Ustashi* (Fascist) regime of Croatia during World War II; (iii) Serbian nationalists, including royalists and supporters of the *Chetnik* movement of World War II; (iv) Cominformists, i.e. pro-Soviet Communists opposed to the 1948 break between Yugoslavia and the Soviet Union, and (v) Socialists, either democratic or tending towards the West European "New Left".

For the internal defence of the state the Yugoslav Government has developed two systems: (i) the "General People's Defence" constituted by the regular Army (the country's only truly centralized institution) and territorial units capable of mobilization at short notice, with their own weapons and their own command and embracing practically all men and women capable of bearing arms; and (ii) "Social Self-Protection" aimed at "countering any negative manifestations in political and economic life, in ideology and culture, and also the machinations of foreign information services, diversionary and terrorist attempts, hostile propaganda, corruption and attacks on social and general property", its fundamental function being—as stated in January 1976 by Lazar Kolichevski (then a member of Yugoslavia's collective Presidency)—"to unmask and to prevent hostile activities against our society and the workers".

According to a statement made in May 1981 by Gen. Franjo Herljevic, the Yugoslav Federal Secretary for Internal Affairs, over 600 persons had been arrested since 1974 for "more or less organized political opposition", of whom 89 had until then been convicted.

Albanian Nationalists

Of the more than 1,600,000 Albanians of Yugoslav nationality, about two-thirds live in the autonomous province of Kosovo, where they constitute about 77 per cent of the population, while the remainder live in parts of Macedonia and of Montenegro. The standard of living of Albanians in Yugoslavia has remained among the lowest of any population sector in that country, the average per capita income in Kosovo province being only about one-third of that of the Federative Republic of Serbia. In September 1958 the press in neighbouring Albania alleged that in 1944-48 some 36,000 Albanians had been "massacred" by Tito's agents and the survivors had been "denationalized".

Secessionist or Autonomist Activities of Albanians in Kosovo

In August-September 1966 it was officially disclosed that in dealing with Albanians accused of secessionist activities the security police in what was then the Kosovo-Metohija (or Kosmet) autonomous region had been guilty of irregularities involving the murder and torture of a number of Albanians, and as a result of these disclosures changes were made in the structure of the LCY. In particular, Alexander Rankovic, who had been organizational secretary of the LCY's Executive Committee, was expelled from that body on July 1 and from the LCY on Oct. 4, 1966.

During discussions on constitutional changes in 1968, a minority of the Albanians in Kosovo called for the formation of an Albanian republic based on the Kosmet region as a full constituent member of the Federal Republic of Yugoslavia, while some were said to have called for Kosovo's incorporation into Albania. In student demonstrations in favour of an Albanian republic held in Pristina (the capital of Kosovo) in November 1968, and also in Tetovo (north-west Macedonia) on Dec. 23, 1968, rioters caused damage to property, and the organizers of the Tetovo disturbances were on June 25, 1969, given prison sentences ranging from 18 months to seven years.

Following demonstrations in Pristina in late December 1974 by students and others, calling for a greater Albania incorporating inside Albania not only Kosovo but also other Yugoslav areas inhabited by Moslems of Albanian origin, five persons were on Jan. 14, 1975, sentenced to imprisonment for from three to nine years for "attempting to overthrow the constitutional order and attacking the territorial integrity of Yugoslavia".

On Feb. 7, 1976, a group of 19 men were reported to have been given up to 15 years in prison for "conspiring against the Government and supporting the secession of Kosovo from Yugoslavia". They were said to have tried to recruit followers among the Albanians in Yugoslavia and to have called for the violent overthrow of the Government. On Feb. 27 that year another 12 men were given prison sentences of from 18 months to nine years for anti-Tito activities in December

1974. A further two students were sentenced on March 13 to 12 and six years' hard labour respectively for being members of the Kosovo "nationalist liberation movement".

Following a campaign in the Albanian press during 1979, when Yugoslavia was accused of allowing widespread exploitation of the Kosovo Albanians by other Yugoslav nationalities, disturbances took place in Pristina early in 1980, leading to a number of arrests and to prison sentences ranging from three to eight years being imposed on eight persons on June 9, 1980, and from three to six years imposed on July 7 on three Albanians from Macedonia.

On March 11-12, 1981, some 2,000 (out of a total of 50,000) students at the University of Pristina caused disturbances, and these were resumed on March 25-26 and again on April 1-2, having spread to miners and other workers. As a result, a state of emergency was declared in Kosovo on April 3. It was officially claimed on April 6 that the (Cominformist) Communist Party of Yugoslavia (see below) had been involved in the disturbances, and that the Albanian nationalists had close links with both pro-fascist and Cominformist organizations in Stuttgart (West Germany), Brussels, the United States and elsewhere. Stane Dolanc, a member of the Presidium of the LCY, admitted on the same day that the demonstrators had demanded full republican status for Kosovo, but he declared: "A republic of Kosovo is not possible within the framework of Yugoslavia—neither in terms of our Constitution nor in terms of what was achieved in the national liberation war, especially in view of the fact that the establishment of a republic of Kosovo in Yugoslavia would in essence mean the downfall of Yugoslavia."

Lazar Mojsov (then President of the LCY Presidium) claimed at a meeting of the LCY's Central Committee on May 7, 1981, that the riots in Pristina had been initiated by a clandestine "Albanian Marxist-Leninist Communist Party in Yugoslavia", the aim of which, he said, was the overthrow of the constitutional order in Yugoslavia and the proclamation of an Albanian republic; he maintained that this organization was directed by a "foreign agents' centre", which (he strongly suggested) was close to the Government of Albania.

Gen. Franjo Herljevic (Federal Secretary for Internal Affairs) claimed in an interview published on May 13, 1981, to have "concrete evidence" of the pursuit of pan-Albanian goals in Yugoslavia by official representatives of the Albanian Government, and of the existence of a clandestine "Red Front" closely linked with the ruling Albanian Party of Labour and with the Albanian intelligence services. A formal Yugoslav protest against "gross interference" by Albania in Yugoslav internal affairs was rejected by the Albanian Government on May 15.

Further disturbances took place at the University of Pristina between May 12 and May 19, 1981. Teachers who had supported the students' action and also LCY members and journalists involved in the disturbances were warned that they would be suspended or otherwise disciplined. Gen. Herljevic, reporting to the Federal Assembly on June 8, 1981, stated that during April and May "nationalists and irredentists" had organized 16 mass demonstrations in 11 communes, causing extensive damage to public and private property; that 506 persons had already been convicted of offences connected with the disorders; that 154 persons were accused of belonging to clandestine organizations or of similar offences; and that eight demonstrators and one policemen had been killed and 257 persons injured, including 33 members of the security forces.

In his capacity as Yugoslav Interior Minister, Stane Dolanc stated in a radio interview broadcast on Sept. 29, 1982, that some 700 people had been arrested in Kosovo since March 1982 for activities against the state, and that 320 had been tried for political offences; 55 illegal groups belonging to four different organizations had been uncovered, he said, and over 1,300 people punished. However, the situation in the province remained tense, and despite the improvements brought about mainly by the presence of heavy security reinforcements and the general absence of street violence, there was evidence of continuing and open resistance; for example, 126 attacks on militiamen had been recorded in the province so far in 1982, and, he said, the arrested conspirators had increasingly openly questioned the territorial integrity of Yugoslavia by expressing their support for Enver Hoxha (the First Secretary of the Albanian Party of Labour).

Yugoslavia's 1981 census had shown that 77.5 per cent of the Kosovo population were of Albanian origin, compared with 73.8 per cent in 1971, while 13.2 per cent were Serbs and 1.7 per cent Montenegrins, compared with 18.4 per cent and 2.5 per cent respectively in 1971; the increasing predominance of the Kosovo Albanians was partly due to their high birth rate (thought to be the highest in Europe), but partly also to the emigration of the Kosovo Serbs and Montenegrins, who were in some areas repeatedly harassed by Albanian activists.

The traditional tensions between the Kosovo Serbs and Albanians have been heightened in recent years by the severe economic difficulties experienced by the province. Although the Federal Government had made major investments in Kosovo, the Albanians claimed that these were largely prestige projects or that they otherwise created little local employment. The level of Kosovo's industrial production fell in the 12 months to September 1982 by 4.3 per cent and that of labour productivity by 7.4 per cent, and although the province's income had increased by 18 per cent in cash terms (against inflation rates of some 30 per cent), salaries had risen by 27 per cent.

In the early 1980s the Albanian press maintained a continuing attack on the Yugoslav authorities over a series of arrests and convictions of Albanians in Kosovo, which were variously described as "mass verdicts", as "mounting terror" and as "a real inquisition" which "violated national feelings". Yugoslavia for its part presented a formal note to the Albanian embassy in Belgrade on Dec. 7, 1981, alleging Albanian interference in its internal affairs (although the embassy refused to accept the document). Milos Minic, then a member of the Presidium of the LCY representing Serbia, accused the Albanian secret services, in a speech delivered at Pristina University on Feb. 19, 1982, of direct involvement in the Kosovo disturbances.

During 1981-82 a number of attacks were made on Yugoslav institutions in Brussels and West Germany, where several Yugoslav representatives were killed; in some cases Kosovo Albanians were thought to have been responsible. Strains were accordingly generated in Yugoslavia's relations with Belgium, and on Aug. 26, 1981, the Yugoslav ambassador in Brussels was withdrawn in protest at Belgium's alleged failure to ensure adequate protection for Yugoslav citizens.

Albanians in Other Parts of Yugoslavia

Among the Albanian community in Macedonia (constituting about 20 per cent of the republic's population), five persons were on May 20, 1981, sentenced in Skopje to imprisonment for from seven to 13½ years for creating a "National Party of Labour" to campaign for the secession of the mainly Albanian part of Macedonia.

In other trials of Albanians outside Kosovo, (i) a man was sentenced on July 3, 1981, in Titograd (Montenegro) to two years' imprisonment for "hostile propaganda"; (ii) three soldiers received light or suspended prison sentences on Jan. 26, 1982, in Zadar (Croatia) for belonging to an illegal separatist organization; (iii) an man received a five-year prison sentence in Skopje (Macedonia) on Feb. 16 for selling tape recordings of broadcasts by Radio Tirana (the Albanian state radio); (iv) a man received a two-year sentence in Vranje (Serbia) on March 9 for spreading "hostile propaganda"; (v) another person received a three-year sentence in Macedonia on March 11 for the same offence; (vi) 11 persons were jailed in Vranje on

April 5 for forming an illegal separatist organization, while another four members of an illegal organization were sentenced in the town on May 15 to eight, seven and five years' imprisonment for "hostile activities"; and (vii) a person received a six-year prison sentence in Skopje on May 24 for inciting racial, national and religious hatred.

Croatian Nationalists

Ustashi Movement

The *Ustashi* movement has its origins in the independent state of Croatia set up by Hitler and Mussolini in 1941, and its aim is to restore an independent, anti-communist state in Croatia. Since World War II supporters of this movement have been responsible for numerous murders, bomb attacks and other acts of terrorism in various parts of the world.

According to documents of the Australian Security Intelligence Organization (ASIO) produced in the Australian Senate on March 27, 1972, there existed in Australia, from 1956 onwards, three Croatian terrorist organizations aiming at the overthrow of the Yugoslav Government—(i) the Croatian Revolutionary Brotherhood (HRB), (ii) the United Croatians of West Germany, and (iii) the Croatian Revolutionary Organization—all of which were set up within the Croatian Liberation Movement and the Croatian National Resistance and were supported by two youth organizations, the Croatian Youth and the World League of Croatian Youth.

In Australia members of the *Ustashi* organization were held responsible for two bomb attacks against Yugoslav property in Sydney on Sept. 16, 1972, and according to the Australian police Croatian dissidents had set up a military training camp.

In the Federal Republic of Germany an attack on the Yugoslav trade mission in Bad Godesberg was made on Nov. 29, 1962, by some 25 members of a Croatian "Brotherhood of the Cross" (which was said to have about 200 members and which was banned in Germany on March 12, 1963, as a right-wing extremist organization which had decided on a policy of violence in protest against the existing regime in Yugoslavia). The 25 Croats involved in the attack were on June 25, 1964, given prison sentences, their leader being sentenced to 15 years' hard labour for manslaughter and other offences.

In Sweden two *Ustashi* members temporarily occupied the Yugoslav consulate in Gothenburg on Feb. 10, 1971, and threatened to kill the staff unless the Yugoslav authorities released Miljenko Hrkac (detained in Belgrade in connexion with a bomb attack on a cinema in which one person was killed and 77 were injured). However, on Feb. 11 the two Croats surrendered to the Swedish police and on March 19 they were each sentenced to 3½ years' imprisonment in Gothenburg. (Miljenko Hrkac was on Dec. 26, 1975, condemned to death in Belgrade for terrorist acts, including the above bomb attack.)

On April 7, 1971, the Yugoslav ambassador to Sweden was fatally wounded by *Ustashi* members, and five Croats involved in this act were on July 14, 1971, sentenced to imprisonment ranging from two years to life.

On Sept. 15, 1972, three *Ustashi* members hijacked a Swedish airliner and forced it to land at Malmö airport. They demanded that in return for the release of the aircraft the Swedish Government should hand over to them the seven Croats imprisoned in Sweden as stated above. The Swedish Government acceded to this demand, but only six of the seven imprisoned Croats agreed to be handed over to the hijackers. The airliner was flown to Madrid, where the hijackers surrendered to the police. The Spanish authorities thereupon detained all nine Croats but refused to extradite them to Yugoslavia, as had been requested by the latter.

Croatian nationalists sentenced in Yugoslavia during 1972 included four student leaders given sentences of from one to four years on Oct. 5; seven students sentenced on Oct. 6 to from six months to two years for attempting to overthrow the social order and elected representative bodies; Zlatko Tomicic (former chairman of an independent Writers' Union and former editor of the banned literary review *Hrvatski Knizevsni List)*, sentenced on Oct. 5 to three years' strict imprisonment for extensive subversive activity and collaboration with Croatian political émigrés (this sentence being increased to five years by the Supreme Court of Croatia late in March 1973); four Croats given prison sentences ranging from two to five years on Oct. 10 for "hostile propaganda against the people and the state"; and seven others to from one to 6½ years in strict imprisonment on Nov. 27 for having formed a "terrorist group" and being in contact with *Ustashi* organizations in the Federal Republic of Germany and in Austria.

On June 7, 1973, two *Ustashi* members were sentenced at Tuzla (Bosnia) to 12 and 10 years in prison respectively for involvement in an *Ustashi* attempt to cause disturbances in order to secure the separation of Croatia from Yugoslavia.

Following further incursions by *Ustashi* members, two of them and a policeman were killed south of the port of Rijeka on Oct. 29, 1974, and 10 local sympathizers were on Nov. 20, 1974, reported to have been arrested in the Zagreb area. After a bomb explosion at a Zagreb post office, where one person lost his life, more than 20 people were arrested on Nov. 21.

A group of 15 Croatian nationalists, arrested in Zadar in June 1974, were on Feb. 17, 1975, given prison sentences of from 1½ to 13 years for subversive activities, in particular for having formed, four years earlier, an organization which was to become the basis of a Croatian Liberation Army, and which planned to acquire arms and ammunition, to commit sabotage and to assassinate political leaders, among them Dr Vladimir Bakaric (then the Croatian member of Yugoslavia's collective Presidency). Some of the defendants were also accused of having established links with the *Ustashi* organization abroad and of having adopted a "code of racial purity" banning marriages of Croats with other nationalities. The ultimate aim of the group was said to be the creation of a "great Croatian state" including also Bosnia-Herzegovina and parts of Serbia and Montenegro. The defendants denied that the organization referred to in the indictment existed but affirmed that armed struggle was the only means of attaining "Croatian liberation".

Croatian National Resistance (*Hrvatski Narodni Odbor,* HNO)

Leadership. Stjepan Bilandzic (ch. 1965-78).

This group appears to have been active mainly in the Federal Republic of Germany, where it was banned on June 9, 1976. Stjepan Bilandzic was on June 25, 1964, given a 3½-year prison sentence for his involvement in an attack on the Yugoslav trade mission in Bad Godesberg on Nov. 29, 1962 (when a doorman was killed). On May 25, 1978, he was again arrested and, with others, accused of various crimes against the Yugoslav state, which applied unsuccessfully to the Federal Republic for his extradition to Yugoslavia.

On June 9, 1976, the HNO and also *Drina,* another extreme right-wing Croatian organization, were banned by the German Federal Government because by their constant calls for violent action against Yugoslav institutions and representatives they endangered the internal security of the Federal Republic of Germany.

Croatian Liberation Movement

Leadership. Branimir Peterner.

Established in 1963, this secret organization was accused of conducting Croatian separatist propaganda, collecting military information and seeking to establish contact with Croatian émigrés in the Federal Republic of Germany, with a view to overthrowing the Yugoslav regime by force. At a trial of 13 members of this group, its leader was on Feb. 2, 1966, sentenced to nine years in prison and the other defendants to imprisonment for from two to eight years.

Croatian Liberation Fighters

This underground movement, supporting the creation of a free and independent Croatia, has been responsible for acts of terrorism in the United States, in particular for bomb attacks on a Yugoslav bank in New York on March 17, 1980, and on the house of the Yugoslav chargé d'affaires in Washington, D.C., on June 1, 1980.

Croatian Revolutionary Brotherhood (HRB)

A group of 19 members of this organization, trained in Australia and Austria, entered Yugoslavia (apparently from Austria) in July 1972 but were liquidated by the Yugoslav security forces, who killed 15 of the infiltrators (who in turn had killed 15 members of these forces). Three of the remaining attackers were sentenced to death in Sarajevo in December 1972 and executed on March 17, 1973, and a fourth had his death sentence commuted to imprisonment for 20 years. All the Croats executed, and six of those killed by the security forces, had Australian citizenship.

The HRB was banned in the Federal Republic of Germany in 1968.

Mother Croatia (*Matica Hrvatska*)

Leadership. Dr Dragutin Scukanac.

In December 1971 President Tito accused *Matica Hrvatska,* originally founded in the 1840s as a cultural organization, of being the focus of a Croatian nationalist movement which, he said, threatened the unity of Yugoslavia and was organized by a "so-called revolutionary committee of 50" which had infiltrated the Croatian League of Communists. These and other accusations by President Tito led to a purge and reorganization of the Croatian party and state leadership in the same month and the arrest of 11 leaders of *Matica Hrvatska,* including the editor-in-chief of *Hrvatski Tjednik* (the organization's weekly newspaper, which had attained a circulation of 100,000 copies before ceasing publication in December 1971).

The Zagreb public prosecutor said on April 24, 1972, that *Matica Hrvatska* had been "in permanent correspondence and contact" with groups of émigrés and their "espionage headquarters" in various countries; that it had set up 36 branches abroad (with headquarters in Paris); and that its membership included "notorious *Ustashi*" members.

According to official figures published on Jan. 11, 1972, a total of 554 people had been arrested in connexion with Croatian nationalist activities; 87 of them had been released,

276 fined, 155 sentenced to detention for from two to 60 days, and 36 transferred to an examining magistrate. Of these 36 a number were subsequently sentenced as follows:

Oct. 11, 1972: Dr Scukanac to four years in prison for "gathering information on behalf of a foreign intelligence service"; Ante Bruno Busic (an editor of *Hrvatski Tjednik*) to two years for supplying documents and information to a representative of a foreign power and for publishing "mendacious" allegations of "exploitation and oppression of Croatia"; and Franjo Tudjman (a historian and former general) also to two years for allegedly having collaborated since 1964 with Croatian extremist émigrés known to be "foreign intelligence agents" and to have attempted to make *Matica Hrvatska* into a political party with a nationalist and chauvinist programme.

Oct. 26, 1972: Vlado Gotovac (former editor-in-chief of *Hrvatski Tjednik*) to four years' strict imprisonment and a four-year ban on all public activity, inter alia for misusing his newspaper to propagate Croatian separatism, and Dr Hrvoje Sosic (a former economic science assistant at Zagreb University) to 2½ years' strict imprisonment, also for attempting to separate Croatia from the rest of Yugoslavia (both defendants denying the charges against them).

Nov. 24, 1972: Dr Marko Veselica (a former economics lecturer) to seven years' strict imprisonment, Joza Ivzevic-Bakulic (a law lecturer and former secretary-general of *Matica Hrvatska*) to four years and Zvonimir Komarica (a writer) to two years, all three being also barred for four years from publishing articles in the press or speaking at public gatherings; they were charged with (i) creating within *Matica Hrvatska* "an aggressive opposition (nationalist) political party", (ii) drawing up a list of opponents to be "liquidated", (iii) maintaining close contacts with émigrés, (iv) attempting to transform a 1971 students' strike into a general strike, (v) propagating hatred against the other peoples of Yugoslavia, in particular the Serbs of Croatia, and (vi) drawing up a plan for "an armed struggle and guerrilla warfare". The defendants pleaded "not guilty" and denied having had contacts abroad with persons working against Yugoslavia.

Feb. 23, 1972: Dr Sime Djodan (a law lecturer) to six years' strict imprisonment and a four-year ban on appearing at public meetings or contributing to mass information media, for attempting to overthrow the Government, trying to undermine the economic system, inciting to national intolerance and attempting to change the federal structure of Yugoslavia.

Dr Veselica (given a seven-year sentence on Nov. 24, 1972—see above) was released under an amnesty proclaimed on Nov. 24, 1977.

Serbian Nationalists

A number of Serbian nationalists, in particular former *Chetniks* (i.e. followers of the late Gen. Draja Mihailovic, who had during World War II been opposed by the partisans led by Josip Broz Tito), were dealt with by the courts in 1972-75.

Two Serbian nationalists accused of having, by producing and distributing tracts and books in 1970-71, tried to undermine "the unity and fraternity of the peoples of Yugoslavia" and to bring about "a change of the constitutional order by force" were on June 27, 1972, sentenced to imprisonment for one year and for 14 months respectively, while two others were given suspended sentences.

Dr Djura Djurovic, who had been an aide of Gen. Mihailovic and had been released in 1962 after serving 17 years in prison, was on Oct. 23, 1975, sentenced to five years in prison for anti-Tito articles of his published abroad five years earlier. He was, however, released under the amnesty proclaimed on Nov. 24, 1977.

In February 1976 a group of 17 alleged Serbian nationalists were sentenced at Bosansko Grahovo (central Yugoslavia) to varying terms of imprisonment, some of them for having connexions with the *Chetnik* movement in Western Europe. On June 28, 1976, three Bosnian Serbs were sentenced at Bihac (Bosnia) to 15, nine and seven years in prison respectively for having been in contact with *Chetnik* supporters abroad and for engaging in anti-Yugoslav propaganda.

In Western Europe the *Chetniks* were organized in the *Ravnagora* movement, one of whose leaders (Borivoje Blagojevic) was assassinated in Brussels on March 8, 1975. Other Serbian nationalists murdered in Brussels included the editor of *Vascrc Spoije,* a Serbian royalist anti-Tito newspaper, on May 13, 1975, and two other alleged Serbian royalists, found killed on Aug. 11, 1976.

On the other hand, two members of a "secret Serbian nationalist organization" were held responsible for the murder, on March 29, 1976, of the Yugoslav vice-consul in Lyons (France) whom they claimed to have "executed" as "a traitor for his crimes against the Serbian people in emigration".

Cominformists

Pro-Soviet Communists who opposed the 1948 break between Yugoslavia on the one hand and the Soviet Union and the Cominform (the successor to the Communist International) on the other have frequently attracted the attentions of the Yugoslav authorities. According to Ivo Pervan, Croatian Under-Secretary of the Interior (speaking in November 1975), so-called Cominformists had formed nine secret organizations working in Yugoslavia, committing acts of terrorism and being supported by subversive groups in various countries (notably Australia, Canada, France, the Federal Republic of Germany, Sweden and the Soviet Union). At the end of November 1975 the Croatian security services officially disclosed that they had dossiers on some 2,900 Cominformists, and that there was a network of 29 members intent upon setting up a new Yugoslav Communist Party.

The Communist Party of Yugoslavia was subsequently reported to have been established at a secret conference held in Bar (on the Adriatic coast) during 1974. The party's programme (as published on Feb. 24, 1976, in the *Daily Telegraph* of London) contained a condemnation of President Tito for having "betrayed" the original Communist Party of Yugoslavia and having, by a coup d'état, opened the way to "counter-revolutionary terror" and established "a regime of personal dictatorship" under which "more than 200,000 Communists" had been "expelled and arrested".

The programme declared that the new party was "an inseparable organic part of the international communist movement" and proposed, for a transitional regime leading to "genuine people's democracy", (i) the formation of a united National Front of all socialist and democratic parties and groups opposed to Tito; (ii) the formation of a provisional government of all parties; (iii) the disbandment of the secret police and the counterintelligence organizations in the Army and militia and the abolition of all concentration camps and political prisons; (iv) the abolition of the Presidency of the Republic, dismissal of Marshal Tito from all ruling functions, prohibition of his political activity, and confiscation of the property which he had obtained illegally; (v) the nationalization of the principal means of production; (vi) a new electoral law giving every adult the right to vote, irrespective of his political views, and elections for a constitutional assembly within 12 months; and (vii) Yugoslavia's withdrawal from agreements made with Western governments.

Also during 1974, a total of 32 alleged Cominformists were sentenced, in trials which ended in Pec (Kosovo) on Sept. 18 and in Titograd (Montenegro) on Sept. 20, to prison terms ranging from one to 14 years. One of the principal defendants at the Pec trial, Komnen Jovovic (given 14 years), was released under the amnesty proclaimed on Nov. 24, 1977.

Numerous other alleged Cominformists tried in 1975-78 included several leading figures of this movement, notably Dusan Brkic, a former Deputy Premier of Croatia expelled from the Communist Party of Croatia

in 1950, who was given an eight-year sentence by a Belgrade district court on March 12, 1976.

Vlado Dapcevic, a former colonel and an alleged prominent Cominformist, was condemned to death in Belgrade on July 5, 1976, this sentence being immediately commuted to 20 years in prison. In 1948 he had already been sentenced to 20 years, but had been amnestied in 1956 and had thereupon left the country. On Aug. 9, 1975, he disappeared in Bucharest and was thereafter taken to Belgrade, apparently against his will. At his 1976 trial he was charged with high treason for articles written in 1956-75 calling for the overthrow of the Tito Government; with participation in the creation of the new Communist Party of Yugoslavia in Bar in 1974 (see above); and also with accepting funds from Albania in return for allegedly advocating the surrender of parts of Kosovo and Macedonia to Albania.

Mileta Perovic, a former colonel and former Yugoslav consul in Paris, was on April 13, 1978, sentenced to 20 years in prison for "several grave crimes against the party and the state" committed in 1956-77. In 1949 he had already been sentenced to 18 years in prison but he had been pardoned in 1956 and had left the country in 1958. In Kiev (USSR) he had headed a group of pro-Moscow Yugoslavs and had attempted, with ex-Col. Dapcevic, to set up the (pro-Moscow) Communist Party of Yugoslavia; at the secret congress establishing this party in Bar in 1974, he was, "on his own instructions", elected its secretary-general. The USSR later expelled him and some of his associates, and in 1975 he went to France, from where he was expelled after attempting to set up the party's headquarters in Paris.

Socialist Opposition

Praxis Group

Criticism of the Yugoslav regime from a socialist point of view was expressed, from 1968 onwards, by a number of academics associated with the journal *Praxis,* the organ of the Croatian Philosophical Society. In 1968 contributions to *Praxis* began to reject both capitalism and bureaucratic dogmatism and to criticize what they called the "yawning gap" between Yugoslav doctrine and the real state of affairs in the country. Some of the writers were in contact with "New Left" intellectuals in other countries.

In July 1972 an issue of *Praxis* was banned after Josip Vrhovec, then Secretary of the Croatian League of Communists, had criticized certain articles in it as "anti-Marxist" and "anti-socialist". In January 1975 eight teachers at the University of Belgrade, associated with *Praxis,* were indefinitely suspended for organizing "political opposition in a bid for power" and "preparing a violent change of the Yugoslav system of self-management". In the journal *Komunist* (the central organ of the CLY) they were in the same month accused of "intriguing with others on how to seize power" and of being in touch with a (Trotskyite) Committee for the Reconstitution of the Fourth International, with the Italian extreme left-wing *Manifesto* group (which had seceded from the Communist Party of Italy) and with "other Trotskyites". The eight suspended teachers denied on Jan. 29, 1975, that they were seeking power and claimed that the campaign against them had caused "incalculable damage to the cause of socialism in general".

Of the eight suspended teachers Prof. Mihajlo Markovic expressed the view that bureaucracy was "manifestly in conflict with the fundamental aspirations of all other social strata" and declared: "If the workers are conscious of all the possibilities offered to them by the new historic situation after the elimination of the capitalist class, then their open conflict with the bureaucracy, which blocks the realization of these possibilities, would inevitably take the form of a class struggle". He also stated that the rule of bureaucracy would be seriously threatened if there was free development of critical social thought, which would increase the political consciousness of workers and the young, especially of students.

Praxis ceased publication in February 1975. Nearly three years later, on Jan. 24, 1978, two former editors of *Praxis* and seven of the suspended university teachers were among the signatories of a protest against "severe discrimination against non-members of the LCY" who applied for posts, with the result that employers gave preference to LCY members, which led to "careerism, hyprocrisy and double standards".

Trotskyites

In 1971-72 attempts were made to revive a branch of the Trotskyite Fourth International in Belgrade. On July 21, 1972, three students were given prison sentences ranging from 19 months to two years for attempting to set up a terrorist group and to restore the Trotskyite International. On June 23, 1973, Danilo Udovicki (an architect) was sentenced to two years in prison for having had contacts with two representatives of the Fourth International in Belgrade in 1971-72.

Democratic Socialists

Leading figures among those who advocated democratic socialism for Yugoslavia have been the veteran Communist Milovan Djilas and the (Russian-born) writer Mihajlo Mihajlov.

Milovan Djilas (born in 1911), who had joined the then illegal Communist Party of Yugoslavia in 1938 and had become a member of its Politburo in 1940, held leading positions in the party and the state until Jan. 17, 1954, when he was expelled from the Executive Committee of the LCY because of a number of articles of his which had been published in *Borba* (the organ of the Socialist Alliance of the Working People of Yugoslavia). In these articles he had argued inter alia that the Leninist type of party and state and the work of the LCY were outdated because of the advance of democracy in Yugoslavia; that insistence on dogma was pointless now that socialist consciousness was not confined to the Communists but possessed by the broad masses of society; and that a reprehensible caste system had grown up among leading government and party officials. After he had resigned from the presidency of the National Assembly on Jan. 16, 1954, it was reported on April 21 of that year that he had also resigned from the LCY.

On Dec. 24, 1954, he described himself, in an interview with an *International Herald Tribune* correspondent, as a democratic socialist and stated inter alia that, while he had thought that the Communist Party must permit freedom of discussion, he now saw that this was impossible. He therefore proposed the creation of a new, democratic and socialist party, as the situation was "ripe for political democracy" and the LCY was "depressed and without an ideology". On Dec. 31, 1954, he was expelled from the Socialist Alliance of the Working People, and on Jan. 24, 1955, he was given an 18-months' suspended sentence for "propaganda hostile to Yugoslavia". On Nov. 19, 1956, he was arrested for "spreading hostile propaganda against the state", and on Dec. 12 he was sentenced to two years' hard labour for "supplying enemies of Yugoslavia with material to encourage them to exercise pressure on Yugoslavia" and for alleging that power in Yugoslavia was in the hands of a bureaucratic class. (He was also required to serve one year of his 1955 suspended sentence.) His appeal against the new sentence was rejected by the Supreme Court of Serbia on Jan. 27, 1957.

The book *The New Class,* written by M. Djilas in 1955-56 and published in English in 1957, was banned in Yugoslavia on Sept. 5, 1957, and on Oct. 5 of that year he was sentenced in camera to seven years in prison, to five years' loss of civil rights after his release and to deprivation of all his decorations.

In *The New Class* M. Djilas argued that communism, once it had come to power, tended to develop into a tyranny of expert political managers who, by acquiring exclusive control of the national property, became a new "class"; that communism was therefore doomed to expire; but that Marxism, represented by democratic socialism, was not. In the indictment against him, the prosecutor stated that the book revealed not only the writer's hostile attitude towards socialism and the existing social order in Yugoslavia but also his intention to mobilize all the enemies of that order at home and abroad for action against Yugoslavia.

On Jan. 20, 1961, M. Djilas was released on probation (on his own request) but on April 7, 1962, he was rearrested, and on May 14 he was given a five-year sentence in connexion with his book *Conversations with Stalin* (and was also required to serve the unexpired three years and eight months of his 1957 sentence). The charge on which he was tried was that in his new book (which was published in New York in May 1962) he had disclosed state secrets known to him as a member of Yugoslav government missions to Moscow in 1944-48. He was released from prison under an amnesty of Dec. 31, 1966.

While refraining from further political activity, M. Djilas defended Mihajlo Mihajlov (see below) in a letter published in the *International Herald Tribune* on Nov. 20, 1974, in which he called the latter a supporter of human rights and of spiritual fulfilment and deplored the lack of democracy in the official treatment meted out to M. Mihajlov.

Mihajlo Mihajlov (born in 1935), assistant professor of Slavonic literature at the University of Zadar, Croatia, was on April 30, 1965, sentenced to nine months in prison for insulting the Soviet Union and for publishing material officially banned; he had in fact contended that the Soviet authorities had set up "death camps" long before the Nazis did so. On his appeal the Croatian Supreme Court reversed the conviction on the first charge and suspended the sentence on the second on June 23, 1965. He had been suspended from his post on April 28, but this decision was overruled by the Supreme Court on Jan. 7, 1966.

In an open letter addressed to President Tito (and published in an Italian weekly on July 11, 1966), M. Mihajlov announced his intention to launch *Slobodni Glas* ("Free Voice") as an independent democratic socialist organ which would become the nucleus of a political and social movement "in conformity with Yugoslav law and the Constitution"). However, this proposed journal was never launched, as M. Mihajlov was arrested on Aug. 8, 1966, for "spreading false information about Yugoslavia", and on Sept. 23 he was sentenced to nine months in prison. (Two of his associates had earlier left the country.) At his trial he said inter alia that he could not consider socialist a society in which only six or seven per cent of the people (i.e. the members of the LCY) had all the rights and the great majority did not enjoy even essential rights. (In an interview published in Austria on Aug. 9, 1966, he expressed his belief that President Tito would be succeeded by M. Djilas.)

He was released from prison in March 1970, but on Feb. 28, 1975, he was sentenced in Novi Sad to seven years in prison for "hostile propaganda" (in contravention of Art. 118 of the criminal code), and he was also forbidden to have his works published, to speak in public or to broadcast (for four years after completion of his sentence). Since 1970 publication of his works in Yugoslavia had been forbidden, and those published abroad had been ignored by the Yugoslav authorities.

In articles published abroad M. Mihajlov had maintained inter alia that there existed in Yugoslavia a totalitarian regime without democratic freedom; that its existing one-party system was similar to that of Mussolini's Fascism in Italy; and that after President Tito's death the greatest danger to Yugoslavia would come from the Soviet Union. At the opening of his trial he pleaded "not guilty" and claimed that his articles were aimed at "helping the Yugoslav struggle for socialist self-management" although he believed that this was possible only within a dual-party system.

Exiled Parties

Croatian Peasants' Party

Leadership. Juraj Krnjevic.

The leader of this exiled formation has been officially described in Yugoslavia as a "war criminal", in line with the Government's approach to all manifestations of Croatian nationalism (see separate section above). In August 1977 a Dr Nikola Novakovic was reported to have been sentenced in Sarajevo to 12 years in prison for "counter-revolutionary and nationalist activities" by taking up contact with this party.

Slovene People's Party

This exiled formation is affiliated to the Christian Democratic World Union.

Yugoslav Socialist Party

Leadership. Marko Milunovic (g.s.).

This formation of exiled democratic socialists opposed to what they regard as the illegal assumption of sole power by the Yugoslav Communists after World War II is a consultative member of the Socialist International and a constituent party of the Socialist Union of Central and Eastern Europe (SUCEE).

2. ASIA AND THE FAR EAST

Afghanistan

Capital: Kabul

Pop. 14,000,000

The Democratic Republic of Afghanistan was set up on April 27, 1978, by a Revolutionary Council which established a Government dominated by the (communist) People's Democratic Party of Afghanistan (PDPA) which effectively became the country's sole legal political party. Afghanistan has no parliament. Following massive Soviet intervention from December 1979 onwards, a provisional Constitution (known as the Basic Principles of the Democratic Republic of Afghanistan) was ratified by the PDPA on April 13, 1980, and by the Revolutionary Council on the following day. It laid down inter alia that Afghanistan would proceed "from backwardness to social, economic and cultural progress under the leadership of the PDPA"; that "the sacred and true religion of Islam" would be protected; and that the "traditional friendship and co-operation with the USSR" would be strengthened and broadened. It also provided that a Grand National Assembly or Supreme Council *(Loya Jirga)* would be the highest organ of state power but that pending its election by free and direct vote the Revolutionary Council would hold supreme power.

A National Fatherland Front, a broad alliance of political parties, mass organizations and tribal bodies, formed at a congress on June 15, 1981, with the object of promoting national unity, was to be under the guidance of the PDPA and to have a national congress meeting at least once every five years. This Front was, however, in late 1981 reported to have failed because of dissension between its two factions—the dominant *Parcham* (Flag) faction and the larger but less influential *Khalq* (People) faction.

The rule of the PDPA, and even more so the Soviet intervention in Afghanistan, were violently opposed by a variety of Islamic and tribal movements and alliances (the most important of which are detailed below). Despite overwhelming Soviet superiority in armaments, the guerrillas of these groups, generally referred to as *mujaheddin* (holy warriors), have succeeded in conducting protracted warfare with enormous losses on both sides and causing the exodus of over 2,000,000 refugees, most of them fleeing to Pakistan. From reports on military activities it has not been possible, in most cases, to attribute the activities concerned to specific *mujaheddin* groups. Nor has it been possible to determine the volume or value of external support for the rebels. President Sadat of Egypt disclosed on Nov. 10, 1980, that Egypt was supplying military aid to the *mujaheddin*. In 1981 it was alleged in the United States that the (US) Central Intelligence Agency (CIA) was involved in a covert international operation for the provision of arms to the Afghan rebels, partly paid for by Saudi Arabia. President Sadat said in September 1981 that the United States had since 1979 been transporting arms of Egyptian origin into the hands of the *mujaheddin*.

By mid-1981 fighting by rebel Moslems centred mainly around Kandahar (a city in eastern Afghanistan, long held by the rebels), or areas close to the border with Pakistan, and in Parwan province (north of Kabul), in particular the Panjshir valley. In Kabul heavy fighting and various shootings and bombings took place, involving the killing of the head of the Forces for the Defence of the Revolution and of the deputy head of the secret police (both in April 1981). Prominent among the guerrilla organizations claiming major successes was the Islamic Party *(Hizb-i-Islami)*.

In a speech before the Central Committee of the PDPA on March 14, 1982, President Babrak Karmal stated inter alia that the "fratricidal war", which he attributed to the forces on "imperialism and reaction", had been the main obstacle to the Government's attainment of its economic goals. The Minister of Internal Affairs said in an address to the PDPA conference at the same time that in the past year over 10,000 "counter-revolutionaries" had been killed and over 4,000 weapons captured.

By April 1982 the *mujaheddin* appeared to be stronger than in early 1980 and to control, as before, over 80 per cent of the surface area of Afghanistan, including many large towns. The Afghan armed forces were said to have been reduced from about 100,000 in late 1975 to less than 30,000 (by losses in battle and by large-scale desertions), while the Soviet troops in Afghanistan were thought to number at least 90,000.

Mujaheddin Alliances

Islamic Alliance for the Liberation of Afghanistan (IALA)

Leadership. Prof. Ghulam Abdur Rasoul Sayaf.

This Alliance was formed on Jan. 27, 1980, at an extraordinary meeting of the Foreign Ministers of the Organization of the Islamic Conference in Islamabad (Pakistan) by representatives of the Afghan rebel organizations—the Islamic Afghan Association *(Jamaat-i-Islami Afghanistan)*, the Movement for the Islamic Revolution *(Harkat-i-Inkalab-i-Islami)*, the Afghan National Liberation Front, the Afghan Islamic and Nationalist Revolutionary Council, the faction of the Islamic Party *(Hizb-i-Islami)* led by Gulbuddin Hekmatyar, and the other faction of this party led by Maulavi Mohammad Yunus Khales; the former faction, however, withdrew from the IALA in March 1980 because of disagreement over representation on a proposed Supreme Revolutionary Council (see separate entry).

At the 11th session of the Foreign Ministers of the Organization of the Islamic Conference held in Islamabad on May 17-22, 1980, Prof. Rasoul Sayaf presented a list of demands calling inter alia for (i) the severance of diplomatic relations with the Soviet Union and Afghanistan and (ii) the recognition of the insurgent organizations as the sole legitimate representatives of Afghanistan and their acceptance as a member of the Organization of the Islamic Conference. The meeting, however, adopted a resolution providing for the establishment of a three-member committee to seek "ways and means for a comprehensive solution of the crisis with respect to Afghanistan". (The Islamic Conference Organization had suspended Afghanistan's membership in January 1980 and a number of its member states had provided funds, among them Saudi Arabia, "to assist Afghan insurgents and refugees".)

Talks between the three-member Islamic Conference committee and an IALA delegation, led by Prof. Rasoul Sayaf, in Switzerland on June 20-21, 1980, ended inconclusively. The committee assured the IALA of the moral and political support of the Islamic nations and restated its aim of seeking a peaceful solution to the conflict on the basis of "immediate, total and unconditional withdrawal of Soviet troops from Afghanistan" in order to restore to that country political independence, sovereignty, non-alignment, an Islamic identity and freedom to choose its own form of government as well as political, social and economic system. The IALA delegation, on the other hand, restated their refusal to negotiate with Kabul or Moscow, called for the withdrawal of Soviet troops, demanded the recognition of the *mujaheddin* as the sole legitimate representatives of the Afghan people and their own participation in the committee in this capacity, and pledged that under their leadership Afghanistan would pursue a policy of "active non-alignment" and would decide on its own future freely and without super-power interference. The delegation also called (i) for special UN and Islamic meetings to be held on Afghanistan, (ii) for the Islamic nations to re-examine their relations with the Soviet Union and (iii) for the opening of a special Afghan resistance fund financed partly by members of the Organization of Petroleum Exporting Countries (OPEC).

The IALA was by this time, however, deeply divided. The Hekmatyar faction of the Islamic Party had left the IALA in March 1980. A moderate faction consisted of the Afghan National Liberation Front, the Movement for the Islamic Revolution and the Afghan Islamic and Nationalist Revolutionary Council (also known as National Islamic Front of Afghanistan). Another faction embraced two Moslem fundamentalist groups—the Islamic Afghan Association and the faction of the Islamic Party led by Maulavi Mohammad Yunus Khales.

71

Islamic Unity of the Mujaheddin of Afghanistan

This organization was formed on June 1, 1981, by three Islamic guerrilla groups—the National Islamic Front of Afghanistan led by Sayed Ahmed Gailani, the Afghan National Liberation Front led by the Imam Seghbatullah Mujjaddedi and the Movement for the Islamic Revolution led by Maulavi Mohammadi.

Supreme Revolutionary Council

Leadership. Mohammad Babrak Zai (l.).

This Council was formed in May 1980 at a special tribal meeting *(loya jirga)* in Peshawar (northern Pakistan), attended by delegates from all areas of Afghanistan. The meeting passed a number of "fundamental resolutions" designed to form the basis of a future constitution for Afghanistan, and it also decided that all treaties signed after April 1978, notably the Soviet-Afghan treaty of friendship under which Soviet troops had entered the country, would be considered void.

Those Who Have Sworn to Fight for Islam *(Teiman Atahad-Islami)*

This organization was formed on Aug. 11, 1979, among refugees in Peshawar (northern Pakistan) by a merger of four groups—the Afghan National Liberation Front, the Islamic Afghan Association, the Movement for the Islamic Revolution and the faction of the Islamic Party led by Maulavi Mohammad Yunus Khales. Among its declared objectives was the establishment in Afghanistan of an Islamic republic based on the Koran and Sunna (Moslem "Way of Life", a supplement to the Koran).

Mujaheddin Organizations

Afghan Islamic and Nationalist Revolutionary Council—see National Islamic Front of Afghanistan

Afghan National Liberation Front

Leadership. Imam Seghbatullah Mujjaddedi (l.).

On March 12, 1979, this Front—which also embraced a faction of the Islamic Party *(Hizb-i-Islami)*—called for a *jihad* (holy war) against the Kabul regime. On March 21, 1979, the Imam Mujjaddedi stated in Islamabad (Pakistan) that all Western countries had refused to supply his movement with arms and that the People's Republic of China had made no offer of help, while the Government of Pakistan had prohibited the transit of arms through its territory; he claimed, how-

ever, that Moslem rebels were fighting in eight of Afghanistan's 26 provinces.

On Aug. 11, 1979, the Front joined with three other movements in forming a group called "Those who have sworn to fight for Islam" *(Teiman Atahad-Islami)*, and on Jan. 27, 1980, it took part in the formation of the Islamic Alliance for the Liberation of Afghanistan. On June 1, 1981, however, it formed—together with the National Islamic Front of Afghanistan led by Sayed Ahmed Gailani and the Movement for the Islamic Revolution led by Maulavi Mohammadi—the Islamic Unity of the Mujaheddin of Afghanistan.

Against Oppression and Tyranny *(Setem-i-Melli)*

Leadership. Taher Badakshi (l.).

Members of this group were held responsible for the assassination, on Feb. 14, 1979, of the US ambassador in Kabul, who had been held hostage by four armed men who demanded the release of three "religious figures" said to be held as political detainees, among them Taher Badakshi; the Afghan Government had refused this demand, and the four kidnappers were all killed by police.

This group has expressed opposition to "Pushtu [i.e. Pathan] domination", especially in areas inhabited by ethnic minorities, such as the Tajiks in Badakshan province (north-eastern Afghanistan), who are Shia Moslems (distinct from the Sunni Moslem majority in Afghanistan). (On Oct. 14, 1979, Afghan officials were said to have tacitly admitted that about 1,000,000 Tajik Moslems, who had emigrated to northern Afghanistan after the 1917 Soviet revolution, were in revolt against the Government.)

Alliance of Islamic Fighters *(Hedadia Mujaheddin Islami Afghanistan)*

Leadership. Wali Beg (l.).

This movement, formed in May 1979 among the Hazara tribes of central Afghanistan, was in mid-August 1979 reported to have some 5,000 men under arms. On Aug. 15, 1979, Wali Beg appealed to the UN Human Rights Commission to inquire into the "regime of terror of the Afghan Army unleashed against the Moslem population". He claimed that his movement, fighting against "the regime in power aided by the Soviet Union", controlled 10 per cent of the country's territory. On Aug. 16, 1979, it was reported that 300 Hazara rebels had been executed near Kabul.

Islamic Afghan Association *(Jamaat-i-Islami Afghanistan)*

Leadership. Prof. Ustad Burhanuddin Rabbani (l.).

This movement has been supported by the

Jamaat-i-Islami of Pakistan, a component of the Pakistan National Alliance, members of which have held posts in the Government of President Zia ul-Haq. On Aug. 11, 1979, the movement joined with three other organizations in forming the group of "Those who have sworn to fight for Islam" *(Teiman Atahad-Islami)*. On Jan. 27, 1980, it took part in the formation of the Islamic Alliance for the Liberation of Afghanistan, of which Prof. Ghulam Abdur Rasoul Sayaf (the deputy leader of the *Jamaat-i-Islami Afghanistan*, who had spent six years in prison) became leader on March 19, 1980. The *Jamaat-i-Islami Afghanistan* was held responsible for the killing of the president of Kabul University in mid-March 1982.

On May 29, 1982, Prof. Rabbani (based in Peshawar, northern Pakistan) issued a report claiming that in a major battle in the Panjshir valley (about 60 miles north-east of Kabul), which had been the headquarters of about 1,000 guerrillas of his organization, some 700 Soviet and Afghan troops had been killed and 21 fighter aircraft and helicopters had been knocked out when an attack (said to involve 18,000 Soviet and Afghan troops and 3,000 tanks and aircraft) had been repulsed. The attack was presumed to have been made in retaliation for a rebel offensive early in March 1982 against the Soviet air base at Bagram (north of Kabul).

Islamic Movement Organization of Afghanistan *(Harekat Islami Afghanistan)*

Leadership. Sheik Mohammed Assef Mohseni (l.).

This Movement seeks the establishment of an Islamic Republic of Afghanistan on the model of that of Iran.

Islamic Party *(Hizb-i-Islami)*

Leadership. The party has two factions led respectively by (i) Gulbuddin Hekmatyar and (ii) Maulavi Mohammad Yunus Khales.

The party announced in Islamabad (Pakistan) on July 30, 1978, that it had launched guerrilla attacks against the (communist) Government of President Nur Mohammad Taraki and was the following year reported to be seeking the restoration of the monarchy in Afghanistan. On Aug. 11, 1979, the Yunus Khales faction of the party joined the Afghan National Liberation Front. Both factions of the party joined the Islamic Alliance for the Liberation of Afghanistan formed on Jan. 27, 1980. A strike by shopkeepers in Kabul, later joined by civil servants and office workers, on Feb. 21-27, 1980, was instigated by the Hekmatyar faction of this party, and led to the imposition of martial law and a curfew in the capital on Feb. 22 and to demonstrations on the same day, when at

least 300 civilians and an unknown number of Soviet and Afghan troops were reported killed, and many thousands arrested. Parallel strikes took place in several regional towns.

The Hekmatyar faction withdrew from the Islamic Alliance for the Liberation of Afghanistan in March 1980 because of disagreements over representation on a proposed Supreme Revolutionary Council (see separate entry). In mid-1981 this faction was reported to have begun, in May of that year, to co-operate in guerrilla activities with a local resistance group based near Kabul and known as SAMA, and also to have reached a new agreement with five other Pakistan based groups on the merging of weapons, funds and manpower.

On April 21, 1982, the Islamic Party announced that it had executed a Soviet geologist (whom it had captured in Kabul on Sept. 12, 1981) after negotiations through the International Committee of the Red Cross to obtain the release of 50 imprisoned rebels in exchange for the Soviet geologist had failed.

The Islamic Party was in 1982 thought to be the largest of the *mujaheddin* groups but also to have made demands for a disproportionate degree of influence in various unions of different guerrilla groups. A new such union, reported in mid-March 1982, was said to embrace the two *Hizb-i-Islami* factions, two factions of the Islamic Afghan Association, two factions of the Movement for the Islamic Revolution, and the Afghan National Liberation Front—with the chairman of the new union to be appointed on a rotating basis from among the leaders of the seven groups, and its deputy chairman being Gulbuddin Hekmatyar of the *Hizb-i-Islami*.

On March 21, 1982, *Hizb-i-Islami* spokesmen claimed in Quetta (Pakistan) that the *mujaheddin* were facing opposition from groups of Baluchi guerrillas in Afghanistan (who had fled there because they rejected the 1947 incorporation of much of Baluchistan in the Republic of Pakistan).

Militant Front of Combatants of Afghanistan

This Islamic socialist Front was in 1981 reported to be solely based inside Afghanistan (unlike other resistance movements which were represented in Pakistan).

Moslem Brotherhood *(Ekhwamis)*

In September 1978 the Government of Afghanistan was reported to have declared a *jihad* (holy war) against the Brotherhood. The Moscow daily *Pravda* (organ of the Central Committee of the Communist Party of the Soviet Union) alleged on March 19, 1979, that the ring-leaders of the Moslem Brotherhood had recently held a conference in Peshawar (Pakistan) which had been attended by Gulbuddin Hekmatyar (an Islamic Party leader) and "other Afghan reactionaries'' as well as by a number of foreigners, and at which the question had been discussed of "starting a war against the existing regime of the Democratic Republic of Afghanistan"; the participants in the conference were said to be "relying on the support of certain circles in Pakistan, China and certain Western countries"; the Pakistan Government was accused of being aware of the rebels' activities and of failing to stop them; and some Arab countries, notably Egypt, were said to be "aiding the Afghan counter-revolutionaries"; strong Soviet support was promised to the Afghan Government.

Movement for the Islamic Revolution
(Harkat-i-Inkalab-i-Islami)

Leadership. Maulavi Mohammadi (l.).

This Movement joined with three other organizations on Aug. 11, 1979, in forming an alliance called "Those who have sworn to fight for Islam" *(Teiman Atahad-Islami)*. On Jan. 27, 1980, it joined the Islamic Alliance for the Liberation of Afghanistan, and on June 1, 1981, it formed—together with the Afghan National Liberation Front led by Imam Seghbatullah Mujjaddedi and the National Islamic Front of Afghanistan led by Sayed Ahmed Gailani—the Islamic Unity of the Mujaheddin of Afghanistan.

National Islamic Front of Afghanistan

Leadership. Sayed Ahmed Gailani (l.).

This Front was originally known as the Afghan Islamic and National Revolutionary Council, which took part in the formation of the Islamic Alliance for the Liberation of Afghanistan in January 1980. Later in 1980 it adopted a new title and on June 1, 1981, it formed (together with the Afghan National Liberation Front led by the Imam Seghbatullah Mujjaddedi and the Movement of the Islamic Revolution led by Maulavi Mohammadi) the Islamic Unity of the Mujaheddin of Afghanistan. A spokesman for the organization was on July 5, 1982, quoted as saying that the Soviet military forces in Afghanistan were turning the country into a forward military base for possible moves into South-West Asia (i) by developing a major air base at Shindand (western Afghanistan), (ii) by building a bridge across the Amu Darya river (on Afghanistan's frontier with the Soviet Union) and starting a railway line from the frontier to Kabul, and (iii) by annexing (in 1981) the Wakhan corridor (in north-east Afghanistan, bordering on Pakistan, China and the Soviet Union). (This annexation would deprive Afghanistan of its frontier with China and would give the Soviet Union a common frontier with Pakistan.)

National United Front

This extreme left-wing Front was in 1981 reported to be based solely inside Afghanistan (unlike other resistance groups which were represented in Pakistan).

Shola Javed

Shola Javed is a group of pro-Chinese communists opposed to the Soviet-backed PDPA regime in Kabul and also to the presence in Afghanistan of Soviet military forces.

Bangladesh

Capital: Dhaka (formerly Dacca)   Pop. 93,000,000

The People's Republic of Bangladesh, an independent state within the Commonwealth, has since March 24, 1982, been placed under martial law and ruled by a Chief Martial Law Administrator (Lt.-Gen. Hossain Mohammad Ershad, the Chief of Army Staff). On assuming power he suspended the Constitution, dismissed the President and Vice-President of the Republic, dissolved the Council of Ministers and Parliament, banned all "direct and indirect" political activities and demonstrations, imposed press censorship and forbade all criticism of the martial law regime (infringement of these regulations being punishable by imprisonment for up to seven years). Under Martial Law Order No. 1 issued on March 25, 1982, the Chief Martial Law Administrator was empowered to set up a special military tribunal, special military courts and summary military courts (although these summary military courts might not impose sentences of death or of imprisonment for more than seven years); the accused might not be defended by a lawyer but only helped and advised by a "friend"; and corruption was liable to harsh penalties, including the death sentence.

The Chief Martial Law Administrator also appointed a Council of Advisers (Cabinet) on March 25 and a new President of the Republic (Justice Abul Fazal Mohammad Assanuddin Choudhury, a retired Supreme Court judge) on March 26. Gen. Ershad said on March 24, 1982, that his main objectives were "to hold fair general elections in the country by making the situation suitable as soon as possible", and also to establish a new economic system for which he would have to "create a favourable climate for investment by private enterprise". The Council of Advisers was subsequently enlarged and redesignated Council of Ministers in May 1982. On Oct. 26, 1982, the Council extended Gen. Ershad's term of office as Chief of the Armed Forces by a further two years (from December 1982, when he would have been due to retire).

The ban on political activities in effect suspended (but did not dissolve) the country's political parties (numbering more than 20), of which the three major ones had gained seats (out of 300 elected seats) in the Parliament *(Jatiya Sangsad)* on Feb. 18, 1979, as follows: Bangladesh National Party *(Bangladesh Jatiyabadi Dal)* 207, *Awami League* 40, Bangladesh Moslem League 20, National Socialist Party *(Jatiya Samajtantrik Dal,* JSD) 9, other parties 8 and independents 16.

Prior to the proclamation of martial law, it had been stated in a report based on official sources and published on July 25, 1981, that during the first six months of 1981 there had been 185 political murders, most of them being attributed to the military wing of the JSD and to a Party of the Disinherited of East Bengal, and others to the Liberation Force *(Kader Bahini)*.

Chittagong Autonomists *(Shanti Bahini)*

Autonomist aspirations had already been expressed at the time of the East Pakistan Government (overthrown in 1971) by (mainly Buddhist, Christian or Hindu) tribal people of the Chittagong Hill Tracts. In this area the population had traditionally lived on a "slash and burn" basis (cultivating burnt forest land until it is exhausted, which forces the inhabitants to move elsewhere). Since 1947 the Government had encouraged the tribal people to take up settled farming and had moved in (mainly Moslem) Bengalis, and this process was speeded up in 1978-79 with the result that the proportion of Bengalis in the area rose from 11.6 per cent in 1974 to 39 per cent in 1981.

Guerrilla warfare by Chittagong Hill Tracts tribes began in 1975 under the leadership of Manabendra Larma (a former independent member of the *Jatiya Sangsad*) after appeals for regional autonomy had met with no response from the Government. The guerrillas attacked not only camps for Bengali settlers, many of whom were killed, but also a number of police posts. The guerrilla operations spread to urban areas and included bomb explosions in Chittagong in December 1976. By the end of 1977 some 12,000 soldiers and police were believed to be fighting the guerrillas in the area.

According to a report by officials of the (London-based) Anti-Slavery Society based on statements by Buddhist monks and published on Dec. 15, 1981, the Bangladesh Army had carried out genocide against the Chittagong Hill Tracts tribal people by committing a number of "massacres". Under a Disturbed Areas Bill adopted in December 1980 (with implied reference to the Chittagong Hill Tracts situation) the Government was empowered to declare any part of the country a disturbed area, and police officers and army NCOs were given unlimited authority to fire upon a person or to arrest him without a warrant in such an area.

Nevertheless *Shanti Bahini* operations were intensified in 1981. In one of the guerrillas' attacks (on three villages on Sept. 24) they killed 18 Bengali settlers, while further attacks were made on other villages. Between June and October 1981 troops arrested over 3,000 tribal people. The fighting and army reprisals led to a mass exodus of refugees to the neighbouring Indian state of Tripura; after their number had reached over 19,000, the Bangla-desh Government agreed on Nov. 6 to repatriate them.

Liberation Force *(Kader Bahini)*

Leadership. Abdul Kader Siddiqui (l.).

Abdul Kader Siddiqui had commanded a pro-Bangladesh guerrilla force during the war of independence against the Pakistan Government in 1971. Following the assassination of President Mujibur Rahman (the first President of the independent Republic of Bangladesh) in a military coup in August 1975, A. Kader Siddiqui was reported to be leading several hundred guerrillas allied to Garo tribesmen in the Mymensingh district (northeastern Bangladesh) in an effort to avenge the death of President Mujibur Rahman.

Early in 1976 the strength of his "Liberation Force" was estimated at between 500 and 3,500 men. Some guerrillas captured by security forces alleged that their organization had received support from India. In 1981 the Force was said to consist of about 1,000 "deserters" from the Army and police led by A. Kader Siddiqui in the Mymensingh district.

Among members of the force captured and tried was Biswajit Nandy, a close associate of A. Kader Siddiqui; he was convicted in 1976 of blowing up an army jeep carrying troops and was sentenced to death, but this sentence was commuted to life imprisonment in October 1982. By that time A. Kader Siddiqui was living in exile in India.

Party of the Disinherited of East Bengal

Members of this organization, operating in the Jessore and Faridpur district south-west of Dhaka, were responsible for murdering a number of landlords and distributing their crops among landless peasants, especially during 1981.

Bhutan

Capital: Thimphu   Pop. 1,160,000

The Kingdom of Bhutan has a National Assembly *(Tsogdu),* to which 101 members are elected by direct universal adult suffrage while 10 seats are reserved for Buddhist bodies and the remaining 39 for ministers, officials and the nine members of a Royal Advisory Council. There is also a five-member Council of Ministers. There are no political parties and there has been no evidence of active political opposition.

Brunei

Capital: Bandar Seri Begawan   Pop. 200,000

The Sultanate of Brunei is a sovereign state with full internal self-government but with responsibility for defence and external affairs being held by Britain until the end of 1983, when Brunei is scheduled to attain complete independence, pending which Brunei has a special arrangement for participation in Commonwealth affairs (agreed to in February 1981). The Sultanate has a Privy Council, a Council of Ministers, a Legislative Council of 21 members (six ex-officio, five nominated by the Sultan and 10 elected by and from among the members of the Sultanate's four district councils). No legislative elections have been held since 1965, and the Sultanate's sole legal political organization, the Brunei People's Independence Front, was established only in 1966.

People's Party of Brunei (PRB) *(Party Ra'ayet)*

Established in 1959, the PRB won all elective seats in the Legislative Council in August 1962, but on Dec. 8 of that year a "North Borneo Liberation Army" linked with the PRB carried out a revolt with the object of preventing Brunei's entry into the then proposed Federation of Malaysia. By Dec. 17 the revolt was suppressed with the help of a British task force. A state of emergency had been declared on Dec. 8, the PRB was banned and hundreds of its members were arrested. The Constitution was suspended on Dec. 20, and the Legislative Council was dissolved. Since then the Sultan (who eventually declined in July 1963 to join Malaysia) has ruled by decree.

The PRB subsequently operated from exile in Malaysia, with the use of facilities in Sarawak (East Malaysia). In 1976 there were still 37 political detainees in Brunei, most of them PRB members arrested in 1962. At the United Nations the PRB has been one of several petitioners for the granting of "the inalienable right of the people of Brunei to self-determination and independence". In a resolution initiated by Malaysia and adopted by the UN General Assembly on Nov. 28, 1977 (with Britain not participating in the vote), the British Government was called upon "to facilitate expeditiously the holding of free and democratic elections in Brunei and the lifting of the ban on all political parties and . . . the return of all political exiles to Brunei".

Burma

Capital: Rangoon   Pop. 34,200,000

The Socialist Republic of the Union of Burma is, under its Constitution approved in a referendum in December 1973, a one-party socialist state with a People's Assembly whose 464 members have been approved by the ruling Burma Socialist Programme Party (Lanzin Party). The country has a President (who is chairman of a State Council) and a Cabinet (Council of Ministers) elected by the People's Assembly and headed by a Prime Minister. Of Burma's population about 71 per cent are Burman. The principal ethnic minorities are the Karen (about 11 per cent of the total population) in southern and eastern Burma, the Shans (Thai in origin) on the eastern plateau; and the Chins, Kachins, Mons and Arakanese (totalling about 1,000,000) in the north and north-east. There are also some 400,000 Chinese and 120,000 Indians and Pakistanis, mainly in the urban areas. By May 1976 the Government's military campaign against communist and tribal rebels was estimated to have caused, during its 13-year duration, the death of some 25,000 rebels, while 50,000 others had been captured or had surrendered, and government losses had been 10,000 men.

An alleged conspiracy by army officers to kill the country's leading personalities and to "destroy the economy", uncovered on July 2, 1976, led to the trial of six officers (including Gen. Tin U, who had resigned in March 1976 as Minister of Defence and Chief of Staff), who were sentenced on Jan. 11, 1977, one of them to death and the others to imprisonment ranging from five years to life. Their plot was said to have been planned in the name of "joint venture capital" with the aim of restoring Burma's socialist economy to private enterprise.

On May 28, 1980, the Government decreed an amnesty for political detainees and insurgents who surrendered within 90 days; prison sentences were reduced and persons under sentence of death were reprieved. It was officially claimed that 2,198 persons had accepted the amnesty, among them U Nu (who had been Prime Minister in 1948-62, had left Burma after his overthrow, had been associated with Burmese living in Thailand and been held responsible for a number of bomb attacks in Rangoon, and who had later lived in India) as well as Bo Thet Tun, a member of the central committee of the Burma Communist Party.

Arakan Liberation Party

This party advocates the secession from Burma of the region of Arakan (bordering on southern Bangladesh), which is largely inhabited by Moslems, whereas the majority of Burma's inhabitants are Buddhists. It superseded a Moslem Mujahid movement which had conducted guerrilla operations in 1952-54 but by 1961 had been reduced to insignificance. The party's armed wing, established in 1974 and known as the Arakan Liberation Army, has engaged in intermittent clashes with government troops, in one of which its leader, Khaing Mo Lin, was killed on June 3, 1977. Meanwhile, the party itself had agreed in May 1975 to join other national minority movements in a Federal National Democratic Front (see separate entry).

On Feb. 23, 1976, four men charged with involvement in an attempt to establish a separate independent state of Arakan (two of whom were said to have been in contact with the Bangladeshi military attaché in Rangoon) were condemned to death and two others to life imprisonment and 10 years in prison respectively; the death sentences were carried out shortly afterwards.

The Burmese Government stated on April 29, 1978, that in a census operation begun in 1977 it had been found that there had been massive illegal immigration into Burma, particularly from Bangladesh into Arakan; the following month it was claimed that over 100,000 people had left the towns of Buthidaung and Maungdaw in Arakan to "escape an immigration check", most crossing the border into Bangladesh and others going into hiding in the jungle.

The Government of Bangladesh had earlier claimed that thousands of Moslems had been expelled from Burma and on June 6, 1978, gave the number of Moslem refugees from Burma in Bangladesh as 167,000. After this situation had caused serious strains in relations between the two countries, an agreement providing for the repatriation of the refugees to Burma was eventually reached on July 9, 1979.

Burma Communist Party (BCP)—("White Flag" Party)

Leadership. Thakin Ba Thein Tin (ch. of central committee).

Having been established in August 1939, the Communist Party in 1946 divided into (i) the Stalinist "White Flag" Communists led by Thakin Than Tun and (ii) the Trotskyist "Red Flag" Communists (see separate entry). The "White Flag" BCP became a powerful force partly owing to its alliance with militant Kachins and Shans and partly because of the overt support which it received from China following its gravitation to a pro-Chinese orientation. Having previously operated mainly in the Arakan and Pegu mountains and in the Irrawaddy delta, the BCP transferred its headquarters to the Chinese border area in 1968. There was heavy fighting throughout 1970 in Shan state (bordering on China, Laos and Thailand); after the establishment of friendly relations between Burma and China in 1971 there were few reports of insurgent activities but in 1973 hostilities revived in Shan state. (For Shan secessionist movements, see separate entries below.)

Of the 22 members of the BCP's central committee elected in 1962, only two were still at large in Burma in 1975. The former chairman, Thakin Than Tun, was assassinated in 1968 by one of his followers. Four central committee members were murdered in a purge in 1967-68; seven were killed in action; one had died of natural causes; one had been captured; two had surrendered, and four were outside the country. Of the later office bearers, Thakin Zin and Thakin Chit, respectively chairman and general secretary, were killed in a clash with troops in the Pegu Yoma mountains (north of Rangoon) on March 15, 1975. On May 17, 1975, the central committee announced that Thakin Ba Thein Tin, the head of the party's delegation in Peking, had been elected chairman.

An army spokesman claimed on March 20 1975, that the communist rebellion in central Burma had been crushed and that during the previous two years 172 communists had been killed, 146 had been captured and 500 had surrendered (the Army's casualties being given as 135 killed and 143 wounded). The communist rebels, however, remained active in Shan state, near the Chinese border, where, according to an army communiqué of June 28, 1975, a total of 120 communists and 32 soldiers were killed within a week.

During a visit to China in November 1975 by Gen. Ne Win, then Chairman of Burma's State Council, it was agreed that neither side would engage in any aggressive move against the other. Nevertheless the Chinese Communist Party continued to give support to the BCP and its forces in rebellion against the Government of Burma. Burmese official announcements on the fighting were made on Jan. 7, 1976 (to the effect that in four major battles and more than 40 skirmishes in November-December 1975 in eastern Burma, 216 communist rebels and Shan tribesmen had been killed and 43 rebels had surrendered or been captured), and on March 26, 1976 (stating that on March 16-21 a total of 1,200 communists and 300 other rebels had been repulsed at Mong Yang, 20 miles from the Chinese border). On April 11, 1976, the Government announced that in clashes in eastern Burma on March 22-26 its troops had killed 96 communist rebels and wounded 150, with 35 soldiers being killed and 62 injured in these engagements. In Rangoon, 47 party members were arrested in August-September 1976, for distributing anti-government publications.

The BCP's radio station, the "Voice of the People of Burma" (VOPB), repeatedly made claims of successful communist military operations, and on Dec. 10, 1980, it summed up its findings for the period from November 1979 to December 1980, stating that 772 battles during that period in northern and north-eastern regions and in central Shan state had resulted in the death of 1,908 soldiers, injury to 3,341 others and the capture by communists of 320 men.

Following the expiry of an amnesty offered on May 28, 1980, to insurgents who surrendered within 90 days, the Government proposed to Thakin Ba Thein Tin that talks should be held to "end the internal strife"; that a ceasefire should be effected by both sides; and that negotiations should be started but be kept secret for the time being. The BCP refused to effect a ceasefire but agreed to secret talks, at which the BCP proposed that the BCP and its armed wing should be allowed to exist and the BCP should also be allowed to use the border area (where it was located) as its base area. (The BCP had earlier warned the Burmese Government against "the threat of Soviet social-imperialism and its invasion of Afghanistan" and also against the "hegemonist" aspirations of Vietnam in South-East Asia.) The Burmese Government in turn proposed that BCP members could join the ruling Burma Socialist Programme Party and take part in elections at various levels to the people's councils; that BCP soldiers could join the government security and police forces; and that BCP members could help to solve the country's internal problems.

The BCP subsequently proposed in draft form (i) that, as the party had never wanted Burma to be divided, the "liberated" areas should be recognized as an autonomous region under a single government; that the BCP's People's Army should be recognized as a military unit controlled by a state defence council under the single government with one or two representatives from either the BCP or its army sitting on that council; and (ii) that the BCP should be permitted to continue to exist. However, Gen. Ne Win, disclosing the talks on May 14, 1981, declared that the demands of the BCP should not be honoured and would not be met, and that the Government had therefore decided to stop the negotiations completely. Thakin Ba Thein Tin thereupon denounced the Government (in a statement broadcast by the VOPB on June 14, 1981) as being responsible for unilaterally breaking off the negotiations, and as "obstructors of democratic rights" and "destroyers of national unity".

On Nov. 22, 1981, a VOPB report on nine months of fighting claimed that up to Sept. 30, 1981, the People's Army of the BCP had fought 30 battles against government forces in central Shan state, killing 40 soldiers and injuring 57, while in battles fought elsewhere another 10 soldiers were killed and six wounded. In February and March 1982 the VOPB reported various People's Army guerrilla attacks from the Kengtung area (eastern Shan state) and other parts of Shan state.

In late 1982 the BCP was thought to have between 10,000 and 15,000 men in the field and to be the strongest of Burma's various insurgent movements.

Communist Party of Burma—"Red Flag" Party

This Trotskyist party was formed in 1946 as a result of a split in the (then Stalinist) Burma Communist Party (see entry above). It conducted its own guerrilla operations but by 1961 its strength was offically estimated at no more than about 500 men, with this number declining further as two of the party's leaders had surrendered. Between Aug. 15 and 19, 1963, inconclusive talks between the ruling Revolutionary Council (under Gen. Ne Win, who had come to power in 1962) and a delegation led by Thakin Soe (general secretary of the party, which then had its headquarters in Arakan state) failed to end in agreement, the Revolutionary Council stating that the "Red Flag" Communists did not have "any honest and sincere desire to restore internal peace". Thakin Soe was captured in 1970 and condemned to death on Sept. 10, 1973 (after a nine-month trial). The party later ceased to exercise any considerable influence on events in Burma.

A group of Arakan "Red Flag" Communists, which demanded the establishment of a "Republic of Arakan with the right to secede from the Union of Burma", had unsuccessful talks on the restoration of peace with the Revolutionary Council, which were broken off on Nov. 18, 1963, because the Council could not accede to the Communists' demand.

Federal National Democratic Front (FNDF)

Leadership. Mahn Ba Zan (pres.); Bo Mya.

This Front was formed on May 27, 1975, by five insurgent organizations of national minorities—the Karen National Union, the Karenni National Progressive Party, the New Mon State Party, the Shan State Progress Party (the political wing of the Shan State Army) and the Arakan Liberation Party—with the object of overthrowing "Ne Win's one-party military dictatorship" (which had come to power in 1962) and establishing in Burma a federal union based on national self-determination. By May 1976 the FNDF was said to have been joined by four other organizations.

The Front superseded an earlier National Democratic United Front (NDUF), led by Mahn Ba Zan, which had been deserted by many Karens in 1968 because their allies in this front, the ("White Flag") Burmese Communists, were allegedly fanatically emulating the "Cultural Revolution" of China; Mahn Ba Zan had himself left this Front in late 1969.

The NDUF had been an alliance comprising the "White Flag" Burma Communist Party, the Karen National Union Party led by Mahn Ba Zan, the New Mon State Party, the Karenni National Progressive Party, and the Chin National Progressive Party. Negotiations designed to restore internal peace between the country's Revolutionary Council and the NDUF were broken off by the former on Nov. 14, 1963, because accession to the NDUF's demand for the recognition of "liberated areas" might eventually lead to Burma "being rent asunder like Korea or Vietnam".

Kachin Independence Army (KIA)

This movement based in the Kachin ethnic minority in northern Burma had been conducting guerrilla operations before the military coup of 1962, which brought a Revolutionary Council led by Gen. Ne Win to power. Negotiations between the Revolutionary Council and the KIA, designed to restore peace in the country, broke down on Nov. 15, 1963, because no agreement could be reached on a ceasefire. In 1970-73, when the KIA began co-operating with the "White Flag" Communists and the Shan State Army, it was said to consist of some 3,000 to 4,000 guerrillas and is thought to have maintained its strength at about this level.

On Aug. 20, 1975, it was reported that three of the KIA's leaders—Saw Seng, his brother Saw Thu and Pon Shwe Saw Saing—had been killed by their followers at a camp in northern Thailand in a dispute about funds obtained by various means. Another brother of Saw Seng was said to have been killed on March 1, 1975, by communists in the northern part of Shan state.

In operations against the KIA and other rebels on Sept. 12-26, 1975, troops destroyed an opium refinery and seized a large quantity of ammunition in the southern part of Shan state. Troops were also engaged in operations against the KIA in northern Burma in June 1976.

Karen National Liberation Front (KNLF)— see Karen National Union (KNU)

Karen National Union (KNU)

Leadership. Bo Mya (pres.).

Established in 1948, the KNU has a long history of guerrilla warfare against the Burmese Government through its armed wing, the Karen National Liberation Front (KNLF), in pursuit of its aim of setting up a separate Karen state. Among the various ethnic guerrilla organizations the KNU has been the strongest and leads the Federal National Democratic Front formed in 1975 (see separate entry). In 1971 the KNU's then president claimed that his organization's armed forces consisted of 16,000 men, including 4,000 regulars, and by 1974 they were said to control considerable areas in south-east Burma. The KNU was financing its activities by levying a 5 per cent tax on goods brought into the area under its control from Thailand by smugglers supplying the black market in Rangoon.

On June 20, 1975, the Army was reported to have launched a major offensive against the KNLF, but this did not end the latter's activities. On April 26, 1976, Karen rebels attacked a ferry off Burma's southern coast, killing 45 and injuring 75 people.

On March 24, 1980, it was reported that an assault by Burmese troops had driven over 2,000 Karen refugees across the border into the Mae Sor district in Thailand. The Burmese Government announced on March 25 that two KNU camps on the Thai border had been destroyed. Further fighting was reported in March and on April 15, when another 1,500 Karens were said to have crossed the border into north-eastern Thailand. In response to the amnesty offered on May 28, 1980, to insurgents who surrendered within 90 days, several KNU leaders returned to Burma from Thailand. On Sept. 22-27, 1980, another 1,000 Karen civilians were reported to have escaped to Thailand after Burmese troops had launched another major offensive against the KNLF at Kawkareik (east of Moulmein and about 20 miles from the Thai border). On Nov. 23, 1981, some 1,000 Karen rebels ambushed about 500 Burmese troops near the Thai border north-east of Rangoon and killed or wounded at least 100 of these troops. KNU guerrillas were also responsible for blowing up a passenger train between Rangoon and Moulmein, killing three persons and injuring 19, in February 1982. In late-1982 the active strength of the KNU was estimated at between 5,000 and 8,000 men.

In late September 1982 a five-man group of heavily-armed KNU insurgents mounted what was thought to be the first Karen attack on Rangoon. After the group had been intercepted by security forces two were killed (including the leader, Mahn Ngwe Aung) and three captured.

National Liberation Front (NLF)

Leadership. Gen. Bo Let Ya.

This Front was formed in June 1970 under an agreement signed by U Nu (the former Prime Minister overthrown in 1962), who had established the Parliamentary Democracy Party (with a military wing called the Patriotic Liberation Army), and the Karen National Union and Mon rebel leaders. The agreement envisaged the restoration of parliamentary democracy in Burma and the establishment of a federal form of government under which the national minorities would enjoy complete autonomy, including the right to control their own police force and armed militia. In March 1973 U Nu was reported to have resigned as leader of the NLF in favour of Gen. Bo Let Ya (a former Defence Minister) because of disagreement over demands made by the national minorities' leaders.

The Front's activities seriously affected relations between Burma and Thailand. On Jan. 2, 1973, the Burmese Government announced that it had sunk 12 Thai boats carrying arms for the NLF, and on Feb. 14 a Thai police helicopter (carrying four police officers and three Americans, including a US embassy official) was reported to have been shot down over Burmese territory. The Thai Government later gave an assurance that it would not support any rebel forces seeking to overthrow the Government in Rangoon. By September 1973 the NLF's strength was reported to have declined to less than 1,000 men.

U Nu returned to Burma from India on July 29, 1980, in response to the amnesty offer of May 28, 1980, to rebels who surrendered within 90 days.

New Mon State Party

Based in the Mon ethnic minority of northern Burma, the New Mon State Party joined with other secessionist organizations to form the Federal National Democratic Front in May 1975 (see separate entry). An earlier movement of Mon insurgents was said to have been "practically eliminated" by 1961, when only about 40 were left. The surrender of a leader of the New Mon State Party at Moulmein was officially announced on June 6, 1980.

Patriotic Liberation Army (PLA)

The PLA, the military arm of the Parliamentary Democracy Party (founded by U Nu, the former Prime Minister overthrown in 1962, and later superseded by the People's Patriotic Party) was said to have increased its strength from about 1,200 in October 1970 to between 3,000 and 5,000 by August 1971. Equipped with US arms obtained on the black market in Thailand, the PLA confined its activities to the Thai border areas. In July 1972 it called for an insurrection, and on Nov. 17 of that year a government spokesman alleged that a plot to assassinate cabinet members had been uncovered and that the PLA had intended to blow up buildings, but that some 500 PLA supporters had been arrested in various cities during October 1972. There have been no reports of PLA activities since 1975.

People's Patriotic Party (PPP)

Leadership. Bo Let Ya; U Thwin ("Gen." Thwin).

This party in 1975 superseded the Parliamentary Democracy Party (PDP) which had earlier been founded by U Nu (the former Prime Minister overthrown in 1962) and had been allied, within a National Liberation Front (see separate entry) formed in June 1970 with the Karen National Union and Mon insurgents. Factions which had seceded from the PDP were the Union Solidarity Party led by Tin Maung Win and the Anti-Fascist People's Unity Party led by Bo Hmu Aung and Kyaw Din. (Three smaller underground factions were called the Kawthulay Insurgents, the Mon Patriotic Group and the Expatriate Faction.)

On Oct. 2, 1975, it was reported that the PPP had earlier that year expelled "Gen."

Yan Naing and his troops from the southern command of its armed wing, the Patriotic Liberation Army, because they had attacked the allied Kawthulay insurgents. Leaders of the PPP who returned to Burma from exile in response to the amnesty offer of May 28, 1980, to insurgents who surrendered within 90 days included Brig. Gen. Saw Kya Doe (a former deputy chief of staff), Bo Hmu Aung (who had been Minister of Defence in 1958) and Gen. Yan Naing.

Shan State Army (SSA)

Leadership. Hso Lane (ch.).

The SSA was formed in the mid-1960s by various insurgent groups which had been active since the Shan revolt of 1958, when a 10-year trial period of Shan participation in the Union of Burma had expired and the central Government had moved to curtail the traditional autonomy of the Shan tribespeople on the eastern Burmese plateau (who are Thais by ethnic origin). By the early 1970s the SSA, which has close links with the Burma Communist Party (BCP) and the Kachin Independence Army (see separate entries) and is equipped with Chinese weapons, was reported to consist of some 4,000 guerrillas. Apart from fighting government troops, the SSA has been engaged since 1972 in a struggle for supremacy in the Shan region with the anti-communist Shan United Revolutionary Army (see separate entry).

Based in strongholds on the western side of the Shan plateau, the SSA also has considerable support among the Palaung tribes further north (the SSA leader himself being half-Palaung). In May 1976 the SSA's political wing, the Shan State Progress Party, participated with other ethnic minority organizations in the formation of the Federal National Democratic Front (see separate entry).

According to the BCP's radio station, the Voice of the People of Burma (VOPB), broadcasting on Jan. 6, 1980, the SSA had killed 34 soldiers in attacks in the area northeast of Mandalay, while on April 3, 1980, the VOPB claimed that Mu-Se (in northern Shan state, near the Chinese border) had been captured by rebels. On April 15, on the other hand, 80 Shan rebels were reported to have crossed into Thailand to escape Burmese troops.

In response to the government amnesty offered on May 28, 1980, to insurgents who surrendered within 90 days, several rebel leaders from eastern Shan state, notably Lo Hsi Ming, returned to Burma from exile.

Shan State Nationalities Liberation Organization (SSNLO)

The Voice of the People of Burma (VOPB) radio station of the Burma Communist Party

82

(BCP) reported on Nov. 22, 1981, that the SSNLO was undertaking combined guerrilla operations with units of the People's Army of the BCP and also of the Kayah New Land Revolutionary Council (a local organization in Kayah state, north-east of Rangoon). This combined force was said to have fought, in the first nine months of 1981, a total of 49 battles in southern Shan state, killing 131 soldiers and wounding 98.

Shan United Revolutionary Army (SURA)

Leadership. Moh Heng (ch.); Kan Jate (vice-ch.); Chau Nor Fah (s.g.).

The SURA was formed in January 1969 by Shan insurgents opposed to the communist-backed Shan State Army (SSA—see separate entry), its original nucleus being the forces of veteran rebel Chau Noi (who later abandoned his role in the insurgency). The SURA chairman, Moh Heng, fought the Japanese during World War II and joined the Burma Communist Party (BCP) in 1952, but left in 1956 in disagreement with its land policy and communization of Shan village life; in the early 1960s he lost his left arm while leading an attack on a Burmese Army garrison.

Strongly anti-communist and equipped with US-made weapons, the SURA became engaged in open conflict with the SSA from 1972 and was on the defensive until 1975. More recently it appears to have consolidated its influence in the southern-central region of Shan state and during 1982 claimed to have received a growing number of high-ranking defectors from both the BCP and the SSA. Its current active strength is estimated at between 2,000 and 3,000 guerrillas in the field, with a further 8,000 trained reservists being available when needed. In its struggle with communist elements, the SURA has received backing from the remnants of the Kuomintang Third Army led by Gen. Li Wen-han, whose forces settled in Burmese border areas after fleeing from China in 1949.

Basing its strategy on a combination of political propaganda and guerrilla warfare, the SURA seeks to appeal to both the nationalistic and the religious sentiments of the Shan people. Its constitution advances the principles of federalism among tribal groups, parliamentary democracy and preservation of the tribal religious and cultural heritage. The SURA's Shan soldiers are required to observe Buddhist precepts and practices (although many of its Kachin recruits are Christian, and are allowed to practise their faith).

Like other insurgent armies in Burma, the SURA derives most of its income from taxes on households in its area of control and from levies on cross-border trade, notably the substantial traffic in precious stones such as jade. The movement is strongly opposed to the growing of opium poppies (a traditional source of income for the Shan people) and disclaims any involvement in the narcotics trade; at the same time, it recognizes that, given the depressed state of the Shan region (which it attributes to government neglect), many inhabitants have few alternative means of livelihood in the short term.

China

Capital: Beijing (Peking)   Pop. 1,008,175,288

The People's Republic of China is, under its Constitution of 138 articles adopted by the Chinese National People's Congress on Dec. 4, 1982, "a socialist state under the people's democratic dictatorship led by the working class and based on the alliance of workers and peasants" in which "all power belongs to the people" and "the organs through which the people exercise state power are the National People's Congress (NPC) and the local people's congresses at different levels". The NPC consists of deputies elected for a five-year term "by the provinces, autonomous regions and municipalities directly under the central government and by the armed forces". The NPC and its permanent body, the Standing Committee, "exercise the legislative power of the state". The Standing Committee inter alia supervises the work of the State Council, i.e. "the central people's Government" and "the executive body of the highest organ of state power".

Contrary to the 1978 Constitution, the 1982 Constitution contained no references to the Chinese Communist Party (CCP), to Marxism-Leninism or to Mao Zedong Thought in any of its articles, although in its preamble there were several references to "the Chinese people of all nationalities under the leadership of the CCP and the guidance of Marxism-Leninism and Mao Zedong Thought". The preamble also referred to the existence of "a broad patriotic united front" under the leadership of the CCP and "composed of democratic parties and people's organizations" and embracing "all socialist working people, all patriots who support socialism and all patriots who stand for reunification of the motherland" (i.e. for the incorporation of Taiwan in the Republic of China). Eight existing minor political parties date back to before the proclamation of the People's Republic on Oct. 1, 1949, and are composed mainly of intellectuals.

Regulations on state secrets adopted in 1951 were reissued on April 10, 1980, when such secrets were defined as secret information on virtually all aspects of military, political and economic affairs, and punishment as a counter-revolutionary was provided for anyone who sold or divulged such information to "enemies at home or abroad" or to "domestic and foreign profiteers".

The power struggle within the CCP which followed the death of Chairman Mao in September 1976 was accompanied by various manifestations of opposition to the Government, although organized groups were largely confined to those seeking full observance of human rights in China. The conviction in January 1981 of the so-called "gang of four" radicals and six former associates of the late Marshal Lin Biao demonstrated the victory in the party power struggle of the "reformist" faction led by Deng Xiaoping, which was further consolidated at the 12th CCP congress held in September 1982. However, while vigorously denouncing the "leftist deviation" of the "gang of four" and their followers, those controlling the country also took steps to clamp down on other forms of opposition which were seen as challenging the leading role of the CCP.

The Communist regime in Peking is faced with no serious external threat from opposition groups, even though two potential centres for such opposition exist close to China's borders, namely the British colony of Hong Kong and the island of Taiwan. As regards Hong Kong, anti-communist sentiments among its predominantly Chinese population of some 4,500,000 (including substantial numbers of refugees from Communist China) have been moderated by the colony's close economic ties with the mainland and by its military vulnerability to China. Moreover, the Kuomintang regime in Taiwan, while continuing to claim that it is the legitimate government of the whole of China, has generally confined concrete expressions of this claim to the receiving of individual defectors from the People's Republic.

Internal Opposition Groups

New regulations announced on July 15, 1980, required all publications to be registered with the local authorities, forbade printing works to do business without the local authorities' consent, and banned the supply of paper and other printing material to unlicensed printing works. These measures led to the virtual disappearance of the human rights organizations which had emerged in the late 1970s (see below). On Aug. 31, 1980, the editors of four unofficial publications were arrested in Canton, and the last unofficial periodical appearing in Peking (a non-political literary magazine called *Today*) was suspended by police in September 1980.

Under an amendment to the 1978 Constitution, adopted by the NPC in September 1980 and incorporated into the 1982 Constitution, the rights of citizens "to speak out freely, air their views fully, hold great debates and write big-character posters" was deleted, although this did not affect the guarantees in the same article of freedom of speech, correspondence, the press, assembly, association, procession and demonstration, and the freedom to strike. The display of posters had been severely restricted by the Peking municipal authorities on Dec. 6, 1979, and authors were not only required to register their names, addresses and places of work, but were also to be held responsible for the contents of posters.

In February 1981 the Communist Party was unofficially reported to have issued two directives (i) insisting that literature and art must conform to official policy and (ii) calling for a total ban on unofficial publications and organizations. Between April and June 1981 at least 25 editors and publishers of unofficial journals were arrested, and several others in July and August, and all such journals ceased to appear after March 1981.

April 5 Group

This human rights group was formed in March 1979 and named after the date on which riots broke out in 1976 in Tien An Men Square in Peking directed against the radical wing of the Communist Party leadership and in support of Deng Xiaoping; it published an unofficial organ, the *April 5 Tribune,* until April 1980. On July 30, 1980, Liu Qing, as editor of the *April 5 Tribune,* who had been arrested for selling a transcript of the trial of Wei Jingsheng, the editor of *Exploration* (see separate entry for the Society of Light), was sentenced to three years of "re-education through labour". Two former editors of the *April 5 Tribune* were arrested on April 10, 1981 (with four other dissidents associated with unofficial publications being also arrested in the same month).

Association for the Study of Scientific and Democratic Socialism

This Association convened a meeting in Tien An Men Square (Peking) on Sept. 13, 1979 (attended by about 1,000 people), when speakers protested against the plight of peasants and others who had staged demonstrations seeking redress for their grievances, and also against the privileges of party officials.

Chinese Democratic Party

An opposition party of this name was alleged to have been formed by three printing workers, two of whom were sentenced to three years in prison, and the third to two years, on Feb. 26, 1981.

Chinese Revolutionary Party

This strongly anti-Maoist formation of dissidents, many of them disillusioned former Red Guards, claimed to have a membership of "hundreds" by late 1982, organized in cells in the major cities, especially Shanghai. Regarding the present Communist leadership as essentially repressive despite its liberal façade, the group advocates the establishment of a multi-party parliamentary democracy in China.

Human Rights Alliance

Leadership. Ren Wanding (founder).

This Alliance was responsible for the publication on Jan. 5, 1979, of a manifesto containing 19 demands, including the removal of Chairman Mao's body from its mausoleum, the re-establishment of friendly relations with the Soviet Union, the release of all political prisoners, a constitutionally-guaranteed right to criticize state and party leaders, representation of non-communist parties in the National People's Congress, open sessions of the Congress and freedom to change one's work and to travel abroad. The Alliance's founder was arrested on April 4, 1979, during a period of official reaction to dissident activities in favour of greater democracy, but the Alliance's manifesto was again displayed on a poster on Sept. 23, 1979.

National Committee of Democratic Journals

This group was reported to be "engaged in increasingly co-ordinated" activities by editors of various unofficial publications in late 1980.

Society of Light

This Society was formed in November 1978 in Guizhou (Kweichow) province, and a Peking branch of it was formed on Jan. 21, 1979. Wei Jingsheng, the editor of *Exploration* (a magazine of the Society's Peking branch), had been responsible for displaying, on Dec. 5, 1978, a poster in which he complained that wages had not kept pace with prices, and called for "the fifth modernization—democracy" (to complement the "four modernizations of agriculture, industry, national defence and science and technology" advocated by the Communist Party since 1975). He also published on March 3, 1979, a poster denouncing the treatment of political prisoners.

Wei Jingsheng was arrested on March 29, 1979, and his assistant editor on May 22. The publication of *Exploration* was suspended between April and September 1979. On Oct. 16, 1979, Wei Jingsheng was sentenced to 15 years in prison, to be followed by three years' deprivation of political rights, for supplying a foreigner with military intelligence and carrying out "counter-revolutionary agitation", his assistant editor having given evidence against him; the defendant's appeal against the judgment was rejected on Nov. 6.

During his trial Wei Jingsheng said that the information which he had passed to a foreigner was based on hearsay and not on official documents and could not have caused any harm to the military situation; he denied that his writings were counter-revolutionary; and he insisted that their central theme was that without democracy there could be no four modernizations, that his criticism had been directed against those who used Marxism as "the pretext for enslaving people", and that *Exploration* was a journal of theoretical investigation on public sale and had never aimed at the overthrow of the Government.

Several persons were subsequently arrested for selling a transcript of Wei Jingsheng's defence, and a man who put up posters in Xinxiang (Hsin-hsiang) was on Dec. 9, 1979, sentenced to eight years' imprisonment and 13 years' deprivation of political rights. On Jan. 12, 1980, it was reported that a supporter of Wei Jingsheng had been sent to prison for eight years in Central Henan province for his alleged "counter-revolutionary" activities.

Xinjiang Dissidents

On Oct. 9, 1980, a secretary of the Communist Party of the Uighur autonomous region (Xinjiang, previously Sinkiang) confirmed that there had been "events harmful to unity between nationalities and between the Army and the people". According to earlier unofficial reports there had been armed clashes between (Moslem) Uighurs and Chinese officials and soldiers in April 1980, apparently caused by Uighur resentment against mass immigration of Chinese into the region. In the Hong Kong newspaper *Zheng Ming* it was alleged in September 1981 that a conspiracy be dissident Uighurs for a rising against Chinese rule had been discovered by the authorities.

External Opposition

Nationalist Party of China (*Chung-kuo Kuo-min-tang* or Kuomintang, KMT)

This party, now the ruling party of Taiwan, was originally founded in November 1894 as the *Hsing Chung Hui* by Dr Sun Yat-sen. It played a major role in the overthrow of the Manchu regime in 1911 and was renamed the Kuomintang in October 1919. Under President Chiang Kai-shek it united most of China by 1927, when it was purged of Communists. During part of the war with Japan which began in 1931 the KMT co-operated with the Communists, but civil war which broke out between the KMT and the Communists after the end of World War II ended with victory for the latter in 1949, when the KMT leadership withdrew to Taiwan.

Parts of the KMT's armed forces, however, fled into Thailand and Burma. These included the KMT Third Army, led by Gen. Li Wen-han, which gave support to the (nationalist and anti-communist) Shan United Revolutionary Army (see separate entry under Burma) by assigning to this movement three brigades to assist it in its struggle against pro-communist Shans. However, by 1982 these two brigades had been reduced to about 200 men, while the whole of the remaining KMT Third Army numbered no more than 3,000.

In recent years the Taiwan Government has consistently rejected overtures from Peking for negotiations on peaceful reunification, detailed proposals for which have been put forward from time to time by Chinese Government spokesmen. In June 1982 it was officially announced in Communist China that the last batch of soldiers and officials of the former Kuomintang regime (numbering 4,237) had been released after 33 years in prison.

In the first hijacking attempt ever officially acknowledged by the Chinese authorities, five men tried unsuccessfully on July 25, 1982, to force an airliner on a Chinese domestic flight to divert from Shanghai to Taiwan. Responsibility for the attempt—reportedly one of several during 1982—was officially attributed to demobilized soldiers whose parents were senior CCP cadres.

India

Capital: New Delhi   Pop. 672,000,000

The Union of India is, under its Constitution with amendments which came into force on Jan. 3, 1977, "a sovereign socialist secular democratic republic" (and a member of the Commonwealth) with a Parliament consisting of the President, the Council of State and the House of the People *(Lok Sabha)*, the latter House having 544 members elected by universal adult suffrage for a five-year term (and up to 20 members representing union territories and up to two additional members nominated by the President). The latter is elected for a five-year term by the elected members of Parliament and of the Legislative Assemblies of the states; he appoints a Prime Minister and, on the latter's advice, other ministers, all of whom are responsible to Parliament.

As a result of general elections held on Jan. 3 and 6, 1980, the 544 seats in the *Lok Sabha* were distributed as follows: Congress (I) and four allied parties 374, *Lok Dal* (Janata Secular Party) 41, Janata Party and four allied parties 34, Congress 13, Left Front (consisting of the Communist Party of India/Marxist, the Communist Party of India and three other parties) 54, three other parties (one each) 3, independents 6, vacant 19.

There is in India a profusion of legal political parties both at national and at state level; divisions of existing parties, defections from these parties and formations of new parties have been frequent. Illegal movements are mainly communal, separatist or extreme left-wing organizations.

Hindu Movements

All-Assam People's Struggle Council *(Gana Sangram Parishad)*

This organization was set up to oppose the inclusion of "aliens" (i.e. Moslems who had fled from East Pakistan in 1971, when that territory seceded from Pakistan and became Bangladesh) in the electoral registers of Assam.

National Union of Selfless Servers *(Rashtriya Swayam Sewak Sang,* RSSS)

Leadership. M. S. Golwalkar.

This paramilitary Hindu organization was founded in 1925 by Dr K. B. Hedgewar, who in 1940 appointed M. S. Golwalkar as its leader. It was banned in 1948 after the assassination of Mahatma Gandhi, but the ban was lifted in 1949 after M. S. Golwalkar had given an assurance that it would adhere to its original non-political character and function only as a cultural organization. In 1968, however, government employees were forbidden to take part in its work.

According to its principles, laid down in M. S. Golwalkar's book *A Bunch of Thoughts,* Indian nationality is founded on Hinduism, and Moslems, Christians and communists are "internal threats" and can qualify for Indian nationality only by breaking away from their "external moorings" and learning to respect Hindu traditions. In 1970 the RSSS was said to have 300,000 members spread all over India, and its influence was held responsible for communal riots in various parts of Maharashtra in May 1970 in which over 60 people, mainly Moslems, were killed.

The RSSS was again banned between July

1975 and March 1977, and clashes which broke out between Hindus and Moslems in Uttar Pradesh, Bihar and elsewhere between August 1978 and August 1979, when several hundred people were killed, were also attributed to the RSSS, which was reported to be rapidly increasing in membership (estimates varying from 1,000,000 to 10,000,000).

Path of Eternal Bliss *(Anand Marg)*

Leadership. Prabhat Ranjan Sarkar (1.); Sarveshwarananda Avadhoot (g.s.).

This organization, founded in 1955 and with headquarters in Bihar, is a fanatical Hindu religious and political movement whose leader has developed a "progressive utility" theory and is regarded by his followers as an incarnation of God. Combining the worship of Kali (the Hindu goddess of destruction) with extreme right-wing political views, the movement claimed to have 1,900,000 members in India and 400,000 abroad by the late 1970s.

In 1974-75 the *Anand Marg* supported the agitation of Jaya Prakash Narayan against corruption and in favour of electoral, educational, and other reforms. When 25 organizations were banned on July 4, 1975, the *Anand Marg* was included in the ban for "creating conditions of violence and chaos in the country" and for planning to assassinate prominent leaders. On Nov. 1, 1976, three *Anand Marg* members involved in throwing hand grenades at the car of the Chief Justice of India on March 20, 1975, were sentenced, two of them to 10 years' imprisonment each for attempted murder and to seven years each for criminal conspiracy (the sentences to run consecutively), and the third to four years in prison.

P. R. Sarkar, who had been imprisoned since 1971, and four others (including the general secretary of the *Anand Marg*) were on Nov. 29, 1976, given life sentences for murdering six former members of the sect who had defected from it in 1970; however, on July 4, 1978, the Patna High Court allowed an appeal by the five defendants against their conviction for murder, on the grounds that the charge had not been proved beyond reasonable doubt; P. R. Sarkar, and S. Avadhoot, against whom other charges were pending, were released on bail on Aug. 2, 1978. The ban on the sect (and on the other organizations prohibited in 1975) was revoked on March 22, 1977 (and state governments were directed to release all detainees).

After the *Anand Marg* had launched a protest campaign against the life sentence passed on its leader, it carried out, between March 1977 and August 1978, a number of attacks on Indian diplomats in Australia; in particular, it was suspected of involvement in the killing of two persons and the injuring of

seven others on Feb. 12, 1978, by a bomb thrown at an hotel in Sydney which housed delegates to a conference of Asian and Pacific Commonwealth heads of government. In Bangkok (Thailand) two Australians and an American woman (all three *Anand Marg* members) were given six-month prison sentences on Aug. 10, 1978, for illegal possession of explosives.

After rumours had spread in early 1982 that the *Anand Marg* was kidnapping children, 17 of its members were stoned or stabbed to death or soaked with petrol and burned to death in Calcutta on April 30, 1982. The rumours were attributed to the fact that members of the public had received letters from the sect asking them to donate one or two of their children for "mission work". The police arrested 106 people in connexion with the latest killings and on May 4 the West Bengal state government appointed a judicial commission headed by a high court judge to inquire into them.

Universal Proutist Revolutionary Party

This party was generally regarded as the political wing of the Path of Eternal Bliss *(Anand Marg)* sect (see separate entry); spokesmen for the latter denied any connexion between the two organizations, but admitted that their aims were similar. The party was banned between July 4, 1975 and March 22, 1977 (as was the *Anand Marg*). It claimed responsibility for a terrorist campaign in favour of the release from life imprisonment of the *Anand Marg* leader, P. R. Sarkar, involving attacks on Indian diplomats in Australia. The party had also threatened to blow up an Air India airliner which in fact exploded in the air off Bombay on Jan. 1, 1978, when all 190 passengers and 23 crew members were killed.

The name of the party ("Proutist") is derived from the "progressive utility" theory developed by P. R. Sarkar.

Left-wing Movements

Naxalite Movement

Originating from an armed revolutionary campaign launched in 1965, the Naxalite movement took its name from Naxalbari, a town in the Darjeeling district of West Bengal, where a peasant revolt broke out in March 1967 under the local leadership of the (pro-Chinese) Communist Party of India (Marxist) or CPI(M). The movement was started in Siliguri (a town south of Darjeeling), where the CPI(M) committee called for the arming of peasants and the setting-up of rural bases in preparation for armed struggle—the committee being opposed to the policy of the CPI(M) of entering into coalition governments in West Bengal and Kerala, and being itself supported by the Communist Party of China (where the Naxalites were hailed as a "spring thunder over India"). The CPI(M), however, expelled the leaders of the revolt, which was suppressed by the Indian Army by August 1967.

On July 2, 1968, supporters of the expelled leaders of the revolt founded a new Revolutionary Communist Party, which was opposed to any participation in parliamentary activities. Naxalites continued their activities during that year, their number being estimated as about 17,000 (6,000 in Andhra Pradesh, 5,000 in West Bengal, and 4,000 in Kerala). Kanu Sanyal, the leader of the Naxalbari revolt, continued to call for the formation of village guerrilla units (even if armed with only bows and spears) to create "free zones", but he was arrested on Oct. 31, 1968. Following his release on April 9, 1969, he announced on May 1 that a new "truly revolutionary party", the Communist Party of India (Marxist-Leninist) or CPI(ML) had been formed on April 22, its programme being "to liberate the rural areas through revolutionary armed agrarian revolution, to encircle the cities and finally to liberate the cities and thus to complete the overthrow throughout the country". Early in 1970 Charu Mazumdar, the party's chief theoretician, called on peasants to murder local landowners and thus to become "the sole authority in settling all their local affairs".

The CPI(ML) was officially supported by the Chinese Communist Party, but not by all Indian Maoists. The new party in turn supported tribal rebellion such as that of the Girijan tribesmen in the Srikakulam district (on the border between Andhra Pradesh and Orissa), which had first broken out at the end of 1967 and had continued since then; on Aug. 17, 1969, about 2,000 Naxalites were reported to have been arrested in Srikakulam.

During 1970 Naxalite activities spread in many Indian states. In West Bengal between 10,000 and 20,000 Naxalites, about half of them in the Greater Calcutta area, were reported to have launched a "cultural revolution" on the Chinese model; between April 1 and Oct. 31, 1970, they were responsible for 108 murders and 1,373 acts of lawlessness.

At its first congress held secretly in Calcutta on May 15-16, 1970, the CPI(ML) decided to build up a strong "People's Liberation Army" and to create "innumerable points of guerrilla struggle throughout the countryside", to form "red bases through annihilation of class enemies and overthrowing the forces of suppression". However, of the party's leaders many were subsequently killed or arrested. In Andhra Pradesh it was officially stated on June 21, 1970, that in the past 18 months Naxalites had committed 55 murders and 104 armed robberies. However, in this state, and also in Orissa, Naxalite activities were to a considerable extent brought under control, and they were kept in check in Assam, Bihar, Maharashtra, Punjab and Uttar Pradesh.

Charu Mazumdar, then general secretary of the CPI(ML), was expelled from the party on Nov. 7, 1971, for pursuing "a Trotskyite adventurist line", after he had been attacked by Ashim Chatterjee (a Naxalite campaign leader in a West Bengal district). The latter had inter alia demanded that, in accordance with the Chinese Communist Party's policy, the CPI(ML) should actively support the Pakistan regime of President Yahya Khan and should act against the *Mukti Bahini* movement fighting for the independence of East Pakistan (Bangladesh). The expulsion of Charu Mazumdar and his replacement as general secretary of the CPI(ML) by Satya Narain Singh led to divisions of the movement into factions attacking each other and to a general decline in Naxalite activities. In February 1972 the numbers of Naxalites serving prison sentences was given as about 4,000 in West Bengal, over 2,000 in Bihar, about 1,400 in Andhra Pradesh and 1,000 in Kerala, Uttar Pradesh and other states; many disillusioned CPI(ML) members were returning to other communist parties.

Charu Mazumdar was arrested in Calcutta on July 16, 1972, and died on July 28 of that year. The faction which had followed him was later divided into two groups—(i) one which supported criticism of his policies by the Chinese Communist Party and in particular of his endorsement of individual terrorism and his opposition to participation in other organizations, and (ii) another which continued his policies, supported Marshal Lin Biao's theory that guerrilla warfare was "the only way to utilize and apply the whole strength of the people", and rejected as "revisionism" the Chinese party's criticism of Mazumdar's views. This second group was, however, according to the police in Bihar, almost "wiped out" by mid-1975.

The CPI(ML) led by S. N. Singh, which rejected terrorism, advocated a combination of legal and illegal activities and also participation in mass movements launched by other left-wing parties; it worked for the unification of the extreme left and claimed in August 1974 to have enrolled 90 per cent of the members of the Revolutionary Communist Party in Andhra Pradesh.

At Cochin (Kerala) on Dec. 14-15, 1974, however, dissident members of the CPI(ML) formed the Centre of Indian Communists (as the fourth Communist Party in India). It rejected the "right-wing opportunism" of the Communist Party of India, the "left-wing opportunism" of the Communist Party

(Marxist) and the "adventurism" of the CPI(ML); it declared that it would follow the Chinese party's line in ideological struggles while taking local conditions into account in applying it; and it defined its aims as the establishment of a people's government by organizing an armed revolution of the working class and the peasants.

During this year (1974) Naxalite activities increased again, especially in West Bengal and Bihar. Officially it was stated that on Sept. 17, 1974, there were in West Bengal 592 Naxalite detainees and 1,017 prisoners convicted of, or awaiting trial for, Naxalite activities. On June 7, 1975, the general secretary of the Communist Party of India alleged that "cold-blooded murder" of Naxalites by both landlords and some members of the police force had been "going on everywhere".

The CPI(ML) was banned on July 4, 1975, under emergency powers, but this ban was revoked on March 22, 1977. Following a series of meetings in April 1977 between S. N. Singh (the party's general secretary) and Charan Singh (the newly-appointed Indian Home Affairs Minister) the former gave an assurance that the party had renounced violence and terrorism and wished to participate in democratic processes. Charan Singh thereupon agreed to release all Naxalite detainees irrespective of the nature of their offences or group affiliations.

However, in West Bengal the CPI(ML) faction formerly led by Charu Mazumdar had the greatest following of all the Naxalite groups and rejected all talk of reverting to parliamentary politics. The third CPI(ML) group, led by Ashim Chatterjee and Kanu Sanyal, had before the general elections of March 1977 (won by the Janata Party) issued a statement calling on the people to vote against the Congress (which was defeated in these elections). It was officially stated on May 24, 1977, that some 550 Naxalites detained in West Bengal had been released unconditionally.

In February 1979 Naxalite guerrilla activities were reported to have intensified in West Bengal, Andhra Pradesh, Bihar, Punjab and Kerala and to have spread to Uttar Pradesh, Maharashtra, Tamil Nadu and Assam, with the total strength of the movement being estimated at 15,000. A secret conference of leaders of 13 Naxalite groups held on Jan. 30-Feb. 2, 1981, agreed to abandon terrorist methods and to concentrate on public political agitation. Nevertheless guerrilla activities continued in several states and increased in particular in Kerala and West Bengal.

In Tamil Nadu the leader of an "annihilationist" group named as Kannamani was killed on Dec. 28, 1980, this group being held responsible for several murders and armed

robberies; another three of its members were killed by police on Aug. 24, 1981. In Andhra Pradesh a Naxalite faction known as the People's War group was involved in fighting in a village on April 20, 1981, when 13 tribesmen and one policeman were killed. In West Bengal, the pro-Lin Biao faction of the CPI(ML)—led by Nisith Bhattacharya and Azizul Haque—continued to murder policemen, landowners, small businessmen and shopkeepers and to steal arms, while in Bihar the Naxalites were principally involved in an armed struggle between landowners · and landless labourers agitating for higher wages.

Home Ministry sources stated on April 13, 1982, that 92 people had been killed in 1981 in 324 violent incidents inspired by Naxalites (compared with 84 killed in 305 incidents in 1980), the states most affected being Andhra Pradesh, West Bengal and Bihar. During the campaign for the May 19 state elections in West Bengal Naxalites carried out attacks on offices of the CPI(M), which nevertheless won the elections at the head of a Left Front. Following these and other attacks on police targets in the state, Nisith Bhattacharya was captured with six of his followers in Bihar on May 27 and two days later the police announced that they had raided the group's hideout in Calcutta and seized three printing presses.

A 164-page document issued in Trivandrum (Kerala) in December 1982 by the "central reorganization committee" of the CPI(ML) gave an analysis of the experiences of the Naxalites over the past 15 years as a contribution to the process of rebuilding the movement for a "new phase" of activities. Entitled "Towards a New Phase of the Spring Thunder", the document said that despite the "serious mistakes" committed under Charu Mazumdar's leadership the revolutionary programme evolved by him should still form the basis of the movement's political and organizational line. Analysing the causes of the recent setbacks and fragmentation suffered by the Naxalites, it said that the movement's line had deviated to the left in dealing with specific issues, notably in respect of the relationship between armed struggle and other forms of struggle. Whereas in the beginning the armed struggle was seen as being complemented by other forms of action, a gradual shift took place towards a "one-sided emphasis on armed struggle and neglect of other forms of struggle"; this in turn had resulted in a neglect of mass movements, with the result that the Naxalites became "isolated" from the people, making it all the more easy for the state to launch "a massive encirclement and suppression campaign".

The document continued that the movement had failed to produce a concrete political, economic and agrarian programme to back up its armed struggle and had placed one-sided emphasis on "annihilation of class enemies", with the result that the concept of "political power at the local level" had degenerated into an "abstract, hollow slogan" and the annihilation campaign into "isolated killings". It therefore urged as the theoretical basis for reunification of the movement the upholding of both armed struggle and all other forms of struggle as complementary to it, as well as the upholding of the proletarian revolutionary line of Charu Mazumdar. It also proclaimed support for "Marxism-Leninism-Mao Zedong thought" and opposition to the "Deng-Hua" clique which had "usurped" power in China after Mao's death.

Dalit Panthers

Leadership. Raja Dhale (founder).

This movement took its name from the word *dalit* (meaning "oppressed") and the (US) Black Panther movement, which it regarded as its model. It was set up in 1972 to defend the interests of the Harijans ("untouchables") who formed 9 per cent of the population of the state of Maharashtra. Its members were involved in clashes with caste Hindus, and it called for a boycott of a by-election for the Bombay Central seat in the Lok Sabha on Jan. 14, 1974, with the result that only 38 per cent of the electorate voted, as against 65 per cent in 1971. Later the movement spread from Maharashtra to Gujarat, where upper-caste militants objected to the reservation of government jobs and university places for Harijans and launched, early in 1981, an agitation which led to riots in which over 40 people were killed. The Dalit Panthers were also active in encouraging conversions of Harijans to Islam (as a means of escaping from the caste system), and in this connexion at least 23 Dalit Panthers were arrested under the National Security Act in Kanpur (Uttar Pradesh) in August 1981. The Government, however, took the line that a ban on conversions would be unconstitutional.

Separatist Movements

KASHMIR

Jamaat-i-Tulaba

Leadership. Sheikh Tajamul Islam (pres.).

This student wing of the *Jamaat-i-Islami* (a pro-Pakistan political party) announced on Aug. 5, 1980, that it was planning "an Iran-type revolution for the liberation of Kashmir from illegal occupation and enslavement by India". This was followed by the arrest of 24 Moslem leaders in Jammu and Kashmir. An

international youth conference convened by the organization for Aug. 22, 1980, was banned by the Government, and Sheikh Tajamul Islam was arrested on that day. (There had been attacks on a police station and on the homes of Hindus in Srinagar on Aug. 17, with the police opening fire and killing five persons.) An ordinance issued on Aug. 23 made incitement of hatred between religious communities a criminal offence.

MANIPUR

People's Liberation Army (PLA)

Leadership. Biseswar Singh (C.-in-C.).

The PLA is a Maoist organization operating mainly in Manipur but advocating independence for the whole north-eastern region of India. It draws support from the Meteis, a tribal people of the plain of Manipur, many of whom have rejected Hinduism as a faith identified with New Delhi's cultural domination, and were held responsible for destroying temples and images. Members of the PLA killed four soldiers of the border security force on April 26, 1979, in Imphal (the state capital), and other violent incidents occurred in September and October of that year, and again in the first four months of 1980. Guerrillas of the PLA carried out armed robberies of banks and government offices to obtain funds for the purchase of arms and ammunitions in Thailand and China, and they were believed to have received training from Chinese in Tibet. On Sept. 8, 1980, the state of Manipur was declared a disturbed area.

The PLA continued to be active in 1981, even after its C.-in-C., Biseswar Singh, was captured and seven of his followers killed in a gun battle near Imphal on July 6. It began to co-operate with the National Socialist Council of Nagaland (see separate entry), carrying out what was reported to be its first combined operation with the latter organization on Feb. 19, 1982, when an army convoy was ambushed on the Kohima-Imphal road and 20 soldiers were killed. On April 13, 1982, nine PLA men were killed in an exchange of fire with security forces near Imphal, the dead including Kunj Behari Singh, who had commanded the PLA since Biseswar Singh's arrest.

The PLA had been declared an illegal organization on Oct. 26, 1981, under the 1967 Unlawful Activities (Prevention) Act, together with the People's Revolutionary Party of Kungleipak (see entry below).

People's Revolutionary Party of Kungleipak (Prepak)

Like the People's Liberation Army (see entry above), the Prepak has been active in the state of Manipur, whose secession from the Union of India it seeks. It was in 1980 divided into two factions (i) led by Maipak Sharma, and having as its C.-in-C. Leishabi Singh (who was killed in a battle with police on July 23, 1980), and (ii) led by Rajkumar Tulachandra Singh, who was captured by government forces in February 1980 and later issued a statement calling for suspension of insurgent operations pending negotiations with the State Government; he was thereupon expelled from the organization by his own followers. The Prepak operated in a similar fashion as the People's Liberation Army and its guerrillas were also believed to have been trained in Tibet, but by June 1981 it was believed to have largely disintegrated. It was declared an illegal organization on Oct. 26, 1981, under the 1967 Unlawful Activities (Prevention) Act, together with the People's Liberation Army.

The Prepak has advocated an independent state of Manipur.

MIZORAM

Mizo National Front (MNF)

Leadership. Laldenga (pres.).

In the Mizo Hills District, then the southernmost part of the state of Assam, the MNF gained one seat on the district council in elections held in 1962 (three years after the Front's formation in 1959), and another two seats in a by-election in 1963. At that time the MNF demanded the secession of the contiguous Mizo areas of India, East Pakistan and Burma to form an independent state (of about 10,000 square miles and a population of some 500,000). Early in March 1966 the MNF launched a revolt, which was suppressed by Indian Army units by March 17. The rebels were said to have formed a government with Laldenga as "president" and with eight "secretaries"; subsequently, guerrilla activities continued even though the revolt had been crushed and the MNF had been banned under emergency regulations. In October 1966 the guerrillas' strength was estimated at 10,000 men and in November of that year they were said to be in complete control of about 700 villages.

Early in 1967 some 50,000 Mizos were removed to "protected or progressive villages", but numerous clashes continued between guerrillas and troops, with the former being reported to have decided to obtain weapons from China (with the co-operation of rebels in Nagaland). By 1969 over half the Mizo population was settled in "protected villages".

At the end of 1971 Mizo guerrilla activity subsided, especially as the secession of Bangladesh (East Pakistan) from Pakistan meant the loss of MNF bases in East Pakistan, where about 2,000 MNF rebels

were taken prisoner by Indian and Bangladeshi forces in December 1981. Laldenga had fled the country and the leadership was taken over by a national emergency committee headed by S. Lianzuala (who, however, surrendered to the Indian security forces in June 1973). Meanwhile, Mizoram had become a Union Territory (separate from Assam) in January 1972, and in the first Mizoram Legislative Assembly (elected on April 18, 1972) the MNF exercised some influence through the (opposition) Mizoram Congress.

In the first half of 1974 the MNF continued its terrorist activities, some 600 or 700 MNF guerrillas being reported to have re-entered Mizoram from their bases in the Arakan and Chin Hills of Burma (where they had been under pressure from Burmese troops operating against communists). In the territory occupied by these guerrillas "Major" Kapchhunga ran a parallel administration from Aizawl (the capital of Mizoram); this administration collected its own taxes and also ordered action against informers or other "offenders", of whom 16 were killed in the first nine months of 1974, while Mizoram was under emergency rule. Talks held in April 1974 between the Chief Minister of Mizoram and the chairman of the MNF's "national emergency committee" led to no agreement.

In December 1974 the MNF ordered all non-Mizos to leave Mizoram by the end of the year or "face the consequences". On Jan. 13, 1975, MNF members killed the three highest ranking police officers in the territory; although the MNF commander in Aizawl was arrested on Jan. 28 and his successor (suspected of being responsible for the murder of the three police officers) was killed in an encounter with security forces on March 6, guerrilla activities continued with at least two more policemen being killed. However, on Nov. 22 it was officially stated that since the beginning of 1975 a total of 326 rebels had surrendered. The MNF was again banned on Aug. 6, 1975, and a scheme for the rehabilitation of former rebels was announced on Sept. 14.

Following peace talks between an MNF delegation headed by Laldenga (who had returned from exile in West Germany) and the Indian Home Secretary, which began on Feb. 18, 1976, an agreement was signed on July 1, whereby the MNF acknowledged that Mizoram was an integral part of India and undertook to hand over its arms and ammunition within a month and to seek a solution of Mizoram's problems within the framework of India's Constitution. All operations by the security forces were on July 7 suspended for three months except against those attempting to cross the international border or to disturb law and order.

On March 22, 1977, the ban on the MNF (and on all other organizations proscribed in 1975) was revoked (and state governments were directed to release all detainees). Charan Singh, then Indian Minister of Home Affairs, confirmed on April 18, 1977, that Laldenga (with whom he had a meeting on that day) had in 1976 clearly acknowledged that Mizoram was an integral part of India and had undertaken to abjure violence; on July 27, however, Charan Singh accused Laldenga of trying to "wriggle out" of the peace agreement which he had made with the Government in April, as further guerrilla activities had taken place, another policeman being killed on June 30. A total of 62 rebels had, however, surrendered on June 9, 1977. Further talks between Laldenga and the Union Government were broken off by the latter on March 18, 1978.

Later in 1978 a conflict developed between the moderate and the extremist elements of the MNF. Laldenga, the MNF president, was in June replaced by Biakchhunga, commander of the "Mizo National Army", and on Oct. 27 Laldenga, then under house arrest in New Delhi, was expelled from the MNF, but his supporters later persuaded the movement to readmit him in January 1979, and in February of that year he was re-elected president in absentia.

On June 2, 1979, the pro-Laldenga leadership issued an ultimatum ordering all non-Mizos to leave Mizoram by July 1. Following the killing of a Bengali civil servant on June 14, riots broke out in which two Mizos were killed, and on June 17 and 19 attacks were made on the houses and shops of non-Mizos in Aizawl, and a curfew was imposed on the town; at the same time, some 200 non-Mizos were removed to a preponderantly non-Mizo area (from which hundreds of Mizos had fled to Aizawl). Some 150 extremist Laldenga supporters (who had entered Mizoram from their headquarters in the Chittagong Hills Tract in Bangladesh) were held responsible for various acts of violence, in which two central reserve police constables were killed on July 1. On July 7, 1979, the MNF was declared an unlawful organization under the Unlawful Activities (Prevention) Act, which banned organizations advocating the secession of any part of India. Laldenga was arrested in India on July 8 and was charged with conspiracy, waging war against India and sedition after documents had been seized showing that he had recently sent messages to the MNF inciting its members to carry on an armed struggle. He was subsequently placed under house arrest in New Delhi.

Biakchhunga and 100 members of the MNF's moderate faction, including four members of its underground "government", laid down their arms on Aug. 1, 1979, on the grounds of the agreement signed by Laldenga on July 1, 1976 (see above), while Malsawma Coloney (who had been vice-president of the MNF under Biakchhunga), surrendered on Sept. 27, 1978. Other MNF guerrillas, however, carried on their acts of violence during August, killing a policeman on Aug. 20. Sporadic MNF acts of violence were committed in late 1979 and early 1980, involving some 28 killings in 1980 alone.

Having been released from house arrest following Indira Gandhi's return to power in January 1980 (when the charges against him were withdrawn), Laldenga stated on June 25, 1980, that the national council and executive committee of the MNF had agreed on June 13-14 to a ceasefire and the withdrawal of its notices ordering all non-Mizos to leave Mizoram. On July 30, it was announced in the *Lok Sabha* that following talks between Indira Gandhi and Laldenga it had been agreed that the MNF would cease all underground activities so that the security force would suspend operations against the MNF from midnight on the following day.

Although the MNF suspended its military activities after the ceasefire, it did not surrender its arms and continued to recruit and collect "taxes". In particular, it succeeded in infiltrating the Mizo Students' Association, in which connexion serious student riots occurred in Aizawl in October 1981.

While Laldenga was again in New Delhi early in 1982 to negotiate with the Union Government, nine of his supporters were arrested, and in an official statement issued on Jan. 21, 1982, the Government accused the MNF of having attacked security forces as well as representatives of the Mizoram administration, and it again outlawed the organization as well as the Mizo National Army. During the talks Laldenga demanded statehood for Mizoram, special constitutional provisions guaranteeing the state's complete autonomy, the dismissal of Brig. T. Sailo's People's Conference Ministry in Mizoram (dating from June 1978), the dissolution of the Assembly, the appointment of a council of advisers to the Governor headed by himself pending fresh elections, and the inclusion in Mizoram of areas of Manipur with a Mizo population. The Government accepted the demand for statehood but insisted that the Governor must retain special powers over finance and law enforcement.

A Home Ministry spokesman stated on Jan. 22, 1982, that Laldenga had used the talks as a cover to undermine the lawfully constituted authority in Mizoram and that his intransigence had made it clear that he did not wish to have a peaceful settlement unless his untenable and unconstitutional demands were met. For his part, Laldenga said on Feb. 21 that the national council of the MNF had reversed an earlier resolution committing it to find a solution to the insurgency problem within the framework of the Indian Constitution. After being ordered to leave the country, the MNF president flew to London on April 21, 1982.

About 490 MNF members were reported on May 27, 1982, to have surrendered or been arrested since Jan. 20, but few of those who surrendered brought their arms with them. About 600 rebels were at that stage believed to be in two camps in the Chittagong Hill Tracts area of Bangladesh, and two clashes with troops stationed on the border took place in May when small groups tried to cross into India. The MNF resumed guerrilla activities in June 1982, during which an editor, an Assembly member and a teacher were murdered. After the MNF had issued a notice warning all non-Mizos to leave Mizoram by June 21, four non-Mizo road-workers were shot dead in the first week of July 1982 and thereafter tensions associated with rebel activity mounted.

NAGALAND

Naga Separatist Movement

Leadership. Angami Zapu Phizo (1.).

The Naga separatist movement has had a history of armed and non-violent resistance to the incorporation of Nagaland in the Union of India, of which that territory became a constituent state in 1972. A Naga National Council (NNC), formed in 1946, agreed upon the achievement of independence by India in 1947 to accept Indian suzerainty for a period of 10 years, but in 1949 it adopted a policy of non-co-operation with the Indian Government. Certain Naga extremists began a campaign of violence in 1952, but Angami Zapu Phizo, president of the NNC, disclaimed any connexion with the disturbances caused by these extremists. However, following the murder of the leader of a faction opposed to A. Z. Phizo in January 1956, the Naga movement was split. A. Z. Phizo dissolved the NNC in May 1956, and formed a "federal Naga government" with its own "parliament". His supporters embarked on an armed rebellion which led to widespread destruction of villages. After the rebels' main forces had been subdued by troops, rebel attacks on loyal villages and other acts of violence continued for many years. A. Z. Phizo left the country, living first in Pakistan and, from June 12, 1960, in London.

Attempts to achieve a negotiated settlement between the Government and the rebels met with little success for many years. On Nov. 10-11, 1975, however, agreement was reached in Shillong between the Governor of Nagaland and a delegation of six representatives of the underground Naga movement led by Kevi Yalay Phizo (a minister in the "federal government" and a brother of A. Z. Phizo), whereby (i) the Naga delegation unconditionally accepted the Constitution of India (and thus the status of Nagaland as part of India); (ii) the underground Nagas would deposit their arms at places agreed upon; and (iii) the Naga representatives would have reasonable time to formulate other terms for discussion on a final settlement. A. Z. Phizo, however, repudiated this agreement on Dec. 1, 1975 (while he was in self-imposed exile in London). On May 8, 1976, it was announced that all political prisoners who had accepted the Shillong agreement had been released, among them "Gen." Mowu Angami and 137 of his followers who had surrendered on March 16 after returning from China on Feb. 26.

On Sept. 9, 1976, it was officially stated that Nagaland was now free from all traces of insurgency; that since March 1975 a total of 1,356 underground Nagas had "come overground" voluntarily; that 134 prisoners under trial and 75 detainees had been released; that unserved portions of 87 sentences had been remitted; that 126 cases had been withdrawn; that rehabilitation grants had been made to ex-underground Nagas and released prisoners; and that grants had also been paid to the families of victims of the insurgency and to the families of officials who had died on counter-insurgency duties.

In June 1977 Morarji Desai, then Indian Prime Minister, had talks with A. Z. Phizo in London, during which he assured the Naga leader that if he accepted the present state of affairs and the agreements made with the Nagas (including the 1975 Shillong agreement), he and the other exiles were welcome to return to Nagaland and he could become Chief Minister of Nagaland if the people wished it. A. Z. Phizo, however, had refused to accept Indian citizenship, and in a statement issued in his name later it was said that the activities of the separatist movement would be intensified.

Raids by Naga guerrillas in January 1979 were not officially attributed to the underground separatist Naga movement. There were, however, still Chinese-trained underground Nagas based in Burma, who were believed to be responsible for an ambush in which seven Indian soldiers were killed on March 27, 1979. On Aug. 8, 1980, a total of 474 Nagas from Burma were officially stated to have taken refuge in the Tuengsang district of Nagaland, and during the later months of 1980 and in 1981 attacks continued to be made by separatists operating in areas near the Burmese border. Three soldiers of the Assam Rifles were killed in an ambush on Dec. 18, 1980, and a Congress (I) member of the state Assembly and two other people were killed on April 27, 1981. About 100 rebels stormed an army outpost in Tuengsang district on May 12, 1981, killing seven soldiers and burning down the camp before withdrawing over the Burmese border.

By the early 1980s the main rebel forces were divided into two mutually hostile groups: those supporting the exiled leader A. Z. Phizo on the one hand and the adherents of the National Socialist Council of Nagaland (see separate entry) on the other. A third faction, hostile to both main groups, had also emerged under the leadership of "Gen." Mowu Angami. In a night attack on a Burmese village near the Nagaland border on Sept. 27, 1980, pro-Phizo forces killed 75 National Socialists and the following year were reported (in August 1981) to have recently co-operated with the Burmese security forces in an attack on a National Socialist camp.

National Socialist Council of Nagaland (NSCN)

Leadership. Muivah Tangkul; Issak Swu.

The NSCN was formed in 1978 by a Maoist breakaway faction of the Naga separatist movement led by A. Z. Phizo (see separate entry) and by 1980 was reported to have seized control of the Naga rebel forces in Burma. In July 1980 NSCN followers were said to have killed 200 pro-Phizo rebels and to have burnt down 150 villages, to which pro-Phizo forces responded by killing 75 NSCN followers on Sept. 27 and subsequently by co-operating with the Burmese security forces in operations directed against the NSCN.

In February 1982 the NSCN began carrying out combined operations with the People's Liberation Army active in Manipur (see separate entry) but by September 1982 was reported to be in disarray following the surrender of several of its leading members, notably "Maj." Ithoku Sema. The latter was quoted as having informed the Governor of Manipur after surrendering that life in the Naga underground had become "miserable beyond words" and as having urged the youth of Nagaland not to join the rebel forces.

All-Nagaland Communist Party

This Maoist party was said at the time of its creation in 1979 to have close connexions with a force of up to 600 separatist Nagas who had been reported in August 1977 as being encamped in the Kachin area of Burma after returning from military training in China, and also with Naga and Arakanese separatist organizations which have been active in Burma.

PUNJAB

National Council of Khalistan

Leadership. Balbir Singh Sandu (l.).

Prior to the formation of this organization in 1972, a demand for an independent Sikh state ("Khalistan") had first been put forward by Dr Jagjit Singh, then general secretary of the *Akali Dal* (the Sikh political party), who stated in London on Dec. 2, 1971 (a day before war broke out between India and Pakistan), that President Yahya Khan of Pakistan had promised his support for the secession of Punjab from India and the establishment of an independent Sikh state and had allowed the Sikhs to open a broadcasting station in West Pakistan; however, the *Akali Dal*'s working committee expelled Dr Singh from the party on Dec. 29 for his "anti-national" activities, and he did not return to India. His followers formed the National Council of Khalistan, which from its headquarters in the Golden Temple in Amritsar (the central Sikh shrine) issued "Khalistan" passports, postage stamps and currency notes.

A youth organization, the *Dal Khalsa,* was founded in 1979 under the leadership of Gajendra Singh, who with four other members of the organization hijacked an Indian airliner on Sept. 29, 1981, forcing the pilot to land at Lahore (Pakistan) and demanding the release of arrested Khalistan supporters by the Indian Government and payment of $500,000 ransom while they held 45 passengers as hostages; however, Pakistan commandos overpowered the hijackers on Sept. 30, and freed the hostages, whereupon nearly 100 extremist Sikhs, mainly *Dal Khalsa* members, were arrested in India.

Among critics of the Khalistan movement, Lala Jagat Narain (a newspaper editor) was shot dead on Sept. 9, 1981. On the other hand members of a fundamentalist Sikh sect regarded as sympathetic to the Khalistan movement were suspected of responsibility for the murder in April 1980 of the leader of another sect regarded as heretical.

Violence continued in November 1981, when two policemen were shot dead in the Ludhiana district of Punjab on Nov. 19 and three people killed on Nov. 29 by a bomb explosion in the temple of the Sikh religious leader, Sant Jarnail Singh Bhindranwale. On April 27, 1982, fighting broke out between Hindus and Sikhs in Amritsar after severed cows' heads had been discovered outside two Hindu temples. Responsibility for the desecration was claimed by the *Dal Khalsa,* which declared that it would be repeated until its demand for a total ban on smoking and cigarette sales in Amritsar was conceded (the use of tobacco being forbidden to Sikhs). The rioting spread to Chandigarh, Patiala and about 20 other towns in the state and continued for several days. Sikhs burned down cigarette shops and slaughtered cattle in front of Hindu temples, while in Chandigarh Hindus invaded a Sikh temple and tore up a copy of the Sikh scriptures. In all about 600 people were arrested in the disturbances, which resulted in both the National Council of Khalistan and the *Dal Khalsa* being banned on May 1, 1982, under the 1967 Unlawful Activities (Prevention) Act.

Further airliner hijacks or attempted hijacks by Sikh extremists in August-September 1982 were accompanied by mounting tension in the Punjab as *Akali Dal* leaders launched a new campaign for an autonomous state of Punjab (similar in status to Kashmir), enlarged to include adjacent Sikh-populated areas, and also in support of various religious demands. Although these demands stopped short of the full independence demanded by the Khalistan movement, secessionists participated in the widespread agitation and demonstrations which developed, to which the authorities responded by arresting thousands of Sikh activists. In a serious incident in New Delhi on Oct. 11 four Sikhs were killed and about 60 injured when police opened fire on armed protesters who were trying to storm the parliament building. Talks between the Government and Sikh leaders towards the end of 1982 failed to produce any agreement on the Sikhs' political demands, although the Prime Minister on Nov. 25 made concessions to their religious demands by announcing that Amritsar would be declared a holy city and that the sale of tobacco and liquor would be banned within its walls.

Sikh League

Leadership. Sukhjinder Singh (1.).

This Sikh separatist organization was formed in late 1981, its leader being a former Education Minister of Punjab who had been expelled from the *Akali Dal* (the main Sikh political party). Having been prominent in the Sikh agitation which developed in mid-1982, Sukhjinder Singh was arrested on Nov. 23, as was Balwant Singh, a former state Finance Minister.

TRIPURA

Tripur Sena

Leadership. Vijoy Rankal (1.).

This separatist and anti-Bengali organization is thought to be an extremist faction of the Tripura Tribal Youth Organization *(Tripura Upajaty Juba Samity)*, a legal autonomist organization represented in the Legislative Assembly of the state of Tripura.

It was on Oct. 29, 1979, officially reported to be involved in a conspiracy (in collusion with the Mizo National Front in the neighbouring union territory of Mizoram—see separate entry) to establish an independent state of Tripura by force; it was also held responsible for acts of terrorism and armed robbery, in collaboration with the Mizo National Front, inside Tripura; for an attack on a police camp on Nov. 9, 1979, in which two members of the border security forces and a civilian were killed; and for an exchange of fire with police on Feb. 25, 1980.

In protest against mass immigration of Bengalis, especially from Bangladesh, which had reduced the tribal population of Tripura to a minority of about 30 per cent, a tribal rising broke out in southern and western Tripura on June 6-10, 1980, leading to the murder of up to 2,000 Bengalis (described as the worst massacre in the history of independent India); the Army was called in to restore order; South and West Tripura were on June 9 declared a disturbed area; over 200,000 people who had lost their homes had to be accommodated in government relief camps; and about 40,000 tribal people were said to have fled to the forests to evade arrest. In mid-June posters appeared in many areas ordering all non-tribal people to leave by June 26, failing which they would be exterminated. Armed clashes continued during July 1980; the security forces arrested 134 suspected extremists on July 9 and another 175 on July 10.

Bands of tribal separatists operating from the Chittagong Hill Tracts area of Bangladesh made frequent raids into border areas of Tripura in late 1980 and throughout 1981, and according to unofficial reports had set up a "revolutionary government-in-exile". They were reported on Dec. 12, 1980, to have killed at least 20 people in the previous five months and on June 26, 1981, to have recently killed at least 12 local tribal leaders and members of the ruling CPI(M).

Army of Tripura People's Liberation Organization (ATPLO)

Leadership. Vijaya Hrankhale; Chuni Koloi; Binanda Jamatiya.

This Organization of hardcore armed separatists was formed in 1982 by young extremists who had participated in the tribal rising of June 1980 (see separate entry for Tripur Sena) and had then gone underground. The principal ATPLO leader, Vijaya Hrankhale, had been arrested after the June 1980 disturbances but had subsequently broken bail to join an estimated 350 other armed extremists campaigning for an independent Tripura. In the latter part of 1982 the ATPLO was thought to be responsible for a series of attacks on policemen in northern Tripura and for the seizing of substantial quantities of arms and ammunition from government forces. On the political front it urged the people of Tripura to boycott the state Assembly elections of January 1983.

Indonesia

Capital: Jakarta   Pop. 150,000,000

The Republic of Indonesia is a unitary state with an executive President who governs with the assistance of a Cabinet appointed by him and who is elected (and is re-eligible) by a 920-member People's Consultative Assembly, the highest authority of the state. Of the Assembly's members, 460 are from the House of Representatives, the country's legislature, to which 364 members are elected for a five-year term by direct universal adult suffrage and the remaining 100 are appointed. The Assembly's other 460 members are government appointees, delegates of regional assemblies, and representatives of parties and groups (appointed in proportion to their elective seats in the House of Representatives).

As a result of elections held on May 4, 1982 (when 91.4 per cent of the registered electorate was officially stated to have voted), the elective seats in the House of Representatives were distributed as follows: Joint Secretariat of Functional Groups (Golkar) 246, Moslem United Development Party 94, Indonesian Democratic Party 24.

Following the abortive Communist-backed coup attempt in 1965 and the subsequent accession to power of Gen. Suharto in place of President Sukarno, effective power passed to a small group of military officers around President Suharto and to the *Kopkamtib* internal security organization, which conducted a country-wide campaign of repression against suspected Communists and other left-wing elements. In October 1977 Amnesty International estimated that there were at least 55,000 and probably about 100,000 political prisoners (known as *"tapols"*), many of them having been held without trial since the 1965 coup attempt (after which—again according to Amnesty International—at least 500,000 persons had been killed and 700,000 arrested).

By December 1979 the Government claimed to have released all political detainees except 61 "category A" prisoners described as hard-core Communists (who were to be brought to trial the following year). However, in December 1981 the Home Affairs Minister stated that there were 249 "category A" political detainees, while a further 36,648 persons were classified as "category B" (against whom there was no evidence but who were nevertheless considered dangerous) and 1,536,936 as "category C" (released detainees).

Apart from the internal security threat posed by the Indonesian Communists, the Suharto regime has come under challenge from Moslem fundamentalist movements, which have gained increasing support within a population which is 90 per cent Moslem for their aim of transforming the existing secular Republic into an Islamic state. The regime has also continued to be confronted with secessionist movements in outlying regions of the Indonesian polity.

Communist Party of Indonesia (CPI)

Founded in May 1920, the CPI was involved in an unsuccessful rising against Dutch rule (in the Netherlands East Indies) in 1926-27, whereafter it went underground. In the 1930s it took part in the establishment of an anti-fascist front which during World War II opposed the invading Japanese forces. After the proclamation of Indonesia's national independence on Aug. 17, 1945, the CPI took part in the Government but in September 1948 this Government was overthrown in a right-wing coup, which led to the killing of numerous CPI leaders and to the temporary return of Dutch rule until Dec. 27, 1949, when sovereignty was transferred to the Republic of the United States of Indonesia. The CPI was re-constituted, and in elections held in 1955 it became one of the country's four major parties, while in local elections held in 1956 it polled the greatest number of votes.

In subsequent years there was discussion on strategy within the party, whose seventh congress held in 1962 advanced the thesis that "the national interest is above class interest" (to some extent reflecting the strongly nationalist Marxism espoused by President Sukarno). The pro-Chinese faction in the CPI gained in influence, and in 1965 the party led the "30th September Movement" in support of a group of young army officers who staged a coup to prevent a planned right-wing coup. The young officers' attempt was defeated, however, and right-wing generals led by Gen. Suharto installed a military regime; thereafter the CPI and other left-wing forces were vigorously suppressed, with Communists and alleged sympathizers being killed or detained.

The CPI nevertheless claimed to have re-constituted itself in the 1960s and 1970s, with the pro-Moscow wing defining its position in three documents—"The Correct Road of the Indonesian Revolution" (1966), "Pressing Tasks of the Communist Movement in Indonesia" (1969) and "For Democracy, Social Justice and People's Prosperity" (1975)—with the aim of creating a front of national unity and eventually an "anti-imperialist, democratic government as the prelude to advancing to socialism". For its part, the pro-Chinese wing issued a statement on the 60th anniversary of the party in May 1980 declaring its support for an Indonesian application of "Marxism-Leninism-Mao Zedong thought" and also calling for vigilance in confronting "Soviet and Vietnamese hegemonism". The statement was signed by Jusuf Adjitorop, who was identified as "secretary-general of the central committee and member of the political bureau of the CPI central committee".

Whereas the Government claimed in December 1979 to have released all but the hard-core elements detained since the 1965 coup attempt, arrests of Communists continued thereafter and the party remained banned. The former strength of the PCI was indicated by the Home Affairs Minister in December 1981, when the total number of Indonesian nationals "involved in the Indonesian Communist Party-affiliated 30th September Movement" was put at 1,580,020. In the same statement the Home Affairs Minister made it clear that over 40,000 ex-detainees who had been adherents of the PCI would have no voting rights in the May 1982 elections.

Case of Pramudya Ananta Toer

Pramudya Ananta Toer, a writer of international repute detained without trial in 1965-79 (mainly on Buru Island) on the grounds that he had been a member of Lekra, a cultural organization supporting the Communist Party of Indonesia, was on May 30, 1981, forbidden to publish his works after his novel *Bumi Manusia (This Earth of Mankind)* had been published in August 1980 and had led the authorities to accuse him of "subtle propaganda for a banned ideology"—i.e. Marxism-Leninism—and a second book, *Anak Semua Bangsa (Child of All Nations)* had also appeared. In October 1981 it was reported that 10,000 copies of the books, returned on orders of the prosecutor-general, had been burned.

Moslem Fundamentalist Movements

Abode of Islam *(Dar-ul-Islam)*

Leadership. Daud Baruah (l.).

The *Dar-ul-Islam* movement, although banned, was active in Indonesia from the early 1950s onwards as a movement aiming at the violent overthrow of the secular Republic and its replacement by an Islamic state. Revolts organized by it broke out (i) in South Celebes (Sulawesi) in 1951, involving 40,000 to 50,000 rebels, leading to the temporary establishment of an "Islamic Indonesian state" in part of Celebes and lasting until 1956, when it was finally suppressed by government forces, and (ii) in Atjeh province (northern Sumatra) on Sept. 23, 1953, causing many hundreds of casualties before being suppressed a few months later. On April 22, 1977, the police announced the arrest of six former *Dar-ul-Islam* members on a charge of plotting to blow up a power station in West Java.

The *Dar-ul-Islam* movement has its main strength in Atjeh (Aceh), where its Islamic fundamentalism provides the ideological basis for the strong separatist tendencies of the province (see separate entry for Free Aceh Movement). In November 1981 the *Dar-ul-Islam* leader, Daud Baruah, was reported to be under house arrest in Jakarta, but in Atjeh the movement continued to run a parallel administration as the effective government of the province, particularly in matters of law and order. When in late 1981 militant Moslems in Banda Aceh (the main city) launched a series of violent attacks on the local Chinese community, government troops were sent from Jakarta to quell the disturbances only after a delay of several days, apparently because of official wariness about intervening in this traditionally autonomous area.

Holy War Command *(Jihad Komando)*

Leadership. Imran Mohammad Zain.

This group, advocating the creation of an Islamic state in Indonesia, has been held responsible for a number of acts of violence. Grenade attacks made in Medan (North Sumatra) on Dec. 25-26, 1976, were officially attributed to this group, which, it was said, intended to prevent the holding of elections, to overthrow the Government and to establish a new state based on Islamic principles. During the trial of a leading member of the group, condemned to death on March 8, 1978, for causing the Medan explosion, it was alleged that the group had tried to obtain arms and funds from the Libyan embassy in Kuala Lumpur (Malaysia). Other leaders of the group had on Feb. 3, 1977, been reported to have been arrested in Java and Sumatra. At this stage the Command appeared to be directing its activities principally against the Moslem United Development Party (PPP), the legal opposition Moslem coalition formation, and some PPP members claimed that it was being secretly encouraged by the security services to create a pretext for a general clamp-down on Moslem activists.

A group of five Moslem extremists said to be members of the Command hijacked an Indonesian airliner on March 28, 1981, and forced it to be flown to Bangkok, demanding that the Indonesian Government should release some 80 detainees and also expel all Jews from the country: four of the hijackers were killed on March 30 by Indonesian troops who stormed the airliner at Bangkok airport (with permission from the Thai authorities) and the fifth subsequently died from injuries received, as did the airliner's pilot. Five of the 80 detainees whose release was demanded by the hijackers had been among 42 persons arrested by the security forces following an attack by Command members on a Bandung police station on March 11, 1981, in which three policemen were killed.

The Indonesian security authorities announced on April 20, 1980, that the organization presumed responsible for the hijacking had been dismantled and its leader arrested, the latter being named as Imran Mohammad Zain and identified as head of the "Indonesian Islamic Revolutionary Council" (apparently the political counterpart of the Holy War Command). In March 1982 a Jakarta court passed a death sentence on Imran Mohammad Zain (who was said to have been in contact with Ayatollah Khomeini of Iran) after finding him guilty of "subversive acts" (including involvement in the hijacking); it was reported on April 13, 1983, that Imran Mohammad Zain had been executed in accordance with the sentence passed on him the previous year.

Secessionist Movements

Free Aceh Movement

This Movement aspires to independence for Atjeh (Aceh), the north-westernmost province of Sumatra, and is closely orientated to the Islamic fundamentalist ideology of the Abode of Islam *(Dar-ul-Islam)* movement (see separate entry). Arrests of activists charged with plotting to set up such an independent state have been reported periodically. In 1980 the Government claimed that the Movement had been suppressed and its leader, Hasan de Tiro, was said to have been killed in October of that year. The Movement was nevertheless believed to be continuing its war of independence on a small scale in the early 1980s, assisted by the limited extent of central government authority in the province.

The Moslems of Aceh have been characterized for centuries by their extreme orthodoxy and separateness, their traditionally closed society being regarded as perhaps the most fully Islamic society anywhere in the Moslem world. They agreed to become part of the new Indonesian state after World War II only after being assured of full local autonomy and the supremacy of Islamic law, customs and social mores (notwithstanding the secular principles officially embraced by Indonesia as a whole).

Papua Independent Organization (*Organisasi Papua Merdeka,* OPM)

Leadership. Elky Bemei.

This movement was founded by educated Papuans who went into exile in 1963, when Irian Jaya (formerly Dutch New Guinea and known as West Irian until 1973) was incorporated in Indonesia. Members of the movement later returned to the territory to lead a tribal revolt in areas bordering on Papua New Guinea. The original leaders of the movement, regarded as pro-Dutch, were later replaced by new leaders who in 1971 formed a "Provisional Revolutionary Government of West Papua New Guinea" which proclaimed the independence of the territory and which had as its president "Brig.-Gen." Seth Rumkorem (a former major in the Indonesian Army). In 1976 these insurgents claimed to control a number of "liberated zones" covering 15 per cent of the territory.

The "Provisional Government", with headquarters in the Netherlands, also set up information offices in Dakar (Senegal) and Stockholm, and President Léopold Sédar Senghor of Senegal stated during a visit to Paris in March 1976 that he had allowed that Government to set up an office in Dakar because the (Melanesian) Papuans were Blacks, differing in race and culture from the Indonesians, and Senegal supported all movements by Black people to assert their national identity. The movement, which claimed to control an armed force of 10,000 men, was believed to be responsible for a rebellion in April-May 1977, which was crushed by Indonesian troops after six weeks of fighting in which over 250 people (including nine soldiers and policemen) were killed.

The Government of Papua New Guinea agreed in January 1977 that it would not allow its territory to be used as a base for incursions into Irian Jaya by subversive elements or "dissidents", and early in 1978 Papua New Guinea had, according to the Indonesian Minister of Information, assured Indonesia that all anti-Indonesian movements in Papua New Guinea were banned and that only those members of the OPM who had good intentions (e.g. of seeking work in Papua New Guinea) would be admitted to the country. Nevertheless, relations between the two countries have been periodically strained by the Irian Jaya situation (notably by reported Indonesian cross-border incursions in pursuit of OPM guerrillas), while in Papua New Guinea itself there exists a substantial body of pro-OPM opinion which regards Indonesia as expansionist.

In 1977 "Brig.-Gen." Rumkorem was succeeded by Jacob Prai as president of the "Provisional Government", which included 10 persons formerly resident in Irian Jaya but currently holding either Papua New Guinea citizenship or residence permits. At a meeting held in Port Moresby (Papua New Guinea) on April 14-16, 1978, between senior ministers and officials of Papua New Guinea on the one hand and J. Prai and "Brig.-Gen." Rumkorem on the other, the latter were warned that Papua New Guinea would "not at any stage allow itself to be used as a sanctuary for subversive activities against Indonesia". In April 1978 it was reported from Papua New Guinea that over 5,000 guerrillas and civilians, as well as 3,500 Indonesians, had been killed in fighting in Irian Jaya since the beginning of 1976; the Indonesian Government, however, described this fighting as a tribal war and consistently referred to OPM guerrillas as "wild gangs".

In June-July 1978 Indonesian military activity increased greatly along Irian Jaya's border with Papua New Guinea, following an ambush by OPM units of an Indonesian helicopter carrying senior military and civilian personnel, seven of whom the OPM seized as hostages. The Indonesian counter-

action was informally supported by the Papua New Guinea Defence Forces. These operations caused some 650 refugees to leave Irian Jaya for Papua New Guinea. In September 1978 J. Prai and his "defence minister" (Otto Ondawame) were arrested as "illegal immigrants" in Papua New Guinea and subsequently sentenced to imprisonment; they later obtained sanctuary in Sweden, where they were taken in February 1979 with two other senior OPM members.

Among the reasons for the Papua New Guinea Government's firm anti-OPM measures at this time (which included the signing of a border security agreement with Indonesia in 1979) was its discovery that leaders of the movement were seeking to obtain support from Communist-bloc countries.

Martin Tabu, then described as leader of the movement, was on April 19, 1980, reported to have surrendered near Jayapura (in Irian Jaya). The military commander of Irian Jaya province stated on March 4, 1981, that no military force would be used against OPM rebels, but only persuasion, which had already led to the surrender of hundreds of OPM members and their leaders; that this policy would be pursued until the OPM had been eliminated; but that stern measures would be taken against OPM members refusing to give themselves up.

"Brig-Gen." Rumkorem, describing himself as "President" of the "Republic of West Papua", reappeared in Rabaul (Papua New Guinea) in September 1982, and was arrested for illegal entry.

Revolutionary Front for the Independence of East Timor (Fretilin)

Fretilin superseded a Timorese Social Democratic Association (ASDT) formed after the 1974 revolution in Portugal and advocating full independence for East Timor (then a Portuguese province). As a pro-communist (and anti-Indonesian) revolutionary movement, Fretilin was opposed by the other political parties formed in East Timor in 1974 and was soon involved in civil war with them. By Sept. 8, 1975, it claimed to have gained complete control of East Timor; it also announced that it had dropped its original demand for complete independence from Portugal and that it wished to move gradually towards self-government, with the installation of a provisional government early in 1976, the election of a constituent assembly and independence within a few years. The Indonesian Government, however, made it clear that it was opposed to a Fretilin government.

On Nov. 28, 1975, Fretilin declared East Timor independent as the "Democratic Republic of East Timor" and claimed that it had the support of 50 Afro-Asian countries. The pro-Indonesian parties, however, declared on Nov. 29, 1975, that as *Fretilin*'s action had "removed the last remains of Portuguese sovereignty" the territory was now part of Indonesia, and on Dec. 7 Indonesian forces began to occupy East Timor. *Fretilin*'s armed forces were forced to withdraw to remote areas, and the territory was formally incorporated in Indonesia on Aug. 17, 1976. While *Fretilin* continued to offer resistance, the Indonesian Government claimed in mid-1978 that about 60,000 *Fretilin* supporters had surrendered in response to an Indonesian amnesty offer of Aug. 16, 1977—such people being resettled in lowland coastal areas controlled by government forces. Those who surrendered included a former president of *Fretilin* and President of the "Democratic Republic of East Timor", Francisco Xavier do Amaral, who had on Sept. 13, 1977, been replaced by Nicolau dos Reis Lobato (who was killed in battle on Jan. 1, 1979); the former *Fretilin* president was later appointed deputy governor of the new province, now called Loro Sae.

Fretilin nevertheless continued not only to retain some bases inside the territory but also, through its "Government of the Democratic Republic of East Timor" (in exile but enjoying recognition by numerous third-world governments and in particular of those of all the former Portuguese provinces in Africa), to take part in negotiations at the United Nations on the future of East Timor, the occupation of which by Indonesia was condemned by the UN Security Council and the UN General Assembly.

Abilio Araujo, a member of *Fretilin*'s central committee and resident in Lisbon, said in London early in May 1982 that resistance in East Timor had been growing since 1980 and that on Dec. 31, 1981, *Fretilin* had carried out a series of attacks in the eastern zone of East Timor, which had resulted in a mutiny of East Timorese soldiers against their Indonesian officers, who had to escape by helicopter. However, in April 1982 an Indonesian military commander in the eastern zone estimated *Fretilin*'s strength at only 130 persons split up into small groups and supported by some 200 sympathizers or sympathizing families; this followed a major Indonesian offensive in July-September 1981 against *Fretilin*'s remaining mountain strongholds (in which unarmed civilians had been used under army supervision to encircle rebel positions), as a result of which some 4,000 inhabitants of the area had been removed to the island of Atauro (off Díli, the capital of East Timor).

In the light of a general improvement in the security situation, the Government from mid-1982 began to allow some people to move back to the mountain areas of East Timor from lowland resettlement villages.

Japan

Capital: Tokyo   Pop. 116,500,000

The Empire of Japan is a constitutional monarchy in which the Emperor, as head of state, has no governing power. Executive power is vested in a Cabinet and legislative powers in a bicameral Diet consisting of (i) a 252-member House of Councillors and (ii) a 511-member House of Representatives, both Houses being elected by universal adult suffrage of citizens above the age of 20 years; 126 members are elected to the House of Councillors every three years—76 in single-member constituencies and 50 in a national constituency of the whole electorate. The members of the House of Representatives are elected for a four-year term in multi-member constituencies of greatly varying sizes. All organizations wishing to nominate candidates for public office have to be registered as political parties; there are over 10,000 such parties but the vast majority of them are of significance only at local or regional level.

Elections to the House of Representatives held on June 22, 1980, resulted in the following distribution of seats: Liberal-Democratic Party 284, Japan Socialist Party 107, *Komeito* ("Clean Government Party") 33, Japan Communist Party 29, Democratic Socialist Party 32, New Liberal Club 12, Social Democratic Federation 3, independents 11.

Acts of politically-motivated violence have been carried out both by extreme right-wing and by extreme left-wing groups. In March 1977 the police estimated that there were perhaps 40 extreme right-wing formations with a total membership of fewer than 3,000 and advocating a totalitarian government as the best solution to overcome corruption, exploitation and "unequal treaties" with foreign powers. Some of the extreme left-wing groups extended their operations to targets outside Japan, and under a law enacted on May 12, 1978, and entering into force on June 5 of that year the death penalty was extended to hijackers and anyone seizing diplomatic establishments, while the penalty for taking hostages was raised from five years to life imprisonment.

Whereas until 1977 the Japanese Government had repeatedly acceded to demands made by hijackers of aircraft (with the then Prime Minister, Takeo Fukuda, stating on Sept. 29, 1975, that human life was "more precious than the earth"), it was reported in June 1978 that the Government had mapped out a new policy whereby no further demands by terrorists would be complied with, even if lives had to be sacrificed.

Several left-wing groups were repeatedly involved in violent clashes with each other, and up to 1980 some 80 members of such groups had been killed, and 4,500 wounded, in ideological feuds.

Extreme Right-wing Organization

Youth League for the Overthrow of the Yalta and Potsdam Structure

Two members of this group were among four armed men who on March 3, 1977, entered the headquarters of Keidanren (the Japanese Federation of Economic Organizations) in Tokyo and temporarily seized about a dozen leaders of the Federation as hostages; at the same time they distributed leaflets denouncing big business for "poisoning Japan's post-war society and its landscape" and also for corruption. However, they surrendered to the police on March 4, all hostages being released unharmed. The other two members of the four-man group had been members of the Shield Society *(Tatenokai)*, an extreme right-wing organization which had been disbanded after the suicide of its leader, the well-known writer Yukio Mishima, in November 1970. The leader of the four men, Shusuke Nomura, had earlier served a 12-year sentence for burning down the house of a conservative politician and was quoted as saying that he regarded as political enemies all who had dominated Japan in the last 30 years; that the Liberal-Democratic Party and the Communist Party were "equally guilty"; and that Japan could not be rescued unless all was destroyed.

The League is opposed to the Allied decisions arrived at during the Yalta and Potsdam conferences in 1945 which it regarded as having destroyed Japan's political independence. (Opposition to the Yalta and Potsdam decisions had first been expressed in slogans of right-wing students in Japan after World War II.)

Extreme Left-wing Groups

East Asia Anti-Japanese Armed Front

In a statement issued in 1976 this Front denounced "Japanese imperialists" for occupying Hokkaido Island (the most northerly of Japan's four main islands) and demanded that this island should be returned to the original inhabitants, the Ainu (of whom there were only about 5,000 among Hokkaido's total population of 5,300,000). The Front also claimed to fight for the rights of the Okinawan, Korean, Taiwanese, Buraku (social outcasts) and other Asian peoples.

Members of the Front were responsible for a bomb attack on the Mitsubishi Heavy Industries headquarters in Tokyo on Aug. 30, 1974, in which eight persons were killed and over 300 injured. There followed further bomb attacks, among them one on the headquarters of the Mitsui trading company in Tokyo on Oct. 14 and one on a Korean research institute in Tokyo on April 19, 1975; of two suspects arrested subsequently one admitted, as claimed by the police on May 26, 1975, being the leader of one of three radical cells and being responsible for nine explosions. The cells were named as "Wolf", "Fangs of the Earth" and "Scorpion", all thought to be part of the East-Asia Anti-Japanese Armed Front, whose policy was to attack the offices of large business companies said to be exploiting underdeveloped Asian nations. The Front itself claimed responsibility for the bombing, on March 2, 1976, of a government building in Sapporo (the capital of Hokkaido) on Aug. 10, 1976, in which two persons were killed and nearly 200

injured. In a trial of four members of the Front two were on Nov. 12, 1980, sentenced to death for their involvement in the attack of Aug. 30, 1974, and for conspiring to assassinate the Emperor Hirohito in 1974.

Fourth (Trotskyist) International—Japanese Section

The Japanese section of the Fourth (Trotskyist) International played a leading role among the radical groups which from 1971 onwards actively opposed the construction and opening of a new international airport at Narita (about 40 miles north-west of Tokyo). Demonstrations by local farmers, left-wing student groups and environmentalists led to several years' delay in the completion of the airport. During disturbances in February-May 1978 four policemen and one civilian died and several hundred persons were injured. On March 26, 1978 (two days before the official opening date), radical groups occupied the air control tower, destroyed vital radar and communications equipment and rendered the airport inoperative; some 14,000 riot police were deployed over the area, 115 persons were arrested and many more were injured. On May 28 police also arrested 50 occupants of a tower-like structure built by opponents of the airport near the proposed main runway and demolished it in a prolonged battle. The Government stated on May 28 that the "acts of violence by extremists" had "nothing to do with the anti-airport movement of some local farmers" but were "a serious challenge to democracy". Under new legislation which came into force on May 13, 1978, the Minister of Transport was empowered to remove any structure within two miles of the airport which might be used for sabotage. Although the airport was officially opened on May 20, attacks on its communications and other installations continued until July 1978.

Middle-Core Faction *(Chukaku-Ha)*

This Marxist breakaway group from the National Federation of Students' Organizations was created in 1960 to oppose the security treaty concluded between the United States and Japan.

Members of the Faction were repeatedly involved in violent clashes with members of the rival *Kakumaru-Ha* movement (see separate entry for Revolutionary Marxist Faction); in such clashes eight persons were killed in March-June 1975; and on Oct. 30, 1980, *Chukaku-Ha* members were reported to have beaten to death five *Kakumaru-Ha* members as an act of revenge for the murder of a leftist leader four years earlier.

Members of the Faction were involved in protest demonstrations against a visit to

Okinawa on July 17, 1975, by the Crown Prince and Princess, who narrowly escaped injury when a Molotov cocktail was thrown at them. In an explosion at a flat at Yokosuka (south-west of Tokyo) on Sept. 4, 1975, three members of the faction and two other persons were killed. On May 7, 1982, the *Chukaku-Ha* claimed responsibility for several attempts to set fire to Self-Defence Force (i.e. Army) facilities and to the Imperial Palace in Tokyo.

Okinawa Liberation League

The League has expressed its opposition to the rule of the Imperial family and "the imperialist bourgeoisie of Japan" over Okinawa (the largest of the Ryukyu Islands) and the use of the island as a military base and terminal station for oil storage.

The alleged leader of the *Ikemiyagusuku* faction of this group was arrested on July 17, 1975, in connexion with the throwing of a Molotov cocktail at the Crown Prince and Princess then visiting Naha (Okinawa).

Revolutionary Marxist Faction *(Kakumaru-Ha)*

As another breakaway group from the National Federation of Students' Organizations, this Faction was involved in clashes with members of the rival Middle-Core Faction *(Chukaku-Ha)*—see separate entry—and also in protest demonstrations against the visit to Okinawa by the Crown Prince and Princess on July 17, 1975.

United Red Army (URA) *(Rengo Sekigun)*

Leadership. Miss Fusako Shigenobu (supreme commander).

The URA was formed in 1969 by a merger of the Red Army Faction *(Sekigunha)*, which was an offshoot of the (Trotskyist) Communist League, and the Keihin Joint Struggle Committee against the US-Japan Security Treaty *(Keihin Anpo Kyoto)* to launch an armed campaign for revolution. In February 1972 some of its militants "executed" 14 alleged "deviationists" and for six days resisted police action against them.

In a document issued in May 1977 the URA declared that it would continue to fight for the materialization of a people's republic of Japan by uniting and joining forces with the "oppressed people, comrades and friends in confrontation with Japanese imperialism". During its early operations the URA had stressed the "need to fight against Zionism" and for "the just cause of the Palestinians", but during the hijacking of an airliner to Dacca in 1977 (see below) the URA affirmed the need of a revolution in Japan, its

solidarity with the Japanese people in their struggle against the monarchy and the growing "imperialism", the economic exploitation of South Korea by Japan, the construction of the Narita airport and corruption in general. In December 1977 the URA called for the formation of a revolutionary council in Japan in order to prepare for a revolutionary government-in-exile.

Major terrorist operations in which URA members took part have included the following:

(1) The hijacking, on March 30, 1970, of a Japan Air Lines (JAL) airliner and its diversion to Seoul (South Korea) by nine URA members who intended to fly to North Korea; after intervention by the Japanese Deputy Minister of Transport the 103 passengers of the airliner were released on April 3 and the airliner was flown to North Korea, where the hijackers were allowed to stay while the airliner was returned to Japan on April 5. (On June 15, 1980, the nine hijackers were reported to be still living near Pyongyang, the North Korean capital.)

(2) A massacre at Lod airport (Tel Aviv) on May 30, 1972, when three URA members opened fire indiscriminately and killed 26 persons (mainly Roman Catholics from Puerto Rico) and wounded 78 others; of the three gunmen, one committed suicide, one was killed by Israeli police and a third (Kozo Okamoto) was captured. Responsibility for the operation was claimed by the Popular Front for the Liberation of Palestine (PFLP) in Beirut on May 31, stating that the three Japanese had come "to take part with the Palestinian people in the struggle against the power of Zionism and imperialism". Okamoto was sentenced to life imprisonment on July 17, 1972.

(3) The hijacking on July 20, 1973, of a JAL airliner flying from Paris to Amsterdam (and thence bound for Tokyo) and its diversion to Dubai, where it remained for three days, and on July 24 to Benghazi (Libya) where, after the passengers and crew had left it, it was blown up by the hijackers who had identified themselves as "Palestinian commandos and members of the Japanese Red Army" and also as members of the "Sons of the Occupied Territories". A statement issued by this group on July 26 described the action as retaliation against the Japanese Government for having paid compensation to Israel for the Lod massacre, and promised "cruel punishment" and further operations against Japan.

(4) An attack on a Shell oil refinery in Singapore on Jan. 31, 1974, when four attackers, claiming to be members of the PFLP and the URA and to be acting in solidarity with the "Vietnamese revolutionary people", seized as hostages the five-member crew of a ferry and demanded safe passage

out of Singapore. While negotiations proceeded between them and the Singapore authorities, with the assistance of the Japanese ambassador to Singapore, five armed men occupied the Japanese embassy in Kuwait on Feb. 6 and held the entire staff as hostages; these armed men, claiming to act for the PFLP, the URA and the "Sons of the Occupied Territories", demanded from the Japanese Government that it should send an aircraft to take the URA members from Singapore to Kuwait. The Japanese Government agreed to this demand, and eventually all hostages, both in Singapore and in Kuwait, were released and all the guerrillas were flown to Aden (South Yemen) on Feb. 8.

(5) The occupation of the French embassy in The Hague on Sept. 13, 1974, by three URA members who took 10 persons, including the ambassador, as hostages and demanded the release of Yutaka Furuya, a URA member detained at Orly airport (in France) in late July 1974; after protracted negotiations the hostages were released in exchange for Furuya, and an aircraft carried him and the guerrillas to Damascus on Sept. 18.

(6) The seizure of the US consulate and the neighbouring Swedish embassy in Kuala Lumpur (Malaysia) on Aug. 4, 1975, by five URA members who took 52 persons hostage and demanded (in return for the latter's release) the release of seven URA prisoners held in Japan—failing which the consulate and embassy buildings would be blown up. The Japanese Government agreed on Aug. 5 to release the seven prisoners, of whom only five agreed to be thus released, and these were flown to Kuala Lumpur on the same day in a Japanese airliner which was, on Aug. 7, flown to Tripoli (Libya) with the five attackers, the five released prisoners and four new hostages (two Malaysian and two Japanese officials, who had replaced 15 of the original hostages, most of whom had been released earlier). In Tripoli the 10 URA members surrendered to the Libyan authorities; and the Malaysian and Japanese officixls returned to their countries in the same airliner on Aug. 10.

(7) The hijacking of a JAL airliner on a flight from Paris to Tokyo after taking off from Bombay on Sept. 28, 1977, by a five-member "Hidaka commando" of the URA, who forced it to land in Dacca (Bangladesh) and demanded the release of seven URA prisoners held in Japan and of two common criminals convicted of murder, and also payment of US$6,000,000. The URA prisoners included Junzo Okudaira, who had taken part in the occupation of the French embassy in The Hague in September 1974 and of the US consulate in Kuala Lumpur in August 1975, had been arrested in Jordan (where he had arrived from Libya), and been extradited to Japan, which he had reached on Oct. 14, 1976, together with the body of Toshihiko Hidaka, who was suspected of being involved in the Kuala Lumpur attack and had committed suicide while under arrest abroad. On Sept. 29 the Japanese Government agreed to these demands "in principle", but their fulfilment was delayed, particularly in that only six of the named prisoners agreed to be released. After most of the hostages had been released the airliner left Dacca on Oct. 2 with 29 passengers, the Japanese pilot, two other members of the original crew and four fresh crew members, as well as the five hijackers, the six ex-prisoners and the ransom; after the release of seven passengers in Kuwait and another 10 in Damascus, the airliner (on Oct. 3) reached Algiers, where the remaining 12 passengers and the crew were released and the hijackers and the ex-prisoners were taken to an unknown destination. A Japanese plea for the extradition of the hijackers and the surrender of the ex-prisoners and the ransom was rejected by Algeria on Oct. 5; according to the Japanese police the hijackers included one wanted in connexion with the 1972 Lod massacre and three exchanged in August 1975 for hostages seized in Kuala Lumpur (see above).

(8) The seizure of a bus with at least 15 passengers in Nagasaki on Oct. 15, 1977, by a two-man "suicide commando" of the URA, who threatened to explode 37 bombs throughout Japan unless their demands for ransom and for talks with the Minister of Justice were met; in this case, however, the authorities made no concessions to the attackers; police stormed the bus on the following day and killed one and seized the other terrorist (while several passengers were slightly injured).

No further URA operations were reported after the above. In July 1978 the National Police Agency estimated that under the leadership of Fusako Shigenobu (who had been resident in Lebanon since early 1971) the URA had 30 members (10 more than in 1977) and was supported by more than 100 sympathizers. In May 1979 the URA issued statements in which it announced its decision to "solidify internationalism and work out our own salvation with our own efforts" and to "properly eliminate inconsistencies in the establishment of socialism".

In May 1982 Fusako Shigenobu was quoted as saying that the URA had abandoned terrorism because it had failed to win international support. She also stated that "under the new situation in the world" it was "important to unify all anti-imperialist forces and to consolidate the movement to build a bigger base". She admitted that URA members were continuing to receive military training in Lebanon but gave no further details. According to the Japanese police, the remnants of the URA had set up their head-quarters in a Palestinian refugee camp on the outskirts of Beirut.

In addition to its involvement in the Palestinian cause and its close links with the Popular Front for the Liberation of Palestine (PFLP), the URA also had ties with revolutionary groups in other countries, notably in West Germany and Spain. In connexion with the URA attack on the French embassy in The Hague in 1974, grenades were found which had disappeared from an army munitions depot in Kaiserslautern (Rhineland-Palatinate) said to have been raided in 1971 by members of the Red Army Faction

(Baader-Meinhof Group). The Madrid daily *Arriba* claimed on Aug. 13, 1975, that three commandos of the URA, consisting of nine men and three women, had arrived in Spain to work for the liberation of arrested members of the Basque separatist movement ETA and the left-wing revolutionary FRAP. On July 23, 1977, the Japanese daily *Sankei Shimbun* reported that the URA had combined with radical groups abroad to form an international terrorist organization called the United World Revolutionary Force with headquarters in Zurich and with groups in Canada, West Germany, Ireland, Japan, Spain, Turkey, Uruguay and Yugoslavia.

Kampuchea

Capital: Phnom-Penh   Pop. 6,000,000

The People's Republic of Kampuchea (PRK, formerly Cambodia) is a (communist) one-party state ruled by a People's Revolutionary Council set up in January 1979 by members of the central committee of a Kampuchean National United Front for National Salvation (KNUFNS), whose "Kampuchean Revolutionary Army" had, with strong support from regular forces of the Socialist Republic of Vietnam, overthrown the regime of "Democratic Kampuchea" led by Pol Pot. Elections to a 117-member National Assembly, which were contested by 148 candidates of the KNUFNS, were held on May 1, 1981, and were officially stated to have shown that 99.17 per cent of the 3,417,339 electors had taken part in the vote. In December 1981 the KNUFNS was officially renamed the Kampuchean United Front for National Construction and Defence.

The country's sole legitimate party is the Kampuchean People's Revolutionary Party (KPRP), founded in February 1951 (when the Indo-Chinese Communist Party formed in 1930 by Ho Chi Minh was divided into independent communist parties for Kampuchea, Laos and Vietnam). It changed its name to Communist Party of Kampuchea at a secret congress held in Phnom-Penh in 1960 and was subsequently divided into supporters of North Vietnam and a Maoist faction led by Pol Pot (then known as Saloth Sar). Though the two factions were reunited during the civil war of 1970-75, Pol Pot began in 1973 to purge the pro-Vietnamese faction, most members of which sought refuge in Vietnam and subsequently held, with defectors from Pol Pot, a "reorganization congress" in January 1979 (after the overthrow of the Pol Pot regime), their party reverting to its original name of KPRP.

The various forms of government which Kampuchea has had since it was formally declared independent (as Cambodia) in 1953 can briefly be defined as follows: (i) from 1953 to 1970, a neutralist Government under Prince Norodom Sihanouk; (ii) from 1970 to 1975 a right-wing Government (of the Khmer Republic) under Gen. (later Marshal) Lon Nol; (iii) from 1975 to the end of 1978 a (pro-Chinese) communist Government installed by the Red Khmers *(Khmers Rouges)*, with Prince Norodom Sihanouk as head of state until April 1976 and thereafter effectively led by Pol Pot as Prime Minister; (iv) since January 1979 a (pro-Soviet) communist Government supported by the forces of the Socialist Republic of Vietnam and opposed by the Red Khmers and various groups of (non-communist) Free Khmers *(Khmers Serei)*.

Communist Movements

Communist Party of Kampuchea (CPK)

As explained in the introduction above, the pro-Chinese CPK originated from the formation in February 1951 of the Kampuchean People's Revolutionary Party (KPRP), which was taken over by the Maoist faction led by Pol Pot in 1960 and renamed. The party came to power in April 1975 when its armed wing (the Red Khmers) overthrew the right-wing Lon Nol regime but was itself overthrown at the end of 1978 by Vietnamese-backed communists, who re-established the KPRP as a pro-Soviet ruling party on attaining power. Thereafter the CPK-led "Government of Democratic Kampuchea" continued to regard itself as the legitimate government of the country (and was recognized as such by most UN members), while at the same time seeking to overthrow the new regime by force.

In its quest to regain effective power the CPK Red Khmers in September 1979 announced the formation of a Patriotic and Democratic Front of the Great National Union of Kampuchea, the purpose of which was to rally all elements opposed to the Vietnamese-backed KPRP regime in Phnom-Penh. In the light of the creation of this Front, the CPK central committee announced on Dec. 6, 1981, that it had been decided at a party congress on Sept. 3-6, 1981, to dissolve the party "in order to conform with the new strategic line which does not pursue socialism and communism". (Fuller details of post-1975 Kampuchean developments are given below in the entry for Red Khmers—*Khmers Rouges*.)

Red Khmers *(Khmers Rouges)*

Leadership. Pol Pot (C.-in-C.); Khieu Samphan (Prime Minister of Red Khmer Government).

The Red Khmers (Khmers being the people of Kampuchea and eastern Thailand) were set up in 1967 as the armed wing of the Communist Party of Kampuchea (CPK)—see separate entry—then led by Pol Pot (earlier known as Saloth Sar), which was the pro-Chinese (and anti-Soviet) faction of the original Kampuchean People's Revolutionary Party (or *Pracheachon*). In 1968 the Red Khmers began an armed struggle against the Government of Prince Norodom Sihanouk, and by the end of that year they were active in 11 out of the country's 19 provinces, allegedly with the support of the *Viet Cong* (the communist armed forces of South Vietnam). When, after his deposition as head of state and the replacement of his Govern-

ment by the (right-wing) Lon Nol regime on March 18, 1970, Prince Norodom Sihanouk proclaimed in Peking on March 23 that he would form a Government of National Union, a National Liberation Army and a United National Front, three Red Khmer leaders—Khieu Samphan, Hon Youn and Hu Nim—stated on March 26 that they would give unreserved support to the Prince's proclamation.

During the ensuing month the Red Khmers supported the gradual penetration of Kampuchea by Viet Cong forces, which led to temporary US intervention in Kampuchea in May-June 1970 and to the proclamation of martial law on May 22.

A Royal Government of National Union, which had been formed by Prince Norodom Sihanouk in exile on May 5, 1970, with the participation of three Red Khmers, was on Aug. 21, 1970, enlarged by new appointments which gave the Red Khmers a majority in it; in particular Khieu Samphan, until then Minister of Defence, became Deputy Premier.

During the civil war of 1970-75 between Marshal Lon Nol's forces and the supporters of Prince Norodom Sihanouk, the Red Khmers were said to number only about 3,000 (out of a total of 65,000 pro-Sihanouk troops, of whom 50,000 were North Vietnamese). Following the conclusion of a peace agreement in January 1973 between the United States, North and South Vietnam and the Provisional Revolutionary Government of South Vietnam, Prince Norodom Sihanouk criticized the Red Khmers in October 1973, alleging that they were reducing their military action in order not to provoke the United States to intervene again in Indo-China.

In November 1973 most of the ministries of the Royal Government were transferred from Peking to Kampuchea, of which Sihanoukists claimed to "control 90 per cent". On April 17, 1975, the civil war ended with the occupation of Phnom-Penh by pro-Sihanouk forces. The Red Khmers thereupon assumed power, with Prince Norodom Sihanouk remaining head of state as "a symbol of national unity" (despite his disagreements with the Red Khmers) until April 1976, when he resigned and was succeeded as head of state by Khieu Samphan, and a new Government was formed under Pol Pot, with Ieng Sary as Deputy Premier and Foreign Minister. The CPK thereupon carried out the most radical communist policy programme ever implemented anywhere, involving the forcible removal of the country's urban population to the rural areas and mass executions of alleged reactionaries.

In 1976-77 a number of dissident Red Khmer leaders were alleged to have been involved in a conspiracy, inspired by Vietnam, against Pol Pot and his pro-

Chinese policy; the pro-Vietnamese elements were, however, said to have been eliminated in the early months of 1977, many of them by execution. From 1977 onwards Vietnamese forces invaded Kampuchea, and Kampuchean counter-attacks were made into Vietnam in 1978. Vietnamese proposals for a peace settlement were rejected by the Pol Pot regime in Kampuchea which claimed (on April 12, 1978) that Vietnam had since 1975 "conducted subversion and infiltration and interfered in Kampuchea's internal affairs" and also "prepared to stage a coup d'état in order to topple Democratic Kampuchea". In a note of May 15 Kampuchea demanded inter alia that Vietnam should "abandon definitively the strategy aimed at putting Kampuchea under the domination of Vietnam in an 'Indo-China federation'". After further Kampuchean allegations concerning a new Vietnamese attempt to stage a coup, broadcast on June 27, 1978, all denied by Vietnam on June 27, 1978, as well as various reports of unsuccessful risings against the Pol Pot regime, it was claimed in Vietnam early in August that Sau Phim, a former deputy chief of staff of the Red Khmers, who also had held high posts in the party and the administration, was leading a resistance movement (with other political leaders), the strength of which was estimated at between 25,000 and 30,000 men.

While conflicting reports appeared in June-August 1978 about further fighting between Vietnamese and Red Khmer forces, Vietnam suggested that Chinese military aid to Kampuchea was responsible for the war, and Hanoi stated on June 21: "On the orders of a foreign country Pol Pot and Ieng Sary have murdered the Kampuchean people." Among other communist countries only China and North Korea supported the Pol Pot regime, while Vietnam was supported by the Soviet bloc and Albania, with Laos, Romania and Yugoslavia remaining neutral.

Eventually the Red Khmer regime of Pol Pot was defeated by the Vietnamese-backed forces of the supporters of the pro-Vietnamese Communists, who had formed a Kampuchean National United Front for National Salvation in December 1978, and who assumed power in January 1979, establishing the People's Republic of Kampuchea (PRK).

The new regime was recognized by the members of the Soviet bloc and a number of non-aligned countries but the Red Khmers, although no longer in control of any substantial part of the country and strongly criticized for their violation of human rights while in power, continued to be recognized as the legitimate rulers of Kampuchea by the vast majority of UN member countries on the basis of the principle of non-intervention in the affairs of another state—a principle said to have been violated by Vietnam's action in invading Kampuchea.

Prince Norodom Sihanouk stated in Peking (where he was living in exile) on Jan. 8, 1979, that he strongly condemned both the Vietnamese invasion and Pol Pot's internal policy; that he nevertheless regarded Pol Pot as the "legal leader of Democratic Kampuchea" and that he had agreed to represent Kampuchea at the United Nations. On Jan. 20, 1979, he revealed that he had refused an invitation from the PRK Government to become President of the PRK, but on March 19 he stated that he would no longer represent Pol Pot's Government. He had earlier proposed that Kampuchea's fate should be decided at a Geneva conference leading to a ceasefire, and general elections open to all Kampuchean parties.

Inside Kampuchea Red Khmer forces continued to resist the Vietnamese army. According to their radio station (believed to broadcast from southern China), "The Voice of Democratic Kampuchea" (VODK), a national conference attended by 400 leaders on Feb. 1-2, 1979, had adopted a policy of "harassment, hit-and-run and attrition" to be used against the Vietnamese forces; while fighting took place in January-April 1979 there was reported to be widespread hostility against the Red Khmers, who were accused of committing several massacres. On April 5 it was claimed by the Vietnam News Agency that Pol Pot's headquarters at Ta Sanh (about 10 miles from the frontier) had been captured in a four-day battle, in which 1,000 of the defenders had been killed or taken prisoner.

In the fighting during 1979 the Red Khmer forces were generally forced to retreat, often into Thailand. Prince Norodom Sihanouk estimated on Nov. 27, 1979, that 60 per cent of Kampuchea was under Vietnamese control, and the remaining 40 per cent either under Red Khmer or Free Khmer control or a no man's land. Among the numerous refugees who entered Thailand, reaching a total of 130,000 by May 1979, the Red Khmers exercised a certain amount of control and attempted to compel refugees to re-enter Kampuchea and to join the Red Khmer forces.

In Phnom-Penh a "people's revolutionary tribunal" on Aug. 19, 1979, sentenced Pol Pot and Ieng Sary to death in absentia on charges concerning a long list of crimes, among them mass killings, displacement of the population (over 2,000,000 from Phnom-Penh alone on April 17, 1975), repression and coercion to work, the abolition of all social relationships, religion and culture, ill-treatment of children and the use of terrorism. The PRK Foreign Minister called on China (on Oct. 4) to cease all protection, shelter and support for Pol Pot and Ieng

Sary, as required by the 1948 Convention on Genocide.

Ieng Sary, however, declared in an interview (published in *Le Monde* on June 1, 1979) that the Red Khmer Government was prepared to collaborate with Prince Norodom Sihanouk, the Free Khmers and Marshal Lon Nol in order to establish an independent, united and non-aligned Kampuchea; that even the Government of the PRK could join the national community if it ceased to collaborate with Vietnam; and that the Communist Party (the KPRP) was prepared to step aside and to accept "a mixed economy and the existence of a bourgeoisie".

On Sept. 6, 1979, the Red Khmers' "ambassador" in Peking released the draft political programme of a "Patriotic and Democratic Front of the Great National Union of Kampuchea" to be formed by the Red Khmers. The aim of this new organization included the expulsion of the Vietnamese from Kampuchea, the overthrow of the PRK Government, the establishment of freedom of speech and the press, freedom to choose one's residence and religious freedom, of a National Assembly to be chosen in free elections under UN supervision, and the formation of a government of representatives of all organizations, strata and individuals opposed to the Vietnamese; and an economy based on "individual or family productive activity" with private property being guaranteed and a national currency being reintroduced (the use of money having been abolished under the Pol Pot regime).

A joint congress of the Standing Committee of a "Kampuchean People's Representative Assembly", the Red Khmer Government and representatives of the Red Khmer forces and government ministries held in the Cardamom Mountains (west of Phnom-Penh) on Dec. 15-17, 1979, adopted the political programme of the Patriotic and Democratic Front (see above) and elected Khieu Samphan as chairman of the Front and as Prime Minister, and he formed a partly reconstructed Government (with Pol Pot, the outgoing Prime Minister, being appointed C.-in-C. of the armed forces).

Khieu Samphan and Ieng Sary admitted on Feb. 27 and March 2, 1980, that the Pol Pot regime had committed political errors, and they called for national independence and free elections under UN supervision as the Red Khmers' prime objectives. Huang Hua, then Foreign Minister of the People's Republic of China, declared on March 19, 1980, that China would continue to give "full armed support" to the Red Khmers.

Fighting between Vietnamese and PRK troops on the one hand and Red Khmers (and Free Khmers) on the other continued in the first half of 1980, mainly near the border with Thailand, with the PRK Government accusing the Thai Government on Feb. 26 of allowing the Red Khmers and Free Khmers to use its territory as a sanctuary. The Red Khmer forces were believed to number between 20,000 and 35,000 men (of whom 15,000 were operating in the western provinces of Battambang, Pursat and Koh Kong, and the rest elsewhere in small guerrilla groups), facing (according to a Red Khmer statement of July 16, 1979) 180,000 Vietnamese and 20,000 PRK troops, as well as some Laotian troops in the northern provinces.

In the second half of 1980 the Red Khmers continued their guerrilla activities in various areas but according to *The New York Times* of Nov. 25, 1980, the Pol Pot forces controlled only enclaves in formerly uninhabited areas and the Vietnamese occupation troops controlled "all of populated Kampuchea". Mutual accusations of border-violations continued to be made by the PRK and Thai Governments.

At the United Nations, however, the General Assembly rejected, on Oct. 14, 1980, by 74 votes to 35 with 32 abstentions, a proposal not to recognize the credentials of the Red Khmers' delegation. On Oct. 22 the General Assembly approved, by 97 votes to 23 with 22 abstentions, a call (by members of the Association of South East Asian Nations—ASEAN, viz. Indonesia, Malaysia, the Philippines, Singapore and Thailand) for an international conference in 1981 to bring about the complete withdrawal of Vietnamese forces from Kampuchea and free elections under UN supervision.

In 1981 the UN General Assembly again approved the Red Khmer delegation's credentials (on Sept. 18 by 77 votes to 37 with 17 abstentions). Ieng Sary (the Deputy Premier and Foreign Minister of the Red Khmer's Government) said in Jakarta (Indonesia) on Nov. 23, 1980, that his Government was willing to let Prince Norodom Sihanouk play a more active role and exercise more power if he accepted that the top priority was the expulsion of the Vietnamese. Ieng Sary also said that his Government was ready to associate itself with Son Sann (of the Khmer People's National Liberation Front—see separate entry) on the same condition.

During 1981 the Red Khmers continued their guerrilla warfare but from October onwards they were less successful than before, with the Red Khmers' forces having fallen to about 25,000 and increasing numbers having surrendered—even though they had reportedly received large arms supplies from China through Thailand.

While defectors from the Red Khmers to the PRK were promised employment and full political rights by the Government in Phnom-Penh, and rewards were offered to those who eliminated their commanders, destroyed their bases or brought back weapons and equipment, or persons who had been kidnapped, others were given prison sentences on various occasions. On April 10, 1981, two Red Khmers were sentenced to imprisonment for life and 20 years respectively for "armed activities against the revolution", and on Oct. 23 six charged with causing explosions in public places were given prison sentences of from two years suspended to life.

In early 1982 the Red Khmers succeeded in retaining a stronghold along the southern part of Kampuchea's border with Thailand, despite massive Vietnamese attacks in the Phnom Malai mountain area. The VODK radio claimed on May 12 that during the current dry season Red Khmer forces had killed or put out of action 21,958 Vietnamese troops, had destroyed 19 Vietnamese tanks, 168 transport vehicles, 50 boats and two aircraft. A Thai officer, on the other hand, estimated that during the current Vietnamese offensive each side had suffered between 100 and 1,000 casualties. On June 27 Red Khmer guerrillas claimed to have killed 20 Soviet advisers and technicians in the Kampong Sila district (as announced by the VODK). (In October 1980 they had claimed to have killed 25 Soviet officials in the same area.)

After protracted negotiations a coalition agreement was signed in Kuala Lumpur (Malaysia) on June 22, 1982, by Khieu Samphan (as Prime Minister of the Red Khmer "Government"), Prince Norodom Sihanouk (as leader of the *Moulinaka* movement) and Son Sann (leader of the Khmer People's National Liberation Front, the strongest Free Khmer grouping).

Under the agreement Prince Norodom Sihanouk became president of the coalition government, Khieu Samphan vice-president with responsibility for foreign affairs, Son Sann Prime Minister and Ieng Sary Deputy Premier; below them were four co-ordinating committees (for defence, finance, education and health); the separate identities of the three coalition parties were maintained, as were the constitutions of the Red Khmer government; all decisions required the unanimous approval of all three parties; and guerrilla resistance to the PRK was to be co-ordinated.

The PRK Government condemned the coalition government on June 27 as "the brainchild of the United States and China", and its formation as interference in the internal affairs of Kampuchea. The US States Department declared immediately after the signing of the coalition agreement that the United States had "granted political and moral support to the Kampuchean non-communist movements" but would "not grant any kind of support whatever to the Red Khmers".

Non-communist Movements

Free Khmers *(Khmers Serei)*

Leadership. (1970) Son Ngoc Thanh (l.); (1979) Van Saren (l.).

The term *Khmers Serei* has been used for a number of different groups of non-communist organizations in Kampuchea. Originally Free Khmers were recruited from among the Kampuchean community in South Vietnam, and these carried out raids (in 1965-67) into Kampuchea then under the neutralist government of Prince Norodom Sihanouk, which the Government of South Vietnam accused of allowing (communist) *Viet Cong* forces to operate from bases inside Kampuchean territory. Many Free Khmers were arrested, and their leaders went into exile in Thailand. However, after the overthrow of Prince Norodom Sihanouk in 1970, the arrested Free Khmers were released, and on May 16, 1970, it was announced that the Free Khmers had rallied to the support of the (right-wing) Government of Gen. Lon Nol. Son Ngoc Thanh—who had been head of a puppet government of Cambodia under Japanese occupation in World War II and had in 1959 been sentenced to death in absentia for involvement in an anti-government conspiracy—returned from exile in Thailand in 1970, when he was appointed (on March 18) Prime Minister under the Lon Nol regime.

After the overthrow of that regime in 1975, Free Khmers fighting against the Red Khmer Government were active in the areas on the border with Thailand, conducting raids into Kampuchea and smuggling wealthy Kampucheans out of the country.

In 1979 the term *Khmers Serei* was applied to several movements (for some of which see separate entries) opposed to both the Vietnamese and the Red Khmers—(i) the Khmer People's National Liberation Armed Forces formed in March 1979 by Gen. Dien Del (a former army officer under the Lon Nol regime), claiming to command over 2,000 men; (ii) the Khmer People's National Liberation Front (KPNLF) led by Son Sann; (iii) the National Liberation Movement of Kampuchea *(Moulinaka)* led by Prince Norodom Sihanouk; (iv) the "Liberation National Government of Kampuchea" formed on Oct. 3 1979, with Van Saren as "Prime Minister"; and (v) the National Liberation Movement led by In Sakhan. The total strength of these groups was believed to be not more than 6,000 men, who were said to observe an informal truce with the Red Khmers, with many of them being compelled to retreat into Thailand.

Between December 1979 and July 1980 fighting occurred between rival Free Khmer groups, in disagreement partly over their attitude to the Red Khmers and partly over the distribution of food supplied by international relief organizations.

The "Liberation National Government" of Van Saren was reported to be selling such food in Thailand and Kampuchea. There were clashes between Van Saren's followers, the *Moulinaka,* the National Liberation Movement of In Sakhan, and a *Khmer Serei* group led by Mitr Don, who had been a lieutenant of Van Saren. The last-named, however, fled to Thailand in April 1980, after his camp had been destroyed by Red Khmer forces collaborating with breakaway Free Khmer guerrillas.

Khmer Serei forces located in a camp at Non Makmora (the site of which was variously described as being in Thailand, as straddling the border and as being in Kampuchea) were attacked on June 23-24, 1980, by Vietnamese forces and PRK troops who also raided another *Khmer Serei* camp. In Thailand it was claimed that Thai forces had repulsed the Vietnamese on June 24. (The incident was followed by a strong public condemnation of Vietnam's "act of aggression" at a meeting of Foreign Ministers of the Association of South-East Asian Nations—ASEAN, i.e. Indonesia, Malaysia, the Philippines, Singapore and Thailand, who reaffirmed their continued recognition of the "Democratic Kampuchean Government" of the Red Khmers, and also by a US decision to accelerate the delivery of military equipment to Thailand.)

(For Free Khmer participation in the coalition agreement of anti-PRK forces signed in June 1982, see separate entry for Red Khmers.)

Confederation of Khmer Nationalists (CNK)

Leadership. Prince Norodom Sihanouk (l.).

The CNK was set up at a conference held on Sept. 28, 1979, in Pyongyang (the capital of North Korea, where Prince Norodom Sihanouk was then living in exile) and attended by 38 representatives of refugee groups. It included also two former leading members of the Lon Nol regime—In Tan (a former Foreign Minister) and Cheng Heng—while Marshal Lon Nol stated later that he considered himself to be a member of the CNK. The General Association of Khmers Overseas, however, announced on May 2, 1980, that it was withdrawing from the CNK because Prince Norodom Sihanouk had on April 2 stated his readiness to co-operate with the Government in Phnom-Penh under certain conditions. (For apparent successor organization to the CNK, see separate entry for National United Front for an Independent National, Peaceful and Co-operative Kampuchea.)

Independence *(Sereika)*

Leadership. Hem Kroesna.

This group was set up in January 1979 with the aim of opposing both the PRK Government and the Red Khmers, and it formed a "provisional government". However, the group's leaders were arrested in the summer of 1979. At the ensuing trial of 16 members of the group, Hem Kroesna stated that the accused had maintained contact with Son Sann (the leader of the Khmer People's National Liberation Front, KPNLF); had established tentative contacts with the Red Khmers; and had set up autonomous units in the seven south-eastern provinces. The accused were on June 7, 1980, sentenced to imprisonment for from three to 20 years.

Khmer People's National Liberation Front (KPNLF)

Leadership. Son Sann (pres.).

The KPNLF was established in France in October 1979 as a democratic and non-communist movement with the object of uniting all non-communist resistance to the Vietnamese-backed regime in Phnom-Penh. Initially it condemned the Red Khmers and demanded that Red Khmer leaders should go into exile and that the KPNLF should have a majority in an anti-Vietnamese coalition government. Son Sann, who had been Prime Minister under Prince Norodom Sihanouk in 1967, stated on Sept. 9, 1980, that the Front would fight the Vietnamese separately on condition that the Red Khmers would not attack KPNLF forces or their supply routes. By 1981 the Front claimed to control 9,000 armed men (although other estimates ranged from 3,000 to 6,000) and to have received arms from China. The KPNLF was also equipped with US-made weapons (believed to have come from the Thai Army).

During the early part of 1982 the forces of the KPNLF were temporarily dislodged from their strongholds near the Thai border but by June 1982 they were re-establishing themselves in that area. (For KPNLF's participation in the anti-PRK coalition agreement signed in June 1982, see separate entry for Red Khmers.)

National Liberation Movement

Leadership. In Sakhan (l.).

Established in 1979, this movement was regarded as a Free Khmer *(Khmer Serei)* group. In July 1980 it lost control of a camp at Nong Samet to the forces of Mitr Don, the leader of another *Khmer Serei* group. On April 15, 1981. In Sakhan announced his support for the *Moulinaka* movement (see separate entry).

111

National Liberation Movement of Kampuchea *(Moulinaka)*

Leadership. Prince Norodom Sihanouk (l.).

This (Free Khmer) movement established in August 1979 was originally led by Kong Sileah (a supporter of Prince Norodom Sihanouk), who had political disagreements with Gen. Dien Del (leader of the Khmer People's National Liberation Armed Forces (see Free Khmers). In 1980 *Moulinaka* units were involved in clashes with Free Khmers following Van Saren. After the death of Kong Sileah on Aug. 16, 1980, *Moulinaka* agreed to co-operate with the Khmer People's National Liberation Front (KPNLF) of Son Sann. On Dec. 1, 1980, it was reported that the first joint military operation by *Moulinaka* and the Red Khmers had been launched on Nov. 28. At a meeting held in Singapore on Sept. 2-4, 1981, Prince Norodom Sihanouk agreed with Khieu Samphan (the Red Khmer leader) and Son Sann (leader of the Khmer People's National Liberation Front, KPNLF) on the formation of a tripartite coalition government (for the creation of which in June 1982 see separate entry for Red Khmers).

National United Front for an Independent National, Peaceful and Co-operative Kampuchea (FUNCINPEC)

Leadership. Prince Norodom Sihanouk (l.).

Prince Norodom Sihanouk announced on March 25, 1982, that he would form FUNCINPEC as his own political party with its own armed forces (and apparently in replacement of the Confederation of Khmer Nationalists—see separate entry).

The Nationalists *(Neak Cheat Niyum)*

Leadership. Vann Sao Yuth (l.).

A total of 17 members of this group said to have their headquarters in Thailand run by Son Sann and Dien Del (the leaders respectively of the Khmer People's National Liberation Front and the Khmer People's National Liberation Armed Forces), were tried in Phnom-Penh on Nov. 26-28, 1980, when Vann Sao Yuth (tried in absentia) was given a life sentence and 14 others prison terms of from two to 20 years (with another defendant being discharged and Princess Botum Bopha, a daughter of Prince Norodom Sihanouk, being given a suspended two-year sentence).

Democratic People's Republic of Korea

Capital: Pyongyang   Pop. 18,700,000

The Democratic People's Republic of Korea (or North Korea) is, under its Constitution adopted on Dec. 27, 1972, "an independent socialist state" in which the working people exercise power through the Supreme People's Assembly, elected by universal adult suffrage, and also through people's assemblies at lower level. The Supreme People's Assembly elects the country's President, and he convenes and presides over an Administrative Council (Cabinet). For elections to the Assembly a single official list of candidates is submitted by the Democratic Front for the Reunification of the Fatherland (i.e. of both North and South Korea), which consists of the country's leading party, the Korean Workers' Party (KWP) and also two small parties—the (religious) Chondoist Chongo (officially stated to comprise former Buddhist believers) and the Korean Social Democratic Party (known until January 1981 as the Korean Democratic Party), both formed in 1945. The General Secretary of the KWP's Central Committee is also head of state and supreme commander of the armed forces.

In general elections to the Supreme People's Assembly held on Feb. 28, 1982, it was officially claimed that all votes had been cast for the 615 candidates on the sole official list.

Reports of Internal Dissent

Reports of dissension inside North Korea have usually had their source among émigrés or defectors living in Japan or in South Korea. In particular, it was asserted by Koreans in Japan in early 1982 that (Mrs) Kim Song Ae, the second wife of Marshal Kim Il Sung (who has been in undisputed power since 1958), opposed the proposed designation, as the Marshal's successor, of Kim Chong Il, his eldest son by his first wife.

In June 1982 it was reported from Japan that a considerable number of North Korean military officers, including more than 10 generals, had defected to mainland China because they also objected to the appointment of Kim Chong Il as the next North Korean leader, and they had, in addition, called for the modernization of the country's armed forces.

South Korean intelligence officials claimed on April 10, 1982, that there were in North Korea at least 105,000 political prisoners serving life sentences in concentration camps of varying sizes referred to as "special dictatorship target areas", this information being later confirmed by defectors from North Korea and also by US reconnaissance photos.

Republic of Korea

Capital: Seoul   Pop. 38,200,000

The Republic of Korea (South Korea) has under its Constitution (which was over-whelmingly approved in a referendum on Oct. 22, 1980, and came into effect on Oct. 27) a President elected for a single seven-year term by a 5,000-member electoral college itself elected by universal adult suffrage and a National Assembly (also elected by universal adult suffrage, but for four years). The President is empowered to take emergency measures only in time of armed conflict or a similar emergency, and such measures must be approved by the National Assembly; he can also dissolve the Assembly, with the Cabinet's approval, but not within the first year after the Assembly's election, and not twice for the same reason.

Under an electoral law there are 92 electoral districts, each returning two members, with no party being allowed to nominate more than one candidate in each district; the party winning the largest number of seats obtains a further 61 seats and 31 other seats are distributed, in proportion to the number of seats won, among other parties which win more than five seats. No party can therefore win more than 153 of the 276 seats in the Assembly; constitutional amendments require a two-thirds majority, i.e. approval by at least two parties. Under a Political Parties' Law parties which fail to win a seat or at least 2 per cent of the valid votes cast are dissolved.

As a result of elections held on March 25, 1981, the distribution of seats in the National Assembly was: Democratic Justice Party 151, Democratic Korea Party 81, Korean National Party 25, Democratic Socialist Party 2, Civil Rights Party 2, New Political Party 2, Democratic Farmers' Party 1, *Anmin* Party 1, independents 11.

Since the assassination of President Park Chung Hee in October 1979 and the accession to power of President Chun Doo Hwan in September 1980, the previous ban on political activities was relaxed and a system of party pluralism began to operate within certain prescribed limits. Outside the registered opposition parties, dissident opinion and activities continued to be channelled principally through student movements and the Christian churches, there being some 8,500,000 Protestants and 1,500,000 Catholics in South Korea in a total population of over 38,000,000.

The continuing division of Korea and the existence since 1946 of a communist regime in North Korea have made successive South Korean governments very sensitive to the threat of internal communist subversion. Although an Anti-Communist Law of July 1961 was revoked in December 1980, many of its provisions were incorporated in an amended National Security Law providing inter alia for increased penalties for forming or joining "anti-state organizations" and for a minimum of two years' imprisonment for the circulation of "groundless rumours" by members of such organizations. Meeting or communicating with persons in "non-hostile" communist countries ceased to be an offence, however, this change being intended to facilitate trade with East European countries.

The South Korean Central Intelligence Agency (KCIA) was renamed the Agency for National Security Planning in January 1981, a government spokesman explaining that the change had been introduced because the KCIA had been guilty of "absurdities and irrational practices" in the past.

Korean Christian Action Organization

This inter-denominational body has been prominent in a recent growth of anti-US sentiments among a small but growing minority of the population, arising mainly from a belief that US support for President Chun constitutes an obstacle to the development of democracy in South Korea. In a statement issued on April 15, 1982, the Organization called for the withdrawal of the US ambassador, Richard Walker, who was said to have described student demonstrators as "spoiled brats" (although he claimed to have been misquoted), and also of Gen. John A. Wickham, then commander of the UN forces in Korea (i.e. head of the combined US-South Korean Command). Gen. Wickham, who was regarded as a strong supporter of President Chun, had incurred opposition criticism for releasing regiments under his command for security work at the time of the Kwangju rising in May 1980 (see separate entry for Kwangju Citizens' Committee) and for a controversial suggestion in August 1980 that Koreans were not ready for democracy. (Gen. Wickham was replaced in June 1982.)

The issuing of the April 15 statement resulted in several leaders of the Korean Christian Action Organization being briefly detained, amid a wider sweep by the authorities against suspected dissidents arising from an arson attack on the US cultural centre in the southern port city of Pusan on March 18, 1982. After police investigations in late March in which several thousand people were detained for questioning, a total of 16 people were arrested and formally charged on April 29, including Father Choi Ki Shik, a priest at a Roman Catholic centre at Wonju, who was accused of harbouring the principal suspects. Kim Hyong Jang, who was allegedly responsible for planning the operation, was said to have been staying at the Wonju centre since 1980; he was also wanted by the police in connexion with the Kwangju uprising. Two Protestant theology students charged with carrying out the Pusan attack, Moon Bu Shik and Miss Kim Un Suk, had apparently sought refuge afterwards at Wonju, although Father Choi was believed to have advised them in their subsequent decision to surrender to the authorities.

Whereas the Government drew public attention to the role of the Christian churches in the Pusan arson case, leaders of both the Protestant and the Catholic communities contended that Father Choi had simply acted within the Christian tradition of providing refuge. Demonstrations held after a mass at Myongdong Cathedral in Seoul on April 26, 1982, were broken up by police, as were demonstrations in Kwangju on May 18. Calls made by Protestant leaders on this latter occasion for the resignation of President Chun were reiterated by the Catholic Council for Justice and Peace on June 4 and at student demonstrations during the same period.

Kim Hyong Jang and Moon Bu Shik were both sentenced to death on Aug. 11, 1982, for planning and implementing the Pusan arson attack, while Miss Kim was sentenced to life imprisonment, Father Choi to three years' imprisonment and the other 12 defendants to terms of between two years and life. During the trial several defendants alleged that evidence had been obtained from them under duress. Moon Bu Shik in particular claimed that he had been tortured into giving a false statement confessing to communist sympathies, whereas it was his true belief in democracy which led him to oppose the US role in Korea.

Kwangju Citizens' Committee

Leadership. Mgr Yoon Kong Hie, Roman Catholic Archbishop of Kwangju (ch.).

This Committee, including religious leaders, professors and students, was formed to negotiate with the local martial law commander in Kwangju (the capital of South Cholla, a poor and over-populated province noted for the radicalism of its inhabitants) on the demand made by a mass movement which had erupted in a popular rising on May 19, 1980. This revolt had its origins in a student protest which had begun in March 1980 and had led to the extension of martial law throughout the country on May 17, the banning of all political activities and the arrest of many anti-government politicians.

The demands of the Committee submitted on May 22 were said to include the removal of the head of the Army Security Command, the lifting of martial law, the formation of an interim government led by democratic politicians, the release of all political detainees, freedom of the press, and full compensation for the families of those killed and wounded during the rising in Kwangju. (The Committee stated later that 261 dead bodies had been found, of which 100 had not been identified; according to an official statement of May 31 the casualties were 144 civilians, 27 soldiers and four policemen killed, and those arrested numbered 1,740 of whom 1,010 had been released.)

The negotiations between the Committee and the martial law commander were unsuccessful as the latter rejected all political demands. On May 27 tanks and infantry moved into Kwangju which had until then been occupied by the rebels whose number had risen to about 200,000 or a quarter of the city's population. The rising also spread to many other areas.

115

On Oct. 25, 1980, five alleged participants in the Kwangju revolt were sentenced to death, and the martial law authorities confirmed that seven other persons had been sentenced to life imprisonment and 163 to prison terms of from five to 20 years. However, under an amnesty of May 2 and another of May 11, 1981, all those connected with the Kwangju revolt were released from prison or had their sentences reduced.

The Case of Kim Dae Jung

Kim Dae Jung, who as candidate of the opposition New Democratic Party in the 1971 presidential election had been defeated by President Park Chung Hee, thereafter campaigned against President Park's regime in Japan and in the United States. On Aug. 8, 1973, he was abducted in Tokyo and taken to South Korea, where he was temporarily placed under house arrest. The kidnapping led to a dispute between South Korea and Japan, where responsibility for the action was attributed to the South Korean Central Intelligence Agency (KCIA); the dispute was settled on Nov. 1, inter alia by South Korea agreeing that no legal action would be taken against Kim Dae Jung for his political activities abroad unless he committed "anti-state acts again in the future".

Kim Dae Jung's kidnapping was also followed by a fusion of student and Christian protest movements against President Park's regime. He was a co-signatory of a declaration read at an ecumenical mass in Seoul's Roman Catholic cathedral on March 1, 1976, calling for the resignation of President Park and the restoration of democracy; on Aug. 28, 1976, he and three other signatories of the declaration were sentenced to eight years in prison (and 14 others to prison terms of from two to five years) for violating an emergency decree of May 1975. On appeal the sentences were reduced on Dec. 29, 1976—Kim Dae Jung's from eight to five years; on Dec. 19, 1977, he was transferred from prison to a hospital, and on Dec. 27, 1978, he and 105 other persons imprisoned under emergency decrees were released under an amnesty.

Although subsequently placed under house arrest, Kim Dae Jung issued, on Nov. 2, 1979 (after the assassination of President Park by the director of the KCIA on Oct. 26), a statement calling for direct elections of a new President and National Assembly. Following the election of President Choi Kyu Hah on Dec. 6, 1979, Kim Dae Jung was released from house arrest on Dec. 8, and his political rights were restored on Feb. 29, 1980. However, under martial law imposed on Oct. 27, 1979, Kim Dae Jung and six others were arrested on May 18, 1980, for "inciting student and labour unrest", and on Sept. 17 of that year he was sentenced to death for plotting rebellion and violating various laws. He admitted that he had been associated with a left-wing movement in 1946, but denied ever having been a communist; he also admitted that he had founded (in the United States in 1973), in collaboration with North Korean sympathizers, a National Congress for the Restoration of Democracy and the Promotion of the Unification of Korea (*Hanmintong*) and for the formation of a similar organization in Japan to oppose "the dictatorial regime of Park Chung Hee", which had, however, not been founded until after his kidnapping in Japan; but he categorically denied having plotted to overthrow the Government, advocated the use of violence or encouraged student demonstrations.

On appeal the death sentence passed on him, and prison sentences given to 16 other defendants, were upheld on Nov. 3, 1980. Although his further appeal against the death sentence was rejected by the Supreme Court on Jan. 23, 1981, the Cabinet later the same day commuted the sentence to life imprisonment, and under an amnesty of March 2, 1982 (which benefited 2,863 persons), his life sentence was reduced to 20 years in prison. On Dec. 16, 1982, he was released from prison and allowed to travel to the United States for medical treatment.

Laos

Capital: Vientiane   Pop. 3,450,000

The People's Democratic Republic of Laos was established in December 1975 by the *Neo Lao Hakset* (Lao Patriotic Front or *Pathet Lao*), whose chairman became President of the Republic, while the General Secretary of the Lao People's Revolutionary Party (LPRP, the Laotian Communist Party, which is the country's sole legal political organization) became Prime Minister. (The name of the Lao Patriotic Front was in February 1979 changed to Lao Front for National Construction.) A People's Congress of 264 representatives elected by local authorities met in December 1975 and appointed a 45-member Supreme People's Council, which was inter alia to draft a new Constitution. There have been no general elections since the establishment of the LPRP's regime.

Between 1975 and 1981 refugees estimated at up to one-tenth of the country's population left Laos, with 100,000 of them reaching the United States, over 105,000 remaining in refugee camps in Thailand and some 100,000 believed to have settled illegally in the Lao-speaking provinces of north-eastern Thailand. No precise figures are available of political prisoners (mainly members of former administrations, but also "elements corrupted by the international reactionaries", i.e. the Chinese) or of persons held in "re-education camps".

Following the invasion of Kampuchea by (pro-Soviet) Vietnamese forces in December 1978, relations between Laos and China broke down early in 1979, when Laos effectively suspended its aid agreements with China, alleged that China was concentrating troops on its .border with Laos, and admitted (for the first time) that Vietnamese troops were stationed in Laos.

Resistance to the LPRP's regime and the Soviet and Vietnamese presence in the country by right-wing groups and (pro-Chinese) communists supported by the Red Khmers of Kampuchea took the form of sporadic guerrilla operations which did not appear to constitute a serious threat to the regime, even though one of its principal opponents, Gen. Phoumi Nosavan, in August 1982 announced that an anti-communist and anti-Vietnamese "Royal Lao Democratic Government" would shortly be set up inside Lao territory.

Lao National Liberation Front

This organization was reported to have conducted guerrilla operations in southern Laos in 1980, with fierce fighting in July and various raids in September, November and December being reported by Kampuchean Red Khmer sources.

Lao Socialist Party

Leadership. Gen. Kong Lae (l.).

In a broadcast of May 17, 1979, by the "Voice of Democratic Kampuchea" (the Red Khmer radio station believed to operate from southern China) this party was described as "the spokesman of the true Lao patriots who are waging a struggle against the Vietnamese aggressors and Vietnam's Lao stooges" (i.e. the ruling Lao People's Revolutionary Party).

Meo Tribesmen

Meo (i.e. barbarian) tribesmen, who called themselves Hmong, or "free men", maintained guerrilla resistance against the LPRP regime from its establishment in 1975. By October 1977, however, the Meo forces were said to have disintegrated into small bands. On Aug. 30, 1978, it was alleged by Hanoi radio that the creation of a Meo kingdom in Laos and northern Vietnam had been discussed in Peking between Chinese leaders and Gen. Vang Pao (who had commanded a Meo force financed by the US Central Intelligence Agency until he had fled to the United States in 1975). In 1980-82 Meo guerrillas operating in northern Laos were said to be receiving aid from China.

According to a statement made in Peking on Dec. 15, 1981, by Dr Khamsengkeo Sengsthith (a former senior official in the Laotian Ministry of Health who had defected to China), chemical weapons were being used in Laos against Meo tribesmen by Vietnamese troops (the number of the latter in the country being put at 50,000 in late 1982 by Prince Souvanna Phouma, the former Prime Minister currently acting as a government adviser). Maintaining that Vietnamese colonialism had plunged Laos into unprecedented terror and anxiety, Dr Khamsengkeo asserted that the use of chemical weapons was part of "a policy of genocide towards national minorities" and that in economic terms Laos had become "a sea of misery", with international relief supplies being plundered by Vietnamese troops.

Royal Government of Free Laos

This "government" was set up on Oct. 14, 1978, at Perpignan (France) by nine exiled right-wing politicians led by Phoui Sananikone, who had been Prime Minister in 1958-59. The French Government disapproved of the formation of this "government" and there have been no reports of its activities.

Royal Lao Democratic Government

Leadership. Gen. Phoumi Nosavan ("head of government").

Gen. Phoumi Nosavan (the former right-wing Deputy Premier who had fled into exile after an abortive coup attempt in 1965) announced in Bangkok (Thailand) on Aug. 18, 1982, that he had formed an anti-communist and anti-Vietnamese "Royal Lao Democratic Government". He subsequently confirmed on Oct. 23 that this "government" had been established in southern Laos with himself as head of government, minister of defence and C.-in-C. of the "Army of Lao Liberation". His declared intention was to overthrow the existing communist regime and to drive out the Vietnamese, acting in co-operation with guerrilla forces currently fighting the Vietnamese-backed regime in Kampuchea.

Gen. Phoumi's initiative was, however, condemned by other prominent exiles and resistance fighters within the United National Front for the Liberation of Laos (formed in September 1980—see separate entry).

United National Front for the Liberation of Laos

Leadership. Sisouk Na Champassak (spokesman of "executive directorate").

This Front was formed on Sept. 15, 1980, at a conference in Champassak province by four anti-Vietnamese movements representing the right-wing forces, neutralists and tribal people opposed to the LPRP regime. At a meeting held in Kampuchea on Nov. 3-4, 1980, officials of the United National Front agreed with Son Sen, "defence minister" in the Kampuchean Red Khmer "government", to co-operate with the Red Khmers. On Jan. 5, 1981, it was reported that 1,000 Lao guerrillas trained in Yunnan (China) were operating in northern Laos; that the Red Khmers had trained two groups of 500 each, which had recrossed the border into Champassak and Sithandone provinces; and that a third group was being trained in northern Kampuchea.

Gen. Phoumi Nosavan (who had been a right-wing Deputy Premier before he had fled from Laos after an abortive coup in 1965) announced on July 24, 1981, that at a meeting of exiled Lao politicians in New York he had accepted the leadership of the United National Front. However, Gen. Phoumi's announcement in August 1982 of the formation of an anti-communist and anti-Vietnamese "Royal Lao Democratic Government" (see separate entry) appeared not to have the support of other exiles and resistance fighters within the Front. In a statement issued in Bangkok on Aug. 27 Sisouk Na Champassak (the Defence Minister of Laos until 1975, when he had left the country and been sentenced in absentia to life imprisonment) described himself as spokesman for the "executive directorate" of the Front and announced that Gen. Phoumi had excluded himself from the organization.

The statement said that Gen. Phoumi's proposed government was neither valid nor representative and that it had been rejected by "all Lao patriots" who were fighting against the Vietnamese forces in Laos in the name of the Front. The statement named nine exiled Lao leaders associated with the Front who were said to have disavowed the Phoumi government even though their names had been included in it.

Reports persisted in 1982 of Chinese support and training for Lao forces opposing the Vientiane regime, whose relations with China were severely strained in consequence. The Lao Government also protested to China on March 25, 1982, over an alleged cross-border incursion by Chinese troops in Phong Saly province on March 18-20.

Malaysia

Capital: Kuala Lumpur   Pop. 13,600,000

The Federation of Malaysia, consisting of Peninsular Malaysia, Sabah and Sarawak, is an independent member of the Commonwealth and a parliamentary monarchy, whose Supreme Head of State is elected for five years, from among themselves, by the nine rulers of the Malay states. Malaysia's Parliament consists of (i) a 58-member Senate—26 of its members being elected (for six years) by the 13 state Legislative Assemblies and 32 appointed by the head of State, and (ii) a 154-member House of Representatives elected (for five years) by universal adult suffrage. The country's Cabinet, headed by a Prime Minister, is appointed by the head of state and responsible to Parliament.

In federal general elections held in April 1982 parties obtained seats in the House of Representatives as follows: National Front 132, Democratic Action Party 9, Pan Malayan Islamic Party 5, independents 8. The National Front embraces 10 political formations (the leading party being the United Malays National Organization) representing all the main ethnic communities; nevertheless, the Government's policy of promoting ethnic Malay economic interests has been criticized by non-Malay groups amid continuing underlying inter-communal tensions.

Under Essential (Security Cases) Regulations promulgated by the Government on Oct. 4, 1975, all acts affecting security were to be tried by a single judge (sitting without a jury); appeals would be limited to cases involving severe penalties; there would be no recourse to the Privy Council; the judge was bound to impose the maximum penalty; and suspects could be arrested without warrant and be kept in preventive custody for 75 days. The Minister of Justice confirmed later that the regulations abolished the principle of the onus of proof of culpability lying with the prosecution, and that guilt was presumed until innocence was proved.

According to an Amnesty International report of Aug. 29, 1979, over 1,000 persons were being held without trial, 53 of them for over eight years. On July 30, 1981, the Government announced the release of 21 such detainees, among them four politicians arrested on Nov. 4, 1976, in connexion with alleged communist subversion, a former deputy minister and member of the United Malays National Organization (the country's dominant political party), the chairman of the (opposition) Malaysian People's Socialist Party, and four members of the (opposition) Democratic Action Party re-elected to the federal House of Representatives in 1978 (notwithstanding their detention). On Feb. 4, 1982, it was officially announced that the total number of releases had reached 168, leaving 444 persons still held without trial—although further arrests were made under internal security provisions later that month.

Under a Societies (Amendment) Bill passed by the federal House of Representatives on April 9, 1981, all clubs, societies and associations were required to register as either political or non-political bodies, and the Registrar of Societies was empowered to take action against any society registered as non-political which was deemed to have involved itself in political affairs, without any appeal being possible except to the Minister of Home Affairs.

Communist Parties

Communist Party of Malaya (CPM)

Leadership. Chin Peng (s.g.).

Established in 1930, the CPM was banned on July 23, 1948, after becoming engaged in an armed insurrection in the Federation of Malaya, which became an independent state within the Commonwealth on Aug. 31, 1957. The insurrection was not finally suppressed (with the help of British, Australian and New Zealand forces) until July 31, 1960, when a 12-year state of emergency was ended. According to official statements the insurrection had resulted in the death of 11,048 persons—6,710 communist guerrillas, 1,865 soldiers and police and 2,473 civilians—in addition to which 510 civilians were listed as missing.

The CPM, which initially had some 15,000 fighters in the field, was largely composed of ethnic Chinese (who form about 35 per cent of Malaysia's population), and followed the policy of the Communist Party of China, by which it was supported. From 1966 onwards a Malayan National Liberation Army (MNLA), organized by the CPM, carried on guerrilla activities near Malaysia's border with Thailand, and it had its own radio station, the "Voice of the Malayan Revolution".

During communal rioting between Malays and ethnic Chinese in Kuala Lumpur in May 1969, the authorities announced, on May 16-18, the arrest of 93 "communist terrorists" and of another 60 "dangerous communists". (The state of emergency imposed during the riots was maintained until Feb. 19, 1971.) During the latter half of 1969 CPM guerrilla activity increased near the border with Thailand, where an estimated 1,000 guerrillas were engaged in fighting under the leadership of Chin Peng (a CPM leader who had fled to southern Thailand after the end of the Malayan emergency in 1960).

Agreement on Thai-Malaysian co-operation against the MNLA was first reached in July 1968 and was confirmed in a military co-operation agreement signed on March 7, 1970. Protracted fighting between guerrillas and Malaysian troops (supported by Thai forces) continued until June 1971, when the Malaysian Government announced the formation of a National Action Committee to cope with "the serious and growing communist threat" and to induce the people of the rural areas to side with the Government and not to allow themselves to be recruited by the MNLA.

In 1971, however, China began to improve its relations with Malaysia and gave progressively less publicity to MNLA operations. When the two Governments decided, on May 31, 1974, to establish diplomatic relations with each other, China undertook to "respect Malaysia's independence and sovereignty" and to enjoin those Chinese in Malaysia who retained their Chinese nationality of their own will "to abide by the laws of the Government of Malaysia".

Although there had been a lull in MNLA activities in 1972-73, communist guerrillas began in 1974 to carry out a number of attacks on troops and workers engaged on building a dam and on a road-building project. A new CPM offensive began on April 1, 1975, when rockets were fired at the Kuala Lumpur air base and bombs exploded near several army camps; seven soldiers were killed on April 7 in four different ambushes in Perak and Kedah states; a special branch detective was shot dead and another near Ipoh on May 17; another detective was shot dead at Ipoh on June 20, and three policemen in an ambush near the Thai border on Aug. 14; on Aug. 30 it was reported that a police supply boat had been ambushed in North Perak and two police killed: and in a grenade attack on the Kuala Lumpur headquarters of the paramilitary field force police on Sept. 3 two policemen were killed and over 40 injured. During the first half of October 1975 a joint Thai-Malaysian suppression force captured three CPM guerrilla camps, when occupants were driven into the jungle.

By 1980 communist guerrillas in Malaysia were said to have been reduced to about 3,000, split into the three factions (CPM, CPM-ML and CPM-RF), with 12 army brigades being deployed in the border area. In November 1980 Musa bin Ahmad (described as chairman of the CPM), who had resided in Peking for 25 years, defected to the Malaysian authorities, and on Jan. 6, 1981, he alleged in a broadcast that China still intended to turn Malaysia into one of its satellites.

The "Voice of the Malayan Revolution" radio station ceased broadcasting on July 1, 1981, but was on July 4 of that year replaced by the "Voice of Malayan Democracy", which announced on June 20, 1982, that the MNLA had been renamed the Malayan People's Army (*Tentara Rakyat Malaya*). According to a statement by the Malaysian Deputy Inspector-General of Police on Oct. 28, 1981, there were only about 230 insurgents still operating in the jungles of Pahang, Perak and Kelantan.

In a new party constitution adopted on April 29, 1980, by the "12th enlarged plenum of the central committee" of the CPM (and broadcast by the "Voice of the Malayan Revolution" on May 20 and 22, 1980), the party was described as "a proletarian party guided by Marxism-Leninism-Mao Zedong thought", whose revolution could "never attain victory by taking the road of parliamentary democracy, armed uprising in the cities or urban guerrilla war" but only by "using the countryside to encircle the cities and seize political power by armed force".

Communist Party of Malaya—Marxist-Leninist (CPM-ML)

The CPM-ML emerged in 1970 as a splinter group from the CPM, from which it differed in advocating the use of urban guerrilla warfare rather than reliance on the rural areas (as practised by the Maoist CPM).

Communist Party of Malaya—Revolutionary Faction (CPM-RF)

The CPM-RF seceded from the CPM in 1970 mainly because of the latter's Maoist policy of using rural areas to encircle the cities—a policy which the CPM-RF considered unworkable in Malaysia, where the majority of the population were Malays. The CPM-RF tried to recruit followers among the Chinese population in the towns and to conduct urban guerrilla warfare. An ambush in the state of Kedah on June 18, 1975, when three government surveyors and eight soldiers were killed, was attributed to this faction by the Minister of Home Affairs.

Malayan People's Army—see under Communist Party of Malaya (CPM)

North Kalimantan Communist Party (NKCP)

This party, operating through its armed wing, the North Kalimantan People's Guerrilla Force (NKPGF), was closely allied to the CPM and was in 1980 said to have some 100 fighters active in the first division of Sarawak. Indonesian and Malaysian security forces had early in 1975 co-operated in disrupting the NKPGF guerrillas' communications along the Sarawak-Kalimantan border.

The Sarawak Chief Minister stated on March 4, 1974, that during the previous five months 482 of the guerrillas (or about three-quarters of their number) in the state had laid down their arms.

Moslem Fundamentalist Groups

Abim

This Moslem fundamentalist group came into conflict with the Government in 1980-81. Some Moslem fundamentalists were reported to have harassed non-Moslems, in particular Indians and Chinese.

Crypto

Nine leaders of this grouping, which was described by the authorities as a "deviant Islamic cult", were arrested under the Internal Security Act on March 27, 1982, after evidence had come to light of its extremist political teachings.

Dakwah (Missionary) Moslem Movement

This Movement, said to have grown significantly in 1978-80, was involved in violent clashes with police in South Johore in August 1980, when about eight persons were killed and 23 injured and a curfew was imposed in Batu Pahat. The *Dakwah* advocated inter alia the destruction of symbols of modern or Western life, such as television sets, and the exclusion of women from higher education (such education of women being regarded as contrary to the Koran). Militant Moslems were also responsible for the destruction of temples of the 700,000-strong Hindu community.

Imbo

This obscure group claimed responsibility for an assassination attempt on the Soviet ambassador in Kuala Lumpur in early January 1983, carried out in protest against the Soviet occupation of Afghanistan.

Mongolia

Capital: Ulan Bator Pop. 1,650,000

The Mongolian People's Republic is "a sovereign democratic state of working people" in which "supreme state power" is vested in the People's Great *Hural* (Assembly) elected for a four-year term by universal adult suffrage and in which effective political power is held by the (communist) Mongolian People's Revolutionary Party (MPRP), the First Secretary of whose Central Committee is head of state and Chairman of the Assembly's Presidium. There is also a Council of Ministers as the country's highest executive power.

In elections held in June 1981 the Assembly's 370 seats were filled by candidates elected unopposed from lists of the MPRP and of a "non-party bloc". There has been no evidence of organized political opposition.

Nepal

Capital: Katmandu Pop. 17,000,000

The Kingdom of Nepal is, under its 1962 Constitution, a "constitutional monarchical Hindu state". Political parties have been banned since Jan. 5, 1961; the "basic units of democracy" are elected village and provincial councils (*panchayats*); under amendments to the Constitution approved in a referendum (which rejected the restoration of political parties) on April 2, 1980, 112 members of the country's National Assembly are elected by direct adult suffrage and another 28 members are nominated by the King; and the Prime Minister is appointed by the King on the recommendation of the National Assembly to which the Council of Ministers (Cabinet) is responsible.

A general amnesty, announced by the King on April 13, 1980, for all who were accused of political offences, was thought to affect between 200 and 300 people, half of them in prison in Nepal and the remainder in exile, mainly in India, where many opponents of King Birendra have lived since the latter's father, King Mahendra, abolished parliamentary democracy in December 1960.

Communist Party of Nepal

The party was declared illegal on Jan. 25, 1952, on the ground that it had been involved in an attempted revolt with other left-wing groups, including dissidents of the Nepalese Congress Party. On July 30, 1952, it was reported that 14 Nepalese Communists had been arrested after returning from Tibet where they were said to have been in contact with the Chinese Communist Party. On April 15, 1956, the ban on the party was lifted after it had given a written assurance that it would

conduct its activities peacefully and constitutionally and that it acknowledged the King as the constitutional head of state. In the 1959 elections the party gained four seats (out of 109) in the Lower House of Parliament, but in January 1961 it was banned again, together with all other political parties.

There were few reports of communist activities in later years. In 1968 pro-Chinese Communists led by Gopal Parsai were said to be engaged in guerrilla warfare in the Jhapa district (south-east Nepal), where they co-operated closely with the Naxalites of India, responsible for the 1967 Naxalbari revolt; Gopal Parsai was on Dec. 1, 1968, reported to have been arrested. In January 1973 members of the Maoist faction of the party were said to have fled to West Bengal (India).

In November 1978, a representative of the pro-Moscow Communist Party (named as Raymajhi) signed a declaration issued by four banned parties and calling for the establishment of a constitutional monarchy, the readmission of political parties and the restoration of "human rights denied to the people for 17 years".

Nepali Congress Party (NCP)

Leadership. K. P. Bhattarai (acting pres.).

The NCP was founded in Calcutta in 1946 under the leadership of Bisheshwar Prasad Koirala (who had been active in the Indian Congress Party and its struggle for Indian independence). In 1947 the left wing of the NCP broke away to form a Nepali National Congress. In March 1950 the NCP absorbed the Nepali Democratic Congress founded by Mahendra Bikram Shan (a member of the Nepali royal family). On Sept. 29, 1950, it was announced in Katmandu that NCP supporters had plotted to assassinate the Prime Minister, and in November-December 1950 NCP followers were involved in a revolt against the Government which induced the latter to introduce constitutional reforms. The NCP thereupon took part in the form-ation of an interim Government on Feb. 12, 1951. Following a cabinet crisis a new Government was formed on Nov. 16, 1951, with Matrika Prasad Koirala (then president of the NCP and a brother of B. P. Koirala) as Prime Minister.

In July-August 1952 M. P. Koirala and his supporters left or were expelled from the NCP and formed a National Democratic Party. In January 1955 the NCP launched a civil disobedience campaign, inter alia with the aim of enforcing the holding of a general election, and it also boycotted a nominated Advisory Assembly convened in April because the representation of parties in it bore "no relation to political realities".

In the country's first elections, held in February-April 1959, the NCP gained 74 of the 109 seats in the Lower House of Parl-iament, and B. P. Koirala thereupon formed a Government which was sworn in on May 27, 1959. However, on Dec. 15, 1960, King Mahendra abolished parliamentary govern-ment, dissolved all political parties and arrested most of their leaders, including B. P. Koirala, who remained imprisoned until Oct. 30, 1968, when he was released after the NCP had, on May 15, 1968, offered the King its "loyal co-operation". On the following day

NCP leaders living in exile in India were pardoned.

The state of emergency imposed by the King had been ended in April 1963 with the introduction of the *panchayat* system of indirect representation, under which political parties remained banned. Ramraja Prasad Singh, a leading member of the NCP who had been elected to the National *Panchayat* early in 1971, was arrested on July 19 of that year and was given a 2½-year prison sentence for alleged anti-state activities, having declared his opposition to the *panchayat* system; however, the King pardoned him on Aug. 25, 1971, and directed that he should be allowed to take his seat in the Assembly from which the Speaker had barred him.

B. P. Koirala, who was then living in exile in India, had threatened King Mahendra with armed struggle against his regime, but to King Birendra (who succeeded to the throne at the death of his father, King Mahendra, on Jan. 31, 1972) he offered co-operation in building "a progressive democratic and prosperous Nepal". However, a number of acts of terrorism which were committed in Nepal in 1973-74 were attributed to NCP members. In connexion with a court case concerning the smuggling of grenades into Nepal, warrants were issued for the arrest of two NCP leaders then in exile in India. On the other hand, Sarod Prasad Koirala (a brother of B. P. Koirala) was assassinated in Bihar (India) on Oct. 18, 1973.

On Dec. 16, 1975, some 50 political prisoners were reported to have been released, among them several former NPC members. B. P. Koirala returned to Katmandu from India on Dec. 30, 1976, but was arrested, with several other NPC followers accompanying him, for "anti-national activities". He had, while in India, stated (on May 26, 1975) that he wanted to carry on "peaceful agitation" for the establishment of democratic institutions in Nepal, and had claimed that the NPC was leading "a big democratic movement" inside Nepal, which was attempting to counter "pro-Chinese communist influence" in that country.

On Feb. 23, 1977, two of B. P. Koirala's supporters were reported to have been condemned to death for "crimes against the state"—one for trying to assassinate the King on March 16, 1974, and the other for leading guerrillas in eastern Nepal before 1975.

On June 9, 1977, it was announced that B. P. Koirala had arrived in New Delhi en route for New York for medical treatment, but that he himself had declared that he would definitely return to Nepal (where he was to face charges under the State Offences Act). On his return to Nepal on Nov. 8, 1977, he was rearrested but on Feb. 23, 1978, a special tribunal cleared him of three charges of treason and sedition, and on March 3 he was acquitted of other charges. After undergoing further medical treatment in the United States he returned to Katmandu on Aug. 20, 1978. He was received by the King on Oct. 30 and said afterwards that in his view a policy of national conciliation would lead to unity and was desirable. An earlier call made by him to party workers to cease all political activities was, however, received with dismay by the central working committee of the NCP, which declared on Oct. 30, 1978, that the party's fight for the restoration of civil and human liberties had been "utterly belied by the betrayal of B. P. Koirala". (His call had also been condemned by the Nepalese Communist Party in September 1978.)

Following the outbreak of student unrest in April 1979 B. P. Koirala was placed under house arrest and three other NCP leaders—Ganesh Man Singh (deputy leader of the NCP), Krishna Prasad Bhattarai (acting president of the NCP and former Speaker of Parliament) and Gokal Prasad (former editor of a government-controlled newspaper)—were taken into custody on April 27, 1979. However, after the Indian Government had reportedly advised the King to come to an understanding with the NCP leaders, the above three and 61 other political leaders were released on May 9, 1979. B. P. Koirala said after his release that the King should not delude himself that he could keep the throne by sheer armed force, and he later welcomed the King's decision to hold a constitutional referendum. However, in this referendum held in May 1980, the policies of the NCP for a restoration of party pluralism were rejected (by 2,443,452 votes to 2,007,452, with about 372,000 spoilt or invalid ballot papers). The first direct parliamentary elections held on May 9, 1981, were boycotted by B. P. Koirala, who died in Katmandu on July 21, 1982. In December 1982 the NCP held its first open conference since 1959 in the capital.

In a manifesto issued in January 1956 the NCP defined its aim as the achievement of socialism by peaceful and democratic methods and of a government which would be a constitutional monarchy on the British model, with a cabinet responsible to the people's representatives and a unicameral legislature elected by universal adult suffrage, a foreign policy based on neutrality and coexistence, industrialization and state planning of the national economy.

Public Welfare League

Nine leaders of this underground political party were on Sept. 29, 1974, reported to have been arrested. The League aimed at the establishment of a democratic socialist regime.

Pakistan

Capital: Islamabad   Pop. 82,700,000

The Islamic Republic of Pakistan is ruled by a national law administration set up in July 1977 and headed by President (Gen.) Zia ul-Haq. Under martial law imposed by the latter, Parliament was dissolved and some provisions of the 1973 Constitution were suspended. Political parties were declared dissolved on Oct. 16, 1979, but remained active. An interim Constitution promulgated on March 24, 1981, provided inter alia that, when political activity was permitted by the President, only those parties which were registered with the Election Commission on Sept. 30, 1979, would be entitled to function. All other parties were dissolved and their property was confiscated; new parties could be formed only with the Chief Election Commissioner's permission, and the President was empowered to dissolve any party "operating in a manner prejudicial to the Islamic ideology or the sovereignty, integrity or security of Pakistan".

As at Sept. 30, 1979, there existed about 80 political parties; 56 of these had registered with the Election Commission, and 44 had submitted their accounts (as required under the amended Political Parties Act); but the Commission announced on Oct. 2, 1979, that only 16 had been granted registration, and that unregistered parties would not be allowed to contest elections. The country's two most influential parties had refused to register, viz. the (democratic socialist) Pakistan People's Party (of the late Zulfiqar Ali Bhutto) and the (Islamic) Pakistan National Alliance (with the exception of the *Jamaat-i-Islami,* one of its six constituent parties). (The official result of the last general elections held in Pakistan, on March 7, 1977—to a National Assembly which never met, owing to the imposition of martial law on July 5—was widely regarded as "rigged"; it showed the distribution of seats as being: Pakistan People's Party 155, Pakistan National Alliance 36, Qayyum Moslem League 1, independents 8.)

On Dec. 24, 1981, President Zia announced the formation of a Federal Advisory Council (of not more than 350 members, who would be appointed by the President), which would act as a bridge between the present martial law administration and a future Islamic democratic government, advising on the form which the latter should take. In an inaugural address to the Council on Jan. 11, 1982, the President said that it was not a substitute for parliament and would cease to exist when an elected National Assembly came into being, although he added that elections could not be held under present circumstances without endangering the country's security and integrity. The country's main political parties, however, regarded the formation of the Council as an unacceptable measure and continued to call for an end to martial law and for the holding of democratic elections under the 1973 Constitution.

Party Alliances

Movement for the Restoration of Democracy (MRD)

This Movement was formed on Feb. 5, 1981, as an alliance of seven political parties—the Pakistan People's Party (PPP), the *Tehrik-i-Istiqlal,* the National Democratic Party, the Pakistan Republican Party, the *Jamaat-i-Ulema-i-Pakistan,* a faction of the Moslem League led by Khwaja Khairuddin, and the Kashmir Moslem Conference—whose leaders signed a declaration calling for the immediate lifting of martial law, President Zia's resignation, fair and free elections to the National and Provincial Assemblies within three months and restoration of the 1973 Constitution. On Feb. 6, 1981, the declaration was also signed by leaders of the National Liberation Front and the Labourers' and Farmers' Party.

Following student unrest and the arrest during February 1981 of numerous opposition leaders—Maulana Fazlur Rahman of the *Jamiat-i-Ulema,* Nasrullah Khan of the Pakistan Democratic Party, Mian Mahmud Ali Kasuri of the *Tehrik-i-Istiqlal,* Lt.-Gen. Tikka Khan, Aftaab Sherpao and Maj.-Gen. Nasirullah Babar (all three of the PPP)—the action committee of the Movement for the Restoration of Democracy met in Lahore on Feb. 23-24 and issued a call for a civil disobedience movement to remove the Government, beginning with a day of protest on March 2 and culminating in a general strike on March 23. The *Jamiat-i-Ulema-i-Pakistan,* however, was not represented at the Lahore meeting and subsequently withdrew from the alliance.

Seven of those who took part in the meeting were afterwards arrested, among them Begum Bhutto (the widow of Zulfiqar Ali Bhutto, the former Prime Minister hanged in 1979 for "conspiracy to murder"). The planned day of protest, however, received only limited support, partly as a result of the arrests of political leaders in the wake of the hijacking of a Pakistani aircraft by members of the militant movement *Al Zulfiqar* (see separate entry).

Following President Zia's creation at the end of 1981 of an appointed Federal Advisory Council to act as a bridge between the present martial law administration and a future Islamic democratic government, the MRD leaders described the Council as an undemocratic attempt to "hoodwink the nation and the outside world" and maintained that it had been created only because of international concern about the military regime. In the course of 1982 the MRD also condemned President Zia's proposal of May 6 for the creation of a "Higher Command Council" to give a permanent role to the armed forces in decision-making and also the idea of holding elections on a non-party basis. At the same time it pressed for the release of political detainees, claiming in a statement issued in early June 1982 that 5,000 political workers were in detention and that 300 had been tortured.

Pakistan National Alliance (PNA)

Leadership. Maulana Mufti Mahmud (pres.); Prof. Ghafoor Mufti Ahmad (g.s.).

This Alliance was formed on Jan. 11, 1977, by nine opposition parties for the purpose of jointly contesting the general elections of

March 7, 1977, on the basis of a democratic and Islamic platform. The parties were the *Tehrik-i-Istiqlal* (a liberal party led by Air Marshal Mohammed Asghar Khan), the National Democratic Party (formed in 1976 by Sherbaz Khan Mazari and regarded as the successor to the left-wing National Awami Party banned in 1975), the Moslem League, the Pakistan Democratic Party, the Moslem Conference, the *Jamaat-i-Islami,* the *Jamiat-i-Ulema-i-Pakistan* (whose leader, Maulana Mufti Mahmud, was elected president of the PNA) and the Pakistan Khaksar Party. The PNA stood for lifting the state of emergency, restoration of the freedom of the press, a reduction in public expenditure, a land reform policy more radical than that of Z. A. Bhutto's Government, some denationaliz-ation measures, the abolition of income tax, strict neutrality in foreign policy (including withdrawal from CENTO), as well as "the purification of society according to Islamic tenets".

However, the PNA gained only 36 out of the 200 general seats in the National Assembly elected on March 7, 1977, mainly in the North-Western Frontier Province and in Karachi, where its election campaign had been received with great enthusiasm. The PNA thereupon denounced the elections as "rigged", and there followed protest demonstrations and strikes leading to rioting in many localities until May 20, with about 350 people being killed. The PNA boycotted the provincial elections held on March 10, when almost all seats in the Provincial Assemblies were taken by the ruling Pakistan People's Party. Z. A. Bhutto rejected the PNA's charges and maintained on March 8 that it had been defeated because the "medieval views" of some of its leaders had "alienated all classes". However, the elected PNA members refused to take their seats in the National Assembly and between March 31 and April 20, 1977, the Election Commission declared void elections in six Punjab con-stituencies because of grave irregularities and ordered fresh elections to be held. In the opposition press it was claimed that the Chief Election Commissioner had said that he was convinced that the elections had been massively rigged in more than half the con-stituencies. During the continuing unrest martial law was imposed on April 21 in Karachi, Hyderabad and Lahore. A general strike called by the PNA was observed in all the major towns on April 22, and many persons were killed in clashes with police and troops. As most of the PNA leaders were arrested on April 24, 1977, the PNA general council elected the Pir of Pagaro (a religious leader and president of the Moslem League) as its acting president.

On April 23, 1977, Z. A. Bhutto was reported to have agreed to new parliamentary and provincial elections under the control of the judiciary and the Army. The Pir of Pagaro was allowed to have talks with the imprisoned PNA leaders and stated on April 27 that the PNA would agree to Z. A. Bhutto's remaining in office as head of a government of national unity pending new elections, provided that the PNA was given two-thirds of the portfolios. On the other hand Air Marshal Asghar Khan said (in a statement smuggled out of prison on May 1) that the PNA would not compromise on its demand for Z. A Bhutto's resignation and for new elections, and he appealed to the Army to refuse to obey orders from the "illegal" Government. There followed inconclusive negotiations between Z. A. Bhutto and the PNA leaders, among whom the Pir of Pagaro was placed under house arrest on May 14, but was released on May 19, as were other arrested PNA leaders during the next few weeks

The negotiations having failed to lead to an agreement, the Army carried out a blood-less coup in Rawalpindi on July 5, 1977 (arresting Z. A. Bhutto and several members of his Government, as well as the most prominent members of the PNA except Begum Wali Khan).

Of the PNA's leaders, the Pir of Pagaro and Mian Tufail Mohammed (of the *Jamaat-i-Islami*) were soon released. The new military regime of Gen. Mohammed Zia ul-Haq introduced inter alia some of the traditional Koranic punishments advocated by the religious wing of the PNA (such as whipping or amputation of the left hand for certain offences).

In the election campaign which led to the indefinite postponement of the general elections by Gen. Zia on Oct. 1, 1977, the PNA leaders were said to have pleaded for the postponement because their alliance had failed "to bring out the crowds" (whereas the Pakistan People's Party appeared to have mass support). However, Maulana Mufti Mahmud, the restored president of the PNA, denied on Nov. 4 that the PNA had requested the postponement and said that, unless elections were held in March 1978, Pakistan would be plunged into chaos. Requests from the PNA that the elections should be held in March and normal political activities, which had been banned on Oct. 1, should be permitted, were rejected by Gen. Zia on Dec. 1, 1977. Air Marshal Asghar Khan, the leader of the *Tehrik-i-Istiqlal,* announced on Nov. 11, 1977, that his party had withdrawn from the PNA.

A new development took place in 1978, when Prof. Ghafoor Mufti Ahmad, the PNA's general secretary, announced on Aug. 6 that the PNA had decided to join the Government, whereupon the National Democratic Party, opposing this decision, broke away from the PNA. The all-civilian Government formed by President Zia on Aug. 23 accordingly included representatives of four of the original PNA member parties—the Moslem League (which had already been represented in a Cabinet formed on July 5, 1978), the *Jamiat-i-Ulema-i-Islam,* the *Jamaat-i-Islami* and the Pakistan Democratic Party (but not of the Moslem Conference or the Khaksar). The *Jamiat-i-Ulema-i-Pakistan* had by then also withdrawn from the PNA. However, on April 15, 1979, the PNA ministers resigned from the Government, although the Alliance undertook to give qualified support to the Government from outside.

At a demonstration at Mirpur (Azad Kashmir) on April 27, 1980, PNA leaders (together with leaders of the Moslem League and the Kashmir Moslem Conference) called for President Zia's resignation and for free elections, and on Oct. 7 of that year Nasrullah Khan (the PNA's vice-president) announced that a 10-party declaration was to be issued calling for civilian rule and general elections; however, the publication of the declaration was delayed owing to dissension between the parties on the method of transition to democracy.

Left-wing Movements

Al Zulfiqar

Leadership. Murtaza Bhutto (l.).

This movement, named "Sword" (*Zulfiqar,* the first name of Z. A. Bhutto, the former Prime Minister who was hanged in April 1979), was established in February 1981 by the late Z. A. Bhutto's elder son, Murtaza Bhutto. The latter had in 1978 sought support for his father, then under arrest and being tried for "conspiracy to murder". After his father's execution, M. Bhutto finally settled in Kabul (Afghanistan), where he established the headquarters of a Pakistan Liberation Army (PLA), an organization dedicated to the overthrow of President Zia. The PLA was divided into a political wing led by Raja Anwar, a former adviser on student affairs to the Pakistan People's Party (PPP), and a military wing composed largely of students and trained by dissident Pakistan Army officers, which began operations in December 1979 and which during 1980 claimed responsibility for numerous acts of terrorism and sabotage.

In December 1980 12 members of the military wing arrested inside Pakistan were tried by a military court in Peshawar for subversion, sabotage and attempting to wage war against Pakistan, with 12 others, among them Murtaza Bhutto, being tried in absentia. In February 1981 Raja Anwar was found to be a government agent and was sentenced to death at a secret trial in Afghanistan. M. Bhutto agreed, at the request of his mother (Begum Nusrat Bhutto) to dissolve the PLA but after visiting Libya for talks with Col. Kadhafi, the Libyan leader, he reorganized the PLA as *Al Zulfiqar.*

On March 2, 1981, *Al Zulfiqar* claimed responsibility for the hijacking (by three armed men) of a Pakistan International Airlines aircraft flying from Karachi to Peshawar. The hijackers, who diverted the aircraft first to Kabul and then to Damascus, demanded the release of 92 political prisoners from Pakistan, but did not attain their objectives, mainly because the Libyan Government withdrew from an agreement to receive both the hijackers and the prisoners to be released by Pakistan. The hijackers killed one of the passengers (a second secretary of the Pakistan embassy in Tehran) and demanded the release of 92 political prisoners from Pakistan. The Pakistan Government eventually agreed to release 55, of whom 54 reached Damascus on March 14, whereupon the hijackers released the aircraft, crew and remaining passengers. The released prisoners included Dr Ghulam Husain, former general secretary of the PPP, and Munir Ahmad Warraich, a former naval officer sentenced to 14 years in prison on undisclosed charges. M. Bhutto claimed in Bombay on April 19 that he had no previous knowledge of the hijacking, as members of *Al Zulfiqar* had been authorized to undertake actions on their own initiative. He denied that his organization had any connexion with the PPP or any other political party, and he said that his mother and sister disapproved of his activities.

In Pakistan it was officially claimed on April 29, 1981, that almost all *Al Zulfiqar* members inside the country had been arrested, but a month later there was said to be rising terrorist activity in Sind province. *Al Zulfiqar* claimed on May 26 to have bombed the Rawalpindi residence of President Zia's Chief of Staff and to have executed a member of a commando sent to assassinate its leaders. On July 8 M. Bhutto and four others charged with complicity in the hijacking were sentenced to terms of hard labour ranging from 10 to 14 years by a military court in Peshawar. The hijacking had also been followed by the arrest of several hundred opposition leaders on March 8-12, 1981.

Al Zulfiqar claimed responsibility for the murder in Lahore on Sept. 25, 1981, of Chaudhri Zahur Elahi, a leader of the Moslem League and a former member of President Zia's Cabinet, and for the injuring in the same attack of Mushtaq Hussain, the presiding judge at Z. A. Bhutto's trial in 1977-78. There were concurrently a number of reports of operations against *Al Zulfiqar* by Pakistani security authorities, while according to Pakistani guerrilla sources in Kabul government security forces conducted secret attacks on their headquarters inside Afghanistan in July and October 1981. Police in Lahore announced on Nov. 29, 1981, that about 100 suspected members of *Al Zulfiqar* had been arrested, and further arrests and discoveries of weapons and explosives were reported in late December in Lahore and Rawalpindi. The Interior Minister said on Jan. 14, 1982, that 481 suspects were in custody out of 1,000 originally sent for guerrilla training in Afghanistan, while the Governor of the Punjab said in August 1982 that a total of 177 people had been arrested in the province in connexion with "the anti-state activities of a Kabul-based terrorist group".

Communist Party of Pakistan

There have been few reports of the activities of this pro-Soviet party. In a press statement issued in Karachi on March 1, 1982, the party's central committee denounced the "Zia ul-Haq military dictatorship"; appealed to "the progressive and democratic forces of the world to raise their voice in militant solidarity with the just struggle of the people of Pakistan" to save "the lives of the political workers in torture chambers" and to secure the "release of thousands of detainees"; and declared that it was "only through the united struggle of the patriotic and democratic forces" that the country could get rid of the military junta and "have a democratic government".

Jamaat-i-Ulema-i-Pakistan

Leadership. Maulana Shah Ahmad Noorani (pres.); Maulana Abdus Sattar Niazi (s.g.)

Established in 1968 by left-wing mullahs, this progressive fundamentalist party gained seven seats in the 1970 National Assembly elections (in the North-West Frontier Province and Baluchistan). In 1977 it became one of the original members of the Pakistan National Alliance (see separate entry) opposed to the then ruling Pakistan People's Party led by Z. A. Bhutto, but broke away from it in July 1978. It was one of the three major parties which registered with the Election Commission by Sept. 30, 1979, as required under an amended Political Parties Act announced by President Zia on Aug. 30, 1979. Originally a member of the Movement for the Restoration of Democracy (see separate entry) founded in February 1981, it withdrew from this movement in the following months.

On March 2, 1982, Maulana Shah Ahmad Noorani claimed that 10,000 people had recently been arrested, the majority of them political activists, and that many had been tortured at camps in Lahore and Karachi. A government spokesman responded that there was no basis for the allegation of torture and that the number of people detained had been grossly exaggerated.

Labourers' and Farmers' Party

Leadership. Fatheyab Ali Khan.

This rurally-based party was a signatory of the declaration issued on Feb. 6, 1981, at the establishment of the Movement for the Restoration of Democracy (see separate entry), in whose subsequent campaign for a return to parliamentary government it played a full part. Fatheyab Ali Khan was one of several opposition leaders arrested on March 22, 1982, and temporarily detained in a move by the authorities to forestall demonstrations on Pakistan's national day (March 23).

National Awami Party (NAP)

Leadership. Khan Abdul Wali Khan (pres.).

In the 1970 general elections the pro-Soviet faction of the NAP (led by Khan Abdul Wali Khan) won six seats (out of the 291 contested) in the National Assembly (three each in Baluchistan and the North-West Frontier Province, NWFP). A pro-Chinese faction of the NAP, led by Maulana Bhashani, did not contest the elections. On the accession of Z. A. Bhutto to the presidency of Pakistan in December 1971 (i.e. after the secession of East Pakistan as Bangladesh) the NAP promised support to the new Government but in January 1972 the NAP (and its ally, the *Jaamat-i-Ulema-i-Pakistan*—see separate entry) criticized President Bhutto's refusal to end martial law and declined his invitation to join the Government. The NAP also demanded that new governors for Baluchistan and the NWFP should be chosen from the NAP (as the largest party in both provinces).

Following a rebellion in Baluchistan in 1973-74 (when the NAP had its own militia) and the assassination of Hayat Mohammed Khan Sherpao, Home Minister of the NWFP, on Feb. 8, 1975, the Pakistan Government declared the NAP illegal on Feb. 10, 1975. This order was unanimously upheld by the Supreme Court on Oct. 30, 1975, on the grounds that the NAP had never reconciled itself to the existence and ideology of Pakistan; had attempted to bring about the secession of the NWFP and Baluchistan through insurrection, terrorism and sabotage; had, to destroy the idea of a single Moslem nation, promoted the concept that Punjabis, Pathans, Baluchis and Sindhis constituted separate nations, each of which had the right of self-determination; and had attempted to propagate hatred of Punjab in the other provinces. However, Khan Abdul Wali Khan, who had been arrested when the party was banned, was released on Dec. 9, 1977 (i.e. after the July 1977 military take-over), and Gen. Zia, the Martial Law Administrator, said on Jan. 1, 1978, that all charges of conspiracy against him and 15 other former NAP members had been withdrawn. Meanwhile, elements of the banned NAP had in 1976 formed the National Democratic Party (see separate entry).

On April 16, 1982, Khan Abdul Wali Khan had talks with President Babrak Karmal of Afghanistan in Kabul, after which he expressed his support for the (communist) regime in Afghanistan and his "concern over the war of fratricide among Pashtuns in their own territory which has been instigated by imperialism and the regional reaction".

The NAP was a left-wing party seeking to represent the interests of workers and peasants. It was a remnant of the Bangladesh National Awami Party, which also had a pro-Soviet and a pro-Chinese wing.

National Democratic Party (NDP)

Leadership. Sherbaz Khan Mazari (pres.); Zahorul Heque (s.g.).

The NDP was formed in 1976 as a successor to the banned National Awami Party (NAP—see separate entry), which represented peasant and worker interests and had taken a pro-Chinese line. The banning of the NAP was due to its alleged involvement in terrorist activities in favour of the secession of Baluchistan and the North-West Frontier Province. Having been a member of the Pakistan National Alliance formed in January 1977 (see separate entry), in February 1981 the NDP joined with other parties to form the Movement for the Restoration of Democracy (see separate entry) and has been active since in campaigning for early elections.

In March 1982 a leader of the NDP, Khan Abdul Wali Khan, was detained for three days along with others after attempting to organize a protest meeting in Peshawar over the murder on March 7 of Ardab Sikandar Khan Khalil, a prominent NDP member whose assailant was believed to have been a right-wing extremist. It was subsequently reported in May 1982 that the entire NDP leadership had been arrested at a meeting in Lahore.

Pakistan Musawat Party

Leadership. Mohammad Haneef Ramay (ch.).

This left-wing party was established in 1978 to advance the cause of the "rule of the people". The party's chairman was a former left-wing member of the Pakistan People's Party (PPP) who had in 1975 gone into opposition and joined the Moslem League in November 1975; on Sept. 21, 1976 he was given a prison sentence for creating disaffection against the Bhutto Government and making a speech calculated to damage Pakistan's relations with other countries and to cause disaffection among the armed forces.

Pakistan National Party (PNP)

Leadership. Mir Ghaus Bakhsh Bizenjo (ch.); Syed Qaswar Gardezi (s.g.).

This party broke away from the National Democratic Party (see separate entry) on June 1, 1979. Its chairman had been a leading member of the National Awami Party (see separate entry) and had been Governor of Baluchistan under Z. A. Bhutto's regime in 1972-73. The PNP refused to register with the Election Commission by Sept. 30, 1979, as required by an amended Political Parties Act announced by President Zia on Aug. 30, 1979.

The PNP stands for increased decentralization, with complete autonomy for Pakistan's four provinces and the federal Government retaining responsibility only for defence, foreign affairs and communications.

Pakistan People's Party (PPP)

Leadership. Begum Nusrat Bhutto (ch.); Dr Ghulam Hussain; Gen. (retd.) Tikka Khan (secs.-g.).

At its foundation on Dec. 1, 1967, the PPP described its policy as one of Islamic socialism, democracy and independence in foreign affairs. It was established by Zulfiqar Ali Bhutto, who had been Minister of Foreign Affairs in 1963-66 and had earlier held other ministerial appointments since 1958. Although he served under President Ayub Khan, he disagreed with the President over the terms of the 1966 Tashkent Declaration which ended the 1965-68 war between India and Pakistan and which Z. A. Bhutto regarded as a surrender to India. After leaving the Government in June 1966 he denounced the President's rule as "a dictatorship under the label of democracy" and, having failed to persuade the existing opposition parties to accept his programme, decided to form his own party. As a result of his propaganda campaign, which was accompanied by student unrest, he was arrested on Nov. 13, 1968, under emergency regulations, together with other persons, including seven members of the PPP and five of the left-wing National Awami Party.

He was released on Feb. 14, 1969 (with over 200 other political detainees), and the state of emergency was ended as from Feb. 17. He did not, however, take part in talks between a Democratic Action Committee (formed by eight other opposition parties) and the Government of President Ayub Khan. The East Pakistan section of the PPP was dissolved on March 3, 1969, because Z. A. Bhutto had failed to support East Pakistan's demand for full autonomy, but on March 10 he entered into a political alliance with the pro-Chinese wing of the National Awami Party led by Maulana Abdul Hamid Khan Bhashani, who had wide support in East Pakistan.

Following the breakdown of law and order throughout Pakistan, the resignation of President Ayub Khan on March 25, 1969, and the proclamation of martial law by Gen. Yahya Khan on the same day, the Constitution was abrogated, the National and Provincial Assemblies were dissolved, the activities of political parties were restricted by a ban on public meetings, and Gen. Yahya Khan assumed the office of President on March 31, 1969. Full-scale political activity was resumed on Jan. 1, 1970, but under a regulation which laid down inter alia that "no political party shall propagate opinions or act in a manner prejudicial to the ideology, integrity or security of Pakistan"; persons carrying arms would not be permitted to participate in political processions or public meetings; and no person should obstruct or disturb any meeting or procession of a political nature. In the first general elections held in Pakistan on the basis of "one man, one vote" on Dec. 7, 1970, the PPP gained 81 out of the 291 contested seats of the National Assembly (all but one of them in Punjab and Sind provinces) and became the strongest party in West Pakistan.

Following the secession of East Pakistan (as Bangladesh) in December 1971, Z. A. Bhutto succeeded Gen. Yahya Khan as President of (West) Pakistan and, in a Cabinet of civilians formed on Dec. 24, took responsibility for Foreign Affairs, Defence, the Interior and Interprovincial Co-ordination, with most other portfolios being held by PPP members. While martial law was maintained, the PPP Government introduced numerous reforms in the social, educational and economic fields and also a new interim Constitution (approved by the National Assembly on April 17, 1972), under which Z. A. Bhutto was sworn in as President on April 21—martial law having ended on the previous day when it had been declared illegal by the Supreme Court. In October 1972 the PPP reached agreement with the other political parties on a new Constitution providing for a federal and parliamentary form of government, and such

a Constitution was adopted by the National Assembly on April 10, 1973 (with all-party support). Under this Constitution Z. A. Bhutto relinquished the office of President on Aug. 13, having been elected Prime Minister by the National Assembly on the previous day. In the Senate, newly elected in July, the PPP held 35 of its 45 seats.

In a Cabinet reorganized on Oct. 22, 1974, Z. A. Bhutto remained Prime Minister and Minister of Foreign Affairs and Defence. During 1975, however, the PPP was weakened by the defection of a number of its leading members; among them, Ghulam Mustafa Khar, former Governor and Chief Minister of the Punjab, resigned from the PPP on Sept. 24, accusing Z. A. Bhutto of imposing a dictatorship on the country. Altogether two members of the National Assembly and 15 of the Punjab Assembly resigned from the PPP in September 1975. Others who resigned from the PPP were Mohammad Haneef Ramay (former Chief Minister of Punjab) on Oct. 15, and Rasul Bakhsh Talpur (former Governor of Sind) on Oct. 17; like G. M. Khar they had been founder members of the PPP. Nevertheless, in the general elections held on March 7, 1977, the PPP gained 155 of the 200 general seats in the National Assembly.

M. H. Ramay, who had joined the Moslem League, was on Sept. 21, 1976, sentenced to 4½-years' imprisonment (and a fine of Rs 50,000 or £3,000) for creating disaffection against the Government and making a speech calculated to damage Pakistan's relations with foreign countries and to cause disaffection among the armed forces. G. M. Khar later rejoined the PPP and was, in June 1977, appointed political adviser to Z. A. Bhutto, then Prime Minister.

The rule of Z. A. Bhutto came to an end in July 1977 when, after his conflict with the Pakistan National Alliance (PNA—see separate entry), his Government was overthrown by a bloodless coup by the Army under the leadership of its Chief of Staff, Gen. Mohammed Zia ul-Haq. Under the military regime a number of Z. A. Bhutto's political opponents were released from prison, among them J. A. Rahim (released on July 23).

The PPP's central committee then decided on Aug. 3, 1977, to participate in the general elections which were planned for Oct. 18, 1977 (but in fact never took place). Also during August 1977, several leading PPP members withdrew their support from Z. A. Bhutto, among them Mir Taj Mohammad Khan Jamali (former Minister of Health), who announced on Aug. 13 that he was forming an independent group which would contest the elections in Baluchistan in co-operation with the PNA, and also Rana Mohammad Hanif Khan (former Minister of

Local Government) and Syed Nasir Ali Rizvi (deputy general secretary of the PPP), who resigned from the PPP on Aug. 17.

On Sept. 3, 1977, Z. A. Bhutto was arrested on a charge of conspiracy to murder: he was found guilty and sentenced to death, with four other men, on March 18, 1978. Gen. Zia stated on Sept. 6 that Z. A. Bhutto was "an evil genius" who had been "running this country on more or less Gestapo lines, misusing funds, blackmailing people, detaining them illegally and even perhaps ordering people to be killed". On Sept. 17 ten other leading members of the PPP were arrested, among them four members of Z. A. Bhutto's last Cabinet. The arrest of Z. A. Bhutto was followed by demonstrations in his favour, in particular in Punjab and Sind. On Oct. 1, Gen. Zia postponed the proposed elections indefinitely mainly on the grounds that the election campaign had resulted in "a state of confrontation . . . between the political parties". Foreign observers, however, took the view that the real reason for the postponement was Gen. Zia's fear that the PPP would win the elections.

Despite mass arrests of PPP supporters, including the intermittent detention, or house arrest, of Z. A. Bhutto's wife and daughter, pro-PPP demonstrations continued during the next few months, and the death sentence imposed on Z. A. Bhutto was followed by numerous protest demonstrations. The military authorities arrested a number of PPP supporters, among them three former ministers and four former members of the National Assembly who were on April 6, 1978, officially stated to have plotted to blow up the Lahore High Court (where Z. A. Bhutto had been tried) and other public buildings.

Despite widespread international criticism, especially by other Islamic governments, of the death sentence imposed on Z. A. Bhutto, an appeal by him against his conviction and sentence was dismissed by the Supreme Court on Feb. 6, 1979 (with four of the seven judges rejecting his appeal and three upholding it). On March 24 the court implicitly recommended that the death sentence should not be carried out; nevertheless, and despite numerous international appeals for clemency, President Zia refused to commute the sentence and Z. A. Bhutto was hanged on April 4, 1979.

Following Z. A. Bhutto's execution, the Government then temporarily adopted a conciliatory attitude to the PPP, releasing some of its leaders from detention and lifting the censorship on its newspaper, *Musawat*. However, Miss Benazir Bhutto (Z. A. Bhutto's daughter) and Lt.-Gen. Tikka Khan immediately launched an anti-government campaign, and pictures and tape recordings of speeches of Z. A. Bhutto were sold freely.

Leadership of the PPP thereafter passed to Z. A. Bhutto's widow, Begum Nusrat Bhutto.

On July 25, 1979, the four men condemned to death with Z. A. Bhutto were also hanged. (Miss Bhutto alleged—as revealed on July 12—that her father had not been hanged but had died by accident in a struggle with officers who had offered that his life would be spared if he signed two documents admitting that he was responsible for the loss of East Pakistan in 1971 and that he had invited Gen. Zia to take power in 1977—documents which he had refused to sign. These allegations were dismissed by a government spokesman on Aug. 20.)

In elections to municipal and district councils held in Punjab, Sind, the North-West Frontier Province (NWFP) and Baluchistan between Sept. 20 and 27, 1979, candidates were forbidden to identify themselves with political parties, but those supported by the PPP were reported to have won between 60 and 80 per cent of the seats in Punjab and the NWFP, and to have been returned unopposed to many seats in Sind. In Rawalpindi, 31 of the 50 seats were won by PPP-supported candidates, most of whom had been imprisoned or flogged under President Zia's regime.

The PPP was one of Pakistan's four major parties (the others being the Pakistan National Alliance, the National Democratic Party and the Pakistan National Party) which refused to register by Sept. 30, 1979, under an amended Political Parties Act announced by President Zia on Aug. 30, 1979. On Oct. 16, 1979, the President finally announced that the proposed general elections had been postponed indefinitely, and all political parties were dissolved. The announcement was followed by the arrest of numerous political leaders (officially stated on Oct. 21 to number 372) and the banning of the PPP newspapers *Musawat* and *Sadaqat*.

A petition by members of the PPP seeking a declaration that elections to the National and Provincial Assemblies would be held under laws in force before 1977, power would be transferred to elected representatives of the people, and fundamental rights would be restored and military courts abolished was dismissed by the Supreme Court on April, 27, 1981. Meanwhile, Begum Bhutto and her daughter were detained in mid-March 1981, the former being released from prison and placed under house arrest in Larkana in July, as was the latter in December 1981. Gen. Tikka Khan, the PPP secretary-general who had been arrested in February 1981, was among eight politicians released to mark Independence Day on Aug. 14, 1981. Later that year the Government initiated legal proceedings against the Bhutto family for the recovery of approximately 5,000,000 rupees which had allegedly been misappropriated by Z. A. Bhutto for personal and PPP use during his period of office. In November 1982 a government medical board approved Begum Bhutto's request to be allowed to leave Pakistan to seek treatment abroad for suspected lung cancer.

From February 1981 the late Z. A. Bhutto's son Murtaza established a militant movement named *Al Zulfiqar* (see separate entry) to mount a guerrilla campaign against the Zia regime, but this organization operated independently of the PPP, which disclaimed any connexion with guerrilla activities.

Progressive People's Party

Leadership. Maulana Kausar Niazi (ch.)

This party broke away from the Pakistan People's Party (PPP) in 1978. Its chairman had held ministerial office in PPP administrations in 1972-77, when he was regarded as being conservative.

Islamic Fundamentalist Parties

Islamic Democratic Revolutionary Party

Leadership. Maj.-Gen. (retd.) Tajammal Hussain (founder).

The party was formed in 1979 with the object of contesting general elections planned for November 1979 and cancelled on Oct. 16 of that year. On March 6, 1980, Gen. Hussain was arrested and charged with attempting to induce members of the armed forces to rise against the Government. In a message smuggled out of prison he claimed that his "only attempt to change the Government was through legal means, by planning an Islamic revolution in Pakistan on the pattern of the Iranian revolution". On Feb. 14, 1981 he was sentenced by a military court to 14 years' hard labour, and his son and nephew (both serving officers) to 10 years each.

Jamaat-i-Islami

Leadership. Mian Tufail Mohammad (pres.); Qazi Hussain Ahmad (s.g.).

Dating from 1941, this lower middle-class, extreme right-wing and ultra-orthodox Islamic party advocates the establishment of an Islamic state in Pakistan. It won four seats in the 1970 general election (in Punjab, Sind and the North-West Frontier Province) and contested the 1977 election as part of the Pakistan National Alliance (PNA—see separate entry) opposed to the then ruling Pakistan People's Party led by Z. A. Bhutto. Following the military takeover of July 1977

it supported the police under President Zia's regime in their repression of anti-Bhutto demonstrators. Expelled from the PNA in 1979 (when it accepted representation in President Zia's Government), the *Jamaat-i-Islami* was one of three major parties which registered with the Election Commission by Sept. 30, 1979, as required under an amended Political Parties Act announced a month earlier.

Following President Zia's decision of Oct. 16, 1979, to postpone elections and to ban party political activity, *Jamaat-i-Islami* pressed for early elections and the ending of martial law while continuing to give broad support to the regime's objectives. In April 1982 a party spokesman said that co-operation with the Zia regime hitherto had been based on the expectation that democracy would eventually be restored. (For the activities of the party's militant student organization, see separate entry for *Jamiat-i-Talaba*.)

Jamiat-i-Talaba (JIT)

Leadership. Shabbir Ahmed.

The JIT, as the youth wing of the *Jamaat-i-Islami* (see separate entry), has sought to expand its influence in the universities, often by enforcing its views at gunpoint, and has been in conflict with other student groups in a struggle for control of the universities. The JIT is a rigidly orthodox right-wing Islamic fundamentalist organization strongly opposed to the emancipation of women and to liberal and Western influences in education. It stands for Islamic emphasis in the teaching of economics, history and other subjects. The organization is based on elitist principles, full members being known as "the pure ones".

In late 1981 and early 1982 the JIT was involved in serious clashes between rival groups at Karachi, Lahore and other universities, following which the organization's leader, Shabbir Ahmed, was arrested in April 1982 while boarding an internal flight in possession of a loaded pistol. In protest against the reporting of this arrest, JIT followers on April 23 ransacked the offices of two Lahore newspapers.

Jamiat-i-Ulema-i-Islam

Leadership. Maulana Fazlur Rahman (pres.); Maulana Mufti Mahmud (l.).

This fundamentalist party advocates a constitution in accordance with Islamic teachings. Formerly allied with the National Awami Party (which was banned in 1975), the *Jamiat-i-Ulema-i-Islam* was a founder member in January 1977 of the Pakistan National Alliance (see separate entry) formed to contest the March 1977 general elections against the then ruling Pakistan People's Party led by Z. A. Bhutto, its leader becoming president of the Alliance. Following the military takeover of July 1977, the party accepted representation in President Zia's Government in 1979 but continued to press for an early end to martial law and the holding of democratic elections.

Solidarity Party *(Tehrik-i-Istiqlal)*

Leadership. Air Marshal Asghar Khan (pres.); Ashaf Vardag (acting pres.); Musheer Ahmad Pesh Imam (s.g.).

Founded in 1968, on a platform of maintaining both Islamic and democratic values, the *Tehrik-i-Istiqlal* was one of the three major parties which registered with the Election Commission by Sept. 30, 1979, as required under the amended Political Parties Act announced by President Zia on Aug. 30, 1979. Previously it had been a constituent party of the Pakistan National Alliance (see separate entry) formed in January 1977 but had withdrawn in November of that year.

Although the *Tehrik-i-Istiqlal* was banned, like all other parties, in October 1979, its central working committee met in Lahore on April 5-6, 1980, and demanded the immediate ending of martial law, elections to the National and Provincial Assemblies and the release of political prisoners. Air Marshal Asghar Khan was released from house arrest on April 18, 1980, but was again placed under house arrest on May 29 after making speeches denouncing the martial law regime. On Aug. 8, 1980, Ashaf Vardag called for a *jihad* (holy war) against the Government and said that the only way to end the martial law regime was by co-operation between all parties opposed to it, including the Pakistan People's Party.

At a meeting in Lahore on April 5-6, 1980, the central committee of the *Tehrik-i-Istiqlal* demanded the immediate ending of martial law, elections to the National and Provincial Assemblies and the release of political prisoners.

In February 1981 the *Tehrik-i-Istiqlal* joined with eight other parties in the Movement for the Restoration of Democracy (see separate entry) to campaign for an end to martial law and a return to parliamentary democracy. Following President Zia's creation at the end of 1981 of an appointed Federal Advisory Council to act as a bridge between the martial law administration and a future Islamic democratic government, Mian Manzoor Ahmed Watoo (a leading member of the party) said that the formation of the Council was "a bogus stunt devoid of all meaning and content" and that only an elected assembly could have a mandate for constitutional change.

Other Parties

Moslem League

Leadership. The Pir of Pagaro (pres.).

This party, earlier referred to as the "Conventionist" Moslem League, was one of three groups into which the original Moslem League (which claimed independence for Pakistan in 1947) was divided in 1962. It continued to hold a dominant position under the regime of President Ayub Khan, who joined it in May 1963 and became its leader. However, in the 1970 elections, the League gained only two seats (in Punjab) out of the 291 contested seats of the National Assembly. Following the July 1977 military takeover, the Moslem League took a restrained line in calling for a return to parliamentary government and in July 1978 accepted representation in President Zia's Government.

In 1979 a faction known as the Chatta group, led by Khwaja Khairuddin, seceded from the Moslem League and joined, in 1981, the Movement for the Restoration of Democracy (MRD—see separate entry). Khwaja Khairuddin had, as senior vice-president of the League, publicly criticized the Government of Z. A. Bhutto and had thereupon been expelled from Pakistan, being regarded as a citizen of Bangladesh, where he had his origin, although he had opposed the creation of Bangladesh. While the Khairuddin group subsequently participated in the MRD's campaign for a return to parliamentary democracy, the Pir of Pagaro's followers expressed opposition to the holding of early elections on the grounds that circumstances were not propitious.

Pakistan Democratic Party (PDP)

Leadership. Nawabzada Nasrullah Khan (l.); Sheikh Nasim Hasan (s.g.).

The PDP was formed on June 24, 1969, by a merger of four previous right-wing parties, as announced by these parties' then leaders— Air Marshal Asghar Khan of the Justice Party, Nurul Amin of the National Democratic Front (and Leader of the Opposition in the previous National Assembly), Chaudri Mohammad Ali of the *Nizan-i-Islam* party (and Prime Minister from August 1955 to August 1956), and Nawabzada Nasrullah Khan of the West Pakistan Awami League (and convenor of a Democratic Action Committee earlier in 1969). In the 1970 elections it gained only one seat in the National Assembly (in East Pakistan). In 1977 it joined the Pakistan National Alliance (see separate entry). Nawabzada Nasrullah Khan, the PDP leader, was one of three opposition leaders arrested on Feb. 16, 1981, in a move by the authorities to prevent exploitation of student riots then in progress throughout Pakistan.

Pakistan Khaksar Party

Leadership. Mohammad Ashraf Khan (l.).

Established in 1947, this party became a member of the Pakistan National Alliance (see separate entry) formed in January 1977. Unlike some other Alliance parties, it did not become represented in government following the military takeover of July 1977. One of the features of the programme of this Islamic party is its advocacy of military training for everyone.

Pakistan Liberation Movement (PLM)

Leadership. Brig. Usman Khalid; Lt.-Col. Mohammed Ilyas Shamim (founders).

The formation of the PLM was announced at a press conference in London on Sept. 20, 1979. Lt.-Col. Shamim claimed on Oct. 26, 1979, that about 400 officers had resigned in the past month, and that the majority of the Army was opposed to President Zia. The PLM's aims were defined as being the ending of military rule and the restoration of democratic government.

Qayyum Moslem League (QML)

Leadership. Khan Abdul Qayyum Khan (l.).

This party was one of the three factions into which the original Moslem League (which achieved independence for Pakistan in 1947) was divided in 1962. In the 1970 general elections the QML obtained nine of the 291 contested seats in the National Assembly (seven of them in the North-West Frontier Province, NWFP). Under the regime of Z. A. Bhutto, leading members of the QML held high office; after being Chief Minister of the NWFP, the QML leader was a minister in various cabinets from March 6, 1972, to Jan. 12, 1977; Aslam Khattak, who had been Speaker in the NWFP Assembly, was appointed Governor of the NWFP on Feb. 13, 1973; and Jam Ghulam Qadir became Chief Minister of Baluchistan on April 27, 1973. In the elections of March 9, 1977, however, the QML retained only one seat in the National Assembly (which was subsequently dissolved under the martial law regime of Gen. Zia ul-Haq on July 5, 1977). On Nov. 15, 1977, the QML's leader declared that it had decided to co-operate with the Solidarity Party (*Tehrik-i-Istiqlal*—see separate entry).

At the outbreak of the 1971 civil war, which led to the breakaway of East Pakistan (as Bangladesh), the QML supported "maximum provincial autonomy consistent with a viable centre" but rejected any arrangement which jeopardized the country's integrity.

Separatist and Minority Movements

BALUCHISTAN

Shortly before the establishment of an independent Pakistan all the tribal chiefs of British Baluchistan decided on June 29, 1947, to join Pakistan, although Kalat (the largest Indian state in Baluchistan) was not represented at the meeting which took this decision. By June 1954 all parts of Baluchistan were merged under one central administration. However, from 1963 onwards there was widespread unrest and armed opposition to the Federal Government, which sent in troops to restore order. A Pakhtoonkhawa National Awami Party (PNAP), formed by Abdus Samed Khan Achakzai, took one seat in the Baluchistan Provincial Assembly election on Dec. 17, 1970, but the PNAP leader was assassinated on Dec. 3, 1973, his death being followed by riots which were suppressed by troops.

A rising took place in Baluchistan from April 1973 onwards, under the leadership of the National Awami Party (see separate entry) led by Khan Abdul Wali Khan. Although the rising was suppressed by military forces of the Federal Government by May 1974 and an amnesty granted to all persons detained in the province except those accused of serious crimes, the civil war continued and the Pakistan Government repeatedly accused the Government of Afghanistan of supporting the rising in Baluchistan.

During the first half of 1975 large numbers of rebel Baluchis surrendered to government troops, but the continuation of guerrilla warfare resulted in the province being placed under Governor's rule on Dec. 31, 1975. In April 1976 the *sardari* system in Baluchistan (and the North-West Frontier Province) was officially abolished, i.e. the rule of tribal chiefs with private armies and the power to administer justice and raise taxes was ended. Nevertheless, guerrilla warfare by tribesmen in Baluchistan continued in subsequent years, with six army divisions fighting against some 20,000 armed guerrillas (as reported in September 1976). Governor's rule was ended in December 1976 when a new Government drawn from Z. A. Bhutto's Pakistan People's Party was formed in Islamabad.

Baluchistan Liberation Front (BLF)

The existence of this armed group seeking the creation of an independent state of Baluchistan (one of Pakistan's four provinces and containing a population of about

3,000,000) was reported in February 1973. It was said to have an office in Iraq and a clandestine radio operating from that country, and to be supplied with finance and guerrilla training for separatist activities in Baluchistan. On Feb. 10, 1973, the Pakistani authorities seized some 300 sub-machine guns, 60,000 rounds of ammunition, 40 incendiary grenades and other military equipment at the Iraqi embassy in Islamabad, although it was not clear whether these arms were intended for the BLF or for a similar Baluchi movement in the south-east of Iran (see pages 168-69). The Government of Iraq subsequently emphasized its respect for Pakistan's sovereignty and territorial integrity.

Baluchi Students' Organization (BSO)

This banned militant separatist movement also stands for the creation of an independent state of Baluchistan. According to an Amnesty International report of November 1981, a leader of the BSO, Abdul Hamid Baluch, was hanged on June 11, 1981, although his appeal against a conviction for murder had yet to be heard. The trial had attracted particular attention because of changes in the prosecution case when the alleged victim of a shooting incident was found to be alive and well, his name being then replaced by another in the indictment.

Popular Front for Armed Resistance

Members of this Front conducted guerrilla warfare in Baluchistan province from 1973 onwards against the Government. In January 1975 the strength of these guerrillas was estimated at between 6,000 and 8,000 men who were opposed by up to 100,000 troops which held some 7,000 prisoners in camps. On Oct. 15, 1974, Z. A. Bhutto, then Prime Minister, claimed that organized insurgency in Baluchistan was over and announced a pardon for over 5,000 guerrillas who had been captured or had surrendered. In a Government White Paper issued on Oct. 19 it was stated that 241 guerrillas had been killed; the main cause of the insurrection was alleged to be the resistance of feudal chiefs (sardari) to the introduction of civil administration and social and economic reforms, and the rebels were said to have received support from "outside forces" (i.e. Afghanistan) seeking to cause Baluchistan to secede from Pakistan. Guerrilla activities increased again in Baluchistan from August 1975 onwards, and on Dec. 31, 1975, the province was placed under the rule of the Governor, and in April 1976 the sardari system was abolished. Nevertheless guerrilla warfare by rebel tribesmen continued in Baluchistan during 1976. By September of that year some 20,000 armed tribesmen were reported to be opposed by six army divisions.

"PATHANISTAN"

A claim to separate nationhood for the Pathans was first made in 1946 by political leaders of the then Indian North-West Frontier Province (NWFP) who strongly objected to a British proposal to group the NWFP with the Punjab. Among these leaders, Nawebzade Allah Nawez Khan, Speaker of the NWFP Legislative Assembly, declared on Dec. 16, 1946: "We frontier Pathans are a nation of 3,000,000, with our distinctive culture, civilization, language, literature, names and nomenclature, legal codes, customs and calendar, history and traditions, aptitudes and ambitions." However, the tribal assemblies of the leading tribes in the NWFP assured the British Governor that they were part of Pakistan, and a referendum in July 1947 resulted in an overwhelming majority in favour of union with Pakistan (and not with India).

The Government of Afghanistan had earlier asked the British Government to give the inhabitants of the NWFP (and also of Baluchistan) an opportunity to decide whether they would join Afghanistan or India, or whether they aspired to complete independence. On the other hand, Mohammed Ali Jinnah, the leader of the Moslem League, was strongly opposed to the idea of an independent Pathan state (and also to union with Afghanistan). The July 1947 referendum was therefore confined to the question of Pathan union either with Pakistan or with India, and it was boycotted by the autonomist Redshirt movement led by Khan Abdul Ghaffar Khan. The latter and also the Fakir of Ipi, a tribal leader in Waziristan in the NWFP, subsequently campaigned for autonomy, some of their followers being arrested in mid-1948; Khan Abdul Ghaffar Khan was sentenced to three years in prison on June 16 and the Redshirt organization was banned on Sept. 16, 1948. Following elections held in the NWFP in November-December 1951, in which the Moslem League gained an overwhelming majority, the provincial Minister of Education observed that the result had "buried the myth of Pathanistan for all time".

During later years the Government of Afghanistan pursued its claims to the Pathan-inhabited parts of the NWFP on the grounds that Pathanistan had "historically always been part of Afghanistan"; it also demanded, with Soviet support, that the principle of self-determination should be applied to the issue. In the 1970s responsibility for promoting the idea of separate nationhood for the Pathans was attributed in particular to the National Awami Party (see separate entry).

SHIA MOSLEMS

Shia Moslems constitute more than a quarter of Pakistan's population and have frequently been in conflict with the central Government on various issues. A Shia convention meeting in Islamabad in defiance of a government order issued on July 4, 1980, condemned *zakat*—a 2½ per cent tax on wealth levied under Islamic law on June 20, 1980, on all savings and deposit accounts of more than Rs1,000 (over $100), securities, annuities and life insurance policies—as contrary to Shia teachings. The convention led to a demonstration and a clash with police in which at least one man was killed and 13 were injured. On July 6 President Zia agreed to amend the tax laws, and on Sept. 15 it was announced that, although tax already paid would not be refunded, Shias would be allowed to claim exemption by means of a sworn affidavit before a magistrate.

Philippines

Capital: Quezon City (Manila)   Pop. 49,000,000

The Republic of the Philippines is ruled by a President who holds wide-ranging executive powers and is elected (under constitutional amendments approved in a referendum on April 7, 1981) for a six-year term by universal adult suffrage of all citizens above the age of 15 years. Legislative power is held by an interim National Assembly elected on April 17, 1978, by universal adult suffrage, with 165 elective seats being won as follows: New Society Movement (*Kilusan Ng Bangong Lipunan,* KBL) 151, *Pusyon Bisaya* Party 13, Mindanao Alliance 1; a further 27 seats were filled by 14 representatives of sectoral organizations and 13 cabinet ministers. A United Democratic Opposition was formed on Feb. 12, 1980, by moderate organizations including the Liberal Party, the *Pusyon Bisaya* Party, the Mindanao Alliance, the National Union for Liberation (NUL) and the Concerned Citizens' Group of Zamboanga City. Other political parties include the Nationalist Party (which had been the President's party before the formation of the New Society Movement formed in 1978) and the People's Power Movement—Fight (*Lakas ng Bayan—Laban*).

Legal opposition by moderate liberal groups has been increasingly ineffective, as these groups failed to nominate a candidate to oppose President Ferdinand Marcos in presidential elections held in June 1981 and unsuccessfully boycotted them. The two principal guerrilla organizations which, though not constituting an immediate threat to the regime, have in recent years engaged almost the full strength of the country's armed forces, have been the (Moslem autonomist or secessionist) Moro National Liberation Front and the (Maoist) New People's Army.

In a US State Department statement issued on Feb. 9, 1978, the Government of President Marcos was accused of using torture and "severe intrusions on individual rights", in that the imposition of martial law (on Sept. 21, 1972, but lifted on Jan. 17, 1981) had resulted in "the suspension of democratic forms of government and in the severe curtailment of human rights of individual citizens", and torture had continued although it had "declined in frequency". The US Government nevertheless continued its military and economic aid to the Philippines, and was also entitled to use its military bases in the Philippines (though under Philippine sovereignty) "without any limitations on their military operations".

A Committee for Political Prisoners in the Philippines announced on Feb. 18, 1982, that in the 1975-80 period there had been 307 summary executions and 268 "disappearances"; that despite the lifting of martial law in January 1981 "arbitrary arrests, torture, summary executions and disappearance of opponents" of the regime had continued; and that in December 1981 there were still 1,332 political prisoners.

Moro National Liberation Front (MNLF)

Leadership. Nur Misuari (pres. of central committee); Hashim Salamat (head of political committee).

The MNLF was established in 1968 as a militant Moslem organization in rebellion against the central Government with the particular objective of achieving independence or autonomy for the Moslem population of the Philippines within a defined geographical area.

Islam had been introduced into parts of the Philippines in the 14th century, mainly by Malays and by the Dayaks of Borneo, and it might have spread to the whole of the archipelago if the latter had not been colonized by Spain in the 16th century, when the Philippine Moslems were called Moros (after the Moslem Moors in Spain) and were ruthlessly suppressed. According to the 1970 census there were then 2,100,000 Moslems (out of a total Philippine population of 38,000,000) concentrated in the four southern provinces of Cotabato, Lanao del Norte, Lanao del Sur and Sulu; they were generally an underprivileged minority, inadequately schooled and poorly represented in public offices; only 29.1 per cent of them regarded themselves as Filipinos, and 21.2 per cent favoured secession from the Philippines.

In 1971 the *Manila Times* estimated that 800,000 Moslems were refugees evicted from their land by Christians. Up to September 1971 over 1,800 people were said to have been killed in clashes between Christians and Moslems within 18 months. During that period a Moslem "Blackshirt" movement was involved in clashes with armed Christians, but following an ultimatum issued by the military commander in Cotabato on Aug. 10, 1971, an agreement was reached on Aug. 19 under which the Blackshirts laid down their arms and Moslems previously expelled from the town of Baliton were resettled there after Christians had been removed from the town.

During this period of massacres and atrocities committed by extremists among Christians and Moslems, the MNLF emerged as a unified Moslem movement. The conflict was exacerbated by army intervention, and in particular by the massacre of 40 unarmed Moslems by army units at Tacub (Lanao del Norte) in 1971. This incident led to accusations of "genocide" made against the Philippine Government in the Moslem world, with Libya taking the lead in a movement to defend the Moslem cause in the Philippines.

The first armed units of the MNLF were said to have been trained in Sabah (Malaysia), whose Chief Minister (Tun Datu Haji Mustapha) was a native of Sulu, with Libya giving material aid. There were said to be between 15,000 and 20,000 Philippine Moslems as refugees in Sabah.

After it had been claimed by the Philippine Government on Dec. 18, 1972, that a peaceful settlement had been reached between Moslem rebels and the armed forces, a meeting took place on Jan. 3, 1973, between the President and some 300 Moslem leaders, after which the President ordered the cessation of military operations (except in self-defence) to enable dissident Moslems to take advantage of a selective amnesty and economic benefits under an offer due to expire on Feb. 26, 1973.

On an official Libyan initiative, the fourth conference of Foreign Ministers of the Organization of the Islamic Conference, meeting in Benghazi (Libya) on March 24-27, 1973, decided inter alia to appeal to the Philippine Government (i) to end immediately the reported repression and mass extermination of Moslems in the southern Philippines and (ii) to take prompt measures to provide protection and security for the Moslem minority and to resettle the thousands of refugees in their homes. The conference also appointed a five-nation delegation consisting of the Foreign Ministers of Afghanistan, Libya, Saudi Arabia, Senegal and Somalia to discuss the issue with the Government in Manila (which agreed to allow the delegation access to all areas of the Philippines to investigate allegations of persecution of the Moslem minority).

After the delegation had visited refugee camps and the scenes of recent incidents in the Philippines, President Marcos announced on Aug. 18, 1973, the creation of new administrative divisions in Mindanao (the southernmost of the main islands of the Philippines and the principal area of Moslem population) and the establishment of a council to help displaced people. Other government measures to end hostilities between Christians and Moslems included provisions for the teaching of Arabic to Moslem children, the codification of Moslem laws and the establishment of a Moslem bank and a number of cultural institutions.

Fighting nevertheless continued during late 1973 and early 1974. Following incidents in Cotabato province on Dec. 31, 1973, some 10,000 people were said to have fled from

137

their homes; 4,000 had been evacuated and another 2,000 had left from other areas while 3,800 refugees were reported to be concentrated at government relief centres in Cotabato and Zamboanga del Sur. On Feb. 11, 1974, one-third of Jolo City was reported to have been burned down, with up to 10,000 people having been killed or being unaccounted for.

At the fifth conference of Foreign Ministers of the Organization of the Islamic Conference, held in Kuala Lumpur on June 21-25, 1974, it was disclosed that Islamic oil producers had contributed aid to Moslems in the Philippines and that the Libyan Government in particular had been supplying funds to the Moslem rebels. In a resolution adopted on June 25 the ministers called on President Marcos to halt all operations against the Moslem rebellion and to negotiate a political solution with representatives of the MNLF, i.e. to go beyond the "socio-economic measures proposed by the Philippine Government" and to achieve "a just solution within the framework of the national sovereignty and territorial integrity of the Philippines".

In January 1975 talks were held in Jeddah (Saudi Arabia) between a delegation led by Nur Misuari of the MNLF and representatives of the Philippine Government, with the executive secretary of the Organization of the Islamic Conference presiding. However, on Feb. 3, 1975, President Marcos described the negotiations as fruitless and declared that his Government would never agree to the MNLF's demand for an autonomous state of Mindanao.

Although President Marcos had stated on March 18, 1973, that the Moslem rebellion had been "practically crushed", this claim was contradicted by later announcements. In April 1973 it was officially stated that in Mindanao 276,487 persons had been evacuated before advancing rebels, and at the end of that month the President himself said that "nearly a million people" had abandoned their homes in Mindanao. A conditional amnesty offer made earlier in the year was abandoned in mid-April for lack of response by the rebels. The government's forces were strengthened by various measures, including the setting-up of armed "self-defence units" by civilians and the introduction of military service for up to 12 months. According to the Roman Catholic bishops the rebels were fighting not only against the Christians but also against the Moslem feudal leaders (apparently supported by the Government) and for the redistribution of their lands.

During 1974-75 fighting continued, especially in Cotabayo province, in Lanao del Sur, near Zamboanga City and on Jolo Island. On June 24, 1974, the President announced a broad amnesty for Moslems who were prepared to give up fighting, and

also the appointment of a number of Moslems to national and municipal government posts, some of the appointees being former rebel leaders. On Nov. 1 he ordered troops to cease hostilities for two months in Lanao del Sur and Lanao del Norte. On Nov. 3 he offered an amnesty to "ideological subversives", including also persons who might have "committed illegal acts to promote political beliefs or enhance views about the social order, the economic system or the form of government"; those surrendering were required to give up their weapons and pledge their loyalty to the Government. On Feb. 10, 1975, he announced that he had ordered a ceasefire throughout the southern provinces of the Philippines. (By Sept. 16, 1974, about 1,000 Moslems were said to have surrendered in Mindanao.)

The MNLF subsequently boycotted talks between the Government and about 140 leaders of 27 different Moslem groups, which opened in Zamboanga City on April 17, 1975. The MNLF had stated on March 31 that the rejection of its demand for an autonomous Moslem state had closed the door to further negotiations; it regarded the Moslem leaders involved in the new talks as being "already in the service of the Marcos Government". In a statement issued on April 19, the Moslem participants in the talks rejected partition of the Philippines as a solution to the rebellion and presented a list of demands for reforms designed to bring about peace.

On April 21 President Marcos agreed to integrate former rebels in the armed forces, and he announced the establishment of two regional offices in Mindanao and Sulu under Moslems who would take over government administration in those areas, and also the allocation of US$7,000,000 for development projects in Mindanao. (The Islamic Development Fund of the United Arab Emirates allotted, in April 1975, $350,000,000 for development projects in Mindanao.) Some 500 rebel leaders met government representatives for further talks in Marawi City on May 11, 1975.

On Aug. 14, 1975, it was officially stated that Abdul Hamid Lukman (a former judge and legal adviser to the MNLF) had accepted a government ceasefire offer on behalf of the MNLF, and at the end of August President Marcos announced that successful peace negotiations had been concluded with A. H. Lukman, who had been appointed assistant regional commissioner for Zamboanga City, Basilan, Sulu and Tawi Tawi. Nur Misuari had, however, disowned A. H. Lukman on Aug. 19, when he stated in Tripoli (Libya), where he was living in exile, that the MNLF would not accept a ceasefire unless the armed forces withdrew from the south and that any agreement reached between A. H. Lukman and the Government would not be binding on the MNLF.

While numerous clashes between rebels and government forces continued between February and August 1975, the Government on Sept. 6 ordered a halt to operations against rebels in the south in order to negotiate the surrender of further insurgent leaders. On Nov. 10 another MNLF leader and 1,000 MNLF rebels were officially stated to have surrendered, the total of those who had surrendered since April 1975 being given as 9,000 (out of an estimated total of 16,000 MNLF forces). President Marcos stated on Jan. 22, 1976, that in 39 months of fighting 2,000 government troops had been killed and 4,000 injured. After more fighting had taken place near Zamboanga City and in Lanao del Sur, nearly 30,000 inhabitants were said to have fled from their homes by the end of March 1976.

During 1976 the MNLF denied involvement in the hijacking of two aircraft by Moslem rebels—(i) on April 7, when three men claiming to be MNLF members seized a Philippine Airlines DC-8 and eventually diverted it to Benghazi on April 8, and (ii) on May 21, when six men claiming to be MNLF supporters forced an airliner to land at Zamboanga City where, however, it was stormed by troops on May 23, with the result that the airliner was destroyed and 16 people, including three of the hijackers, were killed and 19 injured. The remaining three hijackers were condemned to death on Nov. 4, 1976.

Although further major guerrilla attacks occurred in June-October 1976, the acting chief of staff of the Philippines armed forces claimed on Oct. 28 that the situation was "under control". During that period 35 Japanese and at least four other foreigners were kidnapped by guerrillas who demanded ransom to pay for food and supplies.

Talks between the Philippine Government and the MNLF—arranged in November 1976 by Mrs Imelda Marcos (the President's wife) with Col. Kadhafi (the Libyan leader)—took place in Tripoli in December 1976 and led, under the auspices of the Organization of the Islamic Conference, to an agreement in principle, reached on Dec. 30, on the granting of a degree of autonomy to 13 provinces in Mindanao, the Sulu archipelago and Palawan Island and to the establishment of a ceasefire, to be effected gradually between Dec. 24, 1976, and Jan. 20, 1977. President Marcos announced on Jan. 4 that a referendum would be held in 13 provinces to determine which of them wished to be part of an autonomous Moslem region within the Philippines—but the holding of such a referendum was rejected by the MNLF. After diplomatic relations had been established between Libya and the Philippines early in January, talks were

resumed in Tripoli on Feb. 7, 1977, but were suspended on March 3 as no agreement was reached on which of the provinces were to be included in the proposed autonomous region. The Moslems were said to have demanded that it should incorporate three predominantly Christian provinces (Palawan, South Cotabato and Davao del Sur) because of potential oil reserves off Palawan and the rich agricultural land of the two other provinces, and also the formation of their own army and the right to their own flag.

After talks between Col. Kadhafi on the one hand and Imelda Marcos, Juan Ponce Enrile (the Philippine Defence Secretary) and Estelito Mendoza (Philippine Solicitor General) on the other had begun on March 10, 1977, and a three-stage peace plan proposed by the Libyan leader had been accepted, President Marcos proclaimed, on March 26, an autonomous region of 13 southern provinces (including the three predominantly Christian ones mentioned above) and announced the creation of an administration to govern the area provisionally and to supervise the referendum which was to decide on administrative arrangements for autonomy, to be followed by the election of a regional assembly. (On April 12 the President also announced that Nur Misuari, the MNLF leader, could return from exile in Libya to take part in the organization of a provisional government.)

The referendum, held on April 17, 1977, was on April 23 officially stated to have resulted in 97.93 per cent of the total votes cast in the 13 southern provinces (in a poll of about 75 per cent of the registered voters) having been in favour of rejecting autonomy for the region under MNLF rule. The MNLF had boycotted the referendum on the ground that no such consultation had been provided for in the first Tripoli agreement (of December 1976).

New talks which were begun in Manila on April 24, 1977, broke down on May 1 with each side accusing the other of trying to discard the first Tripoli agreement. Gen. Carlos P. Romulo (the Philippine Foreign Secretary) said on May 6 that the major obstacles which had resulted in the impasse were the MNLF's demands for complete control of the region, for the establishment of a separate army of 15,000 men and for the regional (i.e. not national) auditing of finance, as well as the question of MNLF representation in the Cabinet and in the Supreme Court.

A provisional regional government formed by President Marcos (under the provisions of a law of February 1977 dividing the Philippines into 12 partly autonomous regions) met in Zamboanga City on May 10, the MNLF having refused to take up the 15 seats (out of a total of 29) offered to it by the President.

At the eighth conference of Islamic

Foreign Ministers (in Tripoli) on May 16, 1977, the MNLF was "as an exception" granted observer status at the Organization. In its final communiqué issued on May 22, the conference expressed concern at the Philippine Government's policy towards the Moslems and charged its five-nation committee with pursuing "its mission of mediation between the MNLF, which is the legitimate representative of the Moslem people in the southern Philippines, and the Philippine Government". The conference also proposed the creation of a fund, to be financed by all Moslem nations, to assist Philippine Moslems.

Nur Misuari (the MNLF president) was at the same time quoted as saying that the MNLF had decided to revert to its original demand for total independence for the southern Philippines, a demand which (he said) it had abandoned "in a spirit of reconciliation" after the fifth conference of the Islamic Foreign Ministers in 1974. He added that the MNLF was prepared to resume fighting with the 50,000 men at its disposal; that it received no aid from Cuba, China or the Soviet Union but only from Moslem countries (whereas, he claimed, the Philippine Government was aided mainly by the United States and Israel); and that the MNLF was "a Moslem nationalist movement trying to free a Moslem country from the Philippine colonial yoke".

The ceasefire of December 1976 held for most of the year 1977, although both sides accused each other of violations, the MNLF being alleged to have violated the ceasefire 300 times and the Army 703 times, killing over 600 people. More incidents occurred later in 1977, with government forces launching on Sept. 20 a three-front initiative north of Zamboanga City, on Basilan and on Jolo. Two high-ranking army officers were killed on Oct. 10 and 13 respectively, and on Oct. 21 the MNLF claimed that the Army had massacred 400 civilians in retaliation, but this was officially denied. On Nov. 7, 1977, President Marcos announced that since 1973 from 30,000 to 50,000 civilians had lost their lives and 500,000 had been rendered homeless as a result of this conflict. In February 1978 the Defence Ministry stated that during 1977 over 800 people had been killed in various clashes, and in April 1978 the Ministry reported that over 2,000 people had been killed or injured in January-March 1978 in violations of the ceasefire.

During 1980 MNLF guerrillas continued to be involved in a number of raids and ambushes of government troops, while the Government claimed that several MNLF leaders had surrendered with their followers. These leaders were said to include Amelil Malaquiok (Commander Rony), who surrendered in March and was on April 1 appointed chairman of the standing committee of the executive council of Mindanao's autonomous region No. 12, and Jamil Lucman, who surrendered on Sept. 2 and was also appointed a government official. After the lifting of martial law on Jan. 17, 1981, restrictions still remained in force in several southern provinces where clashes continued to occur between MNLF forces and government troops. However, on Feb. 23, 1982, it was officially claimed that since 1973 a total of 46,000 Moslems had "turned their backs" on the rebellion.

Earlier the MNLF was reported to have split into three factions—(i) the main faction led by Nur Misuari, supported by Libya and with its main base in the Sulu archipelago, (ii) another faction led by Hashim Salamat, supported by Egypt and based on the province of Lanao del Sur (Mindanao), and (iii) a minor faction supported by Saudi Arabia. By late 1982 several leaders of the Nur Misuari faction were reported to have moved from Tripoli to Tehran (where the MNLF office had been granted embassy status in 1980) in view of what they regarded as Col. Kadhafi's lukewarm support for their cause. In the course of 1982 Nur Misuari himself spent much of his time in the Iranian capital and was assured by President Khamenei in June of Iran's full political, economic and moral support for the MNLF.

New People's Army (NPA)

As the military wing of the pro-Chinese faction which broke away from the Communist Party of the Philippines (PKP) in 1968, the NPA thereafter intensified guerrilla warfare against government forces, whereas the *Hukbalahap* (originally organized by the PKP as an anti-Japanese army during World War II) was subdued by government forces in the 1970s. The NPA was first set up by about 60 fighters in northern Luzon (the largest and most northerly of the main Philippine islands) led by José Maria Sison (who became chairman of the Maoist PKP).

In a report of Sept. 6, 1971, a Senate committee stated that the armed strength of the NPA was only 350 men and posed "no real military threat". However, on Nov. 13, 1971, President Marcos announced that 63 persons would be tried for attempting to overthrow the Government and to set up "a communist regime under foreign domination", and on July 9, 1972, he ordered a full-scale military offensive against the NPA in the Palanan area, about 200 miles north of Manila. Fighting between communists and army units continued in both northern and southern Luzon, and a number of bomb explosions in Manila during August 1972 were attributed to communist agents. The

President thereupon declared on Sept. 4, 1972, that his military commanders had warned him that, unless the national forces (including 618,000 men in the Army) were appreciably strengthened, the communist movement could overwhelm them within two years; that the communists were "eroding the will to resist of local authorities by political assassinations"; and that out of fear many people were contributing funds to the communists' "invisible government".

Further bomb explosions occurred in the Manila area on Sept. 12 and 19, 1972, and in a report published on Sept. 20 Juan Ponce Enrile, then Secretary of Defence, claimed that the NPA was planning to bomb the presidential palace and thus to initiate a revolution. After the President had, on Sept. 21, signed a decree proclaiming martial law, he was on Sept. 24 reported as asserting that the NPA had 10,000 "active guerrillas" and 100,000 sympathizers and was fighting on both major islands of the Philippines (Luzon and Mindanao). According to the Foreign Secretary (Gen. Carlos P. Romulo) the NPA and other left-wing organizations were "winning the sympathy of the masses" by "manipulating students and other young people by exploiting subjects such as imperialism, fascism, feudalism, partiality of judges, low wages, unemployment and even the distribution of aid".

According to an armed forces report of Jan. 12, 1974, the communists in the Philippines were then divided into three forces—the NPA, the traditional (pro-Soviet) Communist Party (which was recognized as a legal party in October 1974) and a remnant of the *Hukbalahap*; of these the NPA was regarded as the strongest and most active, having expanded its operations from the Cayagan river valley (northern Luzon) to the Visayan Islands, Mindanao, Panay and Negros. However, at the end of 1974 large numbers of communists were said to have surrendered as a result of a conciliation campaign by President Marcos, notably 1,700 communist insurgents during November, over 1,400 NPA members in early December and 1,200 PKP members at the end of December.

On Aug. 27, 1976, President Marcos and military leaders presented 25 captured rebel leaders, among them Bernabé Buscayno, the leader of the NPA, and Victor Corpuz, the NPA's guerrilla training chief, both of whom were sentenced to death on Nov. 8, 1977. José Maria Sison, the founder of the NPA, was captured on Nov. 8, 1977, in La Union province (125 miles north of Manila). It was stated at the same time that a more militant element had taken over the leadership of the NPA and wished to form a united front against the Government with the help of the "Christian left". The NPA was also believed to have a tactical alliance with the Moro National Liberation Front (MNLF—see separate entry).

(The "Christian left" consisted mainly of a minority of Roman Catholic clergy and lay-workers who sympathized with the NPA's policy of support for the country's peasants. On Dec. 23, 1973, a pastoral letter initiated by a "20-23 movement" among the clergy was read out in churches, protesting against arrests of Roman Catholic priests, nuns and lay-workers and warning the Government not to bypass basic human rights and due processes of law in its "current striving to bring about a new society". Further church protests were made against the arrest of a Jesuit priest and 20 of his students on Aug. 24, 1974, and against the conditions of detention and interrogation used in military camps against alleged Communists on Aug. 29, 1974, and Jan. 2, 1975. When President Marcos imposed, on Nov. 3, 1975, a total ban on strikes and lock-outs, he also prohibited foreigners, i.e. foreign priests and missionaries, from taking part in labour protests; this ban was opposed by over 3,000 nuns and priests in a letter in which they rejected compulsory arbitration as the only means of solving labour disputes and expressed their objection to the ban on strikes as a "violation of the basic rights of workers".)

In April 1978 the NPA began to instruct its unarmed supporters to seize weapons from government forces and to hand them over to NPA units, and in the following year it was reported to be extending its operations northwards from central Luzon and also to Samar (where, according to church sources, the NPA was tacitly supported by about two-thirds of the population) and to other adjacent islands. The NPA had also, in 1979, infiltrated the area of the Kalinga tribe, which it supported in opposing a hydro-electric project on the Chico River (a tributary to the Cagayan) in northern Luzon.

During 1981 the NPA extended its activities to further areas in various parts of the country, claiming to have 10,000 armed men, including 2,500 hardcore regulars; they were not known to receive any assistance from outside, and captured or bought their arms from police or army units. In the same year the government forces resorted to applying the "strategic hamlets" concept (first used by the British in Malaya in the 1950s and later by the United States in Vietnam), which involved the uprooting of families from their homes and lands and the relocation of about 250,000 people (mainly in the three Davao provinces in Mindanao); although the Defence Minister ordered the reversal of this policy in March 1982, there was no evidence that the hamlets had been dismantled. While the strategic hamlets exposed and immobilized some guerrilla forces by depriving them of their mass base, they also increased anti-government sentiments among the people.

In April 1982 the strength of the NPA in southern Mindanao alone was officially put at 1,300 regulars, 1,800 active support elements and 18,400 mass base sympathizers. The NPA itself claimed to have a mass base of 9,000,000 sympathizers throughout the Philippines. By May 1982 it was apparent that the NPA had not only extended the area of its activities but had also intensified its "liquidation campaign", in which nearly 150 local councillors had been murdered.

Philippine Communist Party (*Partido Komunista ng Pilipinas,* PKP)

Originally founded in 1930, the PKP was split in 1968 when the Maoist faction broke away from the pro-Soviet wing and set up as its military arm the New People's Army (NPA—see separate entry). It was officially announced on Jan. 7, 1973, that the police had on Dec. 26, 1972, foiled a plot against the President and high-ranking military officers by the central committee of the Maoist PKP and had arrested 31 party activists who had been operating from 20 different "underground houses" in Greater Manila.

Whereas the pro-Soviet PKP achieved legal recognition in October 1974, the pro-Chinese faction continued its underground activities and set up a front organization called the National Democratic Front which brought together Roman Catholic Church members (including many priests and nuns) and other progressive elements opposed to the Marcos regime. The leader of the Front, Sixto Carlos, had been officially listed for arrest after the proclamation of martial law in September 1972 but went underground and was in fact not arrested until April 1979, when he was accused of being a member of the NPA.

Smaller Opposition Groups

April 6 Liberation Movement

This Movement was named after the date of an anti-government demonstration held in Manila on the eve of the elections to the interim National Assembly on April 7, 1978. The Movement claimed responsibility for bomb explosions in Manila on Aug. 22, Sept. 12 (when five persons were killed and 10 injured) and Oct. 4, 1980. According to a statement by the Philippine Minister of Defence on Oct. 24, 1980, the group was part of a church-orientated opposition organization directed by the Movement for Free Philippines based in the United States (see separate entry).

Christian Community Movement

This small non-violent Movement was established in 1978 by members of the Roman Catholic Church in remote areas which had no priests or churches; some of its lay-workers became involved in the defence of the rights of subsistence farmers without legal title to their land and exposed to displacement by sugar planters. A number of the Movement's members were found killed, with charges of murder being laid against certain officials and soldiers.

Christian People's Army

The alleged leader of this group, Innocencio Espinosa ("Big Boy"), was killed, with three other members of the group, in a gun battle in Negros Occidental province on Jan. 18, 1980, when three further members were captured.

Hardcore

This terrorist group was accused of plotting to assassinate President Marcos, and its alleged leader, Prof. Ali Macaraya, was on June 24, 1981, reported to have been arrested.

Light a Fire Movement

According to a statement made on Oct. 24, 1980, by the Philippine Minister of Defence, this group was a member of a church-oriented opposition movement, directed by the Movement for Free Philippines (see separate entry) and was responsible for causing a series of fires in Manila during 1979.

Movement for Free Philippines

Leadership. Raul Manglapus (l.).

According to an armed forces report of Jan. 12, 1974, Raul Manglapus, a former Christian Democrat senator, was one of a group of right-wing opposition members who had set up a government-in-exile in the United States and who were "influencing foreign governments' relations with the Philippines". Following an explosion at a congress of US travel agents in Manila, attended by President Marcos and the US ambassador, on Oct. 19, 1980, the President ordered the arrest of Manglapus, whose Movement was said to have directed this and other bombings. On Nov. 3, 1980, Manglapus was charged with having conspired with others, said to be members of Democratic Forces, to overthrow President Marcos and to have planned to return to the Philippines to lead a "revolutionary government".

Movement for Independence, Nationalism and Democracy

This Movement was in 1981 reported to have agitated for a boycott of elections. During a demonstration in June 1981 four of its alleged supporters were killed by troops. Two of its officials—J. Antonio Carpo and Grace Vinzons Magana—were on July 4, 1981, reported to have been arrested.

National People's Democratic Socialist Party

This party had an armed wing called the Sandigan Filipino National Liberation Army. The Philippine Minister of Defence (Ponce Enrile) described the party in November 1978 as a "third force" underground movement which was winning a broad following among students, intellectuals and labour groups, using the New People's Army (see separate entry) to carry out various anti-government activities, and responsible for armed encounters with government forces in some areas of the central and southern Philippines.

Philippine Liberation Movement

The existence of this Movement was announced on Feb. 18, 1982, when the Philippine authorities accused it of being linked with the New People's Army (see separate entry), of being responsible for the killing of six policemen and of intending to assassinate President Marcos.

Philippines Civil Liberties Union (ULC)

Leadership. José W. Diokno (l.).

The leader of the ULC had been a senator, had resigned from the Nationalist Party on Aug. 31, 1971, and was arrested on the proclamation of martial law on Sept. 23, 1972, and held without trial until Sept. 11, 1974. In September 1975 the ULC issued a statement condemning the policies of President Marcos and the imposition of martial law, demanding that the latter should be lifted as soon as possible because it had worsened the political, economic and social situation, had reduced the country to financial "slavery" with a foreign debt of over \$4,000 million, and had led to the "dictatorship" of one man—the President.

Sandigan Filipino National Liberation Army—see National People's Democratic Socialist Party

Singapore

Capital: Singapore   Pop. 2,400,000

The Republic of Singapore, an independent member of the Commonwealth, has a unicameral Parliament of 69 members elected by universal adult suffrage for five years. Parliament elects a President of the Republic (for a four-year term) who appoints the Cabinet headed by a Prime Minister and responsible to Parliament. In elections held on Dec. 23, 1980, all 67 seats in Parliament were retained by the People's Action Party. Parties which unsuccessfully contested the elections were the *Barisan Sosialis* (Socialist Front), the Singapore Democratic Party, the Singapore Justice Party, *Pekemas* (Singapore Malay National Organization), the United Front, the United People's Front and the Workers' Party—whose secretary-general, however, won a parliamentary seat in a by-election on Oct. 31.

The leader of the People's Action Party, Lee Kuan Yew, has been Prime Minister since 1959. During the 1976 parliamentary election campaign the opposition parties began to allege that the Government had become authoritarian and repressive in character and that Singapore had become "a police state", but the ruling party stressed in its campaign that the Government had given Singapore the highest living standard in Asia after Japan and that the Internal Security Act had normally been used only against subversive elements known to be connected with communist organizations.

The Government stated on March 31, 1980, that only 34 persons were then detained under the Internal Security Act. Among detainees released earlier were two—Dr Lim Hock Siew and Said Zahari—who had been arrested on Feb. 2, 1963, for alleged "pro-communist agitation" and whose detention was suspended under an order (announced on Nov. 17, 1975) confining them to two different islands where they were free to work and live with their families and receive visitors other than former political detainees.

Communist Party of Malaya (CPM)

Originally established in 1930, the CPM was proscribed in July 1948 but pursued an armed insurrection in the Federation of Malaya until 1960, whereafter it conducted sporadic underground activities both in Malaysia (see separate entry under that country) and in Singapore (which seceded from the Malaysian Federation in 1965).

Five alleged members of the CPM were arrested in Singapore early in August 1975, when police seized a quantity of weapons. On Oct. 3, 1975, the Government announced the arrest of six members of a Mao Zedong Thought League, said to have been formed in 1970 by an underground group of CPM followers and to be in contact with the Malayan National Liberation Front (MNLF—see separate entry).

On May 27, 1976, it was officially announced that the police had uncovered a communist attempt to launch a new phase of "subversion and terrorism" in Singapore and that since January 1976 a total of 56 people had been arrested under the Internal Security Act, of whom 23 had been released after interrogation, 10 had been handed over to the Malaysian authorities, and 17 continued to be detained. The communist movement's branches abroad were said to have been established to recruit students from Singapore and Malaysia, and those detained were alleged to have links with an organization in Kuala Lumpur (Malaysia), with training camps in Johore (Malaysia) and with guerrilla groups in southern Thailand.

On Sept. 6, 1976, the Government announced that it had broken up an underground communist cell and arrested four alleged members of the Malayan Communist Youth League (affiliated to the CPM). In 1978 the CPM was reported still to be operating underground in Singapore.

Malayan National Liberation Front (MNLF)

Following the assassination in June 1974 of the Malaysian police chief, it was officially announced on June 21, 1974, that 30 suspected saboteurs and members of the MNLF (described as a branch of the Communist Party of Malaya, CPM) had been arrested. The MNLF advocated the re-integration of Singapore in Malaysia (which would be communist and pro-Chinese).

People's Liberation Organization of Singapore

Leadership. Zainul Abiddin bin Mohammed Shah (l).

It was officially announced on Jan. 10, 1982, that 10 members of this "Moslem extremist" organization had been arrested for attempting to overthrow the Government by force of arms (with the alleged support in men and funds of foreign powers) and that they would be detained under the Internal Security Act providing for internment without trial for an indefinite period. The movement's leader was said to be a member of the Workers' Party of Singapore (which had won its first parliamentary seat in a by-election on Oct. 31, 1981).

Sri Lanka

Capital: Colombo   Pop. 14,471,000

The Democratic Socialist Republic of Sri Lanka (formerly Ceylon) is an independent state within the Commonwealth with a multi-party system and parliamentary democracy. It has an executive President elected for a six-year term by universal adult suffrage; he is head of state and President of the Government and appoints (or dismisses) the Prime Minister and members of the Cabinet. He is also empowered to dissolve Parliament (a 168-member Assembly similarly elected for a six-year term under a system of modified proportional representation).

As at December 1981 seats in Parliament were distributed as follows: United National Party 140, Tamil United Liberation Front (TULF) 18, Sri Lanka Freedom Party 8, Ceylon Workers' Congress 1, independent 1. Legal parties not represented in Parliament are the Communist Party of Sri Lanka, the Democratic Workers' Congress, the People's Liberation Front (*Janatha Vimukhti Peramuna,* JVP), the People's United Front and the Sri Lanka Equal Society Party (*Lanka Sama Samaja* Party). Of these, the JVP led by Rohana Wijeweere had been banned after leading an attempt to overthrow the Bandaranaike Government in April 1971 but had regained its legal status in February 1977 and subsequently received formal recognition from the Election Commission in mid-1982.

In recent years extra-parliamentary dissidence in Sri Lanka has been mainly related to the grievances and demands of the minority Tamil community, against a background of frequent outbreaks of serious inter-communal tension between the Tamils and the Sinhalese majority (the latter comprising 70 per cent of the population).

The Tamil Minority

The minority Tamil community in Sri Lanka consists of (i) about 1,400,000 "Ceylon Tamils" established on the island for many centuries, who are centred around Jaffna in the north and among whom there has been widespread agitation for autonomy or the establishment of "Tamil Eelam", i.e. a separate Tamil state, and (ii) over 1,000,000 "Indian Tamils", descendants of workers on the tea estates, many of them being stateless, pending either repatriation or the granting of Sri Lankan citizenship under agreements between India and Sri Lanka not yet fully implemented: these "Indian Tamils" are largely unpoliticized.

In view of acts of terrorism committed by Tamil militants such as the "Liberation Tigers" (see below) the Sri Lanka Parliament passed, on July 19, 1979, by 131 votes to none, a Prevention of Terrorism Bill making murder, kidnapping and abduction punishable by life imprisonment. The Act was amended under a bill passed by Parliament on March 11, 1982, empowering the Minister of Justice to detain suspected terrorists for up to 18 months without a remand order from a magistrate. (The International Commission of Jurists, however, had on Dec. 14, 1981, described the Prevention of Terrorism Act as a violation of the International Covenant on Civil and Political Rights, and as unjustified by "political terrorism by a small group of Tamil youths".)

Liberation Tigers

This Tamil guerrilla movement has been active mainly in northern Sri Lanka. In 1978 it claimed responsibility for an attempt on the life of a politician (who had defected from the TULF) in February, and for the killing of four policemen on April 7 and of a police inspector in Jaffna; on Sept. 7, 1978, members of the movement destroyed Air Ceylon's only airliner at Katunayake airport (near Colombo). Following the arrest of a number of Tamils suspected of association with the Liberation Tigers and the surrender of others (including the president of the TULF Youth Front), Parliament passed, on

May 19, 1978, a bill banning the Liberation Tigers and empowering the President to proscribe any organization which advocated the use of violence and which was directly or indirectly connected with any unlawful activity. On July 11, 1979—by which time Liberation Tigers had murdered 14 policemen—a state of emergency was declared in Jaffna district and at two airports near Colombo; under the emergency regulations arson and attempts to overthrow the Government by illegal means were made punishable by death; however, the state of emergency expired on Dec. 27, 1979.

Tamil guerrilla warfare nevertheless continued in 1980; in the 10 days ended on Aug. 17, 1980, there occurred (according to government statistics) 196 incidents of arson, 35 of looting and 15 of robbery. A new state of emergency was declared on that day (Aug. 17), and 300 persons were arrested during the next two days. The state of emergency was, however, lifted on Jan. 16, 1982.

In May 1982 several alleged members of the Liberation Tigers were arrested in Tamil Nadu (southern India) in connexion with a shooting incident between rival guerrilla factions. Other incidents took place in Sri Lanka in June and July 1982, a leading member of the Liberation Tigers being arrested on June 15 and four policemen being killed and another three injured in northern Sri Lanka on July 2.

A nationwide state of emergency was reimposed on Oct. 21, 1982, at the end of voting in an election in which President Jayawardene was re-elected for a six-year term. In an attack on a police-station in the Jaffna area on Oct. 28 Tamil guerrillas killed two policemen and three civilians, bringing the official death toll of policemen at the hands of secessionists to 28 over the last four years. The state of emergency was lifted on Jan. 20, 1983, when six people, including two Roman Catholic priests and a Methodist minister, were charged with harbouring Tamil guerrillas in Jaffna.

Tamil Co-ordination Committee

This Committee, based in London, was in December 1981 alleged to be preparing a unilateral declaration of Tamil Eelam (i.e. an independent Tamil state) and the establishment of its own autonomous provincial government.

Taiwan

Capital: Taipei   Pop. 18,000,000

Taiwan, officially the Republic of China, has a President elected (and re-eligible) by the National Assembly for a six-year term. The National Assembly, the vast majority of whose members are life members elected in mainland China in 1948, has limited powers. The country's highest administrative organ is the Executive *Yuan,* whose Council (the Cabinet) is responsible to the Legislative *Yuan* composed of elected members. The Legislative *Yuan* is controlled by the Nationalist Party (Kuomintang) and the great majority of its members are mainland Chinese who have held their seats since 1948 (although some Taiwanese have since been elected to fill vacancies in it). In addition to the ruling Kuomintang, there are two minor legal parties—the China Democratic Socialist Party and the Young China Party.

The Kuomintang's approach to internal security questions has been largely conditioned by Taiwan's position vis-à-vis the People's Republic of China, where the Communists are regarded as having usurped the Nationalists' rightful authority over the whole of China in 1948. Mainly to guard against the threat of internal communist subversion, fundamental constitutional liberties have remained suspended under a state of siege which is to stay in force as long as "the Communist rebellion" continues on the mainland; thus public meetings, strikes, demonstrations, petitions and the "spreading of rumours" are forbidden. Although executions on political charges, which had been numerous in the 1950s and 1960s, became less frequent in the 1970s, several hundred people were still detained for political reasons in the early 1980s, including alleged "communist agents" as well as "rebels" of the Formosan Independence Movement.

In the late 1970s the Government adopted a more liberal internal policy, notably by holding elections to regional assemblies in which large numbers of independent candidates were returned. Nevertheless, the growth of opposition activities gave the authorities cause for considerable concern, and elections to the National Assembly and the Legislative *Yuan* scheduled for December 1978 were postponed until December 1980 (when the successful independent candidates included the wives of two recently-imprisoned dissident leaders). During this period resentment of the political domination of Taiwan by immigrants from the mainland (who formed only 13 per cent of the population) led to demands both for the democratization of the regime and for acceptance that Taiwan was now a state independent and separate from mainland China. The demand for Taiwanese independence has received strong support from the Presbyterian Church (with about 200,000 members), while in the absence of legal party opposition, pro-democratization opponents of the Kuomintang regime have grouped themselves around a number of anti-government magazines, notably the monthly review *Formosa*.

Communist Party of China (CPC)

With regard to Taiwan, the object of the CPC ruling in Peking has always been the incorporation of the island in the People's Republic of China (whereas the object of Taiwan's ruling party, the Kuomintang, has been its own return as the government of mainland China). Alleged agents of the CPC were arrested in Taiwan and sentenced to death or imprisonment on various occasions (pro-communist activities being a capital offence under Taiwan's Constitution), although the party does not appear to have any substantial underground organization on the island. On the other hand, a number of prominent persons have over the years defected from Taiwan to the People's Republic.

In August 1970 a military court in Taipei sentenced two brothers—Quintin and Rizal Yuyitung—respectively to two and three years "re-education" in prison for "spreading communist propaganda" during 20 years while they were publisher and chief editor respectively of the Manila-based *Chinese Commercial News* (by publishing reports of the New China News Agency and pictures of Mao Zedong); although born in the Philippines, they had been deported to Taiwan on May 5, 1970.

On Dec. 13, 1970, it was confirmed that a deputy director of the Broadcasting Corporation of China (i.e. Taiwan) had been arrested and had confessed to having been one of Communist China's principal agents in Taiwan for 20 years; on Dec. 10, 1971, he was sentenced to life imprisonment, while a leader-writer for the *China Daily News,* arrested with him, was given a five-year prison sentence, also for "communist propaganda".

Further trials of alleged communist agents in the late 1970s included that of Wu Chun-fa, who was sentenced to death in April 1979 and executed the following month, while 13 of his suspected associates received prison sentences ranging from two years to life.

Democratic Coalition Movement—see Formosa Group

Formosa Group

Leadership. Huang Hsin-chieh (publisher); Shih Ming-teh (general manager).

A monthly magazine called *Formosa* (this being the original Portuguese name for Taiwan) was founded in August 1979 by a number of opposition leaders (including democrats, socialists, feminists and supporters of Taiwanese independence) who had earlier in the year joined forces in a "Democratic Coalition Movement". Quickly reaching a circulation of over 100,000, *Formosa* pressed for a representative parliament, a free press, an amnesty for political prisoners and the ending of martial law; it also publicized the grievances of factory workers, farmers and fishermen. Its general manager, Shih Ming-teh, had been arrested in 1962 for his political activities inside the student movement and had served 15 years in prison before being released in 1977.

The magazine opened offices in all major cities of Taiwan, and the authorities regarded these offices as "cells" for recruiting activities with a view to obtaining political power; it was also claimed by the Government that members of the *Formosa* group had communist connexions. An application by the group to hold a mass rally of native-born Taiwanese in Kaohsiung (Taiwan's second largest city and its southern port) in December 1979 was refused by the authorities, but the rally was nevertheless held on Dec. 10 and led to riots, in which 182 civil and military police were injured. The authorities thereupon arrested members of the staff of *Formosa* and banned the magazine; by the

147

end of January 1980 a total of 65 persons said to have been involved in the riots were under arrest.

Eight of those arrested following the Kaohsiung disturbances were brought to trial before a Taipei military tribunal in March 1980, the state prosecutor demanding the death sentence for all of them. They were sentenced on April 18—Shih Ming-teh to life imprisonment, Huang Hsin-chieh (the publisher of *Formosa* and also a member of the Legislative *Yuan*) to 14 years and six others (including two members of the Taiwan Provincial Assembly) to 12 years each. The defendants (who claimed that their purported "confessions" had been extracted under duress) denied that they had attempted to overthrow the Government (a charge on which they were convicted) and that they wished to promote independence for the Taiwanese; they admitted, however, that they had organized the rally and that they favoured the replacement of the existing one-party state by a multi-party system. The judge stated inter alia that those who advocated Taiwanese independence were committing a seditious crime.

A total of 31 alleged participants in the riots were on June 2, 1980, given prison sentences ranging from 10 months to six years, and on June 5 the executive secretary of the Taiwan Presbyterian Church was sentenced to seven years in prison for having sheltered Shih Ming-teh before his arrest in Taipei on Jan. 8, 1980, while 10 other church members were given prison sentences ranging from two to seven years.

Taiwan Independence Movement

This Movement, mainly based abroad and regarded as subversive by the Taiwan Government, stands for an independent Taiwan ruled by Taiwanese (and not by the Kuomintang regime dominated by Chinese who came from the mainland in 1948). It advocates self-determination for the people of Taiwan and repudiates "all forms of dictatorship—Chinese Communist or Nationalist".

It was responsible for bomb explosions at the US Information Service office at Tainan in 1970 and at the Bank of America in 1971, and also for an incident in October 1976 in which Hsieh Tung-min (then Governor of Taiwan and since 1978 Vice-President) had his left hand blown off by a letter bomb. Although the Movement was effectively suppressed in Taiwan, it was reported in 1978 to be supported by many Taiwanese in Japan (where it had some 10,000 members) and in the United States.

The American section of the Movement—United Formosans for Independence—was believed to be responsible for bomb explosions in 1979 at offices of China Airlines and the Washington office of the Co-ordination Council for North American Affairs (the Taiwan Government's semi-official representative in the United States). It does not appear to have been active in recent years, however.

United Formosans for Independence—see Taiwan Independence Movement

Thailand

Capital: Bangkok   Pop. 47,800,000

The Kingdom of Thailand is a constitutional monarchy with a bicameral Parliament consisting of (i) a 225-member Senate appointed by the King on the recommendation of the Prime Minister and (ii) a 301-member House of Representatives elected by universal adult suffrage, and with a Cabinet headed by a Prime Minister appointed by both Houses of Parliament meeting jointly. The country has been under military rule since October 1976, with the principal cabinet posts being held by officers of the armed forces.

Elections to the House of Representatives held on April 22, 1979, when not more than 25 per cent of the electorate took part in voting, resulted in seats being distributed as follows: Social Action Party 82, Thai Nation Party 38, Democratic Party 32, Thai People's Party 32, *Seritham* Party 21, other parties 33, independents 63. Of the 301 members of the House of Representatives, 49 were on Sept. 9, 1981, stated to have been co-founders (with 42 other persons) of a new National Democracy Party (*Chart Prachitippatai*).

A 1952 act banning communist activities under pain of imprisonment for from 10 years to life was reinforced on Oct. 17, 1976, by an order defining "communist activities" as "any activities aimed at undermining national security, religion, the monarchy, and the democratic form of government with the King as head of state", nationalizing private property without fair compensation or setting up a social system under which all property was held to be common property; the order also empowered the Prime Minister inter alia to declare any area communist-infested and to prohibit people from entering or living in such an area; measures could also be taken to prevent food and other commodities from reaching communist organizations.

Left-wing Movements

Committee for the Co-ordination of Patriotic and Democracy-loving Forces (CCPDF)

Leadership. Udom Sisuwan (ch.); Bunyen Wothong (vice. ch.); Thirayat Bunmi (g.s.).

The CCPDF was formed in 1977 by the Communist Party of Thailand (CPT) (which then had a guerrilla force estimated of up to 14,000, as well as 15,000 members of village militia groups) and former members of the Socialist Party and the United Socialist Front (see separate entries). Its members included two former Socialist members of the House of Representatives, a former leader of the Nationalist Students' Centre of Thailand, a trade union leader and a peasant leader. After the invasion of Kampuchea by Vietnam in December 1978, and the resultant fall of the Pol Pot regime in Kampuchea, with China diverting its aid from the Thai Communists to the (Pol Pot) Red Khmer

guerrillas, fighting broke out in April 1979 between a pro-Chinese and a pro-Vietnamese faction of the CCPDF, with members of the latter seeking refuge in Laos in June 1979 with the object of setting up a rival communist party.

Communist Party of Malaya (CPM)

Activists of this Maoist party, mainly Chinese from Malaya who had entered southern Thailand, were by 1970 said to consist of about 400 guerrillas in Thailand's southern provinces (notably Pattani, Yala and Narathiwat) and 1,200 on the border with Malaysia. In these areas they were able to win the support of the Moslem community (constituting about 40 per cent of the population in four provinces). By the end of 1975 there were said to be about 3,500 communist guerrillas in the above-named provinces, some 1,000 of them being Moslem separatists. Military operations against the

149

guerrillas resulted inter alia in the occupation by troops of a camp for some 400 guerrillas on Oct. 1, 1975; guerrillas, on the other hand, destroyed, in May 1976, a camp for training village defence volunteers, killing 15 persons, and also attacked a police camp. On July 15, 1976, guerrillas raided Trang, a provincial capital some 80 miles from the Malaysian frontier.

On Nov. 10, 1976, a Thai-Malaysian general border committee decided in Pulau (Penang, Malaysia) to organize joint operations against the Malaysian guerrillas in Thailand's extreme south, and on Jan. 14, 1977, some 2,000 Malaysian troops entered Thailand for joint operations with the Thai Army in Songkhla province; most guerrillas were, however, said to have evaded contact with the joint force whose operation was concluded on Feb. 6 with the withdrawal of the Malaysian troops.

Under a revised border agreement signed in Bangkok on March 4, 1977, details were laid down for further joint Thai-Malaysian operations against the guerrillas. In a second such operation (in the Sadao district of Songkhla province) from March 14 to April 20, 1977, eight permanent guerrilla camps were officially stated to have been destroyed (one of them capable of accommodating up to 400 people). Further joint operations began (i) on July 4 in the Betong salient (projecting into the Malaysian state of Perak), a guerrilla stronghold since 1961, and (ii) on July 7 further east, after which it was announced on July 13 that the headquarters of the CPM had been captured. Although the Betong salient operation was ended on Aug. 10 guerrillas continued to be active in that area. Renewed joint Thai-Malaysian operations against the guerrillas were conducted in April-May 1978 and in February 1979. During 1978 the number of Malaysian Communist guerrillas operating in southern Thailand was estimated at 2,500.

Communist Party of Thailand (CPT)

Leadership. Udom Sisuwan (s.g.).

Established in 1952, the (pro-Chinese) CPT began guerrilla activities in 1965 in the north-eastern province of Thailand (on the border with Laos), spreading to the northern provinces and being supported by Meo tribesmen. In 1970 it was estimated that between 1,000 and 1,600 CPT guerrillas were operating in the north and some 1,500 in the north-east; they achieved a number of successes—killing 17 policemen and officials (whereafter the construction of a strategic road near the Burmese border was abandoned in July 1970) and also the governor of Chiang Rai province on Sept. 20, 1970. While in March 1970 there had been no evidence that they were receiving significant supplies of arms from China or

North Vietnam, their arms supplies greatly increased in 1971 when they began to use mortars, and their strength in the north-eastern provinces alone was said to have risen to between 4,000 and 5,000 men. These guerrillas also made raids on US air bases (used by aircraft bombing North Vietnam) between July 1968 and January 1970, in January 1972 and in June-October 1972.

On Sept. 17, 1974, the CPT claimed for the first time to have established "liberated zones" or "bases" but did not give details of their whereabouts. In October-November 1974 the CPT guerrillas claimed to have killed over 40 soldiers in the north-eastern provinces and to have destroyed four military posts, but the military authorities stated on Dec. 21, 1974, that 215 of the guerrillas had surrendered. It was, however, officially admitted in February 1975 that government forces' losses exceeded those of the guerrillas. In March 1975 martial law was imposed for one year in 28 provinces bordering Laos and Kampuchea, and this was extended for another year on March 9, 1976 (and reimposed on April 12, 1976, in four provinces where it had been lifted in December 1975).

On Aug. 5, 1975, the guerrillas' strength was variously estimated at between 5,500 and 8,000 men. On April 30, 1976, an army spokesman stated that in the past year about 500 members of the armed forces and the civil service had been killed by guerrillas in all areas. The CPT's radio station, broadcasting as the "Voice of the People of Thailand" (VOPT), it was believed from Yunnan in southern China, claimed on June 27, 1976, that in 1975 the CPT guerrillas had shot down or damaged 18 helicopters. Bangkok radio had, however, announced earlier that a fighter-bomber shot down on June 11, 1976, was the first Thai aircraft thus lost in peacetime. In heavy fighting between June 14 and July 4, 1976, government losses were given as 28 soldiers killed and 85 seriously wounded, and guerrilla losses as over 150 dead. On July 7, 1976, guerrillas made their first raid in the central plains area, overrunning an army outpost in Nakhon Ratchasima province (150 miles north-east of Bangkok).

After the coup of Oct. 6, 1976 (when the military National Administrative Reform Council assumed power) Communist guerrilla activity increased greatly; in December 1976 there were said to be 2,000 guerrillas in the north, 3,500 in the north-east, 400 in the central provinces and 2,000 in the south—all having been strengthened by former members of moderate left-wing parties. The VOPT claimed on Oct. 16, 1977, that in the year since the 1976 coup the guerrillas had carried out 717 attacks (compared with 450 in the previous year); had killed 1,475 government troops; and had shot down three helicopters and two other aircraft.

On June 14, 1976, the Thai Defence Minister estimated the total of Communist guerrillas at between 8,000 and 9,000. In an earlier government document of September 1976 it had been asserted that since 1966 over 1,100 guerrillas had received political and military training in Vietnam, Laos or China. By 1978 it was believed that some 1,500 Thai guerrillas were operating at least 15 bases inside Kampuchea with the active support of the Kampuchean Army (of the Pol Pot regime). Thai insurgents co-operating with the Kampuchean Army were said to have been responsible, between June and October 1978, for 42 per cent of all guerrilla incidents in Thailand and for more than half the civilian casualties.

However, as a result of the growing conflict between Vietnam on the one hand and China and Kampuchea on the other, aid to the CPT guerrillas in Thailand from all these outside sources was greatly reduced during the latter part of 1978. The CPT at first attempted to maintain a neutral position between China and Vietnam, with the party's leadership (many of whose members were ethnic Chinese) taking a pro-Chinese line, whereas many of the Socialists who had joined the guerrillas in 1976-77 adopted a pro-Vietnamese attitude. Some 1,000 pro-Chinese Thai Communists were on June 21, 1979, reported to have been expelled from Laos since March, while several hundred pro-Vietnamese CPT members sought refuge in Laos where they subsequently set up the *Phak Mai* (New Party—see separate entry). These developments weakened the Thai guerrillas, of whom 500 were on July 10, 1979, reported to have surrendered in the past three months.

The VOPT adopted, in a broadcast on June 7, 1979, a pro-Chinese attitude, accusing Vietnam of preparing to invade Thailand and calling on the entire Thai people, including all insurgents, to unite against Vietnamese "aggression". Further such broadcasts, calling for the formation of "a broad national united front" against the "Vietnamese regional hegemonists and their masters, the Soviet social imperialists", continued until July 10, 1979, when they were suspended without any reason being given. The Thai Government rejected the call for a united front on July 11 as an attempt to bring about a conflict between Thailand and Vietnam made solely to serve the ends of the CPT.

According to a report by the Bangkok correspondent of *Le Monde,* published on Feb. 23, 1980, the pro-Chinese CPT had condemned the policies of the Pol Pot regime in Kampuchea (which it had previously supported) and had implied that in the conflict with Vietnam (which had invaded Kampuchea in December 1978) Kampuchea had been the aggressor. On July 25, 1980, it was reported that many pro-Soviet Thai Communists (previously trained in Laos) had returned to Thailand. Altogether about one-half of the students and intellectuals who had joined the guerrillas since 1976 returned to Bangkok in 1979-81 as a result of disillusionment with the Chinese-dominated CPT. Udom Thonguai, a leading member of the CPT, surrendered in Bangkok on Dec. 22, 1980.

Despite these divisions and setbacks, guerrilla activities continued in various areas of Thailand. Heavy fighting took place in 1979 in Chiang Rai province (northern Thailand) where over 1,000 troops supported by artillery and aircraft launched an offensive on July 4, in which, it was claimed on Aug. 3, at least 100 guerrillas were killed or wounded, against 200 soldiers killed and 103 wounded; 35 other soldiers were, however, killed in a guerrilla attack on Aug. 25.

The CPT itself claimed in January 1980 that its forces had fought 518 battles with Thai security forces in 1979, especially in north and north-east Thailand and also south of the Isthmus of Kra. By September 1980 CPT guerrillas were said to be operating in 50 of the country's 71 provinces and to number between 8,000 and 15,000. Government forces' losses were given as 544 killed in 1979 (the lowest figure for four years) and 512 in 1980, whereas insurgents' losses in 1980 were stated to be 310 killed and 115 captured (with 1,372 having surrendered), including large-scale surrenders in Uthai Thani province, about 120 miles north of Bangkok, announced on Oct. 4.

The main areas of fighting were (i) in 1980 the southern provinces, where government forces were in August said to have gained full control of the Banthat mountain range and where joint Thai-Malaysian operations were conducted in the Songkhla border province against Malayan Communist guerrillas, and (ii) in February-May 1981 the highlands of Phetchabun (about 200 miles north of Bangkok).

On Dec. 22, 1980, Government forces had been reported to have seized the north-eastern headquarters of the CPT and its satellite camps. The VOPT resumed its broadcasts from southern China to CPT groups in south and south-eastern Thailand on Dec. 31, 1980. On Jan. 13, 1982, Gen. Saiyud Kerdpo, Supreme Commander of the Armed Forces, gave the total strength of communist insurgents in Thailand as about 7,000 men.

The commander of the 4th (southern) Army Region affirmed on April 18, 1982, that he would continue his campaign to destroy the CPT in that region, where he estimated the guerrillas to number 3,000 (and where government casualties in the previous two months had amounted to at least 40 killed and 200 wounded); he added that he would later move the forces to the extreme south "to neutralize Islamic separatist groups and Thai-based elements of the Communist Party of Malaya".

According to government sources quoted in November 1981 and March 1982, the CPT's main base for guerrilla warfare, established in Nan province (in northern Thailand near the border with Laos) in 1952, had been moved to Tak province (near the Burmese border), and Udom Sisuwan had been elected secretary-general of the CPT.

The Thai Army commander, Gen. Arthit Kamlang-ek, claimed on Jan. 23, 1983, that the communist insurgency in north-eastern Thailand had been virtually brought to an end. He was speaking at a ceremony in which nearly 500 CPT guerrillas plus several hundred dependants and sympathizers in Mukdahan province formally defected to the Government—this being the second such mass defection in the area within two months. Thai military officials claimed that the latest surrenders had reduced the number of CPT insurgents in the north-east to about 250 and represented a major success for the Government's new approach of using political persuasion rather than military force.

New Party (Phak Mai)

Leadership. Thoetphum Chaidi, Bunyen Wothong (leaders).

This pro-Vietnamese Communist Party was formed in 1978 by Thai Communists who had sought refuge in Laos after the split of the Communist Party of Thailand (see separate entry). The party's two leaders were respectively a former trade union leader and a former Socialist (and vice-chairman of the Committee for the Co-ordination of Patriotic and Democracy-loving Forces, CCPDF—see separate entry). By November 1979, however, the *Phak Mai* was reported to be divided into a pro-Soviet, a pro-Chinese and a non-aligned faction, and Thoetphum Chaidi returned to Thailand in late 1980.

On Jan. 27, 1981, *Phak Mai* guerrillas were said to have taken control of areas in and around the southern province of Nakhom Phanom. On Feb. 27 it was claimed that the *Phak Mai*'s headquarters ("Office 75") were at Wattai airport in Vientiane (Laos). The party's strength was variously estimated at between 200 and 1,000 members. The party was, however, reported to have been dissolved in September 1982 owing to mass defections.

Socialist Party

Leadership. Col. Somkid Srisangkhom (l.); Khaisaeng Suksai (deputy l.).

Until October 1976 the Socialist Party was a legal party which, in the January 1975 elections, had obtained 15 out of the 269 seats in the House of Representatives (but only two in the April 1976 elections). Composed largely of students and intellectuals, the party advocated land reform, the setting-up of co-operatives, state control of key services and industries, and the withdrawal of all US forces from Thailand. Following the assumption of power by the National Administrative Reform Council on Oct. 6-7, 1976, when all political parties were dissolved, numerous Socialists were arrested and some party leaders fled the country. Four of these, among them Khaisaeng Suksai, declared in Laos on Oct. 14, 1976, that, while the party had previously used only constitutional and parliamentary methods, this was no longer possible and that, since the "enemies of the people" had "first resorted to violent means to suppress and persecute the people", the Socialists were determined to wage an armed struggle until victory was achieved and were prepared to join with any "patriotic and democratic parties and mass organizations". This declaration was broadcast by the "Voice of the People of Thailand" (VOPT) radio station of the Communist Party of Thailand (CPT) on Oct. 21, 1976. Socialists subsequently joined the guerrilla forces of the CPT and also the Committee for the Co-ordination of Patriotic and Democracy-loving Forces (see separate entry).

United Socialist Front (USF)

Leadership. Klaew Norpati (l.).

Until October 1976 the USF was a legal political party which in elections to the House of Representatives. gained 10 seats in June 1975 but only one in April 1976. Support for the USF came mainly from the impoverished north-eastern provinces, and its aims were similar to those of the Socialist Party, with which it had an electoral agreement after the coup of Oct. 6, 1976, and on Feb. 10, 1977, a statement (similar to that of the Socialist Party of Oct. 14, 1976) issued in the name of the USF declared its readiness to wage an armed struggle against the military regime.

Former USF members subsequently took part in the formation of the Committee for the Co-ordination of Patriotic and Democracy-loving Forces (CCPDF—see separate entry). However, certain former USF members formed, together with former members of the Socialist Party, a Social Democratic Party of which Klaew Norpati became the leader and which was the only left-wing party to take part in the elections of April 22, 1979, to the 301-member House of Representatives provided for under a new Constitution which was approved on Dec. 18, 1978.

Right-wing Organizations

Nawapon

Leadership. Dr Watama Keovimal (l.).

This extreme right-wing Buddhist nationalist movement was in March 1976 reported to claim 500,000 members, to be supported by wealthy businessmen and politicians and to have links with the National Security Council and Thai military intelligence. During the election campaign of February-April 1976 members of *Nawapon* were involved in violent action against left-wing parties and moderate politicians. On Oct. 6, 1976, thousands of members took part in an attack on left-wing students at Thammasat University (Bangkok), which led to the arrest of some 3,000 students and the death of about 40 of them and to the proclamation of martial law, the annulment of the 1974 Constitution and the assumption of power by a National Administrative Reform Council consisting of high-ranking officers of the armed forces.

Red Bulls *(Gaurs)*

Leadership. Maj.-Gen. Sudsai Hasdin (l.).

This extreme right-wing organization, mainly of technical college students, was involved in numerous acts of violence against members of the left-wing National Student's Centre during the election campaign of February-April 1976, and in particular in a bomb attack on Feb. 14 on the headquarters of the New Force Party (a left-wing party formed in 1974 by a group of intellectuals opposed to the military regime). On Aug. 21, 1976, hand grenades thrown into the buildings of the Thammasat University by Red *Gaurs* killed two and wounded 36 persons. Red *Gaurs* were also involved in the storming of the university on Oct. 6, 1976, which led to the assumption of power by the National Administrative Reform Council. On March 11, 1981, the organization's leader, who was also the leader of the extreme right-wing Mass Line Party, was appointed as minister attached to the office of the Prime Minister, Gen. Prem Tinsulanond.

Secessionist Movements

Pattani United Liberation Organization (PULO)

Established in 1960, this Moslem secessionist movement conducted operations in the far south of Thailand, where Moslems constituted up to 40 per cent of the population in three provinces (Pattani, Yala and Narithawat). On Dec. 4, 1975, a bomb was thrown at a Moslem demonstration at Pattani, killing 11 and wounding 44 people; as the perpetrators of this attack were not arrested, PULO sent threatening letters to leading members of the government and to Thai embassies abroad. After serious unrest had continued in the three provinces the Government agreed on Jan. 24, 1976, to take action against alleged murderers; anti-government demonstrations nevertheless continued to be mounted until March 4 of that year.

On Oct. 9-10, 1977, four PULO members were arrested and confessed to being members of a PULO sabotage unit and to causing an explosion near the King and Queen at Tambon Sateng (Yala province) on Sept. 22, when 47 people were injured. During 1980 PULO terrorist activities, including arson, bombing and kidnapping, increased markedly; on June 7 PULO activists were reported to have killed five Buddhists in Mayo district; on June 30 PULO claimed responsibility for bomb explosions in Bangkok which injured 40 persons; and on July 19 PULO announced the start of a campaign against Thai embassies abroad. In a letter published on the same day in the *Bangkok Post* PULO accused the Thai armed forces of committing "genocide and massacres" against Moslems in Pattani and threatened further acts of violence, including the hijacking of aircraft. At the same time PULO was reported to have united with two other Moslem secessionist groups. On June 6, 1981, over 50 persons were injured in three explosions caused in Bangkok by PULO members.

PULO has demanded complete independence for those southern provinces of Thailand (inhabited by Moslems of Malay stock) which had been independent until they were conquered and annexed by Thailand (then Siam) in the 19th century. In 1980 PULO was estimated to have in the region of 3,000 members.

Sabillillah Movement

This Moslem secessionist group has demanded independence for Thailand's southern provinces with a substantial Moslem population. After a bomb had exploded at Bangkok airport on June 24, 1977, literature signed by members of the Movement were found in a suitcase containing a further bomb, which was defused.

Shan United Army

Leadership. Khun Sa (Chang Shi Fu) (l.).

This organization, its leader's private army, has been concerned mainly with heroin trafficking and related activities, but has also propagated independence for the Shan people of eastern Burma (a Thai people who had ruled most of Burma in 1287-1531). Military operations against its forces, said to number several thousand men, were carried out in northern Thailand in October 1981 and in January-February 1982, when one of its strongholds with a large arsenal of weapons was seized and over 200 of its members were killed.

Thai Moslem People's Liberation Armed Forces

This organization was formed in August 1977 as an armed wing of the Communist Party of Thailand (CPT) and as a separate organization from the Pattani United Liberation Organization (PULO)—for both of which see separate entries.

Vietnam

Capital: Hanoi

Pop. 60,000,000

The Socialist Republic of Vietnam (proclaimed after North Vietnam-backed Communist insurgents had effectively reunified the country by overthrowing the Government of South Vietnam in 1975) is, under its 1980 Constitution, "a state of proletarian dictatorship" in which the Communist Party of Vietnam is "the only force leading the state and society". It has a Council of State (the collective presidency of the Republic) elected for a five-year term by the National Assembly from among its members. The National Assembly itself is elected, also for five years, by adult suffrage. A Council of Ministers headed by a Prime Minister and also elected by the National Assembly is responsible to that Assembly. In elections to the National Assembly held on April 21, 1981, 496 candidates were elected (in a 97.96 per cent poll as officially announced on May 17, 1981), in 93 constituencies for which the Vietnam Fatherland Front (consisting of the political parties—i.e. the Communist, Socialist and Democratic parties, Catholics and Buddhists, trade unions and mass organizations) had nominated 614 candidates. (The Socialist Party, formed in 1951, consists mainly of intellectuals; the Democratic Party, founded in 1944, officially represents the middle classes and intelligentsia.)

According to a defector quoted on Feb. 2, 1980, there were some 700,000 political prisoners in Vietnam, among them many former South Vietnamese political figures held in re-education camps which in 1981 were said to contain some 20,000 people. Those in prison were said (on Feb. 5, 1981) to include 77 Roman Catholic priests.

Since 1975 an increasing number of Vietnamese have left their country as refugees, largely as a result of political persecutions, food shortages and the removal of much of the urban population of South Vietnam to "new economic zones" in which living conditions were, according to refugees, "appalling". Late in 1980 the Government was reported as regarding at least 750,000 Vietnamese as "unwanted", and by 1982 the total of those who had fled from Vietnam was said to exceed 500,000.

Front of the People and the Army for National Salvation

At a trial in Hue, which ended on March 6, 1980, a former Vietnamese soldier was sentenced to death, two others were given life sentences and unspecified numbers of defendants were sent to prison for from eight to 20 years for founding this organization, conducting propaganda and persuading people to flee the country.

National Front for the Liberation of the Central Highlands

The formation of this Front was reported from Thailand on July 21, 1981. It was said to have its own provincial government (the "Dega") inside Vietnam; to be composed of Rhade tribes from Dac Lac province and of other Vietnamese, Kampuchean and Lao hill tribes; and to be aided by China by way of groups opposed to the Vietnam Government operating from the territory of Kampuchea and Laos.

National Restoration Movement

According to a US intelligence assessment released on April 30, 1980, this anti-communist Movement existed throughout South Vietnam but was weak in numbers and without effective leadership.

National Salvation Committee

Leadership. Truong Nhu Tang (l.).

The formation of this Committee was announced in Paris in January 1981 by Truong Nhu Tang with the object of bringing together all elements opposed to the Vietnamese Government, including supporters of the former Saigon regime; he added in his announcement that the Chinese Government, with which he had had discussions in September 1980, had promised him unconditional aid. Also present at these discussions had been Hoang Van Hoan, a former member of the Political Bureau of the Communist Party of Vietnam who had defected to China in 1979 and had in absentia been sentenced to death for high treason by the Vietnamese Supreme Court in June 1980.

Truong Nhu Tang had been Minister of Justice in the South Vietnamese Provisional Revolutionary (i.e. Communist) Government from 1969 to the reunification of Vietnam in 1976, had fled from Vietnam in September 1979 and had reached France in March 1980. At a press conference in Paris on June 9, 1980, he said inter alia that he wished to fight against both "American intervention and the despotism of a corrupt Government"; that the (Communist) National Liberation Front, which he had joined, had intended to build "an independent, democratic, peaceful, neutral and prosperous South Vietnam" before unifying the country step by step; and that the North Vietnamese leaders had "rushed" the unification and had "instead of a policy of reconciliation and national accord conducted a policy of vengeance and repression".

Truong Nhu Tang declared that the (pro-Soviet) Vietnamese leadership was faced with four basic dilemmas—(i) ideologically, it was pursuing "a Marxist-Leninist brand of working-class communism" (although Vietnamese communism was a peasant movement) and had carried out a massive purge of peasant elements in the party, describing them as "Maoists"; (ii) economically, it claimed to be able to "build an advanced socialist society without passing through the capitalist stage" in the absence of any industrial basis; (iii) politically, it had committed "serious strategic and tactical errors"; and (iv) socially, the "party state"

was producing "a class of corrupt bureaucrats that broadens the gulf between the party and the people". He admitted that there was no resistance inside Vietnam worthy of the name and that the population of the south, although disillusioned, confined themselves to passive opposition; he nevertheless expressed the hope that he would be able to contribute to the development of a resistance movement which would accept "friendly aid free from political conditions" from the United States and China.

National Salvation Front

Members of this Front, said to have been set up in 1975 as an underground organization by officers and officials of the former South Vietnamese regime and by Chinese "reactionary capitalists", were tried in 1979 for conducting propaganda, plotting murders of government officials, hoarding weapons and forcing many Chinese to emigrate. Two persons, including the alleged chairman of the Front, were sentenced to death and 18 others to prison terms of from two to 20 years in Ho Chi Minh City (Saigon) on July 13. Another member of the Front was sentenced to death and 10 other defendants to prison terms of from 12 to 20 years at Cam Ranh on Nov. 28 (inter alia for organizing armed groups and enticing people to escape abroad).

United Buddhist Church

The acting president of this Church, Thich Thieu Minh, whose group at the An Quang pagoda in Saigon had opposed the South Vietnamese regime—without supporting the (Communist) National Liberation Front seeking to overthrow it—had been imprisoned by President Nguyen Van Thieu's Government in 1969. Following the Communist victory in 1975, he was arrested in April 1978 and was on Oct. 25 of that year reported to have died in a re-education camp. Seven members of the An Quang pagoda, arrested in April 1977, were tried in Ho Chi Minh City (Saigon) on Dec. 8-9, 1978 for "agitating against the military service law, and other social duties, discouraging Buddhist believers from joining revolutionary organizations and discriminating against participants in patriotic organizations". Three of the accused were given seven, three and two years' prison sentences respectively, and among the others the vice-chairman of the Institute for the Propagation of the *Dharma* (the United Buddhist Church's organization dealing with secular affairs) was given a two-year suspended sentence. The Paris office of the United Buddhist Church stated on Jan. 17, 1979, that 37 monks were known to be in prison in Vietnam.

A spokesman for the Church said in Paris in November 1981 that its leaders had been under pressure to join a new Buddhist Church of Vietnam established on Nov. 7, 1981, at a Conference for the Reunification of Vietnamese Buddhism. (The new Church committed itself to work for national unity within the framework of the Vietnam Fatherland Front.) On Feb. 25, 1982, both the vice-chairman and the secretary-general of the Institute for the Propagation of the *Dharma* were again arrested.

United Front for the Struggle of the Oppressed Races (FULRO)

This Front was set up as the political organization of the tribal people of the Central Highlands of Vietnam, known as the Montagnards, and has demanded autonomy for the 12 northern provinces of South Vietnam. The Montagnards had repeatedly risen in revolt against the Government of South Vietnam, notably in September 1964, when they hoisted a red flag with three yellow stars as the symbol of their autonomist move-ment, and in December 1965, when they temporarily seized several towns. In March 1975 FULRO forces led a Communist attack on South Vietnamese forces—the Provisional Revolutionary Government (PRG) of South Vietnam having promised the Montagnards local autonomy. By the end of the Vietnamese war on April 30, 1975, most new officials appointed in the Central Highlands by the PRG were said to have been drawn from FULRO. However, early in 1976 FULRO groups were offering armed resistance to the communist regime, and some groups of FULRO members were still engaged in guerrilla activities in 1979.

United Organization of Free Vietnamese in Europe

This Organization has claimed to represent 16 Vietnamese émigré groups. A spokesman for the organization declared in January 1981 that it would never recognize Truang Nhu Tang (the founder of the National Salvation Committee—see separate entry) as its leader.

3. MIDDLE EAST AND ARAB WORLD

Algeria

Capital: Algiers (El Djezaïr)   Pop. 20,000,000

The Democratic and Popular Republic of Algeria is, under its 1976 Constitution, a one-party state in which the ruling party is the National Liberation Front (FLN). There are an executive President (nominated by the FLN and elected, and re-eligible, for a five-year term by universal adult suffrage), a Cabinet headed by a Prime Minister, and a 281-member National People's Assembly elected by universal adult suffrage, also for five years, on a sole list of the FLN. In elections held on March 5, 1982, when three candidates were nominated for each seat, 136 sitting deputies sought re-election but only 68 of them were successful.

Internal unrest in recent years has been caused mainly by the activities of (i) Berbers opposing the Government's Arabization policy and (ii) Arab nationalists or Moslem fundamentalists.

Berber Cultural Movement

The Berbers, as the oldest inhabitants of Algeria, make up almost a quarter of the country's population, with a distinct language (Kabyle) and culture. Militant Berber students, protesting against the alleged repression of Berber culture, took strike action in March-April 1980 at Algiers University. Their action spread to other centres and culminated in a general strike on April 16. In counter-action taken by security forces against students at the Tizi-Ouzou University on April 20 and ensuing riots, up to 200 people were injured and 32 killed. The Government subsequently announced measures designed to appease the militant Berbers, promising in particular to create a chair of Kabyle studies at Tizi-Ouzou University and to restore such a chair which had previously been abolished at Algiers University.

Although continuing with its Arabization programme—designed to replace the hitherto French-oriented Algerian society but in effect giving advantages, especially in employment, to Arab speakers rather than speakers of other languages such as Kabyle—the Government announced in September 1981 that special courses on the Kabyle language and popular Algerian Arabic would be instituted at four universities, but not at Tizi-Ouzou.

On Oct. 28, 1981, one-year prison sentences were imposed on three members of the Berber cultural movement, arrested on May 23 and charged with rioting, while 19 others were given shorter sentences or were released.

Front of Socialist Forces (*Front des Forces Socialistes,* FFS)

Leadership. Dr Hocine Aït Ahmed (l.).

Dr Aït Ahmed was a leading Berber figure in the Algerian war of independence (1954-62) but later instigated an unsuccessful revolt in Kabyle against President Ben Bella in September 1963. In February 1964 the newly-formed FFS announced that it was resuming the armed struggle against President Ben Bella's "dictatorship". However, in this attempt it also failed. Dr Aït Ahmed was arrested on Oct. 17, 1964, and was on April 10, 1965, condemned to death, this sentence being commuted to life imprisonment. However, on May 1, 1966, he escaped from prison and he subsequently reached France, from where he repeatedly called for a "democratization" of Algeria's institutions.

In 1980 the Algerian state-controlled media asserted that the current Berber agitation against the Government's Arabization measures had been organized by "external influences", France and French-based organizations, in particular the FFS.

International Communist Party

Four men arrested in November 1978 were in December 1980 convicted of having formed a cell of this party within the Army, with the support of unspecified left-wing movements in European countries, and were sentenced to from three to six years in prison. The alleged leader of the group, Mohammed Benssada,

158

had fled to France and was given a 10-year sentence in absentia.

Moslem Fundamentalists

Towards the end of 1982 it emerged that Moslem fundamentalists (or "integrationists") enjoyed a measure of support among students in Algiers. In a clash between some of these students and others, mainly "progressive" secularists and Berbers, a young man (though not a Moslem fundamentalist) was killed on Nov. 2 and 29 people were thereupon arrested, most of them being Moslem fundamentalists. To protest against these arrests some 5,000 people rallied in the centre of Algiers on Nov. 12. In mid-December 23 Moslem fundamentalists were arrested and charged with subversion by distributing pamphlets deemed to be "against the national interest" and forming an organization aimed at destabilizing the state. On Dec. 19-20 some 30 people were arrested when they were found in possession of stolen explosives, bombs, firearms and false documents and administrative seals; in the government newspaper *El-Moudjahid* it was stated on Dec. 21 that these people had armed themselves to "fight progress by fire and blood" and that they had sought to "restore a medieval era and stop our people's march towards progress and prosperity".

Socialist Vanguard Party (*Parti de l'Avant-Garde Socialiste,* PAGS)

This party has replaced the Algerian Communist Party (banned since the country achieved independence in 1962). It has given qualified support to the Government since 1971, and from early 1979 onwards the Government tolerated its existence. In September 1981 the PAGS proclaimed a 10-point programme which included the "defence of the state sector" of the economy, the ending of "anti-democratic measures", the strengthening of co-operation with socialist states and an end to attempts to buy weapons from "imperialist countries". However, in April 1982 the ruling National Liberation Front (FLN) accused members and supporters of the PAGS of having infiltrated the National Union of Algerian Youth (*Union Nationale de la Jeunesse Algérienne,* UNJA), a congress of which, held on March 15, 1982, had been followed by demonstrations in Oran by students protesting against examination procedures.

The PAGS is recognized by the Soviet-bloc Communist parties.

Other Movements

The following clandestine opposition movements, set up in 1965-67, have not been reported to have been active in recent years.

Organisation de la Résistance Populaire (ORP), a left-wing group established in July 1965.

Organisation Clandestine de la Révolution Algérienne (OCRA), established in April 1966.

Rassemblement Unitaire des Révolutionnaires, established in 1967.

Mouvement Démocratique de Renouveau Algérien, established in October 1967 by Krim Belkacem.

Bahrain

Capital: Manama   Pop. 373,000

The Amirate of Bahrain, which has no Parliament and no political parties, is ruled by the Al-Khalifah dynasty, who are Sunnite Moslems, whereas the majority of the population are Shi'ite Moslems. Following the establishment of the (Shi'ite) Islamic Republic of Iran in 1979, Shi'ites in Bahrain were called upon to demonstrate against their Government by Shi'ites in Iran, some of whom claimed that Iran held sovereignty over Bahrain. The authorities of Bahrain thereupon deported a number of leading Shi'ites who supported the Islamic revolution in Iran, the influence of which is regarded by the Government as the principal current threat to Bahrain's internal security.

Al-Sanduq Al-Husseini Society

Some 50 members of this Society were arrested on June 22, 1980, after demonstrations to mark the end of 40 days of mourning for a Shi'ite leader alleged to have been killed in Iraq. The Society claimed, however, to be strictly non-political and to be concerned with purely religious purposes only.

Islamic Front for the Liberation of Bahrain (IFLB) *(Al-Jabihah al-Islamiyah Litahrir al-Bahrain)*

In a statement issued in Beirut and broadcast from Tehran on Jan. 15, 1980, the Tehran-based IFLB affirmed the independence of Bahrain as an Islamic state but denounced the Al-Khalifah Government for having had close ties with the former regime of the Shah and for having adopted an antagonistic position towards the Islamic revolution in Iran and its leader. The statement listed a number of measures alleged to have been taken by the Bahraini authorities against supporters of the Islamic revolution and Iranian interests; it accused these authorities of allowing the United States to use Bahrain's civil airport as a base for US military aircraft; and it called "on all Moslems to support the Moslem Bahraini masses in their struggle against the US and Zionist oppressors".

Between Dec. 13 and 19, 1981, the Bahraini authorities announced that 60 members of the IFLB had been arrested (comprising Bahraini citizens and other Gulf nationals) who had come to Bahrain after receiving military training in Iran and in order to carry out sabotage and create anarchy. On Dec. 30 it was reported that this sabotage plan had been masterminded by Hojatoleslam Hadi al-Mudarasi, who had earlier been deported from Bahrain and had thereafter been appointed director of a "Gulf affairs section" of the Iranian Government. The trial of 73 people charged with involvement in the plot (60 Bahrainis, 11 Saudi Arabians, one Kuwaiti and one Omani) subsequently opened on March 13, 1982, and concluded on May 23 with the conviction of all the defendants, three of whom were sentenced to life imprisonment and the remainder to terms of between seven and 15 years.

National Liberation Front of Bahrain

This Front has maintained close relations with the Communist parties of the Soviet-bloc countries.

Djibouti

Capital: Djibouti   Pop. 250,000

The Republic of Djibouti has a President (elected for a six-year term by universal adult suffrage), a Prime Minister who heads a Cabinet, and a 65-member Chamber of Deputies (also elected by universal adult suffrage). In elections held on May 21, 1982, all 65 candidates were elected to the Chamber on a list of the ruling *Rassemblement pour le Progrès* (RPP); the list did not contain the names of 10 previous members of the Chamber who had, in August 1981, been involved in the formation of a new opposition party, the *Parti Populaire Djiboutien* (PPD). Most of the PPD members belonged to the Afar minority (constituting about 35 per cent of the population); an attempt by the PPD to be officially registered was nullified by the adoption by the Chamber on Oct. 19, 1981, of a law providing for the adoption of a one-party system, which was implemented under a further law according the RPP the status of the country's sole legal party.

The two illegal parties mentioned below, both based on the Afar minority, do not appear to have been active in recent years.

Democratic Front for the Liberation of Djibouti (*Front Démocratique pour la Libération de Djibouti,* PDLP)

Leadership. Mohamed Kamil Ali (sec.).

This illegal Front was formed in 1979 by a merger of two Afar groups—the Popular Liberation Movement (*Mouvement Populaire de Libération,* MPL) and a faction of the *Union Nationale pour l'Indépendance* (UNI), which party had been in office until 1977. The MPL, a Marxist-Leninist movement among the Afar minority and based in Ethiopia, had been involved in violent action inside Djibouti, especially in 1977. At the achievement of Djibouti's independence on June 27, 1977, the MPL and the UNI held a celebration separate from that of the Government. On Dec. 16, 1977, the President of Djibouti claimed that the Government of Ethiopia was responsible for arming Afar terrorists in Djibouti, and he announced that the MPL had been banned.

There have been no reports of further activities of this Front since it was banned by the Government in December 1977.

Movement for the Liberation of Djibouti (*Mouvement pour la Libération de Djibouti,* MLD)

Leadership. Shehem Daoud (l.).

Established in 1964, this illegal Afar party, operating from Dire Dawa (Ethiopia), was, from its early days, supported by Ethiopia; during the French colonial period, the latter country had maintained a territorial claim against Djibouti. Together with the (Marxist-Leninist) *Mouvement Populaire de Libération* (see under Democratic Front for the Liberation of Djibouti) the MLD boycotted a conference held in Paris in February-March 1977 to prepare for Djibouti's independence (which was achieved on June 27, 1977). Nevertheless, the MLD agreed in principle, at a conference held in Accra (Ghana) on March 28-April 1, 1977, to the formation of a United Patriotic Front by five of the territory's major political groups—later established as the *Rassemblement Populaire pour l'Indépendance,* the only organization presenting candidates for subsequent elections to the Chamber of Deputies.

Egypt

Capital: Cairo

Pop. 42,636,000

Under its 1971 Constitution as subsequently amended, the Arab Republic of Egypt is "a democratic and socialist state" with a limited system of party pluralism. There is a People's Assembly of whose 392 members 382 are directly elected by universal adult suffrage (and the remaining 10 are appointed by the President of the Republic), and in which the ruling National Democratic Party (NDP) obtained 330 seats in the 1979 elections (while the principal opposition party, the Socialist Labour Party, gained 28 seats, of which 13 were lost to the party by the defection of its members on Nov. 27, 1980). There is also a Consultative Council in which the NDP holds all 140 elective seats (another 70 being filled by the President). The franchise was restricted under a set of principles approved in a referendum in May 1978, providing that the right to belong to political parties and engage in political activities did not apply to those who had "participated in the corruption of political life" before the 1952 revolution or to those convicted of political offences or proved to have "carried out actions tending to corrupt political life or to subject the national unity or social peace to danger".

Under a code of ethics ("law of shame") approved by the People's Assembly on April 29, 1980, newly defined punishable offences included the inciting of opposition to the state's economic, political and social system and the dissemination of "false" or "extremist" statements deemed to have endangered national unity or social peace. Penalties proposed were imprisonment, fines, house arrest, suspension from political activity, dismissal from employment in the service of the state and restrictions on overseas travel.

Among groups opposing the Egyptian regime, the Moslem Brotherhood has been the most powerful, and its Islamic fundamentalism has been supported also by many small militant groups intent upon the violent removal of the state's leadership, one of them being held responsible for the assassination of President Sadat in October 1981. Communist and other left-wing groups have also been involved in acts of violence, particularly in protest against the Government's post-1977 policy of rapprochement with Israel. In addition, the Government has been faced with hostility by groups of former politicians and military men calling for the abandonment of Egypt's pro-Western policies and a return to closer relations with the Soviet Union. Moreover, in 1981 President Sadat was also in conflict with the leading clergy of the Coptic Orthodox Church.

Moslem Fundamentalist Groups

Moslem Brotherhood *(Ikhwani)*

Leadership. Omar Telmessani ("supreme guide").

Founded in Ismailia in 1928 by Shaikh Hassan Al-Banna as a society of religious resurgence, the Moslem Brotherhood claimed, in the early 1950s, a membership of 2,000,000 throughout the Arab world. At that time it was said to have a terrorist wing known as the Secret Organ. In Egypt the Brotherhood was suppressed in 1948 by the then Prime Minister, Nokrashy Pasha, who was subsequently assassinated by one of its members. Shaikh Al-Banna was himself murdered in 1949, allegedly by agents of King Farouk of Egypt.

The Brotherhood was legalized by the Wafdist Government in 1951. In the following year it welcomed the officer's coup which overthrew the monarchy but it later adopted an increasingly hostile attitude to the Neguib Government. On Jan. 13, 1954, the Govern-

162

ment ordered the dissolution of the Brotherhood and temporarily arrested some 450 of its members, among them Dr Hassan el-Hodeiby, its supreme guide, after clashes between Brotherhood supporters and pro-government demonstrators. The Brotherhood's dissolution was, however, revoked on July 8, 1954.

Following an unsuccessful attempt to assassinate Gamal Abdel Nasser on Oct. 26, 1954, the Brotherhood was again dissolved on Oct. 29 and death sentences were passed on Dec. 4 of that year on seven of its leading members, among them Dr el-Hodeiby (whose sentence was commuted to life imprisonment), and six other members of the Brotherhood's executive were given life sentences. On Dec. 12, 1954, four more members were condemned to death for complicity in the plot to overthrow the Government and in terrorist activities, and another 26 were given hard-labour sentences ranging from 10 years to life (the death sentences being later commuted to life imprisonment). Meanwhile, President Neguib had been deposed by Nasser on Nov. 14, 1954, after it had been alleged that he had been involved in a conspiracy by the Moslem Brotherhood. Between Dec. 14, 1954, and Jan. 19, 1955, another 15 members of the Brotherhood were condemned to death and over 300 to imprisonment for from five years to life—but all the death sentences were commuted to life imprisonment. At the same time thousands of its supporters were said to have been imprisoned or interned without trial.

In 1964, however, an amnesty was declared and Brotherhood adherents (as well as communists) were released. In order to counteract the influence of communists, a number of Brotherhood members were appointed to official posts, and some of these played a leading role in anti-government plots uncovered in 1965 and followed by a new wave of trials and wholesale arrests between July 1965 and January 1966. The trials, one of them on charges of plotting to assassinate President Nasser, resulted in numerous sentences of death or imprisonment but only three of the death sentences were eventually carried out.

In the wake of Egypt's defeat by Israel in 1967, the Moslem Brotherhood was revived in Egypt, and President Sadat (who succeeded President Nasser in 1970) gradually came to regard it as a natural ally against the Nasserite socialists and the communists. After the 1973 war, however, President Sadat reorientated his policies, adopted the "open door" approach to Western investors and a policy of political alignment with the United States, leading eventually to the signature of a peace treaty with Israel in 1979. These changes provoked renewed opposition by all Islamic fundamentalist organizations, among which the Moslem Brotherhood in particular published increasingly harsh criticism of the President's policies and offered a detailed political alternative based on Islamic law.

The Moslem Brotherhood was able to rally considerable support, particularly in the universities, and openly called for the creation of an Islamic government. Its influence was further strengthened by the social disruption caused by the increasing Westernization of Arab countries, the growing strength of the Arabs through oil wealth and later the Islamic revolution in Iran. The Brotherhood also infiltrated the Egyptian Army, where its strength was, however, estimated not to exceed 1 per cent of the forces. No Moslem Brotherhood candidates were allowed to take part in the People's Assembly elections of October-November 1976 or in those of June 1979.

After the assassination of President Sadat in October 1981 and the arrest of many hundreds of Islamic fundamentalists, suspected Brotherhood sympathizers were purged from the armed forces, 30 officers and 104 conscripts being transferred to civilian posts (as announced on Oct. 19, 1981). Thereafter security clamp-downs on Islamic fundamentalists tended to be concentrated on an array of smaller groupings rather than on the Brotherhood as such, and from mid-1982 there were indications that the Government had adopted a policy of encouraging the Brotherhood as a moderate alternative to the more extreme fundamentalist groups.

Atonement and Holy Flight from Sin (Al Takfir Wal Hijira)

Leadership. Shukri Ahmed Mustapha (founder).

This movement was established in 1971 after breaking away from a clandestine Islamic Liberation Party active in several Arab countries. Following an attack on the Egyptian Military Academy in Heliopolis in 1974, *Al Takfir Wal Hijira* was accused of having organized an attempted coup to overthrow the Government of President Sadat. In 1975 a number of its members were arrested after burning Moslem shrines in the Nile delta. In August 1976, when it was estimated to have 500 members, the movement was said to have been dismantled by the police. However, it was thought to have participated in the food riots of January 1977—the most serious disturbances since 1953, causing at least 79 deaths—which were in part directed against luxury establishments disapproved of by strict Moslems.

On July 3, 1977, the movement claimed responsibility for the assassination of Dr Mohammed el-Dahabi (a former Minister of Islamic Affairs), and several of its members were subsequently hanged, while its founder was given a six-month prison sentence. It was also held responsible for planting bombs at Dr Dahabi's funeral on July 6 and at Mansura (in the Nile delta) on July 14-15, 1977. The Egyptian Government claimed on July 20, 1977, that the movement had received money and arms from Libya for the abduction and murder of prominent persons and members of President Sadat's Government, but this was officially denied in Libya.

Those arrested in connexion with the assassination of President Sadat on Oct. 6, 1981, were said to be members of a group (*Al-Jihad* or "Holy War"—see separate entry) loosely associated with *Al Takfir Wal Hijira*, 230 suspected members of which were subsequently detained for planning assassinations and other acts of violence, including an uprising in Asyut on Oct. 8-11, when 50 people were reported killed and some 100 injured. Further arrests of members of the movement were announced by the Government in mid-1982, it being officially stated on June 13 that the security forces had broken up over 30 fundamentalist groups over the previous few months.

Islamic Groupings *(Al-Gamaa Al-Islamiya)*

This group, closely associated with the Moslem Brotherhood and said to have received funds from Saudi Arabia, was particularly strong at the universities of Cairo and of Asyut. It was held responsible for attacks on Christians early in 1978 and for involvement in a protest by some 5,000 demonstrators at Asyut on March 30, 1980, against the arrival in Egypt of the former Shah of Iran. The aim of the group is to replace the existing secular regime in Egypt by one based on strict Islamic doctrine as well as morality and respectability in public and private life.

Holy War *(Al-Jihad)*

Leadership. Mohammed Abdel-Salam Faraq (l.).

This extremist Moslem fundamentalist group was loosely associated with the *Al Takfir Wal Hijira* movement, and its earlier leader, Ali Mustafa al-Mughrabi, died in hospital on Jan. 22, 1980. On Aug. 28, 1977, some 80 members of the group were reported to have been arrested. In November 1981, its leader and 23 other members of the group were charged with involvement in the assassination of President Sadat on Oct. 6, and also with attempting to overthrow the Government by force and with other offences.

Sheikh Omar Abdel Rahman, a blind mufti from Asyut University who was described as the group's ideologue and was said to have been named as temporary leader of a regime which would replace the Government, was reported to have issued a religious decree giving permission to the fundamentalist conspirators

to kill all officials taking part in the funeral of the late President Sadat on Oct. 10, 1981, and on Oct. 26 he was reported to have been arrested.

At the trial of 24 defendants said to have been involved in the assassination of the President, the four men charged with murder pleaded "not guilty" but their leader, Lt. Khalid Hassan Sharfiq Islambouli, told the court on Nov. 30, 1981, that he had killed the President and was proud of it. One of the defence counsels said on the same day that the case did not concern "premeditated murder" but "an ideological process" in which no accusation should be made against the defendants; he pointed out that one of the defendants (presumed to be Sheikh Omar Abdel Rahman) had called for a "holy war" against "a deprived and apostate society".

The trial concluded on March 6, 1982, with the conviction of 22 of the 24 defendants—Mohammed Abdel-Salam Faraq, Lt. Islambouli and his three associates being sentenced to death (and executed the following month) and the other 17 to prison terms ranging from five years to life. Sheikh Omar Abdel Rahman and another theologian from Asyut University, Ismail Salamuni, were acquitted but were quickly rearrested and charged with membership of *Al-Jihad*.

Left-wing Movements

Egyptian Communist Party (ECP)

Leadership. Abderrahman Khmissi.

This illegal party has maintained close relations with other pro-Soviet Communist parties and has posed a security threat to Egyptian governments in periods when the latter have pursued a Western-aligned foreign policy. On Oct. 31, 1957, 13 of its members were sentenced to prison terms of from one to seven years for conspiring to overthrow the Government by force, and all property belonging to organizations of the ECP was ordered to be confiscated. Following President Nasser's adoption of a pro-Soviet stance, it was announced on April 25, 1965, that the proscribed ECP had dissolved itself and had merged with the Arab Socialist Union (then the country's sole legal political organization).

After President Sadat had broken with the Soviet Union in the earlier 1970s, an underground ECP became active again, and on Jan. 26, 1977, the Prosecutor-General claimed that it had been "smashed"; in July of that year prison sentences were imposed on a number of persons accused of having taken part in the creation of the ECP with the object of overthrowing the regime. However, between Aug. 16 and the end of September 1979 some 60 alleged activists of the ECP were temporarily detained.

Gen. Mohammed Nabawi Ismail (then Deputy Prime Minister and Minister of the Interior and Services) stated on Sept. 29, 1980, that "leaders and cadres" of a subversive communist organization "working with the Soviet Union" had been arrested during the past two days, but it was not clear whether he referred to the ECP. On March 1, 1981, President Sadat stated that no known communist would be permitted to hold a post in the country's press and information organizations.

Egyptian Communist Workers' Party (ECWP)

This party was founded as an offshoot of the Egyptian Communist Party (ECP). It was said to have links with the ruling National Liberation Front (later the Yemen Socialist Party) of South Yemen and with the Palestinian "Rejectionist Front" led by Dr Georges Habash's Popular Front for the Liberation of Palestine. On Jan. 26, 1977, the Egyptian Prosecutor-General claimed that the ECWP had been "smashed", and in July of that year a number of ECWP members were sent to prison for taking part in the creation of the ECWP with the aim of overthrowing the Egyptian regime; the court also declared that its verdict dissolved the secret ECWP and provided for the "confiscation of all seized books, leaflets and publications".

Nevertheless, arrests and trials were periodically reported in the late 1970s and early 1980s of alleged activists of the ECWP, often in conjunction with members of the (legal) National Progressive Unionist Party.

Other Organizations

Front for the Liberation of Egypt

The discovery of this organization was officially announced on May 27, 1978, when it was alleged that it was financed by Libya to carry out a campaign against the Egyptian Government through the press and radio. On July 22, 1977, President Sadat had accused Col. Kadhafi, the Libyan leader, of having promoted sabotage operations in Egypt during the previous three years. Similar claims were made by the Egyptian Government in later years.

National Coalition

In mid-February 1981 this group issued a statement signed by some 100 leading Egyptian personalities accusing President Sadat of failing to fulfil the peace promise which he had given in signing the peace treaty with Israel in March 1979. The statement said that the treaty had neither brought prosperity to Egypt nor reduced military spending nor strengthened the country's political and economic independence but had "isolated Egypt from the Arab and Islamic worlds without contributing to the achievement of a comprehensive settlement of the Arab-Israeli conflict". The statement also called for the convening of "an informal Arab conference as a first step towards reconciliation between Egypt and the Arab world". Its signatories included Dr Aziz Sidky (who had been Prime Minister in 1971-73), Ismail Fahmi (Foreign Minister in 1973-77) and Dr Mohammed Abdel Salem el-Zayat (who had been a minister in the early 1970s).

National Front

Leadership. Lt.-Gen. Saadeddin Shazli (founder).

The formation of this Front was announced in Damascus in March 1980 by Lt.-Gen. Shazli, who had been Army Chief of Staff from 1971 to December 1973. Later appointed ambassador in London and thereafter in Lisbon, he was on June 20, 1979, suspended from the latter post but refused to return to Egypt to face disciplinary action for alleged "gross violation of his duties" by having, in a letter to the Portuguese press on June 19, described President Sadat as a dictator who had severely weakened the power of Egypt's armed forces. Lt.-Gen. Shazli also claimed that Arab solidarity was at its lowest point for 30 years, that Egypt's role in the Third World had been diminished and that it had been a mistake to exchange Soviet support for closer links with the United States. He later lived in exile in Algeria and offered his military services to the Palestine Liberation Organization.

Upon the Front's foundation Lt.-Gen. Shazli defined its aim as being to unite all opposition forces for the overthrow of the Sadat regime.

New Wafd Vanguard

The re-launching of the *Wafd*—one of Egypt's strongest parties in the pre-Nasser era—was reported in October 1980, when it was said that a younger generation of activists calling themselves the New *Wafd* Vanguard had drawn up a new programme to meet new conditions and intended to set up local party organizations and to start a new newspaper. Two members of the group were arrested in Cairo the following month for mounting an unauthorized demonstration.

The original *Wafd* had been founded as a broad-based progressive movement in 1918 to negotiate with the British over Egypt's independence; it played a prominent role in Egyptian politics (both in power and in opposition) until the overthrow of King Farouk in 1952. Although the party itself was abolished in 1953, many adherents maintained their allegiance to its principles under the de facto leadership of Fuad Serageddin (a former Interior Minister).

In February 1978 the *Wafd* became the first Egyptian party to be legally recognized since the 1952 revolution apart from the then ruling Arab Socialist Union. However, following the enactment on June 1, 1978, of legislation designed to consolidate the Government's internal position by excluding "undemocratic" elements from public life, the *Wafd* announced its dissolution the following day in protest against the new measures.

Socialist Arab Nasserist Party

On Oct. 9, 1981, it was reported from Baghdad that this party had issued a call on all factions of the Egyptian nationalist movement to draw up a joint working plan to continue the struggle which had led to the assassination of President Sadat.

The Coptic Orthodox Church

Leadership. Pope Shenouda III.

This Church, with 6,000,000 members in Egypt and 16,000 elsewhere, is the largest Christian Church in Egypt. Hostility between Moslems and Copts has led to numerous clashes resulting in casualties. On Sept. 28, 1978, a Coptic priest was reported to have been killed at Samalout (about 200 km south of Cairo) by extremist Moslems, and during Christian-Moslem clashes in March 1979 two churches in Asyut and one in Cairo were destroyed by fire.

On May 14, 1980, President Sadat accused Pope Shenouda III and other Coptic clergy of seeking to partition Egypt and to set up a Christian state with Asyut as its capital, but this charge was strongly denied by the Coptic leaders. Following further sectarian clashes between Moslems and Christians in June 1981 (when at least 10 persons died) and a bomb attack on a Coptic church in Cairo on Aug. 3 (when three people were killed and over 50 injured), security measures led to the arrest of 1,536 people by Sept. 7, 1981. Pope Shenouda himself was placed under restriction and his temporal powers were transferred to a five-member committee appointed by the Government (although he remained spiritual leader of the Copts).

Iran

Capital: Tehran Pop. 39,097,000

The Islamic Republic of Iran is ruled by a Council of the Revolution consisting of (Shi'ite) Islamic spiritual leaders following the fundamentalist tenets of Ayatollah Ruhollah Khomeini, the "guardian of the state". There is a 270-member Parliament *(Majlis)* elected by direct universal suffrage, with the majority of seats being held by the Islamic Republican Party, a religious alliance. There are also a directly-elected President of the Republic (without real power) and a Cabinet. Political parties and other organizations enjoy freedom as long as they do not infringe "the principles of independence, freedom, national unity and the bases of the Islamic Republic".

Opposition to the regime has come not only from supporters of the late Shah of Iran (who was overthrown in February 1979) but also from liberal politicians, non-fundamentalist Moslem groups and militant members of ethnic minorities, in particular Arabs, Azerbaijanis, Baluchis, Kurds and Turkomans. In the suppression of armed opposition a special role has been played by the Revolutionary Guards *(Pasdaran),* directly responsible to the Council of the Revolution. The outbreak in September 1980 of open warfare between Iran and Iraq encouraged some of the minority groups to intensify their guerrilla activities against government forces. Under the jurisdiction of the Islamic Republic some 4,000 persons were executed during the three years from February 1979 to February 1982, some 2,500 of the executions being carried out within eight months from June 1981 to February 1982, mostly of political opponents of the regime.

Separatist Movements

Arab Front for the Liberation of Ahvaz

Leadership. Sayyid Hashim Sayyid Adnan (ch.); Mahmud Husain al-Jari (sec.).

The declared aim of the movement (founded in 1981) is to "liberate" the people of Ahvaz province from (Iranian) occupation, said to have existed for more than 58 years, with aid from the Iraqi Government of President Saddam Hussein.

Arab Political and Cultural Organization (APCO)

Leadership. Shaikh Mohammed Taher Shobeir Khaghani.

The Arab minority of some 2,000,000 people in Khuzestan province claimed that it represented about 80 per cent of the province's population and that the remaining 20 per cent, who were Iranians, had settled there only after oil had been found in the province (called Arabistan by the Arabs). The Iranian Government, on the other hand, claimed that only 40 per cent of the province's inhabitants were Arabs, and that unrest in the province was "inspired from abroad". The Arabs were, however, the underprivileged section of the population.

The APCO, formed in 1979 by various political and cultural societies, announced its demands in April 1979, when Shaikh Khaghani had several talks with Ayatollah Khomeini, who agreed to the formation of a provincial council with limited autonomy and also made other minor concessions such as were to be introduced in other provinces. Clashes occurred, however, during the early months of 1979 between followers of Shaikh Khaghani and Revolutionary Guards (and other supporters of Ayatollah Khomeini), especially in Khorramshahr.

Following Arab complaints of harassment by members of armed revolutionary committees the Governor-General of Khuzestan (Rear-Adml. Ahmad Madani) on May 18, 1979, dissolved these committees in Korramshahr, but he also ordered the Arabs to surrender their weapons by May 25. This order caused further clashes between Arabs and Revolutionary Guards supported by troops and Iranian residents, and by May 31 up to 200 people had been killed in fighting which the Government attributed to "a minority backed by foreign powers and forces still loyal to the Shah". A state of emergency was enforced in Khorramshahr from May 30 to June 4, as the unrest continued.

A settlement was reported to have been reached on June 6, 1979, inter alia granting freedom to the APCO to continue its activities. However, as more arrests and cases of persecution of Arabs occurred and the Government was seen to fail to fulfil the terms of the settlement and announced on June 13 that only people "faithful to the revolution" would be allowed to carry arms into Khorramshahr, Shaikh Khaghani was on June 29 quoted as saying that the agreement of June 6 was no longer valid. He claimed in particular that the Government had failed to release Arabs taken prisoner during the May disturbances and to bring to trial those involved in assaults on Arab property; he warned the Government that Arab militants might "take matters into their own hands" unless Arab demands were met. He subsequently denounced repeated acts of sabotage by Arab extremists, especially against oil installations. Among these extremist groups were (i) a "Black Wednesday" organization claiming responsibility for a bomb explosion at the Abadan refinery on June 14, 1979, and a pipeline explosion on July 10, and (ii) a Liberation Front of South Arabistan.

After an explosion at Korramshahr's main mosque on July 15, 1979, when 11 people were believed killed and more than 50 injured during a memorial service for a Revolutionary Guard killed earlier, Shaikh Khaghani's home was attacked by Revolutionary Guards and other Islamic gunmen, who killed four of his bodyguards and took him away. At the end of July he was reported to be under house arrest in Qom (the home town of Ayatollah Khomeini). Also on July 15 three Arabs were executed for involvement in the attack on the mosque, and two others on July 16. Further unrest followed and numerous Arabs were arrested; on July 24 two were executed for planting bombs and a third for "acting against the Islamic Republic". Other acts of sabotage were committed in Khuzestan in September-October 1979 and early in 1980, some 12 pipelines being blown up in March alone. Four alleged saboteurs were executed on April 17 and another four on July 23. Bomb blasts in Ahvaz on June 26 and July 30 caused some 20 deaths. Over 90 people were killed in an explosion at Gatscharah (southern Khuzestan) on Aug. 18. Numerous other acts of sabotage were committed in subsequent months, especially against pipelines.

The Khuzestan Arabs were supported by certain other Iranian opposition movements. In particular, the Kurdish Democratic Party sent, in mid-1979, several of its members to Khorramshahr with the aim of forming some kind of alliance with the militant Arabs. Of the Socialist Workers' Party of Iran, 11 members who had expressed their support for the Arab nationalists were arrested in June 1979 and tried in camera in August for "counter-revolutionary activities".

In London six Iranian Arabs, calling themselves the Group of the Martyr, seized the Iranian embassy on April 30, 1980, taking 26 hostages and demanding that in return for their release 91 Arabs imprisoned in Iran should be set free. After the six had killed two of the hostages, members of the British Special Air Service (SAS) penetrated into the embassy, killing five of the Arabs and seizing the sixth, who was sentenced to life imprisonment on Jan. 22, 1981.

Arab Popular Movement of Arabistan

Two uniformed members of this Movement were produced by the Iraqi authorities in Baghdad on Dec. 23, 1980. According to Abu Karama, a spokesman for the Movement, it was fighting for autonomy for Khuzestan "even if only within the framework of a democratic Iranian state" (i.e. not within the existing Islamic Republic).

Azerbaijani Autonomist Movement

The Azerbaijanis, variously estimated at between 5,000,000 and 10,000,000 people and forming the largest ethnic minority group in Iran, were mainly Shi'ite Moslems acknowledging as their spiritual leader Ayatollah Kazem Shariatmadari. Many of them had taken an active part in religious opposition to the Shah's regime and played an important part in the Islamic revolution. Ayatollah Shariatmadari, however, rejected the supremacy of Ayatollah Khomeini and the involvement of the clergy in the running of the country. In this he was supported by the (Azerbaijani) Moslem People's Republican Party (MPRP) led by Abdolhassan Rostamkhani. Although Ayatollah Shariatmadari had supported a draft Constitution in June 1979, some 80 per cent of the Azerbaijanis followed his call to boycott the referendum held on Dec. 2-3, 1979, to approve the Constitution of the Islamic Republic and thereafter he was confined under virtual house arrest in Qom.

Following an attack on Ayatollah Shariatmadari's home in Qom, a rebellion broke out on Dec. 5, 1979, which spread to Tabriz (the capital of East Azerbaijan), where Azerbaijani autonomists took control and called for self-rule for themselves and for other minorities. Ayatollah Khomeini thereupon requested Ayatollah Shariatmadari to order the disbandment of the MPRP but the latter refused to do so. On Dec. 13 about 700,000 demonstrators expressed their support for Ayatollah Shariatmadari in Tabriz and endorsed a 10-point programme emphasizing the primacy of their spiritual leader and demanding that he should be allowed to approve the appointment of local officials.

There followed clashes between supporters of the two Ayatollahs both in Tabriz and in Qom during December 1979 and January 1980; on Jan. 11 Revolutionary Guards were reported to have seized the headquarters of the MPRP in Tabriz, where four people were killed and 25 MPRP members were disarmed;

11 of them were summarily tried on various charges, including "subversion with guns" and "waging war on God and his messenger", and were executed early on Jan. 12. On Jan. 19 the arrest was reported of 25 members of the Air Force in Tabriz who were charged with plotting a coup and supplying arms to the MPRP; four of them were later reported to have been executed on Jan. 26. On May 23, 1980, A. Rostamkhani and another MPRP member were executed for their involvement in the rebellion of December 1979.

Although it was reported in early 1980 that Ayatollah Shariatmadari had ended his support for the MPRP in an effort to prevent further violence, unrest continued in East Azerbaijan, where on Sept. 11, 1981, Ayatollah Assadollah Madani, a close aide of Ayatollah Khomeini's who had been personally appointed by the latter to lead Friday prayers in Tabriz, was killed instantly by a "suicide bomber".

Following the announcement on April 11, 1982, that a plot to kill Ayatollah Khomeini had been uncovered and that Sadeq Qotbzadeh (a former Foreign Minister) and others had been arrested in this connexion, it was subsequently officially disclosed that Ayatollah Shariatmadari was implicated in the plot. Appearing on Iranian television on May 2 Ayatollah Shariatmadari admitted that he had been aware of the conspiracy, although he asked forgiveness for not having reported it and promised to oppose such actions in the future. (Sadeq Qotbzadeh was subsequently found guilty of conspiring to overthrow the Government and to assassinate Ayatollah Khomeini and was executed on Sept. 16, 1982.)

Baluchi Autonomist Movement

Leadership. Mowlawi Abdul-Aziz Mollazadeh (l.).

In Iran's south-eastern province of Baluchistan and Sistan, Baluchis form the majority of the 550,000 inhabitants and are predominantly Sunni Moslems and also speak their own language. The Sistans, numbering about 110,000, are mainly Shi'ite Moslems and enjoy a higher standard of living than the Baluchis. Baluchi demands for limited autonomy within Iran and economic concessions have been largely ignored. The posting in the province of Revolutionary Guards from other parts of Iran aroused much hostility among Baluchis.

In December 1979 the Baluchis largely boycotted the referendum on the Constitution, and some acts of violence took place at the time. On Dec. 20-22 fighting occurred between Baluchis and Sistans (supported by Persians) in which at least 14 persons were thought to have been killed and some 80 injured. A state of emergency was declared in Zahidan (near the Afghan and Pakistani border) on Dec. 22, when a ceasefire was agreed and Revolutionary Guards were withdrawn to designated areas. Ayatollah Khomeini blamed the violence on "foreigners and troublemakers"; a religious leader of the Sistans said it was the work of "American and communist agents-provocateurs"; but Mowlawi A.-A. Mollazadeh attributed it to the Revolutionary Guards, supported by "vicious elements" among the Sistans, and emphasized that Persians, Baluchis and Sistans were "all brothers". Further incidents nevertheless occurred between Sunni and Shia Moslems in Zahidan in January 1980. Later in that year Baluchi separatists were reported to be intensifying their guerrilla activities.

Black Wednesday—see under Arab Political and Cultural Organization

Group of the Martyr—see under Arab Political and Cultural Organization

Komaleh—see under Kurdish Sunni Moslem Movement

Kurdish Democratic Party of Iran (KDPI)

Leadership. Dr Abdel Rahman Qasemlu (g.s.).

The KDPI was originally formed as an illegal organization after World War II out of an Association for the Resurrection of Kurdistan but was practically liquidated when a Kurdish rebellion in Iran was crushed in 1966-67. Dr Qasemlu—who had been a member of the (communist) *Tudeh* party—was, at a secret KDPI conference held in Baghdad after 1973, elected the party's secretary-general, and he returned from exile to Iran shortly after the February 1979 Islamic revolution.

On Feb. 19, 1979, Kurdish leaders placed their autonomy demands before a government delegation but the new regime took no steps towards accepting these demands. The KDPI thereupon boycotted the March 1979 referendum on the establishment of an Islamic Republic in Iran, largely because the form of the question put to voters, in the KDPI's view, compelled them to vote in favour.

A number of violent incidents led to the outbreak in March 1979 of a Kurdish rebellion in Sanandaj (in the mountainous western part of Iran), involving the loss of between 100 and 200 lives. On March 25 the Government announced a detailed autonomy plan for the Kurds, but this plan was not implemented, partly because Turkomans in north-eastern Iran were pressing for similar autonomy, and the Prime Minister (then Dr Mehdi Bazargan) declared on April 4 that autonomy would be granted only on a national basis and not to individual ethnic groups. By this time Kurdish armed groups (*Pesh Merga* or "Forward to Death" fighters) were in control of the principal Kurdish towns in the western mountains.

Fighting also took place between KDPI supporters and Azeri-speaking Shi'ite Moslems in West Azerbaijan (who supported Ayatollah Khomeini) on April 20-26, 1979, when hundreds of people were killed before government troops succeeded in restoring calm. Further fighting occurred towards the end of June 1979, when farmers, with the support of the KDPI (and also of the Kurdish Sunni Moslem Movement led by Shaikh Hosseini—see separate entry) sought to take possession of land from landowners who had been armed by the Government and tried to regain possession of land seized by Kurdish peasants after the Islamic revolution. On June 26 the KDPI demanded to know from Ayatollah Khomeini why his regime had armed landowners who had "backed the Shah to the very end" and why the local revolutionary committees had been agitating against the Kurds.

When troops, Revolutionary Guards and police tried to remove the armed Kurds from towns and villages, heavy fighting ensued in July 1979, especially in Marivan (West Azerbaijan), but under an agreement reached on Aug. 5 unarmed Kurds were left in control of Marivan. On Aug. 14 some 2,000 armed Kurds attacked military positions at Paveh (Kermanshah province) and within two days gained control of the town. However, after Ayatollah Khomeini had declared himself C.-in-C. of the Armed Forces and had taken over direct command, this insurgency was put down with up to 400 people being killed and 29 Kurds being executed by firing squad on Aug. 19-21. At the same time government forces also regained control of Sanandaj.

Meanwhile the KDPI had boycotted the elections to a Constituent Council of Experts on Aug. 3, 1979; although Dr Qasemlu was nevertheless elected to the Council, he did not take his seat because on Aug. 19 a government spokesman announced that the KDPI had been declared illegal with immediate effect on the grounds that it had "instigated bloody incidents" in various Kurdish areas. Ayatollah Khomeini denounced the rebel Kurds as "communist-backed enemies of the revolution" and branded Shaikh Hosseini and Dr Qasemlu as "traitors". The KDPI was also officially accused of receiving aid from abroad (i.e. by implication from the Soviet Union, Iraq, Israel and supporters of the former Shah).

Dr Qasemlu, alleging that the Ayatollah was gradually restoring Iran to "a religious dictatorship of the Middle Ages", appealed, on Aug. 19, 1979, to world leaders to save the

Kurdish people from "genocide". In nine major Kurdish towns mass demonstrations took place in support of the Kurdish leaders, many of whom were subsequently arrested. On Aug. 22 Ayatollah Khomeini offered a "pardon" to all Kurds (but not to Dr Qasemlu and Shaikh Hosseini) who "returned to the road of Islam" and surrendered their weapons. He also promised that the equivalent of about $70,000,000 would be made available for the development of the Kurdish region if the rebellion ceased, and he offered a large reward to those who would hand over the Kurdish leaders.

Further clashes nevertheless took place on Aug. 22-26, 1979, in Saqqez (north of Sanandaj) on Aug. 22-26, with 300 arrests being made on Aug. 27 and nine military men, accused of siding with the enemy, being executed. A new peace plan submitted by the Kurdish head of the Mahabad municipal council on Aug. 27, 1979, was rejected by Ayatollah Khomeini on the following day, when he sent a special envoy to the Kurdish areas with instructions to "crush" the Kurds and not to negotiate with them. In anticipation of a government offensive (which began on Sept. 3) the KDPI moved its headquarters from Mahabad to Sardesht (near the Iraqi border) and withdrew its armed forces first from Mahabad and later also from Sardesht, and a few days later Iranian troops were in control of most major Kurdish towns.

Dr Qasemlu, however, declared from his hideout (in an interview published in Paris on Sept. 10, 1979) that the rebellion was not ended and that guerrilla war would be pursued. By Oct. 20 Kurdish fighters were reported to have regained control of Mahabad. The Government thereupon showed readiness to negotiate with the Kurds, and at a meeting with Dariush Foruhar (then newly-appointed Minister of State) on Oct. 16 Shaikh Hosseini handed over an eight-point plan signed by himself, the KDPI, and also the *Komaleh* faction of Marxist-Leninist Kurds. On Dec. 17 the Government in turn presented an outline plan for self-government to be applied to all "self-governed regions" of Iran.

However, during December 1979, when the ethnic minorities had largely boycotted the referendum on the country's new Constitution, the Government reinforced its military presence in the Kurdish areas. Violent incidents again occurred there (as well as in areas inhabited by Azerbaijanis, Baluchis and Turkomans). The KDPI also announced that it would boycott the presidential elections to be held on Jan. 25, 1980. Dr Qasemlu warned Ayatollah Khomeini on Feb. 3, 1980, that civil war might break out as the armed forces were using heavy weapons against the population, including women and children, and destroying houses.

Early in 1980 the KDPI continued its guerrilla operations, and its followers clashed with Revolutionary Guards, with the result that these guards were in February 1980 withdrawn from Mahabad, Sanandaj and Kamyaran (western Iran) and a measure of regional autonomy was introduced in the Kurdish areas. As Kurdish rebels continued to be active, a new government offensive was launched in April 1980, when more than 1,000 Kurds and 500 government troops were said to have lost their lives. Meanwhile, elections to the Iranian Parliament (held in two rounds on March 4 and May 9) had been cancelled in at least three Kurdish towns because of the presence of "armed gangs". Following the withdrawal of the Kurds a ceasefire was negotiated between President Bani-Sadr of Iran and the KDPI in July 1980 but was overruled by Ayatollah Khomeini. In August 1980 government forces were said to have retaken Mahabad (the principal Kurdish city and headquarters of most Kurdish organizations).

After the outbreak of war between Iran and Iraq in September 1980 the KDPI leaders initially declared that they would not hinder the Iranian war effort against Iraq; in fact they intensified their struggle and were reported to be in receipt of substantial aid from the Iraqi Government (while the Iranian Government supported pro-Iranian Kurds in Iraq). By October 1980 a unified Kurdish council had been formed with other organizations and large-scale Kurdish attacks began against Iranian army units. Government forces responded by launching periodic offensives against Kurdish positions, using helicopter gunships and heavy artillery; extensive casualties were reported to have been sustained by both sides in the frequent engagements. By mid-August 1982 it was estimated that over one-third of the Iranian Army (including several thousand Revolutionary Guards) was fighting in Kurdistan, while the strength of *Pesh Merga* forces was given by Dr Qasemlu (in March 1982) as 12,000 backed up by up to 60,000 armed peasants. During this period Kurdish forces increasingly mounted joint operations with guerrillas of the *Mujaheddin Khalq*.

The KDPI claimed in August 1982 that the Government had started to imprison or resettle hundreds of Kurdish families and that a recent Iranian offensive against Iraq was in fact a manoeuvre to encircle the Kurds; it was also claimed by Kurdish and *Mujaheddin* sources that the Army had used incendiary and chemical bombs on Kurdish villages. A further government offensive in October 1982 was reported to have provoked the four main Kurdish tribes (Harkis, Shakkak, Bagzadeh and Simko) into united resistance. A particular cause of tension was said to be the arrival of large numbers of Shi'ite mullahs in the Kurdish region, whose action in offering cash rewards to converts had angered Kurdish Sunni ayatollahs.

In November 1981 it had been announced that the KDPI had joined the National Council of Resistance for Liberty and Independence, which had been set up in France earlier in the year by ex-President Bani-Sadr and other exiled opponents of the Khomeini regime.

Kurdish Sunni Moslem Movement

Leadership. Shaikh Ezzedin Hosseini (l.).

Shaikh Hosseini was the acknowledged leader of the Kurdish Sunni community and as such opposed to the domination of the state by the Shi'ite clergy. His Movement boycotted the referendum on the country's Constitution held in March 1979 and also the presidential elections of Jan. 25, 1980, condemning in particular the disqualification as a presidential candidate of Massoud Rajavi, the leader of the *Mujaheddin Khalq* movement. In making proposals on Kurdish autonomy to the Government of Ayatollah Khomeini, he repeatedly co-operated with Dr Qasemlu, the secretary-general of the Kurdish Democratic Party and, like him, was denounced by the Ayatollah on Aug. 19, 1979, as "seditious" and "corrupt on earth".

This Movement incorporates various left-wing Kurdish groups, notably the (Marxist-Leninist) *Komaleh* faction, which on June 8, 1980, rejected any negotiations on a cease-fire. Speaking in Paris on Feb. 19, 1982, a member of *Komaleh*'s executive bureau, Djaffar Chafii, said that his movement was seeking a social revolution in Iran and stressed that only armed struggle would be able to bring about the overthrow of the present regime.

Liberation Front of South Arabistan—see under Arab Political and Cultural Organization

Turkoman Autonomists

In north-eastern Iran the predominantly Sunni Moslem Turkomans called, immediately after the revolution of February 1979, for concessions involving (i) the redistribution of land owned by supporters of the former Shah; (ii) the right to set up their own police force; (iii) the official recognition of their language; and (iv) representation in the local revolutionary committees dominated by Shi'ite Moslems.

Unrest broke out partly after seizure by Turkomans of disputed land, mainly farmed by absentee landlords, and partly over the alleged intransigence of the republican regime in regard to Turkoman demands (including the renaming of Bandar Shah, a town on the Caspian Sea, as Bandar Islam instead of as Bandar Turkoman, as demanded by the Turkomans). In fighting which broke out on March 26, 1979, Turkoman rebels were supported by members of the (left-wing) *Fedayeen el-Khalq*; at least 50 people were killed and over 300 injured before the rebels withdrew in the face of government forces on April 3. The Government claimed that this rebellion had been the result of large-scale aid from the Soviet Union, but this was denied by the rebels, who refused to agree to a ceasefire. Army units, said to be assisted by (Moslem) *Mujaheddin Khalq* guerrillas, advanced towards the Soviet border while the rebels handed in their weapons at local mosques.

Dr Mehdi Bazargan, then Prime Minister, stated on April 4, 1979, that there would be no settlement between the Government and those who demanded regional self-rule or advocated separatism. Through their Turkoman Political and Cultural Society, the Turkomans had earlier inter alia called for a boycott of the referendum of March 30-31 on the new Constitution of Iran.

Unrest occurred again in 1980, when Turkoman *Fedayeen el-Khalq* followers clashed with Revolutionary Guards at Gonbad-e-Qavus on Feb. 9-12 and as many as 32 people were killed, and also at Gorgan (75 miles south-west of Gonbad-e-Qavus), where Revolutionary Guards and troops suppressed a rebellion.

Left-wing Movements

Forqan

Leadership. Akbar Goudarzi (l.).

As an extreme Islamic socialist group opposed to the assumption of a political role by the Moslem clergy, *Forqan* follows the teachings of the late Dr Ali Shariati, who had been a close friend of President Boumedienne of Algeria and had died in London in 1977. The group has claimed responsibility for the assassination of several leading members of the Islamic Republic's regime, including Gen. Mohammed Vali Qarani, the Republic's first Armed Forces Chief of Staff (killed on April 23, 1979), Ayatollah Morteza Motahari, a member of the Revolutionary Council (murdered on May 1, 1979), the head of religious broadcasts (shot dead on July 21, 1979) and the finance director of the daily newspaper *Kayhan* (assassinated on Aug. 26, 1979). The group also claimed to have killed the finance director of the (West German) Merck Pharmaceutical Company in Tehran on Oct. 14, 1979.

The Prosecutor-General's office in Tehran announced on Oct. 17, 1979, that the group's leader had posed as a mullah and had infiltrated revolutionary circles. On Dec. 18, 1979, Dr Mohammed Mofateh, a former member of the Revolutionary Council and of the central committee of the ruling Islamic Republic Party, was also killed by *Forqan* members. Following the arrest, on Jan. 8, 1980, of 16 of the group's members, including its leader, two *Forqan* members were executed on Jan. 25 and another seven on March 2, 1980, in connexion with the above murders. *Forqan* claimed responsibility for a Tehran bomb attack on June 27, 1981, which injured Hojatolislam Seyed Ali Khameini (who later became President)—this attack being also claimed by the external Party of Equality.

National Democratic Front (NDF)

Leadership. Hedayat Matine-Daftari (l.).

The NDF was established in 1979 as a left-wing secular party by its leader, a grandson of Dr Mohammed Mossadeq, who had been the leader of a left-wing National Front and whose Government had been overthrown in 1953. The NDF did not take part in the March 1979 referendum on the establishment of an Islamic Republic in Iran because it considered it "anti-democratic" to ask voters to decide between a government overthrown by them and another as yet unknown. The NDF also called for a boycott of the August 1979 elections to a Constitutional Council of Experts. During 1981 the NDF was increasingly regarded as "counter-revolutionary", and in mid-December Matine-Daftari left Iran for Paris, where he announced his support for the National Council of Resistance of ex-President Bani-Sadr and Massoud Rajavi. Shokrollah Paknejad, a founder-member of the NDF, was executed in January 1982.

People's Crusaders *(Mujaheddin Khalq)*

Leadership. Massoud Rajavi (l.).

This left-wing Islamic movement, which attracted support from the educated middle classes and the young, had been active in opposing the Shah's regime for many years. In the initial stages of the Islamic regime it set up, in February 1979, with the *Fedayeen el-Khalq,* a joint committee to co-ordinate and supervise the use of arms confiscated from the Shah's supporters. It took part in the elections of a Constituent Council of Experts on Aug. 3, 1979, when its leader was elected to that Council. He was, however, not allowed to stand as a candidate in the presidential elections of Jan. 25, 1980, on the grounds that he had not endorsed the country's new Constitution.

During the parliamentary elections held in March-May 1979, the *Mujaheddin Khalq* lodged complaints against alleged irregularities, and its leader called for the elections to be annulled. In subsequent months members of the organization were involved in clashes with pro-Khomeini groups, in particular the extremist fundamentalist *Hezbollahi* (Children of the Party of God). In June 1981 the *Mujaheddin Khalq* began to support President Abolhassan Bani-Sadr in his opposition to the rule of the doctrinaire fundamentalist clergy *(Maktabi),* who made use of the *Hezbollahi* to disrupt anti-government demonstrations.

After the dismissal of President Bani-Sadr on June 21, 1981, the *Mujaheddin Khalq* were exposed to a rigorous government campaign against all opposition. They claimed in particular that a bomb which was exploded in Qom on June 23, killing eight persons and injuring over 50, had been planted by the Islamic authorities to serve as a pretext for the wave of repression against opponents. Following another bomb explosion in Tehran on June 28 (killing 72 leading politicians), for which Ayatollah Khomeini held the *Mujaheddin Khalq* responsible, the latter were also accused of having drawn up death lists including the names of the governor of the Evin prison in Tehran and the Tehran's revolutionary prosecutor.

Numerous *Mujaheddin Khalq* members were subsequently executed, and on July 29, 1981, M. Rajavi arrived in Paris with ex-President Bani-Sadr, and on Oct. 1 he announced that he had formed a provisional government-in-exile (see separate entry for National Council of Resistance for Liberty and Independence). In Iran itself, *Mujaheddin* forces were said to have majority support in the traditionally left-wing strongholds in the northern provinces bordering the Caspian Sea. Moussa Khiabani, described as the most senior *Mujaheddin* leader inside Iran, was killed by Revolutionary Guards in Tehran on Feb. 8, 1982, together with his wife and that of M. Rajavi (then in Paris), and he was succeeded by Ali Zarkesh.

With a membership estimated (in September 1981) at 150,000, the *Mujaheddin Khalq* continued to be the most active opposition group within Iran during 1982. Despite a fierce campaign waged against them by the Revolutionary Guards and despite extensive arrests and executions of their members, they carried out repeated attacks and assassinations of government leaders, including Hojatoleslam Mohammed Ali Amininejad, the head of the Navy's political-ideological office, who was killed on June 11, 1982; Ayatollah Mohammed Sadduqi, a member of the *Majlis* and a close associate of Ayatollah Khomeini's, who was killed in Tehran on July 2; and Ali Mahlojes, a high-ranking member of the ruling IRP, whose assassination was claimed by the *Mujaheddin* on Sept. 2. On Sept. 5, 1982, the *Mujaheddin Khalq* claimed to have killed over 100 Revolutionary Guards in Tehran in the past week alone.

People's Fighters (Fedayeen el-Khalq)

Leadership. (Miss) Ashraf Deghan (l.).

This militant Marxist guerrilla movement was responsible for numerous acts of violence committed under the Shah's regime with the purpose of hastening its overthrow. It supported the Islamic revolution in its early stages but on March 18, 1979, a spokesman for the movement said that before a constitutional referendum was held the country should be given democratic institutions. The organization took part in the elections to a Constituent Council of Experts on Aug. 3, 1979, but on Aug. 21 of that year Ayatollah Khomeini ordered the closure of its newspaper. Later the *Fedayeen* were involved in clashes with Revolutionary Guards, in particular at Gonbad-e-Qavus on Jan. 9, 1980, when 14 persons were killed and 65 injured.

After the outbreak of war between Iran and Iraq the *Fedayeen* initially strongly supported the Iranian war effort and called for "the defence of the revolution and independence of the country in the face of attacks from the Iraqi fascist regime". However, by mid-1981 elements aligned to the (communist) *Tudeh* party (see separate entry) formed the predominant political current within the *Fedayeen*, which accordingly came to echo *Tudeh*'s opposition to the war.

People's Party (Tudeh)

Leadership. Noureddin Kianouri (first sec.).

This Communist party had its origins in the Iranian Social Democratic Party *(Adalat)* which had arisen out of a social democratic group founded in 1904. Established in 1920 as the Communist Party of Iran, it was banned in 1931 and forced to continue its work illegally. In 1941 it was reorganized as the *Tudeh* party of Iran, which was itself repressed and officially declared illegal in 1949. In 1965 the party was divided into three factions—respectively of pro-Soviet, Maoist and Castroite orientation—but the first of these remained the official *Tudeh* party. In 1973 it adopted a new programme with the object of uniting all democratic forces by means of "flexibility, initiative and consistency".

From its base in exile in East Germany, the party welcomed the Islamic revolution of 1979 and pledged full support for its "anti-imperialist and democratic" aims. Allowed to operate once again under the new Islamic revolutionary regime, it called in particular for an alliance of all socialist forces which would enjoy the support of the Soviet Union. However, *Tudeh*'s support for the new regime waned as the latter became more committed to clerical fundamentalism; the party also opposed the Iran-Iraq war which broke out in September 1980. In August 1982 the ruling Islamic Republican Party published a strong critique of the policy of *Tudeh* and of the dominant pro-*Tudeh* faction of the *Fedayeen el-Khalq* (People's Fighters—see separate entry), attacking in particular their opposition to the war.

The *Tudeh* party opposed Iran's participation in the Gulf War because (i) it had the effect of strengthening Iraq's relations with conservative Gulf regimes, (ii) it involved the Iranian Government in heavy expenditure on arms to the detriment of the masses and (iii) increasing popular discontent with the war could lead to counter-revolution.

Peykar

This small pro-Chinese communist formation has actively opposed the Khomeini regime which came to power in 1979, although in May 1982 the Iranian security authorities claimed to have smashed its entire leadership in a series of raids in the southern town of Bandar Abbas. Arrested members of the group who recanted their beliefs were reportedly often forced to join the firing squads for their former colleagues.

Union of Communists

This small pro-Chinese formation has actively opposed the Khomeini regime which came to power in 1979, but by mid-1982 the Iranian authorities were claiming to have virtually destroyed it as a significant force. At the end of August 1982 official sources stated that 183 members of the Union had been arrested in Khuzestan and that large arsenals of firearms and explosives had been discovered.

Monarchist Groups

Since the 1979 revolution the Iranian authorities have announced on several occasions that plots against the Government had been uncovered, those involved being army officers and other members of the armed forces intent upon restoring the monarchy. The same aim has also motivated the activities of a number of organized groups, as detailed below.

Armed Movement for the Liberation of Iran

Leadership. Princess Azzadeh (a niece of the late Shah).

This Movement, established in 1979 and based in Paris, claims to represent the monarchist opposition to the Tehran regime. It was supported by Princess Ashraf, the late Shah's twin sister, who from Paris issued an open letter to the United Nations Secretary-General on Dec. 23, 1979, accusing the Khomeini regime of having executed over 700 people whose only crime, she said, was that they had "co-operated with the old regime"; she added that thousands of others had been "butchered and lynched in all corners of Iran".

Azadegan

On Aug. 13, 1981, some 15 members of this group seized the *Tabarzin,* one of three French-built Iranian gunboats sailing past the Spanish port of Cadiz, and declared this ship the seat of an *Azadegan* government-in-exile. However, on Aug. 19 they handed the vessel over to the French authorities in Toulon, and on Aug. 28 it left Toulon with an Iranian crew after it had been restored to Iranian control, the hijackers having been offered political asylum in France. Although *Azadegan* expressed support for the Iranian monarchy, it was not recognized by Reza Cyrus (the late Shah's son).

Pars Group

In May 1981 a total of 18 members of this Group were arrested in connexion with an alleged plot to restore the monarchy, with the authorities accusing the Group of having links with Dr Shapour Bakhtiar, the leader of the National Resistance Movement (see separate entry) then living in France, and with certain members of the late Shah's family. On Aug. 10, 1981, four members of the Group were executed. The Pars Group itself claimed responsibility for a bomb explosion outside a Revolutionary Guards barracks in Tehran on Feb. 22, 1982, when 15 people were killed.

External Movements

Iranian National Front (INF)

Leadership. Dr Karim Sanjabi (l.).

The INF was established in December 1977 as a Union of National Front Forces comprising several earlier organizations opposed to the Shah's "dictatorship". At first it advocated a return to constitutional monarchy but in 1978 it called for the abolition of the monarchy and the return from exile of Ayatollah Khomeini. Dr Sanjabi was temporarily Minister of Foreign Affairs in the Government of Dr Mehdi Bazargan (appointed by Ayatollah Khomeini in February 1979) but resigned in April 1979 because he was disappointed with the Government's lack of power. In the March 1979 referendum on the establishment of an Islamic Republic the INF called for a "yes" vote but it boycotted the August 1979 elections to a Constituent Council of Experts.

On Aug. 21, 1979, Ayatollah Khomeini ordered the closure of the INF's newspaper, and the INF was thereafter in open conflict with the Ayatollah's regime. In July 1981 an INF member, Karim Dastmaltchi, was executed, inter alia for providing "financial support for the counter-revolution" and giving interviews to the foreign press. The INF

also called for a boycott of presidential elections held on July 24, 1981 (after the dismissal of President Bani-Sadr), leading to the election as President of Mohammed Ali Radjai (until then Prime Minister).

National Council of Resistance for Liberty and Independence (NCR)

The NCR was set up in 1981 by ex-President Abolhassan Bani-Sadr and Massoud Rajavi, the leader of the *Mujaheddin Khalq,* both of whom had reached Paris on July 29, 1981. Bani-Sadr, who had been a close associate of Ayatollah Khomeini, had been elected as first President of the Islamic Republic of Iran on Jan. 25, 1980, but he was later in disagreement with the Ayatollah over the question of the President's powers. After he had refused to sign bills passed by Parliament and had also been criticized for his conduct of the war against Iraq, he was on June 10, 1981, ordered by Ayatollah Khomeini to be dismissed from the post of C.-in-C. of the Armed Forces (to which he had been appointed on Feb. 19, 1980).

On June 12, 1981, he attacked the rule of the Islamic Republican Party as having "worsened the condition of the country day by day", and Parliament thereupon, on June 21, declared him incompetent (by 177 votes to one with one abstention) and on the following day Ayatollah Khomeini formally dismissed him as President, whereupon he disappeared from public life until his arrival in Paris. On Nov. 6, 1981, it was announced that as a result of negotiations with Dr Saeed Badal, a member of the central committee of the Kurdish Democratic Party of Iran, this party had formally joined the NCR.

National Resistance Movement

Leadership. Dr Shapour Bakhtiar.

Dr Bakhtiar had been a supporter of Dr Mossadeq, the (left-wing) Prime Minister of Iran who was overthrown in 1953, and as a leading member of the National Front he was an outspoken critic of the Shah. As the latter's last Prime Minister in January-February 1979, Dr Bakhtiar had a programme of liberalization, including the dissolution of the Shah's secret police and the granting of a greater role to the Moslem religious leaders in drafting legislation. His Government was, however, condemned by Ayatollah Khomeini as "a betrayal of our cause" and was eventually brought down by the Ayatollah's followers on Feb. 11, 1979. Dr Bakhtiar subsequently left Iran and settled in France, where he set up his opposition movement.

On May 13, 1979, Ayatollah Khalkhali, then head of Iran's revolutionary courts, declared that Dr Bakhtiar was among those former Prime Ministers on whom sentences of death had been passed under "religious laws''. On June 10 and July 12, 1980, the Iranian Government announced that a conspiracy by military men to restore Dr Bakhtiar to power had been uncovered and that some 300 persons had been arrested in this connexion. By Sept. 3, 1980, a total of 96 of them, including two generals, had been executed. In Paris Dr Bakhtiar escaped an assassination attempt on July 18, 1980, when three persons were killed and one injured. Ali Tabatabai, a former press attaché at the Iranian embassy in Washington, who was described as a supporter of Dr Bakhtiar and who had been head of a Freedom Foundation (aimed at restoring "a democratic regime" in Iran), was killed in Washington on July 22.

Whilst Dr Bakhtiar had announced the formation of his National Resistance Movement on Aug. 8, 1980, he denied on Sept. 26 that he had formed a government-in-exile in Paris; on Sept. 29 he also denied that he had armed supporters waiting to invade Iran.

Nationalist and Revolutionary Front of Iran

This Front was established in Paris in April 1982 by Mozaffar Firouz (a nephew of the late Dr Mossadeq, the left-wing Prime Minister overthrown in 1953, and the person who had negotiated the withdrawal of Soviet troops from northern Iran in 1947), as well as by Amir Bahman Samsam Bakhtiari (a leader of the Bakhtiari tribe), Prof. Fariborz Nozari and Gen. Jahangir Qaderi (who had been a member of the general staff and of the Imperial Guard under the Shah). The Front issued a statement declaring that it was "loyal to the great Iranian revolution" which it considered to have "lost its true and natural direction"; that, while adhering to the Islamic faith, it regarded religion as being confined to spiritual and moral aspects of life; and that in foreign policy all countries should be called upon to "respect the independence, sovereignty and territorial integrity as well as the non-alignment and neutrality of Iran".

Party of Equality

Leadership. Gen. Moukhtar Karabagh (l.).

This organization, established in August 1980 and based in Turkey, claimed responsibility for a bomb attack in Tehran on June 27, 1981, severely injuring Hojatoleslam Seyed Ali Khameini (who represented Ayatollah Khomeini on the Supreme Defence Council and was subsequently elected President in October 1981). It also claimed responsibility for another bomb attack, also in Tehran, on June 28 killing 72 leading politicians, among them Ayatollah Mohammed Hossein Beheshti (Chief Justice of the Supreme Court and leader of the ruling Islamic Republican Party), four cabinet ministers, six deputy ministers and 27 parliamentary deputies. (Ayatollah Khomeini, however, said on June 30 that the *Mujaheddin Khalq* were responsible for the attack on June 28.)

Religious Minorities

The main religious minorities in Iran are the Bahais (numbering 450,000), Christians (200,000), Jews (60,000) and Zoroastrians (20,000). The last three of these groups are officially recognized in the Constitution, whereas the Bahais are not and have been subjected to considerable repression since the 1979 revolution, before which they had held many senior posts under the Shah.

Bahai Community

The Bahai movement was founded in the mid-19th century by Mirza Husain Ali (who called himself Baha'ullah or the Glory of God) in an attempt to save an earlier movement known as Babism. Sayyid Ali Muhammad had, in 1844, proclaimed himself the Bab (Gate) through which Shi'ite Moslems were to communicate with their "Hidden Imam" (which he himself later claimed to be); Babism became a movement trying to overthrow not only the orthodox Moslem religion but also the social order, if necessary by violence. The Bab was subsequently convicted of heresy and was executed in 1850, his movement being suppressed and over 3,000 of its followers being executed in later years.

Baha'ullah, however, developed the Bahai religion as a peaceful movement, whose members would not belong to political parties or secret societies and were required to respect the authority of the state in which they lived; at the same time the Bahais aspired to the establishment of a world government to be achieved gradually by peaceful means. Nevertheless, Baha'ullah was exiled from Iran in 1853 and later settled at Acre (then in Turkish Palestine and later in Israel).

At the establishment of the Islamic Republic in 1979 there were some 450,000 followers of the Bahai religion in Iran, and many of them had held senior posts under the Shah. Ayatollah Khomeini had already declared before his return to Iran that the Bahais were "a political faction" and "unlawful" and that they would "not be accepted". (For orthodox Moslems any person who claimed to be a successor to the Prophet Mohammed, as Baha'ullah had done, was guilty of collective apostasy punishable by death, whereas religions founded before Islam, such as those of the Jews, Christians and Zoroastrians, were recognized in Iran.) In the Islamic Republic the Bahais were considered not only heretical but also unrevolutionary (since they were non-political) and pro-Zionist (since they had their headquarters in Israel).

During 1980 many Bahais were dismissed from their posts, their property was confiscated, their main investment company was closed down and their shrines were desecrated—without their having any redress against action taken against them by Islamic zealots. Bahais arrested included nine members of their spiritual assembly, seized on Aug. 21, 1980, and at least 10 others were subsequently executed for alleged involvement in a planned coup. Seven Bahais were executed on spying charges in Yazy (central Iran) on Sept. 8 and two others assassinated in Nook (Khorassan) on Dec. 17, 1980.

By May 1982 it was reported that about 100 Bahais had been killed since February 1979, of whom some had been executed after being charged with espionage and some for allegedly seeking to establish a dissident

movement within the Bahai community.

Jewish Community

The situation of the Jewish community in Iran became precarious following the advent in February 1979 of a regime imbued with Islamic fundamentalist zeal and one which declared its full support for the cause of the Palestinian people. Considerable restrictions were placed on the free movement of Jews within the country, while a number seeking to emigrate to Israel were prevented from doing so on the grounds that such emigration was a "Zionist act". According to Western press reports in June 1980, between 50 and 70 Jews had been arrested in Iran since the revolution and a small number were thought to have been executed.

Iraq

Capital: Baghdad   Pop. 13,596,000

The Republic of Iraq is, under its 1968 Constitution, a popular democratic and sovereign state with Islam as its state religion and its economy "based on socialism". It is ruled by a Revolutionary Command Council (RCC) headed by a President (Saddam Hussein Takriti) and a Vice-President, and dominated by the *Baath* Arab Socialist Party of Iraq. In 1973 a National Progressive Front was formed by the *Baath* party with the participation of a faction of the Democratic Party of Kurdistan and the Iraqi Communist Party (ICP), but in 1978 the Government began to eliminate communist influence, and the ICP thereupon went into opposition to the regime.

In elections to a (legislative) National Assembly held on June 20, 1980, the 250 members elected by direct suffrage did not identify themselves with political parties, but the *Baath* party exercised control as all candidates had to express their belief in the principles of the 1968 revolution (which had brought the party to power). A Kurdish Legislative Council of 50 members was elected on Sept. 19, 1980, with limited powers (to pass legislation for the Kurdish region on social, cultural and economic development as well as on health, education and labour matters), but this Council was not supported by a majority of Kurds, whose ultimate aim was full autonomy or even complete independence for Kurdistan.

In addition to the Kurds and the ICP, the predominantly Sunni Moslem regime in Baghdad has encountered strong opposition from militant elements of the Shi'ite Moslem community (constituting more than half of Iraq's population), the latter being in sympathy with and supported by the regime of the Islamic Republic of Iran (with which Iraq has been at war since September 1980). The Iraqi *Baath* party has also been actively opposed by dissident Baathists supported by the Government of Syria.

Arab Opposition Groups

Dawah Party

The *Dawah* party has been the militant organization of the Shi'ite community in Iraq and has been aligned with the Iranian Islamic revolution led by Ayatollah Khomeini (an Islamic Liberation Movement with such ties having first been set up in 1979). At the end of March 1980 the Iraqi Government announced that the death sentence would be imposed on persons affiliated to the *Dawah* party. An Iraqi *mujaheddin* group, presenting itself as being linked to the *Dawah* party, claimed responsibility for a number of acts of violence during 1980, including a grenade attack which slightly wounded Tariq Aziz, a Deputy Prime Minister, on April 1, the shooting of an Iranian embassy employee in Rome on June 4, the killing of an Iraqi diplomat in Abu Dhabi on July 27, and the murder of a leading member of the pro-Iraqi Lebanese regional council of the *Baath* party on July 28.

Ayatollah Bakr al-Sadr, the spiritual leader of the Iraqi Shi'ite community, who had been placed under house arrest on June 1, 1979, was, together with his sister, executed on April 9, 1980. During 1980 the Iraqi Government was reported to have deported some 40,000 Shi'ite Moslems to Iran and to have executed 96 others. Iran's support for the militant Shi'ite Moslems in Iraq is said to have taken the form of the training of a group of Iraqi exiles near Damascus (ostensibly to aid Palestinians in Lebanon) and their infiltration into Iraq to commit acts of sabotage. Their reported actions included an attempt to assassinate President Hussein on June 4, 1980.

Unrest in Iraq's southern area inhabited by Shi'ite Moslems continued in the latter part of 1980. On Aug. 27 it was reported from Tehran that the *Dawah* party had stated in a communiqué that Iraqi forces had attacked a village in which units of the party's *mujaheddin* had sought refuge, that 26 government soldiers had been killed, but that in a retaliatory strike on Aug. 13 some 5,000 government troops had surrounded the village and killed all its inhabitants.

Further deportations of Shi'ite Moslems from Iraq to Iran were reported in 1981-82, while in February 1982 Tehran radio reported that Iraqi *mujaheddin* had mounted a successful attack on a military convoy of arms in transit from Saudi Arabia to Iraq. Iraqi fears that Shi'ite unrest might affect the capability of its Army (in which a majority of other ranks were Shi'ites) were reflected in a new policy adopted from mid-1982 of seeking to accommodate Shi'ite aspirations, notably by the inclusion of five Shi'ites in the Cabinet on June 27, 1982. Nevertheless, the *Dawah* party

remained unreconciled to the regime and claimed responsibility for a car bomb explosion at a Baghdad government building on Aug. 1 in which 30 people were killed and also for a bomb attack on an airline office the following month.

Dissident Baathists

Although not organized in a party or group of their own, Baathists opposed to the Iraqi *Baath* Arab Socialist Party have generally been either in sympathy with or directly linked to the *Baath* party of Syria.

On July 28, 1979, it was officially announced in Baghdad that a plot had been uncovered, involving members of the RCC and two cabinet ministers. Immediately afterwards 28 alleged participants in the plot were tried, and on Aug. 7 a special court passed sentences of death on 22 of them (one of them in absentia) and prison sentences ranging from one to 15 years on 33 others, while the remaining 13 defendants were released. Those condemned to death included not only former cabinet ministers but also a former secretary-general of the RCC (who was a Shi'ite Moslem) and the commander of one of Iraq's three army corps. The plot was said to have been aided by Syria with the object of removing the dominance of President Hussein's family, promoting union between Syria and Iraq and ending the suppression of dissident members of Iraq's Shi'ite community. The execution of 21 defendants condemned to death was carried out on Aug. 8 in the presence of President Hussein and the remaining members of the RCC.

Following the outbreak of the Iran-Iraq war in September 1980 few detailed reports were allowed to emerge on political developments inside Iraq. It did appear, however, that a major cabinet reshuffle on June 27, 1982, and a reduction in the size of the RCC the same day were part of a wider purge of Baathist dissidents within the political and military leadership. According to Western reports, President Hussein had come under increasing criticism from such elements not only for his conduct of the war but also for his alleged departure from Baathist "socialist orthodoxy" in his conduct of economic policy.

Iraqi Communist Party (ICP)

Leadership. Aziz Mohammed (first sec.).

Founded in 1934, the pro-Soviet ICP had a substantial following until 1963, when it was severely repressed and many of its supporters were executed. After coming to power in 1968, the Iraqi *Baath* party took steps to achieve a reconciliation with the ICP, of which two members joined the Government in 1972. In 1973 the ICP was admitted to the recently established National Progressive Front. However, from 1975 onwards (i.e. after the collapse of Kurdish resistance to the Government) the *Baath* party began to impose restrictions on the ICP. Between 1975 and 1977 a number of ICP members were tried for forming secret cells in the armed forces in contravention of a 1971 law which allowed only *Baath* party members to engage in political activities within the armed forces, the police and the secret service. In May 1979 21 Communists condemned to death on such charges were hanged, while other persons sentenced in this connexion had to serve terms of imprisonment.

In Kuwait it was reported in May and June 1978 that there had been mass arrests of ICP members and of military personnel in Iraq, and that about 1,000 people had been detained and at least another 18 Communists had been executed (in addition to the 21 mentioned above). The Communist press in Iraq had at the same time begun to criticize certain government attitudes and had in particular rejected the Iraqi Government's disapproval of the Soviet Union's support for Ethiopia in the latter's campaigns against Somalia and Eritrean secessionists; it also opposed the Government's anti-Syrian propaganda and called for "more realistic" autonomy for the Kurds in Iraq (whom a number of Communists were said to have joined in renewed fighting against government forces).

In January 1979 the Communist parties of nine Arab states issued a manifesto denouncing the Government of Iraq for its treatment of the ICP. In reply the Iraqi *Baath* party published an anti-communist book alleging that the entire communist movement in the Arab world had been founded by Jews from Palestine. Early in that year Mohammed Aziz, the ICP's first secretary, left Iraq, as did hundreds of other party members, and in mid-March the ICP announced that it had terminated its membership of the National Progressive Front. The two Communist members of the Government were subsequently dismissed—a Minister of State on April 25 and the Minister of Transport on May 5, 1979. On July 11 the National Progressive Front accused the ICP of having links with "imperialist and Zionist forces".

During the Iran-Iraq war (which broke out in September 1980) the ICP sided with Iran and in particular looked to Syria as an ally in its fight against the regime of President Saddam Hussein. It condemned Jordan's support for Iraq, and at a meeting between President Assad of Syria and the ICP's first secretary on Feb. 14, 1982, the two sides agreed that the Iran-Iraq war tended to "divert the Arab states and peoples from their battles against the Zionist enemy and its supporters" and had caused "weakness in the anti-imperialist and anti-Zionist front".

National Democratic and Pan-Arab Front
(Al-Jabham al-Wataniyah al-Qawmiyah ad-Dimuqratiyah fi al-Iraq)

This Front was set up in Damascus (Syria) in November 1980 by seven Iraqi opposition groups, including the Democratic Party of Kurdistan led by Masoud Barzani, the Kurdish Socialist Party (Bassok) led by Mahmoud Othman, opposition sections of the Iraqi *Baath* party led by Bakr Yassin (and backed by Syria) and exiled Shi'ite Moslem leaders in touch with Iranian mullahs. Each member of the Front was to retain its own ideological, political and organizational independence and independent activities. (The formation of an Iraqi Islamic Front comprising Shi'ite Moslems, Kurds, dissident Baathists and other émigrés opposed to the regime of President Hussein of Iraq had earlier been reported on Aug. 18, 1979.)

In its charter published in the Syrian press on Nov. 13, 1980, the Front's aim was stated to be to overthrow the existing "dictatorial regime" in Iraq and to establish a national coalition government which would achieve democracy for Iraq and self-rule for Kurdistan "within the framework of Iraqi national sovereignty". The charter described the Front as "part of the Arab liberation movement and the world revolutionary movement" and as aiming at "an alliance of the working class, the peasants, the petty bourgeoisie in the cities and the progressive patriotic factions among the bourgeois middle-class". The Front was to "participate in the pan-Arab battle against imperialism and Zionism" and "to liberate all occupied and usurped Arab and Palestinian territories", to bring Iraq into the pan-Arab "front of steadfastness and confrontation" and to intensify the Arab struggle to nullify the Camp David peace agreement between Egypt and Israel. The Front was also to work for providing the requisites for Iraq's accession to the Syrian-Libyan unitary state.

Supreme Council of the Islamic Revolution of Iraq

Leadership. Hojatoleslam Seyyed Mohammed Bakr Hakim.

The formation of this organization was announced in Tehran (Iran) on Nov. 17, 1982, with the aim of providing a focal point for Iraqi Shi'ite opposition to the prosecution of the war with Iran. Its leader had been banished from Iraq soon after the outbreak of hostilities in view of his dedication to the overthrow of the Hussein regime and its replacement by an Islamic republic led by a theologian on the Iranian model. The Council's inaugural statement denounced the Iraqi Government as a "Zionist regime" and condemned the deportation of Shi'ites from Iraq to Iran; it also alleged that 100,000 people had so far been killed in "an unwanted war".

Kurdish Movements

Democratic Party of Kurdistan (DPK) *(Al-Hizb ad-Dimuqraati al-Kurid)*

Leadership. Masoud Barzani.

Founded in 1946, the DPK was originally led by Mullah Mustapha Barzani who, for over 30 years, led the struggle for autonomy of the Kurds in Iraq. This struggle came to a temporary end in 1975 after the Shah of Iran had ceased to support the Kurds and had concluded a treaty with the Government of Iraq. Mullah Barzani died in exile in the United States on March 1, 1979. From 1977 onwards, however, the DPK resumed the armed struggle against Iraqi government forces.

On Jan. 10, 1977, the DPK provisional leadership disclosed that its fighters had seized six technicians, including five Poles, as hostages and had, through one of them whom they released, put forward demands for the return to their homes of all Kurds previously deported from the mountainous northern areas of Iraq, especially the wives, mothers and children of *Pesh Merga* ("Forward to Death") guerrillas (these dependants being held in special camps or prisons); later the DPK also demanded the release of all political prisoners in Iraq. However, on March 29, 1977, the DPK's provisional leadership announced that these and other hostages held by its fighters had been released "on purely humanitarian grounds" following "informal representations" by the Governments concerned and by the United Nations; at the same time the DPK appealed for international support for its struggle. According to an unconfirmed report of May 3, 1977, the Iraqi authorities had allowed 40,000 of those interned to return to the north.

The DPK's provisional leadership—headed by M. M. (Sami) Abdulrahman, a former Communist who had joined the DPK in 1960—was, in the first half of 1977, accused by the Patriotic Union of Kurdistan (PUK), led by Jalal Talabani, of having links with the (US) Central Intelligence Agency, of receiving funds from Israel and of having bases among Kurds in Turkey. Clashes between the two parties in mid-June 1977 were said to have led to the death of about 400 Talabani supporters and the capture of 400 of his guerrillas, including Ali Askeri, their supreme military commander.

A DPK spokesman said on Aug. 15, 1977, that numerous Kurdish villages had been destroyed in terms of a warning by an RCC member that a 25-mile strip along the Turkish border would be cleared of people. The spokesman also said that 16 Kurds from Halabja (south of Sulaymaniyah) had been condemned to death by a special court and executed. In the first few months of 1979 more Kurds were reported to have been forcibly removed from their homes in northern Iraq. On April 20, 1979, the Turkish and Iraqi Governments concluded an agreement designed to crush Kurdish guerrilla activities. Thereupon the Turkish martial law authorities effectively ensured that Kurds in Iraq no longer received supplies from villages in Turkey, while the Iraqi Government continued its policy of deporting Kurds from the mountainous northern border area, where *Pesh Mergas* were still carrying on their operations.

In mid-1979 Masoud Barzani (a son of Mullah Barzani) returned to Iraq from Iran (where he had lived since 1975), and in July he was quoted as saying that he and his supporters would intensify their fight in the north "to rescue the Kurdish people from persecution" and "to gain real autonomy for the Kurdish people within a democratic and prosperous Iraq". In August of that year he claimed that there were some 5,000 *Pesh Mergas* fighting in northern Iraq. At the first congress of the newly organized DPK's central committee in November 1979 differences arose between traditionalists led by Idris Barzani (elder brother of Masoud Barzani) and the "intellectual" wing of the party led by M. M. Abdulrahman.

In a message to Ayatollah Khomeini of Iran, Masoud Barzani declared on April 9, 1980, that he fully supported Iran's struggle against the Iraqi *Baath* regime. During the month of April the Iraqi authorities expelled Kurds from Iraq to Iran at the rate of about 2,000 a day. (The Iraqi Kurds, or Faili, had emigrated to Iraq during the first half of the 19th century from Ilan province in Iran.)

By 1981 the DPK had its own radio station, the "Voice of Iraqi Kurdistan", which, on Aug. 12, denounced co-operation between the regimes of Iraq and Turkey against "democratic and national movements" in both countries, and in particular against the DPK and its *Pesh Merga* forces, and also opposed these two Governments' joint action against "revolutionary Iran". On Aug. 16, 1981, the DPK received a message of support from the (illegal) Kurdish Socialist Party of Turkey.

At the second congress of the DPK's central committee held between July 21 and Aug. 1, 1981, the party's leadership declared that the DPK was part of the world liberation movement, and it reaffirmed its determination to "intensify efforts to pool all the national, democratic and Islamic forces that oppose Saddam Hussein's fascist regime in the . . . Iraqi National and Patriotic Front" (see separate entry for National Democratic and Pan-Arab Front) and to "further friendly relations with the glorious revolution of the

Iranian peoples under the leadership of Imam Khomeini'', with the Arab national liberation movement and with ''the progressive regime of the Syrian Arab Republic''.

Kurdish Socialist Party (Bassok)

Leadership. Dr Mahmoud Othman, Rasoul Hamand.

This group, an offshoot of the Democratic Party of Kurdistan (DPK), and engaged in armed resistance against government forces in Kurdistan, was responsible for the seizure of a British engineer early in 1981. In return for his release, it demanded the freeing of imprisoned Kurdish families and a ransom of £500,000, to be used for the purchase of medical supplies (as reported on Jan. 24, 1982). In November 1980 Bassok had joined with other Iraqi opposition groups to establish the Damascus-based National Democratic and Pan-Arab Front (see separate entry) of forces seeking to overthrow the regime.

Patriotic Union of Kurdistan (PUK)

Leadership. Jalal Talabani.

This group was set up in July 1975 by a merger of a Kurdistan National Party, the Socialist Movement of Kurdistan and an Association of Marxist-Leninists of Kurdistan. It has been engaged in sporadic attacks on government forces, partly from Iranian territory, in support of its demand for complete autonomy for Kurdistan. In a statement issued in Beirut (Lebanon) on Dec. 24, 1977, the PUK announced that the Iraqi Government had tortured and executed more than 96 Kurds since September 1977 and was planning to dislocate 1,000,000 Kurds from their lands and to send them to the southern parts of Iraq in a continued drive towards Arabizing the Kurdish regions of northern Iraq. Later the PUK was in conflict with the Democratic Party of Kurdistan (DPK—see separate entry), and in October 1978 the PUK claimed in Stockholm that the DPK had executed three PUK members a year earlier.

Israel

Capital: Jerusalem (not recognized as such by the United Nations)   Pop. 3,900,000

The State of Israel is a parliamentary democracy with a President elected for five years by a single majority of Parliament, a Government under a Prime Minister and a unicameral 120-seat Parliament *(Knesset)* elected for four years by universal adult suffrage under a system of proportional representation. There are numerous legal political parties and a few political organizations not recognized by the Government.

Elections to the *Knesset* held on June 30, 1981, and contested by 31 lists resulted in the following distribution of seats: *Likud* 48, Labour Alignment 47, National Religious Party 6, *Agudat Israel* 4, Democratic Front for Peace and Equality (mainly the pro-Soviet New Communist Party) 4, *Tehiya* 3, *Tami* 3, *Telem* 2, *Shinui* 2, Civil Rights Movement 1.

The overriding security problem of Israel has arisen out of the Arab-Israeli conflict and the occupation by Israeli forces of large areas inhabited by Arabs (see main section on Palestinian Movements, pages 196-214).

Jewish Defence League

Leadership. Rabbi Meir Kahane.

The League was established in New York in 1968 as an extremist right-wing organization intent upon conducting counter-terrorist operations against militant Palestinians and also advocating the removal from the occupied West Bank and Gaza Strip of the Arab inhabitants unless they swore allegiance to Israel. During a United Nations Security

Council debate on the Arab-Israeli conflict in January 1976 an offshoot of the League, calling itself the ''Jewish Armed Resistance Strike Unit'', claimed responsibility for the planting of several bombs at the UN building in New York in protest against the anti-Zionist stance of the UN majority.

Rabbi Kahane unsuccessfully contested the 1977 general elections in Israel under the banner of a *Kach* movement. In April 1977 he announced that he would establish a Jewish settlement in Nablus (in the occupied West Bank) but the Israeli authorities subsequently banned him from entering the West Bank. On Aug. 29, 1979, he was sentenced to one year in prison for entering Hebron (on the West Bank) illegally, but nine months of this sentence were suspended.

Early in 1980 groups led by Rabbi Kahane were held responsible for acts of vandalism against the property of Christian churches in Jerusalem. On May 13, 1980, he was detained, together with Baruch Green, a leading member of the *Kach* movement, under emergency powers following reports that he was setting up an underground army to attack Arabs on the West Bank. Although on Aug. 6, 1980, the Prime Minister (Menahem Begin) lifted the detention order against him (though not that against B. Green), he continued to serve a prison sentence on charges of provoking disturbances until he was released on Dec. 12 of that year. Some of his followers had earlier been involved in a bomb attack on the New York offices of the (Soviet) Aeroflot airlines, and in order to enforce his release from prison in Israel four of his organization's members on June 17, 1980, occupied the New York offices of the *Herut* party (M. Begin's wing of the *Likud* front).

The League was strongly opposed to the Israeli withdrawal from Sinai under the 1979 peace treaty with Egypt and participated with other groups such as the *Gush Emunim* extremist settler movement in unsuccessful efforts to prevent the final withdrawal from northern Sinai in April 1982, on the grounds that the area in question had become Israeli territory by right of conquest and settlement.

Naturei Carta

Leadership. Rabbi Moshe Hirsch (sec.).

In October 1980 this anti-Zionist Jewish orthodox sect (which claimed to have 5,000 followers in Jerusalem alone) distributed leaflets urging members of the orthodox community to resist state tax collection and even to murder tax collectors. In March 1981 hundreds of members of the sect were involved in street battles with police in Jerusalem. At the same time the sect sent a letter to the United Nations Secretary-General appealing for UN protection of the Jewish holy places in Jerusalem which, the sect claimed, were being subjected to "Zionist oppression".

In a pamphlet published by the sect it was explained that its members refused to accept any monetary benefit—social or religious—offered by the Zionist secular state and that they preferred to use the Yiddish language, not "the spoken secularized Hebrew language of Zionism—a tool of nationalism".

Redemption of Israel

Leadership. Yoel Lerner, Armand Azran.

On Aug. 8, 1978, a group of 10 members of this small organization were charged in Jerusalem with plotting to overthrow the Government and to replace it with one functioning in strict accordance with Jewish religious law, and also with planning to commit murder and arson against Arabs in East Jerusalem "with intent to incite hatred". Yoel Lerner had previously been an aide to Rabbi Meir Kahane, the leader of the Jewish Defence League (see separate entry).

Jordan

Capital: Amman   Pop. 3,104,000

The Hashemite Kingdom of Jordan has no elected Parliament and there have been no legal political parties since the abolition of a semi-official Arab National Union in 1976. There is a National Consultative Council of 60 members appointed by the King on the recommendation of the Prime Minister and on the basis, inter alia, of their "loyalty to the homeland, nation and Constitution".

Although the life of the King has repeatedly been threatened by militant Palestinians and the Moslem Brotherhood is represented in his country also, Jordan has generally been regarded as one of the politically most stable countries in the Arab world. An attempt to assassinate the King was made on Oct. 6, 1969, by members of an Islamic Liberation Party *(Tahrir)* which had been founded in the 1930s by Shaikh Takieddin Nabhani; it advocated a return to the Caliphate and government based on Koranic law, and was banned in all Arab countries.

Jordanian Communist Party (JCP)

Leadership. Arabi Awad (member of politburo).

Originally established in 1943 as the National Liberation League, the pro-Soviet JCP adopted its present name in September 1951. In July 1967 the party's central committee specified the main lines of its "struggle to eliminate the effects of Israeli aggression" and of "resistance to imperialism". In August 1973 it played a leading role in the formation of the Palestine National Front of the occupied territories (see page 213). The JCP has published illegal newspapers from time to time.

Moslem Brotherhood

Members of the Moslem Brotherhood found asylum in Jordan at the time of the movement's suppression by President Nasser of Egypt. It is represented in Amman by a spokesman for its international organization (while its headquarters have remained in Egypt), who stated in an interview (published in *Le Monde* on Feb. 28, 1980) that nobody in Jordan was perturbed by the movement. Nevertheless, the Moslem Brotherhood has supported the Iranian revolution whereas the Jordanian Government has backed Iraq in its war against Iran and has on several occasions extradited Moslem Brotherhood members to Syria (where they were wanted on criminal charges).

In the same interview the Brotherhood spokesman dismissed differences between Sunni and Shi'ite Moslems as "theological quarrels" which were "completely outdated". He also defined the essence of the Moslem Brotherhood as constituting "a protest against the failure of the Arab world", in particular its failure to resolve the Palestinian problem, to resist Western encroachment on Moslem civilization and "to wipe out corruption and chaos".

Kuwait

Capital: Kuwait   Pop. 1,355,827

The Emirate of Kuwait has a National Assembly *(Majlis)* directly elected by some 43,000 registered voters, or about 3 per cent of the country's total population. (Some 41 per cent of the population are Kuwaiti citizens, and among those excluded from the franchise are not only immigrants, but also all women, members of the armed forces and all those who cannot trace their ancestry in the state back to 1920.) At the elections of February 1981 there were 450 candidates for 50 seats in 25 constituencies, with their political aims ranging from Islamic fundamentalism to the collectivist left, while political parties remained banned. The elections resulted in the defeat of all left-wing and most right-wing candidates in a moderate poll, and most of the successful candidates were middle-class professional men.

Kuwait is the only Gulf state with diplomatic relations with the Soviet Union (which it has had since 1963), and it has advocated the establishment of such relations by all Gulf states both with the USSR and with the entire Soviet bloc.

Moslem Fundamentalists

Sporadic political opposition has come from Moslem fundamentalists, especially under the influence of the (Shi'ite) Islamic revolution in Iran. Between 20 and 30 per cent of Kuwaiti citizens are thought to be Shi'ites.

Abbas al-Mokhri (said to be the son of the Shi'ite leader in Bahrain) was arrested on Sept. 11, 1979, for making seditious political speeches in mosques after he had been warned not to sow sedition and foment feuds; later he and his family were deprived of their Kuwaiti citizenship and deported to Iran, while three other Shi'ites were similarly deprived of their nationality.

Lebanon

Capital: Beirut   Pop. 3,000,000

The Republic of Lebanon has an executive President (customarily a Maronite Christian) elected by a 99-member Chamber of Deputies which is itself elected for a four-year term by universal adult suffrage. The President appoints a Cabinet, which is customarily headed by a Sunni Moslem Prime Minister. The allocation of top political, administrative and military posts has been subject to the unwritten "National Covenant" of 1943, which also provides that there must be six Christians to every five Moslems in the Chamber; a strict grouping according to party affiliation is therefore not possible. In view of the internal security situation there have been no general elections since April 1972 and the life of the Chamber elected then has been repeatedly extended since the expiry of its term in 1976.

In the post-war period tensions between Lebanon's various ethnic and religious communities have regularly erupted into open hostilities between the assorted militia groups maintained by the contending factions. From the early 1970s the situation became additionally complex as a result of Lebanese Christian hostility to the presence in the country of large numbers of Palestine Liberation Organization (PLO) guerrillas, who were accused of having established a "state within a state" which threatened Lebanon's political integrity as well as its national security vis-à-vis Israel. Serious clashes in April 1975 steadily escalated into a fullscale civil war by September of that year, with predominantly right-wing Christian forces ranged against a leftist alliance of Lebanese Moslems and Palestinian guerrillas.

In a move to halt the civil war the Arab League (of which Lebanon is a member) decided in October 1976 to set up a 30,000-man Arab Deterrent Force (ADF) nominally controlled by the Lebanese President and charged with achieving and maintaining a ceasefire. Consisting mainly of Syrian troops from the outset, the ADF brought about a cessation of general hostilities by the end of November 1976; but in the absence of real stability the other Arab League members gradually withdrew their contingents, so that the ADF eventually became a purely Syrian force under the effective control of the Damascus regime. In view of continuing inter-communal hostilities and also of Israeli intervention in southern Lebanon the United Nations decided in March 1978 to establish a UN Interim Force in Lebanon (UNIFIL) to assist the Lebanese Government in "ensuring the return of its effective authority in the area". Meanwhile Christian forces in southern Lebanon, led by Maj. Saad Haddad and supported by Israel, gradually set up, from 1978 onwards, a de facto independent enclave later known as "Haddadland".

In order to eliminate the persistent threat to Israel's northern border areas posed by PLO forces in southern Lebanon, Israel launched a fullscale invasion of Lebanon in June 1982. This resulted in the Israeli occupation of most of Lebanon's southern half, the penetration of Beirut by Israeli forces and the eventual withdrawal of PLO and ADF forces from the Lebanese capital by Sept. 1 (although not from other parts of the country). Israeli forces nevertheless remained in military occupation of most of the southern half of Lebanon.

The Lebanese Chamber of Deputies subsequently elected (on Aug. 23, 1982) a new President of the Republic in the person of Bashir Gemayel, the leader of the Christian Phalangist militia. However, the new President-elect was killed in a bomb explosion in Beirut on Sept. 14, whereupon his elder brother, Amin Gemayel, was elected President on Sept. 21 (by 77 out of 80 votes cast by deputies). In the intervening few days Phalangist militiamen were held directly responsible for a heavy massacre of Palestinian inhabitants of two Beirut refugee camps on Sept. 16-18. Although the new Lebanese Government was on Nov. 9 granted emergency powers, little progress had been made towards re-establishing central government authority by the end of 1982; moreover, the direct Israeli-Lebanese talks which opened on Dec. 28 quickly became deadlocked over Israel's insistence that its troops would be withdrawn from Lebanon only in the context of a general withdrawn of all non-Lebanese Arab forces coupled with the creation of a demilitarized zone in southern Lebanon.

The 1943 "National Covenant" according the Lebanese Christians a dominant political role was drawn up on the basis of a 1932 census which had shown the Christians to be in a majority, i.e. 56 per cent of the total population. However, by the mid-1970s it was generally accepted, in the absence of any later official figures, that the Moslems had come to form the majority and therefore had some justification for their demand for fundamental changes in the country's political and economic structure. Of some 20 recognized religious communities, the Christian ones are, in descending order of numerical strength, the Maronites (over 25 per cent of the total population), Greek Orthodox (10 per cent), Greek Catholics, Armenian Orthodox, Armenian Catholics, Protestants, Syrian Catholics, Latin Catholics, Syrian Orthodox and Chaldeans; of the Moslems, the Sunnites form the largest community, followed by the Shi'ites and the small Druse community (an offshoot of the Shi'ites).

Most of these communities have their own militia forces independent of the central Government.

The Maronites (one of the largest Eastern-rite communities of the Roman Catholic Church) trace their origin to St Maron, a Syrian hermit of about AD 400, and St John Maron, Patriarch of Antioch in 685-707, under whose leadership the Maronites became a fully independent people. The Maronite Church has been in communion with the Roman Catholic Church since the 17th century; its head, the Patriarch of Antioch, is elected by its bishops and approved by the Pope.

(Details of the various Palestinian guerrilla organizations with bases in Lebanon are given in a separate section on Palestinian Movements—see pages 196-214.)

Christian Groups

Armenian Community

The Armenian community in Lebanon, estimated to total some 250,000 people, remained neutral during the 1975-76 civil war. The newspaper *Al-Amal,* the organ of the Phalangist Party, alleged on Sept. 12, 1979, that the Armenians were seeking to establish an "autonomous zone" in Bourg Hammoud and Nabaa (in east Beirut). The Armenians, on the other hand, claimed that there was an organized campaign by some parties "to repress their community and to force them to change their policy of neutrality".

For activities of the Armenian Secret Army, established in Beirut on Oct. 22, 1975, see entry under Turkey (page 490).

Cedar Guardians

Leadership. Saïd Akl.

This extreme right-wing group based in the Christian heartland in the mountains north of Beirut was active during the 1975-76 civil war. In mid-1979 it was also involved in clashes with the Tiger Militia of the National Liberal Party led by former President Camille Chamoun. (The green cedar tree is regarded by Christians as the national emblem of Lebanon.)

Haddad Christian Militia

Leadership. Maj. Saad Haddad (commander).

This militia force was set up during the civil war in Lebanon in order to defend Christian-inhabited areas in southern Lebanon against Syrian forces which had entered Lebanon and also against Palestinian guerrillas. In February 1978 Maj. Haddad called for the establishment of a "government-in-exile" in the south, which would declare the Syrians to be invaders. These areas were occupied by Israel in March 1978 but were left under Christian Militia control after Israel had, in June 1978, withdrawn from southern Lebanon, sectors of which were then occupied by units of the UN Interim Force in Lebanon (UNIFIL) pending the arrival of Lebanese Army units.

In a report by Dr Kurt Waldheim (then UN Secretary-General), approved by the UN Security Council on Dec. 8, 1978, it was stated that Israel had (in June 1978) handed over control to "de facto armed groups" (i.e. the Christian Militia of Maj. Haddad). By April 1979 Maj. Haddad's forces were in control of an eight-mile-wide strip along the entire border of Lebanon with Israel and prevented the Lebanese Army from occupying this area. On April 18 Maj. Haddad declared it "an independent free Lebanese state", called on the Lebanese President (then Elias Sarkis) to resign, declared the Lebanese Parliament to be illegal, and added that no elections would be held in his zone because of the military situation.

Maj. Haddad's declaration was not explicitly supported by Israel, and the Lebanese Government accused him of treason and discharged him from the Lebanese Army. His declaration was also rejected by France, the United Kingdom, the United States and the Arab states. On April 20, 1979, Maj. Haddad stated that he had set up a military council in his zone to carry out the functions of a government, but he stressed that his forces were still part of the Lebanese Front (an alliance of Lebanon's Christian parties).

From then onwards Maj. Haddad's Militia was involved in several clashes with UNIFIL units. In August 1979 Maj. Haddad accused the United States of supporting the Palestinian guerrillas by seeking to put an end to pre-emptive strikes against them by Israel, and he added that his own forces had been "abandoned by the Christian world" for economic reasons. Close co-operation continued, however, between Maj. Haddad's Militia and Israel, which in April 1980 denied having set up military positions in his proclaimed "independent" state. The UN Security Council repeatedly condemned the actions of the "de facto force". A demand made on March 18, 1981, by the UNIFIL commander (Maj.-Gen. William Callaghan of Ireland) for the ending of Israel's assistance in the Christian-held area was rejected by the head of Israel's northern command.

On Nov. 8, 1981, Maj. Haddad expressed the hope that his "free Lebanon" would "spread and extend to cover all the Lebanese territory", since this was, he claimed, "the wish of every honest Lebanese". Following the June 1982 invasion of Lebanon by Israel, the Israeli Prime Minister announced on June 7 that the extent of "Haddadland" would be enlarged by the area of Beaufort Castle (a crusader fortress which had been a PLO command centre about five kilometres north of Israel's border). In the direct negotiations which opened between Israel and Lebanon at the end of December 1982, the Israeli side demanded that Maj. Haddad's forces should be given a recognized security role in the demilitarized zone sought by Israel in southern Lebanon in return for an undertaking to withdraw its troops.

Marada Militia

Leadership. Soleiman Frangié (l.).

The family of Soleiman Frangié, who was President of Lebanon in 1970-76, has traditionally controlled a Christian area centred around Zghorta (northern Lebanon). The ex-President has always retained good relations with the Syrians, and in May 1978 there was an open reconciliation between him and a leading Sunni Moslem, Rashid Karami, who had held numerous posts in Lebanese Governments and had been Prime Minister in 1975-76. He thus incurred the enmity of the (extreme right-wing Christian) Phalangists. On June 13, 1978, Phalangist forces, intent upon extending their control to the northern Christian areas, killed the ex-President's eldest son Tony, the latter's wife and his daughter at Ehden (south-east of Tripoli). In ensuing fighting between Phalangists and Frangié's supporters, then organized as the Zghorta Liberation Army, numerous casualties were suffered by both sides.

Followers of Soleiman Frangié, by now organized in the Marada Militia, subsequently fought back against the Phalangists, attacking in particular the family of their leader, Pierre Gemayel. They kidnapped a Phalangist member of Parliament on Feb. 13, 1980, but released him on March 9 after an exchange of prisoners held by the two sides had taken place on March 5. In May 1980 Marada militiamen unsuccessfully attempted to occupy several Phalangist-held villages near Batroun (on the coast, about 25 miles north of Beirut), and over the following two years relations between these two Christian movements remained tense.

Maronite League

This extremist "Phoenician nationalist" group, linked to the Maronite Organization led by Dr Fouad Chemali, is thought to have had considerable influence within the larger militant Christian movements such as the Phalangists, particularly during the period of the 1975-76 civil war.

Organization of Revolutionaries of the North (ORN)

This Organization, believed to be closely associated with the Phalangist militia and opposed to Soleiman Frangié, claimed on Oct. 10, 1979, to have assassinated five Frangié followers whom it had abducted on Oct. 9.

Phalangist Militia *(Kataëb)*

Leadership. Fadi Frem (commander).

This militia force is the military arm of the Phalangist Party, which was established in 1936 as a right-wing Maronite Christian formation under the leadership of Pierre Gemayel. In more recent years the Phalangists have been the strongest partner in the Lebanese Front of conservative Christian forces and have been the most active Christian grouping in the country's long-running inter-communal strife. A particular object of Phalangist hostility has been the presence in the country of guerrilla forces of the Palestine Liberation Organization (PLO), which was accused of forging an alliance with leftist Moslem groups intent on overthrowing Lebanon's established political and economic structure (under which Christians had enjoyed a traditional ascendancy).

Following serious fighting between the (Christian-officered) Lebanese Army and Palestinian guerrillas in April-May 1973, the Phalangists took the lead among Christian groupings in building up unofficial armed militia units to counterbalance the PLO presence. During this period Christian leaders repeatedly condemned the alleged intervention of the Palestinians in internal Lebanese affairs. Pierre Gemayel in particular demanded a national referendum to decide whether the guerrillas should continue to operate from Lebanon and also called on the Government to repudiate the Cairo agreement of 1969 under which the Palestinians had been authorized to establish camps in Lebanon and conduct military actions against Israel.

Following further heavy fighting between the two sides in mid-1974, the escalation of hostilities into a virtual civil war began in mid-April 1975 when Phalangist militiamen clashed with Palestinian guerrillas in the Beirut area. According to PLO sources, armed Phalangists on April 13 ambushed a bus returning a group of Palestinians to the Tal Zaatar refugee camp on the outskirts of Beirut as it passed through the suburb of Ain Rumaneh (a Phalangist stronghold in the eastern sector of the capital), killing 27 men, women and children. On the other hand, Phalangist spokesmen claimed that the fighting had started when guerrillas opened fire from a car on a church in Ain Rumaneh in which Pierre Gemayel was attending mass; according to this account, Palestinian reinforcements had quickly arrived in a bus and a shoot-out had occurred between the guerrillas and "the population of the area". Whatever the actual circumstances of this incident, it marked the onset of general hostilities between the Phalangists and other Christian militia groups on the one hand and an alliance of leftist Moslems and their Palestinian allies on the other.

Under the leadership of Bashir Gemayel (the youngest son of Pierre Gemayel), the Phalangist Militia played a major role on the Christian side in the ensuing civil war, which was eventually brought to a precarious ceasefire in late 1976 through the intervention of a predominantly Syrian Arab Deterrent Force (ADF). A feature of the latter stages of the 1975-76 conflict was the support which Syrian forces gave to the Lebanese Christians in their successful counter-offensive against the Moslem-Palestinian side, after the latter had appeared to be gaining the upper hand militarily. This Syrian alignment on the side of the Christians reflected the interest of the Damascus regime in restoring a stable central government in Lebanon under pro-Syrian Christians such as the then President, Soleiman Frangié, and with the continued participation of moderate Moslem leaders. For their part, the Phalangists regarded the alliance with the Syrians as a short-term expedient to facilitate the defeat of the Moslem-Palestinian leftists, and remained hostile to Syrian aspirations to hegemony over Lebanon.

Although making common cause with other Christian factions in the struggle against the Moslem-Palestinian leftists, the Phalangist Militia was, for much of the civil war and subsequently, also in conflict with the militia forces of the National Liberal Party (NLP) led by Camille Chamoun. Periodic clashes also occurred in the late 1970s between the Phalangists and the Lebanese Armenian community, which had remained neutral during the civil war. Following particularly heavy clashes between the NLP and Phalangists in Beirut in May 1979, the two sides announced the creation of a joint military command, but this agreement failed to prevent the outbreak of further fighting between the two factions. On July 7, 1980, the Phalangists launched an attack on the offices and strongholds of the NLP in east Beirut and defeated the NLP's militia. In October 1980 the Phalangists went on the offensive in Ain Rumaneh (the east Beirut suburb now nominally controlled by the Lebanese Army but still containing remnants of the NLP militia), and on Oct. 29 the Phalangists claimed to have purged Ain Rumaneh of NLP groups.

The Phalangists thus established control over much of east Beirut and the Christian enclave north of the capital (except areas held by the militia of ex-President Frangié and by the Armenians), where they took over responsibility for levying taxes and customs duties. They were said to have spent large sums of money on light and medium-sized weapons from France, Britain and West Germany and were also in receipt of arms supplies (including heavy weapons) from the Israelis, as confirmed by Israel for the first time in April 1981. Also in April 1981 the Israelis for the first time intervened directly on the side of the Phalangists when they shot down two Syrian helicopters which were involved in an assault by ADF forces on Phalangist positions in Zahle (20 miles to the east of Beirut).

Following the June 1982 Israeli invasion of Lebanon, Phalangist forces were reported to have co-operated closely with the Israelis in actions to eliminate the military presence of the PLO from Beirut. Immediately after the assassination of President-elect Bashir Gemayel on Sept. 14, 1982, Phalangist militia units carried out an operation (approved and sponsored by the Israelis) designed to "purge" the Chatila and Sabra refugee camps in west Beirut of PLO guerrillas who had remained in hiding since the general evacuation of Palestinian and ADF forces from the capital during late August. This operation (on Sept. 16-18) in effect became a massacre of civilians including women and children—the number of dead being variously given as less than 500 and more than 1,200—and was widely condemned by the international community and within Israel itself. An Israeli independent judicial inquiry into the massacre found, in its report published on Feb. 8, 1983, that the killings had been carried out by the Phalangists but that various Israeli political and military leaders bore varying degrees of indirect responsibility for its occurrence, notably in that the Phalangists had been allowed to enter the camps without direct Israeli supervision. Phalangist leaders themselves, on the other hand, have consistently refused to accept any responsibility for the September 1982 Beirut atrocities.

Tiger Militia

This Militia was formed as the military wing of the National Liberal Party led by former President Camille Chamoun and constituting the second strongest group in the (Christian) Lebanese Front after the Phalangists (see separate entry). After the Tiger Militia groups had been attacked and largely defeated by Phalangists, Dany Chamoun (their leader) accused the Phalangists (on July 8, 1980) of treachery and of attempting forcibly to create a single party for the Christians of Lebanon; he also announced his resignation as leader of the Tiger Militia but stated later that he would move to west Beirut to continue his struggle against the Phalangists, whom he described as "blood-thirsty madmen".

Moslem Movements

Al-Mourabitoun Militia

Leadership. Ibrahim Koleïlat (l.).

Members of this left-wing (Nasserite) Moslem group were reported to have been involved in a clash with guards of Dany Chamoun, then leader of the Tiger Militia of the (Christian) National Liberal Party (NLP) while he was visiting the Saudi Arabian ambassador in hospital on Dec. 15, 1978. In February 1980 *al-Mourabitoun* took control of most government buildings in the southern coastal port of Sidon after Syrian troops had withdrawn from them.

Fighting took place in west Beirut in November 1980 between *al-Mourabitoun* members and followers of the (pro-Syrian) Syrian Nationalist Social Party—also known as the Syrian Popular Party and standing for a Greater Syria, to include also Lebanon.

On April 26, 1981, *al-Mourabitoun* units attacked the port of Jounieh (north of Beirut), the headquarters of the Phalangist Christian militia, and in this attack military equipment supplied by Libya was used; it was also reported that some 300 Libyans had been attached to the *al-Mourabitoun* militia. In June 1981 *al-Mourabitoun* members were also involved in fighting with Kurdish activists.

Amal ("Hope")

Leadership. Shaikh Muhammad Mandi Shams ad-Din (principal controller of Command Council); Sadr ad-Din as-Sadr (ch.).

Amal was set up in 1979 as the military wing of the political movement of the Shi'ite Moslem community (a traditionally poor and underprivileged section of the population). Largely under the influence of the Islamic revolution in Iran and of the disappearance of the Shi'ite spiritual leader, Imam Moussa Sadr, at the end of a visit to Libya in August 1978, *Amal* began to launch actions against Palestinian and Lebanese leftists supporting Iraq. A large number of Shi'ite Moslems lived in the "independent" Christian enclave of Maj. Saad Haddad in southern Lebanon.

In March 1980, when *Amal* had organized demonstrations against the disappearance of the leader of some 6,000,000 Shi'ite Moslems in Iraq (Ayatollah Mohammed Bakr al Sadr), fighting broke out between *Amal* followers and those of the Arab Liberation Front, said to be backed by the pro-Iraqi faction of the *Baath* party in Lebanon. Further fighting between *Amal* supporters and pro-Iraqi Lebanese and Palestinians broke out at the end of June 1980 and again in March 1981.

Of the members of a new Cabinet appointed on Oct. 25, 1980, three Shi'ite Ministers of State resigned on Dec. 4, 1980, in response to pressure from *Amal* which refused to accept them as representatives of the Shi'ite community. However, despite a call by *Amal* to boycott cabinet meetings, the ministers complied with a request from the Prime Minister to continue in office (in mid-December).

During August 1981 *Amal* forces were involved in clashes with left-wing and Palestinian groups, in particular with the (pro-Soviet) Lebanese Communist Party and also the Organization of Communist Action in Lebanon.

By mid-1982 *Amal*'s forces had grown to about 30,000 fighters, which made them the largest (non-Palestinian) fighting force in Lebanon after the Phalangists. In March 1982 *Amal* proclaimed the Ayatollah Ruhollah Khomeini (the spiritual leader of Iran's Shias) the Imam of all Moslems throughout the world.

Front for the Liberation of Lebanon from Foreigners

A group of this name claimed responsibility for planting two car bombs in west Beirut on Feb. 23, 1982 (as well as for a serious bomb attack in Damascus, Syria, on Nov. 29, 1981, when at least 90 people were killed and over 135 injured, and also for the bombing of the office of the Ministry of Information, including the office of the *Al-Baath* newspaper, in Damascus on Feb. 18, 1982).

Lebanese National Movement

Leadership. Walid Jumblatt (l.).

This left-wing Moslem alliance arose out of an agreement concluded on Sept. 12, 1977, by Walid Jumblatt, chairman of the Progressive Socialist Party, with the pro-Syrian *Baath* party organization in Lebanon. (Walid Jumblatt's father, Kamal, had led a similar coalition of pro-Palestinian leftist Moslem groups during the 1975-76 civil war but had been assassinated in March 1977.) The objectives of the Movement were "the abolition of political confessionalism in state institutions and services, the creation of a Lebanese Army capable of restoring security, of safeguarding the unity of the country and of participating in the national struggle against the Zionist enemy, co-operation at the highest level between Lebanon and Syria and the application of the Lebanese-Palestinian agreements".

Jumblatt being a Druse, units of the movement were repeatedly involved in clashes of

Moslem Druses with Christian militias. In 1979 the Movement opposed the deployment of Lebanese Army units in southern Lebanon on the ground that the Army was then "an instrument in the hands of the Christians". According to the Lebanese authorities, 170 persons were killed in fighting between units of the Movement and Christian militia groups in October-December 1982.

Lebanese Revolutionary Party (LRP)

The leader of this right-wing group, Capt. Samir al-Ashqar, was killed with 15 of his supporters in a gun battle with regular Lebanese Army soldiers on Nov. 1, 1978. An unsuccessful attempt on the life of Fuad Boutros, the Lebanese Foreign Minister, made on the following day, was attributed to members of the LRP.

Organization of Holy Struggle

The Organization claimed responsibility for planting two car bombs in west Beirut on Feb. 23, 1982 (for which the Front for the Liberation of Lebanon from Foreigners also claimed responsibility). A spokesman for the Organization described the attack as the start of a fierce war against Syrian forces "in reply to the extermination to which our beloved families in Tripoli were subjected". This was a reference to fighting on Feb. 19-21, 1982, between Alawite and Sunni Moslems in the northern city of Tripoli, involving the Syrian-backed Arab Democratic Party and the (Sunni) Popular Resistance Movement, said to be backed by *Al-Fatah*, the Palestinian guerrilla movement.

Sons of Imam Moussa Sadr

A group of 12 Shi'ite gunmen, using the above name and apparently being supporters of *Amal* (see separate entry), seized a Kuwaiti aircraft at Beirut airport on Feb. 24, 1982, and demanded that it should be taken to Tehran (this being the eighth hijack attempt to secure the release from alleged captivity in Libya of the Imam Moussa Sadr—see under *Amal*). However, on Feb. 25 the hijackers surrendered to Lebanese army units, freeing the 125 passengers involved, and without the hijackers being detained (their leader having led six of the previous hijacks without ever being prosecuted).

Other Moslem Groups

Other Moslem groups which have been active in Lebanon include the following:

Alawite Youth, a pro-Syrian group with a militia in northern Lebanon.

Arab Liberation Party, led by Rashid Karami (who had been Prime Minister from

June 1975 to December 1976) and based in Tripoli (northern Lebanon).

Fityân Ali Organization, a Shi'ite Moslem formation led by Ahmed Safouan.

Islamic Group, associated with the Moslem Brotherhood and centred on Tripoli (Lebanon).

Pioneers of Reform, led by Saeb Salam (who had been Prime Minister from October 1970 to April 1973).

Left-wing Movements

Lebanese Armed Revolutionary Factions

Members of this group made an attempt to kill the US chargé d'affaires in Paris (Christian Chapman) in November 1981, when it accused the United States of leading "a fascist, Zionist, reactionary alliance against the Lebanese people", and it later claimed responsibility for killing the US deputy military attaché in Paris (Lt.-Col. Charles Ray) on Jan. 18, 1982.

Lebanese Communist Party (*Parti Communiste Libanais,* PCL)

Leadership. Nicolas Chaoui (s.g.).

Formed in October 1924, the PCL began its activities by fighting against the French occupation of Lebanon (under a League of Nations mandate) and for national independence, democratic freedoms and social and economic demands of the working people. In 1925 it became affiliated to the Communist International (Comintern). It achieved a measure of legality in 1936 and was recognized by law in 1970. In 1965 it formed part of a National Progressive Front and on the outbreak of civil war in April 1975 it joined the alliance of pro-Palestinian Moslem leftists in the struggle against the Lebanese Christians.

The objectives of the PCL within the leftist Lebanese National Movement reconstituted in September 1977 have been to safeguard the unity of the people, the territorial integrity of Lebanon and its Arab character, to defend its independence and sovereignty, to liberate southern Lebanon from Israeli occupation, and to strengthen co-operation with Arab countries, in particular with Syria, and with the Soviet Union, other socialist countries and the non-aligned and third-world countries. The final aim of the (pro-Soviet) PCL is to establish a national democratic regime to open the road to transition to socialism. It issues several publications, in particular the daily *An-Nida.*

Lebanese Red Brigades

This group was reported to have claimed responsibility for the killing of the French ambassador in Beirut (Louis Delamare) on Sept. 4, 1981.

Other Left-wing Groups

Other left-wing groups which have been active in Lebanon in recent years include the following:

Organization of Communist Action in Lebanon (OCAL), led by Mohsen Ibrahim.

Workers' League *(Ligue Ouvrière),* led by Ryad Rahd.

Libya

Capital: Tripoli

Pop. 3,075,000

The Popular Socialist Libyan Arab *Jamahiriyah* ("State of the Masses") has, under its Constitution of March 1977, a General People's Congress assisted by a General Secretariat as its executive and also a General People's Committee acting as a Cabinet. However, effective power is held by Col. Moamer al-Kadhafi, and there are no political parties.

Reports of continuing internal opposition to the regime and of attempts to overthrow it (e.g. by an unsuccessful army revolt in Tobruk in mid-August 1980, when several hundred people were reported to have been killed) have consistently been dismissed by the Libyan regime as being inspired from abroad, especially by Egypt. Opposition to Col. Kadhafi by exiles has been fragmented into groups of Arab nationalists, Islamic fundamentalists and liberals, all of whom have published leaflets and magazines which they have tried to smuggle into Libya through sympathizers in the customs service, armed forces and police. Several such external groups have received support from neighbouring Arab states opposed to the Kadhafi regime in Libya.

Col. Kadhafi stated on April 27, 1980, that all Libyans living in exile would have to return to Libya by June 11, 1980, failing which they would be killed abroad. The secretary of the Libyan "people's bureau" (i.e. embassy) in London stated publicly on June 12, 1980, that Libyan "revolutionary committees" based in Britain had passed death sentences on two opponents of the Libyan regime then living in London (after two other Libyans had already been murdered in London on April 11 and 25 respectively), and that he approved of this decision, whereupon he was expelled from Britain. Other Libyans were assassinated in Italy during March-June 1980, in the Federal Republic of Germany on May 10, in Greece on May 21 and also in Lebanon. From the United States a number of Libyans were expelled in April-May 1980, among them two members of the "people's bureau" in Washington who had distributed leaflets calling for the elimination of "enemies of the revolution" abroad, and also four members of a Libyan "people's committee".

On June 11, 1980, Col. Kadhafi instructed his "revolutionary committees" to halt their overseas assassination campaign except in the cases of "those who are convicted by a revolutionary court" and "those who have been proved—by any means, even if not by a revolutionary court—to have had dealings with the Egyptian, Israeli or US authorities". More assassinations and attempts on the lives of Libyan exiles were made in Europe, the Middle East and the United States during 1981.

External Opposition

Libyan Democratic Movement

Numerous victims of the official Libyan assassination campaign were thought to have been members of this Movement, which was established in 1977 by exiled opponents of the Kadhafi regime.

Libyan National Association

Leadership. Mustafa al-Barki (ch.).

This Association was formed in Cairo in December 1980 to encompass the Libyan community in Egypt (said to number about 25,000 people), and to serve the social and humanitarian needs of those who had "escaped from Kadhafi's terror". At its foundation it was announced that a political department was to be formed within the Association "to carry out various forms of opposition to Kadhafi".

Libyan National Salvation Front *(Al-Jabah al-Wataniyah li inqadh Libya)*

Leadership. Dr Mohammed Yusuf al-Magariaf (spokesman).

The creation of this Front was announced in Khartoum (Sudan) on Oct. 7, 1981, its avowed aim being to "liberate Libya and save it from Kadhafi's rule"; to find "the democratic alternative"; and to unite "all nationalist elements inside and outside Libya in an integral programme of action and struggle" in order to replace the existing regime by a constitutional, democratically-elected government. This was to consist of a presidential council and a provisional administration with a term of office of up to one year, during which it would establish constitutional rule; a national constituent assembly, to be elected in a general election, was to draft a constitution for submission to a national referendum; under this constitution presidential elections would be held and power would be transferred to elected institutions; there would also be legislative elections.

The Front claimed to have contacts with high-ranking Libyan officials and supporters within Libya's armed forces. It was affiliated to an "Afro-Arab International Committee against Kadhafi". (There were said to be about 100,000 Libyans living in exile.) Dr Magariaf had been Libya's ambassador to India until his resignation from government service in mid-1980.

It was reported from Saudi Arabia on April 22, 1982, that a spokesman for the Front, Ahmed Ibrahim Ahwash, had stated that there was no hope of any dialogue with the current Libyan regime and that Col. Kadhafi was "internally isolated" in the face of "economic collapse, administrative anarchy and political muddle, in addition to popular indignation at all levels and in all sectors". It was further reported from Riyadh on April 28, 1982, that the Front had issued a plea to Libyans to bring Col. Kadhafi and his regime to trial for "crimes" committed against "innocent citizens, against the Arab and Islamic nation and against human rights and justice", and had reiterated its denunciation of his foreign activities.

Warriors for Imam Moussa Sadr

This organization was formed by Shi'ites in Lebanon with the object of obtaining the release of the Imam Moussa Sadr, who had been the spiritual leader of the Shi'ites in Lebanon. He had disappeared after a visit to Libya in August 1978 and was believed to be held captive in that country, although the Libyan Government had repeatedly denied having any knowledge of his whereabouts. The Warriors organization, as the military arm of the Lebanese Shi'ite *Amal* ("Hope") movement, repeatedly hijacked airliners in order to draw attention to the case of the Imam but in all such cases the hijackers eventually surrendered and released the aircraft concerned. In particular a Libyan airliner hijacked on a flight from Zurich on Dec. 7, 1981, was eventually released in Beirut by the five members of the organization concerned, after they had been refused landing rights in Iran.

Internal Opposition

Libyan Baathist Party

One of the founders of this party, Amer Taher Dgaies, died in police custody on Feb. 27, 1980, and his funeral on the following day led to anti-Kadhafi demonstrations by several thousand people in Tripoli.

Mauritania

Capital: Nouakchott

Pop. 1,650,000

The Republic of Mauritania (a member of the Arab League) is ruled by a Military Committee of National Salvation (CMSN) of 27 members, headed by a chairman who is President of the Republic (posts held by Lt.-Col. Khouna Ould Haidalla since January 1980). There is also a civilian Council of Ministers headed by a Prime Minister, but there is neither a parliament nor a legal political party. Under a Constitutional Charter published on July 28, 1978, executive power was given to the Chairman of the Military Committee of National Recovery (which was superseded by the CMSN on April 6, 1979); the Charter was to remain effective "until new democratic institutions are established".

On Dec. 19, 1980, the CMSN published a draft Constitution providing inter alia that Mauritania should be "an Islamic, parliamentary, indivisible and democratic republic" with a President elected for a (non-renewable) six-year term and a National Assembly which would be elected for a four-year term. Political parties were to be permitted (although not the Mauritanian People's Party, which had been the country's sole legal party until July 1978).

Former President Ould Daddah, overthrown in July 1978, and resident in France since October 1979, was on Nov. 21, 1980, reported to have been sentenced in absentia to hard labour for life on charges of high treason, violating the Constitution and damaging Mauritania's economic interests. Over the following two years other leading members of former regimes were prominent in various opposition groups (mostly operating in exile) and at least two attempts were made to overthrow the Government—in March 1981 and February 1982. As a result of the latter attempt 10-year prison sentences were passed on Col. Mustapha Ould Mohamed Salek (who overthrew President Ould Daddah in 1978 and effectively led the Mauritanian regime until mid-1979) and on two former ministers.

Alliance for a Democratic Mauritania
(Alliance pour une Mauritanie Démocratique, AMD)

The AMD was established in 1980 as an opposition front sympathetic to former President Ould Daddah of Mauritania (overthrown in July 1978). It was based in Paris, with active branches in Senegal (known as the Movement of Free Officers) and in Morocco (the Islamic Party and the Movement of National Unity), and it appeared to be supported by the Mauritanian Democratic Union and the (Haratine) "Free Man" Movement (see separate entries). It was also said to have links with pro-Iraqi or pan-Arab elements in the Mauritanian Government.

In June 1980 the Movement called for the overthrow of the military regime in Mauritania, but an attempt to bring this about was foiled on March 16, 1981, when an attempted coup led to the death of 28 people, including 13 civilians, and to 60 arrests. The leaders of this attempt—Lt.-Col. Mohamed Ould Ba Ould Abdelkader and Lt.-Col. Ahmed Salem Ould Sidi, both former members of the CMSN and founder members of the AMD—were, with two lieutenants, condemned to death on March 24, 1981, for "high treason, desertion, murder and intelligence with the enemy" (i.e. Morocco) and executed on March 26. Five other defendants were given life sentences and three more were later sentenced to death in absentia.

Free Man Movement

This Movement aims at representing the interests of the (mixed-race) Haratines who have complained of forced Arabization and of discrimination based on colour. The Haratines are the descendants of freed Black slaves who adopted Moorish (Arab-Berber) customs and the local Hassaniya Arabic dialect, continued to perform menial work and are still in many cases regarded as the property of their Arab-Berber employers. Many Haratines are workers on land owned by absentee landlords, and the official abolition of slavery on July 5, 1980, was widely regarded as a first step towards land reform.

Early in 1980 the clandestine "Free Man" Movement distributed tracts denouncing the ruling armed forces as having a "shady rascist side" and alleging that the Haratines were "oppressed because of the colour of their skin". A number of the Movement's leaders were arrested and tried at Rosso (near the border with Senegal).

Mauritanian Democratic Union (*Union Démocratique Mauritanienne*, UDM)

The UDM was established in Senegal and inter alia called for a joining of forces between Black Africans (making up about one-third of Mauritania's population) and the (half-caste) Haratines (almost equal in number to the Black Africans) to confront the country's dominant Arab Berbers.

Walfougi Front

The formation of the Armed Front for the Self-determination of the Black African Population of the Southern Mauritanian Regions of Walo, Fouta and Guidimalia (or Walfougi Front) was announced in March 1979 in a letter to foreign ambassadors accredited in Dakar. In leaflets distributed in early 1979, Black Africans criticized the military Government and Mauritania's membership of the Arab League, and a number of Blacks were arrested in this connexion.

The Black community has also opposed the imposition of Arabic as the main national language and called for the continued use of French and the numerous tribal languages. The Blacks have also called for an even distribution of posts in the administration between the country's ethnic communities and supported the cession of the southern half of Western Sahara to the Saharan Arab Democratic Republic (of the Polisario Front).

Morocco

Capital: Rabat   Pop. 21,274,000

The Kingdom of Morocco is "a sovereign Moslem state" and "a constitutional democratic and social (hereditary) monarchy", with the King appointing, and presiding over, the Cabinet. There is a unicameral Chamber of Representatives, the 264 members of which are elected for a six-year term—176 of them by direct universal adult suffrage and 88 by an electoral college consisting of local councillors and representatives of professional and employees' organizations. In the elections of June 1977 seats were won by seven political parties and two trade unions.

Although all political parties supported the Moroccan Government in its annexation of Western Sahara, members of left-wing parties were on a number of occasions detained or tried. In September 1981 three leaders of the Socialist Union of Popular Forces were sentenced to a year in prison after issuing a statement criticizing some aspects of an Organization of African Unity resolution on a referendum to be held in Western Sahara, but on Feb. 26, 1982, the King granted them a pardon and they were released. Extra-parliamentary opposition to the regime comes mainly from left-wing organizations, in particular of students, although in the early 1980s incidents related to the activities of Moslem fundamentalists also began to be reported.

Forward Movement *(Ilal Amam)*

This Movement emerged in 1974, when a large number of persons were arrested between March and September for distributing "seditious literature" and forming three ex-treme left-wing groups—*Ilal Amam*, the 23rd March Group and *Al-Moutakalinine* ("Rally")—which were to be merged in a Marxist-Leninist front with a "Red Army". Their declared objective was to set up a "people's democratic republic'' to be headed by Abraham Serfaty, an anti-Zionist Jewish engineer who had been a member of the Moroccan Communist Party (banned in 1952) and of the Party of Liberation and Socialism (which existed in 1968-69) and who was said to have Maoist views. On Feb. 15, 1977, a total of 176 of the arrested persons were sentenced to terms of imprisonment, 44 of them for life, among them A. Serfaty. On Feb. 23, 1980, three students were given prison sentences for attempting to reconstitute *Ilal Amam* and for disturbing the public order. (The present-day continuation of the former Communist and Liberation and Socialism parties is the pro-Soviet Party of Progress and Socialism, a legal formation represented in the Moroccan Parliament.)

National Union of Moroccan Students (*Union Nationale des Etudiants du Maroc,* UNEM)

This student organization was officially banned in January 1973 after it had for years agitated for educational reforms and for certain rights such as co-determination and dispensation from military services (rights which were granted in April 1972) and had also organized protest demonstrations against the detention in Casablanca of a group of students and teachers on charges of having established ''Marxist cells'' and thus endangered internal security. Despite the ban the UNEM remained active, and its leaders were on several occasions detained for demonstrating and distributing anti-government leaflets. In 1976 three of them were said to have died in prison.

The ban on the UNEM was lifted in November 1978 but the union's members continued to protest against the authorities allegedly preventing them from conducting normal activities among students. In 1980 they also agitated for the release of political prisoners, and a strike call by the UNEM in February 1981 was reported to have been followed by a majority of Morocco's 12,000 university students, mainly in protest against delay in implementing university reforms decreed in 1975. At that time the majority of the members of the UNEM's executive committee were affiliated to the (left-wing) Socialist Union of Popular Forces (USFP) and the remainder to the (communist) Party of Progress and Socialism (PPS).

Western Sahara

Popular Front for the Liberation of Saguia el Hamra and Rio de Oro, or Polisario Front (*Frente Polisario,* PF)

Leadership. Mohamed Abdelazziz (s.g.).

The PF was established in May 1973 as a national liberation movement in the (then Spanish) Western Sahara. After the Governments of Morocco and Mauritania had, under an agreement concluded in Madrid with Spain in November 1975, divided the Western Sahara between themselves, the PF decided to take up its armed struggle against both these Governments as from November 1975, with the support of the Government of Algeria. In February 1976 the PF proclaimed a Saharan Arab Democratic Republic (SADR).

Following the overthrow of the Mauritanian Government of President Mokhtar Ould Daddah in July 1978, the PF declared a ceasefire in its military operations against Mauritania, and this decision was followed by a peace agreement between the PF and the new Goverment in Mauritania on Aug. 5, 1979, and the withdrawal of Mauritanian forces from the Western Sahara. The territory vacated by Mauritania was, however, formally annexed by Morocco on Aug. 11-12, 1979.

Heavy fighting between PF and Moroccan forces took place in the second half of 1979 and in 1980, with both sides making conflicting claims of successes. While the PF repeatedly asserted that it controlled large areas of the Western Sahara, Morocco retained full control over what it called the ''useful triangle'' near Bou Craa, the centre of the phosphate mines (although these were closed between 1977 and July 1982). By 1981 Morocco had built a wall of fortifications across the desert to protect the most important localities, but its defence expenditure had risen to about one quarter of its annual budget. It was increasingly supplied with sophisticated arms by the United States and was also reported to receive financial support from Saudi Arabia. On the other hand, it has been claimed in Morocco that the PF has been supported not only by Algeria and Libya but also by the Soviet Union, which was said to have supplied the Front with tanks, heavy artillery and ground-to-ground missiles in 1982.

Efforts to find a peaceful solution to the conflict, made by the Organization of African Unity (OAU), have been unsuccessful. An offer to hold a referendum in the Western Sahara, made by the King of Morocco at the OAU Assembly of Heads of State and Government in June 1981, has not been implemented because no agreement has been reached on the modalities of such a referendum; in particular, Morocco has refused to accept any of the preconditions advanced by the PF, including Morocco's prior withdrawal from the territory.

The SADR was admitted to the OAU in February 1982, at the instigation of the OAU's Secretary-General and on the ground that 26 of the 50 OAU member states had recognized the SADR. However, under the OAU's Charter, a quorum of two-thirds of its members was required for any decision on whether the SADR was an independent sovereign state entitled to OAU membership (which was denied by Morocco and other member states supporting the latter); during 1982 it emerged that no such quorum was obtainable and that the OAU was divided into a majority "radical" section (which favoured admission of the SADR) and a minority "moderate" section (which opposed it). The "Foreign Minister" of the SADR reaffirmed on Dec. 20, 1982, that the PF intended to participate in all future meetings of the OAU.

A PF congress held in October 1982 elected the PF's secretary-general Mohamed Abdelazziz, as President of the SADR, which also had a "Cabinet" headed by a "Prime Minister". Over 50 countries which had by then recognized the SADR as "a sovereign and independent state" included not only the majority of the OAU member states, but also those member states of the Arab League which were opposed to the Egyptian-Israeli reconciliation as well as Cuba and Iran.

Oman

Capital: Muscat   Pop. 591,000

The Sultanate of Oman is ruled by decree, with the advice of an appointed Cabinet and a 45-member State Consultative Assembly consisting of members of the Government and appointed citizen's representatives. There are no recognized political parties.

The main threat to Oman's internal security has come from the Popular Front for the Liberation of Oman operating principally in Dhofar province on Oman's western border with South Yemen. For almost 10 years the Front conducted warfare against the forces of Oman (which were supported by a small British contingent, including military advisers, in 1972-77, by forces of the Shah of Iran, and by other assistance from the United States, Jordan and other Arab states), but appeared to be practically defeated by 1976. Omani casualties in 1971-76 were given as 196 men killed and 584 wounded, while Iranian losses were said to have been much greater. The number of PFLO casualties was not known.

Popular Front for the Liberation of Oman (PFLO)

The PFLO had its origins in a Popular Front for the Liberation of the Occupied Arabian Gulf formed with the object of overthrowing the Sultan of Oman and also other "conservative" regimes in the Gulf Area. At its second congress, held in Aden in 1968, this organization's leadership was taken over by Marxists-Leninists. In February 1972 it merged with a National Democratic Front for the Liberation of the Occupied Arabian Gulf to form the Popular Front for the Liberation of Oman and the Arabian Gulf (PFLOAG). In its activities it had the support of the People's Democratic Republic of Yemen (South Yemen), from whose territory it conducted most of its operations, and also of China (until 1973) and later of the Soviet Union.

After a meeting between PFLOAG spokesmen and delegates of the Communist parties of Iraq and the Soviet Union in Aden in March 1974, the organization changed its name to "Popular Front for the Liberation of Oman", thus indicating that it was to be a national liberation movement fighting against British and Iranian "occupation armies" in Oman, and not a revolutionary organization trying to overthrow governments in the Gulf area. Efforts to achieve a ceasefire between Oman and the PFLO made by an Arab League conciliation commission, set up in March 1974, remained ineffective.

In addition to the casualties caused by the protracted warfare, a number of "rebels" were condemned to death in Oman between 1973 and 1975. In a trial held on June 15-17, 1973, a total of 19 PFLOAG members were condemned to death, 23 were given life sentences and 24 others were imprisoned for from one to 12 years. Of those condemned to death 10 were executed on June 20 and the nine others had their sentences commuted to life imprisonment. On June 30, 1974, a PFLOAG member extradited to Oman by the United Arab Emirates (UAE) was condemned to death for murdering a UAE government employee, and 37 others were given prison sentences. On April 16, 1975, four PFLO members were sentenced to death and nine others to imprisonment for plotting assass-inations and armed revolution.

A ceasefire between Oman and South Yemen, negotiated by Saudi Arabia, came in-to force on March 11, 1976, when the Sultan of Oman offered an amnesty to all Omani rebels who surrendered by May 11, 1976. Although a number surrendered, a hard core of PFLO members continued their fighting inside Dhofar province (western Oman), but there were only sporadic clashes until June 1979, when new PFLO attacks were reported. Nevertheless, surrenders of leading PFLO members to the Omani authorities continued to be announced from time to time.

A delegation of the PFLO was present at a summit meeting held in Aden on Aug. 17-19, 1981, by the leaders of Ethiopia, Libya and South Yemen, who agreed to conclude a tri-lateral treaty of friendship and co-operation providing for closer political and economic co-ordination between their Governments.

An agreement on the normalization of relations between Oman and South Yemen came into effect on Nov. 15, 1982, and ap-peared to bring a formal end to 15 years of hostility between the two states. It was noted, however, that the "Voice of Oman Revolu-tion" radio station operated from Aden (South Yemen) by the PFLO continued to broadcast material strongly critical of the Omani regime. In a gesture towards former rebels who had taken refuge in South Yemen, the Omani Government on Jan. 3, 1983, pro-clamed a further amnesty for "all Omani citizens who are still in South Yemen", offer-ing them a four-month "period of grace" to return to Oman, where "all measures" would be taken to receive and settle them.

Palestinian Movements

After World War I Palestine—which had been part of the Ottoman Empire (one of the central powers defeated in the war)—became a British mandate under League of Nations auspices. However, in the Balfour Declaration published in November 1917 the British Government had stated that it viewed "with favour the establishment in Palestine of a national home for the Jewish people, . . . it being clearly understood that nothing shall be done which may prejudice the civil and religious rights of existing non-Jewish communities". In the Middle East this declaration was strongly opposed by the Arabs, in particular those in Palestine.

In September 1921 the British Government promulgated a constitution providing for the setting-up of a Palestinian state, but this instrument was never implemented because the Arabs were unwilling to accept the concessions made in it to Zionism. In 1929 there occurred the first large-scale clashes between Jews and Arabs in Jerusalem. Following increased Jewish immigration from Europe (after the advent to power of Hitler in Germany in 1933) an Arab High Committee was formed in 1936 to unite Palestinian Arabs in opposition to the Jews, and there followed a three-year civil war between them. A British report (of the Peel Commission) published in July 1937 recommended the partition of Palestine, but this was rejected by the Arabs. In the same year the British Government outlawed the Arab High Committee and arrested or exiled its leading members. A new British proposal, reducing the size of the proposed Jewish state from that envisaged by the Peel Commission, was rejected by both Zionists and Arabs in 1938.

In a White Paper published in May 1939 the British Government declared that there would be no partition; that it was not British policy that Palestine should become either a Jewish or an Arab state; that an independent Palestinian state should be set up within 10 years; that meanwhile Jews and Arabs should be asked to take an increasing share in the country's administration; and that Jewish immigration into Palestine should be limited to 75,000 persons during the next five years, after which there was to be no further immigration without Arab consent. By 1939 the Jewish population in Palestine had risen to 445,457 or 30 per cent of the country's total. The progress of the war in Eastern Europe and mass liquidation of Jews by the Nazis brought about massive illegal immigration into Palestine by Jews from many parts of Europe.

By the end of World War II the Jewish Agency was ready to ensure the provisional government of a Jewish state through the Jewish National Council representing local Jews; on the other hand, the League of Arab States formed in March 1945 proclaimed its intention of defending the Arab cause in Palestine. Amid a serious deterioration of the security situation, various new partition proposals failed to move the Arab side from its demand for a unitary Palestinian state based on majority rule; accordingly, the British Government decided in February 1947 to refer the Palestine question to the United Nations (as the successor to the League of Nations for the purposes of the mandate). On the basis of recommendations by a UN special committee, the UN General Assembly on Nov. 29, 1947, took its historic decision in favour of partition (and thus in favour of the creation of a Jewish state) by 33 votes to 13 with 10 countries abstaining and one being absent.

The UN decision was opposed by the Arabs, who declared their determination to resist it by force. Nevertheless, the military forces of the Jews moved to establish full control over the area of the proposed Jewish state, which was officially proclaimed as Israel on May 14, 1948, a few hours before the termination of the British mandate at midnight. Simultaneously, the unco-ordinated armies of Egypt, Transjordan, Syria, Lebanon and Iraq (backed by Saudi Arabian units) invaded the new state with the declared objective of establishing the independence of Palestine for its lawful inhabitants on the basis of majority rule. However, initial Arab advances were quickly stemmed by Israeli forces, who in a successful counter-attack not only secured virtually all of the territory allotted to the Jews under the UN partition plan but also took control of substantial additional areas. Under separate armistices signed in early 1949 between Israel on the one hand and Egypt, Transjordan, Syria and Lebanon on the other (but not Iraq), the Jewish state was left in control of three-quarters of the territory of Palestine. Of what remained in Arab hands, the southern coastal strip around the town of Gaza came under Egyptian administration, while the central area of Palestine west of the Jordan river (including the Old City of Jerusalem) was incorporated into the Hashemite Kingdom of Jordan (as Transjordan was renamed in June 1949).

During the 1948-49 hostilities, between 700,000 and 900,000 Arabs either fled or were expelled from Jewish-held territory, leaving the State of Israel with a substantial Jewish majority. Most of the refugees were housed in refugee camps in the West Bank and Gaza Strip, which thus became the centres of a burgeoning Palestinian Arab nationalism having as its fundamental aim the recovery of the homeland which the Jews were seen as having expropriated. Palestinian *fedayeen* (lit. "martyrs") groups responsible for many attacks on Israeli territory during the 1950s developed into well-organized guerrilla movements, which in 1964 came together in the loose framework of the newly-formed Palestine Liberation Organization (PLO). During this period the broader tensions arising from unremitting Arab hostility to the Jewish state had erupted into a second fullscale conflict, fought between Israel and Egypt in late 1956.

In the third Arab-Israeli war (of June 1967) Israel extended its control of territory to the whole of the area of Palestine by capturing the Gaza Strip from Egypt and the West Bank (including east Jerusalem) from Jordan, while at the same time also taking the Golan Heights from Syria and overrunning the Egyptian Sinai peninsula. The hostilities resulted in a further exodus of Arab refugees, principally to Jordan and Lebanon, but the bulk of the Palestinian inhabitants of the West Bank and Gaza stayed put under Israeli military administration. The Palestinian guerrilla movements, operating at this stage mainly from Jordan and Syria, were thus deprived of their natural bases within the confines of Palestine and found it even more difficult to penetrate to targets in Israel proper, especially after King Hussein had expelled the guerrillas from Jordan in 1970-71. Thereafter, Lebanon became the main centre of Palestinian military activities against Israel, while militant PLO factions increasingly resorted to terrorist attacks on Israeli targets outside the Middle East theatre of conflict.

The outcome of the 1967 war set a new tone for the Arab-Israeli conflict, which for some years thereafter revolved less around the fundamental Palestinian Arab challenge to the legitimacy of Israel and more around the quest of Egypt, Syria and Jordan for the recovery of their lost territories. The crucial outcome of the fourth Arab-Israeli war (of October 1973) was that Egypt re-established control of the eastern side of the Suez Canal (this being the first territory wrested from Israel by military force since its creation in 1948) and was thus psychologically enabled to move towards a rapprochement with the Jewish state. This process got under way with President Sadat's historic visit to Jerusalem in November 1977, which was followed by the conclusion of the Camp David framework agreements in September 1978 and ultimately by the signature of a full peace treaty between Egypt and Israel in March 1979. For the Egyptians the importance of the peace treaty was that Israeli-controlled Sinai would be restored to Egyptian control by April 1982. For the Palestinians, on the other hand, the whole Camp David peace process represented a betrayal of the Arab cause (a view widely shared in the Arab world), particularly because it did not provide for the genuine self-determination of the Palestinian people in their own land.

The PLO and all Arab states except Egypt therefore refused to participate in the US-sponsored negotiations with Israel on the granting of some form of "autonomy" to the Palestinian inhabitants of the West Bank and the Gaza Strip, as envisaged under one of the Camp David agreements. For this and other reasons these negotiations had made virtually no progress by early 1983 (nearly four years after their commencement), during which period Palestinian opposition to the process was strengthened by the oft-repeated claim of the Begin Government that Israel possessed an historic right to sovereignty over the whole of the biblical "Land of Israel" *(Eretz Israel)*—i.e. including the West Bank, Gaza and the Golan Heights. In pursuance of this aspiration, the Israelis not only greatly expanded Jewish settlement of the occupied territories (especially the West Bank) but also passed new legislation in July 1981 strengthening the status of Jerusalem as the "indivisible" capital of Israel (as first proclaimed immediately after the June 1967 war); moreover, in late December 1981 Israel effectively annexed the Golan Heights.

Meanwhile, the Palestinian guerrilla organizations had become increasingly embroiled in the internal hostilities which broke out in Lebanon in 1975, and thereafter their virtually autonomous activities in Lebanon were viewed with increasing concern by Israel. During the late 1970s numerous military interventions were carried out by the Israelis to counter the threat to Israel's northern border area posed by the PLO presence in southern Lebanon; at the same time Israel gave active support to the Lebanese Christians in their continuing struggle with the Palestinian-backed Lebanese Moslem factions. Eventually, some six weeks after completing their withdrawal from Sinai, the Israelis launched a fullscale invasion of Lebanon in June 1982 with the declared objective of eliminating the military presence of the PLO from that country. After a two-month Israeli siege of Palestinian positions in west Beirut, an agreement was eventually reached under which PLO units withdrew from the Lebanese capital by early September, together with Syrian troops of the Arab Deterrent Force stationed in Lebanon since late 1976. But although the PLO had suffered heavy losses during the Israeli campaign, it subsequently became clear that the various Palestinian guerrilla movements remained operational notwithstanding the dispersal of many activists to a number of Arab countries. Moreover, on the political and diplomatic front the PLO continued to play a prominent role in Arab opposition to any Middle East peace settlement which did not provide for the establishment of a sovereign Palestinian state.

At all stages of the Arab-Israeli conflict the presentation of statistics relating to the Palestinians has been fraught with controversy, particularly in respect of refugee numbers resulting from the successive wars. As regards the total number of people who regard themselves as Palestinians, the PLO currently puts the figure at 4,721,000, about 500,000 higher than the official estimate of the US State Department. Of these, according to the PLO, 1,826,000 reside in "Palestine" (818,000 in the West Bank, 477,000 in the Gaza Strip and 531,000 in Israel proper), an overall figure with which the Israeli estimate nearly concurs but with a different distribution (725,000 in the West Bank, 450,000 in Gaza and 653,000 within Israel itself); the corresponding estimate of the US State Department is 1,650,000 (700,000 in the West Bank, 450,000 in Gaza and 500,000 in Israel proper).

As regards Palestinians living outside the territory of Palestine, both the PLO and the US State Department agree that Jordan east of the Jordan river has the highest number (their estimates being 1,161,000 and 1,000,000 respectively), representing over half the total population of the Hashemite Kingdom. Elsewhere the largest concentrations of Palestinians are to be found in Lebanon (600,000 according to the PLO, 400,000 according to the US State Department and 347,000 according to the Israelis), Kuwait (279,000 according to the PLO and 320,000 according to the US State Department) and Syria (216,000 according to the PLO and 250,000 according to the US State Department). As at June 30, 1982, a total of 1,925,726 Palestinians (in the Israeli-occupied territories, Jordan, Lebanon and Syria) were registered as refugees with the United Nations Relief and Works Agency for Palestine Refugees in the Near East (UNRWA).

The highest policy-making body of the dispersed Palestinian people is the Palestine National Council (PNC), a "parliament-in-exile" which meets at regular intervals to determine overall strategy and which also elects the executive committee of the PLO. Politically and diplomatically the PLO is itself regarded as the sole legitimate representative of the Palestinian people by the Arab states and much of the Third World, and also by the Soviet-bloc countries.

Umbrella Organization

Palestine Liberation Organization (PLO)
(Munazamat Tahrir Falastin)

Leadership. Mohammed Abed Arouf (Yassir) Arafat—code-named Abu Ammar (ch. of executive committee); Mohammed Affani—code-named Abu Mutasem (chief of staff).

An Iraqi proposal for the creation of a "Palestinian entity" was adopted at a meeting of the Council of the Arab League in Cairo on Sept. 16-19, 1963. At an Arab League summit meeting held in Cairo on Jan. 13-16, 1964, it was decided, on an initiative sponsored by President Nasser of Egypt, to set up the PLO under the leadership of Ahmed Shukairy (previously spokesman for Palestinian affairs at the United Nations). The inaugural session of what later became known as the Palestine National Council (PNC)—the Palestinian "parliament-in-exile"—was held

in the then Jordanian part of Jerusalem in May-June 1964 and decided (on May 28) to form the PLO as "the only legitimate spokesman for all matters concerning the Palestinian people". The PLO was to be financed by the Arab League and to recruit military units among Palestinian refugees to constitute a Palestine Liberation Army (PLA) which was to be "the vanguard for the liberation of the usurped parts of Palestine" taken by Israel in 1948 (but not of the parts of Palestine then controlled by Egypt and Jordan).

The Jerusalem meeting also adopted (on June 2, 1964) the Palestine National Charter (or Covenant) as the basic statement of Palestinian aims, this document being regarded by the Israelis as enshrining the PLO's objective of destroying the Jewish state. As amended in 1968 and reaffirmed subsequently, the 33-article Charter states inter alia that "Palestine is the homeland of the Palestinian Arab people . . . [and] is an indivisible part of the Arab homeland" *(Art. 1)*; that "Palestine, within the boundaries it had during the British mandate, is an indivisible territorial unit" *(Art. 2)*; that "the Palestinian Arab people possess the legal right to their homeland and have the right to determine their destiny after achieving the liberation of their country in accordance with their wishes and entirely of their own accord and will" *(Art. 3)*; that "the Palestinians are those Arab nationals who, until 1947, normally resided in Palestine regardless of whether they were evicted from it or have stayed there" and also all those born after that date of a Palestinian father "whether inside Palestine or outside it" *(Art. 5)*; that "the Jews who had normally resided in Palestine until the beginning of the Zionist invasion will be considered Palestinians" *(Art. 6)*.

The Charter also declares that "armed struggle is the only way to liberate Palestine" *(Art. 9)*; that "the liberation of Palestine, from an Arab viewpoint, is a national duty", involving the repelling of "Zionist and imperialist aggression against the Arab homeland" as well as "the elimination of Zionism in Palestine" *(Art. 15)*; that "the liberation of Palestine, from a spiritual point of view, will provide the Holy Land with an atmosphere of safety and tranquillity, which in turn will safeguard the country's religious sanctuaries and guarantee freedom of worship and of visit to all, without discrimination of race, colour, language or religion" *(Art. 16)*; that "the partition of Palestine in 1947 and the establishment of the state of Israel are entirely illegal, regardless of the passage of time, because they were contrary to the will of the Palestinian people and to their natural right in their homeland, and inconsistent with the principles embodied in the Charter of the United Nations, particularly the right to self-determination" *(Art. 19)*; that "the Balfour declaration, the mandate for Palestine and everything which has been based on them are deemed null and void" on the grounds that "claims of historical or religious ties of Jews with Palestine are incompatible with the facts of history and the true conception of what constitutes statehood" *(Art. 20)*; that "the Palestinian Arab people . . . reject all solutions which are substitutes for the total liberation of Palestine and reject all proposals aiming at the liquidation of the Palestinian problem or its internationalization" *(Art. 21)*; that "Zionism is a political movement originally associated with international imperialism and antagonistic to all action for liberation and to progressive movements in the world [and] is racist and fanatic in its nature, aggressive, expansionist and colonial in its aims and fascist in its methods" *(Art. 22)*; and that "the Palestine Liberation Organization . . . is responsible for the Palestinian Arab people's movement in its struggle—to retrieve its homeland, liberate and return to it

and exercise the right of self-determination in it—in all military, political and financial fields and also for whatever may be required by the Palestine case on the inter-Arab and international levels" *(Art. 26)*.

From the outset King Hussein of Jordan refused to allow the PLA to train forces in Jordan or the PLO to levy taxes from Palestinian refugees in his country. By 1966 the PLA had a detachment in Syria and in December of that year Shukairy concluded an agreement on co-operation between the PLA and Yassir Arafat's *Al-Fatah,* the main Palestinian guerrilla organization. When the Six-Day War broke out in June 1967, Shukairy placed the PLA under the "national command" of Egypt and Syria (but not Jordan); however, the PLA units were scattered by Israeli forces on the first day of the war, with the result that the PLO and PLA took no effective part in the hostilities and were largely discredited in Arab eyes. At the end of 1967 Shukairy was replaced as leader of the PLO by Yehia Hammouda.

At a meeting in Cairo in February 1969 the PNC unanimously adopted a plan of action stating inter alia that peace would be possible only "in a democratic free Palestinian state where all Palestinians, Christians, Moslems and Jews will be equal and free from Zionist racism" and that it would oppose all attempts to impose "peaceful settlements" contrary to the rights of the Palestinian people. The meeting expressed particular opposition to the terms of Resolution 242 unanimously adopted by the UN Security Council on Nov. 22, 1967, because it made no reference to the rights of the Palestinian people.

(Resolution 242 had emphasized "the inadmissibility of the acquisition of territory by war" and had affirmed that the requisites for a just and lasting peace in the Middle East included "withdrawal of Israeli armed forces from territories occupied in the recent conflict" [i.e. the June 1967 war] as well as "termination of all claims or states of belligerency and respect for an acknowledgment of the sovereignty, territorial integrity and political independence of every state in the area and their right to live in peace within secure and recognized boundaries free from threats or acts of force". It referred only indirectly to the Palestinians, in affirming the necessity "for achieving a just settlement of the refugee problem".)

Having become de facto leader of the PLO in February 1969 by virtue of *Al-Fatah's* dominance, Arafat proceeded to form a Palestine Armed Struggle Command (PASC), which by the end of that year had been joined by all Palestinian guerrilla organizations including the Syrian-backed *Al-Saiqa.* Following the expulsion of Palestinian guerrillas from Jordan in late 1970 and early 1971—see under separate entry below for the Movement for the National Liberation of Palestine *(Al-Fatah)*—the main centre of PLO military activities became Lebanon, particularly the hilly Arqoub region around Mount Hermon in the south-east adjoining the Israeli-occupied Golan Heights (and extending into Syrian territory), where *Al-Fatah* and *Al-Saiqa* guerrillas had first established a presence in 1969. Palestinian guerrilla operations against northern Israeli settlements, mounted from that area and other parts of southern Lebanon, provoked direct Israeli cross-border retaliatory raids, giving rise in turn to increasing concern on the part of the Lebanese Government.

As early as November 1969 the Lebanese authorities had, through Egyptian mediation, entered into the "Cairo agreement" with Palestinian guerrilla leaders with the aim of regulating their military activities on Lebanese territory. Regular clashes nevertheless continued to occur between guerrillas and the Lebanese armed forces seeking to apply the agreement. A direct Israeli commando raid in Beirut on April 10, 1973, in which three top-ranking guerrilla leaders were assassinated served to fan Lebanese resentment at the Palestinian presence. Although a further agreement was reached by the two sides in May of that year underlying tensions remained acute and were a major cause of the eventual outbreak of fullscale civil war in Lebanon in 1975.

From the early 1970s the PLO issued numerous statements condemning individual guerrilla actions outside Palestine, particularly airliner hijackings, asserting that they harmed the Palestinian cause and that those responsible (notably militants of the Popular Front for the Liberation of Palestine—PFLP) would be tried before Palestinian tribunals. On the other hand, the PLO has not condemned raids on Israeli territory (even where they resulted in civilian casualties) or attempts to kill "reactionary" Arab leaders.

A summit meeting of Arab heads of state held in Algiers on Nov. 26-28, 1973, recognized the PLO as the sole legitimate representative of all Palestinians, the only dissenter being King Hussein of Jordan, who would not agree to the PLO representing Palestinians in Jordan. However, at a further meeting of Arab heads of state held in Rabat (Morocco) on Oct. 26-29, 1974, the Arab leaders affirmed "the right of the Palestinian people to establish an independent authority under the leadership of the PLO as the sole legitimate representative of the Palestinian people in all liberated Palestinian territory" and undertook to "support this authority upon its establishment in all respects and degrees".

The UN General Assembly decided on Oct. 14, 1974, to invite the PLO to take part in a debate on the Palestine question, and Arafat accordingly addressed the Assembly as the first speaker in this debate on Nov. 13, when he appealed for international support for the PLO. He said inter alia that he had come "bearing an olive branch and a freedom fighter's gun"; that in "the Palestine of tomorrow" Jerusalem would "resume its historic role of a peaceful 'high place' for all religions"; that the PLO included in its perspective "all Jews who at present live in Palestine and who choose to live here with us in peace and without discrimination"; and that he appealed to every Jew individually to "turn away from the illusory promises made by the Zionist ideology and the Israeli leaders" who had "nothing to offer to Jews but blood, wars and distress". He asserted that the Palestinian revolution was not animated by racial or religious motives and that its target had never been the Jew as an individual but "racialist Zionism and open aggression", adding: "We make a distinction between Judaism and Zionism; while maintaining our opposition to the colonialist Zionist movement we respect the Jewish faith."

The permanent representative of Israel at the United Nations declared in reply that Israel would "not allow the establishment of the authority of the PLO in any part of Palestine" and that the PLO would "not be imposed on the Palestinian Arabs" and "not be tolerated by the Jews of Israel". He claimed that it was not true that the Palestinians had been deprived of a national state or had been uprooted, saying: "Jordan is Palestine, geographically, ethnically and historically, and without the Palestinians, who constitute the majority of its population, Jordan would be a state without people." He declared that Israel was determined "to pursue the murderers of the PLO and to destroy their bases".

At the end of the debate the UN General Assembly adopted, on Nov. 22, 1974—against the votes of Israel, the United States and some other states—two resolutions (i) recognizing the PLO as the representative of the Palestinian people, who were "a principal party" in the establishment of a just and durable peace in the Middle East and who had the right to regain "their rights by all means in accordance with the purposes and principles of the UN Charter", and (ii) granting the PLO permanent observer status at the UN General Assembly and at international conferences sponsored by the United Nations.

The PLO thereafter obtained recognition as the representative of the Palestinian people from a number of international organizations. It became a full member of the movement of non-aligned countries in August 1975 and a member of the movement's Co-ordinating Bureau in August 1976. In February 1975 the Council of Ministers of the Organization of

African Unity (OAU) decided during a meeting in Addis Ababa to grant "token aid" to the PLO and recommended that Arafat should address the next OAU summit (which he did in July 1975). In August 1976 the PLO became, as the representative of Palestine, a full member of the Arab League. It also became a member of the Organization of the Islamic Conference. In addition, the PLO has been authorized to set up representative offices in many of the world's capitals, some of these missions being accorded full diplomatic status by the host government.

In the civil war in Lebanon in 1975-76 the militant PLO guerrilla factions sided with the left-wing Moslem groups against the right-wing Maronite Christian militias. In May 1976 an attempt by Syria to impose a cease-fire was strongly opposed by most Palestinian leaders and the Lebanese National Movement (of left-wing Moslems), whereas *Al-Saiqa* and some PLO units supported Syria and fought against forces of the Movement. On June 4, 1976, Palestinian and left-wing Lebanese forces formed a "joint general command" (although *Al-Saiqa* did not participate) and succeeded in preventing the Syrian Army from gaining control of key positions north of the Damascus-Beirut highway. In view of the continuing warfare in Lebanon Arafat called on all Arab heads of state to halt a "new massacre against the Palestinian revolution", and on July 7, 1976, he announced that the headquarters of the PLA (the PLO's armed wing) were being moved from Damascus to Beirut in order to detach them from close Syrian control. The civil war was brought to a ceasefire by the occupation of Beirut and other towns in late 1976 by an Arab Deterrent Force (ADF), nominally of mixed Arab composition but in fact overwhelmingly (and later exclusively) made up of Syrian troops; nevertheless, no lasting solution had been achieved of Lebanon's deep-seated internal divisions, and particularly of the antagonisms arising from the substantial Palestinian presence in that country.

While the Lebanese conflict was at its height the PLO achieved a significant political success when PLO-backed National Bloc candidates achieved a substantial victory in municipal elections held in the Israeli-occupied West Bank on April 12, 1976. The success of the National Bloc lists—consisting of pro-PLO and *Rakah* (New Communist) candidates, other Arab nationalists and pro-Syrian Baathists—was accompanied by an escalation of serious unrest among the Palestinian inhabitants of the West Bank, setting the pattern of frequent anti-Israeli and pro-PLO demonstrations which by the late 1970s were taking a steady toll of lives on both sides. Since the April 1976 victory of the National Bloc the Israeli authorities have allowed no further elections to take place in the West Bank.

At a conference of heads of state and government of African and Arab states held in Cairo in March 1977, King Hussein of Jordan and Arafat, who had not met since the September 1970 action by Jordan against Palestinian guerrillas, were publicly reconciled with each other. Thereafter, Arafat and the majority PLO wing pursued a policy of close co-operation with Jordan on the Palestinian question.

At a meeting of the PNC held in Cairo on March 12-20, 1977, the delegates were divided into a majority "moderate" group consisting of *Al-Fatah, Al-Saiqa* and the Popular Democratic Front for the Liberation of Palestine (which later dropped the word "Popular" from its title) on the one hand, and on the other the "rejection front" led by the PFLP and also including the PFLP-General Command, the Arab Liberation Front (ALF) and the Popular Struggle Front (PSF). The "moderates" were said to favour the establishment of a Palestinian state in any part of Palestine which could be "liberated", the PLO's participation in Middle East peace talks and the creation of the Palestinian government-in-exile, while the "rejectionists" (backed by Iraq and Libya) opposed any negotiations involving Israel and any "partial" settlement implicitly accepting the existence of a Jewish state and also called for continued armed struggle until the whole of Palestinian territory had been liberated.

At the Cairo session the PNC adopted a new programme and decided to unify all Palestinian combat forces under a supreme military council commanded by the chairman of the PLO's executive committee (i.e. Yassir Arafat), to be financed by the Palestine National Fund. The PNC had, at this session, received a message of support from "the mayors of all West Bank municipalities".

The US State Department declared (for the first time) on Sept. 2, 1977, that Palestinian participation in a settlement of the Palestine question was necessary to ensure the successful outcome of an international peace conference. Arafat welcomed this statement on Sept. 13 as a positive step confirming that the Palestinian cause was "the essence of the conflict in the Middle East" and also confirming "the correctness of the stand adopted by the PLO". A PLO spokesman said in Beirut at the same time that the PLO would continue to reject Resolution 242 of the UN Security Council because it referred to the Palestinians as a refugee problem and not as "a national people with rights to an independent state". The US statement was, however, rejected as inadequate by Zouheir Mohsen (then the *Al-Saiqa* leader) and by Dr Georges Habash of the PFLP on Sept. 14.

Israel consistently refused any negotiations

with the PLO, then and subsequently. On Sept. 1, 1977, the *Knesset* (Israel's Parliament) resolved by 92 votes to four with six abstentions that Israel would "not negotiate with representatives of the PLO". Israel also rejected the inclusion of any reference to the PLO or any Palestinian entity in a programme for an international peace conference.

Following the visit to Jerusalem by President Sadat of Egypt on Nov. 19-21, 1977, the PLO and the Syrian Government issued a joint statement on Nov. 23, condemning the visit and calling for the convening of a pan-Arab people's conference to dissuade Egypt from its course of rapprochement with Israel. At a meeting held in Tripoli (Libya) on Dec. 2-5, 1977, by the PLO and five Arab states (Algeria, Iraq, Libya, Syria and South Yemen), the factions of the PLO asked for the establishment of an "Arab resistance and confrontation front" and reaffirmed their rejection of UN Security Council Resolutions 242 and 338 (the latter having been adopted on Oct. 22, 1973, at the end of the fourth Arab-Israeli war) and of any international conference based on them; they also called for the establishment of an independent Palestine state "without reconciliation, recognition or negotiation with the enemy". The meeting eventually adopted, without Iraq's concurrence, a "Tripoli declaration" which stated that the four states and the PLO would form the nucleus of a pan-Arab front for resistance and confrontation which would be open to other Arab countries; that they would "freeze" their diplomatic relations with Egypt and boycott Egyptian companies and persons conducting business with Israel, and also meetings of the Arab League held in Egypt. The PLO also joined the permanent secretariat of an Arab People's Conference (in Tripoli, Libya) comprising representatives of Algeria, Iraq, Libya, Syria, South Yemen, the Lebanese National Movement and Egyptian opposition groups. Early in February 1978 it was stated in Algiers that the PLO and Syria had secretly agreed to re-open the PLO bases in Syria which had been closed during the civil war in Lebanon in 1976.

The Camp David agreements signed by Israel and Egypt in September 1978 were strongly condemned by Arafat on Sept. 19 as "a dirty deal which the Egyptian people will reject and which does not decide our destiny". He accused President Sadat of Egypt of having "traded Arab Jerusalem for the Sinai desert", and he warned President Carter of the USA and "US interests in the Middle East" that they would "pay" for the Camp David decisions. On the West Bank, 19 of the 29 municipalities called (on Oct. 1) for the establishment of an independent Palestinian state under the leadership of the PLO.

An Arab summit conference held in Baghdad on Nov. 2-8, 1978, rejected the Camp David agreements and agreed inter alia that "all the Arab countries" should "give all forms of support and aid and facilities to the Palestinian resistance's struggle in all its forms through the PLO as the sole legitimate representative of the Palestinian people within and outside the occupied Arab territories for the sake of their liberation and the recovery of their legitimate national rights".

At a meeting between King Hussein and Arafat on March 17, 1979, the King agreed to the opening of a PLO political office in Amman but he was reported to be still opposed to the re-establishment of Palestinian camps in Jordan. At a further Baghdad Arab summit conference on March 27-31, 1979 (after the signature in Washington of the peace treaty between Egypt and Israel on March 26), the PLO sided with Iraq, Libya and Syria in taking a hard line against Egypt, which became subject to an Arab diplomatic and economic boycott which included suspension of Egypt's membership of the Arab League. In February 1979 Arafat asked OPEC member countries to "exert economic pressure on the United States in order to bring about changes in US policies towards the Middle East". Thereafter the PLO and other Arab League members refused to participate in the US-sponsored negotiations between Egypt and Israel on the granting of "autonomy" to the West Bank and Gaza Palestinians, as envisaged under the Camp David agreement.

Meanwhile, the Israelis had been taking an increasingly vigorous line against the PLO guerrilla presence in southern Lebanon, while at the same time consolidating a buffer zone under the control of Maj. Saad Haddad's anti-PLO Lebanese Christian forces immediately to the north of the border. The Israelis were concerned not only to prevent direct Palestinian attacks on northern Israel, but also to forestall any penetration further south of the Syrian ADF forces. In March 1978 a major Palestinian raid on Israel was immediately followed by an Israeli invasion of southern Lebanon with the aim of clearing the area of PLO bases. This led directly to the deployment of a UN peace-keeping force (UNIFIL) in two border areas; but this force proved largely powerless to control the situation after Israeli troops withdrew in June 1978, especially since the more radical PLO factions insisted on continuing the military campaign.

Early in 1979 the PLO resumed its attacks on Israeli positions from Lebanon and these again led to counter-action by the Israelis, their Prime Minister (Menaham Begin) declaring in April of that year that pre-emptive strikes would be used by Israeli forces at any time and in any place rather than in retaliation for specific actions; this policy was formally agreed to by the Israeli Cabinet on July 1. The PLO and the Lebanese National Movement had earlier, on June 6, agreed to withdraw from southern Lebanon to "deprive Israel of any possible pretext for continuing its attacks on civilian targets". The PLO subsequently closed down its headquarters in Tyre and withdrew also from Nabatiyeh (north-east of Tyre), and on Oct. 4, 1979, the PLO announced a unilateral ceasefire in Lebanon, entailing the cessation of PLO guerrilla action against Israel from Lebanese territory, but not elsewhere. (The PFLP dissociated itself from this decision on Oct. 5.) In June 1980 Arafat announced that he had ordered the closure of all guerrilla offices in Sidon and their withdrawal to refugee camps.

A further escalation of tensions occurred in April 1981 when Israeli planes for the first time intervened directly in support of Lebanese Christian Phalangists then under attack by the Syrians, who responded by deploying surface-to-air missiles in the Bekaa Valley in eastern Lebanon. During the subsequent Israeli-Syrian crisis major Israeli air strikes were mounted on PLO positions throughout Lebanon, including a heavy raid on west Beirut on July 17 (the first since December 1974) in which, according to Israeli sources, the headquarters of two Palestinian organizations were destroyed. Palestinian guerrillas, by now regrouped in southern Lebanon, responded by launching heavy rocket attacks on northern Israeli settlements in the second half of July 1981. Through US mediation a ceasefire came into effect on July 24, 1981, inaugurating a period of several months of relative stability in the border area; nevertheless, Arafat's insistence that the ceasefire applied only to cross-border hostilities (on which grounds he reserved the right to continue military operations within Israel and also against the Haddad enclave) and the rejection of the ceasefire by some PLO militants ensured that tensions remained acute.

From November 1981 Israeli spokesmen frequently accused the PLO of violating the ceasefire by moving supplies and reinforcements into the border area and by harassing Christian positions in the Haddad enclave. A resumption of Israeli air strikes on PLO positions in April 1982 was followed by a steady build-up of tension during May and further PLO rocket attacks on northern Israel. After the attempted assassination of the Israeli ambassador in London on June 3, Israeli forces on June 6 launched a fullscale invasion of Lebanon code-named "Peace for Galilee" with the declared objective of destroying the military capability of the PLO in that country and creating the conditions for a restoration of effective central government authority.

In their rapid advance up Lebanon's western coastal roads Israeli forces cut off and eventually overran Palestinian bases in Tyre, Sidon, Saadiyat and Damour. Meanwhile, a second Israeli force crossed the central sector of the border and quickly captured the PLO's mountain fortress of Beaufort Castle (which was handed over to Maj. Haddad's forces) as well as Nabatiyeh further north. A third Israeli advance from the Golan Heights in the east rapidly penetrated the PLO-held Arqoub region on the slopes of Mount Hermon. By mid-June Israeli forces had completely encircled the Lebanese capital, in the western area of which large numbers of PLO fighters as well as substantial contingents of Syrian ADF troops found themselves trapped.

There followed two months of intensive negotiations in which US and other mediators eventually established the basis for an evacuation of the PLO and Syrian forces trapped in Beirut (which was the scene of further heavy fighting during this period as Israeli forces closed in on Palestinian refugee camps harbouring PLO guerrillas). The evacuation plan (which did not have the status of a legal agreement in view of Israel's refusal to sign any formal pact to which the PLO was a party) applied only to the Palestinian and Syrian forces in Beirut and not to those elsewhere in Lebanon. As carried out from Aug. 21, the withdrawal took place in daylight, partly by sea and partly overland by way of the Beirut-Damascus highway (the land route being used in particular by the Syrian ADF forces and the Palestine Liberation Army); Palestinians evacuated by sea (mainly to a staging-post in Cyprus) were transferred later to various Arab countries which had agreed to receive them. Those evacuated were permitted to.take with them light weapons only and the whole process was supervised by a newly-deployed international peace-keeping force of US, French and Italian soldiers, assisted by the regular Lebanese Army.

The evacuation was completed on Sept. 1, 1982 (some three days ahead of schedule), by which time the official Lebanese total of evacuees (including regular Syrian troops and several hundred Palestinian women and children) was 14,656, whereas the Israeli count put the corresponding total at 14,847. The Lebanese count gave the number of regular Syrian evacuees as 2,700, whereas the Israelis put the figure at 3,500; both accounts agreed that over half of all those leaving Beirut went to Syria. Other Arab destinations of Palestinian guerrillas were Tunisia, South Yemen, Algeria, Jordan, Sudan, North Yemen and Iraq. Arafat himself left Beirut on Aug. 30 bound for Greece, where he was welcomed by Greek Prime Minister Andreas Papandreou.

On leaving the Lebanese capital the PLO leader vowed that the Palestinian struggle would be continued "so that we can win the war''; on arriving in Greece he denied that the Palestinian withdrawal from Beirut represented a defeat, adding that he was proud to have been instrumental in preventing a full Israeli assault on the Lebanese capital. Arafat's decision to go to Greece from Beirut was said by a PLO spokesman on Sept. 1 to signify his disappointment over the lack of general Arab support for the Palestinians during the recent Lebanon crisis. Following the withdrawal from Beirut, the main PLO headquarters became Damascus (the Syrian capital).

The PLO suffered heavy losses as a result of the Israeli invasion of Lebanon, in terms of military infrastructure, arms and personnel; by mid-August 1982 the Israelis had captured some 6,000 Palestinian guerrillas (and had killed at least 1,000 others), who were placed in special internment camps and denied prisoner-of-war status because as "terrorists" they did not conduct their operations "in accordance with the rules of war". Nevertheless, the PLO retained a substantial military presence in northern and eastern Lebanon, and many guerrillas evacuated from Beirut to Syria in August 1982 were later reported to have moved back across the Lebanese border. By late 1982 the Israeli authorities estimated that there were 7,000 PLO guerrillas in Lebanon and insisted that they must be withdrawn as a necessary pre-condition for an eventual Israeli withdrawal jointly with Syrian troops.

Suspecting that some 2,000 heavily-armed PLO fighters remained in hiding in Palestinian refugee camps in Beirut, the Israelis in mid-September 1982 sponsored an operation by Lebanese Christian Phalangist militiamen designed to clear guerrillas from the Chatila and Sabra camps in west Beirut; however, this operation on Sept. 16-18 turned into a wholesale massacre of civilian occupants including women and children—the total number of deaths being later estimated at between 700 and 800. The atrocities provoked almost universal international condemnation as well as a major political crisis in Israel itself, while for his part Arafat claimed that not only Israel but also the United States bore responsibility in that President Reagan had guaranteed the security of Palestinian civilians in Beirut under the August 1982 evacuation agreement.

As regards the Israeli role, an official Israeli inquiry under Chief Justice Itzhak Kahan found in a report published on Feb. 8, 1983, that the actual massacre had been perpetrated by Phalangist militiamen but that certain Israeli political and military leaders bore varying degrees of indirect responsibility. Particular censure was directed against Defence Minister Ariel Sharon for having allowed the Phalangists to enter the camps without direct Israeli supervision.

On the broad diplomatic front, President Reagan's new Middle East peace plan of Sept. 1, 1982—envisaging in particular the granting of self-government to the West Bank and Gaza Strip Palestinians in some sort of federation with Jordan—led to divisions within the PLO, although the precise alignment of the various factions remained unclear. Whereas the "rejectionist" wing condemned the Reagan plan as running counter to the PLO's commitment to a fully independent Palestinian state, the moderate wing appeared unwilling to reject it outright and Arafat himself entered into exploratory talks on the federation concept with King Hussein of Jordan in late 1982.

Shortly after the appearance of the new Reagan proposals Arafat subscribed on behalf of the PLO to a new Middle East peace plan issued on Sept. 9 by a summit conference of the Arab League in Fez (Morocco) and envisaging inter alia the establishment of an independent Palestinian state coupled with the issuing of "peace guarantees" by the UN Security Council to "all countries in the region". However, this apparent willingness to give implicit recognition to Israel found no favour with the militant Palestinian factions, which condemned "all forms of recognition, negotiation and making peace with the expansionist Zionist state".

At a session held in Algiers on Feb. 14-23, 1983, the Palestine National Council adopted a resolution recording its refusal to consider the Reagan peace plan as a "sound basis for a just and lasting solution to the Palestinian problem and the Arab-Israeli conflict". However, at the instigation of Arafat (who was re-elected chairman of the PLO executive committee at the Algiers meeting) the PNC resolution appeared to stop short of a total rejection of the US plan.

Main PLO Factions

Movement for the National Liberation of Palestine *(Tahir al-Hatani al-Falastini)* or Conquest *(Al-Fatah)*

Leadership. Mohammed Abed Arouf (Yassir) Arafat—code-named Abu Ammar (l.); Salah Khalaf—code-named Abu Iyad (deputy l.).

Al-Fatah (which is a reversed acronym of the full Arabic title of the organization as given above) was formed in the late 1950s by Palestinian students, including Yassir Arafat, at foreign universities. Having its origins in the Moslem Brotherhood (of which Arafat himself became a member while studying engineering at Cairo University), *Al-Fatah* was intended from the outset to be a Palestinian national movement not tied to or influenced by any Arab government.

205

Arafat had his first base in the Gaza Strip, where he decided to maintain a Palestinian force outside President Nasser's direct control (Gaza then being under Egyptian administration). After Algeria had achieved its independence in 1962 *Al-Fatah* established training camps in that country (and also in Kuwait), but with limited success. In 1964 *Al-Fatah* was allowed to establish itself in Syria, which supplied it with training facilities and enabled it to form storm troops known as *Kuwat al-Asifa* which, operating from Jordan, carried out its first raids into Israel in January 1965. According to Israeli sources there were 31 *Al-Fatah* raids during 1965—27 from Jordan and four from Lebanon. The first Israeli reprisal took place on May 27 of that year against *Al-Fatah* staging camps in Jordan.

Following the access to power of an extreme left-wing Government in Syria in 1966, *Al-Fatah* came under Syrian control, and it published its own newspaper (*Saut al-Asifa* or "Voice of the Storm") in Damascus. From the end of 1966 its incursions into Israel increased greatly and led to Israeli reprisals against Syria. When the June 1967 Arab-Israeli war broke out, *Al-Fatah*'s fighting strength was about 500 men, but most of its forces trained in Algeria arrived too late to take part in the fighting. After the war Arafat and the Syrian Chief of Staff worked out plans for subversive warfare inside Israel, but by November 1967 most of *Al-Fatah*'s forces on the Israeli-occupied West Bank had been killed, captured or repulsed.

In response to *Al-Fatah* incursions from Jordan, Israeli forces attempted in March 1968 to attack an *Al-Fatah* base at Karameh (in Jordan) but succeeded only partly in the face of fierce resistance by Palestinian guerrillas backed by Jordanian forces. *Al-Fatah* thereupon moved its headquarters from Damascus to Amman, where it greatly expanded it strength, accepting also former members of the Moslem Brotherhood (as a result of which it was regarded with suspicion by President Nasser and the Baathist Government in Syria).

Arafat had earlier begun moves to unify the diverse Palestinian guerrilla organizations. At a meeting convened by him in Cairo on Jan. 20, 1968, in which the Palestine Liberation Organization (PLO) did not take part, the organizations represented agreed that their objective was to regain by force of arms the whole of Palestine. At a meeting of the Palestine National Council (PNC)—the Palestinian "parliament-in-exile"—held in Cairo on Feb. 1-5, 1969, and attended by representatives of most of the guerrilla organizations and of the PLO, *Al-Fatah* gained virtual control of the PLO by obtaining four seats on its 11-member executive committee, of which Arafat himself was elected chair-

man. In 1969 President Nasser allowed *Al-Fatah* to use a Cairo radio station for broadcasts by the "Voice of *Fatah*" (*Saut al-Fatah*).

Of *Al-Fatah*'s guerrilla members (*fedayeen*), then numbering between 20,000 and 25,000, some 10,000 were located in bases and staging camps in Jordan, over which King Hussein gradually lost control. In November 1968 Arafat had been the principal negotiator of an agreement with King Hussein, under which Palestinian guerrillas in Jordan had to carry identity cards, conform to certain rules in their operations against Israel and not wear uniforms or carry arms in the towns—but they retained their weapons and were free to make their own decisions. This agreement was followed by increased *Al-Fatah* guerrilla activities which led to Israeli attacks on Iraq and Jordan.

The Israelis estimated that there were in 1969 some 7,500 trained Palestinian guerrilla fighters along their borders with Jordan, Syria and Lebanon. However, the guerrillas did not succeed in their objective of causing the Arab population in the occupied territories to rise against Israeli rule, nor had the Arab states any intention of allowing the *fedayeen* to build up strong conventional forces on their territory which would have attracted Israeli reprisals and constituted an internal danger to themselves.

During 1969 *Al-Fatah* (and also the Syrian-backed *Al-Saiqa*) established a strong base in southern Lebanon, where the Lebanese Army had difficulty in containing them within the few square miles which they were originally allocated. Their raids into Israel led to Israeli reprisal action against Lebanese territory. After armed clashes between Lebanese Army units and Palestinian guerrillas, a ceasefire was signed in Cairo on Nov. 2, 1969, when the "Cairo agreement" was concluded, under which a Higher Committee for Lebanese Affairs was set up by both Lebanese and guerrillas (who had found no mass support in Lebanon). The guerrillas, however, continued their military operations until early in 1970, when a 10,000-strong Christian militia in southern Lebanon gained the upper hand over them. Israeli forces made a strong attack against guerrillas in Lebanon on May 12, 1970.

In Jordan a conflict arose in 1970 between the Palestinian guerrillas and the Government, which on Feb. 10 issued decrees forbidding the carrying of weapons in public in Amman and other towns and villages, the storage of arms and ammunition and activities of political parties. When the Palestinians defied these decrees, the King suspended them and serious hostilities developed between the guerrillas and the Jordanian armed forces, interspersed with periods of ceasefire. King Hussein announced on Aug. 29 (after he had had talks with President Nasser) that he was accepting a US peace initiative, and he warned the Palestinian guerrillas that his Army was exercising its absolute right to military movement throughout the country. This announcement was followed by further fighting between Palestinians and Jordanian forces in and around Amman (the Jordanian capital) and the hijacking of several airliners by the Popular Front for the Liberation of Palestine (PFLP), which also had a guerrilla presence in Jordan. On Sept. 16 King Hussein placed Jordan under military rule, whereupon the guerrillas appointed Arafat as "general commander of all the armed forces of the revolution". They also declared a general strike and demanded the establishment of a national government in Jordan.

After Arafat had rejected an order by the Jordanian military governor that the guerrillas should surrender their weapons and also an ultimatum ordering them to leave Amman, the Jordanian Army began to eject them forcibly in the course of what the Palestinians came to call the "Black September" of 1970. This operation was completed within 10 days, after the guerrillas had failed to obtain any support from other Arab states (although Syrian forces gave them limited support in northern Jordan until being finally expelled from Jordan by Sept. 23). The fighting was ended by an agreement concluded in Cairo on Sept. 27, 1970, by King Hussein, Arafat and Arab heads of state and providing that both Jordanian troops and guerrillas would be withdrawn from population centres; that Jordan would return to civilian rule; and that a ceasefire would be supervised by an Arab truce commission. On Oct. 13, 1970, the Cairo agreement was enlarged by a further agreement signed in Amman by King Hussein and Arafat, stipulating that the guerrillas' camps should be sited along the Israeli border and not around Jordan's main population centres (as had been demanded by Arafat), with the King abandoning his demand for control of the guerrillas' militia. Jordan returned to civilian government on Oct. 16.

The Jordanian Government led by Wasfi Tell, which took office on Oct. 28, 1970, was, however, intent upon a complete removal of the Palestinian guerrillas from Jordan. On Dec. 10 Wasfi Tell and Arafat signed an agreement providing that the militias of both the Palestinians and of Jordan should hand in their weapons, and by January 1971 the Jordanian Army had cleared the Palestinians from all areas adjoining Israel. The result of these developments was that many Palestinian guerrillas took refuge in Syria, where President Hafez Assad assumed presidential powers on Feb. 22 and promised support for their armed struggle against Israel.

In April 1971 the guerrillas once again tried to fight back against the Jordanian Army, and *Al-Fatah* subsequently openly called for the overthrow of King Hussein, whereupon Wasfi Tell accused it on June 2 of plotting to set up a breakaway state in Jordan. On July 13 the Jordanian Army moved in force against the Palestinians, and on the next day Arafat declared war on the Jordanian Government. The latter thereupon declared, on July 16, all previous agreements to be null and void. Many guerrillas crossed into Israel and gave themselves up, and by July 20 Jordan was cleared of hostile Palestinians.

Arab heads of state meeting in Tripoli (Libya) on July 30, 1971, condemned King Hussein but took no action against him, except that Libya and Syria broke off diplomatic relations with Jordan. During the whole of 1971 about 9,000 Palestinian guerrillas escaped from Jordan, mainly to Syria, where the Government kept them under tight control, with the result that many moved to Lebanon, whose Army confined them to a restricted area in the south-eastern Arqoub region on the slopes of Mount Hermon, which became known as "Fatahland". By 1972 there were some 4,000 guerrillas in this area, from which they conducted raids into Israel which were usually followed by Israeli counter-action.

Mgr Hilarion Capucci, the Greek Catholic Archbishop of Jerusalem, was on Dec. 9, 1974, sentenced to 12 years' imprisonment by an Israeli court for smuggling arms and explosives into Israel on behalf of *Al-Fatah*. His release was repeatedly called for by Palestinian guerrillas carrying out hijacking and other operations, and he was eventually released in November 1977 upon a request by the Vatican.

The first attack on Israel from the sea was launched by eight *Al-Fatah* guerrillas on Tel Aviv on March 5-6, 1975, when altogether 18 persons were killed and one of the guerrillas was captured alive. Another group of 11 *Al-Fatah* members, wishing to demonstrate that there would be no peace settlement without the Palestinians, invaded Israel from the sea on March 11, 1978, and killed 34 Israelis and a US citizen and injured over 70 Israelis before nine of them were killed and the two others captured. According to Israeli officials the raid had been organized by Halil al-Wazir (Abu Jihad), the head of *Al-Fatah*'s military wing, whom they considered also responsible for the (Black September) massacre at the 1972 Olympic Games in Munich.

The Israeli Prime Minister (Menahem Begin) said on March 13, 1978, that "dozens of training courses" had been conducted for *Al-Fatah* and other PLO members in the Soviet Union and other East European countries, and he called on West European governments to close PLO offices in their countries. On March 14-15, 1978, Israel launched a major military intervention in Lebanon designed to ensure that Palestinian guerrillas would no longer strike at Israel; however, no lasting solution was achieved to Israel's security problem. (For subsequent developments leading to the Israeli invasion of Lebanon in June 1982, see under Palestine Liberation Organization above.)

Since Yassir Arafat became leader of the PLO in 1969, *Al-Fatah* has been the leading "moderate" Palestinian faction, and by virtue of its status as by far the largest guerrilla movement has generally been able to exercise a controlling influence over the PLO's policy line. Describing itself as an "Arab nationalist organization". *Al-Fatah* encompasses a broad political spectrum within its membership and has accordingly sought to transcend dissension within Palestinian ranks over ideological orientation. The movement has informed the United Nations that its objectives are (i) to liberate the whole of Palestine from "foreign occupation and aggression" and (ii) to form an independent, democratic, sovereign Palestinian state where all legitimate and legal inhabitants would share equal rights, irrespective of religion or language (but with Jews being limited to those living in Palestine since before 1917 and their offspring).

The *Al-Fatah* leadership has consistently condemned Palestinian military operations directed against civilians, particularly those mounted outside the Middle East theatre and involving innocent neutrals. It has also endeavoured, in the interests of good relations with all Arab states, not to get involved in the internal political disputes of Arab League members. For example, whereas the radical Palestinian factions fought on the Moslem leftist side throughout the 1975-76 civil war in Lebanon, *Al-Fatah* guerrillas refrained from active involvement in the conflict in its early stages, and Arafat himself sought to play a mediatory role; not until the Syrians became heavily involved from mid-1976 on the side of the Lebanese Christians did *Al-Fatah* guerrillas enter the hostilities, and then principally in defence of Palestinian refugee camps.

Following the trauma of the PLO's enforced evacuation from Beirut in August 1982, support for *Al-Fatah*'s policy line within the PLO appeared to diminish. Two factions previously belonging to the "moderate" PLO wing, *Al-Saiqa* and the Democratic Front for the Liberation of Palestine, increasingly associated themselves with the "rejectionist" camp led by the PFLP, particularly in opposition to President Reagan's new peace plan of Sept. 1, 1982, envisaging the creation of a self-governing Palestinian political entity linked to Jordan—an option which Arafat himself was ready to explore with King Hussein. Nevertheless, Arafat and *Al-Fatah* retained their dominance of the PLO at the session of the Palestine National Council held in Algiers in February 1983, when the "rejectionists" failed to commit the PLO to total opposition to the Reagan plan.

Popular Front for the Liberation of Palestine (PFLP) *(Al-Jabha Al-Shabiyya li Tahrir Falastin)*

Leadership. Dr Georges Habash (l.).

After the 1948 war Dr Habash (a Christian Arab) moved from Palestine to Lebanon, where in 1959 he founded an Arab Nationalist Movement (ANM)—*Haraka al-Quamiyyin al-Arab* or *Haraka*—as a pro-Nasserite organization with Marxist leanings. After the 1967 war Dr Habash moved to Jordan and formed the PFLP as the guerrilla organization of the ANM, with headquarters in Amman. Whereas *Al-Fatah* is a broad-based nationalist movement, the PFLP is a Marxist-Leninist organization which considers itself to be conducting "a class struggle against Zionism and imperialism" and to be "an important cadre of organic rapport between the Palestinians and international revolutions".

From its training camps in Jordan the PFLP began in 1968 to commit acts of violence against targets in Israel and the occupied territories and also against Israeli airliners, in reprisal for which Israel destroyed 13 Arab airliners in Beirut on Dec. 28, 1968. During this early phase probably the best known PFLP activist was Leila Khaled, who was responsible for the hijackings of a US airliner to Syria in August 1969 (by the "Che Guevara commando unit" of the PFLP) and of an Israeli airliner over England in September 1970 (which resulted in her arrest).

Dr Habash was quoted at this time as saying that the PFLP was justified in killing civilians travelling to Israel on the following grounds: "We have no control over the land that was stolen from us and called Israel . . . ; whoever goes to Israel should ask for our permission. . . . Our struggle has barely begun, the worst is yet to come. And it is right for Europe and America to be warned now that there will be no peace until there is justice for Palestine. . . . We will never agree to a peaceful settlement. If the Arab countries think they can gang up and make peace over our heads, they are mistaken. All we have to do is to assert our power in one country and the rest will lose their resolve. . . ."

The PFLP's policy of mounting terrorist attacks on Israeli targets anywhere in the world came under strong criticism from the PLO mainstream led by Yassir Arafat, it being repeatedly stated by the PLO leadership that those responsible for such actions would be brought to trial before Palestinian tribunals. At a congress in Tripoli (Lebanon) in March 1972 the PFLP announced that it had given up hijacking because the practice tended to create a "revolutionary élite" at the expense of enabling the masses to participate in the liberation of Palestine. Nevertheless, the PFLP and its various offshoots continued to be identified with extremist Palestinian terrorist operations.

In furtherance of its aims, the PFLP established close links with revolutionary groups in other countries, notably the Japanese Red Army and the West German Red Army Faction. Both of these organizations were represented at a conference of Palestinian and other groups convened by Dr Habash in northern Lebanon in May 1972, when it was reportedly agreed that each of the movements would participate in terrorist attacks on behalf of any of the others. The first fruit of this agreement was the attack carried out by three young Japanese at Lod airport in Israel on May 30, 1972, in which many civilians and two of the attackers were killed (see entry for United Red Army under Japan on pages 104-06).

Together with the Japanese Red Army, the PFLP was responsible for an attack on a Shell refinery and ferry in Singapore on Jan. 31, 1974, by four terrorists who were, however, seized and held in Singapore until Feb. 7, when they were handed over to Japanese Foreign Ministry officials. The latter took them to Kuwait, where a group of PFLP and Japanese Red Army members had seized the Japanese embassy on Feb. 6 and were holding its staff as hostages until their colleagues from Singapore were released. The PLO condemned these operations of the PFLP on Feb. 8 and expressed regret that they had taken place.

During 1973 PFLP members had been involved in arms smuggling operations by the left-wing Turkish People's Liberation Army; the PFLP also claimed responsibility for an attempt on the life of Joseph Edward Sieff (later Lord Sieff), a prominent Zionist and businessman in London, in December 1973. For these and other operations Dr Habash came to be regarded as an "arch-killer" by the Israelis, who made an abortive attempt to capture him in August 1973 by intercepting an Iraqi airliner over Lebanon in the mistaken belief that the PFLP leader was on board.

The PFLP had also, in 1970, recruited the international revolutionary "Carlos Martínez" (Ilich Ramírez Sánchez), a Venezuelan who was subsequently held responsible for numerous acts of terrorism in various countries. These included the temporary seizure—carried out by a self-styled "Arm of the Arab Revolution"—of several ministerial representatives of the Organization of Petroleum Exporting Countries (OPEC) in Vienna in December 1975.

On June 27, 1976, a "Haifa section" of the PFLP (including two West Germans) hijacked an Air France airbus (with 247 passengers and a crew of 12) and diverted it to Entebbe (Uganda). A PFLP spokesman in Beirut, however, denied on June 28 that his organization was in any way involved. The hijackers demanded the release of prisoners held not only in Israel but also in West Germany (i.e. members of the Red Army Faction), Switzerland, France and Kenya (i.e. PFLP members arrested there in January 1976 for planning to attack an Israeli airliner). The hijack operation was ended by the intervention of some 200 airborne Israeli commandos on July 3-4, though not without casualties.

Following their expulsion from Jordan in 1970-71 (along with other Palestinian guerrilla units), PFLP adherents became increasingly active in Lebanon not only in organizing anti-Israeli operations but also in supporting leftist Lebanese Moslem groups in their developing internal conflict with the dominant Maronite Christians. On May 1, 1973, PFLP guerrillas kidnapped two Lebanese Army corporals and held them hostage against the release of PFLP members arrested earlier for attempting to plant bombs. This incident led to intense fighting between Palestinians and Lebanese troops and the declaration of a state of siege in Lebanon from May 7 to 23, 1973, and contributed to the steady escalation of Palestinian-Lebanese tensions which were one of the underlying causes of the civil war of 1975-76.

Within the broad Palestinian liberation movement the PFLP has been the leading opponent of any "partial" solution to the Palestinian question (i.e. any settlement which falls short of the establishment of a state based on majority rule in the whole of Palestine). In September 1974 the PFLP representative withdrew from the PLO executive committee, accusing the PLO leadership of having secret contacts with the US Secretary of State (then Dr Henry Kissinger) and preparing for a peace settlement which would guarantee the existence of Israel and increase US influence in the Middle East. Although the PFLP remained a member of the PLO as such through its continued participation in the Palestine National Council, it was thereafter the leading faction within the "rejection front" of militant Palestinian groups who opposed any compromise on the basic aims of the PLO as enshrined in the Palestine National Charter.

Democratic Front for the Liberation of Palestine (DFLP)

Leadership. Nayef Hawatmeh (s.g.).

The Popular Democratic Front for the Liberation of Palestine (as the DFLP was originally known) seceded from the Popular Front for the Liberation of Palestine (PFLP) in February 1969 on the grounds that the

PFLP had developed bourgeois tendencies. Hawatmeh, a Christian Arab, is a Marxist who has close links with the Soviet-bloc countries. In accordance with its policy of carrying out increased passive and active resistance to Israeli rule in the occupied territories, it has mounted raids into these territories from Lebanese and Jordanian territory, in particular in 1974. In that year Hawatmeh stated (on May 16) that a PDFLP action (which resulted in the death of 20 Israeli children and injury to over 70 others at Maalot, northern Israel) had been a deliberate attempt to sabotage a United States peace mission in the Middle East. This action was followed by massive Israeli attacks on Palestinian camps in Lebanon, causing large numbers of casualties.

In 1978 the PDFLP was reported to be among those guerrilla groups which had set up cells in the West Bank territory, and in 1979 it claimed responsibility for another attack on Maalot. At the same time, it sought to develop relations with left-wing Israeli groups prepared to recognize the claim of the Palestinians to basic political rights. Since the early 1980s the designation "Popular" has been dropped from the Front's official title.

The DFLP is a Marxist-Leninist movement standing for the establishment of a binational state of Palestine for both Jews and Arabs. As a member of the PLO it formed, with *Al-Fatah* and *Al-Saiqa,* the majority "moderate" wing of that organization during the 1970s, in part because of close personal relations between Hawatmeh and the PLO leader, Yassir Arafat. However, the setbacks suffered by the Palestinian movement in Lebanon during 1982 and Arafat's policy of rapprochement with Jordan contributed to the DFLP's gravitation into the "rejectionist" camp led by the PFLP. In late 1982 and early 1983 the DFLP associated itself in particular with condemnations by the militant PLO factions of the new US peace plan announced by President Reagan on Sept. 1, 1982, envisaging the creation of a self-governing Palestinian entity in the West Bank and Gaza Strip which would be linked to Jordan.

Popular Front for the Liberation of Palestine—General Command (PFLP-GC)

Leadership. Ahmed Jabril (l.).

Established in 1968 by dissident members of the Popular Front for the Liberation of Palestine (PFLP), this guerrilla group was subsequently responsible for a series of terrorist acts. These included the blowing-up of a Swiss airliner in February 1970 (when 47 persons were killed), an attack on an Israeli school bus in May 1970 (when 12 children and several adults died) and the killing of 18 Israelis (among them 12 children and five women) at Kiryat Shemona in northern Israel in April 1974.

The PFLP-GC was held responsible for the kidnapping in Beirut on June 29, 1975, of a Black US colonel, who was released after the US embassy had paid for 10 tons of food and clothing to be distributed among the poor affected by the fighting in Beirut. It also claimed responsibility for an explosion in Jerusalem on July 4, 1975, when 13 people (including four Arabs) were killed and over 70 injured.

In 1977 a pro-Iraqi faction led by Abul Abbas broke away from the (pro-Syrian) PFLP-GC and formed the Palestine Liberation Front. On March 16, 1979, Salem Ahmad Hassan, a self-confessed "soldier" of the PFLP-GC, was sentenced to life imprisonment in London for killing Col. Abdul Razzak al-Nayef (a former Iraqi Prime Minister) on July 9, 1978—the defendant having called him "a traitor" who deserved to die. The PFLP-GC was also reported to have a strong group in Uppsala (Sweden), where some of its members were charged with illegal activities in 1980. Other PFLP-GC members had been killed in a bomb explosion near Tel Aviv on May 23, 1979.

As part of the "rejection front" within the PLO, the PFLP-GC stands for the destruction of Israel and the "liberation" of the whole of Palestine. Together with other militant Palestinian factions, it has therefore strongly opposed all moves towards a "partial" settlement of the Palestinian question.

The Storm *(Al-Saiqa)*

Leadership. Issam al-Qadi (l.).

Formed in 1968 by the Syrian Baathist Government as a counter-balance to *Al-Fatah, Al-Saiqa* was recruited from among Palestinian Baathists in refugee camps and was led by regular Syrian Army officers. The movement was originally the military wing of the Vanguards of the Popular War for the Liberation of Palestine. Operations carried out by *Al-Saiqa* have included the action taken on Sept. 23, 1973, by two of its members calling themselves "Eagles of the Palestine Revolution", who had entered Austria from Czechoslovakia and seized two Jews (who had just arrived from the Soviet Union) and an Austrian customs officer; they demanded, in return for the release of these hostages, the closure of an Austrian transit camp for Jews from the Soviet Union wishing to reach Israel. The Austrian Federal Chancellor (Dr Bruno Kreisky) acceded to their demand and was thereupon intensely criticized by Israel, whose Prime Minister (then Golda Meir) called his decision "the greatest encouragement to terrorism throughout the world".

In 1978 *Al-Saiqa* was among the Palestinian groups which set up resistance cells on the Israeli-occupied West Bank, and it also had bases in Lebanon, where it became a major arm of Syrian intervention in the 1975-76 civil war and was temporarily in conflict with other Palestinian groups in that country, notably *Al-Fatah*. On Dec. 23, 1981 four self-confessed members of the "Eagles of the Palestine Revolution" were sentenced to death in Ankara (Turkey) for an attack on the Egyptian embassy in that city in July 1979, when an embassy official and two Turkish policemen lost their lives.

Within the PLO *Al-Saiqa* was during the 1970s generally regarded as part of the "moderate" wing led by *Al-Fatah*; however, following the events in Lebanon during mid-1982 *Al-Saiqa* increasingly associated itself with the "rejectionist" factions led by the Popular Front for the Liberation of Palestine (PFLP) in opposition to any compromise on basic Palestinian demands.

Arab Liberation Front (ALF)

Leadership. Abdel Rahim Ahmad (l.).

The ALF was established in April 1969 by the Baathist Government of Iraq as the sole Palestinian guerrilla group to be permitted in that country (as a counterweight to the Syrian-backed *Al-Saiqa*). With its headquarters being in Lebanon (where it was backed by the pro-Iraqi faction of the Lebanese *Baath* party), the ALF was in 1978 and 1980 involved in raids against targets in Israel and in the latter year also in clashes with (Shi'ite Moslem) *Amal* forces and with Israeli troops. The ALF's then leader, Dr Abdel Wahab Kayyale, was assassinated in Beirut in December 1981.

The pro-Iraqi Baathist ALF is a member of the "rejection front" within the PLO. Militant offshoots of the Front have been involved in terrorist actions in Western Europe, notably the attack on Orly airport (Paris) in January 1975.

Popular Struggle Front (PSF)

Leadership. Bahjat Abu Gharbiyya; Samir Ghosheh.

This Iraqi-backed group was originally formed in Jordan in 1968 by members of the Popular Liberation Forces (the commando wing of the Palestine Liberation Army). Closely identified with *Al-Fatah* in the early 1970s, the small PSF later became part of the "rejection front" within the PLO.

Palestine Liberation Front (PLF)

Leadership. Abul Abbas (l.).

Formed in 1977, this breakaway group from the Popular Front for the Liberation of Palestine—General Command has received backing from Iraq. In August 1978 over 180 people died in a bomb explosion which destroyed the PLF's headquarters in Beirut. Four of its members raided Nahariya in northern Israel on April 22, 1979—allegedly to emphasize the Front's rejection of the March 1979 Egyptian-Israeli peace treaty. Israeli forces thereupon attacked Palestinian positions in Lebanon for four days, during which about 60 people were killed, including 27 Palestinians. The PLF is part of the "rejection front" within the PLO.

Other Palestinian Groups

Apart from the main PLO factions described above, the past decade has witnessed the proliferation of a complex array of other Palestinian groups and sub-factions—many of them formed as splinter groups of the larger movements. Often identifying themselves in connexion with specific terrorist actions, such groups have been denounced by the official PLO leadership when they mounted attacks on civilian targets (especially those outside Palestine). On the other hand, the Israeli authorities have always maintained that the tactical purpose of such groups is to divert responsibility from the PLO itself.

Abu Nidal Group

Leadership. Sabri Khalil al-Banna—codenamed Abu Nidal (l.).

This militant faction, which broke away from *Al-Fatah* in 1973, was based in Iraq and was supported by that country's Government, although in the late 1970s it appeared to come under the influence of Syria. Because of his association with extremist actions, including attacks on "moderate" Palestinian leaders, Abu Nidal was sentenced to death in absentia by a PLO tribunal.

The Group was held responsible for the killing of the secretary-general of the Afro-Asian People's Organization (a former Egyptian minister) in Nicosia (Cyprus) on Feb. 18, 1975—an assassination which was strongly condemned by the PLO's executive committee. There followed a gun battle between Egyptian commandos sent to Cyprus and Cypriot forces (the latter being supported by Palestinians, according to Egypt), and the Egyptian Government decided on Feb. 27 to revoke all special privileges granted to Palestinians in Egypt (estimated at between 39,000 and 50,000).

The Abu Nidal Group has also been held responsible for a series of attacks on, and assassinations of, "moderate" PLO representatives—such internecine conflict also involving Iraqi diplomats abroad, several of whom were attacked in various capitals in the mid-1970s in what the Iraqi regime regarded as retaliatory action by the PLO leadership. Two self-confessed followers of Abu Nidal murdered the PLO representative in Paris on Aug. 3, 1978—although responsibility was also claimed by the "Rejectionist Front of Stateless Palestinians". Abu Nidal was also believed to be behind the Black June militant Palestinian movement which appeared in late 1976.

After some years of apparent inactivity, the Abu Nidal Group re-emerged in the early 1980s and was believed to have carried out—through a grouping identifying itself as *Al-Asifa*—an attempt on the life of the Israeli ambassador in London on June 3, 1982.

Al-Asifa—see under Abu Nidal Group

Al-Seeir

Of the self-confessed members of this breakaway group from *Al-Fatah,* Mrs Khouloud Moghrabi (18) was sentenced in London on May 15, 1979, to 12 years' imprisonment for conspiring to murder the Iraqi ambassador in London.

Arab Nationalist Movement *(Haraka)*—see under Popular Front for the Liberation of Palestine (PFLP)

Arab Nationalist Youth Organization for the Liberation of Palestine

This Organization which had broken away from the Popular Front for the Liberation of Palestine (PFLP) in 1972, was responsible for an attack on the Israeli ambassador in Nicosia (Cyprus) in April 1973 and for a number of hijack operations in 1973-75 (after *Al-Fatah* had officially abandoned such operations in 1973). The Nicosia attack was followed by a raid on Beirut on April 10, 1973, by Israeli commandos, who killed a number of prominent PLO leaders—notably Mohammed Yussef Najjar (Abu Yussef), second-in-command of *Al-Fatah*; Kamal Adwan, *Al-Fatah* spokesman and member of the PLO's executive committee; and Kamal Nasser, an official PLO spokesman.

The group stated on March 5, 1974, that its actions were directed in particular against Britain because of the latter's "crimes against the Palestinian people, from the Balfour Declaration onwards". It has supported the PLO's "rejectionist" wing.

Arab Revolutionary Army—Palestine Command

This group claimed responsibility for the poisoning by "oppressed workers" on the West Bank of oranges exported to Western Europe in 1978. The Israeli authorities contended that the poisoning had been carried out in Europe.

Black June Movement

This grouping took its name from the Syrian intervention in the civil war in Lebanon in June 1976, after which the Palestinian-backed Lebanese Moslem leftists were defeated by the combined forces of the Syrians and the Lebanese Christians. On Sept. 27 of that year three members of the Movement were tried and hanged for an attack on an hotel in Damascus on the previous day with the object of enforcing the release of a number of persons arrested on charges of having committed acts of violence. The leader of the group was killed by Syrian troops, and four persons held hostages also lost their lives in the attack. The group was said to have been trained in Iraq.

Three members of the Movement were killed in a gun battle with Jordanian troops in Amman on Nov. 17, 1976, when they had tried to seize hostages at an hotel.

Black June also claimed responsibility for an unsuccessful attack, on Dec. 1, 1976, on the life of Abdel Halim Khaddam, the Syrian Deputy Prime Minister and Minister of Foreign Affairs.

Black September Group

Leadership. Abu Daoud.

This Group, which took its name from the month in which *Al-Fatah*'s forces were defeated by Jordanian troops in 1970, broke away from *Al-Fatah* because it disagreed with the latter's emphasis on the need for political action as a "national liberation movement". The Black September Group belonged to the minority grouping of "avenging" Palestinians, members of which committed individual acts of violence.

It was held responsible for the killing of Wasfi Tell (the Jordanian Prime Minister) in Cairo on Nov. 28, 1971 (in revenge for the killing of its former leader, Abu Ali Iyad, in July 1971). However, Abu Daoud, the group's leader, was said to have stated later that *Al-Fatah* had been responsible for the assassination of Wasfi Tell, which, he said, had been organized by Abu Yussef (Mohammed Yussef Najjar), then a member of the PLO's political department and chairman of the Higher Committee for Palestinian Affairs in Lebanon (who was killed by Israelis raiding Beirut on April 10, 1973).

Other acts of violence attributed to the Black September Group included the hijacking of a Sabena airliner at Lod (Israel) in May 1972; the murder of 11 Israeli athletes at the Olympic Games in Munich on Sept. 5, 1972; the seizure of the Israeli embassy in Bangkok in March 1973; and the murder in Khartoum of the US ambassador and the Belgian chargé d'affaires at the Saudi Arabian embassy on March 1, 1973.

In August 1973 two members of the Group made an attack at Athens airport, killing five people and injuring 55 others; they were sentenced to death in Athens, as confirmed by the Greek Supreme Court on March 9, 1974. Their sentences were, however, commuted to imprisonment after three members of the (Pakistani) Moslem International Guerrillas had on Feb. 2 seized a Greek cargo ship in Karachi and had held the ship's first officer and chief engineer hostage pending the release of the two Black September members. However, after the latter's death sentences had been commuted, the Pakistanis released their hostages and were themselves flown to Libya.

Abou Daoud, the Group's leader, was among the 1,000 political prisoners released by King Hussein of Jordan under an amnesty in September 1973, most of them having been held since the 1970-71 Jordanian action against Palestinian guerrillas. On March 24, 1973, he was reported to have stated that the Black September organization was actually part of *Al-Fatah* and that its operations in Amman and in Munich had been planned by Salah Khalef, the second-ranking leader of *Al-Fatah*; that Black September received its orders from the *Al-Fatah* leadership; but that he was not certain that Yassir Arafat himself was in control of these orders.

On Jan. 7, 1977, Abu Daoud was arrested in Paris, where he had arrived as a member of a PLO delegation attending the funeral of Mahmoud Saleh, a PLO representative in Paris who had been killed on Jan. 3. However, a French court released Abu Daoud on Jan. 11 after the West German authorities had not immediately made their request for his extradition on charges of his involvement in the attack on the Israeli athletes in Munich in 1972 and as Israel was considered to have no right to ask for his extradition. Abu Daoud said after his arrival in Algiers that he was "a revolutionary Palestinian" but "not a terrorist" and he added that he was innocent of the charges raised against him in West Germany.

Black September—June Organization

This group was described as a merger of the Black September and Black June organizations and the Abu Nidal Group led by Sabri Khalil al-Banna (Abu Nidal). It claimed responsibility for the killing of a Minister of State for Foreign Affairs of the United Arab Emirates in Abu Dhabi on Oct. 25, 1977, when the killer had aimed at Abdel Halim Khaddam, the Syrian Deputy Prime Minister and Minister of Foreign Affairs, who was then visiting Abu Dhabi. The assassin, who was said to have been supported by the Iraqi regime, was condemned to death and executed on Nov. 16, 1977. His action was con-demned by Yassir Arafat and by the central committee of *Al-Fatah*.

Eagles of the Palestine Revolution—see under The Storm *(Al-Saiqa)* above

Moslem Brotherhood

Early in 1982 the Moslem Brotherhood was reported to have many adherents among young Arabs on the Israeli-occupied West Bank who were disappointed with the failure of the PLO (or any other Arab organization) to find a solution to the Palestine problem; such adherents opposed the establishment by the PLO of a secular state in Palestine and advocated instead an Islamic state based on the Koran in accordance with the principles of the Moslem Brotherhood (for the origins of which, see entry under Egypt, pages 162-63).

In the first few months of 1982 violent clashes took place between PLO and Brotherhood supporters both on the West Bank and in the Gaza Strip, leading to the closure of the university at Nablus and the burning in Gaza of a library closely associated with the PLO. At the University of Bir Zeit, where a Brotherhood-dominated Islamic Bloc held more than 40 per cent of the votes on the student council, courses were suspended for two months from mid-February after clashes between students and an Israeli official.

Palestine National Front (PNF)

According to Israeli sources the PNF—formed in 1974—was the first serious resistance group formed on the occupied West Bank since 1967, its core being the Jordanian Communist Party. Three of its leaders were on Nov. 4, 1974, deported to Lebanon by the Israeli authorities after they had called on the Arabs on the West Bank to support the PLO. More alleged PNF members were deported after violent incidents in November 1974.

Palestinian Communist Party (PCP)

The PCP was established in Beirut in February 1982 to include Communists of the Israeli-occupied West Bank and the Gaza Strip, the Palestinian members of the Jordanian Communist Party living outside Jordan, and the members of the Palestinian Communist Organization in Lebanon.

The immediate objective of the PCP is to fight for the withdrawal of Israel from all territories seized in 1967, the creation of an independent Palestine and the return of the Palestinian refugees to their homeland in conformity with UN decisions. The PCP also supports Soviet initiatives on the Palestinian problem and the Middle East conflict and the convocation of an international conference to search for ways of establishing a just and lasting peace in the Middle East. It considers the PLO as the sole legitimate representative of the Palestinian people and claims the right to be represented within the PLO (membership of which has nevertheless been exclusively of guerrilla movements rather than parties).

Popular Front for the Liberation of Palestine—Special Operations

Leadership. Dr Wadie Haddad.

This Baghdad-based organization was formed in 1975 as a splinter group of the Popular Front for the Liberation of Palestine (PFLP). On Oct. 27, 1977, it was reported to have claimed responsibility for the hijacking of a West German Lufthansa airliner with the object of holding its passengers and crew hostages until the release of Red Army Faction members held prisoners in West Germany and of two Palestinians held in Turkey. The airliner was eventually diverted to Mogadishu (Somalia), where it was (on Oct. 18) stormed by a West German border guard commando who killed three of the hijackers and captured the fourth. (Responsibility for the kidnapping had earlier, on Oct. 13, been claimed by the "Struggle against World Imperialism Organization".) Among other acts of which the Front claimed responsibility was an attack on an El Al (Israeli airline) bus in London on Aug. 20, 1978.

Punishment *(Al-Eqab)*

Five members of this group seized the Saudi Arabian embassy in Paris on Sept. 5, 1973, in an attempt to enforce the release of Abu Daoud, the Black September leader then held in prison in Jordan. The five men were subsequently allowed to take five Saudi Arabian diplomats to Kuwait in an aircraft placed at their disposal, but in Kuwait they surrendered to the authorities and their hostages were released. (Abu Daoud was released under a Jordanian amnesty in the same month.)

Rejectionist Front of Stateless Palestinians—see under Abu Nidal Group

Sons of the Occupied Territories

This group was responsible for the diversion, on July 20, 1973, of a Japanese airliner from Amsterdam to Benghazi (Libya), where they blew it up on July 24 after all passengers and crew members had been allowed to leave it. The hijacking was described by the group as retaliation for the payment of compensation to Israel by Japan for the Lod massacre of May 1972 attributed to the Popular Front for the Liberation of Palestine (PFLP).

Vanguards of the Popular War for the Liberation of Palestine—see under The Storm *(Al-Saiqa)*

Qatar

Capital: Doha   Pop. 270,000

The state of Qatar has a Council of Ministers appointed by and presided over by the head of state (the Amir) and assisted by a 30-member Advisory Council appointed for a three-year term. There is no Parliament and there are no official political parties. Although at least 70 per cent of the population are immigrants (including many from the Indian sub-continent) and there is a Shi'ite minority, there have been few signs of internal political tension.

Saudi Arabia

Capitals: Riyadh (royal capital),
      Jeddah (administrative capital)

Pop. 10,200,000

The Kingdom of Saudi Arabia is under the direct rule of the King, who is also the Prime Minister and who presides over a Council of Ministers. There is no Parliament nor are there any legal political parties.

Opposition to the regime has come mainly from some Shi'ites and Moslem fundamentalists inside the country and from other (mainly left-wing) groups based outside Saudi Arabia.

Committee for the Defence of the Rights of Man in Saudi Arabia *(Comité de Défense des Droits de l'Homme en Arabie Saoudite)*

This Committee was set up in Paris in 1972 by representatives of clandestine parties in Saudi Arabia—including the (Arab nationalist) Party of Labour, the *Baath* party of Saudi Arabia, the Communist Party of Saudi Arabia (see separate entry), the (Shi'ite) Organization of the Islamic Revolution and the (Sunnite) *El-Salaf El-Saleh.* A spokesman for the Committee announced in Paris in January 1983 that during the past few months some 150 persons, most of them favouring the establishment of a constitutional and democratic regime, had been arrested in Saudi Arabia without any charges being laid against them.

Communist Party of Saudi Arabia

Representatives of this (pro-Soviet) party, which has never been legal in Saudi Arabia, took part in a conference of the *World Marxist Review (Problems of Peace and Socialism)* held in Prague on Nov. 24-27, 1981.

Moslem Revolutionary Movement in the Arabian Peninsula

Leadership. Mohammed ibn Abdullah al-Qatani ("Mahdi"); Juhayman bin Mohammed bin Seif al-Oteibi (l.).

Established in 1974, this Movement of only a few hundred members was built up by its leader and found support in Egypt and some of the Gulf states. It was aimed at obtaining universal Moslem recognition of Mohammed al-Qatani as the expected "Mahdi" or prophet (as prophesied by certain Mahdist sects). On Nov. 20, 1979, some 200 armed members of the organization took over the Grand Mosque in Mecca with the object of forcing the congregation (of some 50,000 Moslems) to recognize their "Mahdi". The Government announced on Nov. 25 that the Ulema (the supreme body of Islamic jurisdiction) had decided to lift the Koranic ban on the use of weapons in the mosque, and about 2,200 troops thereupon entered the mosque, taking until Nov. 3 to overcome all resistance by the intruders. The Movement had, on Nov. 27, declared that it was responsible for the action at the mosque and that it was directed against the Saudi Arabian royal family, whom it denounced as "corrupt".

On Jan. 9, 1980, a total of 63 of the intruders were executed by being beheaded on instructions of Saudi religious courts; 19 other death sentences were commuted to terms of imprisonment and 22 women and children were sent to corrective institutions. Of the insurgents, 102 were said to have died during or after the occupation of the mosque, while troop casualties were officially given as 127 dead and 451 injured, and civilian casualties as 26 dead and 109 injured. The "Mahdi" was reported to have been killed in the fighting. Those beheaded included not only Saudi Arabians but also Egyptians, Yemenis and Kuwaitis. In some other Islamic states, including Iran, responsibility for the Mecca attack was attributed to the United States and to Zionism; accordingly, anti-American demonstrations and riots took place in several such countries.

From the writings of the organization's leader it appeared that it condemned all current rulers of Islamic states as not upholding the religion of Islam which laid down that obedience was owed "only to those who lead by God's book" and not to those who had made religion into a way of satisfying their materialistic interests.

215

Popular Front for the Liberation of the Arabian Peninsula

In a statement referred to in a broadcast from Tripoli (Libya) on Nov. 18, 1982, this Front condemned the "despotic" rulers of Saudi Arabia as being responsible for "the sell-out of the Palestinian cause" and the use of American aircraft "to defile the Arabian peninsula's sky"; it called for these rulers to be brought to trial and for the establishment of an Islamic administration "to preserve the sanctity of God's House" in Arabia.

Shi'ite Moslem Fundamentalists

Saudi Arabia's Shi'ite minority, concentrated in the oases of Qatif and Hasa, in the Eastern province, form an' underprivileged section of the population and constitute about one-third of the workforce in the country's oil production. Its younger generation has been greatly influenced by the Islamic revolution in Iran. Pro-Iranian demonstrations in the Eastern province in November-December 1979 (also described as an "uprising") were put down by troops, and there was further loss of life when troops intervened to disperse a Shi'ite demonstration in Qatif in February 1980 to celebrate the first anniversary of the Iranian revolution. The Government, however, responded to the unrest by devoting increased resources to material improvements in Qatif.

Union of the People of the Arabian Peninsula

Leadership. Nasser al-Said (l.).

This left-wing underground organization expressed sympathy with the action taken against the Grand Mosque in Mecca on Nov. 27, 1979, by the Moslem Revolutionary Movement in the Arabian Peninsula (see separate entry) and called it "a spontaneous response to social injustice under the rule of the monarchy". The organization's leader also alleged that over 7,000 sympathizers with the action in Mecca had been arrested throughout the country.

Somalia

Capital: Mogadishu   Pop. 3,530,000

The Somali Democratic Republic (a member of the Arab League) is ruled by the leadership of the Somali Revolutionary Socialist Party (SRSP), whose secretary-general, Gen. Mohammed Siyad Barreh, is head of state and directs the Government with the assistance of an appointed Council of Ministers. Although there is an elected People's Assembly, there are no legal political parties other than the SRSP.

The defeat of Somalia's forces in the hostilities, conducted since 1977 over Somali claims to territory under Ethiopian control—a defeat resulting in part from massive Soviet and Cuban support for Ethiopia—brought about serious internal difficulties in Somalia by 1980. On Oct. 21 of that year a state of emergency was declared "to deal with hostile elements in the country and attacks from Ethiopia". A series of bomb explosions in Mogadishu in January 1981 was followed by the arrest of suspected Soviet sympathizers. The general state of emergency was eventually lifted on March 1, 1982—although it was reimposed in the "battle zones" on the Ethiopian border on Aug. 15.

A general amnesty was announced on Feb. 21, 1981, for any Somali who had committed an offence against the state before Feb. 14, 1981, and who returned to the country within three months. The number of political detainees in Somalia was, in April 1981, thought to be between 5,000 and 10,000. On Oct. 20, 1981, it was announced that an amnesty involving the release of over 5,000 prisoners did not cover those convicted of crimes against the sovereignty, security and unity of the state. Earlier, on May 8, 1981, four persons had been condemned to death for grave crimes against the state alleged to have been committed on behalf of "foreign powers".

Democratic Front for the Liberation of Somalia—see Democratic Front for the Salvation of Somalia

Democratic Front for the Salvation of Somalia (DFSS)

Leadership. Col. Abdullahi Yusuf Ahmad (ch.); Said Jana Husayn (vice-ch.); Abder Rahman Aidid Ahmad (sec. for information)—members of 11-member committee.

The DFSS was set up at a conference held from Sept. 19 to Oct. 5, 1981, by representatives of the Somali Salvation Front (SSF—see separate entry), the Democratic Front for the Liberation of Somalia (led by A. R. Aidid Ahmad) and the Somali Workers' Party (led by Said Jana Husayn). Its formation was announced by Radio Kulmis, broadcasting from Ethiopia and describing itself as "the mobile station of the DFSS", having previously called itself "the voice of the SSF". On Oct. 27, 1981 the DFSS claimed in a further broadcast that it had achieved "major victories" on the battlefield against President Siyad Barreh's regime and that hundreds of soldiers had been deserting him and joining the DFSS forces; the broadcast also called on Western nations to cease their aid to President Siyad Barreh and to adopt a neutral attitude to Somalia.

On Nov. 1, 1981, five Somali officials were reported to have sought political asylum in Libya and to have decided to join the DFSS. On Nov. 25, 1981, it was reported that five members of the President's regime (including a former Minister of Information and two former members of the SRSP's central committee) had announced in Beirut that they had decided to join the DFSS.

At its foundation the DFSS announced its policies as including the destruction of Siyad Barreh's regime; the establishment of a democratic system under a new constitution; the holding of free elections for a people's parliament; the removal of all US air, naval and ground bases from Somalia; the pursuit of a non-aligned, neutral policy and good-neighbourly relations with East African countries, in particular in the Horn of Africa; support for the Arab people in their opposition to the 1979 peace treaty between Egypt and Israel; and support for the Palestine Liberation Organization and all liberation movements fighting against apartheid.

In October 1982 it was announced that the DFSS had formed a joint military committee with the Somali National Movement (see separate entry) as well as another committee which would seek to establish the basis for an eventual unification of the two movements.

Somali National Movement (SNM)

Leadership. Ahmad Ismail Abdi (s.g.); Hassan Adan Wadadid (spokesman).

The SNM was founded in London in April 1981 by Somali exiles in Europe and the United States, most of them Issaqs from northern Somalia opposed to President Siyad Barreh's Government strongly based on southerners. At its foundation the SNM declared its aim to be to organize "internal resistance" with a view to overthrowing the Siyad Barreh regime "by any means, including force of arms" and to restore Somalia's "former neutrality". The Movement subscribes to a moderate form of Islamic nationalism and to the concept of the mixed economy.

The SNM began guerrilla operations inside Somalia during 1982 and in early January 1983 mounted a successful attack on a prison at Mandera (south of the port of Berbera), freeing over 700 prisoners, including several political detainees.

It was reported from Ethiopia on April 15, 1982, that at a meeting held between March 29 and April 8 delegates from the SNM and the Democratic Front for the Salvation of Somalia (DFSS—see separate entry) had decided in principle to implement the unification of the two movements into "one organization with a clear national democratic programme". It was subsequently announced in October 1982 that the DFSS and the SNM had established a joint military committee to facilitate operations against government forces as well as a separate committee charged with elaborating the basis for an eventual union of the two movements.

Somali Salvation Front (SSF)

Leadership. Col. Abdullahi Yusuf Ahmad (l.).

Founded in February 1979, the SSF superseded a Somali Democratic Action Front established in 1976 with Osman Nur Ali (a former minister in President Siyad Barreh's first Cabinet formed in 1969) as secretary-general and based in Rome. While President Siyad Barreh is of the Marrehan tribe (part of the Darod confederacy of southern Somalia), the SSF was based mainly on the rival Mijertein tribe (of the same confederacy), which had been dominant in Somalia's Government until Gen. Siyad Barreh came to power in 1969.

The SSF was based mainly in Ethiopia but also had representatives in Kenya and South Yemen. In 1980 it claimed to have its headquarters at Warder, near which a Somali army unit was defeated (as announced on Aug. 6, 1980). It also claimed to have inflicted heavy casualties on Somali troops, in particular on Feb. 8 (52 soldiers killed) and on July 2-3, 1980 (72 soldiers killed). It was supplied with weapons by Libya and conducted further hit-and-run operations against the Somali Army from March 1981 onwards, claiming to have 10,000 active members. In October 1981 the SSF became a founder member of the broader-based Democratic Front for the Salvation of Somalia (see separate entry).

At a news conference in Washington (reported by Radio Kulmis, Addis Ababa, on Jan. 30, 1981), the SSF leaders set out their aims as being (i) "to liquidate the fascist rule" in Mogadishu; (ii) to form a provisional government in which all Somalis would "participate equally and by right"; (iii) to draw up a constitution within 12 months; (iv) to form a democratic government and to hold free and independent elections; (v) to be non-aligned in foreign affairs; and (vi) to support liberation fronts against colonialism and apartheid as practised in Africa and elsewhere.

Somali Workers' Party—see Democratic Front for the Salvation of Somalia

Sudan

Capital: Khartoum Pop. 19,028,000

The Democratic Republic of the Sudan has an executive President, who is nominated by the Sudanese Socialist Union (SSU), the country's sole legal political organization, and who is also Prime Minister (although he may appoint another person to this post). There is a People's Assembly of 304 members, of whom 30 are appointed by the President and 274 are elected by universal adult suffrage, all candidates having to be approved by the SSU. (The Moslem Brotherhood, which in other Arab countries is in opposition, is represented in the Government by its secretary-general and "supreme guide", Dr Hassan Abdallah al Turabi, who is the country's Attorney General.) For the country's Southern Region there are a separate High Executive Council and a Regional People's Assembly.

The regime of President Jaafar Mohammed al-Nemery has repeatedly been threatened by attempted coups allegedly planned by Sudanese exiles supported by certain Arab countries, in particular Iraq and Libya. With the latter country the Sudan's relations became particularly strained in 1979, after President Nemery had attacked Libya's alleged "expansionist policies" in Africa in a speech at the Assembly of Heads of State and Government of the Organization of African Unity in Nairobi on June 26.

In April 1981 President Nemery said that all means necessary would have to be used to remove Col. Moamer al-Kadhafi, the Libyan leader, from his position. Late in 1981 there were reports of Libyan air raids on Sudanese territory and of preparations for a Libyan invasion of the Sudan, for which Col. Kadhafi was said to be organizing a Sudanese Liberation Army in October 1981, while in the Sudan some 10,000 people were reportedly arrested as a precaution against Libyan-inspired subversion.

Baath Arab Socialist Party

Alleged members of this party, which has been banned since 1969, continued to be tried in the late 1970s and early 1980s.

Council for the Unity of Southern Sudan

Leadership. Clement Mboro (ch.). Samuel Aru Bol (deputy ch.); Joseph Adohu (sec.).

This Council, formed in late 1981 by a number of leading politicians of the Southern Region, objected to the Government's 1981 programme for decentralization of the Sudan's administration. They claimed that this programme, involving the division of the country's Southern Region, was contrary to the Addis Ababa agreement of 1972 under which the Southern Region had been established (following a protracted civil war between the Northern and the Southern Sudan). The Council protested in particular against the Government's announcement that a referendum on decentralization would be held only in Equatoria (and not in the Region's other two provinces of Bahr el Ghazal and Upper Nile).

On Jan. 4, 1982, a total of 21 leading southern politicians (among them 17 former ministers and two former Speakers of the Southern Regional People's Assembly) were arrested and charged with having formed the Council as an illegal organization. The interim President of the Southern Region's High Executive Council was reported at the same time as stating that this illegal organization had received financial and moral aid from abroad and was backed by Libya, and that under the Constitution there could be no other political party or organization outside the SSU. By Jan. 6, 1982, all of those arrested except five (including the office bearers listed above) had been released from detention.

Democratic Unionist Party (DUP)

Leadership. Hassan M. Randach; Toujami M. Moussa.

This party was formed in December 1967 by a merger of the National Unionist Party and the People's Democratic Party (which had been formed by the religious *Khatmiyya* group). With the advent of President Nemery to power in May 1969 the DUP ceased to be a legal party, but it has been active in exile since then. The party's then leader, Hussein el-Sharif el-Hindi, died in exile in January 1982; he had operated outside the country since 1969 (mainly within the Sudanese National Front—see separate entry) and had been accused by the Government of involvement in an apparent assassination attempt on President Nemery in May 1980 and of working against the Nemery regime from Iraq.

Sudanese Communist Party (SCP)

Established illegally in August 1946 in Khartoum as a Sudanese Movement for National Liberation, which adopted the name of Sudanese Communist Party (SCP) in 1956, the party defined its task as being to carry out a national-democratic revolution. It was active in fighting against the military dictatorship in 1958-64 but became legal thereafter and took part in government from October 1964 to February 1965. In general elections held in northern Sudan in April-May 1965 the SCP gained 11 of the 173 seats contested but on Dec. 9, 1965, it was banned after a Communist student had made derogatory remarks about Islam and clashes had occurred between Communists and members of the Moslem Brotherhood. An appeal against the ban was upheld by the Sudanese High Court but the Government nevertheless declared on Jan. 2, 1967, that the ban would remain in force. It had banned the SCP's newspaper at the end of 1966 after the failure of an attempted coup which was officially attributed to the Communists but in which any involvement by the SCP was denied by the party's secretary-general, Abdel Khaliq Mahgoub. The latter was elected, as the sole successful Communist candidate, to a new Constituent Assembly in May 1968.

After the assumption of power by (the then Col.) Jaafar Mohammed al-Nemery on May 25, 1969, Communists were again admitted to the Government. However, following the failure of an attempted coup by left-wing officers on July 19-22, 1971, President Nemery ordered the arrest of all persons suspected of involvement in the attempt and also of all known Communists, of whom over 2,000 were subsequently detained. Although pleading "not guilty", Abdel Khaliq Mahgoub was condemned to death on July 27 and executed the next day. At the same time all Communist-led organizations were officially dissolved. Since then the (pro-Soviet) SCP has operated illegally and a number of its members were brought to trial in the late 1970s and early 1980s.

Sudanese National Front (SNF)

Leadership. Dr Sadiq el-Mahdi (l.).

The SNF was set up in 1969 in London (after the coup which brought President Nemery to power) by exiled members of the centre and right-wing parties which had taken part in previous governments. Dr Sadiq el-Mahdi, who had been the leader of the *Umma* (People's) Party and Prime Minister in 1966-67, was arrested on June 5, 1969, and the following month it was officially stated that the Government had foiled an attempted coup aimed at setting up a government to be led by Dr el-Mahdi.

Dr el-Mahdi, who was released from detention in April 1974, stated in Paris on July 10, 1976, that a Libyan-inspired attempt to overthrow President Nemery was "a popular insurrection". In the Sudan both he and other former ministers were officially accused of complicity in the attempt, and on Sept. 30, 1976, Dr el-Mahdi was condemned to death in absentia. On Jan. 1, 1977, President Nemery accused the Ethiopian Government of giving support to the SNF since the latter had set up training camps for its fighters in Ethiopia, which (the President said) had been visited by Dr el-Mahdi in December 1976.

Shortly afterwards, however, talks began in London between Dr el-Mahdi and the Sudanese Minister of the Interior on a possible national reconciliation. In an interview published on Sept. 13, 1977, Dr el-Mahdi developed his policies as including the ending of Sudanese support for Eritrean separatists in Ethiopia, "friendly and equidistant relations" of the Sudan with both the United States and the Soviet Union, and the economic development of the Sudan on socialist lines. He returned to the Sudan on Sept. 28, 1977.

Under a national reconciliation agreement subsequently signed in London on April 12, 1978, it was provided inter alia that the SNF would be dissolved, all its members were to return to the Sudan, their training camps would be abolished and their arms and equipment were to be handed over to the Sudanese armed forces. Some of the SNF's leaders, including Dr el-Mahdi, were thereupon admitted to the central committee of the ruling Sudanese Socialist Union. The agreement was, however, not accepted by some SNF components, and Dr el-Mahdi resigned from the SSU central committee two months after his appointment because he disagreed with President Nemery's support for the Egyptian-Israeli peace initiative.

The SNF subsequently continued its opposition to President Nemery's regime, and Dr el-Mahdi stated in a programme in February 1982 that the dangerous instability in the Sudan could be ended by a transitional government supported by the people and the Army; such a government would carry out an economic salvation plan, a return to "the line of Islamic identity" and a truly democratic regime based on a "socialist economic order", with an "Arab" foreign policy with close relations with African states and internationally "neutralist".

Sudanese Socialist Popular Front *(Al-Jabhah ash-Shabiyah al-Ishtirakiyah as-Sudaniyah)*

Leadership. Mahgoub Elfil.

According to a broadcast from Tripoli (Libya) on Jan. 7, 1982, this organization had issued a statement calling on all members of the Sudanese armed forces and police to join in one front with the popular masses to destroy the existing "regime of terrorism, domination and treason" and to establish "the authority of the masses". The statement also described Col. Kadhafi, the Libyan leader, as "the defender of freedom and the popular masses" of the people of the Sudan and the "commander of their revolution".

Syria

Capital: Damascus   Pop. 8,800,000

The Syrian Arab Republic is, under its 1973 Constitution, a "socialist popular democracy" with an executive President, who is secretary-general of the *Baath* Arab Socialist Party and also president of the National Progressive Front (NPF) embracing the country's five legal parties—the *Baath*, the (Nasserite) Socialist Unionist Movement, the (also Nasserite) Arab Socialist Union, the (anti-Egyptian) Arab Socialist Party and the Syrian Communist Party. There is a legislative People's Council, in which all parties and also independents are represented. The Government, the *Baath* party and the armed forces are dominated by members of the minority Alawite sect of the Shi'ite Moslem community (constituting only about 12 per cent of the country's population, whereas some 70 per cent are Sunni Moslems).

Sunni Moslems have strongly opposed the 1973 Constitution and have demanded that it should recognize Islam as the state religion, but an amendment to the Constitution adopted in February of that year stated merely that the President must be a Moslem. Serious disturbances occurred at the time, and in a referendum held in March 1973 to approve the Constitution many Sunni Moslems abstained or voted against its adoption.

The principal opposition to the regime of President Hafez al-Assad (as leader of the Syrian *Baath* party) has come from Moslem extremists within the Sunni community, their strongest organization being the Moslem Brotherhood; violent actions against his regime have also been carried out by dissident Baathists supported by the *Baath* party of Iraq.

Moslem Brotherhood

Leadership. Shaikh Bayanouni (spiritual l. and s.g.); Issam al-Attar (l. based in Aachen, West Germany).

Deriving from the historic movement originally founded in Egypt (see pages 162-63), the Syrian offshoot of the Moslem Brotherhood has in recent years been engaged in a bloody struggle for supremacy with the regime of President Assad. Although most of its members are Sunni Moslems, the Moslem Brotherhood of Syria shares many objectives with the Shi'ite revolutionaries who came to power in Iran in February 1979. In Syria the Brotherhood not only propagates Islamic fundamentalist tenets but also demands free elections, a more liberal economy and an end to Alawite dominance. According to Shaikh Bayanouni, the Islamic state which it wishes to establish in Damascus will not take away the religious rights of Christians and other non-Moslems and will create "a political movement which will satisfy all the people"; however, full rights will be accorded only to those whose ideologies do not contradict that of Islam.

The Moslem Brotherhood is well-organized not only in Syria, where it is said to have cells in the armed forces and publishes an underground journal called *Al-Nazeer* ("The Herald"), but also in many other countries, including Austria, West Germany, the United Kingdom and the United States, where there are Syrian émigrés and where funds are collected on its behalf. According to the Syrian Government, the Moslem Brotherhood is supplied and encouraged by the country's enemies, including Israel, the United States, Jordan, Iraq, the Phalangists in Lebanon and also Egypt.

Acts of violence committed by its members in Syria in their struggle against the regime of President Assad began to escalate in 1978, when "extremist Moslems" were officially held responsible for the death of a Soviet adviser to the Syrian Air Force in February and for a number of assassinations during March of that year. In an attack on an artillery school at Aleppo on June 16, 1979, a total of 63 army cadets (believed to have been Alawites) were killed, and the Government held the Moslem Brotherhood responsible.

The Minister of the Interior stated on June 22, 1979, that the United States and Israel had "reactivated" the Brotherhood "in an attempt to weaken Syria's opposition to Egypt's peace treaty with Israel"; he also accused the Brotherhood of having instigated earlier attacks on prominent Alawites and Baathists, and he promised that the Government would "liquidate" the movement. On June 24 it was announced that a group of 14 men had been sentenced to death (12 of them in absentia) for their part in the Aleppo killings. Among another 200 Brotherhood members arrested after these killings, 18 were sentenced to death for murder and other acts of violence, 15 of them were hanged on June 28 and the three others had their sentences commuted to life imprisonment.

Early in August 1979 Husni Mahmoud Abou, the leader of the Aleppo faction of the Moslem Brotherhood, was arrested (together with his deputy); early in September he ap-

peared on television, saying that his organization had planned a wave of assassinations and bombings aimed at causing civil war in Syria; and on Dec. 26, 1979, he and four other Brotherhood members were executed in Damascus for alleged participation in the Aleppo killings.

Among other acts of violence attributed to the Moslem Brotherhood was the killing of an Alawite religious leader on Aug. 30, 1979, which led to fighting between Alawites and Sunnites in Latakia, where 12 persons were killed, and to bombings and assassinations in Damascus. During September 1979 Abdul Satar al-Zaim, a leading member of the Brotherhood, was killed in a gun battle some 40 miles north-east of Damascus. Further clashes involving Moslem Brotherhood members took place in Aleppo in November and December 1979.

Early in February 1980 it was reported that since the beginning of that year Moslem Brotherhood activists had assassinated at least 12 Soviet military advisers. Late in February the Syrian security forces launched an offensive against the Brotherhood, which led to the outbreak of a general insurgency on March 8 in Aleppo and other northern cities. Violence and general unrest subsequently spread to a wide area of northern Syria, as a result of which the Government withdrew heavy armoured brigades from the Syrian-Israeli front to use them against the Moslem extremists, of whom about 100 were said to have been killed (against some 80 government or party officials). Further clashes occurred during May and June, when the authorities claimed that Capt. Ibrahim Youssef, the presumed leader of the insurgency in Aleppo in June 1979, had been killed on June 2.

Following an attempted assassination of President Assad on June 26, 1980, the People's Council approved, on July 7, a law instituting the death penalty for membership of the Moslem Brotherhood, with the proviso that those who left it within a month would be pardoned. This amnesty was later extended to Aug. 27, when the Government claimed that several hundred Brotherhood members had surrendered to the authorities; violent clashes nevertheless continued during July and August in northern Syria, with several hundred Brotherhood or other opposition activists being killed, summarily executed or arrested. According to a government statement the military leader of the Brotherhood, Hisham Jumbaz, was killed at Homs on Aug. 16 (with five other Brotherhood members). Of those who had surrendered, some 200 Brotherhood members were (as claimed in the Western press early in September) massacred by security forces at a camp east of Aleppo on Aug. 14, 1980.

On June 1, 1981, Moslem Brotherhood

gunmen were reported to have killed 15 soldiers, three intelligence service members and four boys in Aleppo after the Army was said to have killed 50 people in the previous week. Later in 1981 the Syrian authorities continued their "suppression campaign" against internal opponents and in particular the Moslem Brotherhood, with arrests inside Syria and assassinations outside it (including that of the wife of Issam al-Attar, reported on Sept. 27). Widespread unrest was reported on Oct. 8, 1981, from Aleppo, Homs and Hama, a senior Syrian officer being killed by a Moslem Brotherhood follower on Oct. 6. On Nov. 29 a bomb said to have been planted by the Moslem Brotherhood in Damascus killed 64 people and injured 135 others.

Battles between Moslem Brotherhood and army units continued in Aleppo and Hama (which was cut off from the rest of Syria for five days in mid-December), with Communists being said to be in league with the Moslem Brotherhood. By January 1982 some 35,000 Syrians were said to have disappeared as a result of continued fighting, and on Jan. 18 it was reported that several hundred army officers had been arrested on charges of carrying out hostile activities against the Syrian regime and plotting a coup, apparently in association with the Moslem Brotherhood. On Jan. 25, 1982, it was reported that after the Moslem Brotherhood had warned Soviet experts to leave Syria about 100 Soviet military experts had repatriated their families.

In early February 1982 an armed insurrection by Brotherhood activists broke out in the northern city of Hama, apparently after a newly appointed military governor had employed forceful methods in trying to curb the movement. Clashes between Brotherhood members and security forces seeking illegal arms in Hama led to a declaration of rebellion from two of the city's mosques on Feb. 3, the inhabitants being told that they had been "liberated" from the Assad regime. A communiqué issued on Feb. 10 by a group called "the command of the Islamic revolution in Syria" stated that the rebels had raided the arsenal of the local headquarters of the Baath party and occupied the police station and the governor's office; it also claimed that many units of regular Syrian forces had defected to fight alongside the rebels.

The Syrian security forces responded by encircling Hama with tanks and heavy artillery and mounting a prolonged bombardment of the city in which much of it was destroyed. The Government made repeated claims after Feb. 12 that Hama had been brought under control, but it was not until late February that the rebels appeared to have been overcome. In reducing the insurgency the Syrian security forces inflicted large numbers of casualties, the number of dead being estimated by Western sources as running into many thousands, most of them civilians.

In a speech on March 7, 1982, President Assad attributed the insurgency to the Moslem Brotherhood, claiming that it had "transformed mosques and houses of God into warehouses to stockpile ammunition" and used them as barricades from which rebels had "opened fire and killed citizens". He also claimed that the Brotherhood had the backing of Israel (suggesting that the uprising had been timed to divert Syrian attention from the Israeli annexation of the Golan Heights in December 1981) and that it had been armed by the United States and Iraq.

National Alliance for the Liberation of Syria

Leadership. Hammoud el-Shufi (spokesman).

This Alliance was formed in March 1982 by about 20 political and religious groups with the aim of consolidating opposition to the Assad regime from within Syria and abroad. The announcement of its formation was made in New York on April 3 by Hammoud el-Shufi, who said that it included the Moslem Brotherhood and the closely related Islamic Front in Syria, as well as dissident members of the ruling *Baath* party, such as himself (see entry below for Baathist Dissidents).

The aims of the Alliance as set out in its charter included the forcible overthrow of the Assad Government and its replacement by a constitutional, elective system in which freedom of faith, expression and association would be guaranteed. Islam would be the country's religion and the *Sharia* (Islamic law) would be the basis of legislation, but the rights of non-Moslems would be protected. On matters of external policy the Alliance would support "the liberation of Palestine from the Zionist occupation", work for Arab unity and abide by the principles of the non-aligned movement.

Other Movements

Arab Communist Organization

On July 29, 1975, the Supreme State Security Court in Damascus sentenced 14 members of this Organization for a series of acts of sabotage, including the bombing of Egyptian, Jordanian and US diplomatic or information offices. The court imposed sentences of death on four Palestinians and three Syrians (two of the latter death sentences being commuted to life imprisonment), of life imprisonment on two Palestinians and a Syrian, and of 15 years' hard labour on two Palestinians and two Syrians.

Baathist Dissidents

Syria became the main power base of the *Baath* Arab socialist movement in 1963, and the *Baath* party of Syria, as the left wing of the movement, was thereafter separated from the right-wing "historic" *Baath* party of Iraq under the leadership of the movement's founder, Michel Aflaq.

Early in April 1975 about 200 members of the Syrian party, who were understood to be supporters of the Iraqi party, were arrested on charges of plotting against the Government. The sixth congress of the Syrian party, held on April 9, 1975, denounced the Iraqi party as "a rightist clique" in alleged collusion with Iran and a traitor to "the cause of the Arab nation". The assassination of a member of the *Baath* Party's pan-Arab command in Syria (who was of Iraqi origin) on July 10, 1976, was officially attributed to Iraqi Baathists.

A former secretary-general of the Syrian *Baath* party until 1964, Hammoud el-Shufi resigned as Syria's permanent representative at the United Nations on Dec. 27, 1979, declaring that he hoped to participate in the formation of a new opposition front in exile "to defend the democratic aspirations of the Syrian people". He accused the Syrian regime of having mounted an "impossible degree of repression" in 1979 and of having imprisoned "former Presidents, Prime Ministers and army officers by the hundreds"; he also denounced "the real monopoly of political power and economic wealth" of the Alawite minority.

A group calling itself "the Vanguard of the Arab Revolution" claimed on Feb. 8-9, 1981, to have been involved in heavy fighting with Syrian army units in Aleppo where it attempted to storm a prison in order to release Salah Jadid, a former Syrian chief of staff and senior *Baath* party member; the group also claimed to have "executed" a Syrian secret agent in Kuwait "in revenge for the execution of Salah al-Bitar". (The latter had been co-founder of the *Baath* party, had been Prime Minister of Syria between 1963 and 1966 and had later lived in exile after his right-wing *Baath* faction had been finally ousted by the left wing, which has since then remained in power in Syria. Known to be seeking to set up an opposition front Bitar was assassinated in Paris on July 21, 1980, in the course of an "assassination campaign" against external opposition members, as expressly confirmed by President Assad on July 24, 1980.)

Another Baathist dissident group, known as the "National Salvation Command", claimed responsibility for bomb explosions at the Prime Minister's offices in Damascus on Aug. 17, 1981, and at the *Baath* party's headquarters (also in Damascus) on Sept. 12; the latter explosion resulted in the death of the three members of a "Martyr Kamal Jumblatt group" who had caused the explosion, and also of about 43 persons working at the party headquarters. (Kamal Jumblatt, a Druse who had been the leader of the Progressive Socialist Party of Lebanon, had been assassinated in March 1977.)

In March 1982 exiled Baathist dissidents participated in the formation of the National Alliance for the Liberation of Syria (see separate entry) together with the Moslem Brotherhood and other political and religious opposition groups.

Islamic Front in Syria—see under National Alliance for the Liberation of Syria

National Salvation Command—see under Baathist Dissidents

Party of Communist Action

In March and April 1982 several members of this independent communist formation were arrested in Syria, including one of the party's founders, Fateh Jamous, who had been wanted by the authorities since 1976. Several of the party members arrested were later found dead.

Vanguard of the Arab Revolution—see under Baathist Dissidents

Tunisia

Capital: Tunis

Pop. 6,554,000

The Republic of Tunisia has an executive President and a National Assembly, both elected for five-year terms by universal adult suffrage. The ruling Destour Socialist Party (PSD), called the Neo-Destour Party until 1964, was for many years the country's sole legal party, until it decided in April 1981 in favour of a pluralist system. The first multi-party elections since independence in 1956 were subsequently held on Nov. 1, 1981, and were contested by three opposition parties as well as by a National Front alliance of the PSD and *Union Générale des Travailleurs Tunisiens* (UGTT) trade union federation. The National Front won all 136 Assembly seats and the three opposition parties all failed to attain the minimum 5 per cent share of the vote which the Government had earlier specified as a requirement for eventual legal recognition. One of these, the (pro-Soviet) Tunisian Communist Party, had been restored to full legality in July 1981 (after being banned since 1963) without conditions being attached as to performance in the elections; but the Movement of Socialist Democrats (MDS) and the Movement of Popular Unity (MUP) remained officially unrecognized.

In moving to a limited form of party pluralism the Government made it clear that it did not intend to grant recognition to Tunisia's emerging Moslem fundamentalist groups. In December 1979 the Prime Minister had issued a strong warning that it would not allow the country's mosques to be transformed into political tribunes "sowing hatred and encouraging fanaticism"; moreover, in July 1981 he denounced those who were "spreading sedition inside God's houses" and called on all officials and national organizations to protect the mosques against those who "don religious attire to further political ends".

Serious challenges to the Government of President Bourguiba in recent years have included (i) a one-day general strike called by the UGTT on Jan. 26, 1978, which led to serious civil disorder and widespread arrests of union activists, and (ii) an attack on the central Tunisian town of Gafsa in January 1980 by Libyan-backed insurgents. In both cases government authority was quickly re-established, and in the early 1980s the Bourguiba regime has appeared to be under no serious internal or external threat. As indicated above, a full rapprochement was achieved between the PSD and the UGTT by the time of the November 1981 elections.

Arab National Rally (*Rassemblement National Arabe,* RNA)

Leadership. Bechir Essid.

The formation of the RNA was announced on May 15, 1981, by Bechir Essid, a Tunis barrister, who stated that the party sought the "development and expansion of the Arabic-Moslem personality of the Tunisian people" and would campaign for "the total unity of the Arabic countries". It was noted by Western press sources that the new party appeared to be differentiating itself from the main Moslem fundamentalist current in Tunisia and that the phraseology of its programme echoed precepts subscribed to by the Libyan regime. The RNA did not contest the November 1981 general elections and has not been legally recognized (fundamentalist movements being ineligible for registration as parties).

Islamic Progressive Movement (*Mouvement Islamique Progressiste,* MIP)

This small Moslem fundamentalist group stands to the left of the more substantial Islamic Trend Movement (see separate entry).

Islamic Trend Movement (*Mouvement de la Tendance Islamique,* MTI)

Leadership. Rachid Ghanouchi (pres.); Abdel Fatah Mourou (s.g.).

After the establishment of the Islamic Republic of Iran in February 1979, the Moslem fundamentalist (or "integralist") movement greatly increased its following in many Arab countries, including Tunisia, in particular among students. Before the creation of the MTI in 1981, Abdel Fatah Mourou was, together with Hasen Ghodbani, among the leaders of the Khwanyia Movement, whose publication, *Al Moujtamaa,* was banned for three months early in December 1979, when legal proceedings were instituted against its editor and director.

Violent incidents at a number of colleges and schools during February 1981 were officially attributed to activists of the newly formed MTI, but early in May 1981 the MTI leaders rejected such allegations, claiming that the authorities were mounting a campaign against the MTI to deny it legal existence. On July 11-18, 1981, large-scale arrests took place of Moslem fundamentalists, among them the MTI's president and secretary-general. Following protests against these arrests by the MTI and other opposition groups, the Minister of the Interior stated on July 30 that they were the result of an attempt by Islamic fundamentalists at M'Saken (100 miles south of Tunis) to replace by their own nominee a government-appointed imam (Moslem priest). Referring also to other incidents, the Minister claimed that the group had "contacts with foreign quarters with expansionist aims". On Sept. 4, 1981, a total of 99 Islamic fundamentalists were sentenced (many of them in absentia) to prison terms ranging from one to 11 years, the heaviest sentences being imposed on the MTI's president (11 years) and its secretary-general (10 years). On appeal the president's sentence was, on Oct. 3, 1981, reduced to 10 years.

On Sept. 14, 1981, it was reported that, following demonstrations in support of Ayatollah Khomeini, the Iranian leader, 140 persons had been detained, among them leaders of the MTI. The Movement then boycotted general elections held on Nov. 1, 1981, mainly because it objected to the provision that no party gaining less than 5 per cent of the votes would be entitled to official recognition.

The MTI unsuccessfully demanded that all restaurants should be closed for Ramadan, and it was strongly opposed to tourism and the establishment of Western-type boutiques. Calling the Tunisian President a "despot", the Movement issued, in October 1981, a statement calling for the "resuscitation of the Islamic personality of Tunisia so that it can recover its role as a great home of Islamic civilization in Africa and put an end to the situation of dependency, alienation and decay".

Movement of Socialist Democrats (*Mouvement des Démocrates Socialistes,* MDS)

Leadership. Ahmed Mestiri (s.g.).

The MDS came into being in 1971 when "liberals" within the ruling PSD called upon the Government to liberalize and modernize the country's political life and institutions. Mestiri was expelled from the PSD in January 1972, as were seven other liberals in 1974. During 1977 the Movement began to establish itself as a significant opposition group and in June 1978 formally constituted itself into a political party. However, it met with strong criticism from the Government and its repeated requests for legal recognition were rejected.

The MDS refused to seek participation in the November 1979 elections notwithstanding the Government's decision that each seat would be contested by two candidates. In March 1980 the PSD political bureau rescinded the expulsions of Mestiri and the other seven liberals in a move, partly successful, to attract prominent members of the Movement back into the ruling party; but the faction led by Mestiri continued to oppose the Government and was one of three opposition parties which contested the November 1981 elections, in each case unsuccessfully.

In that it obtained only 3.3. per cent of the vote, the MDS failed to attain the 5 per cent share which the Government had earlier specified as a requirement for eventual legal recognition of the unofficial parties such as the MDS.

Popular Revolutionary Movement (*Mouvement Populaire Révolutionnaire,* MPR)

On Nov. 12, 1982, the Tunisian security services announced that about 10 "terrorists" belonging to this organization had been arrested as they were "preparing criminal acts against certain institutions in the capital and its suburbs".

Popular Unity Movement (*Mouvement de l'Unité Populaire,* MUP)

Leadership. Ahmed Ben Salah (s.g. of external faction).

The MUP was formed in 1973 by followers of the former Economy and Finance Minister, Ahmed Ben Salah, who had originally been a leading theorist of the ruling PSD but had been dismissed and sentenced to 10 years' imprisonment in 1970. After escaping from prison in 1973, Ben Salah later reappeared in exile and as leader of the newly formed MUP campaigned against the Bourguiba regime, with some support within the country.

After the MUP had refused to seek participation in the November 1979 elections, a split developed within the party in early 1981 when President Bourguiba on Feb. 13 granted an amnesty to all MUP members still subject to restrictions or exile, with the specific exception of Ben Salah himself. The amnesty decision was taken after a meeting between the President and MUP activists opposed to the leadership of Ben Salah, this group having the previous month been suspended from MUP membership for entering into contacts with the Interior Ministry for the party's legalization without reference to the official party leadership.

Subsequently, both factions of the party made official applications for legal registration, each claiming to be the authentic MUP. Moreover, the internal MUP faction participated in the November 1981 general elections, whereas the Ben Salah faction continued the party's established policy of boycotting such polls. The internal MUP obtained only 0.8 per cent of the vote in the election and thus failed to attain the 5 per cent share which the Government had earlier specified as a minimum requirement for eventual legal registration.

Progressive Nationalist Front for the Liberation of Tunisia (*Front Nationaliste Progressiste pour la Libération de la Tunisie,* FNPLT)

Leadership. Mahvez Saadawi (s.g.).

The illegal FNPLT comprises the *Union Socialiste Arabe de la Tunisie* (of Nasserites), the *Mouvement Socialiste* (of Baathists) and Youssefists. (The last-named are followers of the late Salah Ben Youssef, who had been secretary-general of the Neo-Destour Party and a rival of President Bourguiba; condemned to death in absentia in December 1958 for organizing, with Egyptian help, a plot against President Bourguiba which was uncovered in March 1958, he was murdered in the Federal Republic of Germany in August 1961.) The Youssefists were also alleged to have been involved in a plot against President Bourguiba uncovered on Dec. 19, 1962. On June 30, 1979, a number of persons were sentenced to prison terms for membership of the FNPLT, which thereafter appeared to have fallen into relative inactivity.

Revolutionary Party of the Tunisian People (*Parti Révolutionnaire du Peuple Tunisien,* PRPT)

A number of persons were on June 30, 1979, sentenced to varying terms of imprisonment for membership of this illegal left-wing party, which subsequently appeared to have no significant presence.

Tunisian Armed Resistance (*Résistance Armée Tunisienne,* RAT)

According to the Tunisian authorities, this organization was established among Tunisians working in Libya, where they had been given military training. On Jan. 28, 1981, the movement claimed responsibility for an attack launched on the previous day by some 50 armed men from Algerian territory against the Tunisian town of Gafsa, this attack being intended as "the starting point of a movement whose final aim is the liberation of our people from the dictatorship of the *Parti Socialiste Destourien* and from neo-colonialist domination". The Tunisian Government regarded the attack as having been planned and organized in Libya (while the Algerian Government disclaimed any involvement in it), and it was repulsed with heavy losses and numerous insurgents being arrested.

Of those involved in the attack, 15 were on March 27, 1981, condemned to death (two of them in absentia) and 24 were given prison sentences ranging from six months to 20 years (five in absentia). The 13 men hanged on April 17 included Ezzedine Sharif (the alleged organizer of the attack, who had previously served a prison sentence for involvement in the December 1962 assassination plot against President Bourguiba) and Ahmed Mergheni (the military commander of the attack).

The Tunisians involved in the attack were, (according to *The Sunday Times* of Feb. 17, 1980) part of a "force of 7,000 volunteer soldiers and terrorists currently training in 20 Libyan camps" and recruited from Egypt, Tunisia, Algeria, Morocco, Mali, Niger, Chad, Guinea, Senegal and the Ivory Coast, and also from South Yemen, Pakistan, the Philippines and North Korea, and including some members of the Irish Republican Army (IRA). These men, described by Col. Kadhafi, the Libyan leader, as "the liberators of the Third World", were said to be receiving training from "several thousand Soviet, Cuban and East German instructors", with planning for guerrilla operations being carried out by a "Bureau for Exporting the Revolution" *(Maktab Tasdir Athaoura)* supervised by Col. Kadhafi.

Tunisian Communist Party (*Parti Communiste Tunisien,* PCT)

Leadership. Mohamed Harmel (s.g.).

The PCT held its first congress in 1937, and during World War II it contributed to Tunisian resistance to the Italian and German occupation of the country. Later, and especially during 1952-54, it supported Habib Bourguiba's Neo-Destour Party in its "national" struggle against colonialism. The party later took part in various elections without gaining any seats, i.e. as the sole opposition party in Tunisia's first general election to a Constituent Assembly on March 25, 1956; in municipal elections in May 1957; and in National Assembly elections in November 1959 (when in presidential elections it supported President Bourguiba as the sole candidate of the Neo-Destour Party). Although it had strongly condemned an attempt to assassinate the President, the party was informed in January 1963 that it must cease all its activities; the party's weekly paper had already been banned on Dec. 31, 1962, but it was stated that the PCT was not formally banned as it had "never been legally recognized since independence" was achieved (in 1956).

The party later gave conditional support to the "progressive" economic policies of the Tunisian Government until 1969, whereafter it openly opposed the Government and was formally banned. However, after the move to limited party pluralism in April 1981, the PCT was accorded full legal recognition on July 18, 1981, and participated as one of three opposition parties in the November 1981 general elections, obtaining only 0.8 per cent of the vote and no seats.

The TCP has maintained close relations with other pro-Soviet Communist parties.

United Arab Emirates

Capital: Abu Dhabi   Pop. 920,000

The United Arab Emirates (UAE) are a federated state of seven sheikhdoms without parliament or political parties.

Joint Opposition Front

At a meeting held in London in November 1980, agreement was reached by various opposition leaders on the formation of a united political opposition front and the establishment, as its military arm, of a movement for the liberation of the UAE. In its manifesto the meeting called for the overthrow of the existing regime, the establishment of a democratic and popular regime, the control of national wealth and its use in the interests of the country's citizens, and the use of all forms of struggle to recover the three Gulf islands seized by Iran at the end of November 1971 (i.e. Abu Musa and the Greater and Lesser Tunbs).

Yemen Arab Republic

Capital: Sana'a Pop. 7,080,000

The Yemen Arab Republic (North Yemen) is under military rule. It has no elected assembly and no political parties. There is a Presidential Council formed by a Constituent Assembly set up in February 1978 and enlarged in May 1979. The Government's policies have been influenced by the need to maintain friendly relations with the country's powerful neighbour (Saudi Arabia) and by its relations with the People's Democratic Republic of Yemen (South Yemen), with which agreements on eventual unification have been concluded on several occasions. The Government has, as a result, been faced with political opposition from traditional forces (said to have support from Saudi Arabia) and from left-wing forces supported by South Yemen. There have been many incidents involving political violence, and two of the Republic's Presidents have been assassinated—the pro-Saudi Lt.-Col. Ibrahim al-Hamadi in October 1977 and his successor, Lt.-Col. Hussein al-Ghashmi, in June 1978.

Under a decree of Feb. 7, 1979, all political prisoners detained in the past five years were pardoned, and 494 were subsequently released. On March 15, 1979, a general amnesty was granted to all opponents of the regime who declared their loyalty and surrendered their arms. Under a further decree of Aug. 20, 1979, the President pardoned a number of political prisoners, including those sentenced to death, who were released.

Islamic Front

Leadership. Shaikh Abdullah Bin Hussein al-Ahmar.

This Front was described as a pressure group consisting of conservative tribes in remote mountain regions supported and financed by Saudi Arabia to oppose North Yemen's proposed merger with South Yemen. Its leader was a member of the country's Consultative Council and also the head of the Hashed tribal confederation (centred around Sada'a, in the northern part of the country). In July 1977 he led an unsuccessful insurrection aimed at the establishment of a strict Moslem regime in North Yemen.

National Democratic Front (NDF)

Leadership. Sultan Ahmed Omar (l.).

The NDF, consisting mainly of North Yemeni tribesmen, was formed in 1977 with headquarters in Aden (South Yemen). In February the Front launched an attack from South Yemen on North Yemeni territory and gained control of an area along the two countries' border. In North Yemen the attack was described as having been launched by regular South Yemeni troops supported by

East German and Soviet advisers, but this was denied in South Yemen.

Following mediation by the Governments of Iraq, Jordan and Syria, a ceasefire was agreed for March 3, 1979, but fighting nevertheless continued while the Arab League Council of Ministers, meeting in Kuwait on March 4-6, worked out a plan to restore peace and involving the withdrawal of the forces of both sides within 10 days. At the same time the NDF issued an appeal over South Yemen's radio to North Yemeni soldiers to revolt against their regime, and on March 6 it announced the killing by "revolutionary forces" of a tribal leader loyal to the North Yemeni regime.

In the light of further reports of alleged Cuban and Soviet involvement in South Yemen, the US Government—which had announced on Feb. 28 that it would speed up the delivery of arms ordered by North Yemen—ordered (as announced on March 6) a US naval task force to head for the Arabian peninsula and disclosed (on March 9) that it had approved delivery of further arms (including jet fighters and tanks) to the area as a "co-operative venture" with Saudi Arabia, which would receive and pay for the arms.

The United States also decided to send military advisers to North Yemen.

Meanwhile, NDF forces had occupied further areas, including the towns of Qataba and Al-Bayda. A ceasefire was not observed until March 16, 1979, and by March 19 the withdrawal of troops, including those of the NDF, was completed under supervision by an Arab League commission.

At a meeting held in Kuwait on March 28-30, 1979, the Presidents of North and South Yemen provisionally agreed to unite their two countries in a People's Republic of Yemen. Further talks on the subject were, however, not held until early in 1980, when an agreement was signed (in mid-February) by the Government of North Yemen and the NDF on the establishment of a coalition government in North Yemen, the holding of free elections and the promulgation of a new Constitution for North Yemen, as well as guaranteed political and trade union rights and the adoption of a non-aligned, independent foreign policy.

Following Saudi Arabia's failure to supply further arms to North Yemen (to whose unification plans Saudi Arabia was strongly opposed), arms were delivered to North Yemen by the Soviet Union under an agreement concluded in mid-1979. At the same time the NDF was reported to have infiltrated certain tribes in North Yemen traditionally opposed to that country's regime and previously backed by Saudi Arabia, and to have wrested control of some villages from ruling shaikhs and to have begun to administer them on South Yemeni lines. NDF units were also involved in a number of clashes with North Yemeni troops. On Aug. 28, 1980, it was reported that three NDF leaders—Dr Abdul

Salam al-Dumaini and his two brothers—had been killed in Sana'a while they were officially "trying to negotiate unification of the two Yemens". An NDF conference was said to have been held inside North Yemen on Dec. 9-10, 1980.

However, on Jan. 26, 1981, it was reported from Kuwait that a three-week offensive by North Yemeni government forces had defeated the NDF "once and for all" and had forced it to withdraw to South Yemen. The Government of North Yemen subsequently emphasized its close relations with Saudi Arabia, and at the end of a meeting of a Saudi-North Yemeni Co-ordination Council on April 14, 1981, it expressed its satisfaction at "the continuous support" which Saudi Arabia was giving to the Government and the people of the Yemen Arab Republic in a number of fields.

Party of Popular Yemenite Unity (PPYU)

According to a statement by Dr Abdul Karim Ali al-Iryani, the Prime Minister of the Yemen Arab Republic, reported early in May 1982, the PPYU was "a 100 per cent Marxist-Leninist organization" and constituted the strongest and most active of the opposition forces in his country; he said that its headquarters were in Aden, received weapons via South Yemen and had guerrillas crossing the frontier from that country. He also claimed that the PPYU was not distinct from the Yemen Socialist Party (YSP), the sole legal party of South Yemen, and that three of the PPYU's leaders, whom he named as Yehya el-Chami, Mohammed Kassem el-Thawr and Jarallah Omar, were members of the YSP's political bureau.

People's Democratic Republic of Yemen

Capital: Aden   Pop. 1,950,000

The People's Democratic Republic of Yemen (South Yemen) is ruled by the 11-member Presidium of the (Marxist-Leninist) Yemen Socialist Party (YSP), constituted as the country's sole legal party in October 1978, following the overthrow and execution of Salem Rubayya Ali (the head of state), who was accused inter alia of having wished to reduce Soviet influence in South Yemen and to improve relations with other (including conservative) Arab states. There is a 111-member People's Supreme Assembly elected on a list of the YSP.

Although firmly tied to the Soviet Union by a treaty of friendship and co-operation concluded in October 1979 (which was said to entitle the USSR to station up to 25,000 troops in South Yemen) and the only Arab country to express support for the Soviet intervention in Afghanistan in December 1979, South Yemen has since then made efforts to expand its relations with other countries, including North Yemen and Saudi Arabia.

Opposition groups established outside the country in recent years are not considered to constitute a serious challenge to the regime.

National Grouping of Patriotic Forces of South Yemen

Leadership. Abdul Qawee Mackawee (s.g.).

This Grouping was established in March 1980 in Baghdad, the Iraqi capital.

A. Q. Mackawee had been the leader of the Front for the Liberation of Occupied South Yemen (FLOSY), one of the two movements fighting for the establishment of an independent South Yemen (the other being the National Liberation Front, which later became the ruling YSP); he had also briefly been Chief Minister of Aden in 1965. Following the establishment of the Democratic People's Republic under the control of the National Liberation Front in November 1967, A. Q. Mackawee left the country and in August 1972 established in North Yemen a United National Front of South Yemen, which comprised most of the leading opponents of the Aden regime. However, this movement was banned by the Government of North Yemen on Dec. 2, 1972, after an agreement had been concluded in Tripoli (Libya) on Nov. 28 of that year on the proposed establishment of a united Yemeni Republic to be based on Islamic socialism.

At a conference held in Cairo on Feb. 10, 1981, A. Q. Mackawee described his organization's case as one which should be supported by all members of the Islamic Arab nation, who should resist the advance of in-

ternational communism (as in Afghanistan). He said that more than half of South Yemen's people had fled the country "in search of security, peace and a decent living", and he declared that South Yemen was not only a Soviet colony but "a springboard for communism" which threatened the security, safety and stability of all the Arab and Moslem countries.

The Grouping has declared its objectives as being to bring together all "progressive national and patriotic forces" opposed to what it calls "the puppet fascist regime" in South Yemen. It has undertaken to fight against "all forms of foreign presence in South Yemen", to liberate the country from "the authority of the secessionists and their overlords" and to unify the two Yemens.

National Liberation Army

Several men claiming to be members of this group were among 13 South Yemenis sentenced in Aden on April 7, 1982 (12 of them to death and the other to 15 years in prison) for "plotting" to sabotage South Yemen's economic and oil installations after being allegedly trained by the (US) Central Intelligence Agency (CIA) in Saudi Arabia and having brought explosives into the country. Of the death sentences two were on April 12 commuted to 15 years' imprisonment, whereas the other 10 were carried out on April 22, 1982.

South Yemen Liberation Front

This Front was established in Cairo (Egypt) in July 1980. It has defined its aims as being "to put an end to Marxist influence in South Yemen, using all legal means and methods, to put an end to subservience to anti-Arab and anti-Islamic forces and to establish a national democratic regime which democratically represents the people through honest, free elections". (A Yemeni National Unity Front had earlier been set up in Cairo by Mohammed Ali Haithem, who had been Prime Minister of South Yemen in 1969-71 and who escaped an assassination attempt in Cairo in October 1975. The Egyptian capital has become a haven for South Yemeni exiles.)

4. CENTRAL, EAST AND WEST AFRICA

Benin

Capital: Porto Novo   Pop. 3,600,000

The People's Republic of Benin (formerly Dahomey) is ruled by a (military) National Council of the Revolution which takes decisions in conformity with those of the central committee of the left-wing Benin People's Revolutionary Party (*Parti de la Révolution Populaire du Bénin,* PRPB), the country's sole legal political organization. There is a National Revolutionary Assembly of 336 People's Commissioners elected by direct universal suffrage on Nov. 20, 1979, on a list of PRPB candidates. The Assembly elects the President of the Republic, who is head of state and of the Executive Council (Cabinet).

Dahomey Liberation and Rehabilitation Front (*Front de Libération et de Réhabilitation du Dahomey,* FLRD)

This illegal organization was established in France after the military takeover on Oct. 26, 1972, bringing to power the left-wing military regime which has been in office since then. The object of the FLRD has been the return to a democratic government in Benin. Among the personalities joining it was Gratien Pognon, who until August 1975 was Dahomey's ambassador in Belgium and at the European Communities.

Several unsuccessful attempts to overthrow the regime in Benin have not been expressly attributed to the FLRD. Following the discovery of one such plot in February 1973, another was foiled on Jan. 21, 1975, and resulted in death sentences being passed on March 17 by a "national revolutionary tribunal" on seven men alleged to have been involved. These included Dr Emile Derlin Zinsou (President of Dahomey in 1968-69 and resident in France since 1970), who was sentenced in absentia, while life sentences were passed on five army officers and 15-year prison sentences on two civilians. The uncovering of a further plot was announced on Oct. 18, 1975, and attributed to Dr Zinsou, who denied its existence; 11 persons accused of involvement in it were on Feb. 3, 1976, condemned to death by the National Council of the Revolution (sitting as a special court), three others to life imprisonment and one to 20 years' hard labour; those sentenced to death included a former Minister of Information under Dr Zinsou.

On the other hand, an invasion by some 100 armed men (about 40 of them White)—who arrived at Cotonou airport in a DC8 aircraft on Jan. 15, 1977, but were repulsed with losses—was on Jan. 24 specifically attributed to the FLRD, and in particular to Dr Zinsou and 11 other persons. A UN Security Council mission sent to Benin in February 1977 to investigate the attempted coup stated in its report (submitted to the UN Secretary-General on March 8, 1977) that the operation had been staged by a French colonel engaged by the FLRD. Allegations made in this report of involvement by France, Gabon, the Ivory Coast, Morocco and Senegal were rejected by the Governments of all these countries as being untrue.

On May 25, 1979, it was officially announced that the National Council of the Revolution, constituted as a revolutionary court, had condemned to death in absentia a total of 100 persons alleged to have been involved in the invasion, with three other defendants being given prison sentences ranging from five to 10 years. Those sentenced to death included 11 Benin citizens described as "traitors", among them Dr Zinsou and Gratien Pognon, as well as 62 European mercenaries; the latter group included the French colonel referred to by the UN mission, who was identified as Col. Bob Denard (who had led various other mercenary operations in Africa).

Burundi

Capital: Bujumbura   **Pop. 4,200,000**

The Republic of Burundi has an executive President elected by universal adult suffrage for a five-year term, the sole candidate for this office being the president of the *Union pour le Progrès National* (Uprona, the country's only legal political organization) and a 65-member National Assembly, to which 52 members are elected for a five-year term by universal adult suffrage and 13 are nominated by the President. In parliamentary elections held in October 1982 each elective seat was contested by two Uprona candidates.

Although no organized opposition groups appear to exist in Burundi, in the period since independence the Government has been faced with a major internal security problem in the shape of serious ethnic tensions between the minority Tutsi tribe (forming about 15 per cent of the population) and the majority Hutu (about 84 per cent). These tensions developed into an open conflict in 1972 resulting in substantial loss of life, in the light of which the regime of President Bagaza (who came to power in 1976) has officially proscribed any reference to Tutsi or Hutu and declared all inhabitants to be Burundi, i.e. one nation of Burundi. On another plane, the Bagaza regime has experienced conflict with the country's Roman Catholic Church, which the President in 1979 described as forming "a hierarchy parallel to that of the state and the party"

Cameroon

Capital: Yaoundé   **Pop. 8,600,000**

The United Republic of Cameroon has an executive President elected for a five-year term by universal adult suffrage (and re-eligible) and a Cabinet headed by a Prime Minister and consisting of ministers who are not members of Parliament. The country's 120-member National Assembly is elected also by universal adult suffrage and for a five-year term from a list submitted by the Cameroon National Union (*Union Nationale Camerounaise,* UNC), the country's sole legal political party.

Signs of internal opposition to the regime have in recent years been confined to the distribution of leaflets deemed to be subversive. Under laws promulgated in July 1980 the authorities were empowered to seize and destroy such leaflets. After Amnesty International had alleged that there were some 200 political detainees, it was officially stated on Feb. 13, 1980, that there were only four in Cameroon. Externally, several opposition groups based in Paris have made statements about their policies and activities.

Army of the Black People of Cameroon

On July 10, 1980, an anonymous caller claiming to speak for this organization accepted responsibility for a bomb attack on the Paris office of the German Federal Railways, declaring that this attack marked the start of an "offensive against German imperialism in Africa".

National Union of Cameroon Students (*Union Nationale des Etudiants de Kamerun,* UNEK)

Leadership. Albert Moutoudou (ch. of executive committee).

This Union has held annual congresses in Paris. On Dec. 28, 1976, a "group of militants" of the UNEK issued a document alleging that since July 1976 "hundreds of young people—pupils, students and workers"—were being "detained in Yaoundé without being tried" and that many of them had been tortured; the document listed some 30 political detainees.

Albert Moutoudou stated in January 1977 that, although the UNEK was "not a movement in opposition to the Yaoundé regime", its demands were not separable from "the global struggle of the people of Cameroon for independence, peace and social well-being". He also supplied a list of 118 political detainees held in Cameroon.

Union of Cameroonian Peoples (*Union des Populations Camerounaises,* UPC)

Leadership. M. Woungly-Massaga (l.).

This clandestine party based in Paris was banned in Cameroon in 1955, when it was regarded as communist-led and responsible for riots which had occurred in Douala in May of that year. The party took no part in elections held on Dec. 23, 1956, for a 70-member Legislative Assembly for the then French Cameroons. The UPC was thereafter divided into a Marxist wing led by Dr Félix Moumié (then in Cairo) and a nationalist wing led by Ruben Um Nyobé, who led a rebellion inside Cameroon but was killed by security forces in September 1958. Many members of this wing thereupon surrendered, and in April 1959 a UPC leader was elected to the Legislative Assembly as a member of the "legal opposition".

Dr Moumié, however, announced in June 1959 that the "revolution" would continue, and guerrilla warfare followed. On Aug. 18, 1959, he and André-Marie M'Bida (a former Premier of the Cameroonian Government) issued a warning that "revolutionary action" would continue until the French Government agreed to abolish the existing institutions in Cameroon, to annul the decree banning the UPC, and to convene a round-table conference to be followed by general elections as essential prerequisites for real independence. While UPC guerrilla activities continued, Dr Moumié died in Geneva on Nov. 3, 1960, after he had alleged that he had been poisoned by the "Red Hand", a French organization engaged in counter-terrorist activities against the Algerian nationalists.

In post-independence Cameroon the UPC was held responsible for protracted unrest until 1970, when its leader, Ernest Ouandié, was captured by security forces. He was later tried for "attempted revolution" and other crimes, together with the Roman Catholic bishop (Albert Ndongmo) and 25 other defendants; on Jan. 5, 1971, he and two other accused were sentenced to death and the bishop to life imprisonment (after he had admitted that he had sometimes given material aid to the UPC), while 13 other defendants were given prison sentences of from five to 20 years. However, at a second trial on charges of having plotted the assassination of President Ahmadou Ahidjo of Cameroon, the bishop and two other defendants were sentenced to death on Jan. 6, 1971, when prison sentences ranging from five years to life were imposed on 58 further defendants. Ouandié and two others were executed on Jan. 15, but the sentence on the bishop was commuted to life imprisonment; he was subsequently allowed to leave the country, and was officially reprieved on May 17, 1975.

According to a statement made in April 1975 by Ouandié's successor as leader of the UPC, Woungly-Massaga, the widow of Ouandié was, after being extradited from Equatorial Guinea, being held in Cameroon in detention without trial.

Cape Verde

Capital: Praia   Pop. 310,000

The Republic of Cape Verde is, under its Constitution approved on Sept. 7, 1980, a "sovereign, democratic, unitary, anti-colonialist and anti-imperialist republic". It has a National People's Assembly, an executive President and a Cabinet headed by a Prime Minister. The President is also the secretary-general of the country's sole legal political party, the African Party for the Independence of Cape Verde (PAICV), established on Jan. 20, 1981, as the successor to the Cape Verde branch of the African Party for the Independence of Guinea-Bissau and Cape Verde (PAIGC), whose Government in Guinea-Bissau was overthrown on Nov. 14, 1980. The 56-member National Assembly elected on Dec. 7, 1980, is composed exclusively of members elected on the PAIGC list, which was said to have obtained 93 per cent of the votes cast in a 75 per cent poll.

There are said to be no political prisoners in the Cape Verde Islands. Three members of the Government who resigned during 1979 were expelled from the PAIGC as "Trotskyites".

Independent Democratic Union of Cape Verde (UCID)

This clandestine opposition movement was opposed to the ruling PAIGC's policy of eventual union between Cape Verde and Guinea-Bissau, on the grounds that such a union would extend Soviet influence in the region. Since the successor party to the PAIGC, the PAICV, has declared itself in favour of an independent state of Cape Verde, the UCID's influence has declined. It has admitted that its organization exists only among emigrant Cape Verdian communities overseas, who are opposed to a governmental land reform involving the expropriation of land owned by absentee landlords. In June 1982 prison sentences were imposed by a military court on 16 defendants alleged to be linked to the UCID and charged with attempting to alter the Constitution of Cape Verde by violence; in particular, they were said to have incited rebellion on San Antão island against the implementation of the land reform during August 1981, when at least one person was killed in riots which were quelled by the security forces.

Central African Republic

Capital: Bangui

Pop. 3,200,000

The Central African Republic has been under military rule since Sept. 1, 1981, when President David Dacko was deposed and the Constitution and the country's political parties were suspended. Legislative and executive powers were assumed by a new Military Committee for National Recovery (CMRN) whose chairman, Gen. André Kolingba (Army Chief of Staff), became Chief of the General Staff of the Armed Forces, head of government and Minister of Defence.

The political parties legalized under the Constitution promulgated on Feb. 6, 1981, but subsequently banned or suspended (finally in September 1981) are described below.

Central African Democratic Union (*Union Démocratique Centrafricaine,* UDC)

Leadership. David Dacko (l.).

The UDC was established in March 1980 by President Dacko as the country's sole legal party to serve as his power base until elections were held. Dacko had first become head of the Central African Government in 1959 and head of state on independence in 1960; although overthrown in 1966 by President Bokassa (who later became Emperor), he was appointed as the latter's personal adviser in September 1976; three years later he overthrew the Emperor's regime and restored, with French help, the Central African Republic. In the presidential elections of March 15, 1981, Dacko was officially stated to have received 50.23 per cent of the valid votes cast in a 77 per cent poll (but this result was contested by the opposition parties which considered the elections to have been fraudulent).

Central African Movement for National Liberation (*Mouvement Centrafricain de Libération Nationale,* MCLN)

Leadership. Rodolphe Idi Lala (l.).

Rodolphe Idi Lala founded the MCLN after being excluded from the Oubangian Patriotic Front led by Dr Abel Goumba (for which he had been spokesman) in August 1980. In a statement issued from Nigeria on July 16, 1981, the MCLN claimed responsibility for a bomb explosion at a cinema in Bangui on July 14, when three persons were killed and 32 others injured. Lala later threatened to commit further acts of violence unless President Dacko formed a unity government comprising all political parties

and also arranged for the repatriation of the French troops stationed in the Central African Republic. The pro-Libyan MCLN was officially banned on July 18, 1981.

Central African People's Rally (*Rassemblement du Peuple Centrafricain*)

Leadership. Gen. Sylvestre Bangui (l.).

Gen. Bangui had been ambassador of the Central African Empire in France until May 22, 1979, when he resigned in protest at a massacre of school children (committed with Emperor Bokassa's participation) and founded a Oubangian Liberation Front; on Sept. 11, 1979, he announced (in Paris) the formation of a provisional government-in-exile of the "Republic of Oubangui" with the aim of overthrowing the Emperor, drafting a new constitution and holding elections to a new National Assembly within 18 months. After the overthrow of the Emperor on Sept. 21, 1979, he returned to Bangui and subsequently was Deputy Prime Minister with responsibility for Foreign Affairs until Nov. 12, 1980, when this post was abolished. The following month he announced the formation of the *Rassemblement du Peuple Centrafricain.*

Central African Socialist Party (*Parti Socialiste Centrafricain,* PSC)

Leadership. Jean Tandalet Ozi Okito (l.).

This party's leader stated on Feb. 21, 1981, that the presidential elections scheduled for March 15 were premature, that proper electoral lists needed to be prepared and that he was withdrawing his candidature.

238

Independent Grouping of Reflection and Action (*Groupement Indépendant de Réflexion et d'Action,* GIRA)

Leadership. François Pehoua (l.).

Standing as an independent in the presidential elections of March 15, 1981, François Pehoua, a banker and former minister, advocated democracy and a liberal economic policy leading to self-sufficiency in food production; however, he obtained only 5.33 per cent of the valid votes cast (according to the official results). The GIRA was one of the four parties which formed a "provisional political council" seeking (according to a statement issued in Paris on July 25, 1981) the resignation of President Dacko and the establishment of a national council charged with setting up a "provisional government of national unity"; the four parties also reaffirmed their determination to work for peace and "true democracy" in the Central African Republic.

Movement for Democracy and Independence (*Mouvement pour la Démocratie et l'Indépendance,* MDI)

Leadership. François Guéret (l.).

François Guéret was a member of the Cabinet under President Dacko from September 1979 until March 1980, when he was dismissed after having prepared, as Minister of Justice, a report on crimes of the Emperor Bokassa's regime; in this report he had incriminated various members of President Dacko's regime (in particular Henri Maidou, who had been Prime Minister under the Emperor and later was Vice-President under President Dacko). Guéret established the MDI in 1981.

Movement for the Liberation of the Central African People (*Mouvement de Libération du Peuple Centrafricain,* MLPC)

Leadership. Ange Patasse (l.).

Ange Patasse was Prime Minister from September 1976 to July 1978 (when he was replaced by Henri Maidou, later the leader of the Republican Progress Party). After he had left the country he stated in Paris on June 7, 1979, that a "committee of national union" was being formed to speed up the liberation of the country from the Emperor, whom he accused inter alia of being responsible for numerous summary executions and of trying to poison him (Patasse). While in exile he set up the MLPC, which rejected the Government of President Dacko established in September 1979; Patasse was nevertheless allowed to return to Bangui in October of that year. On Nov. 3, 1979, however, he was arrested for "fomenting unrest", and he was not released until Nov. 24, 1980. By that time the MLPC had obtained widespread support in the country, and in the presidential elections of March 15, 1981, A. Patasse came second with 38.11 per cent of the valid votes (according to the official results).

The MLPC was suspended on July 18, 1981, but was on Aug. 10 of that year allowed to resume its activities. It was one of the four parties which formed a "provisional political council" and which (in a statement issued in Paris on July 25, 1981) called for the resignation of President Dacko and the establishment of a national council charged with setting up a "provisional government of national unity".

However, on March 6, 1982, the MLPC was banned after a number of its members and several army officers had been arrested in connexion with an unsuccessful attempt to overthrow the military Government on March 3. Ange Patasse took refuge in the French embassy in Bangui on March 6, and on April 13 he was flown to Togo (where he was granted political asylum).

Oubangian Patriotic Front—Party of Labour (*Front Oubangais Patriotique—Parti du Travail,* FOP-PT)

Leadership. Dr Abel Goumba (l.); Patrice Endijimongou (s.g. for external relations).

Dr Goumba had been an opponent of David Dacko (then President) since 1959. He was leader of a *Mouvement d'Evolution Démocratique d'Afrique Centrale,* which was officially accused of being based on tribalism and which was dissolved in February 1961, when Dr Goumba and other leaders of the movement were placed under house arrest. He was later allowed to leave the country and became an official of the World Health Organization. From the Congo he set up an Oubangian Patriotic Front, which in a statement issued in January 1980 rejected the Government of President Dacko, and called for the departure of French troops from the country and for a general election to bring about the restoration of free democracy.

After 17 years in exile Dr Goumba returned to Bangui in February 1981 and stood as a candidate for the FOP-PT in the presidential elections of March 15, 1981, but obtained only 1.42 per cent of the valid votes (as officially stated). The FOP-PT was banned on July 18, 1981, but was allowed to resume its activities on Aug. 10 of that year. However, after the coup of Sept. 1, 1981, it was suspended with all other political parties.

The FOP-PT had been one of the four parties which formed a "provisional political council" and which (in a statement issued in Paris on July 25, 1981) called for the resignation of President Dacko and the establishment of a national council charged with setting up a "provisional government of national unity".

However, on Aug. 30, 1982, the authorities of the Central African Republic announced that "subversive documents" had been found three days earlier in the possession of the banned party's secretary-general for external affairs at Bangui airport, and that both he and Dr Goumba, who had supplied the documents, had been arrested. The authorities also claimed to have formal evidence of the existence of close ties between Dr Goumba and the leader of an unnamed foreign political party (believed to be the French Socialist Party).

Republican Progress Party (*Parti Républicain du Progrès,* PRP)

Leadership. Henri Maidou (l.).

Although Henri Maidou had been Prime Minister under the Emperor Bokassa, he served as Vice-President under President Dacko from September 1979 to Aug. 23, 1980, when he was dismissed and placed under house arrest for a month, having been incriminated (in a report of Jan. 19, 1980, by François Guéret, then Minister of Justice) of involvement in the imprisonment of school children and misappropriation of public funds under the Emperor. In the presidential elections of March 15, 1981, he obtained only 3.23 per cent of the valid votes as the candidate of the newly-formed PRP, which called for representative democracy and free debate.

The PRP was one of the four parties which formed a "provisional political council" and which (in a statement issued in Paris on July 25, 1981) called for the resignation of President Dacko and the establishment of a national council which would be charged with setting up a "provisional government of national unity".

Chad

Capital: N'Djaména   Pop. 4,490,000

The Republic of Chad is ruled by a Council of State (consisting of 18 commissioners and 12 vice-commissioners) drawn from the members of the Armed Forces of the North (*Forces Armées du Nord,* FAN), which came to power (through civil war) in June 1982 and whose leader, Hissène Habré, became the official head of state in Chad on June 19, 1982. By early September 1982 the new Government was in control of all 14 administrative centres in the country.

Of the principal political factions opposed to the regime of Hissène Habré and described below, only the National Peace Government with its "National Liberation Army" was by early 1983 still a fighting force.

Chad Armed Forces (*Forces Armées Tchadiennes,* FAT)

Leadership. Lt.-Col. Wadal Abelkader Kamougue (commander).

Established in 1975, the FAT were originally the armed forces loyal to President Félix Malloum (in office from April 1975 until March 1979). They represented mainly the Black Christian and animist south of the country against the Moslem north. At the same time the FAT opposed the various factions of the Chad National Liberation Front (Frolinat). Having continued their armed resistance beyond the assumption of power by Hissène Habré in June 1982, the FAT were then gradually defeated by Habré's FAN, which took Moundou (Lt.-Col. Kamougue's stronghold) on Aug. 27, 1982. The latter had ruled a region in the south since 1978 by means of a "permanent committee", but after the fall of Moundou he fled the country. A large part of the FAT forces had earlier defected to the *Forces Armées du Nord* (FAN), and on Dec. 25, 1982, it was reported that FAN and FAT had combined to form the basis of a new national army known as *Forces Armées Nationales Tchadiennes* (FANT).

Democratic Revolutionary Council (*Conseil Démocratique Révolutionnaire,* CDR)

Leadership. Acheikh Ibn Oumar (l.).

Established in 1979, the CDR (also known as the New Volcano Army) was one of the numerous factions of the Chad National Liberation Front (Frolinat). As such it took part in the formation of a transitional Government of national unity (GUNT) set up in November 1979 under President Goukouni Oueddei. The CDR had its base in the extreme north of Chad and partly also in the south-east. Its leader at the time, Acyl Ahmat, was said to have negotiated an agreement between Chad and Libya on Jan. 6, 1981, when the two Governments announced their decision to work for "full unity" between their two countries—an agreement which was opposed by Hissène Habré and also by certain members of the GUNT. The latter included (i) Lt.-Col. Wadal Abdelkader Kamougue, the leader of the Chad Armed Forces (FAT); (ii) Dr Abba Sidick, the founder of the original Frolinat; and (iii) Moussa Medela Mahamat, the leader of another Frolinat faction known as the *Forces Armées Occidentales* (FAO); all three resigned from the GUNT in July 1981.

In the armed struggle of the CDR, Acyl Ahmat headed a *Front d'Action Commune* (FAC), supporting the Popular Armed Forces (FAP) of President Goukouni Oueddei against Habré's Armed Forces of the North (FAN). Acyl Ahmat opposed President Goukouni Oueddei's call for the withdrawal from Chad of all Libyan troops, which had first entered Chad in April 1979, partly in support of Lt.-Col. Kamougue's "permanent committee" set up in southern Chad (see separate entry for Chad Armed Forces). Upon the assumption of power by Habré, Lt.-Col. Kamougue rejected the new President's call to disarm his forces, but on July 19, 1982, he was killed in an accident. His successor, Acheikh Ibn Oumar, had been Minister of Defence in Goukouni Oueddei's last Government, and before that Minister of Education. The CDR forces were, however, decisively defeated in the battles which led to the fall of Moundou, the stronghold of Lt.-Col. Kamougue's Chad Armed Forces, in August 1982.

National Peace Government

Leadership. Goukouni Oueddei (1.).

Goukouni Oueddei had headed a Transitional Government of National Union (GUNT) between November 1979 and June 1982, when it was overthrown by the forces of Hissène Habré. The formation of the National Peace Government at Bardei (northern Chad) on Oct. 28, 1982, was announced in Libya and was stated to have been the result of a meeting in Algiers early in October of the leaders of eight of the 11 factions which had composed the GUNT; the objectives of the National Peace Government were declared to be the overthrow of "the terrorist FAN regime" of Hissène Habré and the restoration of "peace and unity" in Chad. The National Peace Government formed a "National Liberation Army" which, according to Libyan sources, fought several successful battles against the forces of Hissène Habré's Government in January-March 1983. H. Habré, however, stated that the National Peace Government was "nothing more than an instrument used by our enemies" (i.e. Libya).

New Volcano Army—see Democratic Revolutionary Council (CDR)

Congo

Capital: Brazzaville   Pop. 1,500,000

The People's Republic of the Congo has been ruled by a Military Committee of the Congolese Party of Labour (*Parti Congolais du Travail,* PCT) since the assassination of President Marien Ngouabi on March 18, 1977, whereafter the Constitution was suspended and the National Assembly dissolved. Under a new Constitution approved in a referendum on July 8, 1979, provision was made for a popularly elected National People's Assembly consisting of members nominated by the PCT. The congress of the PCT appoints the country's President, who presides over a Council of Ministers headed by a Prime Minister. In elections to the People's National Assembly held on July 8, 1979, over 90 per cent of the voters were stated to have approved the PCT's official candidates.

Under an amnesty declared by President Denis Sassou-Nguesso on Aug. 14, 1979, a number of political prisoners were released, including those implicated in the assassination of President Ngouabi and Cardinal Biayenda in 1977 and in an attempted coup of Aug. 14, 1978; at the same time all Congolese opposition members abroad, especially in France, were not to be prosecuted and were enabled to "return to their country without fear". Under a further amnesty announced on Aug. 24, 1980, the penalties of most prisoners (except those tried for economic sabotage or embezzlement of public funds) were reduced—death sentences to hard labour for life, and life sentences to 30 years' imprisonment.

Patriotic Armed Group of the Congo
(Groupe Armé Patriotique du Congo)

This Group surfaced in March 1982 when a telephone caller in Paris identified himself as a member and reportedly stated that an earlier explosion in a Brazzaville cinema was due to a terrorist action which had killed 15 persons (and not five, as officially reported). He stated that his Group wanted clarification of the murder of President Ngouabi and also of the imprisonment of President Joachim Yhombi Opango in 1979 after he had relinquished power to Col. Sassou-Nguesso.

(An unknown gunman had previously fired shots at the first secretary at the Congolese embassy in Brussels on Jan. 29, 1980, and a bomb had exploded on Feb. 20, 1983, outside the building housing that embassy.)

Equatorial Guinea

Capital: Malabo Pop. 320,000

The Republic of Equatorial Guinea is ruled by a Supreme Military Council headed by Lt.-Col. Teodoro Obiang Nguema Mbasago and in power since Aug. 3, 1979, when it overthrew the dictatorial regime of President Francisco Macias Nguema. There is no Parliament nor are there any legal political parties. A new Constitution approved by 95 per cent of the voters in a referendum on Aug. 15, 1982, provided for Lt.-Col. Obiang Nguema to remain head of state for a further seven years, after which there would be presidential elections by direct popular vote. The Constitution also provided for elections to a National Assembly with a five-year term and for the formation of a Council of State.

Opposition to the regime has been directed by groups in exile. An attempt to overthrow the Government was reported to have been made on April 10, 1981, and between 60 and 180 persons were estimated to have been arrested in this connexion, among them two former ministers of the Macias Nguema regime. On June 13 of that year a court-martial sentenced one soldier to death and seven others and four officials to 30 years in prison each inter alia for acting against the process of "national reconstruction".

Command Council of the Revolution

This Council was established in August 1981 at a secret congress held in mainland Equatorial Guinea, with the reported support of two exile opposition groups—the National Alliance for the Restoration of Democracy (ANRD) and the Revolutionary Front of Equatorial Guinea. The ANRD, established in 1974, and based in Spain, had claimed in August 1979 that Lt.-Col. Obiang Nguema Mbasago (who had on Aug. 3 overthrown the regime of President Macias Nguema) had been responsible for the killing of several of his military colleagues before the coup.

The change of regime was, in the view of the ANRD, merely a palace revolution unless all political prisoners were released; all exiles were allowed to return; national independence and integrity were safeguarded; a date was set for an end to military government; slavery, forced labour, deportations, arbitrary arrests and other outrages against the population were ended; the repressive bodies of the former regime were dissolved; and all those responsible for atrocities under the former regime were brought to trial. The ANRD also protested against the introduction of the new Constitution approved in August 1982, which it regarded as merely a manoeuvre to attract foreign aid and capital to Equatorial Guinea.

Democratic Movement for the Liberation of Equatorial Guinea (RDLGE)

Leadership. Manuel Rubén Ndongo (l.)

This Movement expressed doubts about the authenticity of the official result of the referendum of Aug. 15, 1982, approving the country's new Constitution, but it later accepted the Constitution itself.

National Alliance for the Restoration of Democracy (ANRD)—see under Command Council of the Revolution

Revolutionary Front of Equatorial Guinea—see under Command Council of the Revolution

Sole Bloc of Guinean Democratic Forces (Bloque Unico de las Fuerzas Democráticas Guineas)

This organization was set up in Paris in September 1981 by Daniel Oyono, a nephew and protégé of the late President Nguema (executed on Sept. 29, 1979). The announcement of its foundation was followed by the arrest in Equatorial Guinea on Sept. 16 of 20 persons, of whom 19 were released on the following day, but not Luis Nguema Oyono, a brother of Daniel Oyono.

Ethiopia

Capital: Addis Ababa   Pop. 31,000,000

Ethiopia is a republic ruled by a Provisional Military Administrative Council (PMAC or *Derg*), whose Chairman (Lt.-Col. Mengistu Haile Mariam) is head of state and chairman of a Council of Ministers. A Commission for Organizing the Party of the Working People of Ethiopia (COPWE) was set up in December 1979, but by the end of 1982 this Commission had not yet developed into a political mass party on the Soviet model, despite the country's close ties with the Soviet Union and the latter's allies, notably Cuba.

The most serious threats to the continued unity of the Ethiopian state are the separatist movements in Eritrea and the Western Somali Liberation Front (supported by the Government of Somalia). The regime has also faced opposition from political movements opposed to its pro-Soviet policies and from sections of the Protestant Church in Ethiopia. In the face of such challenges, however, the regime has shown no indication of being prepared to make concessions and has in particular deployed massive military forces against the separatists.

Eritrean Separatists

Now Ethiopia's most northerly province, Eritrea had been an Italian colony until World War II and was in 1952 placed by the United Nations under Ethiopian sovereignty with a federal arrangement whereby the province retained its own government, administration and flag. However, under Ethiopia's Constitution of 1955 the country became a unitary state, and by 1956 the Ethiopian authorities had established de facto control of Eritrea's administration. In 1962 Eritrea became de jure one of Ethiopia's 13 provinces. Of its inhabitants rather more than half are Moslems (with certain ties to Moslems in Arab Countries) and most of the remainder are Christians.

The first Eritrean liberation front was founded in 1956, initially with the object of achieving some measure of autonomy and later increasingly calling for complete independence for Eritrea. New liberation movements were formed subsequently, some of them being Marxist rather than traditionalist pro-Arab. Efforts to forge a unitary liberation movement were not successful, however. After the secessionists had gained control of most of Eritrea's countryside through their warfare against Ethiopian forces, the latter gradually gained the upper hand from 1975 onwards, largely as a result of massive military aid from the Soviet Union and Cuba.

Eritrean Liberation Front—Popular Liberation Forces (ELF-PLF)

Leadership. Osman Saleh Sabeh (s.g.).

An Eritrean Liberation Front (ELF) was set up in 1958 in Cairo and was, from 1961 onwards, increasingly active in preparing for armed struggle inside Eritrea with weapons brought in from the Sudan (although the Government of that country officially did not allow Eritrean refugees to engage in subversive activities against Ethiopia). In 1969 and 1971 ELF members committed a number of acts of sabotage and hijacking of Ethiopian airliners. The ELF also undertook guerrilla warfare inside Eritrea, with the result that a partial curfew was imposed by the Ethiopian Army in 1969 and a state of emergency was declared in the greater part of the province on Dec. 16, 1970, by which time the ELF forces were estimated at between 1,500 and 2,000 men equipped with small-arms from Libya. However, claims of spectacular ELF successes, made by Osman Saleh Sabeh in Damascus, were categorically denied by the Ethiopian authorities, which claimed to have the situation under control.

In the following years ELF guerrilla activities increased greatly; by 1974, when the ELF claimed to be in control of certain areas in Eritrea, its forces were estimated at between 5,000 and 10,000 men. Nevertheless, after the deposition of Emperor Haile Selassie by Ethiopia's armed forces in September 1974, the ELF reduced its military activities and indicated its willingness to negotiate a peaceful settlement with Ethiopia's military rulers provided they recognized the ELF as the sole legitimate representative of the Eritrean people.

A Popular Liberation Front (PLF) had earlier been set up as a more radical liberation movement than the ELF. At a conference held in Rome early in July 1974 the PLF claimed that in the 10-year "liberation war" against the Ethiopian "occupation" of Eritrea 20,000 Eritreans had died and 70,000 had fled to the Sudan. The PLF asserted that Ethiopia and Eritrea were two separate countries, different at every level—historically, ethnically and culturally. It also expressed readiness to negotiate with the Ethiopian Government provided the latter recognized the PLF as the sole legitimate representative of the Eritrean people and also their right to self-determination and independence (i.e. not a return to federal status, which was out of the question).

In the latter part of 1974 both the ELF and the PLF intensified their military activities and greatly increased their influence in the countryside, holding two mass meetings near Asmara (the Eritrean capital), the second of which (on Oct. 13) was said to have been attended by between 20,000 and 30,000 people. Tentative talks between government representatives and ELF and PLF leaders, however, remained inconclusive. Early the following year (1975) the ELF and PLF reached agreement (at a conference in Coazien) on the formation of a common front, and thereafter the two organizations gradually coalesced into a unitary movement based on non-Marxist principles.

On Jan. 28, 1975, the military Government declared that it had "come to the end of its patience" with the Eritrean rebels and would launch an all-out offensive against them. The Army thereupon cleared Asmara on Feb. 2 of guerrillas who had infiltrated it; the ELF appealed to "the conscience of the world" to "stop the bombardment of residential parts of Asmara" and the "war of extermination". On Feb. 4 the ELF appealed to "all other liberation movements in Ethiopia" to cooperate with it, and it claimed to have received "generous assistance" from Arab states, including arms supplies from Libya worth $5,000,000.

In view of continued heavy fighting, during which ELF units freed about 1,000 prisoners held in and near Asmara, the state of emergency was on Feb. 15, 1975, extended to the whole of Eritrea. By that time casualties caused in the Asmara area were given as over 2,000 secessionists, at least 1,500 government troops and up to 2,000 civilians killed. However, between March and June 1975 the Ethiopian Army regained full control over Erit-

rea's three main cities of Asmara, Keren and Massawa while secessionist forces largely retained control over the countryside. During the period, joint ELF-PLF operations were carried out against US citizens in Ethiopia in retaliation for the supply of American arms to Ethiopia's armed forces.

An offer of "immediate autonomy" for the people of Eritrea and the lifting of the state of emergency was made on May 16, 1976, by the then chairman of the PMAC (Brig.-Gen. Teferi Benti) but was rejected by O. S. Sabeh. The latter was on July 8 reported to have said in Baghdad that his organization maintained "our right to full national independence" and to have claimed that the "Eritrean revolution" would now set up "a provisional government on more than 80 per cent of Eritrea's land". A "Voice of the Eritrean Revolution", a Baghdad radio station claiming to be the organ of the ELF-PLF, was first heard in August 1976.

A proposal for a ceasefire made by the rival (Marxist) Eritrean People's Liberation Front (EPLF) on Nov. 24, 1980, was opposed by the ELF-PLF, on whose behalf O. S. Sabeh recommended a united EPLF and ELF-PLF approach to negotiations with the Ethiopian Government. However, no such rapprochement took place and by August 1981 the EPLF claimed to have demolished the ELF-PLF, with the latter's remaining guerrillas having been forced to retreat across the border into the Sudan.

Owing to a rapprochement between the Governments of Ethiopia and the Sudan in 1980, the latter's Government in August 1981 extended its restriction on the movement of Eritrean refugees (estimated at 450,000) to control the movement of Eritrean guerrillas along the border and inside the Sudan. On Aug. 25 the ELF-PLF stated that its offices in Khartoum and other Sudanese cities had been closed. Other sources indicated that ELF-PLF arsenals near the border had been confiscated, that guerrillas had been disarmed and that some had been arrested.

In May 1980 the ELF-PLF had split into two factions when a group led by Osman Agyp (who was based in Iraq) broke away in opposition to the leadership of O. S. Sabeh (who was based in Egypt and Dubai). Osman Agyp was, however, assassinated in Khartoum on Nov. 15, 1980, by an unknown assailant. Shortly after the murder, the Sudanese Government expelled the Cuban chargé d'affaires in Khartoum.

Eritrean Liberation Front—Revolutionary Command (ELF-RC)

Leadership. Ahmed Muhammad Nasser (ch.).

This organization was set up at a national council meeting called in December 1971 by a

"General Command" which had itself been formed in August 1969 as a breakaway group from the Eritrean Liberation Front (ELF). The ELF-RC was to have its own People's Liberation Army organized on a socialist basis. In 1972 the ELF-RC was in open conflict with the Popular Liberation Forces (which later joined the ELF), but in September 1975 it was reported from Beirut that the ELF-RC and the ELF had, at a meeting in Khartoum (Sudan), agreed in principle on forming "a unified national democratic front with one liberation army". On Oct. 20, 1975, an agreement was signed between the ELF-RC and the Eritrean People's Liberation Front (EPLF) to set up joint co-ordination committees.

At the end of April 1978 the ELF-RC claimed that there were 115,000 Ethiopian troops ready for an offensive against the Eritrean liberation movements. Lt.-Col. Mengistu Haile Mariam (the Ethiopian head of state) said on June 7, 1978, that until then 13,000 soldiers and between 30,000 and 50,000 civilians had lost their lives in 13 years of fighting in Eritrea, and that 200,000 people had fled the country; after stating that mediation efforts by both socialist and Arab states had failed, he declared that the "socialist, democratic and progressive forces" had "the revolutionary duty of siding with us in the struggle to safeguard the unity and revolution of Ethiopia". However, an offer made by him to grant both an amnesty and a measure of internal autonomy was rejected by the EPLF and the ELF-RC, who declared that the autonomy stage had long since passed and the struggle was now for independence.

An attempt by Ahmed Muhammad Nasser to dissuade the Soviet Union (which he was said to have visited in the second week of June 1978) from intervening in Eritrea appeared to have failed. In fact Soviet pressure on Iraq, Libya and Syria was said to have resulted in the cessation of aid to the Eritrean movements by these countries.

After suffering some severe military setbacks in mid-1978, the ELF-RC agreed the following year on the establishment of a joint command with the EPLF; both organizations remained committed to a demand for recognition as the sole legitimate representatives of the Eritrean people and acceptance of Eritrea's right to self-determination. Later, however, the ELF-RC was in conflict with the EPLF, and it suffered a decline; it rejected a ceasefire proposal made by the EPLF on Nov. 24, 1980 (and ignored by the Ethiopian Government).

In the course of 1981 the ELF-RC was reported to have been obliged to surrender territory to the forces of the EPLF. It was also reported to have suffered a depletion of its fighters as a result of desertion to the EPLF or to the Ethiopian Army.

Eritrean People's Liberation Front (EPLF)

Leadership. Ramadan Mohammed Nur (s.g.).

This Front was established in 1970 as a breakaway organization from the Eritrean Liberation Front (ELF) by Issaias Afewerki, who defined its object as "a national democratic revolution without ethnic or religious discrimination", a "state at the service of the people" and "an independent nation" which would be "nobody's satellite". At a congress held in January 1977 the EPLF elected a 43-member central committee and a 13-member political committee (comprising six Moslems and seven Christians).

A movement well organized on Marxist-Leninist lines, the EPLF regarded the Eritrean Liberation Front—Popular Liberation Forces (ELF-PLF) of Osman Saleh Sabeh as reactionary and anti-Marxist, and it broke all links with this organization on March 22, 1976. By May 1977 the EPLF, which was active mainly in the areas bordering the Red Sea, had some 12,000 fighters and was in control of most of Sahel province, having taken Nakfa, its chief town, on March 24.

The EPLF claimed further military successes in 1977, capturing numerous towns, among them Keren in July 1977; by December 1977 Ethiopian forces in Eritrea were left in control only of Asmara, Barentu, Massawa and Assab. The EPLF had set up its own administration and also claimed to hold between 4,000 and 5,000 Ethiopian prisoners (although this was denied by the Ethiopian Government). However, from 1978 onwards the Soviet Union was giving massive support to the Ethiopian forces (on the grounds that the secessionists were "objectively helping the realization of imperialist designs" to weaken Ethiopia and deprive it of its outlets to the Red Sea).

On April 25, 1978, it was reported from Agordat (northern Eritrea) that the EPLF and the ELF—Revolutionary Command (of Ahmed Muhammad Masser), also regarded as Marxist, had agreed to join forces and to merge their various committees administering large parts of Eritrea, in order eventually to set up an independent state.

From July 1978 onwards, however, a government offensive succeeded in retaking some 30 towns from secessionist movements—although Keren, where the EPLF had established its headquarters after capturing it in 1977, did not fall to the superior Ethiopian forces until Nov. 27, 1978. According to EPLF sources, the town's inhabitants had previously been evacuated; an estimated 100,000 people had withdrawn towards the northern mountains and the Sudanese border; and 13,000 civilians had been killed in the fighting in the area. I. Afewerki, by then EPLF deputy secretary-general, said in mid-

December 1978: "We are no longer fighting the *Derg*; now it is the Soviet Union."

While the earlier agreements between the EPLF and the ELF-RC had largely remained ineffective, the two organizations concluded a new agreement in Khartoum on Jan. 27, 1979, providing for the setting up of a unified delegation with common political programmes for any future negotiations and for a joint military headquarters and a unified command; the formation of this command was announced in Paris on April 10 and that of a joint political command in Kuwait on May 19.

During 1979 the EPLF still held Nakfa (whose 40,000 inhabitants had been evacuated in February) and maintained its links with the Sudan through the border town of Karora. An EPLF radio station, "The Voice of the Broad Masses of Eritrea", broadcasting from "liberated areas of Eritrea", was first heard on Aug. 11, 1980.

An EPLF proposal for a ceasefire made on Nov. 24, 1980—and to be followed by a referendum offering a choice between independence, a return to Eritrea's federal status or regional autonomy within the Ethiopian state—was ignored by the Ethiopian Government.

By February 1981 the latter's forces were firmly in command of all major towns in Eritrea except Nakfa, which was still held by the EPLF (by then the strongest of the Eritrean liberation movements). Towards the end of November 1981 the EPLF claimed to have extended the area under its control by repelling an Ethiopian force near Afabet (not far from the Red Sea) and also taking territory from ELF-RC units (some of which had deserted to the EPLF and others to the Ethiopian Army). The EPLF also claimed to have repulsed a further Ethiopian offensive on Dec. 16, 1981.

Between August 1981 and January 1982 the EPLF made several attacks on Ethiopian forces. Having claimed to have taken as many as 8,000 Ethiopian prisoners since 1976 the EPLF announced on Nov. 30, 1981, that it had decided to release 3,000 Ethiopian Army prisoners. Owing to the rapprochement between the Governments of Ethiopia and the Sudan in 1980, the office of the EPLF in Khartoum was closed between August and November 1981; it was reopened thereafter.

Other Separatist Movements

Afar Liberation Front (ALF)

Leadership. Sultan Ali Mirah Hanfare (1.).

The leader of this Front, which had been engaged in guerrilla warfare against the forces of the Emperor Haile Selassie,

declared in October 1974 that he fully supported the New Ethiopian military regime, claiming that the former Government had condemned the Afars to a perpetual nomadic existence. Nevertheless, by May 1975 open conflict had developed between the Sultan's followers and government forces. The Sultan was said to have demanded to be exempted from the land reform and new taxes decreed by the military regime, and to have fled to Djibouti on June 2, while some 5,000 armed Afar warriors had attacked troops and militia on June 3-12; this action in turn led to the killing of some 2,500 civilians and the partial destruction of the town of Aisaita (near the Djibouti border) by government troops.

Afar resistance continued intermittently in subsequent years, notably in early 1977, when the ALF claimed to have killed 200 Ethiopian soldiers. In September 1977 ALF units blew up a bridge on the road from Addis Ababa to the port of Assab. In recent years calls have been made by Eritrean separatists for co-operation with the ALF, but with little apparent result.

Oromo Liberation Front (OLF)

This Front, set up among the Oromo (Galla) people in the southern provinces of Shoa, Hararghe, Bale and Sidamo, was trained by the Eritrean People's Liberation Front (EPLF). Although in June 1976 separatists were said to control much of the countryside in Bale province, the OLF did not appear to play an important role. It set up an office in Mogadishu (Somalia) in January 1980, which enabled it to co-operate more closely with the Western Somali Liberation Front (WSLF). On April 27, 1981, the OLF alleged that between 2,000 and 3,000 people had been killed or wounded in the first Ethiopian air raids in the Oromo tribal area on March 19-21 of that year.

Somali Abo Liberation Front (SALF)

This Front operated in close co-operation with the Western Somali Liberation Front (WSLF) in favour of autonomy for the Abo people of Bale province (in south-eastern Ethiopia). Its units were involved in a number of guerrilla attacks in the Ogaden area in 1980.

Tigre People's Liberation Front (TPLF)

The TPLF was set up in 1976 under the auspices of the Eritrean People's Liberation Front to further separatist aspirations among the people of Tigre province (south-west of Eritrea). Its forces were involved in fighting against peasants mobilized by the military regime for supporting the country's regular forces in a march into Eritrea in 1976.

In 1979 the Government announced that the forces of the TPLF had been destroyed in a four-month campaign in the western and central parts of Tigre province. The TPLF, however, claimed to have launched a successful counter-offensive in July-August 1979, capturing the Amba-Alagi pass on the road from Addis Ababa to Asmara (the capital of Eritrea); in September 1979 the TPLF claimed to have taken the airport at Axum (northern Tigre). During 1980 the TPLF extended its guerrilla operations, capturing a number of towns between January and August and claiming control of most of the countryside in Tigre province. The TPLF made numerous further guerrilla attacks in September-October 1980, and a spokesman for the Front stated in Khartoum on Sept. 29 that Ethiopian troops had displaced 80,000 people and destroyed churches, schools and mosques in retaliation for guerrilla attacks. On March 2, 1981, the spokesman claimed that the TPLF had killed about 420 Ethiopian soldiers and trapped 4,000 others involved in a new offensive.

Between August 1981 and May 1982 the TPLF claimed to have carried out numerous further actions against Ethiopian forces, to have taken several towns and to have carried the struggle into Wollo province. The TPLF also claimed to control 90 per cent of the countryside in Tigre province and to have received the surrender of hundreds of "government agents". In the Western press the TPLF's success was attributed to failure of the *Derg* to extend its political re-education programme to the rural areas of Tigre, demoralization of Ethiopian ground forces and massive support from the EPLF.

Western Somali Liberation Front (WSLF)

Leadership. Abdullahi Hassan Mahmud (or Abdi-Nasir Sheikh Abdullahi) (s.g.).

The first congress of the WSLF was held by some 500 participants in 1975 at Badhiweyne (on the Somali side of the border between Ethiopia and Somalia), the Front's aim being to implement self-determination for the Somalis living in Ethiopia. In Somalia's 1960 Constitution it was stated that the Somali Republic would "provide, by all legal and peaceful means, the union of all Somali territory" (which in the official Somali view included the Ogaden region of Ethiopia). In the 1969 Revolutionary Charter of Somalia it was proclaimed as one of the objects of the revolution to "fight for the unity of the Somali nation".

A member of the WSLF's central committee stated on Aug. 25, 1977, that it would be for the people of the Ogaden region (called Western Somalia by the Front) to decide whether the region should become part of Somalia. The WSLF's secretary-general (and military commander) said on Sept. 4, 1977, that the WSLF claimed all territory east of the line running from Moyale (on Ethiopia's border with Kenya) through Awash (about 100 miles east of Addis Ababa) to El Adde (on the border with Djibouti); he claimed that this area of 240,000 square miles (625,000 sq. km.) was "inhabited by 10,000,000 ethnic Somalis".

The WSLF has issued a journal, *Danab* ("Lightning"), and its radio station, the "Voice of the Western Somali and Somali Abo Liberation Front" based in Mogadishu (Somalia), was first heard in December 1978.

The WSLF's secretary-general claimed in Mogadishu late in May 1977 that WSLF forces active inside the Ogaden region of Ethiopia had, between September 1976 and early May 1977, taken control of seven towns, had "destroyed" six Ethiopian battalions and had "put out of action" 11 Ethiopian tanks and 16 armoured personnel carriers. During the following months the WSLF disrupted the Addis Ababa-Djibouti railway line and attacked Ethiopian garrisons, and by August 1977 the WSLF claimed to have captured about 85 per cent of the provinces of Bale and Sidamo, killing or taking prisoner at least 23,000 Ethiopian troops. While the Government of Somalia consistently denied any involvement of regular Somali forces in the fighting, the Ethiopian Government produced some evidence of such involvement.

In the second half of August 1977 the Somali advance was halted by Ethiopian forces east of Dire Dawa and Harar. The WSLF nevertheless rejected, late in September, any ceasefire unless the Ethiopian Government recognized "the people's right to self-determination", and it reaffirmed its determination to "liberate" Dire Dawa and Harar and to advance as far as Awash (about halfway between Dire Dawa and Addis Ababa). In October and November 1977 the WSLF first reported the presence of Cuban advisers and troops supporting the Ethiopian forces (and on Nov. 13 of that year the Somali Government decided, as a result of Soviet and Cuban aid given to Ethiopia, to abrogate its existing treaty of friendship with the Soviet Union and demanded the withdrawal of all Soviet personnel then stationed in Somalia).

Notwithstanding the withdrawal of Somali forces from Ethiopia before a joint Cuban and Ethiopian offensive in March 1978, WSLF guerrillas continued their activities. On May 29, 1978, the WSLF (and the Somali Abo Liberation Front, SALF) were reported to have concluded an agreement with the Eritrean Liberation Movement—Popular Liberation Forces (ELF-PLF) to join forces against the intervention of the Soviet Union, Cuba and other socialist states in the Horn of Africa.

With the WSLF reportedly in control of 90 per cent of the Ogaden area, heavy fighting continued during 1979-80. Conflicting claims of successes were made by the Ethiopian Government and the WSLF, the latter claiming on June 29 to have killed over 8,000 Ethiopian and Cuban troops in the Ogaden area in April and May, but admitting also a marked increase in the number of Ethiopian troops involved in the fighting. The WSLF also referred to a "scorched-earth policy" of Ethiopia intended to expel the Somali inhabitants of the Ogaden region.

In the second half of 1980 the WSLF suffered severe reverses as it was inferior in manpower and equipment to the Ethiopian Army supported by heavy artillery and (Soviet-built) MiG-21 and MiG-23 fighters and Mi-24 helicopters. By the end of 1980 Ethiopian forces had reoccupied almost all territory of the Ogaden area up to the border with Somalia.

In view of this situation, the WSLF held a congress in February 1981 (according to its own claim "somewhere in the liberated area" but in fact inside Somalia some 30 kilometres, or 18 miles, from Mogadishu), when it elected a new and younger central committee and declared that it was fighting for the creation of an independent state in the Ogaden area (and not for the transfer of the area to a "greater Somalia"). Nevertheless, Somalia remained, together with Egypt, Iraq and Pakistan, the principal supplier of arms to the WSLF. On July 8, 1981, its secretary-general reaffirmed its determination to escalate the armed struggle to end what it called "Ethiopian colonialization".

Opposition Movements

Ethiopian Communist Party (ECP)

The ECP was a pro-Chinese and anti-Soviet party which, on its establishment in August 1976, condemned the *Derg* for having replaced feudalism by a "petty-bourgeois system". The party demanded the election of a people's assembly and the formation of a government controlled by this assembly, and also freedom of the press, the right to strike and to form trade unions and political parties, and the right to self-determination (which might lead to secession by different nationalities). By early 1977 the ECP was illegal and apparently completely suppressed.

Ethiopian Democratic Front

This Front was on Jan. 8, 1982, reported (from Abu Dhabi, United Arab Emirates) to have been formed the previous November by Ethiopian opposition parties, among them the Ethiopian People's Revolutionary Party (EPRP), the Ethiopian Democratic Union (EDU) and a number of left-wing Ethiopian parties.

Ethiopian Democratic Union (EDU)

Leadership. Gen. Iyassu Mengesha (l.); Tesfai Woldemichael (s.g.).

In March 1975 the EDU, led by liberal opponents of the regime of the Emperor Haile Selassie and also of the succeeding *Derg,* formed a 17-member supreme council, set up its headquarters in London and issued a manifesto propagating "an enlightened, progressive and democratic regime" for Ethiopia; it also called for unity among the various resistance movements and a "sincere and credible" political solution in Eritrea. In May 1976 the EDU claimed to have started large-scale guerrilla operations in Ethiopia's northern provinces. In 1977 its forces, said to number between 10,000 and 15,000 men, had some success (temporarily occupying the town of Humera, on the Sudanese border, from Jan. 13 to June 10, and also Metemma from April 5).

In July 1977 the EDU leaders decided to move the organization's headquarters from London to Khartoum and to recognize the Eritrean independence movements. Although the movement achieved no spectacular military successes from 1978 onwards, its leaders repeatedly reaffirmed their hostility to the *Derg* and their determination not to negotiate with it. In the course of the "red terror" mounted by the Ethiopian People's Revolutionary Party (see separate entry) in 1978 numerous EDU members were arrested by the military regime in May and September of that year, and later in 1979 a number of EDU units surrendered to government forces. Since then the EDU's military activities have been in decline. In November 1981, however, the EDU joined the Ethiopian Democratic Front (see separate entry).

Ethiopian People's Revolutionary Party (EPRP)

In 1976 the EPRP described itself as Marxist and denounced the military regime as "fascist", whereupon the Government, describing the EPRP as "anarchist", began to conduct an intensive campaign against its members. On Sept. 11 of that year the EPRP was officially condemned as "subversive and anti-revolutionary", guilty of "economic and industrial sabotage" and allied with "imperialists" and Eritrean secessionists. On Sept. 20 some 100 EPRP supporters were arrested in connexion with illegal strikes; the party was also held responsible for a bomb attack on the headquarters of a *Derg* secretariat on Oct. 25; and on Nov. 2 it was reported that 21 EPRP members had been condemned to death and executed, four of them for attempting to assassinate (on Sept. 23) Lt.-Col. Mengistu Haile Mariam. In October 1976 an EPRP emissary claimed in London that the *Derg* had murdered 1,225 of its opponents and had tortured hundreds more in concentration camps. In November 1976 the EPRP's military branch, the "Revolutionary People's Army", was said to be fighting in several provinces.

Early in 1977 the EPRP, as a party which rejected the Government's thesis that a people's revolution would emanate from a military takeover, was involved in mutual mass killings between supporters and opponents of the regime. The EPRP was held responsible for the killing of a number of high-ranking officials late in 1977 and early in 1978. The EPRP itself claimed in Khartoum on Jan. 30, 1978, that during the previous three years the PMAC had "assassinated 3,500 persons" and that in Addis Ababa alone about 8,000 had been arrested and deported to the countryside. In the Western press it was reported that the "red terror" of the EPRP had been countered by the "white terror" of the Ethiopian military regime. Further arrests of EPRP members were announced in May and on Sept. 27, 1979, and the execution of Berhane Meskel Reda Wolde (one of its leaders captured in March 1979) was confirmed on July 12, 1979. By that time the EPRP appeared to have been effectively liquidated by the regime, although in 1981 the party was reported to have joined the Ethiopian Democratic Front (see separate entry).

Marxist All-Ethiopian Socialist Movement (MAESON)

In February 1977 the MAESON was described as the *Derg*'s political organization, in that it consisted of intellectuals who took the line that a people's revolution could emanate from a military takeover and who therefore gave critical support to the *Derg*. In April 1977, however, some 50 of its members decided to change to "revolutionary opposition" to the *Derg* because they opposed the exclusively pro-Soviet line taken by the regime.

From July 1977 onwards the MAESON—which had played a leading role in the elimination of the (also Marxist) Ethiopian People's Revolutionary Party (EPRP)—was itself discarded by the regime, and many of its leading members went into hiding. The members of the executive committee of the All-Ethiopian Trade Union, who were said to have called for the return to power of MAESON members, were all dismissed on May 26, 1978, for alleged "political sabotage, corruption and misuse of power".

Protestant Church Opposition

Alleged opponents of the regime arrested in the second week of October 1978 included Pastor Gudina Tumsa, secretary-general of the (Lutheran) Mekane Yesus Church (of some 400,000 members); he was released on Nov. 14, 1979, but was again detained and questioned (with over 170 members of his Church) in June 1979. On July 28 he was abducted by unknown armed men, and so was his wife in February 1981. On Nov. 16, 1981, government officials seized the headquarters of the Church, and on Jan. 6, 1982, the Ethiopian Foreign Minister claimed that the building had been used for the "preparation and dissemination of anti-Ethiopian and anti-revolutionary tracts and leaflets" and that Lutheran officials had, in the western Walaga province (i.e. near the Sudanese border), fomented "antagonism between tribes and ethnic groups in Ethiopia".

It was also reported that the Government had accused some church officials of terrorist activities, that 175 Ethiopian pastors had been imprisoned, that the military authorities had closed 180 out of some 600 Lutheran churches in the provinces of Sidamo and Walaga, and that a building (in Addis Ababa) belonging to the Emmanuel Baptist Church had been expropriated by the Government.

Revolutionary People's Army—see under Ethiopian People's Revolutionary Party (EPRP)

Gabon

Capital: Libreville   Pop. 700,000

The Gabonese Republic has an executive President who is elected for a seven-year
term by universal adult suffrage and who is head of state and of the Government,
presiding over a Cabinet under a Prime Minister. There is a 93-member National
Assembly, elected also for a seven-year term by universal adult suffrage, with all candidates being members of the Gabonese Democratic Party (*Parti Démocratique
Gabonais,* PDG). President Omar Bongo was on Dec. 30, 1979, re-elected with 99.85
per cent of the votes cast (as officially announced), and in February 1980 a total of 84
PDG candidates were elected to the National Assembly and another nine were
nominated by the President. The Government has resisted demands from some opposition quarters for the ending of Gabon's one-party system.

Movement for National Renewal (Morena)

This Movement was named as the leading
opponent of the regime among students at
the Omar Bongo National University in
Libreville, which was closed from Dec. 14,
1981, to Jan. 11, 1982, because of a student
strike begun on Dec. 5. Morena had claimed
that the regime was corrupt and had failed to
promote the country's development. During
the disturbances caused by the student strike
leaflets were distributed calling for the creation of a second political party (in addition to
the ruling Gabonese Democratic Party).
Among persons arrested at the time was the
rector of the university, who was dismissed
from his post. President Bongo said on Feb.
20, 1982, that the Constitution did not allow
for a multi-party system and that the only
way in which Morena could come to power
was through a coup d'état.

The Gambia

Capital: Banjul   Pop. 670,000

The Republic of The Gambia, a member of the Commonwealth, has a President who
is elected by direct universal adult suffrage and is head of state as well as of
government. There is a House of Representatives with 35 elective seats and eight other
seats filled by four nominated members and four head chiefs (elected by the country's
Chiefs in Assembly). Both the President and the House of Representatives are elected
for five-year terms. As a result of elections held on May 4-5, 1982, the elective seats in
the House of Representatives were distributed as follows: People's Progressive Party
(PPP) 27, National Convention Party 3, independents 5 (who were former PPP
adherents not nominated by that party).

On Feb. 1, 1982, The Gambia joined the Republic of Senegal in a Confederation of
Senegambia, in which both states retained their independence and sovereignty, but
agreed on the integration of their armed forces and security forces, economic and
monetary union, and co-ordination in the fields of external relations,
communications and other fields in which the confederal state might agree to exercise
joint jurisdiction. The Confederation was to have a President (the President of

Senegal), a Vice-President (the President of The Gambia), a Council of Ministers and a Confederal Assembly (one-third of its members to be chosen by the Gambian House of Representatives and two-thirds by Senegal's National Assembly).

Prior to the establishment of the Confederation, Senegalese forces had in July 1981, played a key role in overcoming an attempted coup in The Gambia by left-wing elements opposed to the Government of President Sir Dawda Jawara.

Gambian Socialist Revolutionary Party (GSRP)

Leadership. Pingon Georges (l.).

The GSRP was banned on Nov. 1, 1980 (together with the Movement for Justice in Africa—see separate entry). President Jawara described it as a "terrorist organization" advocating the use of violence and as "too small" to be a political party.

Movement for Justice in Africa (Moja-Gambia)

Leadership. Koro Sallah (founder).

Established in 1979, this Movement took its name from a Liberian formation then in opposition to the Government of President William Tolbert (although it was not clear whether there were any organizational links between the two movements). The Moja-Gambia accused the Government of President Sir Dawda Jawara of nepotism, corruption, patronage, political intimidation and increasing repression, and it stated as its main aims (i) free political activity and mass control of the political institutions, (ii) the ending of "foreign economic and military control" and (iii) full employment and equal development of all languages and cultures. The Government banned the Movement on Nov. 1, 1980, and later that month the President described it as a "terrorist organization" which was under investigation in connexion with the burning of boats in Gambian ports.

National Liberation Party

This small left-wing opposition party was formed in October 1975 and was an unsuccessful contender in the 1977 general elections. Its leader, Cheyassin Papa Secka, was one of five people sentenced to death on June 18, 1982, after being found guilty of participating in the unsuccessful coup attempt of July 1981 led by the Socialist and Revolutionary Labour Party (see separate entry).

Socialist and Revolutionary Labour Party (SRLP)

Leadership. Kukli Samba Sanyang (l.).

This party's leader had unsuccessfully contested the 1977 general elections as a candidate of the (opposition) National Convention Party before he became a Marxist-Leninist and founded the SRLP in 1978 as a vehicle for revolutionary change. In the absence of President Sir Dawda Jawara in London (for the wedding of Prince Charles) the SRLP, supported by elements of the paramilitary Field Force, staged a coup on July 29-30, 1981, and formed a National Revolutionary Council (NRC) consisting of nine SRLP members and three Field Force officers. On July 30 the NRC announced the suspension of the Constitution; accused the President's Government of "corruption, tribalism, social oppression and creating a bourgeois class"; and added that there was to be a "dictatorship of the proletariat" led by a "Marxist-Leninist party".

The rebels also freed and armed prisoners from the prison in Banjul, and this action was followed by looting (especially of shops owned by Lebanese and Indian traders) and indiscriminate killing, whereby the rebels lost much of the initial support they had gained in Banjul. On July 30 the President invoked a mutual defence agreement with Senegal, and a Senegalese task force, eventually 2,700 men strong, subdued the rebellion within a week and released hostages taken by the rebels, who fled. A state of emergency having been declared on Aug. 2, a total of 814 persons, including some opposition politicians, were arrested. In trials held later in 1981 and the first half of 1982, a total of 27 Gambians were sentenced to death for high treason (by participating in the attempted coup); they included three members of the NRC. Kukli Samba Sanyang and nine of his supporters, who had fled to Guinea-Bissau, were later expelled from that country (as announced by the President of Guinea-Bissau on April 6, 1982), but it was not stated which country had received them.

Ghana

Capital: Accra   Pop. 11,600,000

The Republic of Ghana, a member of the Commonwealth, is ruled by a Provisional National Defence Council (PNDC) which came to power on Dec. 31, 1981, overthrowing the existing parliamentary regime, suspending the Constitution and proscribing all political parties. On Jan. 21, 1982, the PNDC appointed a civilian Government which included a number of established political figures, although effective power remained in the hands of the PNDC chairman, Flt.-Lt. Jerry Rawlings. Under the PNDC's programme the basic unit of the state structure became the "people's defence committee" (PDC) which was to be "an organizing centre for the revolution" to enable the PNDC to remain aware of popular aspirations and needs throughout the country.

Campaign for Democracy in Ghana

This organization was launched in London in April 1982 by various members of Ghana's banned political parties, who issued a statement claiming that the regime of the Provisional National Defence Council was "an instrument of terror" which had violated human rights and destroyed the freedom of the press. On May 5, 1982, Lagos radio reported that the Campaign had been formed in the Nigerian capital as a forum for all Ghanaians opposed to the existing military regime in Ghana and that it would "employ all legitimate means to ensure that democracy and constitutional order were restored in the country".

Guinea

Capital: Conakry   Pop. 5,400,000

The People's Revolutionary Republic of Guinea is a "democratic republic" with an executive President elected by popular vote for a seven-year term and re-eligible, and with a 210-member Popular National Assembly similarly elected (also for seven years) on a national list of the *Parti Démocratique de Guinée* (PDG), which has "sovereign and exclusive control of all sections of national life". There is a Cabinet headed by a Prime Minister.

The regime of President Ahmed Sekou Touré, in power since 1956 despite numerous attempts to overthrow him, has been widely condemned for alleged violations of human rights, in the face of which some 2,000,000 Guineans are thought to have fled the country since independence. The principal opposition movements in exile are described below.

Association of French Wives of Political Prisoners in Guinea (*Association de Femmes Françaises de Prisonniers Politiques en Guinée*)

Leadership. Mme Nathalie Barry (pres.).

This organization staged a demonstration in protest against an official visit to Paris by President Sekou Touré on Sept. 16-20, 1982. The Guinean President admitted on this occasion that eight Guinean husbands of French-women had been executed as "traitors" in Guinea in 1971, but he refused to give Mme Barry any information concerning her husband, Abdullah Barry, of whose fate no official announcement had ever been made.

253

Diallo Telli Committee

This Committee was named after the former Secretary-General of the Organization of African Unity and former Guinean Minister of Justice, who had died, or been killed, in prison in Guinea in 1977. It was set up in France for "the defence of all political prisoners and of democratic rights in Guinea". It issued a statement in July 1977 claiming that there were then more than 3,000 political prisoners in Guinea.

Guinea People's Union (*Union des Populations de Guinée,* UPG)

Leadership. Maj. Diallo (1.).

This Union has claimed to have many followers among Guinean exiles in France. On Feb. 20, 1977, it signed a declaration on a joint action programme with three other Guinean opposition movements.

Organization of Guinean Unity (*Organisation de l'Unité Guinéenne,* OUG)

Leadership. Ibrahima Kaké (1.).

During a visit to Paris by President Sekou Touré on Sept. 16-20, 1982, five Guineans attempted to kidnap Ibrahima Kaké, but French police prevented them from doing so.

Rally of Guineans Abroad (*Regroupement des Guinéens à l'Exterieur,* RGE)

Leadership. Siriadou Diallo (1.).

The RGE, as the principal organization of Guineans in exile, claimed in September 1971 to have several thousand members in the Congo, the Ivory Coast, Liberia, Senegal, Sierra Leone and several European countries; it declared at the same time that it would use force to overthrow President Sekou Touré.

From time to time the RGE reported on defections from the Sekou Touré regime, e.g. that of seven Guinean ambassadors on Oct. 3, 1973. On Feb. 20, 1977, the RGE signed a declaration on a joint action programme with three other Guinean opposition movements.

Unified Organization for the Liberation of Guinea (*Organisation Unifiée de Libération de la Guinée,* OULG)

On Jan. 2, 1978, the OULG stated in a letter to President Giscard d'Estaing of France (who was then planning a visit to Guinea) that a change of regime in Guinea was "not only possible but inevitable" and expressed the hope that the French Government would give "active, direct and discreet support" to "the current stage" of the OULG's struggle. The letter also accused the French parties of the left of having been the "unconditional advocates and supporters" of President Sekou Touré, described as "the Guinean dictator". On Feb. 20, 1977, the OULG signed a declaration on a joint action programme with three other Guinean opposition movements.

Union of Guineans in Senegal (*Union des Guinéens au Sénégal,* UGS)

This Union signed, on Feb. 20, 1977, a declaration on a joint action programme with three other Guinean opposition movements. However, following the conclusion of a treaty of friendship and co-operation between Guinea and Senegal on May 7, 1978, and the failure of a conspiracy against President Sekou Touré in August 1979 (in which Senegal-based Guinean exiles were reported to have been involved), the activities of the UGS were severely restricted.

Guinea-Bissau

Capital: Bissau   Pop. 793,000

The Republic of Guinea-Bissau is ruled by a predominantly military Revolutionary Council (composed almost exclusively of Guinean Blacks) which overthrew the Government of President Luis de Almeida Cabral, a Cape Verdian *mestiço* (half-caste), on Nov. 14, 1980, and dissolved the institutions of that Government. The leaders of the new regime (Maj. João Bernardo Vieira, previously Prime Minister, and Vítor Saúde Maria, previously Foreign Minister) declared after their assumption of power that they intended to pursue the political programmes of the (Marxist) *Partido Africano da Independência da Guiné e do Cabo Verde* (PAIGC), whose principles, they claimed, had been betrayed by President Cabral.

Front for the Fight for Guinea-Bissau's National Independence (*Frente da Luta pela Independência Nacional da Guiné "Portuguesa"*, FLING)

The FLING was recognized by Senegal in May 1964 as a national liberation movement on an equal footing with the PAIGC, as both claimed to have guerrilla forces active in the then Portuguese Guinea. However, the Foreign Minister of the Republic of Guinea announced on March 17, 1965, that the Council of Ministers of the Organization of African Unity had recognized the PAIGC as the only liberation movement of Portuguese Guinea and had decided to give no further aid to the FLING (which subsequently denied that such as decision had been taken).

Benjamin Pinto Bull, the president of the FLING, claimed on Feb. 13, 1967, that during 1966 the guerrillas of his organization had killed 554 Portuguese soldiers and wounded 319, their own losses being 65 dead, 125 wounded and 17 missing. Claims of rather greater successes were at that time being made by the PAIGC guerrillas, and it was the PAIGC which on Sept. 24, 1975, proclaimed the "Republic of Guinea-Bissau", which within weeks gained widespread international recognition. The FLING thereafter remained in existence as a party in exile (based in Paris and Senegal) opposed to the PAIGC's policy of ultimate union between Guinea-Bissau and the Cape Verde Islands. After the assumption of power by the Revolutionary Council in November 1980 a leading FLING associate inside Guinea-Bissau, Rafael Barbosa (a dissident former PAIGC member said to be supported by right-wing elements in Lisbon), was released from prison but was rearrested shortly afterwards. The new regime thus indicated that it did not identify itself with the aims of the FLING.

Ivory Coast

Capital: Abidjan   Pop. 9,000,000

The Republic of the Ivory Coast has an executive President elected for a five-year term, and re-eligible, by universal adult suffrage. He appoints, and presides over, a Cabinet, while legislative power is held by a 147-member National Assembly also elected for five years by universal adult suffrage from a list submitted by the *Parti Démocratique de la Côte d'Ivoire* (PDCI), the country's sole political party. In elections to the National Assembly held in two rounds on Nov. 9 and 23, 1980, the 147 seats were contested by 649 PDCI candidates, of whom 121 were elected to the Assembly for the first time.

No organized opposition movements have emerged in the Ivory Coast, which is one of the most prosperous and stable states of Black Africa. Nevertheless, attempts to overthrow the Government of President Félix Houphouët-Boigny have been made by groups of individual conspirators, notably one in 1973 by 12 former army officers. Moreover, in the early 1980s journalists and other workers have been imprisoned for trade union activities, while in early 1982 there were student demonstrations in Abidjan accompanied by a teachers' strike which resulted inter alia in the withdrawal of official recognition of their union.

Kenya

Capital: Nairobi   Pop. 16,000,000

The Republic of Kenya, an independent state within the Commonwealth, has an executive President who serves a (renewable) five-year term and is nominated by the Kenya African National Union (KANU), the country's sole legal political party; unless he is the sole candidate he is elected by popular vote. He appoints, and presides over, a Cabinet, and there is also a Vice-President. The unicameral National Assembly consists of 158 members elected for five years by universal adult suffrage and of 12 further members nominated by the President. Elections to the National Assembly held on Nov. 8, 1979, were contested by 742 KANU members, and almost half the members of the previous Assembly failed to be re-elected.

The Government has repeatedly acted against those whom it has described as "dissidents", in particular against students who in May 1982 issued a statement claiming that Kenya was still legally a multi-party state. President Daniel Arap Moi alleged on June 6, 1982, that students had plotted to obtain guns "from outside sources, including certain neighbouring countries", and he also attacked lecturers who, he said, were "teaching subversive literature" aimed at creating disorder in the country.

December 12 Movement

This Movement made its appearance with the publication of a pamphlet called *Pambana* ("Struggle") in February 1982. (Dec. 12 was the date of Kenya's attainment of independence in 1963.) In this pamphlet the

Movement criticized "high-level corruption" and foreign influence on Kenya's economy and politics.

Kenya People's Redemption Council

This Council was, according to Nairobi University students, an organization of members of the Kenyan Air Force who attempted to carry out a "1st August Revolution" in 1982 to overthrow the Government of President Arap Moi—this attempt being foiled by loyal sections of the armed forces. The Air Force rebels had stated that their aim was to end corruption and mismanagement and to respond to a call by the people "to liberate the country". They announced that the Constitution had been suspended, that a "National Liberation Council" had been set up and that all political prisoners were declared free. They also stated that it was "not the intention of the military to stay in power indefinitely".

The attempt, which was accompanied by widespread looting, was rapidly suppressed, although some rebel members of the Air Force were not apprehended until September 1982. The Air Force itself was officially disbanded in order to be replaced by a new one. Nairobi University was closed down and President Moi announced on Oct. 20 that it would be restructured before it was reopened. According to a government statement made early in September, 160 people had died as a result of the attempted coup.

During trials of over 700 Air Force members by a special court-martial it emerged that the plotters' organization had been infiltrated by an agent of the security services' special branch, and that Maj.-Gen. Peter Kariuki, who had been commander of the Air Force at the time of the attempted coup, had been given prior warning of it; on Jan. 18, 1983, he was sentenced to four years in prison for having failed to prevent the attempt. While some of those tried were merely dismissed from the Air Force, many others were given prison sentences of up to 25 years and 11 former Air Force members were condemned to death (between Nov. 24, 1982, and March 9, 1983), although no executions were carried out. President Moi announced on Feb. 22, 1983, that of those arrested 412 former servicemen and 61 university students had been pardoned and would be released.

Liberia

Capital: Monrovia   Pop. 1,900,000

The Republic of Liberia is ruled by a Military People's Redemption Council (PRC) which, under the leadership of Master Sergeant (later C.-in-C.) Samuel K. Doe, assumed power on April 12, 1980, and holds all legislative and executive power.

Several attempted counter-coups were reported in April-May 1980, following which two further attempts to overthrow the PRC Government were made in May and August 1981. In connexion with the May 1981 attempt 13 men were condemned to death by a special court-martial board and executed in June, while the August 1981 plot resulted in the execution of five leading members of the PRC (including its co-chairman and deputy head of state).

Of the leaders of political parties which had been in opposition to the previous regime of President William Tolbert but who had rallied to the PRC Government, (i) Dr Togba-Nah Tipoteh, former leader of the Movement for Justice in Africa (Moja), resigned as Minister of Planning and Economic Affairs on Aug. 27, 1981, after being accused of being implicated in the attempted counter-coup earlier that month, and (ii) Gabriel Bacchus Matthews, former leader of the (socialist) Progressive People's Party, was dismissed as Minister of Foreign Affairs on Nov. 20, 1981, for anti-government remarks and actions. Matthews was thought to have reservations about the Government's gravitation towards the United States, the closure of the Libyan embassy in Liberia in May 1981, and the expulsion of a number of Soviet diplomats on May 12; on March 26, 1982, however, he was appointed Director-General of the Cabinet.

On Dec. 23, 1981, C.-in-C. Doe, as head of state, announced the release of all remaining political prisoners held since the military takeover and declared a general amnesty for all Liberians living in exile, except Bennie D. Warner, the former Vice-President, who had set up a government-in-exile in April 1980.

Liberian Government-in-Exile

Leadership. Bennie D. Warner (founder).

The establishment of this government-in-exile was announced in the Ivory Coast on April 28, 1980, by the former Vice-President under President William Tolbert (overthrown and killed on April 12, 1980). He said that he had initially sympathized with the aims of the coup of April 12, but had been repelled by the executions and imprisonments carried out by the new regime, and that he was therefore organizing opposition to it. He was specifically excluded from a general amnesty for Liberian exiles announced by the head of state on Dec. 23, 1981.

Mali

Capital: Bamako

Pop. 6,900,000

Since 1968 the Republic of Mali has been ruled by a Military Committee of National Liberation (MCNL) with an executive President (Brig.-Gen. Moussa Traore), who is head of state and government, as well as secretary-general of the *Union Démocratique du Peuple Malien* (UDPM), the country's sole legal political party. An 82-member National Assembly was elected for a four-year term by universal adult suffrage on a list of the UDPM on June 19, 1979 (but under a constitutional amendment of September 1981 the Assembly was in future to be elected for a three-year term).

The President has repeatedly promised a return to civilian government, but this has been confined to the appointment of civilians to the Cabinet. Opposition to the regime has come from certain officers of the armed forces, students and trade unionists as well as Malians in exile. In recent years, attempted coups have been foiled by the regime in October 1978 and in December 1980.

Committee for the Defence of Democratic Liberties in Mali (*Comité de Défense des Libertés Démocratiques au Mali,* CDLDM)

This Committee based in Paris has been one of several exile organizations in France and Senegal opposed to the existing military regime in Mali and attempting to present a united anti-government front.

National Union of Pupils and Students of Mali (*Union Nationale des Elèves et Etudiants du Mali,* UNEEM)

This Union broke away from the youth movement of the ruling UDPM in 1978 and was ordered by the Government to disband in January 1979. It nevertheless continued its activities, in the first place to resist educational measures such as the raising of pass standards in public service and other examinations, and also to propagate a return to the "scientific socialism" of the late President Modibo Keita (overthrown in 1968).

A strike called by the UNEEM on Nov. 16, 1979, led to the closure of secondary and higher educational institutions on Dec. 6, to clashes with the security forces, and (after schools and colleges had been reopened on Jan. 14, 1980) to the arrest of several hundred students after a demonstration on March 9. A new strike broke out after the reported death of the UNEEM's secretary-general in custody, allegedly after torture. Amnesty International referred, on March 15, 1980, to a report that at least 18 persons had been shot, stabbed or tortured to death by security forces.

After the President had announced on March 29, 1980, that all detained students would be released, classes resumed on March 31. On July 10, 1981, clemency was granted by the President to all persons involved in the 1979-80 disturbances.

Niger

Capital: Niamey   Pop. 5,600,000

The Republic of Niger is ruled by a Supreme Military Council which, on assuming power in April 1974, suspended the Constitution and dissolved the National Assembly and the *Parti Progressiste Nigérien,* until then the country's sole legal political organization. The President of the Supreme Military Council, Lt.-Col. Seyni Kountché, heads a (largely civilian) Council of Ministers, to which a Prime Minister was first appointed on Jan. 24, 1983.

Following an alleged attempted coup of March 15, 1976, it was officially announced on April 10 of that year that a court-martial had passed death sentences on nine persons involved, and also 22 life sentences, five of five years', two of two years' and one of one year's imprisonment; of those sentenced to death, seven were executed on April 21, among them four military men and the former secretary-general of the Niger National Union of Workers.

Sawaba Party

Leadership. Djibo Bakary (l.).

The Sawaba Party was set up as the Niger section of the (federalist) *Parti du Regroupement Africain* (PRA) founded in July 1958, when it represented the ruling parties in Dahomey (later called Benin), Niger and Senegal. Djibo Bakary, the leader of the Sawaba Party and then Prime Minister, advocated a vote for independence in the 1958 referendum (in which the Constitution of the Fifth French Republic was approved), but in general elections held on Dec. 14, 1958, the Sawaba Party was defeated by an alliance dominated by the *Rassemblement Démocratique Africain* (RDA). The results in the six seats which the Sawaba Party won (out of a total of 60) were later annulled, and in subsequent elections these seats went to the RDA alliance, whose leader, Hamani Diori, was elected Prime Minister in December 1958.

The Sawaba Party was officially dissolved in December 1959. Djibo Bakary lived in Guinea until 1974, when he was allowed (by the new military regime) to return to Niger on condition of not engaging in political activities. On Aug. 2, 1975, it was announced that he had been arrested, with two other men, for "attempting to divide the people and to set up an ideological clique with the object of seizing power". He was not released from detention until April 14, 1980.

Nigeria

Capital: Lagos (new capital, Abuja, under construction)　　　　Pop. 84,700,000

The Federal Republic of Nigeria, an independent state within the Commonwealth, consists of 19 federative states and a federal capital territory and is, under its Constitution which came into force on Oct. 1, 1979, "based on the principles of democracy and social justice". It has a President elected by universal adult suffrage for a four-year term; he is Chairman of a Council of State, presides over the federal Cabinet and has powers to appoint federal ministers; a Vice-President is elected as his "running mate". The federal National Assembly consists of (i) a Senate of five members from each state and (ii) a House of Representatives of 450 members—each House being elected for a four-year term by universal adult suffrage. Each state has its own similarly elected House of Assembly.

In elections to the House of Representatives held on July 14, 1980, seats were won by five registered parties as follows: National Party of Nigeria 168, Unity Party of Nigeria 111, Nigerian People's Party 78, People's Redemption Party 49, Greater Nigeria People's Party 43; one seat remained vacant.

The democratic Constitution under which Nigeria returned to civilian rule in October 1979 (after nearly 14 years of military government) provided for freedom of assembly and association, including the right to form or belong to a political party; but with a view to overcoming ethnic and regional divisions, which have bedevilled the country since independence, parties were required to avoid the use of any names, emblems or mottos with religious or ethnic connotations and their activities could not be confined only to one part of Nigeria. Nevertheless, an echo of past instabilities was provided by the return to Nigeria in June 1982 of Odumegwu Ojukwu, the former Ibo leader of the secessionist state of "Biafra". After his defeat in the civil war of 1967-70, he had lived in exile in the Ivory Coast, but on May 18, 1982, he received a presidential pardon; after his return it appeared that he still enjoyed widespread support among the Ibo population.

The discovery of an alleged plot to overthrow the Government of President Shagari (in power since October 1979) emerged when it was announced that Alhaji Zama Bukar Umoru Mandara, a contractor, had been arrested on Feb. 6, 1982, for "conspiring to commit a felony by the incitement of soldiers to commit a mutinous act". On Feb. 26 of that year it was announced that in this connexion nine military men had been detained for interrogation.

Yen Izala

This sect of dissident Moslem fundamentalists was led by Alhaji Mohammadu Marwa (alias Maitatsine), who originally came from Northern Cameroon and who preached a revolutionary version of Islam which rejected the prophet Mohammed as a Moslem leader; the sect opposed all official authority and demanded absolute loyalty to Mohammadu Marwa as its leader. Believed to have some 3,000 members, the sect was responsible for serious riots in Kano (northern Nigeria) between Dec. 18 and 31, 1980, which were forcibly suppressed by the Nigerian Army. According to an official inquiry, a total of 4,177 persons lost their lives in the riots; these included the leader and numerous other members of the sect and also large numbers of civilians killed as "infidels" by members of the sect and of other civilians killed by police or army action. The inquiry attributed the growth of the sect to religious intolerance, widespread urban unemployment among recent arrivals in Kano from the countryside, lax immigration control and the erosion of the traditional Moslem rulers' authority.

Renewed riots in Kano on July 10, 1981, when the building of the State Legislative Assembly was destroyed and other buildings housing ministries were badly damaged, were also attributed to Moslem fundamentalists, who opposed the proposed removal from office of the Emir of Kano (the state's traditional ethnic leader).

Further riots by followers of the late Alhaji Marwa (Maitatsine) broke out in Maiduguri (north-eastern Nigeria) on Oct. 26, 1982, and in simultaneous riots in Kaduna (south-west of Kano) 39 members of the sect were killed by vigilantes on Oct. 29. The total death toll of these riots, as officially stated in Lagos on Nov. 10, 1982, was 188 civilians and 18 policemen (including 133 civilians and 16 policemen in Maiduguri), and the number of persons arrested as 635.

The sect was officially banned on Nov. 18, 1982, and its adherents were made liable to imprisonment.

Rwanda

Capital: Kigali   Pop. 5,200,000

The Rwandese Republic is, under its Constitution approved in a referendum on Dec. 17, 1978, "a democratic, social and sovereign republic based on government of the people, by the people and for the people". It has an executive President, elected for a five-year term by the people and re-eligible, and a (legislative) National Development Council. The latter body has 64 seats filled (also for five years) by direct elections by universal adult suffrage from a list of 128 candidates who are members of the *Mouvement Révolutionnaire National pour le Développement*, the country's sole legal political organization (founded in 1975). The first such elections were held on Dec. 28, 1981.

The Government of President Juvénal Habyarimana (in power since 1973) surmounted a challenge to its authority in May 1980 when a number of prominent officials were arrested for allegedly plotting against the security of the state. These included Maj. Théonaste Lizinde, described as former chief of security and presidential adviser on foreign affairs. Of those arrested, 25 persons were sentenced on Nov. 25, 1981, by a state security court—the "principal instigators" of the attempted coup, Maj. Lizinde and Alphonse Kazenga, receiving the death sentence and the 23 others terms of imprisonment ranging from two to 23 years. Nevertheless, no organized opposition movements have appeared in Rwanda to date.

São Tomé and Príncipe

Capital: São Tomé   Pop. 87,000

The Democratic Republic of São Tomé and Príncipe is an "independent, unitary and democratic state" in which "the leading force" is the Movement for the Liberation of São Tomé and Príncipe (*Movimento de Libertação de São Tomé e Príncipe,* MLSTP). The supreme organ of the state is a 33-member People's Assembly consisting of the Political Bureau of the MLSTP, the Government and other members chosen by the MLSTP. The Assembly, appointed for four years, elects the President of the Republic for the same term of office.

Following the appearance of pamphlets distributed by separatists calling for the independence of Príncipe because food supplies were being withheld from that island by the authorities in São Tomé, disturbances occurred on Dec. 26-27, 1981, when several people were injured. The Government attributed the unrest to "internal reactionary forces" and "enemies of the revolution".

Senegal

Capital: Dakar   Pop. 5,900,000

The Republic of Senegal has an executive President elected by universal adult suffrage for a five-year term and re-eligible. He chooses and appoints a Cabinet headed by a Prime Minister responsible to a 120-member National Assembly elected at the same time as the President. (For creation of Confederation of Senegambia see under The Gambia, page 251.)

Under constitutional amendments made in 1976, 1978 and 1981, a total of 14 political parties (including several extreme left-wing groups) have been registered (although no party is allowed to be identified with a race, a religion, a sect, an ethnic group, a sex, a language or a region). Until 1978 the country had in effect been a one-party state. In elections to the National Assembly held on Feb. 27, 1983, and contested by eight parties, the ruling Socialist Party obtained 111 seats, the Democratic Party eight and the National Democratic Rally one (in a 56 per cent poll). Parties which contested the elections without gaining any seats were the Democratic and Popular Movement, the Democratic League—Movement for the Party of Labour, the Independence and Labour Party, the African Independence Party and the Senegalese People's Party. Another six legalized parties took no part in the elections.

With most shades of opposition to the Government of President Abdou Diouf being channelled through legal opposition parties, extra-parliamentary dissidence has in recent years been confined to small groups variously espousing leftist, Islamic fundamentalist and separatist objectives.

African Independence Party (*Parti Africain de l'Indépendance,* PAI)

Leadership. Amath Dansokho; Maguette Thiam (leaders of illegal faction).

This party, established in 1957, was officially legalized under the leadership of Majhemout Diop and Bara Goudiaby in 1976, but there remained a clandestine faction of the party, whose leaders were in March 1980 detained on charges of inciting workers to strike. Amath Dansokho was in 1981 named as one of the leaders of the legalized (pro-Soviet Marxist-Leninist) *Parti de l'Indépendance et du Travail.*

Movement of the Democratic Forces of the Casamance (*Mouvement des Forces Démocratiques de la Casamance*)

In pamphlets distributed in Dakar (the capital of Senegal) on Dec. 26, 1982, this Movement called for the complete independence of the region of the lower Casamance (situated to the south of The Gambia). On the same day several hundred pro-independence demonstrators attempted to replace Senegalese flags on official buildings at Ziguinchor (the regional capital) by their own; they were prevented from doing so by police, who arrested three leading demonstrators (among them the Rev. Augustin Diamankoun Senghor) and some 50 others, who were taken to Dakar for trial before the State Security Court. A mass demonstration in favour of maintaining the unity of the state of Senegal, held at Ziguinchor on Dec. 29 by the ruling Socialist Party, was supported also by the (opposition) Senegalese Democratic Party. The independence movement thus appeared to have only limited support in the region.

Rally for National Salvation (*Rassemblement pour le Salut National,* RSN)

Leadership. Sidi Lamine Niasse (liaison officer).

The RSN declared in a statement published on July 28, 1981, that it took its inspiration for action from the principles of Islam. Sidi Lamine Niasse's brother, Ahmed Khalifa Niasse, also known as "the ayatollah of Kaolack" (a town to the south-east of Dakar), had earlier called for the establishment of an Islamic state in Senegal, but had left the country in 1979 to go to France, and

to Libya in February 1980. In October 1980 the Government of The Gambia accused Libya of financing the recruitment of Gambian nationals for military training in Libya by A. K. Niasse; the latter later went to Niger, from which country he was extradited to Senegal in January 1982. He was, however, released from detention late in March 1982, after he had called on his followers in Libya to return to Senegal and to refrain from all subversive activities. He claimed on April 3 that his call had been obeyed by some 15 of his supporters; but on May 24, 1982, he was rearrested after expressing his opposition to a visit to Senegal by the French (Socialist) President, François Mitterrand. An application for registration of the RSN as a political party was reported to have remained unsuccessful because of its Islamic fundamentalist character and its leader's close relations with Libya.

Revolutionary Movement for New Democracy (*Mouvement Révolutionnaire pour la Démocratie Nouvelle,* MRDN)

In tracts distributed by this extreme left-wing Movement in May 1982, during a visit to Senegal by President Mitterrand of France, the latter was accused of directing "neo-colonialism under the colours of social democracy"; the ministers in President Mitterrand's Cabinet were condemned as "revisionists".

Roots of the Nation (*Rénu Rewni*)

On April 2, 1975, the State Security Court passed sentences of from three months to five years in prison on 13 persons accused of attempting to set up an illegal left-wing opposition party under the above name, and of distributing *Xaré Bi,* an unauthorized cyclostyled newspaper. Another group of nine persons were given shorter prison sentences on Oct. 20, 1975, for belonging to an illegal party named as "Let Us Struggle Together" *(Andjet),* said to be identical with the *Rénu Rewni.*

Sierra Leone

Capital: Freetown   Pop. 3,600,000

The Republic of Sierra Leone is an independent state within the Commonwealth. Under a 1978 Constitution approved in a referendum in June of that year it is a one-party state, with the All-People's Congress (APC) as the country's sole legal party. It has an elected executive President serving a seven-year term, a First and a Second Vice-President and a Cabinet appointed by the President and presided over by him. There is a House of Assembly of 85 elective constituency seats, 12 seats held by elected paramount chiefs and up to seven seats filled by persons appointed by the President.

The existence of plots to overthrow the government was officially implied in announcements made (i) in September 1981 concerning the discovery of a large cache of arms and ammunition in Freetown, and (ii) in February 1982 of the compulsory retirement of five army officers after a shooting incident near the President's residence in late January. Following the introduction of the one-party Constitution in 1978, several opposition groups were established outside Sierra Leone and were still active in 1982.

National Alliance Party

This left-wing group was set up by exiles in the United States.

Sierra Leone Alliance Movement (SLAM)

Leadership. Ambrose Ganda.

This Movement, based in Britain and led by Ambrose Ganda (a barrister), has published a newsletter, copies of which were said to circulate within Sierra Leone. It has advocated "national recovery" for Sierra Leone in terms similar to those previously propagated by *The Tablet,* an independent biweekly newspaper which had criticized alleged official corruption and mismanagement and whose printing machinery was destroyed by gangs in Freetown on Sept. 1, 1981, whereafter its editor had left the country in order to recommence publication in the United States.

Sierra Leone Freedom Council

The Council was founded by former members of the Sierra Leone People's Party (SLPP), which had been the country's opposition party before the establishment of a one-party system in 1978 (whereupon all SLPP members of the House of Assembly had joined the ruling All-People's Congress).

Tanzania

Capital: Dar-es-Salaam (to be replaced by Dodoma)   Pop. 17,800,000

The United Republic of Tanzania, a member of the Commonwealth, has an executive President who is elected for a four-year term by universal adult suffrage and is re-eligible; he is the head of state and of the Government. There is a Vice-President who is the head of the Executive of the islands of Zanzibar and Pemba. The Cabinet is headed by a Prime Minister, and the separate Executive in Zanzibar deals with internal Zanzibari affairs under the control of a Revolutionary Council of Zanzibar. Legislative power is vested in a National Assembly, partly elected in mainland Tanzania for a five-year term by universal adult suffrage and partly appointed by the President. All candidates must be approved by the country's sole legal political organization, the Revolutionary Party *(Chama Cha Mapinduzi),* but voters may have a choice between two or more candidates in any one constituency.

According to an official statement issued in Zanzibar in July 1980, a coup had been attempted against the President of Zanzibar (who, as stated above, is also Vice-President of Tanzania), in which connexion 16 persons were arrested. The announcement of these arrests followed the appearance of posters in which the regime was criticized for seeking increased union with the Tanzanian mainland and for allowing Zanzibar's economic situation to deteriorate. However, the President of Zanzibar announced on April 26, 1981, that the people arrested had been pardoned and were to be released immediately.

Tanzanian Youth Democracy Movement

Leadership. Moussa Membar (founder).

Five members of this Movement, demanding the resignation of President Nyerere, hijacked a Tanzanian airliner on an internal flight on Feb. 26, 1982, and diverted it to Stansted (Essex, England), where the five men surrendered on Feb. 28 after intervention by Oscar Kambona, a former Tanzanian minister who had lived in exile in London since 1967 (but who disclaimed any prior knowledge of the hijack or of the hijackers' Movement). The five men were, in London on Sept. 17, 1982, sentenced to imprisonment for from three to eight years (under a 1971 Hijacking Act). Moussa Membar, described by the judge as the group's leader, said during the trial that the Movement had been set up by himself in 1979 with the object of returning Tanzania to democracy, and that it had 3,000 members and also many sympathizers among Tanzanian officials. The Government had not demanded the extradition of the five men during the proceedings in London.

Togo

Capital: Lomé   Pop. 2,600,000

The Togolese Republic is ruled by an executive President who is head of state and of the Government (which has no Prime Minister). He is elected by universal adult suffrage for a seven-year term on the proposal of the *Rassemblement du Peuple Togolais* (RPT), the country's sole legal political organization. There is a 67-member Parliament similarly elected on a list proposed by the RPT.

In 1970, and again in 1977, it was officially announced that the authorities had foiled coup plots by followers of the former Togolese President Sylvanus Olympio, who was overthrown and killed on Jan. 13, 1963, and for whose death President Gnassingbe Eyadema (who came to power in January 1967) personally accepted responsibility. The alleged leader of the first attempt (made in August 1970), Noë Kutuklui, was on Dec. 1, 1970, sentenced in absentia to 20 years' detention. The 1977 plot was said to have involved a number of mercenaries and eventually resulted in the conviction of 15 alleged ringleaders in August 1979, when 10 were sentenced to death (eight in absentia). The two defendants sentenced to death who were present in court, a Maj. Sanvi and Emmanuel de Souza, were subsequently pardoned by the President, who also rehabilitated other members of the de Souza family who had been deprived of their nationality.

Togolese Movement for Democracy (*Mouvement Togolais pour la Démocratie,* MTO)

This Movement, based in Paris, claimed on Jan. 15, 1980, that (contrary to an announcement by President Gnassingbe Eyadema to the effect that there were only 11 political prisoners in Togo) several hundred political prisoners were "languishing in Togo's prisons" because they had shown opposition to the regime.

Uganda

Capital: Kampala   Pop. 14,000,000

The Republic of Uganda, a member of the Commonwealth, has a President elected by the members of a 126-member National Assembly, which is elected by universal adult suffrage. The President is head of state and of the Government, which also has a Vice-President and a Prime Minister. In elections to the National Assembly, held on Dec. 10, 1980, the Uganda People's Congress led by Dr Milton Apollo Obote obtained an overall majority (according to official results announced on Dec. 14), and Dr Obote was accordingly elected President of the Republic. His Government, which had come to power some 20 months after the overthrow (in April 1979) of President Idi Amin Dada by a Ugandan National Liberation Front (UNLF) and Tanzanian armed forces, has been faced with opposition not only in Parliament—from the Democratic Party (DP), which challenged the official election results—but also outside it, partly by supporters of ex-President Amin and partly by movements conducting guerrilla warfare.

At international level the Obote regime has been charged with violations of human rights, arising partly from undisciplined actions of the country's Army. According to senior officials of the International Committee of the Red Cross (ICRC) there were, in August 1981, some 2,000 political detainees in Uganda, most of them imprisoned since President Obote's return to power in 1980. Amnesty International appealed to the Ugandan Government on April 15, 1982, to halt what it called widespread "extra-legal executions, torture, killings of people in detention and abductions". The Government thereupon published, on May 16, 1982, a list of 237 persons detained indefinitely without trial. However, a further Amnesty International report of Sept. 1, 1982, listing several accounts of group killings by the Army, was rejected by the Government on Sept. 2. At the same time it was announced that between October 1981 and August 1982 over 3,500 detainees had been released in stages, including numerous former soldiers loyal to ex-President Amin and also members of the Democratic Party.

Movement for the Struggle for Political Rights (Mospor)

This Movement, set up in February 1981, claimed responsibility for a number of acts of violence committed in March 1981, especially against Tanzanian and Ugandan soldiers and against a police post.

National Resistance Army (NRA)

Leadership. Yoweri Museveni.

The NRA, at first known as the People's Revolutionary Army, was set up by Yoweri Museveni, who had been Minister of Defence and acting President under the interim regime of President Godfrey L. Binaisa (June 1979 to May 1980) and who had thereafter formed the Uganda Patriotic Movement (see separate entry). The avowed aim of the NRA was the overthrow of the Obote regime. By August 1981 it was said to have received its first supplies of arms from Libya, Israel and European arms dealers, and in September 1981 it claimed to have launched several guerrilla attacks in the Kampala area.

In mid-May 1982 the NRA asserted that since August 1981 it had killed 480 Ugandan soldiers, destroyed two police stations, eight lorries and a tank, and seized arms and ammunition. In mid-July of that year Museveni claimed that his guerrillas had killed 118 Ugandan soldiers and destroyed vehicles and equipment within two weeks in June, and on Oct. 4 the NRA claimed further successes in an area north of Kampala, involving the killing of 25 soldiers and rocket hits on eight military vehicles.

The political wing of the NRA is the London-based National Resistance Movement led by Prof. Yusufu K. Lule (see separate entry).

National Resistance Movement (NRM)

Leadership. Prof. Yusufu K. Lule (ch.).

The NRM was set up as the political wing of the National Resistance Army (NRA—see separate entry). Prof. Lule, a former vice-chancellor of Makerere University (Kampala), had been the leader of the Ugandan National Liberation Front (UNLF) set up by representatives of 18 Ugandan exile groups in Moshi (Tanzania) in March 1979; after the overthrow of President Amin, he had become President and head of a new provisional Government on April 11, 1979. However, a National Consultative Council (formed as a provisional Parliament) removed him from office on June 20, 1979, and replaced him by Godfrey L. Binaisa (who had been Attorney General under President Obote until 1967).

Although Prof. Lule claimed to be still President of Uganda, he left the country, first for Kenya and thereafter for London, where he arrived on July 9, 1979. From his exile he called, on Nov. 19, 1980, for the dissolution of the UNLF Military Commission which had taken power in Uganda on May 12, 1980, and for the postponement of elections scheduled for Dec. 10 of that year until the registration of voters (which had reportedly already taken place) was repeated under impartial supervision.

In a letter published in *The Times* on July 12, 1982, Prof. Lule stated that the resistance of the Ugandan people to the Obote regime was largely due to the "dubious" elections of 1980 which were "the total negation of a carefully defined and organized democratic process"; he asserted that President Obote was carrying out "repression and dictatorship" by means of an army "built purely on tribal lines"; he referred to "endless reports of officially sanctioned atrocities"; and he condemned the British Government for giving support to the Obote regime.

Uganda Democratic Union (UDU)

This Union was set up in November 1979 as a political party with the object of challenging the dismissal of President Yusufu Lule by the then existing National Consultative Council on June 20, 1979. Prof. Lule had been dismissed for allegedly making decisions without prior consultation of the Uganda National Liberation Front and for ignoring democratic methods of making decisions. The UDU advocated inter alia a return to Uganda's independence Constitution of 1962.

Uganda Freedom Movement (UFM)

Leadership. Balaki K. Kirya (ch.); Dr Lukatome Andrew Kayiira (military commander).

This Movement was formed by various opponents of President Obote, including several prominent politicians who had held office prior to his election to the presidency in December 1980. In addition to Balaki K. Kirya and Dr Kayiira (the latter having fled to Kenya in August 1979 after holding office under President Lule), the UFM executive also includes Francis Bwengye (former secretary-general of the Democratic Party), Samuel Sebagereka (former Minister of Finance under President Lule), Grace Ibingira (a former minister under President Obote in 1962-66, in detention in 1966-71, permanent representative of Uganda at the United Nations under President Amin for two years, and briefly a minister under President Lule in June 1979) and Dr Arnold Bisase (a former Minister of Health under President Lule).

The UFM called on all farmers and traders not to sell coffee to the Obote Government, advocated a general economic and moral boycott of the Government and requested all foreign firms and banks to cease supporting the Government.

Its military activities were initiated by Dr Kayiira in February 1981. UFM guerrillas were responsible for killing, on April 16, 1981, the member of Parliament who had defeated F. Bwengye in the election of Dec. 10, 1980, and for attempting to kill the Minister of Animal Industries on April 27 of that year. The UFM also claimed responsibility for an assault on the Malire barracks in Kampala on Feb. 23, 1982, after which the Ministry of Defence stated that at least 67 guerrillas had been killed and 10 wounded, whereas the UFM claimed to have caused 300 casualties. Army reprisals which followed this attack resulted in the death of numerous civilians and (according to a DP spokesman) the arrest of some 500 persons in a round-up of suspects. During March and April several thousand other alleged suspects were temporarily detained.

The Minister of Internal Affairs claimed on July 5, 1982, that the arms used in the Malire attack had been of Libyan origin, and he accused the Libyan Government of giving financial support to opposition guerrillas in Uganda to enable them to move to Libya for military training; the UFM, however, denied on July 8 that it had received aid from Libya. On Oct. 9 it was reported that the Libyan Government had agreed to cease supplying arms to anti-government guerrillas in Uganda.

The UFM and the National Resistance Movement had earlier, on April 10, 1982, issued a joint statement in which they condemned the conduct of the Ugandan Army and police and at the same time denied that they were planning to stage a coup. The UFM's chairman, Balaki K. Kirya, was arrested at Toro (near the Kenyan border) and was, on July 27, 1982, charged with treason. According to his wife, however, he had been taken from his home in Kenya and transported across the border against his will.

Early in December 1982 the UFM claimed responsibility for an attack on the India high commission in Kampala, in which one man was killed; the UFM stated that the attack had been made in retaliation for India's support for President Obote.

Uganda National Rescue Front (UNRF)

Leadership. Brig. Moses Ali (ch.).

Brig. Ali had been Minister of Finance under the Amin regime until his dismissal in July 1978; he established the UNRF in 1980 and the Front subsequently opposed the Government of Dr Milton Obote following the latter's election as President in December of that year.

In connexion with a reported invasion of Uganda's Western Nile district by several thousand followers of ex-President Amin, entering the district from Zaïre and the Sudan and said to be led by Maj.-Gen. Isaac Lumago (a former Chief of Staff of the Armed Forces under President Amin until April 1978), Brig. Moses denied on Oct. 13, 1980, that the UNRF was in any way connected with the events in the Western Nile district, although it advocated that all exiles should be allowed to return to Uganda. Despite this denial, on May 1, 1981, the UNRF was reported to have occupied parts of the Madi and Western Nile districts (in north-western Uganda), although Brig. Moses denied that his forces supported ex-President Amin.

Uganda Patriotic Movement (UPM)

Leadership. Yoweri Museveni (pres.); Jabeli Bidandi Sali (s.g.).

The UPM was established as a political party in June 1980 with a view to contesting the general elections of Dec. 10, 1980, in which, however, it gained only one of the elective seats in the National Assembly. The UPM thereupon called for new elections under the supervision of a neutral body. As this call met with no response, the UPM threatened to overthrow President Obote's regime (established as a result of the elections) by force.

The UPM had numerous supporters at Makerere University (Kampala), many of whom fled in February and March 1981 to escape arrest by the Obote authorities. Of a number of UPM office bearers who were arrested, several were later reported to have died or been killed in prison. Yoweri Museveni himself went into hiding and set up his own guerrilla organization, at first known as the People's Revolutionary Army and later as the National Resistance Army (see separate entry). On the other hand, Jabeli Bidandi Sali (who had been arrested on Feb. 10, 1981) was unconditionally released on Oct. 30 of that year.

Uganda Popular Front (UPF)

It was announced in London on Jan. 7, 1982, that this Front had been formed by all Ugandan exile groups except the Ugandan National Liberation Front (UNLF). The declared aim of the UPF was to co-ordinate all opposition groups and to overthrow the Obote Government by force, since in the view of the UPF no negotiation was possible with it.

Signatories to the agreement to form the UPF included (i) Maj.-Gen. Ibrahim (Emilio) Mundo (a former Minister of Defence under President Amin), who had regrouped his guerrilla forces north of Arua (in the Western Nile district); (ii) several exiled Democratic Party (DP) leaders, among them ex-President Yusufu Lule (chairman of the National Resistance Movement), Balaki K. Kirya (leader of the Uganda Freedom Movement) and Francis Bwengye (former secretary-general of the DP); (iii) Yoweri Museveni (leader of the National Resistance Army) and (iv) Brig. Moses Ali and Felix Onama (leaders of the Uganda National Rescue Front).

It had earlier been reported in mid-September 1981 that a co-ordinating council had been formed in Nairobi (Kenya) to link the NRA, the UFM and the guerrillas led by Maj.-Gen. Mundo.

Upper Volta

Capital: Ouagadougou   Pop. 5,700,000

The Republic of Upper Volta is ruled by a People's Salvation Council (*Conseil du Salut du Peuple,* CSP) headed by Maj. Jean-Baptiste Ouedraogo and described as the state's "supreme political body". It came to power in a coup on Nov. 7, 1982, as the People's Provisional Salvation Council, and on Nov. 26 it announced the formation of a permanent secretariat of the CSP and of a predominantly civilian Government. On Jan. 10, 1983, the CSP elected a Prime Minister, namely Capt. Thomas Sankara, who was described as one of the "brains" behind the November 1982 coup.

The country has no other political institutions, since its 1977 Constitution and also all its political parties were suspended in a previous military coup on Nov. 25, 1980.

Zaïre

Capital: Kinshasa   Pop. 29,000,000

The Republic of Zaïre is a "united, democratic and social state" with an executive President elected for a seven-year term (and re-eligible); he is head of state, head of the National Executive Council (Cabinet) and leader of the Popular Revolutionary Movement (*Mouvement Populaire de la Révolution,* MPR), the country's sole legal political organization, whose political bureau he appoints. There is a National Legislative Council of 268 members elected by universal adult suffrage for a five-year term on a list of the MPR.

In April 1980 President Mobutu Sese Seko signed ordinances replacing the existing National Documentation Centre by a National Intelligence Service (SNI) with responsibility for external security and by a National Research and Investigations Centre (CNRI) with responsibility for internal security.

External Opposition

A number of organizations hostile to the regime of President Mobutu have been founded by Zaïreans in exile, mainly in Brussels. There have been several attempts to overthrow the regime. In Rwanda it was reported in June 1979 that seven Belgians had been sentenced to imprisonment for up to 10 years for alleged involvement in an attempted anti-Mobutu coup in February 1979.

Action Movement for the Resurrection of the Congo (*Mouvement d'Action pour la Résurrection du Congo,* MARC)

Leadership. Monguya Mbenge (ch.).

This Movement, set up in Brussels in 1974, has used its present name since 1976. It was held responsible for planning a coup d'état for February 1978, and in this connexion its founder, Kanyonga Mobateli, as well as Monguya Mbenge (a former governor of Shaba province) and two other MARC leaders, were condemned to death in absentia on March 16, 1978. Since then the MARC has tried to win the confidence of Western governments which would enable it to gain power by means of a coup. The MARC's declared aim is "to end the neo-colonialist regime of Mobutu".

Congolese Front for the Restoration of Democracy (*Front Congolais pour le Rétablissement de la Démocratie*)

Leadership. Nguza Karl I Bond (l.).

This Front was established in Brussels in October 1982 as an alliance of a number of rival opposition groups. Nguza had had a long diplomatic and political career during which he was State Commissioner for Foreign Affairs in 1972-74 and 1974-77, a member of the political bureau of the ruling MPR in 1972-77 and its director in 1974-77, Vice-President of the National Executive Council (Cabinet) and State Commissioner for Foreign Affairs and International Co-operation from February 1976 to August 1977.

He was arrested on Aug. 13, 1977, and on Sept. 13 he was condemned to death for undermining Zaïre's external security (by failing to reveal his knowledge of the impending rebel action in Shaba by the Congolese National Liberation Front—see separate entry), a charge to which he pleaded not guilty. The death sentence was on Sept. 15 commuted to life imprisonment, and on July 14, 1978, he was released under an amnesty declared by President Mobutu. On March 6, 1979, he was reappointed State Commissioner for Foreign Affairs and International Co-operation, and on Aug. 27, 1980, he was given the post of First State Commissioner (Prime Minister). His resignation from this post was announced on April 17, 1981, when he was in Belgium, where he stated that his return to Zaïre would mean his return to prison.

Nguza subsequently strongly attacked President Mobutu's regime, stating on June 25, 1981, that he was "pro-Western" and shared the West's valid concern for "keeping Zaïre out of communist hands" but that the "human rights violations, the economic misery" in Zaïre and "the President's pilfering of state coffers" were equally important. Before a US House of Representatives' subcommittee on Africa he stated on Sept. 15, 1981, that the West should abandon its "blind and uncritical support" for President Mobutu and that the situation in Kinshasa was ripe for uprisings.

Congolese National Liberation Front (*Front de Libération Nationale Congolais,* FLNC)

Leadership. Lt.-Gen. Nathaniel Mbumba (l.).

The FLNC was set up by former Katangese gendarmes who had fled to Portuguese Angola after the collapse of Moïse Tshombe's secessionist regime in Katanga in 1964. In 1965 they were joined by other Katangese gendarmes who left their country after the dismissal of Tshombe as Prime Minister of the Congo-Kinshasa. After serving as mercenaries in the Portuguese forces in Angola, they fought (following the departure of the Portuguese in 1975) alongside the Popular Movement for the Liberation of Angola (MPLA) in the latter's successful struggle for control of the country.

By 1977 the FLNC forces were said to number between 5,000 and 7,000 men. An invasion of the province of Shaba (formerly Katanga) launched by the FLNC in March 1977 was repelled by May of that year after Zaïre had received military aid from Moroccan troops airlifted to Zaïre by France and also military equipment supplied by the United States. President Mobutu denounced the invasion as a Soviet and Cuban attempt to destabilize Zaïre. (In the aftermath of this attempt, deserters from the Zaïrean Army staged a rebellion in the Kwilu area in December 1977 and January 1978, which was suppressed with great loss of life and with 14 rebel leaders being condemned to death and executed.)

A second invasion of Shaba province was launched from Angola by the FLNC in May 1978 and penetrated as far as Kolwezi (on the Copperbelt) before being repulsed with the aid of French and Belgian paratroopers sent "to protect French and other foreign residents of Kolwezi and to restore security there". The FLNC described its action as an intensification of the war against the Mobutu regime, with which the Zaïrean population was said to be "discontented". The numerous casualties caused by this action included some 150 Europeans killed or missing. President Agostinho Neto of Angola was at the end of June 1978 reported to have ordered the FLNC to pull back from the border area and to be disarmed. An amnesty offered by President Mobutu on June 24, 1978, for refugees and exiles who returned to Zaïre was rejected by the FLNC. In July 1980 the FLNC joined the Council for the Liberation of the Congo-Kinshasa (see separate entry).

Congo National Movement—Lumumba (*Mouvement National du Congo—Lumumba,* MNC-Lumumba)

Leadership. Paul Roger Mokede (pres.).

This Movement was named after Patrice Lumumba, the first (and left-wing) Prime Minister of the independent Republic of the Congo (proclaimed on June 30, 1960), who was murdered in February 1961. After giving a press conference in Brussels during the second invasion of Shaba province by forces of the Congolese National Liberation Front, in May 1978, Paul Roger Mokede was expelled from Brussels to Paris. President Mobutu had previously protested to the Belgian Government against its toleration of active Zaïrean opposition groups in Belgium.

Congolese Progressive Students (ECP)—see under Council for the Liberation of the Congo-Kinshasa

Congolese Socialist Party (PSC)—see under Council for the Liberation of the Congo-Kinshasa

Council for the Liberation of the Congo-Kinshasa (*Conseil pour la Libération du Congo-Kinshasa,* CLC)

Leadership. Mungul Diaka (pres.).

The CLC was established in Brussels in July 1980 as a merger of various exile groups in opposition to the Mobutu regime—(i) the National Front for the Liberation of the Congo (FNLC), (ii) the National Movement for Union and Reconciliation in Zaïre (MNUR), (iii) the People's Revolutionary Party (PRP), (iv) the Congolese Socialist Party (*Parti Socialiste Congolais,* PSC) and (v) the Congolese Progressive Students (*Etudiants Congolais Progressistes,* ECP).

Mungul Diaka had a varied career under President Mobutu. Having been appointed Minister of Education in October 1967, he was dismissed on July 5, 1968, for alleged "grave shortcomings incompatible with the revolutionary objectives of the new regime"; on Feb. 11, 1972, he was sentenced to 10 years in prison for plotting against President Mobutu, but he was later reprieved, and in March 1979 he was appointed State Commissioner for Higher Education and Scientific Research. He held this post until January 1980, when he was stated to have fled to Brazzaville (Congo) after a judicial inquiry had begun into alleged fraud and maladministration. In December 1980 some 30 distributors of CLC pamphlets were reported to have been arrested in Kinshasa, while Mungul Diaka stated that three Zaïrean parliamentarians were being interrogated on suspicion of having helped him to flee Zaïre.

The declared aim of the CLC is the restoration of democracy and fundamental human rights in Zaïre.

National Movement for Union and Reconciliation in Zaïre (*Mouvement National pour l'Union et la Réconciliation au Zaïre,* MNUR)

Leadership. Mbeka Makosso (founder).

This Movement was set up in Brussels by Mbeka Makosso (formerly Joseph Mbeka), who had been Minister of the Economy under President Mobutu from November 1969 to February 1972 and later ambassador in Washington and Tehran. It subsequently joined the Council for the Liberation of the Congo-Kinshasa (CLC) on its formation in July 1978 (see separate entry).

Internal Opposition

Internal opposition to President Mobutu found expression in a parliamentary report completed by a five-member committee in October 1980 and revealing substantial foreign currency deals by the Mobutu family and outside interests. The five members of

the committee were all arrested on Dec. 31, 1980, and on Jan. 2, 1981, a total of 13 people's commissioners (i.e. members of the National Legislative Council) were deprived of their parliamentary immunity because they had, as officially stated, "carefully prepared a 50-page pamphlet . . . denigrating established institutions, harming the head of state's reputation, creating confusion in people's minds and inciting them to revolt". The lifting of the 13 members' immunity was opposed by 17 members of the Legislative Council, while 22 others abstained from voting.

National Conscience Party (*Parti pour la Conscience Nationale,* Pacona)

Leadership. Tharcisse Mutena Mbaw'O-Mpyp (pres.).

This party was set up in Kinshasa in 1977 with the object of replacing the Mobutu regime by a bicameral parliamentary system incorporating recognition of the authority of traditional chiefs. The party has also called for the rehabilitation of Christian churches in Zaïre (where all non-recognized religious sects were on Jan. 3, 1979, forbidden to practise their cult).

People's Revolutionary Party (*Parti de la Révolution Populaire,* PRP)

Leadership. Laurent Kabila (1.).

The PRP is a remnant of the *Comité National de Libération* which in 1964 conducted insurrectional activities under the leadership of Pierre Mulele. Since 1967 the PRP has held guerrilla strongholds in the Fizi Baraka area (on the western shore of Lake Tanganyika). It was responsible for the kidnapping of four students from the United States in Tanzania on May 19, 1975, and for their release in July 1975 upon payment of ransom by the students' parents. Action taken against the PRP guerrillas by Zaïrean Army units has failed to eliminate them. The PRP was reported to have refused to support the 1977 invasion of Shaba province by forces of the Congolese National Liberation Front. In July 1980 the PRP joined the Council for the Liberation of the Congo-Kinshasa (see separate entry).

Union for Democracy and Social Progress (*Union pour la Démocratie et le Progrès Social*)

The creation of this Union as a second political party (in opposition to the ruling MPR) was discussed in 1982 by a group of politicians including 13 people's commissioners (i.e. members of the National Legislative Council) who drew up a clandestine manifesto calling for an end to President Mobutu's "arbitrary'' rule and claiming that in the event of free elections the MPR "would not win a single seat". At the end of 1980 these 13 people's commissioners had made allegations of irregular financial dealings by President Mobutu's family (see above).

On March 15, 1982, the President alleged that they had attempted "to create a new political party" by agreeing to set up "a tribalist and ethnic cartel aimed at creating restlessness among men and women MPR sympathizers"; he emphasized at the same time that Zaïre would remain a one-party state as laid down in the 1978 Constitution.

On July 1, 1982, the State Security Court imposed sentences of 15 years' imprisonment on each of the 13 people's commissioners as well as on 25 other persons.

5. SOUTHERN AFRICA AND INDIAN OCEAN

Angola

Capital: Luanda   Pop. 6,658,000

The People's Democratic Republic of Angola is a one-party state, its sole legal party being the (Marxist-Leninist) Popular Movement for the Liberation of Angola—Party of Labour (MPLA-PT). This party is responsible for the political, economic and social leadership of the nation, and its president is also President of the Republic. The supreme state body is a National People's Assembly elected every three years by colleges composed of representatives chosen by all "loyal" citizens over 18 years old. There is a Government presided over by the head of state. The 206-member National People's Assembly was first elected in the latter half of 1980 and installed on Nov. 11 of that year.

The end of Portuguese colonial rule in 1975 was followed by a fierce struggle for power in Angola between the three principal liberation movements, from which the MPLA (as it was then known) emerged victorious, mainly due to military backing from Cuban "volunteers" and Soviet advisers. Nevertheless, the Government of President José Eduardo dos Santos (who succeeded Antônio Agostinho Neto in 1979) has faced a continuing security threat from the two movements in question, notably from the National Union for the Total Independence of Angola (UNITA) operating in southern Angola with the backing of South African forces based in Namibia. Moreover, in the north separatist forces have continued to be active in the enclave of Cabinda, regarded by the Government as an integral part of Angola.

Military Council of Angolan Resistance
(*Conselho Militar de Resistência Angolana,* Comira)

This organization was set up in August 1980 to replace the National Front for the Liberation of Angola (FNLA), whose leader, Holden Roberto, had been overthrown by his own military commanders. In December 1981 it was reported from Portugal and from Angola that Comira, which was said to be well established in northern and central Angola, had some 2,000 insurgents in training in Zaïre with the intention of invading northern Angola. The Council was said to have been formed in liaison with the US Government in order to "put into practice the United States' need to set up a new counter-revolutionary movement capable of co-ordinating and organizing subversive action in northern Angola" and to replace the "demoralized" FNLA. The US Congress had, however, refused in December 1981 to rescind the so called "Clark Amendment" of Feb. 10, 1976, under which the United States had ceased to give military aid to Angolan movements opposed to the ruling MPLA (later renamed the MPLA-PT).

The FNLA had been formed in April 1962 by the merger of an Angolan People's Union (*União das Populações de Angola,* UPA) led by Holden Roberto and a Democratic Party of Angola, and on April 5 of that year Roberto announced in Léopoldville (later Kinshasa, Zaïre) the formation of a Revolutionary Angolan Government-in-Exile (*Govêrno Revolucionario de Angola no Exilio,* GRAE) with himself as "Prime Minister". The UPA had in March 1961 begun a rebellion against Portuguese rule in Angola, causing thousands of casualties and widespread destruction in northern Angola, but by January 1963 the Portuguese authorities claimed to have regained control of the situation.

The GRAE was formally endorsed by a Foreign Ministers' conference of the Organization of African Unity (OAU) in February 1964; but in November 1964 the OAU also decided to give aid to the MPLA, which was supported by the Soviet Union and its allies. In December of that year the People's Republic of China decided to support the FNLA and to cease its aid to the MPLA. In June 1965 dissidents within the GRAE raided the organization's offices in Léopoldville and destroyed its records, accusing Roberto of having embezzled funds and of failing properly to organize the fight against the Portuguese. GRAE forces had in fact been in conflict with units of the MPLA, but on Oct. 15, 1966, the two organizations agreed to cease all hostile propaganda against each other. Although GRAE forces continued guerrilla warfare during the next few years, the OAU withdrew its recognition of the FNLA and the MPLA as "freedom fighter" movements.

About its military activities the GRAE made claims which were generally regarded as greatly exaggerated—viz. to have killed 1,684 Portuguese and destroyed 113 vehicles and 20 aircraft in 1971 and to have killed more than 1,600 Portuguese and destroyed 14 helicopters and three other aircraft during 1972.

In 1972 the FNLA and the MPLA attempted a reconciliation, and under an agreement signed in Kinshasa on Dec. 13 the two organizations were to merge in a "Supreme Council for the Liberation of Angola" (CSLA), in which the FNLA was to name the head of a political council (responsible for propaganda, diplomatic activities and the administration of liberated areas). However, after the overthrow of the Caetano regime in Portugal in April 1974 the FNLA and the MPLA signed separate ceasefire agreements with Portugal on Oct. 11 and 21 respectively.

On Jan. 9, 1975, the FNLA was recognized by the OAU liberation committee as one of Angola's three official liberation movements, together with the MPLA and Dr Jonas Savimbi's National Union for the Total Independence of Angola (UNITA—see separate entry). But although all three movements took part in the formation of a transitional Government in Angola on Jan. 31, 1975, fighting continued between MPLA and FNLA forces, leading to considerable loss of life. Even after the signing of a truce agreement providing for the integration of MPLA, FNLA and UNITA troops into a combined force on March 28 (as laid down in the independence agreement), fighting continued between units of the three movements and in particular the MPLA and the FNLA, with the result that virtual martial law was declared on May 15, 1975. Nevertheless, the three movements decided, under an agreement signed in Nakuru (Kenya) on June 21, 1975, to renounce the use of force, to carry out elections to a constituent assembly and to guarantee each other the right to free political activity in all parts of the country.

The agreement, however, soon broke down and new hostilities began on June 23, 1975. On July 12 the FNLA headquarters in Luanda were destroyed by MPLA units; and by Aug. 10-11 all remaining FNLA (and UNITA) forces were withdrawn from Luan-

da. While the MPLA proclaimed the independence of the People's Republic of Angola in Luanda on Nov. 11, 1975, Holden Roberto declared in Ambriz (north of Luanda) on the same day that the country would be known as the Democratic People's Republic of Angola. After the MPLA had formed a Government in Luanda on Nov. 14, the FNLA and UNITA established, on Nov. 23, 1975, a separate coalition government with two prime ministers (one from each organization) and with Roberto and Dr Savimbi as joint military chiefs of staff.

Early in 1976 the FNLA forces were driven northwards towards the Zaïre border by Soviet-equipped MPLA forces, and also southwards (together with UNITA forces), with the result that on Feb. 24, 1976, the FNLA announced that it would resort to guerrilla warfare. The MPLA Government was thereupon recognized by numerous African and European governments, and it became a member of the OAU on Feb. 23, 1976.

In the context of its guerrilla warfare the FNLA claimed in Paris on June 28, 1976, to have launched a "systematic sabotage campaign" against the MPLA regime. On Oct. 21 of that year Roberto claimed in Brussels that the FNLA and UNITA controlled two-thirds of Angola (while the number of Cubans sent to Angola to aid the MPLA was given as 30,000); he also said that the FNLA had established a new political and military structure and that its aim was to "bring about free elections so that the Angolan people can choose its leaders".

The South African Government claimed in an official statement of Feb. 3, 1977, that it had during 1975 acted in an advisory capacity to the FNLA but that Holden Roberto had scorned South African advice and had engaged in unsuccessful attacks, with "disastrous" results for the FNLA. During 1975 the FNLA, which had a training camp in Zaïre, had already lost the support of President Mobutu of Zaïre (Holden Roberto's brother-in-law), and under an agreement concluded between the Governments of Angola and Zaïre in Brazzaville on Feb. 28, 1976, each side undertook not to allow on its territory any military activity against the other; on May 5 Zaïre closed the FNLA headquarters in Kinshasa. Holden Roberto, however, did not leave Zaïre finally until Nov. 12, 1979 (after a non-aggression pact had been concluded between Angola, Zaïre and Zambia on Oct. 12, 1979).

Daniel Chipenda (a former leader of a dissident MPLA faction and later secretary-general of the FNLA) claimed on Nov. 11, 1977, that the FNLA's 18,000 men controlled large areas of northern Angola and also said that the FNLA was "ready to ask South Africa" for military help against "a common enemy'' and that, if victory became imminent, the FNLA would join forces with UNITA. However, on March 7, 1980, Holden Roberto was reported to have sought political asylum in France.

National Front for the Liberation of Angola (FNLA)—see under Military Council of Angolan Resistance (Comira)

National Union for the Total Independence of Angola (*União Nacional para a Independência Total de Angola,* UNITA)

Leadership. Dr Jonas Savimbi (pres.); Miguel N'Zau Puna (s.g.).

This organization, established in 1966 and based mainly on the Ovimbundu and Chokwe tribes of central and southern Angola (constituting about 40 per cent of Angola's population), was one of the three original Angolan liberation movements (with the MPLA and the National Front for the Liberation of Angola, FNLA). UNITA's president (Dr Jonas Savimbi) had been ''Foreign Minister'' in the Revolutionary Angolan Government-in-Exile (GRAE) formed in 1962 by the FNLA, but he resigned this post on July 18, 1964, stating that the Portuguese had eliminated all significant groups of Angolan nationalist guerrillas and that there could be no successful offensive by ''freedom fighters'' until all political groups (then said to number about 17) had formed a common front. He subsequently established UNITA, at first with headquarters in Lusaka (Zambia) and later in Cairo. By 1970 his guerrillas were active in south-eastern Angola, and in 1973 he was said to be the only guerrilla leader actually inside Angola.

After the overthrow of the Caetano regime in Portugal in April 1974, UNITA signed a separate ceasefire agreement with Portugal on June 17 of that year. On Jan. 9, 1975, UNITA was recognized by the liberation committee of the Organization of African Unity (OAU) as one of Angola's three official liberation movements (together with the MPLA and the FNLA). UNITA also agreed to take part, with the two other movements, in independence negotiations with Portugal (which regarded the FNLA as right-wing, UNITA as centrist and the MPLA as ''progressive'' or left-wing), and the Angolan independence agreement was thereupon signed on Jan. 15, 1975, by the leaders of the three movements together with Portuguese ministers. On Jan. 31 of that year UNITA also took part in the formation of a transitional Government of Angola by the three movements.

UNITA initially stood apart from the fighting which nevertheless continued between the MPLA and the FNLA, until in August 1975 it began to operate jointly with the FNLA in the southern half of Angola. During the weeks leading up to the achievement of Angola's independence (on Nov. 11, 1975) each of the three liberation movements intensified its efforts to consolidate its military position. In November 1975 the South African Government admitted that its troops and military advisers were actively supporting the FNLA-UNITA forces in southern Angola. The South Africans officially stated on Feb. 3, 1977, that they had acted on an appeal by UNITA and the FNLA; that in October-December 1975 South African battle groups had captured numerous Angolan towns (including Sá da Bandeira, Moçamedes, Benguela, Lobito and Novo Redondo); and that the 2,000 South African troops involved could have captured the whole of Angola had not Dr Savimbi insisted that he was interested only in controlling the traditional UNITA area because he wanted ''to reach a settlement with the MPLA to the advantage of the whole of Angola''. South African troops were therefore withdrawn early in 1976.

At the achievement of independence UNITA had held six of the provincial capitals in southern Angola, and it held a separate independence celebration on Nov. 11, 1975, in Huambo (formerly Nova Lisboa, south of Luanda), where a ''Joint National Council for the Revolution'' was formed by UNITA and the FNLA. Early in 1976, however, UNITA's forces were driven southwards by the Cuban-supported MPLA. The UNITA headquarters were moved from Huambo to Bié (Silva Porto, 100 miles east of Huambo) and on Jan. 19 UNITA leaders appealed for military help from ''any country willing to provide such assistance''. By February 1976 UNITA had been forced to move its headquarters again, to Serpa Pinto (over 200 miles south of Bié); and later that month UNITA was forced to evacuate the last of its positions and to resort to guerrilla warfare in the bush.

Despite its military defeat UNITA issued on May 10, 1976, a manifesto drawn up at a congress at Cuanza (central Angola), calling for an intensification of the armed struggle ''against the regime imposed by the Cubans and Russians'', and stating there would be no dialogue with the MPLA as long as it was supported by foreign troops. It threatened to attack the Benguela railway (running from Lobito to Zaïre via the border town of Dilolo) and to sabotage all other forms of communication; it also proposed to reorganize its own military and political structure and create an armed people's militia.

Subsequent clashes between MPLA and UNITA forces in southern and eastern Angola led to widespread losses and chaotic conditions, especially in the south. In November 1976 Dr Savimbi claimed to have 6,000 men at his disposal and gave the number of

Cubans in Angola as 15,000, plus 4,000 administrative personnel carrying out local defence duties. On Dec. 28, 1976, it was reported in Lusaka that UNITA had been prohibited from using Zambian territory as a base for military activities against the MPLA Government and that its officials had been expelled from Zambia (which formally recognized the MPLA Government on Jan. 6, 1977).

While UNITA forces continued their guerrilla activities during 1977, Dr Jorge Sagumba (UNITA's external affairs spokesman) claimed in London on Nov. 3 that UNITA controlled 10 of Angola's 16 provinces and had established almost 900 schools there, but added that there could be no negotiation with the MPLA to form a coalition government before some 24,000 Cuban and 3,000 Soviet military personnel were removed from Angola. He also said that UNITA had since the end of the war with Portugal received no material aid from South Africa (and was receiving none from Israel), but that South Africa wanted UNITA to win.

UNITA's information secretary claimed in London on April 4, 1978, that UNITA was having "steady success" against MPLA and Cuban forces in the province of Cuando-Cubango (south-east Angola), where 580 MPLA and Cuban troops and 78 UNITA guerrillas had been killed during February 1978. According to other UNITA claims made on June 15, a Cuban offensive had been "routed". On Nov. 10, 1978, UNITA claimed to have wrecked 37 miles of the Benguela railway, and on Jan. 18, 1979, the information secretary of UNITA declared in London that the railway would not be allowed to function against the will of UNITA or to be used to transport Cuban troops; he added that UNITA was ready to talk to the MPLA, though not until all Cuban forces had been withdrawn from Angola. Dr Savimbi stated on Feb. 1, 1980, that 20,000 Angolan troops spearheaded by 5,000 Cubans had been attacking UNITA forces on four fronts in the provinces of Benguela, Huambo, Bié and Moxico to allow the Benguela railway to be reopened.

The Angolan authorities, on the other hand, claimed in July 1980 to have made considerable advances against UNITA forces, of whom more than 1,000 were said to have surrendered. It was also stated officially that some 800,000 peasants, who had fled into the bush because they distrusted the MPLA, had re-emerged since the beginning of 1980. During that year a number of UNITA members were tried for various acts of violence; on July 29, a total of 16 were sentenced to death and seven others to imprisonment for between 12 and 24 years for bombing acts in Luanda, Huambo and elsewhere in the previous two years (the death sentences being carried out

on Aug. 5); on Aug. 24 nine others, condemned to death in Huambo on Aug. 21, were also executed, five others having been given prison sentences ranging from two to 20 years; on Dec. 1 four were sentenced to death for sabotage in Cuito, and three to imprisonment; and on Dec. 8 three were condemned to death for sabotage in Lobito, where fuel tanks and harbour installations had on Aug. 11 been reported to have been destroyed. After the August executions, UNITA announced that its "tribunal of resistance" had condemned to death and executed 15 prisoners belonging to the government armed forces.

By January 1981 the Angolan authorities were reported to have displaced some 467,000 persons to "protected villages" in central Angola in order to keep UNITA guerrillas away from the population. During 1981 UNITA units, apparently better armed than before, continued their attacks on the Benguela railway, of which the majority of engines and weapons were put out of action, with the result that within 18 months only 18,000 tonnes of manganese were transported to Lobito from Zaïre (compared with the normal quota of 40,000 tonnes a month).

On March 8, 1981, it was officially announced that another 18 UNITA members had been sentenced to death for participating in bomb attacks. UNITA, on the other hand, claimed on Nov. 30 that its underground cells in Luanda were responsible for a major fire at the state-run oil refinery in Luanda on that day. Notwithstanding this escalation in the civil war between UNITA and the MPLA forces (supported by Cuban units), Dr Savimbi said in an interview (published in *The Observer* of London on Jan. 24, 1982) that he was "very interested" in the possible establishment of a "government of national reconciliation" and that UNITA had established unofficial contacts with the MPLA-PT.

A UNITA congress held at Mavinga (south-eastern Angola) at the end of July 1982 and attended by some 1,500 delegates issued a "Mavinga Declaration" stating inter alia (i) that UNITA was now willing to negotiate with the MPLA without any prior conditions (such as the withdrawal of Cuban troops from Angola) as a first step towards the formation of a government of national union—although the latter would not be possible until all foreign troops were withdrawn; (ii) that any ceasefire in Namibia would be valid only if it involved the departures of Cuban forces from Angola (without their replacement by other foreign troops); and (iii) that all foreigners should leave the country, of whose 16 provinces 10 had been declared zones of war.

In a South African government newspaper, Dr Savimbi described himself (on Aug.

27, 1982) as having ties with South Africa; he also pointed out that a takeover of Namibia by the South West Africa People's Organization (SWAPO) would expose UNITA to attack on two fronts, in the north by the MPLA and in the south by SWAPO. (In the light of the Angolan Government's backing for SWAPO, South African forces carried out several major military incursions into southern Angola in the late 1970s and early 1980s.)

In the ensuing months UNITA claimed to have inflicted heavy losses on government forces. Col. Juan Bock, head of UNITA logistics, stated on Sept. 21, 1982, that during the previous 12 months UNITA had killed about 1,500 Cubans and 3,000 MPLA soldiers. Allegations by the Angolan news agency that UNITA had massacred about 150 villagers (as reported on Oct. 6) and another 300 and 150 respectively on two other occasions (reported on Oct. 11) were denied by UNITA on Oct. 19.

According to a report in the *International Herald Tribune* on Nov. 30, 1982, UNITA's forces were then larger and better equipped than in 1980. In large areas outside the principal towns in southern Angola, UNITA guerrillas were roaming freely and had made roads and the Benguela railway unusable.

Further UNITA claims concerning a battle fought on Dec. 6-17, 1982, and allegedly resulting in heavy losses by the government forces involved, were disputed by the Angolan news agency on Jan. 7, 1983; the agency admitted, however, that UNITA's forces fighting in south-eastern Angola were stronger than they had been in 1975-76.

Cabinda Separatists

Armed Forces for the Liberation of Cabinda (FALC)—see under Popular Movement for the Liberation of Cabinda

Front for the Liberation of the Enclave of Cabinda (*Frente de Libertação do Enclave de Cabinda,* FLEC)

Leadership. Francisco Xauter Lubota (commander of operations).

FLEC was set up in 1963 as a separate national liberation movement of the enclave of Cabinda (bordering on the Congo and Zaïre, but with no common border with Angola). In a statement broadcast by Brazzaville (Congo) radio on Jan. 12, 1975, FLEC rejected any attempt to integrate Cabinda with Angola and declared that during the past 14 years no Angolan political organization had succeeded in establishing itself in Cabinda. However, the independence agreement signed on Jan.

25, 1975, by the three then existing Angolan liberation movements stated in Article 3 that Cabinda was "an integral and inalienable part of Angolan territory".

By this time FLEC was divided into three factions—one in Cabinda led by Augusto Techioufouj, another in Kinshasa (Zaïre) led by Luis de Ganzaga Ranque Franque and a third in Angola. On July 25, 1975, a further faction of FLEC announced in Paris that a provisional revolutionary government of Cabinda had been formed, with Henrique N'Zita Tiago (described as vice-president of FLEC) as president, in a FLEC-controlled zone in Cabinda on July 16. This announcement was, however, immediately condemned by the Kinshasa headquarters of FLEC.

On Aug. 13, 1975, it was announced that an independent government of Cabinda had been formed by L. de G. Ranque Franque as president and Francisco Xauter Lubota (a former secretary-general of the National Front for the Liberation of Angola, FNLA) as prime minister. In a further announcement made in Kampala (Uganda) on Nov. 1, 1975, L. de G. Ranque Franque declared Cabinda to be independent. From early November 1975 onwards heavy fighting took place in Cabinda between forces of FLEC and of the (Marxist) Popular Movement for the Liberation of Angola (MPLA), and during 1976 FLEC was reported to be offering resistance to some 3,000 Cubans then present in Cabinda.

On May 2, 1977, FLEC again announced in Paris that the "first provisional government of the Republic of Cabinda" had been established with H. N. Tiago as "head of state". At the same time FLEC claimed that it had forced Cuban troops to abandon an air base at Belize (in Cabinda) and that it controlled two-thirds of Cabinda, but added that it needed arms to consolidate its gains. A congress held in the "liberated zone" of Safica on Feb. 15-20, 1979, confirmed H. N. Tiago as president of FLEC, but on Dec. 21 of that year he was mortally wounded in a clash with Cuban forces.

Francisco Xauter Lubota claimed in Brussels in June 1979 that FLEC forces of about 7,000 men held 30 per cent of the territory of Cabinda; that there were 8,000 Cubans, 2,000 Angolan soldiers and 400 Hungarian military personnel in Cabinda; and that 150,000 Cabindans (half the enclave's population) had fled to Zaïre since 1975.

On May 21, 1981, it was reported in Lisbon that six men had been condemned to death in Angola on charges of belonging to FLEC and of having carried out bomb attacks. FLEC itself claimed that its saboteurs had exploded bombs at Cabinda's only airport on Dec. 13, 1981, and had totally destroyed the state oil installation in the enclave on Dec. 16.

Military Command for the Liberation of Cabinda

Leadership. Maj. Luis Matos Fernandes; Lt.-Col. Marcelino Tumbi.

This Command was formed in November 1977 by the above officers of the Cabindan armed forces with the aim of reorganizing "on a new democratic foundation" the Front for the Liberation of the Enclave of Cabinda (FLEC), which they regarded as having failed to "initiate political action capable of winning international support for the just demands of our people".

Movement for the Liberation of Cabinda (*Movimento para a Libertação de Cabinda,* Molica)

Leadership. João da Costa (1.).

This group was formed from an offshoot of the Front for the Liberation of the Enclave of Cabinda (FLEC).

Popular Movement for the Liberation of Cabinda (*Movimento Popular de Libertação de Cabinda,* MPLC)

Leadership. Maj. Vicente Balenda (head of executive committee).

This Movement was established on June 1, 1979, as a splinter group of the Front for the Liberation of the Enclave of Cabinda (FLEC) by the "Armed Forces for the Liberation of Cabinda" (FALC). The MPLC described itself as a "progressive" Movement not hostile to the West but rejecting FLEC as "irresponsible and overtly imperialistic" and as exploiting Cabinda's resources.

A MPLC does not appear to have made any real challenge to FLEC's position as the principal Cabindan separatist movement.

Botswana

Capital: Gaborone   Pop. 937,000

The Republic of Botswana, a member of the Commonwealth, has an executive President responsible to a 38-member National Assembly, of which 32 members are elected for a five-year term by universal adult suffrage, four are nominated by the President and two are ex-officio members. There is also an advisory 15-member House of Chiefs. In general elections held on Oct. 20, 1979, parties gained elective seats in the House of Assembly as follows: Botswana Democratic Party 29, Botswana National Front 2, Botswana People's Party 1. The (left-wing) Botswana Independence Party gained no seats. There has been no evidence of extra-parliamentary opposition in Botswana.

Comoros

Capital: Moroni (on Njazidja or Grand Comoro)   Pop. 370,000 (excluding Mayotte)

The Federal and Islamic Republic of the Comoros has, under its Constitution approved in a referendum on Oct. 1, 1981, a President elected for a six-year term by universal adult suffrage and a 39-member Federal Assembly elected similarly for a five-year term. There is a Cabinet headed by a Prime Minister appointed by the President, who shares with the Assembly the power to dismiss him. For the elections to the Federal Assembly held in December 1978 no political parties had been formed. However, following the Assembly's decision in January 1979 that a one-party system should be established for 12 years, the Comorian Union for Progress (*Union Comorienne pour le Progrès,* UCP) was formed as the country's sole political organization.

Within what it regards as its own borders, the Government of President Ahmed Abdallah has no authority over the island of Mayotte, whose population has opted by a substantial majority to remain under the sovereignty of France (the former colonial power in the Comoro Islands). Apart from Mayotte separatism, organized opposition to the Government has consisted mainly of groups based abroad, in particular in France. Internally, more than 40 people arrested on the island of Grand Comoro (known as Njazidja since 1980) in mid-February 1981 were accused of planning to overthrow the Government after some of them had been found in possession of arms originating from the armoury of the presidential guard.

National Committee of Public Salvation
(Comité National du Salut Public)

Leadership. Saïd Ali Kemal (founder).

The formation of this Committee was announced in Paris on Oct. 14, 1980, by Saïd Ali Kemal, a former ambassador of the Comoros to France, who had in July 1980 declined to accept a post in the Cabinet under President Ahmed Abdallah; at the same time he had resigned as ambassador, accusing the President of corruption and calling for his resignation, the establishment of a government of national unity, a general amnesty, land reform and a just distribution of wealth, and in foreign affairs a policy of non-alignment and a rapprochement with Madagascar. He also contended that the President had sought to pass on to him responsibility for dealing with embarrassing problems concerning political prisoners in the Comoros. (In January 1981 a Paris advocate, who had acted as defence counsel for former army officers found guilty of crimes committed under the left-wing regime of President Ali Soilih—overthrown in May 1978, stated that there were about 100 former supporters of that regime in detention; however, on Jan. 27, 1982, it was reported that 14 political prisoners had been released.)

Union for a Democratic Republic of the Comoros *(Union pour une République Démocratique des Comores)*

Leadership. Mouzaoir Abdallah (founder).

The creation of this Union was announced early in August 1981 by Mouzaoir Abdallah, who had been Foreign Minister under the left-wing regime of President Ali Soilih in 1976-78; thereafter he had been under house arrest for nearly three years, had fled the country in June 1981 but had returned after declaring that he had been in contact with a number of friendly and neighbouring states including France, Madagascar, Seychelles and Tanzania. On Nov. 7, 1981, he was arrested and accused of being engaged in subversive activities in the company of Yves Lebret, a former roving ambassador. On May 19, 1982, he was given a suspended two-year prison sentence but on May 28 he was pardoned.

United National Front of the Comoros *(Front National Uni des Komores,* FNUK)

Leadership. Abubakar Ahmed Burdin (l.).

Based in Dar-es-Salaam, this Front of supporters of the former left-wing regime of President Ali Soilih issued in June 1980, an open letter to President Ahmed Abdallah, accusing him of "tyranny" and "despotism", especially in his treatment of political prisoners and of the press through censorship, and also in gaining profits for politicians. By 1982 the FNUK was allied, under the leadership of Abubakar Ahmed Burdin, with the Association of Comorian Trainees and Students *(Association des Stagiaires et des Etudiants Comoriens)* in an organization referred to as FNUK-UNIKOM.

Lesotho

Capital: Maseru   Pop. 1,500,000

The Kingdom of Lesotho is a hereditary monarchy in which power is held by the leadership of the Basotho National Party, the Constitution having been suspended after alleged irregularities in elections to the National Assembly in 1970. An interim National Assembly appointed in April 1973 contained also members of three opposition parties. In subsequent years the regime was threatened by the activities of a faction of the Basotho Congress Party.

Basotho Congress Party (BCP)—Dissident Faction

Leadership. Ntsu Mokhehle (1.).

The BCP was originally founded in 1952 (as the National Basutoland Congress) by Ntsu Mokhehle. It gained 25 out of the 60 seats in the first general elections to a National Assembly held in 1965. In elections held in 1970 the BCP claimed to have gained a majority of votes and seats, but the Government suspended the Constitution and the BCP refused to co-operate with the regime. In 1973, however, the BCP was split—one section of it accepting seats in an appointed National Assembly and the other remaining, under the leadership of Mokhehle, in opposition and making an unsuccessful attempt to overthrow the Government in 1974. On March 10, 1975, prison sentences ranging from four to nine years were imposed on 15 BCP members for high treason. Mokhehle and other leaders of his faction had earlier left the country.

In 1979-80 heavy fighting occurred in parts of Lesotho. Mokhehle stated on Dec. 8, 1979, that guerrilla forces of the BCP, whom he described as the Lesotho Liberation Army (LLA), were active in the country, and on Dec. 14 he claimed that the LLA had 65 Libyan-trained guerrillas and 500-1,000 other men in training in secret mountain camps. In one of the clashes between Lesotho police and BCP members, eight of the latter were said to have been killed on June 2, 1980.

The Government of Lesotho claimed that many of the guerrilla attacks were made from bases outside Lesotho, in particular from

South Africa. The South African Government denied this and Naleli Ntlama, described as political commissar of the LLA, asserted on Nov. 17, 1980, that his organization operated entirely from bases in Lesotho and was not assisted by South Africa but bought its weapons from private gun-runners and smuggled them into the country, or captured them from government forces. In September-November 1981 the LLA made a number of attacks involving the use of bombs, mortars and machine-guns, causing several deaths.

During 1982 the LLA intensified its guerrilla operations, which included the laying of landmines and resulted, inter alia, in the killing on July 5 of a former BPC leader who had returned to Lesotho from exile under an amnesty, and of the Minister of Works on Aug. 7. The Lesotho Government alleged that those responsible for the death of the Minister had been trained by the South African police, and similar accusations against South Africa were made by the Prime Minister on Aug. 14, but were categorically rejected by the South African Minister of Foreign Affairs. The BCP's representative, in a statement on Dec. 9, 1982, accused the Prime Minister of Lesotho of having disregarded the national interest by allowing the Communist Party of South Africa to establish "anti-South African military bases on the sovereign territory of the Kingdom of Lesotho" (but this and other similar allegations were all refuted by the Government of Lesotho). Concerning the objective of the BCP dissidents, Mokhele had stated on Dec. 8, 1980, that it was to enable the Basotho people "to free themselves from [Prime Minister] Leabua Jonathan's illegal rule of repressive terror".

Communist Party of Lesotho (CPL)

This party was formed in May 1962 mainly by migrant workers employed in the Republic of South Africa. In 1967 it was split, when a left-wing group opposed to the policy of co-operation with national democratic forces was expelled from the main body of the CPL. It was the only legal party of its kind in southern Africa until it was banned in February 1970 (when the Prime Minister, Chief Leabua Jonathan, suspended the Constitution and declared that his fight was "against the threat of international communism and its agents in Lesotho"). The CPL has nevertheless continued its activities.

The CPL has defined its immediate task as the struggle, in the framework of a national liberation front, for the establishment of a national democratic state, and its ultimate aim as the setting-up of the dictatorship of the proletariat and a socialist society. The CPL is officially recognized by the Communist parties of the Soviet-bloc countries.

Lesotho Liberation Army (LLA)—see under Basotho Congress Party (BCP)—Dissident Faction

Madagascar

Capital: Antananarivo   Pop. 9,000,000

The Democratic Republic of Madagascar has an executive President elected for seven years by universal adult suffrage. He is also Chairman of a Supreme Revolutionary Council which is "the guardian of the Malagasy Socialist Revolution" and the members of which are, as to two-thirds, nominated by the President and, as to the other third, chosen by him from a list presented by the National People's Assembly which is elected by universal adult suffrage, normally for five years. The Government headed by a Prime Minister appointed by the President is responsible to the National People's Assembly.

Elections for the 137 seats in the Assembly, held on June 30, 1977, were conducted on a sole list of the National Front for the Defence of the Malagasy Socialist Revolution *(Front National pour la Défense de la Révolution Malgache),* from which seats were allotted to four parties as follows: President Didier Ratsiraka's Vanguard of the Malagasy Revolution (Arema) 112, Congress Party for Malagasy Independence (AKFM) 16 Popular Impulse for National Unity (VONJY) 7 and Christian Democratic Party (Udecma-KMPT) 2. Three radical left-wing parties are currently outside the National Front while retaining the status of legal political formations, namely (i) the Movement for Proletarian Power, (ii) the National Movement for the Independence of Madagascar (Monima) and (iii) the *Vondrona Sosialista Monima* (which broke away from Monima to support the National Front). Assembly elections which had been due in 1982 were postponed for a year, although presidential elections were held in November 1982 and resulted in the re-election of President Ratsiraka.

Although the organized opposition or semi-opposition parties referred to above have generally pursued their political objectives within the framework of the existing system, the National Movement for the Independence of Madagascar (Monima) has been particularly associated with manifestations of political dissent in recent years. Frequent demonstrations and disturbances by students and unemployed young people discontented with the Ratsiraka regime have often taken the Monima leader, Monja Jaona, as a rallying figure, and Jaona himself has frequently attacked what he describes as the repressive approach of the security authorities to such dissent.

Partly in the light of such unrest, Monima was admitted to the National Front in March 1981 and Jaona himself was reported (in August of that year) to have been appointed to the Supreme Revolutionary Council (SRC). However, at a Monima Congress held in Toliary (Tuléar, southern Madagascar) on July 25, 1982, Jaona accused the Army and police of carrying our "massacres" in various localities in southern Madagascar, involving inter alia the killing of 50 members of Arema (the President's party).

Jaona later decided to oppose President Ratsiraka in presidential elections, which were held on Nov. 7, 1982, and resulted in the re-election of the President by about 80 per cent of the voters taking part in an 86.6 per cent poll. Jaona thereupon called (on Dec. 14) for a general strike, apparently with the object of obtaining annulment of the elections. However, on Dec. 15 he was dismissed from the SRC and on the following day was warned not to take part in any political activity; later he was reported to be in detention in a military camp in southern Madagascar.

Meanwhile, allegations of the discovery of an anti-government plot and the subsequent arrest of several priests and military officers were made on Jan. 24, 1982, by Fr Richard Andriamanjato, the leader of the Congress Party for Malagasy Independence (AKFM), who said that mercenaries were involved in this plot. It was later reported that the plotters were believed to have connexions with South African mercenaries.

Malawi

Capital: Lilongwe   Pop. 6,200,000

The Republic of Malawi, a member of the Commonwealth, has an executive President appointed for life. He is also the head of the Government. Of the members of the National Assembly, 87 are elected for a five-year term by universal adult suffrage from candidates nominated by district committees of the Malawi Congress Party (MCP)—the country's sole legal political organization—and approved by the President, who may appoint up to 15 additional members to the Assembly. The leader of the MCP is Dr Hastings Kamuzu Banda, who has led Malawi since independence in 1964 and who was made Life President in 1971.

There has, in recent years, been little evidence of political dissent inside Malawi, partly as a result of stringent internal security measures. The entry of foreign journalists has, with a short interruption, been banned since 1974.

In October 1976 Albert Muwalu Nqumayo (until then Minister without Portfolio, and secretary-general and administrative secretary of the MCP) was expelled from the party. Together with Focus (Martin) Gwede (a former senior police officer of the Special Branch), he was on Feb. 14, 1977, condemned to death for high treason, specifically by conspiring to overthrow the lawfully constituted Government of

Malawi and by procuring arms for the purpose. It was officially stated that both had intended to set up a communist state in Malawi; both pleaded not guilty. The death sentence imposed on Gwede was later commuted to life imprisonment, whereas that passed on Nqumayo was not.

Gwanda Chakuamba, who had been dismissed on Feb. 29, 1980, as Minister of Youth and Culture and Minister for the Southern Region, was also expelled from the MCP on March 19, 1980, and was on March 20, 1982, sentenced to 22 years in prison for sedition. He had been charged inter alia with trying to raise popular disaffection against the Government, and also with possession of political publications, including photographs of exiled former ministers. The defection of a number of members of the armed forces was reported during 1980—that of 12 army officers to Zambia during October and that of two Malawi Air Force officers (with a transport aircraft) to Tanzania on Nov. 6—all of them having sought political asylum.

The three opposition movements in exile described below have never appeared to constitute a serious threat to the regime, and the opposition of members of the Jehovah's Witnesses sect has apparently been forcibly subdued.

Congress for the Second Republic

Leadership. M. W. Kanyama Chiume (l.).

M. W. K. Chiume was dismissed as Minister of External Affairs on Sept. 7, 1964 (i.e. shortly after Malawi had become independent in July of that year). Dr Hastings Banda (then Prime Minister) accused him in particular of having been "under the steering hand of the Chinese ambassador in Dar-es-Salaam", who was said to have offered Malawi a loan of £18,000,000 if in return Malawi granted diplomatic recognition to the People's Republic of China. Chiume admitted on Sept. 9 that such a loan had been offered but claimed that he had reported the offer to Dr Banda who, he said, had asked him to lead a delegation to Peking; he denied that he was a communist supporter. Chiume left Malawi for Lusaka (now in Zambia) on Oct. 5, 1964, and later reached Dar-es-Salaam, where he set up the Congress for the Second Republic. Dr Banda alleged on Oct. 10, 1965, that the People's Republic of China was supporting Chiume with funds and guns and was training infiltrators (against whom military operations were conducted in Malawi in April-November 1965).

Thereafter, nothing was heard of any activities by Chiume or his followers until May 1, 1976, when Dr Banda (who had become President of the Republic of Malawi in 1966) announced the arrest of a "group of agents" who had, he said, been sent by Chiume and had confessed that their mission had been to assassinate him (the President). On June 2, 1976, the President stated that Chiume had (in a letter in the President's possession) admitted that he had attempted to overthrow the Government of Malawi and that he had been refused help to this end by a communist country which he had approached (but which the President did not name); he also said that

followers of Chiume who had fled to Zambia were living there as "outcasts".

Malawi Freedom Movement (Mafremo)

Leadership. Orton Chirwa (l.).

Orton Chirwa was dismissed on Sept. 7, 1964 (i.e. shortly after Malawi had become independent in July of that year), as Minister of Justice and Attorney General—Dr Hastings Banda (then Prime Minister) having accused him and other ministers of wanting "to introduce bribery and corruption into ministerial posts". Chirwa had previously criticized Dr Banda's foreign policy as "fascist and dictatorial". He left the country for Tanganyika on Oct. 30, 1964, and was admitted to Britain as a political refugee on Dec. 8 of that year.

In 1977 he founded Mafremo in Dar-es-Salaam with the aim of restoring "democracy, justice and liberty" in Malawi. In the second half of 1981 he attempted, as reported in *The Guardian* on Jan. 19, 1982, to strengthen Mafremo and to forge some kind of unity with the Congress of the Second Republic (also based in Dar-es-Salaam) and the Socialist League of Malawi (based in Maputo, Mozambique). On Jan. 6, 1982, it was officially announced in Lilongwe that he and his wife and son had been arrested in Central province: it was later said that he had been connected with the murder of a chief (a supporter of Dr Banda) in 1964.

During the trial on charges of treason of Chirwa and his wife Vera, the prosecution produced on Aug. 6, 1982, inter alia 1,277 Mafremo membership cards allegedly brought into the country by the accused, a letter from Chirwa to an alleged national chairman of Mafremo in Malawi, the alleged Mafremo master plan of how to overthrow the Government, and the text of an oath of secrecy and allegiance of Mafremo members. Chirwa claimed on Aug. 12, however, that the alleged membership cards were forged, and he also claimed to have been arrested in Zambian territory in violation of international law. On Sept. 1 the prosecution also produced parts of an alleged agenda of a Mafremo conference held in Mbeya (Tanzania) on May 2, 1981, at which an attempt to unite all exiled Malawi political groups was said to have failed.

During the trial it emerged (on Sept. 6, 1982) that with the permission of the authorities Chirwa and his wife had been taken (partly by air) to three regions of the country and shown the development taking place in the country with a view to convincing them that their wish to overthrow the Government was not justified.

During subsequent trial proceedings, Chirwa denied in November 1982 that Mafremo intended to overthrow President Banda's Government and claimed that the meeting which he had convened in Tanzania in 1981 was merely meant to unify dissident political movements; later he reaffirmed, as reported on Nov. 26, his belief in political freedom, multi-party democracy and regular parliamentary elections. Late in February 1983 the court postponed its judgment "until further notice".

People's Liberation Army of Malawi—see under Socialist League of Malawi (Lesoma)

Socialist League of Malawi (Lesoma)

Leadership. Dr Attati Mpakati (or Mphakathi) (l.).

This organization was established in Maputo (Mozambique) and has claimed to have the support of Cuba and the Soviet Union. In 1979 Dr Mpakati was reported to have received a parcel bomb which blew his hands off, and in March 1979 President Banda of Malawi had "claimed credit" for this assassination attempt. In 1980 Lesoma was said to have formed a People's Liberation Army of Malawi, but there have been no reports of activities of such a force.

Jehovah's Witnesses

The sect of Jehovah's Witnesses (the Watchtower Bible and Tract Society, whose members are opposed to military service) was outlawed as a subversive organization by the Government of Malawi in October 1967. The police announced on Nov. 8 of that year that about 3,500 members (out of an estimated total of 18,000 in Malawi) had surrendered after being told that they would face up to seven years in prison unless they abandoned the sect. Four White missionaries of the sect were deported on that day and four others left the country of their own accord.

The Jehovah's Witnesses were nevertheless allowed to practise their religion and by 1972 they were said to number more than 20,000. On Sept. 17, 1972, President Banda declared at a congress of the Malawi Congress Party (MCP) in Zomba that members of the sect were "Devil's Witnesses" who neither believed in the Government nor wanted to pay tax. The congress thereupon adopted a resolution under which members of the sect would be deprived of their livelihood and expelled from their villages unless they joined the MCP. There followed violent action by members of the MCP's youth section and the paramilitary Young Pioneers against sect members failing to produce MCP membership cards, resulting in the flight of some 20,000 of them to Zambia.

Under an agreement between Zambia and Malawi announced on Dec. 6, 1972, and with the help of officials of the UN High Commissioner of Refugees, most of them were repatriated by Dec. 20, 1972 (while 342 had died and others had fled into the bush). In September-October 1975 between 3,000 and 4,000 members of the sect again fled to Zambia, but on Nov. 3 of that year it was officially stated in Zambia that they had all been repatriated.

The society's president (in Tulsa, Oklahoma) alleged in November 1975 that 30,000 members of his society were undergoing "severe and unjust persecution" in Malawi. From South Africa it was reported in December 1975 that some 18,000 Witnesses expelled from Mozambique (since this country achieved independence on June 25, 1975) had been moved to Malawi, but on March 17, 1976, it was reported that more than 12,000 had fled back to Mozambique (where 18,000 were held in a detention camp), and 3,000 were in a camp north of Lilongwe (Malawi's capital).

Maldives

Capital: Malé   Pop. 150,000

The Republic of Maldives, a special-status member of the Commonwealth, has an executive President elected for a five-year term by universal adult suffrage, a Cabinet presided over by the President and a 48-member People's Council (*Majlis*) to which 40 members are similarly elected for five years and the remaining eight are appointed by the President. There are no political parties and no organized dissident groups, although the Government of President Maumoon Abdul Gayoom (in power since November 1978) has found it necessary to take action against certain members of the former regime of President Ibrahim Nasir.

During 1979 the Government launched an investigation into the activities of officials of the former regime, in particular of Abdul Hanna, former Minister of Public Safety, who was charged with political persecution. The ex-minister was subsequently banished to a remote island of the Maldives archipelago, while 20 officials were sentenced to up to four years' banishment to such islands. On April 1, 1980, Mrs Moomina Ismail, former Minister of Health, was banished for four years for sedition (on a charge of inciting people to act against the Government).

On April 27, 1980, Ahmed Naseem (brother-in-law of ex-President Nasir) and two other men were given life sentences after being accused of plotting against President Gayoom with the aid of foreign mercenaries. The plot, it was alleged, had been foiled in February 1980 and had been masterminded by ex-President Nasir (who from his residence in Singapore denied all involvement in the alleged conspiracy). President Gayoom stated in Parliament on the same day that nine European mercenaries, led by a former Irish Republican Army chief, had been hired to assassinate him, and that Ahmed Naseem had been instrumental in preparing the plot. However, all the mercenaries involved, including nine former members of the British Special Air Services (SAS), had managed to leave Malé before being apprehended.

During a subsequent visit to Colombo (Sri Lanka), President Gayoom reiterated that ex-President Nasir had masterminded the February 1980 plot, and he added that the former President was to have arrived in Maldives on Feb. 15 to take over power from the existing regime.

Mauritius

Capital: Port Louis   Pop. 970,000

Mauritius is an independent state within the Commonwealth, with the British monarch as head of state being represented by a Governor-General. It has a Cabinet headed by a Prime Minister and a Legislative Assembly with 62 elective seats and additional seats (four in 1982) filled by the Supreme Court from among unsuccessful candidates with the greatest number of votes.

As a result of elections held on June 11, 1982, seats in the Legislative Assembly were distributed as follows: Mauritian Militant Movement (MMM) 42, Mauritian Socialist Party (PSM) 18, Organization of the People of Rodrigues (OPR) 2, Labour Party 2, Mauritian Social-Democratic Party (*Parti Mauricien Social-Démocratique*) 2. The elections were contested by a total of 34 parties, and the voting turnout was estimated at about 90 per cent.

Internal unrest in Mauritius has arisen mainly in connexion with labour disputes, in particular a general strike from Aug. 13-24, 1979, which led to the burning by strikers of some 30,000 tonnes of sugar and 2,000 acres of cane, but which was ended by an agreement on working hours and increased pay. There appears to be no organized extra-parliamentary opposition to the left-wing MMM-led Government in power since the overwhelming defeat of the longstanding Labour-led coalition in the June 1982 elections.

Mozambique

Capital: Maputo   Pop. 12,000,000

The People's Republic of Mozambique is, under its 1975 Constitution, "a sovereign, independent and democratic state" in which "power belongs to the workers and peasants united and led by Frelimo"—the Front for the Liberation of Mozambique—which is "the leading force of the state and society". The president of Frelimo is also head of state and of the Council of Ministers. The state's supreme organ is the People's Assembly of 226 members indirectly elected (by an intricate system leading to the election of provincial councils which elect, from among themselves, the Assembly's members, all candidates having been chosen from a list drawn up by Frelimo).

On Feb. 28, 1979, the People's Assembly passed a law providing for the imposition of the death penalty for certain crimes against the security of the people and the state and for those whose reintegration into society appeared impossible. Revolutionary military courts were set up under a law of March 30, 1979. The main threat to the Government of President Samora Machel has come from an anti-communist national resistance movement alleged to receive South African support—if only as a means of "destabilizing" the rule of Frelimo.

Mozambican National Resistance (*Resistência Nacional Moçambicana,* RNM)

Leadership. Afonso Dlakama (pres.); Evo Fernandes (director of planning and spokesman in Lisbon).

This organization was set up mainly by Mozambicans who had fled to Rhodesia to escape the Frelimo regime, and with the alleged help of the Smith regime in Rhodesia. From 1976 onwards, RNM guerrillas were active in Mozambique, at first near the Rhodesian border, but by 1979 they had penetrated further into Manica and northern Sofala provinces. During that year 36 persons were sentenced to death by Mozambican revolutionary military courts for treason and sabotage (attributed not only to RNM guerrillas but also to Rhodesian agents, the Government alleging in September 1979 that rebel activity inside Mozambique was due to a combination of Rhodesian officers, mercenaries and traitors).

In May 1980 the Government of Mozambique accused South Africa of supplying the RNM and of having set up a base for training its members in the northern Transvaal. On May 13, 1980, RNM members attacked a dam near Mavuze, destroying two turbines and cutting off power to Beira for 14 hours. On July 10, 1980, Mozambique claimed that 272 rebels had been killed and over 300 captured in an attack on the RNM's main camp in western Manica province on June 30. During the latter part of 1980 and in 1981 the RNM guerrillas extended their activities, destroying villages south of the Beira-Umtali (Mutare) railway line, which was closed between Sept. 21 and Oct. 3, 1980, after the RNM had derailed a train.

On Nov. 29, 1980, RNM guerrillas attacked one of the stations at the Cabora Bassa hydroelectric complex on the Zambezi River, cutting off power supplies to South Africa, and a further such attack was made on April 10, 1981; supplies were not resumed until November 1981. In June 1981 the RNM attacked communal villages set up by Frelimo. The RNM further cut power lines, road and rail links and the oil pipeline from Mozambique to Zimbabwe between August and October 1981. RNM action also temporarily destroyed eight channel marker buoys in Beira harbour on Nov. 13, 1981.

According to Mozambican official statements made on several occasions during 1981, the RNM was then supported not only by former members of the Rhodesian secret service but also by the South African Defence Force, which was alleged to have supplied both arms and military instructors to the RNM guerrillas. The Mozambican news agency AIM claimed in particular that Mozambican forces, capturing a major RNM base in Manica province on Dec. 7, had found documentary evidence of such support. However, both South Africa and the RNM categorically denied that such aid had been given.

By June 1982 the RNM claimed that the area of its activities covered more than half of Mozambique's 10 provinces, and that the "rapid advance towards our ultimate goal of shaking the parasite Frelimo yoke imposed on the nation could not have been achieved without the widespread and spontaneous support of the population". The RNM also gave a warning that it would treat as enemies any Portuguese military personnel sent to Mozambique as advisers at the request of the Government of Mozambique. The RNM claims were, however, challenged by Western observers, according to whom the RNM guerrillas operated only in rural areas inhabited by less than a quarter of the country's population, and they had only about 3,000 trained fighters (with more than that number still being trained). Nevertheless their frequent sabotage actions disrupted transport in important areas, which included parts of the Niassa and Zambezi provinces (where a separate organization known as *Africa Livre,* established in 1965, had been engaged in sabotage with varying success).

The numerous guerrilla actions carried out by the RNM from late 1981 to early 1983 included the abduction of foreigners (among them a British ecologist held by the RNM from Dec. 17, 1981, to May 24, 1982); sabotage of the Maputo to Zimbabwe railway line and of power lines from the Cabora Bassa hydroelectric complex in December 1981 (and of the latter also on Aug. 14, 1982); attacks on traffic between Malawi and Mozambique; the seizure of six Bulgarian road engineers (who were freed on Nov. 2, 1982); and the destruction of several months' oil supplies in the oil depot in Beira on Dec. 8, 1982. After the last-named attack five Mozambicans were sentenced to death and a British shipping agent to 20 years in prison for involvement in sabotage and terrorism (as reported from Maputo on Feb. 22, 1983).

In September 1982 Mozambican officials claimed that RNM forces were operating from bases in Malawi. On the other hand RNM activities were obviously inflicting great damage on the economy of Malawi, and following a visit to Malawi by the Foreign Minister of Mozambique on Oct. 17, 1982, it appeared that facilities for the RNM in Malawi had been closed down.

On the question of alleged South African support for the RNM, conflicting statements were made during the second half of 1982. A member of the RNM's executive council said on Aug. 23 (before setting out on a visit to Europe) that he hoped to dispel the RNM's image as a guerrilla band used by South Africa, and he claimed that its 12,000 members obtained their weapons from the West and not from South Africa. On the other hand, a British mercenary stated on Nov. 3 that South Africa was recruiting and training mercenaries from several countries to fight with the RNM, and that these were being infiltrated into Mozambique by the South African Defence Force (which, however, denied this allegation).

On March 17, 1983, the RNM's radio station—*Voz da África Livre* ("Voice of Free Africa", said to be broadcasting from South Africa)—announced that the first assembly of military and political cadres of the RNM had been held in Geneva; it was also claimed that a government-in-exile had been set up with a six-member cabinet.

The RNM had occasionally published a journal. *A Luta Continua* ("The Struggle Continues"), in Cascais (Portugal). It has set

out its aim as the establishment of an independent, non-communist Mozambique which would not favour development projects of foreign concerns.

United Mozambique Front (*Frente Unida Moçambicana,* FUMO)

Leadership. João Khan (pres.).

This Front was set up in 1974 by Portuguese business elements with a view to protecting their interests in an independent Mozambique. During 1980 FUMO, then based in Portugal, was reported to be making efforts among émigrés from Mozambique to set up forces to fight the Frelimo regime; FUMO leaders refused, however, to cooperate in any way with the Mozambican National Resistance (RNM).

Namibia

Capital: Windhoek   Pop. 1,037,000

The territory of Namibia (South West Africa), a former League of Nations mandate administered as an integral part of South Africa, was in October 1966 declared to be under United Nations responsibility; in fact, however, it continued to be under the control of the Republic of South Africa. The latter appointed, on July 6, 1977, an Administrator-General for a transitional period which was to lead to the territory's independence. The South African Government took further steps, without United Nations consent, (i) by holding elections (by universal adult suffrage) in December 1978 of a 50-member Constituent Assembly which was, in May 1979, converted into a National Assembly with legislative powers (and with the addition of 15 nominated members); (ii) by creating, on July 1, 1980, a 12-member Council of Ministers with executive powers in internal matters (subject to the veto of the Administrator-General, and with the South African Government retaining responsibility for constitutional matters, foreign affairs and overall security), while with effect from Aug. 1, 1980, the Council of Ministers also controlled a defence force, the "South West African Territorial Forces", and from Sept. 1, 1980, the police (except the security police); and (iii) by holding elections for Administrative Assemblies in eight of the territory's ethnic areas in November 1980. The elections for the National and the Administrative Assemblies were contested by a number of political parties, among which the (multiracial) Democratic Turnhalle Alliance (DTA) held an absolute majority in the National Assembly. All elections were boycotted by the South West Africa People's Organization (SWAPO), the territory's liberation movement.

However, on Jan. 18, 1983, the National Assembly was dissolved after the Council of Ministers had resigned following the failure of the president of the DTA (Peter Kalangula) to convert the Alliance into a unitary party, as well as serious disputes between the DTA and the Administrator-General. The latter thereupon took over the government of the territory until an independence plan could be agreed.

People's Liberation Army of Namibia (PLAN)—see under South West Africa People's Organization (SWAPO)

South West Africa People's Organization (SWAPO)

Leadership. Sam Nujoma (pres.); Moses Garoeb (admin. sec.); Daniel Merero (nat. ch.); Theo-Ben Gurirab (representative at the United Nations).

SWAPO was founded in June 1960 by Hermann Toivo ja Toivo (who later received a 20-year prison sentence in 1968 for offences under the South African "Terrorism Act" of 1967). It replaced an earlier Ovamboland People's Organization (created in 1957) with the object of gaining support from ethnic groups other than the Ovambos. SWAPO gradually absorbed smaller parties from various parts of the territory, among them the Caprivi African National Union. By 1976 the 14-member internal executive of SWAPO comprised seven Hereros, five Ovambos, a Rehoboth Baster and a Coloured (mixed-race) woman, while the external executive included three Damaras, a Herero, a Nama and an East Caprivian.

In its early years SWAPO sent petitions to the United Nations in order to gain that organization's support. These petitions asked the United Nations to terminate immediately the League of Nations mandate, to entrust the temporary administration of the territory to a UN commission composed of African states, to arrange for free general elections to enable South West Africa to accede to (i) self-government immediately through the establishment of a democratic African government based on the principle of one man, one vote, and (ii) independence not later than 1963. The UN General Assembly and various UN committees passed successive resolutions condemning South Africa's policies in the territory. Sam Nujoma addressed the UN Special Committee of 24 (on the ending of colonialism) in May 1964 and specifically opposed the implementation of the "Odendaal Report", a South African plan to divide the territory into distinct ethnic areas.

SWAPO's guerrilla operations, supported from the outset by the liberation committee of the Organization of African Unity (OAU) as a means of furthering the eventual independence of South West Africa, began in September 1965. In August 1966 conflicting statements were made by SWAPO and the South African authorities on the nature of, and casualties caused in, clashes between guerrillas and South African armed forces. The South African Deputy Minister of Justice said on Sept. 22, 1966, that documents found on arrested guerrillas showed that SWAPO was part of a communist conspiracy. The first mass trial of SWAPO guerrillas ended in

Pretoria on Feb. 9, 1968, when 30 men were sentenced to imprisonment—19 of them for life, nine to 20 years each (among them H. Toivo ja Toivo) and two to five years each—on charges of taking part in a SWAPO conspiracy to overthrow the Government of South West Africa. On appeal five of the life sentences were on Nov. 22, 1968, reduced to 20 years in prison.

After SWAPO guerrilla activities had continued (especially in the Caprivi Strip) during 1968, another trial of alleged guerrillas ended in Windhoek on Aug. 22, 1969, when five Ovambos were sentenced to life imprisonment for conspiracy with 96 accomplices to overthrow the Government and replace it with a SWAPO-led regime.

At the United Nations the Security Council called, on March 20, 1969, for South Africa's immediate withdrawal from Namibia, the voting being 13 to none, with Britain and France abstaining. At a meeting with a special representative of the UN Secretary-General early in October 1972 Nujoma reiterated SWAPO's demand for South Africa's "immediate and total withdrawal" from South West Africa. SWAPO also insisted on the territory's independence as a unitary state. It therefore opposed South African measures whereby Ovamboland became the first self-governing territory of South West Africa on May 1, 1973, and SWAPO also boycotted elections held to elective seats in an Ovamboland Legislative Council on Aug. 2-3, 1973.

Before the UN Council for Namibia (created in May 1967), Nujoma declared in May 1973 that the people of Namibia rejected further diplomatic contacts (which had failed to lead to any agreement on eventual independence for Namibia) and that an "intensification of armed liberation struggle" was "the only language" which the South Africans understood. On Dec. 11, 1973, the UN General Assembly passed a resolution, by 107 votes to two (Portugal and South Africa) and with 17 abstentions, recognizing SWAPO as the "authentic representative of the Namibian people".

As more and more SWAPO followers were being arrested in South West Africa, a growing number of Africans, notably Ovambos, left the territory for Angola, where a UN High Commissioner for Namibia had assumed office on Feb. 1, 1974.

In December 1974 the British Government decided to develop contacts with SWAPO, and on Jan. 1, 1975, the British Prime Minister (James Callaghan) had talks with a SWAPO delegation in Lusaka (Zambia), during which he expressed the hope that the talks would help in moves to full independence for Namibia, while SWAPO leaders expressed appreciation of financial aid received from Britain.

SWAPO again boycotted elections in Ovamboland, held on Jan. 13-17, 1975, to fill 42 elective seats in an enlarged Legislative Council. The result of the election, in which 55 per cent of the voters were officially stated to have taken part, was interpreted by the South African authorities as a "rejection of SWAPO".

Nujoma issued a statement on Jan. 17, 1975. offering to negotiate with the South African Government on six preconditions, failing acceptance of which SWAPO would renew its guerrilla warfare. The conditions were that (i) South Africa publicly recognized the right of the Namibian people to independence and national sovereignty; (ii) Namibia's territorial integrity was inviolate and respected; (iii) SWAPO was recognized and accepted as the only authentic representative of the Namibian people; (iv) all political prisoners in Namibia and South Africa were released; (v) all Namibians in exile were allowed to return without fear of arrest or victimization; and (vi) South Africa undertook, before any talks began, to withdraw all troops and police from Namibia.

The South African Prime Minister (B. J. Vorster) had said on Dec. 31, 1974, that SWAPO was not South West Africa and that its so-called leaders outside the territory were "neither the natural nor the elected leaders of any of the peoples" and would "not be imposed upon them by any outside organization".

As a result of a meeting between 800 and 1,000 delegates held at Katatura, Windhoek, at the end of February 1975, SWAPO formed, with three other parties, a new Namibian National Convention, while a minority remained within the existing National Convention (of two Herero groups and the chiefs of the Nama people).

On April 18, 1975, B. J. Vorster said that he would ask leaders of non-White organizations in South West Africa to join in talks with the African chairman of the UN Council for Namibia or with the special committee of the OAU on the future of South West Africa—but he made it clear that he would not include SWAPO because it had been "fathered in 1957 by four [South African] Communists" and its aims were to unite the inhabitants of the territory in one political organization, establish independence "with the co-operation of freedom movements" and confiscate the lands of Blacks and Whites who did not support SWAPO.

On May 20, 1975, B. J. Vorster again made it clear that he could not accept the role proposed for SWAPO by the United Nations and the OAU (which had, on April 11, 1975, demanded that South Africa should recognize SWAPO as the sole representative of the Namibian people).

SWAPO also boycotted a constitutional conference called by the South African administration and held at the Turnhalle in Windhoek beginning on Sept. 1, 1975. On that date SWAPO released its own proposals for a Namibian constitution, under which Namibia was to become a republic with a president elected by the people and a cabinet chosen from a single-chamber legislature. On Dec. 2, 1975, the Government of the neighbouring Republic of Botswana recognized SWAPO as the only legitimate representative of the people of Namibia.

The continuation of SWAPO guerrilla activities in Ovamboland led to the proclamation of new emergency regulations on May 19, 1976, and to the establishment of a 1,000-metre wide strip as a specially prohibited area along the border with Angola.

On Aug. 2, 1976, it became clear that dissenting members of SWAPO had been expelled from the movement, when Nujoma declared in Lusaka (Zambia) that "agents of the South African regime and imperialists" had been "rooted out of our movement". It had earlier been revealed (in May 1976) that at least 40 SWAPO members, among them Andreas Shipanga (the Organization's secretary for information), were being held in a camp by the Zambian authorities, and on July 28 it was disclosed that 11 of them (including Shipanga) had been moved to Tanzania on July 18. However, in May 1978 he and other former SWAPO members were released and returned to Namibia, where Shipanga formed a new party, the SWAPO-Democrats, during the following month. Like SWAPO, this new party also boycotted the elections to a Constituent Assembly in December 1978.

On Aug. 10, 1976, a SWAPO delegation reached Moscow for talks with Soviet leaders on the future of Namibia, and in October 1976, Nujoma had talks with Dr Fidel Castro, the Cuban leader, after which he stated (on Oct. 3) that Cuba was giving SWAPO "political, material, diplomatic and political support". SWAPO's administrative secretary confirmed on Oct. 20 that SWAPO needed more weapons, which it would get from "friends" who supported its stand. SWAPO also received material aid, though not weapons, from Scandinavian countries and the European Commission.

After SWAPO had rejected the constitutional proposals made at the Turnhalle negotiations, the information and publicity secretary of SWAPO's internal wing (Daniel Tjongarero) said on Aug. 30, 1976, that SWAPO insisted on the holding of elections on the basis of one man, one vote for political parties rather than ethnic groups, and only after withdrawal of South Africa's "occupying forces". He also declared that the United Nations had entrusted SWAPO with "the sole responsibility for liberating the country'' but did not regard SWAPO as the only political force in Namibia; he added that SWAPO envisaged no direct takeover of the territory, which should be handed over to the United Nations for a transitional period, during which other political groups would also play a major role.

The UN General Assembly decided on Dec. 20, 1976, to grant SWAPO observer status and to invite it to participate in the Assembly's sessions and in the work of all international conferences convened under the Assembly's auspices. In October-November 1976 and April 1977 SWAPO was strengthened by the accession of six political groups until then considered to be moderate, viz. four Nama breakaway groups, the Namibian African People's Democratic Organization (NAPDO) and a Herero royalist association.

By 1977 the armed wing of SWAPO was known as the People's Liberation Army of Namibia (PLAN), its supreme commander being named as Dimo Hamamba. At that time the guerrillas engaged not only in the laying of land mines but also in the abduction of young Ovambos from mission schools who were taken to Angola for training. Even before the South African-sponsored constitutional (Turnhalle) conference had decided (in March 1977) to set up an interim Government, SWAPO had declared that it had no alternative but to fight on the battlefield "however long it might take" and that only an international conference would eventually bring the war to an end. Of SWAPO's aims, Nujoma said on Feb. 4, 1977: "We are an African party which believes in neutrality and non-alignment." He admitted that SWAPO was receiving "large donations from Soviet Russia" but added that this did not mean that SWAPO automatically followed Soviet foreign and international policy.

On June 17, 1977, Nujoma declared his support for the efforts of five Western member states of the UN Security Council (Britain, France, Canada, the Federal Republic of Germany and the United States) to find a peaceful way of bringing Namibia to independence; he also said that, although he did not accept a South African-appointed Administrator-General for the territory, he would accept one appointed by the UN Council for Namibia; that SWAPO would take part in free elections as long as all South African troops were first withdrawn; and that SWAPO would accept the presence of a UN peacekeeping force during the interim period before independence.

Following the assumption of office by the territory's first (South African) Administrator-General on Sept. 1, 1977, SWAPO and other opposition groups were allowed to hold political meetings, and the emergency regulations in force in the three northern "homelands" (Ovambo, Kavango, and East Caprivi) were repealed. SWAPO, however, declined to have any discussions with the Administrator-General (whom it regarded as illegal) on SWAPO participation in general elections, and at the end of September 1977 SWAPO's central committee decided to reject "bogus elections under the armed forces with a view to installing a puppet neo-colonial Turnhalle regime" and to continue and intensify the armed struggle.

At that time South African estimates of the strength of SWAPO's guerrilla forces were of some 300 in Ovamboland, 2,000 in Angola and 1,400 in Zambia (north of the Caprivi Strip). From September 1977 onwards the guerrillas' activities increased significantly, and conflicting claims were made on both sides regarding the number of casualties inflicted.

The South African Prime Minister (B. J. Vorster) said in September 1977 that, if SWAPO did not agree to a ceasefire involving an end to hostilities and the dismantling of landmines already laid, elections would be held without SWAPO participation. SWAPO, on the other hand, announced on Oct. 15, 1977, that it would not accept any settlement plan which did not include (i) a total withdrawal of South Africa's troops (as a precondition) and (ii) the retention of the port of Walvis Bay as part of Namibia (whereas the South African Government had proclaimed its resumption of control, with effect from Sept. 1, 1977, over Walvis Bay as part of the Cape Province, which it had been until 1922).

In early 1978 the external and internal branches of SWAPO issued conflicting statements about SWAPO's aims. Nujoma declared on Feb. 26 inter alia that "majority rule" was "out", stating: "We are not fighting for majority rule. We are fighting to seize power in Namibia for the benefit of the Namibian people. We are revolutionaries, we are not counter-revolutionaries." The publicity secretary for SWAPO's internal branch, however, said on Feb. 28 that SWAPO wished "to establish in Namibia a democratic secular government founded on the will and the participation of all the Namibian people"; that it was prepared to test its strength in "free and fair elections"; and that it would accept the same restrictions on the movements of its active forces in northern Namibia as those applying to the South African troops, and also the presence of a "token force" of 1,500 such troops in Namibia up to the elections. The South African Government in principle accepted the Western powers' proposals on April 25, 1978.

During February-March 1978 there were serious clashes between SWAPO and Democratic Turnhalle Alliance (DTA) supporters, leading inter alia to the death of an Ovambo minister and to that of Chief Clemens Kapuuo (president of the DTA). Among persons detained under a new internal security proclamation in April 1978 were nine of the 13 members of the executive committee of SWAPO's internal wing.

On May 4, 1978, the South African Minister of Defence (then P. W. Botha) announced that in a "limited operation" against SWAPO forces South African troops had invaded Angola, and according to Angolan sources they had reached Cassinga (a town 115 miles north of the Namibian border) and hundreds of persons, mainly Namibian refugees, had been killed. SWAPO announced in New York on May 8 that in view of the "grave situation" created by the South African invasion of Angola SWAPO would take no further part in negotiations with the five Western powers. Nevertheless SWAPO endorsed the five-power agreement (providing for Namibia's independence to be achieved by Dec. 31, 1978) on July 12, and the UN Security Council endorsed the plan on July 22. On the other hand, the question of Walvis Bay remained unresolved, with the South African Government making it clear that it would break off all discussions if the UN Security Council insisted that Walvis Bay should be reintegrated in Namibia (as demanded by SWAPO and also the five Western powers). After the UN Security Council had passed, on July 27, 1978, two resolutions—the second of which (adopted unanimously) declared that Walvis Bay must be reintegrated within Namibia—the South African Government decided on July 31 to withhold its final approval of the UN plan for transition to independence, based on the Western powers' proposals and containing no reference to the Walvis Bay question.

New proposals made by the UN Secretary-General on the basis of a report by the UN Commissioner for Namibia (who had visited the territory in August 1978) were approved by SWAPO on Sept. 4, 1978, but rejected by the South African Government on Sept. 20, when it was announced that elections would be held (without UN supervision) to a Constituent Assembly on Nov. 20-24, 1978; any participation in these elections was immediately rejected by SWAPO on Sept. 22. After further negotiations the South African Government agreed on Oct. 19 that the proposed elections—then rescheduled for Dec. 4-8, 1978—were to be followed by UN-supervised elections at a later date. SWAPO strongly opposed this compromise and called for a UN Security Council meeting to improve "comprehensive mandatory economic sanctions" on South Africa, but no such resolution was in fact passed.

The South African-organized elections, in which 80.2 per cent of the electorate was officially stated to have taken part, gave the DTA an overwhelming overall majority (of 41 out of 50 seats) in the Constituent Assembly. At a closed session the Assembly agreed, on Dec. 21, 1978, in principle to the holding of UN-supervised elections in 1979—but only provided several conditions were met.

The then vice-chairman of SWAPO's internal wing, Daniel Tjongarero, said on Jan. 4, 1979, that SWAPO would take part in the proposed UN-supervised elections provided no changes were made in the UN Secretary-General's independence plan. The central committee of SWAPO's external wing, however, made no such statement but reiterated on Jan. 9 that it would continue its armed struggle as the only means of achieving genuine liberation for Namibia.

Renewed SWAPO attacks on South African military camps in Ovamboland in February 1979 induced R. F. Botha, the South African Foreign Minister, to point out to the UN Secretary-General that "the whole delicate edifice of agreement" on a Namibian settlement was "in danger of collapse". He said that SWAPO was seeking to block the settlement, especially by making "outrageous demands"—including the establishment (by SWAPO) of five armed bases inside South West Africa, the complete withdrawal of South African troops and the refusal to place SWAPO forces under UN monitoring.

In the absence of any final agreement on the modalities of achieving a transition to independence, the South West African Constituent Assembly decided on May 2, 1979, to set itself up as a National Assembly (with the addition of up to 15 nominated members) with wide-ranging legislative powers. S. Nujoma thereupon declared in Luanda on May 15 that this step had virtually destroyed efforts to solve the Namibian problem through negotiation. In the meantime South African forces had carried out more raids on targets in Angola and Zambia, claiming on March 11 to have destroyed more than 12 SWAPO bases.

In view of SWAPO activities inside South West Africa, 39 SWAPO officers were detained under internal security regulations while, of its leaders, Tjongarero and Mokganedi Thlabanello (publicity and information secretary) had left the territory before these arrests. SWAPO's offices in Windhoek were demolished on May 6, allegedly by members of a White Resistance Movement. According to P. W. Botha (speaking in the Cape Town House of Assembly on May 11), 61 civilians, 11 Defence Force members, five home guard members and one policeman had been killed by "terrorists" since the beginning of 1979. In a report to the UN Security Council during July 1979 the Government of Angola claimed that South African incursions had caused damage estimated at $293,000,000, the death of at least 530 Angolans and injury to 594 others. The report also referred to three South Africans killed and eight wounded, 198 Zimbabweans killed and 600 wounded, and 612 Namibians killed and 611 wounded.

Following the destruction of SWAPO's offices in Windhoek, Tjongarero dissolved the organization's national executive branch within Namibia (of which he had been the leader) in June 1979, but in August of that year SWAPO's central committee decided in Angola that he had acted unconstitutionally and declared his action null and void, and he was relieved of his position in September 1979. On July 22, 1980, the central committee expelled three of its members and six other officials (all from the Caprivi Strip) for alleged counter-revolutionary and secessionist activities aimed at dismembering Namibia's national territory by accepting separate independence for the Caprivi Strip. Those expelled included Mishake Albert Muyongo (acting vice-president of SWAPO), who announced in Lusaka (Zambia) on Aug. 6 that he would reassert the separate existence of the Caprivi African National Union (CANU, which had been one of SWAPO's constituent parties); however, the Zambian Government did not allow CANU to be established in Zambia, and it was officially alleged in Windhoek that numerous Caprivians were being detained in Zambia.

In the absence of any agreement between the United Nations, the five Western members of the UN Security Council, the South African Government and SWAPO on the modalities of transition to independence for Namibia, the armed struggle between SWAPO units and South African forces continued during 1980. It was marked by further South African raids into Angola in November-December 1979 and June-August 1980. According to official figures released by the military authorities in Windhoek on Jan. 6, 1981, a total of 1,467 SWAPO guerrillas were killed in 1980 (nearly three times as many as in 1979), and South African casualties had been 72 in all. In mid-1981 the number of SWAPO guerrillas inside Namibia was estimated (in *The Times* of July 15) at about 600, but there were between 6,000 and 8,000 based in Angola (according to the *International Herald Tribune* of June 8).

So-called "hot pursuit" operations by South African and territorial forces invading Angola in May-August 1981 resulted in some 1,000 deaths (according to South African military sources, which claimed on July 30 that South African forces had shattered the command structure of two out of three regional SWAPO headquarters). The Angolan President denied on Sept. 10, 1981, that South Africa had directed its attack against SWAPO and declared that the raid had been "an attack on the defenceless Angolan population and against our regular forces", and

that South Africa was strengthening the (Angolan opposition) National Union for the Total Independence of Angola (UNITA) to "make the settlement of the Namibian problem more difficult".

During their mid-1981 operation South African forces captured one Soviet officer and killed four others, and claimed to have discovered an "enormous amount of Soviet propaganda material", in connexion with which Gen. Magnus Malan, the South African Minister of Defence, stated on Sept. 1, 1981, that there could be no doubt that SWAPO was "directly controlled and given ideological and material support by the Soviet Union". The Angolan ambassador to France admitted on Sept. 2 that there were Soviet experts and advisers in Angola, as they were needed for training Angolans in the use of sophisticated Soviet equipment, but he denied that Soviet troops were working with SWAPO (and this was also denied by Sam Nujoma in Luanda on Sept. 5, 1981).

Further South African incursions into Angola on Nov. 1-20, 1981, resulted, according to South African sources, in the destruction of SWAPO's central headquarters at Chitequeta (some 140 miles north of the Namibian-Angolan border) and in the shooting-down of a MiG-21 fighter by the South African Air Force on Nov. 6, as well as in the death of 71 SWAPO guerrillas (against the loss of four South African soldiers' lives). The Angolan news agency claimed that nine Angolan soldiers and 33 Angolan citizens had also been killed during this action.

According to a South African statement made in January 1982, a total of 1,494 SWAPO insurgents had died in fighting with security forces in 1981 (excluding the raid into Angola in August of that year), against 72 security forces casualties and 172 civilians killed. The General Officer Commanding the South West African Territorial Forces, however, conceded on April 20, 1982, that SWAPO infiltration had been in greater numbers over a greater area and with stronger weapons and more attacks (the weapons used having included SAM-7 missiles and RPG-7 rocket launchers).

Further South African raids were undertaken into Angola in March-May 1982, and on Aug. 11 a spokesman for the South African Defence Force claimed that 314 SWAPO guerrillas had been killed in a major battle on the border; he admitted that a South African helicopter had been shot down with the loss of 15 lives. The Angolan Defence Ministry claimed on Aug. 28 that 5,500 South African troops were operating in southern Angola, while another 30,000 were massing on the Namibian border in preparation for an invasion.

The Chief of the South African Defence Force declared on Dec. 2, 1982, that South

Africa was "capable of maintaining the situation for a long time to come or until a lasting solution is arrived at". SWAPO, on the other hand, asserted that its guerrillas were operating in most of the northern half of Namibia, where they had launched "more than 800 attacks against military targets".

Casualty figures for the year 1982, as given officially in South Africa on Dec. 29 of that year, were 1,268 SWAPO guerrillas, 77 members of the security forces and at least 2,139 civilians killed in the fighting. Among those killed by an anti-tank mine in Ovamboland on Nov. 25 was Pastor Cornelius Ndjoba, former president of the DTA and former chairman of the Ovambo Executive Committee. SWAPO, however, rejected the official South African casualty figures and claimed that most of the persons killed by South African forces were Namibian or Angolan civilians.

In South African church circles it is believed that SWAPO enjoyed wide support among the people of Namibia. Bishop Desmond Tutu, secretary-general of the South African Council of Churches (SACC), declared after a visit which he had paid to Namibia in February 1982 as participant in an SACC delegation that in the view of all but one of the church leaders to whom the delegation had spoken SWAPO had the support of the majority of the people of Namibia. The Most Rev. Denis Hurley, Roman Catholic Archbishop of Durban, presenting a report of the Southern African Catholic Bishops' Conference, claimed on May 14, 1982, that the majority of the Namibians regarded the South African Army as an army of occupation, but he added that atrocities had been committed by both SWAPO and South African forces.

With regard to SWAPO's international connexions, R. F. Botha, the South African Minister of Foreign Affairs, said on Nov. 1, 1978, that external aid to SWAPO from the five Western members of the UN Security Council, the Scandinavian countries, the Netherlands and Belgium (i.e excluding financial aid and military equipment supplied by the Soviet Union and its allies), amounted to $79,000,000 a year in direct or indirect contributions, the latter through an international fund from which SWAPO drew or was given certain amounts. On Feb. 23, 1979, R. F. Botha stated that during 1978 the United Nations and its agencies had given SWAPO $5,935,380. SWAPO became a full member of the movement of non-aligned countries on Oct. 2, 1978. It is also a member of the International Labour Organization, and has had permanent observer status at the United Nations since 1976.

The UN Council for Namibia has set up, in Lusaka (Zambia), a UN Institute for Namibia for the training in development studies and management of officials for a future SWAPO Government in Namibia.

Seychelles

Capital: Victoria (on Mahé)   Pop. 66,000

The Republic of Seychelles, a member of the Commonwealth, has an executive President elected by universal adult suffrage at the same time as a National Assembly (to which 13 members are elected on a list presented by the Seychelles People's Progressive Front, the country's sole legal political organization, and another two members are appointed to represent small islands without fixed population). The President is head of the Cabinet and also holds portfolios while there are seven other ministers.

Since the overthrow of President James Mancham in June 1977, the left-wing Government of President France Albert René has survived two major coup attempts involving foreign mercenaries. On Nov. 16, 1979, it was announced that a plot "sponsored from abroad with the co-operation of mercenaries" standing ready in Durban (South Africa) had been uncovered and that a number of persons had been arrested; several French nationals said to have been involved in the plot were recalled by the French Government and others were deported. A further attempt to overthrow the Seychelles Government was made on Nov. 25, 1981, by a group of mercenaries led by Col. Michael Hoare (who had been a leader of mercenaries in the Congo in 1964-65) and consisting mainly of South Africans. The coup was foiled by the

Seychelles Defence Force, and seven of the mercenaries were arrested in Seychelles while 45 of them returned to South Africa in an Indian airliner which they had commandeered.

On July 6-7, 1982, a court presided over by the Chief Justice of Seychelles sentenced four of the mercenaries to death and two others to 20 and 10 years in prison respectively on a charge of treason and illegal import of firearms. In Pietermaritzburg (South Africa) the Natal Supreme Court sentenced, on July 29, 1982, a total of 42 of the mercenaries, among them Col. Hoare, to effective prison terms ranging from six months to 10 years on charges arising from the hijacking of the Indian airliner. During the trial the South African Government admitted that members of the South African Defence Force had been involved in the attempt but stated that neither the Government nor the State Security Council had been aware of it.

Movement for Resistance (*Mouvement pour la Résistance*)

Following student protest demonstrations held on Oct. 11-12, 1979, against government plans to introduce compulsory national service for young people above the age of 15 years, the Movement for Resistance distributed leaflets calling for the resignation of the Government, the withdrawal of Tanzanian troops (which had been present in Seychelles since 1977, when the regime of President James Mancham was overthrown) and the holding of elections under international control.

Paul Chow, a spokesman for the Movement, claimed in London on Nov. 28, 1981, that it consisted of people who had been "forced into exile by the illegal and oppressive regime of France Albert René" and intended to achieve "the restoration of democracy in Seychelles"; he also said that the Movement's first choice as President of Seychelles would be ex-President Mancham, but denied that the latter was involved in the South African-backed attempt to overthrow the Seychelles Government in November 1981. On the other hand, Chow claimed on Nov. 29, 1981, that some 100 Seychelles exiles had backed the attempted coup with finance and other help.

Seychelles Liberation Committee

This Committee was established in 1979 by exiles in Paris with the aim of seeking the overthrow of President France Albert René and the abolition of the one-party system.

Seychelles Popular Anti-Marxist Front (SPAMF)

It was reported by Johannesburg radio on Dec. 3, 1981, that the SPAMF had disclosed that it had had prior knowledge of the abortive coup led by Col. Michael Hoare the previous month but had decided not to participate because it regarded the plan as unworkable and foolhardy. However, a SPAMF spokesman also revealed that his group had sought the backing of the South African Government for a large-scale coup attempt of its own but had been turned down because the South African authorities stated that they could not afford to be involved in such adventures.

South Africa

Capitals: Pretoria (administrative)   Pop. 24,700,000
              Cape Town (legislative)
              Bloemfontein (judicial)

The Republic of South Africa is a unitary independent state in which the right to vote for and to be elected to Parliament and any of the four Provincial Councils is reserved for White citizens above the age of 18 years. There is a unicameral Parliament, the House of Assembly, consisting of (i) 165 members elected for a five-year term by direct popular vote of Whites and (ii) 20 members appointed by the State President, who is himself elected for a seven-year term by an electoral college consisting of the members of Parliament. The State President is assisted by a Vice State-President and by an advisory 60-member President's Council comprising White, Coloured (i.e. mixed-race), Indian and Chinese (but not African) representatives.

At the end of 1982 political parties held elective seats in the House of Assembly as follows: National Party 118, Progressive Federal Party 26, Conservative Party of South Africa 18, New Republic Party 8. Of parties not represented in the House, the strongest is the Reconstituted National Party *(Herstigte Nasionale Party),* which in the 1981 elections obtained 13.8 per cent of the valid votes but no seats.

The fundamental political issue in South Africa has been, and remains, the lack of political representation both at provincial and at national level of the non-White population, representing about four-fifths of the total, not including the inhabitants of the four "independent" Black homelands of Bophuthatswana, Ciskei, Transkei and Venda (whose population is excluded from the South African total given above). Among organizations campaigning for political rights of the non-Whites (and not only for the removal of all discrimination against them in the fields of rights of residence, employment and education, and for freedom of association and movement), the strongest is the African National Congress. Since 1960 there has been a growing tendency, especially among young Africans, to abandon non-violent means of political struggle and to resort to armed action, sabotage in the first instance and major guerrilla operations more recently, to destabilize the White regime. The South African authorities have responded with the introduction of ever more severe internal security laws and with a major defence effort. The Government has also in recent years taken increasingly severe measures against the leaderships of the rapidly growing trade union movement among non-White workers.

Internal security legislation introduced since 1950 was consolidated and amended in a new Internal Security Act which came into force on July 2, 1982, and which provided inter alia (i) that "terrorism"—i.e. the commission of, or intent to commit, an act of violence—was liable to the death penalty; (ii) that "subversion" and "sabotage" carried a maximum sentence of 20 years' imprisonment; and (iii) that suspects could be detained without trial but could be visited by an inspector of detainees and could not be held in detention for more than six months without a ministerial decision based on the report of a board of review, to which the police would have to submit reasons for the continued detention of the detainee concerned.

Since 1960 the South African Government has built up the strongest military force of any country in Africa in preparation for an anticipated low-intensity guerrilla war of long duration conducted by African nationalist infiltrators from abroad, and also for any major onslaught. South African defence measures have included the erection of defensive fences along the country's northern border and the extension of compulsory military service by White men to two years full-time followed by a total of 720 days over a 12-year period in the "Citizen Force"; thereafter White males are liable to service in commando units (for some categories of men for up to 1,000 days over a 20-year period).

Anti-Apartheid Movements

African National Congress (ANC)

Leadership. Nelson Mandela (pres., in prison); Oliver Tambo (acting pres.); Alfred Nzo (s.g.); Johnstone Maketini (chief representative at the United Nations and in the United States).

The ANC was founded on Jan. 8, 1912, as the South African Native National Congress at a conference held in Bloemfontein by representatives of the African peoples of Southern Africa (i.e. then the Union of South Africa, the Rhodesias, Basutoland, Bechuanaland and Swaziland). The principal object of the conference was to unite all the African people as a unified nation, overcoming tribal and ethnic divisions and opposing British colonialism and the British and Boer (Afrikaner) domination in the Union of South Africa established in 1910. Before World War I the organization worked mainly through petitions to the authorities but later it began to organize Black labourers brought into the towns with the development of industry. It changed its name to African National Congress in 1925.

Following the advent of the (White) nationalist Government in South Africa in 1948, the ANC sought co-operation with the South African Indian Congress (SAIC), the (White) Congress of Democrats and the Coloured People's Organization—with members of the Communist Party of South Africa being prominent among the leaders of these organizations.

After the introduction in the House of Assembly on Feb. 20, 1950, of a Population Registration Bill providing for the classification of South Africa's population in race groups, the ANC's council of action decided on March 4, 1950, to cease all co-operation with the Government. A civil disobedience campaign against "unjust laws"—a campaign involving deliberate violation of the apartheid laws—was organized jointly by the ANC, the SAIC and the Coloured People's Organization. The campaign began on June 26, 1952, and lasted to the end of that year; it led to the arrest of some 8,500 people for disobeying apartheid laws, and those arrested included a few Whites, among them Patrick Duncan (later an office bearer of the Pan-Africanist Congress).

The ANC repeatedly condemned the use of violence as "damaging the cause of the Africans themselves" (especially after riots in Port Elizabeth had led to the deaths of at least 12 people on Oct. 18, 1952). On April 20, 1953, the ANC, the SAIC and their joint "franchise action committee" reaffirmed their belief in "non-violent struggle against the injustice of White supremacy and apartheid" and for "the fundamental human rights of freedom of speech, association and movement" and called on the non-Whites "to make the policy of apartheid unworkable in every sphere of life".

A milestone in the history of the ANC was reached at a Congress of the People, which ended at Kliptown (Johannesburg) on June 26, 1955, with the adoption of a Freedom Charter, which was conceived by Prof. Z. K. Matthews, a leading ANC member, and which in effect became the political platform of the ANC. The Charter opened with the following sentence: "We, the people of South Africa, declare for all our country and the world to know: that South Africa belongs to all who live in it, Black and White, and that no Government can justly claim authority unless it is based on the will of all the people." The Charter included the following demands: (i) "every man and women shall have the right to vote for and to stand as candidates for all bodies which make laws"; (ii) "the national wealth of the country, the heritage of all South Africans, shall be restored to the people"; (iii) "the mineral wealth beneath the soil, the banks, and monopoly industry shall be transferred to the ownership of the people as a whole"; (iv) "restriction of land ownership on a racial basis shall be ended and all the land redivided among those who work it, to banish famine and land hunger".

In the Transvaal the ANC executive subsequently declared that the ANC aimed at replacing the Government of the few by a government of people's democracy in which the power of the state would be exercised by the working people of all colours, together with all other democratic classes who would work for the changes set out in the Freedom Charter.

The absence from the Freedom Charter of any reference to African liberation and to Pan-Africanism eventually led to the breakaway of the Africanists from the ANC, who had already objected to the ANC's decision to co-operate with non-African and pro-communist organizations and who in 1959 formed the Pan-Africanist Congress (see separate entry).

The ANC also opposed the Bantu Education Act (which came into force on April 1, 1955, and which placed the education of all African education under the control of one government department) and called on all African parents to withdraw their children from school indefinitely—a call which was, however, not followed.

In December 1956 a total of 156 prominent anti-apartheid activists were arrested—among them three ANC leaders (ex-Chief Albert Luthuli, president-general since 1952; Oliver Tambo, then general secretary; and Walter Sisulu, a former secretary)—on charges of high treason or of contravening the Suppression of Communism Act, in particular by campaigning against government legislation, convening the Congress of the People, adopting the Freedom Charter and advocating in it the establishment of a communist state. However, the case against ex-Chief Luthuli and the majority of those arrested was withdrawn or quashed, and the remaining 28 defendants were found "not guilty" on March 29, 1961, after the court had found that the ANC did not have a policy of violence.

An All-African People's Conference held in December 1958 adopted a resolution proposed by the ANC, calling for the imposition of an economic boycott against South Africa, and this call was taken up by the sixth world congress of the International Confederation of Free Trade Unions (ICFTU) and by trade unions in a number of countries. The ANC received further international recognition when the 1960 Nobel Peace Prize was awarded to ex-Chief Albert Luthuli for his persistent opposition to racial violence. Ex-Chief Luthuli had been dismissed from his post as tribal chief in September 1952 after he had rejected a government demand that he should relinquish the presidency of the ANC. In a speech made on April 28, 1959, he had declared: "We of the ANC have no desire to dominate others by virtue of our numerical superiority. We are working for a corporate multiracial society. We are prepared to extend the hand of friendship to White South Africans who are our brothers and sisters." On May 22, 1959, he was banned from attending meetings for five years and confined to a district in Natal. In 1960 he was fined for publicly burning his pass, and later he was sentenced to imprisonment. On May 23, 1964, he was confined to his home for another five years on the ground that he had engaged in "activities furthering the cause of communism". He died in July 1967.

However, the ANC abandoned its non-violent policy in 1961 as a result of the shooting at Sharpeville (near Vereeniging,

Transvaal) on March 21, 1960, when police killed 69 Blacks (among them women and children) and wounded 180 during a protest demonstration against the pass laws called by the Pan-Africanist Congress (PAC—see separate entry). After the Sharpeville shooting both the ANC and the PAC were declared unlawful organizations on April 5, 1960. The ANC, however, refused to disband and went underground, while several hundred of its members went abroad and ANC offices were established in various African capitals and also in Moscow.

A strike called for the end of May 1961 by an all-African congress held in Pietermaritzburg (Natal) on March 25-26, 1961, in protest against the introduction of a republican Constitution (approved in a referendum in which non-Whites had taken no part) was suppressed by police action, and early in June 1961 the ANC leadership decided that it would be unrealistic and wrong to continue preaching peace and non-violence at a time when the Government met the ANC's demands with force. On Dec. 16, 1961, the ANC published the manifesto of *Umkhonto we Sizwe* ("Spear of the Nation") in which it declared: "We shall not submit and we have no choice but to hit back by all means in our power in defence of our people, our future and our freedom." *Umkhonto,* described as "the nucleus of an army of national liberation" and founded already in November 1960, was to conduct acts of sabotage as "properly controlled violence" without loss of life (i.e. with the consent of the ANC). In fact, however, *Umkhonto* began immediately to send volunteers abroad to be trained in guerrilla warfare.

The principal organizer of the May 1961 strike had been Nelson Mandela, a member of the executive of the ANC (which did not itself support the strike call), who had earlier been subjected to various restrictions. In February 1962 he attended a meeting in Addis Ababa of the Pan African Freedom Movement for East, Central and Southern Africa (PAFMECSA, superseded in 1963 by the liberation committee of the Organization of African Unity), at which the ANC was accepted as a member of this organization. Arrested in South Africa on Aug. 5, 1961, Mandela was on Nov. 7, 1961, sentenced to five years for inciting the May strike and for leaving the country without valid documents.

Umkhonto began its campaign by exploding bombs at public buildings, blowing up power pylons, cutting telephone lines, attempting to derail trains and committing widespread arson (500,000 tons of sugar cane being destroyed by fire in Natal during 1962). A "Sabotage Act" enacted on June 27, 1962, laid down a minimum penalty of five years' imprisonment and the death penalty as a maximum for acts of sabotage; it also provided for new restrictions on suspects without any right of appeal to a court. *Umkhonto* was officially banned on May 10, 1963.

This period of ANC activities came to an end with the discovery by the police of the "high command" of *Umkhonto* in Rivonia (Johannesburg) in July 1963, which led to the trial of eight alleged *Umkhonto* leaders, beginning in October 1963. In documents produced by the prosecution, the *Umkhonto* leaders claimed that they could obtain "almost unlimited assistance" from "friendly governments" for the execution of a revolutionary plan called "Operation *Afrika Mayibuya*" (or "Africa come back"). The plan allegedly envisaged that four groups totalling 3,000 men, each armed and equipped to be self-sufficient for a month, would be landed in South Africa from the sea and would be joined by 7,000 local guerrillas to embark on "a massive onslaught on selected targets", while a political authority would be set up in a neighbouring country to control operations and eventually to become the provisional revolutionary government.

During the trial Mandela (one of the eight defendants) said on April 20, 1964, that he himself was not a communist, but that the communists were "great allies of the ANC". On the same day Walter Sisulu (a member of the ANC since 1940) said that he had advocated keeping communists out of the ANC; that he had gone overseas inter alia to seek facilities for military training, for which the first recruits had left South Africa in 1962; and that there had never been any agreement between the ANC and African states on the question of armed intervention in South Africa or on the supply of arms. The eight defendants in the Rivonia trial were sentenced to life imprisonment on June 12, 1964.

Umkhonto suffered further setbacks with the trial of alleged members for sabotage, notably (i) 18 Africans sentenced in Port Alfred (Cape Province) on March 16, 1964—three of them to death for murdering (at the direction of a regional committee of *Umkhonto*) a state witness, all three of them being executed in Pretoria on Nov. 6, 1964, and the remaining 15 being given prison sentences totalling 174 years; (ii) eight Africans sentenced in Pretoria on Sept. 18, 1964, to from five to 15 years in prison; and (iii) five persons sentenced on Dec. 18, 1964, to from 12 years' to life imprisonment, among them Ian David Kitson, a White engineer sentenced to 20 years and described as an "unrepentant" communist who had, after the Rivonia trial, formed a new revolutionary "high command" with the four other defendants.

On March 24, 1969, a total of 11 persons were given prison sentences ranging from five to 20 years in Pietermaritzburg for having conspired in 1962-68 with the South African Communist Party, *Umkhonto we Sizwe* and the ANC, some of them having undergone military training in the Soviet Union and also in Ethiopia under the auspices of *Umkhonto*. On May 10, 1971, the Natal Supreme Court in Pietermaritzburg gave a 15-year prison sentence to a Coloured man convicted of undergoing guerrilla training as a member of the banned ANC and *Umkhonto*. On Nov. 23, 1972, an African was sentenced in Pietermaritzburg to 15 years in prison for belonging to the banned ANC and *Umkhonto* and taking part in "terrorist activities" in 1962 and 1972 after receiving military training in China, the Soviet Union and East Germany.

The General Officer Commanding South African police counter-insurgency forces claimed in November 1972 that the Black nationalist intruders had suffered "severe defeats" and that since April 1968 they had lost 28 men killed and many more captured.

During a trial which ended on June 20, 1973, when the Supreme Court in Pretoria passed sentences ranging from five to 15 years in prison on six defendants (four Africans and two Whites), witnesses described the unlawful activities of the ANC as including the training of guerrillas in the Soviet Union and their illegal entry into South Africa; they stated that the ANC consisted not only of young members "prepared to fight" but also of many thousands of others who wanted to achieve the ANC's aims by non-violent methods. One of the White defendants, Alexandre Moumbaris, escaped from prison in Pretoria on Dec. 11, 1979, and succeeded in fleeing the country.

At a party congress of the Coloured Labour Party, held in Upington, Cape Province, on Jan. 6-7, 1976, it became apparent that the ANC exerted a strong influence on sections of the party, with the leader of its left wing, the Rev. Alan Hendrickse, calling for a union of "all those who are oppressed" and demanding that Coloured people should "stop selfishly seeking privileges for themselves and identify with the common struggle of the Blacks".

Raymond Sorrell Suttner, a senior law lecturer at the University of Natal, was sentenced in Durban on Nov. 13, 1975, to 7½ years in prison for recruiting two persons for unlawful activities; he said on Nov. 6 that neither the ANC nor the Communist Party, whose aims he had furthered, was anti-White or terrorist, and he claimed that in acting "for freedom and equality, for an end to racial discrimination and poverty", he had the support of "the over-whelming majority of our people".

Of three other Whites accused of activities encouraging the ANC (among other banned organizations) two were given prison sentences of seven and 10 years respectively in Cape Town on Sept. 29, 1976. The chief accused, Dr David Rabkin, pleaded guilty and declared on Sept. 28 that in his view the ANC and the Communist Party held "the only hope for the channelling of the energies, talents and aspirations of all our people".

A White poet, Breyten Breytenbach, sentenced to nine years' imprisonment in Pretoria on Nov. 26, 1976, admitted during the trial that as an active supporter of the ANC he had (with four co-conspirators not present at the trial) formed a White ANC wing (later called *Okhela*) aimed at the overthrow of the White Government of South Africa and its replacement by a Black one. It was later stated that according to Breytenbach the *Okhela* group was "an attempt by the ANC leadership, notably Oliver Tambo, to break the stranglehold of the South African Communist Party over the ANC".

In 1977 the South African authorities announced a number of successful counter-insurgency operations. J. T. Kruger, then Minister of Justice and the Police, said on Jan. 25 that 65 Africans trained abroad had been arrested and that a quantity of weapons had been seized; he also said that the ANC had instructed detainees to commit suicide rather than "betray the cause" under interrogation. On Aug. 27 the South African police claimed (i) to have foiled a massive terrorist plan by the ANC and the Communist Party to invade South Africa and (ii) to have "wiped out" several "terrorist" bases near Durban as well as several more near Johannesburg.

Africans tried for recruiting people for military training or themselves undergoing such training included (i) five given life sentences in Pietermaritzburg on July 25, 1977, when four others were given sentences ranging from seven to 18 years, and (ii) one sentenced at Malmesbury (Cape Province) on Sept. 14, 1977, to seven years in prison—a state witness having alleged during the trial on Aug. 18 that in the early 1960s a total of 55,000 Black South Africans had undergone guerrilla training in the "army" of the ANC. Acts of sabotage continued, however, to be carried out in growing numbers, mainly in the Transvaal and also in Port Elizabeth in November-December 1977.

On April 7, 1978, six ANC members were sentenced in Pretoria to prison terms ranging from seven to 18 years for revolutionary ANC activities over a period of 15 years. An ANC member who had infiltrated the police force was on Oct. 27, 1978, sentenced to six years in prison.

Solomon Mahlangu, who had admitted receiving insurgency training as an ANC member in Angola, was on March 2, 1978, sentenced to death for murder and other crimes after being arrested in a shooting incident in Johannesburg in June 1977, when two White bystanders were killed. He was ex-ecuted on April 6, 1979, despite numerous international pleas for clemency.

According to the chief of the South African security police, quoted on June 2, 1978, there were at that time an estimated 4,000 Black South Africans undergoing military training in Angola, Mozambique, Tanzania and Libya. The South African Terrorism Research Centre stated a year later that in the 31 months up to June 1979 there had been 91 violent incidents involving 110 bombs, hand grenades or firebombs, and in the previous three years eight persons had been killed and 142 wounded in urban terrorist incidents (of which 31 had taken place in the Johannesburg district, 11 in Cape Town, five in Durban and four each in Pretoria and Port Elizabeth).

ANC members who fled to the neighbouring states of Lesotho or Swaziland (to escape the South African security police) could not legally be politically active in those countries whose Governments did not allow the establishment of guerrilla bases (whereas those of Angola, Mozambique and Zambia tacitly allowed such bases, even if officially describing them as refugee camps). On Aug. 21, 1979, the number of trained insurgents captured in South Africa since October 1976 was officially given as 170, while there had been 48 guerrilla attacks, including 18 against railway lines and five on police stations.

There was an escalation of ANC guerrilla activities in 1979 and early 1980, including several attacks on police stations (notably in Soweto in May and November 1979, at Soekmekaar in the northern Transvaal on Jan. 3, 1980, and in a White suburb of Johannesburg on April 4, 1980) and the temporary seizure of a bank and 25 hostages at Silverton, near Pretoria, on Jan. 25, as well as an attack on the SASOL I fuel plant complex (for distilling petrol from coal) at Sasolburg, Transvaal, on June 1 (when the damage caused was estimated at about £3,000,000). According to Tambo (the ANC's acting president) attacks made on SASOL II had been "unsuccessful". All three ANC guerrillas involved in the Silverton incident were killed by police, while two of the hostages also lost their lives. On Nov. 20, 1980, three ANC members were condemned to death for murder and robbery as participants in the Soekmekaar attack, and on Nov. 26 six others were given prison sentences ranging from 10 to 20 years for high treason on charges arising out of the Silverton attack. The State President, however, commuted the three death sentences to life imprisonment on June 2, 1982.

In a treason trial of ANC members concluded on Nov. 15, 1979, one of the accused, James Mange, was sentenced to death and 11 others received prison sentences ranging from 13 to 15 years; on appeal the death sentence against Mange was overruled on Sept. 11, 1980, and he was instead given a 20-year prison sentence.

In February 1980 the South African Defence Force took over from the police responsibility for the security of northern Natal, where a major guerrilla arms cache was discovered early in February. An even larger cache was later found near Springs (Transvaal), as announced on March 3.

Dr Renfrew Christie, a White academic, was on June 6, 1980, sentenced to 10 years in prison for allegedly having supplied to ANC members information concerning South Africa's nuclear programme and having exposed vital installations to the danger of sabotage by guerrillas.

On June 16, 1980, the ANC (in Lusaka, Zambia) called for the further intensification of the "liberation struggle" on all fronts. However, from South African official announcements made in 1981 and 1982 it emerged that many ANC actions had been foiled by South African security forces.

During 1980 it appeared that Chief Gatsha Buthelezi (the Chief Minister of KwaZulu) was anxious to maintain good relations with the ANC. At a meeting of the central committee of *Inkatha* (Chief Buthelezi's Zulu movement) the Chief read a letter which he had written to Tambo as acting president of the ANC expressing misgivings about recent hostility shown by ANC leaders towards *Inkatha* and accusing Tambo of creating discord among the Black community.

Announcing the arrest of an alleged Soviet spy (Maj. Alexei Mikhailovich Kozlov) on Jan. 28, 1981, the Prime Minister (P. W. Botha) said that "three volumes of evidence" had been extracted from that officer on the Soviet Union's active support for revolutionary movements such as the ANC (and also SWAPO in Namibia).

On Jan. 30, 1981, the Chief of the South African Defence Force announced that a South African commando had attacked and destroyed "the planning and control headquarters" of the ANC at Matola (a suburb of Maputo, Mozambique) where, he said, "numerous terrorists" had been killed and a large quantity of weapons, sabotage equipment and documents had been seized. On April 2, 1981, the police announced the discovery of further arms caches near Johannesburg, intended for use by ANC infiltrators from Mozambique via Swaziland. Further death sentences were passed on ANC members in 1981 and 1982—(i) on three men on Aug. 19, 1981, for involvement in the Sasolburg action (see above) and (ii) on three others on Aug. 6, 1982, for attacks on police stations in 1979 and 1981.

Among ANC members sentenced to imprisonment was Khotso Seatlholo, a former president of the (banned) Soweto Students'

Representative Council, who was said to have taken over, in July 1979, the leadership of a South African Youth Revolutionary Council founded in Kenya in April 1979 by exiled South African students; on March 11, 1982, he was sentenced to 15 years in prison at Vanderbijlpark (Transvaal).

The head of the South African security police claimed on Aug. 18, 1982, that in the past 18 months over 35 insurgents had been arrested or "otherwise neutralized" and that the number of guerrilla attacks had risen from 19 in 1980 to 55 in 1981. During 1981 there had been a rocket attack on the Voortrekkerhoogte military complex near Pretoria on Aug. 12 and another on a police station near Pretoria on Dec. 26, leading to the discovery of an arms cache near Hammanskraal (now in Bophuthatswana). ANC attacks launched in 1982 included one on a fuel depot and transformers at a coal mine near Paulpietersburg (Transvaal) in May 1981.

A number of leading ANC members were assassinated outside South Africa. These included Joe Gqabi, a senior member of the ANC executive, killed in Harare (Zimbabwe) on July 31, 1981; Petrus Nyaose, a senior ANC member, and his wife, killed by a car bomb in Swaziland on June 4, 1982; and Dr Ruth First, research director of the Centre for African Studies at the University in Maputo (Mozambique), the wife of Joe Slovo (another ANC member) and also a member of the South African Communist Party, killed by a letter bomb on Aug. 17, 1982.

On Dec. 9, 1982, South African commandos raided the homes of alleged ANC members in Maseru (Lesotho) in an action in which 42 people were killed—30 of them being reported to have been South African refugees and the others civilians. The Chief of the South African Defence Force said on the same day that, while some women and children had been killed in "cross-fire", the 12 targets of the raid had been the planning and control headquarters for ANC guerrilla activities against South Africa, and that a number of trained "terrorists" had during the past month arrived in Maseru with orders to assassinate leaders of the Ciskei and Transkei Black homelands. The Maseru raid was unanimously condemned by the UN General Assembly on Dec. 14 and by the UN Security Council on the following day. King Moshoeshoe II of Lesotho said before the Security Council that his Government had dealt firmly with those few ANC "freedom fighters" whom it had found to be armed but that it would continue to refuse to hand them over to the South African authorities.

Further explosions attributed to the ANC were those of four bombs at South Africa's first nuclear power station (under construction at Koeberg, north of Cape Town) on

Dec. 18-19, 1982, and of others in central Johannesburg on Dec. 31 and in Bloemfontein on Feb. 18, 1983 (when 86 persons were injured).

The Minister of Law and Order stated on March 3, 1983, that during 1982 large quantities of arms and explosives, mainly of communist origin by the ANC, had been brought into the country by the ANC, had been seized at 29,000 different road blocks.

Since its banning in 1960, the ANC seems to have retained, and perhaps even increased, its popularity among Blacks, at least among those in urban areas. This was demonstrated in a survey, published in *The Star* of Johannesburg late in 1981, of Africans in three major urban areas who had been asked to choose between four Black organizations—the ANC, the Pan-Africanist Congress (these two being illegal), the *Inkatha* movement of Chief Gatsha Buthelezi and the Azanian People's Organization (a Black Consciousness movement); of the respondents some 40 per cent stated that in a general election they would vote for the ANC, and some 76 per cent regarded Nelson Mandela as the most popular leader. The ANC colours (black, green and gold) have continued to be displayed in public on numerous occasions, including funerals of prominent opponents of apartheid.

Initiatives taken at the United Nations by the ANC to counter "the grave threat to peaceful relations between ethnic groups" constituted by apartheid in South Africa met with growing response among the international community from 1952 onwards. The ANC was also instrumental in the setting-up of a liberation committee by the Organization of African Unity (OAU) created in 1963, and the ANC was subsequently recognized by the OAU as a national liberation movement qualifying for the receipt of official OAU support.

Regular publications issued by the ANC include the *ANC Weekly News Briefing* (London) and *Sechaba* (monthly official journal).

African National Congress of South Africa (African Nationalists)

Leadership. Jonas Matlou (ch. of four-member executive).

This organization was established in London in August 1978 as a breakaway group from the African National Congress (ANC), which it criticized as being excessively influenced by communists, including Whites. It has expressed its allegiance to Nelson Mandela (the ANC president serving a life sentence since 1964) and envisages the possibility of unity between itself and the Pan-Africanist Congress of Azania (PAC).

African People's Democratic Union of South Africa (Apdusa)

Leadership. I. B. Tabata (ch.).

Formed in 1958, Apdusa was a breakaway group from the Non-European Unity Movement. During the trial of 13 defendants accused inter alia of being members of the banned Apdusa it was stated in Pietermaritzburg on Nov. 15, 1971, that I. B. Tabata had reported at a meeting in Cape Town in 1963 that he had visited the Organization of African Unity in order to obtain recognition of his movement and that he had been promised "arms, soldiers and money" by the then President of Algeria (Ahmed Ben Bella). It was also alleged that Apdusa had tried to recruit men to go to Zambia for training in order to establish Apdusa's standing in the eyes of the OAU and that such recruiting had still been carried out in 1970.

Azanian People's Liberation Army—see under Pan-Africanist Congress of Azania (PAC)

Azanian People's Organization (Azapo)

Azapo was set up in September 1979 as a new Black consciousness movement (in succession to the banned Black People's Convention, BPC) and had African as well as Coloured and Indian members (Azania being the African nationalists' name for South Africa). At its inaugural conference it elected Curtis Nkondo (chairman of a Soweto Teachers' Action Committee) as president and adopted the slogan "One Azania, one people" (formerly used by the BPC).

Azapo also declared itself opposed to all institutions created by the Government and to the principle of ethnically-based institutions, and advocated the setting up of a single parliamentary state as well as of a common education system for all races. Many Azapo office bearers were subsequently placed in detention, among them Curtis Nkondo on April 23, 1980 (although he had been suspended as president of Azapo in January 1980).

African Resistance Movement (ARM)

This Movement, established in Johannesburg in May 1962 as the National Council of Liberation and incorporating the African Freedom Movement, the National Liberation Committee and the Socialist League, consisted mainly of Whites, some of whom had previously held office in the National Union of South African Students (NUSAS) or in the (legal) Liberal Party. The ARM was held responsible for the blowing up of three power pylons near Cape Town immediately after the end of the Rivonia trial (of alleged ANC or *Umkhonto we Sizwe* members) on June 12, 1964.

Following the explosion of a bomb at the Johannesburg central railway station on July 24, 1964, for which an ARM member (Frederick John Harris) was sentenced to death on Nov. 6, 1964, numerous other ARM members were arrested and tried on charges arising out of unlawful ARM activities. Several prominent ARM members succeeded in fleeing the country. One of these, Robert Watson, stated in London on Dec. 31, 1964, and Jan. 13, 1965, that for 2½ years he had trained ARM members in the use of explosives, but only for the demolition of property; that "at the height of its powers the ARM had enough explosives and trained saboteurs to have brought South Africa to its knees economically and politically by the end of 1964"; but that the Movement had failed because its leaders were "inadequate for the task" as they had been totally opposed to the taking of life and had wanted to attack minor targets purely as a form of political protest, whereas he himself had "wanted to inflict real damage on installations vital to the economy".

The ARM was officially declared an unlawful organization on Sept. 25, 1964, on the ground that it had directly or indirectly carried on some of the activities of the banned African National Congress.

Black People's Convention (BPC)

Leadership. Sipho Buthelezi (s.g.).

The BPC held its first national congress at Hammanskraal (Transvaal) on Dec. 16, 1972, when it limited its membership to non-Whites (Africans, Coloureds and Indians) and declared in its constitution that it intended to "unite and liberate Blacks from psychological and physical oppression". It also aimed to "preach and popularize the philosophy of Black consciousness and Black solidarity, create and maintain an egalitarian society and unite South African Blacks in a political organization which will articulate their aspirations and seek their freedom". When two men closely associated with the BPC were placed under banning orders, Sipho Buthelezi (the BPC secretary-general) declared that Blacks were used to "these intimidatory actions" through restrictions "by job reservation, influx control, house permits, lack of freehold rights, poor wages, disease, poverty and squalor". By October 1973 three leading BPC members were banned under the 1950 Suppression of Communism Act, which meant that they could no longer be politically active, and by November 1974 some 20 BPC members were being detained under the "Terrorism" Act.

Widespread riots began in Soweto (the country's largest concentration of Africans) near Johannesburg on June 16, 1976, the immediate cause being protest demonstrations by school children against the use of the Afrikaans language as a medium of instruction. The riots led to the death of 176 persons (all but two of them being Blacks), injury to 1,228 persons (among them 22 policemen), the arrest of 1,298 persons and material damage estimated at up to £35,000,000. Hlaku Kenneth Rachidi, the national president of the BPC, declared on June 27, 1976, that "a new era of political consciousness" had dawned for Black people in South Africa; but he said that the disturbances had become "a generalized expression of revulsion by the Black community against their political powerlessness and dehumanization under the apartheid system"; and he appealed for consultation between White and Black leaders to find ways and means of getting out of the situation of confrontation in which the country was placed.

After unrest among Blacks had continued in Soweto and elsewhere until August 1976, causing the death of another 84 persons, numerous members of the BPC and of the South African Students' Organization (SASO—see separate entry) were arrested.

In December 1976 the BPC strongly attacked the Black United Front (see separate entry) formed on Nov. 29 by three Black "homelands" leaders, including Chief Gatsha Buthelezi (Chief Minister of KwaZulu); the BPC declared that it would have nothing to do with these homelands leaders and that if the latter wished to become leaders in the "liberation struggle" they would have to "show their credentials by getting out of the oppressive Bantustan [i.e. Black homelands] scheme".

Rachidi was arrested on Oct. 19, 1977, when the BPC was (together with 17 other organizations including its welfare arm, the Black Community Programme) declared unlawful. Rachidi was released from detention on Oct. 27, 1978, but on Dec. 18 of that year he was placed under a five-year banning order. Similar orders were imposed on several other BPC members. Nevertheless the Black consciousness movement retained its influence among younger Black people who were opposed to the African National Congress on the grounds that it was under the influence of White leaders of the South African Communist Party and that its strategy meant that after inadequate training its youngest recruits were being sent on "suicide missions" in its sabotage campaign.

Black United Front (BUF)

Leadership. Dr Sipho Nyembezi (ch.).

The BUF was formed in November 1976 as a political party on an instruction by Chief Gatsha Buthelezi, Prof. Hudson Ntsanwisi and Dr Cedric Phatudi (Chief Ministers respectively of the Black "homelands" of

KwaZulu, Gazankulu and Lebowa). Chief Buthelezi stated at the party's foundation that it would not be "anti-White" but "pro-South African, Black and White" and that it would attempt to establish a non-racial political system involving an end to the pass laws, to influx control (to keep Blacks out of "White areas"), to migratory labour, to the Bantu education system and to the home-lands policy, with the existing homelands to become provincial bodies.

At a conference held at Seshego (near Pietersburg, Transvaal) on March 5, 1977, the BUF committed itself to work for a united South Africa with "free association across colour lines" and instructed Dr Phatudi to tell the South African Prime Minister: "We do not wish to retaliate for the deprivation which we have suffered but to go forward to build a peaceful new South Africa."

National Liberation Front (NLF)

Leadership. Dr Neville Edward Alexander (l.).

On April 15, 1964, a Cape Town court sentenced 11 persons (10 Coloureds and one African) to terms of imprisonment for from five to 10 years for conspiracy to commit sabotage. The accused, most of them teachers, were said to have discussed "the elimination of the [White] *Herrenvolk* of South Africa" and to have planned the introduction of techniques of armed insurrection for which they had in 1962 formed a Yu Chi Chan Club (YCCC), later named National Liberation Front (NLF), as a paramilitary organization "aimed at the overthrow of the Government". In the NLF's illegal newspaper *Liberation* they expressed the intention of taking over from the Pan-Africanist Congress which was said to have failed with its anti-pass campaign.

Non-European Unity Movement (NEUM)

The NEUM was established in 1943 by Coloured (mixed-race) people in the Cape Province with the aim of obtaining a multi-racial franchise. Some of its leaders, mainly teachers, had Trotskyist leanings and were at odds with the Communist Party of South Africa and also with the African National Congress. On April 6, 1972, the Natal Supreme Court in Pietermaritzburg sentenced 13 alleged members of the NEUM or the African People's Democratic Union of South Africa (see separate entry) to imprisonment for from five to eight years, inter alia for having joined a conspiracy to overthrow the Government by force of arms and for recruiting South Africans between 1963 and 1970 for military training abroad for that purpose. Since then there has been little evidence of NEUM activities.

Pan-Africanist Congress of Azania (PAC)

Leadership. John Nyati Pokela (ch.); D. Mantshontsho (admin. sec.).

The establishment of the PAC in April 1959 was strongly influenced by the emergence of the pan-African idea as an intellectual and political movement among Afro-Americans and Africans who regarded Africa and peoples of African descent as homogeneous and who advocated the political unity of Africa, or at least close collaboration among African states in one form or another. Their object has been to modernize Africa on the basis of equality of rights and the principle of "Africa for the Africans".

A first pan-African conference was convened in London in 1900 by Henry Sylvester Williams. Among Afro-Americans a split subsequently developed between Marcus Garvey, who called for the goal of "Africa for the Africans" to be achieved by people of African descent through their personal endeavour, and Dr W. E. B. duBois, who believed that co-operation with White liberals was essential in the African's struggle to achieve equality, and who organized four pan-African congresses after World War I. Garvey's attacks on duBois as a "White man's nigger" and "traitor to the race" were later reflected in the South African PAC's attacks on the multiracial African National Congress (ANC).

At the fifth pan-African congress, held in Manchester in 1945, a strong influence was exerted by George Padmore, a pro-Marxist West Indian, while others who attended the congress included Peter Abrahams of South Africa, Kwame Nkrumah of the Gold Coast (later Ghana) and Jomo Kenyatta of Kenya. The congress issued the slogan "Colonial and subject peoples of the world unite" and laid the basis for an African nationalist liberation movement fighting against racialism, colonialism and imperialism and to bring about decolonization.

The pan-African movement, however, did not become a reality until Ghana achieved independence in 1957 and two conferences were held in Accra in 1958—(i) a Conference of Independent African States (in April), at which Dr Nkrumah emphasized the responsibility of these states "to hasten the total liberation of Africa, the last stronghold of colonialism", and (ii) an All-African People's Conference (in December), to work out a strategy of "African non-violent revolution" and to set up a permanent secretariat in Accra. These conferences were attended by delegates from African as well as Arab states, and pan-Africanism was then given a strong multi-racial colour.

The PAC founded in South Africa succeeded an Africanist movement formed earlier by Anton Lembede, who was one of

the founders of an African National Congress Youth League (ANCYL) in 1944. The
ANCYL had embraced various tendencies,
among them an African nationalist group (including A. P. Mda and Oliver Tambo), who
stood for "African political assertion" but
wanted to avoid "extremist and inward-
looking nationalism", and an Africanist
group (including Anton Lembede, Peter
Raboroko and Walter Sisulu). After Lembede's death in 1948 A. P. Mda became
president of the ANCYL, taking the line that
"African nationalism only hates White oppression and White domination, and not the
White people themselves".

The founding conference of the PAC of
South Africa (in April 1959) was attended by
nearly 300 Africans who had been expelled
from the ANC, or had left it in protest
against its policy of alliance with left-wing
Whites and Indian organizations. The PAC
stood for "a government of the Africans for
the Africans", an African being "everybody
who owes his only loyalty to Africa and who
is prepared to accept the democratic rule of
an African majority"; it guaranteed "no
minority rights" because minorities thought
"in terms of individuals—not groups"; and
Whites and upper-class Indians were excluded
from those deemed to owe their first loyalty
to Africa. The PAC rejected multiracial co-
operation on the ground that it was a way of
"safeguarding White interests", and it
regarded South Africa as an integral part of
Africa and as incapable of solving its problems in isolation. The PAC also rejected
both communism and liberalism. The conference elected Robert M. Sobukwe as first
PAC president and Potlako K. Leballo as national secretary. Sobukwe defined the PAC's
aims as "the overthrow of White domination
and the maintenance of the right of self-
determination for the African people", the
attainment of these objects by 1963 and the
ultimate establishment of a United States of
Africa.

On Feb. 14, 1960, the PAC announced that
on March 21 of that year it would launch a
non-violent campaign against the pass laws
(first introduced in the 19th century and later
consolidated, with the effect that from 1952
Africans were required to produce on demand
a reference book which normally included a
residence permit, an employer's certificate, a
tax receipt and a curfew pass). The campaign
began peacefully in most towns but led to a
confrontation between some 20,000 Africans
and the police at Sharpeville (north of
Vereeniging, Transvaal), where the police
opened fire, killing 69 Africans and wounding
180. A state of emergency was declared on
March 30 (and remained in force until Aug.
31, 1960); over 1,900 persons of different
races were arrested; and under a bill passed
by Parliament on April 5 both the APC and

the ANC were banned. In protest against
numerous arrests at Langa (Cape Town) some
30,000 Africans led by Philip Kgosana went
on strike and marched towards police headquarters in Cape Town on March 30, but
turned back peacefully after the police had
promised Kgosana an interview with the
Minister of Justice. However, when Kgosana
presented himself for the interview he was arrested, and during the next few days the
police forcibly ended the strike. Among 19
PAC members sentenced to imprisonment on
May 4, 1960, for inciting Africans to support
the PAC's campaign was Sobukwe, who was
given a three-year sentence.

Having been banned, the PAC activated its
underground organization known as Poqo
("Alone, for Africans only"), which was
responsible for numerous acts of violence in
1961-63, involving the killing of at least three
tribal chiefs and an unsuccessful attempt on
the life of Chief Kaiser Matanzima of the
Transkei. Potlako K. Leballo, acting president of the PAC since the imprisonment of
Sobukwe, stated in Maseru (Basutoland—
now Lesotho) on March 25, 1963, that Poqo
had been a slogan since 1950 and more
especially since 1960; that the PAC had more
than 150,000 members; and that its "revolutionary council" was discussing the timing
and manner of action for a rising to be launched in South Africa in 1963.

Poqo was organized in a system of cells of
10 members each with one leader, and no
women or non-Africans were admitted as
members (while the PAC also excluded communists from membership); Poqo members
were enjoined to infiltrate all spheres of life
and to further the aims of Poqo in any organization of which they were members; they
were to await instructions from the national
committee before acting to "achieve freedom
in 1963 for the African people" by overthrowing the Government and murdering all
Whites and African chiefs and headmen who
supported the Government.

A number of serious attacks by Poqo members during 1962 were later described as having
been premature, i.e. carried out without the
national committee's instructions. These attacks involved the killing of Whites at Paarl
(where six Africans were killed by police
retaliating against the Poqo attack on Nov.
22), at Queenstown, in the Transkei and elsewhere. Six Poqo members who murdered a
chief on Oct. 29, 1962, were sentenced to
death at Umtata (Transkei) on Oct. 29, 1962.

Poqo's intentions were, however, thwarted
when the Lesotho police searched the PAC
offices in Maseru (from which Leballo had
fled) early in April 1963 and found a list of
between 15,000 and 20,000 names of alleged
Poqo members, and also detained 13 PAC
members. In South Africa police arrested 15
PAC "ringleaders" and Leballo's secretary,

who was carrying letters with instructions to PAC cell leaders to rise against the Whites within two weeks. Sobukwe, whose prison term was due to expire, was affected by a General Law Amendment Act (which came into force on May 2, 1963) providing that any person serving a prison sentence for sabotage or similar crimes could be detained, after expiry of the sentence, for an indefinite period (and that any suspect could be detained for 90 days, renewable for a further 90 days "as required", without any court having powers to order that person's release).

On June 20, 1963, the Minister of Justice (then B. J. Vorster) gave the number of suspected *Poqo* members arrested during the previous 12 months as 3,246, and on June 13, 1964, it was officially announced that 162 *Poqo* members had been charged and convicted of various crimes, and that the "mopping-up" of *Poqo* had been completed. Trials of alleged PAC or *Poqo* members led to death sentences imposed in Cape Town for murder on one African on Oct. 20, 1966, on nine Africans on Dec. 14, 1966, on four others on Jan. 31, 1976 (all these murders having been committed in 1962), and on two Africans on April 19 and June 17, 1967, respectively.

In 1964 the PAC had adopted the name of PAC of Azania—Azania being an African name for South Africa. (In his book *Black Mischief* Evelyn Waugh used Azania as the name of an ancient East African Kingdom.)

The only known White member of the PAC, Patrick Duncan (son of a former Governor-General of the Union of South Africa), who had lived in Basutoland, was on June 4, 1963, banned by the British Colonial Office from any of the three High Commission Territories (Basutoland, Bechuanaland and Swaziland). In March 1964 he was appointed PAC representative in Algiers; on June 30, 1965, however, he was dismissed from his PAC post by Leballo, and in July 1965 he was deprived of his South African citizenship.

Leballo, who left Basutoland on Aug. 21, 1965, continued to be acting president of the PAC, with headquarters in Dar-es-Salaam (Tanzania). Sobukwe was released from detention on May 13, 1969, but was thereafter restricted to the municipal area of Kimberley, and he died on Feb. 26, 1978. Shortly afterwards a PAC meeting attended by some 100 members at Arusha (Tanzania) elected Leballo as president in succession to Sobukwe. The meeting also expelled from the PAC seven members of its central committee for alleged dishonesty (and after it had been reported that a power struggle had taken place at the PAC headquarters in Dar-es-Salaam during the preceding six months).

In Swaziland the authorities arrested, in April 1978, some 50 PAC officials at Manzini, among them Joe Mkwanazi, the chief official

who had sought refuge in Swaziland in 1963; those arrested were said to have been involved in the training of guerrillas and in tribal faction fighting.

Changes in the PAC leadership took place in 1979, when Lancelot Dube (described as the commander of the PAC's Azanian People's Liberation Army) was killed in a car accident in January, and Leballo resigned the PAC presidency on May 2. He was succeeded by a three-member presidential council consisting of David Sibeko (previously PAC representative at the United Nations), Vusumzi Make and Elias Ntloedibe. However, on June 12, 1979, Sibeko was killed and Make wounded in an attack for which six PAC members were, on June 15, 1981, sentenced by the Tanzanian High Court to 15 years in prison for manslaughter—the court having rejected the government prosecutor's argument that there had been a conspiracy against Sibeko by elements within the ANC's military wing.

By 1982 it appeared that the influence of the APC among South African Blacks was far inferior to that of the ANC or the various organizations of the Black consciousness movement. The PAC was granted observer status by the UN General Assembly in September 1974.

Port Elizabeth Black Civic Organization (PEBCO)

Leadership. Thomazile Botha (ch.).

This Organization was established in 1979. Its chairman and three members of his executive were detained by the security police on Jan. 11, 1980, after they had opposed the removal of Blacks from a township at Walmer, Port Elizabeth, to a new site 12 miles away. Thomazile Botha was released on Feb. 28 but he and the three others were served with five-year banning orders; he fled to Lesotho on May 3-4, 1980.

South African Communist Party

Leadership. Dr Yusuf Dadoo (ch.).

A Communist Party of South Africa (CPSA) was established in Cape Town in July 1921 by a merger of several Marxist groups, including the International Socialist League created in 1915 after the South African Labour Party had abandoned its internationalist stand and had from then on increasingly represented the interests of White workers. A 1924 CPSA congress decided not to return to the Labour Party but to concentrate on the interests of African workers. In the period following World War II some of the party's leading members held office in the African National Congress (ANC), the South African Indian Congress and a number of trade unions (mainly of non-White workers), and four leading members were elected (as "Native Representatives") to the House of Assembly and the Cape Provincial Council respectively.

However, the party decided to dissolve itself on June 20, 1950, on which date the House of Assembly passed the third reading of a Suppression of Communism Bill, which came into force on July 17, 1950. The Act, which effectively banned the CPSA, was amended by a further act which came into force on July 23, 1951, but with retroactive effect from July 17, 1950, which inter alia provided for the "naming" as a communist any person who had professed communism before July 17, 1950, for the unseating of Communist members of Parliament or Provincial Councils, and for making private (as well as public) advocacy of communism a punishable offence.

The CPSA was reconstituted in 1953 as the South African Communist Party, led by a central committee based in London. At a congress held in 1962 it adopted a programme, "The Road to South African Freedom", which defined as the party's foremost task the building and strengthening of a united front of national liberation. The party was strengthened by the arrival in Britain of several leading Communists who had fled South Africa or had, in 1963, been allowed to leave that country on exit permits (excluding any legal return to South Africa).

The Communist Party co-operated closely with the ANC, although it regarded the latter's Freedom Charter of 1955 as merely a short-term programme and only the beginning of the party's programme of establishing a Marxist state. A number of Communists served on the ANC's national executive (notably Albert Nzula and Moses Kotane, both former CPSA secretaries, and J. B. Marks, a former member of the CPSA central committee). The party supported the sabotage campaign of the ANC but (according to the testimony of Ahmed Mohammed Kathrada, a prominent party member and one of the defendants in the Rivonia trial, speaking on April 20, 1964) it did not consider guerrilla warfare to be feasible and did not regard sabotage as a substitute for "mass action", without which no freedom could be obtained.

During a trial of 12 party members (who were sentenced in Johannesburg on April, 2, 1965, to imprisonment for from one to five years) it emerged that the party had been infiltrated (as had other organizations such as the ANC) by a secret agent of the South African security police. Several other party leaders were tried and sentenced during 1966; they included two party members sentenced in Pretoria on May 6 to five and 15 years in prison respectively, the 15-year sentence be-

ing imposed on Michael Dingaka for having procured persons for training abroad for the Communist Party, the ANC and its armed wing, *Umkhonto we Sizwe.*

Former leaders of the CPSA sentenced in 1966 included Advocate Abram Fischer and Fred Carneson (a former Cape Provincial councillor). Fischer, who had at times acted as chairman of the party's central committee, was on May 9, 1966, sentenced to life imprisonment on charges of conspiracy with the ANC and *Umkhonto we Sizwe* to commit sabotage, and to 24 years in prison on six counts of Communist Party membership. He denied, however, that he had been involved in the creation of *Umkhonto we Sizwe* which, he claimed, had never reported to the party's central committee nor received orders from it. (He died on May 8, 1975.) Carneson was on May 25, 1966, sentenced to five years and nine months in prison for membership of the party's central committee, for participation in the party's activities and for planning activities of *Umkhonto we Sizwe.*

During a trial of four Indians in Pretoria (who were on Nov. 1, 1972, given five-year prison sentences) the judge found that Ahmed Timol, an alleged co-conspirator and leader of the "main unit" of the Communist Party of South Africa, had stayed in England in 1966-70 in contact with known Communists; he further found that Timol had after his return been charged with organizing groups of Communist supporters and had on his arrest been found in possession of Communist Party and ANC pamphlets and of copies of secret correspondence with the party's central committee in London. (Before being brought to trial Timol committed suicide by jumping from the 10th floor of the Johannesburg police headquarters.)

The South African Government has repeatedly denounced the South African Communist Party as its principal enemy intent upon organizing a "total onslaught" on the Pretoria regime. At the same time it has expressed confidence in its ability to deal with any communist threat. J. T. Kruger, the Minister of Justice and the Police, assessing the prospects of communism in South Africa, said on Sept. 8, 1976, that Communist activities in South Africa would continue for some years but that he wished to tell the party's leaders in London that as long as their party lived South Africa would continue to beat it.

The party's quarterly journal, *African Communist,* is published in London. The party's leadership has co-operated closely with that of the Communist Party of the Soviet Union. After a meeting in Moscow between a delegation led by Dr Yusuf Dadoo and Soviet party officials, it was announced on Nov. 18, 1975, that the Soviet side had reaffirmed its "firm support for the just efforts" of the South African party.

South African Indian Congress (SAIC)

The SAIC was preceded by a Natal Indian Congress which was founded in 1894 to fight discrimination against Indians in South Africa, and which conducted a campaign of non-violence *(satyagraha)* under the leadership of Mahatma Gandhi (who lived in South Africa in 1893-1914 and later practised *satyagraha* in India). A passive resistance campaign was also conducted in the Transvaal in 1906 against the pass laws which forced Indians to carry certificates of registration at all times; Indians who refused to register were sent to prison (among them Mahatma Gandhi), and many Indians were deported to India.

The SAIC became active after World War II. On May 28, 1950, its then president, Dr G. M. Naicker, issued a statement describing as "a serious challenge to world peace" the South African Government's policy of apartheid, as expressed inter alia in the Population Registration Bill introduced in the House of Assembly on Feb. 20, 1950; he appealed to the United Nations to outlaw the South African Government "from the family of democratic nations". (At the United Nations the Government of India was the prime mover of initiatives against South Africa's apartheid policies.)

The SAIC has co-operated with the African National Congress (in the Congress Alliance) while stressing that it adhered to methods of non-violence or passive resistance. At the abortive 1959-61 treason trial I. A. Cachalia (a former executive member of the SAIC) said that it was the duty of resisters not to fight back against violence used by police and that for the SAIC to abandon extra-parliamentary and occasionally unlawful methods would simply mean the abandonment of its struggle.

South African Students' Organization (SASO)

SASO was set up in 1968 as the student section of the Black consciousness movement, of which the Black People's Convention (BPC)—see separate entry—became the overall political organization. A SASO conference held at Hammanskraal (Transvaal) on July 5, 1972, expressed the Organization's total rejection of the South African Government's policies of separate development and its opposition to the Black homelands' leaders whom SASO's leaders regarded as having themselves allowed to become involved in the government system. SASO also refused to enter into any dialogue with White students (including the "liberal" National Union of South African Students, NUSAS). The conference accordingly deposed SASO's current leader, Temba Sono, who had recommended co-operation with homelands and other apartheid organizations in order to convert them to SASO's thinking.

The emergence of SASO brought with it an entirely new development in that members of the Coloured (mixed-race) population groups combined with Africans, identifying themselves as Blacks, and no longer as a separate group standing somewhere between Whites and Blacks—as had been the view of most Coloured people and that of practically all Whites. In the view of SASO's Coloured members, they and Africans were equally disenfranchised and discriminated against and should join together in the struggle for their rights.

In 1973 the authorities held SASO responsible for student riots, especially at the University of the Western Cape (for Coloureds) in Bellville (near Cape Town), at the (African) University of Fort Hare and at the Bethesda Teacher Training College (near Pietersburg, Transvaal). On March 2, 1973, it was announced that banning orders had been issued against six SASO leaders (two of them being placed under 12-hour house arrest). On July 26, 1973, Henry Isaacs (a student at the University of the Western Cape, newly elected president of SASO), was restricted to the magisterial district of Pietermaritzburg (Natal) after students at his university had demanded to be taught by Black lecturers "with whom we can communicate meaningfully and share our aspirations as members of an oppressed community". There were then 70 White and only 12 non-White teachers at that university.

Abraham Tiro, a SASO leader expelled for his political activities at the (Black) university at Turfloop (Transvaal) in 1972, was killed by a parcel bomb sent to him near Gaborone (Botswana) on Feb. 1, 1974. Nine Africans, most of them members of SASO, were sentenced in Pretoria on Dec. 21, 1976, to imprisonment for five or six years for organizing illegal rallies to express support for the assumption of power by Frelimo (the Mozambique Liberation Front) in September 1974 and for "conspiratorial agreement" aimed at "a total change in South Africa". Those sentenced to six years in prison included Justice (Muntu) Myeza (former national president and secretary-general of SASO), and Phandelani Nafolovhodwe (former SASO president), while a five-year sentence was imposed on Strinivasa Moodley (former SASO publications director). Two former officebearers of the Black People's Convention among those sentenced were Dr Nchaupe Aubrey Mokoape (six years) and Absolom Zitulele Cindi (five years).

The cause of SASO received worldwide publicity through the death in police custody in Pretoria on Sept. 12, 1977, of Steven Biko, who had been the founder of SASO, its president in 1968-69, and later honorary president of the BPC and also an executive member of the Black Community Programme (set up to implement the self-help ideas of the Black Consciousness Movement). He had first been restricted to King William's Town in 1973, had later been in detention until Nov. 30, 1976, and was finally rearrested on Aug. 19, 1977, and he was the 20th political detainee to die in custody in South Africa within 18 months. According to the findings of an inquest concluded on Dec. 2, 1977, he died of intensive brain injuries but "the available evidence" did "not prove that death was brought about by an act of omission involving an offence by any person, i.e. any particular person . . . or persons . . .". No prosecution followed these findings at the inquest.

SASO was one of the 18 organizations banned on Oct. 19, 1977. Barney Pityana, its secretary-general, was arrested at the same time; on his release from detention on Aug. 10, 1978, he was placed under a banning order, but later he and his family escaped via Lesotho to Britain, where they were granted refugee status in October 1978.

South African Youth Revolutionary Council—see under African National Congress (ANC)

Soweto Students' Representative Council—see under African National Congress (ANC)

Spear of the Nation (Umkhonto we Sizwe)—see under African National Congress (ANC)

Transvaal Indian Congress (TIC)

A Transvaal British Indian Association was first founded in 1902 by Mahatma Gandhi (see also under South African Indian Congress). In the 1940s the TIC was taken over by its radical members who participated in a 1952 defiance campaign against "unjust laws". The TIC was a signatory of the 1955 Freedom Charter (see under African National Congress) but after the bannings which followed the Sharpeville shootings of 1960 (see under Pan-Africanist Congress) its leaders were banned or went into exile. The TIC was, however, reactivated on April 30, 1983, when it reaffirmed its commitment to the Freedom Charter and to the Congress Alliance in which the African National Congress was the senior partner.

White "Backlash" Movements

Afrikaner Resistance Movement (*Afrikaanse Weerstandsbeweging,* AWB)

Leadership. Eugene Terre'Blanche (l.).

This Movement was established with the avowed object of maintaining White supremacy in South Africa by all possible means. To this end the AWB has called for the abolition of all political parties, for the right to vote to be restricted to White Christians approved as eligible by a special court (thus excluding Jews) and for a Government controlled by an AWB Higher Council *(Opperraad).* The AWB was organized on paramilitary lines, and had a swastika-like emblem as well as a blackshirt youth movement.

The AWB has been responsible for a number of threats and acts of violence against persons advocating racial desegregation, and on June 29, 1978, a group of 10 of its members were fined for assaulting a university professor. On Dec. 11, 1982, it was officially announced that the AWB's leader had been arrested with eight other members of the Movement, after the police had uncovered illegal arms caches in different parts of the country, mainly weapons and explosives hidden in metal containers.

After AWB members had disrupted meetings of the ruling National Party in April 1983, the Prime Minister ordered an investigation into its activities. Under standing orders of the Commissioner of Police members of the police force were forbidden to become members of the AWB. However, an application by the AWB to be registered as a political party under the name of White People's State Party was reported to have been granted.

White Commando *(Wit Kommando)*

Established in May 1980, this group is officially regarded as a White "underground terror movement" opposed to the policies of the Government of P. W. Botha, which it regards as "a Marxist set-up" likely to convert South Africa from a well-developed country to "a state of chaos"; its members declared themselves ready to "take up arms to force Whites not to serve Blacks". The movement claimed responsibility for a number of bomb attacks, e.g. against the offices of an adviser to the Prime Minister and of a non-racialist White councillor in Durban. Its declared policy was "to warn first, and later to eliminate, if necessary, all persons, institutions and organizations promoting racial integration and Black rule in South Africa".

After a number of members of the Commando had been arrested, South Africa's Director of Security was on March 8, 1981, quoted as saying that they were "part of an international right-wing network", some of them being of Italian origin and linked with European extremists. The Commando is said to have about 500 members; although it has an Afrikaans name, it also admits non-Afrikaners to membership.

Swaziland

Capital: Mbabane Pop. 510,000

The Kingdom of Swaziland is ruled by a Paramount Chief (Ngwenyama) as King, who exercises authority through a Cabinet headed by a Prime Minister. The Parliament (consisting of 110 members elected by an elected college, itself elected by popular vote and with a majority of members of the Imbokodvo National Movement, and of a Senate consisting of 10 members elected by the electoral college and another 10 nominated by the King) has purely advisory functions. All political parties were banned under the repeal of the 1968 Constitution in the new Constitution proclaimed on Oct. 13, 1978.

Following the death of King Sobhuza II on Aug. 21, 1982, his senior widow was appointed Regent for an indefinite period.

Ngwane National Liberatory Congress

Leadership. Dr Ambrose P. Zwane (l.).

In general elections held on May 16-17, 1972—the first to take place since Swaziland became independent in September 1968—this party—founded in 1962—obtained three of the 24 elective seats as the only opposition party to be represented in Parliament. The party was, however, officially disbanded in 1973 under the new Constitution which banned all political parties.

Dr Zwane was repeatedly placed in deten-tion (where he could be kept for up to 60 days, under a law introduced in April 1973) for "behaving as if the party still existed". Of the decision taken by King Sobhuza II in March 1977 to abandon all attempts to work out a "Western-type" constitution for a parliamentary regime and to resort instead to a government based on traditional tribal communities, Dr Zwane said that it had "put our country back a thousand years".

The Ngwane National Liberatory Congress has consistently called for a return to parliamentary democracy in Swaziland.

Zambia

Capital: Lusaka   Pop. 5,800,000

The Republic of Zambia, a member of the Commonwealth, has an executive President elected by universal adult suffrage for a five-year term (and re-eligible). He appoints a Prime Minister and a secretary-general of the United National Independence Party (UNIP), of which he is the president and which is the country's sole legal political party. He also appoints the Cabinet, which is subordinate to UNIP's central committee. There is a National Assembly to which 125 members (chosen from candidates approved by UNIP local committees) are elected at the same time as the President and 10 additional members are nominated by the President.

During the year 1980 two attempts to overthrow President Kenneth Kaunda's regime were reported to have been foiled. The first of these, reported on Feb. 22, related to an alleged attempt to assassinate the President in January 1980 by nine army officers who were captured, interrogated and hanged. The second attempt, which was confirmed by President Kaunda on Oct. 27, was made on Oct. 16 when Zambian security forces put to flight some 200 men, mainly Katangese gendarmes (who had been involved in secessionist activities in Zaïre—see page 271) said to be in the pay of Zambian dissidents supported by South Africa. In connexion with this attempt, seven men were on Jan. 20, 1983, condemned to death for treason (among them Valentine Musakanya, a former governor of the Bank of Zambia, and four Zaïreans) and an eighth defendant was given a 10-year prison sentence, all of them having pleaded "not guilty". A further alleged conspirator, Pierce Annfield, was said to be in hiding in South Africa.

On June 23, 1981, it was reported that another alleged plot had been uncovered on June 14, when a group of Zambians, South African mercenaries and Katangese gendarmes were said to have planned to overthrow the Government on June 17 and to liberate 13 persons detained in connexion with the attempt of October 1980.

Zimbabwe

Capital: Harare (formerly Salisbury)   Pop. 8,500,000

The Republic of Zimbabwe, an independent state within the Commonwealth, has a President chosen by the Legislature and required to act on the advice of the Prime Minister and the Executive Council (Cabinet). The Legislature consists of (i) a House of Assembly of 100 members, 80 of whom are elected by universal adult suffrage on a common roll and 20 on a roll for Whites, Coloureds and Asians; and (ii) a Senate of 40 members, 10 of whom are chosen by the White members of the House of Assembly, 14 by Black members of the House, 10 by a Council of Chiefs and six by the President on the advice of the Prime Minister.

In elections held on Feb. 14, 1980, for the 20 non-Black seats in the House, all 20 were taken by the Rhodesian Front, which changed its name to Republican Front in June 1981 and of whose members nine decided in March 1982 to sit as independents. In elections to the 80 common-roll (Black) seats held on Feb. 27-29, 1980, the result was as follows: Zimbabwe African National Union—Patriotic Front (ZANU-PF) 57, Patriotic Front—Zimbabwe African People's Union (PF-ZAPU) 20, United African National Council 3.

Internal unrest which has persisted since 1980 has been due mainly to a conflict between ZANU-PF led by Robert Mugabe (the Prime Minister) and PF-ZAPU led by Joshua Nkomo and their respective former armed forces, the Zimbabwe African National Liberation Army (ZANLA) and the Zimbabwe People's Revolutionary Army (ZIPRA); the former are based mainly on the majority Shona population group and the latter on the Ndebele people of Matabeleland (south-western Zimbabwe). Clashes between members of these two armies, which were in principle to be merged in one national Army, and also involving dissidents who recognized neither ZANLA nor ZIPRA, led to the death of hundreds of people in 1980-82 and also to the periodic renewal of regulations under an Emergency Powers Act of 1965.

Following the discovery of large quantities of arms in Matabeleland which, according to the Government, had been hidden in caches by guerrillas loyal to Joshua Nkomo in preparation for a military coup, the President of the Republic issued on Feb. 16, 1982, a proclamation declaring that 11 companies owned by Nkomo and other leading ZAPU members were illegal organizations and that they had been seized by the state; he explained that in the light of the arms finds they were "likely to endanger, disturb or interfere with defence, public safety or public order". The Prime Minister announced on Feb. 17 that he had relieved Nkomo and three other ZAPU members of their responsibilities in the Government. Senior military advisers to Nkomo, as well as former ZIPRA members said to have undergone secret military training in Matabeleland, were arrested during March 1982.

Several talks between Mugabe and Nkomo failed to achieve a peaceful solution of the conflict, which was, early in 1983, greatly exacerbated by the intervention of the fifth brigade of Zimbabwe's Army which had been trained by North Korean instructors and was said to be totally committed to the Prime Minister. According to Nkomo and numerous observers, this unit was guilty of terrorizing the Ndebele people and of committing atrocities. Nkomo, feeling threatened with arrest, secretly left the country for Britain in March 1983.

6. LATIN AMERICA AND THE CARIBBEAN

Antigua and Barbuda

Capital: St John's

Pop. 74,500

Antigua and Barbuda, consisting of the Caribbean islands of Antigua, Barbuda and Redondo (the last-named being uninhabited) became an independent state within the Commonwealth on Nov. 1, 1981, with the British monarch as head of state, represented by a Governor-General. It has a bicameral Parliament consisting of (i) a House of Representatives (currently of 17 members) elected for five years by universal adult suffrage and (ii) a Senate to which 11 members are appointed on the advice of the Prime Minister, four on the advice of the Leader of the Opposition, one on the advice of the Barbuda Council and one at the Governor-General's discretion. The Prime Minister and the Cabinet are collectively responsible to Parliament.

In general elections held on April 24, 1980, the Antigua Labour Party gained 13 seats, the Progressive Labour Movement three seats and an independent representing Barbuda the remaining seat. The (new left) Antigua Caribbean Liberation Movement received less than 1 per cent of the vote.

As regards political dissent, the new state has been faced in particular with agitation for a separatist state of Barbuda.

Barbuda People's Movement (BPM)

This Movement gained control of the Barbuda Council established in 1976 as the local government body of the 1,500 inhabitants of Barbuda. Notwithstanding concessions made in the independence negotiations in December 1980 in response to demands by the Barbudan delegation for increased autonomy for the island, the BPM declared that the people of Barbuda had three choices: (i) separate colonial status, (ii) separate associate status or (iii) separate independence with a view to forming an "association with other friendly nations".

In addition, a majority of the island's inhabitants signed a "Barbuda Declaration" in which they stated their intention to establish a separate territory upon Antigua's attainment of independence. The islanders' aspirations were, however, explicitly rejected by the central Government, mainly on the ground that their grievances were being exploited and manipulated by foreign criminal interests, including US drug traffickers.

Argentina

Capital: Buenos Aires   Pop. 27,600,000

The Republic of Argentina has since March 1976 been ruled by a three-man military junta whose membership has changed from time to time. There is a President of the Republic, whose functions were separated from those of the junta in 1978, but who remained responsible to it, and a Cabinet chosen by the President. After assuming power the junta dissolved the existing bicameral National Congress, formally outlawed the left-wing political parties and suspended the activities of all other parties and of the trade unions.

The assumption of power by the junta was also followed by the arrest of about 3,000 former ministers, labour leaders and trade union officials, as well as the freezing of the assets of the (Peronist) General Confederation of Labour (CGT), of the major trade unions and of some 150 former leading personalities, including ex-President Isabel Perón. On June 2, 1976, a total of 48 parties, trade unions and other organizations were declared dissolved. On Sept. 10, 1976, severe penalties were laid down for employers who caused lock-outs of workers and for any person inciting strikes. Under a law of Dec. 13, 1976, trade union privileges as well as workers' benefits were drastically reduced.

As from July 15, 1976, the Government provided for the imposition of the death penalty (which had been reintroduced in 1970 for the first time since 1886), or life imprisonment, for attacks against members of the security forces or the judiciary and public officials on duty, as well as for kidnapping and disrupting of transport if it had subversive motives or resulted in death or serious injury. Under a law approved by the Government on April 21, 1980, all political and trade union activity was forbidden in universities; no senior university staff was allowed to hold political posts in parties or trade unions, or to make political statements in public; students had to pay their own course fees; and anything which could be regarded as "propaganda, indoctrination, political campaigning or agitation of either a political or a trade union nature, and also the dissemination or support of totalitarian or subversive political ideas" was banned from the university campus.

On July 14, 1981, a national front known as the *multipartidaria* was formed by five of the political parties suspended in 1976, namely the Radical Civic Union (*Unión Cívica Radical,* UCR), the Justicialist National Movement *(Movimiento Nacional Justicialista),* the Intransigent Party (*Partido Intransigente,* PI), the Christian Democratic Federation *(Federación Cristiana Demócrata)* and the Movement for Integration and Development *(Movimiento de Integración y Desarrollo).* On Dec. 16, 1981, this organization issued a statement calling for national reconciliation and in particular for immediate measures such as the lifting of the ban on political and trade union activities, the application of an existing statute on political parties, and the holding of general elections without restrictions; in addition it called for an official explanation of the fate of those who had disappeared *(los desaparecidos),* said to number up to 15,000. The statement also defined the task of the armed forces as being to consolidate and preserve the national decision-making process under the authority of an elected government.

Following the repossession by British forces of the Falklands Islands, which Argentina had seized in April 1982, an entirely new military junta took power in

June-September of that year and Gen. Reynaldo Benito Antonio Bignone, as nominee of the Army, assumed office as President on July 1. The new President had a week earlier met representatives of 14 political parties, including the *multipartidaria,* and had undertaken to lift the ban on political activities and to hold elections before March 1984. The *multipartidaria* had, on June 21, put forward a "national reconstruction programme" which included demands for the restoration of constitutional rights, the lifting of the state of siege and the release of all political prisoners.

Under a statute promulgated on Aug. 26, 1982, all political parties were required to re-register within eight to 13 months, and to obtain official recognition each party was to have at least 35,000 members and adequate representation in at least five provinces, while all parties which denied human rights or advocated "the replacement of the democratic system, the illegal and systematic use of force and personal concentration of power" were prohibited.

Human Rights Issues

President Jorge Rafael Videla declared on Dec. 10, 1977, that the campaign against armed terrorist groups in Argentina was nearing its end and that the terrorists retained only 15 per cent of their former strength. He also said: "This is really a war. In a war there are survivors, wounded, dead, and sometimes people who disappear." He admitted that some of the missing persons "might have disappeared as a result of repression" but that repression was "directed against a minority whom we do not consider Argentinians". On Jan. 28, 1978, the Minister of the Interior gave the number of imprisoned "subversive criminals" as 3,472.

The question of alleged violation of human rights by the Argentinian Government was taken up by the Inter-American Commission on Human Rights (ICHR) of the Organization of American States (of which Argentina is a member). The ICHR visited Argentina for two weeks in September 1979 and reported later on "grave violations of fundamental human rights" in Argentina, where it had documented more than 6,000 cases of persons who had disappeared—cases which had not been clarified by the authorities—as well as instances of torture and deprivation of legal rights; the ICHR concluded that most of the missing persons were dead and had been buried secretly. It was reported that on Aug. 10, 1979 (i.e. before the ICHR's visit), that police had raided the offices of three human rights organizations in Buenos Aires and had removed files on some 5,000 missing persons which were to have been submitted to the commission.

In a report of June 30, 1979, by the Minister of the Interior it had been stated that between November 1974 and June 28, 1979, a total of 8,713 persons had been arrested for subversive and terrorist activities; that 5,913 of them had been released; and that 2,800 had not been released—713 of them having been allowed to emigrate, 192 having been expelled, 160 freed under supervision and 12 placed under house arrest; and that since 1974 a total of 3,876 people had appeared in court, of whom 592 had been sentenced. No mention was made of missing persons.

A five-member working group of the UN Human Rights Commission investigating the fate of missing persons in Argentina and 14 other countries prepared a report, which was debated by the Commission in February 1981 and in which it was stated that initial evidence seemed to indicate that about 9,000 people had disappeared in Argentina—including children, adolescents, pregnant women and babies born in prison—and that the vast majority of the missing people had been arrested, detained or abducted by members of "organs of the executive power or of bodies controlled by the Government or acting in open or tacit complicity with it". The Buenos Aires daily *La Prensa,* on Dec. 18, 1981, published a list of 1,898 missing persons.

During the latter part of 1982 the Government announced the release of several hundred political prisoners, including some who had been held without trial since 1976 as well as many who had been convicted and sentenced by military courts for alleged subversive activities. These releases were said by the Government to indicate its intention to free all political detainees in due course and as circumstances permitted.

However, with reference to those who had allegedly "disappeared", the new military junta declared at the end of September 1982 that all operations against "terrorists" in the 1970s had been "carried out in conformity with plans approved and supervised by the armed forces", and at the same time the Government prohibited the coverage by the media of cases of missing persons, activities of the "Mothers of the Plaza de Mayo" (see below) or "anything connected with subversion".

Human Rights Groups

Grandmothers of the Plaza del Mayo (Abuelas de la Plaza del Mayo)

This group, an offshoot of the Mothers of the Plaza del Mayo (see separate entry), was formed in August 1981 to press for information about children who had been abducted with their parents or had been born in prison. In December 1981 a committee of support for the group was set up under the chairmanship of Ernesto Sabato.

Mothers of the Plaza del Mayo (Madres de la Plaza del Mayo)

Members of this group have held a weekly vigil in the Plaza del Mayo in Buenos Aires in protest against the absence of any official explanation of those thousands of persons who had disappeared over several years during the repression of supporters of left-wing movements. In 1982 these vigils developed into more pronounced anti-government demonstrations.

Left-wing Organizations

Communist Party of Argentina (Partido Comunista de Argentina, PCA)

Leadership. Athos Fava (g.s.).

The PCA was founded on Jan. 6, 1918, by the Marxist faction of the Socialist Party of Argentina. It was illegal from 1966 to May 1973, when it was legalized, though without being granted electoral rights. Two of its members had earlier in 1973 been elected to Parliament as candidates of an *Alianza Popular Revolucionaria*. By 1975 it claimed to have 145,000 members organized in almost 4,000 branches, while its Young Communist Federation was said to have 68,000 members. It was, however, believed to have little working-class support. In 1982 it welcomed the political programme of the *multipartidaria* five-party alliance (see above).

The Moscow-line PCA is recognized by the Communist Party of the Soviet Union.

Fifth of April (Cinco de Abril)

This little-known left-wing group carried out a bomb attack on June 8, 1980.

Montoneros

Leadership. Mario Eduardo Firmenich (l.).

The discovery of a nationwide network of alleged pro-Castro "terrorists" was first announced in July 1964 by the counter-espionage service of the (anti-Peronist) Government of President Arturo Illia. One of the "terrorists", however, alleged that many of the terrorist acts committed were part of a plan of the (Peronist) General Confederation of Labour (CGT) designed to create chaotic conditions in which ex-President J. D. Perón, then in exile in Spain, might be received as the only possible "pacifier".

As an openly left-wing Peronist urban guerrilla group, the *Montoneros* began their operations in 1970. They took their name from half-Indian cavalry forces of the 19th century who fought against Buenos Aires troops. The first major action carried out by the *Montoneros* was the abduction of Lt.-Gen. Pedro Eugenio Aramburú (who had been President of Argentina in 1955-58) on May 29, 1970, and his "execution" on June 1 by a "revolutionary court" on the grounds (i) that he had ordered the execution, on June 9, 1956, of Peronist leaders, including Gen. Juan José Valle, who had unsuccessfully tried to restore Gen. Perón to power, and (ii) that he had been guilty of "271 crimes" during his presidency.

In a message found on June 11, 1970, the *Montoneros* called on the people of Argentina to resist the Government and to support the return of Gen. Perón. The Government, however, had reacted on June 2 by the introduction of the death penalty (which had not existed in Argentina since 1886) for persons who murdered or seriously injured victims of kidnapping or who used a service uniform while committing a crime (as two of the kidnappers had done) and the provision of prison sentences for kidnapping.

After the election of the (Peronist) President H. J. Cámpora in April 1973, the *Montoneros* and the Revolutionary Armed Forces (see separate entry) declared that they would respect the new Government even though only a battle had been won and the "war" was "not finished". On June 26, 1973, it was reported that the *Montoneros* had decided to lay down their arms and to support President Cámpora. At a mass rally organized near Ezeiza international airport for the reception of Gen. Perón on his return from exile in Spain on June 20, 1973, armed clashes took place between *Montoneros* and members of the Revolutionary Armed Forces on the one hand and traditionalist Peronists on the other, with at least 34 people being killed and 342 injured.

The strength of support for the *Montoneros* among Peronists in 1974 became evident at a May Day rally addressed by President J. D. Perón, who strongly condemned left-wing extremists, calling them "stupid, treacherous and mercenary", with the result that some 30,000 *Montoneros* supporters, or about half his audience, left the rally in protest.

In the circumstances the *Montoneros'* period of peaceful coexistence with the Government was shortlived. In a statement read out at a secret press conference in Buenos Aires on Sept. 6, 1974, they declared that they were returning underground to fight "a popular war" against the Government and that they would use arson, assassination, sabotage and bombings. They explained that this decision was due to "aggression by police and para-police groups against the people's forces". The decision was not approved by other left-wing Peronists, however, and on Sept. 10 over 60 orthodox Peronist organizations published a declaration stating that the *Montoneros* had been unmasked as "a band of delinquents . . . damaging the process of reconstruction and liberation which Gen. Perón had left as an essential mandate".

Among the first major actions of the *Montoneros* after their decision to resume warfare was the kidnapping of Jorge and Juan Born (two brothers) of the firm Bunge y Born (one of Argentina's largest grain dealers) on Sept. 19, 1974. The brothers were released on June 20, 1975, on payment of US$60,000,000 in ransom and after distribution of $1,000,000 worth of food and clothing to the poor "as a punishment for shortages inflicted on the people" by the company, and also the publication of a lengthy *Montoneros* statement in two international newspapers, in which the *Montoneros* undertook to continue "without truce the resistance to the present Government, laying bare its antipopular, repressive and pro-imperialist essence . . . until we achieve its annihilation".

Later in 1975 the *Montoneros* launched the largest guerrilla operations ever undertaken in Argentina (i) by blowing-up, on Aug. 2, a Navy missile-launching frigate near La Plata on Aug. 22; (ii) by planting a bomb in the path of an Air Force transport aircraft carrying 114 soldiers (for anti-guerrilla operations) at Tucumán on Aug. 25, causing four deaths and injury to 25 people; and (iii) by seizing the airport at Formosa (near the border with Paraguay) on Oct. 5, and hijacking an airliner which took about 20 guerrillas to Rafaele (Santa Fé province) from where they escaped by road. At least 30 soldiers and guerrillas were killed in the last-named operation, and about 30 of the guerrillas were captured by the armed forces on Oct. 7, 1975.

Targets of *Montoneros'* other actions in 1975-76 included kidnappings and assassinations of foreign business executives in Argentina and an attack on a police academy in La Plata on Feb. 1, 1976, in which numerous *Montoneros* lost their lives. Later in 1976 *Montoneros* were responsible for a number of other attacks on military targets or police premises. On Sept. 29, 1976, five *Montonero* leaders were killed in Buenos Aires and M. E. Firmenich narrowly escaped arrest. Norma Arrostito, a founder-member of the *Montoneros* involved in the kidnapping of ex-President Aramburú in May 1970, was killed by security forces on Dec. 3, 1976; in reprisal, *Montoneros* killed 14 people and injured 20

by exploding a bomb in a Defence Ministry lecture hall on Dec. 15.

On April 20, 1977, it was officially confirmed that a group of Argentinian financiers headed by David Graiver had been financing the *Montoneros* by investing about $17,000,000 and securing interest of about $130,000 a month for the *Montoneros*. D. Graiver was alleged to have been killed in an aircrash in Mexico in August 1976 (although there were rumours to the contrary). On Dec. 9, 1977, a military court imposed prison sentences of 15 years each on David Graiver's father, brother and widow, and of five years on his mother, for having "knowingly aligned themselves with the ranks of the self-proclaimed *Montoneros,* whom the nation has decided to annihilate in order to save its traditions and way of life based on freedom and human dignity".

Also in April 1977 Jacobo Timerman, editor of the daily *La Opinión,* was detained in Buenos Aires on suspicion of being connected with *Montonero* guerrillas; in December 1977 he was deprived of his political rights and his property was confiscated; on April 17, 1978, he was placed under house arrest, from which he was released on Sept. 25, 1979, when he was deprived of his Argentine nationality and expelled from the country (whereupon he joined his family in Israel). The Supreme Court had ruled twice—in July 1978 and again on Sept. 20, 1979—that he should be freed as there was no basis for his continued house arrest.

M. E. Firmenich announced in Rome on April 20, 1977, that the *Montoneros* and the Authentic Peronist Party (*Partido Auténtico Peronista,* PPA) had merged and established a Supreme Council of the Peronist *Montoneros (Consejo Supremo de Montoneros Peronistas).* He also announced an eight-point pacification and liberation programme which, he said, was "not a surrender or a truce but an appeal to the common sense of all national forces" and did not mean the abandonment of the armed struggle. The programme called inter alia for a new economic policy favouring national and popular interest, the restoration of constitutional rights and guarantees, the rehabilitation of all political parties, the liberation of all political prisoners and the closure of "concentration camps", the institution of proceedings against those responsible for torture, kidnappings and murder, the rehabilitation of trade unions and the holding of general elections.

The PPA had been established on March 12, 1975, with Dr Oscar Bidegain (a former Governor of Mendoza province) as its president, to "fight monopolies, promote worker participation in the planning and control of the national economy, and denounce the compromise (of the Government) with imperialism to the detriment of the people". Some of the founders of the PPA, including its president, were expelled from the Justicialist Liberation Front (*Frejuli,* the overall Peronist organization) on April 4, 1975, and on Sept. 21 the PPA created its own national council. At its first national congress, held in Córdoba on Nov. 16-23, 1975, the PPA called for the resignation of President Isabel Perón and the holding of elections. On Dec. 24, 1975, the PPA was officially banned, together with its newspaper, *El Auténtico,* after arms and ammunition had been found at two ranches belonging to Dr Bidegain. The PPA had earlier experienced right-wing attacks against its officials.

By 1980 the *Montoneros* were thought to have been reduced to about 350 active members, and there were few reports of any activities by *Montoneros* in Argentina. According to Arab sources, a small number of *Montoneros* were being trained in guerrilla warfare in camps of the Palestine Liberation Organization in Syria and Lebanon.

People's Revolutionary Army (*Ejército Revolucionario del Pueblo,* ERP)

Leadership. Luis Mattini (l.).

The ERP was formed in July 1970 as the armed wing of the (nominally Trotskyist) Workers' Revolutionary Party (*Partido Revolucionario de los Trabajadores,* PRT). It had affiliations with the *Tupamaro* guerrillas in Uruguay. Its first major operation was the abduction, on March 21, 1972, of Dr Oberdán Sallustro, director-general of the Fiat Concord company, and his assassination on April 10 after he had, according to an ERP statement, been tried by a "people's court". His kidnappers had put forward demands, inter alia, for gift parcels of food, clothing and classroom equipment worth $1,000,000 to be distributed among children in nearly 800 schools, the release of prisoners, the reinstatement of dismissed workers and payment of an indemnity to the ERP. The Government, however, ordered Fiat not to take any action which could be construed as assisting the guerrillas, with the result that Dr Sallustro's life was not saved.

Also on April 10, 1972, the ERP, in cooperation with the Revolutionary Armed Forces (see separate entry), killed Gen. Juan Carlos Sánchez, commander of the Second Army in Rosario. The General had previously claimed to have "smashed" 85 per cent of the urban guerrillas in Rosario.

On Aug. 15, 1972, a group of 29 detained members of the ERP, the Revolutionary Armed Forces and the *Montoneros* (see separate entry) overpowered their guards at Rawson (Patagonia), killing one of them. The ex-detainees thereupon occupied the nearby naval air base at Trelew, where 10 of them (including Roberto Mario Santucho, the founder of the ERP) forced the crew of an airliner to take them to Chile, where they were accepted as "political refugees" on Aug. 24 but from where they left for Cuba on Aug. 25. Of the other 19 ex-detainees, who had meanwhile surrendered to Argentinian troops, 16 were killed by security forces on Aug. 22 (allegedly while trying to escape).

The ERP subsequently abducted and/or killed numerous businessmen as well as officers of the armed forces and newspaper publishers, and was also responsible for the hijacking of an Argentinian airliner on July 4, 1973, and its diversion to Havana (Cuba), from where the aircraft with its passengers and crew was returned to Argentina on July 6 after the hijackers' extradition had been unsuccessfully demanded by Argentina.

Following the 1973 election victories of the (Peronist) Justicialist Liberation Front *(Frejuli)*—leading to the election of Dr Hector José Cámpora as President on April 26—the ERP stated on May 27, 1973, that it would not attack the Government unless the latter attacked the people or repressed the guerrillas, but that it would pursue "the hostilities against foreign and national enterprises and against the counter-revolutionary armed forces". It demanded the nationalization of all foreign enterprises and land reform and on May 30 it declared that Dr Cámpora's Government could not, and would not, "by its methods and its composition, effectively pursue the revolutionary struggle".

After the assassination on Sept. 25, 1973, of José Ignaci Rucci, secretary-general of the (Peronist) General Confederation of Labour (CGT), the ERP was on the same day declared unlawful. The ERP claimed on Sept. 27 that it was in no way responsible for J. I. Rucci's death and the ban did not diminish its violent activities, which continued with further kidnappings of foreign business executives and attacks on military targets. The ERP was in particular held responsible for the murder of Dr Arturo Mor Roig, a former Minister of the Interior, on July 15, 1974, a total of 28 ERP members being detained for complicity in the assassination.

During 1974 the ERP was particularly active in Catamarca and Tucumán provinces (north-western Argentina), where late in September it accused the armed forces of having summarily executed 16 guerrillas who had surrendered; the ERP thereupon decided to "execute" a similar number of members of the armed forces in retaliation, and in fact two officers (one of them being the commander of a division of the Third Army) were killed on Sept. 25 and another on Oct. 7 in Buenos Aires. On the other hand the police discovered, on Sept. 7, 1974, the printing press of the ERP near Buenos Aires, where the ERP's organ, *Estrella Roja* ("Red Star"), had been produced.

On Oct. 8, 1974, the ERP notified the Government that it was "disposed to an armistice" on condition that all political prisoners were freed, repressive legislation was repealed and the decree outlawing the ERP was revoked. The Government, however, ignored this initiative, and in the following years it became obvious that the security forces had gained the upper hand over the ERP.

In an ERP attack on police headquarters in Córdoba on Aug. 20, 1975, seven persons were killed and at least 20 injured. However, a co-ordinated ERP attack made on military targets in the Buenos Aires area on Dec. 23-24, 1975, was decisively defeated by the armed forces, using heavy artillery and helicopter gunships, with over 160 persons being killed. A further ERP attack on an army communications base at La Plata was similarly repulsed on Dec. 27, 1975. On July 19, 1976, Roberto Mario Santucho, the ERP's leader, was killed with several others near Buenos Aires. By 1977 the ERP's activities in rural areas of Tucumán province were repressed, but arrests and trials of ERP supporters continued in later years. According to the Paraguayan police, ERP members were responsible for the assassination in Asunción on Sept. 17, 1980, of ex-President Anastasio Somoza Debayle of Nicaragua.

Although originally Trotskyist, the ERP broke off all relations with the Fourth (Trotskyist) International in 1973, as the latter had not approved the ERP's guerrilla warfare strategy. In February 1974 the ERP set up a *Junta Coordinadora Revolucionaria* (JCR), which provided links with the National Liberation Army (ELN) of Bolivia, the Revolutionary Left Movement (MIR) of Chile and the National Liberation Movement (MLN) of Uruguay.

Revolutionary Communist Party

This Maoist offshoot of the Communist Party of Argentina (see separate entry) has experienced particular opposition from right-wing paramilitary movements such as the Argentina Anti-communist Alliance (AAA—see separate entry).

17 October Montoneros *(Montoneros 17 de Octubre)*

Leadership. Miguel Bossano (l.).

This group was formed in April 1980 as a dissident faction of the Peronist *Montoneros* movement (see separate entry), and was named after the date of the mass mobilization which started the Peronist movement in 1945. The group has described itself as "completely committed to insurrection".

Trade Unions

General Confederation of Labour *(Confederación General del Trabajo,* CGT)

Leadership. Saúl Ubaldini (s.g.).

The CGT was the Peronist trade union council until March 1973, when it was placed under military control. Although it was officially dissolved in 1979, it remained active and still called for strikes, though with limited success (e.g. on July 22, 1981), in protest against unemployment and low wages.

United Leadership of Argentinian Workers *(Conducción Unica de los Trabajadores Argentinos,* CUTA)

The CUTA was formed on Sept. 10, 1979, by a union of the National Commission of Workers *(Comisión Nacional del Trabajo,* CNT, formed in 1978) and the Committee of 25 (a grouping of orthodox Peronist unions not placed under military control). The CUTA intended to oppose the military junta with the support of the Church and to work for the immediate restoration of the law on collective labour agreements, the return to normal of unions placed under military control and the release of union leaders detained without charge or trial. (On July 27, 1979, the Argentine bishops' conference had issued a statement in support of trade union freedom.) Later in 1980, however, the CUTA was reported to have experienced a split.

Workers' Revolutionary Party—see under People's Revolutionary Army

Right-wing Organizations

Argentinian Anti-Communist Alliance *(Alianza Anticomunista Argentina,* AAA)

Established in 1973, this organization took violent action not only against communists but also against other politicians whom it regarded as leftists. On Nov. 21, 1973, a senator of the (opposition) *Unión Cívica Radical* (UCR) was injured by a car bomb said to have been placed by AAA members. On July 31, 1974, an extreme left-wing deputy and co-editor of the Peronist journal *Militancia* was assassinated by AAA members; at his funeral on Aug. 2 the police arrested some 350 left-wing demonstrators.

Following the death of President Juan Perón on July 1, 1974, the AAA began, in September 1974, to publish lists of persons whom it intended to kill, with the result that a number of those listed, notably left-wing academics, left the country. Further murders attributed to the AAA occurred nevertheless, the victims being known left-wingers prominent in public life.

On June 1, 1975, the AAA announced that in response to an appeal by the Minister of the Interior it would observe a 90-day truce. It had earlier been alleged by some Peronists that the "intellectual author and instigator" of the AAA had been José López Rega, who had for many years been a close adviser to Gen. Perón and his wife Isabel, and who left Argentina in July 1975. J. López Rega had also incurred growing hostility within the armed forces. On April 2, 1975, opposition leaders in the Chamber of Deputies had asked (i) why security forces had neglected to investigate murders by right-wing extremists and (ii) why no official investigation had been carried out into the AAA.

Later in 1975 the AAA resumed its killings, and in November of that year it claimed to have killed some 30 left-wing personalities during the previous three months. Early in February 1976, the AAA issued a warning of the imminent assassination of leaders of the (pro-Soviet) Communist Party, the (Maoist) Revolutionary Communist Party, the Authentic Peronist Party, Marxist-Leninist guerrillas and the Radical Revolutionary Youth (a left-wing branch of the UCR) and also of "progressive" priests. However, since the introduction of military rule in March 1976, AAA activities have declined.

Argentinian National Socialist Front (*Frente Nacional Socialista Argentino,* FNSA)

This anti-semitic organization was held responsible for bomb explosions at several synagogues in Buenos Aires in August 1976, after which the Jewish community made representations to the Government. The latter responded by publishing on Sept. 13, 1975, a decree banning the publication, distribution and export of anti-semitic literature (until then freely circulated in Argentina, mainly from the Editorial Milicia publishing house). The Front attributed the cause of Argentina's problems to "Jewish-Bolshevist plutocracy".

Bahamas

Capital: Nassau (on New Providence Island)   Pop. 225,000

The Commonwealth of the Bahamas, a member of the Commonwealth, with the British monarch as head of state represented by a Governor-General, has a bicameral Parliament consisting of (i) a 43-member House of Assembly elected for five years by universal adult suffrage and (ii) a 16-member Senate to which nine members are appointed on the advice of the Prime Minister, four on that of the Leader of the Opposition and three at the Governor-General's discretion. The Prime Minister and his Cabinet are collectively responsible to Parliament.

In elections to the House of Assembly held on June 10, 1982, the ruling Progressive Liberal Party gained 32 seats and the Free National Movement the remaining 11. Parties which unsuccessfully contested the elections were the Vanguard Nationalist and Socialist Party, the Workers' Party and the Commonwealth Democratic Party.

The Government of the Bahamas has consistently refused to allow opponents of the Duvalier regime in Haiti to settle in the Bahamas. There have been no reports of activities by extra-parliamentary opposition groups.

Barbados

Capital: Bridgetown   Pop. 250,000

Barbados, a member of the Commonwealth with the British monarch as head of state being represented by a Governor-General, has a 27-member House of Assembly elected for five years by universal adult suffrage and a 21-member Senate appointed by the Governor-General (12 senators on the advice of the Prime Minister, two on that of the Leader of the Opposition and seven at the Governor-General's discretion). The Prime Minister and his Cabinet are collectively responsible to Parliament.

In elections to the House of Assembly held on June 18, 1981, the Barbados Labour Party gained 17 seats and the Democratic Labour Party 10. The elections were not contested by a ("new left") Movement for National Liberation.

There have been no signs of internal political opposition outside existing legal parties or pressure groups.

Belize

Capital: Belmopan   Pop. 150,000

Belize became, on Sept. 21, 1981, a "sovereign democratic state" and an independent member of the Commonwealth as a constitutional monarchy with the British monarch being head of state and represented by a Governor-General, who acts on the advice of a Cabinet headed by a Prime Minister. There is a bicameral National Assembly consisting of (i) a House of Representatives of up to 29 members, elected by universal adult suffrage, and (ii) a Senate of eight members (five appointed by the Governor-General on the advice of the Prime Minister, two on the advice of the Leader of the Opposition and one on that of a Belize Advisory Council). Cabinet ministers are appointed similarly from among the members of the National Assembly.

In elections to the House of Representatives held on Nov. 21, 1979, the People's United Party gained 13 seats and the United Democratic Party (UDP) the remaining five. One of the UDP members resigned from the party in December 1982 to sit in the House as an independent. The UDP, which gained 47 per cent of the votes in the 1979 elections, has opposed the terms under which Belize was granted independence on Sept. 21, 1981, and has unsuccessfully called for a referendum on the independence issue. Both parties have strongly rejected Guatemalan claims to the whole or part of Belize's territory.

Anti-Communist Society (ACS)

This Society was founded in 1980 by Santiago Perdomo, who resigned as Minister of Trade, Industry and Consumer Protection in December 1978. The ACS was suspected of involvement in attacks during 1980 on left-wing politicians, including members of the ruling People's United Party, and of being pro-Guatemalan.

Belize Action Movement (BAM)

This Movement was launched by extremist members of the United Democratic Party (the official opposition), which had unsuccessfully called for the holding of a referendum on the question of independence and whose leader (Theodore Aranda) had in September 1981 stated that "polarization of opinion" in Belize was now such that there was "no way in which peace could be maintained and independence could survive". Clashes between BAM members and the police had led to the introduction of public safety regulations on July 28, 1981, including restrictions on public meetings.

Bolivia

Capital: La Paz   Pop. 5,900,000

The Republic of Bolivia has an executive President elected for a four-year term by universal adult suffrage and a 157-member Congress consisting of a 130-member House of Representatives and a 27-member Senate similarly elected for four years.

In elections held on June 29, 1980, parties provisionally gained aggregate seats in Congress as follows: Democratic Popular Unity (UDP) 57, National Revolutionary Movement—Historic Faction (MNR-H) 44, National Democratic Action (ADN) 30, Socialist Party—One (PS-1) 11. In presidential elections held on the same day the UDP candidate, Dr Hernán Siles Zuazo, obtained the highest number of votes, but not an absolute majority. As a result, there followed a military take-over on July 17, 1980, in response to which Dr Siles Zuazo the following month formed a clandestine government.

More than two years later, the armed forces announced on Sept. 17, 1982, a return to civilian rule, whereupon the electoral court decided on Sept. 23 that the June 1980 elections were valid. Accordingly, the Congress on Oct. 5 elected Dr Siles Zuazo as President of the Republic, and the latter proceeded to appoint a Cabinet of UDP ministers, including two Communists. The constituent parties of the UDP are the Leftist Revolutionary Nationalist Movement (MNRI), the Movement of the Revolutionary Left (MIR) and the (pro-Soviet) Bolivian Communist Party (PCB). Altogether 18 different parties were represented in Congress.

Bolivian politics have in recent years been dominated by frequent government changes, many of them due to military intervention by either right-wing or left-wing officers; many leading politicians have from time to time been arrested or sent into exile by their opponents in power. Internal unrest has been caused by a number of unsuccessful attempts to overthrow the government of the day, and also by mass action by workers organized in trade unions as well as by sections of the peasantry.

Bolivian Workers' Revolutionary Party (*Partido Revolucionario de Trabajadores Bolivianos,* PRTB)

Leadership. Antonio Peredo (l.).

This party was established in 1972 as the political front of the National Liberation Army (ELN—see separate entry) with the object of constituting "a wide resistance movement combining legal, semi-legal and clandestine organizations". The party was not officially recognized, and it was engaged in only limited activities in 1979-80.

Che Guevara Brigade

This group claimed responsibility for the assassination in Paris on May 11, 1976, of Gen. Joaquín Zenteno Anaya, then Bolivian ambassador to France; he had been a local commander of the forces which had killed Che Guevara in October 1967, had briefly been Foreign Minister in 1964 and commander of the armed forces in 1971-73, whereafter he had resigned because of differences of opinion with President Banzer. The group was also reported to have claimed that in its attack on the General it had used the weapon with which the Spanish military attaché had been wounded in Paris on Oct. 8, 1975. However, in the Paris left-wing *Le Nouvel Observateur* it was claimed in May 1976 that the General had been murdered by the Bolivian secret service because leading exiles had charged him with forming a new government for Bolivia.

National Committee for the Defence of Democracy (CONADE)

This group was formed in April 1980 by representatives of the Roman Catholic Church, trade unions, certain political parties and several newspapers after a Jesuit journalist (Fr Luis Espinal) had been kidnapped and murdered by armed men on March 21, 1980.

National Liberation Army (*Ejército de Liberación Nacional,* ELN)

The ELN was founded in 1967 by Ernesto "Che" Guevara, who was born in Argentina but left that country (after graduating in medicine in 1952) to devote himself to left-wing activities in Bolivia, Peru, Ecuador, Costa Rica and Guatemala (where he held a minor post in the left-wing Government of President Arbenz Guzmán, overthrown with US help in August 1954). In 1956 he escaped to Mexico and joined Dr Fidel Castro, becoming the latter's chief aide and taking part in the struggle for power which led to the setting-up of the Castro regime in Cuba on Jan. 1, 1959.

In 1965, however, Che Guevara withdrew from public life and in 1966 he left Cuba with the aim of implementing his theory that "given suitable operating country, land hunger and injustices, a hard core of 30 to 50 men" would be "enough to set off armed revolutions in any Latin American country". He chose Bolivia for this purpose. However, he failed to obtain support from Bolivia's trade unions, from the (pro-Soviet) Bolivian Communist Party or from Bolivia's peasants—although some unions and students staged demonstrations in his support. Bolivian armed forces, trained and equipped with US help, succeeded in October 1967 in surrounding Guevara's small guerrilla band. He himself was wounded on Oct. 8 and died the following day in captivity; other members of his group were also killed in the engagement.

Che Guevara had explained his theories in the book *Guerrilla Warfare* (1960) and had described his impression of Dr Castro's campaign in Cuba in 1956-58 in *Passages of Revolutionary War*. His *Bolivian Campaign Diary* was published in Spanish in Havana on July 1, 1968 (a copy of the original text having been smuggled out of Bolivia with the connivance of President René Barrientos Ortuño); an English edition appeared in New York on July 2 of that year.

Of Guevara's supporters, Jules Régis Debray (a French journalist and revolutionary philosopher) had been arrested in Bolivia on April 20, 1967, and was sentenced to 30 years' imprisonment on Oct. 31, 1967, for subversive activities. During his trial his book *Revolution in the Revolution?* was used in evidence against him; he himself expressed pride in being a guerrilla and leader of a liberation movement but denied having been a member of the ELN. On Dec. 23, 1970, however, J. R. Debray was released (together with Ciro Bustos, an Argentine painter sentenced with him in 1967) and flown to Chile on orders from (the left-wing) President Juan José Torres of Bolivia. (More than a decade later Debray became a special adviser to President Mitterrand following the latter's election to the French presidency in May 1981.)

On Nov. 7, 1970, the Bolivian Government also expelled to Chile two ELN leaders (Oswaldo "Chato" Peredo and Mario Suárez Moreno) who had been involved in July 1970 in an ELN raid on a gold mine north of La Paz, where they had seized two German technicians as hostages but had released them unharmed after the Government had, on July 22, acceded to their demand for the release of 10 political prisoners (all former ELN supporters). "Chato" Peredo and M. Suárez Moreno had been captured after eight members of their group had been killed by security forces on July 30, 1970.

After the advent to power of the right-wing Government of President Hugo Banzer Suárez in August 1971, thousands of left-wing militants went into exile; among the few who were tried in court Luis Alberto Morant, an ELN guerrilla leader, was condemned to death and executed.

On Dec. 20, 1972, President Banzer stated that four foreigners linked with the ELN had been arrested in connexion with a conspiracy to assassinate him; the Minister of the Interior alleged on the same day that Dr Castro had contributed $300,000 towards the cost of a planned invasion of Bolivia from neighbouring countries. On May 14, 1973, it was officially announced that security forces had on the previous day shot dead two ELN members who had entered the country to revive the ELN; they were named as Osvaldo Ucasqui Urval and Monika Ertl Frielo (a German-born woman suspected of having assassinated the Bolivian consul-general in Hamburg in April 1971). Eleven other ELN members were on June 11 reported to have been captured at Cochabamba. Since then no further ELN activities have been reported.

Revolutionary Anti-imperialist Front *(Frente Anti-imperialista Revolucionario)*

This organization, based in Cuba, was stated to have organized the escape from Bolivia of numerous left-wing activists after the advent to power of President Hugo Banzer Suárez in August 1972.

Single Federation of Peasant Workers *(Federación Unica de Trabajadores Campesinos, FUTC)*

This left-wing peasant pressure group was active in land occupations and other operations, mainly in the Oruro department during 1980.

Brazil

Capital: Brasília   Pop. 130,000,000

The Federative Republic of Brazil consists of 22 states, one Federal District and four territories. Legislative power is exercised by a National Congress consisting of (i) a Chamber of Deputies of 479 members elected for four years by universal adult suffrage and (ii) a Senate of 69 members elected for eight-year terms by direct secret ballot (each state being represented by three senators), one-third of its members being elected after four years and the other two-thirds after another four years. Executive power is exercised by the President, aided by ministers of state; he is elected for six years by an electoral college consisting of all members of the National Congress and delegates appointed by the state legislatures. A Vice-President is elected similarly.

Brazil has been under effective military rule since 1964 and until late 1979 had a limited party system under which, in addition to the government party, only one opposition formation was officially authorized. A reform bill approved by Congress on Nov. 22, 1979, provided for the dissolution of the two official parties and laid down rules for the introduction of a multi-party system under which new parties would be permitted provided that they guaranteed their allegiance to the "democratic system"; any party found guilty of "racial, religious or class bias" or having links with "foreign governments, bodies or parties" would not be recognized. In order to be formally constituted any new party has to win 5 per cent of the vote at the next elections spread over at least nine states, or have the support in Congress of 10 per cent of the members of each House; the formation of alliances is permitted.

In elections held on Nov. 15, 1982 (the first full multi-party contest to be held since 1962), parties gained seats in the Chamber of Deputies as follows: Social Democratic Party 234, Party of the Brazilian Democratic Movement 200, Democratic Labour Party 24, Brazilian Labour Party 13 and Workers' Party 8.

In a document issued on Oct. 8, 1979, by a Brazilian amnesty committee and compiled with the assistance of the Archbishop of São Paulo and the president of the Brazilian press association (who was a member of the opposition Brazilian Democratic Movement) the names were given of 179 persons who had allegedly died at the hands of the police and security forces between 1964 and 1979 (excluding 45 killed in guerrilla activities in the Araguaia region in the early 1970s); dossiers were also presented on 53 cases of missing persons, covering in particular the 1969-74 period.

The various left-wing guerrilla groups active until the early 1970s have since then been suppressed, and Brazil's only remaining political prisoner was reported to have been released on Oct. 8, 1980.

Right-wing Movements

Brazilian Anti-Communist Alliance (*Aliança Anticomunista Brasileira,* AAB)

This organization was held responsible for planting a bomb at the headquarters of the Brazilian press association in September 1976; for beating up the Bishop of Nova Iguacu (who, they claimed, was a communist); and for other acts, including the planting of car bombs and telephone threats against churchmen who were alleged to have left-wing tendencies.

Death Squad *(Esquadrão da Morte)*

This organization was founded in 1964 by policemen who wished to avenge the death of one of their colleagues at the hands of a criminal; by 1970 its members were estimated to have killed 1,000 or more alleged criminals and other "undesirables", marking their victims with a skull and crossbones. From 1968 onwards the Death Squad openly claimed credit for numerous killings, and early in 1970 a newspaper received by telephone a list of persons whom the Death Squad had "condemned to death". After the murder of a police inspector on July 18, 1970, a total of 11 persons were found killed during the next few days, among them a leader in the left-wing underground movement suspected of having killed the inspector.

The suspected head of the Death Squad was Police Commissioner Sergio Paranhos Fleury, who was taken into custody on several occasions but did not face charges until 1979, when he died on May 1 as the result of an accident.

In 1972-76 a number of former policemen were sentenced to imprisonment for up to 198 years on murder charges. Following 23 murders in Rio de Janeiro attributed to the Death Squad, six policemen were arrested in May 1976. In 1980 alone 12 Death Squad victims were discovered in Rio de Janeiro on Feb. 5-6; another 10 on March 21 (bringing the total to 148 since Jan. 1, 1980); 215 victims in February-March, according to the Rio newspaper *Ultima Hora*; another 10 found in Rio on Sept. 15; another 19, also in Rio, on Dec. 13; and five others killed in Rio on Dec. 25.

Lieutenant Mendes *(Tenente Mendes)*

This right-wing terrorist group was responsible, inter alia, for placing a time bomb (defused on Jan. 18, 1980) designed to kill Leonel de Moira Brizola (who later founded the Democratic Labour Party). Other attacks by the group were directed mainly against newspapers which were deemed to have taken a left-wing political line.

New Fatherland Phalange (*Falange Patria Nova,* FPN)

Members of this group (which emerged in 1980) were responsible for a number of bomb attacks, including one on a news stand in Brasília on Aug. 11, 1980, and three in Rio de Janeiro, which killed one person and injured seven others, on Aug. 27, 1980.

Vanguard of the Commando for Hunting Communists (*Vanguarda de Comando de Caça aos Comunistas,* CCC)

This group was in 1980 held responsible, together with the Death Squad (see separate entry), for the death of about 100 people a month. On Aug. 28, 1980, CCC members bombed a school in Rio de Janeiro (causing no injuries).

Left-wing Movements

Brazilian Communist Party (*Partido Comunista Brasileiro,* PCB)

Leadership. Giocondo Dias (s.g.).

This party, established on March 25, 1922, as the Communist Party of Brazil, was banned shortly after its formation. In November 1935 it was involved in an armed rising, which was suppressed and led to the imprisonment of Luis Carlos Prestes, who remained its secretary-general until May 1980. At the end of World War II the party was legalized, and in general elections held in 1945 it gained about 10 per cent of the votes and 17 seats in the Chamber of Deputies. After being banned again in 1947, the party did not regain semilegal status until 1960, when it changed its name to Brazilian Communist Party.

Following the military coup of 1964 the party reverted to illegality. A number of party members were arrested in later years, especially in 1974, when some were reported to have been missing since 1973. In the general elections of Nov. 15, 1974, the party supported the Brazilian Democratic Movement (then the sole legal opposition party). On March 23, 1975, prison terms ranging from seven months to five years were imposed on 23 persons for trying to reorganize the party.

Although the police had discovered the party's printing presses in Rio de Janeiro and São Paulo in January 1975, the party's newspaper, *Voz Operaria,* reappeared in April and in August 1976; it claimed that half the party's leaders had been killed and others had been imprisoned and tortured in the past two years; the paper also called upon the people to vote, in the 1976 municipal elections, against the "dictatorship" of the Government. Early in August 1976 another 17 Communists were sentenced to imprisonment for from two to three years, and for eight of them their civil rights were withdrawn for from five to eight years.

L. C. Prestes returned from exile (with several other party members) under an amnesty signed by the President of the Republic on Aug. 29, 1979. *Voz Operaria* resumed publication on Oct. 2, 1980, but the party as such has not received legal recognition. Having under the previous two-party system given tacit backing to the opposition Brazilian Democratic Movement, the PCB gave unofficial support to the trade union-based Workers' Party in the November 1982 election.

During the party's seventh congress in São Paulo on Dec. 13, 1982, the federal police arrested the entire central committee and about 80 ordinary members of the party but released all but seven of them on the following day.

A Moscow-line party recognized by the Communist Party of the Soviet Union, the PCB gravitated towards the "Eurocommunist" tendency espoused by the Italian and Spanish Communist parties in the 1970s.

Communist Party of Brazil (*Partido Comunista do Brasil,* PCdoB)

This party broke away from the Brazilian Communist Party in 1961 and took a pro-Albanian line. During a raid by security forces in São Paulo on Dec. 16, 1976, three members of the party's central committee, among them Pedro de Araujo Pomar, the party's founder, were killed and six others were arrested. Certain members of the party were allowed to return to Brazil from exile under an amnesty signed by the President of the Republic on Aug. 28, 1979. The party, has, however, remained illegal.

National Liberation Alliance (*Aliança Libertadora Nacional,* ALN)

The ALN was set up in 1968 under the leadership of Carlos Marighella by dissidents from the (pro-Moscow) Brazilian Communist Party. It was responsible for several hundred armed attacks carried out until 1971, together with the Popular Revolutionary Vanguard (VPR—see separate entry), involving the appropriation of the equivalent of £1,000,000 in bank raids, the killing of 13 persons and injury to 26 others.

In particular, an ALN *Comando Juarez Guimarães de Brito* claimed to have carried out what it called the *Operação Joaquim Câmara Ferreira* on Dec. 7, 1970, by abducting the Swiss ambassador to Brazil; the ambassador was, however, released on Jan. 16, 1971, after the Brazilian Government had, as demanded by the ALN, released 70 persons from detention, all of them being sent to Chile (then under the Socialist Government of President Allende). The 70 ex-detainees included 26 members of a *Movimento Revolucionario de 8 Outubro* (MR 8, named after the date of the mortal wounding of the revolutionary activist Che Guevara in Bolivia in 1967); members of MR 8 had earlier been responsible for the abduction on Sept. 4, 1969, of the US ambassador to Brazil who had been released three days later after the Brazilian Government had agreed to an MR 8 demand by flying to Mexico 15 political prisoners—among them Gregorio Becerra (76), a pro-Moscow Communist sentenced to 19 years in prison in 1964, and also several left-wingers in sympathy with the MR 8, two of whom had admitted killing a US officer in São Paulo in 1968.

The names used by the ALN Commando referred to (i) Guimarães de Brito, a deputy leader of the VPR, who had committed suicide on May 30, 1970, as he was about to be captured by security forces, and (ii) J. Câmara Ferreira, a member of the ALN, who had died on Oct. 23, 1970, after being captured (and allegedly tortured) by police.

Carlos Marighella was killed in a gun battle in a suburb of São Paulo on Nov. 4, 1970. On March 23, 1975, a total of 27 alleged ALN members, arrested five years earlier with 92 others, were given prison sentences ranging from 15 months to 33 years for subversive activities.

In a handbook of urban guerrilla warfare (published in English in 1971 as *For the Liberation of Brazil*), C. Marighella gave detailed instructions on how this warfare should be conducted in Brazil. He stated that bank raids were "the most popular form of action" and had been made "a kind of entrance exam for apprenticeship in the technique of revolutionary war". A revolutionary, he said, must take care not to be confused with bandits or with right-wing counter-revolutionaries and must therefore make clear the purpose of his action (i) by refusing to take any money or personal possessions from customers in banks, and (ii) by writing slogans on the walls and handing out explanatory leaflets or pamphlets. He also gave details of whom to kidnap and hold as hostages—"policemen, North American spies, political figures or notorious enemies who are a danger to the revolution". He added: "Kidnapping American personalities who live in Brazil, or who have come to visit here, is a most powerful form of protest against the penetration of US imperialism into our country." Moreover, he advocated the sabotage of transport and of oil pipelines, the destruction of food supplies and a "scorched-earth strategy", assuming that the masses would blame the Government (and not the guerrillas) for the calamities resulting from such actions.

Palmares Revolutionary Armed Vanguard
(Vanguarda Armada Revolucionária-Palmares)

This group was responsible, inter alia, for the killing of a British sailor in Rio de Janeiro on Feb. 5, 1972.

Popular Revolutionary Vanguard *(Vanguarda Popular Revolucionária,* VPR)

This Castroite movement has co-operated closely with the National Liberation Alliance (ALN—see separate entry). It was responsible, inter alia, for the kidnapping of the Japanese consul-general in São Paulo on March 11, 1970, and his release on March 15 after the Brazilian Government had allowed five political prisoners to leave for Mexico (as demanded by the kidnappers). Its leader, the former army captain Carlos Lamarca, organized the kidnapping, on June 11, 1970, of the West German ambassador to Brazil, who was released on June 17 after the Brazilian Government had acceded to a demand by the kidnappers for the release of 40 political prisoners. (They were flown to Algiers, where several of them displayed the effects of torture, which, they alleged, they had suffered while in prison.)

In a manifesto issued jointly by the VPR and the ALN, and published in the Brazilian press and broadcast by the Brazilian radio on June 13 (as demanded by the kidnappers), the Government was accused, inter alia, of having imprisoned "thousands of freedom fighters" and of having tortured and murdered political prisoners (in particular nine "revolutionaries" whose names were given) and a call was made for the overthrow of the "dictatorship" and its replacement by a "people's government".

C. Lamarca was killed in a shoot-out with police at Pintada (Bahia state) on Sept. 17, 1971. Another six members of the VPR were shot dead by police at Paulista (near Recife) on Jan. 8, 1973. Although no further VPR activities were reported, arrests of suspected members continued until 1978. In 1979 it was reported that a number of VPR members were receiving guerrilla training in camps of the Palestine Liberation Organization in Lebanon.

Revolutionary Communist Party of Brazil
(Partido Comunista Revolucionário do Brasil)

This Maoist party broke away from the (pro-Moscow) Brazilian Communist Party in March 1967 and its founders included Mário Alves de Souza Vieira (who died in detention in March 1970, allegedly as a result of torture), Carlos Marighella (who in 1968 organized the National Liberation Alliance— see separate entry) and Apolonio de Carvalho. The last-named was, with others, released from detention in March 1970 in exchange for the release of the West German ambassador to Brazil by the Popular Revolutionary Vanguard (see separate entry).

Revolutionary Tiradentes Movement *(Movimento Revolucionário Tiradentes,* MRT)

This group was responsible for acts of urban guerrilla warfare in 1970-71. One of its founders, José de Carvalho, was killed by police in São Paulo on April 5, 1971. Following the murder of a Danish businessman on April 15, 1971, the police announced on April 19 that the MRT leader Dimas Antônio Cassemiro and another MRT member had been shot dead.

Chile

Capital: Santiago   Pop. 11,200,000

The Republic of Chile has since the overthrow of its parliamentary Government on Sept. 11, 1973, been ruled (under emergency provisions) by a four-member junta of the commanders of the armed services and the para-military police, who dissolved the National Congress, banned the countries' Marxist parties, placed all other parties into "indefinite recess" and prohibited all political activities. All remaining political parties were also banned on March 12, 1977. The head of the junta, Gen. Augusto Pinochet Ugarte, has since June 26, 1974, been Supreme Chief of State (or President) responsible for the administration of the country, while the agreement of the junta has been required for the appointment of ministers and other high-ranking officials and of generals.

In September 1975 Gen. Pinochet announced that two or three parties might be allowed, one of them being the *Movimiento de Unidad Nacional,* founded in April 1975, which he described as an "apolitical civic movement assigned to giving us support, without any privileges in return".

Under a new Constitution which entered into force on March 11, 1981, President Pinochet was enabled to remain in office at least until 1989. In the latter year the junta would nominate a single presidential candidate who, if confirmed by plebiscite, would remain in power until 1997, when free presidential elections would take place; if the candidate was rejected President Pinochet would remain in office for another one year but would call for such elections within that year. The Constitution (which had been approved in a national plebiscite on Sept. 11, 1980, by 67.04 per cent of the votes cast, with 30.14 per cent against it) also provided for elections to a Chamber of Deputies and a Senate at the end of 1989.

The Chilean Government announced in August 1978 that the secret police organization DINA *(Dirección de Inteligencia Nacional)* had been dissolved and replaced by a new military intelligence body called the National Information Centre (CNI). It was stated that DINA (formed in 1974) had "completed the delicate functions of national security for which it was created" and that the CNI would have reduced powers, notably excluding the power of arrest, and would be principally concerned with gathering information for security purposes.

Human Rights Issues

In a document published on Oct. 14, 1976, by the UN Commission on Human Rights the Chilean junta was charged with systematically extending its suppression of human rights from the political to other sectors of the population including the Church, trade unions, academics and professional groups; other Governments were urged to exert economic pressure on Chile to cease arbitrary arrests, torture and deportations; Oswaldo Romo was named as a "leading torturer"; and it was proposed that he should be tried by the international community. The UN General Assembly has also repeatedly condemned "constant and flagrant violations of human rights and fundamental freedoms" in Chile and censured the Pinochet Government for refusing to co-operate with the Human Rights Commission.

President Pinochet claimed (after the release of the Communist Jorge Montes on June 19, 1977) that there were no more political prisoners in Chile. Amnesty International had stated on March 16, 1977, that at least 1,500 political prisoners had disappeared since September 1973; that many of them were being held in secret detention centres in remote parts of the country: and that it possessed complete documentation on 500 people whom the Chilean police claimed not to have arrested but who were in fact in detention. The Chilean Government announced on May 22, 1977, that it had pardoned 918 Chileans living in exile after being convicted on various charges by military courts; it subsequently claimed that it was authorizing the selective return of up to 1,000 exiles a year.

Under a general amnesty decreed by the junta on April 19, 1978, all crimes against "national security" committed since September 1973 were erased. It was officially stated that the decree affected 2,071 persons, of whom 1,021 were living in exile and would be allowed to return to Chile on signature of an undertaking not to engage in political activities. The amnesty did not apply to persons detained or serving sentences for common and economic crimes, nor to those expelled from Chile without being charged or sentenced—in particular the secretaries-general of the Communist Party (Luis Corvalán Lepe), the Movement of the Revolutionary Left (MIR, Andrés Pascal Allende) and the Socialist Party (Carlos Altamirano).

In a further report of Feb. 21, 1979, a working group of the UN Commission on Human Rights stated that from January to October 1978 a total of 378 persons had been arrested in Chile for political or "national security" reasons (compared with 346 in 1977 and 582 in 1976); the group also claimed to have firm proof of the disappearance of over 600 people, and it demanded that those responsible for the torture and death of detainees should be tracked down and punished. The Minister of the Interior stated on July 15, 1978, that he had no evidence that any of the missing persons were in Government custody but he admitted that some of them might have been killed in clashes with the security forces. Unmarked graves were subsequently found in and near Santiago, over 600 of them in the city's main cemetery in November 1979, and others elsewhere.

In the early 1980s international and national human rights bodies have continued to censure Chile for alleged arbitrary arrests, secret police activity against dissidents and increasingly brutal forms of torture. In July 1981 a "Group of 24" Chilean lawyers and academics directed particular criticism against the broad powers wielded by the Government under transitional Clause 24 of the 1981 Constitution, giving the Government extensive powers to act without reference to the judiciary. The Group said that since March 1981 the clause had been used to arrest 158 people, although most of them had been released within a short time; that seven of the detainees were to be tried for breaking the ban on political activity; and that 62 of the 158 claimed to have been maltreated and seven to have been tortured.

According to an Amnesty International assessment issued on Sept. 9, 1981, there had been only sporadic reports over the past year of abductions or killings after arrest, as opposed to the "epidemic of disappearances" of earlier years. Nevertheless, said Amnesty, torture "still appears to be a systematic part of official policy" and several deaths had been reported under torture in 1979-80. Although measures such as short-term detentions and internal exile made it difficult to estimate the numbers of political prisoners, Amnesty believed that 2,700 people had been arrested on political grounds in 1980 and that all but 100 had been released shortly afterwards.

A report presented on Nov. 18, 1981, by a special UN rapporteur on Chile (who had been appointed by the UN Commission on Human Rights in March 1979) found that the Chilean authorities were "systematically refusing to respect the rights of their opponents to liberty, physical and moral integrity and personal security"; torture was still routine during interrogation, said the report, and the international community should continue to press for the full restoration of human rights in Chile.

Political Opposition

Christian Democratic Party (*Partido Democrático Cristiano,* PDC)

Leadership. Gabriel Valdés (pres.).

The PDC was created in 1957 as the successor to a National Falange founded in 1934; as a democratic reform party, it advocated a new social doctrine based on Christian humanism to overcome Chile's poverty and economic underdevelopment. The PDC's leader, Dr Eduardo Frei Montalva, was President of the Republic from 1964 to 1970, when he was succeeded by the Socialist, Dr Salvador Allende Gossens, whose regime was strongly opposed by the PDC. The party at first gave tacit support to the military junta which had seized power in 1973 but by 1974 many PDC leaders increasingly opposed the regime. In effect, the PDC became divided, as members of its right wing began to cooperate with the junta whereas what appeared to be the party's main body opposed it and took part in meetings and initiatives outside Chile organized by the Popular Unity alliance of left-wing parties (see separate entry).

At a secret congress held in March 1975 the PDC issued a declaration describing the ruling military junta as a "right-wing dictatorship with fascist manifestations" and their policies as "erroneous, unjust and incompatible with our principles regarding human rights, economic orientation and the situation of the workers". On the other hand, the congress rejected any liaison with "clandestine organizations".

On March 28, 1975, the Christian Democratic broadcasting station, Radio Balmaceda, was closed for 10 days by order of the junta for having allegedly undermined the security of the state and endangered peace and national harmony. The radio had reported the resignation from administrative posts of three Christian Democrats and also the seizure of a book on European fascism written by Claudio Orrego, a former Christian Democratic deputy known as a firm opponent of Dr Allende.

Dr Frei Montalva declined to become a member of a consultative Council of State established on Dec. 31, 1975, on the grounds that the Council had no juridical basis and that the Government would in no way be bound by its advice. On the other hand, the authorities allowed "as an exception", on Jan. 23, 1976, the publication of a booklet by Dr Frei, criticizing various aspects of the military junta and pleading for a "democratic alternative" to its totalitarian rule.

The Christian Democratic Weekly *Ercilla* was suspended on March 23, 1976 (the party's daily *La Prensa* having been forced to close in September 1973). Radio Balmaceda was closed indefinitely on Jan. 27, 1977, under a decree prohibiting political parties from operating radio stations.

On March 12, 1977, plans of two Christian Democrats—Andrés Zaldívar Larrain and Tomás Reyes—were published in the Santiago press, in which the co-operation of all political forces was called for in order to achieve a peaceful gradual transition to democracy. The Secretary-General to the Cabinet said that such plans would be "called subversive in any country", and on the same day the junta issued a decree banning all the remaining parties, i.e. the Christian Democrats, the National Party, the Radical Democrats and the Radical Left on the grounds that there was a Christian Democratic plot to overthrow the Government.

In a document released in Venezuela on Oct. 17, 1977, the PDC proposed that a "national movement of democratic restoration" should be created to replace Chile's military Government and demanded the convocation of a directly elected constituent assembly leading to an eventual full return to parliamentary democracy with an elected President; as an immediate step it proposed the lifting of the state of siege in force since September 1973 and renewed from time to time.

On Dec. 27, 1977, the PDC issued a statement urging the electorate to vote "no" in a plebiscite called for by President Pinochet (for Jan. 4, 1978) to endorse a declaration of support for the President and for the "legitimacy" of the Government. The PDC condemned the holding of the plebiscite while the country was still under a state of siege and personal and press freedoms were still restricted; stated that the result would have no validity; and added that the plebiscite confused the concepts of fatherland and government and sought to divide Chileans between patriots and non-patriots. In the event, however, 75.3 per cent of the valid votes were reported to have been "yes" votes and only 20.39 per cent "no" votes.

On Jan. 14, 1978, a military court ordered the indefinite exiling to remote villages in the northern Andes of 12 leading Christian Democrats (including Tomás Reyes, the party's vice-president) arrested with several others on Jan. 13 for indulging in political activity by holding a meeting. On Jan. 17, 1978, the PDC claimed that 60 of its members had been arrested, mistreated or banished. On Jan. 30 the federal court of appeals decided that the authorities could not deprive persons of their liberty unless they were convicted of a crime, and that the 12 persons exiled on Jan. 14 would have to be transferred to a hotel in Arica (a port near the border with Peru)—exile from one province to another being permitted. The 12 were, however, allowed to return to Santiago on March 2, 1978.

Ex-President Frei, addressing an authorized meeting on Aug. 28, 1979, called for the formation of a civilian-military transitional government to restore full democracy within the next two to three years. The meeting, however, turned into an opposition demonstration which was broken up by police. Other such demonstrations took place that year.

On Oct. 16, 1980, the junta announced that A. Zaldívar Larrain, then PDC president touring Europe, would not be allowed to re-enter Chile unless he signed a document accepting the results of the plebiscite of Sept. 11, 1980, approving the new Constitution and the authority of the Government and the Constitution. He was inter alia accused of making denigratory statements about Chile to a Mexican newspaper and of thus threatening Chile's internal security. The PDC presidency was subsequently assumed by Gabriel Valdés.

Ex-President Frei died in Santiago on Jan. 22, 1982, when President Pinochet declared three days of official mourning; a government memorial service was held on Jan. 25 but later on the same day a main ceremony held by the family was addressed by Cardinal Raúl Silva Henríques (Archbishop of Santiago and Primate of Chile) and was heard by thousands of mourners.

Four exiled Christian Democrats who were not allowed to enter Chile for ex-President Frei's funeral included Jaime Castillo Velasco, president of the Chilean human rights commission, who had been expelled in

August 1981 with three other prominent opposition figures after they had been accused of violating the ban on political activity and showing a "defiant attitude". In his capacity as a lawyer, Jaime Castillo Velasco had been acting for the family of Orlando Letelier, the former Chilean ambassador in Washington and minister in the Allende Government, who had been murdered in the US capital in 1976 by Chilean secret agents.

Christian Left

The small Christian Left formation was formed by elements of the Christian Democratic Party (PDC) which supported the candidacy of the Socialist leader, Dr Salvador Allende Gossens, in the November 1970 presidential elections. As part of the Popular Unity alliance (see separate entry), the Christian Left was banned by the military junta which seized power in September 1973. Since then it has participated in the anti-junta activities of the alliance and has in particular acted as a bridge between the Popular Unity parties and the left-wing section of the PDC itself.

Communist Party of Chile (*Partido Comunista Chileno,* PCC)

Leadership. Luis Corvalán Lepe (s.g.).

A Socialist Workers' Party founded in 1912 decided at its fourth congress held in Rancagua in January 1922, to affiliate with the Third International and to change its name to Communist Party of Chile. By 1970 the PCC was the third largest among pro-Moscow Communist parties (after those of France and Italy) outside the Communist-ruled countries. In congressional elections held on March 2, 1969, the PCC gained 22 out of the 150 seats in the Chamber of Deputies; in the presidential elections of Nov. 4, 1970, it was part of the Popular Unity alliance, whose candidate, the Socialist Dr Salvador Allende Gossens, was elected President with 36.3 per cent of the votes cast. In the Popular Unity Cabinet formed subsequently, the PCC was given ministerial posts. On Dec. 3, 1971, the party (then claiming to have 150,000 members) set up a Revolutionary Workers' Front which established "anti-fascist brigades" in the factories.

On Jan. 16, 1972, the PCC criticized the "sectarian extremism" of the Revolutionary Movement of the Left (MIR) which had "alienated middle sectors" of the population, and it emphasized that the "correct strategy" was to divide the opposition by attracting "progressive" sections of the Christian Democratic Party which supported economic and social change. In June 1972 Luis Corvalán Lepe, the PCC's secretary-general, publicly called for the consolidation of socialist gains and for slowing down further progress towards socialism in order to reassure public opinion and to win the congressional elections in 1973. In these elections the Popular Unity alliance gained 43.39 per cent of the votes cast for candidates for the Chamber of Deputies, against 54.70 per cent gained by the (opposition) Federation of Democratic Parties; in consequence, the Popular Unity alliance gained only 63 of the 150 seats in the Chamber (with the PCC gaining 25).

Following the banning of the PCC by the junta which took power on Sept. 11, 1973, the party went underground, carrying out secret activities despite serious losses resulting from the arrest or death of many of its members. The party claimed at the end of October 1973 (in *La Stampa* of Turin, Italy) that "a communal struggle" was being prepared "for the overthrow of the military regime". Thereafter the party co-ordinated its anti-junta activities in exile within the framework of the Popular Unity alliance (see separate entry). On Nov. 2, 1975, the Government alleged that Communists, of whom 15 had been arrested on Sept. 19, had planned to assassinate President Bordaberry of Uruguay during a state visit to Chile in September.

On Dec. 18, 1976, Luis Corvalán Lepe (former secretary-general of the PCC, held in detention in Chile since September 1973) was exchanged at Zurich airport against Vladimir Bukovsky (the Soviet dissident imprisoned in the Soviet Union since 1972). L. Corvalán Lepe was taken to the Soviet Union, where he made several statements on the policy of the PCC, notably one on Dec. 30, 1976, when he alleged that there were 3,300 political prisoners in Chile and that another 2,000 persons had disappeared. (On June 19, 1977, Jorge Montes—a PCC leader detained in Chile since July 1974—was released in exchange for the release of 11 German political prisoners held in the German Democratic Republic.)

On Jan. 4, 1977, L. Corvalán Lepe called (in Moscow) for the formation of a united front of all democratic forces, including the Chilean Christian Democrats, against the "military dictatorship" in Chile; at the same time he declared that the PCC firmly adhered to the principles of "proletarian internationalism" and of the "dictatorship of the proletariat", claiming that the latter concept was more democratic than "any bourgeois form of government", although in Chile its implementation was a problem to be solved at a later stage. On Jan. 12, 1978, he appealed to the Chilean Christian Democrats for the setting-up of a "government of democratic union" which should speedily replace the military junta; he claimed that the majority of the military and the police in Chile wished to end repression and the existing situation.

In 1982 the PCC's political commission

issued a renewed call for unity of all opposition strata seeking the overthrow of the military regime in Chile.

Javier Carrera Popular Resistance Commando (*Comando de Resistência Popular Javier Carrera,* CRP)

This group, which carried out two guerrilla operations in 1980 following its establishment in April of that year, was thought to be an offshoot of the Movement of the Revolutionary Left (MIR—see separate entry).

Movement of the Revolutionary Left (*Movimiento de la Izquierda Revolucionaria,* MIR)

Leadership. Andrés Pascal Allende (s.g.).

Under the Christian Democratic Government headed by President Eduardo Frei Montalva (in 1964-70) the MIR, established in 1965 as an extreme left-wing group committed to guerrilla activities, was illegal. It gave conditional support to President Allende after the latter's election in 1970, but repeatedly called for much more radical revolutionary procedures than those of the Government. On Nov. 1, 1971, its secretary-general at the time (Miguel Enríquez) demanded the abolition of Parliament, its replacement by a "people's assembly" and the takeover of farms and factories without compensation.

After the assumption of power by the military junta the MIR was in open conflict with the regime. An offer of a truce, said to have been made by the Armed Forces Intelligence Service, was publicly refused by the MIR on Sept. 10, 1974. On Oct. 5, 1974, M. Enríquez was killed in a gun battle with troops in Santiago. On Jan. 8, 1975, a group of 12 army officers were given prison sentences of up to 15 years for collaboration with the MIR. On Nov. 10, 1975, the Government announced that it had arrested 15 MIR members in connexion with an "operation red boomerang" designed to infiltrate 1,200 extremists into southern Chile from Argentina in collaboration with the Argentinian People's Revolutionary Army (ERP); the organizers of this operation were said to include A. P. Allende.

In January 1976 safe-conducts out of Chile were issued for four leading MIR members who had been involved in a gunfight with police on Oct. 15, 1975, when another MIR leader had been killed; the four men included A. P. Allende, who arrived in Costa Rica on Feb. 2, 1976, when he claimed that since 1973 there had been over 150,000 political prisoners in Chile, of whom 40,000 had died under torture.

In October 1977 the MIR claimed responsibility for a series of bombings in Santiago, in particular of government buildings on Oct. 14-16, thought to have been made in retaliation for the suicide in Havana of Beatriz Allende, a daughter of the late President.

In February 1981 the MIR claimed to have carried out more than 100 attacks during 1980, including the assassination of the head of the army intelligence school and his driver on July 15, after which several hundred persons were detained for questioning and a number of people were attacked or kidnapped by right-wing groups.

In military operations against MIR forces in Valdivia province (500 miles south of Santiago) in July-September 1981, seven guerrilla suspects were killed by security forces as they were preparing to attack the Foreign Minister's residence, and on Nov. 18 three policemen were killed in a gunfight outside the house of the presidential chief of staff. In a number of other incidents during 1981-82 three MIR suspects were killed on May 9, July 17 and Jan. 16, 1982. A secret police agent was killed by the MIR on July 6, 1981, and nine MIR members were expelled from Chile on Nov. 22. On Nov. 27, 1982, the second-in-command of the MIR, Dagoberto Cortes Guajardo, was killed in a shoot-out with security forces in Santiago.

On the political front, the exigencies of the anti-junta struggle have impelled the MIR to reconcile its differences with the parties of the Popular Unity alliance (see separate entry). A communiqué issued to the press in Santiago in mid-January 1981 said that the MIR leadership had joined with exiled leaders of the Popular Unity formations in signing a declaration of unity providing for joint opposition to the Pinochet regime.

Multipartidaria Alliance

This broad opposition coalition was launched in March 1983 with the signature of a "democratic manifesto" by (i) the majority *Partido Republicano* faction of the National Party (the main right-wing democratic party); (ii) the Christian Democratic Party; (iii) the three main factions of the Socialist Party; (iv) the Radical Party; and (v) some social democratic elements previously within the Radical Party. The Communist Party remained outside the new alliance, principally because of opposition to its participation from the Christian Democrats.

The new coalition comprised as its information and publicity department a group of former right-wing politicians and trade union leaders calling themselves *Proyecto de Desarrollo Nacional* (Proden). The Government was reported to have agreed to study charges brought by the Alliance against a former Minister of Finance and the Economy and also its proposal for constitutional reform.

Popular Unity *(Unidad Popular)*

Leadership. Dr Clodomiro Almeyda Medina (first sec. of executive committee).

Set up in 1969 as an electoral alliance of left-wing parties, which led to the election of the Socialist Dr Salvador Allende Gossens as President on Nov. 4, 1970, the Popular Unity was deprived of all power through the military coup of Sept. 11, 1973 (on which day President Allende committed suicide). A secretariat of the Popular Unity was thereupon set up in Rome (Italy) by the Communist ex-Senator Volodia Teitelboim on Sept. 18, 1973. The secretariat later disseminated news of persecution and repression of President Allende's supporters in Chile, claiming in November 1973 that more than 3,000 officers and men of the armed forces, loyal to Dr Allende, had been executed, and that others condemned to death had included leading Communists. Many of those sent to Dawson Island (off Tierra del Fuego) for detention had died, according to other sources. On May 1, 1974, all constituent parties of the Popular Unity issued a declaration calling for the formation of an "anti-fascist front" in order to end "illegal detention, tortures and summary executions" and to "regain democratic rights".

A meeting of leaders of the Popular Unity parties and the left wing of the Christian Democratic Party was held in July 1975 in Caracas (Venezuela), where they decided to work together for the restoration of "a just and socialist democracy in Chile"; at a further meeting in East Berlin in August 1975 they published a joint programme aimed at resisting the military regime and restoring democratic freedoms; and in October they met in London to discuss the establishment of unified headquarters. A further meeting of Popular Unity parties' leaders and left-wing Christian Democrats was held in New York in September 1976, whereafter Dr Almeyda Medina (who had been expelled from Chile on Jan. 11, 1975) declared again that the aim of the Popular Unity was to establish an "anti-fascist" front with the participation of the Christian Democrats.

In a communiqué issued to the press in Santiago in mid-January 1981 it was announced that the parties constituting the Popular Unity alliance—the Communist Party, the Radical Party, the two wings of the Socialist Party, the Christian Left, the Unified Popular Action Movement and the latter's Workers and Peasants offshoot—had joined with the Movement of the Revolutionary Left (MIR) to sign a declaration of unity providing for joint opposition to the Pinochet regime.

Anti-government demonstrators in Santiago in March 1983 used the Popular Unity slogan 'bread, justice, work and liberty'.

Radical Party *(Partido Radical)*

Leadership. Anselmo Sule (ch.).

Founded in 1906, the Radical Party became Chile's main reformist party by the 1930s and held the presidency both before and after World War II. Strongly anti-communist in the 1940s and 1950s, it later gravitated to the left and in 1969 joined the Popular Unity alliance (see separate entry) which secured the election of the Socialist leader, Dr Salvador Allende Gossens, to the presidency in November 1970. Radicals held ministerial posts in successive Popular Unity administrations, although the party was weakened by breakaways of elements opposed to its espousal of Marxism in 1971. Within Chile the Radical Party has its main strength among white-collar workers and public officials.

Together with the other Popular Unity formations, the Radical Party was banned by the military junta which seized power in September 1973. Since then it has co-ordinated its efforts to overthrow the Pinochet regime within the Popular Unity alliance, with the particular role of ensuring liaison between the alliance and democratic socialist forces in other countries. The party is a member of the Socialist International, of which organization its chairman is a vice-president.

Socialist Party *(Partido Socialista)*

Leadership. Carlos Altamirano (s.g.).

The Socialist Party is one of the constituent parties of the Popular Unity *(Unidad Popular)* alliance (see separate entry), which came to power when the Socialist leader, Dr Salvador Allende Gossens, was elected President of the Republic in November 1970. In his election programme Allende had made radical proposals, inter alia to replace the existing Parliament by an "assembly of the people", to nationalize all major foreign-owned companies and the banks and to develop close ties with Communist countries. After the overthrow of his regime on Sept. 11, 1973, the Socialist Party was banned (with all other member parties of the Popular Unity); of its members, many were sentenced to terms of imprisonment in 1974 and thereafter.

Party members were also involved in legal proceedings arising from an alleged conspiracy to infiltrate Socialists into the armed forces under President Allende's regime which a military court (which was trying them) deemed to have been illegal; four defendants were sentenced to death for "treason and sedition" on July 30, 1974, but these sentences were, on Aug. 5, commuted to 30 years' imprisonment: 52 other defendants were given prison sentences of up to 20 years.

In 1977 a split occurred in the party in exile, when Pedro Vuskovic (who had been Minister of Economic Affairs under President Allende in 1970-72 and had gone into exile after the military coup of September 1973) was expelled from the Socialist Party in July 1977 for "activities tending to divide the party". He did not agree with the main body of exile opinion that the Chilean military regime could be overthrown with help from abroad, and in mid-October 1977 he claimed in London that the Popular Unity and the Christian Democrats aimed at "reconstituting the bourgeois democracy" which had previously existed in Chile, and that the increasing consumer capitalism in Chile and other Latin American countries was incompatible with democracy, which could only be achieved under a reconstructed Socialist Party.

Of Socialist leaders imprisoned ex-Senator Erich Schnake, given a 20-year sentence for conspiracy on July 30, 1974, was released on Dec. 23, 1977, on condition that he left the country. He said in Madrid early in January 1978 that he owed his release to Felipe González, secretary-general of the Spanish Socialist Workers' Party (PSOE), who had visited him in prison in August 1977.

At a meeting in Algeria in March 1978, delegates both from within Chile and from the party in exile elected a single party leadership and reaffirmed the unity of the party within the Popular Unity alliance and its increased co-operation with the Christian Democratic Party against the junta. Nevertheless, in the early 1980s the leadership of Carlos Altamirano came under challenge from two smaller Socialist Party factions led respectively by Clodomiro Almeyda and by Raúl Ampuero.

Unified Popular Action Movement (*Movimiento de Acción Popular Unida,* MAPU)

Leadership. Jaime Anselmo Cuevas Hormazábal (l.).

MAPU was one of the constituent parties of the Popular Unity alliance in power under President Allende in 1970-73. After the military coup of Sept. 11, 1973, when it had been banned, it engaged in underground activities. Its leader was arrested in April 1980. Like its small Workers and Peasants offshoot, MAPU has co-ordinated its anti-junta activities within the Popular Unity alliance (see separate entry) since the 1973 coup.

Workers and Peasants—see Unified Popular Action Movement

Trade Union Opposition

In November 1977 President Pinochet confirmed that seven trade union leaders (among them Juan Manuel Sepúlveda Malbrán), who were "agitators and agents of an international campaign" against the Chilean regime, had been exiled to remote mountain villages in the region of Putre (northern Chile); this order was on Dec. 20, 1977, reported to have been revoked, but J. M. Sepúlveda Malbrán subsequently went into exile.

Following increased opposition trade union activity in 1981, Tucapel Jiménez, veteran leader of the union of public employees, was found killed outside Santiago on Feb. 25, 1982, after he had announced a week earlier that he and other trade union leaders proposed to establish a broadly-based trade union movement to oppose the Government's economic policies which, he said, had led to the dismissal of 68,000 public sector employees within the past 14 months.

National Trade Union Co-ordinating Body (*Co-ordinadora Nacional Sindical,* CNS)

Leadership. Juan Manuel Sepúlveda Malbrán (l.).

This body was set up in 1978 as a left-orientated trade union organization by a number of trade unions including the Ranquil National Peasants' and Indians' Confederation, Peasant-Worker Unity (UOC) and five textile, construction, engineering and mineworkers' confederations, all of which the Government described as "Marxist" and banned on Oct. 19, 1978. After petitioning the Government for basic changes in economic and social policies, trade union liberties and wage increases, 11 leading members of the CNS were temporarily detained from July 6, 1981, onwards. The CNS leader, who had earlier left the country, was on Aug. 13, 1981, prohibited from returning to Chile.

Church Opposition

On March 27, 1977, the permanent committee of the (Roman Catholic) episcopal conference published a document in which it described the existing Government as unrepresentative and declared that a suitable political system could only emerge as the result of "a free national consensus, expressed in a legitimate manner". The document requested President Pinochet to investigate the cases of those persons who had disappeared since September 1973 and criticized the lack of freedom of expression. It also stated: "We do not believe that human rights will be guaranteed until the country has a Constitution and as long as laws are dictated by those who are not the legitimate representatives of the people and all organs of state are not subject to the Constitution and the law." The church leaders were thereupon strongly criticized by the Minister of Justice who, however, resigned on April 21, 1977.

On Nov. 16, 1977, police broke up a meeting held in a Dominican convent; in reply to a complaint by Cardinal Raúl Silva Henríquez (Archbishop of Santiago and Primate of Chile), President Pinochet maintained that the meeting had been a clandestine political gathering and part of a plot to create social agitation with those attending having included the president and the vice-president of the Christian Democratic Party and two trade union leaders.

The Roman Catholic bishops decided at a meeting on Dec. 30, 1977, to call for the postponement of the plebiscite called for by President Pinochet (for Jan. 4, 1978) to endorse his Government. In a statement also signed by Cardinal Silva Henríquez, the bishops complained that the wording of the plebiscite question was confusing and that the existing state of siege prevented freedom of expression.

Committee of Co-operation for Peace in Chile

This inter-church organization of Roman Catholic, Protestant and Jewish clergy compiled, in May 1974, a report accusing the junta of torturing political prisoners, based on the testimony of hundreds of victims. This report, published in *Excelsior* (a leading Mexican newspaper) on May 16, 1974, was originally intended solely for the attention of church leaders. It alleged that before being released victims were forced to sign declarations stating that they had been well treated. A junta spokesman (on May 17) condemned reports of torture as "a grave distortion of reality".

On Nov. 4, 1975, the Government accused the Roman Catholic Church, and in particular the Committee of Co-operation for Peace, of protecting "Marxist elements, including leaders of the Revolutionary Movement of the Left". Nine members of the Committee were subsequently arrested, and on Nov. 17 President Pinochet requested Cardinal Silva Henríquez to dissolve the committee in order to "avoid serious conflicts between Church and State". The Cardinal, however, stressed in reply that the Committee's involvement in human rights questions would continue within other church organizations. (Bishop Helmut Frenz, head of the Evangelical Lutheran Church in Chile and co-president of the Committee, had on Oct. 3 been refused re-entry into Chile after a visit to Geneva; he was accused of "antinational activities".)

The Committee was formally closed down on Dec. 31, 1975, but was subsequently replaced by a "Vicariate of Solidarity" (see separate entry). On April 12, 1976, the former head of the Committee's human rights department was expelled from Chile after he had, among others, spoken to a visiting US congressional delegation concerning alleged Chilean violations of human rights.

Vicariate of Solidarity

The Vicariate was set up in January 1976 by the Roman Catholic bishops' conference to replace the Committee of Co-operation for Peace in Chile (see separate entry), which was formally closed down on Dec. 31, 1975. In January 1977 the Vicariate demanded that the Supreme Court should appoint a special judge to investigate the disappearance of 415 people up to August 1976. The demand was rejected, but in February a judge was appointed to look into 15 cases of alleged disappearance. In November 1977 President Pinochet accused the Vicariate of helping to finance labour unrest.

In January 1982 the Vicariate reported that there had been a return to particularly brutal forms of torture, a growth in "secret group activity" against political dissidents and a number of political killings which amounted to virtual executions.

Right-wing Movements

Avengers of the Martyrs Commando (*Comando Vengador de Mártires,* Covema)

This right-wing group claimed responsibility for a number of attacks made from July 1980 onwards, including the temporary kidnapping of the journalists connected with church radio stations and of six students, one of whom died of wounds inflicted by the kidnappers.

Popular Nationalist Movement (*Movimiento Nacionalista Popular,* MNP)

Leadership. Roberto Thieme.

This right-wing Movement was established in 1980 by Roberto Thieme, a former military officer who had, as general secretary of the neo-fascist *Patria y Libertad* group, been involved in attempts to subvert the left-wing Government of President Allende in the early 1970s. Initially a supporter of the military regime which seized power in September 1973, Thieme later broke with President Pinochet and organized the MNP in his base of Temuco in the south, where it received some support from dissident farmers.

In October 1982 Thieme mounted an unsuccessful attempted coup against the Pinochet regime, claiming that the latter had betrayed the "nationalist revolution" in Chile by encouraging foreign (notably US) interests to increase their influence over the country's affairs. Thieme, who left Chile thereafter to live in Argentina, declared his admiration for the achievements of the military regime of Gen. Juan Velasco Alvarado which held power in Peru after 1968.

Colombia

Capital: Bogotá   Pop. 27,000,000

The Republic of Colombia has an executive President elected by direct popular vote for a four-year term and a bicameral Congress consisting of a 114-member Senate and a 199-member House of Representatives, both elected for four-year terms by universal adult suffrage. In elections held on March 14, 1982, seats in the House of Representatives were gained in a 45 per cent poll as follows: Liberals 114, Conservatives 84, Democratic Unity of the Left 1. In presidential elections held on May 30, 1982, however, the Liberal vote was split by the emergence of a New Liberalism faction, with the result that the Conservative candidate was elected, gaining 46.8 per cent of the vote, against 41 per cent gained by the Liberal candidate and 10.9 by the New Liberalism candidate; only 1.2 per cent was obtained by the candidate of the Democratic Unity of the Left, this alliance consisting of the Communist Party of Colombia, the *Firmes* Movement, the Socialist Revolutionary Party and the Colombian Labour Party. The elections were also contested by the (Workers') Movement of the Revolutionary Left (MOIR), whose presidential candidate, however, withdrew from the contest.

Political violence has a long tradition in Colombia. During the period of Colombia's history between 1946 and 1953, known as "La Violencia", about 180,000 Colombians were killed in acts of violence due to banditry as well as to civil war. In later years many thousands of others lost their lives, largely as a result of guerrilla warfare and acts of terrorism. For the year 1977 kidnappings were officially given as 87 and political murders as 133. On Oct. 22, 1980, the Minister of Defence stated that in the past three years guerrillas had killed 128 members of the security forces and 417 peasants; had attacked 83 military bases and 152 banks; and had obtained $4,000,000 through 88 kidnappings and 10 cases of extortion; he also said that 1,830 guerrillas were still at large while 1,027 were in captivity. According to police statistics, the total of persons kidnapped in 1981 was 100 (63 by guerrillas and 37 by common criminals), of whom 44 had been freed, nine had been killed, and 47 remained in the hands of their abductors.

Shortly before he relinquished office, President Turbay Ayala on June 20, 1982, lifted the state of siege which had been in force almost continuously for 34 years and at the same time abrogated over 30 emergency decrees. His successor as President, Dr Belisario Betancur Cuartas, undertook at his inauguration on Aug. 7 to pursue his predecessor's efforts to achieve an amnesty with the country's left-wing guerrilla groups. The most active of the latter are effectively the military wings of the (pro-Soviet) Communist Party of Colombia (CPC) and the (pro-Chinese) Communist Party of Colombia (Marxist-Leninist).

Right-wing Groups

Death Squads *(Escuadrones de la Muerte)*

These right-wing terror groups have been held responsible for numerous killings of alleged left-wing militants. According to a police report of Sept. 14, 1980, the Death Squads had killed 560 persons in Pereira (Risaraldas department) alone in January-August 1980. On Oct. 27, 1980, courts in Medellín reported that Death Squad activities

Medellín reported that Death Squad activities had claimed 60 lives. On Nov. 24, 1980, another 11 Death Squad victims were discovered in Medellín. A secret service officer who had denounced the existence of Death Squads sought asylum at the British embassy in Bogotá on Feb. 22, 1980.

Death to Kidnappers (*Muerte a los Secuestradores,* MAS)

This group emerged early in 1982, its avowed aim being to act against guerrilla groups which carried out abductions to finance their operations. Its victims included not only suspected guerrillas but also trade union leaders; it was also responsible for the death of a leading defence lawyer for left-wing defendants in March 1982. The newly-elected Conservative President, Dr Belisario Betancur Cuartas, ordered the security forces to investigate and break up the MAS. According to a report submitted to the President and the Minister of Defence at the end of January 1983 by the office of the procurator-general, MAS had close links with a number of senior army officers, although this was denied by the Minister of Defence.

Left-wing Movements

April 19 Movement (*Movimiento 19 de Abril,* M-19)

Leadership. Dr Carlos Toledo Plata; Jaime Bateman Cayón.

Formed in 1974, the M-19 took its name from the date on which ex-President (Gen.) Gustavo Rojas Pinilla, the leader of the National Popular Alliance (*Alianza Nacional Popular,* ANAPO), had been defeated in presidential elections in 1970. The M-19 claimed to be the armed wing of ANAPO, although the latter rejected this claim. While ANAPO was a hierarchically-organized party standing for "Colombian socialism" on a Christian social basis, the M-19 came, by the end of the 1970s, to be regarded as left-wing and Marxist, and its leaders declared as its aim the achievement of a democratic and ultimately socialist state by political means.

The first operation of the M-19 was the theft from a museum outside Bogotá of the sword and spurs of Simon Bolívar (the liberator of Spanish America) in January 1974. There followed other acts of violence. These included the kidnapping on Feb. 15, 1976, of the president of the Colombian Confederation of Workers (CTC), José Raquel Mercado, whom the M-19 accused of being a traitor to the working class and for whose release it demanded inter alia the reinstatement of dismissed workers and the release of a number of political prisoners; the Government, how-

ever, refused to negotiate with the M-19, and J. R. Mercado was "executed" by the M-19 on April 19.

On Aug. 28, 1978, the M-19 was reported to have "declared war" on the (right-wing Liberal) Government of President Julio César Turbay Ayala, which had introduced increased penalties for acts of violence such as armed rebellion, kidnapping and bombing. During the next few weeks the M-19 was (together with the Colombian Revolutionary Armed Forces) responsible for the death of over 40 people, and in January 1979 M-19 members stole 5,000 weapons from an army arsenal north of Bogotá (but the Army claimed later to have recovered most of these arms); about 150 M-19 suspects were subsequently arrested in January-February 1979, among them several Argentinians, Uruguayans and West Germans.

Major M-19 operations in 1980 included the temporary occupation of the embassy of the Dominican Republic in Bogotá from Feb. 27 to April 27, 1980, when M-19 guerrillas seized 57 hostages including the ambassadors of 14 countries—among them those of Israel, Mexico and the United States—as well as the papal nuncio. The guerrilla group was led by Rosemberg Pabón Pabón (a former university professor). The demands originally made by the kidnappers for the release of the hostages were, in protracted negotiations involving among other intermediaries the Inter-American Human Rights Commission (IHRC) of the Organization of American States, eventually reduced to payment of a ransom of $10,000,000 and the release of 28 political detainees. President Turbay Ayala insisted that such a release would contravene the Constitution but agreed on March 12 to appoint a team of lawyers to investigate ways of accelerating the trial of 219 M-19 detainees which was due to go on for another year. The guerrillas accepted assurances that the M-19 trials would be monitored by IHRC observers, and left by air for Havana on April 27, taking with them 12 remaining hostages (who were later released in Cuba); all other hostages had been freed in stages during the negotiations, and one of the guerrillas was killed in a shooting incident at the beginning of the action. It was believed that the ransom actually paid amounted to $2,500,000.

Later in 1980 the M-19 continued to be engaged in numerous acts of violence, including bomb attacks on the Costa Rican and Uruguayan consulates in Cali on March 30; the temporary occupation of the US cultural centre in Medellín on May 8; the planting of a bomb at the US consulate in Cali on May 11, when two M-19 members were killed by the bomb; the temporary occupation of a naval vessel in Cartagena on June 29; the interruption of television broadcasts on Sept. 14; and the hijacking of an aircraft to Cuba with 65 hostages and the occupation of a radio station in Cali (to broadcast a message) on Dec. 15.

By September 1980 the M-19 was officially regarded as the second strongest guerrilla organization with 531 active members. J. Bateman Cayón announced on Jan. 12, 1981, that he intended to contest the 1982 presidential elections, but in fact the M-19 did not take part in these elections.

The abduction of a US citizen (Chester Allen Bitterman), accused of being a "spy" of the (US) Central Intelligence Agency (CIA), on Jan. 19, 1981, and his later killing, were attributed to a radical faction of the M-19 (see below). After an attack on March 11 by M-19 guerrillas on the town of Mocoa (southern Colombia), in which 11 persons were killed, the Army launched major anti-guerrilla operations in southern Colombia, where 19 guerrillas were reported killed and 26 captured. Among 50 others who had fled to Ecuador (but were arrested in that country and handed over to the Colombian authorities) were Dr Toledo Plata and Rosemberg Pabón Pabón. The Army subsequently claimed that the guerrillas involved had been part of an invasion force which had entered Colombia by boat from Cuba via the Panama Canal in March 1981, and in June 1981 a military court found 15 people guilty of being members of the M-19 and of taking part in the invasion attempt; they were sentenced to prison terms totalling 330 years.

President Turbay Ayala announced on March 23, 1981, that his Government was severing its diplomatic relations with Cuba on the grounds that the latter was arming and aiding the M-19; but Cuba denied the following day that it had directly or indirectly aided the M-19 or any other-revolutionary organizations in Colombia.

When President Turbay Ayala proposed an amnesty bill, which was finally approved by the Senate on March 4 and signed by the President on March 13, 1981, the M-19 was already divided into two factions, the major one of which (led by J. Bateman Cayón, Dr C. Toledo Plata and Ivan Marino Ospina) favoured a legal political role, as was offered in the President's amnesty bill to all guerrillas who laid down their arms within four months. The smaller faction constituted itself as the *Coordinadora Nacional de Bases* (CNB), which rejected peaceful negotiations and the amnesty (which inter alia specifically excluded all those guilty of murder, kidnapping and extortion) and called for the continuation of the armed struggle.

On the expiry of the amnesty on July 23, 1981, the M-19 reiterated its earlier peace proposals for a general amnesty without exclusions and for the abrogation of the 1978 security legislation. At the same time it intensified its guerrilla operations, partly in collaboration with the Colombian Revolutionary Armed Forces. On July 19, 1981, M-19 guerrillas launched an attack on the presidential palace in Bogotá and another on a police station, where a policeman was killed. Early in October 1981 the armed forces claimed to have uncovered an M-19 plan to stage an insurrection (to coincide with a general strike), and they placed Bogotá under military control. The strike, staged on Oct. 21, was not widely followed, but owing to continued student unrest the universities in Bogotá, Medellín and Baranquilla were temporarily closed in October. On Nov. 14 a coaster was sunk by the Navy off the Pacific coast on suspicion of carrying arms for the M-19, four people being killed, 20 reported missing and five arrested.

On the recommendation of a peace commission set up by President Turbay Ayala in October 1981, the Government announced, on Feb. 19, 1982, a second amnesty (for two months, later extended to June 19, 1982) for all those who had committed "rebellion against the state" (but again not those who had carried out murders and kidnappings). However, the amnesty was rejected by most guerrillas. Recommendations by the peace commission that the Government should enter into direct negotiations with the M-19 leaders were rejected by the Government (owing to opposition by the armed forces and certain political sectors), and when the Government rejected another recommendation by the peace commission (to suspend sentences imposed on guerrillas) five of the commission's members resigned.

The M-19 had meanwhile continued its violent activities, in particular by hijacking another Colombian airliner on Jan. 27, 1982; most of the passengers and crew were released at Cali on Jan. 28 in exchange for a free passage of the seven hijackers to Havana.

A further presidential amnesty offer came into effect in November 1982, with the major crimes to which it would not be applicable being limited to "premeditated murder and murders which take advantage of the inferior strength of the victim"; this amnesty therefore also covered acts of sedition, rebellion and conspiracy. As a result the seven-member political command of the M-19 had talks with the Minister of the Interior with a view to obtaining a guarantee of "social justice" before the M-19 laid down its arms. J. Bateman Cayón was quoted as saying that a six-month armistice would be needed to ensure the success of the amnesty. In October 1982 he had described the M-19 as being a "nationalist, ideologically pluralist and 80 per cent Catholic" movement.

Despite these efforts to achieve an amnesty agreement M-19 guerrillas continued to be engaged in acts of violence, which included the kidnapping of a banker's daughter in

January 1983, a ransom of US$15,000,000 being demanded for her release.

Colombian Revolutionary Armed Forces (*Fuerzas Armadas Revolucionarias Colombianas,* FARC)

Among several independent republics set up during the period of "La Violencia" (1946-53) was that of Gaitania (later called Marquetalia, in the department of Tolima). It was founded in 1949 by Fermín Charry Rincón (a member of the central committee of the Communist Party and also known as Jacobo Frias Alape), who was killed in January 1960 and was succeeded by Manuel Marulanda Vélez (also called Pedro Antonio Marín or Tiro Fijo—"Sure Shot"). Marquetalia was occupied by the Colombian Army in May 1964, but its guerrillas decided to continue their struggle and set up, in April 1966, the FARC under the leadership of M. Marulanda Vélez and other members of the Communist Party's central committee. On Sept. 14, 1970, M. Marulanda Vélez was reported to have died. During this period the FARC carried on guerrilla activities in the departments of Huila, Tolima, Quindio and Valle.

In July 1976 the FARC was reported to be active in the departments of Chocó and Córdoba, and on July 16 some 40 FARC members temporarily seized the town of Sabane Grande, in Sucre. A US Peace Corps worker (Richard Starr), kidnapped by FARC members on Feb. 14, 1977, was released on Feb. 11, 1980, after money had been borrowed to pay a ransom of $250,000. In an offensive against the FARC in December 1978-January 1979 the Army claimed to have killed more than 200 guerrillas, mainly in the department of Santander.

On Jan. 20, 1980, some 50 FARC members attacked a police station near Algeciras (Huila department), killing three policemen; throughout the rest of the year the movement was involved in numerous other clashes with the security forces (suffering and inflicting many casualties) and significant numbers of its members were arrested and brought to trial. The FARC was also responsible for further kidnappings, including that of a US businessman on Aug. 17, 1980, who was released on Oct. 28 on payment of £820,000 ransom. On the other hand, the Army uncovered FARC arsenals on Oct. 28 and Nov. 4, 1982. The amnesty offer made by President Turbay Ayala was rejected by FARC on June 17, 1980. In September 1980 FARC was officially regarded as the strongest of the guerrilla organizations, with some 770 active members.

FARC guerrillas were still active early in 1983 when a group of 120 men attacked the town of Toribio (Valle department) and killed two officials early in January, and on Feb. 5 other FARC guerrillas ambushed an army patrol, killing eight soldiers and an officer. Nevertheless, FARC showed interest in President Betancur's amnesty offer which came into effect in November 1982, and early in 1983 FARC delegates had talks with a presidential peace commission.

National Co-ordination of Bases (*Coordinador Nacional de Bases,* CNB)—see under April 19 Movement

National Liberation Army (*Ejercito de Liberación Nacional,* ELN)

Leadership. Nicolas Rodríguez Bautista.

Established in January 1965, the ELN at first operated in the department of Santander (north-eastern Colombia) under the leadership of Fabio Vásquez Castaño and with the support of a (pro-Chinese) Workers', Students' and Peasants' Movement (MOEC). It repudiated the pro-Soviet Communist Party on Aug. 1, 1967, after that party had condemned guerrilla warfare as "an erroneous form of revolution". Earlier, on Jan. 7, 1966, Fr Camilo Torres Restrepo, a former Dominican priest who had advocated a "Christian revolution" to overthrow the existing social order, disclosed that he had joined the ELN, explaining that as all lawful means of obtaining redress were barred to the people he would pursue the armed struggle in the country until the people had gained power; however, on Feb. 15, 1966, he was killed in a clash between guerrillas and an army unit.

The ELN continued its activities, which included kidnappings, such as that of Dr Fernando Londono y Londono, a former Minister of the Interior, on July 9, 1970; he was, however, released on July 18 after his family had paid his abductors the equivalent of $100,000; he claimed that they had tortured him. During the whole of 1970, a total of 134 guerrillas were said to have been killed and 201 captured.

In June 1975 ELN guerrillas were reported to be active in several departments, and a major military operation was launched against them in the northern Bolívar department, where ELN units had ambushed an army patrol and temporarily occupied three towns.

On Sept. 8, 1975, ELN guerrillas assassinated the Inspector-General of the Army (Gen. José Ramón Rincón Quiñones), who had led major anti-guerrilla operations; over 50 persons, including 12 university professors, were arrested in connexion with this murder, and on Jan. 30, 1976, four ELN members were sentenced to imprisonment for from 24 to 28 years for the general's assassination. The death of a policeman in an explosion at the Spanish embassy in Bogotá during the following night was attributed to retaliation for the sentences.

In September 1976 the ELN confirmed that Fabio Vásquez Castaño had been replaced as leader of the ELN by Nicolas Rodríguez Bautista. During the 1978 election campaign ELN units attacked a police station in Bogotá on June 2, killing one and wounding eight policemen.

By September 1980 the ELN was officially stated to have been reduced to less than 40 active members. However, notwithstanding President Turbay Ayala's amnesty offer of March 1981, the ELN intensified its guerrilla activities near the Venezuelan border in mid-1981. A new amnesty offer, made by President Belisario Betancur and effective from November 1982, was accepted by a number of ELN guerrillas.

ORP

In November 1982 a group using this designation claimed responsibility for the assassination of Gloria Lara de Echeverry (the wife of a former President of Congress), who had been kidnapped on June 23, 1982. Her father, Oliverio Lara Borrero, had been assassinated in Huila in 1975.

Pedro León Abroleda Brigade (PLA)

This Marxist guerrilla group is thought to be an offshoot of the People's Liberation Army and has claimed responsibility for a number of acts of violence, such as the occupation of the Liberal Party's headquarters in Medellín on Jan. 23, 1980. One of its leaders, Maria Isabel Ramírez de Montano, was arrested on May 12, 1980; but in September of that year the PLA was officially stated to comprise 309 active guerrillas.

People's Liberation Army (*Ejercito Popular de Liberación,* EPL)

The formation of the EPL was announced in January 1968 by the (pro-Chinese) Communist Party of Colombia (Marxist-Leninist) which had broken away from the Communist Party of Colombia (CPC) in July 1965. The EPL went into action in the department of Córdoba but it survived severe setbacks inflicted by the Army.

Early in July 1977 EPL members made an unsuccessful attack on the Air Force Chief of Staff (Col. Alvaro Mejía Soto). Carlos Reyes Niño, an alleged EPL member, was in December 1978 sentenced to 14 years in prison for guerrilla activities carried out during 1977.

The EPL was still active in 1980, and on March 17 of that year a total of 14 EPL members were sentenced to altogether 400 years in prison. By September 1980 the EPL was officially stated to consist of only 60 active guerrillas.

A clash between an EPL commando and security forces was reported from Antioquia department in November 1982, and another EPL group was involved in a similar incident in January 1983.

Workers' Self-Defence Movement (*Movimiento de Autodefesa Obrero,* MAO)

Leadership. Oscar Mateus Puerto.

Members of a "Sept. 14 Commando" of this organization killed, on Sept. 12, 1978, Dr Rafael Pardo Buelvas, who had been Minister of the Interior at the time of a 24-hour general strike on Sept. 14, 1974, which had led to widespread clashes and the death of about 18 people. In May 1980 its founder, Armando López Suárez ("Coleta"), and its leader, Oscar Mateus Puerto ("Julian"), were both arrested; and in November 1980 eight MAO members were given lengthy prison sentences for the murder of Dr Parvo Buelvas.

By August 1980 only 20 MAO members were officially considered to be still active. However, by mid-1981 MAO guerrillas were again active in several areas.

Costa Rica

Capital: San José   Pop. 2,250,000

The Republic of Costa Rica is a democratic multi-party state with an executive President elected for four years by universal adult suffrage. He appoints, and presides over, a Cabinet. Legislative power is held by a Legislative Assembly similarly elected by universal adult suffrage.

As a result of elections held on Feb. 7, 1982 (with the participation of 77 per cent of the electorate), seats in the Assembly were distributed as follows: National Liberation Party (PLN) 33, Unity Alliance 18, People United 4, National Movement 1, Alajuela Democratic Party 1. The Unity Alliance consisted of the Democratic Renewal Party, the Christian Democratic Party, the Calderonist Republican Party and the Popular Union. The People United coalition included the (pro-Soviet communist) Popular Vanguard Party. Under its 1949 Constitution Costa Rica has no army, but as a result of border incidents, involving in particular Nicaragua, the Government called, in 1978, for an enlargement of its 6,000-man Civil Guard by 2,500 voluntary trainees.

In connexion with strikes which took place in 1979 and were declared illegal, three Soviet diplomats were expelled from the country on Aug. 19, 1979, when the President called them "international agitators" and referred to "anti-nationalist forces inside and outside the country". On Jan. 11, 1980, the Government expelled six diplomats (three Cubans and one each from Bulgaria, the Soviet Union and Yugoslavia), after a strike in the country's banana plantations which the Government attributed to "communist agitators". Five communist trade unionists were arrested at the same time, and on Jan. 18 a Bulgarian trade union adviser was expelled.

Carlos Argüero Echeverría Commando

This left-wing group, named after a Costa Rican opponent of the Somoza regime in Nicaragua, claimed responsibility for a bazooka attack in which three US marines were injured on March 17, 1981.

Simón Bolívar International Brigade

Two members of this group, named after the liberator of Latin America but of uncertain political orientation, were arrested on March 2, 1980. No precise information has emerged on the group's aims and methods.

Cuba

Capital: Havana   Pop. 10,000,000

The Republic of Cuba has a Government which since December 1961 has been designated as Communist. Under a Constitution approved in a referendum in February 1976 the Republic was defined as "a socialist state of workpeople and other manual and intellectual workers"; the leading role of the Communist Party of Cuba was recognized; and the "fraternal friendship, aid and co-operation of the Soviet Union and other socialist countries" were acknowledged. Under this Constitution a 481-member National Assembly is elected indirectly for a five-year term by delegates elected to municipal assemblies (the basic organs of "people's power") by universal suffrage of citizens above the age of 16 years. Most of the candidates are Communist Party members; they need to obtain an overall majority in a first ballot, failing which a second (run-off) ballot is held. The head of state and government (currently Dr Fidel Castro Ruz, First Secretary of the Cuban Communist Party) is elected by the National Assembly as President of the Council of State, which is the country's highest representative body and which, in addition to its President, five Vice-Presidents and its secretary, has another 23 members. There is also a Council of Ministers headed by an Executive Committee, of which Dr Castro is Chairman. In elections to 169 municipal assemblies on Oct. 11 and 18, 1981, a total of 9,763 delegates were elected in a 97.2 per cent poll in the first ballot and another 10,725 delegates in a 93.6 per cent poll in the second ballot.

Political opposition to the Castro regime has found most of its support among Cuban refugees, of which several hundred thousand have settled in the United States. Following the abortive "Bay of Pigs" invasion attempt in April 1961 (planned by the US Central Intelligence Agency and approved by President Kennedy), various other landings by small groups of Cuban exiles have been reported from time to time, as have plots to assassinate Dr Castro. The Inter-American Human Rights Commission of the Organization of American States (from which Cuba has been excluded since 1962) claimed in a report released in Washington in March 1980, and based largely on evidence of former prisoners, that Cuba ill-treated political prisoners, of whom there were still about 1,000 (some held without trial); the report added that treatment was worst for those prisoners who refused to conform to socialist principles.

Refugee Activities

According to a report by a US Senate intelligence committee, issued on Nov. 20, 1976, Cuban exiles had been involved in plans to assassinate Dr Castro conceived by officials of the (US) Central Intelligence Agency (CIA) between 1960 and 1965, most of these plans being made without the knowledge of the US Government. Between December 1965 and April 1973, a total of 260,737 Cubans entered the United States, most of them by means of airlifts agreed between the two countries. Dr Castro said on Sept. 28, 1968, that "counter-revolutionaries" were active in

Cuba; two men accused of sabotage were executed on Oct. 7, 1968.

Of a group of Cuban exiles who landed near the US base of Guantánamo on May 7, 1969, three were killed, three others were sentenced to 20 years' imprisonment by a military court, and four were shot dead at Santiago de Cuba on Dec. 7, 1969. Of a further group which landed in eastern Cuba in September 1970, and were captured shortly afterwards, five were sentenced to death and two to 30 years in prison in March 1971.

Cuban exiles were also held responsible for a machine-gun attack on two Cuban fishing-boats off Florida on April 6, 1976; the bombing of the Cuban embassy in Lisbon on April 22, when two persons were killed; the bombing of the Cuban mission at the United Nations on July 5; an explosion at an airline office representing the Cuban airline in Barbados on July 10; the kidnapping of two Cuban embassy officials in Argentina on Aug. 9; and the bombing of the Cuban airline office in Panama on Aug. 18.

A new influx of Cubans into the United States began in 1978, when it was disclosed that the Cuban Government had unilaterally agreed to release several hundred Cuban political prisoners to allow them and others freed earlier to leave for the United States. The first group of 66 such Cubans arrived in Miami (Florida) on Oct. 21. Dr Castro announced on Nov. 22, 1978 (after talks with Cuban exiles invited to Havana), that he intended to release some 3,000 political prisoners at a rate of at least 400 a month, provided the United States agreed to accept those who wished to go there. He said that of a total of 4,263 (i.e. 3,238 political prisoners, 600 who had tried to leave Cuba illegally and 425 regarded as war criminals of the pre-1959 Batista era), about 80 per cent would be freed and the remainder would be considered later.

On Dec. 8-9, 1978, President Castro added that an agreement had been signed for the release of 3,000 political prisoners (with 400 of them to be freed immediately); that 12,000 former prisoners and their families would be allowed to leave Cuba for a place of their choice; and that Cubans living abroad would be allowed to visit Cuba as tourists. On June 5, 1979, it was officially announced in Havana that until then 1,900 prisoners had been released, and further releases were announced of 500 on July 24 and of another 400 on Aug. 24 (the latter included Rolando Cubelas, sentenced in 1966 to 25 years in prison for conspiring to kill Dr Castro).

A group of other released political prisoners flown to Costa Rica with their families on Oct. 21, 1979, included Maj. Huber Matos, who had played a leading part in the overthrow of the Batista regime in 1958-59 but had thereafter protested against the rising influence of communism in Cuba and had, at the instigation of Dr Castro, been sentenced late in 1959 to 20 years in prison for treason; during his imprisonment he had refused "political re-education" and therefore had to forgo certain privileges. Maj. Matos stated in Costa Rica on Oct. 23 that he had suffered permanent physical damage from his treatment in prison but that he still believed in the ideals of the Cuban revolution to which, he said, Dr Castro was the real traitor.

Following the release of another 400 political prisoners on Nov. 14, 1979, the Cuban Government claimed that all prisoners (numbered at 3,600) whom it had undertaken to release had by then been freed. However, a new exodus of Cubans to the United States between April and June 1980 resulted in the arrival by boat of 114,475 Cubans in Florida where they joined another 500,000 who had settled there in earlier years. After more than 10,000 Cubans wishing to leave their country had sought refuge in the Peruvian embassy in Havana early in April 1980, Dr Castro let it be understood that Cuban exiles in the United States would be permitted to pick up by boat anyone who wished to leave Cuba. At a meeting of Foreign Ministers of the Andean Pact member states (Bolivia, Colombia, Ecuador, Peru, and Venezuela) on April 9, 1980, it was agreed that several countries would accept certain quotas of these Cuban refugees at the Peruvian embassy, and these were later announced as United States 3,500, Peru 1,000, Venezuela 500, Spain 500, Canada 300, Costa Rica 300, Ecuador 200 and Belgium 150.

On June 3 it was reported that an estimated 100,000 Cubans were still wanting to leave their country, including 5,000 former political prisoners who had registered at the US interest section of the Swiss Embassy in Havana (the United States having broken off diplomatic relations with Cuba in 1961). Political prisoners still detained in Cuba included Armando Fernando Valladares, sentenced in 1961 to 30 years in prison for offences against the state but now in poor physical condition; a campaign for his release was being co-ordinated in Europe by Maj. Matos, who announced in Paris on June 19, 1980, that he was forming an anti-Castro organization.

On Sept. 26, 1980, the Cuban Government ended the exodus of refugees (whose total since April 21, 1980, it gave as 123,000). On Oct. 27 the Cuban Government released all 33 US citizens serving prison sentences in Cuba and allowed 30 of them to fly to the United States (with the remaining three having chosen to stay in Cuba). According to a statement made in December 1980 by the US interests section at the Swiss embassy in Havana, about 100,000 Cubans were still waiting for permission to leave the island. Over the following two years extensive illegal immigration of Cubans into the United States took place, usually by means of small boats.

In October 1980 a conference of anti-Castro elements held in Caracas under the chairmanship of Maj. Matos approved a plan to create the necessary conditions for a rising of the Cuban people against the Government of President Castro.

In the United States it was reported in January 1982 that anti-Castro refugees from Cuba were, in Florida, undergoing clandestine training in guerrilla warfare and use of sophisticated weapons, although under US law they were not allowed to use weapons other than semi-automatic ones.

Exiled Groups

Alpha-66 Group

Leadership. Andrés Nazario Sargen (s.g.); Humberto Pérez Alvarado (chief of military operations).

This Group, set up by 66 Cuban refugees in Miami in 1962 with the aim of overthrowing the Castro regime, was involved in several attempted landings in Cuba. On April 17, 1970, a group of 13 members of the group, led by Col. Vicente Méndez, landed in eastern Cuba, but four of the group were killed and the remainder taken prisoner by Cuban troops (who themselves lost five soldiers killed while one was wounded). Dr Castro refused on May 13, 1970, to exchange those captured against 11 Cuban fishermen held by Alpha-66 members who had sunk two Cuban fishing boats during the previous week.

In 1981 the Group attempted a landing in Matanzas province (east of Havana) with the object of killing Dr Castro and sabotaging industrial installations, but Havana radio announced on July 11 that five "counter-revolutionaries" involved in the attempt had been arrested.

Christian National Movement

Leadership. Capt. Orlando Lorenzo (s.g.).

This exile group, based in Florida, claimed on May 8, 1970, that raiders led by its secretary-general, Capt. Orlando Lorenzo, had landed in Cuba without encountering opposition.

Committee of 75

This Committee was formed in the United States by Cuban exiles who wished to negotiate with the Cuban authorities on the reunification of families, on the lifting of restrictions on Cubans wishing to leave or to enter Cuba, and on the release of political detainees.

Cuban National Revolutionary Council

This Council was formed in New York on March 21, 1961, under the leadership of Dr José Miró Cardona (who had been the first Prime Minister in Dr Castro's Government). The Council embraced various groups opposed to the Castro regime, notably the Democratic Revolutionary Front headed by Dr Manuel Antonio de Varona (a former Prime Minister) and the People's Revolutionary Movement headed by Manuel Ray (a former Minister of Public Works). The Council set up a directing committee, whose members had previously held high offices in Cuba.

In a declaration issued in the name of the Council on April 8, 1961, Dr Miró Cardona accused Dr Castro of betraying the ideals of the revolution and converting Cuba into "a Soviet colony"; he called on the Cuban people to overthrow the Castro regime so that "a democratic regime based on liberty and social justice" could be established in Cuba. Dr Miró Cardona strongly denied that the Council was backed by the (US) Central Intelligence Agency.

An attempt made by a force of Cuban exiles to land in the Bay of Pigs of Cuba on April 17, 1961, was repulsed by the Cuban Army and militia with heavy losses (the Cuban authorities subsequently giving the number of prisoners captured in connexion with the invasion as 1,173). At the same time the activities of anti-Castro guerrillas inside Cuba were also suppressed by Cuban forces.

Since 1961 the Council has not been reported as being active.

Cuban Nationalist Movement (*Movimiento Nacionalista Cubano*, MNC)

Three members of this US-based Movement—Alvin Ross Díaz, Guillermo Novo Sampol and Ignacio Novo Sampol—were sentenced in Washington on March 23, 1979 (the first two to life imprisonment and the last-named to eight years in prison), for complicity in the murder (on Sept. 21, 1976) of Orlando Letelier (a former Chilean ambassador and former minister under President Allende of Chile) and a passenger in his car. Two other Cuban exiles accused of involvement in the murders were believed to be in Nicaragua.

Cubans United (*Cubanos Unidos*)

Leadership. Wilfredo Navarra (s.g.).

This exile group based in the United States sent several boats to the US base of Guantánamo on Cuba during the second half of August 1981 to set up a government-in-exile; however, their attempts were frustrated by a tropical storm as a result of which 60 members of the expedition were shipwrecked while about 16 others were rescued by US Coastguards.

Democratic Revolutionary Front—see under Cuban National Revolutionary Council

El Condor

This group of anti-Castro Cuban exiles claimed responsibility for an explosion on a Cuban airliner off Barbados on Oct. 6, 1976, where 73 persons (including 57 Cubans) were killed.

Omega 7

This terrorist group of Cuban exiles in the United States opposed any negotiations with

349

the Castro regime by Cuban exiles. It was responsible for a bomb explosion in front of the Cuban mission at the United Nations in New York on Sept. 9, 1978, and for bombing the offices of a moderate Cuban exiles' newspaper in New York on Oct. 21 of that year. On March 25, 1979, Omega 7 carried out bomb attacks on Cuban-linked premises in New Jersey and at Kennedy Airport (New York).

Other Omega 7 attacks in 1979 were directed against a member of the "Committee of 75" (see separate entry), and on April 28 it killed (in Puerto Rico) a Cuban travel agent who organized exiles' tours to Cuba.

On Sept. 11, 1980, a Cuban diplomat at the UN mission in New York was murdered by an Omega 7 member. Orlando Bosch, believed to be linked to Omega 7, was one of four men acquitted by a Venezuelan court in September 1980 after being accused of having placed a bomb on a Cuban airliner over Barbados on Oct. 6, 1976, when 73 people were killed (see under separate entry for *El Condor*).

Following the assumption of office by President Reagan in the United States in January 1981, Omega 7 announced a "truce" in its activities, but on Sept. 21, 1981, it announced that it had ended the truce, and it proceeded to bomb Mexican consular premises in Miami and New York in protest against Mexico's friendly relations with the Castro regime.

Organization for the Liberation of Cuba (*Organización para la Liberación de Cuba*, OPLC)

Héctor Fabián, a spokesman for this organization, claimed in January 1982 that it had the backing of the well-to-do Cuban community in Miami and that its activities were not being interfered with by the Reagan Administration, which was said to tolerate the existence of camps for clandestine training in guerrilla warfare.

People's Revolutionary Movement—see under Cuban National Revolutionary Council

United Revolutionary Organization Co-ordination (CORU)

This movement was founded in Chile in 1975 by Orlando Bosch, an anti-communist Cuban, with the object of undermining all links between Cuba and other American states. He was held responsible for a number of acts of violence, including two bombings of the Cuban embassy in Caracas (Venezuela) in 1974, and an explosion at the airport of Kingston (Jamaica) on July 9, 1976.

Dominica

Capital: Roseau   Pop. 76,000

The Commonwealth of Dominica has been an independent republic within the Commonwealth since Nov. 3, 1978. It has a President elected by the House of Assembly, a Government headed by a Prime Minister, and a unicameral House of Assembly with 21 members elected by universal adult suffrage, with 11 Senators being elected or appointed to it in addition. In elections to the House of Assembly held on July 21, 1980, the (conservative) Dominican Freedom Party gained 17 seats, the newly-formed Dominica Democratic Labour Party two and independents two. Parties which contested the elections without gaining seats were the Dominican Labour Party and the ("new left") Dominican Liberation Movement Alliance.

Recent internal instability in Dominica has been principally associated with the activities of adherents of the Rastafarian movement, which originated in Jamaica in the 1960s and subsequently spread to other Caribbean islands.

The Rastafarians

Leadership. Desmond Trotter (spiritual l.).

The Rastafarians, known as "Dreads" in Dominica, originated in Kingston (Jamaica) as a cult of Blacks advocating the return of the Blacks in the Americas to Africa, the use of natural food, the cultivation and smoking of marijuana (cannabis or "pot") and the playing of music. Adherents have made the former Emperor of Ethiopia, Haile Selassie (whose original name was Ras Tafari), the object of a cult and compare the "heaven" of Ethiopia with the "hell" of places such as Jamaica and Dominica.

As some Rastafarians in Dominica had been involved in acts of violence, the Dominican Labour Party Government (of Patrick R. John) passed in 1974 a "Dread Act" under which Rastafarians could be shot on sight. D. Trotter was condemned to death in 1976 but after riots he was released in 1979 (following the removal of P. R. John from office).

In January 1981 two "Dreads" were condemned to death for having killed a farmer in 1980. There followed armed clashes in which the police killed two Rastafarians on Feb. 12, 1981. On the same day a group of armed Rastafarians kidnapped another farmer (whose son was the Government's press secretary) and demanded, in return for his release, the freeing from prison of the two condemned men, an inquiry into an anti-drug squad operation and "an end to police brutality". The Government, however, rejected these demands and declared a state of emergency on Feb. 13. It had earlier been revealed that members of the Dominican Defence Force had traded weapons for marijuana supplied by "Dreads".

On March 7, 1981, the Prime Minister announced that the security forces had uncovered a plot to overthrow the Government, and that six persons had been arrested, among them the leader and another member of the Dominican Labour Party's executive as well as the commander and deputy commander of the Dominican Defence Force (which had in December 1980 been ordered to transfer all its weapons to the police armoury). The Dominican Defence Force was disbanded under a law passed by Parliament in mid-April 1981. Further details of the con-

spiracy, including evidence of a meeting held in a "Dread" stronghold in the mountains in Dominica, where agreement on the execution of the plot was reached (and was said to have been finally signed by P. R. John, who was to be restored to the premiership which he had lost in June 1979), emerged later in trials held in the United States.

The US proceedings included the sentencing in New Orleans on July 22, 1981, of two men linked with the Ku Klux Klan, who were given three-year sentences for violating the (US) Neutrality Act and five years suspended for conspiracy. Five other men were given three-year sentences on July 1; they included Michael E. Perdue, said to be the ringleader of the intended invasion of Dominica. In a further ramification of the conspiracy (Miss) Marian McGuire, a Canadian citizen said to have connexions with the Irish Republican Army and reportedly sent to Dominica by a "grand wizard" of the Ku Klux Klan in Canada to act as a spy for M. E. Perdue, was sentenced to three years in prison in Dominica on Sept. 17, 1981.

A state of emergency was again in force from Dec. 19, 1981, to March 31, 1982, as a result of attacks made on the island's police headquarters and prison with the aim of obtaining the release of four of the six men arrested in March 1981; the attacks resulted in the death of three policemen and three of the attackers. Three surviving attackers were later charged with murder or attempted murder.

The Prime Minister declared on Dec. 19, 1981, that opponents of the Dominican Freedom Party's conservative ideology were acting in concert with criminal elements whose aim was "to have a more pliable government in power that would give the narcotics trade a freer hand".

Dominican Republic

Capital: Santo Domingo Pop. 6,200,000

The Dominican Republic has an executive President elected by universal adult suffrage for a four-year term and a Congress consisting of a 120-member House of Representatives and a 27-member Senate, both similarly elected at the same time as the President. The latter appoints, and presides over, a Cabinet. In congressional elections held on May 16, 1982, a majority of seats was won in both the House of Representatives and the Senate by the (centre-left) Dominican Revolutionary Party, with the principal other parties being the Reformist Party and the Dominican Liberation Party. The elections were also contested by six other parties or alliances—the (right-wing) Quisqueyan Democratic Party, the Social Democratic Alliance, the Progressive National Force, the Christian Popular Party, the (pro-Soviet) Dominican Communist Party (standing jointly with the Movement for Socialism), and the United Left (an alliance of six communist parties and the Anti-Imperialist Patriotic Union).

In September 1979 the Government claimed to have uncovered a plot to overthrow the existing regime, in which context over 100 army officers and civilians were arrested, most of them being connected with the previous regime of President Joaquín Balaguer (of the Reformist Party).

Revolutionary Armed Nationalist Group
(Grupo Armado Nacionalista Revolucionario)

This hitherto unknown Group claimed responsibility for a grenade attack carried out on June 18, 1982, on the premises of the central electoral tribunal, where five people were killed and at least 20 were injured. Three former colonels and a number of civilians were subsequently arrested on suspicion of having been involved in the incident. The precise objectives and orientation of the Group remained unclear.

Ecuador

Capital: Quito

Pop. 8,800,000

The Republic of Ecuador has an executive President elected, together with a Vice-President, for a five-year term by universal adult suffrage. There is a unicameral Congress, to which 57 members are elected on a provincial basis and 12 on a national basis, all by universal adult suffrage for a five-year term. There is a Cabinet presided over by the President.

By November 1981 seats in Congress were distributed as follows: Concentration of Popular Forces (Bucaram faction) 12, Democratic Left (ID) 12, Popular Democracy (DP) 7, Conservative Party 6, Radical Liberal Party 4, Social Christian Party 2, Revolutionary Nationalist Party 2, Democratic Popular Movement (Maoist) 1, Democratic Party (PD) 1, non-aligned 22. Of the non-aligned group, 12 former members of the Concentration of Popular Forces (CFP), led by León Roldos, formed an opposition party which on Nov. 17, 1982, assumed the name of People, Change, Democracy, Roldosist People's Party *(Pueblo, Cambio, Democracia, Partido del Pueblo Roldocista).* During 1980 a Democratic Convergence was formed by an alliance of centre-left parties—the ID, DP, PD, the Roldosist members of the CFP and independents.

Other political formations in existence in Ecuador include two which are not officially recognized, namely: (i) the (centre-right) *Coalición Institucionalista Demócrata*; and (ii) the (left-wing) *Frente Amplio de la Izquierda* (FAD), embracing the (pro-Moscow) *Partido Comunista Ecuatoriano,* the *Partido Socialista Revolucionario,* the *Movimiento para la Unidad de la Izquierda* and the *Movimiento Revolucionario de la Izquierda Cristiana,* as well as the legal *Frente Radical Alfarista* and *Partido Nacional Velasquista.*

Unrest was caused during 1980-82 by student disturbances and strike action by militant trade unions, which led to repeated declarations of a temporary state of emergency and also to some loss of life in clashes with the security forces. Open challenges to the Government have been confined to two minor left-wing direct-action groups.

Astra 18th October Movement of Revolutionary Action (*Movimiento 18 de Octubre de Accion Revolucionaria Astra,* M-18-X)

This leftist Movement first emerged on April 18, 1980, when it temporarily occupied the Colombian consulate in Quito.

Liberation Front of the Poor (*Frente de Liberación de los Pobres,* FLP)

In support of a demand for the repeal of a national security law, members of this Front occupied a Santo Domingo convent on July 7-11, 1980.

El Salvador

Capital: San Salvador Pop. 4,800,000

The Republic of El Salvador has an interim Government under a head of state elected by a Constituent Assembly which was itself elected by universal adult suffrage on March 28, 1982, and which was to draft, by mid-1983, a new Constitution providing for general elections to be held early in 1984. In the Constituent Assembly the 60 seats were distributed as follows: Christian Democratic Party (PDC) 24, National Republican Alliance (Arena) 19, National Reconciliation Party (PCN) 14, Democratic Action (AD) 2, Salvadorean Popular Party (PPS) 1. (The Popular Orientation Party also took part in the elections but gained no seats.) In the "Government of national unity" set up on May 4, 1982, Arena and the PCN (both right-wing formations) each held four ministerial seats, the PDC held three, and the remaining seats were held by independents.

El Salvador, a densely populated country with the highest population growth rate (of 3.5 per cent per annum) in Central America, was for a long time under military rule following the suppression of a peasant rebellion in 1932 (at a cost of 30,000 lives including that of Farabundo Martí, the rebel peasants' leader). After elections held in 1972 and 1977 the opposition (of which the Christian Democrats then formed the major part) claimed that the ruling National Reconciliation Party had carried out massive electoral fraud, and many opposition candidates sought asylum abroad.

Following the overthrow of President Carlos Humberto Romero in October 1979, El Salvador's various left-wing groups became increasingly critical of the alleged right-wing tendencies of the new ruling junta and from 1980 mounted a concerted military and diplomatic campaign to overthrow the Government. Anti-regime guerrilla forces, operating mainly in the northern border region, are grouped within the Farabundo Martí Front for National Liberation (FMLN), the political arm of which, the Revolutionary Democratic Front (FDR), acts as the main umbrella organization of a complex array of left-wing opposition parties and other bodies. The FMLN and the FDR boycotted the March 1982 elections and have repeatedly called on the San Salvador Government to enter into a dialogue with a view to a restoration of "genuine democracy"; at the same time they have rejected the Government's demand that the guerrilla war should be halted as a prelude for negotiations.

Main Left-wing Alliances

Farabundo Martí Front for National Liberation (*Frente Farabundo Martí para la Liberación Nacional,* FMLN)

The late Salvador Cayetano Carpio, hitherto leader of the FMLN, had been secretary-general of the (pro-Soviet) Salvadorean Communist Party (PCS) between 1940 and 1969, when he left that party. The FMLN (named after a peasant leader killed in a 1932 rising) is headed by a unifying revolutionary directorate (DRU) formed in May 1980 with the object of launching a "final offensive" against the Government on the (Marxist-Leninist) theoretical basis of a strategy of "prolonged popular war" or "war of attrition". The stated aim of the FMLN was to create a "proletarian unity party" which would form the basis of a "people's state" after a guerrilla victory. The FMLN's main components are (i) the Communist Party; (ii) the Farabundo Martí Popular Liberation Forces (FPL), themselves the armed wing of the Popular Revolutionary Bloc (BPR); (iii) the Armed Forces of National Resistance (FARN), the armed wing of the Unified Popular Action Front (FAPU); and (iv) the People's Revolutionary Army (ERP), the armed wing of the February 28 Popular Leagues (LP-28).

The FARN leader, Fermán Cienfuegos, stated in December 1980 that the guerrilla offensive should lead to "an irreversible political and military situation in El Salvador" before the assumption of office by President Ronald Reagan in the United States on Jan. 20, 1981; he added that the FMLN and its political wing, the Revolutionary Democratic Front (FDR—see separate entry), would both form part of the future "democratic revolutionary government".

The planned "general offensive for a final onslaught" was started on Jan. 10-11, 1981, with heavy fighting breaking out in many parts of the country. The FMLN took over a radio station and issued a call to arms, whereupon the Government declared martial law and imposed a curfew on Jan. 12; it also linked up all radio stations in order to block guerrilla broadcasts, which were nevertheless continued from two transmitters under the name "Radio Venceremos". On Jan. 12 the guerrillas claimed to have taken four cities but the Army stated that the offensive had already been crushed, and by Jan. 19 the armed forces and the Government claimed to have the country under complete military control, with the Minister of Defence (Col. José Guillermo García) stating that 980 guerrillas and 142 soldiers had been killed (whereas the Red Cross stated that most of those killed had been civilians). Fighting continued, however, between guerrillas and the Army, especially north of San Salvador.

At the end of May 1981 the FMLN claimed to be in control of four provinces and was launching attacks against police and army positions in the capital. On July 2, 1981, Havana radio claimed that the FMLN had inflicted about 900 casualties on the Salvadorean Army during June. During the next few months severe fighting continued in many parts of the country, and on Aug. 15 the FMLN claimed to have established a "revolutionary government" at Perquín (in the Morazán department, eastern El Salvador); however, on Aug. 21 the Government stated that Perquín had been retaken and that there were no prisoners. (The FDR-FMLN office in Madrid stated on the same day that in this operation the Salvadorean Army had been assisted by 500 Honduran soldiers.) The FMLN also conducted an intensive campaign of economic sabotage, with one quarter of the country's electricity pylons being blown up, and 11 bombs exploding within 10 minutes in San Salvador on Aug. 27, 1981.

International attempts to mediate between the warring parties, made during 1981 in particular by members of the Socialist International, were all rejected by the Government of El Salvador, and the idea of negotiating a settlement with the guerrillas was also rejected on July 16 by Thomas O. Enders, US Assistant Secretary of State for Inter-American Affairs.

On the other hand, the Foreign Ministers of France and Mexico, in a joint statement issued in Mexico City on Aug. 28, 1981, recognized the FMLN-FDR alliance as "a representative political force" which was "ready to assume its obligations and exercise the rights deriving from it" and therefore to help establish the framework for a political settlement of the crisis. This decision was supported by the (centre-left) Government of the Netherlands of Sept. 29. On Aug. 29 Yugoslavia had recognized the FMLN-FDR as belligerent forces in the conflict (this being usually the first step towards the recognition of guerrilla movements).

The Franco-Mexican declaration was, however, condemned on Sept. 2, 1981, by the Foreign Ministers of nine Latin American countries—Argentina, Bolivia, Chile, Colombia, the Dominican Republic, Guatemala, Honduras, Paraguay and Venezuela; it was also criticized by the Government of Brazil on the same day. Of the countries in the region, only Cuba, Panama and Nicaragua expressed support for the Franco-Mexican declaration, with Panama offering on Sept. 30 to help solve the conflict.

From October 1981 onwards the FMLN consolidated its positions in the north and north-east of the country. It was then thought to have between 4,000 and 6,000 active guerrillas, with conflicting estimates being published of their losses and of the numbers of troops killed in clashes with them (e.g. the FMLN claimed on Dec. 31, 1981, to have, in the past six months, killed 2,000 members of the security forces and to have lost only 160 of its own men). The FMLN also claimed to have blown up 25 major bridges during 1981.

Prior to the Constituent Assembly elections of March 1982 the FMLN announced in December 1981 that fighting would continue before, during and after the elections but that its leadership was prepared to enter into a dialogue with the Government at any time. In an open letter to President Reagan of the United States (published on Jan. 29, 1982) the leaders of the FMLN's component groups accused the United States of prolonging the civil war in El Salvador and of "sustaining at the peak of power the most repressive elements of the Salvadorean Army", but proposed negotiations without preconditions at any time.

Particularly heavy fighting took place in the Morazán department between December 1981 and February 1982. On Jan. 27 FMLN guerrillas attacked the Ilopango airbase near San Salvador and claimed to have destroyed 28 military aircraft (for the replacement of which the USA allocated $55,000,000 in emergency military aid, as announced on Feb. 1).

After the US Government had repeated its earlier assertion that Nicaragua was supplying the FMLN guerrillas with weapons, President López Portillo of Mexico, on Feb. 21, 1982, proposed a three-point plan to end the war in El Salvador and to settle US differences with Cuba and Nicaragua. The FMLN-FDR accepted the Mexican President's offer of mediation on March 3. In the United States the House of Representatives had on Feb. 3 (by 396 votes to three) urged President Reagan to press for "unconditional discussions among the major political factions in El Salvador in order to guarantee a safe and stable environment for free and open democratic elections".

In February-April 1982 FMLN attacks were reported from numerous towns in northern and central parts of the country. In June fierce fighting took place in Morazán, where the FMLN was temporarily in control of the town of Perquín. With effect from June 23 the FMLN declared a ban on all road traffic and threatened to destroy any moving vehicle. After an apparent lull in FMLN operations in the latter part of 1982, the Government's rejection of a new offer of a dialogue issued by the FDR-FMLN on Oct. 5, 1982, was followed by a renewed guerrilla offensive in northern El Salvador in early 1983.

In the areas which the FMLN controlled it had since mid-1981 set up structures of local popular power (*Poder Popular Local,* PPL), with each PPL having, for about 1,000 persons, an elected junta responsible for administration, social services, education, production and defence. The fighting forces of the FMLN in these areas consisted of frontline fighters with special training and improved weapons, guerrillas operating almost exclusively in the controlled areas and along main roads, and militia for defence measures.

Revolutionary Democratic Front (*Frente Democrática Revolucionario,* FDR)

Leadership. Guillermo Manuel Ungo (ch.).

This Front was set up as the political arm of the Farabundo Martí Front for National Liberation (FMLN—see separate entry), and had Enrique Alvarez Córdova as its first secretary-general. It comprised (i) a Democratic Salvadorean Front (*Frente Salvadoreño Democrático,* FSD) set up earlier in April 1980 and including the National Revolutionary Movement (MNR), the Christian Social Popular Movement (MPSC) then led by E. Alvarez Córdova, and several trade union, student and professional organizations, and also (ii) the Popular Revolutionary Bloc (BPR), the Unified Popular Action Front (FAPU), the February 28 Popular Leagues (LP-28), the People's Liberation

Movement (MPL) and the (communist) National Democratic Union (UDN).

A general strike organized by the FDR for Aug. 13-15, 1980, was intended to be "the commencement of a co-ordinated left-wing effort to ignite a popular insurrection" but it was not widely followed and in clashes with troops at least 40 people were reported to have been killed; the FDR, however, claimed that its "neighbourhood defence organizations" had proved that they could not be neutralized by the military.

On Nov. 28, 1980, six FDR members—including E. Alvarez Córdova and Juan Chacón, leader of the MPL—were found murdered after they had been kidnapped on the previous day; responsibility was claimed by the Maximiliano Hernández Martínez Anti-Communist Alliance (see separate entry). On Jan. 5, 1981, Guillermo Manuel Ungo (the MNR leader, who had briefly been a member of the ruling junta following the overthrow of President Romero in October 1979) was elected as the new leader of the FDR. In support of a military offensive launched on Jan. 10, 1981, by the FMLN the FDR called a general strike for Jan. 13, but it had only limited effect.

On Jan. 14, 1981, the FDR formally announced in Mexico City that it had formed a seven-member diplomatic-political commission which would seek to establish a "democratic revolutionary government". The commission consisted of leading members of the MNR, the MPL, the People's Revolutionary Army (ERP), the FAPU, the Farabundo Martí Popular Liberation Forces (FPL), the UDN and the MPSC. On the same day the FDR called for direct negotiations (leading to a political settlement) between the guerrillas and the United States (which the FDR accused of having "contributed to the radicalization and polarization" of the situation in El Salvador). Although the FDR renewed this call on Feb. 23, it was rejected by the US Administration on Feb. 26, with the advice to turn to the Government of El Salvador.

The US Defence Department at that time assessed the guerrillas' strength at 3,700 full-time and 5,000 part-time fighters against El Salvador's armed forces of about 17,000. The FMLN had earlier claimed to have a guerrilla army of 5,000 active members and 30,000 reservists engaged in political work who could be integrated gradually, as well as militia and self-defence groups.

In a memorandum made public by the US Government on Feb. 19-20, 1981, it was asserted that on the basis of documents captured from guerrillas it was clear that the insurgency in El Salvador had been "progressively transformed into a textbook case of indirect armed aggression by communist power through Cuba". For the FDR, a spokesman had earlier asserted in London that neither the Soviet Union nor Cuba were major suppliers of arms to Salvadorean guerrillas, whose more important suppliers were Algeria, Libya, the Palestine Liberation Organization, Iraq and the US black market; FDR leaders in Mexico pointed out on Feb. 23 that three of the five member-groups of the FMLN were "strongly anti-Soviet". (The Reagan Administration announced on March 2, 1981, that an extra $25,000,000 in military aid had been allocated to the Government of El Salvador for the year up to Sept. 30, 1981—bringing the total for that year to $35,400,000—and that the number of US military advisers would be increased from 34 to 54.) The Cuban Government strongly denied on Sept. 3 that it was sending advisers or Soviet weapons to the guerrillas in El Salvador, as had been alleged by the US authorities.

During October 1981 leaders of the FDR expressed the view that the elections to be held in 1982 could not be conducted democratically because of military pressures and that under the existing conditions elections would merely allow the Government to identify and destroy the opposition. However, the FDR proposed that a dialogue should immediately begin and lead to negotiations between all the forces in the conflict with international mediation, and that no prior conditions should be laid down by any of the parties.

Having boycotted the March 1982 elections, FDR leaders in exile repeatedly called for a dialogue with the new Government in San Salvador, while making it clear that the guerrilla war would continue until a satisfactory agreement for a return to full democracy had been achieved. After one such appeal for negotiations, issued jointly by the FDR and the FMLN in October 1982, had been rejected by the El Salvador Government, a number of prominent "internal" FDR activists were arrested by the security forces.

Guerrilla Movements

Armed Forces of National Resistance (*Fuerzas Armadas de Resistencia Nacional,* FARN)

Leadership. Fermán Cienfuegos (l.).

The FARN group was formed in 1975 as an offshoot of the People's Revolutionary Army (ERP) and was later described as the armed wing of the Unified Popular Action Front (see separate entry). From 1978 onwards the FARN group was responsible for the kidnapping of a number of foreign businessmen in support of demands for ransom as well as for the release of alleged detainees and the publication of FARN statements.

Those kidnapped included a Japanese businessman (abducted on May 17, 1978, and

found murdered on Oct. 13), the Swedish manager in El Salvador of the Ericsson telephone company (kidnapped on Aug. 24, 1978, and released on Aug. 24 after his company had paid for the publication of a FARN manifesto in Swedish and Japanese newspapers and had also paid a ransom); the local manager of the (Dutch) Philips electronics firm (abducted on Nov. 24, 1978, and released on Dec. 30, after payment by Philips for publication of a FARN manifesto in newspapers throughout the world, as well as of a ransom); two British executives of the Bank of London and South America (abducted on Nov. 30, 1978, and released on July 2, 1979, on payment of an undisclosed ransom); and the (Salvadorean) honorary consul for Israel (kidnapped on Jan. 17, 1979, and found murdered on March 22, although the Government had released 22 political prisoners on the previous day). These kidnappings caused a general exodus of foreigners from El Salvador.

In July 1980 some 300 FARN members temporarily occupied San Miguel (El Salvador's third largest town) until they were driven out by troops. The FARN leader Ernesto Jovel was killed in September 1980. By mid-1980 FARN's guerrilla forces were estimated at 800 men and were operating as part of the Farabundo Martí Front for National Liberation (see separate entry).

Farabundo Martí Popular Liberation Forces (*Fuerzas Populares de Liberación Farabundo Martí,* FPL)

This group—regarded as the armed wing of the Popular Revolutionary Bloc (see separate entry)—was an offshoot of the (pro-Soviet) Salvadorean Communist Party (PCS). It first emerged in 1977, when its guerrillas kidnapped the then Foreign Minister (Mauricio Borgonovo Pohl) on April 19 and demanded, in return for his release, that 37 named political prisoners should be set free. The then President (Arturo Armando Molina) declared on April 20 that the Government would not negotiate with the guerrillas and that anyway only three of the 37 named were in fact in detention; and on May 11 the Minister was found shot dead.

The FPL stated after the killing of M. Borgonovo Pohl that its operation had been aimed at achieving the release of 37 political prisoners and was "part of the prolonged war which the FPL is continuing until it achieves an ultimate popular revolution towards socialism". The FPL also claimed responsibility for killing, on July 12, 1977, Col. Osmín Aguirre y Salinas (President of EL Salvador in 1944-45), who as chief of police had in 1932 suppressed the rising in which the peasant leader Farabundo Martí had been killed. On Sept. 16, 1977, the FPL killed the government-appointed rector of the University of El Salvador.

In 1978 the FPL called for a boycott of general and municipal elections (which were held on March 12 with an estimated participation of between 40 and 50 per cent of the registered voters); during the election campaign the FPL committed several bomb attacks.

The FPL also claimed responsibility for the murder of the Minister of Education (Dr Carlos Herrera Rebollo) on May 23, 1979. The FPL was further held responsible for the murder of President Romero's brother on Sept. 6, 1979, whereafter clashes between teenagers and security forces led to the death of 14 people on Sept. 8-9; a demonstration of some 1,000 people was fired on by snipers on Sept. 14, when six people were killed and 21 wounded; and 10 other persons were killed in clashes between FPL members and police as well as National Guards.

The FPL was also responsible for the kidnapping of the South African ambassador (Archibald Gardner Dunn) on Nov. 28, 1979, this action being coupled with demands for the severance of diplomatic relations with Chile, the freeing of political prisoners, the trial of ex-President Romero and of his predecessor (ex-President Arturo Armando Molina). (The Government had broken off its relations with South Africa before the seizure of the latter's ambassador.) On Oct. 9, 1980, however, the FPL announced that the ambassador had been killed because its demands had not been met.

On Jan. 8, 1980, the FPL was joined by Salvador Samayoa, who had six days earlier resigned as Minister of Education. From May 1980 FPL forces conducted operations as part of the Farabundo Martí Front for National Liberation (see separate entry).

Cayetano Carpio (known as Comandante Marcial), the leader of the FPL, was on April 20, 1983, reported to have committed suicide in Nicaragua on April 12 and to have been succeeded by Salvador Guerra Firma.

People's Revolutionary Armed Forces (*Fuerzas Revolucionarias Armadas del Pueblo,* FRAP)

The relatively small FRAP group was formed in 1975 as an offshoot of the People's Revolutionary Army (see separate entry); it later became the armed wing of a Workers' Revolutionary Organization (*Organización Revolucionaria de Trabajadores,* ORT) which has been active since 1979.

People's Revolutionary Army (*Ejército Revolucionario del Pueblo,* ERP)

Leadership. Joaquín Villalobos (l.).

Established in 1972, this extreme left-wing guerrilla group—said to be the armed wing of the February 28 Popular Leagues (LP-28—see separate entry)—was responsible for kidnappings, including that of an industrialist on Jan. 27, 1977, for whose release the ERP collected a ransom of $1,000,000 but of whom it disclosed on Jan. 29 that he had died of gunshot wounds. Bombs planted by the ERP early in February 1979 (in retaliation for the killing of a priest and four youths by security forces on Jan. 20) resulted in the death of 14 National Guards and two civilians and injury to 20 other persons.

The ERP also frequently used bombs, especially against army units, and after the overthrow of President Romero on Oct. 15, 1979, it incited (together with the LP-28) three townships near San Salvador to rise against the new Government; however, this attempt was foiled by the Army.

The ERP was also responsible for the kidnapping on Oct. 31, 1979, of Jaime Hill (a member of one of El Salvador's most powerful "14 families"), who was released on March 15, 1980, after his family had paid for the publication of anti-government statements in foreign newspapers. The ERP claimed responsibility for an attack on the US embassy on Sept. 16, 1980, and in the week ended on Oct. 15 a large-scale military offensive was reported to have been mounted against ERP strongholds in eastern parts of El Salvador.

Although in May 1980 it became a member of the Farabundo Martí Front for National Liberation (see separate entry), the ERP has retained its own strategy aimed at mass insurrection, for which it has propagated armed self-defence by its militants, especially in urban areas, who were in mid-1980 estimated to number 800 men.

Popular Liberation Army (*Ejército Popular de Liberación,* EPL)

This small group was established in November 1979 as an offshoot of the Farabundo Martí Popular Liberation Forces (see separate entry). Its leader, Humberto Mendoza, was killed in November 1980.

Revolutionary Party of Central American Workers (*Partido Revolucionario de Trabajadores Centroamericanos,* PRTC)

The PRTC was said to be the military wing of a group known as the Liberation Leagues (*Ligas de Liberación,* LL). On Sept. 21, 1979, it claimed responsibility for the kidnapping of two businessmen, both of whom were released unharmed on Nov. 7 after their US employers had paid for the publication of a lengthy PRTC manifesto in US, Central American and European newspapers. It was active in subsequent years, also in Guatemala and Honduras.

Unified Popular Action Front (*Frente de Acción Popular Unificada,* FAPU)

This direct action group of activists who broke away from the (pro-Soviet) Salvadorean Communist Party drew its strength from among industrial workers and the lower middle-class; it has remained Marxist, tending towards Leninism, and has had links with the Armed Forces of National Resistance (FARN) and with similar groups elsewhere in Latin America.

From 1979 onwards it was responsible for a number of violent acts. On Jan. 16 of that year some 60 FAPU members occupied the Mexican embassy and the office of the Organization of American States in San Salvador, taking more than 150 hostages, in support of a demand for the release of all political prisoners. President Romero of El Salvador, however, declared that there were no political prisoners in the country and that persons who were alleged to have disappeared had in fact gone underground or left the country. As a result of negotiations between FAPU and the Government, all the hostages were freed on Jan. 18 and the FAPU members concerned were flown to Mexico, where they were granted political asylum.

Other Left-wing Movements

Agricultural Workers' Union (*Unión de Trabajadores Campesinos,* UTC)

This organization was, according to the Ministry of Foreign Affairs, involved in demonstrations for the release of political prisoners on May 1, 1977, when security forces shot dead 10 persons. The UTC co-operated with the Salvadorean Christian Peasants' Federation (see separate entry) in particular in the latter's campaign of 1978. Among four peasants killed by government forces after their arrest on Sept. 29, 1979, was the UTC's secretary-general (Apolinario Serrano).

In the late 1970s and early 1980s the UTC formed part of broader alliances of left-wing opposition forces, notably the Popular Revolutionary Bloc and the Revolutionary Democratic Front (see separate entries).

February 28 Popular Leagues (*Ligas Populares de 28 de Febrero,* LP-28)

The LP-28 adopted their name in 1977 on the occasion of general elections widely regarded as fraudulent. They are supported by urban and rural workers, and most of their leaders and activists are former members of the National Opposition Union defeated in the 1977 elections. The LP-28 have a distinct armed wing known as the People's Revolutionary Army (ERP—see separate entry in previous section).

LP-28 members were said to be involved in bomb attacks at the presidential palace and elsewhere on Sept. 25, 1979, when seven people were reported as having been killed. On Sept. 21-27 of that year LP-28 members occupied the Ministry of Labour in support of their demand for the release of imprisoned leaders of their organization.

After the overthrow of President Romero on Oct. 15, 1979, the LP-28 at first opposed the new Government, as did other left-wing groups, but on Oct. 19 they announced that they had decided to suspend violent activities while continuing to "organize the masses". Nevertheless, the LP-28 continued to be involved in violent clashes with the security forces and in early 1980 they followed other left-wing groups in reverting to a policy of outright opposition to the regime. In April 1980 the LP-28 became a member of the Revolutionary Democratic Front (see separate entry), while the ERP thereafter became part of the Farabundo Martí Front for National Liberation (see separate entry).

The LP-28 were also engaged in actions against several foreign embassies in San Salvador in January-February 1980. By occupying the Panamanian embassy on Jan. 11-15 the LP-28 obtained the release of seven of their members arrested in December 1979; the occupation of the Spanish embassy on Feb. 5 was ended on Feb. 18, by which date several detainees had been released and an investigation into the whereabouts of others had been promised; and a further occupation of the Panamanian embassy on Feb. 13-14 had as its object the release of LP-28 members arrested on Feb. 12 and the handing over of the bodies of dead LP-28 members. (As a result of these incidents, a number of countries withdrew their diplomats from El Salvador—Britain at the end of January, West Germany on Feb. 7 and Israel on Feb. 19.)

Christian Social Popular Movement (*Movimiento Popular Socialcristiano,* MPSC)

Leadership. Roberto Lara Velado (l.).

The MPSC was formed in 1980 as an offshoot of the Christian Democratic Party, and it opposed the participation in 1980 of that party's leader, José Napoleón Duarte, in the junta which took power in October 1979. The MPSC has been joined by other Christian groups and stands for social justice, respect for human life and an equitable distribution of wealth. It is not recognized by the Christian Democratic Organization of America (ODCA).

National Association of Salvadorean Teachers (*Asociación Nacional de Educadores Salvadoreños,* ANDES)

Over 200 members of this organization (which was affiliated to the Popular Revolutionary Bloc) were killed by right-wing groups in June and July 1979.

National Revolutionary Movement (*Movimiento Nacional Revolucionario,* MNR)

Leadership. Guillermo Manuel Ungo (l.).

The MNR is a social democratic party with a programme for the development of a modernized capitalism and radical reformism. All its leaders are in exile in Costa Rica, Mexico, Venezuela or the United States. The MNR is a member of the Socialist International and is recognized by the Democratic Action Party of Venezuela and the National Liberation Party of Costa Rica. The MNR leader, Guillermo Manuel Ungo, became a member of the civilian-military junta formed after the overthrow of President Romero in October 1979 but resigned in early January 1980 in protest against the new regime's alleged "swing to the right". He subsequently became chairman of the Revolutionary Democratic Front (see separate entry) of opposition parties formed in April 1980 as the political arm of the Farabundo Martí Front for National Liberation (see separate entry). In this capacity Guillermo Manuel Ungo has acted as the principal political spokesman of the various forces seeking to overthrow the present regime.

Nationalist Democratic Union (*Unión Democrática Nacionalista,* UDN)

Leadership. Mario Aguiñada Carranza (l.).

The UDN is a socialist and popular democratic party standing for the moderization of capitalism and national democratization. It is supported by workers, trade union leaders, teachers, students and peasants. It has been in alliance with the Salvadorean Communist Party. In January 1981 its leader went underground after he had been the target of an attempt on his life.

In 1980 the UDN became one of the members of the Revolutionary Democratic Front and also of the Revolutionary Co-ordination of the Masses (see separate entries).

People's Liberation Movement (*Movimiento de Liberación del Pueblo,* MLP)

Leadership. Fabio Castillo (l.).

This small militant group was active in 1980 and became a member of the Revolutionary Democratic Front (see separate entry). Its leader was a former rector of the National University of El Salvador.

Popular Revolutionary Bloc (*Bloque Popular Revolucionario,* BPR)

Based on a majority of the country's teachers, as well as members of the revolutionary lower middle-class, radical workers, students and rural workers, the BPR is a Marxist-Leninist formation standing for a revolutionary socialist society independent of Soviet influence. Formed in 1975, the BPR has proclaimed its thesis of a prolonged people's war; it has rejected any alliance with non-proletarian parties and has attracted other sectors taking the same line; and it has become the strongest of the rural guerrilla movements through its armed wing, the Farabundo Martí Popular Liberation Forces (see separate entry).

Although founded as a mainly non-violent movement, the BPR soon engaged in acts of violence. On Nov. 10, 1977, demonstrators led by BPR members occupied the Ministry of Labour in San Salvador and seized at least 86 hostages, among them the Minister of Labour and Social Security and that of the Economy, as an act of support for wage demands by textile and agricultural workers, but after the Government had undertaken to look into these demands the demonstrators agreed to leave the building peacefully on Nov. 12.

Members of the BPR said to consist of some 150 peasants belonging to the Salvadorean Christian Peasants' Federation and the Agricultural Workers' Union on April 11-13, 1978, peacefully entered the embassies in San Salvador of Costa Rica, Panama, Switzerland and Venezuela and also occupied the cathedral in San Salvador, requesting embassy officials to intercede with the Government of El Salvador "to stop the repression of the people and immediately to withdraw the Army, the police and the paramilitary groups from the occupied zone and to allow the peasants who were forced to flee to return to their homes"; they claimed that the military had committed "genocide" and demanded the release of 75 detained peasants. However, on April 19 the BPR members withdrew after mediation by ambassadors, the Red Cross and local representatives of the Church.

During May 1979 the BPR took a number of new violent actions. On May 4 some of its members occupied the Costa Rican and French embassies in San Salvador in support of a demand for the release of five BPR leaders believed to have been arrested recently. The Costa Rican ambassador and four other hostages managed to escape from the Costa Rican embassy on May 8, while three others agreed on May 10 to accept safe-conducts out of the country and left by air for Costa Rica. After two policemen and a guard had been shot dead outside the French embassy, the seizure of the French ambassador and five other persons in the embassy ended on June 1, 1979, after negotiations by a French special envoy, with both the former hostages and 16 BPR members being taken to Panama.

Another group of BPR members had occupied the cathedral in San Salvador on May 4, 1979; when some 100 people out of a crowd of 500 tried on May 8 to join those inside the cathedral, police opened fire, whereupon 23 persons were reported killed and 70 of them wounded. On May 10 some 10,000 people took part in the funeral procession, and Archbishop Romero of San Salvador called on the people "to unite in the face of military repression". On May 11 the Government ordered the release of two imprisoned BPR leaders—Facundo Guardado (secretary-general) and José Ricardo Mena—but denied holding the three others whose release had been demanded. Also on May 11 nine BPR members seized the Venezuelan embassy in San Salvador, taking the ambassador and seven others hostages, but all eight of the latter escaped from the building on May 20. On May 22 a total of 14 people were killed and 20 injured in clashes with security forces facing a crowd calling for the supply of food to the nine BPR members inside the building. The Venezuelan Government thereupon arranged for the immediate evacuation of Venezuelan nationals from El Salvador. A state of siege was proclaimed throughout the country on May 23; the occupation of the cathedral and other churches by BPR militants ended on May 25; and the nine BPR members were evacuated to Panama with the 16 from the French embassy—all of them being subsequently granted asylum in Cuba.

By the middle of 1979 the BPR embraced the following major groups: the Salvadorean Christian Peasants' Federation, the Agricultural Workers' Union, the National Association of Salvadorean Teachers (ANDES), the University Revolutionary Front (FUR-30) based at the University of Central America, the Revolutionary University Students (UR-19) based at the University of El Salvador, the Slum Dwellers Union (UPT) and the Trade Union Co-ordinating Committee (CCS).

After the overthrow of President Romero on Oct. 15, 1979, the BPR declared that it would not accept any truce with the new "counter-revolutionary" Government, and BPR members proceeded to occupy the cathedral in San Salvador on Oct. 22. After similarly occupying the Ministries of Labour and of the Economy on Oct. 24, the BPR demanded a 100 per cent wage increase, freedom for all political prisoners, the dissolution of the security forces, the lowering of basic food prices and compensation for the families of victims of political violence. After four BPR members were shot dead outside the Ministry of Labour, the Government of-fered negotiations on a peaceful solution, and on Oct. 29 the BPR released most of the hostages held by it but retained some, including the two ministers. After further negotiations the occupation of the ministries ended on Nov. 6, when the Government agreed to some of the BPR's demands, in particular to lower certain food prices, to end two labour conflicts in progress since mid-October and to dissolve the extreme right-wing National Democratic Organization (Orden).

From April 1980 the BPR formed part of the Revolutionary Democratic Front (see separate entry) set up by left-wing opposition parties as the political arm of the Farabundi Martí Front for National Liberation (see separate entry).

Revolutionary Co-ordination of the Masses (*Coordinación Revolucionaria de las Masas*, CRM)

This organization was set up on Jan. 10, 1980, as a "revolutionary alliance" of three major left-wing organizations: (i) the Popular Revolutionary Bloc (BPR) with the Farabundo Martí Popular Liberation Forces (FPL) as its armed wing; the February 28 Popular Leagues (LP-28) with the People's Revolutionary Army (ERP) as their armed wing; and (iii) the Unified Popular Action Front (FAPU) with the Armed Forces of National Resistance (FARN) as its armed wing; other participants were the Salvadorean Communist Party and the Nationalist Democratic Union (UDN).

At the end of February 1980 the new alliance announced its aims as the overthrow of the current Government; the installation of a "democratic revolutionary government"; the nationalization of the means of production, the banking and financial system and foreign trade; the creation of a new army; and the investigation of cases of missing persons dating back to 1972. A march held on Jan. 22, 1980, to mark the formation of the new alliance led to an armed conflict in which at least 22 persons were killed and 135 wounded.

Despite a far-reaching land reform programme (announced by the Government between February and April 1980), which would cover 90 per cent of the country and from which 1,250,000 people (80-90 per cent of the rural population) were expected to benefit, the CRM called during March 1980 for a general strike as a sign of opposition to the Government and especially to action taken against peasants by the security forces.

A partly successful general strike was organized by the CRM for June 24-25, 1980, in protest against the imposition of a state of siege in March 1980 and its monthly extension since then. During a meeting of the

CRM at the University of El Salvador on June 26, 1980, at least 50 people were killed and many others injured by troops.

Revolutionary Movement of Salvadorean Students (*Movimiento de Estudiantes Revolucionarios Salvadoreños,* MERS)

Members of this Movement (a component of the Popular Revolutionary Bloc—see separate entry) occupied the Ministry of Education on Feb. 5, 1980, seizing about 400 hostages in support of various educational demands; the occupation ended peacefully on Feb. 12 with agreements being signed with the ministry.

Revolutionary Workers' Federation (*Federación de Trabajadores Revolucionarios,* FTR)

This trade union organization called, upon its formation in December 1980, for its members to be ready for a general strike such as had been planned by the Revolutionary Democratic Front (see separate entry) to paralyse the nation and to facilitate an early opposition takeover.

Salvadorean Christian Peasants' Federation (*Federación de Campesinos Cristianos Salvadoreños,* Feccas)

This organization was, according to the Ministry of Foreign Affairs, "actively involved" in demonstrations for the release of political prisoners on May 1, 1977, when 10 persons were shot dead by security forces. It was subsequently declared illegal on the grounds that it had "communist links" (which it denied). In March 1978 peasant unrest in various parts of the country resulted in the death of 29 people and injury to 50 others, and the Government claimed that Feccas and also the Agricultural Workers' Union (UTC) had attempted to gain control of some areas with the support of "religious organizations", had used violence to try to recruit people into their organizations, and had killed members of the paramilitary progovernment National Democratic Organization (Orden).

Feccas and the UTC in turn declared that they were campaigning for "fair wages, the right to organize and the radical transformation of our society to construct a new society where there is no misery, hunger, repression or exploitation of one group by another"; they accused vigilantes belonging to Orden to have murdered peasants and evicted villagers from their homes. The peasants' stand was supported by Archbishop Romero of San Salvador, who denied that the Church had been behind the incidents of March 1978 but also issued a warning that, if wages were not raised and land

rents lowered, and if force continued to be used against the peasants, violence would spread in the country.

In a demonstration in San Salvador on March 17, 1978, for which Feccas and the UTC were officially held responsible, and which was dispersed by troops, nine people were said to have been killed and 25 injured. On Jan. 20, 1980, Feccas supporters occupied 25 plantations in the country's northern part in support of a 50 per cent pay increase. In the late 1970s and early 1980s Feccas formed part of broader alliances of left-wing opposition forces, notably the Popular Revolutionary Bloc and the Revolutionary Democratic Front (see separate entries).

Salvadorean Communist Party (*Partido Comunista Salvadoreño,* PCS)

Leadership. Jorge Schafik Handal (s.g.).

This party has been illegal for most of the time since its formation in 1930. Although it was not legalized at the time, one of its members briefly was Minister of Labour and Social Welfare in the Cabinet formed on Oct. 22, 1979 (a week after the overthrow of President Romero). However, in January 1980 the PCS joined a left-wing opposition alliance called the Revolutionary Co-ordination of the Masses and subsequently became an influential force in the broader Revolutionary Democratic Front formed in April 1980 (see separate entry). The PCS is also a leading component of the main left-wing guerrilla organization, the Farabundo Martí Front for National Liberation (see separate entry).

The PCS is officially recognized by the Communist parties of the Soviet-bloc countries.

University Revolutionary Front (*Frente Universitario Revolucionario,* FUR-30)

This group, a student branch of the Popular Revolutionary Bloc (BPR—see separate entry), has been active since 1980, as a component of the BPR. On Feb. 15, 1980, members of the group stormed the (Jesuit) University of Central America in San Salvador and seized 60 hostages, including the chancellor (a Spanish Jesuit)—but all were released on Feb. 18.

Extreme Right-wing Groups

Anti-Communist Political Front (*Frente Político Anticomunista,* FPA)

Established in May 1979, this militia has, like others, been active in attacks on alleged left-wing leaders.

Eastern Anti-Guerrilla Bloc (*Bloque Anti-guerrillero del Oriente,* BAGO)

Established in 1980, this group has been responsible for a number of killings and bomb attacks, in particular for the death of 14 alleged left-wing guerrillas on Sept. 24, 1980.

Maximiliano Hernández Martínez Anti-Communist Alliance (*Alianza Anticomunista Maximiliano Hernández Martínez*)

This group was named after President Martínez who was in power in 1931-44 and under whose regime the 1932 peasant rebellion was suppressed. It claimed responsibility for the murder of six leaders of the (left-wing) Revolutionary Democratic Front (see separate entry) in November 1980. This group was also reported to have delivered to a San Salvador radio station (in March 1982) a "death list" of 34 (mainly foreign) journalists alleged to have contacts with left-wing guerrillas.

National Democratic Organization (*Organización Democrática Nacional,* Orden)

Dating from 1968, this mainly rural anti-guerrilla militia was officially disbanded after the October 1979 coup (in which President Romero was overthrown) but members of it have continued their activities since then.

New Death Squad (*Escuadrón de la Muerte Nuevo,* EMN)

This anti-communist execution squad has claimed a membership of 3,000 and has been involved in bombings and killings since September 1980.

Organization for Liberation from Communism (*Organización para la Liberación del Comunismo,* OLC)

This paramilitary group has been active since early 1980. It killed four Popular Revolutionary Bloc (BPR) members on Jan. 29, 1980, and it was reported to have planted bombs which had, on Feb. 18, 1980, destroyed the transmitter of the radio station belonging to the archbishopric of El Salvador and also publishing offices at the (Jesuit) University of Central America.

Salvadorean Anti-Communist Army (*Ejército Salvadoreño Anticomunista,* ESA)

This group was in 1980 held responsible for numerous acts of persecution directed notably against teachers, priests, monks and nuns. On June 29, 1980, the ESA was reported to have dynamited the print shop of the University of El Salvador.

White Warriors' Union (*Unión de Guerreros Blancos,* UGB)

This terrorist organization was responsible for numerous actions against alleged left-wing activists and in particular against Jesuit priests said to be involved in subversive peasant organizations. In revenge for the killing of an industrialist by members of the Farabundo Martí Popular Liberation Forces (FPL) in April 1977, the UGB killed a Jesuit priest and in June of that year it threatened to kill the 47 Jesuits still remaining in the country if they had not left by July 20. The Government, however, subsequently placed these priests under guard. The UGB was also held responsible for the murder of further priests in late June and on Aug. 4, 1979, and for that of 16 garage mechanics in San Salvador on Aug. 16 of that year.

Grenada

Capital: St George's   Pop. 120,000

Grenada is an independent state within the Commonwealth with the British monarch as ceremonial head of state being represented by a Governor-General. It is ruled by a ("neo-left") People's Revolutionary Government (PRG) consisting of a Cabinet of 10 ministers (including a Prime Minister) and by a Revolutionary Council. The country's 1974 Constitution was suspended in March 1979, when the regime of Sir Eric Gairy was overthrown by the New Jewel Movement (NJM, Joint Endeavour for Education, Welfare and Education) under the leadership of Maurice Bishop. There are no other legal parties and there is no parliament.

Since 1980 the PRG has developed close relations with the Government of the Soviet-bloc countries and in particular Cuba. During this period, there have been, according to the PRG, several plots to overthrow the Government and US-inspired "destabilization" efforts, and also sporadic guerrilla activities, in some of which small "counter-revolutionary" groups were said to have been involved. In connexion with a bomb attack on the Governor-General, the Prime Minister and the Cuban ambassador on June 19, 1980 (when two persons were killed and many others injured, and security forces shot dead an army sergeant said to be the leader of the "counter-revolutionaries"), five persons were charged in August 1980.

Following these events, the death penalty was introduced for terrorism on Oct. 3, 1980, and under a preventive detention law promulgated in September 1981 the Minister of National Security was empowered to issue restriction orders (including subjection to house arrest) in the interest of public safety and public order.

Grenada National Party for Recovery and Liberation

On June 19, 1981, the authorities closed down a mimeographed independent newspaper, *The Grenadian Voice*, founded by a group of businessmen, lawyers, professional people and trade unionists. The newspaper's owners were accused of having acted on behalf of the Grenada National Party for Recovery and Liberation by issuing "five counter-revolutionary pamphlets during the past six months" and of having been involved in a destabilization campaign by the (US) Central Intelligence Agency (CIA), for which they were alleged to have planned a dock strike. Four persons were, on July 11, 1981, placed under detention in connexion with an alleged "CIA plot to overthrow the Government".

Patriotic Alliance

Leadership. Dr Stanley Cyrus; James Herry.

This Alliance was formed in August 1981 by exiles opposed to the People's Revolutionary Government (PRG), which accused its two leaders of being "counter-revolutionaries" who had "openly engaged in CIA-sponsored activities involving conspiracy to overthrow the PRG and incite persons to violence".

People's Action Group

Leadership. Winston Whyte.

Established in 1979 as an alliance of smaller right-wing groupings, this movement included members of the United People's Party (which had in 1976 contested elections in alliance with the New Jewel Movement) and two members of a faction of the Rastafarian sect who were hostile to the People's Revolutionary Government (PRG). These two and W. Whyte were, with others, arrested on Oct. 15, 1979, for plotting against the PRG.

(Details on the origins and beliefs of the Caribbean Rastafarian movement are given in the country section for Dominica, on pages 350-51.)

Guatemala

Capital: Guatemala City   Pop. 7,600,000

The Republic of Guatemala has since March 23, 1982, been under the control of military officers who were close to the extreme right-wing anti-communist National Liberation Movement (MNL). On seizing power they suspended the 1966 Constitution and the existing political parties, and also declared null and void the results of presidential and congressional elections held on March 7, 1982. All political parties, however, declared themselves in favour of the new regime. On June 9, 1982, the President appointed by the officers (Gen. Efraín Rios Montt) assumed sole executive and legislative functions as head of state and C.-in-C. of the Armed Forces.

The official results of the 1982 congressional elections showed the distribution of seats in the 66-member unicameral Congress to be as follows: Popular Democratic Front (a conservative alliance of the Revolutionary Party, the Democratic Institutional Party and the Front of National Unity) 33, the (extreme right-wing) National Liberation Movement 21, the (right-wing) National Authentic Central 3, the (centrist) National Opposition Union (comprising the National Renewal Party and the Guatemalan Christian Democratic Party) 2, others 7.

The country's four principal left-wing guerrilla organizations have been active since the 1960s in both rural and urban areas, waging an assassination campaign against government officials, judges and members of the armed forces. In February 1982 they established a "unified military command" and subsequently boycotted the March 1982 elections, declaring on March 27 that they would continue their operations because the military coup of March 23 had produced merely "a change in the façade of the regime" and that no reforms were possible in Guatemala "without revolutionary changes". The new regime under President Rios Montt nevertheless made certain overtures to the guerrillas, who, however, rejected an offer of negotiation (made on April 11). They also rejected an amnesty decreed on May 22 for one month (at the end of which certain areas of the country were to be declared zones of exception and anti-guerrilla operations would intensify, with the assistance of some 25,000 newly recruited and trained paramilitary peasant militias) and another offer to negotiate made on June 15, 1982. Both before and after the March 1982 elections the killings continued unabated.

Left-wing Movements

Christians for Respect for Life

Members of this group kidnapped a nephew of President Rios Montt on Oct. 13, 1982, but six weeks later security forces were able to free him.

Commando of the Popular Forces of the People (*Comando de las Fuerzas Populares del Pueblo*)

This group's formation was announced on Dec. 9, 1981, when it claimed to be "ready for armed action against the Government".

Committee of Peasant Unity (CUC)—see under Guatemalan Committee of Patriotic Unity *and* 31st January Popular Front

Democratic Front against Repression (*Frente Democrático contra la Represión,* FDR)

This Front was formed in March 1979 by over 72 parties and organizations, including the (social democratic) United Revolutionary Front (*Frente Unido de la Revolución,* FUR) established in 1977. The objects of the FDR were defined as the denunciation of national and international level of all repressive actions committed in Guatemala against any popular and democratic sector and the provision of aid to widows and orphans of the victims.

Democratic Socialist Party (PSD)—see under Guatemalan Committee of Patriotic Unity

Federation of Guatemalan Workers (FTG)—see under 31st January Popular Front

Felipe Antonio García Revolutionary Workers' Nuclei—see under 31st January Popular Front

Guatemalan Committee of Patriotic Unity (*Comité Guatemalteco de Unidad Patriótica,* CGUP)

Leadership. Luis Cardoza y Aragón (head of co-ordinating committee).

This Committee was formed on Feb. 16, 1982 (as announced simultaneously in Panama, Paris and Mexico City on Feb. 19), by (i) the Democratic Front against Repression, which had close links with the Revolutionary Organization of the People in Arms (ORPA); (ii) the 31st January Popular Front (FP-31), which was close to the Guerrilla Army of the Poor (EGP); (iii) several members of the (social democratic) United Revolutionary Front (FUR); and (iv) 26 prominent Guatemalan exiles of various political affiliations. These 26 persons signed a founding document and set up an eight-member co-ordinating committee headed by Luis Cardoza y Aragón, a veteran politician who had been a member of the (left-wing) Government of President Arbenz Guzmán, overthrown in June 1954; other members of the committee included Guillermo Toriello Garrido (who had been Foreign Minister under President Arbenz Guzmán), a member of the Committee of Peasant Unity (CUC) and Carlos Gallardo Flores, leader of the Democratic Socialist Party (*Partido Socialista Democrático,* PSD).

The CGUP endorsed the basic programme of the Guatemalan National Revolutionary Unity (URNG—see separate entry), stating that the popular revolutionary war was the only road left open, but that it had no direct links with the guerrillas. The CGUP also denounced the elections to be held on March 7, 1982, as a "farce" on the grounds that "electoral fraud, corruption, persecution and assassination of democratic leaders and of hundreds of party members" had been "the permanent practices of the regime". It declared that the people of Guatemala were carrying on a war aimed at "constructing a new society which responds to its interests and aspirations, confronting the bloodiest dictatorship which Latin America has ever known".

Guatemalan Labour Party (*Partido Guatemalteco del Trabajo,* PGT)

This party was founded as the Communist Party of Guatemala at an underground congress held in September 1949 (after having previously been known as the Democratic Vanguard of Guatemala formed out of various left-wing groups). It was one of the first and best organized communist parties in Central America. In 1954 the party was outlawed; from then on it worked underground; and from 1961 it conducted armed struggle. At its second congress, held in December 1962, it adopted the name of Guatemalan Labour Party.

In 1969 the party adopted a new programme aimed at "the agrarian anti-imperialist revolution" and "the socialist revolution". However, in 1972-74 all members of the party's central committee were executed or murdered. The party subsequently elected a new leadership and decided in favour of a peaceful road to socialism, but it turned out that this decision was endorsed only by a minority of party members (most of whom were killed or went into exile), whereas a majority of members reverted to armed struggle and participated in the formation of the Rebel Armed Forces (FAR—see separate entry).

By 1980 PGT guerrillas were active in Guatemala City and areas to the south and west of it. In February 1982 the guerrilla faction of the PGT joined the unified military command known as the Guatemalan National Revolutionary Unity (URNG)—see following entry.

The PGT is officially recognized by the Communist parties of the Soviet-bloc countries.

Guatemalan National Revolutionary Unity (*Unidad Revolucionaria Nacional Guatemalteca,* URNG)

The formation of this unified military command was announced on Feb. 8, 1982, by the four main guerrilla organizations which had on several earlier occasions (in November 1979, May 1980 and January 1981) declared their intention to unite. They were the Guerrilla Army of the Poor (EGP), the Revolutionary Organization of the People in Arms (ORPA), the Rebel Armed Forces (FAR) and a faction of the (Communist) Guatemalan Labour Party (PGT).

The URNG announced in a statement widely distributed in Guatemala City that it intended to pursue a "popular revolutionary war" as the sole means left to the people "to free themselves from oppression, exploitation, discrimination and dependence on foreign countries". The statement also denounced "the most odious genocide perpetrated in the whole of the western hemisphere", where, it said, on average 36 persons disappeared or were assassinated every day.

Announcing its aims over a number of radio stations which it had seized temporarily the URNG listed as its main objectives (i) an end to repression and a guarantee of life, peace and fundamental human rights for all citizens; (ii) provision for the basic needs of the majority of the people; (iii) equality for the indigenous and the White-descended *(ladinos)* people; (iv) the creation of a new society in which all sectors of the population would be represented in the Government; and (v) non-alignment and international co-operation.

Guerrilla Army of the Poor (*Ejército Guerrillero de los Pobres,* EGP)

This movement emerged in the early 1970s and greatly extended its activities in 1976, with the result that by the end of that year it controlled certain areas in the country's northern mountains. While the EGP was active mainly among the country's landless peasants, some of its members were also involved in incidents in Guatemala City.

On Nov. 6, 1976, the EGP claimed responsibility for the bombing of a hotel in Guatemala City in retaliation for the killings of two EGP members by the hotel owner's bodyguard. In January 1977 the EGP increased its activities in southern Guatemala. On Dec. 31, 1977, EGP guerrillas kidnapped a former minister but released him on Jan. 30, 1978, after they had obtained compliance with their demands for (i) the publication in the press of an EGP manifesto and (ii) the release of an EGP member who had sought refuge in the Costa Rican embassy and who was subsequently flown to Costa Rica; the EGP was also reported to have been paid a large ransom.

Following the use of firearms by the Army against demonstrating peasants at Panzós (north-east of Guatemala City) on May 29, 1978, when it was officially stated that 43 persons had been killed and 17 wounded, President Laugerud García of Guatemala accused both the EGP and Roman Catholic and Protestant clergy of inciting peasants to "invade private estates" and seize land. Following a march in protest at these incidents on June 8, a bomb planted by the EGP killed 14 military policemen in Guatemala City on June 14.

A group of 27 Indian peasants from the department of El Quiché (north-west of Guatemala City) which had been under virtual military occupation since 1975 because of the activities of the EGP (and also of the Revolutionary Organization of the People in Arms, ORPA) occupied the Spanish embassy in Guatemala City on Jan. 31, 1980, taking the ambassador and other people hostages. When the Guatemalan police, against the express wishes of the ambassador, stormed the building, a petrol bomb was thrown by the peasants and in the ensuing fire 39 people lost their lives, the only survivors being the ambassador and one of the peasants—Yuxa Shona, who was, however, killed by a death squad after being abducted from hospital on Feb. 1 (see separate entry for Yuxa Shona Front).

On Sept. 5, 1980, Elias Barahona, press secretary at the Guatemalan Ministry of the Interior, stated at a press conference in Panama that he was a member of the EGP and had infiltrated the Government four years earlier; he alleged inter alia that the right-wing Secret Anti-Communist Army (ESA) and the Death Squad (EM) were directed by the country's President, its Minister of the Interior and a number of generals.

In 1980-81 the EGP operated largely in the northern highlands and also in and around Guatemala City. It has considerable influence among the Indian population and has repeatedly occupied villages temporarily, partly to carry out recruitment. Such action has led to punitive raids by the Army, in which large numbers of people have been killed.

In June 1981 the guerrillas claimed to have extended their "people's war" to 19 of Guatemala's 22 departments and to be concentrating on the Verapaz oil region near the Mexican border in the north-west. In February 1982 the EGP joined the unified military command known as the Guatemalan National Revolutionary Unity (URNG).

People's Revolutionary Movement-Ixim (*Movimiento Revolucionario del Pueblo-Ixim,* MRP)

Members of this Movement kidnapped the daughter of the President of Honduras (Dr Roberto Suazo Córdova) on Dec. 14, 1982, but released her on Dec. 24 after the Guatemalan Government had permitted the publication of an MRP manifesto in local newspapers (this manifesto being also published in newspapers in Mexico and Central America).

Rebel Armed Forces (*Fuerzas Armadas Rebeldes,* FAR)

The FAR, established in December 1962, superseded a 13th November Revolutionary Movement (*Movimiento Revolucionario Trece de Noviembre,* MR-13) which had arisen out of a rebellion by a group of officers on Nov. 13, 1960, and was led by Luis Turcios Lima (who died in 1966), Marco Antonio Yon Sosa ("El Chino", who was killed in a clash with troops in May 1970) and Luis Trejo Esquivel. The FAR was, on its foundation, joined by part of the Guatemalan Labour Party (PGT). From 1970 onwards the FAR went into decline but in 1972 it was reorganized with the aim of constituting a mass party, and later it reverted to armed struggle. By 1980 it operated in northern areas and also near Lake Izabál (in eastern Guatemala).

In February 1982 the FAR joined the unified military command known as the Guatemalan National Revolutionary Unity (URNG).

Revolutionary Organization of the People in Arms (*Organización Revolucionaria del Pueblo en Armas,* ORPA)

The ORPA was established in September 1979 as a political and military movement to be built up secretly, at first in rural areas and later among all sections of the people. It is anti-racialist and stands for the development of the indigenous people's culture.

ORPA guerrillas, who enjoyed considerable support among the Indian population, were in 1980 active mainly in western and central departments but also in Guatemala City and areas to the south of it. In September of that year they occupied tourist-frequented areas on the shores of Lake Atitlán (west of Guatemala City), near which the Army thereupon established a base from which it launched attacks against the guerrillas. In July 1981 security forces destroyed ORPA bases in the capital. The ORPA guerrillas co-operated closely with those of the Guatemalan Labour Party (PGT).

In February 1982 the ORPA joined the unified military command known as the Guatemalan National Revolutionary Unity (URNG).

Rubén García Revolutionary Student Front— see under 31st January Popular Front

31st January Popular Front (*Frente Popular 31 de Enero,* FP-31)

This Front, formed in January 1981, took its name from the date of the 1980 attack on the Spanish embassy in Guatemala City by peasants (see under Guerrilla Army of the Poor, EGP).

Its component parties were the Federation of Guatemalan Workers (FTG), the Committee of Peasant Unity (CUC), the Felipe Antonio García Revolutionary Workers' Nuclei, the Trinidad Gómez Hernández Settlers' Co-ordinating Body, the Vicente Menchu Revolutionary Christians and the Rubén García Revolutionary Student Front. The FP-31 described its aims as "the removal from power of the military, economic and political forces which sustain the dictatorship and the establishment of a revolutionary, popular and democratic government" by means of guerrilla warfare.

On May 12, 1982, a dozen members of the FP-31 and the Committee of Peasant Unity (CUC), claiming to represent people who had been "persecuted" and whose harvests and farms had been burned, and protesting against killings by the security forces in rural areas, seized the Brazilian embassy in Guatemala City and took some 10 persons, including the ambassador, as hostages. However, after the Government had agreed to the occupiers' demand to hold a press conference denouncing the massacres, they were flown to Mexico with some of the hostages who had agreed to guarantee their safety, while the remaining hostages (among them the ambassador) were released unharmed.

Trinidad Gómez Hernández Settlers' Co-ordinating Body— see under 31st January Popular Front

Vicente Menchu Revolutionary Christians— see under 31st January Popular Front

Voluntary Defence Front (*Frente Voluntario de Defensa,* FUD)

This small left-wing guerrilla group emerged in July 1980.

United Revolutionary Front (FUR)— see under Democratic Front against Repression *and* Guatemalan Committee of Patriotic Unity

Yuxa Shona Front *(Frente Yuxa Shona)*

This Marxist-Leninist group, established in March 1980, was named after a survivor of the siege at the Spanish embassy by peasants on Jan. 31, 1980, who was later killed by a death squad on Feb. 1 (see under Guerrilla Army of the Poor, EGP). The group was said to be in sympathy with the Revolutionary Organization of the People in Arms (ORPA), the Rebel Armed Forces (FAR) and the EGP.

Extreme Right-wing Groups

In retaliation for the killings and other acts of violence perpetrated by left-wing guerrillas, numerous extreme right-wing organizations, some of which were alleged to enjoy government support or to work in close association with the police, have in recent years engaged in attacks on left-wing leaders, including journalists, trade unionists and lawyers. The loss of life on both sides in the conflict has run into tens of thousands.

Amnesty International alleged on Dec. 11, 1976, that in the past 10 years over 20,000 people, many of them political dissidents, had been killed or had disappeared without trace in Guatemala as a result of action by government or semi-official forces. According to a conservative Guatemalan newspaper (quoted in *The New York Times* on Nov. 28, 1980) there had been, in the first 10 months of 1980, a total of 3,617 violent deaths (including those of 389 university students, 326 school teachers, 311 peasant leaders, 86 university professors and 12 journalists).

In a further Amnesty International report published on Feb. 18, 1981, it was alleged that the murders were being carried out by the police and the Army and that secret detentions and summary executions were "part of a clearly defined programme of government" and reflected "a pattern of selective and considered official action" based on denunciations and on decisions made by senior officials of the Ministers of Defence and the Interior in consultation with the Army General Staff. A US State Department report issued on Feb. 7, 1982, maintained that in 1981 political killings had attained 250-300 a month (compared with an estimated 70-100 a month in 1980). According to Guatemalan church sources, however, over 11,000 people had lost their lives in political violence during 1981.

Of the political parties which had been legal until March 1982, the Christian Democratic Party (PDC) and the (social democratic) United Revolutionary Front (FUR) lost several of their leading members as a result of killings by extreme right-wing groups, and on June 6, 1982, the PDC announced that it was suspending its activities owing to the security situation; the killings of PDC leaders nevertheless continued.

Details of some of the known extreme right-wing groups active in Guatemala are given below.

Armed Action Forces (*Fuerzas de Acción Armada,* FADA)

This group was responsible, inter alia, for the murder on Jan. 25, 1979, of Alberto Fuentes Mohr, a former Foreign Minister (in 1966-70) and supporter of the (centre-left) National Unity Front (FRENU).

Death Squad (*Escuadron de la Muerte,* EM)

The EM was for many years engaged in killings of alleged left-wing activists or sympathizers. In 1980 alone it was considered responsible for several hundred such deaths every month. According to a statement made in Panama on Sept. 1, 1980, by Elias Barahona, an agent of the Guerrilla Army of the Poor (EGP), the EM was directed by the President, the Prime Minister and a number of generals.

Secret Anti-Communist Army (*Ejército Segredo Anti-Comunista,* ESA)

Established in 1976, this organization was responsible for the killing of numerous politicians and officials as well as trade unionists and student leaders whose names appeared on regularly published "death lists". The ESA was believed to be linked to the extreme right-wing National Liberation Movement (MLN) led by Mario Sandoval Alarcón, who was Vice-President of Guatemala in 1974-78. The ESA was thought to be involved in the killing of the president of the university students' association on Oct. 20, 1978. It was also thought to be one of the organizations responsible for the murder of Manuel Colom Argueta (the country's leading opposition figure and former mayor of Guatemala City in 1970-74) on March 22, 1979.

In a declaration published in a Guatemalan newspaper in January 1980, Jesuits stated that between January and October 1979 ESA death squads had committed 3,252 murders "with absolute impunity". From Rome it was announced on Feb. 13, 1980, that on Jan. 23 the Jesuit Order had received death threats from the ESA against its 52 priests in Guatemala. (It was also reported that a government inquiry had been opened into the activities of foreign Jesuits.)

According to a statement made in Panama on Sept. 1, 1980, by an agent of the Guerrilla Army of the Poor (EGP), Elias Barahona, the ESA was directed by the President, the Prime Minister and a number of generals.

The White Hand (*La Mano Blanca*)

This group has been active since 1970, when its headquarters were said to be in the police building in Guatemala City. It was, in particular, responsible for the killing, on April 8, 1970, of César Montenegro Paniagua, a (pro-Soviet) Communist leader suspected of involvement in the abduction and killing by the Rebel Armed Forces (FAR) of the West German ambassador in Guatemala a week earlier.

The White Hand was reported to be linked to Gen. Carlos Manuel Araña Osorio, who was President of Guatemala in 1970-74 and who was a leading member of the (right-wing) National Liberation Movement (MLN). The White Hand was also believed to be one of the two organizations suspected of involvement in the murder of Manuel Colom Argueta, a leading opposition figure, on March 22, 1979 (the other suspected organization being the Secret Anti-Communist Army, ESA).

Other Right-wing Groups

Other extreme right-wing groups which have been active in recent years include the following:

Armed People's Organized Youth (*Juventud Organizada del Pueblo en Armas,* JOPA), established in March 1980 as an anti-communist execution squad.

Band of the Hawks (*Banda de los Halcones*).

Band of the Vultures *(Banda de los Buitres).*

The Centurions *(Los Centuriones).*

Eye for an Eye *(Ojo por Ojo),* already active in 1970.

15th September Liberty *(Libertad 15 Septiembre).*

Guatemalan Workers' Militia *(Milicias Obreras Guatemaltecas,* MOG), founded in March 1978 and active during 1980.

King's Band *(Banda del Rey).*

New Anti-Terrorist Organization *(Nueva Organización Antiterrorista,* NOA), which emerged in 1982.

North-Eastern Anti-Communist Front *(Frente Anticomunista del Nororiente,* FANO), established on May 8, 1980.

Order of Death *(Orden de la Muerte).*

Organization Zero *(Organización Cero).*

Organized Anti-Communist Movement *(Movimiento Anticomunista Organizado,* MANO).

The Shadow *(La Sombra).*

Southern Anti-Communist Commando *(Comando Anticomunista del Sur,* CADS), established as an execution squad in May 1980.

The Thunderbolt *(El Rayo).*

Guyana

Capital: Georgetown   Pop. 850,000

The Co-operative Republic of Guyana, a member of the Commonwealth, has under its Constitution, which came into effect on Oct. 6, 1980, a popularly elected executive President and a First Vice-President who is also Prime Minister. There is also a National Assembly to which 53 members are elected for a five-year term by universal adult suffrage, while another 12 members are elected by 10 regional democratic councils from among their own members and by a national congress of local democratic organs.

According to the official results of elections held on Dec. 15, 1980, the 53 directly elected members of the National Assembly were distributed as follows: People's National Congress (PNC) 41, People's Progressive Party (PPP) 10, United Force (UF) 2. However, a team of observers led by (the British Liberal) Lord Avebury reported that "massive and blatant fraud" had been committed during the elections. The (co-operative socialist) PNC is supported mainly by the African section of the population, and the (pro-Soviet communist) PPP by the East Indian community. Political parties not represented in the Assembly are the (conservative) Liberator Party, the (left-wing) Working People's Alliance (WPA), the (Maoist) Working People's Vanguard Party and the People's Democratic Movement—the two last-named parties forming, in 1979, a Vanguard for Liberation and Democracy.

The WPA, led by Marxists and Black Power activists, was in 1979-82 kept under close surveillance by the Government; some of its members were sentenced to imprisonment, others were not allowed to leave the country, and several were murdered. Those killed included Dr Walter Rodney, a leading member of the party, who died on June 13, 1980, as the result of a car bomb explosion; he had been regarded as one of the Caribbean region's leading radical historians and the founder of the "New Left" movement in Commonwealth Caribbean politics.

Guyana Human Rights Association

In a statement issued on June 20, 1980, and supported by 22 other organizations (including professional bodies, trade unions and churches of various denominations) this Association called for a return to "democracy and the rule of law" in Guyana; the im-

mediate establishment of an international commission of inquiry into the circumstances of the death of Dr Walter Rodney, the leading member of the Working People's Alliance (who died in an explosion on June 13, 1980); and a commitment by all Guyanese to "work to make this society one based on respect for fundamental human rights and freedoms''. The Association warned the people of Guyana that, if they did not take the opportunity "to reconstruct a peaceful society", they would have "to face the consequences of continuing violence". The authorities, however, ignored this and other appeals for an inquiry into Dr Rodney's death.

House of Israel

Leadership. David Hill—also known as Edward Emmanuel Washington ("rabbi").

Members of this Black supremacist sect were held responsible for acts of violence which led to the death of the deputy editor and a photographer of *The Catholic Standard* (a newspaper which had been critical of the Government's human rights record) during a procession held in Georgetown on July 14, 1979. The procession was conducted by supporters of the (opposition) Working People's Alliance (WPA) in protest against the detention of WPA leaders after the bombing (on July 11) of a building housing the Ministry of National Development and the secretariat of the ruling People's National Congress (PNC). The WPA regarded the House of Israel as "mainly a pseudo-military arm" of the PNC, since it had earlier been involved in strike-breaking and harassment of critics of the Government.

Haiti

Capital: Port-au-Prince   Pop. 5,300,000

The Republic of Haiti has an executive President (appointed for life), who presides over a Council of Ministers appointed by him. There is a unicameral National Assembly of 58 members elected for six years by universal adult suffrage. In an emergency the President is empowered to dismiss the Council of Ministers and the National Assembly and to govern by decree. In elections held on Feb. 11, 1979, the Party of National Unity *(Parti de l'Unité Nationale),* the country's sole legal party, gained 57 seats, while the remaining seat went to an independent.

The Government of Haiti, supported by a special force of National Security Volunteers generally known as the Tontons Macoute, has been repeatedly condemned by the international community for its internal policies as pursued under the presidencies of both Dr François ("Papadoc") Duvalier and his son Jean-Claude Duvalier (who succeeded his father in 1971). Numerous arrests and executions of alleged plotters against the Government were carried out between 1967 and 1970, and several attempts to land in Haiti, made by anti-government Haitian exiles in Florida, were foiled in 1966-67 (some of them by the US authorities). By 1970 there were about 400,000 Haitians living in exile, and numerous political groups formed by them ranged over the whole political spectrum from conservative to communist. Massive emigration from Haiti continued in the 1970s, and during the year 1980 alone over 30,000 further Haitian refugees were said to have reached the United States. Although President Duvalier announced at the end of September 1982 that all Haitians in exile would be allowed to return to their country, only a limited number did so.

Movements in opposition to the regime have been set up both inside and outside Haiti.

Christian Democratic Party of Haiti

Leadership. Dr Sylvio Claude (pres.); Abel Cangé (s.g.).

Dr Sylvio Claude was an unsuccessful candidate in the February 1979 National Assembly elections and was thereafter briefly deported from Haiti before returning to form his party on July 5, 1979. An open-air political meeting organized by him in Port-au-Prince for Aug. 28, 1979, was attacked by some 2,000 people, and on the following day the party's offices were ransacked by the police. He himself, however, managed to deliver a broadcast reporting what had happened, whereupon he was arrested on Aug. 30 with some 200 others, among them Prof. Grégoire Eugène (the leader of the "June 27" Christian Democratic Party of Haiti—see separate entry); he was, however, released on May 2, 1980, after he had been involved in a hunger strike.

On Oct. 13, 1980, Dr Sylvio was rearrested for infringing a press law by asking in his newspaper *La Conviction* how long President Duvalier would still remain dictator, and on Aug. 26, 1981, he was with 21 other persons (including his son and daughter) sentenced to 15 years in prison for "incitement to revolt and attempting to create a climate of disorder and to start fires". However, in February 1982 the President announced that these sentences had been annulled. At a retrial ordered by the Appeals Court on Aug. 27-28 the sentences were reduced to six years each, and at the end of September 1982 all the accused were released subject to being placed under house arrest.

Representatives of the party were present at a continental conference of solidarity with the people of Haiti, held in Panama in September 1981 and attended by about 40 Haitians from nine different countries, where they lived in exile. The conference called for the restoration of democratic freedoms in Haiti, for an amnesty of 90 named political prisoners (such prisoners being officially stated to number only 55, compared with an unofficial estimate of over 300) and for permission for exiles to return to Haiti unconditionally.

Council for the National Liberation of Haiti

Leadership. Roland Magloire (l.).

This organization of Haitian exiles, led by the nephew of a former President (Paul Magloire, 1950-56), was involved in an attempt to invade Haiti from Florida on March 16, 1982, but the 16 mercenaries setting out in two cabin cruisers were arrested by US coast guards.

Haitian Human Rights League

Leadership. Gérard Gourgue (pres.); Lafontant Joseph (s.g.).

Joseph Maxi, a lawyer and founder-member of this movement, was reported to have been arrested after the parliamentary elections of February 1979, together with 12 others, apparently in connexion with an alleged anti-government plot. A meeting of the League in Port-au-Prince in early November 1979 was broken up by police who beat up a number of persons, including personnel from the embassies of Canada, France and West Germany and the US political attaché. Among over 400 people temporarily detained late in November

1979, when it was officially claimed that a plot against the Government had been discovered, was the League's secretary-general.

Haitian National Christian Party

Leadership. The Rev. René des Rameaux (l.).

The formation of this illegal party was announced on Aug. 29, 1979, by its leader in St Louis du Nord.

Hector Riobé Brigade

This group carried out several air attacks on targets in Haiti in mid-1982, among them one on vehicles near the main presidential palace and another on the President's ranch north of Port-au-Prince. It was also responsible for scattering anti-government leaflets from a light aircraft, and for bomb explosions in Port-au-Prince in December 1982 and on Jan. 1, 1983. Late in January 1983 it issued a warning to the papal nuncio to see to it that the forthcoming visit by the Pope (in March 1983) should not be "put to the service of the Duvalier family".

"June 27" Christian Democratic Party of Haiti

Leadership. Prof. Grégoire Eugène (l.).

This illegal party, also referred to as the Social Christian Party, was founded in July 1979 by Prof. Eugène, who had been an unsuccessful candidate in the 1979 parliamentary elections. In his fortnightly journal *Fraternité* he had criticized the regime and on June 27, 1979, he had published in Port-au-Prince a book in which he maintained that the Haitian Constitution allowed the formation of political parties. Prof. Eugène was temporarily detained after an open-air political meeting held on Aug. 28, 1979. After being arrested with some 400 other opposition figures, human rights activists and journalists late in November 1980, Prof. Eugène was, with several others, deported to the United States on Dec. 2 of that year.

National Haitian Popular Party

Leadership. Bernard Sansaricq.

The formation of this party was announced in leaflets signed by Bernard Sansaricq (a right-wing leader of Haitians in exile) and dropped from a light aircraft which flew over Port-au-Prince late in October 1981. In the leaflets a call was made for a rising against the regime of President Duvalier. Shortly afterwards the presidential yacht was said to have been hijacked, and there followed numerous arrests of political and trade union figures.

An invasion attempt co-ordinated by B. Sansaricq (who was said to have been involved in two previous invasion attempts in 1964 and 1968) was launched from the (British) Turks and Caicos Islands on Jan. 9, 1982, but was unsuccessful. The Haitian Ministry of the Interior and National Security stated on Jan. 22 that, of 44 "terrorists" involved, 26 (including B. Sansaricq) had been arrested by the US authorities, eight had been killed and 10 had fled, while four members of the security forces had lost their lives in the course of the fighting.

Progressive Nationalist and Democratic Assembly (*Rassemblement Démocratique Nationaliste et Progressiste,* RDNP)

Leadership. Leslie Manigat.

This organization was founded by Leslie Manigat in Caracas (Venezuela) in March 1981. It was not represented at a continental conference of solidarity with the people of Haiti held in Panama in September 1981 (see under Christian Democratic Party of Haiti for details).

Union of Democratic and Patriotic Forces (*Union des Forces Patriotiques et Démocratiques)*

This organization was one of those represented at the continental conference of solidarity with the people of Haiti, held in Panama in September 1981 (see under Christian Democratic Party of Haiti).

United Party of Haitian Communists (*Parti Unifié des Communistes Haïtiens,* PUCH)

Leadership. Jacques Dosilien (s.g.).

This party was founded in November 1968 by the merger of a Haiti People's Unity Party (formed in 1959) and a People's Party of National Liberation (formed in 1954). It has been illegal under an anti-communist law of April 28, 1969. At a congress held in November 1978 the delegates adopted a new programme demanding inter alia that "imperialist pillage" of Haiti's national wealth should be ended; that the anti-communist law should be abrogated; that the system of hereditary presidency for life should be abolished; and that political prisoners should be released, political émigrés allowed to return unconditionally, and a general amnesty be proclaimed. The congress confirmed the party's loyalty to the principles of Marxism-Leninism and "proletarian internationalism" and condemned the Chinese Communist leadership. The party has published several journals outside Haiti, and it is officially recognized by the Communist parties of the Soviet-bloc countries.

The party also took part, with several associated organizations, in the continental conference of solidarity with the people of Haiti, held in Panama in September 1981 (see under Christian Democratic Party of Haiti).

Workers' and Peasants' Movement (*Mouvement Ouvriers-Paysans,* MOP)

Representatives of the MOP attended the continental conference of solidarity with the people of Haiti in Panama in September 1981 (see under Christian Democratic Party of Haiti).

Honduras

Capital: Tegucigalpa

Pop. 3,500,000

The Republic of Honduras has an executive President who is elected for a four-year term by universal adult suffrage and who presides over a Cabinet. There is a unicameral Congress of 82 members, similarly elected for a four-year term. In elections held on Nov. 29, 1981 (marking the end of almost uninterrupted military rule since 1963), political parties gained seats as follows: Liberal Party 44, National Party 34, Innovation and Unity Party (PINU) 3, Christian Democratic Party (PDC) 1; about 80 per cent of the registered voters took part in the elections.

Unrest in neighbouring countries has not been without effect on the situation in Honduras. Many thousands of refugees from the civil war in El Salvador were by 1982 accommodated in camps just inside Honduras, while former Nicaraguan national guards opposed to the Sandinista regime were reported to have set up training camps inside Honduras. Among violent actions by indigenous Honduran groups, the most serious appear to have been those committed by militant peasants in support of their demands for accelerating the Government's land reform programme.

Left-wing Movements

Chinchoneros National Liberation Movement *(Movimiento de Liberación Nacional "Chinchoneros")*

This Movement was established in 1978 as an offshoot of the (pro-Soviet) Communist Party. It took its name from a former national peasant leader, and its political wing is the Revolutionary People's Union (URP—see separate entry).

In March 1981 members of this Movement hijacked a Honduran airliner with 81 passengers and six crew members, diverted it to Managua (Nicaragua)—where 37 of the passengers were released—and demanded the release from detention of 11 Salvadoreans and two Hondurans, notably of Facundo Guardado, former secretary-general of the Salvadorean Popular Revolutionary Bloc (BPR) who had been arrested in Honduras on Feb. 7, 1981. After the aircraft had been taken to Panama, the Honduran authorities released the detainees to that country; the remaining hostages were released by the hijackers who surrendered to the Panamanian authorities (and were later believed to have flown to Cuba).

The Movement also claimed responsibility for a bomb which exploded in the Constituent Assembly building in Tegucigalpa on Sept. 23, 1981, as part of a protest against imminent joint US-Honduras military manoeuvres.

In September 1982 members of the Movement occupied the chamber of commerce building in San Pedro Sula (north-eastern Honduras) in support of demands which included calls for the repeal of anti-terrorist legislation, the expulsion of military advisers from the USA, Argentina, Chile and Israel and the release of 57 political prisoners (including the leaders of the URP). The Government, however, denied that there were any military advisers from Argentina, Chile or Israel in Honduras, and the police chief stated that there were no political prisoners in the country—which led opponents of the Government to believe that those named had meanwhile been killed.

As a result of negotiations the occupation ended on Sept. 25, 1982, with the release of hostages held and the departure of 12 guerrillas to Panama en route for Cuba (with these guerrillas claiming that they had secured the release of one prisoner). The Movement's action was condemned by a rally of some 30,000 people in San Pedro Sula on Sept. 21.

Communist Party of Honduras (*Partido Comunista de Honduras,* PCH)

Leadership. Rigoberto Padilla Rush (g.s. of central committee).

Established in April 1954, this party has been illegal for most of its life. In 1960 and again in 1965-67 it suffered breakaways of factions opposed to the party's pro-Soviet line. At its second congress, held in April

374

1972, the party reaffirmed its loyalty to Marxism-Leninism and "proletarian internationalism" and adopted a new programme and constitution, defining its tasks as "struggle against the domination of US imperialism and the reactionary bourgeoisie and landowners, and for an anti-imperialist, agrarian, popular and democratic revolution". The PCH is officially recognized by the Communist parties of the Soviet-bloc countries.

Honduran Patriotic Front (*Frente Patriotico Hondureño,* FPH)

Leadership. Mario Orlando Iriarte (pres.).

Founded in October 1979, this leftist alliance included some 50 parties and organizations which were illegal or ineligible to nominate candidates for the Constituent Assembly to be elected on April 20, 1980 (including the pro-Soviet and pro-Chinese Communist parties and the Christian Democratic Party—the last-named being disqualified on a technicality). The Front conducted a campaign for abstention from voting in the elections, but this did not prevent a 75 per cent turn-out of the registered electorate being officially recorded.

Honduran Peasants' National Unity Front (*Frente de Unidad Nacional Campesino Hondureño,* Funacamh)

In 1981 this militant alliance of peasant unions, established in October 1975, embraced six principal peasant unions. The largest of them, with 80,000 members (in 1981), was the National Association of Honduran Peasants (ANACH) led by Antonio Julián Méndez, a PINU member of Congress; the second largest, with 20,000 to 30,000 members, was the National Union of Authentic Peasants of Honduras (UNCAH), which was under the influence of the Revolutionary People's Union (URP).

The other unions which joined the alliance were the National Front of Independent Peasants of Honduras, the Federation of Farming Co-operatives of the Honduran Land Reform (Fecorah), the National Union of Popular Co-operatives of Honduras (Unacooph), and the associated farming enterprises *(empresas asociativas campesinas)* of the areas of Las Isletas and Guayamas.

The Funacamh has co-ordinated a campaign, involving the occupation of land as well as strikes by peasants, with the object of accelerating the execution of the government's land reform programme and of ending abuses. On Feb. 1, 1982, however, it was reported that the ANACH had withdrawn from the Funacamh.

Lorenzo Zelaya Popular Revolutionary Forces (*Fuerzas Populares Revolucionarias Lorenzo Zelaya,* FPR)

The FPR was thought to have its origins in a Maoist Communist Party which broke away from the pro-Soviet Communist Party in 1975. On Sept. 23, 1981, members of this group shot and wounded two US military advisers in Tegucigalpa as part of an "armed struggle against Yankee imperialism". In September 1982 the FPR was reported to have carried out a number of bomb attacks and temporary occupations of buildings in the capital.

Morazanista National Liberation Front (*Frente Morazanista de Liberación Nacional,* FMLN)

Established in September 1979, this Front (named after Francisco Morazán, a 19th-century military leader) was reported to have the aim of pursuing a "revolutionary struggle" after Constituent Assembly elections of April 20, 1980. On Aug. 2, 1980, a spokesman for the FMLN stated that its chief objectives were to give land to the peasants, to eliminate the social and economic problems afflicting the masses and to set up a people's government to carry out this programme.

National Association of Honduran Peasants (ANACH)—see under Honduran Peasants' National Unity Front

National Union of Authentic Peasants of Honduras (UNCAH)—see under Honduran Peasants' National Unity Front

Peasant Alliance of National Organizations of Honduras (*Alianza Campesina de Organizaciones Nacionales de Honduras,* ALCONH)

This Alliance was established on Oct. 10, 1980, as a "revolutionary and belligerent" peasant group under the leadership of Reyes Rodrígues Arevalo, a former leader of the National Association of Honduran Peasants (ANACH).

People's Guerrilla Command

Leadership. José Alberto Munguia Vélez; José Antonio Montalván Munguia.

On July 3, 1981, it was announced that a bomb factory of this group (which was established in April 1980) had been discovered in the Miraflores district of the capital.

Popular Front against Repression (*Frente Popular contra la Represión,* FPR)

This Front was formed at the end of May 1981 by five trade unions—the United Workers' Front of Honduras (FUTH) led by Napoleón Acevedo Granados; the Honduran

Peasants' National Unity Front (Funacamh); the Teachers' Unity Front (FUM); the University Students' Front of Honduras (FEUH); and the Secondary Students' Front (Fese). The FPR has alleged that the aim of government repression of opposition forces is to "delay the Honduran revolutionary process by the physical elimination of leading members of the popular organization" on the Guatemalan model.

Revolutionary People's Union (*Unión Revolucionaria del Pueblo,* URP)

Leadership. Tomás Nativi (pres.); Fidel Martínez (s.g.).

The URP was formed in September 1979 by defectors from the Communist Party and the Socialist Party, with the aim of waging armed struggle with the support of peasants and trade unionists. It was active mainly in the country's northern part and was said to be in sympathy with the Popular Revolutionary Bloc (BPR) of El Salvador. On Aug. 15-16, 1980, a group of 15 URP members temporarily occupied the offices of the Organization of American States in Tegucigalpa, and on Oct. 2 of that year the URP announced the start of its "armed struggle".

Socialist Party (*Partido Socialista,* Paso)

Nine members of this party were arrested in April 1980 (at the time of the election of a Constituent Assembly). Earlier, Paso defectors had participated in the formation of the Revolutionary People's Union (URP) in September 1979.

Extreme Right-wing Groups

Honduran Anti-Communist Movement (*Movimiento Anticomunista Hondureño,* Macho)

This Movement was reported to have issued death threats in 1981 and to have links with organizations in other Central American countries.

The White Hand *(La Mano Blanca)*

This paramilitary organization was reported to have issued death threats to alleged members of left-wing groups and to have carried out some of these threats. It was said to have links with similar groups in other Central American countries.

Jamaica

Capital: Kingston Pop. 2,300,000

Jamaica, a member of the Commonwealth with the British monarch as head of state being represented by a Governor-General, has a bicameral Parliament consisting of (i) a 60-member House of Representatives elected for five years by universal adult suffrage and (ii) a 21-member Senate to which 13 senators are appointed by the Governor-General on the advice of the Prime Minister and the remaining eight on the advice of the Leader of the Opposition. The Prime Minister and his Cabinet are responsible to Parliament. In elections to the House of Representatives held on Oct. 30, 1980, the Jamaica Labour Party gained 51 seats and the People's National Party (PNP) only nine after having been in power since 1972. The PNP received "critical support" from the (pro-Soviet communist) Workers' Party of Jamaica.

The election campaign was marked by unprecedented political violence, with the total of fatal shootings during 1980 being given as 638. The Chief of Staff of the Jamaica Defence Force said in December 1980 that the military were preparing to deal with possible "threats to Jamaica's economic recovery", including "industrial sabotage" and "guerrilla or radical political activity". However, no names have been mentioned of organizations said to be engaged in such activity.

Mexico

Capital: Mexico City   Pop. 77,000,000

The United Mexican States are a federal republic consisting of 31 states and a federal district (around the capital), with an executive President who is elected by universal adult suffrage for a six-year term and who heads a Cabinet. There is a bicameral National Congress consisting of (i) a Federal Chamber of Deputies of 400 members elected by universal adult suffrage for three years, 300 of them by majority vote and the other 100 by proportional representation, and (ii) a 64-member Senate (comprising two senators for each state and for the federal district), also elected by universal adult suffrage for three years. Each state has a governor elected for six years and a Chamber of Deputies elected for three years.

In the elections to the Federal Chamber of Deputies held on July 4, 1982, the ruling Institutional Revolutionary Party (PRI) gained 299 of the 300 seats filled by majority vote, the remaining seat going to the National Action Party (PAN); the 100 seats filled by proportional representation were distributed as follows; PAN 54, United Socialist Party of Mexico (PSUM) 17, Popular Socialist Party (PPS) 11, Socialist Workers' Party (PST) 10, Mexican Democratic Party (PDM) 8. Presidential elections held on the same day were won by the PRI candidate, Miguel de la Madrid Hurtado, who received the support of the PPS and the Authentic Party of the Mexican Revolution (PARM); other candidates were presented by the PAN, the PSUM, the PDM, the PST, the (Trotskyist) Revolutionary Party of Workers (PRT) and the Social Democratic Party (PSD). (The pro-Soviet Mexican Communist Party, which had effectively dissolved itself on Oct. 16-18, 1981, had in August 1981 joined in the formation of the PSUM, together with the Revolutionary Socialist Party and the Socialist Movement for Action and Unity, with the Mexican Movement joining the PSUM in September 1981; on the other hand, the Mexican Workers' Party, led by Heberto Castillo, had not joined the PSUM.)

The most serious disturbances for over 50 years occurred in Mexico City in the summer and autumn of 1968 when a strike by some 150,000 students developed into a full-scale revolt against the "establishment" of the ruling PRI by left-wing (but mainly middle-class) students, which was suppressed by the armed forces with substantial loss of life and hundreds of arrests. Various left-wing guerrilla groups, some of them tracing their origins back to the 1968 events, remained active in subsequent years, in particular in Guerrero state (said to be the poorest of the country's 31 states); trials of captured guerrillas have taken place from time to time.

Left-wing Movements

Independent Peasant Front

This militant pro-communist organization (which formed part of the Ocampo Pact coalition, comprising also pro-government peasant groups) campaigned from 1976 onwards for the early and equitable implementation of the Government's land reform, in particular of a law limiting land ownership to 250 acres (100 hectares) per person (which was often circumvented). The delay in the implementation of the land reform led to a number of strikes and to widespread but illegal occupation of land by peasants.

Permanent Congress of Indigenous Peoples

The representative of this Congress in south-east Mexico (Gaspar Antonio Xiu Cachón) stated in Mérida (Yucatán) on July 17, 1977, that 300 peasants had been detained as "enemies of the state government" and that more than 50 of them had been murdered in Yucatán state in a "wave of repression" against peasants, students and workers who opposed the state government or who denounced corruption and fraud on the part of the state authorities.

Poor People's Party (*Partido de los Pobres,* PLP)

This group was responsible for killing 10 soldiers near Acapulco on June 25, 1972, and for the kidnapping of a senator of the ruling Institutional Revolutionary Party and four aides on May 30, 1974 (all five being, however, freed by army action on Sept. 7, 1974). The party's leader, Lucio Cabañas ("El Professor"), was killed on Dec. 2, 1974, after a five-month operation by the armed forces in Guerrero state, during which at least 800 peasants were reported to have been killed. The PLP does not appear to have been active in recent years.

Popular Revolutionary Armed Forces (*Fuerzas Revolucionarias Armadas Populares,* FRAP)

FRAP first became known through a number of kidnappings for which it was responsible. The first of these was that of the US consul-general in Guadalajara (Jalisco state) on May 4, 1973; the kidnappers demanded the release of 30 named political prisoners and their transfer to Cuba, as well as the publication of a FRAP statement, failing which the US consul-general would be executed by May 6; the Mexican Government accepted the demands on May 5, and on the following day the 30 persons listed reached Cuba in a Mexican Air Force aircraft, while the FRAP statement published in newspapers and broadcast on radio and television called on the people to overthrow the Government by armed struggle; the US consul-general was released on May 7, when it emerged that a ransom of about $80,000 had been paid to FRAP. FRAP was also responsible for the kidnapping on March 22, 1974, of the US vice-consul in Hermosillo (Sonora state, in north-western Mexico), who was found dead on July 8, 1974.

In May 1976 the reported leader of FRAP, Ramón Campana López, was captured by police in Jalisco state. In recent years FRAP appears to have been inactive.

Popular Student Front

On April 28, 1976, students belonging to the Front occupied the University of Puebla but clashed with members of a rival left-wing group from among whom they seized 18 hostages, while demanding the resignation of the rector and an inquiry into accounts kept by him. In the clashes two students were killed and several gravely injured on April 30, 1976.

Revolutionary Action Movement (*Movimiento de Acción Revolucionaria,* MAR)

This Movement, the existence of which emerged after a bank robbery in Mexico City in February 1971, consisted of about 60 men and women trained in communist ideology, sabotage and guerrilla warfare. Some of them had formed the MAR while they were at the Patrice Lumumba University in Moscow, whence they had been sent to North Korea for military training, after which they had returned to Mexico in 1966-67. Further actions attributed to the MAR were assaults and bank robberies in September 1971 and the kidnapping of the Mexican director of civil aviation on Sept. 27, 1971 (the kidnappers releasing him on Sept. 30 upon receipt of the equivalent of £100,000 in ransom). On Oct. 26, 1974, the authorities announced the capture of 27 members of the MAR and other groups. There have been no further reports of MAR activities.

Salvador Allende Movement (*Movimiento Salvador Allende*)

When the Lebanese honorary consul in Guadalajara, who had been kidnapped on June 5, 1974, was found dead on June 8, despite payment of a ransom by his son, this Movement expressed its regret. There have been no further reports of it being active.

September 23 Communist League (*Liga Comunista 23 de Septiembre*)

Leadership. Miguel Angel Barraza García (l.).

This group was said to be the urban guerrilla group of the Poor People's Party (see separate entry). It was responsible for the killing of a wealthy industrialist in September 1973, and for the kidnapping on Oct. 10, 1973, of the British honorary consul in Guadalajara (who was released unharmed on Oct. 14) and of a Mexican industrialist (who was found murdered on Oct. 18). The group also kidnapped an elderly uncle of the Governor of Guerrero in January 1974, who was found murdered in Acapulco the following month. On Dec. 5, 1974, the police captured a member of the group, Miguel Torres Enríquez, who had for five hours held the French consul-general in Mexico City, his deputy and a secretary as hostages while he demanded a safe-conduct out of the country. During a demonstration on Nov. 20, 1975, in Juchitán (south-east of Mexico City) nine persons were killed when four youths, who police claimed were carrying out propaganda for the September 23 Communist League, opened fire on the crowd.

The group was further involved in the killing of nine people (most of them security agents) in a Mexico City suburb on May 6,

1976, and in the temporary kidnapping, on May 25-30, of the Belgian ambassador's daughter, released on payment of $408,000 ransom. In August 1978 its leader at the time, Carlos Jiménez Sarmiento, was killed, and during 1980 further members lost their lives in clashes with police, while others were arrested. Since then the League has declined.

Union of the People (*Unión del Pueblo,* UP)

This organization declared its aims as being to "bring Lenin's revolution" to Mexico and to put an end to "unemployment, hunger and exploitation imposed on the people by the ruling class". It claimed responsibility for the explosion of 23 bombs on Sept. 14, 1977, in Mexico City, Guadalajara and Oaxaca, injuring five people. Police subsequently defused 17 other bombs, and 10,000 troops and police were placed on alert to search for the members of the organization. There has been no further evidence of UP activities.

Human Rights Groups

In response to a campaign by human rights groups in Mexico calling for an amnesty and for information concerning an estimated 367 people said to have disappeared during the past five years, the Attorney General stated on Jan. 24, 1979, that the Government had investigated the cases of 314 missing persons and had found that 154 of them had died during confrontations with the police and the Army, that 89 were known "subversives" in hiding, that 20 had died in fighting between rival groups, that 18 had been killed as "traitors" by their own groups, that three had died naturally and one had been killed by a home-made bomb; and that there was no police record of the remaining 26.

Of the principal human rights groups, the two listed below took action against embassies in support of their demands.

Mexican Committee for the Defence of Political Prisoners, Exiles and Disappeared Persons

A group of 27 members of this Committee occupied the Swiss embassy in Mexico City on Aug. 3-10, 1979, in support of a demand for the release of 153 political prisoners excluded from an amnesty declared in September 1978 and for information on the whereabouts of 553 persons reported as missing during the past 10 years.

Popular National Democratic Front (*Frente Nacional Democrático Popular,* FNDP)

Unarmed members of this Front occupied the Belgian embassy and the lobby of the Danish embassy in Mexico City between Feb. 18 and 24, 1980, and demanded the release of 150 political detainees, as well as information concerning both the fate of 623 persons arrested for political reasons and the distribution of land to peasants. The Government refused to consider these demands, and the occupiers of the embassies were evicted by police after six days. The Secretary for the Interior declared in this connexion that there were no political prisoners in Mexico.

The FNDP was said to be led by Felipe Martínez Soriano, a former (left-wing) rector of Oaxaca University, for whom a warrant of arrest was issued by the police on Feb. 23, 1980.

Right-wing Groups

The Falcons *(Los Halcones)*

This extreme right-wing group was involved in an attack on left-wing students on June 10, 1971, whereafter a student committee claimed that the group had killed 25 students and that 62 others had disappeared. The group was banned in June 1971.

White Brigade *(Brigada Blanca)*

This right-wing militia, allegedly supported by members of the police force, has claimed responsibility for several hundred kidnappings of people considered to have been involved in left-wing activities or to have left-wing sympathies. It was said to have been active since 1976, and in February 1980 seven persons accused it specifically of having inflicted torture on its victims. At the same time the existence of the White Brigade was officially denied.

Nicaragua

Capital: Managua   Pop. 2,600,000

The Republic of Nicaragua is ruled by a junta of national reconstruction which heads a provisional Government installed in July 1979 following the defeat of President Anastasio Somoza Debayle by the forces of the Sandinista National Liberation Front (FSLN) after 18 months of civil war. (Ex-President Somoza was assassinated in Asunción, Paraguay, on Sept. 17, 1980, but the Government of Nicaragua denied any involvement in this murder as had been suggested by the Government of Paraguay.) The FSLN announced on Aug. 23, 1980, that preparations for general elections would not begin until 1984, and under a decree issued on Aug. 27, 1980, all electoral activity was banned until 1984. A Council of State, appointed as an auxiliary legislative body, first met on May 4, 1980; its 51 members included representatives of 32 of the country's political, labour, social and popular organizations and also of the private sector of the economy.

Government parties allied since 1980 in a Patriotic Front for the Revolution (*Frente Patriotico para la Revolución,* FPR) are the FSLN, the Independent Liberal Party (PLI), the Popular Social Christian Party (PPSC) and the (pro-Soviet communist) Nicaraguan Socialist Party (PSN). Other legal parties are the Nicaraguan Democratic Movement (MDN), the (pro-Chinese) Communist Party of Nicaragua (PCN), the Democratic Conservative Party (PCD), the Nicaraguan Social Christian Party (PSC) and the Social Democratic Party (PSD).

During 1980-82 the Sandinista Government was faced with increasing difficulties, partly because its policies (revealing a growing pro-Soviet and pro-Cuban trend) not only led to strained relations with the United States but also alienated those sections of the Nicaraguan people who had hoped for early elections and a return to democratic government. On the other hand several extreme left-wing groups have criticized the Government for not having carried out a true socialist revolution. On Sept. 9, 1981, the Government introduced a state of "economic and social emergency", establishing severe penalties for staging strikes, for occupying land outside the agrarian reform programme, for taking over factories, for obstructing production, and also for "inciting foreign governments to inflict damage on the national economy".

Externally the Sandinista Government has faced a continuing threat from armed "Somocist" groups (i.e. those identified with the former regime), operating from bases across Nicaragua's northern border with Honduras and including many former National Guards who had fled the country in 1979; at the same time, a number of non-Somocist opposition movements have also been seeking the overthrow of the Sandinista regime. The Government has repeatedly claimed that such external groups are in receipt of support from the United States and from neighbouring right-wing regimes.

Anti-Sandinista Movements

Anti-Communist Armed Forces (*Fuerzas Armadas Anticomunistas,* FARAC)

Seven members of FARAC were sentenced to imprisonment on Aug. 20, 1980.

Democratic Armed Forces (*Fuerzas Armadas Democráticas,* FAD)

Leadership. Carlos García Solorzano (l.).

The FAD's leader, who had been head of the National Security Office under President Somoza, was arrested (with several other

380

FAD members) on May 9, 1980, and on Aug. 25 of that year he was sentenced to 14 years' imprisonment. The reputed commander of the FAD, Lt.-Col. Bernardino Larios (a former National Guard under the Somoza regime, who had been appointed Minister of Defence in the first Sandinista Government), was arrested on Sept. 19, 1980, and charged with conspiring to assassinate members of the Sandinista directorate; on Oct. 31 he was sentenced to seven years in prison. At the time of his arrest he alleged that the FAD had received financial aid from Jorge Salazar Argüello, the head of a landowners' organization, who was shot dead on Nov. 17, 1980, by police who regarded him as the ringleader in an anti-government plot. A Spanish diplomat said to be connected with the FAD was expelled from Nicaragua on Oct. 10, 1980.

Democratic Conservative Party (PCD)—see under Nicaraguan Democratic Force

Democratic Revolutionary Alliance (*Alianza Revolucionaria Democrática,* ARDE)

This organization was formed in San José (Costa Rica) in December 1982 by representatives of four groups: (i) the Sandinista Revolutionary Front (FRS) led by Edén Pastora Gómez, who had on July 7, 1981, resigned as Deputy Minister of Defence and head of the Sandinista people's militia; (ii) the Nicaraguan Democratic Movement (MDN) led by Alfonso Robelo Callejas; (iii) the Misurata Indian group led by Brooklyn Rivera; and (iv) the Nicaraguan Democratic Union (UDN) with its armed wing, the Nicaraguan Armed Revolutionary Forces (FARN).

In a statement issued in mid-December 1982 the ARDE called on the Sandinista Government to hold elections before June 1983 so that an end could be put to the continuing violence in the country. A. Robelo was quoted as saying that the ARDE was neither Somocist nor counter-revolutionary; that it would not reject a dialogue with the ruling FSLN but that, if all doors to talks were closed, the ARDE would not abandon its military option and would not surrender.

In a message broadcast on Feb. 5, 1983, by the "Voice of Sandino" (an opposition radio station) A. Robelo declared: "We seek a third way out. . . . We are the force which wants neither to return to the old path nor to fall into totalitarianism. . . . We want to make deep social, political and economic changes in Nicaragua . . . [but] we are democratic revolutionaries. . . . We want the people to choose freely."

National Liberation Army (*Ejército Nacional de Liberación,* ENL)

Leadership. "Juan Carlos" (l.).

This Somocist group operates from Hon-

duras and is composed of former National Guards under President Somoza. Late in 1980 it claimed to have access to 4,000-6,000 armed men inside Nicaragua and several hundred elsewhere. It has also claimed to favour elections, free enterprise and respect for human rights, and to have influence with the autonomist Misurasata organization (see separate entry) on Nicaragua's east coast. The ENL operates independently of the Nicaraguan Democratic Union (UDN) and the Nicaraguan Armed Revolutionary Forces (FARN).

Nicaraguan Armed Revolutionary Forces (*Fuerzas Armadas Revolucionarias Nicaragüenses,* FARN)

This right-wing guerrilla group—the armed wing of the Nicaraguan Democratic Union (see separate entry)—carried out a number of attacks in 1980, by the end of which it claimed to have 2,000 members. Late in March 1981 it claimed that a 600-man "freedom force" was waiting in Honduras and would soon be joined by "thousands of supporters" from Guatemala and Miami (Florida) to carry out an invasion which would cause a popular insurrection to "liberate" Nicaragua with the help of the Governments of El Salvador, Guatemala and Honduras.

Daniel Ortega Saavedra, the co-ordinator of the Nicaraguan junta, alleged in Havana (Cuba) on April 19, 1981, that armed groups had a base in Honduras, near the Nicaraguan border, with a "line of communication which passes through Guatemala" and had a central headquarters in Miami, and that invaders from Honduras had conducted attacks in which they had killed more than 60 Nicaraguans. However, an open conflict between Honduras and Nicaragua was avoided through talks between D. Ortega Saavedra and President Paz García of Honduras at a border post on May 13, 1981.

Nicaraguan Democratic Force (*Fuerza Democrática Nicaragüense,* FDN)

The formation of the FDN as a political-military organization was announced on Nov. 27, 1981, by a clandestine radio station claiming to be inside Nicaragua and declaring that its aim was to "liberate our people from Marxist totalitarianism". The FDN's component groups were given as the "September 15 Legion", the Misurasata Indian movement (see separate entry) and the Nicaraguan Democratic Union. On Dec. 14, 1982, the Government claimed that its forces had, after six days of fighting, repulsed an attempt by FDN units, who had entered the country from Honduras, to establish a "liberated" zone inside Nicaragua.

The FDN had earlier announced the appointment of a new eight-member directorate said to consist of "moderate" anti-

Sandinistas; they included three business-men—Edgar Chamorro Coronel, Alfonso Callejas and Mario Zeledón; an ex-Somocist colonel (Enrique Bermúdez); and Lucia Cardenal, widow of Jorge Salazar, who had been killed in a gun battle with Sandinistas in 1980. On Feb. 9, 1983, the FDN was joined by Adolfo Calerok, the leader of the Democratic Conservative Party (PCD), who declared that armed struggle was "the only road left open".

The FDN had in January 1983 announced that it would cease all action against the Government if the latter agreed to the holding of elections by September 1983 under the supervision of the Organization of American States. The FDN nevertheless continued to be involved in fighting during February 1983, when 55 Somocists were said to have been killed (as against five soldiers).

Nicaraguan Democratic Movement (MDN)— see under Democratic Revolutionary Alliance

Nicaraguan Democratic Union (*Unión Democrática Nicaragüense,* UDN)

Leadership. Edmundo Chamorro Rapaciolli (l.).

The UDN was formed by conservative businessmen; its leader had actively opposed the Somoza regime and had recognized the FSLN, at the time of the overthrow of that regime, as leader of the revolutionary process, but he had since come to criticize it for its undemocratic procedure. He claimed late in 1980 that the UDN and its armed wing, the Nicaraguan Revolutionary Armed Forces (FARN), were fighting not for a return to a right-wing dictatorship but for democracy and they would therefore not accept into their ranks former National Guards who wished to revert to the old ways.

On Aug. 25, 1981, E. Chamorro Rapaciolli was sentenced in absentia with 25 others (of whom only about half were present in court) to prison terms of up to 25 years and the confiscation of their property for subversive activities. In December 1982 the UDN joined the Democratic Revolutionary Alliance (see separate entry).

Nicaraguan Democratic Union Assembly (*Asamblea Nicaragüense de Unidad Democrática,* Anude)

This opposition group was formed in September 1982. Its founders included José Davila, a leader of the exiled section of the Social Christian Party, who was quoted as saying that Anude had offices in Costa Rica, Venezuela and Europe and maintained links with the military forces in Honduras; that one of its aims was to foster the creation of a

united opposition front; and that in his view only violence would remove the Sandinistas. While Anude was said to represent right-wing elements who had opposed the Somoza regime, it appeared at the same time to maintain links with Somocist groups.

Nicaraguan International Rescue from Communism (SINC)

Five members of this right-wing group hijacked a Costa Rican aircraft with 22 persons on board at San José airport on Oct. 29, 1981. The hijackers demanded the release of seven members of SINC who had been imprisoned in December 1980 after attacks on the left-wing Radio Noticias del Continente transmitter (the transmissions of which were suspended by the Costa Rican Government on Feb. 20, 1981). The Government eventually agreed to the release of the seven prisoners, one of whom was, however, reported to choose to remain in prison. The other six, and the five hijackers, were flown to El Salvador, where they were arrested. In November 1981 it was announced that they were all to be returned to Costa Rica, where the hijackers were to face trial.

Sandinista Revolutionary Front (FRS)—see under Democratic Revolutionary Alliance

September 15 Legion—see under Nicaraguan Democratic Force

Left-wing Parties

Communist Party of Nicaragua (*Partido Comunista de Nicaragua,* PCN)

Leadership. Elí Altamirano (g.s.).

This (pro-Chinese) party broke away in 1967 from the original Communist Party founded in 1939 (and still in existence as the Nicaraguan Socialist Party, which is pro-Soviet and part of the Sandinista-led Patriotic Front for the Revolution, FPR). Its trade union wing is the Labour Action and Unity Confederation (CAUS). The PCN was not allowed to participate in the Council of State (as officially stated on April 10, 1980).

On Oct. 20, 1981, E. Altamirano was arrested and charged with violating laws under the economic and social emergency declared on Sept. 9 of that year after the PCN had, on Oct. 6, published a document on "the serious economic crisis and the deviation of the Sandinista revolution". Although the PCN has retained its legal status, D. Ortega Saavedra, the co-ordinator of the junta, said on Oct. 21 that the PCN had for some time been carrying out "organized and systematic sabotage" against the national economy and promoting strikes, work stoppages and land seizures in open challenge to the revolutionary Government. On Oct. 29, 1981, four PCN members were given seven-month prison sentences.

Workers' Front (*Frente Obrero,* FO)

The armed members of the extreme left-wing FO—which was affiliated to the (pro-Chinese) Communist Party (see separate entry)—had before 1979 formed the People's Anti-Somocist Militias (Milpas). The Sandinista Government, however, claimed that the FO and Milpas were threatening production and provoking unrest in some areas by inciting workers to strike and take over land.

By October 1979 some 70 FO members were reported to be under arrest; on Jan. 25, 1980, the Government closed down the daily *El Pueblo,* the mouthpiece of the FO; and on April 10, 1980, a member of the junta declared that neither the FO nor the Communist Party would be allowed to participate in the Council of State.

Autonomist Movement

Misurasata

Leadership. Brooklyn Rivera (l.).

This group, representing the English-speaking Black community and the Miskito, Sumo and Rama Indians in the east coast province of Zelaya (the Mosquito coast), was represented on the Council of State by Steadman Fagoth Müller. The latter was arrested (with about 70 others) in February 1981 and accused of having been a security agent for President Somoza, while two of the others were charged with fomenting a separatist plot. (There had been an autonomist tradition on the Mosquito coast since the 18th century when the British had established a protectorate known as the Miskito Kingdom, which also embraced part of present-day Honduras; however, the Miskito King was deposed in 1894, when most of the area was incorporated in Nicaragua.)

The arrest of the Misurasata leaders was followed by protest demonstrations which led to clashes in which four soldiers and four Miskito Indians were killed on Feb. 21, 1981; the Government thereupon released all those arrested except the three charged as stated above but the unrest continued. S. Fagoth Müller, having been released provisionally, fled to Honduras on May 11, 1981, and on May 21 it was reported that many other Miskito Indians had left Nicaragua to join the 100,000 already living in the Honduran Mosquito region. In December 1982 the Misurasata group joined forces with the Democratic Revolutionary Alliance (see separate entry).

Panama

Capital: Panama City   Pop. 2,000,000

The Republic of Panama is in effect ruled by its National Guard under the command of (the pro-Western and anti-communist) Gen. Rubén Darío Paredes, on whose recommendation the President of the Republic is appointed and forms a Cabinet. A 505-member National Assembly of Community Representatives was elected for a six-year term in August 1978, when no candidate was allowed to represent a political party. A National Legislative Council, to act as an upper chamber, was formed in 1980 of 19 elected members and 37 members appointed from among the members of the National Assembly. In 1978 the then commander of the National Guard, Brig.-Gen. Omar Torrijos Herrera, undertook that free elections should be held in 1984, and this undertaking, involving a democratization of the regime, has since been reaffirmed on several occasions.

Political parties represented in the Cabinet at the end of 1982 were the (official) Democratic Revolutionary Party (PRD) and the Liberal Party (PL). Opposition parties include the Broad Popular Front (Frampo), the Christian Democratic Party (PDC), the Liberal Republican and Nationalist Movement (Molirena), the (pro-Soviet communist) Panamanian People's Party (PPP), the (right-wing) Panameñista Party (PP), the Popular Action Party (Papo) and the Popular Nationalist Party (PNP).

Internal disturbances in recent years have been confined mainly to industrial unrest and student demonstrations, the latter often directed against US policies in Latin American affairs. A more serious threat seemed to be constituted by an alleged right-wing plot, uncovered in October 1979 and attributed to the Panamanian National Front.

Panamanian National Front (*Frente Nacional de Panamá,* FNP)

Leadership. Abraham Crocamo (l.).

It was officially announced on Oct. 24, 1979, that the Government had uncovered a plot to overthrow the existing regime and that this plot was led by Abraham Crocamo (a former National Guard officer later identified as leader of the FNP) and supported by foreign mercenaries and members of the right-wing Panameñista Party (led by Dr Arnulfo Arias Madrid, who had been President of Panama immediately before the 1968 military coup which had brought Brig.-Gen. Omar Torrijos Herrera to power). While several arrests were made in connexion with the alleged plot, A. Crocamo had escaped; on Jan. 16, 1980, he sought political asylum in Costa Rica, but on Feb. 9, 1980, he was deported from that country to exile in Venezuela.

Paraguay

Capital: Asunción   Pop. 3,300,000

The Republic of Paraguay is, under its 1967 Constitution, a "representative democracy" with an executive President elected (and re-eligible) for a five-year term by universal adult suffrage. Since coming to power in a military coup in 1954, President (Gen.) Alfredo Stroessner has been elected for seven successive terms as the candidate of the National Republican Association—Colorado Party, which has been the country's dominant party since 1940. Legislative power is held by a bicameral Congress consisting of a Senate of at least 30 members and a Chamber of Deputies of at least 60 members, both elected for five-year terms by direct adult suffrage. However, the party which gains a majority in parliamentary elections obtains two-thirds of the seats in both Houses of Congress, the remainder of the seats being divided among the minority parties in proportion to their electoral strength.

Under legislation introduced in 1981, parties were prohibited from urging voters to return blank ballot papers or to abstain as a form of protest; in order to be registered, a party was required to have 10,000 members distributed among at least one-third of the country's electoral districts; the Communist Party and any party with "similar aims" remained banned; and other prohibited parties were those with international links and those which preached "racial, religious or class struggle" or "hatred among Paraguayans".

In elections held on Feb. 6, 1983, some 90 per cent of the votes were, according to official results, cast in favour of President Stroessner and his National Republican Association—Colorado Party, while the remaining votes went to the Radical Liberal Party and the Liberal Party (in a 90 per cent poll), all other parties having called for abstention. Unregistered parties include the Christian Democratic Party (PDC), the Authentic Liberal Radical Party (PLRA) and the Popular Colorado Movement (Mopoco)—all of which participated in the formation in 1978 of the National Agreement (AN) as a broad alliance of opposition parties, together with the (registered) Febrerista Revolutionary Party (PRF). The regime has also encountered considerable opposition from within the Roman Catholic Church in Paraguay, while externally its record on human rights has been severely censured by international bodies such as the Inter-American Human Rights Commission.

Unregistered Parties

Authentic Liberal Radical Party (*Partido Liberal Radical Auténtico,* PLRA)

Leadership. Dr Domingo Laino (pres.).

This centre-left party—a faction of the Unified Liberal Party (PLU) which had been formed in January 1977 by majorities of the earlier legal Liberal Radical Party (PLR) and the Liberal Party (PL)—included among its leaders Dr Laino (who had been elected leader of the PLR on Jan. 25, 1974), Carlos Alberto González and Miguel Angel Saguier. Dr Laino (then the party's vice-president) visited the United States in June 1978, when he testified on the human rights situation in Paraguay before the General Assembly of the Organization of American States and recommended that sanctions should be taken against his country. After his return to Asunción he was arrested on July 7 and was charged with subversion and associating with left-wing extremists, but was released on Aug. 9, 1978. He was again temporarily arrested in 1979 and in September-October 1980, but in March 1981 he visited Brazil, where he had contact with Brazilian opposition groups and also with exiled members of the Colorado Popular Movement (Mopoco).

385

Christian Democratic Party (*Democracia Cristiana,* DC)

Leadership. Luis Resck (pres.).

Established in 1960, this party has consistently opposed the Stroessner regime. It boycotted the presidential elections of 1968 (when it demanded the lifting of the state of siege, the release of political prisoners and the return of exiles to Paraguay). In February 1971 the Electoral Commission refused to grant it the status of a political party, and it could therefore not take part in elections. It continued, however, to advocate the boycott of elections. In July 1981 its president was expelled from Paraguay after he had been arrested for alleged terrorist activities against the security of the state and had begun a hunger strike.

The party stands for the creation of a true democracy in Paraguay, transition from underdevelopment to economic development and the maintenance of private ownership and free enterprise. It is affiliated to the Christian Democratic World Union and the Christian Democratic Organization of America.

Popular Colorado Movement (*Movimiento Popular Colorado,* Mopoco)

A leader of this Movement, named as Dr Goiburu, was officially held responsible for an alleged plot to kill President Stroessner and to abduct ministers and other office-bearers of the regime, this plot having been discovered by police after the arrest and interrogation of students in Asunción on Nov. 29, 1974. The plot was said to be supported by the (Argentinian) People's Revolutionary Army (ERP) and to be planned for January 1975. The police announcement was followed by numerous arrests (totalling over 1,000 as stated by the Minister of the Interior in early March 1975). Some Mopoco members were kidnapped while in Brazil but Dr Goiburu escaped a kidnap attempt in Argentina.

Illegal Movements

Agrarian Peasant League (*Liga Agraria Campesina*)

Leadership. Victoriano (Vitor) Centurión (l.).

The leader of this peasant action group was active in the peasant protest movement in 1972 and was held in prison for three years without trial and was later said to have created the Agrarian Peasant League as a radical underground movement. A group led by him hijacked a bus on March 8, 1980, in order to travel to Asunción to put their grievances to the President; however, the

police arrested many of them and others fled, with V. Centurión taking refuge in the Panamanian embassy. The Government stated later that he had sought political asylum but that he was guilty of subversion.

Paraguayan Communist Party (*Partido Comunista Paraguayano,* PCP)

Established in February 1928, the PCP has been illegal except for a short period from August 1946 to January 1947, when it was suppressed after a rising. It nevertheless held a congress in August 1949. In 1967 it was split over the Chinese issue, but in 1971 it held a further congress at which it approved a Marxist-Leninist (pro-Soviet) programme and elected a new central committee.

Dr Antonio Maidana (the PCP's first secretary) and two other PCP leaders, Julio Rojas and Alfredo Acorta (head of the party's foreign department), all of whom had been in prison since 1958, were reported to have been released on Feb. 3, 1977; later Gilberta Verdún, imprisoned in 1968 for belonging to the PCP, was also reported to have been released. Dr Maidana and A. Acorta reportedly went to Moscow via Peru.

Three leading PCP members were, in an Amnesty International report of October 1979, said to have died under torture in police custody. Dr Maidana and Emilio Roa, a member of the PCP's central committee, were later reported to have been kidnapped in Buenos Aires on Aug. 27, 1980 (allegedly in a joint Argentinian-Paraguayan police operation) and to have died in custody.

Politico-Military Organization (*Organización Politico-Militar,* OPM)

According to the Paraguayan Minister of the Interior this guerrilla group had links with Argentinian extremists and had as one of its leaders a Spanish Jesuit (Fr Miguel Sanmarti García). The Minister also said (early in May 1976) that the OPM had been involved in an incident in early April, in connexion with which one French and six Spanish Jesuits had been arrested and expelled from the country for allegedly spreading Marxist propaganda and supporting guerrilla activities against the Government. The police appealed to the public to help find Fr Sanmarti García, whom they described as "a dangerous criminal", but his Jesuit superior claimed that he had been in Spain for the past five months. Police subsequently arrested several alleged OPM members and killed a presumed leader of the organization.

On Dec. 18, 1977, a group of 19 trade unionists (mainly members of the Christian Confederation of Workers and the Christian Agrarian League) were arrested at Ypacarai (near Asunción) on charges of reorganizing the OPM, but nine of them were released on Feb. 11, 1978. The Minister of Justice and Labour said on Jan. 15, when representations on behalf of these detainees were made by US trade union representatives, that there was no evidence that the detainees were guilty of subversion and that they would probably be released after trial.

Peru

Capital: Lima   Pop. 17,800,000

The Republic of Peru has an executive President elected for a four-year term by universal adult suffrage, a Cabinet presided over by a Prime Minister and a bicameral Congress consisting of a 60-member Senate and a 180-member Chamber of Deputies elected similarly and at the same time as the President.

As a result of general elections held on May 18, 1980 (ending 12 years of military rule) seats in the Chamber of Deputies were distributed as follows: Popular Action (AP, centre-right) 98, American Popular Revolutionary Alliance (APRA, centre-left) 58, Christian Popular Party (PPC) 10, National Front of Workers and Peasants (FNTC or Frenatraca) 4, Workers' Revolutionary Party (PRT, Trotskyist) 3, Popular Democratic Unity (UDP, Maoist) 3, Revolutionary Left Union (Unio, also Maoist) 2, United Left (UI) 2. Parties which failed to win seats included the right-wing National Odriista Union (UNO) and the Popular Front of Workers, Peasants and Students (FOCEP).

Other left-wing parties (which had unsuccessfully attempted to form two electoral alliances) were the (pro-Soviet) Communist Party (PC-*Unidad*), the Revolutionary Socialist Party (PRC), the (Trotskyist) Workers' Socialist Party, the (also Trotskyist) Revolutionary Marxist Labour Party and the (Maoist) Anti-Imperialist Revolutionary Forces for Socialism (FRAS).

The Government formed by President Fernando Belaunde Terry after the elections consisted mainly of AP members but also of three retired officers, two PCP members and two independents. In July 1980 the Government returned to their former publishers seven major newspapers expropriated by the military regime in 1974 and declared a general political amnesty and the reinstatement of public sector workers, especially teachers, dismissed under the military regime.

An anti-terrorist law decreed on March 12, 1981 (largely in response to the terrorist activities of the Maoist *Sendero Luminoso* guerrilla movement), provided for prison sentences of up to 20 years for those convicted of terrorism. Over the following two years the Government frequently declared states of emergency in areas of guerrilla activity (notably Ayacucho department in the south) and on Nov. 28, 1982, the President announced that the regular Army would in future be deployed in the struggle against the insurgents.

National Liberation Army (*Ejército de Liberación Nacional,* ELN)

Leadership. Juan Pablo Chang Navarro (l.).

Established in 1962, the ELN was one of several Peruvian guerrilla movements active in the 1960s. In a manifesto issued in 1965 the ELN proclaimed that, for the liberation of the country's workers and peasants, it would pursue both armed struggle and a "policy of unity". However, ELN guerrilla operations begun in the Ayacucho area in September 1965 were successfully suppressed by the Army by December of that year, with the remaining guerrillas withdrawing to Ecuador. A re-organized ELN appeared in September 1980 under the leadership of Juan Pablo Chang Navarro, but its operations appear to have remained insignificant.

Peasant Patrols *(Rondas Campesinas)*

These patrols were active, even before Peru's return to democratic government in 1980, in the illicit occupation of land in the Sierra region. When the Minister of the Interior in the newly-appointed Government refused to legalize the patrols, they decided in September 1980 to declare the entire Chota province (in the Cajamarca department, north-western Peru) an "independent zone". Although they continued their activities they were not a serious challenge to the authorities.

Red Fatherland *(Patria Roja, PR)*

This Maoist group, an offshoot of the (pro-Soviet) Peruvian Communist Party, was reported to have claimed responsibility for an attack by some 150 guerrillas on a prison at Ayacucho on March 2, 1982, when about 250 prisoners, including 54 guerrillas, were freed in a struggle which caused the death of 14 people (seven of the attackers, three policemen and four prison inmates). The PR was also said to have claimed responsibility for a simultaneous dynamite attack on the Supreme Court building in La Libertad department (on the north-west coast).

Later reports, however, attributed these attacks to the Shining Path *(Sendero Luminoso)* movement (see separate entry).

Shining Path *(Sendero Luminoso,* SL)

Leadership. Manuel Abimael Guzmán Renose ("Comrade Gonzalo") (l.).

The SL took its name from the title of one of its first pamphlets, "The Shining Path of Juan Carlos Mariategui". Juan, or José, Carlos Mariategui, 1894-1930, had been the founder of the Peruvian Socialist Party which was formed on Oct. 7, 1928, and later became the Peruvian Communist Party; he had advocated a return to the peasant communes of the Inca empire.

In a 32-page pamphlet published in July 1982, the SL called itself "a new type of Marxist-Leninist-Maoist party" with the aim of waging "a people's war" from the countryside in order to carry it eventually into the cities; claiming that it had already carried out 2,900 attacks, it declared that it would pursue "total war" against the Government until the latter was overthrown. It had broken off relations with Peking in 1979 and called the Chinese Communist leaders "traitors" whose embassy in Peru it did not exempt from its acts of violence against diplomatic missions. Its policy was rejected by all other (legal) left-wing groups in Peru.

During 1980-82 the activities of the SL passed through three stages—(i) acts of sabotage designed to draw attention to the existence of the SL, (ii) attacks on business premises and banks with the object of obtaining funds, and (iii) actions against police posts in remote areas with the aim of seizing weapons. A fourth stage was to lead to the eventual seizure of power.

The SL made great efforts to broaden its base among the peasants, and in this context it proceeded to the public "execution" of a number of mayors summarily tried as "enemies of the people" by so-called "people's courts". However, its support remained largely confined to the Ayacucho department. It succeeded in temporarily cutting off electricity supplies to Ayacucho, to Lima and to eight other cities on Aug. 20, 1982; and again to Lima on Dec. 3, 1982.

Major SL attacks included one on buildings of the University of Ayacucho on Aug. 3, 1982, when a 140-member commando caused damage assessed at $1,400,000 and threatened 50 staff members with death if the destroyed buildings were restored. In another, some 200 guerrillas attacked a civil guard post in Ayacucho province with machine-guns and dynamite on Aug. 22, 1982, when 20 guerrillas and five policemen were killed in a four-hour battle. On Dec. 2 of that year a simultaneous assault was mounted on five villages in Ayacucho province by some 300 guerrillas who carried out "summary trials" of 22 persons.

President Belaúnde Terry stated on Dec. 26, 1982, that the SL had been responsible for the death of 150 persons in 1982 and that it was "a gang of murderers" and not a political party. He appealed to SL members to surrender unconditionally within 48-72 hours to save further loss of life. However, on Dec. 29 the President was reported to have ordered that, since the time limit for a surrender had expired, terrorists were to be attacked immediately and killed (although those who wished to surrender could still do so).

Early in 1983 the SL guerrillas were reported to have extended their activities to new areas, and by Jan. 18 the President had placed eight provinces under military control and troop reinforcements had been sent to the areas concerned. Late in January about 32 SL fighters were said to have been killed in clashes with police and anti-SL peasants, 32 of those killed having tried to destroy a bridge in the province of Apurimac. In February 1983 the security forces claimed that over 100 SL supporters had been killed in clashes north and south of Ayacucho.

Further heavy clashes in the Ayacucho area during April 1983 were said to be the heaviest since the SL began its guerrilla war three years previously. In late April the total death toll in the fighting since the beginning of the year was estimated to be at least 370.

Thereafter the Government took further steps to quell a virtual SL insurrection, but appeared to be making little progress against guerrillas operating in favourable terrain.

Tawantinsuyo Liberation Front

Leadership. Aureliano Turpo Choque-huanca (l.).

This Front was established on Sept. 15, 1981, at a meeting on the shores of Lake Titicaca by representatives of Indians from Bolivia, Ecuador and Peru. Named after the region of the former Inca empire centred on Peru, the Front was aimed at regaining sover-eignty over that region which it regarded as being currently "artificially fragmented" by the frontiers of Peru, Bolivia and Ecuador. (According to a statement made in November 1980 by the director of the Inter-American Indigenist Institute of Mexico, the percentage of Indians of the following countries' population was estimated as follows: Guatemala 59.7; Bolivia 59.2; Peru 36.8; Ecuador 33.9; Mexico 12.0.)

St Lucia

Capital: Castries   Pop. 130,000

St Lucia, one of the Windward Islands, is an independent state within the Commonwealth with the British monarch as head of state being represented by a Governor-General. It has a bicameral Parliament consisting of (i) a 17-member House of Assembly elected for five years by universal adult suffrage and (ii) an 11-member Senate appointed by the Governor-General (six senators on the advice of the Prime Minister, three on the advice of the Leader of the Opposition and two by consultation with religious, economic and social bodies). The Prime Minister and his Cabinet are responsible to Parliament.

In elections to the House of Assembly held on May 3, 1982, the (conservative) United Workers' Party gained 14 seats, the St Lucia Labour Party two and the Progressive Labour Party one seat. There have been no reports concerning activities of extra-parliamentary opposition groups.

St Vincent and the Grenadines

Capital: Kingston   Pop. 120,000

St Vincent and the Grenadines are an independent state with the state of a "special member" of the Commonwealth, with the British monarch as its head of state being represented by a Governor-General. It has a House of Assembly consisting of 13 members elected by universal adult suffrage and six senators appointed by the Governor-General. There is a Cabinet collectively responsible to the House of Assembly. In elections held on Dec. 5, 1979, the ruling St Vincent Labour Party obtained 11 seats in the House, and the New Democratic Party two.

Other opposition parties are the People's Political Party, the United People's Movement (an alliance of the Youlou United Liberation Movement and the *Arwee* rural group), the People's Democratic Movement and the Progressive Democratic Party.

National Committee in Defence of Democracy

This Committee, consisting of members of various opposition parties, trade unions and other representative bodies, organized in May 1981 protest demonstrations against two government bills—a Public Safety and Public Order Bill and a bill to amend the Essential Services Act; as a result the passing of these bills was deferred.

Rastafarians

The Rastafarian sect is traditionally non-political (see also under Dominica, page 350) but members of it gave active support to the coup which brought to power the left-wing Government of Grenada (to the south of St Vincent) in March 1979. On Dec. 7, 1979 (two days after a general election), members of this sect were said to be involved in a rising on Union Island (in the Grenadines), where rebels occupied strategic positions for eight hours in protest at the return of the St Vincent Labour Party Government, which they accused of neglecting the interests of the Grenadines' inhabitants. The rising was suppressed, with a state of emergency being imposed (until May 1980) and with the help of troops from Barbados. While one suspected rebel was killed, 42 were arrested and four others detained in Grenada; these four were later extradited to St Vincent, among them the alleged leader of the rising, Lennox Charles (or Rasta Bomba), who was in mid-1980 sentenced to eight years in prison for robbery and causing an explosion; sentences of from one to four years were given to the other three who were extradited from Grenada.

Suriname

Capital: Paramaribo   Pop. 440,000

The Republic of Suriname has since February 1980 been ruled by a National Military Council (NMC) led by Sgt.-Maj. (later Lt.-Col.) Desi Bouterse, who successively dismissed the country's President and suspended its Constitution (on Aug. 15, 1980); he later announced (in March 1981) that Suriname would strengthen its relations with Cuba and follow "a clear socialist course". The NMC succeeded in foiling several attempts by army officers to overthrow it, and on Nov. 27, 1981, it set up a "Revolutionary Front" including "political parties, progressive organizations and other sectors". On March 31, 1982, a mainly civilian Government was set up. However, as a result of a confrontation between the Government and the country's trade unions in October-December 1982 the NMC on Dec. 8 declared a state of martial law, dismissed the Government and destroyed the headquarters of the opposition media and of the largest right-wing trade union, the *Moederbond*. Lt.-Col. Bouterse stated on Dec. 20 that he intended to form a "truly revolutionary government", and he added on Dec. 30 that there would "never again" be a parliamentary democracy in Suriname of the type in existence until February 1980.

In the dissolved Parliament, seats had been held (as the result of elections held on Oct. 31, 1977) as follows: National Alliance (NPK) 22, United Democratic Parties (VDP) 19; a number of smaller parties had gained no seats. The NPK was by May 1979 reduced to 19 seats, and the ensuing crisis contributed to the seizure of power by the NMC.

Moederbond

This trade union, the largest of the right-wing unions in Suriname, staged a strike at Paramaribo airport on Oct. 28, 1982, in protest against the delay in restoring democratic civilian rule in Suriname. When the *Moederbond,* supported by four other major trade union groupings, called for a general strike with the aim of forcing the Government's hand, this call was widely observed, whereupon the Government agreed on Nov. 4 to implement a timetable for the restoration of parliamentary democracy, starting with the election of a constituent assembly to draft a constitution. The Government also agreed to the release of Cyriel Daal, the chairman of the *Moederbond,* who had been arrested a week earlier.

However, on Dec. 7, 1982, severe disturbances broke out in Paramaribo, where the *Moederbond* headquarters and the offices of a newspaper were burned down, apparently by pro-government forces. These events were followed by the proclamation of martial law on Dec. 8 and an announcement by Lt.-Col. Bouterse on Dec. 9 that he had foiled an attempted coup. On the following day it became known that 17 opposition figures had been executed, among them C. Daal, three former ministers and the leader of a pro-Albanian Communist Party (Bram Behr).

Movement for the Liberation of Suriname

This Movement was-formed in the Netherlands in January 1983 by Dr Henk Chin a Sen (who had been Prime Minister of Suriname from March to December 1980 and its President thereafter until February 1982). On Feb. 6 the Movement's founder defined its aim as being the removal from power of Lt.-Col. Bouterse "by peaceful means, particularly by political, diplomatic and economic pressure".

Trinidad and Tobago

Capital: Port of Spain   Pop. 1,100,000

The Republic of Trinidad and Tobago, a member of the Commonwealth, has a President elected for a five-year term by an electoral college constituted by the members of the country's bicameral Parliament which consists of (i) a 36-member House of Representatives elected for five years by universal adult suffrage and (ii) a 31-member Senate appointed by the President (16 senators on the advice of the Prime Minister, six on the advice of the Leader of the Opposition and nine at his own discretion). The Prime Minister and his Cabinet are collectively responsible to Parliament.

In elections to the House of Representatives held on Nov. 9, 1981, the People's National Movement (PNM) was returned for a sixth consecutive term of office by gaining 26 seats; the United Labour Front (ULF) gained eight seats; and the Democratic Action Congress (DAC) gained the two seats allotted to the island of Tobago. The elections were unsuccessfully contested by the following groups: (i) the Organization for National Reconstruction formed in 1980 by a defector from the PNM; (ii) the Trinidad and Tobago National Alliance formed by three groups—a faction of the ULF, the Tapia House Movement and the Trinidad section of the DAC; and (iii) the National Joint Action Committee, which was led by a former Black Power Movement leader and which had until 1981 operated outside the established political system.

During 1980-81 a number of fire-bomb attacks were carried out against prominent persons, several members of the police force were shot at and some property was destroyed by arson, but no political organizations have been identified as having been responsible for these acts. The Minister of National Security and External Affairs alleged in June 1980 that "high-ranking and respected" Trinidadian citizens were involved in plans to destabilize the Government which, he said, had been discussed in other countries (which he did not name).

Uruguay

Capital: Montevideo Pop. 3,300,000

The "Eastern Republic of Uruguay" has, since February 1973, in effect been under military rule, with the then existing bicameral Congress being dissolved on June 27 and the National Trade Union Confederation (*Confederación Nacional de Trabajadores*) on June 30 of that year. A draft constitution designed to ensure the continued existence of the military regime was, however, rejected by some 60 per cent of the voters taking part in a referendum held on Nov. 30, 1980. On Sept. 1, 1981, the military regime thereupon promised on Sept. 1, 1981, that general elections would take place in 1984 and that power would be transferred to civilians in March 1985.

In preparation for the proposed elections the military Government decided in January 1982 to permit three political groups—the country's two traditional parties, the Blanco (or National) Party (PN) and the Colorado Party, as well as the Civic Union (*Unión Cívica*), a small Roman Catholic conservative group—to nominate candidates for election to 500-member congresses for each group (and also to local representative bodies). The members of these congresses were to nominate candidates for the 1984 general elections. All other parties, in particular those which had in 1971 formed a Broad Front (*Frente Amplio*), remained banned, and all persons who had criticized the military regime were disqualified from standing as candidates. However, opposition was organized within the two traditional parties to the military regime (i) in an alliance of the For the Fatherland (*Por la Patria*) and *Movimiento de Rocha* groups inside the PN and (ii) the *Unidad y Reforma* group within the Colorado Party.

The elections, during the campaign for which the Broad Front had called for the casting of blank votes, were held on Nov. 28, 1982, and produced the following results: PN 46.4 per cent (of which 51 per cent were cast for the opposition alliance); Colorado Party 39.7 per cent (of which 67.5 per cent were for the opposition); and Civic Union 1.1 per cent. The remaining 12.8 per cent were blank or invalid votes and the percentage poll was 60.5.

Recent Security Measures

The military regime, which was established only after a serious internal security threat posed by the *Tupamaro* guerrillas of the National Liberation Movement (see entry below) had been averted, gradually developed into what was widely regarded as the most dictatorial regime in any Latin American state.

Under a presidential decree (known as Institutional Act No. 4) of Sept. 1, 1976, all persons who had presented themselves as candidates for Marxist parties in the 1966 and 1971 elections were deprived of their political rights for 15 years, and so were all persons who had been tried for crimes against the nation, while those who had been candidates for other parties retained their right to vote

but lost all other political rights (also for 15 years), with those currently holding government posts being exempted from these measures which were estimated to affect several thousand people. (Ex-President Juan Maria Bordaberry, elected in 1971 but removed from office on June 12, 1976, and six other politicians had their political rights restored on Oct. 7, 1976.)

Under a further decree (announced on Oct. 21, 1976) any person over the age of 18 years could be declared as being in a "state of danger" on suspicion of subversive activity and could be subjected to imprisonment, house arrest or other restrictions, or deportation, with anyone arrested under the decree having to appear in court within 15 days.

Under a political parties charter published in March 1979 parties were not permitted to maintain ties with any foreign state or organization or to have among their members people involved in any organization aiming to destroy the political structure of the country, and in order to remain officially recognized every party would have to maintain a level of support equivalent to not less than 0.5 per cent of the total number of valid votes cast in the previous general election.

A number of former detainees who managed to leave Uruguay during 1980-81 gave detailed accounts of torture allegedly inflicted on all political prisoners for the purpose of extracting information from them. In mid-1981 there were, according to estimates by human rights organizations, about 7,000 political prisoners in Uruguay (this being the highest proportion of the population in any country of the world), one in every 400 citizens had been tortured, thousands had served terms in concentration càmps, hundreds of others were missing, and thousands were in exile or had emigrated for political reasons. Most of the detainees were held at the prison of La Libertad, some 30 miles from Montevideo.

An amnesty declared in January 1982 for politicians detained or in exile since 1973 affected only some 200 politicians and trade union leaders.

Anti-regime Movements

Broad Front (*Frente Amplio,* FA)

Leadership. Líber Seregni Mosquera.

The FA was formed in 1971 by 17 political groups ranging from Christian Democrats to Communists and including also dissidents from the two traditional parties (the Blanco and Colorado parties), in order to contest the 1971 presidential, congressional and local elections. In the congressional elections it gained almost 19 per cent of the valid votes cast and 18 seats in the 99-member Chamber of Deputies. In the presidential elections its candidate, Gen. Líber Seregni Mosquera (a former member of the Colorado Party), gained the same proportion of votes and thus came third. However, he was held in detention from July 9, 1973, to Nov. 2, 1974, was rearrested on Jan. 12, 1976, and was sentenced, in May 1978, to 14 years in prison for violating the Constitution by participating in a pact among leaders of the armed forces to protect the 1971 elections against the possibility of a coup.

Of other leading members of the FA, Zelmar Michelini was found murdered in Buenos Aires on May 22, 1976, after being kidnapped on May 18 (according to Wilson Ferreira Aldunate, the leader of the For the Fatherland faction of the Blanco Party).

Communist Party of Uruguay (*Partido Comunista de Uruguay,* PCU)

Leadership. Rodney Arismendi (first sec., in exile); Alberto Altesor González (1., imprisoned since October 1975).

The PCU was founded in September 1920 by the left wing of the Socialist Party of Uruguay. In February 1971 it joined, with 16 other political groups, the Broad Front (see separate entry). After the party had been banned on Dec. 1, 1973, and both its newspapers (*El Popular* and *Crónica*) had been suppressed shortly afterwards, Rodney Arismendi was detained from May 1974 to Jan. 4, 1975, and thereafter he left for the Soviet Union.

On Dec. 25, 1975, it was disclosed by military officers that numerous PCU activists had been in detention since early November; they were later said to number more than 500; and another 100 were reported to have been arrested during the following week. Most of some 70 people who had sought refuge in the Mexican embassy in Montevideo were in March 1976 said to be PCU members. Among those arrested in late 1975 was A. Altesor González, one of four former parliamentarians who were in 1978 sentenced to imprisonment for from eight to 12 years; another was Dr José Luis Massera Lerena, also a leading PCU member and ex-Senator, who was still in detention in 1980 without having been tried.

The PCU has condemned the policy of guerrilla warfare, in particular that of the National Liberation Movement (*Tupamaros*). The party is officially recognized by the Communist parties of the Soviet-bloc countries.

Democratic Convergence in Uruguay (*Convergencia Democrática en Uruguay,* CDU)

Leadership. Justino Zabala (1.); Juan Raúl Ferreira (pres.).

The establishment of the CDU was announced in New York in April 1980 and in Madrid on May 19 of that year. Its founders included individual members of the Colorado, Blanco, Communist and Socialist parties and two independent supporters of the Broad Front. Aiming to unite all forces opposed to the dictatorship in Uruguay, the CDU declared on April 22, 1980, that it did not envisage the overthrow of the regime by force but rather "a concerted effort to isolate the present Government and support the struggle of the Uruguayan people". According to the Communist ex-Senator Alberto Suárez (quoted on May 2, 1980) the CDU's objects were "full democratization and a new economic model" for Uruguay.

J. R. Ferreira (the son of ex-Senator Wilson Ferreira Aldunate, former National

Party leader living in exile in London) stated early in April 1981 that after the restoration of a democratic climate in Uruguay the CDU would call for general elections to a constituent assembly; he also said that in the face of terrorism of the state, the Uruguayan people and its forces had chosen "the road of peaceful, democratic and pluralist struggle".

The CDU had earlier set up a permanent information office in Washington (as the only democratic opposition force in Latin America to do so) to keep in touch with the US Government, Congress and trade unions.

For the Fatherland (*Por la Patria*)

Leadership. Wilson Ferreira Aldunate (1.).

This faction of the Blanco (or National) Party (PN) took the line that it would not participate in any legislative body which was not freely elected and would not do so until a genuine liberalization process had begun. It was therefore not invited to talks which began in July 1981 between the Government and politicians from the PN, the Colorado Party and the Civic Union. Its leader, W. Ferreira Aldunate, had unsuccessfully contested the 1971 presidential elections for the PN. After the dissolution of Congress in June 1973 he had left Uruguay for Argentina but on May 28, 1976, he had left that country as a result of the murder of two Uruguayan ex-parliamentarians (including that of Zelmar Michelini of the Broad Front); on June 14, 1976, he stated in London that the Uruguayan regime was collaborating with the Argentine security forces and had ordered these murders.

National Liberation Movement (*Movimiento de Liberación Nacional,* MLN or *Tupamaros*)

Leadership. Raúl Sendic (1.).

The name *Tupamaros* was derived from that of Tupac Amaru, a Peruvian Indian leader, who claimed Inca descent and led an anti-Spanish revolt at the end of the 18th century but was eventually captured and executed. The movement was founded at a time when Uruguay was beginning to face a deepening economic crisis with growing inflation and unemployment. Following the establishment of the Movement in 1962, *Tupamaro* leaders were active among sugar workers in northern Uruguay. From 1963 (when they first seized rifles and ammunition from a rifle club) they extended guerrilla warfare to urban areas on the basis of theories developed by Abraham Güillén, a Spanish ideologist of urban terrorism, who had recommended a strategy of small guerrilla action to compel the security forces to surrender terrain, and also the establishment of small cells which could act without reference to a high command—this strategy to be reinforced by political work in order to gain mass support.

By mid-1972 the *Tupamaros* were said to number about 6,000, recruited mainly from among left-wing students and teachers. Their early actions included robberies, the spoils of which they distributed among the poor, and later they engaged in kidnappings, assassinations, shootings and bombings with the aim of weakening the country's political leadership which they held responsible for the economic crisis. By 1971 it appeared possible that they might seize power, but the Government of President Juan Maria Bordaberry (who was elected in 1971) succeeded in crushing the movement by November 1972 after proclaiming, in April of that year, a "state of internal war" which was repeatedly extended.

Notable victims of *Tupamaro* action were Dan A. Mitrione, a US adviser to the Uruguayan police force, kidnapped on Aug. 2, 1970, and found murdered on Aug. 9 (the Uruguayan Government having refused to accede to a *Tupamaro* demand for the release of all political prisoners); Geoffrey (later Sir Geoffrey) Jackson, British ambassador in Montevideo, seized on Jan. 8, 1971, and released on Sept. 10 of that year (although the Uruguayan Government had refused to negotiate with his captors); and Col. Artiges Alvarez, chief of the civil defence force, killed by *Tupamaro* machine-gun fire on July 25, 1972.

Among others kidnapped by *Tupamaros* was a press photographer, Nelson Bardesio (seized on Feb. 25, 1972), who was said to have confessed that he belonged to an unofficial police group similar to the Brazilian "Death Squad" and involved in killing persons suspected of subversive activities. (There was, in fact, an extreme right-wing group, the "Upstanding Uruguayan Youth" or *Juventud Uruguaya de Pie,* JUP, which was involved in actions against *Tupamaros.*)

The assassination in Paris on Dec. 19, 1974, of Col. Ramón Trabal (Uruguayan military attaché) by members of a "Raúl Sendic International Brigade" was followed by the killing, in Montevideo on the next day, of five former *Tupamaros* (apparently as an act of reprisal) and by the arrest of numerous persons, the rearrest of hundreds of provisionally released political prisoners as well as by dismissals among university staff and sanctions against the press.

Raúl Sendic, the movement's founder, was first arrested in August 1970, but he was among 106 *Tupamaros* who escaped from a maximum security prison in Montevideo on Sept. 6, 1971. He was, however, rearrested on Sept. 1, 1972; after being held in detention without trial, he was eventually, on July 1980, sentenced to 45 years in prison. Other leading *Tupamaros* sentenced to long terms of imprisonment included (i) Antonio Mas Mas, given a 30-year sentence on Feb. 16, 1977, for his involvement in the kidnapping and killing of D. A. Mitrione and in the seizure of the British ambassador, in addition to which he was to be kept in custody for a further 16 years and thereafter to be deported to Spain (as he was a Majorcan); (ii) Eleuterio Fernández Huidobro, who was among 10 *Tupamaros* sentenced to from 4½ to 30 years in prison on May 6, 1982, and (iii) Jorge Amilcar Maneras Lluveres, reported on Aug. 3, 1982, as having been given a 30-year sentence for setting up a criminal organization, conspiracy, armed robbery, the manufacture and storage of bombs and explosives, abduction and "especially aggravated murder".

The head of Uruguay's Supreme Military Court (Col. Silva Ledesma) stated on May 6, 1982, that 992 guerrillas (134 of them women) were still in detention, including most of the members of the *Tupamaro* general staff, and that 3,238 *Tupamaros* had been released, many of them after serving their sentences.

Party for the Victory of the People (*Partido por la Victoria del Pueblo,* PVP)

The PVP was formed as an independent opposition party outside the Broad Front. On Oct. 29, 1976, the security forces announced that 62 members of the PVP had been arrested and that the party had been planning the assassination of many members of the Uruguayan Government and the armed forces, and also terrorist acts. Uruguayan exile groups, however, asserted that many of those arrested had earlier been kidnapped in Argentina and that Uruguayan and Argentine security forces were working in close co-operation against dissidents in both countries.

Popular Union (*Unión Popular,* UP)

Leadership. Ex-Senator Enrique René Erro (l.).

The UP was one of 13 left-wing formations banned by the military regime on Dec. 1, 1973. The leader of the party (which formed part of the Broad Front—see separate entry) was in March 1973 accused of collaboration with the *Tupamaros,* of which his son was suspected of being a member; he left the country for Buenos Aires, shortly before an order was issued late in June 1973 for his arrest for "conspiracy and treason". He later sought political asylum in Argentina, where he set up (in July 1973) a committee-in-exile to organize Uruguayan resistance externally; he emphasized, however, that the necessary changes in Uruguay would have to be carried out in a democratic manner. He was also reported to be co-operating with ex-Senator Wilson Ferreira Aldunate, the leader of the For the Fatherland faction of the Blanco Party. In April 1976, however, he was arrested in Buenos Aires.

Six-Point Movement (*Movimiento de Seis Puntos*)

The existence of this Movement, led by several prisoners in the prison of La Libertad, was referred to by the Commander of the Second Army Division on Nov. 28, 1980. It was said to be named after its programme to constitute a continuation of the *Tupamaro* movement and to have some 500 members.

Unity and Reform Group (*Unidad y Reforma*)

This Group, a faction of the Colorado Party opposed to the military regime, held the first public demonstration since 1973 on Oct. 3, 1982, to inaugurate its election campaign.

Uruguayan Socialist Party (*Partido Socialista Uruguayo,* PSU)

The PSU, a left-wing Socialist party, has been a component part of the Broad Front (see separate entry) and was banned, with other left-wing groups, on Dec. 1, 1973. Its president, José Pedro Cardoso (77), was arrested in Montevideo on Aug. 22, 1980.

Other Banned Movements

In addition to the Communist Party, the Popular Union and the Uruguayan Socialist Party (see separate entries), 10 other left-wing formations banned by the military regime on Dec. 1, 1973, were the following:

Eastern Revolutionary Movement (*Movimiento Revolucionario Oriental*).

Federation of Revolutionary Students (*Federación de Estudiantes Revolucionarios,* FER).

Federation of University Students of Uruguay (*Federación de Universitarios de Uruguay,* FUU).

Groups for Unified Action (*Grupos de Acción Unificadora,* GAU), established in February 1980 and part of the Broad Front (see separate entry).

Movement of March 26 (*Movimiento 26 de Marzo*).

Red Group (*Grupo Rojo*).

Revolutionary Workers' Party (*Partido Revolucionario de Trabajadores,* PRT).

Self-Defence Group (*Grupo de Auto-Defensa,* GAP).

Student Worker Resistance (*Resistencia Obrero Estudiantil,* ROE).

Union of Communist Youth (*Unión de la Juventud Comunista*).

Venezuela

Capital: Caracas   Pop. 15,400,000

The Federal Republic of Venezuela, consisting of 20 autonomous states, a federal district, two federal territories and 72 federal dependencies, has an executive President elected by universal adult suffrage for a five-year term and presiding over a Cabinet appointed by him. There is a bicameral Congress consisting of (i) a Senate to which two senators from each of the 20 states and from the federal district are elected for a five-year term by universal adult suffrage (while additional senators are selected to represent minorities and all former Presidents of the Republic are life members of the Senate) and (ii) a 199-member Chamber of Deputies similarly elected (at least two members for each state and one for each federal territory). The President is not eligible for two consecutive terms.

As a result of elections held on Dec. 3, 1978, seats in the Chamber of Deputies were distributed as follows: Democratic Action (AD) 88, Christian Social Party (COPEI) 88, Movement towards Socialism (MAS) 11, Left Revolutionary Movement (MIR) 4, People's Electoral Movement (MEP) 3 and five other parties 1 each—Common Cause, Communist Vanguard, Movement of National Integration (MIN), Socialist League and Venezuelan Communist Party (PCV). Legal parties not represented in Congress include the Democratic Republican Union (URD), the Nationalist Civic Crusade (CCN), the Nationalist United Front (FUN), National Opinion (Opina), the National Renewal Movement (Morena), the Popular Democratic Force (FDP) and the United Vanguard.

Guerrilla Activities, 1963-77

A major offensive against Venezuela's Government by well-organized left-wing urban guerrillas in the 1960s remained unsuccessful as the result of various factors, including a significant improvement in the country's economy, effective action by the security forces coupled with a policy of pacification by means of offers of amnesties, and disunity among the guerrillas—especially after the Venezuelan Communist Party (PCV) renounced guerrilla warfare in 1967. The remaining left-wing guerrilla groups have been small and of limited effect in recent years.

In the years between 1963 and 1977 urban guerrilla warfare was conducted by the (extreme left-wing) Armed Forces of National Liberation (*Fuerzas Armadas de Liberación Nacional,* FALN), which superseded a large number of separate guerrilla groups and to which the PCV acceded only on condition that a National Liberation Front (*Frente de Liberación Nacional,* FLN) should be established at the same time with responsibility for

political decisions affecting the guerrilla movement. However, a conflict arose in subsequent years between the PCV and Douglas Bravo (the military leader of the FALN) and by 1967 the PCV decided that, as there was no longer a revolutionary situation in Venezuela, it would abandon its armed struggle and would instead contest elections; the party also decided to expel Douglas Bravo from its ranks.

The FALN continued its activities, which included the hijacking of aircraft, kidnappings and assassinations (which the PCV condemned). An amnesty offer made by President Rafael Caldera Rodríguez in March 1969 was spurned by a hard core of the FALN led by Douglas Bravo. Early in 1970. Bravo (whom Dr Fidel Castro, the Cuban leader, had previously acclaimed as "the leader of the Venezuelan revolution") broke with Cuba, accusing it of having abandoned the struggle for the "liberation of the Latin American continent" and of having instead chosen to receive economic aid from the Soviet Union.

By 1975, however, the remnants of the FALN had been subdued by the security forces. Bravo, who had been underground for 18 years, was amnestied on Sept. 24, 1979—all charges previously laid against him being withdrawn. He explained early in 1980 that he no longer believed in armed struggle and was going to be engaged in legal activities within the Revolutionary Party of Venezuela, which he had founded.

Left-wing Guerrilla Groups

Américo Silva Front—see under Red Flag

Argimiro Gabaldón Revolutionary Commando

This Commando was responsible for the kidnapping on Feb. 27, 1976, of William F. Niehous (general manager in Venezuela of the US Owens-Illinois glass firm and its world president). As a condition for his release the group demanded the publication in three international newspapers and in the Venezuelan press of a communiqué attacking the US firm as "one of the many multinationals that plunder the country and submit the working class to overt exploitation" and as having the power to "intervene barefacedly in all of the country's internal affairs".

The demand for publication of the communiqué in the three newspapers outside Venezuela was met on April 6, but its publication inside the country was not permitted by the Venezuelan Government, which also acted to prevent the payment of ransom, as demanded by the kidnappers, to "finance food packages and other forms of social aid". In this connexion several persons were arrested for alleged contact with the kidnappers, among them two opposition deputies and the secretary-general of the Socialist League, Jorge Rodríguez; concerning the latter, the Minister of the Interior admitted on July 26, 1976, that he had been killed at the hands of four policemen acting without orders.

W. F. Niehous was, according to official reports, rescued on June 30, 1979, by police who had discovered his hideout near Ciudad Bolívar (southern Venezuela) and had killed two guerrillas. According to other sources, however, his release was the result of government negotiations with the kidnappers and also of the Government's "pacification policy" under which several guerrillas had been pardoned (among them Douglas Bravo, the commander of the Armed Forces of National Liberation—see above).

International Movement of the Proletariat *(Movimiento Internacional del Proletariado)*

Two alleged members of this (pro-Cuban) Movement hijacked a Venezuelan airliner on Nov. 6, 1980, diverting it, with 55 passengers, to Havana in protest against the acquittal by a Venezuelan court of four men accused of placing a bomb on a Cuban airliner which exploded off Barbados on Oct. 6, 1976, when 73 persons were killed.

M.28

Members of this small left-wing group were in August 1980 reported to be sought by the security forces near Valencia (east of Caracas).

Manuel Rojas Luzardo International Commandos—see under Red Flag

Ramón Emeterio Betance Commando *(Comando Ramón Emeterio Betance)*

This extreme left-wing group, named after a 19th-century Puerto Rican nationalist, claimed responsibility for hijacking, on Dec. 7, 1981, three Venezuelan airliners, and their diversion to Havana. On arrival in the Cuban capital, all the hijackers were taken into custody and all passengers and crew members were released unharmed on Dec. 8, about half the passengers having earlier been set free at successive landings in Colombia, Aruba (Netherlands Antilles), Honduras, Guatemala and Panama.

The hijackers had demanded the release of 23 alleged political detainees in Venezuela and payment of $10,000,000. They had also appealed for solidarity with the guerrillas of El Salvador and distributed leaflets on behalf of a group called Manuel Rojas Luzardo International Commandos, said to be a branch of the Red Flag organization (see separate entry).

Red Flag *(Bandera Roja)*

Leadership. Gabriel Puerte Aponte.

This small Marxist-Leninist group broke away from the Armed Forces of National Liberation (FALN—see above) and was engaged in various guerrilla operations until 1978. Its leaders, the brothers Carlos and Argenis Betancourt, were both arrested in 1977. The group, however, was again active in September 1980, when it seized weapons and the equivalent of £800,000 in a raid in Valencia (east of Caracas).

Gabriel Puerte Aponte, the group's leader, and 10 other members were captured in Caracas on April 9, 1982; three others were arrested in Caracas on May 6; and four members of the group and two policemen lost their lives in a clash some 200 miles east of Caracas on May 12. In fighting by guerrillas against army and police units at Cantaura (150 miles south-east of Caracas) 28 persons (including a policeman) were killed on Oct. 4, 1982, the guerrillas being described as members of the Américo Silva Front *(Frente Américo Silva),* said to be the armed wing of the underground Red Flag organization. A faction called the Manuel Rojas Luzardo International Commandos was also thought to be linked with the Red Flag movement.

Zero Point (*Punta Cero*)

This small Marxist urban guerrilla group was first reported to be active in 1975. It rejected a presidential amnesty offer of December 1979 and was again said to be active in January 1981.

7. WESTERN AND SOUTHERN EUROPE

Austria

Capital: Vienna   Pop. 7,540,000

Under the Austrian State Treaty of May 15, 1955, the Republic of Austria is a "sovereign, independent and democratic state" with a Government "based on elections by secret ballot" and by "free, equal and universal suffrage". There is a bicameral Parliament consisting of a 183-member *Nationalrat* (Lower House) and a 58-member *Bundesrat* (Upper House), the latter being elected by the legislatures of the country's nine federal provinces (*Länder*).

As a result of elections held on April 24, 1983, seats in the *Nationalrat* were distributed as follows: Austrian Socialist Party 90, Austrian People's Party 81, Austrian Freedom Party 12. Among a number of smaller parties without parliamentary representation is the National Democratic Party, whose leader has led a Munich-based South Tirol liberation group; members of this group have been convicted in Italy of terrorist activities, and its followers were still engaged in acts of violence in the Alto Adige-Trentino region of Italy during 1982 (see under Italy, pages 455-56). Two ecologist parties, the United Greens and the Alternative List, failed to gain any seats in the 1983 elections. There has been no political group advocating the use of violence inside Austria itself.

Pro-Vorarlberg

In September 1979 this pressure group published an appeal in which it demanded a special "Vorarlberg Statute" within Austria's federal structure for the *Land* (province) of Vorarlberg. The appeal led to an initiative by the *Landtag* (provincial parliament) based on a 10-point programme and empowering the *Land* Government to conduct negotiations with the central Government on financial and fiscal autonomy, various degrees of regional control of education, commerce, forestry, agriculture and broadcasting, and the right to conclude contracts with neighbouring countries (e.g. on the sale of hydro-electric power to the Federal Republic of Germany, a major source of Vorarlberg's income).

The initiative was supported by the Austrian People's Party, which held 22 seats out of the 36 in Vorarlberg's *Landtag* and which had formed a coalition Government with the Austrian Freedom Party (with four seats); it was approved in a referendum on June 23, 1980, by 69.4 per cent of the valid votes cast in an 88.1 per cent poll. The initiative was, however, opposed by the Austrian Socialist Party, which held power at federal level, on the grounds that no special powers should be granted to any one *Land* to the exclusion of the other eight *Länder* of Austria.

Belgium

Capital: Brussels   Pop. 9,910,000

The Kingdom of Belgium is a constitutional monarchy with a multi-party parliamentary democracy. It has a bicameral Parliament consisting of (i) a 212-member Chamber of Representatives elected for a four-year term by a system of proportional representation and (ii) a 181-member Senate (to which 106 senators are elected directly). As a result of elections held on Nov. 8, 1981, seats in the Chamber were distributed as follows: Christian People's Party (Flemish) 43, Party for Freedom and Progress (Flemish liberal) 28, Socialist Party (Walloon) 35, Socialist Party (Flemish) 26, People's Union (Flemish nationalist) 20, Liberal Reformist Party (Walloon) 24, Christian Social Party (Walloon) 18, Francophone Democratic Front—Walloon Rally 8, others 10.

Devolution plans providing for Belgium to have, in addition to its central Government, separate governments for Brussels, Flanders and Wallonia have been debated for some years but are not yet fully implemented. There have been violent incidents between French- and Flemish-speaking Belgians from time to time, arising out of disputes over the boundaries of the respective language areas. Moreover, several extreme left-wing groups claimed responsibility for acts of violence committed in Belgium between 1979 and 1981.

Commando Andreas Baader

Named after the West German revolutionary extremist who had died in Stammheim prison in October 1977, this Commando was one of three left-wing groups which claimed responsibility for an unsuccessful attempt on the life of the NATO supreme commander in Europe in June 1979 (see under Julien Lahaut Brigade).

Direct Action (*Action Directe*)

This Belgian offshoot of the French Direct Action movement (see entry under France) claimed responsibility for a bomb explosion at a synagogue in Antwerp on Oct. 20, 1981, causing the death of two persons and injury to 98 others. The Belgian authorities, however, attributed this action to a Palestinian splinter group (the Palestine Liberation Organization having condemned it).

Flemish Militant Order (*Vlaamse Militante-norde,* VMO)

The VMO has been involved in militant action against French-speaking groups in various disputes over linguistic areas, in particular in the district of Voeren (Fourons), which was in 1962 transferred from the (Walloon) province of Liège to the (Flemish) province of Limburg. This transfer was opposed by militant Walloon groups, including a "Back to Liège" movement led by J. Happart. Following armed confrontations in the district in August and October 1979, a 1934 law banning the maintenance of uniformed private armies was invoked against the VMO, and on Oct. 14, 1980, 60 VMO members were arraigned on arms charges. The Government confirmed on June 5, 1981, that Voeren would remain part of Flemish territory.

The VMO is a more extreme nationalist organization than the two Flemish nationalist political parties—the People's Union *(Volksunie)* and the more radical Flemish Bloc *(Vlaamse Blok)*.

Julien Lahaut Brigade

This extreme left-wing group claimed responsibility (together with the Commando Andreas Baader and the Vengeance and Liberty faction) for an unsuccessful attempt on June 25, 1979, on the life of Gen. Alexander Haig, who was then retiring as Supreme Allied Commander Europe of the NATO forces. Julien Lahaut, who had been a leading member of the Communist Party of Belgium, was assassinated after the outbreak of World War II.

The Brigade named after him stated in its announcement that the attempt had been aimed at "the most visible representative of the United States' aggressive and military policy" and that it was "up to the Communists of the so-called socialist states to strike blows against leading Warsaw Pact personalities in order to create close connexions among revolutionaries who are sickened by all kinds of dictatorship".

Vengence and Liberty *(Revanche et Liberté)*

This extreme left-wing faction was one of three groups which claimed responsibility for an unsuccessful attempt on the life of the NATO supreme commander in Europe in June 1979 (see under Julien Lahaut Brigade above).

Were Di

This Flemish neo-Nazi group has called for an amnesty for wartime collaborators with the Nazis.

Cyprus

Capital: Nicosia   Pop. 835,000

Since February 1975 the Republic of Cyprus (a member of the Commonwealth) has been de facto divided into two states—the (Greek-Cypriot) Republic of Cyprus and the (Turkish-Cypriot) not internationally recognized Turkish Federated State of Cyprus, created after the occupation by Turkish troops of about 40 per cent of the island's area in July 1974. Both are multi-party states and have an executive President presiding over a Cabinet, as well as unicameral Parliaments elected by universal adult suffrage.

The Greek-Cypriot 35-member House of Representatives has, as a result of elections held on May 24, 1981, a distribution of seats as follows: the (communist) Progressive Party of the Working People (AKEL) 12, Democratic Rally 12, Democratic Party 8 and Socialist Party of Cyprus (EDEK) 3. In the Turkish-Cypriot Legislative Assembly the 40 seats are, as a result of elections held on June 28, 1981, distributed as follows: National Unity Party 18, the (Maoist) Socialist Salvation (Communal Liberation) Party 13, Republican Turkish Party (orthodox Communist) 6, Democratic People's Party 2 and Turkish Unity Party 1.

There has been little evidence of extra-parliamentary opposition to the two Governments in Cyprus in recent years. An alleged (apparently right-wing) conspiracy to overthrow the Greek-Cypriot Government was publicly referred to on July 14, 1978, in connexion with the expulsion from Cyprus of a former counsellor at the West German embassy in Nicosia because of alleged interference in the island's internal affairs. Those charged on July 18-20, 1978, with alleged seditious conspiracy (which was said to have begun in March 1978) included Kikis Constantinou, a former leader of EOKA-B. The latter right-wing organization had, in July 1974, staged a coup against President Makarios, for which Nicos Sampson (the EOKA leader who was President of Cyprus for eight days following the coup) was sentenced to 20 years in prison on Aug. 31, 1976.

Denmark

Capital: Copenhagen   Pop. 5,150,000

The Kingdom of Denmark, a democratic multi-party state, has a monarch who exercises executive power through a Cabinet headed by a Prime Minister, while legislative power lies jointly with the monarch and the Diet (*Folketing*), a unicameral Parliament elected for a four-year term by universal adult suffrage and consisting of 179 members (including two each for the Faroe Islands and Greenland).

As a result of elections held on Dec. 8, 1981, the 175 metropolitan seats in the Diet were distributed as follows: Social Democrats 59, Conservatives 26, Socialist People's Party 21, *Venstre* Liberals 20, Progress Party 16, Centre Democrats 15, Radical Liberals 9, Left Socialists 5, Christian People's Party 4; the two Faroes seats were taken by a Social Democrat and a Union Party member (who joined the *Venstre* Liberal parliamentary group), while the Greenland seats went to an *Atassut* member (who co-operated with the Social Democrats) and a *Siumut* candidate (who associated himself with the Socialist People's Party).

Parties which unsuccessfully contested the 1981 elections were the Single-Tax Party, the Communist Party, the Communist Workers' Party and the Socialist Workers' Party in metropolitan Denmark; the Republican Party, the People's Party, the Home Rule Party and the Progressive and Fishermen's Party in the Faroe Islands; and the *Kandidatforbund* in Greenland. Other parties existing in Denmark included the Schleswig Party (representing the German minority) and, in Greenland, the Eskimo Federation (*Inuit Ataqatigiit*) and the Wage-Earners' Party (*Sulissartut*).

There has in recent years been some evidence of the existence of both right-wing and left-wing extremist groups in Denmark.

Danish National Socialist Alliance

This Nazi organization was in 1980 reported to have links with other similar extreme right-wing groups in Europe, Australia, Canada and Latin America. A commando which daubed the walls of the Copenhagen offices of El Al (the Israeli airline) with swastikas on Jan. 19, 1981, was also held responsible for attacking and seriously injuring the head of these offices. The organization has attracted only minimal support on the extreme right-wing fringe.

"Revolutionary Army" Group

The police announced in Copenhagen on Nov. 13, 1980, that 16 members of this Group had been arrested after being found in possession of drugs (worth the equivalent of £1,400,000), the sale of which was intended to finance its plans to assassinate the Danish royal family and leading politicians and to overthrow Parliament. The police had also found machine guns which had been used against drug dealers who had not paid the Group.

Finland

Capital: Helsinki   Pop. 4,810,000

The Republic of Finland, a democratic multi-party state, has a President elected for a six-year term by a college of 301 electors chosen by universal adult suffrage. He holds supreme executive power and appoints a Cabinet under a Prime Minister which must enjoy the confidence of the 200-member unicameral Parliament (*Eduskunta*) elected for a four-year term by universal adult suffrage. In elections held on March 20-21, 1983, seats in Parliament were gained as follows: Social Democrats 57, Conservatives 44, Centre-Liberal Alliance 38, Finnish People's Democratic League (led by the Communist Party) 27, Rural Party 17, Swedish People's Party 11, Finnish Christian League 3, Ecologists 2, Constitutional Party 1.

Under the 1947 peace treaty with the Soviet Union the Finnish Government was obliged to dissolve all political, military and paramilitary "fascist" organizations and all organizations engaged in propaganda against the Soviet Union and other friendly nations, and also not to tolerate the existence of such organizations in the future (Art. 8). Moreover, it was forbidden to give any military, naval or air instruction to persons other than members of the Finnish Army, Navy or Air Force (Art. 15).

In November 1977 the Government prohibited the activities of four unregistered extreme right-wing organizations (with a total membership of not more than 100).

Patriotic People's Front

Leadership. Pekka Siitoin (l.).

Pekka Siitoin, the alleged leader of this organization (one of the four prohibited by the Government in November 1977), was on Nov. 14, 1979, reported to have been sentenced to five years in prison for involvement in an attempt to set fire to the printing works of two Communist newspapers a year earlier, and also for founding and directing an illegal political organization. Five other persons sentenced to imprisonment at the same time included the "secretary-general" of the proscribed organization, who was given a 3½-year prison sentence.

France

Capital: Paris Pop. 54,000,000

The French Republic has an executive President elected for a seven-year term by universal adult suffrage, a Government headed by a Prime Minister and a bicameral Parliament consisting of (i) a 295-member indirectly-elected Senate and (ii) a 491-member National Assembly elected for a five-year term by universal adult suffrage in single-member constituencies over two rounds of voting. General elections held on June 14 and 21, 1981, resulted in the Assembly seats being distributed as follows: Socialists and associates 285 (including 14 Left Radicals), the (Gaullist) Rally for the Republic (RPR) and associates 88, the (centrist) Union for French Democracy (UDF) and associates 63, Communists and associates 44, unattached 11. There is a multiplicity of other "orthodox" political parties without parliamentary representation, including several on both the extreme left and the extreme right.

Partly in consequence of France's traditional status as a haven for political refugees from other countries, numerous non-French extremist groups have pursued their aims while operating on French soil, notably in the capital, and have posed a major threat to internal security in recent years. Such groups (which are dealt with under appropriate country headings elsewhere in this volume) include Armenian nationalists committed to violent action against Turkish targets, militant Palestinian splinter groups seeking to extend their struggle against Israel and Zionism beyond the Middle East, and various other Arab groups pursuing assorted inter-Arab rivalries. At the same time, numerous specifically French extremist groups are committed to aims and methods which pose a threat to the existing order, those active in recent years encompassing both ends of the political spectrum. The French polity has also been under challenge from various separatist or autonomist movements (notably in Corsica) and from a number of pro-independence groups active in the overseas departments and territories.

The accession to power of the left-wing Government of President François Mitterrand in mid-1981 heralded a significant diminution of the extreme left-wing violence which had been a recurrent feature of French political life over the previous 23 years of right-wing dominance. With a view to promoting political reconciliation the new Government has not only granted amnesties to substantial numbers of political prisoners but has also dismantled parts of the security enforcement apparatus created by previous administrations, notably the State Security Court. Nevertheless, serious violent incidents have continued to take place, mainly associated with the activities of non-French extremist groups but also increasingly with a new militancy on the French extreme right. In the latter context, the early 1980s have witnessed a recrudescence of anti-semitism in France and a sharp rise in the incidence of violent attacks on the French Jewish community.

In view of what it regarded as a deterioration in the internal security situation, the French Government on Aug. 17, 1982, introduced new anti-terrorist measures, including a strengthening of the security forces, tighter controls on illegal border entries and arms trafficking and the installation of more computer capacity in anti-terrorist information units; President Mitterrand also created a new post of Secretary of State for Public Security (entrusted to security specialist Joseph Franceschi) whose principal function was to co-ordinate the new measures. The Government made it clear that its main aim was to curb the current wave of "international" terrorism in France, but also indicated that the new measures reflected its concern over the intensification of anti-Jewish attacks attributed to French extreme right-wing groups.

Extreme Right-wing Movements

Action-Youth Group (Groupe Action-Jeunesse)

This extreme right-wing cell claimed responsibility for a Molotov cocktail attack on the Paris office of a pacifist movement on June 15, 1981. In a message telephoned to the Agence France-Presse the grouping declared itself to be "against cosmopolitanism and internationalism".

Anger of the Legions (Colère des Légions)

This hitherto unknown group was one of several extremist organizations (of both the right and the left) which claimed responsibility for a raid on a military arms depot near Toulouse in November 1981. A considerable number of weapons were stolen in this raid but almost all were subsequently recovered by the police in early January 1982.

Charles Martel Club

Named after the 8th-century Carolingian king who stemmed the Moslem Arab penetration of Europe at Poitiers in 732 AD, this group had its origins in the forces which opposed the granting of independence to Algeria in 1962. Its first violent action was a bomb attack on the Algerian consulate in Marseilles in December 1973, when four people were killed. Among its further actions was a bomb attack on the Algerian consulate in Aubervilliers (Paris) on May 11, 1980.

Civic Action Service (Service d'Action Civique, SAC)

Leadership. Pierre Debizet (s.g.).

The SAC was established in 1958 on the return to power of Gen. De Gaulle to act as the unofficial security arm of the Gaullist movement and as a focus for Gaullist sympathisers outside the orthodox party political framework. It subsequently gained a reputation for using violent methods in pursuit of its aims and for having links with the French underworld.

The organization came into sharp public focus in July 1981 in connexion with the murder in Marseilles of Jacques Massie (a police inspector and former local SAC chief) together with five members of his family. Of about a dozen SAC members subsequently arrested by the police, four reportedly confessed to having participated in the killings, apparently because Massie had refused to surrender documents in his possession which incriminated the SAC.

After a parliamentary investigation committee had recommended the dissolution of the SAC on the grounds of its clandestine criminal activities, the French Cabinet on July 28, 1982, announced the official banning of the organization. A government statement said that "the action of this organization is founded on violence and on practices bordering on banditry, as evidenced by the numerous judicial cases in which certain of its members and leaders have been implicated".

Committee for the French People (Comité pour le Peuple Français)

Leadership. Thierry Colombo (founder).

This Committee was established as a "cultural" organization of supporters of extreme right-wing ideas. Its founder, Thierry Colombo, was sentenced to four years' imprisonment (three suspended) on May 22, 1981, after being convicted of "non-denunciation of criminals" in connexion with the murder in May 1976 of an extreme right-winger who had apparently been regarded as a security liability by his associates. At the same trial two men convicted of being directly responsible for the murder, Serge Devillers and Bernard Lemaître, were sentenced to 15 and four years in prison respectively.

Delta

The Delta organization takes its names from a commando group formed during the Algerian war of independence under the leadership of Roger Degueldre, a former lieutenant in the French paratroops. Degueldre, who at that time was head of the "direct action" branch of the Secret Army Organization (OAS) fighting to maintain French rule in Algeria, was eventually sentenced to death by the State Security Court and executed in July 1962.

Delta resurfaced in 1977 when it claimed responsibility for the killing in Paris on Dec. 2 of Laïd Sebaï, the leader of an Algerian organization in France. It was also believed to have carried out the murder in Paris on May 4, 1978, of Henri Curiel, an Egyptian Jew who had been founder of the Egyptian Communist Party and was later said to have been involved in various left-wing and pro-Arab activities in France.

Delta also claimed responsibility for an incendiary attack on the house of a leading

Communist in a Paris suburb on June 6, 1980, and for an attack on the flat of Henri Curiel's widow in Paris on Aug. 13, 1980. The latter action was carried out by Delta's "Mario Tutti Commando", named after an activist of the extreme right-wing Armed Revolutionary Nuclei (NAR) of Italy, with which Delta was believed to have links.

In early March 1981 Delta claimed responsibility for having sent a parcel bomb (which was defused) to Jacques Fauvet, the director of the daily newspaper *Le Monde*. Subsequently, it was one of several extremist organizations (of both the right and the left) which claimed responsibility for a raid on a military arms depot near Toulouse in November 1981. A considerable number of weapons were stolen in this raid but almost all were subsequently recovered by the police in early January 1982.

European Nationalist Alliances (*Faisceaux Nationalistes Européens,* FNE)

The FNE was formed in September 1980 as the successor to the Federation of National and European Action (FANE—see separate entry) following the banning of the latter organization. It was held responsible for numerous anti-Jewish attacks and incidents, the most serious of which was the explosion of a bomb outside a synagogue in the Rue Copernic in Paris on Oct. 3, 1980, resulting in the death of four people and the injury of many others. (In the absence of any arrests in connexion with the Rue Copernic attack, it was surmised in some quarters that the explosion might have been the work of Palestinian extremists—this view being taken by, among others, the Israeli Government.)

Fascist New Generation—see under Federation of National and European Action

Fascist Revolutionary Action Party (*Parti Fasciste d'Action Révolutionnaire*)

This previously unknown party claimed responsibility for planting a bomb (which was defused) at a Paris court-house on March 11, 1980.

Federation of National and European Action (*Fédération d'Action Nationale et Europeénne,* FANE)

Leadership. Marc Fredriksen (founder and l.).

FANE was formed in 1966 as an amalgamation of two former factions of the extreme right-wing *Occident* movement (itself officially banned in 1968). After the organization had been linked with an intensification of attacks on Jewish and left-wing targets from early 1980, the French Government on Sept. 3, 1980, ordered its dissolution under a 1936 public order act as amended in 1972 to cover the incitement of discrimination, hatred or violence. The banning decision followed an investigation by the Interior Ministry which found that "violent demonstrations were organized by this movement, one of whose expressed aims is the installation of a new Nazi regime".

FANE's founder and leader, Marc Fredriksen (a bank employee), claimed shortly before the banning order that the organization had 60 active members in Paris and 200 in the provinces, but denied that it had been involved in violence against the French Jewish community, which FANE opposed "as a powerful pressure group rather than as individuals". As part of FANE's aim of building a pan-European neo-fascist movement, Fredriksen was known to have established contacts with the extreme right-wing Armed Revolutionary Nuclei (NAR) of Italy.

Six weeks after the banning of FANE, Fredriksen was on Oct. 17, 1980, sentenced to 18 months' imprisonment (with one year suspended) after being convicted in a Paris court of inciting racial hatred and violence and of justifying war crimes and collaboration with Nazi Germany during World War II; he was also fined and ordered to pay damages to five organizations which had sought redress against him. Fredriksen's sentence was subsequently reduced on appeal to a suspended sentence of 13 months' imprisonment, although the financial penalties were upheld.

Shortly before the trial Fredriksen and a political associate had been attacked and injured by a group of young Jewish militants at Rambouillet (near Paris); a subsequent telephone call to the Reuters news agency claimed that the "Jewish Brigades" had carried out the attack as a warning to neo-Nazis that they could not act with impunity.

Former FANE activists brought to trial in 1981 included (i) Marc Gillet, who had formed a branch of the organization in Alpes-Maritimes and who received an 18-month prison sentence (15 suspended) in Nice on May 19 for writing death threats, inciting racial discrimination, hatred and violence, and possessing arms (his sister Marie-France being given a two-month suspended sentence for this last offence); and (ii) Fredriksen's former body-guard, Jean-Yves Pellay, who was given a 12-month suspended prison sentence on Sept. 17 for transporting arms.

Following the banning of FANE its followers regrouped under differently-named organizations, notably the European Nationalist Alliances (FNE) and the New Nazi Front (NFN)—see separate entries. Early in 1981 a grouping calling itself the "Fascist New Generation" issued a text under the ex-FANE symbol proclaiming its belief that "Adolf Hitler is the only god" and listing about 60 Jewish personalities of the Alpes-Maritimes area as apparent potential targets.

French National Liberation Front (*Front de Libération Nationale Française,* FLNF)

This anti-semitic organization became active during 1980 within the context of a sharp intensification of anti-Jewish attacks in Paris and elsewhere.

Honour of the Police (*Honneur de la Police*)

This group, purporting to vindicate the honour of the French police services, claimed responsibility for an attack on the car of a trade union official in 1979; it was also linked with the murder in Paris on Sept. 20, 1979, of Pierre Goldman, a Jewish left-wing extremist who had previously served six years in prison for violent offences.

In the latter part of 1980 and early 1981, allegations were made by the two main French police trade unions and other organizations that the memberships of various extreme right-wing movements included a substantial number of serving police officers. Although such allegations were discounted by the Interior Ministry, left-wing and other groups continued to insist that the existence of right-wing sympathies in the upper echelons of the police forces had effectively sabotaged official investigations into anti-Jewish actions and other attacks attributed to the extreme right.

In August 1981 the Interior Minister, Gaston Defferre, received a death threat signed by Honour of the Police, which apparently regarded the security policy of the new Government as insufficiently vigorous.

The Mongoose (*La Mangouste*)

This hitherto unknown group claimed responsibility for three bomb explosions at left-wing premises in Toulouse in early May 1981, namely the printers of the anarchist review *Basta,* the studio of Radio Barberouge and the local headquarters of the Revolutionary Communist League.

National Socialist Movement (*Mouvement National Socialiste*)

This Movement was one of several extreme right-wing groupings which made their existence known in the context of a sharp intensification of anti-Jewish attacks from early 1980.

National Youth Front (*Front National de la Jeunesse,* FNJ)

This Front maintained that a commando of its members had been responsible for a bomb explosion on the Paris-Moscow express train on April 26, 1980.

New Nazi Front (*Nouvelle Front Nazi,* NFN)

The NFN is believed to be one of the successor groups of the Federation of National and European Action (FANE) created after the banning of the latter in September 1980 (see separate entry). The NFN symbol, together with that of FANE, was found on some of about 70 Jewish tombstones desecrated in a Paris cemetery during the night of April 24-25, 1981. Slogans daubed on the tombstones included "Death to Israel" and "Nuremberg—revenge soon".

Odessa

The clandestine Odessa movement is believed to have originated as an offshoot of the Secret Army Organization (OAS) during the latter's violent campaign to preserve the French status of Algeria. Since Algeria's achievement of independence in 1962 the Odessa network is thought to have continued as a focus of contact between former OAS activists and other right-wing elements.

Order and New Justice (*Ordre et Justice Nouvelle*)

This group claimed responsibility for a bomb attack on a left-wing printing works in Marseilles on Aug. 11, 1980, when 17 persons were injured.

Organization for the Liberation of France (*Organisation pour la Libération de la France*)

This previously unknown group claimed responsibility for a bomb attack on a new mosque in the south-eastern town of Romans-sur-Isère on May 3, 1982.

Peiper Vengeance Group

This clandestine group, named after a former German SS officer, has claimed responsibility for numerous bombings and other assaults on Jewish and Moslem premises in France.

Research and Study Group for European Civilization (*Groupement de Recherche et d'Etudes pour la Civilisation Européenne,* GRECE)

Leadership. Alain de Benoist.

GRECE is the principal intellectual forum of the "New Right" in France, inspired by the ideas developed in the late 1970s by Alain de Benoist, a former student revolutionary of the 1968 generation who subsequently gravitated to the other end of the political spectrum. Concepts propagated by GRECE include anti-Marxism, the rejection of egalitarianism on the grounds that it "ruins what is best in the human race", the importance of hereditary as opposed to environmental factors, the superiority of the Indo-European heritage over Soviet communism or US materialism and its contamination by the "decadent" Judaeo-Christian tradition.

As editor of the GRECE journal *Nouvelle Ecole,* Benoist had claimed to be opposed to totalitarianism and to the violence perpetrated by some extreme right-wing groups; while conceding that his theories of the superiority of European civilization and of the need for a political elite bear similarities with the ideology of the German Nazis, he nevertheless maintains that such ideas were abused and distorted by Hitler. The research sub-group of GRECE, known by the acronym GENE, has in a recent publication asserted that "systematic hybridization can be a privileged route to genocide".

A number of French commentators have drawn attention to links between the GRECE leadership and the *Club de l'Horloge,* founded in 1974 by elite civil servants (although most of this club's members belong to orthodox political parties).

Revolutionary French Brigades (*Brigades Révolutionnaires Françaises,* BRF)

The previously unknown BRF claimed responsibility for the kidnapping of Jean-Edern Hallier, a left-wing literary journalist, in Paris on April 25, 1982. A message from the group stated that Hallier had been abducted "because of his connivance with the Socialist-Communist Government" and continued: "The French people will not submit to the terrorism directed by the Kremlin and carried out by its satellites. We will respond to terror with terror." Conditions for Hallier's release were listed as the dismissal of Communist ministers from the Government, cancellation of natural gas contracts with the Soviet Union, the allocation of national aid to the "resistance of the Afghan people" and the resignation of Gaston Defferre ("a corrupted and incapable politician") as Interior Minister. None of these demands were taken seriously by the Government and Hallier reappeared on May 4.

Subsequently the BRF claimed responsibility for a bomb attack on the Paris flat of Régis Debray, the left-wing writer and former revolutionary who had become a special adviser to President Mitterrand after the latter's election in May 1981 and who was accused by the BRF of being a "collaborator with the Communist International". In a message sent to the Interior and Justice Ministers on July 28, 1982, the BRF issued "a second and final warning" that it would not hesitate "to strike hard" at those whom it deemed responsible for left-wing subversion. Notwithstanding these threats, however, nothing further was heard of the BRF over the following 12 months.

Revolutionary Nationalist Movement (*Mouvement Nationaliste Révolutionnaire,* MNR)

Leadership. Jean-Gilles Malliarkis (l.).

This group claimed responsibility for a bomb explosion caused in Paris (as a protest against "foreign invasion" of the capital) on Oct. 5, 1980, when a Dutch woman tourist was injured. The explosion took place two days after the attack on the Rue Copernic synagogue attributed to the European Nationalist Alliances (see separate entry).

Secret Army Organization (*Organisation de l'Armée Secrète,* OAS)—see under Delta and Odessa

Extreme Left-wing Movements

Action Autonomy—see under Autonomous Movement

Armed Cells for Popular Autonomy (*Noyaux Armés pour l'Autonomie Populaire,* NAPAP)—see under Direct Action

Autonomous Fighters against Capitalism—see under Autonomous Movement

Autonomous Group for Radical Action against Capital—see under Autonomous Movement

Autonomous January 22 Group—see under Autonomous Movement

Autonomous Militant Front (*Front Militant Autonome,* MAF)—see under Autonomous Movement

Autonomous Movement

The so-called Autonomous Movement, comprising a number of separate cells of young extremists influenced by anarchist ideas, came to prominence in early 1979 when a group calling itself the "Autonomous Group for Radical Action against Capital" claimed responsibility for a series of attacks on fashionable shops in Paris and other cities; particular targets of this latter Group were parking meters, many hundreds of which were destroyed in the Paris area alone in the early months of 1979.

In other incidents in this period, (i) members of the "Autonomous January 22 Group" on Jan. 31, 1979, forcibly invaded and ransacked the Paris flat of a public prosecutor in revenge for the passing of prison sentences (on Jan. 22) on four young autonomists; (ii) a bomb attack on the Finance Ministry in Paris on Feb. 27, 1979, was claimed by the "Autonomous Fighters against Capitalism"; and (iii) the "Collective of Autonomous Groupings" claimed responsibility for eight bomb explosions at bank premises in the

411

Paris area during the night of April 10-11, 1979.

Small groups of autonomists also took part in industrial disturbances in early 1979, including clashes between police and workers in the northern steel town of Denain in March as well as May Day incidents in various localities, notably in the eastern steel town of Longwy. In the aftermath of May 1, 1979, the "Revolutionary Co-ordination Group" claimed responsibility for a series of bomb explosions in Paris and Toulouse, while during May Day demonstrations in 1980 autonomist elements were prominent in serious clashes in Paris and elsewhere between the police on the one hand and students and young workers on the other. Further serious violence occurred in Paris on May 14, 1980, when thousands of young leftists demonstrated against alleged police brutality in connexion with the death the previous day of a youth who had fallen through a roof while fleeing from the police.

Meanwhile, (i) a previously unknown group calling itself the "Autonomous Revolutionary Brigades" had claimed responsibility for the fatal shooting of Joseph Fontanet (a former centrist cabinet minister under Presidents De Gaulle and Pompidou) in Paris on Feb. 1, 1980; and (ii) an apparently separate cell known as "Autonomous Revolutionary Action" had admitted responsibility for a bomb attack on a Paris electricity office on March 19, 1980.

Subsequent arrests of suspected activists of the Autonomous Movement included those of (i) Philippe Gobain, who was charged on May 15, 1981, with participation in a Paris hold-up the previous month in which a policeman had been shot dead; and (ii) Oreste Scalzone, an Italian national who was arrested in Paris on Aug. 29, 1982, on suspicion of having sought to establish links between French autonomists and extremist left-wing Italian movements such as the Red Brigades.

Cells of autonomists continued to be active in 1982, notably in Toulouse, where police made a number of arrests of suspected activists on Dec. 14 and where a bomb explosion at the state broadcasting station on Dec. 23 was claimed by the hitherto unknown "Action Autonomy" grouping. Autonomist activities also spread beyond the borders of France itself and included a bomb attack on the French consulate in Amsterdam on Feb. 10, 1983, for which a group calling itself the "Autonomous Militant Front" (*Front Militant Autonome,* MAF) claimed responsibility on the grounds (according to a telephoned message) that "the so-called left-wing Government in France is itself also participating in the arms race".

Autonomous Revolutionary Action—see under Autonomous Movement

Autonomous Revolutionary Brigades—see under Autonomous Movement

Bakunin-Gdansk-Paris-Guatemala-Salvador Group (*Groupe Bakounine-Gdansk-Paris-Guatemala-Salvador,* GBGPGS)

This grouping of militant anarchist activists emerged in the early 1980s when it claimed responsibility for a series of attacks on US-owned multinational companies in France and also on the premises of firms trading with Eastern Europe and Latin America. The title assumed by the movement is believed to indicate the broad international concerns of its members.

The GBGPGS has also mounted attacks on East European trading organizations with offices in Paris, notably those of Poland and the Soviet Union, as well as on South African business premises in the French capital. The Group has expressed particular opposition to the policy of the Socialist-led Government which came to power in mid-1981 of maintaining trading links with South Africa and of continuing to sell armaments to "repressive" third-world regimes.

Committee to Liquidate or Neutralize Computers (*Comité liquidant ou détournant les Ordinateurs,* CLODO)

This grouping of anarchist activists caused damage to the property of the British firm International Computers in Toulouse in May 1980 and was also responsible for other attacks on computer installations, which it regarded as posing a threat to personal liberty and to jobs. Believed in some quarters to be an offshoot of the Direct Action movement (see separate entry), CLODO re-emerged in early 1983 when it claimed responsibility for three bomb explosions at a government computer centre in Toulouse on Jan. 28, 1983.

Direct Action (*Action Directe,* AD)

Leadership. Jean-Marc Rouillan.

AD emerged in 1979 as a new revolutionary movement embracing elements of the anarchist *Groupe d'Action Révolutionnaire Internationaliste* (GARI) and a Maoist formation known as the *Noyaux Armés pour l'Autonomité Populaire* (NAPAP). In the course of 1980 it claimed responsibility for a series of attacks on government buildings and other targets, including a machine-gun assault on the Ministry of Co-operation in Paris on March 18, 1980. After this incident the French security authorities on March 27-28, 1980, carried out a major anti-terrorist sweep in the capital, seizing quantities of arms and explosives and arresting about 30 suspected AD activists, of whom 19 were later charged with various offences. The Paris raids were co-ordinated with similar police operations in

Toulon and Nice in southern France, in which four Italians suspected of being members of the Red Brigades were arrested.

In addition to having contacts with the Italian Red Brigades, AD was also believed to have established a relationship with the militant leftist wing of the Basque separatist movement ETA as well as with militant Palestinian or pro-Palestinian groups operating in France. From late 1980 AD activists were thought to include a substantial contingent of Turkish political refugees who had left their own country following the military takeover of September 1980.

Although the police believed that the AD network had been largely dismantled by the March 1980 operations, the movement subsequently claimed responsibility for a bomb explosion and two rocket attacks on the Transport Ministry in Paris on April 15, 1980; moreover, a series of acts of sabotage on computer equipment in Toulouse in early April 1980 was also attributed to AD or to an apparently connected "Committee to Liquidate or Neutralize Computers" (CLODO—see separate entry).

On Sept. 13, 1980, the presumed leader of AD, Jean-Marc Rouillan, was arrested in Paris together with his female companion Nathalie Ménignon. A few days later, on Sept. 19, AD claimed responsibility for a machine-gun attack on the Military School in Paris, following which the police on Sept. 23 raided a farmhouse in Ardèche (southern France), arrested three people thought to be connected with AD and seized a substantial quantity of explosives. At this stage the French authorities were again convinced that AD had been effectively neutralized.

In May 1981, however, the AD activists then in custody, including Rouillan, benefited from a general amnesty for political prisoners declared by the incoming President Mitterrand, and by the end of the year the movement was again claiming responsibility for bomb attacks on "capitalist" targets in Paris. In early 1982, moreover, AD elaborated its theoretical stance, notably in two documents entitled *Pour un Projet Communiste* and *Sur l'Impérialisme Américain* published in March and April 1982 respectively. At the same time members of the movement followed the anarchist tradition of robbing banks—termed "expropriations"—to finance the organizations's activities.

Renewed arrests of suspected AD members and seizures of arms from AD hideouts in April and May 1982 were accompanied by further bomb attacks in Paris and elsewhere for which the movement claimed responsibility. Several were perpetrated against US targets, while from early August 1982 the movement carried out several attacks on "Zionist" (i.e. Jewish) persons and property. This latter change of emphasis was thought to reflect the existence of links between AD and an extremist group calling itself the Lebanese Armed Revolutionary Factions, which had earlier claimed responsibility for the killings of a US diplomat in January 1982 and of an Israeli diplomat in April 1982—both in Paris.

On Aug. 18, 1982, the French Government announced the formal banning of AD, adherence to which in itself thereby became a criminal offence. This announcement followed the publication in the left-wing newspaper *Libération* of a claim by Jean-Marc Rouillan that AD had been responsible in recent weeks for three attacks on "Zionist targets". Two days before the banning decision the French police had arrested the presumed press spokesman for AD, Helyette Besse. On the day after the banning a bomb attack on the Paris offices of the right-wing journal *Minute* was claimed as the work of AD.

Further arrests of suspected AD activists took place in the latter months of 1982, including those of Michel Camilleri (said to be leader of a hard-line faction within the movement) on Sept. 17 and of Frédéric Oriach (a former NAPAP leader) on Oct. 12. Following the arrest of the latter the French authorities claimed to have firm evidence of links between AD and militant anti-Zionist/pro-Palestinian organizations with a presence in France. Bomb attacks attributed to AD continued to occur in late 1982 and early 1983, by which time AD was thought to have split into several separate factions, each with its own distinct theoretical position.

Enraged Peasants' Movement *(Mouvement des Paysans en Colère)*

Members of this rural Movement bombed an hotel in Bouches-du-Rhône (southern France) on July 12, 1980.

Group of International Revolutionary Action *(Groupe d'Action Révolutionnaire Internationaliste,* GARI)—see under Direct Action

Red Poster *(L'Affiche Rouge)*

This extremist grouping made its existence known when it claimed responsibility for a number of attacks on "capitalist" and other targets in the Lyons area in mid-1982. In a published tract the group identified its targets as "the bastions of colonialism" and warned that further attacks would be directed "against capital and all its patrons".

Regional Movements

ALSACE

Although the long historical chapter of Franco-German rivalry for control of Alsace was finally closed in 1945, the majority ethnic

German population of the region has continued to evince some support for autonomist demands, as propagated by cultural groups and individuals constituting a loose Alsatian autonomist movement. There is, however, no serious challenge to the status of Alsace as an integral part of France, successive governments of which have sought to cater for legitimate regional aspirations within the context of various measures to decentralize powers to all the French regions.

Black Wolves Alsatian Combat Group
(Elsässische Kampfgruppe Schwarze Wölfe)

This small cell of right-wing militant autonomists claimed responsibility for three bomb attacks in 1981, two of them on a Cross of Lorraine monument at Thann commemorating Alsatian resistance to the German Nazis during World War II. The Group announced its intention to combat "French colonialism" and to prevent the subjugation of "our maternal language and our culture".

Of 13 suspected activists detained in October 1981 (including three of German nationality), six were subsequently brought to trial in Mulhouse; five of these—three men and two women—were on July 2, 1982, sentenced to prison terms of from seven months to three years after admitting their involvement in the 1981 bomb attacks. The court refused to recognize that the defendants had any political motivation.

BASQUE REGION

In that the separatist organization called Basque Nation and Liberty (*Euzkadi ta Azkatasuna,* ETA) seeks the establishment of an independent Basque state comprising Basque-populated areas on both the Spanish and the French sides of the Pyrenees, its aspirations pose an implicit threat to the territorial integrity of France. Both the ETA and the associated Enbata Movement have been banned by the French Government—in October 1972 and January 1974 respectively—and their subsequent clandestine activities in French territory have been directed at giving support to Basque activists operating in Spain. (For details of the ETA and other Basque movements within Spain, see pages 469-76.)

Enbata Movement

The Enbata Movement and publication of the same title were founded in April 1963, the name being taken from a storm-bearing sea-wind prevalent in the Basque region. Closely linked to the ETA, Enbata presented candidates in the 1967 and 1968 French general elections, but with no success; thereafter it concentrated on journalistic and propaganda activities and also on providing support and shelter for ETA activists from Spain.

As a result of the assassination of the Spanish Prime Minister by Basque guerrillas in December 1973, the French authorities increased their surveillance of Basque activists operating in France, and on Jan. 30, 1974, the Government announced the official banning of Enbata. In its statement justifying the banning decision the Government asserted that Enbata "supports the use of violence" and that its declarations "give the appearance of a joint association with the commandos operating in Spanish territory".

BRITTANY

Separatist or autonomist sentiments are said by their present-day proponents to have existed in Brittany since the then duchy was incorporated into France in 1532. Societies dedicated to the rediscovery of the popular Celtic culture of Brittany appeared in the 19th century, paving the way for the foundation of *Breiz Atao* ("Brittany Always") in 1919 as the first Breton movement with clear political objectives. Collaboration between *Breiz Atao* and the German Nazis during World War II cast the Breton separatist movement into disrepute in the post-war period, but a new generation of left-wing Breton activists emerged in the 1960s committed to achieving autonomy for Brittany through the agency of a socialist transformation of France as a whole. Two main representative movements were established in this period, namely (i) the Breton Democratic Union (UDB), formed in 1964 as an orthodox political party seeking "a socialist Brittany as the only way of securing self-determination for the Breton people"; and (ii) the Liberation Front of Brittany (FLB), launched in 1965 to resist "French domination" by force and to wage an armed struggle for the eventual "liberation" of Brittany. Nevertheless, the vast majority of Breton voters have continued to give their support to the various national parties, their preferences normally reflecting nation-wide trends.

The FLB carried out its first bomb attack (on a government tax collecting office in Lorient) on Nov. 24, 1967, and thereafter regularly claimed responsibility for explosions at police stations, military camps, radio transmitters and similar "official" targets. By the early 1970s the Front was split into two main factions, both of which were eventually banned by the Government on Jan. 30, 1974. In its statement justifying the banning decision the Government maintained that the FLB "has been inspired from abroad by a person of French origin who has acquired Irish nationality, Yann Goulet" and who had at the same time "maintained relations" with the Irish Republican Army (IRA). (Yann Goulet had led the *Breiz Atao* movement during World War II and had been sentenced to death in 1944 for alleged collaboration with the Germans; having consistently denied such allegations he was permitted to leave France to take up residence in Dublin, where he became an Irish citizen and established the Committee for Free Brittany, which subsequently claimed to exercise a co-ordinating role over militant elements in Brittany.)

Before and after the January 1974 banning of the two FLB wings arrests and trials took place of many Breton activists accused of participation in violent actions; by the end of the decade the French authorities believed that the violent wing of the Breton movement had been effectively dismantled or neutralized. On the political front the advent of a left-wing Government in Paris in mid-1981 was welcomed by the UDB in view of its commitment to major decentralization measures for the French regions. However, these measures are regarded in some Breton quarters as coming insufficiently close to the objective of full autonomy, an aspiration which continues to be espoused by a number of active groups.

The designation commonly used for the totality of parties and movements seeking to further the Breton cause is EMSAV. A major recent focus of Breton activity has been opposition to the proposed construction of a nuclear power station at Plogoff, on the south-western tip of the Brittany peninsula.

Breton Insubordination Movement (*Mouvement d'Insoumission Bretonne,* MIB)—see under Breton Republican Party

Breton Republican Party *(Strolled Pobl Breiz)*

Leadership. Jean-Pierre Le Mat (pres.).

Established in 1980, this small formation propagates the idea of eventual independence for Brittany, on the model of Ireland's achievement of independence after centuries of British rule. The party is closely identified with the Breton Insubordination Movement (MIB), which encourages Breton conscripts to refuse the discipline of the French armed forces. After three members of the party had been apprehended in April 1982 while in possession of "first category" arms, Jean-Pierre Le Mat (the movement's president) was himself briefly detained on suspicion of involvement.

Liberation Front of Brittany—Breton Republican Army *(Front de Libération de Bretagne—Armée Républicaine Bretonne,* FLB-ARB)

The FLB-ARB evolved out of the original Liberation Front of Brittany (established in 1965), of which it became the main faction by the early 1970s. Together with the other main faction, the Liberation Front of Brittany for National Liberation and Socialism (see separate entry), it was banned by the Government on Jan. 30, 1974. A government statement said that after numerous arrests of Breton activists in the late 1960s and early 1970s, the relevant authorities had tried to show clemency by offering amnesties and passing light sentences; but this approach had proved of no avail: "Since then the FLB-ARB has reconstituted new groups which have undertaken violent actions. In 1973 eight attacks were perpetrated and since Jan. 1, 1974, three others have been carried out."

The FLB-ARB remained active after the banning decision, being responsible in particular for demonstrations and also for further bomb attacks. The latter included (i) the blowing up a television mast at Roc-Tredudon on Feb. 14-15, 1974 (when the FLB-ARB called for the recognition of the right of Bretons to be informed in their own language); (ii) an explosion at a radio transmitter near Saint-Mayeux on Feb. 14, 1974; and (iii) attacks on a gendarmerie post in Brest on June 26, 1974, on a naval garage in Brest on Jan. 3, 1975, on a Fokker-27 aircraft at the Quimper-Plugufflan airport on Aug. 6 and on a nuclear power station at Brennilis (Finistère-Nord) on Aug. 14-15, 1975.

By July 1978, however, the police claimed that almost all known FLB-ARB members were in custody or awaiting trial. Those tried by the State Security Court included 13 sentenced on July 23, 1978, to imprisonment for up to eight years for 13 bombing attacks carried out between March 1975 and October 1977; two sentenced on Nov. 23, 1978, to 15 years in prison each for placing a bomb which severely damaged the Palace of Versailles (near Paris) on June 26, 1978; and 18, among them the above two, who were on Oct. 20, 1979, given prison sentences of up to 15 years for bomb attacks carried out in 1974-78 against public buildings and installations.

Other trials of Breton separatists, most of them members of the FLB-ARB, were held in 1980 and ended (i) on June 11, when eight defendants (three of them in absentia) were given prison sentences of up to 12 years for blowing up the villa of a regional police commissioner in Paimpol on May 30, 1979; (ii) on Oct. 20, when six accused (one of them already convicted on June 11) were given sentences of up to eight years for bomb attacks on a police building in Saint-Brieux in May 1979; and (iii) on Dec. 15, when nine defendants (including the one already sentenced on both June 11 and Oct. 20) were given sentences of up to 13 years for bomb attacks on official buildings in 1978-79.

Most of the Breton militants still serving prison sentences were released under an amnesty granted by the incoming President Mitterrand in May 1981; thereafter there was some evidence that former FLB-ARB activists were regrouping within differently-named movements, but the incidence of violent attacks remained minimal as compared with the level of a decade previously. It was reported by a left-wing Paris newspaper in September 1981 that in the early 1970s the FLB-ARB and other Breton movements had been infiltrated by agents of the DST security service, who had acted as *agents-provocateurs* for many of the bomb attacks of that period.

The FLB-ARB has maintained contacts with the Irish Republican Army and the Basque separatist movement, as well as the Corsican and Occitanian autonomist organizations. It has also participated in conferences of representatives of "oppressed" European ethnic groups and supported calls for the dismantling of the centralized state systems of countries such as France and Spain.

Liberation Front of Brittany for National Liberation and Socialism (*Front de Libération de la Bretagne pour la Libération Nationale et le Socialisme,* FLB-LNS)

In March 1973 longstanding ideological differences within the Liberation Front of Brittany—Breton Republican Army (FLB-ARB—see separate entry) led to the splitting away of a left-wing faction known as the FLB-LNS, which described itself as "a socialist revolutionary Breton organization of national liberation". After it had claimed responsibility for bomb attacks in mid-January 1974, the FLB-LNS was banned by the French Government on Jan. 30, 1974, together with the FLB-ARB.

The FLB-LNS continued its operations after the ban, declaring in March 1974 that it would carry on "blow by blow" its activities against the "bourgeois French Government and the French imperialist state" which were continuing their "exploitation of the oppressed Breton people". Nevertheless, most known FLB-LNS activists had been brought to trial by the late 1970s, leaving the French authorities confident that the organization had effectively ceased to exist.

Like the FLB-ARB, the FLB-LNS sought to maintain contact with other like-minded groups in Europe, notably the Spanish Basque separatist movement. Following the assassination of the Spanish Prime Minister by Basque activists in December 1973, a joint communiqué was issued by the FLB-LNS and the Basque ETA on Dec. 26 asserting that "in claiming the right to social, political and cultural liberation the Basque and Breton peoples are simply insisting on their legitimate rights, which have been denied by the capitalist system".

National Liberation Front of Brittany (*Front National de Libération de Bretagne,* FNLB)

In announcing its formation in January 1982, the FNLB declared itself to be a movement for "Bretons above all" without any political affiliation (in contrast to the leftist stance of the other autonomist formations). It called upon the Government to grant a special statute for Brittany rather than more decentralized powers within the existing regional system, and also demanded that certain other urgent measures should be taken, notably the recognition of the Breton language and the reversion of the Loire-Atlantique department to Brittany (this department being currently part of the Pays de la Loire region). The FNLB stated that it did not advocate "violence for its own sake" but warned that it would take violent action if its demands were not met.

Yann Kel Kernaleguen Group

This Group made its existence known when it claimed responsibility for an unsuccessful attempt to place a mortar shell on a railway line at Ingrandes station on Aug. 7, 1982. It takes it name from that of a young Breton activist who was killed in September 1976 when a bomb exploded while still in his possession. In a communiqué issued on Aug. 23, 1982, the Group gave the following warning: "New forms of clandestine Breton action could emerge in Brittany and France if the Socialist Government does not progress rapidly. Jacobin France has many debts to pay to Brittany before there can be reconciliation. . . ."

CORSICA

Over recent years Corsica's internal stability has been seriously threatened by a campaign of violence waged against "French colonial" targets by separatist elements mainly grouped within the Corsican National Liberation Front (FLNC). These elements seek independence for the island (possibly in association with France) and the rehabilitation of the Corsican language and culture, which they regard as having been steadily eroded since the island was purchased for the French crown from Genoa in 1769. Such aspirations have, however, found little support among the 240,000 inhabitants of the island, the political representation of which remains largely in the hands of Corsican sections of the mainland parties favouring the maintenance of Corsica's status as an integral part of France.

The main legal nationalist party is the Union of the Corsican People (UPC) led by Dr Edmond Siméoni, which advocates autonomy for the island within the French Republic. In 1975-76 leaders of the UPC's predecessor, the Association of Corsican Patriots (APC), were involved in a number of violent actions; but since the APC was reconstituted as the UPC in July 1977 the party has repeatedly condemned the use of violence in pursuit of Corsican aims. In contrast, the smaller *Con-*

sulta di i Cumitati Nationalisti (CCN), formed in 1980 as a legal pro-independence movement, has consistently refused to condemn the use of violence, although it stresses that it is committed to "means and objectives significantly different from those of the FLNC".

As part of its major decentralization plan for the whole of France, the left-wing Government which came to power in Paris in mid-1981 enacted legislation in January 1982 elevating Corsica from regional status to that of a "territorial collectivity" *(collectivité territoriale),* with a directly-elected Assembly and significantly increased administrative and economic powers. In the first elections to the new 61-seat Assembly held on Aug. 8, 1982, Corsican offshoots of the left-wing metropolitan parties returned 23 members (including 12 Left Radicals), while the right-wing formations secured 29 seats. The balance of power thus went to the UPC with seven seats (and 10.6 per cent of the popular vote) and the small nationalist *Partitu Populare Corsu* (PPC) with one seat—the remaining elected member being an independent. Divisions within the right subsequently enabled Prosper Alfonis (Left Radical president of the outgoing regional council) to secure election on Aug. 20 to the presidency of the new Assembly and to form a left-wing administration.

Whereas the UPC declared its intention to participate in Corsica's new political structure as a stage towards its goal of eventual autonomy, both the FLNC and the CCN called for a boycott of the elections (in which the actual abstention rate was 31.5 per cent). Shortly after the elections the FLNC officially declared the truce which it had observed in principle since April 1981 (but which had effectively broken down early in 1982) to be at an end, following which there occurred a sharp escalation of bomb attacks and other violent incidents. In the face of a deteriorating situation the Government announced the banning of the FLNC on Jan. 5, 1983, and took steps to strengthen security arrangements for the island.

The extensive use of political violence by Corsican nationalist elements has led to the emergence of extremist pro-French movements which have themselves been prepared to resort to violent methods. Other significant features of the Corsican situation include (i) widespread hostility among the native Corsican population of all persuasions to the presence on the island of French "settlers", including some 17,000 *"pieds-noirs"* from the former French territories of North Africa; and (ii) periodic tensions, often leading to violent incidents, between the local population and immigrant Arab workers. In the latter context, the FLNC has consistently condemned attacks on Arab workers.

Corsican Guerrillas and Partisans (*Francs-Tireurs et Partisans Corses,* FTPC)

The FTPC was reported to have been founded in March 1981 by former members of a National Front of Corsica (an early precursor of the Corsican National Liberation Front—see separate entry) to carry on the tradition of Pasquali Paoli (1725-1807), the founder of Corsican nationalism and the head of a Corsican Republic in 1755-69. The FTPC was held responsible for several acts of violence in mainland France, including a fire at a Total oil depot in Châteauroux on March 14, 1981. However, it denied any responsibility for a bomb explosion at Ajaccio airport on April 16, 1981 (shortly after the arrival of President Giscard d'Estaing on an election campaign visit), and it affirmed that its military objective would "always be to attack targets associated with the economy, the French state, the force of repression and the despoilers of the Corsican people".

Corsican National Liberation Front (*Front de Libération Nationale de la Corse,* FLNC)

Leadership. Yves Stella ("political commissar").

The FLNC was formed in May 1976 by former members of an earlier *Front Paysan Corse de Libération* (FPLC) and the *Ghjustizia Paolina* movement (see separate entry). The FPLC had been responsible for a series of bomb attacks between September 1973 and January 1974, at the end of which month it was officially banned by the French Government; it nevertheless continued its violent activities until being subsumed by the broader FLNC.

The FLNC's programme issued in May 1976 listed as its aims the "recognition of Corsica's national rights, the destruction of all instruments of French colonialism, the setting-up of a people's democracy, the confiscation of all large colonial properties and tourist trusts, the implementation of land reform and the right to self-determination." At a secret press conference on May 5, 1977, the FLNC members present described their movement as being both military and political; claimed that tourism was "ravaging" Corsica; denounced as "treason" the reformist policy of the legal autonomist Association of Corsican Patriots—which was in July 1977 reconstituted as the Union of the Corsican People (UPC); blamed France for having "erased our history in order to impose its own"; and declared their determination to continue military actions, carrying their struggle into French territory. At a further press conference held on Aug. 15-16, 1977, the FLNC declared that it would fight to "disorganize the police apparatus in order to bring about conditions for political negotiations". The FLNC has propagated its views in a clandestine tabloid entitled *U Ribellu* ("The Rebel"), first produced in December 1977.

On May 5, 1976, the FLNC announced that it was responsible for causing 16 explosions in Corsica during the previous night, and also for attacks on the Palace of Justice in Marseilles and an electric relay station in Nice (damage being estimated at the equivalent of more than $1,000,000). It carried out further attacks on the house of a divisional army commander in Corsica (on July 23-24); on the car of a Secretary of State at the Ministry of Agriculture (on Aug. 14); on an Air France Boeing 707 at Ajaccio airport (on Sept. 7); and on the home of the Foreign Legion commander and an ammunition dump—in support of a call for the withdrawal of the Legion from Corsica (on Sept. 26).

During 1977 the FLNC was said to have carried out 63 attacks against property of "colonialists" (i.e. non-Corsican settlers, mainly from Algeria); it was also responsible for explosions at government offices, a railway station, police stations, a tourist camp and a television relay transmitter near Bastia (on Aug. 13, 1977); and on Jan. 14, 1978, it partly destroyed a French Air Force radar station.

In 1979 it was held responsible for 287 bomb explosions, 32 of them in Paris and Corsica on March 9-10, one at the French Foreign Minister's villa in Corsica on March 18, another at the Palace of Justice in Paris on April 25 and a further 30 explosions in Corsica on May 6-7, and also for 22 bombs placed in Paris on May 30-31. Other bombs were planted by the FLNC in Lyons on Sept. 12-13, 1979, and military fuel tanks were blown up north of Paris on Oct. 25, 1979.

In 1980 there were 378 bomb explosions caused by the FLNC in Corsica. It also claimed responsibility for an attack on security forces guarding the Iranian embassy in Paris on May 14, 1980, when four gendarmes were injured. On April 2, 1981, the FLNC announced that it would halt its bombing campaign until after the presidential elections were completed by May 10 (while it called on Corsicans to abstain from voting in these elections).

Meanwhile, a number of FLNC members had been tried by the State Security Court in Paris. On July 11, 1979, the court sentenced 17 members to imprisonment for from five to 13 years for 36 bomb attacks on public buildings in Corsica and Paris in the previous two years; seven of them were in addition sentenced to concurrent prison terms of from five to 10 years for treason committed on March 25-26, 1977, by blowing up a military communications station in Corsica.

Yves Stella, reported to be the FLNC's "political commissar", who had been arrested in June 1978, was on Sept. 29, 1980, given a 15-year sentence for participating in bombings in 1977-78; he was said to have continued to direct FLNC bombing operations from prison for several months after his arrest. On July 9, 1980, another FLNC member was given a 13-year sentence, and two others were sentenced to five years each (with 2½ years suspended) for travelling to Lebanon in March 1978 to obtain arms and training from Palestinian guerrillas.

The FLNC maintained its truce after the election of a left-wing Government in Paris in mid-1981; a number of imprisoned Corsican activists were released under a political amnesty granted by President Mitterrand; and the new Socialist Interior Minister, Gaston Defferre, stated his willingness to enter into a dialogue with the Front and other Corsican nationalist groups with reference to the detailed application in Corsica of the Government's decentralization plans for the French regions. However, although the new political structure for Corsica (which as eventually enacted in January 1982 provided inter alia for the island to became a "territorial collectivity" with a directly-elected Assembly) was given a qualified welcome by the UPC, it was rejected by the FLNC on the grounds that it maintained the island's "colonial" status in all essentials.

Dissension appeared within the FLNC's ranks when on Sept. 19, 1981, militant members publicly denounced the truce being observed by the Front as a "strategic error"; this development was accompanied by a recurrence of bomb attacks in Corsica for which FLNC dissidents claimed responsibility. Following the enactment of the new Corsican political structure in January 1982, the FLNC demonstrated its opposition by carrying out a "blue night" of violence of Feb. 11-12, during which a Foreign Legionnaire was killed and two injured in an attack on a military camp in Corsica, while some 25 bomb explosions caused severe damage to various official buildings as well as to secondary homes.

In claiming responsibility for the new spate of attacks (which continued over the next few days and included some 20 bombings in Paris on Feb. 16), the FLNC said that they were intended as a warning to the French Government that its new measures for Corsica were insufficient. In a communiqué issued on Feb. 12 the Front said inter alia: "Concrete political acts wiping out the symbols of colonialism should have been announced, with their implementation well under way. There has been nothing of the sort. The Front could wait no longer. The new Government must rapidly acknowledge the rights of the Corsican people." The communiqué repeated the FLNC's demands for the immediate withdrawal of the Foreign Legion from Corsica, the departure of all French "settlers", the rehabilitation of the Corsican language and culture, and the dismantling of the "clan" system permeating the public life of the island.

Although the FLNC maintained at this stage that the truce remained technically in effect, the February 1982 violence marked its effective end in Corsica (although there was a further lull in attacks on the mainland). Arrests of supected FLNC activists over the following months were accompanied by a steady escalation of violent incidents, culminating in a major FLNC offensive before and after the August 1982 elections to the new Corsican Assembly in support of the Front's call for a boycott. After 100 bomb explosions marking the election of the Assembly's president on Aug. 20, the FLNC announced at a clandestine press conference during the night of Aug. 24-25 the official "resumption of the armed struggle", which would involve attacks on "continental interests" to bring about "decolonization" and to demonstrate that "the Corsican people and the French colony can no longer cohabit". At the same time, however, the Front declared its intention to maintain the truce on the mainland.

Thereafter the security situation in Corsica rapidly deteriorated, to the extent that by the end of 1982 official statistics gave the number of bomb attacks and other violent incidents for that year at over 800, approaching double the level during 1981; of the 1982 incidents, nearly 50 per cent had been officially claimed by the FLNC. At the end of December 1982 the Front officially confirmed that it was seeking to exact a "revolutionary levy" from residents of mainland origin—several of whom were the subject of attacks after refusing to pay the levy. In the light of this latter development in particular, the French Government on Jan. 5, 1983, announced the official banning of the FLNC (which at that time was officially thought to have only about 30 activists and about 200 supporters).

As well as banning the FLNC the French Government also reinforced the security forces in Corsica and appointed a new police chief with special powers to combat terrorism; the Front responded with further bombings, but by the end of March 1983 the arrest of more than 100 suspected extremists had contributed to a significant reduction in the level of violent incidents attributed to the FLNC. During this period the French authorities were believed to have accumulated evidence of links between the FLNC and other extremist groups such as the Irish Republican Army (IRA) and the mainland Direct Action movement, and also with an international terrorist group led by Ilich Ramírez Sánchez ("Carlos Martínez"), the Venezuelan revolutionary held responsible for numerous acts of terrorism in various countries during the 1970s.

On the political level the FLNC appeared to moderate its demands when at the end of January 1983 it declared itself ready to accept an "association" between an independent Corsica and the French Republic; at the same time, however, the Front warned that lack of immediate progress towards Corsican self-rule would force it to end the mainland truce. After the security offensive of the next three months, this threat was carried out at the end of April, when some 15 bomb explosions in Paris and its environs on April 29 were officially claimed by the FLNC. Immediately after the Paris bombings the French police announced on May 1 the arrest of a cell of Corsican extremists operating in the capital and the seizure of quantities of explosives.

Corsican Revolutionary Action (*Action Révolutionnaire Corse*, ARC)

Established in July 1976, this group declared the following month that it intended to "advance the cause of the Corsican people by showing itself wherever there is evidence of the ideology aimed at digging the grave for our race". It claimed responsibility, inter alia, for a bomb explosion at the Palace of Justice in Vannes (Morbihan, Brittany) on Aug. 7, 1976. The ARC's then leader, Max Siméoni (brother of the leader of the Union of the Corsican People), was released under supervision in December 1977 after being convicted by the State Security Court of participating in an attack on the wine-producing establishment of a French settler of North African origin. He was eventually amnestied in September 1981, by which time the ARC appeared to be defunct.

France-Resurrection *(France-Résurrection)*

This grouping made its existence known on Jan. 9, 1983, when it published a warning to Corsican nationalists in the Paris area that it would take reprisals if attacks continued on residents of mainland origin in Corsica. The group's message contained the names and addresses of four alleged members of the Corsican National Liberation Front (FLNC) living in the French capital and asserted that "they will be the first to pay if the continentals living in Corsica are attacked again". The emergence of the group followed a number of attacks in Corsica on residents who had refused to pay a "revolutionary levy" demanded by the FLNC (see separate entry).

Ghjustizia Paolina

This nationalist grouping was one of the component factions of the Corsican National Liberation Front (FLNC) on its formation in 1976. It claimed responsibility in its own right for a bomb attack on Calvi town hall on Feb. 14, 1982—its re-emergence apparently reflecting internal divisions within the FLNC (see separate entry).

New Action Front against Independence and Autonomy (*Front d'Action Nouvelle contre l'Indépendance et l'Autonomie,* Francia)

During 1977 members of Francia carried out six attacks on property of Corsican nationalists regarded as posing a threat to the island's status as an integral part of France. In 1979 the organization was believed to be responsible for a dozen bomb attacks on property of automonist sympathizers in Corsica. On Jan. 6, 1980, threee armed members of Francia were temporarily held hostages by some 30 members of the extreme right wing of the (legal) Union of the Corsican People. This incident was followed by further action by other separatists, in which three persons (including a police officer) were killed on Jan. 11, 1980.

OCCITANIA

Several groups, some of them prepared to use violence, have campaigned for the achievement of autonomy by "Occitania" (the area between the north-eastern Pyrenees and the mouth of the River Rhône, including Languedoc and Provence).

Red Brigade of Occitania (*Brigade Rouge d'Occitanie,* BROC)

This clandestine group claimed in April 1974 that it was responsible for explosions at a military camp at Larzac in August 1973 and at a paratroop camp in Toulouse and again at the Larzac camp in April 1974 (apparently in protest against expropriations of land for extensions to the camp).

"We Shall Blow Everything Up" *(Farem Tot Petar)*

This group was responsible for 15 explosions carried out in 1974-75. At the time it expressed support for the Corsican and other separatist movements, which it regarded as allies in the opposition to the centralized French state.

French Overseas Departments and Territories

During the early 1980s extremist pro-independence movements have become increasingly active in several of the French overseas departments and territories (DOM and TOM), notably in the two Antilles departments of Guadeloupe and Martinique (in the Caribbean), in the department of French Guiana (on the South American mainland) and in the overseas territory of New Caledonia (in the Pacific). Majority political representation remains largely in the hands of local sections of the metropolitan parties which support the maintenance of French status; but the various pro-independence movements appear to be mounting a growing challenge to the longer-established autonomist parties in favour of a gradual loosening of the French connexion.

Economic grievances have figured prominently in the campaigns of both the autonomist and the pro-independence movements in the DOM and TOM. In French Guiana, Guadeloupe and Martinique particular criticism has been directed not only at the·high level of local unemployment but also at the increasing emigration of local workers to metropolitan France. A further source of tension in these three departments is the growing influx of White French "settlers", who tend to dominate the local tourist industries as well as other important economic sectors.

In a move to cater for legitimate political aspirations in the overseas departments, the left-wing Government which came to power in Paris in mid-1981 eventually secured the enactment in December 1982 of major decentralization measures under which French Guiana, Guadeloupe, Martinique and Réunion (in the Indian Ocean) were each endowed with an Assembly to be elected directly on the basis of proportional representation.

Overseas Departments

FRENCH GUIANA

Increasing unrest in this, the largest overseas French possession (although with a population of only about 60,000), has been mainly associated with the activities of the extremist pro-independence movement described below. By mid-1980 the principal vehicle for non-violent pro-independence opinion in French Guiana was the (Marxist) *Unité Guyanaise* led by Albert Lecante, a former member of the department's Socialist Party (PSG) who had been imprisoned in 1974 for illegal political activities. The PSG responded by radicalizing its traditional autonomist stance into a demand for autonomy as a "necessary and preparatory state" towards the establishment of an independent state.

In the first elections to the new departmental Assembly on Feb. 20, 1983, the PSG-led list secured 14 of the 31 seats, a centre-right list 13, an extreme left-wing list of the (independent) *Union des Travailleurs de Guyane* 3 and an independent associated with the PSG 1.

Boni Liberation Front—see under Guiana National Liberation Front

Guiana National Liberation Front (*Front National de Libération Guyanais,* FNLG)

Leadership. Raymond Charlotte (co-ordinator).

The FNLG leader, Raymond Charlotte, was one of eight French Guiana separatists who were, in December 1974, charged with plotting "to substitute an illegal authority for that of the French state" and were taken to Paris; however, the State Security Court decided on March 12, 1975, to cancel all charges against them, stating inter alia that the authorities in French Guiana had exceeded their powers.

Following bomb attacks at the Kourou space station on April 20, 1980, and a former police building in Cayenne (the capital of French Guiana) on April 22, four suspected FNLG members were on July 15, 1980, flown to Paris to face charges in connexion with these explosions. They included Charlotte and Antoine Aouegui ("Lamoraille"), who had in 1976 helped to form a Boni Liberation Movement to promote nationalist ideas among the Boni people in the Suriname border region. By April 1981 two further pro-independence militants had been arrested and taken to Paris.

Charlotte was released in July 1981 under the terms of a political amnesty granted by the new Socialist President, François Mitterrand, as were the other FLNG detainees in the same period.

GUADELOUPE

A recent campaign of violence associated with some of the pro-independence movements described below has been condemned not only by Guadeloupe's ruling centre-right formations but also by the island's pro-autonomy Communist Party (PCG). In the first elections to the new departmental Assembly on Feb. 20, 1983, the centre-right list won 21 of the 41 seats, the PCG-led list 11 and the local Socialists 9.

Armed Liberation Group (*Groupe de Libération Armée,* GLA)

This extremist pro-independence group was widely believed to be the armed-action wing of the Popular Union for the Liberation of Guadeloupe (UPLG—see separate entry). It was responsible for 11 acts of violence carried out in Guadeloupe between March and December 1980. It warned all French residents (in March 1980) that those of them who did not leave the island by the end of 1980 would be considered "enemies of the Guadeloupe people" and would be treated as such. The victims of GLA attacks included an army sergeant-major killed while he was trying to defuse a bomb on Sept. 17, 1980.

Claiming responsibility for all attacks carried out in 1980, the GLA announced on Jan. 8, 1981, that it would continue its campaign against "French capitalism and colonialism" both on the island and in metropolitian France. After further acts of violence five suspected GLA members were arrested in March and April 1981 and flown to Paris for trial by the State Security Court. On March 21-22 some 5,000 demonstrators protested in Pointe-à-Pitre (the capital of Guadeloupe) against the transfer to Paris of four of the suspects.

All of the detained GLA activists were released by early July 1981 under a political amnesty granted by the new Socialist President, François Mitterrand. In a "warning" to the left-wing Government in Paris the GLA subsequently noted that certain of its members were still due to appear before "colonial tribunals" and continued: "The GLA will oppose any plan supposedly 'specific' to Guadeloupe . . . which seeks to reinforce the eonomic and political departmentalization of Guadeloupe, [which is] the cause of the ruin and degeneration of our country. Only the national independence of Guadeloupe, with a socialist content, will permit recovery of our country's economy, through the taking of control of the affairs of the country by the Guadeloupians themselves." The statement concluded: "For our part, no compromise, no truce should or can be envisaged—our objective, irrespective of the colour of successive governments in France, being the unconditional accession of our country to national independence.''

One of the principal GLA leaders was Luc Reinette, a younger son of a prominent Guadeloupe family, who was one of those detained in Paris in 1981. The following year he announced the formation of his own party, called the Popular Movement for Independent Guadeloupe (see separate entry).

Camus

This clandestine pro-independence cell has claimed responsibility for several violent acts, including the ransacking of government offices in Pointe-à-Pitre.

Committee against Genocide of Blacks by Substitution (Comité contre le Génocide des Noirs par Substitution)

This hitherto unknown group claimed responsibility for starting a fire in the carpark of Pointe-à-Pitre airport during the night of July 30-31, 1982. The group was beieved to be demonstrating its opposition to the extent of the French "settler" presence in Guadeloupe. The Committee's name is taken from a slogan used by Aimé Césaire, leader of the Progressive Party of Martinique.

Metro Clandestine Committee of Resisters (Comité Clandestin des Résistants Métro, CCRM)

This little-known extremist group favouring the maintenance of Guadeloupe's French status has mounted "punitive" attacks on persons identified with the pro-independence movement.

Movement for the Unification of National Liberation Forces of Guadeloupe (Mouvement pour l'Unification des Forces de Libération de la Guadeloupe, MUFLNG)

Leadership. Rosan Mounien (l.).

The MUFLNG was formed in January 1982 as an alliance of pro-independence organizations, notably the Popular Union for the Liberation of Guadeloupe (UPLG—see separate entry), with the aim of "mobilizing the people in joint action to eliminate French colonial domination in Guadeloupe and to attain national independence''.

The other components of the Movement are the Union Générale des Travailleurs de la Guadeloupe (UGTG), the Union des Paysans Pauvres de la Guadeloupe (UPPG), the Syndicat Général de l'Education en Guadeloupe (SGEG), the Syndicat des Instituteurs, Professeurs et Agents de la Guadeloupe (SIPAG), the Association Générale des Etudiants Guadeloupéens (AGEG), the Union Nationale des Elèves et Etudiants de la Guadeloupe (UNEEG) and Chrétiens pour la Libération du Peuple Guadeloupéen (CLPG).

During the night of Feb. 14-15, 1982, the owner of Guadeloupe's largest banana pantation, Max Martin, was assassinated at his residence at Capesterre on the eastern coast of Basse-Terre. One of the UGTG's affiliated unions, the Union des Travailleurs Agricoles (UTA), was at the time involved in a bitter industrial dispute with Martin.

National Liberation Army (Armée de Libération Nationale, ALN)

The previously unknown ALN claimed responsibility for starting a fire at the premises of the Peugeot concessionaire in Point-à-Pitre on April 7, 1982.

Popular Movement for Independent Guadeloupe (Mouvement Populaire pour la Guadeloupe Indépendante, MPGI)

Leadership. Luc Reinette (founder and l.).

This militant pro-independence Movement was launched in June 1982, its founder having earlier been a prominent activist within the Armed Liberation Group (GLA—see separate entry). Two members of the Movement, including Max Safrano (a founding member and prominent trade unionist), were arrested immediately after four bombs had exploded during the night of Aug. 26-27, 1982, causing serious damage to government buildings and other premises.

Popular Union for the Liberation of Guadeloupe (Union Populaire pour la Libération de la Guadeloupe, UPLG)

Leadership. Théodore François (founder).

Established in 1978, this semi-clandestine pro-independence organization succeeded an earlier Groupe d'Organisation Nationale Guadeloupéenne (GONG), which had been founded in 1958 by students from Guadeloupe in Paris and established on the island in 1964. Together with the Communist Party of Guadeloupe, the GONG had formed a short-lived Front Guadeloupéen pour l'Autonomie (which was divided when the Communists supported François Mitterrand in the presidential elections of December 1965, whereas the GONG called for abstention). The GONG was officially dissolved after disturbances in May 1967.

Théodore François carried on clandestine political activities in the 1970s, and in 1973 he founded an Union Générale des Travailleurs de la Guadeloupe (UGTG) as a rival to the (Communist-led) Centrale Générale des Travailleurs Guadeloupéens (CGTG), which, however, remained the island's principal trade union federation. It was initially believed that the Armed Liberation Group (GLA—see separate entry) was the armed wing of the UPLG, but the latter dissociated itself publicly, during 1980, from the GLA's violent actions and claimed that the attacks attributed to the GLA were in fact "police provocations" designed to discredit the independence movement.

In January 1982 the UPLG became a founding component of the broader Movement for the Unification of National Liberation Forces (MUFLNG—see separate entry).

MARTINIQUE

Pro-independence feeling has increased in Martinique in recent years, notably on the left wing of the Progressive Party (PPM) led by Aimé Césaire (one of the department's three deputies in the French National Assembly, where he sits with the Socialist Group). The PPM majority has nevertheless remained committed to the achievement of greater autonomy rather than outright independence as advocated by the groups described below.

In the first elections to the new departmental Assembly on Feb. 20, 1983, the left-wing pro-autonomy formations won a narrow aggregate majority of 21 of the 41 seats (PPM 12, Socialists 5 and Communists 4) against 20 for a list comprising local sections of the centre-right metropolitan parties.

Armed Liberation Group of Martinique (*Groupe de Libération Armée de la Martinique,* GLA-Martinique)

This Group, said to be an offshoot of the GLA of Guadeloupe, claimed responsibility for attacks carried out in December 1980, including one on the headquarters of French television in Martinique.

Martinique Independence Movement (*Mouvement Indépendantiste Martiniquais,* NIM, or *La Parole au Peuple)*

Leadership. Prof. Alfred Marie-Jeanne (l.).

The leader of this Movement, who is Mayor of the town of Rivière-Pilote, declared in March 1980: "It is not through elections that we will take power, but we shall use the *conseil général* and the mayors' offices to help our struggle for revolutionary unity in the Caribbean. We do receive help from other countries (including Cuba and the Soviet Union). . . . Our revolution embraces all solutions, including armed struggle."

The MIM called for abstention in the June 1981 National Assembly elections, regarding the pro-autonomy parties as "using the same language as the departmentalists" and directing particular criticism at Aimé Césaire of the PPM for being the "incorrigible valet of the French state". In the latter part of 1981 there were signs of dissension within the MIM, some members of which resigned in

protest against Prof. Marie-Jeanne's personalized style of leadership.

REUNION

Although pro-independence sentiment exists in Réunion, the main political debate in recent years has been over the degree of local autonomy which is appropriate for the island. In this debate the local sections of the metropolitan left-wing parties have argued for more local self-rule in the context of continued French status, whereas the Réunion centre-right formations have resisted changes in that direction and have in particular opposed the new left-wing metropolitan Government's December 1982 measures creating a departmental Assembly directly elected by proportional representation.

In the first elections to the new Assembly on Feb. 20, 1983, the combined centre-right list obtained 18 of the 45 seats, the Réunion Communists 16, the Socialists 6 and "various right" candidates 5.

Militant Departmentalist Front (*Front Militant Départmentaliste,* FMD)

Leadership. Jean Fontaine (founder and l.).

This Front emerged in December 1981 with the aim of preserving Réunion's departmental status as its then existed and of rallying "all the anti-Marxist family" in this cause. The Front's founder and leader is Mayor of Saint-Louis and an unattached deputy in the French National Assembly.

Movement for the Independence of Réunion (*Mouvement pour l'Indépendance de la Réunion,* MIR)

This Marxist pro-independence grouping was formed in November 1981 as the successor to the *Mouvement pour la Libération de la Réunion* (MPLR), which itself had sprung from the *Organisation Communiste Marxiste-Léniniste de la Réunion* (OCMLR). At its foundation the MIR stated that "the people of Réunion cannot achieve responsibility unless it is . . . totally sovereign" and expressed the view that the Government in Paris "can only perpetuate, with the active complicity of the parties of the presidential majority [i.e. of President Mitterrand], the existing colonial situation".

ST PIERRE AND MIQUELON

Unlike the four overseas departments dealt with above, the population of St Pierre and Miquelon (in the north-west Atlantic) is predominantly of French stock and overwhelmingly in favour of retaining the islands' French status. Nevertheless, the elevation of the islands from overseas territorial to over-

seas departmental status in 1976 has been opposed by substantial sections of the local
population, notably the trade unions, which
have demanded the application of a "special
status" under which St Pierre and Miquelon
would enjoy fiscal and customs arrangements
suited to its geographical situation while remaining an integral part of the French
Republic. Such demands have been pursued
through local sections of the metropolitan
political formations.

Overseas Territories

FRENCH POLYNESIA

Elections to the territorial Assembly of
French Polynesia in May 1977 resulted in the
United Front for Internal Autonomy (FUAI)
retaining its aggregate majority, following
which increased internal autonomy was
granted under a bill enacted by the French
Parliament later in the year and accepted by
both government and opposition parties in
the archipelago. However, the question of
the territory's status was effectively reopened
in late 1978 when John Téariki (leader of the
Pupu Here Aia party, the strongest component of the FUAI) declared his support for an
orderly transition to eventual independence,
whereas the then political head of the
Government Council, Francis Sanford,
stated on behalf of his United Front Party
(*Te Eaa Pi,* the other major component of
the FUAI) that the future should not be risked
with "ill-considered decisions".

In further elections to the territorial
Assembly in May 1982 the pro-autonomy
formations lost their overall majority to the
local section of the metropolitan Rally for the
Republic (RPR, Gaullist), which opposes any
further loosening of the link with Paris. In
the May 1982 elections the left-wing *Ta Mana
Te Nunaa* formation obtained three of the 30
seats on a platform of seeking independence
by way of "class struggle" against "colonialist capitalism"; it has, however, not
associated itself with the extremist pro-
independence groupings described below.

The Ancestors' Blood *(Te Toto Tupana)*

This organization was described as an anti-
French terrorist group with which the (legal)
pro-independence *Te Taata Tahiti Tiama*
party led by Charlie Ching was suspected of
having co-operated in 1978-79.

Maohi Republic Provisional Government
*(Gouvernement Provisoire de la République
Maohi)*

Leadership. Mai Tetua ("President of the
Provisional Government").

This small pro-independence movement
came to prominence when its leader, Mai

Tetua, and 40 of his followers were arrested
on Aug. 15, 1982, after two local policemen
had been briefly held and ill-treated by
members of the group. The latter abductions
had been carried out after police had the
previous day stopped a uniformed group of
the movement's members and confiscated
their banners. On Aug. 17 Tetua and 16
others were charged with premiditated
violence against representatives of public
order and other offences.

NEW CALEDONIA

In elections to the New Caledonian territorial Assembly held in July 1979 the (predominantly Melanesian, or Kanak) pro-independence parties allied within the *Front
Indépendantiste* (FI) retained 14 of the 36
seats, whereas the (Gaullist) Popular Caledonian Rally for the Republic (RPCR) secured
15 and the (autonomist) Federation for a
New Caledonia (FNSC) 7. In that consultation parties favouring the maintenance of the
territory's French status (with varying
degress of internal autonomy) obtained 65.6
per cent of the vote and the pro-independence
formation 34.4 per cent, although the support
of the latter among the Melanesian population
amounted to about 60 per cent of voters. (New
Caledonia's population of about 135,000
comprises some 60,000 Melanesians, 50,000
Europeans and 25,000 Polynesians and
others.)

The metropolitan Government took the
view that on the basis of the July 1979 election
result New Caledonia had the opportunity to
enjoy political stability and economic progress and made it clear that any violent attempt to challenge the existing status of the
territory would be firmly resisted by the
authorities. However, speaking in Paris on
Oct. 29, 1979, the FI leader, Roch Pidjot, denounced "French colonialism and imperialism in the Pacific" and declared that
"by its obstinate refusal to grant the Kanak
people sovereignty in their own country" the
French Government bore full responsibility
for the "inevitable" confrontation to come.

In opposition the FI and its constituent
formations adopted an increasingly radical
approach to the independence issue, including
the drawing up of plans for the occupation of
European-owned plantations by Front supporters with the aim of gaining control of
enough territory in which to make an early
declaration of independence. Moreover, the
most militant of the pro-independence movements, the Kanak Liberation Party (Palika),
has been associated with various acts of
violence, including disturbances during a
demonstration on July 13, 1980, for which
three Palika members were sentenced to imprisonment.

The conflict between those favouring independence (mainly Melanesians) and those opposing it (mainly Europeans and other population groups) was greatly intensified by the assassination on Sept. 19, 1981, of Pierre Declercq, a French Roman Catholic school teacher and secretary-general of the Caledonian Union (UC), the principal party within the FI. A young European was arrested as the suspected murderer but denied any involvement and was later released on bail pending further inquiries. Acts of violence during the ensuing months included an attack on a hotel on the east coast of the main island by some 50 Melanesians on Oct. 10-11, 1981, when three police officers were injured, and incidents in Nouméa (the capital) on Nov. 6-7, involved attacks on Whites, damage to property and looting, with six policemen being injured and 88 people arrested.

On the other hand, Europeans staged demonstrations against a pro-independence administration installed in June 1982 after the FNSC had broken with the RPCR and entered a coalition with the FI under the leadership of Jean-Marie Tjibaou (UC). Europeans also protested against proposed reforms which would give improved economic and social rights to Melanesians and enable officials to expropriate White-owned land for the benefit of the traditional tribal owners. From such a demonstration some 250 Europeans broke away on July 27, 1982, invaded the Assembly and fought with politicians; police intervened and arrested 10 people, while 19 policemen were injured; 17 persons were later charged with possessing arms and other dangerous objects and with using violence against the police force.

In further violence early in 1983, two policemen were killed and four injured when Melanesian tribesmen ambushed a convoy carrying equipment for a timber plant in the La Loa area 60 miles north of Nouméa. On Jan. 13 a total of 18 Melanesians were charged with involvement in the ambush, which was seen as reflecting local concern over environmental damage allegedly being caused by the plant to which the convoy had been proceeding.

Movement for Order and Peace (*Mouvement pour l'Ordre et la Paix,* MOP)

This Movement was founded in 1979 by Europeans in opposition to extremist Melanesian pro-independence elements. Early in January 1980 an off-duty police inspector (who according to pro-independence sources was an MOP member) shot and killed a Melanesian youth—which led to increased unrest among the pro-independence Melanesians.

Socialist Kanak Liberation (*Libération Kanake Socialiste,* LKS)

Leadership. Nidoish Naisseline (l.).

The leader of this movement, one of the most extremist advocates of independence for New Caledonia, declared after the assassination of the secretary-general of the Caledonian Union in September 1981 that his group would continue the struggle for independence, so far waged by the murdered leader, until final victory; he alleged that "fascist groups" were threatening the lives of elected pro-independence representatives. On Nov. 10, 1981, the LKS put demands to the French high commissioner for initiating the process of decolonization, the dissolution of extreme right-wing movements and the requisition of all weapons.

WALLIS AND FUTUNA ISLANDS

There have been no reports of active pro-independence movements in the Wallis and Futuna Islands (a French overseas territory situated in the Pacific north of Fiji and west of Samoa). In the June 1981 French National Assembly elections the one Wallis and Futuna seat was retained by a representative of the local section of the (Gaullist) Rally for the Republic (RPR).

MAYOTTE

Mayotte, one of the four main islands of the Comoros in the Indian Ocean, has a special status virtually equivalent to that of a French overseas department, with a view to the possible attainment of overseas departmental status if its population so decides in a referendum. Mayotte's population had opted to remain within the French Republic following the July 1975 unilateral declaration of independence by the other three Comoro Islands (whose Government has since then claimed sovereignty over the island).

The island's dominant political formation is the *Mouvement Populaire Mahorais* (MPM), whose leader, Younoussa Bamana, in August 1982 launched an attack on what he described as "pro-Comoros intellectuals" resident in metropolitan France for having distributed a tract blaming the French presence for the island's economic and social difficulties. The tract appeared during a general strike called by the *Union des Travailleurs de Mayotte* (UTM).

Federal Republic of Germany

Capital: Bonn   Pop. 61,315,000

The Federal Republic of Germany is, under its Basic Law (Constitution) of 1949, "a democratic and social federal state" whose organs are (i) the Federal Diet *(Bundestag)* elected by universal adult suffrage for a four-year term; (ii) the Federal Council *(Bundesrat)* consisting of 45 members of the Governments of the Republic's 10 *Länder* (constituent states) and of West Berlin; (iii) the Federal President elected for a five-year term by the Federal Assembly *(Bundesversammlung)* consisting of the members of the *Bundestag* and an equal number of delegates nominated by the *Länder* parliaments; and (iv) the Federal Government consisting of the Federal Chancellor elected by the *Bundestag* on the proposal of the Federal President and of ministers appointed by the President upon the proposal of the Chancellor.

Of the *Bundestag*'s 518 members, 248 are elected by simple majority vote in single-member constituencies; another 248 by proportional representation from party lists for each *Land*; and 22 nominated by the House of Representatives of West Berlin (but having no voting rights in the *Bundestag*). To qualify for representation in the *Bundestag* a party must gain at least 5 per cent of the total national votes cast or secure the election of at least three of its candidates by votes in the constituencies. Parties are legally defined as being a constitutionally necessary element of a free democratic order and as contributing to the formation of the national political will, inter alia by influencing public opinion, by encouraging public participation in political life and by training citizens for the assumption of public office.

As a result of elections to the *Bundestag* held on March 6, 1983, parties gained seats as follows: Social Democratic Party 193, Christian Democratic Union 191, Christian Social Union 53, Free Democratic Party 34, and *Die Grünen* (ecologists opposed to all nuclear weapons) 27. Parties which contested the elections without gaining any seats were the National Democratic Party, the (pro-Soviet) German Communist Party, the European Workers' Party, the Christian Bavarian People's Party, the Ecology Economy Party, the Communist Party (Marxist-Leninist), the Independent Social Democrats and the League of Communists of West Germany. Of these parties, the two first-named gained 0.2 per cent of the votes each, and the others less than 0.1 per cent each.

In addition to the various German organizations responsible for causing internal unrest, numerous organizations of foreigners have also been involved in acts of violence in recent years. According to a report by the Federal Ministry of the Interior published in October 1979 there were some 145 extremist organizations of foreigners in the FRG with a total membership of about 93,000. These organizations included (i) the (anti-Shah) Confederation of Iranian Students (CISNU), which was involved in confrontation with police in Frankfurt on Nov. 28, 1978, and in Hamburg on Dec. 10, 1978; (ii) Palestinian groups, among which the General Union of Palestinian Workers (of about 1,000 members) and the General Union of Palestinian Students had been banned on Oct. 4, 1972 (following the murder of 11 Israeli athletes at the Munich Olympic Games by "Black September" followers on Sept. 5 of that year), and other groups which were responsible for planning bomb explosions, for which several persons were sentenced to imprisonment in July 1979 (and also in April 1980); and (iii) Croatian nationalists, the extradition of some of which was requested by the Yugoslav authorities but was refused by the FRG.

Extreme Right-wing Groups

From 1976 onwards there was a marked increase in the number of reported offences by extreme right-wing activists, the annual number of such offences being 616 in 1977, 992 in 1978 and an estimated 1,500 in 1979. On Jan. 19, 1979, television transmitters in Koblenz and Münster were severely damaged by extremists during the transmission of the (US-made) "Holocaust" serial (dealing with the extermination of Jews in the Nazi era). On Jan. 31 of that year the police announced the discovery of an extensive hoard of weapons, explosives and Nazi propaganda material in North Rhine-Westphalia, and added that the arrest of five members of a right-wing group had led to the seizure of 600 kg of explosives in Hesse. On Sept. 13, 1979, a court in Celle (Lower Saxony) sentenced six men to imprisonment for up to 11 years on charges of forming a neo-Nazi terrorist organization to carry out raids on banks and military installations.

On Nov. 2, 1981, it was officially announced that 31 hidden depots of arms and ammunition had been uncovered on the Lüneburg Heath (Lower Saxony) after a list of their contents had been found in the possession of a forestry official, Heinz Lembke, who had committed suicide in prison on Oct. 28, 1981; the latter was a member of the National Democratic Party of Germany (NPD) and was said to have had links with Manfred Roeder of the extreme right-wing German Action Group.

According to official statistics published early in August 1981, there had been 1,824 right-wing offences during 1981, two-thirds of them being of a neo-Nazi character and more than 300 anti-semitic. Gerhart Baum, then Federal Minister of the Interior, stated on Nov. 7, 1981, that there were 75 extreme right-wing organizations in the FRG with a total of 19,800 members, most of them in legal or quasi-legal political or social associations.

Action for German Unity—see under German People's Union

Action Front of National Socialists *(Aktionsfront der Nationalsozialisten)*

Leadership. Michael Kuhnen (l.).

The leader of this group claims to have links with the American Nazi Party (see under United States of America).

Black Forest Combat Group—see under Schlageter Defence Sport Group

Brunswick Group *(Braunschweig Gruppe)*

Five members of this neo-Nazi Group were sentenced in Brunswick on Feb. 20, 1981, to up to 5½ years in prison for being ringleaders in a terrorist organization and for causing and preparing explosions.

Combat League of German Soldiers *(Kampfbund deutscher Soldaten)*

Erwin Ernst Schönborn, a publisher said to be a member of this organization, was on March 25, 1981, sentenced in Frankfurt to two years and eight months for publishing anti-semitic and pro-Nazi propaganda material. Later, however, he was reported to have been arrested in Klagenfurt (Austria) on Feb. 5, 1982, and to have subsequently been deported to Germany as an unauthorized immigrant.

German Action Front *(Deutsche Aktionsfront)*

This group claimed responsibility for causing five explosions between Feb. 2 and Aug. 17, 1980, among them one at an exhibition on the Auschwitz concentration camp.

German Action Group *(Deutsche Aktionsgruppe)*

Leadership. Raimund Hörnle (l.).

The leader of this Group was on Sept. 4, 1980, reported to have confessed that he had prepared bombs for several attacks and had himself thrown a Molotov cocktail at a Hamburg hostel for Vietnamese refugees, two of whom were killed. On June 28, 1981, a court in Stuttgart-Stammheim sentenced four members of the Group as follows: R. Hörnle and Sybille Vorderbrügge each to life imprisonment for having caused the death of two persons and injury to others in bomb attacks on hostels for foreigners; Manfred Roeder, described as the intellectual leader of the Group, to 13 years (he was also the leader of the German Citizens' Initiative—see separate entry); and Dr Heinz Colditz, who had admitted having made two bomb attacks on Feb. 21 and April 18, 1980, respectively, to six years. The court established that Roeder and Dr Colditz had for many years propagated the unconditional struggle against the political system of the Federal Republic of Germany.

German Action Groups *(Deutsche Aktionsgruppen)*

This organization claimed responsibility for an attack on Feb. 22, 1980, on an exhibition on the Auschwitz concentration camp—condemning the exhibition as "anti-German agitation". The organization was also suspected of having been involved in an attack on a hostel in Hamburg housing 211 Vietnamese refugees in August 1980, when one of the refugees was killed and another died later of burns. (Several other bomb attacks obviously also directed against foreigners took place in various localities during 1980.)

German Citizens' Initiative *(Deutsche Bürger-initiative)*

This group was founded as a non-violent organization by Manfred Roeder (see also separate entry for German Action Group), who had in 1976 and 1977 been sentenced to imprisonment for incitement to hatred and anti-constitutional activities and had been barred from practising as a lawyer.

German People's Union *(Deutsche Volks-union, DVU)*

Leadership. Dr Gerhard Frey (ch.).

This neo-Nazi and anti-semitic organization was said to have 1,000 members in Bavaria alone. It has two subsidiary organizations—Action for German Unity *(Aktion Deutsche Einheit,* AKON) and the People's Movement for a General Amnesty *(Volksbewegung für Generalamnestie,* VOGA). Dr Frey is the publisher of a *Deutsche National Zeitung.*

German Workers' Youth *(Deutsche Arbeiter-jugend)*

This anti-semitic group, which has been active in West Berlin, has published a journal, *Deutscher Kurier.* A police raid on the homes of 17 suspected members of the group on Dec. 8, 1982, led to the seizure of ammunition, parts of uniforms and neo-Nazi literature.

Hoffmann Defence Sport Group *(Wehrsport-gruppe Hoffmann)*

Leadership. Karl-Heinz Hoffmann (l.).

Following the establishment of this organization in 1974, Karl-Heinz Hoffmann was in 1977 given a suspended prison sentence for involvement in an attack on left-wing students at Tübingen University; in November 1979 he was convicted of wearing Nazi insignia and an illegal uniform in public. After the organization was said to have conducted paramilitary manoeuvres near Nuremberg as "an element in the formation of an illegal military unit", the Group was banned by the Federal Ministry of the Interior on Jan. 30, 1980. On that day police raided a number of premises in Baden-Württemberg, Bavaria and Hesse and confiscated an armoured vehicle, an anti-aircraft gun and large quantities of firearms, ammunition and other military equipment assembled by the Group.

Members of the Group were suspected of having caused a bomb explosion in Munich on Sept. 26, 1980, when 13 persons were killed and over 200 injured (one of those killed being a member of the Group). On June 23, 1981, it was reported that the Group had planned a kidnapping with the object of en-forcing the release from Spandau prison of Rudolf Hess (the former Nazi leader serving a life sentence for war crimes).

K.-H. Hoffmann was known to have paid several visits to the Middle East for the purpose of buying military-type vehicles. Two other members of the Group—Franz Joachim Bojarsky and Klaus Hubel—were arrested by Italian police on Jan. 18, 1982, at Avellano (Abruzzi), where arms and ammunition were found; the two arrested men were said to have recently returned from Lebanon.

On Jan. 19, 1983, K.-H. Hoffmann was charged with involvement in the murder of Shlomo Levin, a Jewish publisher, and his woman companion in Erlangen on Dec. 19, 1980. The alleged perpetrator of the murders, Uwe Behrend, was reported to have committed suicide in Lebanon in the latter half of 1981.

The Group was estimated to have some 80 active members and 400 sympathizers and to aim at destroying the existing social structure in Germany and replacing it by an authoritarian *("Führer")* state.

National Socialist Anti-Comintern Youth *(Nationale Sozialistische Antikomintern-Jugend)*

This movement was said to have published a monthly bulletin glorifying Hitler and calling for the destruction of parliamentary democracy and the reconstitution of the German Reich. Volker Heidel, an alleged member of the group, was during 1980 twice sentenced to imprisonment (for up to 10 months) for spreading racialist and anti-constitutional propaganda. He was said also to be a member of the Brunswick Group (see separate entry).

People's Movement for a General Amnesty—
see under German People's Unity

People's Socialist Group *(Volkssozialistische Gruppe)*

The alleged leader of this Group, Frank Schubert, had been expelled as unreliable from the People's Socialist Movement of Germany (VSBD—see separate entry). He was involved in numerous violent actions; when he tried to smuggle arms and ammunition from Switzerland to Germany on Dec. 24, 1980, he killed two Swiss border guards and thereupon committed suicide.

People's Socialist Movement of Germany—Party of Labour *(Volkssozialistische Bewegung Deutschlands—Partei der Arbeit, VSBD-PdA)*

Leadership. Friedhelm Busse (ch.).

The organization was founded in 1971 as the Party of Labour (as an offshoot of the

National Democratic Party of Germany, NPD) and adopted its extended name in 1975. It has a youth group known as *Junge Front*. In 1981 Friedhelm Busse was reported to have secretly visited France to meet members of the *Fédération d'Action Nationale Européenne* (FANE) with a view to creating a European Nazi umbrella organization for the various neo-Nazi movements in France, Belgium, Austria, Britain and Switzerland as well as Germany. On Oct. 21, 1981, two alleged members of the party were killed and three others, including its chairman, were arrested while attempting to carry out a bank raid near Munich; four other party members were arrested by police in Belgium on Oct. 22.

The VSBD-PdA was officially banned on Jan. 27, 1982.

People's Socialist Movement of Hesse *(Volkssozialistische Bewegung Hessens)*

The leader of this group, Wolfgang Koch, was in October 1980 believed to have transferred funds to Britain for a resurrection of the newspaper *Völkischer Beobachter* (the former organ of the German Nazi party).

Ruhr Area Defence Sport Group *(Wehrsportgruppe Ruhrgebiet)*

Two members of this organization were sentenced in Kleve (Rhineland) on July 17, 1981, to imprisonment for 6½ and 2½ years respectively for various offences, including armed robbery, theft and violation of arms control legislation.

Schlageter Defence Sport Group *(Wehrsportgruppe Schlageter)*

This Group was in November 1980 said to have been formed by Kay-Uwe Bergmann, Steffen Dupper and Ottfried Hepp. All three disappeared, apparently having left for Lebanon, after Hepp had been found to be connected with the perpetration of the Munich bomb attack of Sept. 26, 1980 (see under separate entry for Hoffmann Defence Sport Group), and had also been named as founder of a Black Forest Combat Group *(Kampfgruppe Schwarzwald)*.

RAF and Related Groups of the Extreme Left

Extreme left-wing groups engaged in acts of violence have, during the past 12 years, had an effect on public life in the Federal Republic of Germany (FRG) quite out of proportion to the numerical strength of their membership. Although they have not succeeded in creating a revolutionary mass party and their sympathizers have never constituted more than a small minority of the population (more particularly among left-wing students), their acts of terrorism have necessitated a considerable law enforcement effort on the part of the state. While at times it appeared that the majority of known left-wing terrorists had been imprisoned or were dead (some of them as a result of suicide) or had abandoned their cause, there was, by early 1983, no certainty that the threat to public order constituted by these groups had been finally eliminated.

In May 1979 the head of the Federal Criminal Office stated that 39 persons, including 31 alleged "hard-core terrorists", were still wanted by the police; that between 75 and 100 persons were thought to make up a "second circle" of assistants to these terrorists by providing cars and accommodation; and that about 1,000 persons were under observation on suspicion of contact with terrorist organizations.

The principal organization of these left-wing guerrillas styled itself the Red Army Faction and was generally known as the Baader-Meinhof Group or Gang. Some of this organization's members formed separate commandos to carry out specific acts of violence and others formed entirely independent groups.

These acts included the assassinations of leading personalities, in particular Günter von Drenkmann (president of the West Berlin Supreme Court) on Nov. 10, 1972; Dr Siegfried Buback (Chief Federal Prosecutor) on April 7, 1977; Dr Jürgen Ponto (chief executive of the Dresdner Bank) on July 30, 1977; and Dr Hanns-Martin Schleyer (president of the Federal Union of German Industry and the Federation of German Employers' Associations) on Oct. 18, 1977.

Red Army Faction *(Rote Armee Fraktion, RAF)*

Leadership (original). Andreas Baader, Ulrike Meinhof.

Established in 1968, the RAF (also known as the Baader-Meinhof Group or Gang) took its name from the Japanese Red Army (for which see under Japan). The history of the RAF can be traced back to a *Sozialistischer Deutscher Studentenbund* (SDS), which had originally been formed in 1946 and enjoyed the support of the Social Democratic Party (SPD) until 1961, when a section of the SDS remained loyal to the SPD and formed a new organization, whereas the SDS became a revolutionary group of some 1,600 members (out of a total student population of some 300,000) and formed the core of the so-called "extra-parliamentary opposition" hostile to the "establishment" and in particular to the "grand coalition" Government formed in 1966 by the SPD and the Christian Democrats.

The SDS's aim was a radical reform of West German society and the setting-up of a communist society, although not in the forms represented in the Soviet Union and the German Democratic Republic. Its ideological mentors were not only Marx, Engels and Lenin but also the dissenting Marxists Rosa Luxemburg, Mao Tse-tung (Mao Zedong) and Prof. Herbert Marcuse; its "heroes" included Ho Chi Minh (the Vietnamese Communist leader), Fidel Castro and Che Guevara. In 1967 the Federal Ministry of the Interior named as the most influential person in the SDS Rudi Dutschke, who described himself as "a professional revolutionary and a Marxist", whose aims were the overthrow of the "corrupt establishment" represented by capitalism in the West and Stalinism in the East, which he hoped to achieve by protest demonstrations and "discussion" rather than violence.

During a riotous demonstration by left-wing students against a visit to West Berlin by the Shah of Iran on June 2-3, 1967, a 26-year-old student, Benno Ohnesorg, was shot dead by a police detective (while 44 persons, including 20 police officers, were injured). On Dec. 17, 1967, the Federal Ministry of the Interior declared the SDS a "danger to the Constitution" because of its stated aim to overthrow the constitutional order and parliamentary democracy. R. Dutschke was severely injured by a right-wing attacker on April 11, 1968, and this attack was followed by violent demonstrations by SDS followers on April 11-15 in West Berlin and many other cities, in particular against premises of the Springer concern which controlled between 30 and 40 per cent of West Germany's total newspaper circulation, and 65-70 per cent of that in West Berlin. The demonstrations led to the deaths of a press photographer and a student in Munich.

The SDS decided on March 21, 1970, to dissolve itself because of dissension among its numerous sections, one of which was the RAF. This group was responsible for arson at a Frankfurt department store on April 2, 1968, for which Andreas Baader was, on May 14, 1968, sentenced to three years' hard labour; he had described his action as an act of "extra-parliamentary opposition to the policy and social order of the Federal Republic". On May 14, 1970, however, he was freed by three RAF members—Ulrike Meinhof, Ingrid Schubert and Irene Görgens—while he was, under escort, visiting an institute in West Berlin to consult some books.

In connexion with this action I. Schubert and I. Görgens were on March 21, 1971, sentenced to six years' imprisonment and four years' juvenile detention respectively (for attempted murder and illegal possession of arms). Horst Mahler, a lawyer and member of a "socialist lawyers' collective" (closely linked with the "extra-parliamentary opposition") was at the same time acquitted on similar charges; however, on Feb. 23, 1973, H. Mahler was sentenced in West Berlin to 12 years in prison on charges of having founded the RAF, of having acted as its ringleader until arrested on Oct. 8, 1970, and of having taken part in three bank raids in West Berlin.

In connexion with bank robberies, car thefts and other crimes committed by alleged members of the Baader-Meinhof group, several of them were killed in clashes with police—notably Petra Schelm in Hamburg on July 12, 1971, Georg von Rauch (who had escaped from detention) in Berlin on Dec. 4, 1971, and Thomas Weisbecker (sought for inflicting grievous bodily harm and committing arson) in Augsburg on March 2, 1972.

Among alleged RAF members tried, Karl-Heinz Ruhland (arrested on Dec. 20, 1970) was sentenced in Düsseldorf on March 15, 1972, to 4½ years in prison for participating in a bank robbery in West Berlin and in two acts of burglary (to obtain documents and rubber stamps for forging identity cards); during his trial he made a detailed confession and named a number of sympathizers.

Bomb attacks attributed to the Baader-Meinhof group took place during May 1972 at the headquarters of the US Army Fifth Corps in Frankfurt (killing an officer and injuring 13 other people) on May 11; at the city police headquarters in Augsburg and at the Bavarian criminal police office in Munich on May 12; on the car of a judge investigating the group in Karlsruhe on May 15; at the headquarters of the Springer publishing group in Hamburg on May 19; and at the US Army's European Command headquarters in Heidelberg on May 24 (when three US servicemen were killed and five other persons injured).

In June 1972 the police arrested several prominent members of the group. A. Baader, Holger Meins and Jan-Carl Raspe were arrested in Frankfurt on June 1; as was Dorothea Ridder the following day near the Bavarian-Austrian border. Gudrun Ensslin was arrested in Hamburg on June 7 (having in October 1968 been sentenced to three years in prison for jointly committing arson with A. Baader in Frankfurt but having disappeared after being provisionally released pending the hearing of her appeal). Also arrested were U. Meinhof near Hanover on June 16 (when she was found in possession of several pistols, a submachine-gun, two home-made hand grenades and a bomb); Gerhard Müller (at the same time and place); Siegfried Hausner in Stuttgart on June 19 (being suspected of being the group's bomb specialist); Klaus Jünschke (thought to have taken over the group's leadership after the arrest of A. Baader and U. Meinhof); and Irmgard Möller in Offenbach on July 8.

A police raid carried out in Hamburg in February 1973 resulted in the seizure of sub-machine-guns, sawn-off shotguns, pistols, explosives and hand grenades of a type used by NATO forces; another raid in Frankfurt (at the same time) produced arms and ammunition, including dum-dum bullets and tear-gas, as well as forged passports and money in various currencies.

H. Meins, an alleged hard-core member of the RAF arrested on June 1, 1972, and awaiting trial for involvement in five murders and 54 cases of attempted murder, died in prison on Nov. 9, 1974, having started a hunger strike on Sept. 14 of that year (as part of a concerted campaign by RAF prisoners awaiting trial). On the following day (Nov. 10) Günter von Drenkmann, president of the West Berlin Supreme Court, was shot dead at his home, with the RAF claiming responsibility for his death "in revenge for the death of H. Meins" (although the victim of this assassination had not been involved in proceedings against the RAF).

The Federal Minister of Justice spoke firmly on Nov. 13, 1974, against sympathy campaigns for RAF prisoners in which they were described as political prisoners suffering "isolation torture or destructive imprisonment"; in the name of the Federal Government he stated that in the FRG no one was persecuted or imprisoned for his political beliefs, that the imprisoned were suspected of serious crimes and that some of them had already been legally sentenced; he added that proceedings were under way against at least 60 accused, of whom 35 were then in detention. On Nov. 29 the Federal Ministry of the Interior released 165 pages of documents to show that the RAF was working for the destruction of the social system in the FRG and that with the help of their lawyers the suspects had been able to establish an effective prison-to-prison communications network. Following an official announcement that the main trial of RAF suspects would begin on May 21, 1975, the hunger strike was called off early in February.

Among RAF members sentenced to imprisonment in 1973-74 were the following: Margrit Schiller (in Hamburg on Feb. 9, 1973 —two years and three months); Carmen Roll (in Karlsruhe on July 23—four years); Marianne Herzog (in Frankfurt on Dec. 17—two years and three months); Rolf Pohle, a lawyer (in Munich on March 1, 1974—six years and five months); I. Schubert (in June —13 years for armed robbery and membership of a criminal organization; she had in May 1971 been given a six-year sentence—see above—and later hanged herself in her cell in Munich-Stadelheim on Nov. 12, 1977); Bernhard Braun and Brigitte Mohnhaupt (in West Berlin on Aug. 30, 1974—4½ years each); U. Meinhof (in West Berlin on Nov. 29—eight years for attempted murder in connexion with the freeing of A. Baader—see above) and H. Mahler (by the same court)—two years as an accomplice, in addition to the 12 years imposed earlier. (By this time, however, H. Mahler had already changed his mind about the RAF, declaring that it had no mass support and that without such support an armed insurrection was impossible; he joined the newly-established Maoist Communist Party of Germany—KPD—and was expelled from the RAF.)

Acts of violence attributed to the RAF in 1974-75 included (i) an unsuccessful attempt made on March 12, 1974, to free three alleged RAF members from prison in Zweibrücken (Saarland); (ii) a bomb explosion on Nov. 20 outside the house of a judge in Hamburg; (iii) an attempt to kill the treasurer of the Christian Democratic Union (Walter Leisler Kiep) near Kronberg (Taunus) on Nov. 30; and (iv) the burning-down of a chalet in Switzerland belonging to Axel Springer (the newspaper magnate) on Jan. 5-6, 1975.

Further prison sentences were imposed in 1975 on RAF members as follows: (i) On Lothar Gend in Bochum on May 21 (15 years, inter alia for shooting and injuring three policemen, having been involved, with Gabriele Kröcher-Tiedemann, in a shooting incident with police) and (ii) on Sigurd Debus (12 years), Karl-Heinz Ludwig (six years), Wolfgang Stahl and Gerd Jürgen Wieland (5½ years each)—in Hamburg on May 30 for four bank raids in which they had stolen DM 600,000.

During the trial of A. Baader, G. Ensslin, U. Meinhof and J.-C. Raspe, which opened in Stuttgart on May 21, 1975, U. Meinhof was found hanging in her cell on May 9, 1976 (a verdict of suicide being pronounced by the Stuttgart public prosecutor on June 13). The trial of the three remaining defendants for their part in four murders, 34 attempted murders and the formation of and membership in a criminal organization ended on April 28, 1977, with life sentences for all three of them. During the trial the defendants generally refused to make any concrete declarations on their actions, but A. Baader said in January 1976 that they were "an urban guerrilla group, a small motor to start up the great revolution by armed force".

The defence lawyers argued on Jan. 20, 1976, that the trial should be terminated and the defendants be treated as prisoners of war as they were engaged in partisan warfare which was recognized in international law; defence counsel had repeatedly but unsuccessfully demanded that the accused should be treated as political prisoners because their actions had been inspired by political motives, and not as common criminals. The authorities, however, refused to acknowledge the existence of political prisoners in the FRG.

G. Ensslin said in a written statement on May 4, 1976, that the accused had been organized in the RAF since 1970 and were responsible for attacks on the headquarters of the (US) Central Intelligence Agency in Frankfurt and the US Army in Heidelberg, and also for an attack on the Springer building in Hamburg; she claimed that their actions should be considered within the context of the Vietnam war which, she said, had taken place not only in the Far East but also in Germany owing to the logistical role of US forces in Europe. Following the death of U. Meinhof the three other defendants made no further appearance in court.

Of RAF members involved in the raid on the office of the Organization of Petroleum Exporting Countries (OPEC) in Vienna in December 1975 (see page 209), Hans-Joachim Klein announced his rejection of terrorism in a letter published in *Der Spiegel* on May 9, 1977, when he stated that the "revolutionary action" of the RAF had been "virtually fascist".

Other prison sentences were imposed on alleged RAF members in 1976 by courts in Hamburg as follows: (i) I. Möller and G. Müller (on March 16)—4½ and 10 years respectively on various charges, including illegal possession of weapons and forging of documents (and complicity in murder in the case of G. Müller, who was a key witness for the prosecution at the trial of A. Baader, G. Ensslin and C.-J. Raspe), and (ii) eight persons (on Sept. 28)—namely Christa Eckes (seven years), Helmut Pohl (five years), Margrit Schiller (four years and eight months), Eberhard Becker (4½ years), Ekkehard Blenck (three years), Ilse Stachowiak and Wolfgang Beer (4½ years' "youth" imprisonment each) and Kay Werner Allnach (two years suspended)—for various offences including membership of a criminal organization, violation of firearms and explosives regulations and forging of documents.

In 1977 Waltraud Boock was sentenced (in Vienna on Feb. 4) to 15 years for aggravated robbery, resisting a state official and contravention of the firearms law. Manfred Grashof and Klaus Jünschke were given life sentences (in Kaiserslautern on June 2) for the murder of a policeman and on other charges, while Wolfgang Grundmann was given four years for unlawful possession of arms and membership of a criminal organization.

Towards the end of 1977 Dierk Hoff (who had given evidence for the prosecution of A. Baader, G. Ensslin, U. Meinhof and J.-C. Raspe) was sentenced (in Frankfurt on Dec. 21, 1977) to four years and eight months for supporting a criminal organization and illegally manufacturing bombs, and Verena Becker was given a life sentence (in Stuttgart on Dec. 28) for the attempted murder of six policemen, membership of a criminal organization and aggravated robbery. V. Becker had earlier been sentenced in December 1974 to six years' "youth" imprisonment for her part in an attack on a British forces yacht club in West Berlin in February 1972 which had caused one death; she had been released in exchange for P. Lorenz in March 1975 (see under separate entry for June 2 Movement).

RAF members also sentenced to imprisonment in 1976-77 were as follows: Peter-Paul Zahl (on March 12, 1976) to 15 years for two cases of attempted murder; Gertraud Will (in Munich on June 15) to two years and 10 months for participating in a criminal organization, using explosives, illegal procurement of arms and aiding and abetting; Irmgard Deschler (on July 12) to five years for preparing an explosives attack, bank robbery, taking a hostage and falsification of documents (this sentence being reduced to 4½ years' "youth" imprisonment on May 12, 1977); Karl-Heinz König (on Aug. 17) to six years for aggravated robbery; Wolfgang Quante (on Nov. 23) to an unlimited term of "youth" imprisonment for membership of a criminal organization (being released on April 4, 1977, having been one of those RAF prisoners whose release was demanded by the attackers of the West German embassy in Stockholm in April 1975); Borvin Wulf and Bernd Geburtig (on March 2, 1977) to 5½ years each for a bomb attack on the house of a former Hamburg Senator of Justice on Oct. 16, 1975, and also for arson, theft, illegal possession of firearms and forgery of documents; Helmut Lülf (in Hamburg on April 28) to four years for membership of a criminal organization, forgery of documents, fraud and aiding and abetting; Dieter Kett (on May 12) to 4½ years on explosives charges (and on May 17 to a further 10 months for insulting the state prosecutor); Robert Jarowoy and Wernfried Reimers (in Frankfurt on June 30) to seven years and three months each on blackmail charges; Rainer and Inge Hochstein (in Hamburg on July 1) to 11 and 10 years respectively for aggravated robbery and membership of a criminal organization; and Uwe Henning (on Oct. 12) to two years and three months for allowing G. Ensslin to use his flat, which served as an RAF hideout and arms store.

Rolf Pohle, another former RAF prisoner exchanged for P. Lorenz, had been arrested in Athens on July 21, 1976, and extradited to the FRG on Oct. 1, 1976; in Munich on March 10, 1978, he was sentenced to three years and three months for extortion (on behalf of the five prisoners exchanged for P. Lorenz, who had been given a total of DM 120,000).

Other RAF members sentenced to imprisonment during 1978 were: Johannes Thimme (in April) to one year and 10 months for membership of a terrorist organization and the construction of explosives; Günter Sonnenberg (in Stuttgart on April 26) to imprisonment for life on two charges of attempted murder on May 3, 1977 (when he had been arrested on the Swiss border with Verena Becker); Kurt Groenewold, a lawyer who had acted as defence counsel for accused RAF members (in Hamburg on July 10) to two years in prison, a fine of DM 75,000 and costs for supporting a criminal organization, in particular by running an information centre of the RAF prisoners to keep terrorist organizations abroad in touch; Klaus Dorff (in Frankfurt on Aug. 2, 1978) to 13 years for two armed attacks on banks in Frankfurt and Dortmund (in which he had stolen DM 225,000); Jürgen Tauras (at the same time) to 7½ years for a bank raid in Hamburg (weapons, ammunition and other equipment having been found in their possession upon their arrest on Feb. 20-21, 1976, in Cologne); Volker Speitel and Hans-Joachim Dellwo (in Stuttgart on Dec. 14, 1978) to respectively two years and two months and two years for supplying a terrorist organization and acting as couriers between lawyers and their imprisoned clients and alleged terrorists outside. Both the last-named had been employed by the law firm of Dr Croissant (see below) and both stated at the trial that they had severed their connexion with the RAF, making full confessions and thus contributing to the prevention of further crimes, in particular by destroying the legend, spread by RAF supporters, that A. Baader, G. Ensslin and J.-C. Raspe had been "murdered" in prison.

Four RAF members—Brigitte Mohnhaupt, Rolf-Clemens Wagner, Sieglinde Hofmann and Peter Jürgen Boock (the husband of Waltraud Boock)—were taken into custody in Zagreb (Yugoslavia) in May 1978 when they were found to carry stolen Liechtenstein passports. The FRG demanded the extradition of these four persons at the same time as the Yugoslav authorities requested the extradition of six Croatians, one Albanian and one Serb—all émigrés in the FRG whom the Yugoslav Government accused of various crimes against the Yugolav state. The West German Government refused the Yugoslav request, mainly on grounds of insufficient evidence regarding the Yugoslavs' alleged involvement in crimes. In Yugoslavia the four West Germans were convicted of using false passports and of entering the country illegally but were all released and left the country in November 1978; the Yugoslav Government had rejected the FRG's request for their extradition on the ground that the legal requirements for their extradition had not been fulfilled.

In Switzerland, Gabriele Kröcher-Tiedemann was on June 30, 1978, sentenced at Porrentruy to 15 years in prison for attempted murder of two border guards and Christian Möller to 11 years for complicity, both having been arrested at Delémont (northwestern Switzerland) in December 1977. Elisabeth von Dyck (wanted inter alia in connexion with the murder of Dr Schleyer and with the attack on the West German embassy in Stockholm) was shot dead by police in Nuremberg on May 6, 1979, allegedly while resisting arrest by drawing a gun.

Dr Klaus Croissant, a lawyer who had acted as defence counsel for various hardcore RAF members, was sentenced in Stuttgart on Feb. 16, 1979, to 30 months' imprisonment for supporting a criminal organization by abusing his status to carry messages between imprisoned terrorists and those still at large; he was also banned from practising as a lawyer for four years. Dr Croissant had been extradited in November 1977 from France where he had sought political asylum in July 1977 after he had been released from investigative custody in West Germany.

Other prison sentences were imposed on RAF members and supporters during 1979 as follows: Christine Kuby (in Hamburg on May 2) to life imprisonment for the attempted murder of two police officers on Jan. 21, 1978 (proclaiming her allegiance to the RAF during her trial); Irmgard Möller and Bernhard Braun, both alleged founder members of the RAF (in Stuttgart-Stammheim on May 31), to life imprisonment and to 12 years respectively for crimes including a bomb attack at the US military headquarters in Heidelberg in May 1972 and an attack on a federal judge (for their earlier sentences, see above); Angelika Speitel, a former employee of Dr Croissant and Siegfried Haag (see under separate entry for Haag-Mayer Group) and described by the prosecution as a particularly active RAF member, (in Düsseldorf on Nov. 30) to two terms of life imprisonment for murder and attempted murder of police officers in September 1978 (being also suspected of involvement in the murders of Drs Schleyer, Ponto and Buback).

Two lawyers who had formerly been employed by Dr Croissant—Arndt Müller and Armin Newerla—were in Stuttgart on Jan. 31, 1980, given prison sentences of four and 3½ years respectively for supporting a terrorist organization and smuggling guns into prison, enabling A. Baader and J.-C. Raspe to kill themselves.

Astrid Proll, one of the founder members of the RAF, was on Feb. 22, 1980, sentenced to five years in prison and a fine of DM 4,500 (the prison sentence being suspended because she had already spent over four years in investigative custody) for armed bank robbery and uttering forged documents. She had been extradited from Britain, where she had gone in 1974 and had married under an assumed name, for which reason she was refused a formal declaration of British nationality; she had repeatedly asserted that she had sincerely changed her attitude towards terrorism.

Gert Schneider and Christof Wackernagel, both RAF members, were in Düsseldorf on Sept. 5, 1980, sentenced to 15 years in prison each for the attempted murder of Dutch policemen in Amsterdam on Nov. 10, 1977. Rolf Clemens Wagner, who had been associated with the RAF since 1975, was sentenced to life imprisonment in Winterthur (Switzerland) on Sept. 26, 1980, for murder committed during a bank raid in November 1979.

During 1981 a number of actions involving the placing or exploding of bombs or the committing of arson were attributed to the RAF. Thus bombs were discovered in two US Army helicopters at Erlensee (Hesse) on Feb. 3; the US military information office in Giessen was bombed on March 29; three Molotov cocktails were thrown into a US Army labour office in Frankfurt on March 30; arson was attempted at the US international school in Düsseldorf on April 6; a bomb was discovered at the US Army administrative office in Wiesbaden on April 16; an explosion took place at the US Andrews Barracks in West Berlin on Aug. 18; an arson attack was made on US barracks in Frankfurt on Aug. 19; seven cars and a motor-cycle were set on fire in a US Army housing estate in Wiesbaden on Sept. 1; an attack was made on the home of the US consul-general in Frankfurt on Sept. 13; and two bombs were discovered on a railway line leading to the US Air Force base near Frankfurt on Sept. 16.

Hans-Christian Ströbele, a lawyer, was in West Berlin on Jan. 19, 1981, sentenced to 1½ years in prison suspended for three years for supporting the criminal RAF. Norbert Kröcher was in Düsseldorf on Feb. 10, 1981, sentenced to 11½ years' hard labour for membership of a criminal association and aggravated robberies and extortion (in particular in Sweden), while Manfred Adomeit was given a 6½-year sentence. Petra (Piccolo-) Krause was in Zurich on March 9, 1981, sentenced to 3½ years' hard labour and expulsion from Switzerland for 15 years for her participation in RAF bomb attacks in Berne and Zurich in June 1974.

Karl-Friedrich Grosser was, in Stuttgart on Oct. 12, 1982, sentenced to three years in prison and Jürgen Schneider to 2½ years, for aiding the RAF. Rolf Heissler, who had been released from prison in 1975 in exchange for the release of P. Lorenz (see under June 2 Movement), was on Nov. 10, 1982, sentenced to life imprisonment for killing two Dutch border guards in 1978 and for other offences.

Following the arrest of three leading RAF members—Brigitte Mohnhaupt and Adelheid Schulz (on Nov. 11, 1982) and Christian Klar (on Nov. 16)—the Federal Minister of Justice appealed to the "remaining hard core" as well as to the sympathizers and supporters of the RAF on Nov. 19, 1982, to cease their criminal activities and to surrender; he added that only those could expect leniency who made efforts to prevent further possible offences by a terrorist association. An RAF arms cache was uncovered at an unspecified locality on Nov. 12, 1982, and on Nov. 28 it was reported that the security forces had found four more arms caches of the RAF, mainly in the Frankfurt area.

In a programme of the RAF called "Urban Guerrilla Concept", first secretly circulated in May 1971 and thought to have been written in part by Ulrike Meinhof, it was stated that the use of violence was the only means of changing society; that legal means to that end, as well as parliamentarianism, were to be rejected; that the "urban guerrillas" were Maoist "Communists" and not anarchists; and that the armed struggle against "American imperialism" could be carried out in Germany or anywhere else. In another 1971 publication, "Concerning the Armed Struggle in Western Europe", believed to have been written by Horst Mahler, instructions were given on how to manufacture weapons and to form commandos; violence was defined as "the highest form of the class struggle"; and it was claimed that "proletarian leadership" could "only be realized by the vanguard", i.e. students. In a 1973 publication the RAF praised the Black September action at the Munich Olympic Games in 1972, in which 11 Israeli athletes were killed, as having been "in memory of the 1936 Olympics" (held in Berlin under Hitler).

During her trial Ulrike Meinhof defined the aims of the RAF (on Sept. 13, 1974) as being the destruction of "imperialism"—(i) internationally the military alliances of the United States throughout the world, and in Germany between NATO and the *Bundeswehr* (the armed forces of the FRG), (ii) nationally the armed formations of the state which "represent the monopoly of power of the ruling class", (iii) in the economic sphere "the power structure of the multinational concerns" and (iv) politically the governmental and non-governmental "bureaucracies, organizations and power structures (parties, trade unions and media) which rule the people".

The RAF has not played any part in the peace movement, the anti-nuclear campaign or action by squatters. In 1981 it reaffirmed its policy of violent action not only against the United States and its armed forces but also against the Government of the FRG (then dominated by the Social Democrats) which the RAF regarded as the USA's executive arm in Europe.

In 1970 a group of RAF members, among them Horst Mahler, Hans-Jürgen Bäcker, A. Baader, U. Meinhof, G. Ensslin, Monika

Berberich and Manfred Grashof, were trained in guerrilla warfare in a camp of the Popular Front for the Liberation of Palestine (PFLP) in Jordan for about two months, where they were taught to handle pistols.

A member of the RAF who was part of the network of the PFLP was the lawyer Wilfried Böse, who was the leader of a group of four hijackers who diverted an Air France airbus to Uganda in June 1976 and who was killed when Israeli commandos recovered the airbus (see page 209).

In connexion with alleged Libyan support for the RAF, the Federal Minister of the Interior (Gerhart Baum) said after talks which he had had with Col. Moamer al-Kadhafi and other Libyan leaders on Nov. 24, 1978, that the Libyan side had repeatedly explained that it had no ties with the German terrorists, whom it regarded "not as freedom fighters but as mentally sick" because they were not fighting for any recognizable revolutionary goal.

Black Bloc *(Schwarzer Block)*

This group, which was active from May 1980 onwards, was suspected of supporting the RAF and of having been involved in arson and bomb attacks. Twenty alleged members of the group were arrested in the Frankfurt area on July 28–29, 1981.

Group of March 6

This group claimed responsibility for bomb explosions at the Paris offices of several West German newspapers (in particular those of the Axel Springer group, which had been the target of RAF attacks on other occasions) and radio stations on March 6, 1975.

Gudrun Ensslin Commando

This commando claimed responsibility for an attack with (Soviet-made) anti-tank grenades on the car of Gen. Frederick J. Kroesen, US Ground Forces Commander in Europe, who was slightly injured, in Heidelberg on Sept. 15, 1981.

Haag-Mayer Group

Leadership. Siegfried Haag, Roland Mayer, Günter Sonnenberg (leaders).

This Group was formed in 1976 around the legal practice of Siegfried Haag with the object of directing the activities of a restructured Red Army Faction (RAF) at the end of the first phase of the RAF's operations marked by the suicides of its leading figures (U. Meinhof on May 9, 1976, followed by A. Baader, G. Ensslin and C.-J. Raspe on Oct. 18, 1977). The principal aims of the Group appeared to be the enforcement of the release of imprisoned RAF members and revenge for the deaths of others, rather than the achievement of a political revolution.

The founder members of the Group were thought to include also Sieglinde Gutrun Hofmann, Stefan Wisniewski, Verena Becker, Rolf Heissler (freed from prison in exchange for Peter Lorenz—see under separate entry for June 2 Movement) and Friederike Krabbe—all of whom were, with S. Haag, said to have spent time at a training camp of the Popular Front for the Liberation of Palestine in South Yemen in 1976. According to documents found in S. Haag's possession on his arrest, Waltraud Boock had been one of the most active acquirers of money for the Group.

On Nov. 30, 1976, S. Haag and R. Mayer were arrested at Butzbach (Hesse), where police found in S. Haag's possession not only bank notes stolen in recent bank raids but also detailed plans of attacks to be carried out by at least 11 persons (including G. Sonnenberg, Christian Klar and Knut Folkerts). On Sept. 30, 1977, S. Haag, R. Mayer, Elisabeth von Dyck and Sabine Schmitz were charged with membership of a criminal organization, and S. Haag and E. von Dyck also with complicity in murder by having procured weapons for the attack on the West German embassy in Stockholm (see separate entry for Holger Meins Commando), and on Feb. 23, 1978, S. Haag was charged with murder in connexion with that attack.

On July 11, 1979, S. Haag and R. Mayer were sentenced in Stuttgart-Stammheim to 14 and 12 years in prison respectively for leading a terrorist organization (i.e. their group) and its involvement in the kidnapping of Dr Hanns-Martin Schleyer (see under separate entry for Siegfried Hausner Commando), while Sabine Schmitz was at the same time given a 32-month prison sentence. On Dec. 19, 1979, S. Haag was given a further 15-year sentence for obtaining weapons used in the attack on the West German embassy in Stockholm.

The Hamburg section of the Haag-Mayer Group was held responsible for the killing of Dr Jürgen Ponto (chief executive of the Dresdner Bank) on July 30, 1977, for which the "Red Morning" group (see separate entry) had claimed responsibility.

Among other members of the Group, Willy Peter Stoll was fatally shot by police in Düsseldorf on Sept. 6, 1978. He had been an assistant of Dr K. Croissant (the defence lawyer of leading RAF members) and had gone underground in 1975. He was said to have joined the Haag-Mayer Group; to have stolen, together with Knut Folkerts, on July 1, 1977, arms which were used against Dr Hanns-Martin Schleyer (see under separate entry for Siegfried Hausner Commando); and to have been involved in the murders of Drs Buback, Ponto and Schleyer.

Uwe Folkerts, brother of Knut Folkerts, was (in Stuttgart on Dec. 19, 1978) sentenced to 16 months in prison for supporting the Group.

Holger Meins Commando

Named after one of the first leaders of the Red Army Faction (RAF), who died in prison as a result of a hunger strike on Nov. 9, 1974, this group admitted responsibility for a bomb attack on the West German consulate in Florence on Nov. 16 of that year and for another on a Mercedes car sales agency in Paris on Feb. 8, 1975. On April 24, 1975, six armed members of this Commando seized the West German embassy in Stockholm and took 12 staff members, including the ambassador, as hostages. Swedish police promptly surrounded the building but were warned by the attackers that, if they did not leave the area, one of the hostages would be shot every hour. The police, however, ignored the warning, whereupon the attackers shot the West German military attaché (who died a few hours later). The attackers demanded the release of 26 persons serving terms of imprisonment or in investigative custody on various charges, including membership of the RAF or other alleged terrorist organizations.

A "crisis staff" formed by the West German Government decided not to accede to the commando's demands, and the latter thereupon killed the economic attaché at the embassy in Stockholm. However, later on April 24 an accidental explosion set the building on fire and killed one member of the commando while the five others were captured by the police, with all remaining hostages escaping alive. Of the five commando members captured, Siegfried Hausner (who had already served a three-year sentence imposed in 1972) was severely injured and died in a prison hospital in Stuttgart-Stammheim on May 4, 1975. The four other commando members—Karl-Heinz Dellwo, Hanna Elise Krabbe, Bernd Maria Rössner and Lutz Manfred Taufer—were each sentenced in Düsseldorf on July 20, 1977, to serve two life sentences for joint murder in two cases.

June 2 Movement *(Bewegung 2. Juni)*

This Movement, established in 1973 and named after the date of the death of a student (Benno Ohnesorg), shot by police during a protest demonstration against a visit by the Shah of Iran in West Berlin in 1967, was formed by members of the Red Army Faction (RAF). Among these, Ingrid Siepmann was on Oct. 18, 1974, sentenced to 12 years in prison for six cases of robbery, and Annerose Reiche to seven years for a bank robbery with violence and the attempted freeing of two

RAF prisoners, Ingrid Schubert and Irene Görgens (see page 430).

On Feb. 27, 1975, Peter Lorenz, the chairman of the Christian Democratic Union (CDU) in West Berlin, was kidnapped by members of the Movement who announced that he would be tried for "his connexions with the economic system, with the bosses and with fascist powers, as a propagandist of Zionism, of the aggressive policy of the State of Israel in Palestine" and for his "participation in the military coup by Pinochet and his accomplices in Chile". They threatened to kill P. Lorenz unless all their demands were fulfilled—in particular the immediate release of all persons arrested in connexion with demonstrations following the death of Holger Meins (see previous entry) and also the release of six RAF members—Verena Becker, Gabriele Kröcher-Tiedemann, Horst Mahler, Rolf Pohle, Ingrid Siepmann and Rolf Heissler, these six to be flown out of the country in the company of Pastor Heinrich Albertz (former Social Democrat Chief Burgomaster of West Berlin at the time of B. Ohnesorg's death).

A government "crisis staff" chaired by the Federal Chancellor, Helmut Schmidt, decided to place the life of P. Lorenz above the interests of the state and to accede to the kidnappers' demands. The West Berlin police announced on Feb. 28 that two demonstrators, imprisoned after the death of H. Meins, would be released on March 1. G. Kröcher-Tiedemann and H. Mahler, however, announced on television towards midnight on March 1 that they did not wish to be flown out of the country in exchange for P. Lorenz. H. Mahler subsequently issued a statement in which he declared inter alia: "The strategy of individual terrorism is not the strategy of the working class and as I dissociated myself during my trial (see page 431) from the strategy of the RAF I refuse to be taken out of the country in this way."

The four other prisoners (V. Becker, R. Heissler, R. Pohle and I. Siepmann) and also G. Kröcher-Tiedemann, who had reversed her earlier decision, accompanied by Pastor Albertz, were flown out of the country and eventually reached the People's Democratic Republic of (South) Yemen, where the former prisoners were granted political asylum on March 4. Following the return to Berlin of Pastor Albertz, P. Lorenz was released by the kidnappers late on March 4.

The Movement was also held responsible for the abduction of a Vienna industrialist, Walter Michael Palmers, on Nov. 9-10, 1977, for whose release on Nov. 13 a sum equivalent to almost $2,000,000 was paid as a ransom. Two heavily-armed members of the Movement—Juliane Plambeck and Wolfgang Beer—were killed in a car crash on July 25, 1980. (J. Plambeck had been arrested on

Sept. 13, 1975, and charged with involvement in the kidnapping of P. Lorenz and the murder of Judge von Drenkmann, but had escaped from investigative custody on July 7, 1976.)

On July 27, 1979, a West Berlin court, in a retrial of six persons tried in June 1976, sentenced to life imprisonment Ilse Jandt and to prison terms of from four to eight years the five other accused, all being found guilty of the murder of a former member of the June 2 Movement who had implicated members of the group in terrorist activities.

For involvement in the abduction of P. Lorenz, Ralf Reinders and Till Meyer were, in West Berlin on Oct. 13, 1980, sentenced to 15 years in prison each; Ronald Fritzsch to 13 years and three months; Gerald Klöpper to 11 years and two months; and Andreas Vogel to 10 years.

Other actions of the June 2 Movement included the explosion of a bomb at the Berlin Kreuzberg town hall on June 12-13, 1980. Of the members of the Movement, Gabriele Rollnik, Angelika Goder and Klaus Viehmann were, in West Berlin on May 15, 1981, sentenced to 15 years in prison each for their part in the kidnapping of P. Lorenz and of W. M. Palmers, and these sentences were confirmed by the Federal Court in Kassel in June 1982. Ingrid Barabas was, in Frankfurt on June 29, 1982, given a four-year prison sentence for membership of the June 2 Movement.

July 4 Movement

This group claimed responsibility for an attack on the office of the Christian Democratic Union in Brunswick on Sept. 7, 1981.

Kaiserslautern Anti-fascist Struggle (*Antifaschistischer Kampf Kaiserslautern,* AKK)

Three alleged members of this group, accused of supporting the RAF and forming a criminal association, were arrested on Feb. 17, 1980.

Red Morning (*Roter Morgen*)

After Dr Jürgen Ponto, chief executive of the Dresdner Bank, had been fatally wounded at his home in Oberursel (near Frankfurt) on July 30, 1977, this group claimed responsibility for his death on July 31, adding that further killings would follow unless "all political prisoners of war" in the FRG were released immediately. While this threat was officially ignored, the Chief Federal Prosecutor (Dr Kurt Rebmann), who had succeeded the late Dr Buback (for whose death see page 439) on June 24, 1977, stated on Aug. 10 that links had been established between the assassinations of Dr Buback and Dr Ponto and that they were part of a plot worked out by the Haag-Mayer Group (see

separate entry), to which all those so far named as suspects belonged.

The group's members included Susanne Albrecht (who had been accepted as a friend by the Ponto family), Silke Maier-Witt, Sigrid Sternebeck, Angelika Speitel and Rosemarie Priess. (Volker Speitel, the husband of A. Speitel, had held an important position in the office of Dr K. Croissant, and R. Priess had worked in the Hamburg office of Kurt Groenewold, another defence lawyer of Red Army Faction members.)

For her part in the killing of Dr Ponto, Sieglinde Hofmann was, in Frankfurt on June 16, 1982, sentenced to 15 years in prison.

Siegfried Hausner Commando

This Commando of the Red Army Faction (RAF)—named after a member of the Holger Meins Commando (see separate entry) who died after being wounded by Swedish police in connexion with the attack on the West German embassy in Stockholm on April 24, 1975—issued a number of threats in a letter posted in Hamburg on May 8, 1975, and addressed to a Stockholm newspaper. The Commando threatened in particular (i) to murder Princess Christina of Sweden and her husband, as well as a minister without portfolio, unless the equivalent of £190,000 was paid to the West German *Rote Hilfe* (Red Aid, an organization for the support of families of "political" prisoners) and (ii) to attack Stuttgart by means of SAM-7 missiles, bombs and mustard gas unless an amnesty was granted to all RAF members and those then awaiting trial were released from custody.

The Commando claimed responsibility for the abduction, near Cologne on Sept. 5, 1977, of Dr Hanns-Martin Schleyer, president of the Federal Union of German Industry and the Federation of German Employers' Associations, with his chauffeur and three police guards being killed. In a letter made public on Sept. 8 the Commando demanded that in return for Dr Schleyer's release 11 prisoners named by it were to be released on Sept. 7, each being handed DM 100,000 and 10 of them being flown to a country of their choice in the company of Pastor Martin Niemöller (who had been held in concentration camps by the Nazis and later was president of the World Council of Churches) and Denis Payot (a Geneva lawyer, former secretary-general of the International Federation for the Rights of Man and then president of the Swiss League for Human Rights).

Those RAF members whose release was demanded were A. Baader, G. Ensslin, J.-C. Raspe, Verena Becker (see under separate entry for June 2 Movement), Werner Hoppe (serving a 10-year sentence imposed in 1972 for three cases of attempted murder of policemen), K.-H. Dellwo, Hanna Krabbe, B. M. Rössner (all involved in the attack on the West German embassy in Stockholm), Ingrid Schubert (who had inter alia taken part in the freeing of A. Baader on May 14, 1970, and had in May 1971 been sentenced to six years in prison for complicity in attempted murder and the freeing of a prisoner and in June 1974 to 13 years for armed robbery and membership of a criminal organization), Irmgard Möller (sentenced to 4½ years in prison in Hamburg on March 16, 1976, for membership of a criminal organization, illegal possession of weapons, forging documents and resisting arrest) and Günter Sonnenberg (a member of the Haag-Mayer Group, who had been arrested on May 3, 1977).

Pastor Niemöller and D. Payot agreed on Sept. 9, 1977, to act as contacts between the kidnappers and the authorities. Although the Federal Government made efforts to find countries which would be prepared to accept the prisoners if they were freed, it emerged later than Algeria, Iraq, Libya, Vietnam and South Yemen had all refused to do so. The release of the 11 prisoners held in Germany was also demanded (together with that of two Palestinians serving life sentences in Turkey for attacking passengers on an Israeli airliner in Istanbul in August 1976) by a group calling itself the "Martyr Halimeh Commando", which had hijacked a West German airliner between Palma de Mallorca and Frankfurt on Oct. 13, 1977, this aircraft being eventually allowed to land in Dubai (United Arab Emirates) on the following day.

However, also on Oct. 13, 1977, a group named as "The Struggle against World Imperialism Organization" claimed responsibility for the hijacking, and on Oct. 14 both this grouping and the kidnappers of Dr Schleyer stated that, if the prisoners did not reach their destination in Somalia, Vietnam or South Yemen by Oct. 16, Dr Schleyer would be killed and the aircraft blown up. Oct. 16, however, passed without any action taking place, and on Oct. 17 the West German airliner flew to Mogadishu (the capital of Somalia), where it was, during the following night, stormed by a West German border guard commando (assisted by two members of the British Special Air Services regiment and using British-made stun grenades) who killed three of the kidnappers and wounded and captured a fourth (a woman).

The pilot of the airliner had been killed by the hijackers on Oct. 17; the crew and passengers of the aircraft and the border guards all returned to the FRG by Oct. 2; and on Oct. 18 the Federal Chancellor (Helmut Schmidt) paid tribute to support given to the rescue operation by Britain, France, Saudi Arabia, Somalia and the United States, stating in particular: "The co-operation between the Somali security forces and our own was excellent and their readiness to help immense. . . . Somalia has set an example for the international co-operation which is indispensable for the fight against terrorism." The Chancellor also noted that Yassir Arafat, the leader of the Palestine Liberation Organization, had clearly dissociated himself from the hijacking "long before it came to an end". Moreover, he expressed appreciation of the willingness of the Soviet Union and the German Democratic Republic to use their "good offices on our behalf" with the Government of South Yemen.

From Beirut it was reported on Oct. 27, 1977, that responsibility for the hijack operation was claimed by the Popular Front for the Liberation of Palestine—Special Operations led by Wadie Haddad (see entry under "Palestinian Movements"). The surviving hijacker (Soraya Ansari) was, in Mogadishu on April 25, 1978, sentenced to 20 years in prison.

A few hours after the storming of the West German airliner in Mogadishu A. Baader, G. Ensslin and J.-C. Raspe were all found dead in their cells at Stammheim prison. Their deaths were followed by the discovery of a sophisticated network of radio equipment, secret hiding places and explosives in the prisoners' and adjoining cells, and this discovery led to the dismissal of the prison's governor and its chief security officer and to the resignation of the Minister of Justice of Baden-Württemberg. A parliamentary commission of inquiry which reported its findings on Feb. 27, 1978, failed to determine how the prisoners had obtained the weapons with which they had committed suicide.

The deaths of the three leading RAF members were followed by numerous attacks made on Oct. 19 on West German property in Italy, France, the Netherlands and elsewhere, and on the same day the dead body of Dr Schleyer was found in Mulhouse (Alsace), while a message from the "Siegfried Hausner Commando, RAF", stated that the kidnappers had ended "the miserable and corrupt existence" of Dr Schleyer; that his death was "in no way commensurate with our pain and anger over the massacre at Mogadishu and Stammheim"; that they would "never forget the blood which has been shed by Schmidt and the imperialists who supported him"; and that the battle was "only just beginning".

However, it has since then been generally accepted that the suicide of the three RAF leaders, following on the failure of the RAF to enforce the release of its imprisoned members, marked the end of the first phase of the RAF's activities, which had failed to evoke a general mobilization of revolutionary forces which might have led to the overthrow of the existing regime in the FRG.

For involvement in the killing of Dr

Schleyer, Stefan Wisniewski was, in Düsseldorf on Dec. 4, 1981, sentenced to life imprisonment; he had earlier, in Frankenthal (Palatinate) on Sept. 4, 1980, been given a six-year sentence for robbery and other charges.

Sigurd Debus Commando

This Commando, named after an imprisoned RAF member who had died as a result of a hunger strike on April 16, 1981, claimed responsibility for two explosions at the US Air Force base at Ramstein (near Kaiserslautern) on Aug. 31, 1981, when 20 persons were injured.

In a statement issued in 1981 the Commando listed among its aims the ending of the "lack of perspective, alienation, dehumanization of labour and the destruction of living standards by the nuclear and chemical industries and by concrete".

Socialist Patients' Collective (*Sozialistisches Patientenkollektiv,* SPK)

Leadership. Dr Wolfgang Huber (head).

The SPK was formed in Heidelberg an antipsychiatry group therapy unit based on the belief that the patient's illness stemmed from capitalism. Working circles of the SPK included one on making explosives (headed by Dr Huber's wife), another on radio transmission and one on judo/karate. A number of student members of the SPK became active RAF members, notably Carmen Roll (sentenced in Karlsruhe on July 23, 1973, to four years in prison for membership of a criminal organization, making preparations for bomb attacks, forging documents, illegal possession of weapons and assault); Siegfried Hausner (who died in connexion with the April 1975 attack on the West German embassy in Stockholm); Margrit Schiller (sentenced in Hamburg on Feb. 9, 1973, to 27 months in prison and again on Sept. 28, 1976, to four years and eight months, inter alia for membership of a criminal organization, arms and explosives offences and forging of documents); and Klaus Jünschke (sentenced in Kaiserslautern on June 2, 1977, to life imprisonment for murdering a policeman in the course of a bank robbery in December 1971). Dr Huber himself was arrested on July 20, 1971, and was subsequently sentenced to seven years in prison for forming a criminal association.

Another former student member of the SPK, Gabriele Kröcher-Tiedemann, became a member of the June 2 Movement (see separate entry); was arrested in July 1973 in connexion with a shooting incident with police, after which she was given an eight-year prison sentence, but was released in exchange for P. Lorenz (seized in West Berlin in February 1975 by the June 2 Movement—see separate entry); was thereafter involved in the seizure of representatives of the member countries of the Organization of Petroleum Exporting Countries (OPEC) in Vienna in December 1975, organized by Ilich Ramírez Sánchez (alias Carlos Martínez) and also in the hijacking of an Air France airbus flying from Tel Aviv to Paris but rescued early in July 1976 by Israeli commandos flown to Entebbe (Uganda)—from which action she escaped alive; and was arrested in Switzerland on Dec. 30, 1977, when she was found in possession of weapons of the type used in the kidnapping of Dr Schleyer (see page 437) and also of currency which was part of a ransom paid for the release of W. M. Palmers, an Austrian industrialist kidnapped on Nov. 9-10, 1977 (see above under June 2 Movement), whereafter a Swiss court sentenced her, on June 30, 1978, to 15 years in prison, inter alia for attempted murder and illegal possession of arms.

Ulrike Meinhof Commando

This Commando of the RAF claimed responsibility for the killing of Dr Siegfried Buback (Chief Federal Prosecutor) and his chauffeur in Karlsruhe on April 7, 1977 (and also of a bodyguard, who died during the night of April 12-13). Dr Buback had been responsible for the co-ordination of measures against espionage and terrorism in the FRG. On April 4, 1977, he had announced the arrest (after extradition from Sweden) of Norbert Kröcher and Manfred Adomeit (two Red Army Faction activists suspected of having planned the kidnapping of a Swedish minister without portfolio in 1975) and had warned the public against the terrorists' ability to plan simultaneous actions in the FRG and abroad.

The Commando issued a statement accusing Dr Buback of being responsible for the "murder" of H. Meins (who had died as a result of a hunger strike on Nov. 9, 1974), Ulrike Meinhof (who had committed suicide in prison on May 9, 1976) and S. Hausner (who was shot by Swedish police during the attack on the West German embassy in Stockholm on April 24, 1975, and who died of his wounds in a German prison hospital on May 4, 1975). Three persons suspected of involvement in the assassination of Dr Buback were Knut Folkerts, Christian Klar and Günter Sonnenberg, all of whom had joined the Haag-Mayer Group (see separate entry) in 1976. K. Folkerts was arrested in Utrecht (Netherlands) on Sept. 22, 1977, after killing a policeman and injuring another, and was on Dec. 20 of that year sentenced to 20 years in prison for murder, attempted murder and illegal possession of weapons. On July 31, 1980, he was sentenced in Stuttgart to life imprisonment for his part in the murder of Dr Buback.

Ulrike Meinhof-Puig Antich Commando

This group incorporated in its name that of the member of the extreme left-wing Iberian Liberation Movement (MIL) who was executed in Barcelona on March 2, 1974, for the killing of a policeman and involvement in a bank robbery—despite widespread protests against his death sentence. It claimed responsibility for a bomb explosion at a nuclear power station construction site at Fessenheim (Alsace) on May 3, 1975, and also for bomb explosions at various offices of Swedish concerns in Paris and at the West German consulate in Nice on May 21, 1975.

Waltraud Boock Liberation Group

This Group was named after Waltraud Boock, a member of the Haag-Mayer Group (see separate entry) who had been arrested on Dec. 13, 1976, and it claimed responsibility for two bomb attacks in Austria. Of the Group's members, Hans Georg Wagner was killed and Peter Hörmann seriously injured in a bomb explosion in Vienna on Jan. 28, 1977. According to the Vienna police these two men had committed both of the two earlier bomb attacks.

Left-wing Organization opposed to RAF

Revolutionary Cells *(Revolutionäre Zellen)*

This movement, established in 1973 as an offshoot of the RAF, was held responsible for some 70 bomb and arson attacks between 1973 and mid-1978, in particular against industrial property in the Ruhr area. An arsenal belonging to this organization was uncovered in Wiesbaden on Sept. 11, 1978, in connexion with which two women—Leila Bocook (a naturalized Turk) and Sylvia Herzinger—were arrested. On March 23, 1980, members of the organization exploded three bombs at the Federal Labour Court in Kassel and on May 23, 1981, the organization accepted responsibility for arson at US barracks in Frankfurt.

The organization also admitted responsibility for the murder, on May 11, 1981, of Heinz-Herbert Karry (Minister of the Economy and Transport in Hesse) but claimed that its members had intended only to maim him. During 1982 the organization claimed responsibility for a bomb attack on July 2 on the US Forces headquarters in Frankfurt and, on July 20, for several bomb attacks on the property of firms building a third runway for Frankfurt airport. (Attacks on US military bases had also taken place early in June 1982, and a further bomb exploded on Aug. 11-12 in a Frankfurt residential area housing US military personnel.)

The Revolutionary Cells consist of small groups independent of each other (without authoritarian structure as in the case of the RAF, which they reject) and modelled on the Italian Red Brigades; they have been estimated to have about 200 members. In contrast to the RAF, the Revolutionary Cells intend to mobilize all "victims of the inhuman society" such as squatters, anti-nuclear militants, prisoners and other social outcasts. They have published, about once a year, a journal called *Revolutionärer Zorn* ("Revolutionary Rage").

Greece

Capital: Athens   Pop. 9,530,000

Greece, or the Hellenic Republic, is a parliamentary democracy with a President as head of state who is elected by Parliament for a five-year term and who exercises legislative power jointly with Parliament and executive power jointly with the Government headed by a Prime Minister. The unicameral 300-member Parliament is elected for a five-year term by universal adult suffrage under a system of reinforced proportional representation. In parliamentary elections held on Oct. 18, 1981, the seats were contested by numerous parties but only three of them obtained more than 2 per cent of the valid votes cast and any seats—the Pan-Hellenic Socialist Movement (Pasok) 172, New Democracy 115 and the Greek Communist Party (KKE Exterior) 13.

In recent years the internal security of Greece has been disturbed by acts of violence committed by members of several extreme right-wing groups and also of numerous small extreme left-wing organizations. An anti-terrorism law passed by Parliament on April 17, 1978 (by 158 votes to 109), provided inter alia for the mandatory death penalty for terrorist acts resulting in loss of life, life imprisonment for such acts carried out without loss of life and up to 10 years' imprisonment for membership of a terrorist organization. For refusing military service members of the Jehovah's Witnesses sect have been given severe prison sentences.

Right-wing Organizations

Fourth of August Movement

This group, named after the date of a military takeover in 1936, was one of several right-wing organizations of which members were arrested in 1977 for alleged terrorist offences and illegal possession of arms and explosives.

New Order

This group, which was affiliated to the Italian *Ordine Nuovo* (banned in Italy in 1973), was used by the military regime (of 1967-74) to intimidate its opponents. It was one of 23 extreme right-wing organizations which in 1974 obtained recognition as legal political parties, subject to the provisos that they did not "disseminate ideas tending to overthrow the existing political order or social system" and that they declared formally that their statutes were "opposed to any action aimed at the violent seizure of power or the overthrow of the free democratic regime". Nevertheless, New Order was said to have carried out a number of subversive activities in 1975-76.

Organization of National Restoration

This Organization claimed responsibility, inter alia, for the detonation of over 40 explosive devices in Athens on Dec. 17, 1978—carried out as an "act of commemoration" of the assassination of a convicted torturer (under the military regime of 1967-74) by left-wing elements on Dec. 14, 1976. The group was said to have been formed by supporters of the former military regime.

Left-wing Organizations

June 1978 Organization

This group, established as an offshoot of the 17th November Revolutionary Organization (see separate entry), claimed responsibility for the assassination of a convicted torturer (in the secret police under the military regime in 1967-74) on Jan. 31, 1979.

New October 80 Revolutionary Organization

This group took its name from the month in which Greece re-entered the military structure of the North Atlantic Treaty Organization (NATO). It was responsible for fire bombs which destroyed two Athens department stores on Dec. 19, 1980.

441

People's Revolutionary Struggle (ELA)

This group, which was an offshoot of the 17th November Revolutionary Organization (see separate entry), claimed responsibility for the destruction of vehicles at an Athens bus depot on Jan. 31, 1979, and for attacks on US premises in Salonika in November 1978 and on an Athens court building in May 1979. Seven members of the group arrested in Crete on Feb. 17, 1980, were charged with acts of terrorism. Other members caused bomb explosions near Athens on Aug. 4, 1980; at Shell and British Petroleum offices in Athens on Aug. 21, 1980; at the US ambassador's residence in Athens on April 1, 1982; at a shop selling US-made computer equipment in Athens on April 25-26, 1982; under a US diplomat's car in Athens on April 28, 1982; and at the American Express office in Salonika on April 30, 1982.

Popular Front Action

This group was established as an offshoot of a Marxist-Leninist People's Power group. When 10 of its members were arrested on Feb. 15, 1980, some of them were said to have been trained in Lebanon by the Popular Front for the Liberation of Palestine (PFLP) and to have planned attacks on various targets, including the US embassy in Athens and the US ambassador's residence.

Revolutionary Anti-Capitalist Initiative

This group claimed responsibility for a fire in which six buildings, including a large department store, were destroyed in Athens on June 3, 1981. Fires were also caused in other areas in July-August 1981.

Revolutionary Left

This group was held responsible for the explosion of four car bombs in Athens on July 16, 1980, and for arson attacks on five cars of the US military mission in Greece on Sept. 16, 1980.

17th November Revolutionary Organization

This group claimed responsibility for the assassination of an alleged UN intelligence officer in Athens on Dec. 23, 1975, and of a convicted torturer (i.e. a former member of the secret police under the military regime in 1967-74) on Dec. 14, 1976. Following the assassination of a deputy riot police chief and his driver on Jan. 16, 1980, nine members of the group were arrested.

Iceland

Capital: Reykjavik   Pop. 235,000

The Republic of Iceland is a multi-party democratic state with a President elected (and re-eligible) for a four-year term by universal adult suffrage. Executive power is held by a Cabinet headed by a Prime Minister, and legislative power by a bicameral 60-member Parliament (*Althing*) similarly elected for a four-year term, consisting of an Upper House constituted by one-third of the whole *Althing*'s members elected at a joint sitting, and the Lower house comprising the remaining two-thirds of its members.

As a result of elections held on April 24, 1983, the seats in the *Althing* were distributed as follows: Independence Party (conservative) 23, Progressive Party 14, People's Alliance (Communist-dominated) 10, Social Democrats 6, New Social Democrats 4, Feminists 3.

There has been no evidence of activities of extra-parliamentary opposition groups in Iceland.

Ireland

Capital: Dublin   Pop. 3,400,000

The Republic of Ireland is, under its 1937 Constitution, "a sovereign, independent democratic state" with a President elected for a seven-year term by universal adult suffrage; he holds specific constitutional powers and is advised by a Council of State. Legislative power is vested in the National Parliament consisting of the President and two Houses—(i) a House of Representatives (*Dail Eireann*) of 166 members elected for a five-year term by adult suffrage (under a complex system of proportional representation) and (ii) a Senate of 60 members (11 nominated by the Prime Minister, six elected by the universities and 43 chosen by representatives of vocational and administrative bodies). Executive power is held by a Government headed by a Prime Minister and responsible to the *Dail*.

As a result of elections held on Nov. 24, 1982, seats in the *Dail* were distributed as follows: *Fianna Fail* 75, *Fine Gael* 70, Labour Party 16, Workers' Party 2, Independent *Fianna Fail* 1, independents 2. Parties not represented in Parliament included the Communist Party of Ireland, the Democratic Socialist Party (which took part in the elections but failed to gain any seats) and the Provisional *Sinn Fein*.

For many years a major security problem has been posed for the Irish Government by extremist Republican movements seeking the integration of Northern Ireland in a united Ireland. These movements are dealt with in the section on Northern Ireland under the United Kingdom (pages 499-503). For its part, the Dublin Government has taken stringent measures of various kinds to suppress the activities of such movements south of the border and has repeatedly declared its belief that the unification of Ireland cannot be achieved by violent means.

The Alliance

This group was said to have been formed inside Portlaoise prison in September 1981 by former members of the Irish National Liberation Army (INLA) and the Provisional Irish Republican Army serving their sentences.

The group appeared to have a paramilitary character and to have organized resistance to searches by prison officers, one of whom narrowly escaped assassination by an alleged member of the group in an attack on March 23, 1983.

Italy

Capital: Rome Pop. 57,100,000

The Italian Republic is, under its 1948 Constitution, "a democratic republic founded on work". It has a bicameral Parliament consisting of a 315-member Senate and a 630-member Chamber of Deputies, the latter being elected for a five-year term by universal adult suffrage; it also has a President elected for seven years at a joint session of both Houses of Parliament and of delegates from 20 regional councils. Any attempts to reconstitute the Fascist Party (which was in power in 1922-43) is prohibited under the Constitution and under a special law passed in 1952. Elections held to the Chamber of Deputies in June 1983 resulted in the following distribution of seats: Christian Democrats 225, Communist Party 198, Socialist Party 73, Italian Social Movement (neo-fascist) 42, Republican Party 29, Social Democratic Party 23, Liberal Party 16, Radical Party 11, Party of Proletarian Democracy 7, others (regional parties) 6.

In recent decades, Italy's society has been exposed to widespread acts of political violence, including murders and kidnappings (although the latter are usually accompanied by demands for ransom and thus by no means all politically motivated). In December 1970 the Prefect of Milan stated that there were "20,000 armed extremists" in the country, and the Ministry of the Interior declared that of 1,290 persons charged with violence in 1970 about two-thirds had been members of "extra-parliamentary movements". On May 18, 1978, the Prime Minister reported to the Chamber of Deputies that the number of political crimes had risen from 1,198 in 1976 to 2,129 in 1977 (i.e. by 77 per cent, with 42 members of the Carabinieri and the police force having been killed).

In view of the rising number of acts of terrorism, the Government repeatedly increased the penalties for such acts. Under a decree which came into force on Dec. 15, 1979, mandatory life sentences were introduced for the murder of policemen, members of the judiciary, lawyers and trade union leaders. President Alessandro Pertini (Socialist) declared in a 1981 New Year message that the "terrorist threat" meant that Italy was "at war"; that in his view the terrorism was being organized from abroad; that the bridge constituted by Italy (between Europe on the one hand and Africa and the Middle East on the other) could be destroyed if Italy's democracy was destabilized; and that this constituted a danger to the whole of Europe.

Official statistics for the years 1978-81 on the activities of organizations described as "terrorist" showed that the number of individual incidents fell from 2,395 in 1978 to 2,366 in 1979, to 1,264 in 1980 and to 848 in 1981; on the other hand, casualties resulting from these incidents rose from 25 killed and 99 injured in 1978 to 120 killed and 288 injured in 1980, thereafter falling to 26 killed and 70 injured in 1981. The large totals for 1980 include casualties resulting from the bombing of Bologna railway station in August, in which 85 persons were killed. A total of 113 different "terrorist" organizations claimed responsibility for 229 of the 848 incidents of 1981, and 91 of these organizations were said to be of the extreme left and most of the remainder of the extreme right.

In a report presented by the Italian police on June 22, 1982, it was stated that between 1969 and March 1982 acts of terrorism had led to the death of 364 persons and injury to 1,075, while 1,414 members of armed left-wing groups and 432 of extreme right-wing groups had been imprisoned.

Under a law (the *Legge Cossiga*) enacted in May 1982 the courts were empowered to give lighter sentences to convicted "terrorists" who confessed or gave information to the authorities. The law expired on Jan. 29, 1983, and according to a spokesman for the Ministry of Justice 389 guerrillas from the Red Brigades and the Front Line group had made use of it—78 of them having actively and continuously co-operated with the police, 134 having confessed their crimes and given some information about them, and 177 having formally renounced their group's actions. At the beginning of 1983 there were some 36,000 people held in Italian prisons, about two-thirds of them awaiting trial (according to the Chief Prosecutor's report for 1982).

Right-wing Movements

Anno Zero

This organization was one of several neo-fascist groups accused by the Minister of the Interior on Aug. 13, 1974, of trying to create chaos by a "strategy of terror" threatening Italy's democratic institutions.

Armed Nazi Cells *(Squadre Nazi Armate)*

This neo-Nazi group was responsible for the firebombing of the home of a Jewish community leader in Livorno on Feb. 17, 1980.

Armed Revolutionary Nuclei (*Nuclei Armati Rivoluzionari,* NAR)

The NAR is a neo-fascist organization which has been held responsible for major bomb explosions and for the killing of a number of its political opponents. Its actions included the causing of a bomb explosion damaging the Capitol in Rome on April 20, 1979; of a bomb attack on the Regina Coeli prison in Rome on May 14, 1979; and of an explosion at the Bologna railway station on Aug. 2, 1980, when 85 persons were killed and 194 injured. The Bologna attack was reportedly carried out "in honour of Mario Tutti", a right-wing extremist serving a life sentence for murdering a policeman and also charged with involvement in an explosion on a Rome-Munich express on Aug. 5, 1974. The NAR later denied any involvement in the Bologna station explosion.

On Feb. 22, 1980, NAR members killed a member of the (left-wing) Workers' Autonomy Group. Four suspected NAR members were arrested on Feb. 28 on charges of illegal possession of arms. On March 12 NAR members bombed a Communist Party office in Naples. The group also accepted responsibility for the killing of a policeman on May 28, of a deputy public prosecutor (investigating right-wing attacks) in Rome on June 23, 1980, and of a policeman in Rome on

Dec. 6, 1981—one day after police had killed Alessandro Alibrandi, an NAR suspect, in a gun battle north of Rome. The NAR also admitted shooting another policeman in Rome on June 24, 1982.

In connexion with the Bologna station bombing, warrants of arrest were issued on Sept. 11, 1982, against five alleged perpetrators of this attack—Stefano delle Chiaie, a former leader of the neo-Nazi National Vanguard (see separate entry), who had fled to South America in 1976; Maurizio Giorgi; Pier-Luigi Pagliai (who was extradited by Bolivia on Oct. 11, arrived in Rome on Oct. 12 but died on Nov. 5, 1982, from wounds received in a gunfight in Bolivia); Joachim Fiebelkorn (a West German who surrendered to the police in Frankfurt on Sept. 13); and Olivier Danet (a Frenchman detained in France for illicit arms trading with Belgium and linked to various extreme right-wing groups). A sixth suspect, Carmine Palladino, had been murdered in prison on Aug. 4, 1982, by Pier-Luigi Concutelli, who had claimed that Palladino was responsible for the death of Giorgio Vale (a long-sought NAR member shot in a gun battle with police in Rome on May 5, 1982) and who had in April 1981 strangled another prisoner, Ermanno Brezza, a neo-fascist who had turned police informer.

Early in October 1982 police in Milan arrested Roberto Frigato, described as the "killer" of a gang led by Gilberto Cavallini and Pasquale Belsito (both of whom had gone underground), who were accused of being involved in the killing of two Carabinieri, various robberies and the Bologna station bomb explosion. Frigato's arrest was made possible through the co-operation with the police of another neo-fascist, and he was also accused of trading in arms and involvement in assassinations and kidnappings in Lombardy and Venetia.

On Feb. 22, 1983, a court in Rome sentenced two NAR members to life imprisonment and two others to terms of 21 years and 15 years and eight months respectively in prison on charges of killing a neo-fascist whom they had mistaken for a police informer. On April 26, 1963, police in Rome arrested Fabrizio Zani, said to be one of the most dangerous right-wing terrorists, with two other persons, all alleged to be members of the NAR, and also uncovered a quantity of weapons, explosives and forged identity documents.

Black Order *(Ordine Nero)*

This group was established in 1974 as a successor to the New Order organization, which was banned in November 1973 (see separate entry). *Ordine Nero* claimed responsibility for a bomb explosion at an anti-fascist demonstration in Brescia on May 28, 1974, when eight persons were killed and 95 injured, and also for an explosion on the Rome-Munich express on Aug. 5 of that year, when 12 persons were killed and 48 injured. On this occasion the group accused the Italian Government of leading the country towards Marxism and asserted that Nazism would "return to save Italy". On Aug. 12, 1974, it warned the Prime Minister that it had condemned him for "exploitation of the Italian people".

Having planted bombs at several other places, *Ordine Nero* claimed responsibility for an explosion at Savona (on the coast west of Genoa) on Nov. 21, 1974 (when one person was killed and eight were wounded), and on Dec. 23 of that year it threatened to place bombs inside churches unless "the Church and the Pope give their immense wealth to the people" and to carry out a "massacre" if "charity institutes refused to accept the sums which the Church will have to give". The group appears to have been dormant since the mid-1970s. Mario Affatigato, a former leader of the group, was extradited from France to Italy on Sept. 7, 1980, being suspected of involvement in the Bologna station explosion of Aug. 2, 1980, attributed to the Armed Revolutionary Nuclei (see separate entry).

Compass Card *(Rosa dei Venti)*

This right-wing movement, supported by some members of the armed forces, was investigated by the authorities in late 1973, when a list of some 2,000 persons was found whom the movement allegedly planned to assassinate after a coup. Andre Mario Piaggio, an industrialist, was arrested on Aug. 24, 1974, on charges of giving financial support to *Rosa dei Venti*.

Ludwig Group *(Gruppe Ludwig)*

This neo-Nazi group has accepted responsibility for killing eight persons, including three priests. One of the latter, Fr Armando Bison, died in Trento on March 8, 1983, of wounds received a fortnight earlier.

Mussolini Action Squads *(Squadre Azione Mussolini,* SAM)

The SAM group was repeatedly reported to have accepted responsibility for bomb attacks on offices of left-wing organizations before 1974. A SAM camp with arms and explosives was discovered at Rieti (north-east of Rome) in June 1974, when a SAM activist was killed and plans were found for the killing of three magistrates and the kidnapping of another. On July 9, 1974, several SAM members were, with other neo-fascists, accused of planning a "strategy of tension" aimed at causing civil war and with conspiracy and attempting to subvert the Constitution.

National Front *(Fronte Nazionale)*

An investigation into an alleged attempt of this organization to carry out a coup d'état was abandoned for lack of evidence in 1972. Its leader, Prince Junio Valerio Borghese (then abroad), was allowed to return to Italy in December 1973. In October 1974, however, Prince Borghese was alleged to have backed a plot which was cancelled at the last moment, and a number of persons were later arrested or questioned in connexion with the planned coup. Prince Borghese, however, had died in Spain in August 1974.

In September 1975 the Attorney-General proposed charges to be brought against 84 people, including Gen. Vito Miceli (a former head of the secret service, SID, arrested on Oct. 31, 1974) and a former military commander (arrested in December 1974 for trying to seize power in 1970 in an operation known as "Tora Tora"). Gen. Miceli was released on bail on April 30, 1975, and was acquitted on July 14, 1978, when 46 other defendants were given prison sentences of from two to 10 years. Those sentenced included Mario Rosa (the only accused held in custody), who was given 10 years, and Sandro Saccucci (who had left the country—see under "New Order"), who was given four years.

On July 14, 1978, a court in Rome decided that National Front members had conspired against the Republic between 1969 and 1972 but had not attempted to stage a coup, and that Italy's democratic institutions had not been seriously endangered.

National Vanguard *(Avanguardia Nazionale)*

This neo-fascist group was one of several accused by the Minister of the Interior on Aug. 13, 1974, of trying to create chaos. It had repeatedly accepted responsibility for bomb attacks on offices of left-wing groups before 1974. One of the group's leading members, Pier Luigi Concutelli, was imprisoned after confessing to having murdered, in Rome on July 10, 1976, Judge Vittorio Occorsi, who had been investigating the activities of the New Order (see below); Concutelli was also said to have been associated with extreme right-wing groups in Spain and to have links with the Propaganda Due lodge (see separate entry).

New Order *(Ordine Nuovo)*

This organization was founded by Tino Rauti, a journalist and former member of the Italian Social Movement (MSI), who was its leader until 1969, when he rejoined the MSI. The organization was banned on Nov. 23, 1973, after 30 of its members (out of an estimated total of 600) had on Nov. 21 been sentenced to from six months to five years in prison for violating the 1952 *"Legge Scelba"* (which provided for imprisonment for from three to 10 years for promoting or organizing under any form the reconstitution of the dissolved Fascist Party). At the same time, all property of the New Order was ordered to be confiscated. The movement had earlier claimed responsibility for attacks on the offices of left-wing organizations.

There followed several trials for alleged New Order activities. On Dec. 3, 1975, Sandro Saccucci (an MSI deputy) was sentenced to four years in prison and barred from public office for five years for forming and organizing the New Order; this sentence was, however, suspended pending an appeal, and during the May 1976 election campaign he left the country while he was being sought in connexion with the shooting of a Communist after an MSI rally near Rome.

The trial of 119 persons, which had begun on July 16, 1974, on charges of trying to reconstitute the Fascist Party and belonging to the New Order, was repeatedly adjourned.

Popular Revolutionary Movement *(Movimento Popolare Rivoluzionario, MPR)*

This neo-fascist group was reported to have been active during 1980.

Propaganda Due (P-2)

Leadership. Lucio Gelli (Grand Master).

The existence of this secret Masonic lodge became known in March 1981 when the police recovered a list of 931 alleged members and other documents showing that the lodge had been involved not only in large-scale crimes but also in right-wing terrorist activities in the late 1960s and early 1970s, including a bomb explosion in Milan in 1969. In a report to the Government by a Milan magistrate in May 1981 it was stated: "The P-2 lodge is a secret sect which has combined business and politics with the intention of destroying the constitutional order of the country and transforming the parliamentary system into a presidential system."

A special commission appointed in May 1981 reported on June 15, 1981, that P-2 presented the characteristics of a "secret society" and could therefore be in breach of the Constitution. On June 20 a total of 22 members of P-2, including a former head of the secret service (SID), were charged with political conspiracy and activities against the state.

The list of alleged P-2 members discovered by the police contained also the names of a number of senior officials and of the editor-in-chief of the Milan *Corriere della Sera,* who were subsequently replaced. Disclosures made during this affair also led to a government crisis and the formation of a largely new administration under the premiership of the leader of the Republican Party (PRI) on June 28, 1981, and to the approval by the Government, on July 29, 1981 of a bill outlawing and dissolving all secret societies.

At the request of the Italian authorities Lucio Gelli, who had fled to Switzerland, was arrested in Geneva on Sept. 13, 1982, and continued to be held pending his possible extradition to Italy. In March 1983 the High Council of Magistratures declared inter alia that the P-2 had directed its efforts towards political changes and interference in the most sensitive affairs of the state. However, it was also decided officially that mere membership of the P-2 did not constitute an offence.

Revolutionary Action Movement *(Movimento di Azione Rivoluzionaria, MAR)*

Leadership. Carlo Fumagalli (l.).

On May 23, 1974, Carlo Fumagalli and 21 other MAR members were arrested after the discovery of an arms smuggling ring linking subversive right-wing movements in the Milan and Brescia regions. The police accused the MAR on July 30, 1974, of having planned to set up, in collaboration with the Compass Card *(Rosa dei Venti)* group (see separate entry), a fascist republic in Italy. On Feb. 2, 1978, Fumagalli was sentenced to 20 years in prison for political conspiracy, while 15 other defendants were given prison sentences of from five to 15 years, and 40 received shorter prison terms.

Young Italy *(Giovane Italia)*

This group was said to consist of "mercenaries" expelled from the Italian Social Movement (MSI) and paid from unknown sources for acts of violence against leftists before 1974.

Youth Front *(Fronte dalla Gioventù)*

This group, standing to the right of the Italian Social Movement (MSI), accepted responsibility for bomb attacks on offices of left-wing organizations before 1974.

Left-wing Movements

Annamaria Ludmann Column—see under Red Brigades

Anti-fascist Nuclei *(Nuclei Antifascisti)*

This small group was reported to be active in 1980 and had, inter alia, bombed the offices of the Italian Social Movement (MSI) in Rome on March 21 of that year.

Armed and Organized Proletarian Group *(Gruppo Armato Organizzato Proletario)*

This group was reported to have been active in Rome during 1980, injuring two night-watchmen by shooting them on May 6.

Armed Communist Squads *(Squadre Armate Comunisti)*

This was one of several small left-wing groups reported to be engaged in terrorist acts in 1980, including the killing of a state prosecutor in Salerno on March 16.

Armed Patrols for Communism *(Ronde Armate per il Comunismo)*

Members of this group were responsible for the bombing of a labour exchange at Rovigo (south of Padua) on Feb. 7, 1980.

Armed Proletarian Nuclei *(Nuclei Armati Proletari,* NAP)

The NAP has been responsible for committing numerous acts of violence since its inception in 1974. These included an attack on a subsidiary of the (US) International Telephone and Telegraph Corporation (ITT) in Milan on Oct. 6, 1974—the ITT being alleged to have played a role in the overthrow of the left-wing Allende Government in Chile in 1973.

In April 1975 the NAP was reported to have planned retaliatory action for an attack on Communists by right-wing extremists in Rome on April 23. On May 6, 1975, the NAP accepted responsibility for the kidnapping of Dr Giuseppe di Gennaro, a Rome judge, who was, however, released on May 11 after the authorities has agreed to transfer three prisoners to a Piedmont prison (in compliance with one of the demands of the NAP). In June 1975 the police discovered seven NAP cells in Rome, arrested six NAP members and recovered part of a ransom paid in December 1974 for the release of a kidnapped industrialist (Giuseppe Moccia).

By January 1977 the NAP was officially held responsible for 30 political crimes, which included the kidnapping of Guido De Martino (a Socialist leader in Naples) who was released upon payment of the equivalent of about $1,100,000. For this kidnapping 15 people were, in Naples on Jan. 9, 1978, given prison sentences of from eight to 14 years. By October 1977 the NAP was believed to have formed a central command with the Red Brigades (see separate entry), and it later claimed responsibility, together with the Red Brigades, for the murder of a prison guard in Udine on June 6, 1978.

Armed Proletarian Power *(Potere Proletario Armato)*

This offshoot of the Red Brigades was responsible for attacking a woman doctor employed at a women's prison in Rome in December 1982 and for killing a woman warder at the same prison on Jan. 28, 1983.

Armed Radical Groups for Communism *(Gruppi Armati Radicali per il Comunismo,* GAR)

Two suspected members of this organization were arrested in Genoa on Dec. 9, 1982, for alleged participation in bomb attacks in Genoa in 1978-80.

Communist Fighting Nuclei *(Nuclei Combattenti Comunisti)*

A group of this name claimed responsibility for causing a bomb explosion which, on Jan. 3, 1982, shattered the outside wall of the prison at Rovigo (40 miles from Venice), which enabled three women members of the Front Line (among them Susanna Ronconi, a former Red Brigades member) and one of the Red Brigades to escape from the prison. (Of the four women, Loredana Biancamano was recaptured on April 15, 1982, and Susanna Ronconi on Oct. 28, 1982.)

On Nov. 23, 1982, a court in Rome sentenced 31 members of the group to imprisonment for from three to 30 years for attempted homicide, kidnapping, robbery, bombing attacks and violation of arms regulations, without leniency being shown to those defendants who had co-operated with the police.

Communist Fighting Organization *(Organizzazione Comunista Combatente)*

This group was active in 1980, attacking in particular a politician in Milan on Feb. 10.

Communist Group for Proletarian Internationalism

This Group claimed responsibility for bomb explosions in Rome on Oct. 23-24, 1981, the targets including the Chilean embassy, the Guatemalan mission to the Vatican and an Argentine government commercial office. On May 26, 1982, the Group also claimed responsibility for an explosion at the offices of the *International Daily News* in Rome.

Communist Nucleus (Nucleo Comunista)

This group accepted responsibility for five bomb explosions which damaged a prison under construction near Pesaro (central Italy) on Sept. 29, 1982.

Communist Patrols for Counter-power (Ronde Comunisti per Contrapotere)

Members of this group were responsible for bombing police barracks in Rome on April 4, 1980.

Continuous Struggle (Lotta Continua)

Leadership. Guido Vale (l.).

Although this Maoist group took part (unsuccessfully), as part of a United Left alliance, in general elections in 1979, some of its members have been involved in acts of violence. Such actions have been directed mainly against right-wing extremists, the targets including the office of the Italian Social Movement (MSI) in Turin on Jan. 27-28, 1973.

An attack by members of the group on the offices of the daily *Corriere della Sera* in Milan on March 11-12, 1973, was followed by fighting with MSI followers and police, at least 50 of whom were injured. The group, which has wide student support and rejects the Communist Party of Italy for "betraying the working classes", believes that it is justified in retaliating against police who fire the first shot.

Front Line (Prima Linea, PL)

Leadership. Sergio Segio (founder); Corrado Alunni (l.).

This organization was established in 1976 as one of the groups of "organized autonomists" (outside the three major trade union federations) with a largely working-class membership. It has been responsible for a number of attacks on industrialists and other persons concerned with production, and it has co-operated with the Red Brigades (see separate entry).

On Oct. 11, 1978, members of the PL killed Alfredo Paolella, a university professor and forensic expert, whom they considered a "state collaborator"; on Nov. 8 of that year a senior magistrate, his driver and his bodyguard were killed by PL members at Patricia (south of Rome). PL members were also responsible for killing a deputy public prosecutor in Milan on Jan. 29, 1979, a Christian Democrat provincial secretary in Palermo on March 9, two policemen in Genoa on Jan. 25, 1980, a Seveso factory executive on Feb. 5, a suspected informer in Milan on Feb. 7, and a magistrate in Milan on March 19. On Dec. 11, 1979, PL members attacked a business school in Turin (where lecturers were employed by Fiat) in retaliation for the dismissal of "troublemakers" and the temporary halting of recruitment at Fiat's plant in Turin.

Marco Donat Cattin (son of the Christian Democrat Senator Carlo Donat Cattin), who was alleged to be a PL member and against whom a warrant of arrest had been issued in May 1980, fled the country after his father had warned him of his impending arrest. On June 21, 1980, a Milan court sentenced 27 alleged PL members to prison terms for murder and kidnapping; those sentenced included Corrado Alunni (the alleged leader of the Red Brigades) sentenced to 29 years in prison to run concurrently with other sentences imposed on him.

Also in 1980 a group of 21 PL members arrested in Paris on July 7 were extradited to Italy on Oct. 26, and the trial of 108 alleged PL members opened in Turin on Dec. 5, 1980. This trial ended on July 29, 1981, when 94 of the defendants were sentenced, among them Susanna Ronconi (to 14½ years in prison, and most others to 14 years each, while 28 received suspended sentences). On June 25, 1982, an appeals court in Turin upheld the convictions of 91 of the accused but reduced some of their sentences, including that of Susanna Ronconi from 14½ to 13½ years.

Three PL members—Maurice Bignami, Roberto Vitelli and Sergio Segio (the founder of the PL, who was still at large)—were sentenced to life imprisonment in Viterbo on Oct. 24, 1981, for killing two policemen in a bank robbery in 1980. On Feb. 11, 1982, an appeal court in Milan sentenced Corrado Alunni (the PL leader) to 29 years and two months in prison and also gave long prison sentences to 29 other defendants. During this trial some of the accused stated that since 1978 there had been links between the PL and the Basque ETA in Spain and that there had been a joint training camp of the two organizations in southern France.

On Aug. 5, 1982, a court in Bergamo sentenced 42 alleged PL members to a total of 467 years in prison. Those sentenced included Sergio Segio and Diego Forestieri, both sentenced in absentia to 24½ and 24 years respectively, Michele Viscardi (12 years and two months) and Marco Donat-Cattin (nine years). Sergio Segio, who had been sentenced in absentia in October 1981 (see above) and was sought in connexion with the killing of Judge Emilio Alessandrini in 1979 and of Judge Guido Galli in March 1980, was arrested in Milan on Jan. 18, 1983. Forestieri, who had escaped from prison in October 1981, was recaptured in Milan on Jan. 27, 1983.

Antonio Pernisco, a PL leader, was on Dec. 19, 1981, reported to have surrendered to the authorities and to have declared that he dissociated himself from the armed struggle which, he said, was "historically defeated" and "ideologically superseded". By Feb. 6, 1982, the police claimed to have "neutralized" 15 PL bases in various parts of the country. In August 1982 former PL members were quoted as having stated that the PL had not approved the action of the Red Brigades (see separate entry) against Aldo Moro, the Christian Democrats' leader, in 1978; that the aim of the PL had been to conduct a social struggle and not to engage in acts of violence for the purpose of obtaining political recognition; and that the Moro affair had been counterproductive as it had revitalized the Italian political system. These former PL members denied that they were committing "political treason" and emphasized that they had only abandoned the armed struggle as a means of expression of the struggle against capitalism; that they wanted a return to the theories of Marx and to the "classical forms of the workers' struggle"; and that terrorism had been "an error".

Front Line Armed Nucleus *(Nucleo Armato dalla Prima Linea)*

This group claimed responsibility for an attack on a police official in Rome on Jan. 6, 1982.

Front Position *(Prima Posizione)*

This group claimed responsibility for killing a Carabinieri officer in Milan on July 16, 1982.

March 28 Column—see under Red Brigades

October 22 Group—see under Red Brigades

Partisan Action Groups *(Gruppi Azione Partigiana,* GAP)

Members of this organization were officially held responsible for a number of acts of violence, notably against NATO installations and also against political opponents, and also for the murder of the Bolivian consul-general in Hamburg in 1971. Giangiacomo Feltrinelli (a publisher whose dead body had been found on March 15, 1972, near a power-line pylon to which explosives had been attached) was on March 21 said to have been an active member of the GAP.

Incriminating material found on April 15, 1972, indicated that Feltrinelli had been involved in organizing a network of left-wing "resistance centres" against a possible right-wing coup, but all charges against several persons suspected of involvement in a conspiracy with Feltrinelli were dropped in October 1973.

Proletarian Squads *(Squadre Proletarie)*

Members of this group were reported to have killed, on Dec. 11, 1980, a Christian Democratic mayor accused of having misappropriated earthquake relief funds.

Red Brigades *(Brigate Rosse,* BR)

Leadership. Renato Curcio (l.); Alberto Franceschini (chief ideologue).

Established in 1969, this organization of Marxist-Leninist urban guerrillas, modelled on the *Tupamaros* of Uruguay, was during the first three years of its existence active mainly in Milan, not only in disseminating Marxist-Leninist propaganda but also in attacks on the property of industrialists and other "enemies of the working class". By 1974 their activities had spread to Genoa and Turin and they had begun kidnapping operations. Since 1976 the BR have operated in most parts of the country, intimidating, wounding or murdering their victims and seeking the greatest possible publicity for their actions. They have published lists of potential victims among factory directors and managers as well as company security guards, and their numerous kidnappings have led to the payment of considerable sums in ransom to them.

The original declared aim of the Red Brigades was to create a situation in which a fascist coup could be provoked; this would lead to a return of the Communist Party of Italy (CPI) to its "revolutionary" role which, the BR asserted, the CPI had abandoned by collaboration with the Government, and to the consequent outbreak of civil war which would bring the left to power. In a statement issued on March 25, 1979, the BR compared its struggle to those of the (Provisional) Irish Republican Army, the (West German) Red Army Faction (Baader-Meinhof Group) and the Palestine Liberation Organization.

In their Journal No. 4 of December 1981 the BR declared that they intended to progress from being a clandestine organization to the stage of a more centralized party which would proclaim "total class war". In another BR communiqué it was stated that their first target would from then on be "the multinational centre of American imperialism". In a further statement issued on Dec. 19, 1981, the BR called for the creation of a "terrorist international" in which the central position would be held by the BR and the West German Red Army Faction, and which the "European revolutionary forces" of the ETA in Spain and the Irish Republican Army could join once they had abandoned "the stifling perspective of nationalism".

The first Red Brigades' terrorist act was the bombing of a Milan electronics firm's premises in 1970. On June 15, 1972, a group of 21 BR members were tried for kidnapping an engineer on March 3 of that year. A Fiat personnel director kidnapped in Turin on

Dec. 14, 1972, was released four days later after he had allegedly supplied the BR with details of Fiat's "espionage system" used against its workers.

On April 18, 1974, BR members abducted Mario Sossi, a senior magistrate in Genoa (who had played an important part in bringing to justice a BR group known as "October 22" responsible for kidnappings in 1972); the BR demanded the release of eight "October 22" members, failing which their victim would be killed; and after a Genoa court had set these men free Sossi was released on May 23. The Government, however, did not give in to other demands made by the BR (for passports and safe conducts to Algeria, Cuba or North Korea for the released eight men), nor was the court order for their release confirmed by the procurator-general or the Supreme Court of Cassation. The BR also claimed responsibility for the murder of two members of the (neo-fascist) Italian Social Movement (MSI) on June 17, 1974.

On Sept. 9, 1974, police arrested Renato Curcio and Alberto Franceschini, who had led the BR since 1972; however, Curcio was liberated from an Alessandria prison on Feb. 18, 1975, by a BR commando including his wife (Margharita Cagol, who was killed in a police raid on June 5, 1975). Curcio was subsequently recaptured in January 1976 and was, on June 23, 1977, sentenced to seven years in prison for wounding a policeman, possessing a firearm and resisting arrest, while four other BR members were given prison sentences of from 2½ to five years. During this trial the BR continued their campaign of intimidation by attacking journalists and threatening to take action against jurors and lawyers' families if the trial were proceeded with.

An earlier trial of Curcio and 52 other BR members for belonging to a subversive organization had opened in May 1976 but was postponed after the assassination of Francesco Cocco (a state prosecutor) by the BR in Genoa, and again after the assassination by BR members on April 28, 1977, of Dr Fulvio Croce, head of the Turin lawyers' association. Another BR member, Carlo Picchiura, was sentenced in Padua on June 1, 1977, to 26 years in prison for killing a policeman and was also ordered to pay compensation to the victim's family.

The BR also claimed responsibility for the mortal wounding, on Nov. 16, 1977, of Carlo Casalegno (deputy editor of *La Stampa* of Turin), who died in hospital on Nov. 29; the killing of Angelo Pistolesi, an extreme right-wing activist, in Rome on Dec. 28; and the murder, on Feb. 14, 1978, of Riccardo Palma, a magistrate in Rome.

On March 16, 1978, members of the BR seized Aldo Moro (61), the president of the Christian Democratic Party (DC), who had been Prime Minister between 1963 and 1976. The BR stated that he would be tried by a "people's court" for being "the most loyal executor of directives laid down by imperialist centres"; they also demanded the release of certain detainees as the price of freeing their hostage. The Italian Government, however, refused to make any concessions to the BR, and this attitude was widely supported, notably by the three major trade union federations, including the (Communist-led) General Confederation of Italian Labour (CGIL).

On April 15, 1978, the BR declared that Aldo Moro had been found guilty and sentenced to death, as his trial by a "people's court" had (they said) exposed "the real and hidden responsibilities in the bloodiest pages of the history of recent years", "the intrigues of those who held power, the conspiracy that covered up murder committed by the state, and the intricate web of personal interests and corruption". On April 20 the BR declared that Aldo Moro would be executed within 48 hours unless an unspecified number of "communist" prisoners was released, and on May 9 Aldo Moro was shot dead by at least two of his kidnappers and his body was found in a car parked in the centre of Rome.

On May 17, 1978, five BR members were arrested, and on June 5 these five—Enrico Triaca, Teodoro Spadaccini, Giovanni Lugnini, Antonio Marini and Gabriella Mariani—as well as a sixth BR member still at large were formally charged with complicity in the murder. Three other suspects were charged on June 6.

When the trial of Renato Curcio and others reopened in Turin on March 9, 1978, one of the defendants, Paolo Ferrari, read out a statement on behalf of the accused, declaring a state of war and threatening further violence against anyone who collaborated with the court. Following the assassination, in Turin on March 10, of a policeman who had taken part in the arrest of Ferrari, the trial was again adjourned until May 20. Meanwhile, a senior prison guard, described as a "torturer" of prisoners, was murdered by BR members on April 20, 1978. Nevertheless, on June 23 Curcio was sentenced (in Turin) to 15 years in prison for forming an armed group to subvert the state and for carrying out political kidnappings; Pietro Bassi was given 15 years, Pietro Bertolazzi 14¾ years, Alberto Franceschini 14½ years and 26 others (some of them in absentia) from 2¼ to 13 years, among them Prospero Gallinari, who was sought in connexion with the murder of Aldo Moro and was given a 10-year sentence in absentia. He was later arrested on Sept. 24, 1979.

On June 24, 1978, Massimo Maraschi, another BR member, was sentenced in Alessandria to 24 years in prison for murder, attempted murder and kidnapping, while Pietro Villa, also a BR member, was given five years in Milan for membership of a subversive organization, robbery and sabotage.

Corrado Alunni, the BR leader who was suspected of having masterminded the kidnapping of Aldo Moro, was arrested on Sept. 13, 1978, was a week later sentenced to 12 years and four months in prison for illegal possession of arms and was on Oct. 28 given an additional seven-year sentence for attempted murder and possession of arms. At the same trial in Milan on Oct. 28 Attilio Casaletti was sent to prison for nine years and eight months, Pierluigi Zuffada for 9½ years and three others for from two years and four months to three years and four months for BR activities.

Renato Curcio was on Feb. 6, 1979, given a further 12-year prison sentence for attempted murder and possession of arms and a six-year sentence on Nov. 1 for his escape from prison in 1975, while nine other BR members were also sentenced for "terrorist activities" to from four months to six years in prison. On Oct. 14, 1979, Curcio received a further 10-year sentence and 13 other BR members were given sentences of from eight to 10 years for insulting the judges and inciting BR followers to insurrection during the 1978 trial.

Further acts of violence had been committed by BR members from October 1978 onwards. Girolamo Tartaglione, a senior official at the Ministry of Justice, was shot dead at his home in Rome by BR members on Oct. 10, 1978. During the May 1979 election campaign BR members carried out many attacks, including one on a Christian Democratic Party office in Rome on May 3, when a policeman was killed and two others were injured, while the building was damaged by bombs and the terrorists escaped unharmed. Other policemen killed by BR members included two in Genoa on Nov. 21, 1979, one in Rome on Nov. 27, another in Rome on Dec. 7, three in Milan on Jan. 8, 1980, two (one of them the police chief) in Genoa on Jan. 25, and three in Turin on March 24. BR members also murdered, on Jan. 29, 1980, a Montedison deputy technical director in Mestre, and on Feb. 12 Vittorio Bachelet, deputy president of the High Council of Magistratures and a leading DC member, on the Rome University campus where he taught.

BR members were also responsible for the killing of the head of the anti-terrorist police in Mestre on May 12, 1980; of a Christian-Democratic regional councillor in Naples on May 19 (for which four BR members were on July 8, 1980, sentenced to life imprisonment); and of Walter Tobagi, a journalist on the *Corriere della Sera* of Milan, killed on May 28 by a "March 28" column of the BR. Tobagi was co-author of a book on the

psychology of terrorism and had, after police had killed four BR suspects on March 28, 1980, written a newspaper article on the "disintegrating myth of the [Genoa] column of the BR".

The Italian police had, in fact, been able to carry out large-scale arrests of BR members (and also of the Front Line organization—see separate entry) during March and April 1980. While Mario Moretti, whom an informer had on Feb. 19, 1980, named as the organizer of the Aldo Moro murder, was still at large, Franco Pinna (described as the BR's military chief) and three other BR members suspected of involvement in that murder, were arrested in France on March 29, 1980.

On Dec. 12, 1980, BR members kidnapped Judge Giovanni D'Urso, who was, however, released by them on Jan. 15, 1981, after the Government had, on Dec. 26, acceded to a BR demand to close a maximum security prison on the island of Asinara (off Sardinia) and three newspapers had published BR documents (as also demanded by the BR). A revolt at the Trani prison (in Apulia), where several BR members were detained, was put down by a Carabinieri unit on Dec. 29. Persons killed by BR members late in 1980 were Renato Briano, a Milan industrialist (on Nov. 12), the director of a Milan steel mill (on Nov. 28) and a prison security chief in Rome (on Dec. 31).

During 1981 BR groups made a number of attacks, inter alia on a transport van of the Italian telephone company on July 29; on an Air Force barracks near Rome, where they seized a quantity of weapons, on Aug. 19; and on a military convoy in Salerno on Aug. 26, when there followed a clash with police in which one officer was killed and eight other persons were injured, while the attackers escaped with several automatic weapons. On Feb. 9, 1982, four BR members overpowered guards at a barracks and seized a vanload of weapons at Caserta (20 miles north of Naples).

At a trial held in Cagliari (Sardinia) two BR members, who had turned state witnesses, were on Nov. 8, 1981, reported to have said that they had met dissident members of the Palestine Liberation Organization in Mestre (near Venice) and had received a shipment of submachine-guns and hand grenades from them.

Brig.-Gen. James L. Dozier (a US Army staff officer and deputy commander of NATO land forces Southern Europe) was abducted in Verona on Dec. 17, 1981, and the BR immediately accepted responsibility for this action. The BR subsequently issued several communiqués, and on Dec. 22 they announced that Gen. Dozier had been found guilty by a "people's court" and would be killed. However, on Jan. 28, 1982, police acting on information received from a suspect freed the general unhurt and arrested the five BR members who were holding him in an apartment in Padua. This police action constituted the first occasion on which Italian police had succeeded in freeing a hostage seized by the BR. The five arrested BR members were said to be members of an Annamaria Ludmann Column which had been active in Venetia. Their names were later given as Antonio Savasta, Cesare Di Lenardo, Giovanni Ciucci, Emilia Libera and Emanuela Frascella. (E. Savasta and E. Libera were, also on Jan. 28, sentenced in absentia to 30 years in prison each for involvement in a gun battle with police in Sardinia in February 1980.)

A court in Verona tried altogether 17 BR members (eight of whom were still at large and were tried in absentia) for involvement in Gen. Dozier's abduction, and on March 25, 1982, the court passed prison sentences totalling over 300 years on the defendants; in particular, C. Di Lenardo was given 27 years and Alberta Biliato 17½ years (both these accused having refused to testify for the state). Antonio Savasta and E. Libera were given 16½ and 14 years respectively after Savasta, who had confessed having committed 17 murders, had co-operated with the authorities and had given information which had led to the arrest of hundreds of BR suspects.

An under-secretary at the Ministry of Information stated on March 16, 1982, that since the abduction of Gen. Dozier 385 persons had been arrested on terrorism charges—340 from the BR and affiliated organizations and 45 from the extreme right; that 35 arms caches and "safe houses" had been found in the past three months; and that of those captured only 10 per cent had refused to co-operate with the authorities, most of the "terrorists" having realized that they had failed to attain their political aims.

Four of the five abductors of Gen. Dozier were on March 7, 1982, reported to have issued an appeal to their fellow-members of the BR to give up the armed struggle which, they claimed, had proved "utterly negative" during the past 10 years. Moverover, Prof. Enrico Fenzi, one of the ideologues of the BR, who had in Genoa in 1981 been sentenced to 7½ years in prison for terrorism, declared early in March 1982 that the BR and the idea of armed struggle had failed and that "ten years of bloodstained struggle" had definitively proved that it could "produce no political programme".

Of the eight defendants tried by the Verona court in absentia, Umberto Catabiani, BR leader in Tuscany, was shot dead by police on May 24, 1982; Marcello Capuano (who had been given a 26-year sentence) was captured by police in Rome on May 29, 1982; and Remo Pancelli, also sentenced to 26 years in prison, was arrested near Rome on June 6, 1982. On Jan. 13, 1983, an appeal court in Venice reduced some of the sentences passed by the Verona court, although only insignificant reductions were ordered in the cases of those who had made no confession.

Antonio Savasta, the prominent BR member who had decided to co-operate with the authorities, was on March 10, 1982, reported to have alleged that the Bulgarian secret service had tried to obtain, through a BR infiltrator in the administration, information from Gen. Dozier about NATO and that the Bulgarians had been ready to give aid to the BR. Moreover, he was said to have referred to BR contacts with the Palestine Liberation Organization, which was interested in destabilizing Italy in order to weaken the United States' ability to give aid to Israel.

Persons killed by BR members during 1981 and 1982 included the following: Raffaele Del Cogliano, a Christian Democratic politician and commissioner of the Campania regional government, shot dead in Naples (with his driver) on April 27, 1981; Roberto Peci, seized on June 10 and found dead on Aug. 3, 1981, after his brother Patricio, who had been arrested in 1980, had given the police information on BR activities; Giuseppe Talierco, an industrial manager, killed in Mestre (near Venice) on July 6, 1981; two anti-drug squad policemen asssassinated in Rome on June 8, 1982; Antonio Ammaturo, head of the Naples mobile police squad, and his driver, shot on July 17, 1982, by terrorists who issued a statement in which they expressed praise of the activities of the Camorra (the criminal Mafia of Naples—see below); and Ennio Di Rocco, a BR member killed in prison at Trani (near Bari) by other prisoners on July 27, 1982. The last-named had been arrested in Rome on Jan. 4 together with Stefano Petrella, and both were said to have supplied information to the police leading to the arrest of Prof. Giovanni Senzani (one of the principal theoreticians of the BR) and to the rescue of Gen. Dozier.

Among persons abducted by BR members was Ciro Cirillo, a Christian Democratic politician from Naples, seized on April 27, 1981, but released on July 24 of that year. He stated in March 1982 that his family and friends had raised 1,500 million lire, or about $1,100,000, paid in ransom to the BR.

The trial of 63 defendants (nine of whom were still at large) for involvement in the abduction and killing of Aldo Moro in 1978 (see above) and in other crimes was held in Rome between April 14, 1982, and Jan. 24, 1983. During the trial Antonio Savasta (one of the defendants who had already been sentenced for involvement in the abduction of Gen. Dozier—see above) made a full confession of all his activities within the BR and stated his conclusion that the BR had failed to realize their aims. On May 3, 1982, he denied that the BR had any links with the Irish Republican Army, the Palestine Liberation Organization, Libya or the Israelis.

Passing judgment, the court imposed life sentences on 32 of the defendants for 17 murders (including that of Moro), 11 attempted murders and four kidnappings during the years 1977-80. Among those imprisoned for life were Mario Moretti, said to have directed the kidnapping of Moro, and Prospero Gallinari, convicted of killing Moro. Two of the accused were given 30-year sentences, and A. Savasta and Emilia Libera each received 16 years, this being the highest sentence given to those who had "repented" of their BR activities, but rather higher sentences were given to those who, while dissociating themselves from the crimes committed by the BR, did not co-operate with the authorities.

On Feb. 26, 1983, a court in Genoa sentenced 10 BR members (among them M. Moretti and P. Gallinari, both already convicted in the Moro murder case) to life imprisonment and four others to prison terms of from seven to 18 years for involvement in the murder of five policemen and a trade union official in Genoa in 1978-80. Among seven defendants acquitted at this trial were Patricio Peci and Antonio Savasta, who had served as informers to the Italian security authorities.

In 1977 the BR were said to consist of cells of from three to five members each, of which only one member was in contact with another cell; several cells constituted a "column" in a city or region. There was also, it was reported, a "strategic directorate". The Red Brigades had an estimated membership in 1980 of about 500 activists, with a further 10,000 supporters.

Thereafter, the active membership of the BR was widely believed to have gone into a significant decline, principally because of the success of the security authorities in penetrating and neutralizing the organization's cells in different parts of the country.

Red Brigades—Fighting Communist Party (Brigate Rosse—Partito Comunista Combatente)

This name was assumed by remnants of the so-called militaristic wing of the Red Brigades (BR) formed after the reverses which the BR had suffered at the hands of the police during 1982. The group assumed responsibility for an attempt to murder a professor of labour law in Rome on May 3, 1983.

Red Squad Organized Comrades (Squadra Rossa Compagni Organizzati)

Members of this group killed an employee of the (neo-fascist) daily Il Secolo d'Italia on March 12, 1980.

Revolutionary Action (Azione Rivoluzionaria)

Leadership. Prof. Gianfranco Faina (l.).

This small group was reported to have been active in 1980, with its alleged members including two Britons. The movement's leader was (in Livorno on June 28, 1980) sentenced to 19¼ years in prison for heading this illegal organization.

Revolutionary Mass Organizations (Organismi di Massa Rivoluzionari)

Four persons suspected of belonging to this group were arrested on March 23, 1983, on charges of involvement inter alia in robbery and illegal possession of arms.

Territorial Anti-fascist Squads (Squadre Anti-fascisti Territoriale)

Members of this group were responsible for a bomb attack on the offices of the (neo-fascist) daily Il Secolo d'Italia in Rome on March 7, 1980.

Territorial Communist Nuclei (Nuclei Comunisti Territoriali)

A member of this group killed a janitor at the Fiat plant in Turin on Jan. 31, 1980. In connexion with arson at the Lancia works and the killing of a nightwatchman in January 1980, a group of 25 suspected members of the group were arrested in Turin on Feb. 6, 1982.

Third Organization (Terza Organizzazione)

As one of the so-called "organized autonomists" (outside the three major trade union federations) with a largely working-class membership, this group advocated indiscriminate attacks on "all enemies of the working class".

Unity of Fighting Communists (Unità Combattenti Comunisti)

Leadership. Antonio Campesi (l.).

This group's leader and seven other members were arrested in Milan on Feb. 19, 1980.

Walter Alasia Column

Leadership. Nicolo Di Maria (l.).

This group broke away from the Red Brigades early in 1980. It was responsible for the abduction of Renzo Sandrucci, an Alfa Romeo executive, on June 10, 1981, near Milan; he was, however, released unharmed on July 23, 1981. On Nov. 25, 1981, a court in Rome sentenced 19 alleged members of the Column to a total of 230 years in prison, among them Nadia Mantovani (the girl friend of Renato Curcio, the Red Brigades' leader), who was given a 17-year sentence.

The police officially claimed on March 1, 1982, that it had broken up the Column after the seizure of four vehicles which the Column had intended to use for an attack on the San Vittore prison (in Milan), where Aurore Betti (the Column's "historic leader") was held; he had been arrested in 1981 and succeeded as leader by Nicolo Di Maria. Early in 1983, however, it appeared that the Column had been reconstituted, as police arrested a number of its alleged members in Milan.

Workers' Autonomy *(Autonomia Operaio)*

This organization was established as a successor to Workers' Power (*Potere Operaio*—see separate entry). Prof. Antonio Negri (a teacher of political science at Padua University) was, upon his arrest in April 1979, charged with membership of this illegal organization, which was said to have links with the Red Brigades. Franco Piperno (a physics teacher at Cosenza and a founder-member of Workers' Autonomy), was arrested in France in August 1979 and extradited to Italy in October of that year on charges of involvement in the Moro murder and other killings; however, he was released for lack of evidence on June 30, 1980.

Workers' Power *(Potere Operaio)*

Leaders of this movement were involved in the students' unrest which began in 1968. Its members were said to be responsible for an attack on the home of a leader of the Italian Social Movement (MSI), in which two of his sons were burnt to death on April 13, 1973. When Prof. Antonio Negri and 24 other left-wing intellectuals were arrested in April 1979, he and several others were known to be members of *Potere Operaio* and were said to have joined the Red Brigades, with Prof. Negri becoming one of the latter's leading ideologues. However, charges brought against him in connexion with the murder of Aldo Moro were dropped on April 24, 1980.

Prof. Negri was in October 1981 reported to have condemned the murder of a factory director by the Red Brigades as a "barbaric" deed and to have argued that a new political generation had arisen which was engaged in "great struggles for the community, for peace and for a new kind of happiness".

Regional Movements

SARDINIA

Sardinian Separatists

Leadership. Bainzu Piliu (l.).

Early in December 1982 a total of 15 suspected members of this group were ar-

rested on charges of planning sabotage at Cagliari airport, the NATO base at Decimomannu and refineries, as well as the abduction of a US officer. Those arrested included several members of the Sardinian Action Party (represented by four members in the Sardinian regional Parliament).

SOUTH TIROL

Association for the Protection of Italians

This hitherto unknown right-wing group admitted responsibility for bomb explosions at eight different localities in Bolzano province (South Tirol) on Dec. 5, 1979. The group appeared to be committed to the use of violence to maintain the Italian status of the predominantly German-speaking South Tirol (ceded to Italy by Austria in 1919, and now part of the autonomous Italian region of Trentino-Alto Adige).

Italian Fighters for Alto Adige

This right-wing movement accepted responsibility for an explosion at Brunico (Bruneck) on Oct. 30, 1979, and it threatened to cause further explosions unless the authorities speedily restored an Italian war memorial which was said to have been destroyed by militant (German-speaking) South Tiroleans. The movement also committed arson near the town of Bolzano (Bozen) on Nov. 22, 1980, said to be in retaliation for attacks by the separatist "Tirol" group (see separate entry).

South Tirol Liberation Committee *(Befreiungsausschuss Südtirol)*

This organization favouring the return of South Tirol to Austria (of which it had been part until the end of World War I) was involved in causing a large number of violent acts (some of which led to loss of life) from 1957 onwards. These acts led to trials of numerous supporters of the Committee, including Germans and Austrians, between 1963 and 1971 by courts both in Italy and in Austria. Those tried included Dr Norbert Burger, who was given a life sentence (in absentia) by a court in Florence on May 14, 1970, and who later became the leader of the (small right-wing) National Democratic Party in Austria. From 1980 onwards the aims of the Committee were pursued by a group calling itself "Tirol" (see separate entry).

Tirol

This group of German-speaking Tiroleans has called for full self-determination for South Tirol and has expressed admiration for the Palestinian liberation movement. It was responsible for a number of explosions late in 1980, in particular the destruction of a power pylon near Merano on Nov. 20 and attacks on cars registered in other parts of Italy; it was also responsible for five explosions in Merano and Bressanone (Brixen) on Nov. 26-27, 1981, and for three other explosions in October 1982.

Organized Crime

The power of organized crime, embodied in the Mafia of Sicily and the Camorra of Naples, has been expressed in numerous assassinations of its opponents, including representatives of the state. The most significant of these murders has been that of Gen. Carlo Alberto Dalla Chiesa (and his wife) in Palermo on Sept. 3, 1982. The General had been co-ordinator of anti-terrorist measures since 1978 and had, since May 1982, been directing operations against the Mafia. He was quoted as having said shortly before his death that the Mafia would have to be fought not just in Palermo but in all major Italian cities where it had made "huge investments in real estate, commerce and perhaps also industry". In the eight months before his death there had been 103 murders which had been attributed to the Mafia. Although the killers of the General were not identified, it was generally believed that the Mafia was responsible for his death. The Prime Minister, Giovanni Spadolini, said on Sept. 3 that the General had been "sent to Palermo as the representative of the Government of the Republic to respond to the mortal challenge against the democratic state".

Official statistics gave the total number of Mafia killings in Palermo in 1982 as 151, while those attributed to the Camorra gang in Naples in the same year were given as 265.

Luxembourg

Capital: Luxembourg-Ville   Pop. 365,000

The Grand Duchy of Luxembourg is a constitutional hereditary monarchy in which the head of state exercises executive power through a Council of Ministers headed by a Prime Minister and also takes part in the legislative process. There is a unicameral Chamber of Deputies elected for a five-year term by universal adult suffrage, and also an advisory Council of State of 21 members appointed for life by the sovereign.

As a result of elections to the Chamber of Deputies on June 10, 1979, seats were distributed as follows: Christian Socials 24, Democratic Party 15, Socialist Workers' Party 14, Social Democrats 2, Communists 2, Independent Socialists 1, *Enrôlés de Force* (a pressure group of Luxembourg citizens forcibly enrolled in the German Army in World War II) 1. Parties which unsuccessfully contested the elections were the Liberal Party, the Communist Revolutionary League, the *Club des Indépendants* and the *Alternativ Lëscht-Wiert Iech* (Self-Defence List).

Although there had been no reports of extra-parliamentary opposition activities, the Chamber of Deputies passed, on July 16, 1982, a Communications Control Bill under which the Prime Minister was, in certain circumstances, empowered to order surveillance by technical means of offences against the security of the state. The Bill, was, however, not approved by the Council of State.

Malta

Capital: Valletta   **Pop. 330,000**

The Republic of Malta is an independent member of the Commonwealth and has a President elected for a five-year term by a 65-member House of Representatives, which is elected, also for five years, by universal adult suffrage. The President appoints a Prime Minister and, on his advice, the other ministers. In general elections held on Dec. 12, 1981, the ruling Labour Party retained its 34 seats and the Nationalist Party the remaining 31 in the House of Representatives (while obtaining 50.9 per cent of the valid votes cast, against Labour's 49.1 per cent). Parties not represented in Parliament are the Communist Party and the Progressive Constitutional Party.

The conflict between the two major parties has deeply divided society in Malta. For more than a year after the 1981 elections the (Christian democratic) Nationalist Party pursued a boycott of Parliament on the ground that the result was due to "gerrymandering"; it has also accused the Labour Party of using dictatorial measures. Against a background of growing political violence in recent years, an attempt was made on the life of Dom Mintoff, the (Labour) Prime Minister, on Oct. 10, 1979; a bomb attack was made on his secretary's home on Aug. 20, 1982; and another bomb exploded outside the Nationalist Party's headquarters at Pietà, near Valletta, on Aug. 22 of that year.

Allegations concerning an alleged plot to seize Mintoff and to dissolve all political parties were made on July 31, 1981, when a Maltese citizen was charged in Valletta with failing to report information in his possession concerning this plot; in a statement made to police and read out in court he was said to have asserted that a Maltese citizen had retained 300 British ex-servicemen to carry out the planned coup "to eliminate the threat of a Soviet takeover" of Malta.

No extra-parliamentary opposition groups have, however, been reported to exist in Malta.

Netherlands

Capital: Amsterdam

Seat of Government: The Hague

Pop. 14,000,000

The Kingdom of the Netherlands (comprising the Netherlands in Europe and the Netherlands Antilles) is a constitutional and hereditary monarchy. The Netherlands in Europe has a bicameral Parliament consisting of (i) a 75-member First Chamber elected by the country's 11 provincial councils and (ii) a 150-member Second Chamber elected by direct universal suffrage and by proportional representation. Executive power rests with the Crown and a Council of Ministers whose members may not be members of Parliament.

As a result of elections held on Sept. 8, 1982, seats in the Second Chamber were distributed as follows: Labour Party 47, Christian Democratic Appeal 45, Party of Freedom and Democracy 36, Democrats-66 6, Pacifist Socialist Party 3, Communist Party 3, State Reform Party 3, Radical Reform Party 2, Reformist Political Federation 2, Centre Party 1, Reformed Political Association 1, Evangelical People's Party 1. Parties which failed to secure representation included the Socialist Party, Democratic Socialists-70 and the Farmers' Party.

There are in the Netherlands few indigenous political groups advocating extra-parliamentary action, although riots have been caused (in particular in Amsterdam) by various groups of the "alternative society" as well as squatters and homeless people, notably at the investiture of Queen Beatrix on April 30, 1980. The most violent incidents were caused in 1966-78 by members of the South Moluccan community who had failed to become assimilated in the Dutch community.

Free South Moluccan Organization

Leadership. Eddie Aponno (l.).

This Organization was set up by South Moluccans, of whom some 15,000 had been brought to the Netherlands in 1951 after the Indonesian Government had, in 1951, incorporated into the unitary Indonesian Republic the state of Negara Indonesia Timur (East Indonesia—one of 16 states making up the Republic of Indonesia), which included a Republic of the South Moluccas (Republik Maluku Selatan, RMS) proclaimed in April 1950. After South Moluccans who had remained in Indonesia had continued their resistance to the Indonesian Government, the "President" of the RMS was arrested in 1963 and executed in 1966, whereafter he was succeeded as "President" of the RMS by Dr Jan Alvares Manusama. The latter was resident in the Netherlands, where certain South Moluccans pursued their aim of restoring the RMS and, to further their aim, resorted to acts of violence—which were, however, not approved by Dr Manusama.

These acts included the setting on fire of the Indonesian embassy in The Hague on July 26-27, 1966; the temporary occupation of the Indonesian ambassador's residence in The Hague on Aug. 31, 1970, to bring about a meeting between Dr Manusama and President Suharto of Indonesia (who was then expected on a visit to the Netherlands); the setting on fire of an Indonesian Airways office and an attempt to kidnap the Indonesian consul-general in Amsterdam in April 1974; and extensive damage caused to the seat of the International Court of Justice in The Hague in December 1974. On April 1, 1975, it was officially announced that 42 South Moluccans had been arrested for planning an attempt to kidnap Queen Juliana, and on June 10 of that year prison sentences were imposed on a total of 17 of these South Moluccans.

Further acts of violence were committed by South Moluccan groups (i) between Dec. 2 and 14, 1975, by seven armed South Moluccans who stopped a train, killing its driver and later a soldier and seizing the passengers (one of whom they also killed), and (ii) between Dec. 4 and 17, 1975, by another seven armed

South Moluccans who occupied the Indonesian consulate-general in Amsterdam and held all persons present as hostages. In both cases the armed attackers eventually surrendered. Of their demands, the Netherlands authorities refused all except that to hold discussions with South Moluccan leaders. The members of the two groups were sentenced (i) to 14 years in prison each on March 26, 1976, and (ii) to six years each on April 8, 1976. Dr Manusama strongly condemned their actions as being harmful to the South Moluccan independence movement. The Netherlands Government, on the other hand, stated on Jan. 17, 1976, that it could not support the political ideals pursued within the South Moluccan community but that it recognized the "existence and gravity" of these ideals. From early 1976 onwards a joint Dutch-Moluccan commission met periodically to discuss relations between the Dutch and South Moluccan communities.

Nevertheless, armed South Moluccans undertook further violent action in 1977. On May 23 two groups attacked a train and a school in the northern Netherlands and took 54 passengers and some 100 school children and teachers as hostages against demands for the release of South Moluccans in prison. Although all the school children and some of the train passengers were subsequently released, the Dutch Government eventually decided to use force and on June 11 troops stormed the train and the school; this action resulted in the death of two hostages and six South Moluccans, among them one who was said to have undergone guerrilla training in South Yemen. These South Moluccan acts were again strongly condemned by Dr Manusama, but the funeral of the six South Moluccans killed was, on June 14, attended by an estimated 5,500 South Moluccans. On Sept. 22, 1977, eight of those who had been involved in the two actions were sentenced to imprisonment for from one to nine years.

During the 1977 trial the instigator of the actions, Willem Soplanit, declared that the attacks had been carried out because the world had ignored the South Moluccan cause after the actions of December 1975 and had "still not understood what we want". While the trial was in progress serious disturbances broke out between members of the South Moluccan community on Sept. 7, and on Sept. 10-11 the police seized machine-guns, pistols and other weapons and made 32 arrests.

On March 13, 1978, three South Moluccan gunmen attacked provincial government offices near Assen (in the northern Netherlands) and seized 71 hostages in an attempt to secure the release of 21 South Moluccans serving prison sentences; they killed a provincial official but were overpowered by marines on March 14, although not without injury to some of the hostages, one of whom died later. The Prime Minister appealed to the public to accept the attempt as an isolated incident not supported by the South Moluccan community in general. During the trial of the three attackers one of them confirmed on June 15, 1978, that, unless they were given a free passage to leave the country, he and his colleagues had fully intended to shoot all the hostages. All three were on June 30 sentenced to 15 years in prison.

In a declaration presented in Parliament on Jan. 26, 1978, the Netherlands Government stated that "for juridical, historic and political reasons" it could not "recognize or support an autonomous South Moluccan republic". The Deputy Prime Minister and Minister of Justice said at the same time that the Government would nevertheless continue to respect the South Moluccans' right to their traditions, religion and language and would carry on its efforts to integrate the community (estimated at about 36,000), if the Moluccans so wished.

Dissensions among the South Moluccan community appeared to continue as two assailants, presumed to be South Moluccans, shot and wounded, in The Hague on Jan. 29, 1978, a prominent member of the community as he was about to pay an "information visit" to Indonesia. A Dutch citizen born in Indonesia was, as announced on June 2, 1978, expelled from Indonesia for "subversive activities" in connexion with alleged support for the formation of an independent republic of the South Moluccas.

Left-wing Groups

Red Aid *(Rood Hulp)*

This group was set up to aid extremist movements in other countries such as the Armenian Secret Army for the Liberation of Armenia, the Irish Republican Army, the Basque separatist ETA and the Red Army Faction in the Federal Republic of Germany.

Red Resistance Front

In May 1980 the Dutch police produced documents to show that this Front was linked with the Basque separatist ETA.

Norway

Capital: Oslo   Pop. 4,080,000

The Kingdom of Norway is a constitutional hereditary monarchy in which the monarch exercises authority through a Council of State (Cabinet) headed by a Prime Minister and responsible to Parliament (the *Storting*) of 155 members elected for a four-year term by universal adult suffrage. The *Storting* divides itself by election into an Upper House *(Lagting)* of 39 members and a Lower House *(Odelsting)* of the remaining 116 members, these two Houses having to consider separately any questions relating to legislation; in the event of disagreement a bill can be approved only by a two-thirds majority of the *Storting* as a whole.

As a result of elections held in September and December 1981, seats in the *Storting* were distributed as follows: Labour Party 66, Conservatives 53, Christian People's Party 15, Centre Party 11, Left Socialists 4, Progressive Party 4, Liberal Party 2. Parties which contested the elections without gaining any seats were the Red Electoral Alliance (incorporating the Workers' Communist Party), the Liberal (formerly New) People's Party and the Communist Party. Other registered parties not represented in the *Storting* are the Lappish People's List, the Norwegian Democratic Party, the Single Persons' Party and the Women's Free Popularly-Elected Representatives. Extreme right-wing groups, which were in 1980 reported to have links with similar groups in other countries, are the National Union (*Natjonal Samling,* NS) and the Norwegian Front (*Norsk Front,* NF).

There also exist in Norway neo-Nazi groups of a paramilitary nature, as described below.

Norwegian-German Army

Leadership. Espen Lund (l.).

According to the prosecutor in a trial held in Oslo in January 1982, this Nazi group was led by Espen Lund (an army sergeant). Together with two other members of the group, Johnny Olsen (a member of the Vigilante group—see separate entry) and Jon Charles Hoff, he was charged with murdering two of their comrades on Feb. 21-22, 1981, in order to prevent them from revealing to the police a large theft of weapons (from a Home Guard depot) and details of their secret organization. On searching the home of Lund in March 1981, the police had found Nazi literature, arms, explosives and a "hit list" of left-wing persons.

Lund was said to have stated that he had been recruited by the Odessa organization (a German organization of former members of the SS); that Odessa had at least 50 members in the Norwegian Army; and that their aim was to train members in sabotage and guerrilla warfare with the ultimate aim of a right-wing takeover in Norway.

On Jan. 26, 1982, the court sentenced Lund and Olsen to 18 years each in prison, and Hoff to 12 years. (Hoff had earlier been questioned in connexion with the wounding of two persons during a May Day demonstration in 1979.) Investigating other thefts of weapons and explosives, the police subsequently arrested several other suspected members of Nazi organizations.

Norwegian National Popular Party

This small group was suspected of being connected with the murder committed in February 1981 by members of the Norwegian-German Army (see separate entry) but denied any involvement.

Vigilante

Members of this group were responsible for attacks on left-wing demonstrators, in particular at May Day celebrations in 1979-82. In March 1981 the police found a large depot of explosives believed to have been assembled by Vigilante members north of Oslo. The group co-operated closely with the Norwegian-German Army (see separate entry).

Portugal

Capital: Lisbon   Pop. 9,900,000

The Republic of Portugal is, under its 1976 Constitution reflecting the aims of the 1974 revolution, "a democratic state based . . . on pluralism . . . with the objective of ensuring the transition to socialism". It has a President elected by universal adult suffrage for a five-year term; an Assembly of the Republic of 250 members elected by universal adult suffrage for a four-year term; and a Government under a Prime Minister appointed by the President. As a result of elections held on April 25, 1983, seats in the Assembly were distributed as follows: Socialists 101, Social Democrats 74, Communists 44, Democratic Social Centre 31. There are also several extreme right-wing and left-wing parties with no seats in the Assembly.

Under a law passed on June 16, 1978, and promulgated on Sept. 19 of that year prison sentences of from two to eight years were provided for leaders of organizations promoting fascism and violence against democratic institutions or national unity and for from one to two years for members of such organizations. In recent years the principal extra-parliamentary opposition to the Government has come from pro-independence movements in the Azores and Madeira and from small extreme left-wing groups.

Independence Movements

AZORES

Azorean Liberation Front (*Frente de Libertação dos Açores,* FLA)

Leadership. José de Almeida (l.).

This movement was formed in mid-1975 to oppose the administration imposed on the Azores from Lisbon after the metropolitan coup which overthrew the Caetano regime in April 1974, and in particular to oppose all influence of the Communist Party of Portugal. Between June and August 1975 the FLA destroyed or closed the offices of left-wing parties in the Azores and enforced the withdrawal of the governors and military commanders sent from Lisbon and the transfer of the administration to Azorean leaders. On Aug. 1, 1975, it was reported in Lisbon that an underground FLA "Government of the Azores" had already been formed, and in September the FLA threatened armed action unless steps were taken towards the independence of the islands.

The granting to the Azores of a regional government and assembly under the Constitution promulgated on April 2, 1976, was eventually accepted by the FLA, but new violence broke out in 1978. On April 15 of that year members of the FLA as well as refugees from the former Portuguese territories in Africa attacked Dr Antônio de Almeida Santos, then (Socialist) Deputy Prime Minister and previously Minister for Inter-territorial Co-ordination, who was visiting the Azores but was forced to leave the capital (Ponta Delgada); further clashes between FLA members and the police followed at the final departure of Dr Almeida Santos from the islands on April 20.

In a statement issued by the Socialist Party in Lisbon it was asserted (on April 21, 1975): "Taking advantage of the passivity of the local authorities (controlled by the centrist Social Democratic Party) the FLA separatists have established a climate of terror in Ponta Delgada; the Socialists and other political forces cannot meet freely, their premises are attacked and invaded, their houses and cars are destroyed and set on fire and even their children are threatened and persecuted." However, a new autonomy statute for the Azores, promulgated on July 25, 1980, was given qualified support by the FLA leader.

In a broadcast in August 1975 the FLA had defined its aim as the creation of a Western-style democracy, the rapid raising of the standard of living, the improved use of human and material resources, the replacement of the existing "provisional Government" by one which would safeguard the democratic exercise of power by means of elections, and respect for the wishes and traditions of the Azorean people. It was also stated that the proposed independent "Democratic Republic of the Azores" could not possibly fit into the Portuguese political framework, which was "clearly communist", and that it would have close relations with the United States.

MADEIRA ARCHIPELAGO

Madeira Archipelago Liberation Front (*Frente de Libertação do Arquipelago de Madeira,* FLAMA)

In August 1975 members of this newly-formed movement were involved in a number of bomb attacks, in particular on the property of its (left-wing) political opponents. On Aug. 29 of that year FLAMA claimed to have set up a provisional government for Madeira. However, after the Portuguese Government had, under its Constitution promulgated on April 2, 1976, given Madeira a regional government and assembly, there was no further evidence of acts of violence committed by the organization.

FLAMA is an anti-communist movement, advocating the separation of Madeira from Portugal and a possible federation of Madeira with the Azores and the (Spanish) Canary Islands.

Left-wing Movements

People's Forces of 25 April (FP-25)

Established on April 30, 1980, this small extreme left-wing group took its name from the date of the 1974 revolution which overthrew the Caetano regime. Members of the group have been involved in bank raids, bombings and extortion. It was responsible for the murder on May 12, 1980, of Clariano Baia, a Lisbon businessman who had refused to pay a "revolutionary tax" equivalent to about £12,000.

Proletarian Revolutionary Party (*Partido Proletariano Revolucionario*)

The military wing of this Maoist formation, the Revolutionary Brigades, based in Algeria before the 1974 revolution, was responsible for a number of bomb attacks carried out under the Caetano regime, in particular for an explosion at the regional army headquarters in Oporto on Oct. 26, 1973. After the revolution of 1974 the party took part in political life without gaining any seats in elections but it also continued its violent activities.

Among six of the party's members who unsuccessfully contested the 1980 parliamentary elections from prison were two of its founders—Dr Isabel do Carmo and Carlos Melo Antunes—who had been arrested in 1978 and were sentenced in Lisbon on April 9, 1980, to prison terms of 11 and 15 years respectively for being morally responsible for a series of bank robberies and the murder of a policeman carried out by the party and its military wing since 1974. At the same trial Maria Fernanda Fraguas was give a 10½-year prison sentence and three others were given prison sentences of from eight to 11 years in absentia.

In a bank raid in Lisbon on Oct. 8, 1980, two members of the Revolutionary Brigades were killed.

Revolutionary Brigades—see under Proletarian Revolutionary Party

Spain

Capital: Madrid   Pop. 37,720,000

The Kingdom of Spain is, under its 1978 Constitution, a "democratic state" and a "parliamentary monarchy" which guarantees the right to autonomy of all "nationalities and regions" of Spain. The country has a Cabinet headed by a Prime Minister and responsible to a bicameral Parliament consisting of a Congress of Deputies of 350 members elected by direct adult suffrage and a 208-member Senate also elected by adult universal suffrage, both for four-year terms. As a result of elections held on Oct. 28, 1982, parties were represented in the Congress of Deputies as follows: Socialists 202, Popular Alliance 106, Union of the Democratic Centre 12, Convergence and Union (Catalonia) 12, Basque Nationalist Party (PNV) 8, Communist Party/Unified Socialist Party of Catalonia 4, Democratic and Social Centre 2, the (Basque extremist) *Herri Batasuna* 2, Catalan Republican Left 1, Basque Left 1.

The granting of autonomy to various regions of Spain has met the aspirations of most autonomist regional parties except in the Basque region (consisting of the provinces of Avala, Guipúzcoa and Vizcaya, but not including Navarra, claimed as "Basque" by many Basque nationalists), where violent resistance to the Spanish regime has been carried out by the pro-independence Basque Nation and Liberty (*Euzkadi ta Azkatasuna*—ETA) and its supporters in several other groups. At the same time internal security has been disturbed by operations of right-wing organizations, involving also some high-ranking officers who had served under the Franco regime and intent upon restoring a traditional authoritarian regime, as well as by extreme left-wing (both anarchist and communist) groups. According to police sources, political violence claimed 123 lives in 1979, 126 in 1980 and 49 in 1981 (31 of the last-named in the Basque region).

In June 1978 the Government banned the wearing of paramilitary uniforms, and in November of that year it decreed that the national flag could not be used by political organizations as their own symbol. On Oct. 29, 1980, the Congress of Deputies passed (by 298 votes to two with eight abstentions) a bill providing inter alia for the suspension of certain fundamental rights in the case of persons suspected of terrorist acts or complicity in or defence of such acts.

Extreme Left-wing Movements

Armed Libertarian Groups (*Grupos Armados Libertarios,* GAL)

The GAL are believed to stand to the left of the anarchist National Labour Confederation (CNT) and to have arisen out of splits in a *Front d'Alliberament de Catalunya* (FAC). The movement was held responsible for many acts of violence, including bank robberies in 1980-81 to provide liquid funds to finance its activities.

Armed Revolutionary Struggle (*Loita Armada Revolucionaria,* LAR)

This group claimed responsibility for four explosions at the port of Vigo on Oct. 1, 1980, when some 30 Citroën cars ready for export were destroyed.

Autonomous Anarchist Groups (GAS)

In December 1979 five GAS members were arrested in connexion with preparations for causing explosions at flats housing some 300 military families in Barcelona.

Autonomist Anti-capitalist Commando (Comando Autónomo Anticapitalista)

On Sept. 29, 1979, the police in San Sebastian announced the detention of four members of this group suspected of being involved in an attack on a municipal office and a bank robbery earlier that month. The police also discovered arms, explosives and other equipment assembled by the group. Members of this group killed a civil guard and a fisherman near San Sebastian on April 6 and a bar owner in Azpeitia (south-west of San Sebastian) on Dec. 7, 1980.

Communist Party (International) (Partido Comunista—Internacional, PC-Internacional)

In September 1980 eight persons presumed to be linked with this illegal party were detained in Barcelona on charges of preparing acts of violence.

First of October Anti-fascist Resistance Group (Grupo de Resistencia Anti-fascista Primero de Octubre, GRAPO)

Leadership. José María Sánchez Casas (l.).

GRAPO took its name from Oct. 1, 1975, the date of Gen. Franco's last political appearance, on which occasion it killed four policemen. It was set up as the armed wing of the (Maoist) Reconstituted Spanish Communist Party (Partido Comunista Español Reconstituido, PCE-R) founded in Galicia in 1963 as an offshoot of an Organization of Spanish Marxist-Leninists (OMLE). The PCE-R never had any mass support and was in some quarters regarded as manipulated and infiltrated by right-wing fascist elements.

On July 18, 1976, GRAPO members carried out bomb attacks in several towns, and between July 28 and Oct. 25 of that year 45 GRAPO members were arrested. On Dec. 11, 1976, a GRAPO commando kidnapped the President of the Council of State and demanded the release of 15 political prisoners and their transfer to Algeria; on Jan. 24, 1977, GRAPO members also kidnapped the President of the Supreme Council of Military Justice (in retaliation for the killing of a student during a demonstration on Jan. 23); and on Jan. 28 GRAPO members killed two policemen and a civil guard in Madrid. However, the two senior officials kidnapped by GRAPO were freed in a police operation on Feb. 11, 1977.

On May 17, 1977, GRAPO bombed the US cultural centre in Madrid. After further acts of violence by the Group, including the murder of two civil guards in Barcelona on June 5 and bomb attacks on French embassy and cultural premises in Madrid on July 11-12, police arrested six GRAPO members on Aug. 6, 1977, in Madrid, three others on Sept. 23 and a further 18 in Barcelona, Beni-

dorm and Madrid early in October 1977. On March 22, 1978, however, GRAPO members killed the director-general of the Spanish prison service in Madrid in revenge for the death, at the hands of prison guards, of an imprisoned anarchist.

GRAPO also claimed responsibility for killing a policeman in Barcelona on Aug. 28, 1978, and a brigadier-general in Madrid on March 5, 1979; it was believed responsible for a bank raid in Barcelona on March 7, 1979, when a policeman was killed, and for killing another policeman in Seville on April 6, 1978. The alleged GRAPO leader, Juan Carlos Delgado de Codex, was shot dead by police in Madrid on April 20, 1978.

GRAPO was also held responsible for a bomb explosion in Madrid on May 26, 1979, when nine persons (said to be right-wing militants) were killed and 61 injured; for the killing of four policemen and civil guards in Seville, León and Madrid in May-July 1979; and for a bomb explosion on July 5 at the Madrid branch of the Banque Nationale de Paris in retaliation for the killing by Paris police on June 28-29 of two members of the PCE-R. Between July and October 1979 police arrested numerous GRAPO suspects, among them two (on July 26) who confessed to involvement in the Madrid bomb explosion on May 26, the killing of the brigadier-general on March 5, and that of several policemen. J. M. Sánchez Casas, who was said to have succeeded J. C. Delgado de Codex as GRAPO leader, was arrested on Oct. 15, 1979.

Various trials of GRAPO members resulted in prison sentences being imposed as follows: 37 years for one GRAPO member, 25 years for another, and from 13 months to 10 years for five others on May 4, 1979—the charges against them including the murder of a police captain on Sept. 27, 1977; 10 years each for five GRAPO members convicted on May 21, 1979, of kidnapping (in December 1976 and January 1977) the two senior officials, mentioned above, with two others being given six-year terms; 25 years each for two men and a woman, sentenced on Jan. 2, 1980, for killing a GRAPO member whom they suspected of giving information to the police; from 17 months to 19 years for eight GRAPO members (on Jan. 8, 1980) for kidnapping a radio technician to broadcast a GRAPO message in July 1977; 10 years (also imposed on Jan. 8, 1980) for six GRAPO members for attacks and robberies in Seville in January 1978; 18, 11, seven and two years respectively for four persons (on March 14, 1980) for crimes including robbery with violence in 1977; two years for each of two GRAPO members (on March 21, 1980) for bomb attacks on the office of the Diario-16 magazine in Madrid in June 1977; 74 years (on June 4, 1980) for a GRAPO member who had killed a civil guard and injured three others in January 1977; 30 years each for two GRAPO members (on July 16, 1980), one of them being J. M. Sánchez Casas, and 18 years for a woman for shooting a civil guard in Barcelona in February 1979; an additional 33 years for J. M. Sánchez Casas (on Nov. 18, 1980) for murdering the brigadier-general on March 5, 1979, with two others receiving 30 years and a woman 20 years for complicity in this crime; 47 years (on Dec. 1, 1980) for a GRAPO member convicted of robbery with violence; 24 years each for two GRAPO members (on Feb. 20, 1981) for murdering a policeman in 1979; and 15 years each for five men and three years each for two women (on March 9, 1981) for planning to murder a general in 1979, with one of the defendants being given an additional 31 years for three other attempted murders.

Meanwhile, GRAPO had continued its campaign of violence during the early 1980s. On July 22 of that year a civil guard was killed and 30 others were injured by a bomb placed under a civil guard bus by GRAPO members in Logroño province (northern Spain). On Sept. 2 GRAPO members killed a general in Barcelona and mortally wounded another, apparently in retaliation for the killing of a leading GRAPO member by police in Madrid on Aug. 29, 1980. On Nov. 23 an Air Force colonel was killed by GRAPO in Saragossa, and on Dec. 12 the secretary-general of the National Youth Front (a more extreme splinter group of the right-wing New Force) was killed by GRAPO members in Madrid. In 1981 a GRAPO member was held responsible for killing a (reputedly liberal) general in Madrid on May 4. Four suspected GRAPO members were shot by civil guards in Catalonia on June 17, 1981.

Among GRAPO members tried in 1981, J. M. Sánchez Casas and Alfonso Rodríguez García were on July 9 each given 270-year sentences and fines of 150,000,000 pesetas ($1,500,000) for the Madrid bomb explosion of May 26, 1977; on Aug. 2 J. M. Sánchez Casas was given a further 26 years for robbery with murder, together with another man given the same sentence and a woman sentenced to 15 years.

One of GRAPO's earlier leaders, Enrique Cedán Calixto, who had escaped from prison in 1979, was killed in a shootout with police in Barcelona on Sept. 5, 1981. Another GRAPO member serving a long sentence for robbery and planting explosives died in a Madrid hospital on June 19, 1981, after starting a hunger-strike on March 14 in protest against prison conditions.

During 1977-79 GRAPO had an active local group known as *Comando Barcelona,* which was responsible (according to the police) for a series of bank robberies, attacks on premises of firms and organizations, and also for murders between February and May 1979.

Iberian Federation of Anarchist Groups (FIGA)

Leadership. Alejandro Mata Camacho (l.).

This small group broke away from the (anarchist trade union) National Confederation of Labour (*Confederación Nacional del Trabajo,* CNT) in 1978. Its leader was, in Madrid on March 11, 1983, sentenced to 33 years' imprisonment for five armed robberies at banks and savings banks and for possession of arms.

Iberian Liberation Movement (*Movimiento Ibérico de Liberación,* MIL)

This somewhat obscure extreme left-wing group has sought to maintain the long Spanish tradition of support for anarchist concepts.

International Revolutionary Action Group (*Grupo de Acción Revolucionaria Internacional,* GARI)

This anarchist group was responsible for the abduction of the director of the Paris branch of the Bank of Bilbao, who was released after 19 days upon payment of a ransom equivalent to £270,000 in May 1974. It also claimed responsibility for bombings along the route of the Tour de France cycle race (in France) in July 1974.

Organization of Spanish Marxist-Leninists (OMLE)—see under First of October Antifascist Resistance Group (GRAPO)

Reconstituted Spanish Communist Party (PCE-R)—see under First of October Antifascist Resistance Group (GRAPO)

Red Guerrillas (*Guerrilleros Rojos*)

This group claimed responsibility on June 27, 1977, for a series of attacks on the cars of French tourists north of Barcelona, these attacks being accompanied by demands for the release of a militant Basque arrested in France on June 2, 1977, on suspicion of involvement in the kidnapping and murder in May-June 1977 of an industrialist and former Mayor of Bilbao by the *Bereziak* wing of the ETA; the Basque in question was freed by a court in Aix-en-Provence on Sept. 6, 1977, subject to certain restrictions, but he later failed to report to police as required under the terms which had been specified by the court in his release order.

Revolutionary Anti-fascist and Patriotic Front (*Frente Revolucionaria Antifascista Patriotica,* FRAP)

Members of this organization, formed in 1973 by various Maoist groups, were responsible for killing a number of policemen and civil guards in 1973-77. According to a Spanish police statement on May 19, 1973, FRAP had in a programme drawn up by a congress in Italy in April 1973 called for the "overthrow of the present regime by means of revolutionary struggle", the establishment of a "popular democratic and federal republic" and the creation of "an army in the service of the people".

On Sept. 12, 1975, a military court in Madrid sentenced three FRAP members to death for murdering a policeman on July 14, 1975, and two other FRAP members to 30 and 25 years in prison respectively. On Sept. 18 the court passed death sentences on five further FRAP members (including two women) and a 20-year prison sentence on another FRAP member for killing a civil guard on Aug. 16 of that year. The death sentences of the two women and that of one of the men sentenced on Sept. 12 were subsequently commuted to 30 years' imprisonment, and the two women were later released under an amnesty of May 1977.

On Sept. 23, 1975, the Public Order Court in Madrid sentenced five FRAP members (including a woman tried in absentia) to from 11 to 18 years in prison for illegal association connected with the killing of a policeman in Madrid on May 1, 1973. On May 9, 1977, a Barcelona industrialist was killed as he tried to dismantle a time bomb strapped to his chest by FRAP members who had demanded a ransom of 500,000,000 pesetas; four persons detained in connexion with this incident were released under an amnesty of November 1977.

Revolutionary Organization of Anti-fascist Spain

This group claimed responsibility for the assassination in Madrid on Sept. 27, 1977, of a police captain—the date of the assassination being the second anniversary of the execution of militants of the Revolutionary Anti-fascist and Patriotic Front (FRAP) and of the separatist Basque National and Liberty (ETA).

Union of Anti-fascist Youth (*Unión de Juventudes Antifascistas*)

In May 1981 a member of this organization was sentenced to 15 months in prison for supplying the First of October Anti-fascist Resistance Group (GRAPO) with information which GRAPO had used to commit acts of violence.

Extreme Right-wing Movements

Almond Trees (*Almendros*)

This name was adopted by a group of officers of the armed forces and civilians who were believed to have planned a right-wing coup for the spring of 1981, communicating with each other through code words in certain publications, including *El Alcázar,* the Civil War veterans' newspaper. Members of the group were among those arrested after an attempted coup of Feb. 23, 1981, by Lt.-Col. Antonio Tejero Molinas, allegedly supported by certain high-ranking military officers, such as Gen. Armada Comyn (Deputy Chief of Staff of the Army) and Lt.-Gen. Milans del Bosch y Ussía (Captain-General of the Valencia military region).

Some of the military leaders associated with the February 1981 coup attempt were also implicated in a further right-wing plot to seize power on the eve of the general elections of Oct. 28, 1982. On Oct. 3, 1982, the Spanish Defence Ministry announced that on the previous day three artillery officers had been detained in connexion with an operation planned against the security of the state, namely Col. Jesús Crespo Cuspinera, his brother Lt.-Col. José Crespo Cuspinera and Col. Luis Muñoz Gutiérrez. It was reported that the activities of certain officers had been monitored for some time and that a decision to act against the plotters had been taken by the Government after confirmation had been obtained that a coup attempt was planned for Oct. 27.

In addition, some of the officers who had been sentenced for their involvement in the February 1981 coup attempt—namely Lt.-Gen. Milans del Bosch, Lt.-Col. Tejero, Gen. Luis Torres Rojas and Maj. Ricardo Pardo Zancada—were held incommunicado from Oct. 2. The latest plot had been uncovered after Col. Muñoz had visited Lt.-Gen. Milans del Bosch in prison in Madrid, while Lt.-Col. Tejero was known to be a close friend of the Crespo brothers.

Documents taken from the home of Col. Muñoz and Col. Jesús Crespo showed that the officers had planned a coup (on the model of the Greek military takeover of 1967) under the codenames "Operation Cervantes" and "Operation Mars". The plan envisaged (i) the occupation of Madrid within three hours on the morning of Oct. 27 and its isolation by a small group of officers, (ii) the seizure of the Zarzuela Palace (the residence of King Juan Carlos) and also of the Moncloa Palace (the office of the Prime Minister), (iii) the "neutralization" of the Government by the detention of the Prime Minister (then Leopoldo Calvo Sotelo y Bustelo) and other senior ministers, and also of the Director-General of State Security and the leaders of the main centre and left-wing parties, (iv) the seizure of the national communications network and (v) the establishment of a junta and the formation of a mixed military and civilian government.

Meanwhile, Lt.-Col. Tejero had formed a new right-wing political party called Spanish Solidarity (SE), though he had been sentenced in June 1982 to 30 years' imprisonment for his role in the February 1981 coup attempt (this conviction being temporarily in abeyance because he was appealing against it). The new party was seen as having been intended to serve as the political "front" for the October 1982 coup attempt; in the Oct. 28 elections it received only 28,451 votes.

As a result of an appeal by the officers against the sentences passed on them in June 1982 and of a counter-appeal by the state, the Supreme Court in Madrid decided on April 28, 1983, to increase several of the prison sentences imposed—notably that against Gen. Armada Comyn (whom the court regarded as a co-leader of the attempted coup) from six to 30 years; that against a divisional chief of staff from three to 10 years; and those against Gen. Torres Rojas and Maj. Pardo Zancada from six to 12 years. The court also confirmed the 30-year sentences imposed upon Gen. Milans del Bosch and Lt.-Col. Tejero.

Anti-communist Apostolic Alliance (*Alianza Apostolica Anticomunista,* AAA)

Members of this organization have been responsible for both threats and acts of violence not only against left-wing activists but also against members of the Government. In December 1976 the AAA issued a warning that "the night of the long knives" would arrive if the President of the Council of State—who had been kidnapped on Dec. 11 by members of the First of October Anti-fascist Resistance Group (GRAPO)—were not released. On Jan. 24-25, 1977, AAA members attacked a meeting of left-wing labour lawyers in Madrid, spraying it with machine-gun fire, killing five people and wounding four. Of several persons arrested in connexion with this attack, some were said to belong to the New Force (see separate entry).

On Feb. 24, 1977, the AAA issued a death threat against the Prime Minister (then Adolfo Suárez González), condemning him as a "traitor". After AAA members had planted a bomb which destroyed the office of a satirical newspaper in Barcelona, killing one and injuring 15 persons (one of whom died later), 12 AAA members were arrested in various cities early in October 1977.

On Sept. 28, 1978, the AAA announced, together with the Anti-terrorist Organization against the ETA and the Warriors of Christ the King (see separate entries) that they had set up a "committee for private justice" to execute the Prime Minister, the Ministers of the Interior and Defence and other "agents of freemasonry, separatism and Marxism". The AAA also claimed responsibility for sending a letter bomb to the Madrid office of the independent daily *El País,* on Oct. 30, 1978, injuring three persons, one of whom died on Nov. 1.

During 1980 the AAA was responsible for causing a bomb explosion in Bilbao on July 23, killing a woman and two children, and for the killing of a club owner at Ondárroa (near Bilbao) on Aug. 31.

Anti-Marxist Commando

This group claimed responsibility for setting fire to the headquarters of the Communist movement in Valladolid on Dec. 9, 1979, when two persons were burnt to death.

Anti-terrorist Organization against the ETA (ATE)

Early in 1976 this Organization was involved in attacks on property of alleged supporters of the separatist Basque Nation and Liberty (ETA) and on bookshops selling "left-wing propaganda". On Sept. 28, 1978, it joined in the formation of a "committee for private justice" with the Anti-communist Apostolic Alliance (AAA) and the Warriors of Christ the King (see separate entries).

Armed Spanish Groups (*Grupos Armados Españoles,* GAE)

Members of this movement, strongly opposed to the Basque separatists, were involved in clashes with Basques in which two of its members were killed by ETA members at Baracaldo (near Bilbao) on Jan. 5 and 23, 1980. GAE members killed a Basque nationalist near San Sebastian on Jan. 16, 1980, and also placed a bomb in a bar at Baracaldo on Jan. 20, which killed four and injured 19 persons; another GAE member was killed by ETA supporters in Baracaldo on Jan. 23, 1980.

Falange

Leadership. Raimundo Fernández Cuesta (l.).

Members of the Falange—which had been the paramilitary mass organization under Gen. Franco's regime—appeared in Madrid in 1979 wearing blue shirts; however, a demonstration planned by them in a traditionally left-wing quarter of the city for May 2, 1979, was prohibited.

On the political level elements seeking a restoration of a traditionalist authoritarian regime have pursued their aims within the *Falange Española de las JONS (Juntas de Ofensiva Nacional—Sindicalista)* and also within the New Force (see separate entry). Both movements joined with other neo-fascist groups within the National Union for the 1979 elections, returning one deputy. The *Falange Española de las JONS* did not contest the October 1982 elections so as to minimize divisions within "the forces opposing Marxism".

Jesús García Command *(Comando Jesús García)*

In January 1980 members of this group threatened to burn down newspaper kiosks selling the magazine *Interviu,* which had named 19 alleged right-wing "troublemakers".

National Revolutionary Youth

Members of this organization were reported to have taken part in a demonstration to celebrate Hitler's birthday on April 20, 1979. At least one of its members was suspected of involvement in the murder of a Communist in Madrid on April 29, 1979, while others were arrested after the police had found an arms cache.

National Youth Front *(Frente Nacional de la Juventud)*

The leader of this organization (Juan Ignacio González Ramírez) was killed by members of the First of October Anti-fascist Resistance Group (GRAPO) in Madrid on Dec. 12, 1980.

Nationalist Syndicalist Trade Union

Leadership. José Antonio Assiego (l.).

This organization was founded as a breakaway movement from the trade union wing of the New Force (see separate entry).

New Force *(Fuerza Nueva,* FN)

Leadership. Blas Piñar (l.); David Martínez (national security head).

The FN was formed in 1976 by right-wing elements seeking a return to an authoritarian regime. On July 18, 1978, Blas Piñar told a rally of 25,000 supporters that Spanish democracy was "a front for vile and bastard interests" and on Nov. 19 of that year he called for a fight against "democracy, pornography and abortion". On Nov. 24, 1978, he expressed his rejection of Spain's new Constitution because it signified to him "the destruction of the nation" and would make it possible for "Marxism to rule here in the near future".

FN members have been involved in numerous clashes with left-wing extremists, one of the latter being killed in a Madrid suburb on Feb. 10, 1980. In a trial which ended on March 4, 1980, two FN members were given prison sentences totalling 193 years each, another 73 years and two others four and one year respectively for the murder of four left-wing labour lawyers and an office employee in Madrid on Jan. 24-25, 1977 (see also under Anti-Communist Apostolic Alliance, AAA); the defendants were also sentenced to pay compensation to the families of the murder victims, but they were ordered to serve no more than 30 years of their sentences.

On Nov. 19-22, 1981, members of the NF and of its youth movement (Young Force, *Fuerza Joven*) were involved in incidents arising out of demonstrations to mark the sixth anniversary of Gen. Franco's death in Madrid on Nov. 19-22, 1981.

Spanish Basque Battalion *(Batallón Vasco Español,* BVE)

During 1980 alone the BVE was responsible for 16 political killings (out of a total of 126 for the whole of Spain). Those killed by BVE members included two members of the Basque separatist ETA (killed in Madrid and San Sebastian respectively on Feb. 2, 1980); two persons killed on Nov. 23 in a bar in Hendaye (France), where 10 others were injured, in an action against Basque separatists; a leading ETA member killed on Dec. 30, 1980, by a car bomb planted by the BVE in Biarritz (France); and two Basque nationalists and a Communist shot dead in Tolosa on June 24, 1981. On March 21, 1981, French police arrested a member of a BVE commando which had attacked three Basque exiles in St Jean-de-Luz (France).

Spanish Catalonian Battalion (PRE)

This previously unknown right-wing group claimed on March 1, 1981, to have abducted a famous football player on the ground that his club (CF Barcelona) was a separatist organization and should not be allowed to become Spain's football champion.

Spanish Circle of Friends of Europe *(Circulo Español de Amigos de Europa,* CEDADE)

This group was founded in 1965 and includes among its members German and Italian exiles (i.e. former leading Fascists and Nazis) and veterans of the Blue Division (the Spanish unit which served on the Nazi side in World War II). It is based in Barcelona.

Spanish Liberation Army

According to an announcement by the police in Barcelona on Feb. 26, 1980, this group was responsible for attacks on left-wing organizations and public buildings, and also for bank robberies; 12 of its members had been arrested, and it was claimed that the group had been "dismantled".

Spanish Solidarity (SE)—see under Almond Trees

United International Secret and Revolutionary Cells

Members of this group claimed responsibility for a bomb explosion at the Cuban national airline office in Madrid on Oct. 27, 1976.

Warriors of Christ the King *(Guerrilleros del Cristo Rey)*

Leadership. Mariano Sánchez Covisa (l.).

In January 1970 this organization declared that its enemies were "the adversaries of the Church and of Spain, principally the progressives, the heretical and subversive Christian movements". In 1975 it embarked on reprisals against members of the Basque separatist ETA and their families, and its activities carried out in early 1976 were said to have led to a temporary decrease in separatist operations. In February 1977 the organization's leader was thought to have co-operated with Italian right-wing extremists, one of whom had been sentenced by an Italian court (in absentia) to 23 years in prison for attempting to attack a train. On Sept. 28 the organization joined the Anti-communist Apostolic Alliance (AAA) and the Anti-terrorist Organization against ETA in forming a "committee for patriotic justice" with the object of "executing" leading figures of the regime.

Separatist Movements

BASQUES

Anti-capitalist Autonomous Command—see under Basque Nation and Liberty (ETA)

Basque Nation and Liberty *(Euzkadi ta Azkatasuna, ETA)*

Leadership. Eugenio Etxebeste (commander).

Basques in Spain have since the late 19th century campaigned for either autonomy within the Spanish state or complete independence for the Basque areas, defined by them as the provinces of Vizcaya, Guipúzcoa, Alava and Navarra; some of them have also campaigned for the inclusion of certain areas of France partly inhabited by Basques, namely Labourd, Basse-Navarre and Soule (all bordering on the Spanish province of Navarra and forming part of the French department of Basses-Pyrénées). Until 1936 the Basques enjoyed a measure of autonomy under the Spanish Republican Government, and during the 1936-39 Civil War the Basque provinces held out for long as a Republican enclave within Nationalist-controlled territory. After the Civil War

militant Basque nationalism was quiescent, until ETA was formed in 1959 as a breakaway group from the Basque Nationalist Party *(Partido Nacionalista Vasco*, PNV), which remained a legal autonomist party opposed to the use of violence.

In 1960 the Spanish Government issued a decree authorizing military courts to try cases of "military rebellion", an offence which included the dissemination of false or tendentious news intended to cause internal disorders, international conflict or loss of prestige to the Spanish state and its institutions, and also the holding of illegal meetings and the fomenting of strikes; penalties included death or life imprisonment for sabotage, causing explosions, arson, kidnapping, armed assault and armed robbery. The decree was later suspended but was reimposed on Aug. 15, 1968, after the head of the political police in Guipúzcoa province had been assassinated on Aug. 2 and a partial state of emergency declared in the province on Aug. 5. Three young men identified as ETA members were each sentenced to 48 years in prison in San Sebastian on Dec. 13, 1968, for arson, terrorism and illegal possession of arms, and a fourth was sent to prison for 12 years.

In June 1969 four Basques were sentenced in Pamplona to 12 years in prison each for terrorism and planting bombs. On June 12 four priests were sentenced by a court-martial in Burgos to from 10 to 12 years in prison for "encouraging separatism and dismemberment of the nation". On Aug. 25 four alleged ETA members were given prison sentences of from six to 16 years for "military rebellion". On Oct. 23 it was announced that the Burgos court had also sentenced four priests and three other persons to prison terms of from two to 10 years for having, inter alia, been post factum accomplices in the shooting of a taxi-driver near Bilbao in gun battles between police and ETA members in April 1969. Early in 1970 about 100 alleged ETA members were arrested, including, it was claimed, the entire "high command" of ETA in Vizcaya.

The opening on Dec. 3, 1970, of the trial in Burgos of 16 Basque separatists (one of them being accused of killing the Guipúzcoa police chief on Aug. 2, 1968) was accompanied by widespread strikes and demonstrations in the Basque provinces on Dec. 3-4. Earlier, a pastoral letter of the bishops of Santander and San Sebastian had been read in all churches of the two dioceses on Nov. 22, appealing for an end to both "subversive and repressive violence", for the holding of the trial by a civilian (and not a military) court and for the commutation of any death sentences passed. The court, however, decided on Dec. 28, 1970, to condemn six of the defendants to death and to sentence nine others to long terms of imprisonment totalling over 700 years (while another defendent, a woman, was acquitted).

The six condemned to death had denied any complicity in the killing of the police chief but five of them had testified that they were Marxist-Leninists. Those sentenced to imprisonment included two priests, one of them a self-confessed ETA member. After the Holy See and the bishops of three Basque dioceses had pleaded for clemency, General-issimo Franco (the head of state) commuted the death sentences to 30 years' imprisonment on Dec. 30. Opposition to the trial had been expressed in many European countries.

In 1971 ETA was reported to have split into two factions: (i) a non-Marxist "military" section, which had attempted to form, with other groups outside ETA, a Basque National Front (*Frente Nacional Vasco,* FNV); and (ii) a Marxist section, trying to set up a mass movement among the Basque working class. The second faction was said to consist of two parts—one known as *Sayoak,* intent upon spreading the Basque struggle to the whole of Spain, and another, *Borriak,* wishing to confine it activities to Spanish and French Basque country. Reference was also made at this time to the existence of a pro-Chinese faction of ETA, named as *Kommunistak.*

Prison sentences were imposed by the Burgos military court on Basque separatists during 1971 as follows: (i) on July 27 a term of 25 years for a woman for participating in an armed attack on a shipyard office in Sestao (near Bilbao) in 1970; (ii) on July 30 a term of 21 years for a man convicted of placing an explosive charge at a television relay station at Zarauz (west of San Sebastian) in August 1968, with five others being sentenced to from 1½ to three years; and (iii) on Aug. 1 terms of from six months to 21 years for 10 members of a dissident ETA group (set up in Guipúzcoa in 1966) for bomb attacks carried out in 1968.

In January 1972 ETA described its objective as being "the reunification of the Basque country north and south of the Pyrenees and the defence of the interests of the working class until it effectively assumes the political, cultural and economic control of Euzkadi" (the Basque country).

ETA activities during 1972 included (i) a gun battle with police near Pamplona on March 17, when three ETA members were involved, of whom one killed himself the following day when he was surrounded by police; (ii) numerous explosions near San Sebastian and Bilbao during August; (iii) a gun battle near Bilbao on Aug. 29, when a policeman was killed; and (iv) another clash with police on Sept. 2, when two ETA members were killed and an arsenal of weapons and Basque nationalist propaganda material were found at Lequeitio (on the coast west of San Sebastian). During the first week of September 1972 at least 130 ETA suspects were arrested. On Dec. 6 ETA claimed responsibility for simultaneous attacks on five offices of the offical syndicate (trade union) organization in Guipúzcoa province.

On March 27, 1972, a Santander military court sentenced two ETA members to 20 years each on charges arising out of a bomb explosion at Eibar (east of Bilbao) in December 1967. On Jan. 25, 1973, a Bilbao military court passed prison sentences of from 12 to 17 years on four alleged ETA members for involvement in the temporary abduction of a prominent industrialist on Jan. 19-22, 1972 (who was released by them after his firm had agreed to ETA demands, notably for the reinstatement of workers dismissed after a strike and for a pay increase).

On Jan. 16-26, 1973, the owner of some 30 industrial enterprises was temporarily held near Pamplona by four armed ETA members, pending compliance with demands made by them for a pay rise, improved conditions and the reinstatement of dismissed workers at the Torfinosa metallurgical works in Pamplona. The Spanish Government, however later revoked the concessions made to the kidnappers by the management. On April 20, 1973, the police announced that Eustaquio Mendizábal, the head of ETA's military wing, sought in connexion with the earlier kidnapping and with other activities, had died in hospital after a gun battle with police near Bilbao. On July 5 eight persons were sentenced in Santander for involvement in the kidnapping of Jan. 16-23, the penalties ranging from 15 to 20 years in prison and including repayment of a ransom of 50,000,000 pesetas.

Other ETA activities in 1973 included (i) numerous bomb explosions in factories in Bilbao on Aug. 7; (ii) involvement in a gun battle with police on Sept. 27, when two members of ETA's military wing were arrested; (iii) an attack on Nov. 26 by six ETA members armed with machine-guns on a yacht club near Bilbao, the building of which was burned down; (iv) a bomb explosion in San Sebastian on Nov. 28 (while two ETA members were killed by their own bomb in a Bilbao suberb); and (v) a bank raid at Lasarte (near San Sebastian) on Dec. 3.

The most spectacular ETA action was the assassination, on Dec. 23, 1973, of Adml. Luis Carrero Blanco, then Prime Minister of Spain, together with his chauffeur and a bodyguard, in an explosion in Madrid. On Dec. 24 the police named seven members of ETA's military wing as being wanted in connexion with the murder, among them Pedro Pérez Beotegui ("Wilson"), who had been expelled from Britain after trying to set fire to the Spanish embassy in London. At a press conference held in south-western France on Dec. 28, four young Basques claimed to have carried out the assassination. A book describing it was banned in France on Sept. 25, 1974.

ETA actions during 1974 included bomb explosions at university institutes in Bilbao and exchanges of fire with police in Pamplona on April 2-3, and the killing of a civil guard officer near Azpeitia (south-west of San Sebastian) on April 3.

Trials of alleged ETA members held in 1974 resulted in prison sentences being imposed as follows: on Feb. 13 (in Madrid)—20 years for a student for illegal propaganda and possession of arms, and from two to seven years for five other defendants; on Feb. 14 (in Burgos)—15 years for an ETA member convicted of robbery; on March 26 (in Madrid)—17 years for an ETA member for illegal association (by taking charge of an ETA recruiting office in Bilbao); on April 2 (in Burgos)—from six to 15 years for four ETA members for blowing up an industrialist's villa near Eibar in February 1973 (three of them having already been sentenced on July 5, 1973, as mentioned above); on April 25 (also in Burgos)—from five to 31 years for four defendants for theft of explosives and the explosion of a device at a civil guards barracks in 1972; on June 11—30 years for two Basques involved in the kidnapping of Jan. 16-23, 1973; on July 24—48 and 21 years respectively for two alleged ETA members for acts of terrorism in 1973; on Sept. 12—15 years for an ETA member for placing explosives at a telephone centre in Burgos on April 29, 1972; on Nov. 12—12½ years for an ETA member convicted of a bank robbery in Berio; and on Nov. 21—78, 53 and 52 years respectively for three ETA members for terrorist offences.

On Dec. 11, 1974, some 200,000 workers in the Basque region held a one-day strike called for by ETA in support of a demand for an amnesty for political prisoners and of a hunger strike by some 150 imprisoned Basques. After several policemen had been killed by ETA supporters early in 1975, the Government declared a state of emergency in Guipúzcoa and Vizcaya, where 152 ETA supporters were subsequently detained, among them six priests alleged to be ETA militants.

On May 1, 1975, it was announced that ETA, the Socialist Party for the National Liberation of the Catalan Lands (SNAP) and the Union of the People of Galicia (UPG) were joining forces and had appealed to all "democratic and revolutionary forces" to support them.

In trials held in 1975 two ETA members were, on May 29, each sentenced in Madrid to 16 years in prison for illegal association and terrorism; five Basques, including a priest, were sentenced in Burgos on June 6 to from six to 23 years for bomb attacks in San Sebastian in 1973; and seven ETA members were sentenced in Burgos on June 20 to from three to 20 years for stealing dynamite in January 1973.

A new anti-terrorist law published on Aug. 26, 1975, laid down the death penalty for terrorist acts causing (i) the death of a member of the police or the armed forces or a state official and (ii) the death or mutilation of a kidnap victim. Under this new law death sentences were passed on Aug. 29, 1975, on two ETA members for killing a civil guard in Azpeitia (Guipúzcoa) on April 3, 1974 (one of these sentences being commuted to 30 years in prison). On Sept. 19 another ETA member was also condemned to death (for murdering a policeman during a bank raid on June 6, 1975)—but this sentence was subsequently also commuted to 30 years' imprisonment. ETA killings of policemen and civil guards nevertheless continued. On Oct. 5, 1975, three civil guards were killed and two seriously injured by an ETA bomb some 60 miles from San Sebastian, and another civil guard was killed at Zarauz on Oct. 18.

After the death of Gen. Franco on Nov. 20, 1975, ETA called on all mayors and members of provincial councils to resign, and on Nov. 25 it claimed responsibility for the murder of the Mayor of Oyarzún (near San Sebastian), whom it described as a police informer. In gun fights with police two suspected ETA members were killed on Dec. 3 and 8 respectively. Continuing their campaign in 1976, ETA members murdered the Mayor of Galdácamo on Feb. 9. On Feb. 18 ETA released the son of a Basque industrialist whom it had kidnapped on Jan. 13, after payment of a ransom of 8,000,000 pesetas ($114,280). Another wealthy industrialist, kidnapped by ETA on March 18, was found murdered on April 8, 1976, the required ransom equivalent to $2,860,000 having remained unpaid.

Between February and April 1976 a total of 16 Basques were sentenced to from three to 16 years in prison for ETA membership, terrorist activities and illegal possession of arms. On March 26 an ETA member was given a 19-year prison sentence for wounding a policeman and for illegal association and possession of arms.

After a leading ETA member, who had been kidnapped on July 25, 1976, was found murdered (allegedly by members of the anti-ETA Spanish Basque Battalion), protest demonstrations took place in the Basque region, during which a young Basque was killed by civil guards in Fuenterrabia (near Irún) on Sept. 8. There followed further strikes and protest demonstrations, in particular a one-day strike observed by some 600,000 people on Sept. 27, 1976. As an act of revenge for the killing of Sept. 8, ETA members shot dead, in San Sebastian on Oct. 4, the president of the Provincial Council of

Guipúzcoa (who was also a member of the Council of the Realm and a member of the Chamber of Deputies), together with three of his bodyguards and his chauffeur.

Earlier, it had been announced at a press conference held in France late in September 1976 that the political-military wing of ETA (ETA-pm) had been formed as a new "nationalist and revolutionary party" which would continue to campaign for the aims of the existing ETA—i.e. the creation of a united and independent Basque state comprising both the Spanish and the French Basque provinces—but would be non-violent and aim at "strengthening the autonomous organs of the Basque people" within the framework of "bourgeois democracy" in Spain. In April 1977 ETA-pm set up the Basque Revolutionary Party (*Euskal Iraultzako Alderdia,* EIA), which was legalized in March 1978.

On March 23, 1977, ETA offered to observe a ceasefire until June 15 of that year (the date of general elections) on condition that the Government agreed to all Basque demands, including the recognition of Basque as an official language, the independence of the Basque provinces, an amnesty for all political prisoners and exiles, and the dissolution of the "repressive" security forces. The Government, for its part, decided on March 20 to offer a choice of voluntary exile to Basque political prisoners, and on May 22 five of them, who had been sentenced to death at the 1970 Burgos trial, were flown to Norway, with the sixth following on June 6, together with another ETA member sentenced to death in Burgos on Aug. 29, 1975. Further ETA members awaiting trial—some of them (including Ignacio Pérez Beotegui) in connexion with the assassination of Adml. Carrero Blanco in December 1973—were flown to Denmark, Austria or Norway on June 9, and some others were released.

However, other ETA groups, in particular the military wing (ETA-m) and *Bereziak* ("Storm Troops", which had split off from ETA-pm), carried on with acts of violence. On May 20, 1977, *Bereziak* members kidnapped an industrialist and former Mayor of Bilbao and, although it was reported that a ransom of 1,000 million pesetas ($15,000,000) had been paid by his family, murdered him on June 23. On Oct. 8, 1977, ETA-m claimed responsibility for the murder in Guernica of the president of the Vizcaya Provincial Council and two of his bodyguards. ETA-pm, on the other hand, on Oct. 13 criticized this murder and two subsequent bomb attacks in Pamplona as acts which contributed nothing to the future of the Basque people. The Bilbao newspaper *Egin* had, on Oct. 2, published a declaration by ETA-pm announcing that the armed struggle would be relegated to a secondary position and that priority would be given to political action, with the practice of extorting "revolutionary taxes" (which had been publicly denounced by the Basque National Party on Sept. 16) being abandoned.

On Nov. 3, 1977, ETA-m claimed responsibility for the murder of a police sergeant near Irún and for a bomb attack on police barracks in Vitoria (Alava) on Oct. 31. On Nov. 12 a car bomb explosion near Bilbao injured three policemen, and on Nov. 26 ETA members killed the police commander of Navarra in Pamplona (as part of a campaign to "rid the Basque country of military occupation forces"). On Dec. 12 an Irún municipal councillor was assassinated, and on Dec. 28-29 ETA members seized two lorry-loads of dynamite between Bilbao and Santander. On Jan. 11, 1978, two ETA members and a police inspector were shot dead in Pamplona; and on Feb. 6 a television station was blown up in Palencia (north of Valladolid).

Following an appeal by all major political parties to ETA to renounce violence as a political instrument, ETA-m stated on Jan. 13, 1978, that it would abandon its terrorist activities provided the Government fulfilled conditions involving the granting of a total amnesty, the unconditional legalization of all political parties and the removal of all state security forces from the Basque provinces. (The Government had already decided, on Oct. 17, 1977, on an amnesty for most political offences committed before June 15, 1977; this applied inter alia to nine suspects detained after a bomb attack in Madrid on Sept. 13, 1974, and to all suspects held in connexion with the assassination of Adml. Carrero Blanco, who were formally amnestied on Jan. 20, 1978.)

Continuing its violent operations, ETA-m on March 1, 1978, attacked the construction site of a nuclear power station at Lemóniz (near Bilbao); on March 17 a bomb explosion at the site killed three people, injured 14 others and caused heavy damage. Two policemen were killed and three injured by ETA members in Vitoria on March 5, and a former civil guard in Aduna (Guipúzcoa) on March 10. ETA-m attacks during April and May 1978 included the blowing-up of a civil guards jeep in Pamplona on May 8 (when two civil guards were fatally wounded) and the killing of two other civil guards in San Sebastian on May 9. On July 21, 1978, two high-ranking army officers were killed by ETA members in Madrid (in revenge for "recent killings" in the Basque region), and ETA also claimed reponsibility for the killing of a civil guard in Mondragón (Guipúzcoa) on Aug. 28. On Sept. 25 two civil guards were shot dead in San Sebastian, and on Dec. 4 two policemen, also in San Sebastian.

Nine other civil guards and two ETA supporters were killed in several shooting and bomb incidents in October-November 1978, and on Nov. 16 ETA-m claimed responsibility for the assassination of a Supreme Court judge and former president of the Public Order Court in Madrid. On Nov. 28-30 ETA-pm temporarily held the provincial delegate of the Education Ministry in Guipúzcoa as part of a protest against the lack of recognition of the Basque language. Other ETA killings during December 1978 included those of a civil guard at Oñate (Guipúzcoa) on Dec. 1; two policemen in San Sebastian on Dec. 5; the former police chief in Santurce (near Bilbao) on Dec. 9; the municipal police chief of Pasajes (near San Sebastian) on Dec. 13; and a retired army colonel in San Sebastian on Dec. 17. On Dec. 21 a leading ETA-m member was killed by a car bomb at Anglet (France).

In 1979 ETA members were responsible for the killing of the adjutant of the military governor of Guipúzcoa on Jan. 2; the fatal wounding of the military governor of Madrid on Jan. 3; the killing of civil guards in Irún on Jan. 3, in Llodio (south of Bilbao) on Jan. 5, at Beasain (south-west of San Sebastian) on Jan. 6 and 13, and near San Sebastian on Jan. 29, a Supreme Court judge in Madrid on Jan. 9, a former Mayor of Echarri Arañaz (Navarra) on Jan. 27, a former civil guard at Andoain (near San Sebastian) on Feb. 3, the Mayor of Olavarría (Guipúzcoa) on Feb. 6, the police chief of Munguía (near Bilbao) on Feb. 12, an army officer in Vitoria on Feb. 14, a civil guard in Iciar (Guipúzcoa) on Feb. 23, a policeman in Pamplona on Feb. 28, the municipal police chief of Beasain on March 9, the president of the Bilbao Civil War veterans' association on March 16, a police inspector in Vitoria on March 23, a civilian in Pamplona on April 6, three policemen in Loyola on April 7, and a civil guard in Villafranca de Ordicia (Guipúzcoa) on April 9.

Notwithstanding its earlier renunciation of violence, ETA-pm conducted in June-July 1979 a bombing campaign designed to disrupt the tourist industry and in support of demands for the replacement of the National Police units by ordinary warders at a maximum security prison in Old Castile holding some 100 Basques and for the transfer of these prisoners to prisons in the Basque region. On July 3 ETA-pm members seriously wounded a deputy of the Union of the Democratic Centre (UCD) in an attempt to kidnap him, and on July 29 ETA-pm caused the death of five persons and injury to 113 others by explosions at railway stations and the international airport of Madrid; however, on Aug. 2 ETA-pm announced that it was ending its campaign because it did not wish to fight against the Spanish people.

Nevertheless, ETA-pm was responsible for the kidnapping, on Nov. 11, 1979, of the UCD spokesman for foreign affairs, whom it released on Dec. 12 after representations had been made on his behalf by the Pope and various other international figures, including Yassir Arafat, the leader of the Palestine Liberation Organization. In response to various demands made by ETA-pm the Congress of Deputies decided unanimously on Dec. 12, 1979, to create a commission to investigate allegations of torture of prisoners, and 14 Basque detainees were released between Dec. 12 and 21.

ETA-m, on the other hand, had meanwhile renewed its attacks on French installations in Spain, partly in protest against the French Government's decision of Jan. 30, 1979, to abolish the political refugee status for Basque refugees from Spain and also against the murder of a Basque from Spain in Bayonne (France) on June 25 by members of the right-wing National Action Group (ANE); this campaign led to bomb explosions on Aug. 21 and 23 and to clashes with police on Sept. 1-3. ETA-m was also responsible for killing the army chief of manpower, with two colonels and a chauffeur, in Madrid on May 25, two army officers in Bilbao on Sept. 19 and the military governor of Guipúzcoa in San Sebastian on Sept. 23. Early in November 1979, however, ETA-m offered a ceasefire provided the Government was willing to negotiate and conceded immediately (i) the legalization of all Basque political parties and (ii) an amnesty for all ETA activists. These two demands had also been made by a Patriotic Socialist Coalition (KAS) of left-wing parties, including *Hasi* and *Laia,* two illegal parties forming sections of the *Herri Batasuna* party, which supported ETA.

Trials of ETA-m members during 1979 resulted in sentences of (i) 12 years in prison imposed on Nov. 27 on an ETA activist for complicity in the murder of the Navarra police commander on Nov. 26, 1977; (ii) 15 years for one and 7½ years and one year respectively for two others (on Dec. 4) for various terrorist activities; and (iii) 34 years in prison, imposed on Dec. 19, on an activist for murdering two civil guards in San Sebastian, with a second defendant being given a seven-year term for conspiracy to terrorism.

During the campaign leading to a referendum which was held on Oct. 25, 1979, and led to approval of a regional autonomy statute for Alava, Guipúzcoa and Vizcaya (by 90.3 per cent of the votes cast in a 58.9 per cent poll), ETA-m staged no major acts of violence from Oct. 4 onwards; nevertheless, it opposed the proposed statute as a barrier to full self-determination for the Baque nation, while the *Herri Batasuna* party called for abstention from voting. ETA-pm, on the other hand, called for a "yes" vote, regarding the proposed statute as a short-term solution which might ultimately lead to independence.

In November 1979, a group styling itself ETA *Autónomo* broke away from ETA-m.

After the election of the first regional Parliament of the Basque region on March 9, 1980, when the *Herri Batasuna* party gained 11 seats (out of the total of 60) and 16.3 per cent of the votes cast, the party declared that it would not take its seats until some 200 imprisoned ETA members had been amnestied. However, the party nominated as its spokesman in Parliament Iñaki Pikabea Burunza, an ETA-m member then on trial for terrorism.

ETA-pm, on the other hand, claimed responsibility for launching an anti-tank grenade at the Prime Minister's residence near Madrid on Feb. 21, 1980, when it announced that it would use its weapons unless the Government (i) ordered that an immediate referendum should be held in Navarra on the question of joining the Basque region (this possibility having been provided for in the statute for the Basque region), (ii) returned all Basque prisoners to Basque prisons, (iii) lifted the extra security measures taken in the region and (iv) ordered the immediate formation of an autonomous police force as provided for in the statute.

During 1980 a large number of further political killings were carried out, the persons killed by ETA-m including the following: two members of the right-wing Armed Spanish Groups at Baracaldo (Vizcaya), one on Jan. 5 and another on Jan. 23; the Alava provincial police chief in Vitoria on Jan. 10; a civil guard at Elorrio (Vizcaya) on Jan. 14; a policeman at Guecho (Vizcaya) on Jan. 19; a New Force grave digger at Vergara (Guipúzcoa) on Jan. 25; a policeman in an attack on a bus near Bilbao on Jan. 27, when five other policemen were injured; six civil guards near Lequeitio on Feb. 1; a major and a policeman in Guipúzcoa on Feb. 8; a retired colonel in San Sebastian on Feb. 20; a private in Madrid on March 18, when ETA-m attempted to assassinate a general and his aide; two men in Durango (Bilbao) and Escoriaza (Guipúzcoa) respectively on March 24; a count in Bilbao on March 25; the Vitoria police chief on April 13; two civil guards in Irún on April 16; a civil guard and a policeman at Oyarzún (Guipúzcoa) on April 28; a retired major in San Sebastian on May 8; a policeman near San Sebastian on May 9; three policemen in San Sebastian on May 15; two civil guards in Pamplona on May 16; an alleged police infiltrator in Bilbao on June 3; a policeman in Pamplona on June 14; a Michelin director in Vitoria on June 25; three persons in Azcoitia (Guipúzcoa) on June 28; three civil guards at Orio (near San Sebastian) on July 13, when two ETA members were also killed; a private in Madrid on July 29 (in an assassination attempt on a general, who was injured); a Communist trade unionist in Eibar on Aug.

2; a customs agent in Irún on Aug. 28; a docker near Bilbao on Sept. 3; four civil guards at Marquina (Vizcaya) on Sept. 20; a UCD official in Vitoria on Sept. 30; a taxi driver in Rentería (east of San Sebastian) on Oct. 2; two security policemen and their driver in Durango on Oct. 3; three civil guards at Calvatierra (Vitoria) on Oct. 4; a tobacconist in Eibar on Oct. 6; a lieutenant-colonel in San Sebastian on Oct. 13; a prospective UCD deputy in Elgóibar (Guipúzcoa) and a telephone company executive in San Sebastian on Oct. 23; another telephone company executive in San Sebastian on Oct. 29; another prospective UCD deputy in San Sebastian on Oct. 31; four civil guards and two civilians in San Sebastian on Nov. 3; a policeman and a civilian in Eibar on Nov. 6; a (centre-right) Popular Alliance official near Bilbao on Nov. 16; a civil guard in La Coruña on Nov. 20; the San Sebastian police chief on Nov. 27; and a policeman in Eibar on Dec. 11.

ETA-m was also responsible for blowing up equipment at a nuclear plant near Vitoria on Feb. 3, 1980; the kidnapping, near San Sebastian on Sept. 22, of an industrialist who was released on Nov. 6; the kidnapping of another industrialist in Bermeo (Vizcaya), who was released on Oct. 26; and a raid on Air Force headquarters in San Sebastian on Nov. 16.

Of ETA members tried in 1980, three were sentenced in Madrid on Feb. 28 to 41, 18 and two years respectively, and two others to one year each, for crimes including the murder of three policemen in San Sebastian in 1978; another member was sentenced in Madrid on June 16 to 19½ years on bombing charges; and four others were on July 9 given 27, 22, 12 and six years in prison respectively for killing the mayor of Echarri Arañaz (Navarra) in 1979.

Of the total of 126 people killed in political violence during 1980, 85 were, according to the police, killed by ETA-m and 33 by other extremists, while eight ETA suspects were killed by the police; ETA-m was said to have raised the equivalent of over £100,000,000 by extortion and robberies in 1980.

During 1981 ETA followers continued to be involved in the killing of policemen, civil guards and retired military officers, as well as in other acts of violence. In particular ETA-m on Jan. 29 kidnapped the chief nuclear engineer at the Lemóniz power station construction site (near Bilbao), demanding in return for his release the commencement within a week of the demolition of the power station. After Iberduero, the company building the station, had refused to negotiate with ETA-m (although it was ready to halt construction work temporarily and to accept the Basque Government's eventual decision on carrying on with the project) and some 10,000 people had demonstrated in Bilbao for the engineer's release, he was found murdered on Feb. 6, 1981.

The murder was condemned by the Premier of the Basque Government and by all parties except the *Herri Batasuna*; trade unions called a 24-hour strike in protest against ETA terrorism for Feb. 9. The Basque Parliament resolved on Feb. 12, 1981 (with only the Basque Left and the *Herri Batasuna* abstaining), that work at Lemóniz should be resumed. ETA-pm had also condemned the murder (on Feb. 11) and had accused ETA-m of leading the region into civil war.

Between June 25 and Aug. 7, 1980, ETA-pm had conducted another bombing campaign at Spanish beach resorts in support of demands for the immediate release of 18 ETA suspects and the setting of a timetable for the incorporation of Navarra in the Basque region. However, on Feb. 28, 1981 (i.e. after an attempted right-wing coup in Madrid involving civil guard and army officers on Feb. 23), ETA-pm announced an indefinite and unconditional ceasefire and urged ETA-m to follow suit. ETA-pm released the honorary consuls of Austria, El Salvador and Uruguay whom it had kidnapped on Feb. 19-20, 1981. At the same time it demanded (i) the broadcasting in full on radio and television of an Amnesty International report on alleged police brutality in Spain and its publication in national and Basque newspapers; (ii) the similar broadcasting and publication of a report by the Basque Parliament of alleged violations of human rights by the police and civil guards; and (iii) the showing on television of photographs of a Basque who died in custody on Feb. 13. Few of the media complied with these demands (most coverage being given to the attempted right-wing coup).

ETA-m, on the other hand, pursued its policy of provoking a right-wing coup or backlash which would lead to a popular rising in the Basque region, and committed further murders—of a police commissioner in Bilbao on March 5; of a lieutenant-colonel, mortally wounded in Bilbao on March 19, 1980; and of a retired lieutenant-colonel in Pamplona on March 21. ETA-m was said at this time to be organized in cells of which only one member communicated with a member of another cell, and to have five operational regions, each under a regional organizer *(herrialdeburu)*. ETA-m cells were believed to exist also outside the Basque region, i.e. in Barcelona, Madrid and Valencia.

ETA activities during 1981 included the kidnapping on Jan. 13 of a wealthy industrialist in Valencia, who was released on April 14, 1981, after payment to ETA-pm of a ransom of 500,000,000 pesetas (about £2,600,000); the killing of three military men and the wounding of Gen. Joaquín de Valen-

zuela (head of the King's military household) on May 7; a bomb explosion which holed a Spanish destroyer in Santander on Oct. 2, with another bomb being found under a naval pier in Santander a week later; and the kidnapping on Dec. 29 of the father of an internationally known singer (but in this case the victim was rescued on Jan. 17, 1982, by police who arrested several ETA members and also seized, on Jan. 20, five tonnes of arms and ammunition, said to represent most of the arsenal of ETA-pm, near Bilbao). On Jan. 5, 1982, ETA-m claimed responsibility for the kidnapping of an industrialist in Bilbao, who was released on Feb. 6 after the reported payment of ransom.

The Spanish Commissioner of Police said on April 30, 1981, that ETA-m activities were being directed by seven of the organization's leaders who were habitually resident in France. Early in May 1981 the police uncovered a plan drawn up jointly by ETA-m, ETA-pm and ETA *Autónomo* to free some 80 ETA prisoners from the Carabanchel prison in Madrid. Among ETA members tried during 1981 was Iñaki Pikabea Burunza, an ETA-m member and spokesman of the *Herri Batasuna* party in the Basque regional Parliament, who was on June 30 given a 33½-year sentence for murdering an Irún municipal councillor on Dec. 16, 1977, and for other offences, with three further defendants being sentenced to a total of 78 years in prison.

Subsequent militant Basque actions in 1982-83 were associated in particular with a group identifying itself as the Anti-capitalist Autonomous Command, which was reported to be an extreme leftist splinter group deriving from ETA.

During its long campaign ETA has had numerous supporters in various countries, notably in France, where the Government banned ETA on Oct. 8, 1972. The French Minister of the Interior stated in November 1972 that the Government would not allow refugee activities "tending to aim a blow at the integrity of the national territory"; that there was no agreement between the French and Spanish Government on this matter; that "Spanish refugees must not take part in any demonstrations which disturb public order"; and that French territory should not be used as a base for activities across the border.

The French Government has not complied with Spanish demands for the extradition of Basque (or other) "terrorists" who had taken refuge in France, the French Prime Minister stating on June 8, 1981, that France was "a country of asylum" and would "not be disposed to grant such extraditions". On the other hand, the French Government agreed on July 29, 1981, to intensify border controls and to give "full support to the Spanish authorities in their fight against terrorism". On

Aug. 3, 1981, the French Minister of Justice confirmed that it was the wish of the French authorities to pursue in France the authors of all crimes committed on French territory and that a new extradition treaty (to replace that of 1877) would be negotiated.

According to the Spanish police magazine *Policia Española* there were, in January 1981, some 200 Basque terrorists living in France (and up to 100 others in Belgium and a similar number in Venezuela); ETA members were being trained in South Yemen, Lebanon, Czechoslovakia, Ireland, Uruguay and Cuba (and had earlier also been trained in Algeria); and Libya, China and the Soviet Union were giving economic aid to ETA.

Spanish Prisoners' Trade Union (COPEL)

Leadership. Daniel Pont (l.).

This illegal organization was alleged to have co-operated with ETA in kidnapping operations, robberies and mutinies in prisons during 1977-80. Its presumed leader and 10 other members were arrested in February 1980, when they were found to be in possession of weapons which were to be smuggled into prisons and to have planned robberies and prison mutinies.

CANARY ISLANDS

Movement for the Self-Determination and Independence of the Canary Archipelago (*Movimiento para la Autodeterminación y Independencia del Archipiélago Canario,* MPAIAC)

Leadership. Antonio Cubillo.

This organization was first established in 1961 as an autonomist movement of the Canaries. It had its headquarters in Algiers, while some of its followers were involved in acts of violence in the Canary Islands. In 1971 the Movement claimed that following the declaration of a state of emergency by the Spanish authorities on Dec. 14, 1970, over 200 persons had been arrested, among them 29 MPAIAC activists—but the Spanish Government later denied this. On Sept. 28, 1976, Antonio Cubillo appealed to the Spanish Government to "avoid recourse to violence" and to recognize the MPAIAC as the legitimate representative of the people of the islands and to commence negotiations in an African country on a timetable for the de-colonization of the Canaries under the auspices of the Organization of African Unity (OAU). In the absence of any response to his appeal, Cubillo ordered the Movement on Nov. 1, 1976, to begin a campaign of "armed propaganda".

After the Spanish authorities had announced on Feb. 26. 1977, that about 20 MPAIAC militants had been arrested and that the Movement was virtually dismantled, Cubillo ordered an armed struggle to begin. On March 25 a teenage militant was shot dead by a soldier while he was allegedly trying to steal arms from a military depot. In revenge the MPAIAC caused a bomb explosion at Las Palmas airport; this led to the diversion of two Jumbo jets to Tenerife where they collided on the runway, causing the death of 582 people.

Cubillo thereupon suspended his Movement's armed activities until April 11, 1977, when his campaign designed to disrupt tourism was resumed, involving some 80 bomb attacks during 1977. On Oct. 12 of that year police defused two bombs wrapped in separatist flags and planted near a place where the Spanish King was due to stand during a ceremony. During demonstrations called on Tenerife in support of a general strike called by the MPAIAC, a student was killed by civil guards on Dec. 12, 1977. On Feb. 24, 1978, a policeman was wounded while defusing a bomb planted by the MPAIAC in Tenerife; he died on March 8. On April 5 an MPAIAC bomb exploded at the civil guard headquarters in Las Palmas (without causing any casualties).

An attempt to assassinate Cubillo in Algiers was attributed by him (on April 10, 1978) to the "Spanish secret service and police" with the co-operation (he alleged) of the Spanish Socialist Workers' Party (PSOE), which had come out strongly in favour of continued Spanish sovereignty over the Canary Islands. On May 7 the Algerian state security court passed sentences of death on two Spaniards (on one of them in absentia) for involvement in the assassination attempt, and a 20-year prison sentence on an accomplice. One of those sentenced to death claimed that he had been sent to Algeria by the (Maoist) Revolutionary Anti-fascist and Pactriotic Front (FRAP), which had described Cubillo as an agent of the (US) Central Intelligence Agency. The Spanish Government denied any involvement in the assassination attempt.

Sentences passed on MPAIAC members included prison terms of four years and two months and one year and two months respectively imposed on April 2, 1979, on two members for an attack on a bank in Tenerife on Dec. 27, 1977, and a 5½-year term for another member on May 22, 1980.

In a programme published in Algiers on Jan. 2, 1973, the MPAIAC listed as its objects (i) the creation of an independent Canary Islands Republic, to be called the Guanch Republic (after the islands' original inhabitants, regarded as being exploited and repressed by Spain); (ii) limited autonomy for each of the seven main islands; (iii) election of a national assembly by universal suffrage; and (iv) restoration of the Guanch language.

The programme also advocated respect for private property, workers' participation and control of foreign interests in the islands. The Spanish Government was called upon to open negotiations on the constitutional proposals contained in the programme. In 1977 the MPAIAC stated that it wanted to make the Canaries Archipelago a socialist African independent republic which would be a member of the OAU.

The liberation committee of the OAU recognized the MPAIAC as a liberation movement in July 1968, and in February 1978 the OAU Council of Ministers supported the committee's recommendation for material and financial aid to be given to the Movement (with only Morocco and Mauritania voting against this decision). The Spanish Government thereupon made great efforts to dissuade African governments from giving such aid. A Spanish parliamentary delegation which had visited nine West African countries reported on May 7, 1978, that only Senegal, The Gambia and Liberia had expressed clear support for continued Spanish sovereignty over the Canary Islands. However, at a further meeting of the OAU Council of Ministers in July 1978, the earlier recommendation was no longer pursued.

The MPAIAC's aims were implicitly rejected at a Council of Europe conference of members of local authorities and regional bodies which declared on Oct. 18, 1979, that the Canary Islands (as also the Azores and Madeira) were "peripheral regions of Europe" in the economic development of which European countries should participate.

The MPAIAC has used a "Voice of the Free Canaries" radio transmitter in Algeria, with the Spanish Government having repeatedly protested to the Algerian Government against its protection of this transmitter.

CATALONIA

Catalan Popular Army (*Ejército Popular Catalan,* EPC)

Leadership. Jaime Martínez Vendrell (l.).

Established in 1967, this movement was said to have been founded by Josep Maria Batista i Roca, who was then living in exile but died in Barcelona in 1978. It leader was arrested in March 1979 when the movement was accused of having murdered a former Mayor of Barcelona and his wife in 1978, but he was released on June 18, 1980.

Free Land *(Terra Lliure)*

This Catalan nationalist group, which demanded equal rights for the Spanish and Catalan languages in Catalonia, claimed responsibility for blowing up an electrical installation (which was to be used by a nuclear plant in Tarragona province) on Aug. 18, 1980. On May 21, 1981, the group claimed responsibility for seizing and injuring a signatory of a "Manifesto of the 2,300" issued by Spanish-speaking intellectuals in Catalonia, complaining of discrimination against them because they did not speak or write Catalan.

Resistance Movement of National Freedom

The Spanish police announced in Barcelona on Feb. 23, 1980, that it had dismantled this left-wing Catalan nationalist movement which had, during two years, been responsible for various bombings, attacks on the police and robberies, and of which six members had been arrested. The movement was said to be a subsidiary of the Reconstituted Spanish Communist Party (PCE-R), whose armed wing was the First of October Anti-fascist Resistance Group (GRAPO—see separate entry).

CEUTA AND MELILLA

Ceuta Liberation Movement (*Movimiento de Liberación Sebta,* MLS)

It was alleged in the daily *Faro de Ceuta* on May 20, 1982, that 200 Moroccan residents of the Spanish enclave of Ceuta had signed a complaint to the Spanish authorities about three members of the Moroccan community in Ceuta whom they identified as Moroccan secret policemen and whom they accused of involvement in activities in connexion with the MLS, including kidnapping and the distribution of clandestine leaflets. The first of the signatories of the complaint had his car set on fire on May 23 and thereupon asked the police for protection.

The MLS stands for the integration of Ceuta into the Kingdom of Morocco.

Moroccan Patriotic Front

This organization stands for the restoration of Moroccan sovereignty over the cities of Ceuta and Melilla. Members were responsible for several bomb attacks in the Spanish enclaves of Ceuta and Melilla (on Morocco's Mediterranean coast) in late 1978 and early 1979 in protest against Spain's insistence on these cities' status as part of the Kingdom of Spain.

GALICIA

Armed Galician League (*Liga Armada Gallega,* LAG)

This separatist group claimed responsibility for killing a civil guard in Santiago de Compostela on Aug. 28, 1978.

Sweden

Capital: Stockholm   Pop. 8,380,000

The Kingdom of Sweden is a parliamentary democracy in which the monarch has purely ceremonial functions as head of state. There is a Cabinet headed by a Prime Minister and responsible to a unicameral Parliament (*Riksdag*) of 349 members elected for a three-year term by universal adult suffrage. As a result of elections held on Sept. 19, 1982, seats in the *Riksdag* were distributed as follows: Social Democratic Labour Party 166, Moderate Party 86, Centre Party 56, Liberal Party 21, Communist Left Party 20. Parties which obtained no seats were the Christian Democratic League, the Communist Party of Sweden, the Ecology Party and the Swedish Workers' Communist Party.

Extremist political activities in Sweden have been largely confined to neo-Nazi groups opposed to the presence of alien communities, members of which (e.g. Iranians and Yugoslavs) have in some cases themselves committed acts of violence directed against the regimes of their countries of origin.

Extreme Right-wing Groups

There is in Sweden a large minority of alien residents, making up (at the end of 1982) about 12 per cent of the total population, or almost 1,000,000 persons, including about 400,000 from Finland and other large groups from Turkey, Yugoslavia and Greece. The presence of these foreigners has led to growing hostility by young Swedes and by at least five extreme right-wing groups calling for the repatriation of these aliens. Although these groups have remained small, several have been reported to have links with neo-fascist groups in other countries; a group mentioned in this context has been the *Nordiska Riks-partiet*.

New Nazi Party

In March 1979 members of this party were responsible for plastering the walls of a comprehensive school at Olofström (a town in southern Sweden with a large immigrant population) with posters demanding the maintenance of racial purity in Sweden. The posters described Hitler as a hero and contained a warning of a coming second "crystal night" (i.e. a pogrom).

Switzerland

Capital: Berne   Pop. 6,360,000

The Swiss Confederation is a republic in which power is held by the electorate which consists of all adult citizens. These elect the Federal Assembly as well as cantonal and local councils and have powers to vote on constitutional amendments and other matters, including international treaties, in a referendum if requested by a fixed minimum of voters. The bicameral Federal Assembly consists of (i) a Council of States composed of two members for each of 20 cantons and one for each of six half-cantons, and (ii) a 200-member National Council elected for a four-year term in proportion to the population of the cantons (each canton or half-canton being represented by at least one member). The President of the Confederation, who is also President of the Federal Council (Government), is elected, together with a Vice-President, for a one-year term by the two Houses of Parliament, which also elect the members of the Government.

In elections to the National Council held on Oct. 21, 1979, parties gained seats as follows: Social Democratic Party 51, Radical Democratic Party 51, Christian Democratic Party 44, Swiss People's Party 23, Independents 8, Liberal Party 8, Evangelical People's Party 3, Party of Labour (communist) 3, Progressive and Autonomist Socialists (consisting of the Autonomist Socialist Party and the Progressive Organizations of Switzerland, POCH) 3, National Action 2, Swiss Republican Movement 1, Ecologists 1, Jura Entente 1, Jura Popular Unity 1. Parties not represented in Parliament are the Political and Social Action Movement and the (Trotskyist) Revolutionary Marxist League.

Switzerland has been the scene of numerous acts of violence committed by political extremists from outside the country, notably Palestinians, Armenians and members and supporters of the West German Red Army Faction. Internally, unrest was caused in the city of Zurich during 1980-81 by groups of young people resorting to violence in the expression of their discontent with the affluent society of Switzerland, but apart from individual leaders no specific organization was held responsible for the violent incidents which occurred. In Lausanne, however, a group calling itself "Red Lausanne" staged an unauthorized demonstration of some 400 people on Oct. 4, 1980, leading to clashes with the police force, three members of which were injured. The group was said to have no proper structure and no clear motives other than dissatisfaction with having to live in a regimented world.

Jura Movements

The canton of Jura was established with effect from Jan. 1, 1979, in the north-western part of the canton of Berne as a canton inhabited overwhelmingly by French-speaking Swiss. The leaders of the newly-established cantonal Government continued to press for the incorporation into their canton of certain areas in the canton of Berne inhabited by French-speaking people. Among the latter, however, there exists a strong movement in favour of remaining inside the canton of Berne.

Béliers ("Rams")

The *Béliers* are the youth movement of the *Rassemblement Jurassien,* an alliance of various political parties in power in the canton of Jura. Members of this movement have repeatedly been involved in clashes with anti-separatist (though French-speaking) Swiss who have opted for their areas to remain within the canton of Berne. Five members of the *Béliers* staged a brief demonstration on Sept. 10, 1982, in the hall of Schönbrunn Palace in Vienna, where the 1815 Treaty of Vienna had been signed, settling inter alia the fate of the Swiss Jura by allotting it to the canton of Berne.

Jurassic Liberation Army

This pro-separatist movement claimed on Sept. 26, 1982, that it was responsible for stealing two ballot boxes at the village of Vellerat while local elections were in progress. Although inhabited by French-speaking people, Vellerat had remained inside the canton of Berne after the establishment of the canton of Jura. The villagers of Vellerat had, on Aug. 14, 1982, declared themselves independent of the canton of Berne.

Sangliers ("Wild Boars")

The *Sangliers* are the youth movement of the *Force Démocratique,* the pro-Berne organization in the southern part of Jura. Members of this movement have on a number of occasions been involved in clashes with (pro-separatist) *Béliers* (see separate entry).

Extreme Right-wing Movement

New Social Order (*Nouvel Ordre Social,* NOS)

This movement was, in 1980, reported to have links with other, mainly neo-Nazi, organizations in various countries of Europe and elsewhere.

Turkey

Capital: Ankara   Pop. 45,500,000

Since Sept. 12, 1980, the Republic of Turkey has been under military rule, which was installed with the object of ending what was termed the country's slide to anarchy through the activities of terrorist groups of both the right and the left, and also of developing a new democratic system based on solid foundations. On assuming power the Chief of the General Staff (Gen. Kenan Evren) and the commanders of the four armed services (Army, Navy, Air Force and Gendarmerie) abolished Parliament, suspended all political activities and set up a National Security Council, which formed a mainly civilian Government and, under a constitutional amendment of Oct. 28, 1980, assumed the functions of Parliament. On Oct. 16, 1981, the military rulers ordered the dissolution of all political parties and the confiscation of their property.

A new Constitution overwhelmingly approved in a referendum held on Nov. 7, 1982, specified that Turkey was a democratic, secular and social state in which legislative power belonged to the Grand National Assembly (Parliament) and in which the President and a Council of Ministers exercised executive power. In addition to nearly 200 main articles, the new Constitution contained a number of "temporary articles", the first of which stated that Gen. Evren was to become President of the Republic for a period of seven years, while the other four members of the National Security Council were assured leading positions in a Presidential Council as the chief advisory body to the President. The process of a gradual return to civilian rule subsequently began on April 24, 1983, when a presidential decree lifted the general ban on political activity, although certain restrictions remained, notably in that about 100 former party leaders continued to be barred from political activity for 10 years.

Prior to the military takeover the 450-member National Assembly (Lower House) had, as a result of general elections held on June 5, 1977, and of subsequent by-elections, been composed as follows: Republican People's Party (RPP) 208, Justice Party (JP) 182, National Salvation Party (NSP) 22, National Action Party (NAP) 17, independents, others and vacancies 21. Since the overthrow of Süleyman Demirel's minority JP Government in September 1980 and the dissolution of all parties in

October 1981, members of some of these formations have been involved in varying degrees of opposition to the Evren regime, which has not only sought to dismantle militant organizations of the extreme left but has also brought many right-wingers to trial in connexion with violent attacks on the left committed before the military take-over.

By early 1981 some 30,000 persons were in detention for suspected terrorist activities, the majority of them being members of some 40 different left-wing groups. On Aug. 14, 1981, the Prime Minister (Adml. Bülent Ülüsü) declared that since the military takeover there had been 459 victims of political violence as against 3,710 in the preceding 21 months. By the end of December 1981 it was officially stated that most terrorist groups in Turkey had been dismantled; that about 45,000 persons had been arrested since Sept. 12, 1980, with about 30,000 of them having been charged with offences, for which 85 death sentences had been passed, of which 11 had been carried out. It was also claimed that no less than 662 organizations were operating against Turkey from abroad; 286 of them were described as extreme left-wing, 17 as separatist and 280 as religious extremist. The National Security Council stated on Jan. 1, 1982, that 7,662 alleged terrorists were still at large, some of them in Europe, and it announced shortly afterwards that since September 1980 a total of 794,661 rifles or pistols and 5,271,000 rounds of ammunition had been seized.

The Turkish news agency Akajans reported on Feb. 12, 1982, that there were 24,377 persons (including 13 former politicians and 64 trade union leaders) under arrest and another 7,034 in detention (for up to 45 days), all officially for "terrorist activities" or for "attempting to overthrow the democratic order by revolutionary struggle under cover of Marxism-Leninism". It also reported that there had been 390 complaints about alleged torture, of which 115 had been rejected for "lack of evidence" and 37 had led to judicial procedure against 65 defendants. A government spokesman admitted on March 16, 1982, that since September 1980 at least 15 persons imprisoned in connexion with political terrorist activities had died in prison after being tortured and that 15 others had died of unspecified causes.

The martial law co-ordination office at the General Staff headquarters reported on June 11, 1982, that by the end of April 1982 the martial law courts had examined 33,782 cases since the declaration of martial law, of which they had completed 27,275 cases (the remaining 6,507 being still in progress). A total of 23,145 defendants had been sentenced on various charges by the courts, and at that time some 19,125 persons were under arrest while a further 1,105 were in detention. An earlier report issued at the beginning of May 1982 had stated that 37 trials involving allegations of torture were then in progress and that another eight had been completed; the latter had led to nine prison sentences being imposed. Altogether 112 security officers had been charged with the use of torture, but 15 had been acquitted, while investigations in connexion with another 125 cases had been dropped. The report claimed that most allegations of torture in Turkish prisons were propaganda intended to discredit the military authorities.

Left-wing Movements

Association of Revolutionary Youth (Dev-Genc)

Established in 1969, this loose grouping of several extreme left-wing factions was held responsible for a number of bank robberies and operations against US military personnel in Turkey. The association was said to have given rise to the creation of the Turkish Peo-ple's Liberation Army (TPLA—see separate entry). Under martial law the organization was banned in several areas of Turkey in April 1971, and on July 1 of that year a former secretary of Dev-Genc was given a 15-year sentence for a bomb attack on the home of a general.

Ertugrul Kurkcu, a former Dev-Genc president, was arrested on March 30, 1972, for alleged involvement in the abduction of two NATO technicians by the TPLA on March

26. Early in February 1973 a group of 14 *Dev-Genc* members were found guilty of trying to set up a Marxist-Leninist social system in Turkey and were given prison sentences ranging from four to 10 years.

Bank—IS

Leadership. Atilla Onur (s.g.).

The secretary-general and 21 other leading members of this small white-collar trade union were sentenced by a military court in Istanbul on March 9, 1982, to imprisonment for up to 10 years and eight months for violating the anti-communist articles of the penal code, and the union's treasurer was given an additional five-year sentence for possessing a pistol and some ammunition. The prosecution alleged that the defendants had taken instructions from the ruling Albanian Party of Labour. The union was officially banned by the military authorities on the same day.

Communist Party of Turkey (CPT)

Communists took part in the Turkish national movement in 1918-22, during which the CPT was founded on Sept. 10, 1920. The party was banned in 1923, and under Articles 141 and 142 of the Turkish penal code of 1926 (modelled on that of Fascist Italy) communist propaganda and activities were prohibited; moreover, any initiatives designed to overthrow the Constitution by force or to set up an association with the object of establishing the domination of one social class by another were made liable to long terms of imprisonment or even the death penalty. The CPT, however, continued its underground activities and, since World War II, has had its headquarters in East Berlin under the auspices of the Socialist Unity Party of East Germany.

Following the military takeover in September 1980, hundreds of alleged party members were arrested, and in September 1981 it was stated in the Turkish press that the party had divided Turkey into six sections and had called for the establishment of a Kurdish state in eastern Anatolia and of an "independent socialist state" without military bases in Cyprus. It was also said to have called for the repeal of Articles 141 and 142 of the penal code to enable it to assume power legally, failing which it would set up a national democratic front as an umbrella organization of all "antifascist" elements. The trial of 205 of the arrested alleged party members opened in Ankara on Feb. 15, 1982.

Publications issued illegally by the CPT from time to time include *Atilim* (the party's central organ) and *Durum* (a news bulletin). The CPT is officially recognized by the Communist parties of the countries of the Soviet bloc.

Confederation of Revolutionary Trade Unions of Turkey (DISK)

Leadership. Abdullah Bastürk (ch.); Fehmi Isiklar (s.g.).

DISK was established in 1967 as a legal trade union organization. Those of its members who had been found guilty of acts of violence before 1974 were amnestied in that year. The organization was involved in numerous strikes and also in a May Day demonstration in Istanbul (where it was banned) in 1978, when troops opened fire and killed about 90 persons, and in another one in 1979 in Izmir (where it was permitted). In September 1980 (when its membership had reached 400,000) DISK's activities were suspended and 156 of its members were tried on charges of attempting to overthrow the Constitution and to set up a Marxist state, with the death penalty being demanded for 56 of them.

Ahmet Isvan, a former Mayor of Istanbul, was arrested in November 1980 on charges of having helped DISK to organize an illegal May Day parade in 1977 (when 36 persons were said to have died). On Jan. 20, 1981, warrants of arrest were issued against 223 DISK members in Istanbul for attempting to set up "a Marxist-Leninist regime" in Turkey, and at the same time a court rescinded an earlier decision to release 426 detained DISK members. By December 1981 some 1,000 DISK members were in detention, and the trial began of 52 members accused of attempting to form a communist state through revolution (although there was said to be no evidence of terrorist activities on their part).

Federation of Turkish Labour in Germany (FIDEF)

This Federation was said to be closely allied with the illegal Communist Party of Turkey (with headquarters in East Berlin) and it was not recognized by the West German trade union movement. It claimed a membership of 20,000.

Marxist-Leninist Armed Propaganda Unit

This grouping, said to be the "hit squad" of the Turkish People's Liberation Party (see separate entry), was held responsible for numerous assassinations, including those of several US servicemen in Turkey, carried out in 1979-80. On June 7, 1979, seven members of the Unit were arrested. On Jan. 2, 1980, members of the Unit killed Abraham Elazar, manager of the Israeli airline El Al in Istanbul. On Sept. 17, 1980, Zeki Yumurtaci, a leader of the Unit awaiting trial on murder charges, was killed in a shooting incident.

On March 5, 1981, a military prosecutor called for the death penalty for 56 alleged members of the Unit (out of a total of 139 arrested) for killing 85 persons and wounding 100 others. Four other members of the Unit, said to have been involved in the killing of 29 persons (also including US servicemen) in May and November 1979, were killed by police in May 1981.

People's Liberators

During September-October 1980 three leaders of this organization were arrested at Elazig (eastern Anatolia).

People's Revolutionary Union—Marxist-Leninist (TKP-ML)

From among the members of this group, 31 alleged activists were arrested in Istanbul on Jan. 27, 1982, for alleged involvement in 18 murders.

Progressive Youth Association *(Ilerici Genclik Dernegi)*

This organization was set up to fight against the commandos of the extreme right-wing National Action Party (see separate entry) after 1975. In April 1981 Erhan Tuskan, editor of a journal connected with the Association, was sentenced in Ankara to nine years and five months in prison for "making communist propaganda, inciting the public to crime and praising extremist activities".

Celal Alter, said to be associated with this group, was one of four persons who hijacked a Turkish airliner to Bulgaria in May 1981, when they demanded the release of 47 political prisoners held in Turkey.

Republican People's Party (RPP) *(Cumhuriyet Halk Partisi)*

The RPP's first chairman from its formation in September 1923 was Kemal Atatürk, the founder of the Turkish Republic, and the party was in power continuously until May 1950. Thereafter it was in opposition until 1961, when it entered a coalition Government with the Justice Party and with Ismet Inönü, then RPP chairman, as Prime Minister. The party was again in opposition from 1965 to January 1974, when it formed a coalition with the National Salvation Party in which Bülent Ecevit (who had succeeded Inönü as RPP chairman in 1972) held the premiership. This Government ended in 1974 and the RPP did not return to power until January 1978, when Ecevit formed a coalition with two smaller parties. This administration lost its parliamentary majority in October 1979, however, and the RPP went into opposition despite being the largest party in the National Assembly.

Ecevit was among a number of party leaders arrested immediately after the military takeover of September 1980. Although released the following month, he maintained open opposition to the Evren regime and has received a number of prison sentences for contravening martial·law decrees banning political activity (in protest against which he had resigned the RPP chairmanship in October 1980). As a social democratic formation, the RPP is affiliated to the Socialist International, member parties of which have repeatedly protested at the Evren regime's treatment of Ecevit and other party members.

Revolutionary Left *(Dev-Sol)*

The *Dev-Sol* was the first extreme left-wing group to pledge itself to public opposition to the military regime set up on Sept. 12, 1980, which it described as "a fascist attack directed particularly against the working class and the rest of our impoverished people". Members of *Dev-Sol* sentenced to imprisonment in 1971-73 had been amnestied in 1974.

In 1980 *Dev-Sol* members were responsible for the assassination of Gun Sazak (deputy chairman of the National Action Party) on May 22; of Dr Nihat Erim (Prime Minister in 1971-72) on July 19; of an intelligence agent in Istanbul on July 30; of two policemen in Ankara on Sept. 1; and of a senior policeman in Istanbul on Sept. 17. One *Dev-Sol* member was killed and 15 were arrested near Fatsa (on the Black Sea coast) on Nov. 5, 1980.

On Jan. 16, 1981, a military prosecutor demanded prison terms of up to 30 years for 43 alleged *Dev-Sol* members charged with conspiring to set up a communist regime in Turkey and with being responsible for killings, bomb attacks, extortion and other crimes. *Dev-Sol* was also held responsible for the murder of a deputy chief of security in Istanbul on Feb. 6, 1981 (this crime being also attributed to the Warriors of the Turkish People's Liberation Front—see separate entry).

On May 1, 1981, it was reported that Mustafa Isik, a *Dev-Sol* member suspected of having killed two security agents, had been shot dead by police. On May 3 a total of 168 Dev-Sol members were arrested in Istanbul and charged with murdering 31 policemen and civilians before Sept. 12, 1980. Edip Erhan Eranil, who was said to be the *Dev-Sol* leader for the Ankara region, was arrested in Burgas (Bulgaria) after an unsuccessful attempt to hijack a Turkish airliner on May 24, 1981.

On July 23, 1981, it was reported that 540 *Dev-Sol* members were being tried and that the death sentence had been demanded for 90 of them. During another trial of 425 alleged *Dev-Sol* members in September 1981 for "breaches of the Constitution" involving murders, bombings and robberies with the object of "setting up a Marxist-Leninist social order'' the prosecutor called for the death sentence for 141 of the defendants. On Nov. 16, 1981, six *Dev-Sol* members were condemned to death for the assassination of Dr Erim in July 1980 and of the Istanbul police chief early in 1981.

In a trial of 428 alleged *Dev-Sol* members, which opened in Istanbul on March 15, 1982, the prosecution demanded death sentences for 146 of the accused, reportedly for more than 90 murders, the victims of which included Dr Erim and also officials and other members of the National Action Party. In another trial on the same day five *Dev-Sol* members were sentenced to death in Izmir for four political murders and ''conspiracy to establish a proletarian dictatorship'', while three other defendants were given life sentences and 43 prison sentences of from two to 15 years (27 being acquitted).

According to government sources *Dev-Sol* had, before the military takeover of Sept. 12, 1980, agreed on co-operation with the Popular Front for the Liberation of Palestine (PFLP) led by Dr Georges Habash, whereby the PFLP would supply *Dev-Sol* with weapons and training and enable it to open an office in Beirut. Since March 1980 the PFLP was said to have supplied *Dev-Sol* with 1,000 pistols, 300 Kalashnikov machine-pistols, 500 hand grenades and 10 small grenade-throwers.

Revolutionary People's Unity

A hideout of this group was reported to have been discovered at Elazig (eastern Anatolia) on Oct. 7, 1980. The trial of 76 alleged members of the group opened in Adana on Jan. 19, 1982.

Revolutionary Pioneers for the People

Four members of this prohibited movement, who were being sought in connexion with the assassination of two policemen at Usak (130 miles east of Izmir), were killed by security forces in Istanbul on March 15, 1981.

Revolutionary Struggle (*Dev-Savas*)

Of this minor group, 35 members were arrested in mid-March 1981.

Revolutionary Sympathizers' Union

This group was officially described as a ''left-wing extremist terrorist group'', and 16 of its members were arrested on April 24, 1981, for murdering four persons.

Revolutionary Vanguard of the People

This organization was one of at least six armed groups which had up to the military takeover in September 1980 been organized in a Front of the Liberation Party of the Turkish People. On Aug. 18, 1981, the military prosecutor in Istanbul called for death penalty for 25 members of the group on charges of ''armed insurrection''.

Revolutionary Way (*Dev-Yol*)

Leadership. (Mrs) Gulten Çayan (based in Paris).

Before the military takeover of September 1980 this organization had held a dominant position in several small towns and had engaged in numerous acts of violence, in particular against political opponents. Under the military regime large numbers of the organization's members were arrested and tried.

On Nov. 25, 1980, it was announced that against 30 out of 74 arrested *Dev-Yol* members the death penalty had been called for by a military prosecutor. On Dec. 27 of the same year it was reported that 43 alleged *Dev-Yol* members had been arrested for alleged involvement in the murder of 23 opponents and in bombings throughout the country. On Jan. 12, 1981, the police gave the total of *Dev-Yol* members arrested during the previous three months as 204 and stated that this had helped to solve 25 murders, 25 armed attacks, eight robberies and 18 bombing incidents; it was also claimed that troops had found, in Ahiboz (a village near Ankara), a file containing the addresses of *Dev-Yol*'s entire membership and also a blacklist of potential targets for kidnapping or murder.

At the trial of 574 leading *Dev-Yol* members the prosecutor demanded, on Feb. 26, 1981, the death penalty for 186 of them and prison terms of from eight to 36 years for the others, saying that the defendants were guilty of 333 murders and a wide range of other terrorist offences. On Nov. 5, 1981, one *Dev-Yol* member was killed by security forces, another was captured and 17 were detained near the Black Sea port of Ordu. A trial of *Dev-Yol* members at Adana resulted on Nov. 10 in seven death sentences, two life sentences and 58 other prison sentences. On Nov. 16 the police announced that 72 *Dev-Yol* members had been arrested and charged with murdering a police officer and four of their political opponents, with setting up shops as front businesses for creating funds for *Dev-Yol*, with illicit possession of arms and with having drawn up a ''hit-list'' of possible candidates for assassination.

On Nov. 29, 1981, a total of 81 suspected *Dev-Yol* members were arrested in Izmir, where a quantity of weapons and explosives were also seized. At the trial of some 800 *Dev-Yol* members in Erzurum, the prosecution demanded the death penalty for 120 of them on Nov. 30, 1981.

By this time *Dev-Yol*'s headquarters were

believed to have been set up in Paris, the organization's six-member committee being headed by Gulten Çayan, whose husband, Mahir Çayan, had been the most influential leader of the Association of Revolutionary Youth (*Dev-Genc*) and a founder-member of the Turkish People's Liberation Army (TPLA). In 1971 he had been tried for conspiring to overthrow the state and for involvement in other crimes, including the murder of the Israeli consul-general in Istanbul in May 1971; during the trial he had escaped from prison in November of that year but had himself been killed, with other TPLA members, on March 30, 1972.

In January 1982 16 activists were arrested in Trabzon for reviving the *Dev-Yol* group under the alleged leadership of Ali Kemal Celik; three other leaders were arrested at Erzincan (eastern Turkey); and for 101 alleged members out of 270 being tried in Adana the death penalty was demanded by a military prosecutor. In June 1982 death sentences were similarly demanded for 259 persons believed to be connected with *Dev-Yol,* who had been brought to trial in Erzincan (eastern Turkey) on charges arising out of an attempt to create a left-wing "liberated zone" at Fatsa on the Black Sea coast; a further 416 persons were reported to have been accused of other offences in connexion with the zone.

Turkish Communist Party—Marxist-Leninist (AKKO)

This Maoist party was formed in 1973 under the leadership of a provisional co-ordinating committee. On Jan. 30, 1980, a total of 98 members of the party were arrested and charged with murder, and by September 1981 there were 178 alleged party members being tried for armed insurrection. The AKKO's principal founder, Ibrahim Kaypakkaya, died in custody following the military takeover of September 1980.

Of the party's "Partisan" faction, 51 alleged members were on Jan. 8, 1981, reported to have been arrested for killing six people, including a policeman, and for committing armed robberies and bombings. On Dec. 6, 1981, it was officially announced that two suspected members of this faction had been killed (together with two security men) in a shoot-out at Tunceli (eastern Turkey) on Dec. 5. Fifty-five members of an "ultra-Maoist" offshoot of the party were arrested on Feb. 19, 1981, at Reyhanli (near the Syrian border). The party also set up a "Turkish Revolutionary Peasants' Liberation Army".

Turkish Communist Workers' Party

Three alleged members of this party were hanged in Izmir on March 12, 1982, after being convicted of having killed the local secretary of the Nationalist Action Party and a building contractor in Izmir in April 1981.

Turkish Labour Party (*Türkiye Isçi Partisi*)

Leadership. (Mrs) Behice Boran (pres.).

After its foundation in 1961, this left-wing socialist party based in the trade unions had 15 Assembly deputies in 1965-69 but as a result of a change in the electoral law retained only two seats in the 1969 general elections. The party opposed the imposition and extension of martial law in 1970-71 and was dissolved by the Constitutional Court in July 1971, following which a number of its leaders received prison sentences for propagating Marxism-Leninism and other offences. They were amnestied in 1975, however, and in May of that year the party was re-established, although without making any electoral impact thereafter.

The party opposed the military takeover of September 1980 and many of its members became active in left-wing movements seeking the overthrow of the Evren regime. In late February 1981 the party's leader, Behice Boran, was deprived of her Turkish citizenship because of her failure to return to Turkey to stand trial; she was nevertheless tried in her absence on charges of distributing communist propaganda.

Turkish Peace Association

Leadership. Mahmut Dikerdem (pres.).

Established in 1977, this Association was officially dissolved shortly after the military takeover of Sept. 12, 1980. On Feb. 26, 1982, 42 of its leading members were arrested, among them Mahmut Dikerdem (a former ambassador), Orhan Apaydin (chairman of the Istanbul Bar Association and chief defence counsel for the accused members of the DISK trade union federation), Niyazi Dalyanci (owner of an independent news agency), Ali Sirmen (columnist for the daily *Cumhuriyet*) and Mrs Reha Isvan (wife of a former Mayor of Istanbul, under arrest since September 1980). On March 3, 1982, a military prosecutor stated that those arrested would be charged with "conspiracy to establish a Marxist-Leninist regime".

The Association was officially regarded as the Turkish section of the World Peace Council founded in Warsaw in 1950 and based in Helsinki.

Turkish People's Liberation Army (TPLA)

Established in 1970, the TPLA first emerged in 1971, when it claimed responsibility for a bank raid (on Jan. 11), the kidnapping of a US sergeant (on Feb. 15) and the temporary seizure (between March 4 and 8) of four US servicemen. The supposed leader of the

TPLA, Deniz Gezmis, was arrested on March 17, 1971. Members of the TPLA were also responsible for the seizure of Ephraim Elrom, Israeli consul-general in Istanbul, on March 17, 1971, and for his murder on March 22.

Gezmis stated after his arrest that he had had guerrilla training with *Al-Fatah* (the Palestinian guerrilla organization) in Syria in 1965 and that his movement hated "all imperialists, including the Soviet Union". On Oct. 9, 1971, he and 17 other TPLA members were condemned to death, and so were five others on Dec. 27, 1971. Three of these death sentences, imposed on women, were subsequently commuted to life imprisonment.

On May 3, 1972, three members of the Association of Revolutionary Youth (*Dev-Genc*)—from which the TPLA was said to have sprung—hijacked a Turkish airliner and diverted it to Bulgaria while demanding the release of Gezmis and two of his accomplices. However, the hijackers surrendered to the Bulgarian authorities on May 4, and the execution of Gezmis and the two other TPLA members was carried out on May 6; it was followed by a number of acts of violence.

Earlier in 1972, two British nationals and a Canadian working as technicians at a NATO base on the Black Sea coast had been seized by TPLA members and were killed by the kidnappers on March 30 when they were surrounded by troops. Another TPLA attack was directed against the C.-in-C. of the Turkish gendarmerie on May 4, 1972. Among the TPLA members killed by troops on March 30, 1972, was Mahir Çayan, a former *Dev-Genc* leader and founder-member of the TPLA.

The TPLA, however, continued its activities in later years. Arrests were announced of seven members on June 15, 1979, and of 55 members in Antalya province in March 1981.

Turkish People's Liberation Party (TPLP or THKP)

During 1980-82 numerous members of this party were arrested and many of them were tried for various offences. They included 18 reported to have been arrested in Izmir on March 28, 1980; 45 members of the "Front Path" faction of the party, whose arrest was announced on April 4, 1980; the local leader of the party at Elazig (eastern Anatolia), arrested shortly after the military takeover of Sept. 12, 1980; 16 members of a faction of the party arrested on Feb. 3, 1981, for attacking a police station and murdering a police officer in Izmir on the previous day; 93 party militants for whom a military prosecutor in Istanbul called, on March 24, 1981, for the death penalty for attempted subversion; and 91 alleged party members being tried in Istanbul at the end of 1981 for involvement in 12 murders and other crimes and for planning a coup to set up a Marxist-Leninist system, with the death penalty being demanded by the prosecution for 25 of them.

Turkish Revolutionary Communist Party (TDKP)

For 11 members of this party the death penalty was demanded by a military prosecutor in Izmir on March 24, 1981. On June 16 of that year a total of 16 members of the party were captured by security forces, who seized a coded list of 247 other members; on July 23, 1981, a group of 34 members were arrested and charged with subversive activities.

Turkish Revolutionary Peasants' Liberation Army—see under Turkish Communist Party —Marxist-Leninist (AKKO)

Turkish Teachers' Union (*Tob-Der*)

Leadership. Gultekin Gazioglu (pres.).

On Dec. 26, 1972, prison sentences of up to eight years and 10 months were imposed on 59 members of the Turkish Teachers' Union for having founded a "secret organization" and carried out communist propaganda and illegal activities (while 93 other members were acquitted). After the military takeover of Sept. 12, 1980, *Tob-Der* was closed down and its property confiscated. Its president left for West Germany soon afterwards and was subsequently deprived of his Turkish nationality. On Dec. 25, 1981, a total of 50 former officials of the union were sentenced to imprisonment for from one to nine years on charges of attempting to overthrow the state.

Warriors of the Turkish People's Liberation Front

Leadership. Omer Faruk Aydin (founder and ch. of central committee).

On Dec. 17, 1980, this Front's leader and five other members were arrested on suspicion of involvement in 35 political murders within three years, including the killing of a US serviceman on May 11, 1979. On Jan. 7, 1981, four members were arrested in Antalya province for killing a US sergeant on April 12, 1979. Of a "liberation faction" of this organization, 10 leaders and over 200 active supporters were arrested later, as announced on Feb. 13, 1981.

Worker-Peasant Party of Turkey (*Türkiye Isçi Köylü Partisi,* TIKP)

Leadership. Dogu Perinçek (ch.).

This Maoist formation was established in January 1978 and was originally legal although not represented in Parliament. Immediately after the September 1980 military takeover Dogu Perinçek and 24 other members were arrested, as were 42 other leading members in November 1980—all being charged with trying to establish an illegal organization aimed at "overthrowing the basic social order".

After the Turkish military Government had threatened to deprive all political refugees of their Turkish nationality, Mustapha Kemal Çamkiran, a leading TIKP member who had fled to West Germany, returned to Turkey in March 1981 but was thereupon detained at a military prison, where he was allegedly ill-treated.

The TIKP is opposed to "imperialism and [Soviet] social-imperialism". In its constitution it has described itself as "the revolutionary political party of the working class of Turkey with the ultimate aim of the realization of the classless society".

Right-wing Movements

Various movements of the extreme right were engaged in violent action against the left in the period before the September 1980 military takeover. Thereafter such movements generally backed the Evren regime in its offensive against the extreme left but were themselves frequently the subject of trials brought by the authorities for illegal activities mainly carried out in the period before September 1980.

Confederation of Nationalist Trade Unions (MISK)

Leadership. Faruk Akinci (g.s.).

On July 17, 1979, the general secretary of this right-wing trade union organization was given a prison sentence for taking part in a bomb attack, in which two persons were killed. The Confederation was banned on Sept. 12, 1980.

Federation of Turkish Democratic Idealist Associations

This right-wing umbrella organization for about 200 allegedly cultural groups of Turks throughout Europe, with headquarters in Frankfurt (West Germany), was said to have been set up by the National Action Party (led by Col. Alparslan Türkes) as a front organization after overseas activities by Turkish political parties had been banned in 1976. Usually known as the Turkish Federation, it has a membership of 50,000 (35,000 of them in West Germany).

Great Ideal Society *(Büyük Ülkü Dernegi)*

This group, which was linked with the National Action Party, has been responsible for a number of acts of violence in recent years.

One of its alleged members was hanged on June 4, 1981, for a murder committed on June 4, 1979, after he had been recruited by the group in 1976.

Idealistic Path *(Ülkü Yolu)*

Members of this (then legal) youth organization were said to have killed at least 23 political opponents during the two years before the military takeover of Sept. 12, 1980. On Jan. 23, 1981, it was reported that 87 of the organization's members had been arrested at Bursa (south-east of the Sea of Marmara) on charges of involvement in 30 murders during the past two years, and that warrants of arrest had been issued against 113 others. On March 19, 1981, it was announced that another 57 members had been arrested.

National Action Party (NAP) *(Milliyetçi Hareket Partisi)*

Leadership. Col. Alparslan Türkes (ch.).

Established in 1948, this right-wing party claimed a membership of over 300,000 prior to the September 1980 military takeover. Formerly known as the Republican Peasant Nation Party, it had taken part in various coalition governments and in the 1977 elections obtained 16 of the 450 Assembly seats. A number of its young militants were involved in acts of violence against left-wing elements, while in July 1980 the party claimed to have raised a militia and to have gained complete control of Yozgat (a town east of Ankara). On the other hand, a number of NAP leaders were killed by political opponents in the course of 1980, notably Gün Sazak (the party's deputy chairman), who was murdered on May 27 of that year.

In its campaign against political extremism of both the left and the right, the Evren regime has taken action against many hundreds of NAP members for alleged political violence, including the murder of left-wing opponents. By August 1981 nearly 600 party activists were on trial, for many of whom the military prosecutor demanded the death penalty; the latter category included Col. Türkes himself, who was charged in a 945-page indictment document of having personally ordered the killing of the police chief in Adana in September 1979 and of a prominent trade unionist in July 1980.

The NAP is strongly anti-communist and nationalist, standing for the defence of freedom and of the interests of the peasantry. It has promoted the formation of various militant right-wing organizations outside its own party framework, such as the Federation of Turkish Democratic Idealist Associations, the Great Ideal Society and the Grey Wolves (see separate entries).

Organization for the Liberation of Enslaved Turks

This underground group was said to be linked wth incidents caused by members of the "Turkish Lightning Commandos" (see next entry).

Turkish Lightning Commandos

Members of this underground group were held responsible for the killing of a mayor and his family by means of a parcel bomb on April 17, 1978, and for rioting (at Malatya, 300 miles south-east of Ankara).

Grey Wolves ("Idealists")

Leadership. Col. Alparslan Türkes (l.).

This organization is the militant youth wing of the extreme right-wing National Action Party (also led by Col. Türkes). Assassinations attributed to Grey Wolves members included that of Abdi Ipekçi (editor of the influential daily *Milliyet* and friend of Bülent Ecevit, the former leader of the Republican People's Party), who was murdered on Feb. 1, 1979. The person convicted of this crime was Mehmet Ali Agca, who was condemned to death in absentia in April 1980 after escaping from prison in November 1979 and fleeing the country.

The sentence was confirmed by the Turkish Consultative Assembly on March 4, 1982, but meanwhile Agca had shot and wounded the Pope in Rome on May 13, 1981, and had been sentenced to life imprisonment by an Italian court on July 22, 1981. A Turkish request for his extradition was refused by Italy. Two alleged Grey Wolves members and accomplices of Agca were arrested in Zürich on Feb. 22, 1982, being identified as Abdullah Catli and Mehmet Sener.

Islamic Fundamentalists

Alevi Moslem Sect

After the Sunni and the (Shi'ite) Alevi Moslem sects in Turkey had for several centuries lived in relative peace with each other, a polarization had begun in 1970, with the Sunnis favouring conservative policies and the generally under-privileged Alevis left-wing ones. In December 1978 fighting broke out between members of the two sects at Kharamanmaras (south-eastern Turkey) and 111 persons were killed and over 900 buildings destroyed. Some 800 persons were subsequently tried, 330 of them for "armed insurrection and murder"; on Aug. 8, 1980, 22 of the defendants were condemned to death, and over 360 other persons received prison sentences of varying lengths.

A further riot at Çorum (northern Anatolia) led to the imposition of a curfew on May 28, 1980, when 22 persons, most of them members of the Alevi sect, were believed to have been killed and mainly Alevi-owned shops and houses had been destroyed. In January 1982 it was reported that a group of left-wing Armenians, led by Garbis Altinoglu, had been involved in the killings at Kharamanmaras in December 1978.

Moslem Brotherhood Union

The principal Islamic fundamentalist party, opposed to the institutionalization of the secular state in Turkey under the 1928 Constitution, has been the National Salvation Party (see separate entry). Islamic fundamentalism has, however, also been propagated by the relatively small Turkish section of the Moslem Brotherhood (deriving from the movement originally formed in Egypt—see page 162).

The police announced on Dec. 20, 1980, that 38 alleged members of the Union had been arrested in Istanbul in connexion with the killing of 20 persons, mainly left-wing terrorists, and with that of an author of a television and radio programme on April 11, 1980. Members of a youth organization of Moslem fundamentalists were in July 1971 tried for attempting to disturb the constitutional order.

Like other Islamic fundamentalist movements, the Turkish Moslem Brotherhood seeks the establishment of a state based on the rule of Koranic law.

National Salvation Party (NSP) *(Milli Selamet Partisi)*

Leadership. Prof. Necmettin Erbakan (ch.).

Founded in October 1972 as the continuation of the proscribed National Order Party, the NSP became the principal political expression of Islamic fundamentalism in Turkey. Having become, with 48 seats, the third strongest parliamentary party in 1973, it entered a coalition Government (led by the Republican People's Party) in January 1974—the first Islamic party to share power since the secularization of the state in 1928. After further governmental participation from March 1975 (this time in coalition with the Justice Party), it gained votes in the June 1977 general elections but saw its representation in the 450-member Assembly halved to 24 seats. It went into opposition in December 1977.

Following the military takeover of September 1980, the NSP came into conflict with the Evren regime and was, together with all other registered parties, officially dissolved in October 1981. The party leader, Prof. Erbakan, had earlier been brought to trial in April 1981 (together with 33 other NSP members) on charges of attempting to create an Islamic state in Turkey. He was eventually sentenced to four years' imprisonment on Feb. 24, 1983, for "anti-laicism".

Turkish Islamic Army

This right-wing group claimed responsibility for the assassination of Kemal Türkler, a co-founder and former chairman of the Confederation of Revolutionary Trade Unions of Turkey (DISK), carried out on July 22, 1980.

Armenian Movements

During World War I the Government of the Ottoman Empire decided in August 1915 to "solve the Armenian question once and for all" by exterminating the (Christian) Armenians. The action which followed and which was later described by Armenians as "systematic genocide" resulted in the death of some 1,400,000 people and the flight of the survivors from Turkey, half of them to the Russian part of Armenia and the remainder to Middle East countries, Europe and North America. In mid-1981 the total number of Armenians was estimated at 6,000,000, of whom some 2,800,000 lived in the Armenian Soviet Socialist Republic, about 200,000 in Lebanon, about the same number in France and some 500,000 in the United States.

While many of these Armenians became assimilated to the peoples of the countries to which they had moved, others maintained their own culture and associations and their adherence to the Armenian Catholic Church. It was only in the third generation since the events of 1915 that a demand was raised by Armenians for the establishment of a united and independent Armenia (which some of them wanted to be socialist). In France a Committee for the Defence of the Armenian Cause (*Comité de Défense de la Cause Arménienne*, CDCA) was set up in 1965, and it has published a journal, *La Cause Arménienne*. In Lebanon Armenians first began to commit acts of violence directly related to their cause in the 1970s.

The organizations subsequently formed to conduct "warfare" against the Turkish authorities (and also those who were deemed to co-operate with them) represented, however, only a minority of the Armenians as a whole; many Armenian organizations repeatedly condemned those of their fellow countrymen engaged in acts of violence. The Turkish Government, on the other hand, has not given in to the demands made by militant Armenians and consistently refuses to accept any responsibility for the 1915 events.

The principal Armenian groups responsible for violent activities are listed below.

Armenian Liberation Army

This guerrilla group claimed responsibility for two bombs placed at Istanbul international airport on May 6, 1979; for three bomb attacks on Turkish institutions in Paris on July 8 of that year; and also for attacks on the Turkish consulate-general in Geneva on Aug. 23 and on the Turkish Airlines office in Frankfurt (West Germany) on Aug. 27, 1979.

The group has described its objective as the restoration of autonomy for the Armenian areas of eastern Turkey.

Armenian Liberation Movement *(Mouvement Libération Arménienne)*

This organization was set up by Armenians in France to support the Armenian Secret Army for the Liberation of Armenia (ASALA—see separate entry). However, in a statement issued on Nov. 17, 1981, it condemned the militant Armenian grouping known as the Orly Organization (see separate entry), calling it "one of the biggest anti-Armenian provocations". The statement added: "Extreme right-wing manipulators in the pay of the Americans and the Turkish fascists [i.e. the Turkish military regime] try to make difficulties for the French Government, to discredit the just Armenian struggle and to create additional conflicts between the Armenian movement and the Mauroy Government [of France]."

Armenian National Liberation Movement

In a radio programme identified as the "Voice of the Armenians of Lebanon" broadcast by the "Voice of the Arab Revolution" on April 10, 1982, it was declared that this Movement believed "in the necessity of armed resistance against the enemy—the Turkish Government". It was claimed that the Movement had reactivated the Armenian armed struggle which had been "buried for 63 years"; that it had "achieved international status along with other revolutionary organizations and struggling peoples"; that it had "forced the Turkish Government to recognize our cause"; and that since 1979 the Armenian people in the diaspora had revised their ideas as a result of the Lebanese civil war, the Iranian revolution and the organization of progressive Armenian youth in Europe and the United States.

The same broadcast asserted that the Movement had entered its second phase, consisting of "heavy attacks against imperialists, Zionists and reactionaries, continuous strikes against our main enemy, direct communication with the Armenian masses and the peoples of the world, and firm relations with revolutionary organizations and joint operations together with the Kurdish Workers' Party"—based on "the natural unity of the Armenian and Kurdish peoples".

Armenian Secret Army for the Liberation of Armenia (ASALA)

Established in 1975, this organization, based in Beirut and consisting of Lebanese of Armenian descent, has directed several hundred violent operations, mainly against Turkish institutions abroad but also against the airlines and other agencies of countries whose governments were considered to be favourably inclined towards the Turkish Government (i.e. notably against targets in Switzerland, Britain, France, Italy and the United States).

Although ASALA's declared objective is the "liberation" and unification of Armenia, a spokesman for the organization has been quoted as saying that the Soviet part of Armenia, i.e. the Armenian Soviet Socialist Republic, is "liberated" and constitutes no problem. ASALA regards itself as part of the worldwide revolutionary movement and thus at peace with the Soviet Union; it is strongly anti-American, has described the Turkish state as having a "fascist regime" and seeks to co-operate with the left-wing Kurdish movement. It regards the Armenian question as a product of "imperialist conflicts" and therefore attacks imperialism wherever it may be (like the Popular Front for the Liberation of Palestine but unlike the Justice Commandos for the Armenian Genocide—see separate entry).

ASALA claimed responsibility for the killing of the Turkish ambassador in Vienna on Oct. 22, 1975, and of that in Paris (with his chauffeur) on Oct. 24, as well as that of the Turkish press attaché in Paris on Dec. 22, 1979. It made similar claims for the bombing of the Turkish Airlines office in Rome on March 3, 1980 (when two passers-by were killed); for the shooting of four persons at the Turkish consulate in Lyons (France) on Aug. 5; for the wounding of the Turkish press attaché in Paris on Sept. 26; and for explosions at the Alitalia office in Madrid on Oct. 5, the Turkish airlines office in London on Oct. 12, the Swissair office in Madrid on Nov. 2, and the Turkish consulate-general in Strasbourg on Nov. 10, 1980.

The following year it was responsible for an attack on a Turkish economic and financial counsellor near Paris on Jan. 13, 1981; for the murder of two Turkish diplomats in Paris on March 4; for an attack on a Turkish diplomat in Denmark on April 2; and for an attack on the Turkish Airlines office in Copenhagen on Sept. 15, 1981. Four ASALA members surrendered to the French police in Paris on Sept. 25, 1981, after they had temporarily seized 50 hostages at the Turkish consulate and had demanded the release of Armenian political prisoners in Turkey, as well as of five Turkish and five Kurdish revolutionaries. The Turkish Government maintained that there were no such prisoners in Turkey.

After Mardiros Jamkodjian, an ASALA member, had been sentenced in Geneva on Dec. 19, 1981, to 15 years in prison following his admission that he had killed a Turkish consular employee in Geneva in June 1980, ASALA threatened action against "all Swiss government and civil institutions and all representatives of the Swiss Government" unless the sentence was reconsidered within a week. However, ASALA's position changed after Max Kilndjian, another Armenian (who had on Dec. 23, 1981, been given a two-year sentence in France for complicity in an attempt to murder the Turkish ambassador in Switzerland on Feb. 6, 1980) had been released on Jan. 29, 1982. (Responsibility for the February 1980 attack had been claimed by the Justice Commandos for the Armenian Genocide.) ASALA declared on the same day that the French Government had complied with its demands (including the granting of political status to the four men arrested in connexion with the action at the Turkish consulate in Paris on Sept. 24-25, 1981) and that further operations against French interests would therefore be halted.

ASALA's operational capability was reported to have been weakened as a result of the Israeli invasion of Lebanon in mid-1982; nevertheless, attacks attributed to its members continued to occur in France and elsewhere in late 1982 and early 1983.

Committee for Aid to Armenian Political Prisoners

This Paris-based organization issued, on July 25, 1981, a statement in which on the one hand it condemned the operations of the Organization of 9th June (see separate entry) as acts of terrorism and, on the other hand, criticized Switzerland as being an ally of Turkey "intent on breaking the resistance of our martyred people" (i.e. by imposing prison sentences on Armenian activists arrested in Switzerland).

Front for the Liberation of Armenia

A group by this name claimed responsibility for the bombing of the Turkish Airlines office in London on Dec. 17, 1979.

Justice Commandos for the Armenian Genocide

Like the Armenian Secret Army for the Liberation of Armenia (ASALA), this organization, established in 1975 and based in Beirut, has claimed responsibility for the deaths of Turkish diplomats in various countries; its victims include the Turkish ambassador to the Holy See (who died on June 9, 1977) and the Turkish consul-general in

Sydney (killed with his bodyguard on Dec. 17, 1980). It has also claimed responsibility for a number of acts of violence such as an attack on the Turkish consulate-general in Los Angeles on Oct. 5, 1980; an explosion at the Turkish diplomatic mission at the United Nations in New York on Oct. 12, 1980; an attack on a Turkish diplomat in Copenhagen on April 2, 1981; another attack on the Turkish consulate-general in Los Angeles on Nov. 20, 1981; and the assassination of the Turkish consul-general in Los Angeles on Jan. 28, 1982.

In 1979 the organization declared that its revolutionary activity would "not cease until the Turkish state as heir to the Ottoman Empire has condemned the Armenian genocide and has entered into negotiations with representatives of the Armenian people with a view to facilitating the restoration of the occupied territories to their rightful owner, the Armenian people" (as envisaged in the 1923 Treaty of Lausanne). The organization has also described its aim as being "to denounce the callous indifference of the so-called civilized world" to the fate of the Armenians and "to give food for thought to the so-called free world, the socialist states and the rulers of the criminal state of Turkey".

New Armenian Resistance Movement

This group has been involved in acts of violence in Switzerland and Italy. In particular, it claimed responsibility for the bombing of British Airways and (Israeli) El Al offices in Rome on Dec. 10, 1979.

Organization of 9th June

This Organization was formed in June 1981 in order to exert pressure on the Swiss authorities to release Mardiros Jamkodjian, arrested for the murder of a Turkish consular employee in Geneva on June 9, 1981 (see also under Armenian Secret Army for the Liberation of Armenia). The Organization claimed responsibility for a number of explosions during 1981, among them those at the Swissair office in Tehran on June 28; at the Swiss *Bundeshaus* (Federal Assembly) building in Berne on July 19; at Zurich international airport on July 20; at a department store in Lausanne on July 21; at Geneva's main railway station on July 22 (killing one person); at the Swissair office in Copenhagen on Aug. 11; at a Swiss precision instruments office in Los Angeles on Aug. 21; at the Swiss embassy in Tehran on Sept. 16; and at the Palace of Justice and the central post office in Geneva on Oct. 4.

Organization of 3rd October

This secret group took its name from the day in 1980 on which two members of the Armenian Secret Army for the Liberation of Armenia (ASALA—see separate entry) were injured at a Geneva hotel while they were preparing a bomb; both were arrested and were subsequently given suspended prison sentences and expelled from Switzerland early in 1981. Following the arrest of the above two Armenians, the group engaged in numerous acts of violence designed to bring about their release.

The group claimed responsibility for explosions at the Swissair office in Beirut on Oct. 8-9, 1980; at the Swiss Centre in London on Oct. 12; at the Swiss travel offices in Paris on Oct. 13 and in London on Oct. 18; at the Palace of Justice in Geneva on Nov. 4; at the Swiss travel office in Rome on Nov. 10; at a Geneva bank on Nov. 25; at the Swissair and TransWorld Airlines (TWA) offices in Madrid on Dec. 29; at the Swissair office and Swiss travel centre in Milan on Jan. 27, 1981; and at the Paris offices of Air France and TWA on Feb. 5.

Later the group also claimed responsibility for explosions at the Paris office of Alitalia on Oct. 20 and at the Olympic travel office in Paris on Aug. 22 (the group objecting to the activities of these offices in promoting emigration of Armenian families from the countries of the Middle East to the United States).

Orly Organization

This group took its name from Orly airport (Paris), where the French authorities on Nov. 11, 1981, arrested a member of the Armenian Secret Army for the Liberation of Armenia (ASALA—see separate entry), who was, however, later released by a French court for lack of incriminating evidence against him. The group claimed responsibility for two attacks on the Air France office and the French Cultural Centre in Beirut on Nov. 15, 1981, and for explosions at the Gare de l'Est in Paris on Nov. 16, at the Air France office in Tehran on Nov. 21, 1981, and again in Paris on Jan. 16, 1982.

Although ASALA denied any connexion with the group, it was widely believed that it had directed its activities. Like ASALA, the Orly Organization declared on Jan. 29, 1982, that it was halting all operations against French interests.

Republican Armenian Army

In a statement issued in Beirut on Oct. 13, 1970, this group called for the liberation of all Armenian areas in Turkey and the Soviet Union and for the creation of an independent Armenian state. The group has also pledged its solidarity with the Palestine Liberation Organization in its struggle for the rights of the Palestinian people.

Suisse XV

This group of Armenian activists claimed responsibility for attacks on targets in Switzerland, notably a match factory at Nyon on Jan. 13, 1982, and on a funicular at Crans-Montana on Jan. 20. These actions were accompanied by calls for the release of Mardiros Jamkodjian, sentenced on Dec. 19, 1981, to 15 years' hard labour for murdering a Turkish consular employee in Geneva on June 9, 1981 (see under Armenian Secret Army for the Liberation of Armenia).

Yaya Kashakan Suicide Squad

Leadership. Wasken Sakaseslian—alias Agop Agopian (1.).

This group of four men, formed within the Armenian Secret Army for the Liberation of Armenia (ASALA—see separate entry), attacked the Turkish consulate-general in Paris on Sept. 24, 1981, killed a guard and took 51 persons as hostages pending the fulfilment of a demand for the release of alleged Armenian political prisoners in Turkey. The Turkish authorities, however, stated that there were only two Armenian political prisoners (both clergymen) in Turkey and refused to negotiate with the attackers. On Sept. 25 the French police stormed the building concerned, setting all the hostages free and arresting the four attackers, who were subsequently charged.

Kurdish Movements

In 1960 the Kurdish minority in Turkey was said to number about 4,000,000 people with their own language and customs, resident mainly in south-eastern Turkey. Of the total of some 8,500,000 Kurds, about 2,500,000 were then resident in western Iran, 1,500,000 in Iraq and 400,000 in Syria (for Kurdish movements in Iran, Iraq and Syria, see under those countries). In the Treaty of Sèvres concluded in 1920 between the Western allies and the Sultan of Turkey, provision was made for an autonomous Kurdistan, but this treaty was superseded by the 1923 Treaty of Lausanne, which practically determined Turkey's present boundaries but contained no mention of special rights for the Kurds.

Except for a brief attempt in Iran in 1945-46, there has never been an independent Kurdistan, and the Turkish Government has never recognized the existence of a Kurdish minority in Turkey. A Kurdish nationalist movement first arose before World War I, and anti-Turkish revolts by Kurds were suppressed in 1908, 1925 and 1930-33. In later years unspecified Kurdish separatist organizations were referred to by the Turkish authorities on several occasions.

On Feb. 6, 1971, police at Erzurum was reported to have broken up a Kurdish separatist organization of left-wing youth elements. At a trial at Diyarbakir (south-eastern Turkey) reported on July 17, 1981, death sentences were called for against 11 Kurdish separatists. The principal Kurdish nationalist or separatist movements active in Turkey are listed below.

Kawa

Numerous members of this left-wing separatist movement of Kurds were arrested in 1981: 302 members of the Ankara branch in mid-March; 47 members in Istanbul on March 23; and 135 in Diyarbakir and 21 in Ankara, as reported on June 18.

Kurdish Democratic Party

Leadership. Pasa Uzun.

Some 200 alleged members of this party were put on trial in November 1980 for establishing a clandestine organization "aimed at secession" and for having committed several assassinations since 1977.

Kurdish Workers' Party (Apocus or PKK)

Leadership. Nemesi Kiliç (s.g.).

Established in 1974, this party was given the name of Apocus after Abdullah Ocalan, a leading Kurdish nationalist who founded the party and some years later fled to Syria and was in December 1981 reported to be in Lebanon. According to a Turkish military prosecutor, the party had been set up as the Ankara Democratic Patriotic Association of Higher Education and had rapidly established regional organizations in eastern and southern Anatolia. It also took part in local elections, gaining second place in mayoral elections in Diyarbakir in 1977.

After September 1980 many hundreds of Apocus members were arrested. They included Kemal Pir, who had been second-in-command to Ocalan, and who, after escaping from prison in September, was arrested near Siverek (southern Turkey) on Dec. 4, 1980; he was said to have been involved in 11 murders in Urfa province. The party was then held responsible for 200 murders as well as hold-ups and kidnappings in eastern Turkey. It had also claimed to have taken part in causing an explosion at the Turkish consulate-general in Strasbourg (France) on Nov. 10, 1980—for which the Armenian ASALA organization had also claimed responsibility.

On April 13, 1981, it was reported that 2,231 active members of the party were in custody awaiting trial for, inter alia, the murder of 243 persons (including 30 members of the security forces) and that in a trial of 447 of these prisoners, among them Mustafa Kiliç (a former minister of state) and several former parliamentarians of the Republican People's party (of Bülent Ecevit), the military prosecutor had called for the death penalty for 97 of them. On Jan. 6, 1982, it was reported that another 65 party activists had been arrested and their weapons had been seized; they were to be charged with "conspiracy to set up a Kurdish state".

On Jan. 15, 1982, it was announced that the party's secretary-general and several dozen other leading members had been arrested. On Feb. 3 the trial opened in Erzurum of 172 alleged Apocus members charged with forming an "underground terrorist organization", with 34 of them facing a possible death sentence. At the trial of 125 alleged Apocus members at Adiyaman (south-eastern Turkey) the prosecution demanded the death sentence for 29 of them on March 15, 1982. The total of Apocus members arrested since September 1980 was officially given as over 2,000.

Revolutionary Cultural Centres of the East

This movement set up cultural centres in Kurdish areas of Turkey from 1969 onwards. It was then associated with the Turkish Labour Party, which was dissolved by the Constitutional Court in July 1971 but was re-established in 1975, The movement was banned under martial law in April 1971, and 70 of its members were on Dec. 12, 1972, given prison sentences ranging from 10 months to 16 years for having founded "a secret society aimed at establishing an extreme left-wing regime in Turkey".

Socialist Party of Turkish Kurdistan

Leadership. Kemal Burkay (1.).

After the military takeover of Sept. 12, 1980, the leader and four other members of the central committee of this party, which had already been a clandestine organization, were reported to have fled abroad, presumably to East Germany. The detention of 31 other members of the party was announced in mid-December 1980. In order to avoid dissolution on charges of separatism, the party had earlier, according to security officials, operated under the name of Socialist Party of Iraqi Kurdistan.

The party is said to seek the establishment of an independent Kurdistan based on Marxist-Leninist principles in its political and social organization.

United Kingdom

Capital: London   Pop. 55,950,000

The United Kingdom of Great Britain and Northern Ireland is a hereditary constitutional monarchy in which the monarch, as head of state, has numerous specific responsibilities. The supreme legislative authority is Parliament consisting of (i) a House of Commons of 650 members elected for not more than five years by universal adult suffrage (and in single-member constituencies) and (ii) a House of Lords with more than 1,000 peers or peeresses having a seat for life (a majority by virtue of heredity). The Government is headed by a Prime Minister who is leader of the party which commands a majority in the House of Commons. There is no written Constitution.

As a result of general elections held on June 9, 1983, seats in the House of Commons were distributed as follows: Conservatives 397, Labour 209, Alliance 23 (i.e. Liberal Party 17 and Social Democratic Party 6), Official Unionist Party (Northern Ireland) 11, Democratic Unionist Party 3, Scottish National Party 2, *Plaid Cymru* (Welsh Nationalists) 2, Ulster Popular Unity Party 1, Social Democratic and Labour Party (Northern Ireland) 1, Provisional *Sinn Fein* (Northern Ireland) 1. Parties which unsuccessfully contested the elections included the British National Party, the (pro-Soviet) Communist Party of Great Britain, the Ecology Party, *Mebyon Kernow* (the Cornish National Movement), the National Front, the National Labour Party, the Socialist Party of Great Britain and the Workers' Revolutionary Party, as well as, in Northern Ireland, the Alliance Party, the Independent Democratic Unionist Party and the Workers' Party. Among parties which did not take part in the elections was the Socialist Workers' Party.

Extreme Right-wing Movements

In addition to the National Front—which despite divisions and defections has remained the major extreme right-wing party in Britain —the following similarly orientated groups have been in existence in recent years.

British Democratic Party

This breakaway faction of the National Front was led by Anthony Read Herbert.

British League of Rights

Established in 1970 by Donald A. Martin, a former member of the Australian League of Rights, this League has had as its official patron Air Vice-Marshal (retd.) Donald Bennett, who has also been involved in an anti-communist New Liberal Party and in an anti-EEC Safeguard Britain Campaign. As a United Anti-Common Market candidate, Bennett gained 6 per cent of the vote in the Cotswolds constituency in the 1979 elections to the European Parliament; he also heads a British Independence Movement. One of the League's objectives has been to influence right-wing Conservatives.

The League has a monthly journal, *On Target,* and a book distribution service, which has distributed anti-semitic and racialist literature. It is said to be federated to the Crown Commonwealth League of Rights, and since 1974 it has been the British chapter of the World Anti-Communist League (under the name of League for European Freedom, in succession to a Foreign Affairs Circle).

British Movement (BM)

Formed in 1968 by Colin Jordan (see also under National Socialist Movement below) and with Michael McLaughlin as chairman, the BM was by 1980 organized in some 25 branches; it has claimed a membership of 4,000 and has a small women's division and two journals—*British Patriot* ("the Voice of White Britain" and *British Tidings* ("Bulletin of the British Movement"). It is an anti-semitic and anti-immigration movement; it encourages military training and has its own Leader Guard providing uniforms and special training.

On Jan. 20, 1981, a BM member (Rod Roberts) was sentenced to seven years in prison for arson, possession of arms and ammunition and an offence against the Race Relations Act, while six other persons were also convicted. Marches planned by the BM in Plymouth and Peterborough were prevented by bans imposed respectively on July 18 and Aug. 25, 1981. The BM has also been reported as having provided mercenary units for foreign wars (e.g. in Angola). It has been considered the second largest extreme right-wing movement in Britain (after the National Front).

British National Party (BNP)

This party was set up in 1960 as an alliance of the League of Empire Loyalists, the White Defence League and the National Labour Party. However, the formation of a paramilitary élite corps, named "Spearhead", under the leadership of Colin Jordan and John Tyndall (a leading member of the National Front), provoked a split in the BNP.

Column 88

This organization was formed in 1970 (the 88 standing for the eighth letter of the alphabet, i.e. H.H. for *Heil Hitler*) by remnants of the National Socialist Movement who objected to Colin Jordan's decision to drop the words "National Socialist" from his organization's name. Membership of Column 88 is said to be highly selective (requiring ideological orthodoxy as well as technical ability in intelligence work, arms handling and the use of explosives) and to have contacts in the regular Army.

Column 88 has carried out a number of postal bomb attacks and raids on left-wing bookshops, and also guerrilla training programmes, inter alia planned for Easter 1977 on Salisbury Plain and for the summer of 1977 in northern Germany. The Column is said to have maintained contacts with active terrorist right-wing groups in Italy, with Palestinian groups and with the *Vlaamse Militantenorde* in Belgium.

Constitutional Movement

This Movement was a 1979 offshoot from the National Front, advocating a more moderate policy in order to increase its popular appeal.

Greater Britain Movement

This Movement was formed in 1964 by John Tyndall, who had until then been a member of the National Socialist Movement and later played a leading role in the National Front.

League of St George

This League was formed in 1974 by several former members of the Union Movement of Sir Oswald Mosley, who regarded the latter's form of anti-semitism as too moderate. The League has issued a bi-monthly *League Review* and has run a book club for the sale of Nazi and racist "classics". Its organization is highly secretive (office-bearers in 1980 being said to include Herbert Grestock as president, Mike Griffin as membership secretary and Steven Brady as international affairs officer). The League has described itself as a "non-party, non-sectarian political club" with the aim of promoting "patriotic" European cultural principles of society against the "communist threat".

The League has undertaken to spread the national socialist ideology, to achieve a European union of "nationalists", to co-ordinate international activities of sympathetic groups, to galvanize the efforts of British fascist groups and to act as an umbrella organization servicing the fascist movement. It practises the Nordic cult of Odinism which is promoted by the Northern League and its publication, *The Northlander,* by the Odinist Committee of London and its publication, *Raven Banner,* and by the Viking Youth (led by Paul Jarvis and publisher of *Young Folk*).

National Labour Party

This party was formed in 1959 by John Bean (a former member of the League of Empire Loyalists) and Andrew Fountaine.

National Party

Leadership. John Kingsley Read (ch.).

This party was formed on Jan. 6, 1976, by former members of the National Front. It stands for "humane repatriation or resettlement abroad of all coloured and other racially incompatible immigrants, their dependants and descendants"; for Britain's withdrawal from the European Communities; for rearmament; and for workers' co-partnership in industry. It has published a journal called *Britain First.*

National Socialist Movement

This Movement was formed by Colin Jordan and John Tyndall, the leaders of the "Spearhead" unit of the British National Party (see separate entry), from which they broke away. It was later joined by Martin Webster (who afterwards played a leading role in the National Front). In 1982 Colin Jordan was proclaimed "World Führer" of a World Union of National Socialists, which included the American Nazi group led by Lincoln Rockwell. In 1968 Colin Jordan, in order to comply with the Race Relations Act, discontinued the use of the words "national socialist".

New National Front

Leadership. John Tyndall (ch.); Dave Bruce (activities organizer).

This Front was formed in June 1980 by John Tyndall, former chairman of the National Front, who claimed that the latter organization was "in ruins" because of expulsions and defections. Marches planned by this Front for London, Coventry, Grimsby and Toxteth (Liverpool) between April and August 1981 were all banned.

SS Wotan 71

This terrorist group, which first became known in 1976, has been active under various names (such as the Adolf Hitler Commando Group, the Iron Guard and the Knights of the Iron Cross) against minorities and the property of left-wing organizations. It has been said to own modern and sophisticated weapons, including anti-tank guns. Its principal organizers have been named as David Wilson and Michael Noonan (a former head of the Leader Guard of the British Movement) and it has produced a monthly journal, *Adler und Kreuz.*

Anarchist Groups

Anarchist Workers' Association

Formed in 1971 as the Organization of Revolutionary Anarchists, this Association stands for "self-activity" on the part of the working class towards a "libertarian communist society". It has issued two newspapers, *Libertarian Struggle* and *Libertarian Communist.*

Angry Brigade

Between 1967 and 1971 a group using this name was responsible for 25 bomb and machine-gun attacks, mainly in the London area. Some of the bombings (such as that on Jan. 12, 1971, on the home of Robert Carr, later Lord Carr, then Secretary of State for Employment) were carried out in protest against an Industrial Relations Bill which had led to protest demonstrations by trade unions. In communiqués issued at the time the group declared that it would "fight back" against the bill and that this "war" would be "won by the organized working class with bombs".

At the end of a lengthy trial four alleged members of the Angry Brigade—John Barker, James Greenfield, Anna Mendleson and Hilary Creek—were sentenced on Dec. 6, 1972, to 10 years in prison each, mainly for conspiring to cause explosions. Among defendants acquitted at this trial was James Stuart Christie, who had on Sept. 1, 1964, been sentenced in Madrid to 20 years in prison for handling explosives on behalf of anarchists, but had been released in 1967. After his return to Britain he had established a "Black Cross" anarchist group, which published *Black Flag* as a journal seeking to aid political prisoners anywhere, especially in Northern Ireland.

The name "Angry Brigade" was again used in 1982-83, when a woman who asserted that she represented the group claimed that she had made a bomb attack on a prison officers' training college in Wakefield in November 1982 and another on the Conservative Party headquarters in Leeds on Jan. 20, 1983.

Black Cross—see under Angry Brigade

Libertarian Communists

This group was earlier known as the Anarchist Workers' Organization and the Organization of Libertarian Struggle. It has produced its own newspaper, *Anarchist Worker*.

Other Extreme Left-wing Groups

In addition to the left-wing parties mentioned in the introduction above, the following groups have existed in recent years.

Anti-Nazi League

This organization was formed in 1975 as a cross-party grouping to counter the rise of the National Front and other extreme right-wing movements. It was sponsored by the Socialist Workers' Party and played an important part in opposing the election campaign of the National Front during the 1979 general elections.

Chartists

A movement of this name was formed in 1970 by members or supporters of the International Marxist Group, the Workers' Revolutionary Party and the Militant Tendency (of left-wing members of the Labour Party) with the object of making the Labour Party accept a "revolutionary programme" and working, inter alia, for the creation of trade unions for the armed forces and for setting up a new Fourth International. The movement temporarily published a quarterly *Chartist International* and *Chartist* (as a newspaper).

Communist League

This small group was established in 1967 as the Marxist-Leninist Organization of Great Britain. It was "anti-revisionist" (i.e. pro-Chinese) and published journals such as *COMbat, COMpas* and *InterCOM*.

Communist Party of Britain—Marxist-Leninist (CPB-ML)

Founded by Reg Birch, the CPB-ML became the largest Maoist party in Britain and was partially recognized by the Chinese. It does not discount the use of armed guerrilla warfare on behalf of the "oppressed working class". In its publication *The Worker* it has violently attacked the concept of "social democracy" and the Labour Party.

Communist Party of England

This Maoist party has been active mainly in labour disputes, i.e. in the "industrial struggle".

Communist Workers' Organization

This small group has published a journal called *The Communist*.

International Communist League (ICC)

Founded in the mid-1960s as Workers' Fight, this group in 1968 joined the International Socialists (IS), which group later became the Socialist Workers' Party. In 1971, however, the League was expelled from the IS, and in 1975 it merged with Workers' Power (which was also expelled from the IS) to form the International Communist League led by S. Matgamna; it has published a monthly called *International Communist*. A new Workers' Power group broke away from the ICC in 1976.

International Marxist Group

This grouping was formed in 1956 by disillusioned supporters of the (pro-Soviet) Communist Party of Great Britain. It adopted the theories of Ernest Mandel, who held that where communism had come to power it had degenerated into the rule of a new bureaucracy. The movement forms the British section of the United Secretariat of the Fourth International (one of the two factions into which the Fourth International was split in 1953) and it has published the weekly *Socialist Challenge* and the occasional *International*.

International Revolutionary Solidarity Movement, First of May Group

On behalf of this group, the Cienfuegos Press has published a booklet entitled *Towards a Citizens' Militia* which gives advice on guerrilla and terrorist tactics.

International Spartacist Tendency

This movement has published a journal called *Socialist Current*.

New Communist Party

Leadership. Sidney French (acting sec.).

This party was established on July 17, 1977, by some of the members of the (pro-Soviet) Communist Party of Great Britain (CPGB) who were opposed to the Euro-communist line adopted by that party. The new party declared inter alia: "Working class power, once gained, can only be held on to and consolidated by a proletarian dictatorship." (The CPGB had, in its draft programme on "The British Road to Socialism", dropped the concept of the dictatorship of the proletariat, and the new party regarded this programme as being social democratic and not communist.) Sidney French later denied that he was a Stalinist and stated that he accepted the criticism of Stalin's life and works by the Communist Party of the Soviet Union. In November 1981 most of the new party's Yorkshire district membership left it in order to join the Labour Party.

Groups with policies similar to those of the new party were formed in Australia and Sweden, and the party received some support from East European countries, in particular from Czechoslovakia.

People's Democracy

This movement, led by Michael Farrell, was set up as a socialist group in 1968, became Marxist in 1972 and adopted Leninism in 1976. Its publication was *Unfree Citizen,* which attacked "British imperialism" in Ireland.

Revolutionary Communist Party

This party has published a weekly known as *The Next Step.*

Revolutionary Communist Party of Britain (Marxist-Leninist)

This pro-Albanian party is hostile to all other communist parties, in particular to both Soviet and Chinese "revisionism". Its publication is the *Workers' Weekly.*

Revolutionary Workers' Party

This party is Trotskyist, of the Posadist school, and has published the newspaper *Red Flag.*

Spartacist League

This League broke away from the Workers' Socialist League in 1978 and has published the monthly *Spartacist Britain.*

Workers' Army

A group of this name was set up by two young men with the object of committing acts of violence to overthrow the state. One of them was on Feb. 11, 1983, sentenced to imprisonment for life for killing a policeman, and the other to 10 years in prison, after both had tried to rob a bank of £5,000 to obtain funds for their group. The principal defendant had also been found in possession of an arsenal of weapons and explosives and of a plan for setting up the Workers' Army as well as a list of target organizations.

Workers' League

This small group has sought to create a broad left front and has called for the "building of a revolutionary socialist workers' organization in Britain" on non-sectarian principles. It has published *Socialist Voice* as its journal.

Workers' Socialist League

This League was established in 1974 by Alan Thornett and consisted of about 200 former members of the Workers' Revolutionary Party who had been expelled from that party and wished to form an "entrist" group (to work inside larger organizations such as the Labour Party and its affiliated trade unions).

Nationalist Groups
ENGLAND

An Gof 1980 Movement

Members of this Cornish nationalist group bombed the magistrate's court at St Austell (Cornwall) on Dec. 8, 1980.

English People's Liberation Army

A group of this name claimed responsibility for sending a parcel bomb (which was defused before it could explode) to the London headquarters of the Campaign for Nuclear Disarmament on March 23, 1983.

SCOTLAND

Army for Freeing Scotland (AFS)

This group of three young men, who were said to have no link with the Army of the Provisional Government of Scotland (the "Tartan Army"—see separate entry) were responsible for placing bombs in Glasgow in June and September 1975 (the latter on the Dumbarton railway line). Two of the men were sentenced, on Jan. 8, 1976, to imprisonment for four and six years respectively, while the third (a boy of 16) was given a one-year suspended sentence.

Army of Gael *(Armach Nan Gaidheal)*

This militant Scottish nationalist group claimed responsibility for starting a fire on Nov. 24, 1982, at an Edinburgh hall where the Prime Minister (Mrs Margaret Thatcher) was due to address Scottish Conservatives two days later. The person who made this claim in a telephone call to a Glasgow newspaper stated that his group would "avenge the savage destruction of Scotland and the crippling of our steel industry" and would "by fire, flames and force of arms . . . smash English rule and free the Scottish nation".

Army of the Provisional Government of Scotland ("Tartan Army")

This extreme Scottish nationalist organization described its aim as being to free Scotland of its "British yoke" by revolutionary means. It claimed responsibility for a bomb attack on the oil pipeline of British Petroleum (BP) between Cruden Bay (north of Aberdeen) and Grangemouth (on the Forth) on Sept. 1, 1973, which coincided within a Scottish National Party campaign on the theme "It's Scotland's oil". Eight of the organization's members were, in April and May 1975, sentenced to imprisonment for up to 12 years on various charges, including conspiracy to rob banks and to break into explosives magazines and military establishments with intent to steal, as well as unlawful possession of explosives.

Two further explosions took place along the above BP pipeline on Sept. 12, 1975, at Crook of Devon (Kinross-shire) and on Sept. 23 near Perth, while another bomb exploded on the Glasgow to Helensburgh railway line on Sept. 16 of that year, the "Tartan Army" claiming responsibility in all these cases.

At the trial of five alleged "Tartan Army" members in Edinburgh, it was stated on Sept. 22, 1976, that the organization was variously known as "the 100 Organization", the "APG", the "Border Clan" and the "Tartan Army". The defendants at this trial had all pleaded "not guilty" to charges of furthering the organization's aims by conspiring to commit thefts, cause explosions and inciting others to do the same. Of the five defendants only two were convicted; Donald Currie, a former local chairman of the Scottish National Party, was sentenced on Oct. 2, 1976, to five years in prison for the two 1975 pipeline bomb attacks and another member of the "Army" was given a 12-month sentence for possessing explosives.

Gaelic Language Defence League (*Ceartas* or Justice)

In a statement issued in March 1981 this organization expressed regret at the defeat of a private member's bill, introduced in the House of Commons by Donald Stewart of the Scottish National Party and designed to give the Gaelic language legal status for the first time. The statement added that the League, having tried "all legal means" to enhance the status of the language, would recommend five steps to be carried out until the authorities agreed to formal bilingualism and a Gaelic radio and television service in Scotland. These steps included the destruction of English road signs and of selected radio and television transmitters.

Demands for legal status for Gaelic have been opposed on the grounds that very few Scots now speak the language.

Scottish National Liberation Army (SNLA)

The SNLA, which was believed to have only a few active members, claimed responsibility, on Nov. 23, 1982, for 10 incendiary bombs during the previous eight months, including one sent to the Queen and another to the then Secretary of State for Defence (John Nott) in July. It was also thought to have made unspecified attacks in protest against proposed steelworks closures in Scotland. In addition it was said to have sent a letter bomb to the Lord Provost of Glasgow in February 1983 and another to the Prime Minister at 10 Downing Street, London, in March of that year.

Scottish Socialist Republican League

Six members of this League were on Oct. 14, 1980, sentenced to imprisonment for from six to 16 years on various bombing charges.

Siol Nan Gaidheal

This paramilitary group of Scottish nationalists was, on two occasions, prohibited by the police from wearing claymores (traditional Scottish Highlanders' swords) and dirks (daggers) at parades in Glasgow in March 1980 and in Aberdeen in November of that year. The Scottish National Party was said to have threatened to expel the group from its ranks because of its alleged militaristic behaviour.

WALES

Cadwyr Cymru

Members of this group were responsible for a fire-bomb attack on the Conservative Party office at Shotton (Clwyd) on March 28, 1980.

College for the Welsh People's Movement (*Mudiad Coeg I'r Cymry*)

On Jan. 21, 1981, this Movement claimed responsibility for forcing doors and damaging a computer at the University College of Wales in Aberystwyth in protest against alleged injustice to Welsh students, constituted by the College authorities' refusal to increase Welsh language education.

Mudiad Amddiffyn Cymru (MAC)

Members of the SMC were responsible for a fire-bomb attack on the Conservative Party office in Cardiff on March 28, 1980.

Remembrancer (*Cofiwr*)

Members of this Welsh historical movement were responsible for several cases of arson at holiday cottages in Wales in 1980 (see also under Welsh Language Society).

Sons of Glyndwr

A group of this name was responsible for a number of attacks on holiday houses in North Wales during 1982 and on one in West Wales on Feb. 17, 1983.

Welsh Language Society *(Cymdeithas yr Iaith Cymraeg)*

Leadership. Wayne Williams (ch.).

Established in 1962, this Society was originally concerned almost exclusively with the defence and expansion of the use of the Welsh language. From its beginnings it campaigned for a separate Welsh television channel and for increased use of the Welsh language in radio broadcasts. However, gradually some members of the society began to use violence, inter alia by destroying cottages owned as second homes by English people, and by removing English-language road signs.

At a conference held in September 1980 the Society decided (i) to continue its campaign for refusing to renew television licences until the precise terms of a Broadcasting Bill then under consideration were known; (ii) to co-operate with groups opposing proposals to bury radioactive waste in rural areas; and (iii) to persuade estate agents not to sell empty houses to second-home buyers.

Between December 1979 and the end of 1982 there were more than 60 arson incidents against second homes in Wales owned by non-residents of Wales. Although the Society condemned such attacks, it sympathized with the motives of those who committed them, on the grounds that the sale of such houses resulted in inflated prices which put housing beyond the means of most Welsh people.

On June 25, 1981, the chairman of the Society was sentenced to nine months in prison for his part in a conspiracy to damage television relay stations in Avon, Somerset and Sussex during 1980 (as part of a campaign for a Welsh television channel) after he had admitted the Society's liability for causing damage worth £43,000.

Welsh Socialist Republican Movement

Eight members of this Movement appeared in black berets and IRA-style uniforms in a procession at Abergele in July 1981 to mark the 12th anniversary of the death of two Welsh nationalists blown up by their own bomb on the eve of the investiture of the Prince of Wales in 1969. A further rally in memory of these two men was held by the Movement in Caernarvon on March 13, 1982, at which support was expressed for the "Troops Out" movement calling for the withdrawal of British forces from Northern Ireland; this rally was also attended (for the first time) by deputations from the Provisional *Sinn Fein* (the political wing of the Provisional Irish Republican Army) and the Irish Republican Socialist Party.

Workers' Army of the Welsh Republic (WAWR)

This group claimed responsibility for a number of bomb attacks in October 1981 during a tour of Wales by the Prince and Princess of Wales and also for one behind government offices in Swansea on Nov. 16, 1982.

Northern Ireland

Capital: Belfast   Pop. 1,550,000

Northern Ireland is a province of the United Kingdom of Great Britain and Northern Ireland. Its population is traditionally deeply divided between (i) a Protestant majority (constituting some 60 per cent of the total population), politically represented mainly by various Unionist parties standing for the maintenance of Northern Ireland's status as part of the United Kingdom, and (ii) a Roman Catholic minority standing for eventual union of Northern Ireland with the Republic of Ireland and politically represented mainly by the Social Democratic and Labour Party (SDLP) and, increasingly in recent years, by the Provisional *Sinn Fein* (the political arm of the Provisional Irish Republican Army). An attempt to bridge the sectarian divide in the province has been made by the constitution of the Alliance Party, which has, however, received only limited support.

All efforts made since the introduction of direct British rule in 1972 to set up a workable democratic government in Northern Ireland based on the principle of power-sharing between the two communities have failed, largely because of Unionist opposition to any power-sharing with Republican parties in Northern Ireland. As a first step towards giving the province a democratic government, elections were held on Oct. 20, 1982, to a 78-member Northern Ireland Assembly, with seats being gained as follows: Official Unionist Party 26, Democratic Unionist Party 21, SDLP 14, Alliance Party 10, Provisional *Sinn Fein* 5, Independent Unionist 1, Ulster Popular Unionist Party 1. (The elections were also contested by some 12 other parties.) The elected representatives of the SDLP and Provisional *Sinn Fein* subsequently refused to take their seats in the Assembly.

Political violence in Northern Ireland, which flared up in August 1969 with clashes between Protestants and Catholics, has induced the British Government sharply to increase its military presence in the province. Enormous damage has been caused to Northern Ireland's infrastructure by arson and bombings, and until June 1981 a total of 2,117 persons had lost their lives as a direct result of the civil unrest. Those killed were 1,213 civilians not believed to be members of paramilitary groups, 456 members of the Army, 151 members of the Northern Ireland police and 151 suspected members of paramilitary organizations; 198 deaths were attributed to army action and 18 to police action. There was a steady decline in casualties caused between 1977 and 1981 but a sharp increase followed during April-September of the latter year. During 1981 alone there were in Northern Ireland 815 shooting incidents, 398 explosions, 132 bombs neutralized, £854,929 stolen from banks, 475 malicious fires and 99 deaths (of 55 civilians, 23 soldiers and 21 policemen).

Republican Movements

Irish National Liberation Army (INLA)

The INLA, with headquarters in Dublin, was set up as the military wing of an Irish Republican Socialist Party (IRSP), which had broken away from the Official Irish Republican Army in December 1974. The IRSP has been a legal political party in the Republic of Ireland with the aim of "ending British rule in Ireland" and establishing "a united democratic socialist republic".

In 1975 the INLA began to conduct armed warfare in order to bring about a British military withdrawal from Northern Ireland which was to be united with the Republic on the basis of "socialist principles". The INLA claimed responsibility inter alia for the murder of Airey Neave, former Conservative spokesman for Northern Ireland affairs in the British House of Commons, in London in March 1979, and of a former police reservist and a police constable in Northern Ireland in July 1979.

On July 2, 1979, the British Government decided to proscribe the INLA, both in Northern Ireland under a Northern Ireland (Emergency Provisions) Act and in the United Kingdom under a Prevention of Terrorism (Temporary Provisions) Act. The INLA, however, continued its bombing campaign and in particular made two bomb attacks on a school of infantry on Salisbury Plain on March 7, 1980. Of INLA members convicted of various offences and held in the Maze prison (Belfast), three (among them one described as the "officer commanding" INLA prisoners), died there between May and August as a result of a hunger strike in support of a demand for "special status" for these prisoners; the INLA, however, ended its use of hunger strikes on Sept. 6, 1980.

In 1982 the INLA claimed responsibility (i) for the killing on June 4 in Dublin of a former director of operations of the Official IRA, who was said to have killed the founder of the IRSP (Seamus Costello) in Dublin in 1977; (ii) for an attack on a Protestant Belfast city councillor on Sept. 1; and (iii) for a bomb explosion which killed a British soldier and two children in Belfast on Sept. 15; and (iv) for several other bomb explosions in Belfast in October.

In the most serious attack against the British forces by the INLA, 11 soldiers and six civilians were killed by a bomb at a public house at Ballykelly (Co. Londonderry) on Dec. 7, 1981.

Leading politicians whom the INLA has attempted to kill include the Rev. Ian Paisley, leader of the Democratic Unionist Party, and several leading members of his party; Harold McCusker, a Unionist member of the British House of Commons; and Gerry Fitt, the West Belfast Socialist MP at Westminster. Three INLA members arrested in Paris on Aug. 28, 1982, were found in possession of arms and explosives and of a list of potential British targets; the French police also believed that they were in touch with the Basque separatist ETA organization in Spain.

There has been no precise indication of INLA membership, which was in early 1982 estimated at between 150 and 200. On Jan. 5, 1982, the Government of the Republic of Ireland declared the INLA to be a proscribed organization.

A member of the INLA's army council, in an interview with a US radio station in mid-January 1983, defended his organization's activities and stated that the INLA would maintain its attacks on police and troops because they represented "the physical oppression of the British presence" and that it would in future "carry out operations against any element within the British Establishment depending on logistics and intelligence available". He also declared that the INLA differed from the Irish Republican Army (IRA) in that it was a revolutionary socialist organization and that, while the IRA was quite likely to lay down its arms when the British withdrew from Ireland, the INLA believed that the resolution of the national question was "just the first stage in the process for establishing a 32-county socialist state". He also envisaged that "at some point in the future the most conscious revolutionary element within the IRA would enter into a broad front with the INLA".

Official Irish Republican Army

The Irish Republican Army had its origins in a National Volunteer Force recruited in the northern counties of Ireland in 1913 as an Irish nationalist group. During the Irish Civil War of 1921-23 the force changed its name to Irish Republican Army, but after 1924 its influence declined. After the IRA had started a bombing campaign as part of its opposition to the Government of Eamonn de Valera (whom it accused of having betrayed the principle of a united Ireland), the IRA was declared an illegal organization by the Dublin Government in June 1939; its leaders were imprisoned. During World War II some of its members were pro-German and were responsible for bomb explosions in England in 1940.

In 1956-62 the IRA conducted a bombing campaign in Northern Ireland, but the authorities were able to confine this action to the border areas. From 1970 onwards the IRA gradually took over the leadership of a Northern Ireland Civil Rights Association, which had been established in 1967 by non-political liberals who wished to improve the status of Roman Catholics. After the breakaway of the Provisional IRA in 1969, the rump of the IRA became known as the Official IRA, whose political wing was the (official) *Sinn Fein,* later *Sinn Fein* the Workers' Party, which in Northern Ireland was known as Republican Clubs. The Official IRA, as a revolutionary republican and Marxist movement, proclaimed that its aim was to unite both Protestant and Catholic workers in an All-Ireland socialist republic.

Members of the Official IRA continued to be involved in acts of violence, which included the bombing of a British Army unit at Aldershot (where a Catholic chaplain and some cleaning women were killed) on Feb. 22, 1972, and the killing of the Northern Ireland Unionist Senator John Barnhill on Dec. 11, 1971, and of the Republican *(Fine Gael)* Senator Billy Fox on March 11, 1974. However, in May 1971 the Official IRA had already condemned the Provisional IRA as "bigots" whose motives were "to set the Protestant and Catholic working class at each other's throats". A clash between the two wings of the IRA in October 1975 resulted in 11 deaths and injuries to 50 persons.

Provisional Irish Republican Army (PIRA or "Provos")

The Provisional IRA broke away from the Irish Republican Army (IRA) in 1969 as a direct-action organization intent upon launching a guerrilla campaign and making Northern Ireland ungovernable by forcing the British Government to withdraw its armed forces and to relinquish all responsibility for the province. At political level the PIRA has operated through the Provisional *Sinn Fein,* which has remained a legal party both in the Republic and in Northern Ireland, whereas the PIRA was declared a proscribed organization under the Prevention of Terrorism (Temporary Provisions) Bill enacted in the United Kingdom on Nov. 29, 1974.

The PIRA is organized on military lines. It has a women's section known as *Cumann Na mBan,* which has been involved in gathering information, planting fire-bombs and providing shelter in "safe houses". The youth wing of the PIRA is known as *Fianna Na h'Eireann,* whose members assist the PIRA in gathering intelligence, acting as lookouts and transporting weapons.

The PIRA began its campaign in Northern Ireland in 1969 by sniping at British soldiers and bombing property; by September 1971 the PIRA was using rocket launchers, and in April 1973 letter bombs appeared, to be followed by parcel bombs sent to senior civil servants. In August 1971 the Northern Ireland authorities introduced internment without trial of suspects, which remained in force for four years despite a civil disobedience campaign called by the Roman Catholic opposition parties in Northern Ireland. Action by British troops against the PIRA led to the death of 13 persons in Londonderry from army gunfire on Jan. 30, 1972, and in a reprisal action for this so-called "bloody Sunday" the British embassy in Dublin was attacked by PIRA members.

By that time a state of confrontation had

been reached between the PIRA on the one hand and, on the other, the British Army, the Ulster Defence Regiment (UDR) and the Royal Ulster Constabulary (the Northern Ireland police), while members of paramilitary Protestant organizations (of which the Ulster Defence Association was the strongest) were responsible for numerous killings (mainly, but not exclusively, of Catholics).

Following a meeting between Protestant churchmen and leaders of the PIRA and the Provisional *Sinn Fein* at Feakle, Co. Clare (in the Republic of Ireland), on Dec. 10, 1974, the PIRA observed a temporary ceasefire from Dec. 22, 1974, to Jan. 16, 1975. Although renewed from Feb. 10, 1975, the ceasefire gradually broke down in the course of 1976. Later PIRA activities in Northern Ireland included several fire-bomb attacks, mainly in Belfast, during August and September 1977, when property worth several million pounds was destroyed. On Jan. 1, 1978, the PIRA admitted that it had been responsible for organizing 46 bombing and shooting incidents since the beginning of the year. On Feb. 17, 1978, a total of 12 people were killed and 30 were injured in a PIRA fire-bomb attack on a restaurant in Co. Down. A new series of fire-bomb attacks was carried out between October 1978 and March 1979.

By that time it was clear that the PIRA was receiving weapons from abroad, including US-made M-60 machine-guns (firing up to 550 rounds a minute) which were first used in January 1978. In the most serious action carried out by the PIRA during 1979 a total of 18 British soldiers were killed by two bombs at Warrenpoint (Co. Down) on Aug. 27.

In the course of a further spate of sectarian killings in Northern Ireland, the PIRA declared on Jan. 21, 1981, that by shooting dead (on that day) a former Speaker of the Northern Ireland House of Commons and his son, also a former member of that House, it had made "a deliberate attempt on the symbols of hated Unionism" in "direct reprisal for a whole series of loyalist assassinations and murder attempts on nationalist people and nationalist activities".

The killing of the Rev. Robert Bradford, an Official Unionist member of the British House of Commons, on Nov. 14, 1981, was described by the PIRA as an "execution" carried out in the course of its campaign against the British presence in Northern Ireland.

In connexion with PIRA activities in the Republic of Ireland, Seamus Twomey, then chief of staff of the PIRA, was in October 1973 sentenced to three years in prison for membership of the proscribed PIRA and for receiving money taken in an armed robbery; he escaped from prison in Dublin shortly afterwards, spent several years in Northern Ireland and was rearrested in Dublin on Dec. 3, 1977. On June 12, 1978, he was given a five-year prison sentence for his escape and a concurrent three-year sentence for PIRA membership.

Among other PIRA prisoners held in the Republic were (i) Dr Bridget Rose Dugdale, sentenced to nine years in prison for her part in hijacking a helicopter in the Republic on Jan. 24, 1974, and forcing it to drop two milk churns filled with explosives over police barracks at Strabane (Co. Tyrone), where, however, they failed to explode; (ii) Kevin Mallon, who had twice escaped from prison and had last been recaptured on Aug. 18, 1974; and (iii) James Hyland, serving a five-year sentence for possessing arms and ammunition. The release of these prisoners was unsuccessfully demanded by a group of PIRA members who kidnapped a Dutch industrialist, Dr Tiede Herrema, on Oct. 3, 1975, but released him on Nov. 7 after they had been surrounded by police to whom they surrendered. On March 1, 1976, four persons were given prison sentences of up to 20 years on charges arising out of this kidnapping, and an additional three men were on March 15, 1977, sentenced to from five to seven years in this connexion.

The most conspicuous operation carried out by PIRA members in the Republic was the killing on Aug. 27, 1979, of Earl Mountbatten of Burma (a cousin of Queen Elizabeth II and uncle of the Duke of Edinburgh) by a bomb placed on his fishing boat. The two alleged perpetrators of this crime were sentenced to life imprisonment in Dublin on Nov. 23, 1979.

In England the PIRA carried out a bombing campaign between March 8, 1973, and May 1976. Of those involved in causing explosions in London on March 8, 1973, eight were sentenced to life imprisonment in Winchester on Nov. 15 of that year, while a ninth defendant was sentenced to 10 years in prison; those given life sentences included Dolours Price, her sister Marion, Hugh Feeney and Gerald Kelly, all of whom were later, with other PIRA prisoners, involved in hunger strikes in support of their demand to be granted special status as "political prisoners". PIRA actions carried out in England in 1974 included a bomb attack on a public house in Guildford (Surrey) on Oct. 5, in which five people were killed; another such attack in Woolwich (London) on Nov. 7, when two persons were killed and 34 injured; and a third one on a public house in Birmingham on Nov. 21, in which 21 persons lost their lives and 120 were injured.

In connexion with the Guildford and Woolwich attacks, life sentences were imposed on Oct. 22, 1975, on four men and a young woman. Numerous other bomb explosions took place in December 1974 and January 1975, and two bomb factories were discovered—one in Southampton in December 1974 and another in Hammersmith (London) on Feb. 27, 1975. For involvement in this PIRA campaign a number of suspected PIRA members were during February and March 1975 sentenced to imprisonment for up to 20 years. A bomb explosion at the Hilton Hotel in London on Sept. 5, 1975, killed two and injured 63 people and was attributed to the PIRA. Prominent persons killed by the PIRA included Ross McWhirter, the publisher who had called for the establishment of a reward fund for information leading to the arrest of bombers and who was shot dead on Nov. 27, 1975. Further bomb explosions took place in February-March 1976 after the death of Frank Stagg, a PIRA member who had been on hunger strike while serving a 10-year sentence for planning to attack targets in Coventry. A number of other alleged bombers were sentenced to imprisonment between May 1976 and January 1977.

Following the suspension of its bombing campaign between May 1976 and January 1977, the PIRA declared in Dublin on Feb. 1 that its "campaign against military and economic targets" would be "maintained" through the coming year both in the six counties (i.e. Northern Ireland) and on the British mainland; "confident of victory", it forecast "a future phase of war which will be more intense than anything experienced to date".

Following a number of sporadic explosions, the PIRA bombing campaign in England was resumed on Dec. 17, 1978, with bombings in London and five other cities and an attack on an oil storage tank at Canvey Island (Essex) on Jan. 17, 1979. Later the PIRA claimed responsibility for shooting, during February and March 1980, three British soldiers in West Germany, one of whom died later of his wounds.

The PIRA was responsible for further bomb attacks in London in December 1980 and January 1981. Another bomb explosion was caused by the PIRA at the Sullom Voe oil terminal (Shetlands), which the Queen was opening on May 9, 1981 (when, however, no injuries were caused). Further PIRA bomb attacks, carried out in London during October and November 1981, resulted in the death of two civilians and a bomb disposal expert and in injury to other persons, among them Lt.-Gen. Sir Steuart Pringle (Commandant-General of the Royal Marines).

After two major bomb attacks carried out in London on July 20, 1982, resulting in the death of 11 soldiers, the PIRA declared that it had carried them out "in accordance with the right of self-defence under Article 51 of the United Nations Charter".

By 1980 it was evident that public support for the PIRA among the Roman Catholic section of Northern Ireland's population was increasing notably, mainly at the expense of the traditional Catholic parties (the largest of which is the Social Democratic and Labour Party). In the Republic, however, the growth of public support for the PIRA was not quite so marked. At funerals of PIRA casualties of the struggle the organization was able to rally thousands of sympathizers.

A number of convicted prisoners from among the many hundreds (of PIRA members and other Republicans), held mainly in the H Blocks of the Maze prison near Belfast, conducted a hunger strike between Oct. 27, 1980, and Oct. 3, 1981, with the object of obtaining special treatment and ultimately the status of political prisoners—a demand which the British Government steadfastly refused to grant. The course of the hunger strike, resulting in the death of many involved in it, appeared to further the cause of the PIRA, as evidenced by several election results.

In a by-election held on April 9, 1981, in Fermanagh and South Tyrone, to a seat in the British House of Commons, Robert Sands, a PIRA hunger striker (serving a 14-year term for arms offences and standing as an Anti-H Block/Armagh, Political Prisoner), won the seat against an Official Unionist (Harry West) by gaining 30,492 votes (a majority of 1,446 votes). However, Sands died in prison on May 5. In a further by-election held on Aug. 20, 1981, the seat was taken by Owen Carron, a member of the Provisional *Sinn Fein*, as the candidate of the same committee which had nominated Sands (the majority being increased to 2,230 votes).

For the general elections held in the Republic on June 11, 1981, the National H Block/Armagh Committee nominated nine prisoners (four of them on hunger strike) and two of these candidates, both being PIRA members, were elected—Paddy Agnew and Kieran Doherty, the latter dying on Aug. 2, the 73rd day of his hunger strike.

Loyalist Movements

Protestant Action Force

This small group emerged in Armagh City in mid-1982 and has been responsible for killing a *Sinn Fein* election worker in October of that year and for other attacks on Catholics in March 1983. The group's name had earlier been used as a cover by the Ulster Volunteer Force (see below).

Red Hand Commandos

This extremist Protestant group, which had emerged early in 1973, was banned in Northern Ireland on Nov. 12, 1973, together with the Ulster Freedom Fighters (see separate entry). A man claiming to represent the group, in a warning issued on May 17, 1974, threatened that more bombs would be exploded in Dublin (after three car bomb explosions in the capital and a fourth in Monaghan had killed 30 people and injured over 150 on the same day).

The Third Force

Plans for the establishment of this Force were revealed by the Rev. Ian Paisley, the leader of the Democratic Unionist Party, at a rally at Newtownards (Co. Down) on Nov. 23, 1981. Dr Paisley had earlier said on Nov. 16 that, in view of official plans to set up an Anglo-Irish Inter-Governmental Council and of the British Government's refusal to establish a third security force (in addition to the Army and the police), Ulster Unionists would make the province of Northern Ireland ungovernable and would demonstrate that such a third force was already in existence. The Newtownards rally was attended by Unionist supporters in paramilitary uniform, but estimates of numbers involved in the parade of the "Third Force" varied between 5,000 and 15,000.

James Prior, Secretary of State for Northern Ireland, had made it clear on Nov. 18, 1981, that private armies had no place in society and that the law did not recognize any distinction between one private army and another, and he added on Nov. 24 that the Government would not allow private armies to take over the work of the police and would "not adopt methods which abandon the rule of law or which are intended to punish the innocent".

Ulster Defence Association (UDA)

Leadership. Andy Tyrie (supreme commander).

The UDA has been regarded as the strongest of various extreme Protestant paramilitary organizations set up in response to the violent activities of the Provisional Irish Republican Army (PIRA). Thomas Herron, then secretary of the UDA, claimed on Oct. 16, 1972, that it had some 50,000 members trained in all aspects of guerrilla warfare. After the PIRA had established "no-go" areas (where the writ of the Northern Ireland Government did not run) in parts of Londonderry, the UDA established its own "no-go" areas in different parts of Northern Ireland in May-June 1972 in protest against the continued existence of the PIRA "no-go" areas; this UDA action led to clashes between UDA members and the Army.

After two UDA leaders had had talks on June 13, 1972, with William Whitelaw, then Secretary of State for Northern Ireland, the UDA agreed to postpone the establishment of further "no-go" areas but stated that if no action had been taken within 14 days to remove the PIRA areas it would put up permanent barricades all over the province. After another meeting with Whitelaw, the UDA declared on June 28 that it would carry out its plan and that some of its barricades would be permanent until the PIRA barricades in Londonderry were taken down. The Army tried in Belfast on July 3, 1972, to prevent the UDA from setting up barricades, but in order to avoid a confrontation the Army agreed that soldiers should set up the road-blocks and that the UDA should be allowed to patrol the streets behind them.

Although the Army had cleared the PIRA's Londonderry areas in a swift operation on July 31, 1972, UDA members continued their activities in Belfast, where clashes between the Army and UDA units occurred on Sept. 7-8, 1972, leading to the death of two UDA members, and again on Oct. 12-13 and Oct. 16; thereafter Herron threatened that the UDA would possibly go over to an offensive against the Army. However, the threat was not carried out and Herron himself was assassinated in September 1973 (it was thought by a member of a rival Protestant group). The UDA itself was held responsible for numerous assassinations, mainly (but not exclusively) of Roman Catholics.

Trials of a number of UDA supporters or members took place in England and Scotland, where the UDA was in 1974 thought to have some 1,000 members. On Dec. 4, 1974, three defendants connected with the Conservative Party were sentenced in Winchester to imprisonment for from five to 10 years for involvement in an attempt to import guns and explosives from Canada for the UDA.

On June 26, 1979, a total of 11 UDA members convicted in Dumfries and Paisley of conspiring to further their organization's aims by unlawfully acquiring guns and ammunition were sentenced in Glasgow to from seven to 16 years in prison; they included the supreme commander in Scotland and the Dumfries and Paisley area commanders of the UDA.

Ulster Freedom Fighters (UFF)

This organization has been said to operate under the aegis of the Ulster Defence Association (UDA—see separate entry), although the latter has on occasion disowned it. In 1973 members of the UFF claimed responsibility for killing two young Catholics, and also for several bombings, in the Belfast area. Late in June 1973 the UFF accepted responsibility for the murder of a Catholic ex-senator and former election agent for the leader of the Social Democratic and Labour Party (SDLP).

The UFF were officially banned in Northern Ireland on Nov. 12, 1973, but nevertheless continued to be involved in assassinations both in the Republic and in Northern Ireland. In particular, the UFF accepted responsibility for killing the (Protestant) *Fine Gael* Senator Billy Fox at Clones (Co. Mohaghan) on March 11, 1974, for which five alleged members of the PIRA were sentenced in Dublin on June 7 of that year to penal servitude for life.

The UFF also claimed responsibility for numerous other murders, mainly of Catholics, in Belfast, between Sept. 16 and Nov. 28, 1974, and in late 1981 and early 1982 for several murders which, the UFF alleged, were in response to the Provisional IRA's campaign during the hunger strike of its prisoners which had cost 64 lives.

Ulster Protestant Action Group

A grouping of this name claimed responsibility for the killing of a number of Catholics, mainly in Belfast, between Sept. 16 and Nov. 28, 1974.

Ulster Volunteer Force (UVF)

The UVF was formed in 1912 as a paramilitary organization to prevent the establishment of a Home Rule Government in Ireland; it was recruited from among Protestants and was armed with rifles and ammunition smuggled in from the continent of Europe; and it was at the time supported by the Conservatives in Britain opposed to the granting of home rule to Ireland. In the 1960s it was revived to take part in the Protestant struggle against the Irish Republican Army (IRA).

Following the killing of a young Catholic by a UVF member (who considered his victim to be a member of the IRA), the UVF was banned in 1966 as the Northern Ireland Government wished to prevent the escalation of sectarian warfare. It was relegalized on May 15, 1974, but was again proscribed in November 1975, after it had been involved in various acts of violence.

A number of alleged UVF members were later sentenced to imprisonment in Scotland. They included one given a seven-year sentence in Dumfries on Nov. 26, 1974, for illegal possession of arms, and nine others sentenced in Glasgow on June 22, 1979, to from 12 to 18 years for conspiring to further the aims of their organization (which was not banned in the United Kingdom) between 1975 and February 1979.

Young Militants

This extremist Protestant group claimed responsibility for killings of Catholics, especially in Belfast, between Sept. 16 and Nov. 28, 1974.

8. NORTH AMERICA

Canada

Capital: Ottawa

Pop. 24,200,000

The Dominion of Canada, a member of the Commonwealth with the British monarch as head of state (represented by a Governor-General), has a Parliament consisting of a 104-member Senate appointed by the Governor-General and a 282-member House of Commons *(Chambre de Communes)* elected by universal adult suffrage for a five-year term. There is a federal Cabinet presided over by a Prime Minister. Of the country's 10 provinces each has its own legislature and government, while the Northwest Territories and the Yukon Territory each have elected Legislative Councils. As a result of general elections held on Feb. 18, 1980, and by-elections held in April and August 1981, seats in the House of Commons were distributed as follows: Liberals 147, Conservatives 102, New Democrats 33.

As a result of the findings (published in August 1981) of a Royal Commission of Inquiry into activities of the Royal Canadian Mounted Police (RCMP) serious irregularities were revealed in the country's police forces, e.g. that in 1966 the RCMP security service had files on more than 800,000 people and that in 1970 the Quebec provincial police had warned Paul Rose, a member of the Quebec Liberation Front, that his telephone was tapped by the RCMP. The Federal Government thereupon decided to set up a new civilian security service which would not abuse its powers nor be abused by the Government.

Separatist Movements

National Indian Brotherhood

Leadership. David Ahenakew (pres.); Wallace Labillois (ch. of council of elders).

The council of elders of this Brotherhood claims to represent 300,000 pure-bred Indians in 50 tribes in Canada. It has worked in co-operation with other associations which claim to represent 1,500,000 "original Canadians", including also Inuit (or Eskimo) and Métis (i.e. half-caste) people.

Wallace Labillois did not accept the official British view that all responsibility for the aboriginal people of Canada was formally handed on by Britain on the attainment of independence by the Canadian Government in 1931 under the Statute of Westminster; in common with other Canadian Indian leaders he maintained the view that the British Crown continued to have the obligation of safeguarding Indian rights. The National Indian Brotherhood in particular claimed in 1981 that the Canadian colonial authorities had a record of broken pledges on aboriginal rights. The Indian demand was for a guarantee of autonomous enclaves in a legally independent Canada, mainly in the area of Prince Rupert Land, around Hudson Bay.

The leader of an Indian delegation, Chief Solomon Sanderson (president of the Federation of Saskatchewan Indians), said in London on Nov. 3, 1981, that the Canadian Indians would fight for their political independence.

Chief Ahenakew, who was also head of the Assembly of First Nations (of status Indians, who live in the reserve), has said that he does not acknowledge the supremacy of the Parliament of Canada, and Chief Max Gros-Louis, leader of the Huron Indians, stated in February 1983 that his group (like the Provincial Government of Quebec) did not recognize the Constitution of Canada. Indians have also claimed that "existing aboriginal rights" as referred to in the Canadian Constitution's Charter of Rights should cover not only the right to "hunting, fishing and gathering" but also ownership of land and its resources.

Quebec Liberation Front (*Front de Libération du Québec,* FLQ)

Leadership. Mathieu Hébert (Pierre Vallières).

The FLQ, founded in 1963, has operated under various names to further its aims of the complete separation of the province of Quebec from the rest of Canada, an end to English-language "colonialist" domination of Quebec and transition to a socialist economy. By 1970 it was held responsible for various terrorist and subversive activities, involving seven deaths, bomb explosions and other acts of sabotage, armed robberies, thefts of weapons and plots to kidnap diplomats or politicians. Within seven years 135 persons had been arrested in Quebec for subversive activities.

On Oct. 5 and 10, 1970, respectively, FLQ members kidnapped the British trade commissioner in Montreal (James Richard Cross) and the Quebec Minister of Labour and Immigration (Pierre Laporte). Demands made by the kidnappers in return for the release of their victims were inter alia for payment of Can. $500,000 to the FLQ, the release of 23 "political prisoners" to be given a safe passage to Algeria or Cuba, the publication of an FLQ manifesto and a ban on any police action against the kidnappers. On Oct. 8 the Canadian Broadcasting Corporation broadcast an FLQ manifesto which praised Dr Fidel Castro, the Cuban leader, and strongly denounced a large number of Canadian politicians and business leaders. Following unsuccessful attempts to achieve negotiations between the Government and the kidnappers, the Federal Government invoked, on Oct. 16, at the request of the Quebec Government, the 1914 War Measures Act providing for emergency powers; on the same day police supported by troops arrested 250 political suspects in 170 separate raids. However, almost all of those arrested were released within weeks.

P. Laporte was found murdered on Oct. 18, 1970, but J. R. Cross was released on Dec. 3 after his kidnappers had accepted a government offer of a safe passage to Cuba. Two alleged murderers of P. Laporte—Paul Rose and Francis Simard—were sentenced to life imprisonment on March 13 and May 20, 1971, respectively. In connexion with the abduction of J. R. Cross, prison sentences were imposed in August and November 1979 on three former FLQ members who had returned to Canada after many years in exile, and a further defendant said to be involved in the Cross case was given a four-year sentence in June 1980. A further former FLQ member involved in the Cross case (Yves Langlois) obtained political asylum in France but returned to Canada on June 9, 1982, to face trial.

Since Le Parti Québecois came to power in 1976 committed to the achievement of political sovereignty for Quebec in an economic association with Canada, there has been an abatement of extremist separatist activity.

Mathieu Hébert is editor of the socialist theoretical journal Révolution Québecoise.

White Supremacy Organizations

Canadian Knights of the Ku Klux Klan

Leadership. James McQuirter ("grand wizard" and national director).

Like the Ku Klux Klan organizations in the United States, this group has been involved in militant actions in support of its advocacy of White supremacy.

Mary Ann McGuire, described as a "grand titan" in the Canadian Klan (and also as a sympathizer with the Irish Republican Army), was arrested in Dominica on April 29, 1981, in connexion with a proposed invasion of the island by US and Canadian mercenaries.

National Association for the Advancement of White People

In August 1980 it was reported that an office had been set up in Toronto under this Association's name by the Canadian Ku Klux Klan.

Western Guard

This group, formerly known as the Edmund Burke Society, stands for White supremacy and is said to have links with the like-minded Canadian Knights of the Ku Klux Klan.

Anti-nuclear Terrorist Group

Direct Action

On May 31, 1982, this group claimed responsibility for a bomb attack on an electric power station under construction on Vancouver Island (British Columbia). On Oct. 20, 1982, the group addressed a nine-page letter to the Toronto left-wing weekly *The Clarion,* claiming responsibility for a bomb explosion on Oct. 14 at a factory of Litton Systems Canada (outside Toronto) engaged in the production of guidance systems for the (US nuclear-armed) cruise missiles. In the letter, in which the group outlined its aims, it expressed its opposition to nuclear weapons but claimed to have no connexion with any of the peace movement organizations which had previously been involved in anti-nuclear demonstrations.

United States of America

Capital: Washington, D.C.   Pop. 232,000,000

The United States of America, consisting of 50 member states with a measure of internal self-government, has an executive President elected for a four-year term by a college of representatives elected directly in each state, and re-eligible once only; he is both head of state and head of the executive, whose other members he nominates. Legislative power is held by Congress consisting of a 100-member Senate and a 435-member House of Representatives. In each state two senators are elected by direct adult suffrage for a six-year term, with one-third of the Senate's membership being renewed every two years. Members of the House of Representatives are similarly elected for a two-year term. There is a traditional two-party system, but the constitutional separation of executive and legislative functions precludes party government in the accepted sense (as the President's party may be faced with a majority of the other party in Congress).

As a result of elections held on Nov. 2, 1982, seats were distributed as follows: (i) in the Senate—Republicans 54, Democrats 46; (ii) in the House of Representatives—Democrats 269, Republicans 166. Parties not represented in Congress include the American Party, the Citizens' Party, the (pro-Soviet) Communist Party of the USA, the Libertarian Party, the National States' Rights Party, the Prohibition Party, the Democratic Socialists of America, the Social Democrats USA, the Socialist Labor Party of America and the (pro-Chinese) US Communist Party (Marxist-Leninist). Other parties which have unsuccessfully contested presidential elections are the American Independent Party, the People's Party, the Socialist Workers' Party and the US Labor Party.

Political organizations outside the legal parties which have taken part in elections have included (i) extreme right-wing organizations, among which the Ku Klux Klan has continued to be involved in violent action in pursuance of its White supremacy policy, while others have acted as pressure groups towards similar objectives; (ii) extreme left-wing organizations, among them the remnants of those movements which had in the 1960s adopted the "Black Power" slogan; and (iii) national liberation movements, among which the Armed Forces of Puerto Rican National Liberation (see below under Puerto Rico) have been responsible for numerous acts of violence in recent years.

Racial riots, often with political implications, have been part of the general climate of violence prevalent in parts of the United States, a country where the possession of firearms is widespread. According to a statement by David Steinberg, executive director of the National Council for a Responsible Firearms Policy, on Nov. 22, 1982, more than 440,000 Americans had been killed by guns in their own country since the assassination of President John F. Kennedy in 1963; more than 1,700,000 were wounded by gunfire and about 2,700,000 were robbed at gunpoint.

Extreme Right-wing Movements

John Birch Society

Leadership. Robert H. W. Welch (pres.).

Established in 1958, this Society was named after the late Capt. John M. Birch, who had carried out behind-the-lines intelligence work in China during World War II and was killed by Chinese Communists 10 days after the end of the war. The Society was founded by Robert H. W. Welch, with the aim of fighting an alleged "communist conspiracy" in the United States, inter alia by operating through front organizations, and of exposing all persons suspected of communist affiliations; among alleged "agents of the Communist Party" it named President Eisenhower and the late John Foster Dulles (former Secretary of State).

The Society inter alia opposed the Civil Rights Act of 1964, US membership of the United Nations and NATO, and all cultural and other exchanges with the Soviet Union. With headquarters in Belmont (Massachusetts), it was reported to be organized in cells, and in 1968 it claimed 100,000 members. In 1961 the Attorney General of California described it as "a monolithic organization with policy dictated from above and no dissent permitted in its ranks".

Publications of the Society are *American Opinion* (monthly), *The Review of the News* (weekly) and *The Bulletin of the John Birch Society* (monthly).

Ku Klux Klan

The first Ku Klux Klan was founded in Tennessee in 1865 and rapidly developed into a political organization with the aim of restoring White supremacy in the South (lost in the civil war) by terrorizing the newly emancipated and enfranchised Negroes; it was banned by special legislation under President Grant in 1871.

A second Ku Klux Klan emerged in Georgia in 1915 as an anti-Negro, anti-Jewish, anti-Catholic, anti-foreign and anti-labour organization, whose members attacked not only the organization's political opponents but also bootleggers, gamblers and wifebeaters. In 1920-24, it grew into a nation-wide movement with between 4,000,000 and 5,000,000 members and politically dominated the southern states and also Indiana, Colorado and Oregon. After 1926 its influence declined, and in 1939 it was discredited by the discovery of its links with the pro-Nazi German-American *Bund*. In 1944 it was disbanded when the Government attempted to collect unpaid taxes of $685,000 owed by Ku Klux Klan business enterprises. Thereafter the Ku Klux Klan was revived in Atlanta (Georgia) by Dr Samuel Green.

The New York Times estimated on April 20, 1965, that there were then about 10,000 active members of about a dozen district Klan organizations and several thousand in allied or front groups, among them the National States' Rights Party in Birmingham (Alabama). It listed the Klan's main organizations as follows:

(i) The United Klans of America Inc., Knights of the Ku Klux Klan of Tuscaloosa (Alabama)—with an estimated 5,000 members and led by its "imperial wizard", who had stated that his organization worked closely with the John Birch Society (see separate entry) and similar groups; three members of this organization were charged with the murder of Mrs Viola Liuzzo, a civil rights worker, on March 25, 1965, and were sentenced to 10 years' imprisonment on Dec. 3 of that year.

(ii) The Original Knights of the Ku Klux Klan in Louisiana—with about 1,000 members.

(iii) The White Knights of the Ku Klux Klan—with about 2,000 members in Mississippi; this group broke away from the Original Knights in February 1964 and was regarded as the most secretive and violent of the Ku Klux Klan organizations.

(iv) The Knights of the Ku Klux Klan of the North Florida Klan at Jacksonville—with about 1,000 members; this group was said to have organized riots at St Augustine (Florida) in 1964.

(v) The Association of South Carolina Klans—with about 500 members.

Smaller Ku Klux Klan groups were said to exist in Georgia, Tennessee and Arkansas.

A sub-committee of the House of Representatives committee on un-American activities found, after a public investigation into the Ku Klux Klan conducted between Oct. 19, 1965, and Feb. 24, 1966, that, as its members had intimidated and done physical violence "to young and old, male and female", its activities should be curbed.

During the 1964-66 civil rights campaign numerous Ku Klux Klan members were involved in acts of violence (including arson and murder) directed against Blacks and White civil-rights workers. The first time an all-White Mississippi jury convicted Ku Klux Klan members of murdering civil rights workers was on Oct. 20, 1967, but the prison sentences imposed on the four defendants ranged only from three to seven years.

Although numerically declining, the Ku Klux Klan has remained active in recent years, mainly in the southern states. Members of the Klan were involved in an attempted invasion of the island of Dominica in early 1981 (purely for gain), and in this connexion Stephen Donald Black (national "grand wizard" of the Klan) and one of his lieutenants were sentenced to three years in prison in New Orleans on July 23, 1981, for plotting to overthrow the Government of Dominica.

An attempted Ku Klux Klan march in Washington (D.C.) on Nov. 27, 1982, was abandoned after violent demonstrations by members of civil rights groups, the (extreme left-wing) Progressive Labor Party, pro-Palestinian groups and other minorities (including Irish Roman Catholics). The leader of the Knights of the Ku Klux Klan of Tuscumbia (Alabama) said that the march was aimed at defeating an immigration bill before Congress which would grant an amnesty to millions of aliens who had arrived before 1977; he added: "The Lord will re-establish the foundation of this nation upon White Christianity and Western civilization."

Minutemen

Leadership. Robert Bolivar DePugh (l.)

Established in 1959, this organization in 1966 stated its aims as being "to resist and expose the spread of communist influence and propaganda; to investigate by means of our own secret memberships the possible infiltration of communist sympathizers into American organizations . . . ; to detect and expose waste, corruption or disloyalty in any American enterprise or activity that might subvert the defence effort . . . ; [and] to resist by all legal means the passage of laws which regulate the private ownership of firearms . . .". The movement was organized in secret groups of from five to 15 members and claimed in 1961 to have about 25,000 members in 40 states.

A district attorney in New York disclosed on Oct. 30, 1966, that police had arrested 20 members of the Minutemen organization, had broken up a right-wing conspiracy to "devastate" three privately-owned camps and had seized arsenals ranging from mortars and machine-guns to home-made bombs and including over 1,000,000 rounds of ammunition; police also stated that Minutemen had tried to infiltrate a reserve army unit in order to learn guerrilla warfare and had distributed racist literature purporting to be from Negro extremists. On Jan. 17, 1967, Robert Bolivar DePugh and two other members were sentenced to imprisonment for up to three years for violating the Federal Firearms Act.

National Socialist German Workers' Party—Foreign Branch (NSDAP-AO)

The existence of this neo-Nazi organization in the United States was referred to by the Bavarian Ministry of the Interior in connexion with the case of Helmut Oxner, an alleged member of the organization, who killed three foreigners and injured two other persons in Nuremberg on June 24, 1982, and who committed suicide before police could arrest him. He had earlier been charged with offensive and threatening behaviour.

National Socialist (Nazi) Party of America

This small party has taken over from the National Socialist German Workers' Party (the NSDAP created and led by Adolf Hitler) not only its insignia (such as the swastika) but also its racialist and nationalist tenets and its hierarchical structure. In 1981 six members of the party were tried for plotting terrorist bombing attacks at Greensboro (North Carolina) between July and November 1980.

In April 1981 two members of the party were said to be involved in an attempt to invade the island of Dominica.

"Black Power" Movement

The slogan "We want Black power" was first used by Stokeley Carmichael, then (the extreme left-wing) chairman of the Student Non-violent Co-ordinating Committee (SNCC), during a march led by Dr Martin Luther King and other civil rights leaders in June 1966 to encourage Negroes to register as voters. Dr King rejected the idea of Black supremacy as "equally as evil as White supremacy", and Carmichael said on June 25 that there was no implied intention of using Black power to lead to Black supremacy.

The Black power principle was endorsed on July 4, 1966, by the Congress of Racial Equality (CORE), whose director, Floyd McKissick, said: "The only way to achieve meaningful change is to take power." On Aug. 21 of that year he listed six "basic ingredients" of Black power—"political power, economic power, an improved self-image of the Black man himself, the development of young militant leadership, the enforcement of federal law (with the abolition of police brutality) and the development of the Black consumer bloc".

The use of violence in pursuance of civil rights for Negroes was condemned by most of the major civil rights movements, notably the National Association for the Advancement of Coloured People (NAACP, established in 1909 and led by Roy Wilkins) and the Southern Christian Leadership Conference (SCLC, founded in 1957 and led by Dr Martin Luther King until his assassination on April 4, 1968, and thereafter by the Rev. Ralph Abernathy).

The principal organizations which have adopted the "Black power" concept or given it a measure of support are listed below.

Black Liberation Army (BLA)

This group, which was believed to have broken away from the Black Panther Party (see separate entry) in 1971, was involved mainly in the killing of policemen. Joanne Chesimard, a reputed BLA leader, was sentenced to life imprisonment for the murder of a New Jersey state trooper in 1973 but escaped from prison on Nov. 2, 1979. Marilyn Buch, who had been in prison on arms possession charges in 1974-77 and who was described as the only White member of the BLA, was one of eight persons charged with involvement in the robbery organized by the Weather Underground (see separate entry) on Oct. 20, 1981, although she had not been captured.

Black Panther Party

Leadership. Elaine Brown (ch. in 1977).

This party, the most influential of the Black power movements, was formed in Oakland, California, in October 1966 by Huey P. Newton and Bobby Seale, who formed armed patrols to protect Negroes against alleged police brutality and who adopted as their symbol the panther (as the animal which, although it does not normally attack first, fights to the death if attacked). The party also organized social service schemes for Negroes and led several successful rent strikes in Harlem (New York).

Eldridge Cleaver, then its leading writer, defined its programme as including full employment or a guaranteed income for the unemployed, housing fit for human beings, exemption of Negroes from military service, education to teach young Blacks their rightful place in society, an end to exploitation by White racist businessmen and "to police brutality and murder of Black people", and the release of all imprisoned Negroes and their retrial by all-Negro juries. The party also proposed the holding of a plebiscite of all US Negroes, under UN supervision, on the question of the establishment of a separate Negro state.

Many leading Black Panther members were imprisoned or shot by the police, or went into exile, from 1968 onwards. The party alleged at the end of 1969 that 28 Black Panthers had been killed by police (who gave the total as only 10), among them Fred Hampton, Illinois deputy chairman of the party, whose death on Dec. 4, 1969, greatly inflamed racial tension in Chicago where Blacks warned Whites not to enter the Negro quarters at night because it would be unsafe for them to do so. (Hampton was killed, with another Black Panther Party member, in a police raid leading to a law suit by survivors and relatives of those killed, which ended in a tentative settlement in October 1982.)

Eldridge Cleaver fled the USA and settled in Algeria in 1968. Bobby Seale, then chairman of the party, was on Nov. 5, 1969, sentenced to four years in prison for contempt of court for his behaviour in court during his trial, with seven others, on conspiracy charges which had arisen out of riots during a Democratic Party convention in Chicago on Aug. 26-28, 1968. The conspiracy charges against him were, however, dismissed on Oct. 19, 1970.

In February 1971 the Black Panther Party was split when Cleaver established an "international section" of the party, with headquarters in Algiers, after he had "expelled" Newton, who had himself earlier "expelled" Cleaver for "counter-revolutionary activities"; the latter had demanded the expulsion from the Black Panthers of David Hilliard, who had assumed the leadership of the party during the imprisonment of Seale and who had expelled two party members who had fled to Algeria in February 1971 while on trial for conspiracy. However, it was announced on Jan. 18, 1972, that Cleaver had resigned as head of the party's "international section" to take up "a new function in the Afro-American Liberation Army".

Newton declared on May 24, 1971, that the Black Panthers would abandon the use of violence and would work within the system to change it, and claimed that only two party branches out of 40 supported Cleaver. After spending three years as a fugitive, Newton arrived (from Cuba) in Canada on June 25, 1977, where he was arrested as an undesirable alien. Two days later he declared that he intended to resume the leadership of the Black Panther Party and to expand its social programme throughout the United States. He returned to the latter country on July 4, 1977, whereafter he proclaimed the party's aim as being "full employment first and socialism based on the American experience at some distant time". On Nov. 5, 1978, he was sentenced to two years' imprisonment on a weapons possession charge. Other trials (of assault and murder) ended in acquittals.

Other Black Panther Party members, however, continued to be involved in violent action. Nathaniel Burns, a former leader of the party, was one of eight persons arrested in connexion with an attack on a security guard organized by the Weather Underground (see separate entry) on Oct. 20, 1981. Three days later two members of the party were involved in a shoot-out with police in Queens (New York), where one of them was killed and the other was arrested.

Meanwhile, Eldridge Cleaver had announced on April 5, 1981 (after returning to the United States and being given a community service sentence for assaulting a police officer in 1968), that he had decided to join the Mormon Church.

Congress of Racial Equality (CORE)

Leadership. Wilfred Ussery (nat. ch.); Floyd McKissick (nat. director).

This movement, founded at Chicago University in 1952 by James Farmer, was prominent in 1960-61 when it supported "sit-in" demonstrations and "freedom rides". In the controversy over the concept of Black power the CORE fully endorsed the demands associated with the movement but without advocating violence. Amending its constitution on July 4, 1967, the CORE defined itself as "a mass membership organization for implementing Black power for Black people" (but it refused to exclude Whites from membership and re-elected its White national chairman). Floyd McKissick considered the

CORE as being "an effective revolutionary movement, the common front for all Black people to unite in". The CORE then claimed a membership of 100,000.

Students' Non-violent Co-ordinating Committee (SNCC)

Leadership. James Forman.

Originally the SNCC, founded in 1960 as a bi-racial student organization, advocated the attainment of racial integration through non-violent means; any of its members possessing a gun was liable to be expelled. However, after the election of Stokeley Carmichael as its chairman in 1966 the SNCC repudiated non-violence, replaced integration by "Black power" as its aim, adopted a black panther as its emblem and advocated "guerrilla warfare in the streets".

In May 1967 Carmichael was replaced as SNCC chairman by Hubert ("Rap") Brown, and during a foreign tour in that year he repeatedly defined his position as a revolutionary. In London he said on July 18 that rebellion was the most effective way of obtaining justice; and in Hanoi (North Vietnam) he said: "We are not reformists; . . . we do not want to be part of the Government of the United States or the American system, we are revolutionaries." In Algiers he said on Sept. 8: "The object of our struggle is the destruction of the imperialist structure of the United States, which has made slaves of us . . . We want to see the Vietnamese win the war, defeat the United States and drive it out of the country."

Brown said in New York on Aug. 6, 1967, that recent riots were "just dress rehearsals for revolution", and on Aug. 27 he called on Negroes in Detroit to arm themselves and make the recent riots in that city "look like a picnic". However, in 1968 the SNCC broke off all relations with Stokeley Carmichael, and Brown, himself disappeared on March 8, 1970, after failing to appear for trial on a charge of inciting a riot in 1967.

Black Separatist Movements

Black Muslim Movement

This sect, formally known as the Nation of Islam, was founded in Detroit by W. D. Fard, who claimed to have come from Mecca but who eventually disappeared. He was succeeded as leader of the sect by Elijah Poole (or Elijah Muhammad), who advocated complete separation for Negroes in a closed economic society to be established in two or three states of the USA. According to *The New York Times* the sect believed that the origin of the US Negroes was in Asia rather than in Africa; that the "Black nation" con-

sisted of all non-Whites; that the White man was "grafted" from the Black and was physically and mentally inferior; and that the day would come when the White man and Christianity ("associated only with Whites") would be destroyed.

A notable member of the sect was Malcolm Little (generally known as Malcolm X)—who, however, resigned from the Movement on March 8, 1964, to form the Organization for African Unity (see separate entry). Another member of the Black Muslims is the former heavy-weight boxing champion Cassius Clay, who took the religious name of Muhammad Ali.

While the Black Muslims had had the reputation of being the most violent of the UN Negro movements, the organization became increasingly conservative after 1964 and took no further part in the civil rights movement but engaged in developing its business interests, selling the produce of its large farms to Negro ghettos in the cities. It established mosques in 42 cities and its membership was estimated at several hundred thousands. Dissident young members of the Movement, who opposed these developments, were responsible for a clash with police on Jan. 10, 1972, leading to the death of two policemen and two Negroes.

Organization for African Unity

This Organization was formed in 1964 by Malcolm Little (Malcolm X)—a former member of the Black Muslim Movement (see separate entry)—and dissidents from other movements. In April 1964 he made a number of speeches advocating the use of violence by Negroes; in May of that year he visited several African countries and in July he attended the Cairo Assembly of Heads of State and Government of the Organization of African Unity. His appeals were followed by outbreaks of racial violence in Harlem (New York) and in the southern states.

Malcolm X was shot dead on Feb. 21, 1965, by three men, two of whom were later identified as members of the Black Muslim sect; all three were sentenced to life imprisonment on April 15, 1966.

Republic of New Africa

This separatist Black organization was founded in March 1968 by Milton Henty at a conference in Detroit, where it was proposed that an independent Afro-American homeland should be established in Alabama, Georgia, Louisiana, Mississippi and South Carolina "through negotiation with the United States, through political activity and secession, or through a combination of these moves supported by appropriate military action".

A national conference on Black power held

in Philadelphia on Aug. 29-Sept. 1, 1968, and attended by over 3,000 delegates endorsed these aims. The movement elected as "president" of the "provisional Government of the Republic of New Africa" Robert Williams, the leader of the Revolutionary Action Movement (see separate entry), then absent overseas. However, after returning to the United States in 1969 Williams resigned this post, stating that he did not believe in separation of races and that he intended to seek support from all groups for the civil rights struggle.

When eight persons were sought for involvement in the armed robbery organized by the Weather Underground on Oct. 20, 1981, those arrested included Cynthia Boston, described as "Minister of Information" of the Republic of New Africa.

Extreme Left-wing Movements

Black Liberation Front

This group was formed in August 1964 by a group of Negroes who had visited Cuba, among them Robert Steele Collier (self-styled leader of the group), who was, with three other persons, arrested (as announced in New York on Feb. 16, 1965) on charges of plotting to dynamite three major historic monuments. Of the four persons arrested, three Negroes were on June 17, 1965, sentenced in New York to 10 years' conditional imprisonment on the evidence of a Black policeman who had infiltrated the Black Liberation Front. The fourth person was a Canadian woman who was given a five-year conditional sentence and was a member of a Quebec separatist *Rassemblement pour l'Indépendance Nationale,* of which another member was, in Montreal on May 11, 1965, found guilty of stealing dynamite and supplying it for the above-mentioned plot.

Land and Freedom *(Tierra y Liberdad)*

This revolutionary movement of Mexican-Americans (Chicanos) has as its aims the mobilization of Chicanos, as part of a Third World Liberation Front with other revolutionary minorities in the United States. It seeks to gain control, by electoral means, of regions where Chicanos are in a majority; to recover land of which they have been expropriated; to boycott "Anglo-American" businesses; and to form Chicano political parties and armed groups to organize countervialence and to carry out "revolutionary justice" on "collaborationists, accommodationists and agents" who played a "neo-colonialist" role.

May 19th Communist Organization

This Marxist-Leninist group, established in 1978, was originally the East Coast faction of the Prairie Fire Organizing Committee, a successor to the Weather Underground (see separate entry). It took its name from the joint birthday of Malcolm X (see under Black Muslim Movement) and Ho Chi Minh (the Vietnamese Communist leader) and had an all-White membership, including some radical feminists. It was, however, said to have received strategic leadership from the revolutionary "Black power" movement.

Revolutionary Action Movement

This Maoist Negro organization was founded by Robert Williams, who fled the country in 1966 and was in 1967 believed to be in China. Members of this Movement were among several Negroes arrested in New York on June 21, 1967, on suspicion of conspiracy to murder moderate civil rights movement leaders and to seize power by force, as arms and explosives had been seized at their homes. (For later activities of Robert Williams see separate entry for Republic of New Africa.)

Revolutionary Fighting Group

This, until then unknown, group claimed responsibility for a bomb explosion on Staten Island, New York, on Jan. 29, 1982, when extensive damage was caused to a building housing an office of the Federal Bureau of Investigation (FBI).

Spartacist League

This Trotskyist group was listed by the California Attorney General as operating in California in 1979; it was said to have several hundred members and to have, in addition, a Spartacus Youth League. The group denied, however, that it advocated the use of violence, as claimed by the Attorney General.

Weather Underground

This movement, at first known as the Weathermen, was founded in June 1969 as an offshoot of the "Students for a Democratic Society" (SDS), a left-wing movement which had in 1964-65 been active in encouraging objection to conscription ("the draft") for military service and in numerous student demonstrations. Under the leadership of Mark Rudd (a student from Columbia University) the Weathermen declared that they as White radicals would violently attack American society to bring about a revolution by fighting in the streets. In order to provoke the authorities into taking repressive action (which would create the appearance that the Weathermen constituted a resistance movement fighting against "the forces of repression"), they took part in some 500 bombing and raiding actions in 1969; in one of these, at the University of Wisconsin, they demanded that the Officers' Training Corps should be disbanded and that imprisoned Black Panther Party (see separate entry) leaders should be released. In October 1969 some 200 Weathermen staged riots in Chicago during four "days of rage". The movement suffered a setback on June 6, 1970, when its store of explosives kept at Greenwich Village exploded and several of its leaders were killed. Mark Rudd went underground in the same year (but surrendered to the police in 1977, was fined and given two years' probation and later became a teacher).

The Weathermen, who subsequently changed their name to Weatherpeople and eventually to the Weather Underground, and who were organized in cells of four or five members, continued to be active between 1970 and 1975 when they were responsible for at least 20 bombings and when the Senate internal security committee identified 37 members as still being active underground. In 1974 the movement published *Prairie Fire,* a guerrilla warfare manual in which it described its members as "communist women and men underground in the United States for more than four years". In November 1978 five Weather Underground members were arrested in Houston (Texas) and were later sentenced to imprisonment for conspiracy to bomb the offices of a Californian state senator. The movement was also said to have inspired the foundation, in 1979, of the May 19th Communist Organization (see separate entry).

Following an armed robbery in New York in which a security guard and two police officers were killed, four alleged members of the movement were arrested on Oct. 20, 1981, among them two leading women members—Judith A. Clark and Katherine Boudin (the latter having lived under an assumed name after escaping from the Greenwich Village explosion in 1970).

Puerto Rico

Capital: San Juan　　　　　　　　　　　　　　　　　　　　　　　　**Pop. 3,300,000**

The Commonwealth of Puerto Rico is, under its 1952 Constitution, "a free state associated with the United States", in which executive power is vested in a Governor who is elected by universal adult suffrage of resident citizens and who presides over an Executive. There is an elected bicameral legislature consisting of a 27-member Senate and a 51-member House of Representatives.

In elections held on Nov. 4, 1980, 25 seats in the House of Representatives were gained by each of two parties—the New Progressive Party (PNP) and the Popular Democratic Party (PPD), with the vacant seat being filled later by a PPD member. Parties not represented in Parliament are three advocating complete independence for Puerto Rico—the Puerto Rican Communist Party (PCP), the Puerto Rican Independence Party (PIP) and the Puerto Rican Socialist Party (PSP).

The PNP has advocated the transformation of Puerto Rico into a state within the United States of America, although in a plebiscite held on July 23, 1967, a majority of Puerto Rico's voters (60.5 per cent of those who took part in the vote) had favoured the retention of the existing commonwealth system, whereas 38.9 per cent had voted for statehood to be given to Puerto Rico and less than 1 per cent had voted for independence (in a 68.5 per cent poll).

The Independence Issue

Political violence in Puerto Rico has come mainly from left-wing groups advocating complete independence for the island on the ground that the existing constitutional system relegates Puerto Rico, in their view, to the status of a US colony. These groups, and the pro-independence parties, have therefore made efforts to set in motion, under United Nations auspices, a "decolonization" process for Puerto Rico.

Acts of violence by pro-independence groups have not been confined to the island;

many have been carried out in the United States, which contains a considerable minority population of Puerto Rican origin. According to the Federal Bureau of Investigation (FBI) there were in 1982 a total of 51 recorded acts of terrorism (against 42 in 1981 and 29 in 1980), of which 25 were ascribed to Puerto Rican independence organizations, 10 of these acts to the Armed Forces of National Liberation (FALN), resulting in three deaths and 19 injuries.

Armed Forces of National Liberation (*Fuerzas Armadas de Liberación Nacional Puertorriqueña,* FALN)

Leadership. Carlos Alberto Torres (1.).

This organization has been involved in acts of violence in various parts of the United States since 1972. By early 1979 it had claimed responsibility for over 100 bombing incidents. On July 3, 1978, two Puerto Rican nationalists attacked and occupied the Chilean consulate in San Juan in support of their demand for the release of Puerto Rican nationalists sentenced in the 1950s (see separate entry for Puerto Rican Nationalist Party), but they surrendered on July 4 without their demand being met.

On April 11, 1979, a FALN member was sentenced to 10 years in prison in New York for unlawful possession of bombs and weapons. In 1980 FALN members attacked both Democratic and Republican party offices during the presidential election campaign. On Aug. 4, 1980, two FALN members were sentenced in Chicago to 30 years in prison, each on conspiracy and illegal possession of arms charges. Early in March 1981 the FALN was reported to have issued bomb threats against army recruiting stations. The FALN also claimed responsibility for four bomb explosions in New York's Wall Street area on Feb. 28, 1982.

Five alleged FALN members arrested by the police refused to give evidence before a New York Federal Grand Jury on Sept. 28, 1982, on the grounds that they did not wish "to collaborate with a tool of coercion aimed at all advocates of Puerto Rican independence". Four further explosions in New York on Dec. 31, 1982, in which three policemen were injured, were also caused by the FALN, according to a telephone caller later identified as Luis Rosado.

The FALN has links with the Puerto Rican Socialist Party (supported by Cuba) and a Puerto Rican Solidarity Committee.

Armed Liberation Commandos (*Comandos Armados de Liberación,* CAL)

This pro-independence guerrilla group was reported to have been active in August 1981.

Armed Pro-Independence Movement (*Movimiento Independentista Armado,* MIRA)

This guerrilla group was also reported as having been active in August 1981.

Full Group of Reflection on Puerto Rico

Leadership. Sarah Sosa (1.).

This Roman Catholic organization, based in San Juan, was in August 1981 reported to have called for the ending of Puerto Rico's status as a "US colony" and for "full transfer of power to the people".

Organization of Volunteers for the Puerto Rican Revolution (*Organización de Voluntarios para la Revolución Puertorriqueña,* OVRP)

This small group was responsible for isolated acts of violence in 1979-80, including an attack on communications installations on July 14, 1980 (causing $800,000 worth of damage).

Puerto Rican Armed Resistance Movement (*Movimiento de Resistencia Armada Puertorriqueña,* MRAP)

This group, an offshoot of the Armed Forces of the National Liberation (FALN—see separate entry), has claimed responsibility for numerous bomb attacks in recent years. including several on the Panam terminal at Kennedy Airport, New York, on May 16-17, 1981, in which a young airport employee was killed. In a communiqué the group threatened to commit further acts of violence against Argentine, Guatemalan, Honduran and US offices.

Puerto Rican Nationalist Party (*Partido Nacionalista Puertorriqueño*)

A Puerto Rican Nationalist Party, founded in 1928 by Dr Pedro Albizu Campos, had called for complete independence for Puerto Rico but received practically no support in elections held in 1932 and thereafter did not take part in further elections. Its founder and other party members were convicted of conspiring to overthrow the US Government in Puerto Rico and served prison sentences in 1937-43, whereafter they spent several years in New York on parole before returning to Puerto Rico in 1948. In an insurrection fomented by the party and carried out on Oct. 30, 1950, a total of 27 people were killed and 51 injured, while hundreds were arrested, among them Dr Campos, who was subsequently sentenced to long terms of imprisonment. Among other party members sentenced 21, found guilty of murdering a policeman, were given life sentences on May 21, 1951.

For an attempt on the life of President Harry S. Truman on Nov. 1, 1950, when a

White House guard was killed, a member of the party was sentenced to death on April 1, 1951 (but the President subsequently commuted this sentence to life imprisonment).

On March 1, 1954, three members of the party shot and wounded five members of the House of Representatives in Washington; the three Puerto Rican nationalists were on July 8, 1954, given prison sentences of up to 75 years. Numerous other party members were arrested in March and May of that year (in New York, Chicago and Puerto Rico), and 13 of these were on Oct. 26, 1954, sentenced to six years in prison each for seditious conspiracy to overthrow the Government.

The four Puerto Rican nationalists sentenced respectively on April 1, 1951 and July 8, 1954, were granted clemency by President Carter on Sept. 6, 1979, and were released. They nevertheless said on Sept. 11 that they hoped to continue the struggle for Puerto Rican independence.

Puerto Rican Popular Army (*Ejército Popular Boricua,* EPB, or *Los Macheteros*)

This clandestine group first claimed responsibility for attacks on 10 aircraft of the US Air Force in January 1981. An explosion, followed by a fire and a second blast at an electric power station at San Juan on Nov. 27, 1981, was also, according to an accompanying telephone call, the work of the *Macheteros* group.

9. AUSTRALASIA AND THE PACIFIC

Australia

Capital: Canberra (ACT)   Pop. 15,000,000

The Commonwealth of Australia (a member of the Commonwealth) is a parliamentary democracy with the British monarch as head of state represented by a Governor-General. It comprises six states as well as the Australian Capital Territory (ACT) and the Northern Territory. Legislative power is vested in a (federal) Parliament consisting of the British monarch, a 64-member Senate whose members serve six-year terms and a 125-member House of Representatives elected for three years by universal adult suffrage. There is a Cabinet headed by a Prime Minister, responsible to Parliament. Five of the constituent states have their own bicameral legislatures, while Queensland and the Northern Territory each have a Legislative Assembly.

As a result of elections held on March 5, 1983, seats in the federal House of Representatives were distributed as follows: Australian Labor Party 75, Liberal Party 33, National Party 17. Among Australia's other political parties, the Australian Democratic Party holds five seats in the Senate. Federally-unrepresented parties include the Australia Party, the Australian Democratic Labor Party, the Communist Party of Australia, the Communist Party of Australia (Marxist-Leninist), the Socialist Party of Australia and the North Queensland Party.

Political violence in Australia has been largely confined to acts by foreigners, in particular by Croatian and Armenian nationalists, in pursuit of their specific political objectives; there are also some political organizations of the extreme right.

Extreme Right-wing Groups

Australian League of Rights

This group has tried to infiltrate so-called "opinion-moulders" into various Australian institutions, including the Liberal Party.

Australian National Front

This Front has been described as a Nazi organization and is a counter-part to the National Front in Great Britain.

Fiji

Capital: Suva   Pop. 660,000

Fiji is an independent state within the Commonwealth, with the British monarch as head of state being represented by a Governor-General. It has a bicameral Parliament consisting of a 22-member Senate and a 52-member House of Representatives. While the senators are appointed for a six-year term, the House of Representatives is elected for five years by universal adult suffrage under a complex system embracing 12 Fijian communal seats, 12 Indian communal seats, three general communal seats, 10 Fijian national seats, 10 Indian national seats and five general national seats.

In elections to the House of Representatives held on July 11-17, 1982, seats were gained as follows: Alliance 28, (the Indian) National Federation Party (NFP) 22 and (the Fijian) Western United Front (allied to the NFP) 2. There is also a Fijian Nationalist Party, which advocates "Fiji for the Fijians".

Although relations between the islands' various racial groups have at times been strained, there have been no reports of organized extra-parliamentary opposition.

Kiribati

Capital: Tarawa   Pop. 57,000

Kiribati (previously the Gilbert Islands) became an independent republic within the Commonwealth on July 12, 1979, with an executive President heading a Cabinet, and a 35-member House of Assembly elected by universal adult suffrage for a four-year term.

A dispute over the island of Banaba, whose inhabitants had in 1980 campaigned for the separation of Banaba from Kiribati or for self-government for the Banabans on Banaba, was settled in April 1982 by an agreement providing for compensation to be paid to the Banabans, with the island remaining part of Kiribati.

Nauru

Capital: Domaneab   Pop. 7,500

The Republic of Nauru, an independent state with special status within the Commonwealth, has a unicameral Parliament of 18 members elected for up to three years by universal adult suffrage and a President elected by Parliament for its duration from among its members. There is a five-member Cabinet consisting of members of Parliament.

A majority of independents in Parliament has supported President Hammer deRoburt, who was re-elected unopposed on Dec. 9, 1980. The opposition is constituted by the Nauru Party, the country's sole political formation.

New Zealand

Capital: Wellington   Pop. 3,200,000

The Dominion of New Zealand, a member of the Commonwealth, is a parliamentary democracy with the British monarch as head of state represented by a Governor-General. It has a unicameral 92-member House of Representatives elected for a three-year term by universal adult suffrage in 88 single-member constituencies and four Maori constituencies. It has a Cabinet headed by a Prime Minister and appointed by the Governor-General.

As a result of elections held on Nov. 28, 1981, seats in the House of Representatives were distributed as follows: National Party 47, Labour Party 43, Social Credit Political League 2. Other political parties in New Zealand are the (pro-Chinese) Communist Party of New Zealand, the New Democratic Party, the (pro-Soviet communist) New Zealand Socialist Unity Party and the New Zealand Values Party.

A Maori "self-government" party, the *Manu Motuhake* (founded in 1979), unsuccessfully contested the four Maori seats in the 1981 elections. There is, among the Maoris (New Zealand's aboriginal population), a protest movement (exemplified by a Waitangi Action Committee in Auckland) against the terms of the Treaty of Waitangi of 1840, under which the Maoris surrendered their lands to White immigrants.

Extreme Right-wing Groups

National Front

This Front has been said to have links with organizations of the same name in Australia and the United Kingdom.

National Socialist Party (NSP)

The NSP is regarded as a Nazi party and is said to have links with similar parties in other countries.

Papua New Guinea

Capital: Port Moresby   Pop. 3,200,000

Papua New Guinea is an independent state within the Commonwealth, with the British monarch as head of state being represented by a Governor-General who is elected by the country's House of Assembly of 99 members elected by universal adult suffrage. Executive power is held by a Cabinet headed by a Prime Minister.

As a result of elections held in June 1982, seats in the House were distributed as follows: Pangu Pati 41, National Party 14, independents (led by Ted Diro, former Defence Force commander) 11, People's Progress Party 10, Melanesian Alliance 8, United Party 6, uncommitted independents 5, Papua Besena 3, vacant (owing to death of candidate) 1.

Parties not represented in Parliament are the Papuan National Alliance (formed in 1980), the People's Christian Alliance (formed in 1981) and three groups associated, as is the Papua Besena, with the republican movement—the Eriwo Development Association, the Papua Black Power Movement and the Socialist Workers' Party.

Inter-tribal Fighting

Hostility between various tribes of Papua New Guinea has led to serious clashes from time to time. It was officially estimated that in the first six months of 1979 at least 35 persons had been killed, 207 had been wounded and over 450 buildings had been destroyed in tribal fighting in the five Highlands provinces, where a state of emergency was declared on July 23, 1979, and the premier of one of the provinces was given a one-year prison sentence in connexion with the establishment of an unofficial police force. In October 1980 the premiers of the five provinces put forward a peace plan for the area, including proposals for constitutional amendments to increase governmental controls over freedom of movement.

Nevertheless, more intense tribal fighting broke out in the Highlands in the second half of 1982 (party owing to population growth, the turning over of farm lands to cash crops such as coffee and tea, and rising unemployment). According to official statements the fighting resulted in the burning of 1,000 houses and 500 stores and the killing of 3,000 pigs, and in the death of at least 13 persons. The Government took steps to end the fighting by inducing local tribal leaders to conclude truce agreements; underlying tensions remained unresolved, however.

Solomon Islands

Capital: Honiara (Guadalcanal)   Pop. 247,000

The Solomon Islands are an independent state within the Commonwealth, with the British monarch as head of state being represented by a Governor-General. Legislative power is vested in a unicameral 38-member National Parliament elected by universal adult suffrage for up to four years. There is a Cabinet composed of a Prime Minister and 14 other ministers and responsible to Parliament.

In a general election held on Aug. 6, 1980, the majority of seats in the National Parliament was won by independents. A Cabinet was thereupon formed by a coalition of independents and the Solomon Islands United Party, but this Cabinet was in September 1981 replaced by a new one composed of independents and members of the People's Alliance Party and the National Democratic Party.

The new Government has issued a programme of action which provides inter alia for constitutional reforms to create a federated republic and (in response to demands for regional autonomy) the transfer to the provinces of responsibilities currently held by the Ministry of Home Affairs.

Tonga

Capital: Nuku'alofa (Tongatapu)   Pop. 104,000

The Kingdom of Tonga is a member of the Commonwealth and has a Cabinet headed by a Prime Minister and also a Legislative Assembly which, in addition to the Speaker and the members of the Cabinet, comprises seven representatives of the nobles and seven of the people, the latter being elected every three years by male literate and tax-paying Tongans and all female literate Tongans (all having to be adults above the age of 21 years). There are no political parties or other political groupings.

Tuvalu

Capital: Fongafale (Funafuti)   Pop. 8,000

Tuvalu (formerly part of the Gilbert and Ellice Islands colony) is an independent state with special statute within the Commonwealth and with the British monarch as head of state being represented by a Governor-General. It has a five-member Cabinet headed by a Prime Minister and a 12-member House of Assembly elected by universal adult suffrage. There are no political parties, but an "opposition group" has been formed in the House of Assembly. No other political organizations have been reported to exist.

Vanuatu

Capital: Port Vila   Pop. 112,000

The Republic of Vanuatu (formerly the British and French condominium of the New Hebrides) is an independent state within the Commonwealth. Its President is elected for a five-year term by an electoral college consisting of Parliament and the presidents of the country's regional councils. The unicameral Parliament is elected by universal adult suffrage for a four-year term. Executive power is vested in the Prime Minister (elected by Parliament from among its members) and a Council of Ministers appointed by him.

In general elections to the then Representative Assembly of 39 members, held on Nov. 14, 1979, the (mainly anglophone) *Vanuatu Pati* (VP) gained 26 seats and the New Hebrides Federal Party (formed as an alliance of mainly francophone "moderate" parties) the remaining 13. Parties not represented as such in Parliament are *Nagriamel, Nakamal,* the *Natatok Efate* Alliance and the *Tan* Union (which in 1979 formed part of the New Hebrides Federal Party).

Secessionist Movements

On May 28, 1980 (i.e. two months before Vanuatu was due to attain independence), some 800 supporters of the secessionist *Nagriamel* movement (which had for many years campaigned for the independence of the island of Santo) captured the British district commissioner and some of his officials and police, occupied the police station and cut off all communications with Port Vila. On June 1 Jimmy Stevens, the leader of *Nagriamel,* announced the formation of a six-member "Provisional Government of the independent state of Vemerana" with himself as "Prime Minister". The action was said to be supported by some French settlers and by US businessmen seeking the establishment of an independent tax-haven country. Some 1,400 people were evacuated from Santo by June 4, and the New Hebrides Government imposed a blockade on Santo. Unsuccessful attempts at secession were made on other islands, notably Aoba, Malekula (Molicollo) and Tanna, during June 1980.

On July 24, 1980, a joint Anglo-French force of 200 men established itself in Santo Town without meeting opposition. Some 150 troops from Papua New Guinea, with Australian support, replaced the Anglo-French forces on Aug. 19. The secessionists were subsequently arrested, among them Jimmy Stevens who was on Nov. 12 sentenced to

14½ years' imprisonment. Some 700 other persons were also tried, and 550 of them were convicted in connexion with secessionist activities. A list of prohibited immigrants published by the New Hebrides Government in October 1980 contained the names of 110 French nationals said to have promoted the secession of Santo.

The methods used to suppress the secession were strongly criticized in a document issued late in 1980 by the Vanuatu Council of Churches, which referred to numerous reports of police brutality in carrying out "massive arrests" and the "detention for long periods of mostly innocent people"; the document called for an immediate end to the "un-Christian tactics" of the Government and an inquiry into the assassination of an opposition deputy, Alexis Yolou. It was reported at this stage that most of the 13 opposition members of Parliament were either living in exile or in prison.

with the disturbances was in January 1981 officially given as 2,274. However, on April 9, 1981, the Government announced that it would not initiate any further prosecutions against persons involved in the rebellion, but would "forgive and forget" it. Jimmy Stevens escaped from prison on Sept. 12, 1982, but was recaptured on the following day; on Oct. 26 he was sentenced to an additional 2¼ years in prison.

Western Samoa

Capital: Apia (Upola) Pop. 159,000

Western Samoa is an independent member of the Commonwealth. Under its Constitution adopted in 1960 the head of state is elected for a five-year term by the Legislative Assembly. (However, the current head of state is holding this office for life.) Executive power is vested in a Prime Minister who must be supported by a majority in the Legislative Assembly and who appoints other ministers. Of the 47 members of the Legislative Assembly, 45 are Samoans elected by about 9,500 clan chiefs, and two are elected by universal adult suffrage on individual voters' rolls (mainly Europeans).

In elections to the Assembly held in February 1982, the Human Rights Protection Party gained 22 seats, while 22 other seats went to opposition members; however, the Supreme Court of Western Samoa, on Sept. 17, 1982, reduced the number of seats held by the ruling party to 21 (on the grounds of electoral fraud in the election of the Prime Minister). A new political group, *Vaega o le Tautua,* was founded in 1981 with the aim of promoting industrialization and private enterprise.

BIBLIOGRAPHY AND INDEXES

SELECT BIBLIOGRAPHY

General

Alexander, Yonah, et al.—*International Terrorism: National, Regional and Global Perspectives*. Praeger, New York, 1976.

Amnesty International Report 1982. Amnesty International Publications, London, 1982.

Annual of Power and Conflict 1980-81 (and previous years). Institute for the Study of Conflict, London, 1981 (and earlier).

Asprey, Robert—*War in the Shadows: The Guerrilla in History*. Macdonald, London, 1976.

Bibliography of Freedom. Centre for Policy Studies, London, 1976.

Blumberg, Herbert H.(ed.)—*Nonviolent Liberation. A Bibliography*. J. L. Noyce, Brighton, 1977.

Buchheit, Lee C.—*Secession: The Legitimacy of Self-Determination*. Yale Univ. Press, 1978.

Carlton, David, and Schaerf, Carlo—*International Terrorism and National Security*. Croom Helm, London, 1975.

Clutterbuck, Richard C.—*Guerrillas and Terrorists*. Ohio Univ. Press, 1982.

Dobson, Christopher, and Payne, Robert—*The Weapons of Terror*. Macmillan, London, 1979.

Fanon, Frantz—*Black Skin, White Masks*. Grove Press, New York, 1962.

Fanon, Frantz—*The Wretched of the Earth*. Grove Press, New York, 1965 and 1968.

Frank, Pierre—*Fourth International: The Long March of the Trotskyists*. Pluto Press, London, 1979.

Gastil, Raymond D.—*Freedom in the World: Political and Civil Liberties*. G. K. Hall, Boston, Mass., 1979.

Hayes, David—*Terrorism and Freedom Fighters*. Wayland, Hove, 1980.

Hyams, Edward—*A Dictionary of Modern Revolution*. Allen Lane, London, 1973.

Janke, Peter (ed.)—*Guerrilla and Terrorist Organizations. A World Directory and Bibliography*. Harvester Press, for Institute for the Study of Conflict, London, 1983.

Laqueur, Walter—*Guerrilla*. Weidenfeld & Nicolson, London, 1977.

Laqueur, Walter (ed.)—*Guerrilla Reader*. Wildwood House, London, 1978.

Laqueur, Walter—*Terrorism*. Abacus Books, London, 1978; Weidenfeld & Nicolson, London, 1979.

Laqueur, Walter (ed.)—*Terrorism Reader*. Wildwood House, London, 1979.

Livingston, Marius H. (ed.)—*International Terrorism in the Contemporary World*. Greenwood Press, London, 1978.

Niezing, Johan (ed.)—*Urban Guerrilla*. Rotterdam Univ. Press, 1974.

Pomeroy, William J. (ed.)—*Guerrilla Warfare and Marxism*. Lawrence & Wishart, London, 1969.

Taber, Robert—*"War of the Flea": Study of Guerrilla Warfare Theory and Practice*. Paladin, London, 1970.

Walter, Eugene Victor—*Terror and Resistance: Study of Political Violence*. Oxford Univ. Press, New York, 1969; Galaxy Books, New York, 1972.

Woddis, Jack—*New Theories of Revolution: A Commentary on the Views of Frantz Fanon, Régis Debray and Herbert Marcuse*. International Publishers, New York, 1972.

Eastern Europe and the USSR

Bahro, Rudolf—*Alternative in Eastern Europe*. New Left Books, London, 1978 and 1981.

Bloch, Sidney, and Reddaway, Peter—*Russia's Political Hospitals*. Gollancz, London, 1977.

Bukovsky, Vladimir—*To Build a Castle: My Life as a Dissenter*. Deutsch, London, 1978.

Djilas, Milovan—*The New Class*. Holt, Rinehart & Winston, New York, 1974.

Djilas, Milovan—*The Unperfect Society. Beyond the New Class*. Allen & Unwin, London, 1972.

Grigorenko, Petro G.—*Memoirs*. Harvill Press, London, 1983.

Labedz, Leopold (ed.)—*Solzhenitsyn—a Documentary Record*. Allen Lane. London, 1970; Penguin, Harmondsworth, 1972.

Kopelev, Lev—*No Jail for Thought*. Secker & Warburg, London, 1975.

Medvedev, Roy A.—*Let History Judge*. Knopf, New York, 1971; Macmillan, London, 1972.

Medvedev, Roy A., et al.—*Détente and Socialist Democracy*. Spokesman Books, Nottingham, 1978.

Medvedev, Roy A.—*On Stalin and Stalinism*. Oxford Univ. Press, 1979.

Medvedev, Roy A.—*Political Essays*. Spokesman Books, Nottingham, 1976-78.

Medvedev, Roy A.—*Samizdat Register: Voices of the Socialist Opposition in the Soviet Union* (2 vols.). Merlin Press, London, 1977-78.

Medvedev, Zhores A.—*The Medvedev Papers*. Macmillan, London, 1971.

Medvedev, Zhores A.—*The Rise and Fall of D. T. Lysenko*. Columbia Univ. Press, New York, 1969.

Medvedev, Zhores A. and Roy A.—*A Question of Madness*. Macmillan, London, 1971.

Mihajlov, Mihajlo—*Underground Notes*. Routledge, London, 1977.

Sakharov, Andrei D.—*My Country and the World*. Collins and Harvill Press, London, 1975.

Sakharov, Andrei D. (ed. Salisbury, Harrison E.)—*Sakharov Speaks*. Harvill Press, London, 1974.

Solzhenitsyn, Alexander (ed. Klimoff, Alexis)—*Alexander Solzhenitsyn Speaks to the West*. Bodley Head, London, 1978.

Solzhenitsyn, Alexander—*Cancer Ward*. Bodley Head, London, 1970.

Solzhenitsyn, Alexander—*Détente: Prospects for Democracy and Dictatorship*. Transaction Books, USA, 1980.

Solzhenitsyn, Alexander—*Gulag Archipelago* (3 vols.). Harvill Press and Fontana, London, 1974-78.

Solzhenitsyn, Alexander—*Mortal Danger*. Bodley Head, London, 1980.

Solzhenitsyn, Alexander—*Nobel Prize Lecture*. Stenvalley Press, 1973.

Solzhenitsyn, Alexander—*One Day in the Life of Ivan Denisovich*. Bodley Head, London, 1971; Panther, 1978.

Solzhenitsyn, Alexander—*Warning to the Western World*. BBC and Bodley Head, London, 1976.

Solzhenitsyn, Alexander, et al.—*From Under the Rubble*. Harvill Press, London, 1975.

Voinovich, Vladimir—*The Ivankiad*. Cape, London, 1978; Penguin, Harmonds-worth, 1980.

Asia and the Far East

Bahadur, Kalim—*The Jama'at i'Islami of Pakistan; Political Thought and Political Action*. South Asia Books, Columbia, Mo., USA, 1977.

Banerjee, Sumanta—*In the Wake of Naxalbari. A History of the Naxalite Movement in India*. Verry, Lawrence Inc., USA, 1980.

Bhutto, Z.—*My Execution*. South Asia Books, Columbia, Mo., USA, 1980.

Chaliand, Gerard—*Report from Afghanistan*. Viking Press, New York, 1982.

Goyal, Des Raj—*Rashtriya Swayamsevak Sangh*. South Asia Books, Columbia, Mo., USA, 1979.

Kerkvliet, Benedict J.—*The Huk Rebellion. A Study of Peasant Revolt in the Philippines*. Univ. of California Press, 1977.

Newell, Nancy P. and Richard S.—*The Struggle for Afghanistan*. Cornell Univ. Press, 1981.

Rosenberg, David A. (ed.)—*Marcos and Martial Law in the Philippines*. Cornell Univ. Press, 1979.

Sayeed, Khalid B.—*Politics in Pakistan: The Nature and Direction of Change*. Praeger, New York, 1980.

Shakir, Moin—*Politics of Minorities*. South Asia Books, Columbia, Mo., USA, 1980.

Singh, Mohinder—*The Akali Movement*. South Asia Books, Columbia, Mo., USA, 1978.

Sturtevant, David R.—*Popular Uprisings in the Philippines*. Cornell Univ. Press, 1976.

The Middle East and Arab World

Dobson, Christopher—*Black September*. R. Hale, London, 1975.

Dobson, Christopher, and Payne, Ronald—*The Carlos Complex: a Pattern of Violence*. Hodder & Stoughton, London, 1977.

El-Rayyes, Riad, and Nahas, Dunia—*Guerrillas for Palestine*. Croom Helm, London, 1976.

Hirst, David—*The Gun and the Olive Branch*. Faber, London, 1977.

O'Ballance, Edgar—*Arab Guerrilla Power, 1967-72*. Faber, London, 1974.

Smith, Colin—*Carlos: Portrait of a Terrorist*. Deutsch, London, 1976.

Africa

Fanon, Frantz—*Toward the African Revolution: Political Essays*. Monthly Review Press, New York, 1967.

Friedland, Elaine Alice—*A Comparative Study of the Development of Revolutionary Nationalist Movements in Southern Africa—FRELIMO (Mozambique) and the African National Congress of South Africa*. Diss., City University of New York, 1980.

Gann, Lewis H., and Duigan, Peter—*South Africa: War, Revolution or Peace*. Hoover Institution Press, Stanford, Calif., 1978.

Geiss, Immanuel—*The Pan-African Movement*. Methuen, London, 1974.

Halliday, Fred, and Molyneux, Maxine—*The Ethiopian Revolution*. New Left Books, London, 1982.

Munslow, Barry—*Mozambique, the Revolution and its Origins*. Longman, London, 1983.

Ottaway, Marina and David—*Ethiopia: Empire in Revolution*. Holmes & Meier, New York, 1978.

Roux, Edward—*Time Longer than Rope: a History of the Black Man's Struggle for Freedom in South Africa*. Univ. of Wisconsin Press, Madison, 1964.

Smaldone, Joseph P.—*African Liberation Movements: an Interim Bibliography*. African Studies Association, Waltham, Mass., 1974.

Latin America

Debray, Régis—*Revolution in the Revolution?* Monthly Review Press, London and New York, 1967.

Dahlin, Therrin C., et al.—*The Catholic Left in Latin America. A Comprehensive Bibliography*. G. K. Hall, Boston, Mass., 1981.

Duff, Ernest A., and McCamant, John F.—*Violence and Repression in Latin America. A Quantitative and Historial Analysis*. Free Press, New York, 1976.

Gheerbrant, Alain—*L'Eglise rebelle d'Amérique Latine*. Seuil, Paris, 1969.

Gott, Richard—*Guerrilla Movements in Latin America*. Nelson, London, 1970.

Gott, Richard—*Rural Guerrillas in Latin America*. Penguin, Harmondsworth, 1973.

Guevara, Ernesto Che—*Guerrilla Warfare*. Monthly Review Press, New York, 1967.

Halperin, Ernst—*Terrorism in Latin America*. Sage Publications, London, 1976.

Hansen, Joseph—*The Leninist Strategy of Party Building: The Debate on Guerrilla Warfare in Latin America*. Path Press, New York, 1979.

James, Daniel—*The Complete Bolivian Diaries of Che Guevara and Other Captured Documents*. Stein & Day, New York, 1968.

Marighella, Carlos—*For the Liberation of Brazil*. Penguin, Harmondsworth, 1972.

Rossi, Ernest E., and Plano, Jack C.—*The Latin American Political Dictionary*. ABC Clio, Oxford, 1980.

Torres, Camilo (ed. John Gerassi)—*Revolutionary Priest*. Cape, London, 1971; Random House, New York, 1971.

Western Europe

Arthur, Paul—*Government and Politics of Northern Ireland*. Longman, Harlow, 1980.

Becker, Jillian—*Hitler's Children*. Michael Joseph, London, 1977; Panther Books, London, 1978.

Carr, Gordon—*The Angry Brigade*. Gollancz, London, 1975.

Clutterbuck, Richard L.—*Britain in Agony: Growth of Political Violence*. Faber, London, 1978; Penguin, Harmondsworth, 1980.

Coogan, Tim Pat—*The I.R.A.* Pall Mall Press, London, 1970; Fontana Books, London, 1980;

McCormick, Paul—*Enemies of Democracy*. M. T. Smith, London, 1979.

Shipley, Peter—*Revolutionaries in Modern Britain*. Bodley Head, London, 1976.

Tomlinson, John—*Left, Right—The March of Political Extremism in Britain*. Calder, London, and Riverrun, New York, 1981.

North America

Bayes, Jane H.—*Minority Politics and Ideologies in the United States*. Chandler & Sharp, Novato, Calif., 1982.

Goldstein, Robert J.—*Political Repression in Modern America. From Eighteen-Seventy to the Present*. Schenkman, Cambridge, Mass., 1981.

Lader, Lawrence—*Power on the Left: American Radical Movements since 1946*. Norton, New York, 1979.

Linedecker, Clifford L.—*The Swastika and the Eagle: Neo-Nazism in America Today*. A. & W. Pubs., New York, 1983.

Lipset, Seymour, and Raab, Earl—*The Politics of Unreason: Right-Wing Extremism in America.* Univ. of Chicago Press, 1978.

Viguerie, Richard A.—*The New Right: We're Ready to Lead.* Caroline House, Aurora, Ill., 1981.

SUBJECT INDEX

Page numbers for countries and for main entries are printed in **bold** figures. *Italics* have been used for the vernacular names of organizations and for publications.

A

A Luta Continua (Mozambique), 291
ABD-Declaration 78 (Bulgaria), 3
Abim (Malaysia), 121
Abode of Islam—*see Dar-ul-Islam*
Abu Nidal Group (Palestine), **211**, 213
Action Autonomy (France), 412
Action Directe (Belgium)—*see* Direct Action
Action for German Unity (Germany, F.R. of), 428
Action Front for the Liberation of the Baltic Countries, 58
Action Front of National Socialists (Germany, F.R. of), 427
Action Group for the Defence of Civil Rights in the USSR, 35
Action Youth Group (France), 408
Adler und Kreuz (United Kingdom), 495
Adolf Hitler Commando Group—*see* SS Wotan 71
Afar Liberation Front (Ethiopia), 247
Afghan Islamic and Nationalist Revolutionary Council—*see* National Islamic Front of Afghanistan
Afghan National Liberation Front, 71, **72**, 73, 74
Afghanistan, **70-74**, 135
Africa Livre (Mozambique), 290
African Communist (London), 310
African National Congress (South Africa) 299, **300-305**, 306, 308, 309, 310, 311
African National Congress of South Africa (African Nationalists), 305
African National Congress Youth League (ANCYL, South Africa), 308
African Party for the Independence of Cape Verde (PAICV), 237
African Party for the Independence of Guinea-Bissau and Cape Verde, 237, 255
African People's Democratic Union of South Africa (Apdusa), **305**, 307
African Resistance Movement (South Africa), 305-306
Afrikaanse Weerstandsbeweging (South Africa), 312
Afrikaner Resistance Movement—*see Afrikaanse Weerstandsbeweging*
Afro-American Liberation Army, 513
Afro-Arab International Committee against Kadhafi, 191
Against Oppression and Tyranny (*Setem-i-Melli*) (Afghanistan), 72
Agrarian Peasant League (Paraguay), 386
Agricultural Workers' Union (UTC, El

Salvador), **359**, 306, 361, 362
Akali Dal (India), 95-96
Alajuela Democratic Party (Costa Rica), 346
Alawite Sect (Syria), 220, 221
Alawite Youth (Lebanon), 189
Albania, **2-3**, 60-62, 66
Albanian Marxist-Leninist Communist Party in Yugoslavia, 61
Albanian Nationalists (Yugoslavia), 60-63
Albanian Party of Labour, 2, 61-62, 482
Alcázar, El (Spain), 466
Alevi Moslem Sect (Turkey), 488
Alfarist Radical Front (*Frente Radical Alfarista*, Ecuador), 353
Algeria, **158-159**. Involvement in: Canaries independence issue, 477; El Salvador, 357
Algerian Communist Party (Algeria), 159
Alianza Popular Revolucionaria (Argentina), 321
All-African People's Conference (Accra, 1958), 301, 307
All-Assam People's Struggle Council (India), 87
Alliance (Fiji), 521
Alliance (Ireland), 443
Alliance for a Democratic Mauritania, 192
Alliance of Islamic Fighters (*Hedadia Mujaheddin Islami Afghanistan*), 72
Alliance Party (Northern Ireland), 493, 499, 500
All-Nagaland Communist Party (India), 95
All-People's Congress (Sierra Leone), 264
All-Russian Social Christian Union for the Liberation of the People (USSR), 55
All-Union Council of Evangelical Christians-Baptists (USSR), 56
Almendros—*see* Almond Trees
Almond Trees (Spain), 466-467
Alpha-66 Group (Cuba), 349
Al-Sanduq Al-Husseini Society (Bahrain), 160
Alternativ Lescht-Wiert Iech (Luxembourg), 456
Alternative List (Austria), 402
Amal (Lebanon), **188**, 189, 191, 211
Amal, Al- (Lebanon), 185
American Independent Party, 510
Agudat Israel, 180
American Indians: Canada, 508; Guatemala, 367; Inter-American Indigenist Institute, 389; Mexico, 377-378; Nicaragua, 383; Peru, 389
American Opinion, 511
American Party (USA), 510
American Popular Revolutionary Alliance (APRA, Peru), 387
Américo Silva Front (Venezuela), 399
Amnesty International. Reports: Brazil (1977, 1981), 333-334; Burundi, 235; Guatemala

537

Druse Community (Lebanon), 184, 188-189
Durum (Turkey), 482

E

Evangelical People's Party (Netherlands), 458
Evangelical People's Party (Switzerland), 479
Expatriate Faction (Burma), 82
Exploration (China), 85, 86
Eastern Anti-Guerrilla Bloc (El Salvador), 363
Eastern Revolutionary Movement (Uruguay), 396
Ecologists (Finland), 406
Ecology Parties: Austria, 402; Finland, 406;
  Germany (F.R. of), 426; Sweden, 478;
  Switzerland, 479; United Kingdom, 493
Ecology Party (Sweden), 478
Ecology Party (United Kingdom), 493
Ecuador, **353**
Ecuadorean Communist Party, 353
Edmund Barke Society—*see* Western Guard
  (Canada)
Egypt, 70, 74, **162-166.** Israel, relations with,
  197-199, 203-205
Egyptian Communist Party, 164-165, 408
Egyptian Communist Workers' Party, 165
Ejército de Liberación Nacional (ELN, Bolivia),
  324, 327, **328**
Ejército de Liberación Nacional (ELN,
  Colombia), 344
Ejército de Liberación Nacional (ELN,
  Peru)—*see* National Liberation Army (Peru)
Ejército Revolucionario del Pueblo (ERP,
  Argentina), **323-324,** 337, 386
Ekhwamis—*see* Moslem Brotherhood
  (Afghanistan)
El Condor (Cuba), 349
El Salvador, **354-363**
Elan Populaire pour l'Unité Nationale—*see*
  Popular Impulse for National Unity
  (Madagascar)
Elsässische Kampfgruppe Schwarze Wölfe
  (France), 414
EMSAV (Brittany, France), 415
Enbata Movement (France), 414
English People's Liberation Army, 497
Enraged Peasants' Movement (France), 413
Enrôlés de Force (Luxembourg), 456
Entebbe, hijack of French airbus to (June 1976),
  209
EOKA-B (Cyprus), 404
Eqab, Al-, see Punishment
Equatorial Guinea, **243**
Ercilla (Chile), 335
Eritrean Liberation Front (ELF), 244-245, 246
Eritrean Liberation Front—Popular Liberation
  Forces (ELF-PLF), **244-245,** 246, 248
Eritrean Liberation Front—Revolutionary
  Command (ELF-RC), **245-246,** 247
Eritrean People's Liberation Front (EPLF), 245,
  246-247
Eriwu Development Association (Papua New
  Guinea), 523
ERP (El Salvador)—*see* People's Revolutionary
  Army (El Salvador)

Estonia, 51-52, 59
Estrella Roja (Argentina), 324
ETA (*Euzkadi ta Azkatasuna*)—*see* Basque
  Nation and Liberty
ETA *Autónomo* (Spain), 474, 475
ETA *militar* (ETA-m, Spain), 472, 473, 474
ETA *politico-militar* (ETA-pm, Spain), 472, 473,
  475
Ethiopia, **244-250**
Ethiopian Communist Party, 249
Ethiopian Democratic Front, 249
Ethiopian Democratic Union, 249
Ethiopian People's Revolutionary Party (EPRP),
  249-250
European Nationalist Alliances (France), 409
European Workers' Party (Germany, F. R. of),
  426
Euzkadi ta Azkatasuna (ETA)—*see* Basque
  Nation and Liberty
Evangelical People's Party (Netherlands), 458
Evangelical People's Party (Switzerland), 479
Expatriate Faction (Burma), 82
Exploration (China), 85, 86

F

Faisceaux Nationalistes Européens (FNE)—*see*
  European Nationalist Alliances
Falange (Spain), 467-468
*Falange Española de las JONS (Juntas de
  Ofensiva Nacional-Sindicalista)*, 467-468
Falange Patria Nova—*see* New Fatherland
  Phalange (Brazil)
FALN (Venezuela)—*see* Armed Forces of
  National Liberation (Venezuela)
FAR (Guatemala)—*see* Rebel Armed Forces
Farabundo Martí Front for National Liberation
  (FMLN, El Salvador), **354-356,** 357, 358, 359,
  360, 362
Farabundo Martí Popular Liberation Forces
  (FPL El Salvador), 354, 356, **357-358,** 360,
  361, 363
Farem Tot Petar ("We Shall Blow Everything
  Up", France), 420
Farmers' Party (Netherlands), 458
FARN (El Salvador)—*see* Armed Forces of
  National Resistance
FARN (Nicaragua)—*see* Nicaraguan Armed
  Revolutionary Forces
Fascist New Generation (France), 409
Fascist Party (Italy), 444, 447
Fascist Revolutionary Action Party (France), 409
Fatah, Al-, 189, 200, **205-208,** 210, 211, 212,
  213, 486
Fatherland Front (Bulgaria), 3
FDR (El Salvador)—*see* Revolutionary
  Democratic Front
Febrerista Revolutionary Party (Paraguay), 385
February 28 Popular Leagues (LP-28, El
  Salvador), 355, 356, 358, **359,** 361
Fedayeen (Palestine), 197
Fedayeen el-Khalq (Iran), 171, 172, **173**

Front of the People and the Army for National Salvation (Vietnam) 154
Front Oubangais Patriotique—Parti du Travail (Central African Republic), 239-240
"Front Path" Faction of Turkish People's Liberation Party, 486
Front Paysan Corse de Libération (Corsica), 417
Front Position (Italy), 450
Fuerza Nueva—see New Force (Spain)
Fuerzas Armadas Revolucionarias (Argentina)—*see* Revolutionary Armed Forces
Full Group of Reflection on Puerto Rico, 517

G

Gaelic Language Defence League (*Ceartas* or Justice, Scotland), 498
GARI—*see Groupe d'Action Révolutionnaire Internationaliste* (France)
GENE—*see under Research and Study Group for European Civilization*
General Association of Khmers Overseas (Kampuchea), 111
Gabon, **251**
Gambia, The, **251-252**
Gambian Socialist Revolutionary Party, 252
General Confederation of Italian Labour (CGIL), 451
General Confederation of Labour (Argentina), 319, 321, 323, **324**
General Union of Palestinian Workers (Germany, F.R. of), 426
Georgian Nationalists (USSR), 53
German Action Front (Germany, F.R. of), 427
German Action Group (Germany, F.R. of), 427
German Action Groups (Germany, F.R. of), 427
German-American *Bund* (USA), 511
German Citizens' Initiative (Germany, F.R. of), 427, **428**
German Communist Party (DKP, Fed. Republic), 426
German Democratic Republic, **15-17**, 301, 336
German People's Union (Germany, F.R. of), 428
German Workers' Youth (West Berlin), 428
Germans in USSR, 53-54
Germany, Federal Republic of, **426-440**
Ghana, **253**
Ghjustizia Paolina (Corsica), 417, **419**
Golkar (Indonesia), 97
Grandmothers of the Plaza del Mayo (Argentina), 321
Grani (USSR), 47-48
GRAPO (Spain)—*see* First of October Anti-fascist Resistance Group
Great Britain—*see* United Kingdom
Great Ideal Society (Turkey), 487
Greater Britain Movement, 494
Greater Nigeria People's Party, 260
GRECE—*see* Research and Study Group for European Civilization
Greece, **441-442**. Relations with PLO, 204-205
Greek Communist Party (KKE Exterior) (Greece), 441

Grenada, **364**
Grenada National Party for Recovery and Liberation, 364
Grenadian Voice, The, 364
Grey Wolves ("Idealists", Turkey), 488
Group for establishing Trust between the USSR and the USA (USSR), 58
Group of March 6 (Germany, F.R. of), 435
Group of the Martyr (Iran), 167
Group of 24 (Chile), 334
Groupe Armé Patriotique du Congo, 242
Groupe d'Action Révolutionnaire Internationaliste (GARI, France), 412
Groupe d'Organisation Nationale Guadeloupéenne, 422
Groupement Indépendant de Réflexion et d'Action (Central African Republic), 238-239
Groups for Unified Action (Uruguay), 396
Guadeloupe Communist Party, 421
Guatemala, **365-370**
Guatemalan Christian Democratic Party, 365, 369
Guatemalan Committee of Patriotic Unity, 366
Guatemalan Labour Party, **366**, 367, 368
Guatemalan National Revolutionary Unity (URNG, Guatemala), **366-367**, 368
Guatemalan Workers' Militia, 370
Gudrun Ensslin Commando (Germany, F.R. of), 435
Guerrilla and Terrorist Tactics, handbooks on—Cienfuegos Press: *Towards a Citizens' Militia,* 496; Marighella, C., *For the Liberation of Brazil* (Penguin, 1971), 331
Guerrilla Army of the Poor (EGP, Guatemala), 366, **367**, 368, 369
Guerrilleros del Cristo Rey—see Warriors of Christ the King
Guiana National Liberation Front (French Guiana), 421
Guinea, **253**
Guinea-Bissau, **255**
Gush Emunim (Israel), 181
Guyana, **370-371**
Guyana Human Rights Association, 370-371

H

Haddad Christian Militia (Lebanon), 185, 203
Haddadland (Lebanon), 184, 185-186, 204
Haag-Mayer Group (Germany, F.R. of), 433, **435-436**, 438-440
Haiti, **371-373**
Haiti People's Unity Party—*see* United Party of Haitian Communists
Haitian Human Rights League, 372
Haitian National Christian Party, 372
Halcones, Los (Mexico), 379
Haratines—*see* Free Man Movement (Mauritania)
Hardcore (Philippines), 142
Harijans (India), 91
Hasi (Spain), 473
Hazara Tribes (Afghanistan)—*see* Alliance of Islamic Fighters
Hector Riobé Brigade (Haiti), 372

Mauritian Socialist Party, 289
Mauritius, **289**
Maximiliano Hernández Martínez Anti-
Communist Alliance (El Salvador), 356, **363**
May 19th Communist Organization (USA), **515,**
516
Mebyon Kernow (Cornish National Movement),
493
Mekane Yesus Church (Ethiopia), 250
Melanesian Alliance (Papua New Guinea), 523
Meo Tribesmen (Laos), 117-118
Metro Clandestine Committee of Resisters
(Guadeloupe), 422
Mexican Committee for the Defence of Political
Prisoners, Exiles and Disappeared Persons,
379
Mexican Communist Party (dissolved 1981), 377
Mexican Democratic Party, 377
Mexican Workers' Party, 377
Mexico, **377-379**. El Salvador, recognition of
FMLN-FDR alliance, 315
Middle-Core Faction—*see Chakaku-Ha* (Japan)
Militancia (Argentina), 324
Militant Departmentalist Front (Réunion,
France), 423
Militant Front of Combatants of Afghanistan,
73
Militant Tendency (United Kingdom), 496
Military Command for the Liberation of
Cabinda (Angola), 281
Military Council of Angolan Resistance
(Comira), 276-278
Military Council of National Salvation (Poland),
19, 25
Mindanao Alliance (Philippines), 136
Minority Rights Group (United Kingdom), 55
Minutemen (USA), 512
Miskito Kingdom (Nicaragua), 383
Misurasata (Nicaragua), 383
Mizo National Army (India), 93
Mizo National Front (India), **92-94,** 96
Mizo Students' Association (India), 93
Moederbond (Suriname), 391
Mon Patriotic Group (Burma), 82
Monarchist Movement (Albania), 2-3
Mongolia, **122**
Mongolian People's Revolutionary Party, 122
Mongoose, The (France), 410
Montagnards (Vietnam), 156
Montoneros (Argentina), **321-323,** 324
Moderate Party (Sweden), 478
Marazanista National Liberation Front
(Honduras), 175
Moro National Liberation Front (Philippines),
136, **137-140,** 141
Moroccan Communist Party, 194
Moroccan Patriotic Front (Spain), 477
Morocco, **193-195**
Moslem Brotherhood: Afghanistan (Ekhwamis),
73; Egypt (Ikhwani), 162; Jordan, 182;
Lebanon, 189, Palestine, 205, **213**; Sudan,
218, 219; Syria, **220-222,** 223
Moslem Brotherhood Union (Turkey), 488
Moslem Fundamentalists: Afghanistan, 71;
Algeria, 159; Egypt, 162ff.; Kuwait, 183;

Malaysia, 121; Nigeria, 260-261; Pakistan,
132-133; Saudi Arabia, 216; Senegal, 263;
Tunisia, 225
Moslem International Guerrillas (Pakistan), 213
Moslem League (Pakistan), 125, 126, **133,** 134,
135
Moslem Mujahid Movement (Burma), 78
Moslem People's Republican Party (Iran), 168
Moslem Revolutionary Movement in the Arabian
Peninsula, **215,** 216
Moslem United Development Party (Indonesia),
97, 99
Mother Croatia (*Matica Hrvatska*), 64-65
Mothers of the Plaza del Mayo (Argentina), 320,
321
Moujtamaa, Al (Tunisia), 225
Moulinaka—see National Liberation Movement
of Kampuchea
Mourabitoun Militia, *Al-* (Lebanon), 188
Moutakalinine, Al- (Morocco), 193
*Mouvement d'Action pour la Résurrection du
Congo* (MARC, Zaïre), 270
*Mouvement de Libération du Peuple
Centrafricain* (Central African Republic), 239
*Mouvement Démocratique de Renouveau
Algérien,* 159
*Mouvement des Forces Démocratiques de la
Casamance* (Senegal), 263
*Mouvement d'Evolution Démocratique
d'Afrique Centrale,* 239
Mouvement National du Congo—Lumumba
(Zaïre), 271
*Mouvement National pour l'Indépendance de
Madagascar* (Monima)—*see* National
Movement for the Independence of
Madagascar
*Mouvement National pour l'Union et la
Réconciliation au Zaïre,* 272
Mouvement Populaire de la Révolution (Zaïre),
270
Mouvement Populaire de Libération (Djibouti),
161
Mouvement Populaire Mahorais (Mayotte), 425
Mouvement pour la Démocratic et l'Indépendance
(Central African Republic), 239
Mouvement pour la Libération de Djibouti, 161
Mouvement pour la Libération de la Réunion,
423
*Mouvement Révolutionaire pour la Démocratie
Nouvelle* (Senegal), 263
*Mouvement Révolutionnaire pour le
Développement* (Rwanda), 261
Mouvement Socialiste (Tunisia), 226
Mouvement Togolais pour la Démocratie, 266
Movement for Free Philippines, 142
Movement for Horizontal Consultations
(Poland), 22
Movement for Independence, Nationalism and
Democracy (Philippines), 143
Movement for Justice in Africa (Moja-Gambia),
252
Movement for Justice in Africa (Moja, Liberia),
257
Movement for National Liberation (Barbados),
326

Movement for National Renewal (Morena, Gabon), 251

Movement for Order and Peace (New Caledonia), 425

Movement for Proletarian Power (Madagascar), 285

Movement for Resistance (Seychelles), 298

Movement for Socialism (Dominican Republic), 352

Movement for the Defence of Human and Civil Rights of Man (Poland), 30

Movement for the Independence of Réunion, 423

Movement for the Islamic Revolution (*Harkat-i-Inkalab-i-Islami,* Afghanistan), 71, 72, 73, **74**

Movement for the Liberation of Cabinda (Molica, Angola), 281

Movement for the Liberation of Suriname, 391

Movement for the National Liberation of Palestine—*see Fatah, Al-*

Movement for the Restoration of Democracy (Pakistan), **125**, 128, 129, 133

Movement for the Self-Determination and Indepence of the Canary Archipelago (MPAIAC, Spain), 476-477

Movement for the Struggle for Political Rights (Mospor, Uganda), 267

Movement for the Unification of National Liberation Forces of Guadeloupe, **422**, 423

Movement for the Unity of the Left (*Movimiento para la Unidad de la Izquierda,* Ecuador), 353

Movement of Free Officers (Mauritania), 192

Movement of March 26 (Uruguay), 396

Movement of National Integration (Venezuela), 397

Movement of National Unity (Mauritania), 192

Movement of Non-aligned Countries: Membership of PLO (August 1975), 201

Movement of Popular Unity (Tunisia), 224

Movement of Socialist Democrats (Tunisia), 224, **225**

Movement of the Revolutionary Left (*Movimiento de Izquierda Revolucionaria,* MIR, Bolivia), 327

Movement towards Socialism (MAS, Venezuela), 397

Movimento de Libertação de São Tomé e Príncipe (MLSTP), 262

Movimento Revolucionario de 8 Outubro (MR8, Brazil), 331

Movimiento de Integración y Desarrollo (Argentina), 319

Movimiento de la Izquierda Revolucionaria (MIR, Chile), 324, 334, 336, **337**, 338, 340

Movimiento de Liberación Nacional (MLN, Uruguay)—*see Tupamaros*

Movimiento de Rocha (Uruguay), 393

Movimiento de Unidad Nacional (Chile), 332

Movimiento Nacional Justicialista (Argentina), 319

Mozambican National Resistance, 290-291

Mozambique, **289-291**. South Africa, training of ANC guerrillas, 303; attacks on alleged ANC headquarters, 304

MPAIAC—*see* Movement for the Self-Determination and Independence of the Canary Archipelago

Mudiad Amddiffyn Cymru (Wales), 498

Mujaheddin (Afghanistan), 70-74

Mujaheddin Group (Iraq), 177

Mujaheddin Khalq (Iran), 170, 171, **172**, 174, 175

Multipartidaria (Argentina), 319, 320, 321

Multipartidaria Alliance (Chile), 337

Musawat (Pakistan), 131

Mussolini Action Squads (Italy), 446

N

Naga National Council (India), 94

Naga Separatist Movement (India), 94-95

Nagriamel (Vanuatu), 525

Nakamal (Vanuatu), 525

Namibia, **291-297**

Namibian National Convention, 293

Namibian People's Democratic Organization (NAPDO), 294

NAPAP—*see Noyaux Armés pour l'Autonomie Populaire* (France)

Natal Indian Congress (South Africa), 311

Natatuk Efate Alliance (Vanuatu), 525

National Action (Switzerland), 479

National Action Group (ANE, Spain), 473

National Action Party (Mexico), 377

National Action Party (Turkey), 480, **487**, 488

National Agreement (Paraguay), 385

National Alliance (Suriname), 391

National Alliance for the Liberation of Syria, 222, 223

National Alliance for the Restoration of Democracy (Equatorial Guinea), 243

National Alliance Party (Sierra Leone), 264

National and European Action (France), 409

National Association for the Advance of White People (Canada), 509

National Association for the Advancement of Coloured People (NAACP, USA), 512

National Association of Honduran Peasants, 375

National Association of Salvadorean Teachers, **360**, 361

National Authentic Central (Guatemala), 365

National Awami Party (Bangladesh), 129

National Awami Party (Pakistan), 126, **128**, 129, 134, 136

National Basutoland Congress—*see* Basotho Congress Party

National Bloc (Israeli-occupied West Bank), 202

National Bloc of Working People, 1945 (Czechoslovakia), 10

National Coalition (Egypt), 165

National Coalition Party (Conservatives, Finland), 406

National Committee for the Defence of Democracy (CONADE, Bolivia), 328

National Committee in Defence of Democracy (St Vincent and the Grenadines), 390

National Committee of Democratic Journals (China), 86

Rassemblement Unitaire des Révolutionnaires
(Algeria), 159
Rastafarians
Dominica, 350-351; Grenada, 364; St Vincent
and the Grenadines, 390
Raúl Sendic International Brigade—*see*
Tupamaros (Uruguay)
Raven Banner (United Kingdom), 495
Ravnagora (Yugoslavia), 65
Rayo, El (Guatemala), 370
Re Patria (USSR), 54
Rebel Armed Forces (FAR, Guatemala), 366,
367-368, 369
Reconstituted Spanish Communist Party (PCE-R,
Spain), 464, 477
Red Aid (*Rood Hulp,* Netherlands), 459
"Red Army" (Morocco), 193
Red Army Faction (Germany, F.R. of), 106,
209, 214, **429-435**, 436-440, 450, 459, 479
Red Army Faction (Japan), 104
Red Brigade of Occitania (France), 420
Red Brigades (Italy), 412, 413, 445, 448, 449,
450-454, 455
Red Brigades—Fighting Communist Party
(Italy), 454
Red Bulls (*Gaurs,* Thailand), 153
Red Cross—*see* International Committee of the
Red Cross
Red Electoral Alliance (Norway), 460
Red Fatherland (*Patria Roja,* Peru), 388
Red Flag (United Kingdom), 497
Red Flag (Venezuela), 398
Red Front (Yugoslavia), 61
Red Group (Uruguay), 396
Red Guerrillas (Spain), 465
Red Hand—*see Main Rouge* (Algeria)
Red Hand Commandos (Northern Ireland), 503-
504
Red Khmers (Kampuchea), 106, **107-110**, 111,
117, 118, 149
"Red Lausanne" (Switzerland), 479
Red Morning (Germany, F.R. of), 435, **437**
Red Poster (*L'Affiche Rouge,* France), 413
Red Resistance Front (Netherlands), 459
Red Squad Organized Comrades (Italy), 454
Redemption of Israel, 181
Reformed Political Association (Netherlands),
458
Reformist Party (Dominican Republic), 352
Reformist Political Federation (Netherlands),
458
Regroupement des Guinéens à l'Extérieur, 254
Rejectionist Front (Palestine), 165, 202, 208, 209,
211
Rejectionist Front of Stateless Palestinians, 212
Religious Opposition—*see* Church Opposition
Rengo Sekigun—see United Red Army (Japan)
Rénu Rewni—see Roots of the Nation (Senegal)
Republic of New Africa (USA), 514
"Republic of the South Moluccas", 458
Republican Armenian Army, 491
Republican Clubs (Northern Ireland), 501
Republican Front (Zimbabwe), 315
Republican Party (Chile)—*see Partido*
Republicano

Republican Party (Faroes, Denmark), 408
Republican Party (USA), 510
Republican Peasant Nation Party—*see* National
Action Party (Turkey), 487
Republican People's Party (Turkey), 480, **483,**
488, 493
Republican Turkish Party (Cyprus, Turkish
Federated State of), 404
Research and Study Group for European
Civilization (*Groupement de Recherche et*
d'Etudes pour la Civilisation Européenne,
GRECE, France), 410-411
Resistance Movement of National Freedom
(Spain), 477
Réunion Communist Party, 423
Revanche et Liberté (Belgium)—*see* Vengeance
and Liberty
Review of the News, The (USA), 511
Révolution Québecoise (Canada), 509
Revolutionärer Zorn (Germany, F.R. of), 440
Revolutionary Action (Italy), 454
Revolutionary Action Movement (Italy), 447
Revolutionary Action Movement (Mexico), 378
Revolutionary Action Movement (USA), 515
Revolutionary Anti-Capitalist Initiative (Greece),
443
Revolutionary Anti-fascist and Patriotic Front
(Spain), 106, **466,** 476
Revolutionary Anti-imperialist Front (Bolivia),
329
Revolutionary Armed Forces (Argentina), 321,
323
Revolutionary Armed Nationalist Group
(Dominican Republic), 352
"Revolutionary Army" Group (Denmark), 405
Revolutionary Brigades (Portugal), 462
Revolutionary Cells (Germany, F.R. of), 440
Revolutionary Communist League (France), 410
Revolutionary Communist Party (Argentina), 324
Revolutionary Communist Party (India), 89
Revolutionary Communist Party (United
Kingdom), 497
Revolutionary Communist Party of Britain
(Marxist-Leninist), 497
Revolutionary Co-ordination Group (France),
412
Revolutionary Co-ordination of the Masses (El
Salvador), 360, **361,** 362
Revolutionary Cultural Centres of the East
(Turkey), 493
Revolutionary Democratic Front (El Salvador),
354, 355, **356-357,** 359, 360, 362, 363
Revolutionary Fighting Group (USA), 515
Revolutionary French Brigades, 411
Revolutionary Front for the Independence of
East Timor—*see* Fretilin
Revolutionary Front of Equatorial Guinea, 243
Revolutionary Left (Greece, 443)
Revolutionary Left (Turkey)—*see* Dev-Sol
Revolutionary Left Movement (Chile)—*see*
Movimiento de la Izquierda Revolucionaria
(MIR)
Revolutionary Left Union (Peru), 387
Revolutionary Marxist Faction (Japan)—*see*
Kakumaru-Ha

565

31st January Popular Front (FP-31, Guatemala), 366, **368**
Those Who Have Sworn to Fight for Islam (*Teiman Atahad-Islam,* Afghanistan), **72**, 73, 74
Tierra y Liberdad—see Land and Freedom (USA)
Tiger Militia (Lebanon), 185, **187**, 188
Tigre People's Liberation Front (Ethiopia), 247-248
Timorese Social Democratic Association, 100
Tirol (Italy), 455
Today (China), 85
Toga, **266**
Tonga, **524**
Transkei, 299, 304
Transvaal British Indian Association—*see* Transvaal Indian Congress
Transvaal Indian Congress, 312
Trade Union Co-ordinating Committee (CCS, El Salvador), 361
Trinidad and Tobago, **392**
Trinidad and Tobago National Alliance, 392
Trinidad Gómez Hernández Settlers' Co-ordinating Body (Guatemala), 368
Tripur Sena (India), 96
Tripura Tribal Youth Organization (India), 96
"Troops Out" Movement (United Kingdom), 499
Tudeh Party (Iran), 173
Tunisia, **224-227**
Tunisian Armed Resistance, 226
Tunisian Communist Party, 224, **226-227**
Tupamaros (Uruguay), 324, 393, 394, **395-396**, 450
Turkey, **480-493**
Turkish Communist Party—Marxist-Leninist (AKKO), 485
Turkish Islamic Army, 489
Turkish Labour Party (*Türkiye Işçi Partisi*), **485**, 493
Turkish Lightning Commandos, 488
Turkish Peace Association, 485
Turkish People's Liberation Army (TPLA), 481, **485-486**
Turkish People's Liberation Party, 482, **486**
Turkish Revolutionary Communist Party, 486
Turkish Revolutionary Peasants' Liberation Army, 485
Turkish Teachers' Union (*Tob-Der*), 486
Turkish Unity Party (Cyprus, Federated State of), 404
Turkoman Autonomists (Iran), 171
Turkoman Political and Cultural Society (Iran), 171
Tuvalu, **524**
20th Century (USSR), 41
23rd March Group (Morocco), 193
"2,000 Words" manifesto (Czechoslovakia), 11-13

U

Uganda, **267-269**
Uganda Domocratic Movement, 268
Uganda Freedom Movement, 268-269

Uganda National Rescue Front, 269
Uganda Patriotic Movement, 367, **269**
Uganda People's Congress, 267
Uganda Popular Front, 269
Ugandan National Liberation Front, 267, 268, 269
Ukrainian Communist Party (USSR), 54
Ukrainian Catholic Church, 55
Ukrainian Herald, The (USSR), 54
Ukrainian Liberation Front, 59
Ukrainian Nationalists (Dr V. Moroz) 43; (G. Snegiryov) 50, **54**, 58, 59
Ulrike Meinhof Commando (Germany, F.R. of), 439
Ulrike Meinhof—Puig Antich Commando (Germany, F.R. of), 440
Ulster Defence Association, 502, **504**
Ulster Freedom Fighters, 504-505
Ulster Popular Unity Party, 493
Ulster Protestant Action Group, 505
Ulster Volunteer Force, 503, **505**
Umkhonto we Sizwe (South Africa), 301, 302, 305, 310
Umma Party (Sudan), 219
UNEM (Morocco)—*see* National Union of Moroccan Students
Unidad y Reforma (Uruguay), 393, **396**
Unified Liberal Party (Paraguay), 385
Unified Popular Action Front (FAPU, El Salvador), 354, 356, 357, **359**, 361
Unified Popular Action Movement (MAPU, Chile), 338, **339**
Unified Socialist Party of Catalonia (Spain), 463
Unión Cívica (Uruguay)—*see* Civic Union (Uruguay)
Unión Cívica Radical (Argentina), 319, 324
Union Comorienne pour le Progrès, 282
Union Démocratique du Peuple Malien, 258
Union des Guinéens au Sénégal, 254
Union des Paysans Pauvres de la Guadeloupe, 422
Union des Populations Camerounaises, 236
Union des Populations de Guinée, 254
Union des Travailleurs Agricoles (Guadeloupe), 422
Union des Travailleurs de Guyane (French Guiana), 421
Union des Travailleurs de Mayotte, 425
Union for French Democracy, 407
Union Générale des Travailleurs de la Guadeloupe, 422
Union Générale des Travailleurs Tunisiens, 224
Union Nationale Camerounaise—see Cameroon National Union
Union Nationale des Elèves et Etudiants du Mali (UNEEM), 258
Union Nationale des Elèves et Etudiants Guadeloupéens, 422
Union Nationale des Etudiants de Kameroun (UNEK), 236
Union Nationale pour l'Indépendance (Djibouti), 161
Union of Anti-fascist Youth (Spain), 466
Union of Christian Democrats of Lithuania, 59
Union of Communists (Iran), 173

US Labor Party, 510
USSR—*see* Union of Soviet Socialist Republics
Ustashi Movement (Yugoslavia), 60, **63-64**

V

Vaega o le Tautua (Western Samoa), 526
Vanguard for Liberation and Democracy
(Guyana), 370
Vanguard Nationalist and Socialist Party
(Bahamas), 325
Vanguard of the Arab Revolution (Syria), 223
Vanguard of the Commando for Hunting
Communists (Brazil), 330
Vanguard of the Malagasy Revolution (Arena),
112
Vanguards of the Popular War for the
Liberation of Palestine, 210
Vanuatu, **525**
Vanuatu Pati, 525
Vascrc Spoije (Yugoslavia), 65
Velasquist National Party (*Partido Nacional
Velasquista,* Ecuador), 353
Venda, 299
Venezuela, **397-399**
Venezuelan Communist Party, 397
Vengeance and Liberty (*Revanche et Liberté,*
Belgium), 403, **404**
Venstre Liberal Party (Denmark), 405
Vicariate of Solidarity (Chile), 340
Vicente Menchu Revolutionary Christians
(Guatemala), 368
Vietnam, **154-156**
Vietnam Fatherland Front, 154
Vigilante (Norway), 460
Viking Youth (United Kingdom), 495
Vlaamse Blok (Flemish Bloc, Belgium), 403
Vlaamse Militantenorde (Flemish Militant Order,
Belgium), **403**, 494
"Voice of Democratic Kampuchea" (VODK),
108, 117
"Voice of Malayan Democracy", 120
"Voice of Oman Revolution", 196
"Voice of Sandino" (Nicaragua), 381
"Voice of the Arab Revolution", 489
"Voice of the Armenians of Lebanon", 489
"Voice of the Broad Masses of Eritrea", 247
"Voice of the Free Canaries", 477
"Voice of the Malayan Revolution", 120
"Voice of the People of Burma" (VOPB),
79-80, 82
"Voice of the People of Thailand" (VOPT),
150-151, 152
"Voice of the Western Somali and Somali Abo
Liberation Front", 248
Vokno ("Window", Czechoslovakia), 9
Völkischer Beobachter (Germany, F.R. of), 429
Volksunie (Belgium)—*see* People's Union
(Belgium)
Vondrona Sosialista Monima (Madagascar), 285
Voluntary Defence Front (Guatemala), 368
VONJY (Madagascar)—*see* Popular Impulse for
National Unity
"*Voz da Africa Livre*" (Mozambique), 291
Voz Operaria (Brazil), 330, 331

W

Watd (Egypt), 165-166
Waitangi Action Committee (New Zealand), 522
Walfougi Front (Mauritania), 193
Walter Alasia Column (Italy), 454
Waltraud Boock Liberation Group (Germany,
F.R. of), 440
Walvis Bay, 294, 295
Warriors for Imam Mousse Sadr (Lebanon), 191
Warriors of Christ the King (Spain), 467, **468**
Warriors of the Turkish People's Liberation
Front, 483, **486**
Wathtower Bible and Tract Society—*see*
Jehovah's Witnesses
Weather Underground (USA), 512, **515-516**
Weathermen—*see* Weather Underground
Wehrsportgruppe Hoffmann—*see* Hoffmann
Defence Sport Group
Welsh Language Society, 498, **499**
Welsh Socialist Republican Movement, 499
Were Di (Belgium), 404
Western Guard (Canada), 509
Western Sahara, 193, 194-195
Western Samoa, **526**
Western Somali Liberation Front (Ethiopia),
244, 247, **248-249**
Western United Front (Fiji), 521
White Brigade (*Brigada Blanca, Mexico*), 379
White Commando—*see Wit Kommando* (South
Africa)
White Defence League—*see under* British
National Party
White Hand, the (*La Mano Blanca,* Guatemala),
369
White Hand, the (*La Mano Blanca,* Honduras),
376
White People's State Party—*see Wit Kommando*
(South Africa)
White Resistance Movement (Namibia), 295
White Warriors' Union (El Salvador), 363
Wit Kommando (South Africa), 312
Women's Free Popularly-Elected
Representatives (Norway), 460
Worker, The (United Kingdom), 496
Worker-Peasant Party of Turkey, 486-487
Workers and Peasants (Chile), 338, 339
Workers' and Peasants' Movement (Haiti), 373
Workers' Army (United Kingdom), 497
Workers' Army of the Welsh Republic, 499
Workers' Autonomy (Italy), 445, **455**
Workers' Communist Party (Norway), 460
Workers' Defence Committee (WDC)—*see* Social
Self-Defence Committee (Poland)
Workers' Fight—*see* International Communist
League (United Kingdom)
Workers' Front (*Frente Obrero,* Nicaragua), 383
Workers' League (Lebanon), 190
Workers' League (United Kingdom), 497
Workers' Movement of the Revolutionary Left
(*Movimento Obrero Izquierdista
Revolucionario,* MOIR, Colombia), 341
Workers' Party (Bahamas), 325
Workers' Party (Brazil), 329, 331
Workers' Party (Ireland), 443
Workers' Party (Northern Ireland), 493, 501

NAMES INDEX

A

Abbas, Abul, 210f.
Abdallah, Ahmed, 282f.
Abdallah, Mouzaoir, 283
Abdelazziz, Mohamed, 194f.
Abdelkader, Lt.-Col. Mohamed Ould Ba Ould, 192
Abdi, Ahmad Ismail, 217
Abduldzhemil (Mustafa Dzhemilev), 53
Abdullahi, Abdi-Nasir Sheikh, 248
Abdulrahman, M. M. (Sami), 179
Abernathy, Rev. Ralph, 512
Abou, Husni Mahmoud, 221
Abrahams, Peter, 307
Acevedo Granados, Napoleón, 375
Achakzai, Abdus Samed Khan, 134
Achtyorev, Pavel, 57
Acorta, Alfredo, 386
Adjitorop, Jusuf, 98
Adnan, Sayyid Hashim Sayyid, 167
Adohu, Joseph, 218
Adomeit, Manfred, 434, 439
Adwan, Kamal, 212
Afewerki, Issaias, 246
Affani, Mohammed, 199
Affatigato, Mario, 446
Aflaq, Michel, 223
Agca, Mehmet Ali, 488
Agnew, Paddy, 503
Agopian, Agop; see Sakaseslian, Wasken
Aguiñada Carranza, Mario, 360
Aguirre y Salinas, Col. Osmin, 357
Agyp, Osman, 245
Ahenakew, David, 508
Ahidjo, Ahmadou, 236
Ahmad, Abdel Rahim, 211
Ahmad, Abder Rahman Aidid, 217
Ahmad, Col. Abdullahi Yusuf, 217
Ahmad, Ghafoor Mufti, 125f.
Ahmad, Musa bin; see Musa bin Ahmed
Ahmad, Qazi Hussain, 132
Ahmar, Shaikh Abdullah Bin Hussein al-, 228
Ahmat, Acyl, 241
Ahmed, Hocine Aït; see Aït Ahmed, Hocine
Ahmed, Shabbir, 132
Ahwash, Ahmed Ibrahim, 191
Aït Ahmed, Hocine, 158
Akinci, Faruk, 487
Akl, Saïd, 185
Alape, Jacobo Frias; see Charry Rincón, Fermin
Alarcón, Mario Sandaval; see Sandoval Alarcón, Mario
Albertz, Pastor Heinrich, 436
Albrecht, Susanne, 437

Aldunate, Wilson Ferreira; see Ferreira Aldunate, Wilson
Alessandrini, Emilio, 449
Alexander, Neville Edward, 307
Alfonis, Prosper, 417
Ali, Chaudri Mohammad, 133
Ali, Mirza Husain, 175
Ali, Mohamed Kamil, 161
Ali, Brig. Moses, 269
Ali, Muhammad (Cassius Clay), 514
Ali, Osman Nur, 217
Ali, Salem Rubayya, 230
Ali Khan, Fatheyab, 128
Alibrandi, Alessandro, 445
Allende, Andrés Pascal; see Pascal Allende, Andrés
Allende, Beatriz, 337
Allende Gossens, Salvador, 331, **334ff.**, 349, 448
Allnach, Kay Werner, 432
Almeida, José de, 461
Almeida Santos, Antônio de, 461
Almeyda Medina, Clodomiro, 338f.
Altamirano, Carlos, 334, **338f.**
Altamirano, Elí, 382
Alter, Celal, 483
Altesor González, Alberto, 394
Altinoglu, Garbis, 488
Alunni, Corrado, 449, 452
Alvarado, Gen. Juan Velasco; see Velasco Alvarado, Gen. Juan
Alvarez, Col. Artiges, 395
Alvarez Córdova, Enrique, 356
Amalrik, Andrei, 38f.
Amaral, Francisco Xavier do, 101
Amarantov, Boris, 36
Amaru, Tupac, 395
Amin, Nurul, 133
Amin Dada, Idi, 267ff.
Amininejad, Hojatoleslam Mohammed Ali, 172
Ammar, Abu; see Arafat, Mohammed Abed Arouf (Yassir)
Ammaturo, Antonio, 453
Ampuero, Raúl, 339
Anaya, Gen. Joaquín Zenteno; see Zenteno Anaya, Gen. Joaquín
Andriamanjato, Fr Richard, 285
Andropov, Yury, 42
Andrzejewski, Jerzy, 31
Angami, "Gen." Mowu, 94f.
Annfield, Pierce, 314
Ansari, Soraya, 438
Antich, Puig, 440
Antunes, Carlos Melo, 462
Anwar, Raja, 127

Aouegui, Antoine, 421
Apaydin, Orhan, 485
Aponno, Eddie, 458
Aponte, Gabriel Puerte; *see* Puerte Aponte, Gabriel
Arafat, Mohammed Abed Arouf (Yassir), 199ff., **205**ff., 438, 473
Aragón, Luis Cardoza y; *see* Cardoza y Aragón, Luis
Arakian, Paruir, 53
Aramburú, Lt.-Gen. Pedro Eugenio, 321f.
Araña Osorio, Gen. Carlos Manuel, 369
Aranda, Theodore, 327
Araujo, Abilio, 101
Arbenz Guzmán, Jacobo, 328, 366
Arevalo, Reyes Rodrígues; *see* Rodrígues Arevalo, Reyes
Argüello, Jorge Salazar; *see* Salazar Argüello, Jorge
Argüero Echeverría, Carlos, 346
Argueta, Manuel Colom; *see* Colom Argueta, Manuel
Arias Madrid, Arnulfo, 384
Arismendi, Rodney, 394
Armada Comyn, Gen. Alfonso, 466f.
Arocená, Juan María Bordaberry; *see* Bordaberry Arocená, Juan María
Arrostito, Norma, 322
Arthit Kamlang-ek, 152
Arutunian, Edvard, 37
Arzhak, Nikolai, *pseud. of* Daniel, Yuli
Asghar Khan, Air Marshal Mohammed, 126, 133
Ashqar, Capt. Samir al-, 189
Ashraf, Princess, 173
Ashraf Khan, Mohammad, 134
Askeri, Ali, 179
Assad, Hafez al-, 178, 207, **220**ff.
Assiego, José Antonio, 468
Atatürk, Kemal, 483
Attar, Issam al-, 220ff.
Avadhoot, Sarveshwarananda, 88
Avebury, Baron, 370
Awad, Arabi, 182
Ayala, Julio César Turbay; *see* Turbay Ayala, Julio César
Aydin, Omer Faruk, 486
Ayub Khan, Field Marshal Mohammed, 129f., 133
Aziz, Mohammed, 178
Aziz, Tariq, 177
Azran, Armand, 181
Azzadeh, Princess, 173

B

Ba Thein Tin, Thakin, 79f.
Baader, Andreas, 403, **429**ff.
Babar, Maj.-Gen. Nasirullah, 125
Babayan, Edvard A., 38
Bachelet, Vittorio, 452
Bäcker, Hans-Jürgen, 434f.
Badakshi, Taher, 72
Badal, Saeed, 174
Badzyo, Yur, 54
Bagaza, Col. Jean-Baptiste, 235
Baha'ullah; *see* Ali, Mirza Husain

Bahro, Rudolf, 16
Baia, Clariano, 462
Bairamoy, Reshat, 53
Bakaric, Vladimir, 64
Bakary, Djibo, 259
Bakhtiar, Shapour, 174f.
Bakhtiari, Amir Bahman Samsam, 175
Balaguer, Joaquín, 352
Balenda, Maj. Vicente, 281
Baluch, Abdul Hamid, 135
Balzer, Herbert, 16
Bamana, Younoussa, 425
Banda, Hastings Kamuzu, 285ff.
Bangui, Gen. Sylvestre, 238
Bani-Sadr, Abolhassan, 170ff., 174
Banna, Shaikh Hassan Al-, 162
Banna, Sabri Khalil al-, 211ff.
Banzer Suárez, Col. Hugo, 328f.
Barabanov, Anatoly, 38
Barabas, Ingrid, 437
Barahona, Elias, 367,369
Barbosa, Rafael, 255
Bardesio, Nelson, 395
Barki, Mustafa al-, 191
Barnhill, John, 501
Barraza García, Miguel Angel, 378
Barreh, Gen. Mohammed Siyad; *see* Siyad Barreh, Gen. Mohammed
Barrientos Ortuño, René, 328
Barry, Abdullah, 253
Barry, Nathalie, 253
Baruah, Daud, 98
Barzani, Idris, 179
Barzani, Masoud, 178f.
Barzani, Mullah Mustapha, 179
Basha i Novosejt, Ydriz, 3
Bassi, Pietro, 451
Bastürk, Abdullah, 482
Bateman Cayón, Jaime, 342f.
Batista i Roca, Josep Maria, 477
Batovrin, Sergei, 58
Battek, Rudolf, 9
Baum, Gerhart, 427, 435
Bäurich, Raimund, 16
Bautista, Nicolas Rodríguez; *see* Rodríguez Bautista, Nicolas
Bayanouni, Shaikh, 220f.
Bayev, Gomer, 53
Bazargan, Mehdi, 169, 171, 174
Bean, John, 495
Beatrix, Queen of the Netherlands, 458
Becerra, Gregorio, 331
Beck, Rev. Klaus-Detlef, 17
Becker, Eberhard, 432
Becker, Verena, 432f., 435f.
Bedranova, Otta, 9
Beer, Wolfgang, 432, 436
Beg, Wali, 72
Begin, Menahem, 181, 198, 203, 207
Beheshti, Ayatollah Mohammed Hossein, 175
Behr, Bram, 391
Behrend, Uwe, 428
Belaúnde Terry, Fernando, 387f.
Belkacem, Krim, 159
Bella, Ahmed Ben; *see* Ben Bella, Ahmed

590

Tun, Thakin Than; *see* Than Tun, Thakin
Turabi, Hassan Abdallah al, 218
Turbay Ayala, Julio César, 341ff.
Turchin, Valentin A., 36, 44
Turcios Lima, Luis, 367
Türkes, Col. Alparslan, 487f.
Türkler, Kemal, 489
Tuskan, Erhan, 483
Tutti, Mario, 409, 445
Tutu, Rt. Rev. Desmond, 297
Tvardovsky, Alexander, 47
Tverdokhlebov, Andrei, 36
Twomey, Seamus, 502
Tyndall, John, 494f.
Tyrie, Andy, 504

U

Ubaldini, Saúl, 324
Ucasqui Urval, Osvaldo, 328
Udom Sisuwan, 149f., 152
Udom Thonguai, 151
Udovicki, Danilo, 67
Ugarte, Gen. Augusto Pinochet; *see* Pinochet
  Ugarte, Gen. Augusto
Uhl, Petr, 9
Ülüsü, Adml. Bülent, 481
Ungo, Guillermo Manuel, 356, **360**
Urval, Osvaldo Ucasqui; *see* Ucasqui Urval,
  Osvaldo
Ussery, Wilfred, 513
Ussia, Gen. Milans del Bosch y; *see* Milans del
  Bosch y Ussia, Gen. Jaime
Uzun, Pasa, 492

V

Vaculik, Ludvik, 11
Valdés, Gabriel, 334f.
Vale, Giorgio, 445
Vale, Guido, 449
Valenzuela, Gen. Joaquín de, 475
Valladares, Armando Fernando, 348
Valle, Gen. Juan José, 321
Vallières, Pierre; *see* Hébert, Mathieu
van der Stoel, Max, 8
Van Saren, 110ff.
Vang Pao, Gen.; *see* Pao, Gen. Vang
Vann Sao Yuth, 112
Vardag, Ashaf, 133
Varona, Manuel Antonio de, 349
Vásquez Castaño, Fabio, 344f.
Velado, Roberto Lara; *see* Lara Velado, Roberto
Velasco, Jaime Castillo; *see* Castillo Velasco,
  Jaime
Velasco Alvarado, Gen. Juan, 341
Vélez, José Alberto Munguia; *see* Munguia Vélez,
  José Alberto
Vélez, Manuel Marulanda; *see* Marulanda Vélez,
  Manuel
Vendrell, Jaime Martínez; *see* Martínez Vendrell,
  Jaime
Verdún, Gilberta, 386
Veselica, Marko, 65
Viana, Ion, 33
Videla, Jorge Rafael, 320

Viehmann, Klaus, 437
Vieira, Mário Alves de Souza, 332
Viera, Maj. João Bernardo, 255
Villa, Pietro, 452
Villalobos, Joaquín, 358
Vins, Pastor Georgi P., 56
Viscardi, Michele, 449
Vitelli, Roberto, 449
Vitkovsky, Dmitri P., 42
Vladimov, Georgy, 36
Vlasov, Gen. Andrei, 49
Vogel, Andreas, 437
Voinea, Eugenie Boeuve, 34
Voinovich, Vladimir, 41
Volokhensky, Lev, 51
Vorderbrügge, Sybille, 427
Vorster, Balthazar Johannes, 293f., 309
Vrhovec, Josip, 66
Vuskovic, Pedro, 339

W

Wackernagel, Christof, 434
Wadadid, Hassan Adan, 217
Wagner, Hans Georg, 440
Wagner, Rolf-Clemens, 433f.
Waldheim, Kurt, 9, 55, 185
Walesa, Lech, 18ff.
Wali Khan, Begum, 126
Wali Khan, Khan Abdul, 128f., 134
Walker, Richard, 114
Warner, Bennie D., 258
Warraich, Munir Ahmad, 127
Washington, Edward Emmanuel ("rabbi"); *see*
  Hill, David
Wasik, Stanislaw, 32
Watama Koevimal, 153
Watoo, Mian Manzoor Ahmed, 133
Watson, Robert, 306
Waugh, Evelyn, 309
Wazir, Halil al-, 207
Webster, Martin, 495
Wei Jingsheng, 85, **86**
Weinhold, Günter, 16
Weisbecker, Thomas, 430
Welch, Robert H. W., 510
Welytschovsky, Most Rev. Basil, 56
West, Henry William (Harry), 503
Whitelaw, William, 504
Whyte, Winston, 364
Wickham, Gen. John A., 115
Wieland, Gerd Jürgen, 431
Wijeweere, Rohana, 145
Wilkins, Roy, 512
Will, Gertraud, 432
Williams, Robert, 515
Williams, Wayne, 499
"Wilson"; *see* Pérez Beotegui, Pedro
Wilson, David, 495
Wisniewski, Stefan, 435, 439
Wojciechowski, Adam, 28ff.
Wolde, Berhane Meskel Reda; *see* Berhane Meskel
  Reda Wolde
Woldemichael, Tesfai; *see* Tesfai Woldemichael
Woungly-Massaga, M., 236

XYZ

X, Malcolm, *see* Malcolm X
Xiu Cachón, Gaspar Antonio, 377

Yahya Khan, Gen. A. M., 89, 95, 130
Yakir, Pyotr, 35f.
Yakoreva, Albina, 51
Yakunin, Fr Gleb, 49, **55**
Yan Naing, "Gen.", 82
Yangelis, Virgilius, 52
Yassin, Bakr, 178
Yermogen, Most Rev. Archbishop of Kaluga, 49
Yessenin-Volpin, Alexander, 35f.
Yolon, Alexis, 525
Yon Sosa, Marco Antonio ("El Chino"), 367
Yoon Kong Hie, Mgr, 115
Yordanov, Kristo Kolev, 4
Youssef, Capt. Ibrahim, 221
Youssef, Salah Ben, 226
Yumurtaci, Zeki, 482
Yussef, Abu; *see* Najjar, Mohammed Yussef
Yuyitung, Quinton, 147
Yuyitung, Rizal, 147

Zabala, Justino, 394
Zahari, Said, 143
Zahl, Peter-Paul, 432
Zai, Mohammad Babrak, 72
Zaim, Abdul Satar al-, 221
Zain, Imran Mohammad, 99
Zaldívar Larrain, Andrés, 335
Zamora Rivas, Mario, 363
Zancada, Maj. Ricardo Pardo; *see* Pardo Zancada, Maj. Ricardo
Zani, Fabrizio, 446
Zarkesh, Ali, 172
Zayat, Mohammed Abdel Salem el-, 165
Zdebskis, Fr Juozas, 55
Zeledón, Mario, 382
Zenteno Anaya, Gen. Joaquín, 327
Zhvaniya, Vladimir, 53
Zia ul-Haq, Gen. Mohammad, 73, 124ff.
Zin, Thakin, 79
Zinsou, Emile Derlin, 234
Zog I, King of Albania, 2
Zuazo, Hernán Siles; *see* Siles Zuazo, Hernán
Zuckermann, B. I., 36
Zuffada, Pierluigi, 452
Zwane, Ambrose P., 313